Uncertain Multi-Criteria Optimization Problems

Uncertain Multi-Criteria Optimization Problems

Editor

Dragan Pamucar

MDPI • Basel • Beijing • Wuhan • Barcelona • Belgrade • Manchester • Tokyo • Cluj • Tianjin

Editor
Dragan Pamucar
Military Academy,
Department of Logistics
University of Defence in
Belgrade
Belgrade
Serbia

Editorial Office
MDPI
St. Alban-Anlage 66
4052 Basel, Switzerland

This is a reprint of articles from the Special Issue published online in the open access journal *Symmetry* (ISSN 2073-8994) (available at: http://www.mdpi.com).

For citation purposes, cite each article independently as indicated on the article page online and as indicated below:

LastName, A.A.; LastName, B.B.; LastName, C.C. Article Title. *Journal Name* **Year**, *Volume Number*, Page Range.

ISBN 978-3-0365-1574-8 (Hbk)
ISBN 978-3-0365-1573-1 (PDF)

Contents

About the Editor

Dragan Pamucar

Dr. Dragan Pamucar is an Associate Professor at the University of Defence in Belgrade Department of Logistics, Serbia. Dr. Pamucar received a PhD in Applied Mathematics with a specialization of Multi-criteria modeling and soft computing techniques, from the University of Defence in Belgrade, Serbia, in 2013, and an MSc degree from the Faculty of Transport and Traffic Engineering in Belgrade, 2009. His research interests are in the field of computational intelligence, multi-criteria decision-making problems, neuro-fuzzy systems, fuzzy, rough and intuitionistic fuzzy set theories, and neutrosophic theory. The fields of application include a wide range of logistics, management, and engineering problems.

Preface to "Uncertain Multi-Criteria Optimization Problems"

Dear Colleagues,

Most real-world search and optimization problems naturally involve multiple criteria as objectives. Generally, symmetry, asymmetry, and anti-symmetry are basic characteristics of binary relationships used when modeling optimization problems. Moreover, the notion of symmetry has appeared in many articles concerning uncertainty theories that are employed in multi-criteria problems. Different solutions may produce trade-offs (conflicting scenarios) among different objectives. A better solution with respect to one objective may be a compromising one for other objectives. There are various factors that need to be considered to address the problems in multidisciplinary research, which is critical for the overall sustainability of human development and activity. In this regard, in recent decades, decision-making theory has been the subject of intense research activities due to its wide applications in different areas. The decision-making theory approach has become an important means to provide real-time solutions to uncertainty problems. Theories such as probability theory, fuzzy set theory, type-2 fuzzy set theory, rough set, and uncertainty theory, available in the existing literature, deal with such uncertainties. Nevertheless, the uncertain multi-criteria characteristics in such problems are yet to be explored in depth, and there is much left to be achieved in this direction. Hence, different mathematical models of real-life multi-criteria optimization problems can be developed in various uncertain frameworks, with special emphasis on optimization problems.

This Special Issue on "Uncertain Multi-Criteria Optimization Problems" aims to incorporate recent developments in the area of applied science. Topics include, but are not limited to, the following:

- Theoretical foundations of MCDM using uncertainty;
- Aggregation operators and application in MCDM;
- Multi-criteria in production and logistics;
- Risk analysis/modeling, sensitivity/robustness analysis;
- Multi-criteria network optimization;
- Mathematical programming in MCDM under uncertainty;
- New trends in multi-criteria decision-making.

Dragan Pamucar
Editor

symmetry

MDPI

Article

Multiple Granulation Rough Set Approach to Interval-Valued Intuitionistic Fuzzy Ordered Information Systems

Zhen Li † **and Xiaoyan Zhang** *,†

College of Artificial Intelligence, Southwest University, Chongqing 400715, China; swulz00@email.swu.edu.cn
* Correspondence: zhangxiaoyan@swu.edu.cn; Tel.: +86-150-2300-2286
† These authors contributed equally to this work.

Abstract: As a further extension of the fuzzy set and the intuitive fuzzy set, the interval-valued intuitive fuzzy set (IIFS) is a more effective tool to deal with uncertain problems. However, the classical rough set is based on the equivalence relation, which do not apply to the IIFS. In this paper, we combine the IIFS with the ordered information system to obtain the interval-valued intuitive fuzzy ordered information system (IIFOIS). On this basis, three types of multiple granulation rough set models based on the dominance relation are established to effectively overcome the limitation mentioned above, which belongs to the interdisciplinary subject of information theory in mathematics and pattern recognition. First, for an IIFOIS, we put forward a multiple granulation rough set (MGRS) model from two completely symmetry positions,which are optimistic and pessimistic, respectively. Furthermore, we discuss the approximation representation and a few essential characteristics for the target concept, besides several significant rough measures about two kinds of MGRS symmetry models are discussed. Furthermore, a more general MGRS model named the generalized MGRS (GMGRS) model is proposed in an IIFOIS, and some important properties and rough measures are also investigated. Finally, the relationships and differences between the single granulation rough set and the three types of MGRS are discussed carefully by comparing the rough measures between them in an IIFOIS. In order to better utilize the theory to realistic problems, an actual case shows the methods of MGRS models in an IIFOIS is given in this paper.

Keywords: granular computing; interval-valued; intuitionistic fuzzy set; multiple granulation; ordered information system

Citation: Li, Z.; Zhang, X. Multiple Granulation Rough Set Approach to Interval-Valued Intuitionistic Fuzzy Ordered Information Systems. *Symmetry* **2021**, *13*, 949. https://doi.org/10.3390/sym13060949

Academic Editor: Dragan Pamucar

Received: 23 March 2021
Accepted: 12 May 2021
Published: 27 May 2021

1. Introduction

For decades, Pawlak [1] has presented the rough set conception, which has become one of the most popular ideas in artificial intelligence litelature. The theory completely subverts the conception of classical sets and has been a soft computing implement to deal with impreciseness, indeterminacy and vagueness in data processing. The theory has been widely used in data mining [2,3], conflict analysis [4–6], patter recognition [7,8] and so on. At present, grest progress has been made in the theoretical basis and applied research of rough set in China, many scholars have published corresponding monographs and hundreds of papers in this field [9,10].

Atanassov [11] proposed the concept of the intuitive fuzzy set [12] on the basis of fuzzy set in 1983, which is an extension of the fuzzy set [13,14]. The intuitive fuzzy set is compatible with information on membership and non-membership [15] and more comprehensive and practical than the fuzzy set in dealing with vagueness and uncertainty. The integration of intuitive fuzzy sets and rough sets pruduces another blending model for processing intuitionistic fuzzy data [16]. For example, Coker first discussed the relationship between intuitive fuzzy set theory and rough set theory. On the basis of the fuzzy rough set given by Nanda, Jena and Chakrabraty put forward different concepts about intuitionistic fuzzy rough set theory. Wu and Liu [17] investigated the intuitionistic fuzzy equivalence relation in intuitive fuzzy system and got upper approximation reduction model in intuitive fuzzy information system. Zhou et al. [18] designed the approximation method of intuitive fuzzy rough set, and further uplifted the algorithm efficiency about intuitive fuzzy rough set approximate representation method in [19]. Zhang [20] researched some properties and conclusions of upper and lower approximation of intuitive fuzzy overlap.

The objects of classical rough set theory is a complete information system [21] which can divide the dominance of discourse through binary indistinguishable relation-the equivalent relation [22], so it can only process discrete data. In reality, however, due to the complexity and uncertainty of the environment, attribute values of a number of objects appear in the form of intuitionistic fuzzy number, and there are advantages and disadvantages among attribute values. To solve this problem, some scholars proposed an extension of rough set model based on dominance relation to replace the equivalence relation, and applied the classcial rough set theory to the ordered information system to research. In recent years, several researchers have been committed to studying the qualities and arithmetics of rough sets based on dominance relations. For example, Xu and Zhang [23] proposed new lower and upper approximations and obtained several important proporties in generalized rough set induced by covering. Xu et al. [24] proposed concepts of knowledge granulation, knowledge entropy and knowledge uncertainty measure in ordered information systems, and investigated some important properties. For an ordered information system, Xu et al. [25] dealed with the problem of attribute reduction with the proof theory. After that, Xu et al. [26] combined the intuitionistic fuzzy set theory with the ordered information system to further expand the inttuitionistic fuzzy set theory.

An equivalence relation on the universe can be regarded as a granulation, from the perspective of granular calculation, divide the domain of discourse into equivalence classes [27]. Hence the classical rough set models can be regarded as based on a granulation that is a equivalence relation. In addition, we can also know that any attributes can induce a equivalence relation in an information system. When based on multiple granulations, we can have the following situations:

Case 1: There exits at least a granulation so that the element must belong to the target concept.

Case 2: There exits at least a granulation so that the element may belong to the target concept.

Case 3: There are some granulations such that the element surely belong to the target concept.

Case 4: There are some granulations such that the element possibly belong to the target concept.

Case 5: All granulations so that the element must belong to the target concept.

Case 6: All granulations so that the element may belong to the target concept.

For case 1, 2, 5 and 6, a multiple source rough set model was proposed by Khan et al. [28]. Qian et al. also made a preliminary exploration of the rough set model from this perspective, defined the upper and lower approximation operators of the optimistic and pessimistic multiple granulation rough set model which are symmetry concepts, gave the properties of these approximation operators and introduced the measure of uncertainty of the target concept. Xu et al. [26] generalized the multiple granulation rough set model to the ordered information system for Case 1, 2, 5 and 6, and established a rough set model based on the ordered information system.

Intervaling intuitionistic fuzzy set can deal with more complex and practical problems [29,30]. How to establish dominant relations on the interval value of attributes about objects has become a hot topic in research. Qian et al. [31] first defined the dominance relation by comparing the upper and lower boundaries of interval values, and used the size of the upper or lower interval to judge the advantage or disadvantage of interval values. Zeng et al. [32] used the radius and center of interval values to define the dominance relation to reduce attributes in the interval-valued ordered information system. Yu et al. considered the dominance relation of two interval values in the intersection by the distribution principle of probability, then upper and lower approximation sets of the interval-valued information system are constructed which are based on this dominance relation. Huang et al. [33] introduced a dominance relation in the framework of interval-valued intuitionistic fuzzy information systems to come up with the concept called a dominance-based interval-valued intuitionistic fuzzy information system, which is used to establish a dominance-based rough set model.

Intervaling the intuitionistic fuzzy set can deal with uncertainty and vagueness in more effectively. This paper draws on the definition of the size between intuitionistic fuzzy numbers in [34]. The interval-valued intuitionistic fuzzy ordered information system [35,36] is obtained by combining the interval-valued intuitionistic fuzzy set [37] with the ordedred information system and extands the single granulation rough set model based on the dominance relation in an IIFOIS to two types of multiple granulation rough set model. In addition, considering that the approximation represention conditions of the two MGRS models for the concept are either too loose or too strict, a generalized multiple granulation rough set model in an IIFOIS is proposed from the perspective of the lower approximation. The rest of the paper is organized as follows. Some basic concepts about the intuitionnistic fuzzy set, the interval-valued intuitionistic fuzzy ordered information system and the rough set theory in an IIFOIS in Section 2. In Sections 3 and 4, for an IIFOIS, two types of MGRS symmetry models are obtained, respectively, where a target concept is approximated from different kings of views by the dominance class induced by multiple dominance relations. In addition, a number of important properties, the rough measure and the quality of approximation of two types of MGRS models are investigated in an IIFOIS. In Section 5, the generalized multiple granulation rough set model based on an IIFOIS is proposed and some important properties are discussed. In Section 6, relationships and differences about the rough set, the rough measure and the quality of approximation are discussed between the single granulation rough set and three types of MGRS models. Finally, the paper is conclued by a summary and outlook for further research in Section 7.

2. Preliminaries

In this section, we will introduce several basic concepts, including the interval-valued intuitionistic fuzzy set (IIFS) and related operations, the interval-valued intuitionistic fuzzy ordered information system (IIFOIS) and the rough set based on the system. More details can be seen in references.

2.1. The Interval-Valued Intuitionistic Fuzzy Set

Let U be the universe , an interval-valued intuitionistic fuzzy set $A^{[\wr]}$ on U is

$$A^{[\wr]} = \{< x, [\mu_A^-(x), \mu_A^+(x)], [\nu_A^-(x), \nu_A^+(x)] > | x \in U\},$$

where $\mu_A^-(x), \mu_A^+(x) : U \to [0,1]$ and $\nu_A^-(x), \nu_A^+(x) : U \to [0,1]$ satisfy $0 \le \mu_A^-(x) \le \mu_A^+(x) \le 1$, $0 \le \nu_A^-(x) \le \nu_A^+(x) \le 1$ and $0 \le \mu_A^+(x) + \nu_A^+(x) \le 1$ for any $x \in U$. $[\mu_A^-(x), \mu_A^+(x)]$, $[\nu_A^-(x), \nu_A^+(x)]$ are called the membership and nonmembership degree interval of x relative to the interval-valued intuitionistic set $A^{[\wr]}$, respectively, where $\mu_A^-(x)$ and $\nu_A^-(x)$ are the lower bounds of the interval, $\mu_A^+(x)$ and $\nu_A^+(x)$ are the upper bounds of the interval. And $IIFS(U)$ represents the class of all interval-valued intuitionistic fuzzy sets on U.

Suppose $A^{[\wr]}, B^{[\wr]} \in IIFS(U), x \in U$. The operations related to the set $A^{[\wr]}$ and $B^{[\wr]}$ are as follows.

(1)$A^{[\wr]} \subseteq B^{[\wr]} \Leftrightarrow \mu_A^-(x) \le \mu_B^-(x), \mu_A^+(x) \le \mu_B^+(x), \nu_A^-(x) \ge \nu_B^-(x), \nu_A^+(x) \ge \nu_B^+(x)$.

(2)$A^{[\wr]} \cup B^{[\wr]} = \{< x, [\mu_A^-(x) \vee \mu_B^-(x), \mu_A^+(x) \vee \mu_B^+(x)], [\nu_A^-(x) \wedge \nu_B^-(x), \nu_A^+(x) \wedge \nu_B^+(x)] > | x \in U\}$.

(3)$A^{[\wr]} \cap B^{[\wr]} = \{< x, [\mu_A^-(x) \wedge \mu_B^-(x), \mu_A^+(x) \wedge \mu_B^+(x)], [\nu_A^-(x) \vee \nu_B^-(x), \nu_A^+(x) \vee \nu_B^+(x)] > | x \in U\}$.

(4)$A^{[\wr]C} = \{< x, [\nu_A^-(x), \nu_A^+(x)], [\mu_A^-(x), \mu_A^+(x)] > | x \in U\}$.
where "$\vee$" and "$\wedge$" represent the operation of max and min, respectively.

2.2. The Interval-Value Intuitionistic Fuzzy Ordered Information System

The interval-valued intuitionistic fuzzy information system (IIFIS) can be recorded as $\mathcal{I}^{[\wr]} = (U, AT, V, f)$, we can know that $U = \{x_1, x_2, \cdots, x_n\}$ represents the whole of objects under discussion, and the class of all subsets of U is denoted by $P(U)$. $AT = \{a_1, a_2, \cdots, a_m\}$ is the collection of all attributes. $V = \cup_{a \in AT} V_a$, V_a denotes that the value domain of objects with respect to the attribute a. $f : U \times AT \to V$, there $f(x, a) =< [\mu_a^-(x), \mu_a^+(x)], [\nu_a^-(x), \nu_a^+(x)] > \in V_a$ for any $a \in AT, x \in U$, where $0 \leq \mu_a^-(x) \leq \mu_a^+(x) \leq 1, 0 \leq \nu_a^-(x) \leq \nu_a^+(x) \leq 1$ and $0 \leq \mu_a^+(x) + \nu_a^+(x) \leq 1$.

If $AT = CT \subseteq DT$, where $CT = \{c_1, c_2, \cdots, c_p\}$ is the collection of all condition attributes, and $DT = \{d_1, d_2, \cdots, d_q\}$ is the collection of all decision attributes, then $\mathcal{I}^{[\wr]} = (U, CT \cup d, V, f)$ is called the interval-valued intuitionistic fuzzy decision information system(IIFDIS). In particular, according to the number of decision attributes, the IIFDIS can be divided into the interval-valued intuitionistic fuzzy single-decision information system($|DT| = 1$) and the interval-valued intuitionistic fuzzy multi-decision information system($|DT| \geq 1$).

Let $\mathcal{I}^{[\wr]} = (U, AT, V, f)$ be an IIFIS, $a \in AT$. According to the domain of the attribute a, for any $x_i \in U$, we can find an object x_j from U such that

$$f(x_i, a)[\wr] \geq f(x_j, a) \Leftrightarrow \mu_a^-(x_i) \geq \mu_a^-(x_j), \mu_a^+(x_i) \geq \mu_a^+(x_j) \text{ and } \nu_a^-(x_i) \leq \nu_a^-(x_j), \nu_a^+(x_i) \leq \nu_a^+(x_j),$$

$$f(x_i, a)[\wr] \leq f(x_j, a) \Leftrightarrow \mu_a^-(x_i) \leq \mu_a^-(x_j), \mu_a^+(x_i) \leq \mu_a^+(x_j) \text{ and } \nu_a^-(x_i) \geq \nu_a^-(x_j), \nu_a^+(x_i) \geq \nu_a^+(x_j).$$

Increasing and decreasing partial ordered relations can be obtained from "$[\wr] \geq$ " and "$[\wr] \leq$ ". In an IIFIS $\mathcal{I}^{[\wr]} = (U, AT, V, f)$, the attribute will be the criterion if and only if the value of objects by the attriibute is partial ordered, so we can get the dominance relation by criterions. In this paper, we only consider the dominance relation by the increasing partial ordered relation. For $x_i, x_j \in U$, $x_i[\wr] \geq_a x_j \Leftrightarrow f(x_i, a)[\wr] \geq f(x_j, a)$ indicates that x_i is superior to x_j with respect to the criterion a, it is also means that x_i is at least as good as x_j about a. For $A \subseteq AT$, $x_i \geq_A x_j$ means that $x_i \geq_a x_j$ for every $a \in A$.

Let $\mathcal{I}^{[\wr]} = (U, AT, V, f)$ be an IIFIS, if all attributes are criterions, then the $\mathcal{I}^{[\wr]}$ is called an interval-value intuitionistic fuzzy ordered information system and recorded as $\mathcal{I}^{[\wr]\geq} = (U, AT, V, f)$. In an IIFOIS $\mathcal{I}^{[\wr]\geq} = (U, AT, V, f)$, $A \subseteq AT$, the dominance relation $R_A^{[\wr]\geq}$ is

$$R_A^{[\wr]\geq} = \{(x_i, x_j) \in U \times U | f(x_i, a) \leq f(x_j, a), \forall a \in A\}.$$

it is obvious that $R_A^{[\wr]\geq}$ is reflective, transtive, but not symmetric, therefore $R_A^{[\wr]\geq}$ is not an equivalence relation.

The dominance class about $x_i \in U$ for A by $R_A^{[\wr]\geq}$ is

$$[x_i]_A^{[\wr]\geq} = \{x_j \in U | (x_i, x_j) \in R_A^{[\wr]\geq}\}.$$

The coverage of U about the attribute set A is

$$U/R_A^{[\wr]\geq} = \{[x_i]_A^{[\wr]\geq} | x_i \in U\}.$$

Proposition 1. *Suppose $\mathcal{I}^{[\wr]\geq} = (U, AT, V, f)$ be an IIFOIS, $A, B \subseteq AT$. Then we have the following results.*

(1) If $B \subseteq A$, then $R_A^{[\wr]\geq} \subseteq R_B^{[\wr]\geq}$ and $[x_i]_A^{[\wr]\geq} \subseteq [x_i]_B^{[\wr]\geq}$, for any $x_i \in U$.

(2) If $x_j \in [x_i]_A^{[\wr]\geq}$, then $[x_j]_A^{[\wr]\geq} \subseteq [x_i]_A^{[\wr]\geq}$ and $[x_i]_A^{[\wr]\geq} = \cup\{[x_j]_A^{[\wr]\geq} | x_j \in [x_i]_A^{[\wr]\geq}\}$, for any $x_i, x_j \in U$.

(3) $[x_j]_A^{[\wr]\geq} = [x_i]_A^{[\wr]\geq}$ *if and only if* $\mu_A^-(x_i) = \mu_A^-(x_j)$, $\mu_A^+(x_i) = \mu_A^+(x_j)$ *and* $\nu_A^-(x_i) = \nu_A^-(x_j)$, $\nu_A^+(x_i) = \nu_A^+(x_j)$ *for* $a \in A$.

Example 1. *Suppose Table 1 is an interval-value intuitionistic fuzzy ordered information system about the information of communities to be sold,* $U = \{x_1, x_2, x_3, x_4, x_5, x_6\}$ *is a universe which consists of 6 communities in one city,* $AT = \{a_1, a_2, a_3, a_4\}$ *is the conditional attributes of the system including location, utility service, type of layout and environment. Decision is the result of excellent student by experts according to the information of these communities, Y express that the community is excellent, and N express the community is not excellent.*

Table 1. An interval-value intuitionistic fuzzy ordered information system.

U	a_1	a_2	a_3	a_4	d
x_1	$< [0.32, 0.37], [0.20, 0.31] >$	$< [0.53, 0.62], [0.10, 0.18] >$	$< [0.26, 0.35], [0.30, 0.38] >$	$< [0.53, 0.62], [0.16, 0.20] >$	Y
x_2	$< [0.39, 0.42], [0.11, 0.12] >$	$< [0.35, 0.37], [0.28, 0.35] >$	$< [0.10, 0.20], [0.50, 0.60] >$	$< [0.47, 0.55], [0.25, 0.32] >$	Y
x_3	$< [0.18, 0.25], [0.39, 0.52] >$	$< [0.30, 0.36], [0.37, 0.42] >$	$< [0.55, 0.62], [0.15, 0.20] >$	$< [0.38, 0.45], [0.30, 0.40] >$	N
x_4	$< [0.27, 0.33], [0.25, 0.35] >$	$< [0.20, 0.32], [0.45, 0.52] >$	$< [0.48, 0.53], [0.17, 0.30] >$	$< [0.30, 0.40], [0.35, 0.45] >$	N
x_5	$< [0.35, 0.40], [0.15, 0.25] >$	$< [0.41, 0.49], [0.25, 0.32] >$	$< [0.30, 0.42], [0.25, 0.33] >$	$< [0.60, 0.82], [0.12, 0.15] >$	N
x_6	$< [0.43, 0.67], [0.08, 0.12] >$	$< [0.45, 0.50], [0.20, 0.24] >$	$< [0.62, 0.72], [0.08, 0.18] >$	$< [0.36, 0.43], [0.30, 0.40] >$	Y

From Table 2, we can know that $U/d = \{D_Y, D_N\}, D_Y = \{x_1, x_2, x_6\}, D_N = \{x_3, x_4, x_5\}$. We can calculate the dominance classes induced by $R_{AT}^{[\wr]\geq}$.

$$[x_1]_{AT}^{[\wr]\geq} = \{x_1\}, [x_2]_{AT}^{[\wr]\geq} = \{x_2\},$$

$$[x_3]_{AT}^{[\wr]\geq} = \{x_3\}, [x_4]_{AT}^{[\wr]\geq} = \{x_4, x_6\},$$

$$[x_5]_{AT}^{[\wr]\geq} = \{x_5\}, [x_6]_{AT}^{[\wr]\geq} = \{x_6\}.$$

Table 2. The support feature function of objects in Table 1.

U	$S_X^{A_1}(x)$	$S_{\sim X}^{A_1}(x)$	$S_X^{A_2}(x)$	$S_{\sim X}^{A_2}(x)$	$S_X^{A_3}(x)$	$S_{\sim X}^{A_3}(x)$	$S_X^{A_4}(x)$	$S_{\sim X}^{A_4}(x)$
x_1	0	0	1	0	0	0	0	0
x_2	1	0	0	0	0	0	0	0
x_3	0	0	0	0	0	0	0	0
x_4	0	0	0	0	0	0	0	0
x_5	0	0	0	0	0	0	0	1
x_6	1	0	1	0	1	0	0	0

Let $A = \{a_1, a_2, a_4\} \subseteq AT$, then we have

$$[x_1]_A^{[\wr]\geq} = \{x_1\}, [x_2]_A^{[\wr]\geq} = \{x_2\},$$

$$[x_3]_A^{[\wr]\geq} = \{x_1, x_2, x_3, x_5\}, [x_4]_A^{[\wr]\geq} = \{x_1, x_2, x_4, x_5, x_6\},$$

$$[x_5]_A^{[\wr]\geq} = \{x_5\}, [x_6]_A^{[\wr]\geq} = \{x_6\}.$$

Obviously, $[x_i]_{AT}^{[\wr]\geq} \subseteq [x_i]_A^{[\wr]\geq}, U/R_{AT}^{[\wr]\geq} = U/R_A^{[\wr]\geq} = \{[x_i]_A^{[\wr]\geq} | x_i \in U\}$

2.3. *The Rough Set in IIFOIS*

Suppose $\mathcal{I}^{[\wr]\geq} = (U, AT, V, f)$ be an IIFOIS, $X \subseteq U$, $A \subseteq AT$. The lower and upper approximation of X with repect to the dominance relation $R_A^{[\wr]\geq}$ are as follows

$$\underline{X}_A^{[\wr]\geq} = \{x \in U | [x]_A^{[\wr]\geq} \subseteq X\},$$

$$\overline{X}_A^{[\wr]\geq} = \{x \in U | [x]_A^{[\wr]\geq} \cap X \neq \emptyset\}.$$

The objects in the lower approximation set $\underline{X}_A^{[\wr]\geq}$ certainly belong to the target set X, while the obiects in the upper approximation set $\overline{X}_A^{[\wr]\geq}$ may be part of the target set X. If $\underline{X}_A^{[\wr]\geq} = \overline{X}_A^{[\wr]\geq}$, we can say that X is a definable set with respect to the dominance relation $R_A^{[\wr]\geq}$, otherwise X is rough. And $Pos(X) = \underline{X}_A^{[\wr]\geq}$, $Neg(X) =\sim \underline{X}_A^{[\wr]\geq}$ and $Bnd(X) = \overline{X}_A^{[\wr]\geq} - \underline{X}_A^{[\wr]\geq}$ are, respecticely, the positive region, negative region and boundary region of X.

Proposition 2. *Suppose $\mathcal{I}^{[\wr]\geq} = (U, AT, V, f)$ be an IIFOIS, $A \subseteq AT$. For any $X \subseteq U$ we have that*
(1) $\underline{X}_A^{[\wr]\geq} \subseteq \underline{X}_{AT}^{[\wr]\geq}$ and $\overline{X}_A^{[\wr]\geq} \supseteq \overline{X}_{AT}^{[\wr]\geq}$.
(2) $X_A^{[\wr]\geq} = X_{AT}^{[\wr]\geq}$ if and only if $\underline{X}_A^{[\wr]\geq} = \underline{X}_{AT}^{[\wr]\geq}$ and $\overline{X}_A^{[\wr]\geq} = \overline{X}_{AT}^{[\wr]\geq}$.

Proposition 3. *Suppose $\mathcal{I}^{[\wr]\geq} = (U, AT, V, f)$ be an IIFOIS, $X, Y \subseteq U$, $A \subseteq AT$. Then we have the following results*
(1L) $\underline{X}_A^{[\wr]\geq} \subseteq X$ (Contraction)
(1U) $X \subseteq \overline{X}_A^{[\wr]\geq}$ (Extention)
(2L) $\underline{\sim X}_A^{[\wr]\geq} =\sim \overline{X}_A^{[\wr]\geq}$ (Duality)
(2U) $\overline{\sim X}_A^{[\wr]\geq} =\sim \underline{X}_A^{[\wr]\geq}$ (Duality)
(3L) $\underline{\emptyset}_A^{[\wr]\geq} = \emptyset$ (Normality)
(3U) $\overline{\emptyset}_A^{[\wr]\geq} = \emptyset$ (Normality)
(4L) $\underline{U}_A^{[\wr]\geq} = U$ (Co-normality)
(4U) $\overline{U}_A^{[\wr]\geq} = U$ (Co-normality)
(5L) $\underline{X \cap Y}_A^{[\wr]\geq} = \underline{X}_A^{[\wr]\geq} \cap \underline{Y}_A^{[\wr]\geq}$ (Multiplication)
(5U) $\overline{X \cup Y}_A^{[\wr]\geq} = \overline{X}_A^{[\wr]\geq} \cup \overline{Y}_A^{[\wr]\geq}$ (Addition)
(6L) $\underline{X \cup Y}_A^{[\wr]\geq} \supseteq \underline{X}_A^{[\wr]\geq} \cup \underline{Y}_A^{[\wr]\geq}$ (F-addition)
(6U) $\overline{X \cap Y}_A^{[\wr]\geq} \subseteq \overline{X}_A^{[\wr]\geq} \cap \overline{Y}_A^{[\wr]\geq}$ (F-multiplication)
(7L) $X \subseteq Y \Rightarrow \underline{X}_A^{[\wr]\geq} \subseteq \underline{Y}_A^{[\wr]\geq}$ (Monotonicity)
(7U) $X \subseteq Y \Rightarrow \overline{X}_A^{[\wr]\geq} \subseteq \overline{Y}_A^{[\wr]\geq}$ (Monotonicity)
(8L) $\underline{(\underline{X}_A^{[\wr]\geq})}_A^{[\wr]\geq} = \underline{X}_A^{[\wr]\geq}$ (Idempotency)
(8U) $\overline{(\overline{X}_A^{[\wr]\geq})}_A^{[\wr]\geq} = \overline{X}_A^{[\wr]\geq}$ (Idempotency)

Let $\mathcal{I}^{[\wr]\geq} = (U, AT, V, f)$ be an IIFOIS, $A \subseteq AT$, $X \subseteq U$. To express the imprecision and roughness of a rough set, the accuracy measure and the rough measure of X by the dominance relation $R_A^{[\wr]\geq}$ are as follows,

$$\alpha(R_A^{[\wr]\geq}, X) = \frac{|\underline{X}_A^{[\wr]\geq}|}{|\overline{X}_A^{[\wr]\geq}|} = \frac{|\underline{X}_A^{[\wr]\geq}|}{|U| - |\underline{\sim X}_A^{[\wr]\geq}|},$$

$$\rho(R_A^{[\wr]\geq}, X) = 1 - \alpha(R_A^{[\wr]\geq}, X).$$

Proposition 4. *Suppose $\mathcal{I}^{[\wr]\geq} = (U, AT, V, f)$ be an IIFOIS, $X \subseteq U$, $A \subseteq AT$. We have the following results.*
(1) $0 \leq \rho(R_A^{[\wr]\geq}, X) \leq 1$.
(2) $\rho(R_A^{[\wr]\geq}, X) = 1 - \frac{|\underline{X}_A^{[\wr]\geq}|}{|\overline{X}_A^{[\wr]\geq}|} = 1 - \frac{|\underline{X}_A^{[\wr]\geq}|}{|U| - |\underline{\sim X}_A^{[\wr]\geq}|}$.

(3) *If* $R_A^{[\wr]\geq} = R_{AT}^{[\wr]\geq}$, *then* $\rho(R_A^{[\wr]\geq}, X) = \rho(R_{AT}^{[\wr]\geq}, X)$.
(4) *If* $B \subseteq A \subseteq AT$, *then* $\rho(R_{AT}^{[\wr]\geq}, X) \leq \rho(R_A^{[\wr]\geq}, X) \leq \rho(R_B^{[\wr]\geq}, X)$.

Let $\mathcal{I}^{[\wr]\geq} = (U, CT \cup \{d\}, V, f)$ be an IIFDOIS, $A \subseteq AT$. The quality of approximation of d by $R_A^{[\wr]\geq}$, also called the degree of dependency, is defined as

$$\gamma(R_A^{[\wr]\geq}, d) = \frac{1}{|U|}\sum_{j=1}^{k}(|\underline{R}_A^{[\wr]\geq}(D_j)|),$$

where $R_d^{[\wr]\geq} = \{(x_i, x_j) \in U \times U | f(x_i, d) = f(x_j, d), U/d = \{D_1, D_2, \cdots, D_k\}$.

Proposition 5. *Suppose* $\mathcal{I}^{[\wr]\geq} = (U, AT, V, f)$ *be an IIFDOIS,* $X \subseteq U$, $A \subseteq AT$. *We have*
(1) $0 \leq \gamma(R_A^{[\wr]\geq}, d) \leq 1$.
(2) *If* $R_A^{[\wr]\geq} = R_{AT}^{[\wr]\geq}$, *then* $\gamma(R_A^{[\wr]\geq}, d) = \gamma(R_{AT}^{[\wr]\geq}, d)$.
(3) *If* $B \subseteq A \subseteq AT$, *then* $\gamma(R_{AT}^{[\wr]\geq}, d) \geq \gamma(R_A^{[\wr]\geq}, d) \geq \gamma(R_B^{[\wr]\geq}, d)$.

Example 2 (Continued from Example 1). *Let* $X = D_Y = \{x_1, x_2, x_6\}$. *Then the lower and upper approximation sets of the concept X by the dominance relation* $R_{AT}^{[\wr]\geq}$ *are as follows.*

$$\underline{X}_{AT}^{[\wr]\geq} = \{x_1, x_2, x_6\},$$

$$\overline{X}_{AT}^{[\wr]\geq} = \{x_1, x_2, x_4, x_6\}.$$

Similarly, the lower and upper approximation sets of the concept X by the dominance relation $R_A^{[\wr]\geq}$ *are as follows.*

$$\underline{X}_{A}^{[\wr]\geq} = \{x_1, x_2, x_6\},$$

$$\overline{X}_{A}^{[\wr]\geq} = \{x_1, x_2, x_3, x_4, x_6\}.$$

Consider rough measures and we can get that

$$\rho(R_{AT}^{[\wr]\geq}, X) = 1 - \frac{|\underline{R}_{AT}^{[\wr]\geq}(X)|}{|\overline{R}_{AT}^{[\wr]\geq}(X)|} = \frac{1}{4}, \rho(R_A^{[\wr]\geq}, X) = 1 - \frac{|\underline{R}_{A}^{[\wr]\geq}(X)|}{|\overline{R}_{A}^{[\wr]\geq}(X)|} = \frac{2}{5}.$$

And

$$\underline{D_Y}_{AT}^{[\wr]\geq} = \{x_1, x_2, x_6\}, \underline{D_N}_{AT}^{[\wr]\geq} = \{x_3, x_5\}.$$

$$\underline{D_Y}_{A}^{[\wr]\geq} = \{x_1, x_2, x_6\}, \underline{D_N}_{A}^{[\wr]\geq} = \{x_5\}.$$

Then

$$\gamma(R_{AT}^{[\wr]\geq}, d) = \frac{|\underline{D_Y}_{AT}^{[\wr]\geq}| + |\underline{D_N}_{AT}^{[\wr]\geq}|}{|U|} = \frac{5}{6}, \gamma(R_A^{[\wr]\geq}, d) = \frac{|\underline{D_Y}_{A}^{[\wr]\geq}| + |\underline{D_N}_{A}^{[\wr]\geq})|}{|U|} = \frac{2}{3}.$$

In that way, we can know that $\rho(R_{AT}^{[\wr]\geq}, X) \leq \rho(R_A^{[\wr]\geq}, X)$, $\gamma(R_{AT}^{[\wr]\geq}, d) \geq \gamma^{[\wr]\geq}(R_A^{[\wr]\geq}, d)$.

3. The Optimistic Multiple Granulation Rough Set in IIFOIS

The above rough set is approximated to the target concept by constructing the upper and lower approximations through a single dominance relation, so it is a single granulation rough set model. However, the granular computing emphasizes observing and solving problems under different granulations which refers to the concept of the multile granulation rough set.

In this section, we will consider the multiple granulation rough set in an IIFOIS from a completely optimistic perspective which means that as long as just one condition is met to accept. We will investigate the representation of the upper and lower approximation operators and discuss two basic mesasures and their properties.

Definition 1. *Let* $\mathcal{I}^{[\wr]\geq} = (U, AT, V, f)$ *be an IIFOIS,* $A_1, A_2, \cdots, A_s \in AT(s \leq 2^{|AT|})$*,* $R^{[\wr]\geq}_{A_1}, R^{[\wr]\geq}_{A_2}, \cdots, R^{[\wr]\geq}_{A_s}$ *be dominance relations, respectively. For any* $X \in P(U)$*, we have the operators* $\underline{OM}^{[\wr]\geq}_{\sum_{i=1}^{s} A_i}$ *and* $\overline{OM}^{[\wr]\geq}_{\sum_{i=1}^{s} A_i}$*:*$P(U) \rightarrow P(U)$*, are as follows:*

$$\underline{OM}^{[\wr]\geq}_{\sum_{i=1}^{s} A_i}(X) = \{x \in U | \bigvee_{i=1}^{s}([x]^{[\wr]\geq}_{A_i} \subseteq X)\},$$

$$\overline{OM}^{[\wr]\geq}_{\sum_{i=1}^{s} A_i}(X) = \{x \in U | \bigwedge_{i=1}^{s}([x]^{[\wr]\geq}_{A_i} \cap X \neq \emptyset)\}.$$

where "$\bigvee$*" means "or" and "*$\bigwedge$*" means "and".* $\underline{OM}^{[\wr]\geq}_{\sum_{i=1}^{s} A_i}(X)$ *and* $\overline{OM}^{[\wr]\geq}_{\sum_{i=1}^{s} A_i}(X)$ *are called the optimistic multiple granulation lower and upper approximation of X by dominance relations* $R^{[\wr]\geq}_{A_1}, R^{[\wr]\geq}_{A_2}, \cdots, R^{[\wr]\geq}_{A_s}$ *in an IIFOIS.*

Similarily, $\underline{OM}^{[\wr]\geq}_{\sum_{i=1}^{s} A_i}(X) = \overline{OM}^{[\wr]\geq}_{\sum_{i=1}^{s} A_i}(X)$, then X is an opetimistic definable set with respect to multiple granulation dominance relations $A_1, A_2, \cdots, A_s (m \leq 2^{|AT|})$, otherwise X is an opetimistic rough set. $Pos^{[\wr]\geq}_{\sum_{i=1}^{s} A_i}(X) = \underline{OM}^{[\wr]\geq}_{\sum_{i=1}^{s} A_i}(X)$, $Neg^{[\wr]\geq}_{\sum_{i=1}^{s} A_i}(X) = \sim \overline{OM}^{[\wr]\geq}_{\sum_{i=1}^{s} A_i}(X)$ and $Bnd^{[\wr]\geq}_{\sum_{i=1}^{s} A_i}(X) = \overline{OM}^{[\wr]\geq}_{\sum_{i=1}^{s} A_i}(X) - \underline{OM}^{[\wr]\geq}_{\sum_{i=1}^{s} A_i}(X)$.

From the above definition, it can be seen that the lower approximation in the optimistic multiple granulation rough set is defined by multiple dominance relations, whereas the rough lower approximation in Section 2.3 is represented via those derived by only one dominance relation. And the operation in the lower approximation is "$\bigvee$". It means that for the object x, as long as the lower approximation condition is met by at least one dominance raltion, it is placed in the lower approximation set. That is what "optimistic" means.

In the following, we will employ an example to illustrate the above concepts.

Example 3 (Continued from Example 1). *In Table 1, we often face the phenomenon that some consumers may prefer some conditions of excellent communities as follows:*
Preference 1: Not only the location and the utility service are better, but also the type of layout is better.
Preference 2: Not only the location and the type of layout are better, but also the environment is better.

From Table 1, we can know that $U/d = \{D_Y, D_N\}, D_Y = \{x_1, x_2, x_6\}, D_N = \{x_3, x_4, x_5\}$*. Let* $X = D_Y = \{x_1, x_2, x_6\}$ *is a set which consists of excellent communities.*

When we only consider one of two preferences, which one must be an excellent community and which one may be an excellent community?

By Preference 1 and 2, we can get that two dominance relations :

$$R_1 = \begin{pmatrix} 1 & 0 & 0 & 0 & 0 & 0 \\ 0 & 1 & 0 & 0 & 0 & 0 \\ 0 & 0 & 1 & 0 & 0 & 0 \\ 0 & 0 & 0 & 1 & 0 & 0 \\ 0 & 0 & 0 & 0 & 1 & 0 \\ 0 & 1 & 0 & 1 & 1 & 1 \end{pmatrix}, R_2 = \begin{pmatrix} 1 & 0 & 0 & 0 & 0 & 0 \\ 0 & 1 & 0 & 0 & 0 & 0 \\ 0 & 0 & 1 & 0 & 0 & 0 \\ 0 & 0 & 0 & 1 & 0 & 0 \\ 1 & 0 & 0 & 0 & 1 & 0 \\ 0 & 0 & 0 & 1 & 0 & 1 \end{pmatrix}.$$

When we consider only Preference 1, we can get that

$$\underline{R}_1^{[\wr]\geq}(X) = \{x_1, x_2, x_6\},$$

$$\overline{R}_1^{[\wr]\geq}(X) = \{x_1, x_2, x_4, x_5, x_6\},$$

and when we consider only Preference 2, we can get that

$$\underline{R}_2^{[\wr]\geq}(X) = \{x_2, x_6\},$$

$$\overline{R}_2^{[\wr]\geq}(X) = \{x_1, x_2, x_4, x_6\}.$$

It means that x_1, x_2, x_6 must be excellent communities and x_1, x_2, x_4, x_5, x_6 may be excellent communities when we consider only Preference 1. And when we consider only Preference 2, it is also easy to find out that x_2, x_6 must be excellent communities and x_1, x_2, x_4, x_6 may be excellent communities.

Now we consider the question: When we consider one of two preferences at least, which one must be an excellent community? When we consider both of two preferences, which one may be an excellent community? We can solve the question according to the definition of the opetimistic multiple granulation rough set. Then we have

$$\underline{OM}_{1+2}^{[\wr]\geq}(X) = \{x_1, x_2, x_6\},$$

$$\overline{OM}_{1+2}^{[\wr]\geq}(X) = \{x_1, x_2, x_4, x_6\}.$$

We can know that the community x_1, x_2, x_6 must be excellent if we consider one of two preferences at least, and the community x_1, x_2, x_4, x_6 may be excellent if we consider both of two preferences. Moreover, we can obtain

$$\underline{OM}_{1+2}^{[\wr]\geq}(X) = \underline{R}_1^{[\wr]\geq}(X) \cup \underline{R}_2^{[\wr]\geq}(X),$$

$$\overline{OM}_{1+2}^{[\wr]\geq}(X) = \overline{R}_1^{[\wr]\geq}(X) \cap \overline{R}_2^{[\wr]\geq}(X).$$

Proposition 6. *Let $\mathcal{I}^{[\wr]\geq} = (U, AT, V, f)$ be an IIFOIS, $A_1, A_2, \cdots, A_s \in AT(m \leq 2^{|AT|})$, $X \in U$, then the following results hold.*

(OL_1) $\underline{OM}_{\sum_{i=1}^{s} A_i}^{[\wr]\geq}(X) \subseteq X$ *(Contraction)*

(OU_1) $X \subseteq \overline{OM}_{\sum_{i=1}^{s} A_i}^{[\wr]\geq}(X)$ *(Extention)*

(OL_2) $\underline{OM}_{\sum_{i=1}^{s} A_i}^{[\wr]\geq}(\sim X) = \sim \overline{OM}_{\sum_{i=1}^{s} A_i}^{[\wr]\geq}(X)$ *(Duality)*

(OU_2) $\overline{OM}_{\sum_{i=1}^{s} A_i}^{[\wr]\geq}(\sim X) = \sim \underline{OM}_{\sum_{i=1}^{s} A_i}^{[\wr]\geq}(X)$ *(Duality)*

(OL_3) $\underline{OM}_{\sum_{i=1}^{s} A_i}^{[\wr]\geq}(\emptyset) = \emptyset$ *(Normality)*

(OU_3) $\overline{OM}_{\sum_{i=1}^{s} A_i}^{[\wr]\geq}(\emptyset) = \emptyset$ *(Normality)*

(OL_4) $\underline{OM}_{\sum_{i=1}^{s} A_i}^{[\wr]\geq}(U) = U$ *(Co-normality)*

(OU_4) $\overline{OM}_{\sum_{i=1}^{s} A_i}^{[\wr]\geq}(U) = U$ *(Co-normality)*

(OL_5) $\underline{OM}_{\sum_{i=1}^{s} A_i}^{[\wr]\geq}(X \cap Y) \subseteq \underline{OM}_{\sum_{i=1}^{s} A_i}^{[\wr]\geq}(X) \cap \underline{OM}_{\sum_{i=1}^{s} A_i}^{[\wr]\geq}(Y)$ *(L-F-multiplication)*

(OU_5) $\overline{OM}_{\sum_{i=1}^{s} A_i}^{[\wr]\geq}(X \cup Y) \supseteq \overline{OM}_{\sum_{i=1}^{s} A_i}^{[\wr]\geq}(X) \cup \overline{OM}_{\sum_{i=1}^{s} A_i}^{[\wr]\geq}(Y)$ *(U-F-addition)*

(OL_6) $X \subseteq Y \Rightarrow \underline{OM}_{\sum_{i=1}^{s} A_i}^{[\wr]\geq}(X) \subseteq \underline{OM}_{\sum_{i=1}^{s} A_i}^{[\wr]\geq}(Y)$ *(Monotonicity)*

(OU_6) $X \subseteq Y \Rightarrow \overline{OM}_{\sum_{i=1}^{s} A_i}^{[\wr]\geq}(X) \subseteq \overline{OM}_{\sum_{i=1}^{s} A_i}^{[\wr]\geq}(Y)$ *(Monotonicity)*

$$(OL_7)\quad \underline{OM}^{[\wr]\geq}_{\sum_{i=1}^{s}A_i}(X\cup Y)\supseteq \underline{OM}^{[\wr]\geq}_{\sum_{i=1}^{s}A_i}(X)\cup \underline{OM}^{[\wr]\geq}_{\sum_{i=1}^{s}A_i}(Y)\qquad \textit{(L-F-addition)}$$
$$(OU_7)\quad \overline{OM}^{[\wr]\geq}_{\sum_{i=1}^{s}A_{i=l}}(X\cap Y)\subseteq \overline{OM}^{[\wr]\geq}_{\sum_{i=1}^{s}A_i}(X)\cap \overline{OM}^{[\wr]\geq}_{\sum_{i=1}^{s}A_i}(Y)\qquad \textit{(U-F-multiplication)}$$

The proof can be found in Proposition A1 of Appendix A.

Definition 2. *Let $\mathcal{I}^{[\wr]\geq}=(U,AT,V,f)$ be an IIFOIS, $A_i\in AT, i=1,2,\cdots,s(s\leq 2^{|AT|})$, $X\in U$, the opetimistic multiple granulation rough measure of X by $\sum_{i=1}^{s}A_i$ is*

$$\rho_o^{[\wr]\geq}(\sum_{i=1}^{s}A_i,X)=1-\frac{|\underline{OM}^{[\wr]\geq}_{\sum_{i=1}^{s}A_i}(X)|}{|\overline{OM}^{[\wr]\geq}_{\sum_{i=1}^{s}A_i}(X)|}.$$

Definition 3. *Let $\mathcal{I}^{[\wr]\geq}=(U,CT\cup d,V,f)$ be an IIFDOIS, $A_i\in AT, i=1,2,\cdots,s(s\leq 2^{|AT|})$. The quality of approximation of d by $\sum_{i=1}^{s}A_i$, also called the opetimistic multiple granulation degree of dependency, is defined as*

$$\gamma_o^{[\wr]\geq}(\sum_{i=1}^{s}A_i,d)=\frac{1}{|U|}\sum_{j=1}^{k}(|\underline{OM}^{[\wr]\geq}_{\sum_{i=1}^{s}A_i}(D_j)|),$$

where $R_d^{[\wr]\geq}=\{(x_i,x_j)\in U\times U|f(x_i,d)=f(x_j,d), U/d=\{D_1,D_2,\cdots,D_k\}$.

Example 4 (Continued from Example 3). *We can obtain the optemistic multiple rough measure of X by the Preferences 1 and 2, as follows*

$$\rho_o^{[\wr]\geq}(1+2,X)=1-\frac{|\underline{OM}^{[\wr]\geq}_{1+2}(X)|}{|\overline{OM}^{[\wr]\geq}_{1+2}(X)|}=\frac{1}{4}.$$

And we have

$$\underline{OM}^{[\wr]\geq}_{1+2}(D_Y)=\{x_1,x_2,x_6\},\underline{OM}^{[\wr]\geq}_{1+2}(D_N)=\{x_3,x_5\}.$$

Then the opetimistic multiple granulation degree of dependency is

$$\gamma_o^{[\wr]\geq}(1+2,d)=\frac{|\underline{OM}^{[\wr]\geq}_{1+2}(D_Y)|+|\underline{OM}^{[\wr]\geq}_{1+2}(D_N)|}{|U|}=\frac{5}{6}.$$

This shows that the degree of uncertainty is $\frac{1}{4}$ by the Preferences 1 and 2 from the optimistic perspective. And the degree of dependence of the attributes including the Preferences 1 and 2 on decision making is $\frac{5}{6}$ from the optimistic perspective.

4. The Pessimistic Multiple Granulation Rough Set in IIFOIS

In this section, we will introduce another the multiple granulation rough set from a completely optimistic perspective which means that accepting only if all conditions are met and some related properties in an IIFOIS. Similarily, two elementary mesasures and their properties are also provided.

Definition 4. *Let $\mathcal{I}^{[\wr]\geq}=(U,AT,V,f)$ be an IIFOIS, $A_1,A_2,\cdots,A_s\in AT(s\leq 2^{|AT|})$, $R_{A_1}^{[\wr]\geq},R_{A_2}^{[\wr]\geq},\cdots,R_{A_s}^{[\wr]\geq}$ be dominance relations, respectively. For any $X\in P(U)$, we have the operators $\underline{PM}^{[\wr]\geq}_{\sum_{i=1}^{s}A_i}$ and $\overline{PM}^{[\wr]\geq}_{\sum_{i=1}^{s}A_i}$:$P(U)\rightarrow P(U)$, are as follows*

$$\underline{PM}^{[\wr]\geq}_{\sum_{i=1}^{s}A_i}(X)=\{x\in U|\bigwedge_{i=1}^{s}([x]_{A_i}^{[\wr]\geq}\subseteq X)\},$$

$$\overline{PM}^{[\wr]\geq}_{\sum_{i=1}^{s} A_i}(X) = \{x \in U | \bigvee_{i=1}^{s} ([x]^{[\wr]\geq}_{A_i} \cap X \neq \emptyset)\},$$

where "$\bigvee$" means "or"and "$\bigwedge$" means "and". $\underline{PM}^{[\wr]\geq}_{\sum_{i=1}^{s} A_i}(X)$ and $\overline{PM}^{[\wr]\geq}_{\sum_{i=1}^{s} A_i}(X)$ are called the pessimistic multiple granulation lower and upper approximation of X.

Similarily, $\underline{PM}^{[\wr]\geq}_{\sum_{i=1}^{s} A_i}(X) = \overline{PM}^{[\wr]\geq}_{\sum_{i=1}^{s} A_i}(X)$, then X is a pessimistic definable set with respect to multiple granulation dominance relations $A_1, A_2, \cdots, A_s (m \leq 2^{|AT|})$, otherwise X is a pessimistic rough set. $Pos^{[\wr]\geq}_{\sum_{i=1}^{s} A_i}(X) = \underline{PM}^{[\wr]\geq}_{\sum_{i=1}^{s} A_i}(X)$, $Neg^{[\wr]\geq}_{\sum_{i=1}^{s} A_i}(X) = \sim \overline{PM}^{[\wr]\geq}_{\sum_{i=1}^{s} A_i}(X)$ and $Bnd^{[\wr]\geq}_{\sum_{i=1}^{s} A_i}(X) = \overline{PM}^{[\wr]\geq}_{\sum_{i=1}^{s} A_i}(X) - \underline{PM}^{[\wr]\geq}_{\sum_{i=1}^{s} A_i}(X)$.

From the above definition, it can be seen that the lower approximation in the pessimistic multiple granulation rough set is defined by multiple dominance relations, whereas the rough lower approximation in Section 2.3 is represented via those derived by only one dominance relation. And the operation in the lower approximation is "$\bigwedge$". It means that for the object x, the lower approximation condition must be met through all dominance raltions before it can be placed in the lower approximation set. That is what "pessimistic" means.

We will illustrate the above concepts through the following example.

Example 5 (Continued from Example 3). *Now we consider another question:When we consider both of two preferences , which one must be an excellent community? When we consider one of two preferences at least, which one may be an excellent community? We can solve the question according to the definition of the pessimistic multiple granulation rough set. Then we have*

$$\underline{PM}^{[\wr]\geq}_{1+2}(X) = \{x_2, x_6\},$$

$$\overline{PM}^{[\wr]\geq}_{1+2}(X) = \{x_1, x_2, x_4, x_5, x_6\}.$$

We can know that the community x_2, x_6 must be excellent if we consider both of two preferences, and the community x_1, x_2, x_4, x_5, x_6 may be excellent if we consider both of two preferences. Moreover, we can obtain

$$\underline{PM}^{[\wr]\geq}_{1+2}(X) = \underline{R}^{[\wr]\geq}_{1}(X) \cap \underline{R}^{[\wr]\geq}_{2}(X),$$

$$\overline{PM}^{[\wr]\geq}_{1+2}(X) = \overline{R}^{[\wr]\geq}_{1}(X) \cup \overline{R}^{[\wr]\geq}_{2}(X).$$

Proposition 7. *Let $\mathcal{I}^{[\wr]\geq} = (U, AT, V, f)$ be an IIFOIS, $A_1, A_2, \cdots, A_s \in AT (m \leq 2^{|AT|})$, $X, Y \in U$, then the following results hold.*

(PL_1) $\underline{PM}^{[\wr]\geq}_{\sum_{i=1}^{s} A_i}(X) \subseteq X$ (*Contraction*)

(PU_1) $X \subseteq \overline{PM}^{[\wr]\geq}_{\sum_{i=1}^{s} A_i}(X)$ (*Extention*)

(PL_2) $\underline{PM}^{[\wr]\geq}_{\sum_{i=1}^{s} A_i}(\sim X) = \sim \overline{PM}^{[\wr]\geq}_{\sum_{i=1}^{s} A_i}(X)$ (*Duality*)

(PU_2) $\overline{PM}^{[\wr]\geq}_{\sum_{i=1}^{s} A_i}(\sim X) = \sim \underline{PM}^{[\wr]\geq}_{\sum_{i=1}^{s} A_i}(X)$ (*Duality*)

(PL_3) $\underline{PM}^{[\wr]\geq}_{\sum_{i=1}^{s} A_i}(\emptyset) = \emptyset$ (*Normality*)

(PU_3) $\overline{PM}^{[\wr]\geq}_{\sum_{i=1}^{s} A_i}(\emptyset) = \emptyset$ (*Normality*)

(PL_4) $\underline{PM}^{[\wr]\geq}_{\sum_{i=1}^{s} A_i}(U) = U$ (*Co-normality*)

(PU_4) $\overline{PM}^{[\wr]\geq}_{\sum_{i=1}^{s} A_i}(U) = U$ (*Co-normality*)

(PL_5) $\underline{PM}^{[\wr]\geq}_{\sum_{i=1}^{s} A_i}(X \cap Y) = \underline{PM}^{[\wr]\geq}_{\sum_{i=1}^{s} A_i}(X) \cap \underline{PM}^{[\wr]\geq}_{\sum_{i=1}^{s} A_i}(Y)$ (*L-F-multiplication*)

(PU_5) $\overline{PM}^{[\wr]\geq}_{\sum_{i=1}^{s} A_i}(X \cup Y) = \overline{PM}^{[\wr]\geq}_{\sum_{i=1}^{s} A_i}(X) \cup \overline{PM}^{[\wr]\geq}_{\sum_{i=1}^{s} A_i}(Y)$ (*U-F-addition*)

(PL_6) $X \subseteq Y \Rightarrow \underline{PM}^{[\wr]\geq}_{\sum_{i=1}^{s} A_i}(X) \subseteq \underline{PM}^{[\wr]\geq}_{\sum_{i=1}^{s} A_i}(Y)$ (*Monotonicity*)

$$(PU_6)\quad X \subseteq Y \Rightarrow \overline{PM}^{[\wr]\geq}_{\sum_{i=1}^{s} A_i}(X) \subseteq \overline{PM}^{[\wr]\geq}_{\sum_{i=1}^{s} A_i}(Y) \qquad (Monotonicity)$$
$$(PL_7)\quad \underline{PM}^{[\wr]\geq}_{\sum_{i=1}^{s} A_i}(X \cup Y) \supseteq \underline{PM}^{[\wr]\geq}_{\sum_{i=1}^{s} A_i}(X) \cup \underline{PM}^{[\wr]\geq}_{\sum_{i=1}^{s} A_i}(Y) \qquad (L\text{-}F\text{-}addition)$$
$$(PU_7)\quad \overline{PM}^{[\wr]\geq}_{\sum_{i=1}^{s} A_i}(X \cap Y) \subseteq \overline{PM}^{[\wr]\geq}_{\sum_{i=1}^{s} A_i}(X) \cap \overline{PM}^{[\wr]\geq}_{\sum_{i=1}^{s} A_i}(Y) \qquad (U\text{-}F\text{-}multiplication)$$

The proof can be found in Proposition A2 of Appendix A.

Definition 5. *Let $\mathcal{I}^{[\wr]\geq} = (U, AT, V, f)$ be an IIFOIS, $A_i \in AT, i = 1, 2, \cdots, s(s \leq 2^{|AT|})$, $X \in U$, the pessimistic multiple granulation rough measure of X by $\sum_{i=1}^{s} A_i$ is*

$$\rho_p^{[\wr]\geq}(\sum_{i=1}^{s} A_i, X) = 1 - \frac{|\underline{PM}^{[\wr]\geq}_{\sum_{i=1}^{s} A_i}(X)|}{|\overline{PM}^{[\wr]\geq}_{\sum_{i=1}^{s} A_i}(X)|}.$$

Definition 6. *Let $\mathcal{I}^{[\wr]\geq} = (U, CT \cup d, V, f)$ be an IIFDOIS, $A_i \in AT, i = 1, 2, \cdots, s(s \leq 2^{|AT|})$, the quality of approximation of d by $\sum_{i=1}^{s} A_i$, also called the pessimistic degree of dependency. It is defined as*

$$\gamma_p^{[\wr]\geq}(\sum_{i=1}^{s} A_i, d) = \frac{1}{|U|}\sum_{j=1}^{k}(|\underline{PM}^{[\wr]\geq}_{\sum_{i=1}^{s} A_i}(D_j)|),$$

where $R_d^{[\wr]\geq} = \{(x_i, x_j) \in U \times U | f(x_i, d) = f(x_j, d), U/d = \{D_1, D_2, \cdots, D_k\}$.

Example 6 (Continued from Example 3). *We can obtain the pessimistic multiple rough measure of X by the Preference 1 and Preference 2, as follows*

$$\rho_p^{[\wr]\geq}(1+2, X) = 1 - \frac{|\underline{PM}^{[\wr]\geq}_{1+2}(X)|}{|\overline{PM}^{[\wr]\geq}_{1+2}(X)|} = \frac{3}{5}.$$

And we have

$$\underline{PM}^{[\wr]\geq}_{1+2}(D_Y) = \{x_2, x_6\}, \underline{PM}^{[\wr]\geq}_{1+2}(D_N) = \{x_3\}.$$

Then the pessimistic multiple granulation degree of dependency is

$$\gamma_p^{[\wr]\geq}(1+2, d) = \frac{|\underline{PM}^{[\wr]\geq}_{1+2}(D_Y)| + |\underline{PM}^{[\wr]\geq}_{1+2}(D_N)|}{|U|} = \frac{1}{2}.$$

This shows that the degree of uncertainty is $\frac{3}{5}$ by the Preference 1 and Preference 2 from the pessimistic perspective. And the degree of dependence of the attributes including the Preference 1 and Preference 2 on decision making is $\frac{1}{2}$ from the pessimistic perspective.

5. The Generalized Multiple Granulation Rough Set in the IIFOIS

In the OMGRS theory and the PMGRS theory, the conditions for approximate description of the target concept are either too loose or too strict to consider the rule of majority. In this section, we will generalize the OMGRS and the PMGRS to the generalized multiple granulation rough set(GMGRS) in an IIFOIS. From the perspective of the lower approximation, the concept of support feasure function will be given. The upper and lower approximation operators and related properties about the GMGRS will be discussed. In addition, two improtaant rough measures of GMGRS are also provided.

Definition 7. *Let $\mathcal{I}^{[\wr]\geq} = (U, AT, V, f)$ be an IIFOIS, $A_i \in AT, i = 1, 2, \cdots, s(s \leq 2^{|AT|})$. For any $X \in P(U)$, $x \in U$,*

$$S_X^{A_i}(x) = \begin{cases} 1, & [x]_{A_i}^{[\wr]\geq} \subseteq X, \\ 0, & otherwise. \end{cases}$$

$S_X^{A_i}(x)$ is called the support feasure function of the object $x \in U$ about the concept X in the dominance relation A_i.

By Definition 7, we can know that $S_X^{A_i}(x)$ expresses whether x accurately supports the concept X or x has a positive description of X with respect to the cover of A_i to U.

Proposition 8. *Let $\mathcal{I}^{[\wr]\geq} = (U, AT, V, f)$ be an IIFOIS, $A_i \in AT, i = 1, 2, \cdots, s(s \leq 2^{|AT|})$, $X, Y \in P(U)$, $x \in U$. The following properties about the support feature function $S_X^{A_i}(x)$ are established.*

(1) $S_{\sim X}^{A_i}(x) = \begin{cases} 1, & [x]_{A_i}^{[\wr]\geq} \cap X = \emptyset, \\ 0, & [x]_{A_i}^{[\wr]\geq} \cap X \neq \emptyset. \end{cases}$

(2) $S_{\emptyset}^{A_i}(x) = 0, S_U^{A_i}(x) = 1.$

(3) $S_{X \cup Y}^{A_i}(x) \geq S_X^{A_i}(x) \vee S_Y^{A_i}(x).$

(4) $S_{X \cap Y}^{A_i}(x) = S_X^{A_i}(x) \wedge S_Y^{A_i}(x).$

(5) $X \subseteq Y \Rightarrow S_X^{A_i}(x) \leq S_Y^{A_i}(x).$

(6) $X \subseteq Y \Rightarrow S_{\sim X}^{A_i}(x) \geq S_{\sim Y}^{A_i}(x).$

The proof can be found in Proposition A3 of Appendix A.

"$\vee$" and "$\wedge$" represent the operation of taking small and taking big, respectively.

Definition 8. *Let $\mathcal{I}^{[\wr]\geq} = (U, AT, V, f)$ be an IIFOIS, $A_i \in AT, i = 1, 2, \cdots, s(s \leq 2^{|AT|})$, $\beta \in (0.5, 1]$. For any $X \in P(U)$, $S_X^{A_i}(x)$ is the support feature function of x, then the lower and upper approximations of X by $\sum_{i=1}^{s} S_X^{A_i}$ are as follows*

$$\underline{GM}^{[\wr]\geq}_{\sum_{i=1}^{s} A_i}(X)_\beta = \{x \in U | \frac{\sum_{i=1}^{s} S_X^{A_i}(x)}{s} \geq \beta\},$$

$$\overline{GM}^{[\wr]\geq}_{\sum_{i=1}^{s} A_i}(X)_\beta = \{x \in U | \frac{\sum_{i=1}^{s}(1 - S_{\sim X}^{A_i}(x))}{s} > 1 - \beta\}.$$

X is called a definable set with respect to $\sum_{i=1}^{s} A_i$ if and only if $\underline{GM}^{[\wr]\geq}_{\sum_{i=1}^{s} A_i}(X)_\beta = \overline{OM}^{[\wr]\geq}_{\sum_{i=1}^{s} A_i}(X)_\beta$; otherwise X is a rough set . The model is the generalized multiple granulation rough set(GMGRS) model, and β is callede information level of $\sum_{i=1}^{s} A_i$.

Different from the optimistic and pessimistic multiple granulation rough sets, the lower approximation in the generalized multiple granulation rough set is defined by the proportion of dominance relations that meet the lower approximation condition. In fact, the GMGRS will degenerated into the OMGRS and PMGRS only when $\beta = \frac{1}{s}$ and $\beta = 1$, respectively.

Proposition 9. *Let $\mathcal{I}^{[\wr]\geq} = (U, AT, V, f)$ be an IIFOIS, $A_i \in AT, i = 1, 2, \cdots, s(s \leq 2^{|AT|})$, $\beta \in (0.5, 1]$. For any $X, Y \in P(U)$, the following results hold.*

(1L) $\underline{GM}^{[\wr]\geq}_{\sum_{i=1}^{s} A_i}(\sim X)_\beta = \sim \overline{GM}^{[\wr]\geq}_{\sum_{i=1}^{s} A_i}(X)_\beta$ *(Duality)*

(1U) $\overline{GM}^{[\wr]\geq}_{\sum_{i=1}^{s} A_i}(\sim X)_\beta = \sim \underline{GM}^{[\wr]\geq}_{\sum_{i=1}^{s} A_i}(X)_\beta$ *(Duality)*

(2L) $\underline{GM}^{[\wr]\geq}_{\sum_{i=1}^{s} A_i}(X)_\beta \subseteq X$ *(Contraction)*

(2U) $X \subseteq \overline{GM}^{[\wr]\geq}_{\sum_{i=1}^{s} A_i}(X)_\beta$ *(Extention)*

(3L) $\underline{GM}^{[\wr]\geq}_{\sum_{i=1}^{s} A_i}(\emptyset)_\beta = \emptyset$ *(Normality)*

(3U) $\overline{GM}^{[\wr]\geq}_{\sum_{i=1}^{s} A_i}(\emptyset)_\beta = \emptyset$ *(Normality)*

(4L) $\underline{GM}^{[\wr]\geq}_{\sum_{i=1}^{s} A_i}(U)_\beta = U$ (Co-normality)
(4U) $\overline{GM}^{[\wr]\geq}_{\sum_{i=1}^{s} A_i}(U)_\beta = U$ (Co-normality)
(5L) $X \subseteq Y \Rightarrow \underline{GM}^{[\wr]\geq}_{\sum_{i=1}^{s} A_i}(X)_\beta \subseteq \underline{GM}^{[\wr]\geq}_{\sum_{i=1}^{s} A_i}(Y)_\beta$ (Monotonicity)
(5U) $X \subseteq Y \Rightarrow \overline{GM}^{[\wr]\geq}_{\sum_{i=1}^{s} A_i}(X)_\beta \subseteq \overline{GM}^{[\wr]\geq}_{\sum_{i=1}^{s} A_i}(Y)_\beta$ (Monotonicity)
(6L) $\underline{GM}^{[\wr]\geq}_{\sum_{i=1}^{s} A_i}(X \cap Y)_\beta \subseteq \underline{GM}^{[\wr]\geq}_{\sum_{i=1}^{s} A_i}(X)_\beta \cap \underline{GM}^{[\wr]\geq}_{\sum_{i=1}^{s} A_i}(Y)_\beta$ (L-F-multiplication)
(6U) $\overline{GM}^{[\wr]\geq}_{\sum_{i=1}^{s} A_i}(X \cup Y)_\beta \supseteq \overline{GM}^{[\wr]\geq}_{\sum_{i=1}^{s} A_i}(X)_\beta \cup \overline{GM}^{[\wr]\geq}_{\sum_{i=1}^{s} A_i}(Y)_\beta$ (L-F-addition)
(7L) $\underline{GM}^{[\wr]\geq}_{\sum_{i=1}^{s} A_i}(X \cup Y)_\beta \supseteq \underline{GM}^{[\wr]\geq}_{\sum_{i=1}^{s} A_i}(X)_\beta \cup \underline{GM}^{[\wr]\geq}_{\sum_{i=1}^{s} A_i}(Y)_\beta$ (L-F-addition)
(7U) $\overline{GM}^{[\wr]\geq}_{\sum_{i=1}^{s} A_i}(X \cap Y)_\beta \subseteq \overline{GM}^{[\wr]\geq}_{\sum_{i=1}^{s} A_i}(X)_\beta \cap \overline{GM}^{[\wr]\geq}_{\sum_{i=1}^{s} A_i}(Y)_\beta$ (L-F-multiplication)

The proof can be found in Proposition A4 of Appendix A.

Proposition 10. *Let $\mathcal{I}^{[\wr]\geq} = (U, AT, V, f)$ be an IIFOIS, $A_i \in AT, i = 1, 2, \cdots, s(s \leq 2^{|AT|})$. For any $\alpha \in (0.5, 1]$, $\beta \in (0.5, 1]$ and $\alpha \leq \beta$, $t \leq s$, $X \in P(U)$, then the following properties hold.*
(1) $\underline{GM}^{[\wr]\geq}_{\sum_{i=1}^{s} A_i}(X)_\beta \subseteq \underline{GM}^{[\wr]\geq}_{\sum_{i=1}^{s} A_i}(X)_\alpha$.
(2) $\overline{GM}^{[\wr]\geq}_{\sum_{i=1}^{s} A_i}(X)_\alpha \subseteq \overline{GM}^{[\wr]\geq}_{\sum_{i=1}^{s} A_i}(X)_\beta$.
(3) $\underline{GM}^{[\wr]\geq}_{\sum_{i=1}^{t} A_i}(X)_\beta \subseteq \underline{GM}^{[\wr]\geq}_{\sum_{i=1}^{s} A_i}(X)_\beta$.
(4) $\overline{GM}^{[\wr]\geq}_{\sum_{i=1}^{s} A_i}(X)_\beta \subseteq \overline{GM}^{[\wr]\geq}_{\sum_{i=1}^{t} A_i}(X)_\beta$.

The proof can be found in Proposition A5 of Appendix A.

Example 7 (Continued from Example 3)**.** *However, some consumers only prefer one of the four community attributes.*
Preference 1:Only the location is better.
Preference 2:Only the unility service is better.
Preference 3:Only the type of layout is better.
Preference 4:Only the environment is better.

By Preference 1, 2, 3, 4, we can get that four dominance relations.

$$R_1 = \begin{pmatrix} 1 & 0 & 1 & 1 & 0 & 0 \\ 1 & 1 & 1 & 1 & 1 & 0 \\ 0 & 0 & 1 & 0 & 0 & 0 \\ 0 & 0 & 1 & 1 & 0 & 0 \\ 1 & 0 & 1 & 1 & 1 & 0 \\ 1 & 1 & 1 & 1 & 1 & 1 \end{pmatrix}, R_2 = \begin{pmatrix} 1 & 1 & 1 & 1 & 1 & 1 \\ 0 & 1 & 1 & 1 & 0 & 0 \\ 0 & 0 & 1 & 1 & 0 & 0 \\ 0 & 0 & 0 & 1 & 0 & 0 \\ 0 & 1 & 1 & 1 & 1 & 0 \\ 0 & 1 & 1 & 1 & 1 & 1 \end{pmatrix},$$

$$R_3 = \begin{pmatrix} 1 & 1 & 0 & 0 & 0 & 0 \\ 0 & 1 & 0 & 0 & 0 & 0 \\ 1 & 1 & 1 & 1 & 1 & 0 \\ 1 & 1 & 0 & 1 & 1 & 0 \\ 1 & 1 & 0 & 0 & 1 & 0 \\ 1 & 1 & 1 & 1 & 1 & 1 \end{pmatrix}, R_4 = \begin{pmatrix} 1 & 1 & 1 & 1 & 0 & 1 \\ 0 & 1 & 1 & 1 & 0 & 1 \\ 0 & 0 & 1 & 1 & 0 & 1 \\ 0 & 0 & 0 & 1 & 0 & 0 \\ 1 & 1 & 1 & 1 & 1 & 1 \\ 0 & 0 & 0 & 1 & 0 & 1 \end{pmatrix}.$$

When we consider at least three of the four preferences, which one must be an excellent community? When we consider at least one of the four preferences, which one may be an excellent community? Unlike the OMGRS and the PMGRS, we can deal with this situation through the GMGRS. The support feature function of objects are in Table 2.

Let $\beta = 0.75$, then we have

$$\underline{GM}^{[?]\geq}_{\sum_{i=1}^{4} A_i}(X)_\beta = \{x_6\},$$

$$\overline{GM}^{[?]\geq}_{\sum_{i=1}^{4} A_i}(X)_\beta = \{x_1, x_2, x_3, x_4, x_5, x_6\}.$$

We can know that the community x_6 must be excellent when we consider at least three of the four preferences, and the community $x_1, x_2, x_3, x_4, x_5, x_6$ may be excellent when we consider at least one of the four preferences.

Definition 9. *Let $\mathcal{I}^{[?]\geq} = (U, AT, V, f)$ be an IIFOIS, $A_i \in AT, i = 1, 2, \cdots, s(s \leq 2^{|AT|})$, $\beta \in (0.5, 1]$. For any $X \in U$. The generalized multiple granulation rough measure of X by $\sum_{i=1}^{s} A_i$ is*

$$\rho_g^{[?]\geq}(\sum_{i=1}^{s} A_i, X) = 1 - \frac{|\underline{GM}^{[?]\geq}_{\sum_{i=1}^{s} A_i}(X)_\beta|}{|\overline{GM}^{[?]\geq}_{\sum_{i=1}^{s} A_i}(X)_\beta|}.$$

Definition 10. *Let $\mathcal{I}^{[?]\geq} = (U, CT \cup d, V, f)$ be an IIFDOIS, $A_i \in AT, i = 1, 2, \cdots, s(s \leq 2^{|AT|})$, $\beta \in (0.5, 1]$. The quality of approximation of d by $\sum_{i=1}^{s} A_i$, also called the generalized degree of dependency, is defined as*

$$\gamma_g^{[?]\geq}(\sum_{i=1}^{s} A_i, d) = \frac{1}{|U|} \sum_{j=1}^{k} (|\underline{GM}^{[?]\geq}_{\sum_{i=1}^{s} A_i}(D_j)_\beta)|),$$

where $R_d^{[?]\geq} = \{(x_i, x_j) \in U \times U | f(x_i, d) = f(x_j, d), U/d = \{D_1, D_2, \cdots, D_k\}$.

Example 8 (Continued from Example 7). *The generalized multiple granulation rough measure of X by $\sum_{i=1}^{4} A_i$ is*

$$\rho_g^{[?]\geq}(\sum_{i=1}^{4} A_i, X) = 1 - \frac{|\underline{GM}^{[?]\geq}_{\sum_{i=1}^{4} A_i}(X)_\beta|}{|\overline{GM}^{[?]\geq}_{\sum_{i=1}^{4} A_i}(X)_\beta|} = \frac{5}{6},$$

and

$$\underline{GM}^{[?]\geq}_{\sum_{i=1}^{4} A_i}(D_Y)_\beta = \{x_6\}, \overline{GM}^{[?]\geq}_{\sum_{i=1}^{4} A_i}(D_N)_\beta = \emptyset,$$

so

$$\gamma_g^{[?]\geq}(\sum_{i=1}^{4} A_i, d) = \frac{|\underline{GM}^{[?]\geq}_{\sum_{i=1}^{4} A_i}(D_Y)_\beta)| + |\underline{GM}^{[?]\geq}_{\sum_{i=1}^{4} A_i}(D_N)_\beta)|}{|U|} = \frac{1}{6}.$$

This shows that the degree of uncertainty is $\frac{5}{6}$ by the Preferences 1 and 2 considering an intermediate situation between the optimistic and the pessimistic. And the degree of dependence of the attributes including the Preferences 1 and 2 on decision making is $\frac{1}{6}$ considering an intermediate situation between optimistic and pessimistic.

6. Differences and Relationships among the Dominance Relation Rough Set, the OMGRS and the PMGRS in an IIFOIS

We have known the definitions and properties of the multiple granulation rough set in an IIFOIS by the above sections. In this section, we will investigate differences and relationships among the dominance relation rough set, the OMGRS, the PMGRS and the GMGRS in an IIFOIS.

Proposition 11. *Let $\mathcal{I}^{[?]\geq} = (U, AT, V, f)$ be an IIFOIS, $A_i \in AT, i = 1, 2, \cdots, s(s \leq 2^{|AT|})$. $X \in P(U)$. Then the following properties hold.*

(1) $\underline{OM}^{[?]\geq}_{\sum_{i=1}^{s} A_i}(X) \subseteq \underline{R}^{[?]\geq}_{\cup_{i=1}^{s} A_i}(X)$.

(2) $\overline{OM}^{[\wr]\geq}_{\sum_{i=1}^{s} A_i}(X) \supseteq \overline{R}^{[\wr]\geq}_{\bigcup_{i=1}^{s} A_i}(X)$.
(3) $\underline{PM}^{[\wr]\geq}_{\sum_{i=1}^{s} A_i}(X) \subseteq \underline{R}^{[\wr]\geq}_{\bigcup_{i=1}^{s} A_i}(X)$.
(4) $\overline{PM}^{[\wr]\geq}_{\sum_{i=1}^{s} A_i}(X) \supseteq \overline{R}^{[\wr]\geq}_{\bigcup_{i=1}^{s} A_i}(X)$.

The proof can be found in Proposition A6 of Appendix A.

Proposition 12. *Let $\mathcal{I}^{[\wr]\geq} = (U, AT, V, f)$ be an IIFOIS, $A_i \in AT, i = 1, 2, \cdots, s (s \leq 2^{|AT|})$, $X \in U$. Then the following properties hold.*
(1) $\underline{OM}^{[\wr]\geq}_{\sum_{i=1}^{s} A_i}(X) = \bigcup_{i=1}^{s} \underline{R}^{[\wr]\geq}_{A_i}(X)$.
(2) $\overline{OM}^{[\wr]\geq}_{\sum_{i=1}^{s} A_i}(X) = \bigcap_{i=1}^{s} \overline{R}^{[\wr]\geq}_{A_i}(X)$.
(3) $\underline{PM}^{[\wr]\geq}_{\sum_{i=1}^{s} A_i}(X) = \bigcap_{i=1}^{s} \underline{R}^{[\wr]\geq}_{A_i}(X)$.
(4) $\overline{PM}^{[\wr]\geq}_{\sum_{i=1}^{s} A_i}(X) = \bigcup_{i=1}^{s} \overline{R}^{[\wr]\geq}_{A_i}(X)$.

The proof can be found in Proposition A7 of Appendix A.

Proposition 13. *Let $\mathcal{I}^{[\wr]\geq} = (U, AT, V, f)$ be an IIFOIS, $A_i \in AT, i = 1, 2, \cdots, s (s \leq 2^{|AT|})$, $X \in U, Y \in U$. Then we have*
(1) $\underline{OM}^{[\wr]\geq}_{\sum_{i=1}^{s} A_i}(X \cap Y) = \bigcup_{i=1}^{s}(\underline{R}^{[\wr]\geq}_{A_i}(X) \cap \underline{R}^{[\wr]\geq}_{A_i}(Y))$.
(2) $\overline{OM}^{[\wr]\geq}_{\sum_{i=1}^{s} A_i}(X \cup Y) = \bigcap_{i=1}^{s}(\overline{R}^{[\wr]\geq}_{A_i}(X) \cup \overline{R}^{[\wr]\geq}_{A_i}(Y))$.
(3) $\underline{PM}^{[\wr]\geq}_{\sum_{i=1}^{s} A_i}(X \cap Y) = \bigcap_{i=1}^{s}(\underline{R}^{[\wr]\geq}_{A_i}(X) \cap \underline{R}^{[\wr]\geq}_{A_i}(Y))$.
(4) $\overline{PM}^{[\wr]\geq}_{\sum_{i=1}^{s} A_i}(X \cup Y) = \bigcup_{i=1}^{s}(\overline{R}^{[\wr]\geq}_{A_i}(X) \cup \overline{R}^{[\wr]\geq}_{A_i}(Y))$.

The proof can be found in Proposition A8 of Appendix A.

Proposition 14. *Let $\mathcal{I}^{[\wr]\geq} = (U, AT, V, f)$ be an IIFOIS, $A_i \in AT, i = 1, 2, \cdots, s (s \leq 2^{|AT|})$, $X \in P(U)$, the lower and upper approximations of the OMGRS and the PMGRS by the support festure function are*
(1) $\underline{OM}^{[\wr]\geq}_{\sum_{i=1}^{s} A_i}(X) = \{x \in U | \frac{\sum_{i=1}^{s} S_X^{A_i}(x)}{s} > 0\}$, $\overline{OM}^{[\wr]\geq}_{\sum_{i=1}^{s} A_i}(X) = \{x \in U | \frac{\sum_{i=1}^{s}(1 - S_{\sim X}^{A_i}(x))}{s} \geq 1\}$.
(2) $\underline{PM}^{[\wr]\geq}_{\sum_{i=1}^{s} A_i}(X) = \{x \in U | \frac{\sum_{i=1}^{s} S_X^{A_i}(x)}{s} \geq 1\}$, $\overline{PM}^{[\wr]\geq}_{\sum_{i=1}^{s} A_i}(X) = \{x \in U | \frac{\sum_{i=1}^{s}(1 - S_{\sim X}^{A_i}(x))}{s} > 0\}$.

The proof can be found in Proposition A9 of Appendix A.

Proposition 15. *Let $\mathcal{I}^{[\wr]]\geq} = (U, AT, V, f)$ be an IIFOIS, $A_i \in AT, i = 1, 2, \cdots, s (s \leq 2^{|AT|})$, $\beta \in (0.5, 1]$, $X \in U$. Then we have*
(1) $\underline{PM}^{[\wr]\geq}_{\sum_{i=1}^{s} A_i}(X) \subseteq \underline{GM}^{[\wr]\geq}_{\sum_{i=1}^{s} A_i}(X)_\beta \subseteq \underline{OM}^{[\wr]\geq}_{\sum_{i=1}^{s} A_i}(X) \subseteq \underline{R}^{[\wr]\geq}_{\bigcup_{i=1}^{s} A_i}(X)$.
(2) $\overline{PM}^{[\wr]\geq}_{\sum_{i=1}^{s} A_i}(X) \supseteq \underline{GM}^{[\wr]\geq}_{\sum_{i=1}^{s} A_i}(X)_\beta \supseteq \overline{OM}^{[\wr]\geq}_{\sum_{i=1}^{s} A_i}(X) \supseteq \overline{R}^{[\wr]\geq}_{\bigcup_{i=1}^{s} A_i}(X)$.
(3) $\underline{PM}^{[\wr]\geq}_{\sum_{i=1}^{s} A_i}(X) \subseteq \underline{R}^{[\wr]\geq}_{A_i}(X) \subseteq \underline{OM}^{[\wr]\geq}_{\sum_{i=1}^{s} A_i}(X) \subseteq \underline{R}^{[\wr]\geq}_{\bigcup_{i=1}^{s} A_i}(X)$.
(4) $\overline{PM}^{[\wr]\geq}_{\sum_{i=1}^{s} A_i}(X) \supseteq \overline{R}^{[\wr]\geq}_{A_i}(X) \supseteq \overline{OM}^{[\wr]\geq}_{\sum_{i=1}^{s} A_i}(X) \supseteq \overline{R}^{[\wr]\geq}_{\bigcup_{i=1}^{s} A_i}(X)$.

The proof can be found in Proposition A10 of Appendix A.

Example 9 (Continued from Example 3)**.** *By computing, we can obtain that approximations of the target set X by $Preference\ 1 \cup Preference\ 2$.*

$$\underline{R}^{[\wr]\geq}_{1\cup 2}(X) = \{x_1, x_2, x_6\},$$

$$\overline{R}^{[\wr]\geq}_{1\cup 2}(X) = \{x_1, x_2, x_4, x_6\},$$

then

$$\underline{PM}^{[\wr]\geq}_{1+2}(X) \subseteq \underline{OM}^{[\wr]\geq}_{1+2}(X) \subseteq \underline{R}^{[\wr]\geq}_{1\cup 2}(X) \subseteq X \subseteq \overline{R}^{[\wr]\geq}_{1\cup 2}(X) \subseteq \overline{OM}^{[\wr]\geq}_{1+2}(X) \subseteq \overline{PM}^{[\wr]\geq}_{1+2}(X).$$

Proposition 16. *Let $\mathcal{I}^{[\wr]\geq} = (U, AT, V, f)$ be an IIFOIS, $A_i \in AT, i = 1, 2, \cdots, s(s \leq 2^{|AT|})$, $X \in U$. Then*
(1) $\rho^{[\wr]\geq}(R^{[\wr]\geq}_{A_i}, X) \geq \rho^{[\wr]\geq}_{o}(\sum_{i=1}^{s} A_i, X) \geq \rho^{[\wr]\geq}(R^{[\wr]\geq}_{\cup_{i=1}^{s} A_i}, X)$.
(2) $\rho^{[\wr]\geq}_{p}(\sum_{i=1}^{s} A_i, X) \geq \rho^{[\wr]\geq}(R^{[\wr]\geq}_{A_i}, X) \geq \rho^{[\wr]\geq}(R^{[\wr]\geq}_{\cup_{i=1}^{s} A_i}, X)$.
(3) $\rho^{[\wr]\geq}_{p}(\sum_{i=1}^{s} A_i, X) \geq \rho^{[\wr]\geq}(R^{[\wr]\geq}_{A_i}, X) \geq \rho^{[\wr]\geq}_{o}(\sum_{i=1}^{s} A_i, X) \geq \rho^{[\wr]\geq}(R^{[\wr]\geq}_{\cup_{i=1}^{s} A_i}, X)$.

The proof can be found in Proposition A11 of Appendix A.

Example 10 (Continued from Example 3)**.** *Computing the opetimistic rough measure of the target set $X = D_Y = \{x_1, x_2, x_6\}$ according to the results in Example 3, it follows that*

$$\rho^{[\wr]\geq}(1, X) = 1 - \frac{|\underline{R}^{[\wr]\geq}_{1}(X)|}{|\overline{R}^{[\wr]\geq}_{1}(X)|} = \frac{2}{5}, \rho^{[\wr]\geq}(2, X) = 1 - \frac{|\underline{R}^{[\wr]\geq}_{2}(X)|}{|\overline{R}^{[\wr]\geq}_{2}(X)|} = \frac{1}{2},$$

$$\rho^{[\wr]\geq}(1\cup 2, X) = 1 - \frac{|\underline{R}^{[\wr]\geq}_{1\cup 2}(X)|}{|\overline{R}^{[\wr]\geq}_{1\cup 2}(X)|} = \frac{1}{4}, \rho^{[\wr]\geq}_{o}(1+2, X) = 1 - \frac{|\underline{OM}^{[\wr]\geq}_{1+2}(X)|}{|\overline{OM}^{[\wr]\geq}_{1+2}(X)|} = \frac{1}{4}, \rho^{[\wr]\geq}_{p}(1+2, X) = 1 - \frac{|\underline{PM}^{[\wr]\geq}_{1+2}(X)|}{|\overline{PM}^{[\wr]\geq}_{1+2}(X)|} = \frac{3}{5},$$

then

$$\rho^{[\wr]\geq}_{p}(1+2, X) \geq \rho^{[\wr]\geq}(1, X) \geq \rho^{[\wr]\geq}_{o}(1+2, X) \geq \rho^{[\wr]\geq}(1\cup 2, X).$$

Proposition 17. *Let $\mathcal{I}^{[\wr]\geq} = (U, CT \cup d, V, f)$ be an IIFDOIS, $A_i \in AT, i = 1, 2, \cdots, s(s \leq 2^{|AT|})$. Then*
(1) $\gamma^{[\wr]\geq}(R^{[\wr]\geq}_{A_i}, d) \leq \gamma^{[\wr]\geq}_{o}(\sum_{i=1}^{s} A_i, d) \leq \gamma^{[\wr]\geq}(R^{[\wr]\geq}_{\cup_{i=1}^{s} A_i}, d)$.
(2) $\gamma^{[\wr]\geq}_{p}(\sum_{i=1}^{s} A_i, d) \leq \gamma^{[\wr]\geq}(R^{[\wr]ge}_{A_i}, d) \leq \gamma^{[\wr]\geq}(R^{[\wr]\geq}_{\cup_{i=1}^{s} A_i}, d)$.
(3) $\gamma^{[\wr]\geq}_{p}(\sum_{i=1}^{s} A_i, d) \leq \gamma^{[\wr]ge}(R^{[\wr]\geq}_{A_i}, d) \leq \gamma^{[\wr]\geq}_{o}(\sum_{i=1}^{s} A_i, d) \leq \gamma^{[\wr]\geq}(R^{[\wr]\geq}_{\cup_{i=1}^{s} A_i}, d)$.

The proof can be found in Proposition A12 of Appendix A.

Example 11 (Continued from Example 3)**.** *Computing the degree of dedpendence by the single granulation and multipe granulations. From Table 2, $U/d = \{D_Y, D_N\}, D_Y = \{x_1, x_2, x_6\}, D_N = \{x_3, x_4, x_5\}$.*

$$R^{[\wr]\geq}_{1}(D_Y) = \{x_1, x_2, x_6\}, R^{[\wr]\geq}_{2}(D_Y) = \{x_2, x_6\}, R^{[\wr]\geq}_{1\cup 2}(D_Y) = \{x_1, x_2, x_6\},$$

$$R^{[\wr]\geq}_{1}(D_N) = \{x_3\}, R^{[\wr]\geq}_{2}(D_N) = \{x_3, x_5\}, R^{[\wr]\geq}_{1\cup 2}(D_N) = \{x_3, x_5\},$$

then we have

$$\gamma^{[\wr]\geq}(1, d) = \frac{1}{|U|}(|\underline{R}^{[\wr]\geq}_{1}(D_Y)| + |\underline{R}^{[\wr]\geq}_{1}(D_N)|) = \frac{2}{3},$$

$$\gamma^{[\wr]\geq}(2, d) = \frac{1}{|U|}(|\underline{R}^{[\wr]\geq}_{2}(D_Y)| + |\underline{R}^{[\wr]\geq}_{2}(D_N)|) = \frac{2}{3},$$

$$\gamma^{[\wr]\geq}(1 \cup 2, d) = \frac{1}{|U|}(|\underline{R}^{[\wr]\geq}_{1\cup 2}(D_Y)| + |\underline{R}^{[\wr]\geq}_{1\cup 2}(D_N)|) = \frac{5}{6}.$$

Moreover,

$$\underline{OM}^{[\wr]\geq}_{1+2}(D_Y) = \{x_1, x_2, x_6\}, \underline{OM}^{[\wr]\geq}_{1+2}(D_N) = \{x_3, x_5\},$$

then we have

$$\gamma_o^{[\wr]\geq}(1 + 2, d) = \frac{1}{|U|}(\underline{OM}^{[\wr]\geq}_{1+2}(D_Y) + \underline{OM}^{[\wr]\geq}_{1+2}(D_N)) = \frac{5}{6}.$$

Moreover,

$$\underline{PM}^{[\wr]\geq}_{1+2}(D_Y) = \{x_2, x_6\}, \underline{PM}^{[\wr]\geq}_{1+2}(D_N) = \{x_3\},$$

then we have

$$\gamma_p^{[\wr]\geq}(1 + 2, d) = \frac{1}{|U|}(\underline{OM}^{[\wr]\geq}_{1+2}(D_Y) + \underline{OM}^{[\wr]\geq}_{1+2}(D_N)) = \frac{1}{2}.$$

Then

$$\gamma_p^{[\wr]\geq}(1 + 2, d) \leq \gamma^{[\wr]\geq}(1, d) \leq \gamma_o^{[\wr]\geq}(1 + 2, d) \leq \gamma^{[\wr]\geq}(1 \cup 2, d).$$

7. Conclusions

The rough set and the intuitionistic fuzzy set are two important tools to describe the uncertainty and vagueness of knowledge, and have been widely applied in the field of granular computing and attribute selection. And intervaling the intuitionisric fuzzy set is very helpful and meaningful. Through this paper, we have gotten a rough set model and three types of the multiple granulation rough set model in an IIFOIS. In addition, we have made the conclusion about differences and relationships among the dominance relation rough set, the OMGRS and the PMGRS in an IIFOIS. In this paper, we introduced two types of MGRS models in the IIFOIS, utilizing which granular structures of the lower and upper approximation operators of the target concept were addressed. Moreover, we investigated a number of improtant properties about the two types of MGRS models and several measures were also discussed, such as the rough measure and the quality of approxiamtion. Futhermore, a more general MGRS was provided and related properties and rough measures were discussed. In addition, the relationships and differences among the single granulation rough set, the three types of MGRS and their measures based on an IIFOIS. In order to help us to apply the MGRS model theory in actual problems, a real example was provided.

The feature selection is a hot research area at present. This paper has established a rough set theoretical model based on the IIFOIS. In our further research, on the basis of what we have done, we can do some related work around the feature selection. On the one hand, we can explore the attribute reduction including the lower and upper approximation reductions based on the rough model we have established in an IIFOIS. On the other hand, we can research dynamic updating approximations utilizing the results of this work. In addition, we can also use the results of this paper to do some works about multiple source information fusion.

Author Contributions: Conceptualization, X.Z.; methodology, X.Z. and Z.L.; investigation,X.Z. and Z.L.; writing Z.L.; supervision, X.Z.; funding acquisition, X.Z. Both authors have read and agreed to the published version of the manuscript.

Funding: This research was supported by National Natural Science Foundation of China (Nos.61976245, 61172002).

Institutional Review Board Statement: Not applicable.

Informed Consent Statement: Not applicable.

Conflicts of Interest: Xiaoyan Zhang has received research grants from National Natural Science Foundation of China(Nos.61976245, 61172002). And this work was supported by these grants. Authors declare that they have no conflict of interest.

Appendix A

In this section, we will give corresponding proofs to some propositions in this article.

Proposition A1. *Let $\mathcal{I}^{[\wr]\geq} = (U, AT, V, f)$ be an IIFOIS, $A_1, A_2, \cdots, A_s \in AT (m \leq 2^{|AT|})$, $X \in U$, then the following results hold.*

(OL$_1$) $\underline{OM}^{[\wr]\geq}_{\sum_{i=1}^{s} A_i}(X) \subseteq X$ *(Contraction)*

(OU$_1$) $X \subseteq \overline{OM}^{[\wr]\geq}_{\sum_{i=1}^{s} A_i}(X)$ *(Extention)*

(OL$_2$) $\underline{OM}^{[\wr]\geq}_{\sum_{i=1}^{s} A_i}(\sim X) = \sim \overline{OM}^{[\wr]\geq}_{\sum_{i=1}^{s} A_i}(X)$ *(Duality)*

(OU$_2$) $\overline{OM}^{[\wr]\geq}_{\sum_{i=1}^{s} A_i}(\sim X) = \sim \underline{OM}^{[\wr]\geq}_{\sum_{i=1}^{s} A_i}(X)$ *(Duality)*

(OL$_3$) $\underline{OM}^{[\wr]\geq}_{\sum_{i=1}^{s} A_i}(\emptyset) = \emptyset$ *(Normality)*

(OU$_3$) $\overline{OM}^{[\wr]\geq}_{\sum_{i=1}^{s} A_i}(\emptyset) = \emptyset$ *(Normality)*

(OL$_4$) $\underline{OM}^{[\wr]\geq}_{\sum_{i=1}^{s} A_i}(U) = U$ *(Co-normality)*

(OU$_4$) $\overline{OM}^{[\wr]\geq}_{\sum_{i=1}^{s} A_i}(U) = U$ *(Co-normality)*

(OL$_5$) $\underline{OM}^{[\wr]\geq}_{\sum_{i=1}^{s} A_i}(X \cap Y) \subseteq \underline{OM}^{[\wr]\geq}_{\sum_{i=1}^{s} A_i}(X) \cap \underline{OM}^{[\wr]\geq}_{\sum_{i=1}^{s} A_i}(Y)$ *(L-F-multiplication)*

(OU$_5$) $\overline{OM}^{[\wr]\geq}_{\sum_{i=1}^{s} A_i}(X \cup Y) \supseteq \overline{OM}^{[\wr]\geq}_{\sum_{i=1}^{s} A_i}(X) \cup \overline{OM}^{[\wr]\geq}_{\sum_{i=1}^{s} A_i}(Y)$ *(U-F-addition)*

(OL$_6$) $X \subseteq Y \Rightarrow \underline{OM}^{[\wr]\geq}_{\sum_{i=1}^{s} A_i}(X) \subseteq \underline{OM}^{[\wr]\geq}_{\sum_{i=1}^{s} A_i}(Y)$ *(Monotonicity)*

(OU$_6$) $X \subseteq Y \Rightarrow \overline{OM}^{[\wr]\geq}_{\sum_{i=1}^{s} A_i}(X) \subseteq \overline{OM}^{[\wr]\geq}_{\sum_{i=1}^{s} A_i}(Y)$ *(Monotonicity)*

(OL$_7$) $\underline{OM}^{[\wr]\geq}_{\sum_{i=1}^{s} A_i}(X \cup Y) \supseteq \underline{OM}^{[\wr]\geq}_{\sum_{i=1}^{s} A_i}(X) \cup \underline{OM}^{[\wr]\geq}_{\sum_{i=1}^{s} A_i}(Y)$ *(L-F-addition)*

(OU$_7$) $\overline{OM}^{[\wr]\geq}_{\sum_{i=1}^{s} A_{i=l}}(X \cap Y) \subseteq \overline{OM}^{[\wr]\geq}_{\sum_{i=1}^{s} A_i}(X) \cap \overline{OM}^{[\wr]\geq}_{\sum_{i=1}^{s} A_i}(Y)$ *(U-F-multiplication)*

Proof. For convenience, we will prove that the results only when $s = 2$, which there are two dominance relations($A, B \subseteq AT$) in an IIFOIS. All terms hold obviously when $A = B$. The following is the proof when $A \neq B$.

(OL$_1$) For any $x \in \underline{OM}^{[\wr]\geq}_{A+B}(X)$, according to the Definition 1 we can know that $[x]^{[\wr]\geq}_A \subseteq X$ or $[x]^{[\wr]\geq}_B \subseteq X$. Besides $x \in [x]^{[\wr]\geq}_A$ and $x \in [x]^{[\wr]\geq}_B$. So we can have that $x \in X$. Therefore, $\underline{OM}^{[\wr]\geq}_{A+B}(X) \subseteq X$.

(OU$_1$) For any $x \in X, x \in [x]^{[\wr]\geq}_A$ and $x \in [x]^{[\wr]\geq}_B$, then $[x]^{[\wr]\geq}_A \cap X \neq \emptyset$ and $[x]^{[\wr]\geq}_B \cap X \neq \emptyset$. It is also to say $x \in \overline{OM}^{[\wr]\geq}_{A+B}(X)$. Therefore, $X \subseteq \overline{OM}^{[\wr]\geq}_{A+B}(X)$.

(OL$_2$) For any $x \in \underline{OM}^{[\wr]\geq}_{A+B}(\sim X)$, we have that

$$\begin{aligned} x \in \underline{OM}^{[\wr]\geq}_{A+B}(\sim X) &\Leftrightarrow [x]^{[\wr]\geq}_A \in \sim X \ or \ [x]^{[\wr]\geq}_B \in \sim X \\ &\Leftrightarrow [x]^{[\wr]\geq}_A \cap X = \emptyset \ or \ [x]^{[\wr]\geq}_B \cap X = \emptyset \\ &\Leftrightarrow x \notin \overline{OM}^{[\wr]\geq}_{A+B}(X) \\ &\Leftrightarrow x \in \sim \overline{OM}^{[\wr]\geq}_{A+B}(X) \end{aligned}$$

Therefore, $\underline{OM}^{[\wr]\geq}_{A+B}(\sim X) =\sim \overline{OM}^{[\wr]\geq}_{A+B}(X)$.

(OU$_2$) For any $x \in \overline{OM}^{[\wr]\geq}_{A+B}(\sim X)$, we have that

$$\begin{aligned} x \in \overline{OM}^{[\wr]\geq}_{A+B}(\sim X) &\Leftrightarrow [x]^{[\wr]\geq}_{A} \cap \sim X \neq \emptyset \text{ or } [x]^{[\wr]\geq}_{B} \cap \sim X \neq \emptyset \\ &\Leftrightarrow [x]^{[\wr]\geq}_{A} \nsubseteq X \text{ and } [x]^{[\wr]\geq}_{B} \nsubseteq X \\ &\Leftrightarrow x \notin \underline{OM}^{[\wr]\geq}_{A+B}(X) \\ &\Leftrightarrow x \in \sim \overline{OM}^{[\wr]\geq}_{A+B}(X) \end{aligned}$$

Therefore, $\overline{OM}^{[\wr]\geq}_{A+B}(\sim X) =\sim \underline{OM}^{[\wr]\geq}_{A+B}(X)$.

Or for any $x \in \overline{OM}^{[\wr]\geq}_{A+B}(\sim X)$, by OL_2 we can know that $\underline{OM}^{[\wr]\geq}_{A+B}(\sim X) =\sim \overline{OM}^{[\wr]\geq}_{A+B}(X) \Leftrightarrow \underline{OM}^{[\wr]\geq}_{A+B}(X) =\sim \overline{OM}^{[\wr]\geq}_{A+B}(\sim X) \Leftrightarrow \overline{OM}^{[\wr]\geq}_{A+B}(\sim X) =\sim \underline{OM}^{[\wr]\geq}_{A+B}(X)$.

(OL$_3$) By OL_1, we can know that $\underline{OM}^{[\wr]\geq}_{A+B}(\emptyset) \subseteq \emptyset$. Meantime, $\emptyset \subseteq \underline{OM}^{[\wr]\geq}_{A+B}(X)$. Therefore, $\underline{OM}^{[\wr]\geq}_{A+B}(\emptyset) = \emptyset$

(OU$_3$) If $\overline{OM}^{[\wr]\geq}_{A+B}(\emptyset) \neq \emptyset$, then there must be a $x \in \overline{OM}^{[\wr]\geq}_{A+B}(\emptyset)$. By Definition 1, $[x]^{[\wr]\geq}_{A} \cap \emptyset \neq \emptyset$ and $[x]^{[\wr]\geq}_{B} \cap \emptyset \neq \emptyset$. It is obvious that this is a contradiction. Therefore, $\overline{OM}^{[\wr]\geq}_{A+B}(\emptyset) = \emptyset$.

(OL$_4$) $\underline{OM}^{[\wr]\geq}_{A+B}(U) = \underline{OM}^{[\wr]\geq}_{A+B}(\sim \emptyset) =\sim \overline{OM}^{[\wr]\geq}_{A+B}(\emptyset) =\sim \emptyset = U$.

(OU$_4$) $\overline{OM}^{[\wr]\geq}_{A+B}(U) = \overline{OM}^{[\wr]\geq}_{A+B}(\sim \emptyset) =\sim \underline{OM}^{[\wr]\geq}_{A+B}(\emptyset) =\sim \emptyset = U$.

(OL$_5$) For any $x \in \underline{OM}^{[\wr]\geq}_{A+B}(X \cap Y)$, we have that $[x]^{[\wr]\geq}_{A} \subseteq (X \cap Y)$ or $[x]^{[\wr]\geq}_{B} \subseteq (X \cap Y)$ by Definition 1. Furthermore, we can get that $[x]^{[\wr]\geq}_{A} \subseteq X$ and $[x]^{[\wr]\geq}_{A} \subseteq Y$ hold at the same time or $[x]^{[\wr]\geq}_{B} \subseteq X$ and $[x]^{[\wr]\geq}_{B} \subseteq Y$ hold at the same time. So not only $[x]^{[\wr]\geq}_{A} \subseteq X$ or $[x]^{[\wr]\geq}_{B} \subseteq X$ hold , but also $[x]^{[\wr]\geq}_{A} \subseteq Y$ or $[x]^{[\wr]\geq}_{B} \subseteq Y$ hold. It is also to say that $x \in \underline{OM}^{[\wr]\geq}_{A+B}(X)$ and $x \in \underline{OM}^{[\wr]\geq}_{A+B}(Y)$. So $x \in \underline{OM}^{[\wr]\geq}_{A+B}(X) \cap \underline{OM}^{[\wr]\geq}_{A+B}(Y)$. Therefore, $\underline{OM}^{[\wr]\geq}_{A+B}(X \cap Y) \subseteq \underline{OM}^{[\wr]\geq}_{A+B}(X) \cap \underline{OM}^{[\wr]\geq}_{A+B}(Y)$

(OU$_5$) For any $x \in \overline{OM}^{[\wr]\geq}_{A+B}(X) \cup \overline{OM}^{[\wr]\geq}_{A+B}(Y)$, we have that $x \in \overline{OM}^{[\wr]\geq}_{A+B}(X)$ or $x \in \overline{OM}^{[\wr]\geq}_{A+B}(Y)$, then $[x]^{[\wr]\geq}_{A} \cap X \neq \emptyset$ and $[x]^{[\wr]\geq}_{B} \cap X \neq \emptyset$ hold at same time, or $[x]^{[\wr]\geq}_{A} \cap Y \neq \emptyset$ and $[x]^{[\wr]\geq}_{B} \cap Y \neq \emptyset$ hold at same time. It is also to say that not only $[x]^{[\wr]\geq}_{A} \cap (X \cup Y) \neq \emptyset$, but also $[x]^{[\wr]\geq}_{B} \cap (X \cup Y) \neq \emptyset$. So $x \in \overline{OM}^{[\wr]\geq}_{A+B}(X \cup Y)$. Therefore, $\overline{OM}^{[\wr]\geq}_{A+B}(X) \cup \overline{OM}^{[\wr]\geq}_{A+B}(Y) \subseteq \overline{OM}^{[\wr]\geq}_{A+B}(X \cup Y)$.

(OL$_6$) Since $X \subseteq Y$, then $X \cap Y = X \Rightarrow \underline{OM}^{[\wr]\geq}_{A+B}(X \cap Y) = \underline{OM}^{[\wr]\geq}_{A+B}(X)$. By OL_5, $\underline{OM}^{[\wr]\geq}_{A+B}(X \cap Y) \subseteq \underline{OM}^{[\wr]\geq}_{A+B}(X) \cap \underline{OM}^{[\wr]\geq}_{A+B}(Y) \Rightarrow \underline{OM}^{[\wr]\geq}_{A+B}(X) \subseteq \underline{OM}^{[\wr]\geq}_{A+B}(X) \cap \underline{OM}^{[\wr]\geq}_{A+B}(Y)$. Therefore, $\underline{OM}^{[\wr]\geq}_{A+B}(X) \subseteq \underline{OM}^{[\wr]\geq}_{A+B}(Y)$.

(OU$_6$) Since $X \subseteq Y$, then $X \cup Y = Y \Rightarrow \overline{OM}^{[\wr]\geq}_{A+B}(X \cup Y) = \overline{OM}^{[\wr]\geq}_{A+B}(Y)$. By OU_5, $\overline{OM}^{[\wr]\geq}_{A+B}(X \cup Y) \supseteq \overline{OM}^{[\wr]\geq}_{A+B}(X) \cup \overline{OM}^{[\wr]\geq}_{A+B}(Y) \Rightarrow \overline{OM}^{[\wr]\geq}_{A+B}(X) \supseteq \overline{OM}^{[\wr]\geq}_{A+B}(X) \cup \overline{OM}^{[\wr]\geq}_{A+B}(Y)$. Therefore, $\overline{OM}^{[\wr]\geq}_{A+B}(X) \subseteq \overline{OM}^{[\wr]\geq}_{A+B}(Y)$.

(OL$_7$) Since $X \subseteq X \cup Y$ and $Y \subseteq X \cup Y$, by OL_6, $\underline{OM}^{[\wr]\geq}_{A+B}(X) \subseteq \underline{OM}^{[\wr]\geq}_{A+B}(X \cap Y)$ and $\underline{OM}^{[\wr]\geq}_{A+B}(Y) \subseteq \underline{OM}^{[\wr]\geq}_{A+B}(X \cap Y)$. Therefore, $\underline{OM}^{[\wr]\geq}_{A+B}(X) \cup \underline{OM}^{[\wr]\geq}_{A+B}(Y) \subseteq \underline{OM}^{[\wr]\geq}_{A+B}(X \cup Y)$.

(OU$_7$) Since $X \cap Y \subseteq X$ and $X \cap Y \subseteq Y$, by OU_6, $\overline{OM}^{[\wr]\geq}_{A+B}(X \cap Y) \subseteq \overline{OM}^{[\wr]\geq}_{A+B}(X)$ and $\overline{OM}^{[\wr]\geq}_{A+B}(X \cap Y) \subseteq \overline{OM}^{[\wr]\geq}_{A+B}(Y)$. Therefore, $\overline{OM}^{[\wr]\geq}_{A+B}(X \cap Y) \subseteq \overline{OM}^{[\wr]\geq}_{A+B}(X) \cap \overline{OM}^{[\wr]\geq}_{A+B}(Y)$. □

Proposition A2. *Let $\mathcal{I}^{[\wr]\geq} = (U, AT, V, f)$ be an IIFOIS, $A_1, A_2, \cdots, A_s \in AT(m \leq 2^{|AT|})$, $X, Y \in U$, then the following results hold.*

(PL$_1$) $\underline{PM}^{[\wr]\geq}_{\sum_{i=1}^{s}A_i}(X) \subseteq X$ *(Contraction)*

(PU$_1$) $X \subseteq \overline{PM}^{[\wr]\geq}_{\sum_{i=1}^{s}A_i}(X)$ *(Extention)*

(PL$_2$) $\underline{PM}^{[\wr]\geq}_{\sum_{i=1}^{s}A_i}(\sim X) =\sim \overline{PM}^{[\wr]\geq}_{\sum_{i=1}^{s}A_i}(X)$ *(Duality)*

(PU$_2$) $\overline{PM}^{[\wr]\geq}_{\sum_{i=1}^{s}A_i}(\sim X) =\sim \underline{PM}^{[\wr]\geq}_{\sum_{i=1}^{s}A_i}(X)$ *(Duality)*

(PL$_3$) $\underline{PM}^{[\wr]\geq}_{\sum_{i=1}^{s}A_i}(\emptyset) = \emptyset$ *(Normality)*

(PU$_3$) $\overline{PM}^{[\wr]\geq}_{\sum_{i=1}^{s}A_i}(\emptyset) = \emptyset$ *(Normality)*

(PL$_4$) $\underline{PM}^{[\wr]\geq}_{\sum_{i=1}^{s}A_i}(U) = U$ *(Co-normality)*

(PU$_4$) $\overline{PM}^{[\wr]\geq}_{\sum_{i=1}^{s}A_i}(U) = U$ *(Co-normality)*

(PL$_5$) $\underline{PM}^{[\wr]\geq}_{\sum_{i=1}^{s}A_i}(X \cap Y) = \underline{PM}^{[\wr]\geq}_{\sum_{i=1}^{s}A_i}(X) \cap \underline{PM}^{[\wr]\geq}_{\sum_{i=1}^{s}A_i}(Y)$ *(L-F-multiplication)*

(PU$_5$) $\overline{PM}^{[\wr]\geq}_{\sum_{i=1}^{s}A_i}(X \cup Y) = \overline{PM}^{[\wr]\geq}_{\sum_{i=1}^{s}A_i}(X) \cup \overline{PM}^{[\wr]\geq}_{\sum_{i=1}^{s}A_i}(Y)$ *(U-F-addition)*

(PL$_6$) $X \subseteq Y \Rightarrow \underline{PM}^{[\wr]\geq}_{\sum_{i=1}^{s}A_i}(X) \subseteq \underline{PM}^{[\wr]\geq}_{\sum_{i=1}^{s}A_i}(Y)$ *(Monotonicity)*

(PU$_6$) $X \subseteq Y \Rightarrow \overline{PM}^{[\wr]\geq}_{\sum_{i=1}^{s}A_i}(X) \subseteq \overline{PM}^{[\wr]\geq}_{\sum_{i=1}^{s}A_i}(Y)$ *(Monotonicity)*

(PL$_7$) $\underline{PM}^{[\wr]\geq}_{\sum_{i=1}^{s}A_i}(X \cup Y) \supseteq \underline{PM}^{[\wr]\geq}_{\sum_{i=1}^{s}A_i}(X) \cup \underline{PM}^{[\wr]\geq}_{\sum_{i=1}^{s}A_i}(Y)$ *(L-F-addition)*

(PU$_7$) $\overline{PM}^{[\wr]\geq}_{\sum_{i=1}^{s}A_i}(X \cap Y) \subseteq \overline{PM}^{[\wr]\geq}_{\sum_{i=1}^{s}A_i}(X) \cap \overline{PM}^{[\wr]\geq}_{\sum_{i=1}^{s}A_i}(Y)$ *(U-F-multiplication)*

Proof. For convenience, we will prove that the results only when $s = 2$, which there are two dominance relations($A, B \subseteq AT$) in an IIFOIS. All terms hold obviously when $A = B$. The following is the proof when $A \neq B$.

(PL$_1$) For any $x \in \underline{PM}^{[\wr]\geq}_{A+B}(X)$, according to Definition 4 we can know that $[x]^{[\wr]\geq}_{A} \subseteq X$ and $[x]^{[\wr]\geq}_{B} \subseteq X$. Besides $x \in [x]^{[\wr]\geq}_{A}$ and $x \in [x]^{[\wr]\geq}_{B}$. So we can have that $x \in X$. Therefore, $\underline{PM}^{[\wr]\geq}_{A+B}(X) \subseteq X$.

(PU$_1$) For any $x \in X$, $x \in [x]^{[\wr]\geq}_{A}$ and $x \in [x]^{[\wr]\geq}_{B}$, then $[x]^{[\wr]\geq}_{A} \cap X \neq \emptyset$ and $[x]^{[\wr]\geq}_{B} \cap X \neq \emptyset$. Besides $x \in \overline{PM}^{[\wr]\geq}_{A+B}(X)$. Therefore, $X \subseteq \overline{OM}^{[\wr]\geq}_{A+B}(X)$.

(PL$_2$) For any $x \in \underline{PM}^{[\wr]\geq}_{A+B}(\sim X)$, we have that

$$\begin{aligned} x \in \underline{PM}^{[\wr]\geq}_{A+B}(\sim X) &\Leftrightarrow [x]^{[\wr]\geq}_{A} \in\sim X \textit{ and } [x]^{[\wr]\geq}_{B} \in\sim X \\ &\Leftrightarrow [x]^{[\wr]\geq}_{A} \cap X = \emptyset \textit{ and } [x]^{[\wr]\geq}_{B} \cap X = \emptyset \\ &\Leftrightarrow x \notin \overline{PM}^{[\wr]\geq}_{A+B}(X) \\ &\Leftrightarrow x \in\sim \overline{PM}^{[\wr]\geq}_{A+B}(X) \end{aligned}$$

Therefore, $\underline{PM}^{[\wr]\geq}_{A+B}(\sim X) =\sim \overline{PM}^{[\wr]\geq}_{A+B}(X)$.

(PU$_2$) For any $x \in \overline{PM}^{[\wr]\geq}_{A+B}(\sim X)$, by PL_2 we can know that $\underline{PM}^{[\wr]\geq}_{A+B}(\sim X) =\sim \overline{PM}^{[\wr]\geq}_{A+B}(X) \Leftrightarrow \underline{PM}^{[\wr]\geq}_{A+B}(X) =\sim \overline{PM}^{[\wr]\geq}_{A+B}(\sim X) \Leftrightarrow \overline{PM}^{[\wr]\geq}_{A+B}(\sim X) =\sim \underline{PM}^{[\wr]\geq}_{A+B}(X)$.

(PL$_3$) By PL_1, we can know that $\underline{PM}^{[\wr]\geq}_{A+B}(\emptyset) \subseteq \emptyset$. Meantime, $\emptyset \subseteq \underline{PM}^{[\wr]\geq}_{A+B}(X)$. Therefore, $\underline{PM}^{[\wr]\geq}_{A+B}(\emptyset) = \emptyset$

(PU$_3$) If $\overline{PM}^{[\wr]\geq}_{A+B}(\emptyset) \neq \emptyset$, then there must be a $x \in \overline{PM}^{[\wr]\geq}_{A+B}(\emptyset)$. By Definition 4, $[x]^{[\wr]\geq}_{A} \cap \emptyset \neq \emptyset$ or $[x]^{[\wr]\geq}_{B} \cap \emptyset \neq \emptyset$. It is obvious that this is a contradiction. Therefore, $\overline{PM}^{[\wr]\geq}_{A+B}(\emptyset) = \emptyset$.

(PL$_4$) $\underline{PM}^{[\wr]\geq}_{A+B}(U) = \underline{PM}^{[\wr]\geq}_{A+B}(\sim \emptyset) =\sim \overline{PM}^{[\wr]\geq}_{A+B}(\emptyset) =\sim \emptyset = U$.

(PU$_4$) $\overline{PM}^{[\wr]\geq}_{A+B}(U)=\overline{PM}^{[\wr]\geq}_{A+B}(\sim\emptyset)=\sim\underline{PM}^{[\wr]\geq}_{A+B}(\emptyset)=\sim\emptyset=U$.

(PL$_5$) For any $x\in\underline{PM}^{[\wr]\geq}_{A+B}(X\cap Y)$, we have that

$$\begin{aligned} x\in\underline{PM}^{[\wr]\geq}_{A+B}(X\cap Y) &\Leftrightarrow [x]^{[\wr]\geq}_{A}\subseteq X\cap Y \; and \; [x]^{[\wr]\geq}_{B}\subseteq X\cap Y \\ &\Leftrightarrow [x]^{[\wr]\geq}_{A}\subseteq X,[x]^{[\wr]\geq}_{A}\subseteq Y,[x]^{[\wr]\geq}_{B}\subseteq X \; and \; [B]^{[\wr]\geq}_{A}\subseteq Y \\ &\Leftrightarrow [x]^{[\wr]\geq}_{A}\subseteq X,[x]^{[\wr]\geq}_{B}\subseteq X,[x]^{[\wr]\geq}_{A}\subseteq Y \; and \; [x]^{[\wr]\geq}_{B}\subseteq Y \\ &\Leftrightarrow x\in\underline{PM}^{[\wr]\geq}_{A+B}(X) \; and \; x\in\underline{PM}^{[\wr]\geq}_{A+B}(Y) \\ &\Leftrightarrow x\in\underline{PM}^{[\wr]\geq}_{A+B}(X)\cap\underline{PM}^{[\wr]\geq}_{A+B}(Y) \end{aligned}$$

Therefore, $\underline{PM}^{[\wr]\geq}_{A+B}(X\cap Y)=\underline{PM}^{[\wr]\geq}_{A+B}(X)\cap\underline{PM}^{[\wr]\geq}_{A+B}(Y)$.

(PU$_5$) For any $x\in\overline{PM}^{[\wr]\geq}_{A+B}(X\cup Y)$, we have that

$$\begin{aligned} x\in\overline{PM}^{[\wr]\geq}_{A+B}(X\cup Y) &\Leftrightarrow [x]^{[\wr]\geq}_{A}\cap(X\cup Y)\neq\emptyset \; or \; [x]^{[\wr]\geq}_{B}\cap(X\cup Y)\neq\emptyset \\ &\Leftrightarrow [x]^{[\wr]\geq}_{A}\cap X\neq\emptyset \; or \; [x]^{[\wr]\geq}_{A}\cap Y\neq\emptyset, or \; [x]^{[\wr]\geq}_{B}\cap X\neq\emptyset or[x]^{[\wr]\geq}_{B}\cap Y\neq\emptyset \\ &\Leftrightarrow [x]^{[\wr]\geq}_{A}\cap X\neq\emptyset \; or \; [x]^{[\wr]\geq}_{B}\cap X\neq\emptyset, or \; [x]^{[\wr]\geq}_{A}\cap Y\neq\emptyset or[x]^{[\wr]\geq}_{B}\cap Y\neq\emptyset \\ &\Leftrightarrow x\in\overline{PM}^{[\wr]\geq}_{A+B}(X) \; or \; x\in\overline{PM}^{[\wr]\geq}_{A+B}(Y) \\ &\Leftrightarrow x\in\overline{PM}^{[\wr]\geq}_{A+B}(X)\cup\overline{PM}^{[\wr]\geq}_{A+B}(Y) \end{aligned}$$

Therefore, $\overline{PM}^{[\wr]\geq}_{A+B}(X\cup Y)=\overline{PM}^{[\wr]\geq}_{A+B}(X)\cup\underline{PM}^{[\wr]\geq}_{A+B}(Y)$.

(PL$_6$) Since $X\subseteq Y$, then $X\cap Y=X\Rightarrow\underline{PM}^{[\wr]\geq}_{A+B}(X\cap Y)=\underline{PM}^{[\wr]\geq}_{A+B}(X)$. By PL_5, $\underline{PM}^{[\wr]\geq}_{A+B}(X\cap Y)=\underline{PM}^{[\wr]\geq}_{A+B}(X)\cap\underline{PM}^{[\wr]\geq}_{A+B}(Y)\Rightarrow\underline{PM}^{[\wr]\geq}_{A+B}(X)=\underline{PM}^{[\wr]\geq}_{A+B}(X)\cap\underline{PM}^{[\wr]\geq}_{A+B}(Y)$. Therefore, $\underline{PM}^{[\wr]\geq}_{A+B}(X)\subseteq\underline{PM}^{[\wr]\geq}_{A+B}(Y)$.

(PU$_6$) Since $X\subseteq Y$, then $X\cup Y=Y\Rightarrow\overline{PM}^{[\wr]\geq}_{A+B}(X\cup Y)=\overline{OM}^{[\wr]\geq}_{A+B}(Y)$. By PU_5, $\overline{PM}^{[\wr]\geq}_{A+B}(X\cup Y)=\overline{PM}^{[\wr]\geq}_{A+B}(X)\cup\overline{PM}^{[\wr]\geq}_{A+B}(Y)\Rightarrow\overline{PM}^{[\wr]\geq}_{A+B}(X)=\overline{PM}^{[\wr]\geq}_{A+B}(X)\cup\overline{PM}^{[\wr]\geq}_{A+B}(Y)$. Therefore, $\overline{PM}^{[\wr]\geq}_{A+B}(X)\subseteq\overline{PM}^{[\wr]\geq}_{A+B}(Y)$.

(PL$_7$) Since $X\subseteq X\cup Y$ and $Y\subseteq X\cup Y$, by PL_6, $\underline{PM}^{[\wr]\geq}_{A+B}(X)\subseteq\underline{PM}^{[\wr]\geq}_{A+B}(X\cap Y)$ and $\underline{PM}^{[\wr]\geq}_{A+B}(Y)\subseteq\underline{PM}^{[\wr]\geq}_{A+B}(X\cap Y)$. Therefore, $\underline{PM}^{[\wr]\geq}_{A+B}(X)\cup\underline{PM}^{[\wr]\geq}_{A+B}(Y)\subseteq\underline{PM}^{[\wr]\geq}_{A+B}(X\cup Y)$.

(PU$_7$) Since $X\cap Y\subseteq X$ and $X\cap Y\subseteq Y$, by PU_6, $\overline{PM}^{[\wr]\geq}_{A+B}(X\cap Y)\subseteq\overline{PM}^{[\wr]\geq}_{A+B}(X)$ and $\overline{PM}^{[\wr]\geq}_{A+B}(X\cap Y)\subseteq\overline{PM}^{[\wr]\geq}_{A+B}(Y)$. Therefore, $\overline{PM}^{[\wr]\geq}_{A+B}(X\cap Y)\subseteq\overline{PM}^{[\wr]\geq}_{A+B}(X)\cap\overline{PM}^{[\wr]\geq}_{A+B}(Y)$. □

Proposition A3. *Let $\mathcal{I}^{[\wr]\geq}=(U,AT,V,f)$ be an IIFOIS, $A_i\in AT, i=1,2,\cdots,s(s\leq 2^{|AT|})$, $X,Y\in P(U)$, $x\in U$. The following properties about the support feature function $S^{A_i}_X(x)$ are established.*

(1) $S^{A_i}_{\sim X}(x)=\begin{cases}1, & [x]^{[\wr]\geq}_{A_i}\cap X=\emptyset,\\ 0, & [x]^{[\wr]\geq}_{A_i}\cap X\neq\emptyset.\end{cases}$

(2) $S^{A_i}_{\emptyset}(x)=0, S^{A_i}_{U}(x)=1$.

(3) $S^{A_i}_{X\cup Y}(x)\geq S^{A_i}_{X}(x)\vee S^{A_i}_{Y}(x)$.

(4) $S^{A_i}_{X\cap Y}(x)=S^{A_i}_{X}(x)\wedge S^{A_i}_{Y}(x)$.

(5) $X\subseteq Y\Rightarrow S^{A_i}_{X}(x)\leq S^{A_i}_{Y}(x)$.

(6) $X\subseteq Y\Rightarrow S^{A_i}_{\sim X}(x)\geq S^{A_i}_{\sim Y}(x)$.

"$\vee$" and "$\wedge$" represent the operation of taking small and taking big, respectively.

Proof. (1) By Definition 7, $[x]^{[\wr]\geq}_{A_i}\subseteq\sim X\Leftrightarrow[x]^{[\wr]\geq}_{A_i}\cap X=\emptyset$ and $[x]^{[\wr]\geq}_{A_i}\nsubseteq\sim X\Leftrightarrow[x]^{[\wr]\geq}_{A_i}\cap X\neq\emptyset$

(2) By Definition 7, for any $x \in U \Rightarrow [x]_{A_i}^{[\wr]\geq} \nsubseteq \emptyset$, it is also to say that $S_{\emptyset}^{A_i}(x) = 0$. For any $x \in U \Rightarrow [x]_{A_i}^{[\wr]\geq} \subseteq U$, it is also to say that $S_U^{A_i}(x) = 1$.
(3) For any $Z \subseteq P(U)$, $Z \subseteq X$ or $Z \subseteq Y \Rightarrow Z \subseteq (X \cup Y)$. So

$$\begin{aligned} S_X^{A_i}(x) \vee S_Y^{A_i}(x) = 1 &\Rightarrow S_X^{A_i}(x) = 1 \text{ or } S_Y^{A_i}(x) = 1 \\ &\Rightarrow [x]_{A_i}^{[\wr]\geq} \subseteq X \text{ or } [x]_{A_i}^{[\wr]\geq} \subseteq X \\ &\Rightarrow [x]_{A_i}^{[\wr]\geq} \subseteq (X \cup Y) \\ &\Rightarrow S_{X \cup Y}^{A_i}(x) = 1 \end{aligned}$$

If $X \cup Y = U$, it is obvious that $S_{X \cup Y}^{A_i}(x) = S_U^{A_i}(x) = 1$, otherwise we have $\sim (X \cup Y) = (\sim X) \cap (\sim Y) \neq \emptyset$. Then

$$\begin{aligned} S_X^{A_i}(x) = 0 &\Rightarrow [x]_{A_i}^{[\wr]\geq} \cap \sim (X \cup Y) \neq \emptyset \\ &\Rightarrow [x]_{A_i}^{[\wr]\geq} \cap [(\sim X) \cap (\sim Y)] \neq \emptyset \\ &\Rightarrow [x]_{A_i}^{[\wr]\geq} \cap (\sim X) \neq \emptyset \text{ and } [x]_{A_i}^{[\wr]\geq} \cap (\sim Y) \neq \emptyset \\ &\Rightarrow S_X^{A_i}(x) = 0 \text{ and } S_Y^{A_i}(x) = 0 \\ &\Rightarrow S_X^{A_i} \vee S_Y^{A_i}(x) = 0 \end{aligned}$$

As a result, for any $x \in U$, $S_{X \cup Y}^{A_i}(x) \geq S_X^{A_i}(x) \vee S_Y^{A_i}(x)$.
(4) For any $Z \subseteq P(U)$, $Z \subseteq X$ and $Z \subseteq Y \Rightarrow Z \subseteq (X \cap Y)$. So

$$\begin{aligned} S_{X \cap Y}^{A_i}(x) = 0 &\Leftrightarrow [x]_{A_i}^{[\wr]\geq} \cap \sim (X \cap Y) \neq \emptyset \\ &\Leftrightarrow [x]_{A_i}^{[\wr]\geq} \cap [(\sim X) \cup (\sim Y)] \neq \emptyset \\ &\Leftrightarrow [x]_{A_i}^{[\wr]\geq} \cap (\sim X) \neq \emptyset \text{ and } [x]_{A_i}^{[\wr]\geq} \cap (\sim Y) \neq \emptyset \\ &\Leftrightarrow S_X^{A_i}(x) = 0 \text{ and } S_Y^{A_i}(x) = 0 \\ &\Leftrightarrow S_X^{A_i} \wedge S_Y^{A_i}(x) = 0 \end{aligned}$$

and

$$\begin{aligned} S_{X \cap Y}^{A_i}(x) = 1 &\Leftrightarrow [x]_{A_i}^{[\wr]\geq} \subseteq X \cap Y \\ &\Leftrightarrow [x]_{A_i}^{[\wr]\geq} \subseteq X \text{ and } [x]_{A_i}^{[\wr]\geq} \subseteq Y \\ &\Leftrightarrow S_X^{A_i}(x) = 1 \text{ and } S_Y^{A_i}(x) = 1 \\ &\Leftrightarrow S_X^{A_i} \wedge S_Y^{A_i}(x) = 1 \end{aligned}$$

As a result, for any $x \in U$, $S_{X \cap Y}^{A_i}(x) = S_X^{A_i}(x) \wedge S_Y^{A_i}(x)$.
(5) If $S_Y^{A_i}(x) = 0 \Rightarrow [x]_{A_i}^{[\wr]\geq} \nsubseteq Y \Rightarrow [x]_{A_i}^{[\wr]\geq} \nsubseteq X \Rightarrow S_X^{A_i}(x) = 0$. If $S_X^{A_i}(x) = 1 \Rightarrow [x]_{A_i}^{[\wr]\geq} \subseteq X \subseteq Y \Rightarrow S_Y^{A_i}(x) = 1$. In that way, $X \subseteq Y \Rightarrow S_X^{A_i}(x) \leq S_Y^{A_i}(x)$.
(6) Similarly, if $S_{\sim X}^{A_i}(x) = 0 \Rightarrow [x]_{A_i}^{[\wr]\geq} \cap X \neq \emptyset \Rightarrow [x]_{A_i}^{[\wr]\geq} \cap Y \neq \emptyset \Rightarrow S_{\sim Y}^{A_i}(x) = 0$. If $S_{\sim Y}^{A_i}(x) = 1 \Rightarrow [x]_{A_i}^{[\wr]\geq} \cap Y = \emptyset \Rightarrow [x]_{A_i}^{[\wr]\geq} \cap X = \emptyset \Rightarrow S_{\sim X}^{A_i}(x) = 1$. Thus, $X \subseteq Y \Rightarrow S_X^{A_i}(x) \geq S_Y^{A_i}(x)$. □

Proposition A4. *Let $\mathcal{I}^{[\wr]\geq} = (U, AT, V, f)$ be an IIFOIS, $A_i \in AT, i = 1, 2, \cdots, s (s \leq 2^{|AT|})$, $\beta \in (0.5, 1]$. For any $X, Y \in P(U)$, the following results hold.*
(1L) $\underline{GM}_{\sum_{i=1}^{s} A_i}^{[\wr]\geq}(\sim X)_\beta = \sim \overline{GM}_{\sum_{i=1}^{s} A_i}^{[\wr]\geq}(X)_\beta$ *(Duality)*

(1U) $\overline{GM}^{[\wr]\geq}_{\sum_{i=1}^{s} A_i}(\sim X)_\beta = \sim \underline{GM}^{[\wr]\geq}_{\sum_{i=1}^{s} A_i}(X)_\beta$ *(Duality)*

(2L) $\underline{GM}^{[\wr]\geq}_{\sum_{i=1}^{s} A_i}(X)_\beta \subseteq X$ *(Contraction)*

(2U) $X \subseteq \overline{GM}^{[\wr]\geq}_{\sum_{i=1}^{s} A_i}(X)_\beta$ *(Extention)*

(3L) $\underline{GM}^{[\wr]\geq}_{\sum_{i=1}^{s} A_i}(\emptyset)_\beta = \emptyset$ *(Normality)*

(3U) $\overline{GM}^{[\wr]\geq}_{\sum_{i=1}^{s} A_i}(\emptyset)_\beta = \emptyset$ *(Normality)*

(4L) $\underline{GM}^{[\wr]\geq}_{\sum_{i=1}^{s} A_i}(U)_\beta = U$ *(Co-normality)*

(4U) $\overline{GM}^{[\wr]\geq}_{\sum_{i=1}^{s} A_i}(U)_\beta = U$ *(Co-normality)*

(5L) $X \subseteq Y \Rightarrow \underline{GM}^{[\wr]\geq}_{\sum_{i=1}^{s} A_i}(X)_\beta \subseteq \underline{GM}^{[\wr]\geq}_{\sum_{i=1}^{s} A_i}(Y)_\beta$ *(Monotonicity)*

(5U) $X \subseteq Y \Rightarrow \overline{GM}^{[\wr]\geq}_{\sum_{i=1}^{s} A_i}(X)_\beta \subseteq \overline{GM}^{[\wr]\geq}_{\sum_{i=1}^{s} A_i}(Y)_\beta$ *(Monotonicity)*

(6L) $\underline{GM}^{[\wr]\geq}_{\sum_{i=1}^{s} A_i}(X \cap Y)_\beta \subseteq \underline{GM}^{[\wr]\geq}_{\sum_{i=1}^{s} A_i}(X)_\beta \cap \underline{GM}^{[\wr]\geq}_{\sum_{i=1}^{s} A_i}(Y)_\beta$ *(L-F-multiplication)*

(6U) $\overline{GM}^{[\wr]\geq}_{\sum_{i=1}^{s} A_i}(X \cup Y)_\beta \supseteq \overline{GM}^{[\wr]\geq}_{\sum_{i=1}^{s} A_i}(X)_\beta \cup \overline{GM}^{[\wr]\geq}_{\sum_{i=1}^{s} A_i}(Y)_\beta$ *(L-F-addition)*

(7L) $\underline{GM}^{[\wr]\geq}_{\sum_{i=1}^{s} A_i}(X \cup Y)_\beta \supseteq \underline{GM}^{[\wr]\geq}_{\sum_{i=1}^{s} A_i}(X)_\beta \cup \underline{GM}^{[\wr]\geq}_{\sum_{i=1}^{s} A_i}(Y)_\beta$ *(L-F-addition)*

(7U) $\overline{GM}^{[\wr]\geq}_{\sum_{i=1}^{s} A_i}(X \cap Y)_\beta \subseteq \overline{GM}^{[\wr]\geq}_{\sum_{i=1}^{s} A_i}(X)_\beta \cap \overline{GM}^{[\wr]\geq}_{\sum_{i=1}^{s} A_i}(Y)_\beta$ *(L-F-multiplication)*

Proof. (1L) By Definition 8, we have that

$$x \in \sim \overline{GM}^{[\wr]\geq}_{\sum_{i=1}^{s} A_i}(X)_\beta \Leftrightarrow \frac{\sum_{i=1}^{s}(1 - S^{A_i}_{\sim X}(x))}{s} \leq 1 - \beta \Leftrightarrow \frac{\sum_{i=1}^{s} S^{A_i}_{\sim X}(x)}{s} \geq \beta \Leftrightarrow x \in \underline{GM}^{[\wr]\geq}_{\sum_{i=1}^{s} A_i}(\sim X)_\beta.$$

(1U) By Definition 8, we have that

$$x \in \sim \underline{GM}^{[\wr]\geq}_{\sum_{i=1}^{s} A_i}(X)_\beta \Leftrightarrow \frac{\sum_{i=1}^{s} S^{A_i}_{\sim X}(x)}{s} < 1 - \beta \Leftrightarrow \frac{\sum_{i=1}^{s}(1 - S^{A_i}_{\sim X}(x))}{s} > 1 - \beta \Leftrightarrow x \in \overline{GM}^{[\wr]\geq}_{\sum_{i=1}^{s} A_i}(\sim X)_\beta.$$

(2L) For any $x \in \underline{GM}^{[\wr]\geq}_{\sum_{i=1}^{s} A_i}(X)_\beta$, we can know that $\frac{\sum_{i=1}^{s} S^{A_i}_X(x)}{s} \geq \beta > 0$. So there must be a $i \leq s$ such that $[x]^{[\wr]\geq}_{A_i} \subseteq X$. Therefore, $\underline{GM}^{[\wr]\geq}_{\sum_{i=1}^{s} A_i}(X)_\beta \subseteq X$.

(2U) By Proposition 9 (1L) and (2L), we have that $\sim \overline{GM}^{[\wr]\geq}_{\sum_{i=1}^{s} A_i}(X)_\beta = \underline{GM}^{[\wr]\geq}_{\sum_{i=1}^{s} A_i}(\sim X)_\beta \subseteq \sim X$. Therefore, $X \in \overline{GM}^{[\wr]\geq}_{\sum_{i=1}^{s} A_i}(X)_\beta$.

(3L), (4L) By Proposition 8, we can know that $S^{A_i}_\emptyset(x) = 0$, $S^{A_i}_U(x) = 1$, then

$$\underline{GM}^{[\wr]\geq}_{\sum_{i=1}^{s} A_i}(\emptyset)_\beta = \{x \in U | \frac{\sum_{i=1}^{s} S^{A_i}_\emptyset(x)}{s} = \frac{\sum_{i=1}^{s} 0}{s} = 0 \geq \beta\} = \emptyset,$$

$$\underline{GM}^{[\wr]\geq}_{\sum_{i=1}^{s} A_i}(U)_\beta = \{x \in U | \frac{\sum_{i=1}^{s} S^{A_i}_U(x)}{s} = \frac{\sum_{i=1}^{s} 1}{s} = 1 \geq \beta\} = U.$$

(3U), (4U) By Proposition 9 (1L) and (1U), we have

$$\overline{GM}^{[\wr]\geq}_{\sum_{i=1}^{s} A_i}(\emptyset)_\beta = \sim \underline{GM}^{[\wr]\geq}_{\sum_{i=1}^{s} A_i}(\sim \emptyset)_\beta = \sim \underline{GM}^{[\wr]\geq}_{\sum_{i=1}^{s} A_i}(U)_\beta = \sim U = \emptyset,$$

$$\overline{GM}^{[\wr]\geq}_{\sum_{i=1}^{s} A_i}(U)_\beta = \sim \underline{GM}^{[\wr]\geq}_{\sum_{i=1}^{s} A_i}(\sim U)_\beta = \sim \underline{GM}^{[\wr]\geq}_{\sum_{i=1}^{s} A_i}(\emptyset)_\beta = \sim \emptyset = U.$$

(5L) For any $x \in \underline{GM}^{[\wr]\geq}_{\sum_{i=1}^{s} A_i}(X)_\beta$, we have $\frac{\sum_{i=1}^{s} S^{A_i}_X(x)}{s} \geq \beta$. By Proposition 8, $X \subseteq Y \Rightarrow S^{A_i}_X(x) \leq S^{A_i}_Y(x)$, then $\frac{\sum_{i=1}^{s} S^{A_i}_Y(x)}{s} \geq \frac{\sum_{i=1}^{s} S^{A_i}_X(x)}{s} \geq \beta \Rightarrow x \in \underline{GM}^{[\wr]\geq}_{\sum_{i=1}^{s} A_i}(Y)_\beta$. Consequently, $X \subseteq Y \Rightarrow \underline{GM}^{[\wr]\geq}_{\sum_{i=1}^{s} A_i}(X)_\beta \subseteq \underline{GM}^{[\wr]\geq}_{\sum_{i=1}^{s} A_i}(Y)_\beta$.

(5U) For any $x \in \overline{GM}^{[\wr]\geq}_{\sum_{i=1}^{s} A_i}(X)_\beta$, we have $\frac{\sum_{i=1}^{s}(1-S_X^{A_i}(x))}{s} > 1-\beta$. By Proposition 8, $X \subseteq Y \Rightarrow \sim Y \subseteq \sim X \Rightarrow S^{A_i}_{\sim Y}(x) \leq S^{A_i}_{\sim X}(x)$, then $\frac{\sum_{i=1}^{s}(1-S^{A_i}_{\sim Y}(x))}{s} \geq \frac{\sum_{i=1}^{s} S^{A_i}_{\sim X}(x)}{s} > 1-\beta \Rightarrow x \in \overline{GM}^{[\wr]\geq}_{\sum_{i=1}^{s} A_i}(Y)_\beta$. Consequently, $X \subseteq Y \Rightarrow \overline{GM}^{[\wr]\geq}_{\sum_{i=1}^{s} A_i}(X)_\beta \subseteq \overline{GM}^{[\wr]\geq}_{\sum_{i=1}^{s} A_i}(Y)_\beta$.

(6L) For any $x \in \underline{GM}^{[\wr]\geq}_{\sum_{i=1}^{s} A_i}(X \cap Y)_\beta$, we have that

$$\begin{aligned} x \in \underline{GM}^{[\wr]\geq}_{\sum_{i=1}^{s} A_i}(X \cap Y)_\beta \Rightarrow \frac{\sum_{i=1}^{s} S^{A_i}_{X\cap Y}(x)}{s} &= \frac{\sum_{i=1}^{s} S^{A_i}_{X}(x) \wedge \sum_{i=1}^{s} S^{A_i}_{Y}(x)}{s} \geq \beta \\ &\Rightarrow \frac{\sum_{i=1}^{s} S^{A_i}_{X}(x)}{s} \geq \beta \; and \; \frac{\sum_{i=1}^{s} S^{A_i}_{Y}(x)}{s} \geq \beta \\ &\Rightarrow x \in \underline{GM}^{[\wr]\geq}_{\sum_{i=1}^{s} A_i}(X)_\beta \; and \; x \in \underline{GM}^{[\wr]\geq}_{\sum_{i=1}^{s} A_i}(Y)_\beta \\ &\Rightarrow x \in \underline{GM}^{[\wr]\geq}_{\sum_{i=1}^{s} A_i}(X)_\beta \cap \underline{GM}^{[\wr]\geq}_{\sum_{i=1}^{s} A_i}(Y)_\beta \end{aligned}$$

Hence, $\underline{GM}^{[\wr]\geq}_{\sum_{i=1}^{s} A_i}(X \cap Y)_\beta \subseteq \underline{GM}^{[\wr]\geq}_{\sum_{i=1}^{s} A_i}(X)_\beta \cap \underline{GM}^{[\wr]\geq}_{\sum_{i=1}^{s} A_i}(Y)_\beta$.

(6U) $\overline{GM}^{[\wr]\geq}_{\sum_{i=1}^{s} A_i}(X \cup Y)_\beta = \sim \underline{GM}^{[\wr]\geq}_{\sum_{i=1}^{s} A_i}[\sim (X \cap Y)]_\beta = \sim \underline{GM}^{[\wr]\geq}_{\sum_{i=1}^{s} A_i}[(\sim X) \cap (\sim Y)]_\beta \supseteq \sim \underline{GM}^{[\wr]\geq}_{\sum_{i=1}^{s} A_i}(\sim X)_\beta \cup \sim \underline{GM}^{[\wr]\geq}_{\sum_{i=1}^{s} A_i}(\sim Y)_\beta = \overline{GM}^{[\wr]\geq}_{\sum_{i=1}^{s} A_i}(X)_\beta \cup \overline{GM}^{[\wr]\geq}_{\sum_{i=1}^{s} A_i}(Y)_\beta$.

Hence, $\overline{GM}^{[\wr]\geq}_{\sum_{i=1}^{s} A_i}(X \cup Y)_\beta \supseteq \overline{GM}^{[\wr]\geq}_{\sum_{i=1}^{s} A_i}(X)_\beta \cup \overline{GM}^{[\wr]\geq}_{\sum_{i=1}^{s} A_i}(Y)_\beta$.

(7L) $X \subseteq X \cup Y$ and $Y \subseteq X \cup Y \Rightarrow \underline{GM}^{[\wr]\geq}_{\sum_{i=1}^{s} A_i}(X)_\beta \subseteq \underline{GM}^{[\wr]\geq}_{\sum_{i=1}^{s} A_i}(X \cup Y)_\beta$ and $\underline{GM}^{[\wr]\geq}_{\sum_{i=1}^{s} A_i}(Y)_\beta \subseteq \underline{GM}^{[\wr]\geq}_{\sum_{i=1}^{s} A_i}(X \cup Y)_\beta \Rightarrow \underline{GM}^{[\wr]\geq}_{\sum_{i=1}^{s} A_i}(X)_\beta \cup \underline{GM}^{[\wr]\geq}_{\sum_{i=1}^{s} A_i}(Y)_\beta \subseteq \underline{GM}^{[\wr]\geq}_{\sum_{i=1}^{s} A_i}(X \cup Y)_\beta$.

So, $\underline{GM}^{[\wr]\geq}_{\sum_{i=1}^{s} A_i}(X \cup Y)_\beta \supseteq \underline{GM}^{[\wr]\geq}_{\sum_{i=1}^{s} A_i}(X)_\beta \cup \underline{GM}^{[\wr]\geq}_{\sum_{i=1}^{s} A_i}(Y)_\beta$.

(7U) $X \cap Y \subseteq X$ and $X \cap Y \subseteq Y \Rightarrow \overline{GM}^{[\wr]\geq}_{\sum_{i=1}^{s} A_i}(X \cap Y)_\beta \subseteq \overline{GM}^{[\wr]\geq}_{\sum_{i=1}^{s} A_i}(X)_\beta$ and $\overline{GM}^{[\wr]\geq}_{\sum_{i=1}^{s} A_i}(X \cap Y)_\beta \subseteq \overline{GM}^{[\wr]\geq}_{\sum_{i=1}^{s} A_i}(Y)_\beta \Rightarrow \overline{GM}^{[\wr]\geq}_{\sum_{i=1}^{s} A_i}(X \cap Y)_\beta \subseteq \overline{GM}^{[\wr]\geq}_{\sum_{i=1}^{s} A_i}(X)_\beta \cap \overline{GM}^{[\wr]\geq}_{\sum_{i=1}^{s} A_i}(Y)_\beta$.

So, $\overline{GM}^{[\wr]\geq}_{\sum_{i=1}^{s} A_i}(X \cap Y)_\beta \subseteq \overline{GM}^{[\wr]\geq}_{\sum_{i=1}^{s} A_i}(X)_\beta \cap \overline{GM}^{[\wr]\geq}_{\sum_{i=1}^{s} A_i}(Y)_\beta$.

□

Proposition A5. *Let $\mathcal{I}^{[\wr]\geq} = (U, AT, V, f)$ be an IIFOIS, $A_i \in AT, i = 1, 2, \cdots, s (s \leq 2^{|AT|})$. For any $\alpha \in (0.5, 1]$, $\beta \in (0.5, 1]$ and $\alpha \leq \beta$, $t \leq s$, $X \in P(U)$, then the following properties hold.*

(1) $\underline{GM}^{[\wr]\geq}_{\sum_{i=1}^{s} A_i}(X)_\beta \subseteq \underline{GM}^{[\wr]\geq}_{\sum_{i=1}^{s} A_i}(X)_\alpha$.

(2) $\overline{GM}^{[\wr]\geq}_{\sum_{i=1}^{s} A_i}(X)_\alpha \subseteq \overline{GM}^{[\wr]\geq}_{\sum_{i=1}^{s} A_i}(X)_\beta$.

(3) $\underline{GM}^{[\wr]\geq}_{\sum_{i=1}^{t} A_i}(X)_\beta \subseteq \underline{GM}^{[\wr]\geq}_{\sum_{i=1}^{s} A_i}(X)_\beta$.

(4) $\overline{GM}^{[\wr]\geq}_{\sum_{i=1}^{s} A_i}(X)_\beta \subseteq \overline{GM}^{[\wr]\geq}_{\sum_{i=1}^{t} A_i}(X)_\beta$.

Proof. It can be obtained easily by Definitions 7 and 8. □

Proposition A6. *Let $\mathcal{I}^{[\wr]\geq} = (U, AT, V, f)$ be an IIFOIS, $A_i \in AT, i = 1, 2, \cdots, s (s \leq 2^{|AT|})$. $X \in P(U)$. Then the following properties hold.*

(1) $\underline{OM}^{[\wr]\geq}_{\sum_{i=1}^{s} A_i}(X) \subseteq \underline{R}^{[\wr]\geq}_{\cup_{i=1}^{s} A_i}(X)$.

(2) $\overline{OM}^{[\wr]\geq}_{\sum_{i=1}^{s} A_i}(X) \supseteq \overline{R}^{[\wr]\geq}_{\cup_{i=1}^{s} A_i}(X)$.

(3) $\underline{PM}^{[\wr]\geq}_{\sum_{i=1}^{s} A_i}(X) \subseteq \underline{R}^{[\wr]\geq}_{\cup_{i=1}^{s} A_i}(X)$.

(4) $\overline{PM}^{[\wr]\geq}_{\sum_{i=1}^{s} A_i}(X) \supseteq \overline{R}^{[\wr]\geq}_{\cup_{i=1}^{s} A_i}(X)$.

Proof. Similarily, we will prove these properties only about two dominance relations $A, B \subseteq AT$ in an IIFOIS for convenience.

(1) For any $x \in \underline{OM}^{[\wr]\geq}_{A+B}(X)$, by Definition 1, we have that $[x]^{[\wr]\geq}_{A} \subseteq X$ or $[x]^{[\wr]\geq}_{B} \subseteq X$. Besides, $A \subseteq A \cup B$ and $B \subseteq A \cup B \Rightarrow [x]^{[\wr]\geq}_{A\cup B} \subseteq [x]^{[\wr]\geq}_{A}$ and $[x]^{[\wr]\geq}_{A\cup B} \subseteq [x]^{[\wr]\geq}_{B}$ by Proposition 1. So $[x]^{[\wr]\geq}_{A\cup B} \subseteq X$, it is also to say that $x \in \underline{R}^{[\wr]\geq}_{A+B}(X)$. Therefore, $\underline{OM}^{[\wr]\geq}_{A+B}(X) \subseteq \underline{R}^{[\wr]\geq}_{A+B}(X)$.

(2) By Proposition 11 (1), we can know that $\underline{OM}^{[\wr]\geq}_{A+B}(\sim X) \subseteq \underline{R}^{[\wr]\geq}_{A+B}(\sim X)$. Then $\sim \underline{OM}^{[\wr]\geq}_{A+B}(\sim X) \supseteq \sim \underline{R}^{[\wr]\geq}_{A+B}(\sim X)$, it is also to say that $\overline{OM}^{[\wr]\geq}_{A+B}(X) \supseteq \overline{R}^{[\wr]\geq}_{A+B}(X)$ by Proposition 3 (2L) and Proposition 6 (OL_2). Therefore, $\overline{OM}^{[\wr]\geq}_{A+B}(X) \supseteq \overline{R}^{[\wr]\geq}_{A+B}(X)$.

(3) For any $x \in \underline{PM}^{[\wr]\geq}_{A+B}(X)$, by Definition 4, we have that $[x]^{[\wr]\geq}_{A} \subseteq X$ and $[x]^{[\wr]\geq}_{B} \subseteq X$. Besides, $A \subseteq A \cup B$ and $B \subseteq A \cup B \Rightarrow [x]^{[\wr]\geq}_{A\cup B} \subseteq [x]^{[\wr]\geq}_{A}$ and $[x]^{[\wr]\geq}_{A\cup B} \subseteq [x]^{[\wr]\geq}_{B}$ by Proposition 1. So $[x]^{[\wr]\geq}_{A\cup B} \subseteq X$, it is also to say that $x \in \underline{R}^{[\wr]\geq}_{A+B}(X)$. Therefore, $\underline{PM}^{[\wr]\geq}_{A+B}(X) \subseteq \underline{R}^{[\wr]\geq}_{A+B}(X)$.

(4) By Proposition 11 (3), we can know that $\underline{PM}^{[\wr]\geq}_{A+B}(\sim X) \subseteq \underline{R}^{[\wr]\geq}_{A+B}(\sim X)$. Then $\sim \underline{PM}^{[\wr]\geq}_{A+B}(\sim X) \supseteq \sim \underline{R}^{[\wr]\geq}_{A+B}(\sim X)$, it is also to say that $\overline{PM}^{[\wr]\geq}_{A+B}(X) \supseteq \overline{R}^{[\wr]\geq}_{A+B}(X)$ by Propositions 3 (2L) and 7 (PL_2). Therefore, $\overline{PM}^{[\wr]\geq}_{A+B}(X) \supseteq \overline{R}^{[\wr]\geq}_{A+B}(X)$.
□

Proposition A7. *Let $\mathcal{I}^{[\wr]\geq} = (U, AT, V, f)$ be an IIFOIS, $A_i \in AT, i = 1, 2, \cdots, s (s \leq 2^{|AT|})$, $X \in U$. Then the following properties hold.*

(1) $\underline{OM}^{[\wr]\geq}_{\sum_{i=1}^{s} A_i}(X) = \bigcup_{i=1}^{s} \underline{R}^{[\wr]\geq}_{A_i}(X)$.

(2) $\overline{OM}^{[\wr]\geq}_{\sum_{i=1}^{s} A_i}(X) = \bigcap_{i=1}^{s} \overline{R}^{[\wr]\geq}_{A_i}(X)$.

(3) $\underline{PM}^{[\wr]\geq}_{\sum_{i=1}^{s} A_i}(X) = \bigcap_{i=1}^{s} \underline{R}^{[\wr]\geq}_{A_i}(X)$.

(4) $\overline{PM}^{[\wr]\geq}_{\sum_{i=1}^{s} A_i}(X) = \bigcup_{i=1}^{s} \overline{R}^{[\wr]\geq}_{A_i}(X)$.

Proof. Without loss of generality, we will prove these properties only about two dominance relations $A, B \subseteq AT$ in an IIFOIS for convenience.

(1) For any $x \in \underline{OM}^{[\wr]\geq}_{A+B}(X)$, we have that

$$\begin{aligned} x \in \underline{OM}^{[\wr]\geq}_{A+B}(X) &\Leftrightarrow [x]^{[\wr]\geq}_{A} \subseteq X \text{ or } [x]^{[\wr]\geq}_{B} \subseteq X \\ &\Leftrightarrow x \in \underline{R}^{[\wr]\geq}_{A}(X) \text{ or } x \in \underline{R}^{[\wr]\geq}_{B}(X) \\ &\Leftrightarrow x \in \underline{R}^{[\wr]\geq}_{A}(X) \cup \underline{R}^{[\wr]\geq}_{B}(X) \end{aligned}$$

Consequently, $\underline{OM}^{[\wr]\geq}_{A+B}(X) = \underline{R}^{[\wr]\geq}_{A}(X) \cup \underline{R}^{[\wr]\geq}_{B}(X)$.

(2) For any $x \in \underline{OM}^{[\wr]\geq}_{A+B}(X)$, we have that

$$\begin{aligned} x \in \overline{OM}^{[\wr]\geq}_{A+B}(X) &\Leftrightarrow [x]^{[\wr]\geq}_{A} \cap X \neq \emptyset \text{ and } [x]^{[\wr]\geq}_{B} \cap X \neq \emptyset \\ &\Leftrightarrow x \in \underline{R}^{[\wr]\geq}_{A}(X) \text{ and } x \in \underline{R}^{[\wr]\geq}_{B}(X) \\ &\Leftrightarrow x \in \underline{R}^{[\wr]\geq}_{A}(X) \cap \underline{R}^{[\wr]\geq}_{B}(X) \end{aligned}$$

Consequently, $\overline{OM}^{[\wr]\geq}_{A+B}(X) = \underline{R}^{[\wr]\geq}_{A}(X) \cup \underline{R}^{[\wr]\geq}_{B}(X)$.

(3) For any $x \in \underline{PM}^{[\wr]\geq}_{A+B}(X)$, we have that

$$\begin{aligned} x \in \underline{PM}^{[\wr]\geq}_{A+B}(X) &\Leftrightarrow [x]^{[\wr]\geq}_{A} \subseteq X \text{ and } [x]^{[\wr]\geq}_{B} \subseteq X \\ &\Leftrightarrow x \in \underline{R}^{[\wr]\geq}_{A}(X) \text{ and } x \in \underline{R}^{[\wr]\geq}_{B}(X) \\ &\Leftrightarrow x \in \underline{R}^{[\wr]\geq}_{A}(X) \cap \underline{R}^{[\wr]\geq}_{B}(X) \end{aligned}$$

So, $\underline{PM}^{[\wr]\geq}_{A+B}(X) = \underline{R}^{[\wr]\geq}_{A}(X) \cap \underline{R}^{[\wr]\geq}_{B}(X)$.

(4) For any $x \in \underline{PM}^{[\wr]\geq}_{A+B}(X)$, we have that

$$\begin{aligned} x \in \overline{PM}^{[\wr]\geq}_{A+B}(X) &\Leftrightarrow [x]^{[\wr]\geq}_{A} \cap X \neq \emptyset \text{ or } [x]^{[\wr]\geq}_{B} \cap X \neq \emptyset \\ &\Leftrightarrow x \in \underline{R}^{[\wr]\geq}_{A}(X) \text{ or } x \in \underline{R}^{[\wr]\geq}_{B}(X) \\ &\Leftrightarrow x \in \underline{R}^{[\wr]\geq}_{A}(X) \cup \underline{R}^{[\wr]\geq}_{B}(X) \end{aligned}$$

So, $\overline{PM}^{[\wr]\geq}_{A+B}(X) = \underline{R}^{[\wr]\geq}_{A}(X) \cup \underline{R}^{[\wr]\geq}_{B}(X)$.

□

Proposition A8. *Let $\mathcal{I}^{[\wr]\geq} = (U, AT, V, f)$ be an IIFOIS, $A_i \in AT, i = 1, 2, \cdots, s (s \leq 2^{|AT|})$, $X \in U, Y \in U$. Then we have*

(1) $\underline{OM}^{[\wr]\geq}_{\sum_{i=1}^{s} A_i}(X \cap Y) = \bigcup_{i=1}^{s}(\underline{R}^{[\wr]\geq}_{A_i}(X) \cap \underline{R}^{[\wr]\geq}_{A_i}(Y))$.

(2) $\overline{OM}^{[\wr]\geq}_{\sum_{i=1}^{s} A_i}(X \cup Y) = \bigcap_{i=1}^{s}(\overline{R}^{[\wr]\geq}_{A_i}(X) \cup \overline{R}^{[\wr]\geq}_{A_i}(Y))$.

(3) $\underline{PM}^{[\wr]\geq}_{\sum_{i=1}^{s} A_i}(X \cap Y) = \bigcap_{i=1}^{s}(\underline{R}^{[\wr]\geq}_{A_i}(X) \cap \underline{R}^{[\wr]\geq}_{A_i}(Y))$.

(4) $\overline{PM}^{[\wr]\geq}_{\sum_{i=1}^{s} A_i}(X \cup Y) = \bigcup_{i=1}^{s}(\overline{R}^{[\wr]\geq}_{A_i}(X) \cup \overline{R}^{[\wr]\geq}_{A_i}(Y))$.

Proof. By Proposition 3 (5L), (5U) and Proposition 12, it can be obtained easily. □

Proposition A9. *Let $\mathcal{I}^{[\wr]\geq} = (U, AT, V, f)$ be an IIFOIS, $A_i \in AT, i = 1, 2, \cdots, s (s \leq 2^{|AT|})$, $X \in P(U)$, the lower and upper approximations of the OMGRS and the PMGRS by the support festure function are*

(1) $\underline{OM}^{[\wr]\geq}_{\sum_{i=1}^{s} A_i}(X) = \{x \in U | \frac{\sum_{i=1}^{s} S_X^{A_i}(x)}{s} > 0\}$, $\overline{OM}^{[\wr]\geq}_{\sum_{i=1}^{s} A_i}(X) = \{x \in U | \frac{\sum_{i=1}^{s}(1 - S_{\sim X}^{A_i}(x))}{s} \geq 1\}$.

(2) $\underline{PM}^{[\wr]\geq}_{\sum_{i=1}^{s} A_i}(X) = \{x \in U | \frac{\sum_{i=1}^{s} S_X^{A_i}(x)}{s} \geq 1\}$, $\overline{PM}^{[\wr]\geq}_{\sum_{i=1}^{s} A_i}(X) = \{x \in U | \frac{\sum_{i=1}^{s}(1 - S_{\sim X}^{A_i}(x))}{s} > 0\}$.

Proof. It can be obtained easily from the definition of the opetimistic multiple granulation rough set, the pessimistic multiple granulation rough set and the support feasure function. □

Proposition A10. *Let $\mathcal{I}^{[\wr]]\geq} = (U, AT, V, f)$ be an IIFOIS, $A_i \in AT, i = 1, 2, \cdots, s (s \leq 2^{|AT|})$, $\beta \in (0.5, 1]$, $X \in U$. Then we have*

(1) $\underline{PM}^{[\wr]\geq}_{\sum_{i=1}^{s} A_i}(X) \subseteq \underline{GM}^{[\wr]\geq}_{\sum_{i=1}^{s} A_i}(X)_\beta \subseteq \underline{OM}^{[\wr]\geq}_{\sum_{i=1}^{s} A_i}(X) \subseteq \underline{R}^{[\wr]\geq}_{\bigcup_{i=1}^{s} A_i}(X)$.

(2) $\overline{PM}^{[\wr]\geq}_{\sum_{i=1}^{s} A_i}(X) \supseteq \overline{GM}^{[\wr]\geq}_{\sum_{i=1}^{s} A_i}(X)_\beta \supseteq \overline{OM}^{[\wr]\geq}_{\sum_{i=1}^{s} A_i}(X) \supseteq \overline{R}^{[\wr]\geq}_{\bigcup_{i=1}^{s} A_i}(X)$.

(3) $\underline{PM}^{[\wr]\geq}_{\sum_{i=1}^{s} A_i}(X) \subseteq \underline{R}^{[\wr]\geq}_{A_i}(X) \subseteq \underline{OM}^{[\wr]\geq}_{\sum_{i=1}^{s} A_i}(X) \subseteq \underline{R}^{[\wr]\geq}_{\bigcup_{i=1}^{s} A_i}(X)$.

(4) $\overline{PM}^{[\wr]\geq}_{\sum_{i=1}^{s} A_i}(X) \supseteq \overline{R}^{[\wr]\geq}_{A_i}(X) \supseteq \overline{OM}^{[\wr]\geq}_{\sum_{i=1}^{s} A_i}(X) \supseteq \overline{R}^{[\wr]\geq}_{\bigcup_{i=1}^{s} A_i}(X)$.

Proof. By Definitions 1 and 4 and Propositions 11 and 12, it can be obtained easily.

It is worth mentioning that there is no clear fixed inclusion relationship between the approximation set $GM^{[\wr]\geq}_{\sum_{i=1}^{s} A_i}(X)_\beta$ and arbitrary $R^{[\wr]\geq}_{A_i}(X)$. □

Proposition A11. *Let $\mathcal{I}^{[\wr]\geq} = (U, AT, V, f)$ be an IIFOIS, $A_i \in AT, i = 1, 2, \cdots, s (s \leq 2^{|AT|})$, $X \in U$. Then*

(1) $\rho^{[\wr]\geq}(R^{[\wr]\geq}_{A_i}, X) \geq \rho_o^{[\wr]\geq}(\sum_{i=1}^{s} A_i, X) \geq \rho^{[\wr]\geq}(R^{[\wr]\geq}_{\bigcup_{i=1}^{s} A_i}, X)$.

(2) $\rho_p^{[\wr]\geq}(\sum_{i=1}^s A_i, X) \geq \rho^{[\wr]\geq}(R_{A_i}^{[\wr]\geq}, X) \geq \rho^{[\wr]\geq}(R_{\cup_{i=1}^s A_i}^{[\wr]\geq}, X)$.
(3) $\rho_p^{[\wr]\geq}(\sum_{i=1}^s A_i, X) \geq \rho^{[\wr]\geq}(R_{A_i}^{[\wr]\geq}, X) \geq \rho_o^{[\wr]\geq}(\sum_{i=1}^s A_i, X) \geq \rho^{[\wr]\geq}(R_{\cup_{i=1}^s A_i}^{[\wr]\geq}, X)$.

Proof. (1) By Propositions 12 and 14, we have that

$$\underline{R}_{A_i}^{[\wr]\geq}(X) \subseteq \underline{OM}_{\sum_{i=1}^s A_i}^{[\wr]\geq}(X) \subseteq \underline{R}_{\cup_{i=1}^s A_i}^{[\wr]\geq}(X),$$

and

$$\overline{R}_{A_i}^{[\wr]\geq}(X) \supseteq \overline{OM}_{\sum_{i=1}^s A_i}^{[\wr]\geq}(X) \supseteq \overline{R}_{\cup_{i=1}^s A_i}^{[\wr]\geq}(X),$$

then

$$\frac{|\underline{R}_{A_i}^{[\wr]\geq}(X)|}{|\overline{R}_{A_i}^{[\wr]\geq}(X)|} \leq \frac{|\underline{OM}_{\sum_{i=1}^s A_i}^{[\wr]\geq}(X)|}{|\overline{OM}_{\sum_{i=1}^s A_i}^{[\wr]\geq}(X)|} \leq \frac{|\underline{R}_{\cup_{i=1}^s A_i}^{[\wr]\geq}(X)|}{|\overline{R}_{\cup_{i=1}^s A_i}^{[\wr]\geq}(X)|}.$$

Therefore, $\rho^{[\wr]\geq}(R_{A_i}^{[\wr]\geq}, X) \geq \rho_o^{[\wr]\geq}(\sum_{i=1}^s A_i, X) \geq \rho^{[\wr]\geq}(R_{\cup_{i=1}^s A_i}^{[\wr]\geq}, X)$ by Definition 2.

(2) By Propositions 12 and 14, we have that

$$\underline{PM}_{\sum_{i=1}^s A_i}^{[\wr]\geq}(X) \subseteq \underline{R}_{A_i}^{[\wr]\geq}(X) \subseteq \underline{R}_{\cup_{i=1}^s A_i}^{[\wr]\geq}(X),$$

and

$$\overline{PM}_{\sum_{i=1}^s A_i}^{[\wr]\geq}(X) \supseteq \overline{R}_{A_i}^{[\wr]\geq}(X) \supseteq \overline{R}_{\cup_{i=1}^s A_i}^{[\wr]\geq}(X),$$

then

$$\frac{|\underline{PM}_{\sum_{i=1}^s A_i}^{[\wr]\geq}(X)|}{|\overline{PM}_{\sum_{i=1}^s A_i}^{[\wr]\geq}(X)|} \leq \frac{|\underline{R}_{A_i}^{[\wr]\geq}(X)|}{|\overline{R}_{A_i}^{[\wr]\geq}(X)|} \leq \frac{|\underline{R}_{\cup_{i=1}^s A_i}^{[\wr]\geq}(X)|}{|\overline{R}_{\cup_{i=1}^s A_i}^{[\wr]\geq}(X)|}.$$

Therefore, $\rho_p^{[\wr]\geq}(\sum_{i=1}^s A_i, X) \geq \rho^{[\wr]\geq}(R_{A_i}^{[\wr]\geq}, X) \geq \rho^{[\wr]\geq}(R_{\cup_{i=1}^s A_i}^{[\wr]\geq}, X)$ by Definition 5.

(3) It can be obtained easily from the information above. □

Proposition A12. *Let $\mathcal{I}^{[\wr]\geq} = (U, CT \cup d, V, f)$ be an IIFDOIS, $A_i \in AT, i = 1, 2, \cdots, s (s \leq 2^{|AT|})$. Then*
(1) $\gamma^{[\wr]\geq}(R_{A_i}^{[\wr]\geq}, d) \leq \gamma_o^{[\wr]\geq}(\sum_{i=1}^s A_i, d) \leq \gamma^{[\wr]\geq}(R_{\cup_{i=1}^s A_i}^{[\wr]\geq}, d)$.
(2) $\gamma_p^{[\wr]\geq}(\sum_{i=1}^s A_i, d) \leq \gamma^{[\wr]\geq}(R_{A_i}^{[\wr]ge}, d) \leq \gamma^{[\wr]\geq}(R_{\cup_{i=1}^s A_i}^{[\wr]\geq}, d)$.
(3) $\gamma_p^{[\wr]\geq}(\sum_{i=1}^s A_i, d) \leq \gamma^{[\wr]ge}(R_{A_i}^{[\wr]\geq}, d) \leq \gamma_o^{[\wr]\geq}(\sum_{i=1}^s A_i, d) \leq \gamma^{[\wr]\geq}(R_{\cup_{i=1}^s A_i}^{[\wr]\geq}, d)$.

Proof. (1) For any $D_j \in U/d = \{D_1, D_2, \cdots, D_k\}$, by Propositions 12 and 14, we have that

$$\underline{R}_{A_i}^{[\wr]\geq}(D_j) \subseteq \underline{OM}_{\sum_{i=1}^s A_i}^{[\wr]\geq}(D_j) \subseteq \underline{R}_{\cup_{i=1}^s A_i}^{[\wr]\geq}(D_j),$$

then

$$|\underline{R}_{A_i}^{[\wr]\geq}(D_j)| \leq |\underline{OM}_{\sum_{i=1}^s A_i}^{[\wr]\geq}(D_j)| \leq |\underline{R}_{\cup_{i=1}^s A_i}^{[\wr]\geq}(D_j)|.$$

Hence, $\gamma^{[\wr]\geq}(R_{A_i}^{[\wr]\geq}, d) \leq \gamma_o^{[\wr]\geq}(\sum_{i=1}^s A_i, d) \leq \gamma^{[\wr]\geq}(R_{\cup_{i=1}^s A_i}^{[\wr]\geq}, d)$ by Definition 3.

(2) For any $D_j \in U/d = \{D_1, D_2, \cdots, D_k\}$, by Propositions 12 and 14, we have that

$$\underline{PM}_{\sum_{i=1}^s A_i}^{[\wr]\geq}(X) \subseteq \underline{R}_{A_i}^{[\wr]\geq}(X) \subseteq \underline{R}_{\cup_{i=1}^s A_i}^{[\wr]\geq}(X),$$

then

$$|\underline{PM}_{\sum_{i=1}^s A_i}^{[\wr]\geq}(X)| \leq |\underline{R}_{A_i}^{[\wr]\geq}(X)| \leq |\underline{R}_{\cup_{i=1}^s A_i}^{[\wr]\geq}(X)|.$$

Hence, $\gamma_p^{[\wr]\geq}(\sum_{i=1}^{s} A_i, d) \leq \gamma^{[\wr]\geq}(R_{A_i}^{[\wr]\geq}, d) \leq \gamma^{[\wr]\geq}(R_{\cup_{i=1}^{s} A_i}^{[\wr]\geq}, d)$ by Definition 6.

(3) It can be obtained easily from the information above. □

References

1. Pawlak, Z. Rough sets. *Int. J. Comput. Inf. Sci.* **1982**, *11*, 341–356. [CrossRef]
2. Chan, C.C. A rough set approach to attribute generalization in data mining. *Inf. Sci.* **1998**, *107*, 169–176. [CrossRef]
3. Kim, D.J. Data Classification based on Tolerant Rough Set. *Pattern Recognit.* **2001**, *34*, 1613–1624. [CrossRef]
4. An, L.P.; Wu, Y.H.; Tong, L.Y. Conflict analysis and negotiation model based on rough set theory. *J. Univ. Sci. Technol.* **2002**, *1*, 91–95.
5. Pawlak, Z. Some remarks on conflict analysis. *Eur. J. Oper. Res.* **2003**, *166*, 649–654. [CrossRef]
6. Sun, B.Z.; Ma, W.M.; Zhao, H.Y. Rough set-based conflict analysis model and method over two universes. *Inf. Sci.* **2016**, *372*, 111–125. [CrossRef]
7. Cyran, K.A.; Mrozek, A. Rough sets in hybrid methods for pattern recognition. *Int. J. Intell. Syst.* **2001**, *15*, 149–168. [CrossRef]
8. Swiniarski, R.W.; Skowron, A. Rough set methods in feature selection and recognition. *Pattern Recognit. Lett.* **2003**, *24*, 833–849. [CrossRef]
9. Miao, D.Q.; Wang, Y. Rough sets based approach for multivariate decision tree contruction. *J. Softw.* **1997**, *8*, 425–431.
10. Wang, Y.; Miao, D.Q.; Zhou, Y.J. A summary of the theory and application on rough set. *Pattern Recognit. Artif. Intell.* **1996**, *9*, 337–344.
11. Atanassov, K.T. Intuitionistic fuzzy sets. *Fuzzy Sets Syst.* **1986**, *20*, 87–96. [CrossRef]
12. Sang, B.B; Zhang, X.Y. The Approach to Probabilistic Decision-Theoretic Rough Set in Intuitionistic Fuzzy Information Systems. *Int. Inf. Manag. Comput. Sci.* **2020**, *12*, 1–26. [CrossRef]
13. Xu, W.H.; Wang, Q.R.; Luo, S.Q. Multi-granulation fuzzy rough sets. *J. Int. Fuzzy. Syst.* **2014**, *26*, 1323–1340. [CrossRef]
14. Zadeh, L.A. Fuzzy sets. *Inf. Control* **1965**, *8*, 338–353. [CrossRef]
15. Coker, D. Fuzzy rough sets are intuitionistic L-fuzzy sets. *Fuzzy Sets Syst.* **1998**, *96*, 381–383. [CrossRef]
16. Sang, B.B.; Zhang, X.Y.; Xu, W.H. Attribute reduction of relative knowledge granularity in intuitionistic fuzzy ordered decision table. *Filomat* **2018**, *32*, 1727–1736. [CrossRef]
17. Xu, W.H.; Liu, Y.F.; Sun, W.X. Upper approximation reduction based on intuitionistic fuzzy T equivalence informatin system. *Rough Sets Knowl. Technol.* **2012**, *4*, 55–62.
18. Zhou, L.; Wu, W.Z. On generalized intuitionistic fuzzy rough approximation operators. *Inf. Sci.* **2008**, *178*, 2448–2465. [CrossRef]
19. Zhou, L.; Wu, W.Z. Characterization of rough set approximations in Atanassov intuitionistic fuzzy set theory. *Comput. Math. Appl.* **2011**, *62*, 282–296. [CrossRef]
20. Zhang, Z.M. Generalized intuitionistic fuzzy rough sets based on intuitionistic fuzzy coverings. *Inf. Sci.* **2012**, *198*, 186–206. [CrossRef]
21. Xu, W.H.; Sun, W.X.; Zhang, X.Y. Multiple granulation rough set approach to ordered information systems. *Int. J. Gen. Syst.* **2012**, *41*, 475–501. [CrossRef]
22. Qian, Y.H.; Liang, J.Y.; Yao, Y.Y. MGRS: A multi-granulation rough set. *Inf. Sci.* **2009**, *180*, 949–970. [CrossRef]
23. Xu, W.H.; Zhang, W.X. Measuring roughness of generalized rough sets induced by a covering. *Fuzzy Sets Syst.* **2007**, *158*, 2443–2455. [CrossRef]
24. Xu, W.H.; Zhang, X.Y.; Zhang, W.X. Knowledge granulation, knowledge entropy and knowledge uncertainty measure in ordered information systems. *Comput. Inform.* **2009**, *9*, 1244–1251.
25. Xu, W.H.; Zhang, X.Y.; Zhong, J.M. Attribute reduction in ordered information systems based on evidence theory. *Knowl. Inf. Syst.* **2010**, *25*, 169–184. [CrossRef]
26. Xu, W.H. The ordered information system and the rough set. Sci. Pre: Beijing/China. 2013. Available online: http://www.ecsponline.com/goods.php?id=154502 (accessed on 22 March 2021).
27. Yao, Y.Y. Granular Computing: Basic issues and possible solutions. *Comput. Inf.* **2002**, *1*, 186–189.
28. Khan, M.A.; Ma, M.H. A Modal Logic for Multiple-Source Tolerance Approximation Spaces. In *Lecture Notes in Computer Science, Proceedings of the Logic and Its Applications, Delhi, India, 5–11 January 2011*; Springer: Berlin/Heidelberg, Germany, 2011.
29. Yu, Y.Y.; Zeng, X.L.; Sun, X.X. Interval-valued information systems based on dominance relation and its attribute reduction.Comput. *Eng. Appl.* **2011**, *47*, 122–124.
30. Zhang, N.; Miao, D.Q.; Yue, X.D.Approaches to knowledge reduction in interval-valued information system. *Comput. Res. Dev.* **2010**, *47*, 1362–1371.
31. Qian, Y.H.; Liang, J.Y.; Dang, C.Y. Interval ordered information systems. *Comput. Math. Appl.* **2008**, *56*, 1994–2009. [CrossRef]
32. Zeng, X.L.; Chen, S.; Mei, L.C.Interval ordered information system and its attribute reduction algorithm. *Comput. Eng.* **2010**, *36*, 62–63.
33. Huang, B.; Wei, D.K.; Li, H.X. Using a rough set model to extract rules in dominance-based interval-valued intuitionistic fuzzy information systems. *Inf. Sci.* **2013**, *221*, 215–229. [CrossRef]

34. Sang, B.B.; Xu,W.H. Rough membership measure in intuitionistic fuzzy information system. In Proceedings of the 2017 13th International Conference on Natural Computation, Fuzzy Systems and Knowledge Discovery (ICNC-FSKD), Guilin, China, 29–31 July 2017.
35. Huang, B.; Zhuang, Y.L.; Li, H.X. A dominance intuitionistic fuzzy-rough set approach and its applications. *Appl. Math. Model.* **2013**, *37*, 7128–7141. [CrossRef]
36. Huang, B.; Li, H.X.; Wei, D.K. Dominance-based rough set model in intuitionistic fuzzy information systems. *Knowl-Based. Syst.* **2012**, *28*, 115–123. [CrossRef]
37. Huang, B.; Guo, C.X.; Zhuang, Y.L. Intuitionistic fuzzy multigranulation rough sets. *Inf. Sci.* **2014**, *277*, 299–320. [CrossRef]

symmetry

MDPI

Article

Risk Assessment of Circuit Breakers Using Influence Diagrams with Interval Probabilities

Jelena D. Velimirovic [1,*] and Aleksandar Janjic [2]

[1] Mathematical Institute of the Serbian Academy of Sciences and Arts, Kneza Mihaila 36, 11001 Belgrade, Serbia
[2] Faculty of Electronic Engineering, University of Nis, Aleksandra Medvedeva 14, 18000 Nis, Serbia; aleksandar.janjic@elfak.ni.ac.rs
* Correspondence: jelena.velimirovic@mi.sanu.ac.rs

Abstract: This paper deals with uncertainty, asymmetric information, and risk modelling in a complex power system. The uncertainty is managed by using probability and decision theory methods. More specifically, influence diagrams—as extended Bayesian network functions with interval probabilities represented through credal sets—were chosen for the predictive modelling scenario of replacing the most critical circuit breakers in optimal time. Namely, based on the available data on circuit breakers and other variables that affect the considered model of a complex power system, a group of experts was able to assess the situation using interval probabilities instead of crisp probabilities. Furthermore, the paper examines how the confidence interval width affects decision-making in this context and eliminates the information asymmetry of different experts. Based on the obtained results for each considered interval width separately on the action to be taken over the considered model in order to minimize the risk of the power system failure, it can be concluded that the proposed approach clearly indicates the advantages of using interval probability when making decisions in systems such as the one considered in this paper.

Keywords: uncertainty; crisp probability; interval probability; influence diagrams; circuit breakers

Citation: Velimirovic, J.D.; Janjic, A. Risk Assessment of Circuit Breakers Using Influence Diagrams with Interval Probabilities. *Symmetry* **2021**, *13*, 737. https://doi.org/10.3390/sym13050737

Academic Editor: Dragan Pamucar

Received: 31 March 2021
Accepted: 18 April 2021
Published: 21 April 2021

1. Introduction

The main goal of every enterprise is to preserve and optimize the quality of its operations and services. Nowadays, the complex power grid is becoming more responsive, safe, and efficient due to large amounts of data that are being collected, stored, and analyzed using new technologies. This analysis provides stakeholders with new insights that are not possible to gain with conventional information technology (IT) and based on which well-informed decisions can be made. Contemporary power systems are coping with serious challenges, such as integration of renewables and active demand and the uncertainty and asymmetric information it brings into the whole system of power operation, planning, and control.

New technologies in the energy sector include risk-based and predictive maintenance to replace aging infrastructure by minimizing its costs, fault detection, fault diagnosis, etc. The technologies can also be applied to monitoring and to routine daily operations, making them more accurate, efficient, and resilient [1].

Maintaining reliability, minimizing operation costs, and making a profit are hard to achieve without proper risk analysis and uncertainty management [2].

Having in mind that a complex power system consists of many interdependent subsystems, analyzing the system's state, keeping reliability at a desired level, and mitigating losses becomes harder than ever [3,4]. That is why new risk assessment methodologies that deal with uncertainty are introduced. The main challenge for this research was to develop a risk assessment methodology when the accurate failure equipment database and the probability distribution of equipment states are missing. For instance, when a group of experts evaluate risk, their evaluation of event probability can be expressed only as an interval value.

Circuit breakers are a vital element of the energy system, which is why there is a need for their continuous improvement through the analysis of increasing reliability and the determination of their remaining life. This is achieved by constant monitoring of work, regular maintenance, and analysis of data from its exploitation.

Another important reason for analyzing them lies in the ability to reduce costs. It is important to know the data of a circuit breaker approaching the end of its life, because it significantly affects the business economy. Therefore, such data make it possible to plan the replacement of the circuit breaker in a timely manner, which is a better scenario in relation to its unplanned failure [5,6].

Regular monitoring of the operation of a circuit breaker, as well as indicators of its condition, provides knowledge of its reliability, i.e., its remaining service life. Based on such data, the cost-effectiveness of the replacement and its scope, as well as the timeframe can be planned [5,6].

Replacing the most risky circuit breakers is a good basis for increasing the reliability of the energy system, reducing the amount of undelivered electricity, and thus eliminating the additional involvement of labor if a circuit breaker is replaced before its unplanned failure. Today, low-oil circuit breakers are replaced with circuit breakers based on modern technologies, such as vacuum and SF6 circuit breakers.

However, despite this, most substations still have a large number of low-oil circuit breakers in operation. With low-oil circuit breakers, there is a need for frequent maintenance, such as changing or refilling oil and lubricating the mechanism, as well as frequent visual inspection.

For these reasons, there is a need to replace old technology circuit breakers, which is why it is necessary to determine the criteria and the pace of their replacement. Analysis of the condition of circuit breakers and determination of risk would provide insight into the number of the most risky circuit breakers. Additionally, from the aspect of energy system stability and business economy, circuit breakers whose failures may produce the greatest consequences would be defined. In this way, the circuit breakers with the highest risk should be proposed for urgent replacement [5,6].

Literature shows different techniques that examine circuit breaker condition analyses. Data mining techniques that include classification techniques and expert opinion, such as fuzzy set theory, are used to examine circuit breakers' lifetime and operation mode [7,8]. Unlike these data-driven prognostics, there is a model-based prognostic that includes engineering knowledge within the considered model [9,10]. Furthermore, literature shows evidence of hybrid prognostic techniques that combine discrete and continuous events within a system. Hybrid approaches comprehensively consider the parameters that affect the operation of a system.

Frequently used hybrid prognostic techniques for circuit breaker analyses are piecewise deterministic Markov processes [11]. In [12,13], it is shown that the use of these models is very suitable for the creation of hybrid prognostic applications. The so-called shock model is a model based on which behavior of a system is modeled during a failure. In [13], a component of the random evolution of the system was added to the shock model, which is described using continuous-time Markov chains.

Additionally, dynamic reliability problems are solved using piecewise deterministic Markov processes [14,15]. In these systems, depending on the operating conditions, it is possible to separately observe and model each component of interest for the reliable operation of the system. In addition to this technique, dynamic Bayesian networks (BNs) [16] are very often used for the problem of dynamic reliability. A new method developed for hybrid prognostics approaches based on a combination of deterministic and stochastic properties called hybrid particle Petri nets is described in [17]. Hybrid bond graphs that form the basis of the model described in [18] represent another tool for hybrid prognostics, which with the help of Monte Carlo simulations enable the determination of variables with constraints in the predictive model.

The necessary conditions for the usage of all previously explained methodologies is an accurate failure equipment database and the already known probability distribution of equipment states. Very few research studies have addressed the uncertainties, accuracy, and confidence of the inspection results, although the simulations and decision models are directly dependent on these results. Probabilistic uncertainties require appropriate mathematical modeling and quantification when predicting a future state of the nature or the value of certain parameters.

The notion of probability is very closely related to the notion of symmetry. Based on symmetry, we can talk about equal conditions for random events. We can extend the notion of probability to interval probabilities, especially when determining the aggregate probability value estimated by several experts and a situation where there is imperfect knowledge (when one party has different information to another).

An integrated framework consisting of intuitionistic fuzzy-failure mode effect analysis (IF-FMEA) and IF-technique for order preference by similarity to ideal solution (IF-TOPSIS) techniques, taking into account the vague concept and the hesitation of experts, was presented in [19]. Similarly, to assess the uncertain and imprecise nature of e-service evaluation in [20], a combination of fuzzy analytical hierarchy process (F-AHP) and fuzzy measurement alternatives and ranking according to compromise solution (F-MARCOS) was used. For the most accurate determination of weights under fuzziness, the fuzzy full consistency method (FUCOM-F) has been proposed in [21]. Additionally, criteria weights have been determined by the fuzzy SWARA (step-wise weight assessment ratio analysis) method, as described in [22]. In [22], for such criteria weights, a combination of fuzzy TOPSIS, fuzzy WASPAS, and fuzzy ARAS methods was used to perform evaluation and selection of suppliers for the considered example. Fuzzy set theory and interval analysis [23] represent one highly performing method for determining parametric uncertainties.

In situations where an estimate needs to be made under uncertain information where attribute values can describe the interval gray numbers, in [24] it is proposed to use a multi-criteria decision-making model that combines the interval gray numbers and normalized weighted geometric Dombi–Bonferroni mean operator.

The origin of the uncertainty in engineering systems come from both aleatoric and epistemic reasons. The review of hybrid uncertainty problems when both of these types are present, including uncertainty modeling, propagation analysis, structural reliability analysis, and reliability-based design optimization, is given in [25].

Probability-boxes (p-boxes) are often used in engineering analysis when the exact probability of a random variable probability distribution is unknown [26]. They offer a mathematically straightforward description of imprecise probabilities, defined via lower and upper bounds on the cumulative distribution function. P-boxes are used in acoustic analysis [27], structural reliability [28], risk analysis [29], and many other engineering fields.

The p-box framework that explains imprecision in stochastic processes by considering additional epistemic uncertainty in the process' autocorrelation structure is described in [30,31]. Surrogate models for propagating probability-boxes include Kriging models [32] and polynomial response surface models [33]. Adaptive schemes based on Gaussian process models that can be applied to parametric and distribution-free p-boxes are given in [34]. Most often, the propagation of p-boxes is analyzed using the Monte Carlo simulation, but the comprehensive review of computational methods for p-boxes propagation in input models is given in [26]. A study of Monte Carlo methods for the general case of propagating imprecise probabilities is described in [35].

Previous methodologies offer a complete solution for the analysis of possible bounds of a certain random variable. However, the practical implementation of these bounds in risk-based decision-making has not been explored so far.

In this paper, authors use a new technique based on influence diagrams (IDs) with interval probabilities for failure prognostics. Based on the derived conclusions on the influence of interval width on the decision-making for the considered scenario, a group of experts evaluated all considered variables with interval probabilities, where the interval width was set in accordance with the previously derived conclusions. We sought to predict the best scenario of replacing the most critical circuit breakers in optimal time.

The novelty of this method is the usage of interval probabilities in standard influence diagrams. Furthermore, the paper examines how the confidence interval width affects decision-making in this context. The method can be easily implemented to any other kind of decision process presented by the influence diagram.

The paper is organized as follows—the second section discusses circuit breaker risk assessment, followed by a section that deals with uncertainty, definition, and properties of BNs and IDs; a case study with results and discussion is given in section four, which is followed by a conclusion.

2. Circuit Breaker Risk Assessment

2.1. Risk Assessment Model

The practice of equipment maintenance in power systems is a combination of corrective maintenance, maintenance at fixed intervals, and maintenance based on monitoring the condition of the equipment. Maintenance at fixed time intervals is defined by statutory deadlines for inspection, testing and inspection of equipment, or manufacturer's instructions regarding when it is necessary to take certain actions on the equipment. Maintenance based on monitoring the condition of the equipment includes visual inspections and audits that are performed on a regular basis, and any repairs or other preventive actions are performed on the basis of audit reports [5,6].

The downside of this approach is that maintenance is performed on the basis of mandatory periodic tests within the deadlines provided by regulations and recommendations, regardless of the condition of the equipment and importance. Existing maintenance practices, however, do not provide an optimal level of maintenance.

All the above facts lead to the conclusion that existing maintenance practice and funds (tangible and intangible) invested in maintenance are not optimal and that a mechanism that would enable the optimization of these funds should be sought [5,6].

Risk-based maintenance is the next generation of reliability centered maintenance (RCM). Like RCM, RBI (risk-based inspection) is a systematic process for optimizing maintenance in technical systems. RBI is very similar to the RCM approach in that its goals are actually the answer to the same questions about system functionality.

For qualitative risk analysis for each component, each part of the system, or the whole system, assessments of the status and correctness of the component or system are formed, or a risk matrix is formed on the basis of which facility and which maintenance actions should be performed, and the actions that should be performed are prioritized. The quantitative approach establishes an analytical link between risk and actions that reduces that risk. Higher risk means less reliability and vice versa [5,6].

Replacing low-oil circuit breakers is not an easy task. First of all, the investment of replacing the circuit breaker in one substation is a big capital endeavor. Next, the time to replace one circuit breaker can take up to 8 h, which in some situations can be a problem if customers cannot be supplied with electricity from another outlet. Replacing circuit breakers in some situations may require replacing or reconstructing other equipment in the cell, such as busbars and circuit breaker stands, then bringing power to the circuit breaker (if the motor power supply differs), which increases investment costs and time [5,6].

Replacing old circuit breakers would reduce the need for frequent maintenance and thus reduce labor engagement, and in addition, the reliability of the system would be increased because even overhauling an old circuit breaker increases its reliability only in a short period because the remaining parts can wear out, fail, and become the cause of a new malfunction, which was previously unpredictable.

2.2. Risk Assessment Using Influence Diagram

Bayesian networks (BNs) and influence diagrams (IDs), as probabilistic methods for uncertain reasoning, are vastly used in complex engineering systems to aid making the best decisions possible in uncertain environments/industries—nuclear, chemical, environmental, maritime, etc. A clear graphical representation sets these methods apart from the others because they show in a very clear and precise way complex causal relationships using simple structures, whereas the main disadvantage is that not every belief can be represented as an exact number or single probability measure. Decision makers are also allowed to represent their imprecise beliefs or knowledge through probability sets, called credal sets [36–39].

A credal network based on credal sets actually represents a graphical probabilistic method by which a belief is displayed using sets of interval probabilities. The use of sets of interval probabilities enables a clearer assessment of epistemic uncertainty, while with the increase of available information, the uncertainty decreases.

The next subsections examine in a more detailed way both BNs and IDs in an environment of uncertainty.

2.3. Definition and Properties of Bayesian Networks

The parents of X_i, according to an acyclic directed graph G, are the joint variable $\Pi_i \subset X$, for $\forall i$, $i = 0, \ldots, n$, where $X := (X_0, X_1, \ldots, X_n)$ represents set of variables that are in one-to-one correspondence with the nodes of G. Set of variables X_i takes its values on the finite set Ω_{X_i}, where Π_i in $\Omega_{\Pi_i} := \times_{X_j \in \Pi_i} \Omega_{X_j}$, for $\forall i$, $i = 0, \ldots, n$. Cartesian set product is marked with $\times$ symbol. As described in [40], any variable is conditionally independent of its non-descendant non-parents given its parents. This means the graph G represents stochastic independence relations if the Markov condition is fulfilled.

The specification of a conditional probability mass function $P(X_i|\pi_i)$ for each $\pi_i \in \Omega_{\Pi_i}$ and $i = 0, \ldots, n$ induces through the graph for each $x \in \Omega_X := \times_{i=0}^{n} \Omega_{X_i}$ the factorization [41]:

$$P(x) := \prod_{i=0}^{n} P(x_i|\pi_i), \tag{1}$$

where the values of x_i and π_i are those consistent with x. Equation (1) and expression $\{P(X_i|\pi_i)\}_{i=0,\ldots,n}^{\pi_i \in \Omega_{\Pi_i}}$ that represent specification of the conditional probability mass functions form BN.

The local models of X_i, $i = 0, \ldots, n$, actually represent the mass functions for X_i written in the form $\{P(X_i|\pi_i)\}_{\pi_i \in \Omega_{\Pi_i}}$. From Equation (1), using the joint probability mass function we establish inference in BN. For example, by summing out other variables from the joint probability, mass function marginal are determined, as described in Equation (2) [41]:

$$P(x_0) = \sum_{x_1 \ldots x_n} \prod_{i=0}^{n} P(x_i|\pi_i), \tag{2}$$

where $x_0 \in \Omega_{X_0}$, whereas instead of $\sum_{X \in \Omega_X}$, $\sum_x$ is used. Additionally, the value from Equation (2) can be calculated in another way using the procedure linear combination of the local probabilities associated with an arbitrary $X_j \in X$:

$$P(x_0) = \sum_{x_j, \pi_j} \left[P\left(x_0 \middle| x_j, \pi_j\right) \cdot P\left(\pi_j\right) \right] \cdot P\left(x_j \middle| \pi_j\right), \tag{3}$$

In this case, from the BN specification the probabilities $P\left(x_j \middle| \pi_j\right)$ are determined, from Equation (2) the unconditional probabilities $P\left(\pi_j\right)$ are obtained, and for the conditional ones $P\left(x_0 \middle| x_j, \pi_j\right) = P\left(x_0, x_j, \pi_j\right) / P\left(x_j, \pi_j\right)$, assuming the condition $P\left(x_j, \pi_j\right) > 0$ is valid. From Equation (3), assuming that $X_j = X_0$ follows:

$$P(x_0) = \sum\nolimits_{\pi_0} P(\pi_0) \cdot P(x_0|\pi_0), \tag{4}$$

For $X_0 \in \Pi_j$, the previous equation becomes:

$$P(x_0) = \sum_{x_j \pi'_j} P\left(x_0, \pi'_j\right) P\left(x_j \middle| x_0, \pi'_j\right),\ \Pi'_j := \Pi_j \backslash \{X_0\}, \tag{5}$$

From the previous expressions it can be noticed that, for example, in the case of determining the marginal, local models do not affect the probability, which means that the local models of X_j have no effect on values of $P(\pi_j)$ and $P(x_0|x_j, \pi_j)$, where $\forall x_j \in \Omega_{X_j}$ and $\pi_j \in \Omega_{\Pi_j}$. Determining $P(\pi_j)$ is not affected by the values of $\{P(X_j|\pi_j)\}_{\pi_j \in \Omega_{\Pi_j}}$, with the condition where for all the variables in Π_j, child is X_j [41].

In case we want to determine a conditional probability, local model can also be irrelevant for a certain part of the calculation; that is, the local models of X_j can be excluded when determining $P(x_0|x_j, \pi_j)$.

ID, as extensions of BN, were proposed in [42] as a tool to simplify modelling and analysis of decision trees. They are a graphical aid to decision-making under uncertainty, representing the causal relationships of possible causes and effects. Unlike a decision tree, an ID shows dependencies among variables more clearly. Thanks to clear links between variables, IDs allow for maximum reduction of a decision maker's confusion during decision-making [43]. Both the BN and the ID are probabilistic networks. The difference is that the BN is used for belief update, while the ID is used for reasoning about decision-making under uncertainty [44].

In addition to the traditional BN, IDs have, besides an external influence (an exogenous variable—a variable whose values are not affected by the decision being made), a decision node; that is, a decision made by the decision maker.

An intermediate variable depicts an endogenous variable whose values are computed as functions of decision, exogenous, and other endogenous variables. A value node (objective variable) is a quantitative criterion that is the subject of optimization. A chance node represents a random variable whose value is dictated by some probability distribution. An arrow shows the influence between variables.

The methods for evaluating and solving IDs are based on probabilities, and efficient algorithms have been developed to analyze them [45–49]. Like in BNs, the input and output values of a node are based on the Bayesian theorem. The use of probability tables with many elements is, however, very difficult because of the combinatorial explosion arising from the requirement that the solution must be extracted by the cross product of all probability tables.

Because it is very difficult to determine the precise probabilities of the remaining lifetime of circuit breakers and the risk they pose to the entire power system, in this paper we introduce a new concept of interval probability in order to find the best strategy for a given circuit breaker set. Namely, based on the collected and available data on circuit breakers, a group of experts evaluated the situation with interval probabilities instead of crisp probabilities.

As described in [50,51], the product of event probability $p(E)$ and its consequence $Cons(E)$ for the considered event E determines the risk associated with that event.

$$Risk(E) = p(E) \cdot Cons(E). \tag{6}$$

In the case where empirical scaling parameters x, y, and w are observed, the previous equation becomes [52]:

$$Risk(E) = p(E)^y \cdot w \cdot Cons(E)^x. \tag{7}$$

In general, for the calculated probabilities described by Equations (1)–(7), the risk can be calculated as follows:

$$R_i = f(C(\pi_i), P(\pi_i)). \tag{8}$$

The risk can also be presented in a table, such as the example given in the Figure 1.

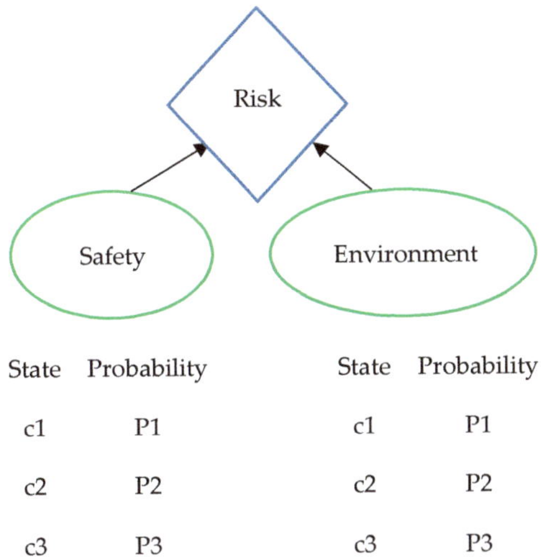

Figure 1. Risk assessment based on two criteria.

Based on the level of these two criteria, the risk can take values in the range from 1 (no risk) to 10 (highest risk). Risk assessment using crisp probabilities for the example given in Figure 1 is shown in Table 1

Table 1. Risk assessment using crisp probabilities for the example given in Figure 1.

Safety	Probability	Environment	Probability	Risk
c1	P1	c1	P1	1
c1	P1	c2	P2	2
c1	P1	c3	P3	3
c2	P2	c1	P1	4
c2	P2	c2	P2	7
c2	P2	c3	P3	6
c3	P3	c1	P1	5
c3	P3	c2	P2	8
c3	P3	c3	P3	10

A complete model of the risk assessment of the circuit breaker maintenance strategy considered in this paper is represented in Figure 2. The graphical symbols in Figure 2 indicate the following: an orange ellipse shows an external influence, i.e., an exogenous variable, the value of which is not conditioned by previous decisions; red and green ellipses denote chance nodes described by random variables defined by discrete probability distributions. The decision is represented by a purple rectangle. Endogenous variables determined as functions of decision and other variables are represented by intermediate variables. The blue diamond represents the subject of optimization and is classified as a quantitative criterion. Influence between variables is described by an arrow.

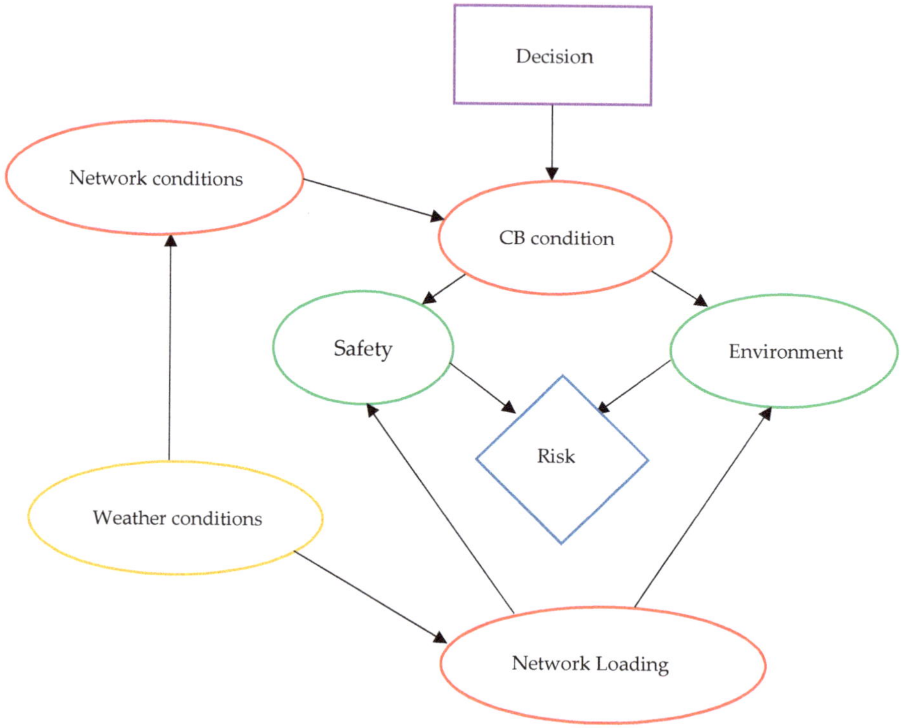

Figure 2. Circuit breaker risk assessment model.

The example shown in Figure 2 was created to assess the risk of a substation with low-oil circuit breakers. The three alternatives that are considered and used for decision-making are do nothing, perform minor interventions, or perform major interventions. Safety and environment are two risk assessment criteria based on which alternatives are assessed. Both criteria are aggregated in the one influence diagram value node, after being assessed according to their risk.

The breaker is in operating conditions (OK), failure to close (FC), and failure to open (FO)—the three modes of operation of the switches that are important in the assessment. Bad weather conditions cause the circuit breakers to be exposed to more difficult operating conditions because the number of failures increases, which leads to a deterioration of the network condition and an increase in the network load. This is further expressed in the case when the distribution network is mostly overhead and when there are frequent power outages. The type of distribution network significantly affects the state of the attachment. The condition of the circuit breaker affects the environment in such a way that oil leaks can have a detrimental effect on the environment. In terms of safety, the condition of the circuit breaker can cause a dangerous effect of electric current on a person, and it can also lead to mechanical injuries, the impact of electromagnetic radiation, and excessive noise.

Due to the uncertainty about the weather forecast—and consequently network technical condition, network maximal demand power (loading) and possible failure modes—probabilities elicited by experts are also uncertain.

According to the diagram presented in Figure 2, the total risk by circuit breakers is calculated as a combination of two individual risks, which are:

- Safety risk, primarily associated to the health and safety of the operators of the substation;

- Environmental risk in terms of spillage of transformer oil into soil or watercourses and ignition of transformer oil and its evaporation.

The components shown in Figure 2 that affect risk and decision-making are described below.

CB condition: the assessment of the condition of this component is based on data from several categories, such as the age of the circuit breaker, i.e., how long the circuit breaker has been in operation, ambient and operational conditions, regularity of maintenance, and test results.

The following scale is used to describe the CB condition:

grade 1: Poor—switch long in operation, under poor ambient and operating conditions, irregular maintenance and testing, poor test results;
grade 2: Medium poor—switch long in operation, under poor ambient and operational conditions, some test results are poor;
grade 3: Medium—switch long in operation, under poor ambient and operational conditions, but regularly maintained and tested, satisfactory results;
grade 4: Very good—newer generation circuit breakers, works under good operating conditions, satisfactory results;
grade 5: Excellent—newer circuit breakers, short in operation, satisfactory test results, regular maintenance and testing.

These ratings for CB condition are actually formed based on the collected data on aging, CB type, and maintenance.

Ageing: A rating in the range of 1 to 5 can be used to estimate the age of the circuit breaker, with lower values indicating better equipment condition ("less is more"). The grade is awarded depending on the range to which the circuit breaker belongs according to its age (<10 years, 10–20 years, 21–30 years, 31–40 years, >40 years).

CB type: The three most commonly used types of circuit breakers in substations are observed: low-oil, vacuum, and SF6 circuit breakers. Depending on the applied technology, each circuit breaker is characterized by a certain intensity of failure, which can be called characteristic and which is a feature of the technology itself. However, the actual intensity of failures depends on many additional factors, of which the two most important are the conditions (operational and ambient) in which the circuit breaker operates and the condition of the circuit breaker itself. Operating conditions refer to load level, protection condition, network condition supplied by this substation. Ambient conditions refer primarily to the temperature in the station itself, which significantly affects the condition of the equipment. As each of these effects is very difficult to quantify, the principle of a correction factor is often adopted, which determines a more realistic value of the failure rate.

Maintenance: Regularity and quality of maintenance are important factors that affect the condition of the equipment itself. The quality of maintenance involves several factors:

- Periodicity and scope of testing;
- Training of maintenance personnel;
- Availability of spare parts;
- Circuit breaker condition monitoring.

The following scale with five rating levels can be used to assess the level of maintenance:

grade 1—Maintenance is performed at regular intervals, all spare parts are easily accessible, there is online monitoring of the condition of the circuit breaker. The staff is well trained. Existing control parameters almost certainly detect a fault;
grade 2—Maintenance is performed at regular intervals, staff is well trained. High probability that the monitored parameters will signal a fault;
grade 3—Moderate probability that the monitored parameters will signal a failure;
grade 4—Low probability that the monitored parameters will signal a failure;

grade 5—No existing monitored parameters can detect a fault. Maintenance is not performed at regular intervals, spare parts are not easily accessible, and there is no online monitoring of the condition of the circuit breaker. The staff is not well trained.

Network conditions and Network loading: The type and load of the network also significantly affect the condition of the circuit breaker. A scale with five levels of assessment can be used for the assessment, where after the assessment of the conditions the value of the correction factor is determined, which is used for further calculations. The description of the grades is as follows:

grade 1—Extremely low load. The distribution network is mostly underground, with short cables and the possibility of reservations;
grade 2—Medium load, average percentage of overhead distribution network, rare power outages;
grade 3—Medium load, higher percentage of overhead distribution network, frequent power outages;
grade 4—High load, especially in winter conditions. High percentage of overhead distribution network representation, frequent power outages;
grade 5—Load extremely high. The distribution network is mostly overhead, with long lines and without the possibility of reservations. The fault occurs without warning.

Weather conditions: Network conditions and loading directly depend on weather conditions. Bad weather conditions correlate with an increased number of failures, which means that circuit breakers will be exposed to more difficult operating conditions because the condition of the network will deteriorate, and the network load will increase. Good weather conditions improve the condition of the network, reduce the load on the network, and provide stable operating conditions for circuit breakers.

Safety and environment criteria evaluations are also expressed in numerical grades (from 1 to 5).

Safety:

grade 1—Very dangerous effect of electric current on humans; toxic and carcinogenic effects of polychlorinated biphenyls (pyralene transformer oil); the danger of mechanical injuries during work on substations is very high if the exposure to danger is very frequent (exposure to danger during one shift of 61–80% of working time); very large impact of electromagnetic radiation on humans; very great influence of noise on the organs of hearing;
grade 2—Dangerous effects of electric current on humans; the risk of mechanical injuries during work on substations is high if the exposure to danger is frequent (exposure to danger during one shift of 41–60% of working time); great influence of electromagnetic radiation on humans; great influence of noise on the organs of hearing;
grade 3—Medium dangerous effect of electric current on humans; the risk of mechanical injuries during work on substations is medium if the exposure to danger is occasional (exposure to danger during one shift of 21–40% of working time); average effect of electromagnetic radiation on humans; moderate impact of noise on the senses of hearing;
grade 4—Low dangerous effect of electric current on humans; the danger of mechanical injuries during work on substations is small if the exposure to danger is very rare (exposure to danger during one shift is less than 20% of working time); small impact of electromagnetic radiation on humans; small noise effect on the senses of hearing;
grade 5—Negligible effect of electric current on humans; the danger of mechanical injuries during work on substations is negligible if the exposure to danger is very rare (exposure to danger during one shift is less than 20% of working time); negligible impact of electromagnetic radiation on humans; negligible effect of noise on the senses of hearing;

Environment:

grade 1—The substation is located in a city center or in a densely populated place, the proximity of watercourses or water supply facilities is less than 10 m, or there are immovable cultural heritage properties, no communal infrastructure, or the road to the substation is not paved;

grade 2—The substation is located on the outskirts of a city (near the substation are mostly small households), distance to watercourses or water supply facilities is 50 m, there are immovable cultural heritage properties, communal infrastructure is partially built, the substation is reached by unpaved road that separates from the local paved road;
grade 3—The substation is located on the outskirts of a city, the populated area is at a distance of 50 m, no endangered plant and animal species, no immovable cultural heritage properties, the proximity to watercourses or water sources is 200 m, an asphalt road that separates from the regional or main road leads to the substation, there is a built communal infrastructure;
grade 4—The substation is outside the settlement, there are individual residential buildings at a distance of 150 m, there are no watercourses or water supply facilities at a distance of 300 m, no endangered plant and animal species, no immovable cultural heritage properties, there is communal infrastructure, an asphalt road (regional or highway) leads to the substation;
grade 5—The substation is outside the settlement, the nearest residential buildings are at a distance of 300 m, there are no watercourses or water supply facilities at a distance of 500 m, no endangered plant and animal species, no immovable cultural heritage properties, there is communal infrastructure, an asphalt road (regional or highway) leads to the substation.

3. Extended Risk Model Based on Interval Probabilities

3.1. Definition and Properties of Interval Probability

The intervals $L = \{L_i = [L(a_i), U(a_i)], i = 1, 2, \ldots, n\}$ represent the interval probability if and only if for any $P(a_i) \in L_i$ there exists $P(a_j) \in L_j$, so the following applies:

$$P(a_i) + \sum_{j=1,2,\ldots,i-1,i+1,\ldots,n} P(a_j) = 1, \quad X \in \{x_1, \ldots, x_n\}, \tag{9}$$

where X—random variable and $\{x_1, \ldots, x_n\}$ finite set [53,54].

In order for L to satisfy the condition described in Equation (9), it must satisfy the following two expressions [53,55–57]:

$$\sum_{\substack{i=1 \\ i \neq j}}^{n} L(a_i) + U(a_j) \leq 1, \tag{10}$$

$$\sum_{\substack{i=1 \\ i \neq j}}^{n} U(a_i) + L(a_j) \geq 1, \tag{11}$$

where $i, j \in [1, \ldots, n]$.

The elicited interval probabilities may or may not satisfy the two previous equations. However, it is not difficult to check whether they satisfy the following inequalities:

$$\sum_{i=1}^{n} L(a_i) \leq 1 \leq \sum_{i=1}^{n} U(a_i), \tag{12}$$

Condition (12) is a necessary but insufficient condition of (10) and (11). The intervals marked with $[L'(a_i), U'(a_i)]$ represent semi-interval probabilities if the condition (12) is fulfilled. Solving the linear programming problem as described with the following function [53]:

$$\begin{array}{l} \max \sum_{i=1,2,\ldots n}^{n} (U(a_i) - L(a_i)) \\ s.t. \sum_{\substack{i=1 \\ i \neq j}}^{n} L(a_i) + U(a_j) \leq 1, \quad \sum_{\substack{i=1 \\ i \neq j}}^{n} U(a_i) + L(a_j) \geq 1 \\ U(a_i) \geq L(a_i),\, U(a_i) \leq U'(a_i),\, L(a_i) \geq L'(a_i) \end{array} \tag{13}$$

enables the selection of interval probabilities from semi-interval probabilities $[L'(a_i), U'(a_i)]$.

3.2. Determining Risk with Interval Probabilities

Rough set theory is one of the important tools with which it is possible, without additional assumptions or some adjustments, to manage uncertain and subjective information [58–60]. To manage uncertain information, determining the lower and upper approximations is a basic task. The lower and upper approximations of X with respect to I, marked with $I_*(X)$ and $I^*(X)$, are defined with the following expressions:

$$I_*(X) = \cup\{X \in U | I(X) \subseteq X\}, \tag{14}$$

$$I^*(X) = \cup\{X \in U | I(X) \cap X \neq \varnothing\}, \tag{15}$$

where $X \subset U$, U is the universe consisting of a non-empty finite set of objects and I is the indiscernibility relation. Ordered pair (U, I) represents the approximation space.

For the lower and upper approximations defined in this way, the boundary region equals:

$$BN_I(X) = I^*(X) - I_*(X), \tag{16}$$

The degree of vagueness is determined by the range of boundary region. Depending on whether the boundary region of X is empty or not, X will be a crisp set or a rough set.

Extended lower and upper approximation and the rough boundary interval described with the previous expressions enables expert evaluation and manipulations in conditions of uncertainty [61].

Definition 1. *Let $R = \{X_1, X_2, X_3, \ldots, X_n\}$ be the set containing n classes of human opinions. The classes are ordered in the manner of $X_1 < X_2 < X_3 < \ldots < X_n$, and Y is the arbitrary object of U, $\forall Y \subseteq U, X_i \subseteq R$, and $i \in \{1, 2, \ldots, n\}$.*

Then, the lower and the upper approximations and the boundary region of X_i can be expressed as

$$I_*(X_i) = \cup\{Y \in U | R(Y) \leq X_i\}, \tag{17}$$

$$I^*(X_i) = \cup\{Y \in U | R(Y) \geq X_i\}, \tag{18}$$

$$BN(X_i) = \cup\{Y \in U | R(Y) \leq X_i\} \cup \{Y \in U | R(Y) \geq X_i\}. \tag{19}$$

The lower and the upper limit, marked with $L(X_i)$ and $U(X_i)$, where rough number (RN) can be a replacement for the class X_i, equals:

$$L(X_i) = \frac{\sum R(Y)}{N_L} | Y \in I_*(X_I), \tag{20}$$

$$U(X_i) = \frac{\sum R(Y)}{N_U} | Y \in I^*(X_I), \tag{21}$$

The number of objects in these approximations are marked with N_L and N_U.

In line with the definition of these limits, expert opinion can be expressed by a rough interval. The degree of preciseness is described with the interval of boundary region (*IBR*). A rough number and an interval of boundary region are equal to:

$$RN_i = [L(X_i)\ U(X_i)], \tag{22}$$

$$IBR_i = U(X_i) - L(X_i), \tag{23}$$

For the two rough numbers RN_1 and RN_2, the following applies (λ is a nonzero constant) [62]

$$RN_1 + RN_2 = [L_1, U_1] + [L_2, U_2] = [L_1 + L_2, U_1 + U_2], \tag{24}$$

$$RN_1 \times \lambda = [L_1, U_1] \times \lambda = [\lambda L_1, \lambda U_1], \tag{25}$$

$$RN_1 \times RN_2 = [L_1, U_1] \times [L_2, U_2] = [L_1 \times L_2, U_1 \times U_2]. \tag{26}$$

In interval mathematics, all the possible relations of different interval numbers are defined, which significantly helps in making decisions based on expert assessment in conditions of uncertainty [63–65].

Definition 2. *Assuming that* $\widetilde{a} = [a^L, a^U]$ *and* $\widetilde{b} = [b^L, b^U]$ *are two interval numbers. Meanwhile, the interval numbers* $\widetilde{a}$ *and* $\widetilde{b}$ *are assumed as the random variables with uniform distributions in their intervals. The probability for the random variable* $\widetilde{a}$ *larger or smaller than the random variable* $\widetilde{b}$ *is expressed as* $P_{\widetilde{b} \geq \widetilde{a}}$ *or* $P_{\widetilde{b} \leq \widetilde{a}}$.

The relationship between $\widetilde{a}$ and $\widetilde{b}$ is described with the following equation.

$$P_{\widetilde{b} \leq \widetilde{a}} = \begin{cases} 1, & b^U \leq a^L \\ \frac{a^U - b^U}{a^U - a^L} + \frac{a^L - b^L}{b^U - b^L} \cdot \frac{b^U - a^L}{a^U - a^L} + \frac{1}{2} \cdot \frac{b^U - a^L}{a^U - a^L} \cdot \frac{b^U - a^L}{b^U - b^L}, & b^L \leq a^L < b^U \leq a^U \\ \frac{a^U - b^U}{a^U - a^L} + \frac{1}{2} \cdot \frac{b^U - a^L}{a^U - a^L}, & a^L < b^L < b^U \leq a^U \\ \frac{1}{2} \cdot \frac{a^U - b^L}{b^U - b^L} \cdot \frac{a^U - b^L}{a^U - a^L}, & a^L \leq b^L < a^U \leq b^U \\ \frac{a^L - b^L}{b^U - b^L} + \frac{1}{2} \cdot \frac{a^U - a^L}{b^U - b^L}, & b^L \leq a^L < a^U \leq b^U \\ 0, & a^U \leq b^L \end{cases}, \tag{27}$$

From the previous Equation (27), we can determine the relationship between $\widetilde{a}$ and $\widetilde{b}$ with the degree α, where $P_{\widetilde{b} \leq \widetilde{a}} = \alpha (0 \leq \alpha \leq 1)$. For the case where $\alpha > .0.5$ means that $\widetilde{a}$ is larger than $\widetilde{b}$, and $\alpha < .0.5$ implies that $\widetilde{a}$ is smaller than $\widetilde{b}$, while $\alpha = 0.5$ represents that $\widetilde{a}$ and $\widetilde{b}$ are equal.

In Figure 3, a risk assessment framework based on expert assessment using interval probability is presented.

The proposed method consists of three main steps. First, data of interest are collected, followed by an assessment of the critical points of the observed system and an analysis of the causes and effects of failures. Then, an expert assessment of the factors influencing the risk by interval probabilities is performed, as well as the formation and calculation of appropriate matrices based on the experts' assessment. Finally, the total risk is calculated and the obtained risks are ranked based on interval probability theory; that is, the minimum risk for the observed case is determined.

Stage 1: Collection of relevant information on the condition of the observed equipment
Step 1. Collect the necessary data to assess the condition of critical equipment
Step 2. Identification of critical points of the observed system
Step 3. Analysis of the causes of failures and the impact of failures

⇩

Stage 2: Risk assessment using interval probabilities
Step 1. Expert assessment of factors influencing risk using interval probabilities
Step 2. Forming the weight matrix of risk factors
Step 3. Calculate the weight of risk factors based on rough set
Step 4. Forming risk assessment matrix with interval probabilities

⇩

Stage 3: Obtain risk priority order for the considered model
Step 1. Calculate risk assessment matrix with interval probabilities
Step 2. Calculate priority order of the calculated risks based on interval probability theory
Step 3. Ranking risks based on calculated priority order

Figure 3. The framework of the proposed model risk assessment using interval probabilities.

4. Case Study

In this case study, two risk calculations were performed based on Figure 4. In the first calculation, crisp probabilities were used for the risk calculation, while in the second calculation the interval probabilities were used.

The decision about the possible replacement of the circuit breaker depends on the calculated risk for keeping the existing breakers in service. The risk consists of safety and environmental risk, characterized with three possible states (denoted with c1, c2, and c3 in Figure 4). Both the safety and environmental impact of the equipment depend on the breaker condition, influenced by the maintenance level (decision node), weather, network condition, and network loading (chance nodes).

As can be seen in Figure 4, regular operating condition (OK), failure to close (FC), and failure to open (FO) represent the three possible states of the considered circuit breakers. The final decision on whether minor maintenance, major maintenance, or do nothing will be applied is made based on two criteria, safety and environment. Based on the level of these two criteria, the risk can take values in the range from 1 (no risk) to 10 (highest risk).

In this paper, for the problem defined in Figure 4, a group of 5 experts was formed who met the following conditions—they were highly qualified for the considered domain, had sufficient experience in assessing the state of a system similar to the observed system, were familiar with probability thinking, and were able to model the system in relation to the available data. We selected 5 experts due to the complexity of the system we were observing and in order to achieve greater overall accuracy during evaluation.

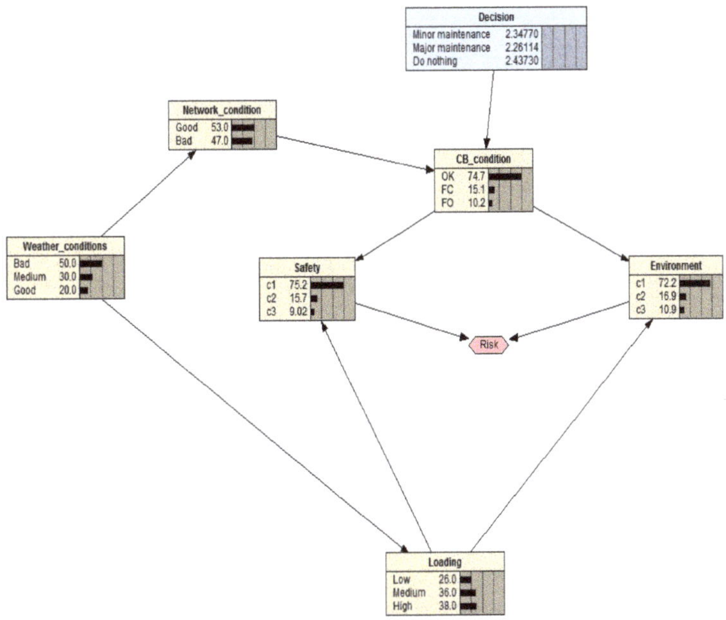

Figure 4. Influence diagram with crisp probabilities.

Based on the experts' opinion and based on previously collected data, the probabilities of the occurrence of each of the conditions were determined: weather conditions, loading and network condition. Additionally, experts determined the conditional probabilities on the basis of which values of the condition in the nodes CB condition, safety, and environment were calculated. The probability values correspond to the mean probability values obtained from the experts. For the probability values shown in Tables 2–7, using Equations (1)–(5), we obtained the results shown in Figure 4.

Table 2. Probability of weather states.

States	Description	Probability [%]
Bad	Severe weather conditions	50
Medium	No extreme temperatures below −20 degree	30
Good	Good weather conditions, no extreme temperatures below −10 degree	20

Table 3. Conditional probabilities of network conditions.

Weather	States	
	Good Conditions, No Increase in Failure Rate [%]	**Bad Conditions—No Maintenance, Increased Number of Failures [%]**
Bad	60	40
Medium	50	50
Good	40	60

Table 4. Conditional probabilities of network loading levels.

Weather	States		
	Low Loading [%]	Medium Loading [%]	High Loading [%]
Bad	10	30	60
Medium	30	50	20
Good	60	30	10

Table 5. Conditional probabilities of CB condition.

Decision	Network Conditions	OK [%]	FC [%]	FO [%]
Minor	Good	70	20	10
Minor	Bad	80	10	10
Major	Good	80	10	10
Major	Bad	90	10	0
Do Nothing	Good	60	20	20
Do Nothing	Bad	70	20	10

Table 6. Conditional probabilities of consequences.

Loading	CB Condition	Safety [%]			Environment [%]		
		c1	c2	c3	c1	c2	c3
Low	OK	90	10	0	80	10	10
Low	FC	80	10	10	80	10	10
Low	FO	70	20	10	70	20	10
Medium	OK	80	10	10	80	10	10
Medium	FC	70	20	10	50	30	20
Medium	FO	60	30	10	60	30	10
High	OK	70	20	10	70	20	10
High	FC	60	20	20	60	30	10
High	FO	50	30	20	50	30	20

Table 7. Safety and Environment criteria grades.

Safety	Probability	Environment	Probability	Risk
c1	[0.752]	c1	[0.722]	1
c1	[0.752]	c2	[0.169]	2
c1	[0.752]	c3	[0.109]	3
c2	[0.157]	c1	[0.722]	4
c2	[0.157]	c2	[0.169]	7
c2	[0.157]	c3	[0.109]	6
c3	[0.090]	c1	[0.722]	5
c3	[0.090]	c2	[0.169]	8
c3	[0.090]	c3	[0.109]	10

Safety and environment criteria evaluations are expressed in numerical grades (from 1 to 10) and represented in Table 7.

Based on Table 7 and Equation (8), the final decision to be taken based on the example given in Figure 4 is shown in Table 8. As can be seen from Table 8, for the crisp values of the variables shown in Figure 4 "Major maintenance" is taken as the final strategy because of the lowest value of risk.

Table 8. Decision values for crisp probability.

Decision	Risk with Crisp Probability	Ranking
Minor maintenance	2.35	2
Major maintenance	2.26	1
Do nothing	2.44	3

In the second case, we worked with interval probabilities. Instead of crisp probability values for the assessment of possible states of the chance nodes, the allowable interval width by which experts assessed the condition was determined by first examining how the interval width affected the final estimate.

The crisp numbers w_{sj}, used to determine risk in case 1, could be transformed into interval numbers form based on Equations (17)–(22):

$$IN\left(w_{sj}^{k}\right) = \left[w_{sj}^{kL}, w_{sj}^{kU}\right], \tag{28}$$

In Equation (28), the lower and upper limits of the interval number are marked with w_{sj}^{kL} and w_{sj}^{kU}, whereas $w_{sj}^{k}(k = 1,2,\ldots,m;\ s = 1,2,\ldots,n;\ j = 1,2,\ldots,l)$ represent kth expert for the sth failure mode with respect to the jth risk factor.

In our case, the interval number matrix is:

$$W_{\text{in}} = \begin{bmatrix} \left[L\left(w_{1j}^{1L}\right), U\left(w_{1j}^{1U}\right)\right] & \left[L\left(w_{1j}^{2L}\right), U\left(w_{1j}^{2U}\right)\right] & \cdots & \left[L\left(w_{1j}^{5L}\right), U\left(w_{1j}^{5U}\right)\right] \\ & \vdots \quad \vdots \quad \vdots \quad \vdots & & \\ \left[L\left(w_{nj}^{1L}\right), U\left(w_{nj}^{1U}\right)\right] & \left[L\left(w_{nj}^{2L}\right), U\left(w_{nj}^{2U}\right)\right] & \cdots & \left[L\left(w_{nj}^{5L}\right), U\left(w_{nj}^{5U}\right)\right] \end{bmatrix}, \tag{29}$$

The average interval number $\overline{IN\left(w_{sj}^{k}\right)}$, $w_{sj}^{k}(k = 1,2,\ldots,m;\ s = 1,2,\ldots,n;\ j = 1,2,\ldots,l)$, based on Equations (24)–(26) is:

$$\overline{IN\left(w_{sj}^{k}\right)} = \left[L\left(w_{sj}^{kL}\right), U\left(w_{sj}^{kU}\right)\right], \tag{30}$$

$$L\left(w_{sj}^{kL}\right) = \left(w_{sj}^{1L} + w_{sj}^{2L} + \ldots + w_{sj}^{kL}\right)/k, \tag{31}$$

$$U\left(w_{sj}^{kU}\right) = \left(w_{sj}^{1U} + w_{sj}^{2U} + \ldots + w_{sj}^{kU}\right)/k. \tag{32}$$

The lower and upper limits of the average interval number are marked with $L\left(w_{sj}^{kL}\right)$ and $U\left(w_{sj}^{kU}\right)$.

In order to enable the experts to have as wide an interval as possible during the evaluation, an analysis was first made of how much the width of the interval influenced the decision for the example given in Figure 4.

The analysis was done so that, in relation to the values of crisp probabilities shown in Figure 4, an interval probability was formed in accordance with Equations (28)–(32), where the values of crisp probabilities represent the center of the newly formed interval.

The analysis was performed for an interval width of 1% to 10%. The obtained results are shown in Table 9.

Table 9. Decision values influenced by interval width.

	1%	**2%**	**3%**	**4%**	**5%**
Minor maintenance	[2.23, 2.43]	[2.14, 2.53]	[2.05, 2.63]	[1.96, 2.76]	[1.84, 2.84]
Major maintenance	[2.14, 2.36]	[2.04, 2.48]	[1.94, 2.60]	[1.87, 2.69]	[1.76, 2.83]
Do Nothing	[2.32, 2.51]	[2.24, 2.61]	[2.16, 2.71]	[2.07, 2.82]	[1.97, 2.89]
	6%	**7%**	**8%**	**9%**	**10%**
Minor maintenance	[1.78, 2.97]	[1.69, 3.08]	[1.60, 3.22]	[1.56, 3.29]	[1.47, 3.48]
Major maintenance	[1.68, 2.95]	[1.57, 3.02]	[1.48, 3.16]	[1.37, 3.31]	[1.33, 3.37]
Do Nothing	[1.88, 2.98]	[1.83, 3.13]	[1.73, 3.23]	[1.60, 3.37]	[1.55, 3.46]

Based on the obtained results, it can be concluded that experts can be allowed to form an interval width from 5% to 10%. This means that experts gave interval probabilities instead of crisp probabilities when evaluating, with the restriction that crisp probabilities were within that interval or represented the lower or upper limit of the interval.

The expert opinion about the circuit breaker condition was obtained from the measurement data covering 42 power stations 35/10 kV and 427 circuit breakers, mounted on 10 kV and 35 kV feeders. Measurement of static resistance of contacts by measuring voltage drop was collected over the past 10 years, with voltage drop measured during every second year.

Other data related to circuit breakers collected for the purposes of analysis were: circuit breaker voltage level, type of terminal, year of production, number of faults, number of short circuit current disconnections, number of consumers at the terminal, and average energy consumption.

The average lifespan of a circuit breaker depends on many factors, such as the intensity of operation, operating conditions, and level of maintenance. The main cause of the deterioration of the circuit breaker is its age, then the number of operations performed at normal load and failure, and operating conditions, such as temperature and environmental pollution.

The resistance of the contacts is an indicator of the general condition of the circuit breaker. It does not depend on environmental conditions until foreign materials penetrate the contact surface. For this reason, any increase in resistance is an indication of the existence of foreign material on the contact surface. This can lead to a local temperature increase and thus to a worsening of the circuit breaker condition.

Measuring voltage drops is equivalent to measuring resistance. Due to the ease of measurement, voltage drop is more often used as a criterion in practice. As for the allowed values of voltage drops, they are more influenced by the height of the rated current of the circuit breaker than the values of its rated voltage.

The permissible values of voltage drops prescribed by the manufacturer are given in the manufacturer's instructions. Permitted overdraft value is + 25%. In the case of a circuit breaker that is already in operation, the permissible voltage drop is 20% higher in than a circuit breaker that is first operated.

The circuit breakers analyzed in this paper were low-oil medium voltage circuit breakers, manufactured by Minel and tested according to the manufacturer's instructions. The test was performed every other year, as defined [66]. This type of maintenance is called time-based maintenance, which is performed according to a predefined schedule at precisely defined time intervals.

In the first step, the state of each circuit breaker was determined depending on whether its voltage drop exceeded the allowable value or not. The year in which they reached this state was determined for the failed circuit breakers. These data were further divided into the following categories:

- circuit breakers mounted on 35 kV terminals
- circuit breakers mounted on 10 kV terminals

- circuit breakers mounted on overhead terminals
- circuit breakers mounted on cable terminals
- all circuit breakers.

From the manufacturer's instructions, the allowable voltage drop depends on the rated current and rated voltage of the circuit breaker, and the manufacturer allows these values to be exceeded by 25%. For this reason, the circuit breakers were also analyzed through the following two criteria: the maximum value of the voltage drop was as in the manufacturer's table and the maximum value of the voltage drop was 25% higher than the value from the table.

In this way, the influence of both criteria on circuit breaker failure was considered. The manufacturer's instructions [66] state that a circuit breaker must be completely repaired after 10–12 years of operation, or 5000 manipulations, or 6 interrupted short-circuit currents, whichever occurs first. Based on these data, the experts assigned interval probabilities first of 5% width, then 6%, and continued up to 10%.

Additionally, values for nodes, such as weather conditions, network condition, loading, safety, and environment, experts assigned on the basis of collected and available data.

It is important to note that experts were not given predefined values of the center of the interval for any node, but they made their assessments of the interval values solely on the basis of the available data and their expertise. As for the risk, the rule used was 1—the lowest risk, 10—the highest risk (as shown in Table 10).

Table 10. Risk assessment using interval probabilities for the example given in Figure 4.

Safety	Interval Probability	Environment	Interval Probability	Risk
c1	[0.71, 0.79]	c1	[0.68, 0.77]	1
c1	[0.71, 0.79]	c2	[0.13, 0.20]	2
c1	[0.71, 0.79]	c3	[0.05, 0.17]	3
c2	[0.12, 0.19]	c1	[0.68, 0.77]	4
c2	[0.12, 0.19]	c2	[0.13, 0.20]	7
c2	[0.12, 0.19]	c3	[0.05, 0.17]	6
c3	[0.03, 0.14]	c1	[0.68, 0.77]	5
c3	[0.03, 0.14]	c2	[0.13, 0.20]	8
c3	[0.03, 0.14]	c3	[0.05, 0.17]	10

Using the previously described methodology for the case of an ID with interval probabilities, based on expert assessments, in combination with Monte Carlo simulation respecting the following condition:

$$\begin{gathered} 0 \le L(a_i) \le p(a_i) \le U(a_i) \le 1 \\ \sum_{i=1}^{n} p(a_i) = 1 \end{gathered} \tag{33}$$

Table 11 includes the obtained results.

Table 11. Risk values obtained by experts' assessment for different interval width.

	5%				
	E1	**E2**	**E3**	**E4**	**E5**
Minor maintenance	[1.91, 2.93]	[1.93, 2.98]	[2.21, 3.36]	[1.78, 2.80]	[1.87, 2.94]
Major maintenance	[1.83, 2.95]	[1.87, 3.02]	[2.12, 3.29]	[1.69, 2.76]	[1.74, 2.88]
Do Nothing	[2.05, 2.99]	[2.08, 3.04]	[2.29, 3.37]	[1.86, 2.79]	[1.95, 2.97]
	6%				
	E1	**E2**	**E3**	**E4**	**E5**
Minor maintenance	[1.93, 3.16]	[2.06, 3.34]	[2.12, 3.47]	[1.85, 3.01]	[1.99, 3.29]
Major maintenance	[1.83, 3.12]	[1.99, 3.32]	[2.04, 3.48]	[1.75, 3.04]	[1.93, 3.29]
Do Nothing	[2.04, 3.21]	[2.11, 3.32]	[2.19, 3.46]	[1.91, 3.05]	[2.02, 3.31]
	7%				
	E1	**E2**	**E3**	**E4**	**E5**
Minor maintenance	[1.73, 3.18]	[1.91, 3.47]	[1.98, 3.51]	[1.88, 3.25]	[1.96, 3.59]
Major maintenance	[1.64, 3.22]	[1.84, 3.56]	[1.90, 3.45]	[1.84, 3.26]	[1.89, 3.58]
Do Nothing	[1.92, 3.24]	[2.14, 3.53]	[2.07, 3.49]	[1.98, 3.27]	[2.07, 3.61]
	8%				
	E1	**E2**	**E3**	**E4**	**E5**
Minor maintenance	[1.73, 3.37]	[1.87, 3.59]	[1.92, 3.62]	[1.88, 3.37]	[1.78, 3.51]
Major maintenance	[1.62, 3.27]	[1.78, 3.55]	[1.82, 3.62]	[1.83, 3.50]	[1.77, 3.50]
Do Nothing	[1.82, 3.36]	[1.97, 3.59]	[1.96, 3.65]	[1.99, 3.43]	[1.89, 3.47]
	9%				
	E1	**E2**	**E3**	**E4**	**E5**
Minor maintenance	[1.71, 3.48]	[1.88, 3.82]	[2.03, 4.06]	[1.86, 3.68]	[1.86, 3.79]
Major maintenance	[1.68, 3.61]	[1.88, 3.89]	[2.00, 4.09]	[1.84, 3.72]	[1.87, 3.82]
Do Nothing	[1.88, 3.50]	[1.97, 3.78]	[2.21, 4.05]	[1.91, 3.71]	[1.97, 3.83]
	10%				
	E1	**E2**	**E3**	**E4**	**E5**
Minor maintenance	[1.81, 3.79]	[2.10, 4.25]	[2.09, 4.09]	[2.02, 4.07]	[2.11, 4.33]
Major maintenance	[1.70, 3.82]	[2.00, 4.36]	[1.98, 4.26]	[2.03, 4.06]	[1.96, 4.34]
Do Nothing	[1.96, 3.86]	[2.21, 4.27]	[2.21, 4.18]	[2.18, 4.25]	[2.17, 4.40]

In this paper, it is proposed that the final decision on which action will be implemented is made by forming an interval based on Equations (30)–(32).

Based on these equations, the final decision on which action will be implemented for each interval range separately is shown in Table 12.

Based on the data presented in Table 12, it can be concluded that the proposed model of determining risk using interval probabilities greatly facilitates the work of experts and gives a very realistic picture of the actions to be taken.

Table 12. Final risk values for each interval range separately.

Decision	5%	6%	7%	8%	9%	10%
Minor maintenance	[1.94, 3.00]	[1.99, 3.25]	[1.89, 3.40]	[1.84, 3.49]	[1.87, 3.77]	[2.03, 4.11]
Major maintenance	[1.85, 2.98]	[1.91, 3.25]	[1.82, 3.41]	[1.76, 3.49]	[1.85, 3.83]	[1.93, 4.17]
Do Nothing	[2.05, 3.03]	[2.05, 3.27]	[2.04, 3.43]	[1.93, 3.50]	[1.99, 3.77]	[2.15, 4.19]

Using Equation (27), we performed a comparison of the interval of different potential decisions to obtain the comparison probability so that we could rank the risk priorities of the considered decisions. The obtained results are given in Table 13. Taking Minor

Maintenance and Do Nothing for 5% interval width as an example, the interval Minor Maintenance is [1.94, 3.00], while FM6 is [2.05, 3.03] based on Equation (27):

$$P_{Do\_not \leq minor} = \frac{1}{2} \times \frac{3.00 - 2.05}{3.03 - 2.05} \times \frac{3.00 - 2.05}{3.00 - 1.94} = 0.43,$$

Table 13. The comparison results for interval decision.

	5%			6%		
	Minor Maintenance	**Major Maintenance**	**Do Nothing**	**Minor Maintenance**	**Major Maintenance**	**Do Nothing**
Minor maintenance		0.55	0.43		0.53	0.47
Major maintenance	-		0.39	-		0.44
Do Nothing	-	-		-	-	
	7%			**8%**		
	Minor maintenance	Major maintenance	Do Nothing	Minor maintenance	Major maintenance	Do Nothing
Minor maintenance		0.52	0.44		0.52	0.47
Major maintenance	-		0.42	-		0.45
Do Nothing	-	-		-	-	
	9%			**10%**		
	Minor maintenance	Major maintenance	Do Nothing	Minor maintenance	Major maintenance	Do Nothing
Minor maintenance		0.49	0.47		0.51	0.45
Major maintenance	-		0.48	-		0.44
Do Nothing	-	-		-	-	

Because $P_{Do\_not \leq minor} = 0.43 < 0.5$, the risk priority of Do Nothing is higher than Minor Maintenance. Similarly, other comparison probabilities are given in Table 13.

Based on the results obtained from the previous table, the following table shows the ranking results of different decisions for each width interval individually.

On the values of the intervals shown in Table 14, it is easy to conclude that the best choice for the observed system is "Major Maintenance" because the risk priority is the highest and it is obtained for this decision for each interval width shown (except for the 9% interval width, where it is second by priority). With this in mind, as well as the result obtained for the crisp values, it can be seen how much better a solution is the decision model applied in this paper. Namely, unlike crisp values, which are very difficult to determine in conditions of uncertainty, allowing experts to assess the state of a system in a wide range of values significantly facilitates proper decision-making. It has been shown that allowing experts to use interval values instead of crisp values, which are very difficult in conditions of uncertainty, can significantly influence the final decision.

Table 14. The ranking results of different decision.

Decision	5%	Ranking	6%	Ranking	7%	Ranking
Minor maintenance	[1.94, 3.00]	2	[1.99, 3.25]	2	[1.89, 3.40]	2
Major maintenance	[1.85, 2.98]	1	[1.91, 3.25]	1	[1.82, 3.41]	1
Do Nothing	[2.05, 3.03]	3	[2.05, 3.27]	3	[2.04, 3.43]	3
Decision	**8%**	**Ranking**	**9%**	**Ranking**	**10%**	**Ranking**
Minor maintenance	[1.84, 3.49]	2	[2.03, 3.48]	1	[2.12, 3.79]	2
Major maintenance	[1.76, 3.49]	1	[2.00, 3.61]	2	[2.03, 3.82]	1
Do Nothing	[1.93, 3.50]	3	[2.21, 3.50]	3	[2.21, 3.86]	3

5. Conclusions

Risk prediction using IDs with interval probabilities is a very popular methodology for determining causal relationships of events in conditions of uncertainty. The knowledge and experience of experts is one of the main links in the formation of the IDs model and the determination of the state of the considered elements for increasing the reliability of power systems. In order to increase the accuracy of the assessment of the state of the considered elements, in this case circuit breakers, in this paper it is proposed to allow experts to use interval probabilities instead of crisp probabilities. An analysis was performed that shows how the width of the interval affects the final decision, and accordingly, the experts were allowed to base their estimates on interval probabilities. The obtained results for the case presented in the paper are also in the form of interval probabilities. Based on the obtained results, it can be concluded that the proposed model of risk prediction using IDs with interval probabilities is an excellent solution for deciding which action should be taken to increase the reliability of circuit breakers. The proposed model of determining risk using interval probabilities greatly facilitates the work of experts and gives a very realistic picture of the actions to be taken. Unlike crisp values, which are very difficult to determine in conditions of uncertainty, allowing experts to assess the state of the system in a wide range of values significantly facilitates proper decision-making.

Although the proposed method shows significant advantages when making decisions in conditions of uncertainty, it can also have certain disadvantages. First, an increase in the number of observed alternatives that affect decision-making can lead to an increase in the required computer power and the required real time to perform computational operations, which can increase the costs and time of decision-making.

The methodology should be tested on high dimension models with a great number of nodes, and this will be the focus of our future research.

Author Contributions: Conceptualization, J.D.V. and A.J.; methodology, J.D.V.; validation, J.D.V. and A.J.; formal analysis, J.D.V.; investigation, J.D.V.; data curation, J.D.V.; writing—original draft preparation, J.D.V.; writing—review and editing, A.J.; supervision, A.J. All authors have read and agreed to the published version of the manuscript.

Funding: This research receive no extra funding.

Institutional Review Board Statement: Not applicable.

Acknowledgments: This work was supported by the Serbian Ministry of Education, Science and Technological Development through the Mathematical Institute of the Serbian Academy of Sciences and Arts.

Conflicts of Interest: The authors declare no conflict of interest.

References

1. Gao, D.W.; Wang, Q.; Zhang, F.; Yang, X.; Huang, Z.; Ma, S.; Li, Q.; Gong, X.; Wang, F.-Y. Application of AI techniques in Monitoring and Operation of Power Systems. *Front. Energy* **2018**, *13*, 71–85. [CrossRef]
2. Peng, C.; Lei, S.; Hou, Y.; Wu, F. Uncertainty Management in Power System Operation. *CSEE J. Power Energy Syst.* **2015**, *1*, 28–35. [CrossRef]
3. Jordehi, A.R. How to Deal with Uncertainties in Electric Power Systems? A Review. *Renew. Sustain. Energy Rev.* **2018**, *96*, 145–155. [CrossRef]
4. Reinders, J.; Morren, J.; Slootweg, J.G. Uncertainty in Power System Planning and Operation: An Integrated Approach. In Proceedings of the IEEE Young Researchers Symposium in Electrical Power Engineering (YRS 2018), Bruxelles, Belgium, 24–25 May 2018.
5. Vachtsevanos, G.; Lewis, F.; Roemer, M.; Hess, A.; Wu, B. *Intelligent Fault Diagnosis and Prognosis for Engineering Systems*; Wiley: Hoboken, NJ, USA, 2006; Volume 456.
6. Daigle, M.J.; Goebel, K. Model-Based Prognostics with Concurrent Damage Progression Processes. *IEEE Trans. Syst. Man. Cybern. Syst.* **2013**, *43*, 535–546. [CrossRef]
7. Strachan, S.M.; McArthur, S.D.J.; Stephen, B.; McDonald, J.R.; Campbell, A. Providing Decision Support for the Condition-Based Maintenance of Circuit Breakers Through Data Mining of Trip Coil Current Signatures. *IEEE Trans. Power Deliv.* **2007**, *22*, 178–186. [CrossRef]
8. Lin, P.; Gu, J.; Yang, M. Intelligent Maintenance Model for Condition Assessment of Circuit Breakers using Fuzzy Set Theory and Evidential Reasoning. *IET Gener. Trans. Distrib.* **2014**, *8*, 1244–1253. [CrossRef]
9. Razi-Kazemi, A.A.; Vakilian, M.; Niayesh, K.; Lehtonen, M. Data Mining of Online Diagnosed Waveforms for Probabilistic Condition Assessment of SF $_ {6} $ Circuit Breakers. *IEEE Trans. Power Deliv.* **2015**, *30*, 1354–1362. [CrossRef]
10. Westerlund, P.; Hilber, P.; Lindquist, T.; Kraftnat, S. A Review of Methods for Condition Monitoring, Surveys and Statistical Analyses of Disconnectors and Circuit Breakers. In Proceedings of the 2014 International Conference on Probabilistic Methods Applied to Power Systems (PMAPS), Durham, UK, 7–10 July 2014; pp. 1–6.

11. Davis, M.H. *Markov Models & Optimization*; CRC Press: Florida, FL, USA, 1993; Volume 49.
12. Lorton, A.; Fouladirad, M.; Grall, A. A Methodology for Probabilistic Model-Based Prognosis. *Eur. J. Oper. Res.* **2013**, *225*, 443–454. [CrossRef]
13. Nguyen, D.N.; Dieulle, L.; Grall, A. Remaining Useful Lifetime Prognosis of Controlled Systems: A Case of Stochastically Deteri-orating Actuator. *Math. Probl. Eng.* **2015**. [CrossRef]
14. Chiquet, J.; Limnios, N. A Method to Compute the Transition Function of a Piecewise Deterministic Markov Process with Ap-plication to Reliability. *Stat. Probab. Lett.* **2008**, *78*, 1397–1403. [CrossRef]
15. Chiacchio, F.; D'Urso, D.; Compagno, L.; Pennisi, M.; Pappalardo, F.; Manno, G. SHyFTA, a Stochastic Hybrid Fault Tree Automaton for the Modelling and Simulation of Dynamic Reliability Problems. *Expert Syst. Appl.* **2016**, *47*, 42–57. [CrossRef]
16. Codetta-Raiteri, D.; Portinale, L. Approaching Dynamic Reliability with Predictive and Diagnostic Purposes by Exploiting Dy-namic Bayesian Networks. *Proc. Inst. Mech. Eng. Part O J. Risk Reliab.* **2014**, *228*, 488–503.
17. Gaudel, Q.; Chanthery, E.; Ribot, P. Hybrid Particle Petri Nets for Systems Health Monitoring under Uncertainty. *Int. J. Progn. Health Manag.* **2015**, *6*. [CrossRef]
18. Daigle, M.; Roychoudhury, I.; Bregon, A. Model-Based Prognostics of Hybrid Systems. *Annu. Conf. Progn. Health Manag. Soc.* **2015**, 18–24. [CrossRef]
19. Kushwaha, D.K.; Panchal, D.; Sachdeva, A. Risk Analysis of Cutting System under Intuitionistic Fuzzy Environment. *Rep. Mech. Eng.* **2020**, *1*, 162–173. [CrossRef]
20. Bakır, M.; Atalık, Ö. Application of Fuzzy AHP and Fuzzy Marcos Approach for the Evaluation of E-Service Quality in the Airline Industry. *Decis. Mak. Appl. Manag. Eng.* **2021**, *4*, 127–152. [CrossRef]
21. Pamucar, D.; Ecer, F. Prioritizing the Weights of the Evaluation Criteria under Fuzziness: The Fuzzy Full Consistency Method-Fucom-F. *Facta Univ. Ser. Mech. Eng.* **2020**, *18*, 419–437. [CrossRef]
22. Petrović, G.; Mihajlović, J.; Ćojbašić, Žarko; Madić, M.; Marinković, D. Comparison of Three Fuzzy Mcdm Methods for Solving the Supplier Selection Problem. *Facta Univ. Ser. Mech. Eng.* **2019**, *17*, 455–469. [CrossRef]
23. Faes, M.; Moens, D. Recent Trends in the Modeling and Quantification of Non-probabilistic Uncertainty. *Arch. Comput. Methods Eng.* **2020**, *27*, 633–671. [CrossRef]
24. Pamucar, D. Normalized Weighted Geometric Dombi Bonferoni Mean Operator with Interval Grey Numbers: Application in Multicriteria Decision Making. *Rep. Mech. Eng.* **2020**, *1*, 44–52. [CrossRef]
25. Jiang, C.; Zheng, J.; Han, X. Probability-Interval Hybrid Uncertainty Analysis for Structures with both Aleatory and Epistemic Uncertainties: A Review. *Struct. Multidiscip. Optim.* **2017**, *57*, 2485–2502. [CrossRef]
26. Faes, M.G.R.; Daub, M.; Marelli, S.; Patelli, E.; Beer, M. *Engineering Analysis with Probability Boxes: A Review on Computational Methods*; ETH Zurich: Zürich, Switzerland, 2021.
27. Chen, N.; Yu, D.; Xia, B.; Beer, M. Uncertainty Analysis of a Structural–Acoustic Problem using Imprecise Probabilities based on P-Box Representations. *Mech. Syst. Signal Process.* **2016**, *80*, 45–57. [CrossRef]
28. Crespo, L.G.; Kenny, S.P.; Giesy, D.P. Reliability Analysis of Polynomial Systems Subject to P-Box Uncertainties. *Mech. Syst. Signal Process.* **2013**, *37*, 121–136. [CrossRef]
29. Montgomery, V.J.; Coolen, F.P.A.; Hart, A.D.M. Bayesian Probability Boxes in Risk Assessment. *J. Stat. Theory Pr.* **2009**, *3*, 69–83. [CrossRef]
30. Dannert, M.M.; Fau, A.; Fleury, R.M.; Broggi, M.; Nackenhorst, U.; Beer, M. A Probability-Box Approach on Uncertain Correlation Lengths by Stochastic Finite Element Method. *PAMM* **2018**, *18*, e201800114. [CrossRef]
31. Faes, M.; Moens, D. Imprecise Random Field Analysis with Parametrized Kernel Functions. *Mech. Syst. Signal Process.* **2019**, *134*, 106334. [CrossRef]
32. Zhang, J.; Xiao, M.; Gao, L. An Active Learning Reliability Method Combining Kriging Constructed with Exploration and Exploitation of Failure Region and Subset Simulation. *Reliab. Eng. Syst. Saf.* **2019**, *188*, 90–102. [CrossRef]
33. Sofi, A.; Muscolino, G.; Giunta, F. Propagation of Uncertain Structural Properties Described by Imprecise Probability Density Functions via Response Surface Method. *Probab. Eng. Mech.* **2020**, *60*, 103020. [CrossRef]
34. Schöbi, R.; Sudret, B. Structural Reliability Analysis for P-Boxes using Multi-Level Meta-Models. *Probab. Eng. Mech.* **2017**, *48*, 27–38. [CrossRef]
35. Troffaes, M.C. Imprecise Monte Carlo Simulation and Iterative Importance Sampling for the Estimation of Lower Previsions. *Int. J. Approx. Reason.* **2018**, *101*, 31–48. [CrossRef]
36. Mancuso, A.; Compare, M.; Salo, A.; Zio, E. Portfolio Optimization of Safety Measures for Reducing Risks in Nuclear Systems. *Reliab. Eng. Syst. Saf.* **2017**, *167*, 20–29. [CrossRef]
37. Yuan, Z.; Khakzad, N.; Khan, F.; Amyotte, P. Risk Analysis of Dust Explosion Scenarios Using Bayesian Networks. *Risk Anal.* **2014**, *35*, 278–291. [CrossRef] [PubMed]
38. Carriger, J.F.; Barron, M.G.; Newman, M.C. Bayesian Networks Improve Causal Environmental Assessments for Evidence-Based Policy. *Environ. Sci. Technol.* **2016**, *50*, 13195–13205. [CrossRef] [PubMed]
39. Zhang, G.; Thai, V.V.; Yuen, K.F.; Loh, H.S.; Zhou, Q. Addressing the Epistemic Uncertainty in Maritime Accidents Modelling using Bayesian Network with Interval Probabilities. *Saf. Sci.* **2018**, *102*, 211–225. [CrossRef]
40. Koller, D.; Friedman, N. *Probabilistic Graphical Models: Principles and Techniques*; MIT Press: Cambridge, MA, USA, 2009.

41. Antonucci, A.; de Campos, C.P.; Huber, D.; Zaffalon, M. Approximate Credal Network Updating by Linear Programming with Applications to Decision Making. *Int. J. Approx. Reason.* **2015**, *58*, 25–38. [CrossRef]
42. Howard, R.A. *Influence Diagrams, The principles and Applications of Decision Analysis, RA Howard and JE Matheson*; Strategic Decisions Group: Menlo Park, CA, USA, 1984; Volume 2.
43. Shachter, R.D.; Peot, M.A. Decision Making Using Probabilistic Inference Methods. In *Computational Morphology—A Computational Geometric Approach to the Analysis of Form*; Elsevier BV: Amsterdam, The Netherlands, 1992; pp. 276–283.
44. Kjaerulff, U.B.; Madsen, A.L. Bayesian Networks and Influence Diagrams. *Springer Sci. Bus. Media.* **2008**, *200*, 114.
45. Shachter, R.D. Evaluating Influence Diagrams. *Oper. Res.* **1986**, *34*, 871–882. [CrossRef]
46. Shenoy, P.P. Valuation-Based Systems for Bayesian Decision Analysis. *Oper. Res.* **1992**, *40*, 463–484. [CrossRef]
47. Jensen, F.; Jensen, F.V.; Dittmer, S.L. From Influence Diagrams to Junction Trees. In *Uncertainty Proceedings 1994*; Morgan Kaufmann: Burlington, MA, USA, 1994; pp. 367–373.
48. Yang, C.C.; Cheung, K.M. Fuzzy Bayesian Analysis with Continuous-Valued Evidence. In Proceedings of the 1995 IEEE International Conference on Systems, Man and Cybernetics, Intelligent Systems for the 21st Century, Vancouver, BC, Canada, 22–25 October 1995; Volume 1, pp. 441–446.
49. Zhang, N.L. Probabilistic Inference in Influence Diagrams. *Comput. Intell.* **1998**, *14*, 475–497. [CrossRef]
50. Janjić, A.; Stanković, M.; Velimirović, L. Multi-Criteria Influence Diagrams—A Tool for the Sequential Group Risk Assessment. In *Granular Computing and Decision-Making*; Springer: Cham, Switzerland, 2015; pp. 165–193.
51. Janjic, A.; Stajic, Z.; Radovic, I. A Practical Inference Engine for Risk Assessment of Power Systems based on Hybrid Fuzzy In-fluence Diagrams. *Latest Adv. Inf. Sci. Circuits Syst.* **2011**, *2011*, 29–34.
52. Zhang, Z.; Jiang, Y.; McCalley, J. Condition based Failure Rate Estimation for Power Transformers. In Proceedings of the 35th North American Power Symposium, Rolla, MO, USA, 19–21 October 2003.
53. Guo, P.; Tanaka, H. Decision Making with Interval Probabilities. *Eur. J. Oper. Res.* **2010**, *203*, 444–454. [CrossRef]
54. Hu, X.; Luo, H.; Fu, C. Probability Elicitation in Influence Diagram Modeling by Using Interval Probability. *Int. J. Intell. Sci.* **2012**, *2*, 89–95. [CrossRef]
55. Tessem, B. Interval Probability Propagation. *Int. J. Approx. Reason.* **1992**, *7*, 95–120. [CrossRef]
56. De Campos, L.M.; Huete, J.F.; Moral, S. Uncertainty Management using Probability Intervals. In *Advances in Intelligent Computing, Proceedings of the International Conference on Information Processing and Management of Uncertainty in Knowledge-Based Systems, Paris, France, 4–8 July 1994*; Springer: Berlin/Heidelberg, Germany, 1994; pp. 190–199.
57. Weichselberger, K. The Theory of Interval-Probability as a Unifying Concept for Uncertainty. *Int. J. Approx. Reason.* **2000**, *24*, 149–170. [CrossRef]
58. Pawlak, Z. Rough Sets. *Int. J. Parallel Program.* **1982**, *11*, 341–356. [CrossRef]
59. Qian, Y.; Liang, J.; Pedrycz, W.; Dang, C. Positive Approximation: An Accelerator for Attribute Reduction in Rough Set Theory. *Artif. Intell.* **2010**, *174*, 597–618. [CrossRef]
60. Zhang, H.; Zhou, J.; Miao, D.; Gao, C. Bayesian Rough Set Model: A Further Investigation. *Int. J. Approx. Reason.* **2012**, *53*, 541–557. [CrossRef]
61. Zhai, L.-Y.; Khoo, L.-P.; Zhong, Z.-W. A Rough Set Enhanced Fuzzy Approach to Quality Function Deployment. *Int. J. Adv. Manuf. Technol.* **2008**, *37*, 613–624. [CrossRef]
62. Wagman, D.; Schneider, M.; Shnaider, E. On the Use of Interval Mathematics in Fuzzy Expert Systems. *Int. J. Intell. Syst.* **1994**, *9*, 241–259. [CrossRef]
63. Ishibuchi, H.; Tanaka, H. Multiobjective Programming in Optimization of the Interval Objective Function. *Eur. J. Oper. Res.* **1990**, *48*, 219–225. [CrossRef]
64. Jiang, C.; Han, X.; Liu, G.R.; Liu, P.G. A Nonlinear Interval Number Programming Method for Uncertain Optimization Problems. *Eur. J. Op. Res.* **2008**, *188*, 1–13. [CrossRef]
65. Ouyang, L.; Zhou, D.; Park, C.; Chen, J.; Tu, Y. Ensemble Modelling Technique for a Micro-Drilling Process based on a Two-Stage Bootstrap. *Eng. Optim.* **2018**, *51*, 503–519. [CrossRef]
66. *Operating Manual for Medium Voltage Medium Oil Circuit Breakers for Internal Assembly*; Minel: Zrenjanin, Serbia, 1984.

symmetry

MDPI

Article

Multi-Criteria Seed Selection for Targeting Multi-Attribute Nodes in Complex Networks

Artur Karczmarczyk [1], Jarosław Jankowski [1] and Jarosław Wątrobski [2,*]

[1] Faculty of Computer Science and Information Technology, West Pomeranian University of Technology in Szczecin, Żołnierska 49, 71-210 Szczecin, Poland; artur.karczmarczyk@zut.edu.pl (A.K.); jaroslaw.jankowski@zut.edu.pl (J.J.)

[2] The Faculty of Economics, Finance and Management of the University of Szczecin, Mickewicza 64, 71-101 Szczecin, Poland

* Correspondence: jaroslaw.watrobski@usz.edu.pl

Abstract: Online environments have evolved from the early-stage technical systems to social platforms with social communication mechanisms resembling the interactions which can be found in the real world. Online marketers are using the close relations between the users of social networks to more easily propagate the marketing contents in their advertising campaigns. Such viral marketing campaigns have proven to provide better results than traditional online marketing, hence the increasing research interest in the topic. While the majority of the up-to-date research focuses on maximizing the global coverage and influence in the complete network, some studies have been conducted in the area of budget-constrained conditions as well as in the area of targeting particular groups of nodes. In this paper, a novel approach to targeting multi-attribute nodes in complex networks is presented, in which an MCDA method with various preference weights for all criteria is used to select the initial seeds to best reach the targeted nodes in the network. The proposed approach shows some symmetric characteristics—while the global coverage in the network is decreased, the coverage amongst the targeted nodes grows.

Keywords: complex networks; social networks; viral marketing; information propagation; MCDA; TOPSIS

Citation: Karczmarczyk, A.; Jankowski, J.; Wątrobski, J. Multi-Criteria Seed Selection for Targeting Multi-Attribute Nodes in Complex Networks. *Symmetry* **2021**, *13*, 731. https://doi.org/10.3390/sym13040731

Academic Editor: José Carlos R. Alcantud

Received: 10 March 2021
Accepted: 16 April 2021
Published: 20 April 2021

Publisher's Note: MDPI stays neutral with regard to jurisdictional claims in published maps and institutional affiliations.

1. Introduction

The analysis of social networks has evolved from early-stage sociograms based on small graphs into mainstream multi-billion node social networks with high business potential [1]. Social platforms let their users easily connect to their friends or acquaintances and easily maintain relationships. These close relations between social network users have been widely used by online marketers to improve the engagement of potential consumers to benefit from their services and products [2]. Viral marketing campaigns in social networks have proven to bring better effects in engaging potential consumers than traditional online advertising [3].

This performance of viral marketing resulted in increased research on information propagation in complex networks. While the majority of the research focuses exclusively on increasing the network coverage with information, as the only factor and performance measure, some works aim their attention at a targeted approach [4,5], also with a focus on user preferences [6]. From a different perspective, other approaches avoid repeated messages due to lowered performance causing a habituation effect [7], information overload [8] or the need for delays between messages for multi-product campaigns [9]. Efforts towards targeting specific users have mainly been focused on single attributes or network metrics for the seed selection [10]. The real-life applications of social networks in viral marketing campaigns are often based on selecting multiple attributes such as age, gender and localization of the target group [11].

To better address the aforementioned needs, the authors' main contribution in this paper is to provide an approach in which multi-attribute targeted groups of users can be reached in social networks by providing the initial seeding information to a limited number of selected network users. In the proposed approach, contrary to other studies, the selection of the seeded nodes of the social network is based on multiple, often conflicting, criteria and nodes' attributes. Moreover, by virtue of the MCDA (Multi-Criteria Decision Analysis) foundations of the proposed approach, the importance of each criterion considered in the selection process can be adjusted to meet the marketer's needs. MCDA tools, such as sensitivity analysis [12], also allow us to further study and understand the effect each seeded nodes' attribute has on the planned viral marketing campaign's capacity to reach the targeted group of the network nodes [13]. Some symmetric characteristics of the proposed approach are assumed—whilst the global coverage in the network can decrease, the proposed approach strives to maximize coverage amongst the targeted nodes.

The paper is comprised of five main sections. After this introduction, the state-of-the-art literature review is presented in Section 2. It is followed by the methodology presentation in Section 3 and the empirical study results in Section 4. Eventually, the paper is concluded in Section 5.

2. Literature Review

The early stage research in the area of information spreading assumed that all nodes within the network have the same interest in the product or the propagated content. The network coverage was the main assumed factor and performance measure for influence maximisation problem identified firstly in [14]. From this point of view, the most central nodes, having a high influence on others, had the highest potential to be selected as seeds. Most of the seed selection methods focused on node network characteristics and heuristics improving the performance [15]. Usually, only the whole network structures are taken into account for seed selection.

While real campaigns take into account various node characteristics, the problem was emphasized by [5] and a targeted approach to viral marketing was proposed. It was based on assigning nodes to a potential market and searching for a local centrality score during the seeding process. For each user, the average importance factor was calculated to determine the impact on target group. Another study focused on targeting with the use of costs assigned to users within the network, together with the benefits related to the user interests [4]. It extends the typical approaches focused on assumption that users are acquired at the same costs with same benefits for marketers. As a result, the authors proposed a cost-aware targeted viral marketing with an effective computational approach, making the seeds selection within billion-scale networks possible. From the perspective of practical applications the authors took into account the number of posts under specific topics are a representation of user interest and potential benefits. While the earlier methods focused on influence maximisation based solely on centralities and influence, the study in [16] distinguished two classes of methods, taking into account more complex structural relations like overlap, and other group focused on user features and social information. They use, among others, trust between the users and cost. The study emphasises the lack of methods taking into account the user interest. The approach is based on the interest in the message. The experimental study was based on randomly assigned interest vectors within well-known datasets, without nodes' attributes. An integrated marketing approach was proposed in [6] for combining targeted marketing with viral marketing. The approach took into account users with revealed preferences and users with potentially high utility scores for the marketer. One of the goals was the maximization of information awareness and constraints focused on reaching the targeted users. The study [17] explored Cost-aware Targeted Viral Marketing model, with focus on the cost of the nodes' acquisition and potential benefits. Integer programming was used with the potential to search for close to exact solutions within large scale networks. From other perspective, the authors of [18] introduced a Targeted Influence Maximization problem, using an objective function and penalization parameter for adoption of non-target nodes. The proposed approaches focused on general target groups characterized by benefits or knowledge acquired from user posts.

While targeting can be based on various performance evaluation criteria and campaign goals it creates space for applications or multi-criteria decision support methods. In the recent years some preliminary research has began in the area of utilising multi-criteria decision analysis (MCDA) techniques in the social network studies. Zareie et al. [19] used the TOPSIS method (Technique for Order Preference by Similarity to Ideal Solution) to reduce overlap and maximize coverage while influencing social networks. Yang et al. [20] used TOPSIS in the Susceptible-Infected-Recovered (SIR) model to dynamically identify influential nodes in complex networks, and in [21] used entropy weighting for setting the weights values. Liu et al. [22] used TOPSIS to evaluate the importance of nodes in Shanxi water network and Beijing subway networks by comparing each node's close degree to an ideal object. Robles et al. [23] used multiobjective optimization algorithms to maximize the revenue of viral marketing campaigns while reducing the costs. Wang et al. [24] proposed a Similarity Matching-based weighted reverse influence sampling for influence maximization in geo-social location-aware networks. Gandhi and Muruganantham [25,26] used TOPSIS to provide a framework for Social Media Analytics for finding influencers in selected networks. Montazerolghaem [27] used separately AHP and TOPSIS to provide rankings of effective factors in network marketing success in Iran. In their prior research, Karczmarczyk et al. [28] used the PROMETHEE II method (Preference Ranking Organization METHod for Enrichment of Evaluations) for evaluation of performance of viral marketing campaigns in social networks, as well as for decision support in the planning of such campaigns.

The up-to-date literature studies show a multitude of available MCDA methods [29]. Some examples of known and widely used MCDA methods include AHP, TOPSIS [30,31], or methods from the ELECTRE and PROMETHEE families [32]. The methods can be divided into three groups, based on the used approach. The first group, also known as the American school of MCDA methods, use the axiom of full variants comparability and two basic relations are available—indifference and preference of variants. The resulting model is aggregated into a single criterion [33]. The methods from the second group, also known as the European school of MCDA methods, are based on the axiom of partial comparability of variants. The aggregation takes place using the outranking relation. The third group consists of methods based on the foundations from both the aforementioned groups. The current taxonomy of the available MCDA methods can be found, for example, in [29,32,34].

The analysis of the existing works shows that among the large number of studies related to the information propagation and influence maximization, only a small fraction is focused on the very common real-life problem of targeting users with specific characteristics. The discussed approaches focused on single attributes and node characteristics for the seed selection to reach the assumed audiences or communities. Nonetheless, the social media skyrocketing is usually based on selection of parameters of the target group with various values of the attributes such as age, gender or localization, with different importance from the perspective of the campaign performance. This forms an interesting research gap, which is addressed in this paper with the proposed new approach. The approach is based on the assumption that, in order to maximize reaching a multi-attribute target group in the network, the seed selection process is also based on a multi-criteria evaluation of nodes. The seed selection process is supported with MCDA methods, allowing us to assign weights to individual attributes of the network nodes and produce rankings of seeds with the potential to increase the coverage in the addressed multi-attribute target group.

3. Methodology

In this section, the methodological framework of the approach proposed in this paper is presented. In Section 3.1, the assumptions regarding the multi-attribute nature of the targeted nodes are presented. Subsequently, in Section 3.2, the problem of multi-criteria seed selection for targeting heterogeneous multi-attribute nodes is explained. Then, in Section 3.3, the MCDA foundations of the proposed approach are presented and the selection of the TOPSIS method is justified. Finally, in Section 3.4 the TOPSIS foundations and its adaptation for seed selection for targeting multi-attribute nodes are presented. The conceptual framework of the proposed approach is also visually presented on Figure 1.

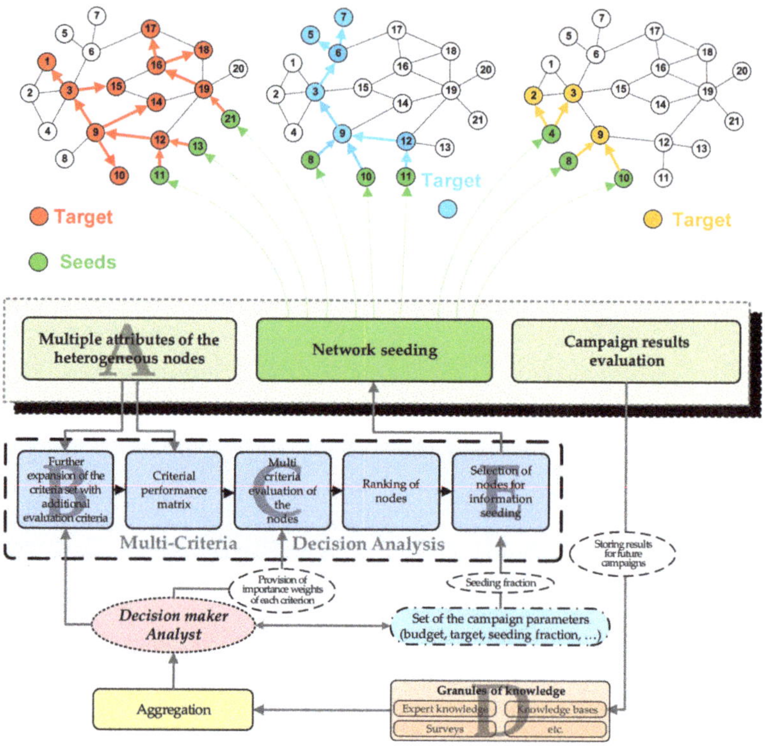

Figure 1. Conceptual framework of the proposed approach. Marks A–E provide anchors to be referred in the main text of the paper.

3.1. Multi-Attribute Nature of the Targeted Nodes

The proposed methodology complements the widely-used Independent Cascade (IC) model [14] for modeling the spread within the complex networks by taking into account the problem of reaching targeted multi-attribute nodes in social networks by the information propagation processes. In the proposed approach, it is assumed that the network nodes are characterized not only by the centrality relations between them and other nodes [35–37], but also by a set of custom attributes $C_1, C_2, \ldots, C_n$ (see Figure 1A).

The values of these attributes for individual vertices can be expressed as precise numerical values, such as age [years] or income [dollars]. Alternatively, if the attributes represent qualitative properties of the nodes, their values can be converted to numeric values with the use of 5-point Likert scale [38,39] (1—strongly disagree, 5—strongly agree) or enumerations (e.g., age: 1—young, 2—midle-aged, 3—old; or sex: 1—male, 2—female).

The nodes can also be characterized by the computed attributes derived from the network characteristics and measures. These include the centrality measures such as degree [35], closeness [40], betweenness [41] or eigenvector [36,37]. Additional attributes can also be derived as a composite of the two aforementioned types of attributes, by computing centrality measures based on limited subsets of the nodes' neighbors (see Figure 1B). For example, if attribute C_i represented the degree of a node, that is, the total count of its neighbors, the C_{i_1} could represent the count of its male neighbors, and C_{i_2} the count of its female neighbors.

The aim of the proposed methodological framework is to reach the targeted network nodes with multi-attribute characteristics, based on the multi-criteria process of selecting nodes for seeding in the process of information propagation.

3.2. Multi-Attribute Seed Selection

As was described in Section 3.1, in the proposed approach an attempt is made to reach the nodes with specific values of the selected attributes. For example, in preventive oncological social campaigns, an attempt is made to reach middle-aged women, that is, aged between 50 and 69.

In the independent cascade model [14], the information propagation process in a complex network is preceded by the selection of seeds. That means choosing a subset of network vertices, to which the information is provided at the beginning of the process, in order for them to pass the information further through the network. Normally, the seeds represent a given fraction of all network nodes. For example, the seeding fraction can be set to 5% of the network. There are numerous approaches to selecting the initial seeds, which generally result in producing a ranking of all network nodes and seeding information to the ones on top of the list.

Whilst other approaches focus on generating the ranking based on a single centrality measure, such as degree [35] or eigencentrality [36], in the authors' proposed approach, multiple attributes are considered in order to select the seeds with the highest potential to eventually propagate the information to the targeted nodes.

It is important to note, that in the proposed approach, the final coverage of the network, i.e., the fraction of nodes to which the information was eventually delivered, can be lower than in case of the traditional centrality-based approaches. However, the proposed method increases the chances to maximize the coverage within the targeted nodes' groups.

3.3. MCDA Foundations of the Proposed Approach and the Research Method Justification

The approach presented in this paper is based on the MCDA methodology foundations [42]. The adaptation of the MCDA methodology for the needs of seed selection resulted directly from the formal and practical assumptions of the research. First, the assumed modeling goal was an attempt to reach only the targeted set of multi-attribute nodes. Therefore, any attempt to obtain the optimal solution in a global sense (such as maximization of the global coverage) was disregarded in this research. Second, the fulfillment of the goals adopted in this research requires considering a number of attributes in the process of seed selection. Third, it was established that a compromise maximizing matching the required goals would be searched for, at the expense of the global network coverage.

The aforementioned premises of the multi-criteria modeling environment and goals, as well as the analysis of the formal components of the MCDA model at the stage of the model structuring and preference modeling, are the starting point for the selection of the appropriate MCDA method. It is worth noting that this is a significant problem, and an improper selection of the MCDA method can lead to incorrect results in the final decision model [29,32].

In this paper, the assumed effect of the construction and operation of the MCDA model is a ranking of variants [43]. The criterial performance of the variants will be expressed on a quantitative scale [44]. The expected result is a complete ranking of variants [45]. The deterministic simulation data environment present in this paper, shows the quantitative character of the input data. The research assumptions require that different weights of the individual criteria are taken into account, and their nature will also be quantitative. There is no need to use relative or absolute weighting criteria [46]. In the modeling process, it was also assumed that due to the deterministic nature of the simulation model being developed, there is no natural uncertainty of the preferential information. In practice, this implies the use of the methods from the "American school" [45]. Based on [29,44], as well as the MCDA methods' set discussed in [32], using the expert system provided in [47], it is easy to show that aforementioned requirements are fully met only by the following set of MCDA methods: MAUT (Multi-Attribute Utility Theory), MAVT (Multi-Attribute Value Theory), SAW (Simple Additive Weighing), SMART (Simple Multi-Attribute Ranking Technique), TOPSIS (Technique for Order Preference by Similarity to an Ideal Solution), UTA (Utilites Additives), VIKOR (VIsekriterijumska optimizacija i KOmpromisno Resenje).

On the foundations of the aforementioned analysis, as well as based on the [32] formal recommendations, two groups of MCDA methods can be indicated as valid for solving the problem stated in this paper. The first one is based on an additive/multiplicative form of a utility/value function (MAUT, MAVT, SAW, SMART, UTA), and the second one is based on reference points (TOPSIS, VIKOR).

The former group of methods is founded on a very trivial mathematical principles—a simple aggregation of data and partial utilities. In practice, this results in transferring into the final models an undesirable effect of linear substitution of criteria. Consequently, this directly implies the possibility of obtaining incorrect rankings (failure to meet the level of individual criteria to a satisfactory degree).

Among the latter group, there is a significant level of similarity between both the TOPSIS and VIKOR methods. They both are based on the same assumptions and differ only in the chosen technique of normalization and aggregation of data. The TOPSIS method assumes minimizing the distance to the ideal solution and maximizing the distance to the anti-ideal solution, whereas in VIKOR only the distance to the ideal solution is minimized.

The principles of the TOPSIS and VIKOR methods, along with the fact that TOPSIS uses vector normalization (compared to linear normalization in VIKOR), expedite the selection of the TOPSIS method as the one which has the best potential in the considered problem of seeds' selection [48]. Consequently, it was the TOPSIS method that was chosen for the further stages of this research. Moreover, it is important to note that the chosen TOPSIS method does not require the attribute preferences to be independent [49–51]. This further strengthens the potential of using this method in the considered problem, in which, due to its preliminary character, we do not yet have full knowledge in the area of dependence or independence of the model attributes.

3.4. Multi-Criteria Seed Selection for Multi-Attribute Nodes Targeting

The Technique for Order Performance by Similarity to Ideal Solution (TOPSIS) is a widely-used MCDA method, originating from the American MCDA school. Originally formed by Hwang and Yoon [52], it is based on the concept that given a set of criteria and their possible values, a positive ideal solution (PIS), and negative ideal solution (NIS) can be indicated. These are a two hypothetical, non-existent, alternatives, whose all values for all criteria are either maximized (PIS) or minimized (NIS). When a set of alternatives are compared, in the TOPSIS method they are ranked based on their relative distance to the PIS and NIS. The best alternative should be as close as possible in terms of criteria values to the PIS, and as far as possible from NIS.

In the proposed approach, the TOPSIS method is used for multi-criteria evaluation of the nodes (see Figure 1C). First of all, the criteria for evaluation of the potential seeding nodes need to be chosen. Then, a decision matrix $D[x_{ij}]$ is built based on the criteria values of all vertices in the studied network, in which the m rows represent the vertices and n columns represent the criteria (see Equation (1)):

$$D[x_{ij}] = \begin{pmatrix} x_{11} & x_{12} & x_{13} & \dots & x_{1n} \\ x_{21} & x_{22} & x_{23} & \dots & x_{2n} \\ x_{31} & x_{32} & x_{33} & \dots & x_{3n} \\ \dots & \dots & \dots & \dots & \dots \\ x_{m1} & x_{m2} & x_{m3} & \dots & x_{mn} \end{pmatrix} \quad (1)$$

In the second step of the algorithm, the decision matrix is normalized. Different formulae are used for the benefit criteria (2) and different for the cost criteria (3):

$$\&r_{ij} = \frac{x_{ij} - min_i(x_{ij})}{max_i(x_{ij}) - min_i(x_{ij})} \tag{2}$$

$$\&r_{ij} = \frac{max_i(x_{ij}) - x_{ij}}{max_i(x_{ij}) - min_i(x_{ij})} \tag{3}$$

The MCDA-based approaches extend the traditional aggregating approaches by the fact that the weights of individual decision attributes can be adjusted to varying values. The analyst adjusts the weights of each decision criterion to the preferences of the decision maker. In the case of the considered problem of seed selection, the marketer adjusts the weights of individual criteria to increase as much as possible the potential to reach to the targeted network nodes through the seeded network nodes. The weights are chosen based on the analyst's knowledge, skills and experience (see Figure 1D). Therefore, in the third step of the TOPSIS algorithm used in the authors' proposed approach, the weights are imposed on the decision matrix and, consequently, a weighted normalized decision matrix is constructed:

$$v_{ij} = w_j \cdot r_{ij} \tag{4}$$

In the fourth step of the algorithm, the positive and negative ideal solutions (V_j^+ and V_j^+ respectively) are computed (Equations (5) and (6)). In the case of the studied seed selection problem, the positive ideal solution would represent a vertex, which for all criteria has the best possible values, whereas the negative ideal solution would be a vertex with the worst possible values for each criterion.

$$V_j^+ = \{v_1^+, v_2^+, v_3^+, \ldots, v_n^+\} \tag{5}$$

$$V_j^- = \{v_1^-, v_2^-, v_3^-, \ldots, v_n^-\} \tag{6}$$

In the penultimate, fifth, step of the TOPSIS method, the Euclidean distances between each network vertex and the positive and negative ideal solutions are computed:

$$D_i^+ = \sqrt{\sum_{j=1}^{n} (v_{ij} - v_j^+)^2} \tag{7}$$

$$D_i^+ = \sqrt{\sum_{j=1}^{n} (v_{ij} - v_j^-)^2} \tag{8}$$

Eventually, the relative closeness of each vertex to the ideal solution is computed:

$$CC_i = \frac{D_i^-}{D_i^- + D_i^+} \tag{9}$$

The obtained CC_i scores are then used to rank the vertices and build the final ranking, which then can be used for selecting the vertices for the initial network seeding (see Figure 1E).

All in all, the MCDA foundations of the proposed approach facilitate obtaining network nodes' rankings with the highest, according to the analyst, potential to reach the targeted nodes in the social network. Moreover, the use of MCDA allows us to study the stability of the obtained ranking with sensitivity analyses. This, in turn, allows us to study the effect of each individual criterion on the final ranking and, therefore, allows us to iteratively improve the obtained solution.

4. Empirical Study

4.1. Real-Life Usage Example

In this section, a brief real-life usage example of the proposed approach will be presented, explaining every step of the proposed framework on a small real network. In further sections, a more in-depth analysis is performed on a larger synthetic network.

The empirical example in this section will be performed on a real network. Enron emails network [53] was selected due to its limited size (143 nodes and 623 edges), which allows us to study in detail the status of every single node of the network. It is important to keep in mind that the proposed approach is intended for networks with nodes characterized by multiple attributes. Due to the fact that the publicly available network repositories principally provide only edge lists of networks, the attributes had to be overlaid on the network artificially. Therefore, artificial values for two attributes were generated for the network, based on [54]: gender (69 nodes male, and 74 nodes female), and age (0–29 years—62 nodes, 30–59 years—55 nodes, over 60 years—26 nodes).

For such a network, for illustrative purposes, two complete scenarios with two different targets will be presented. In both, a constant propagation probability (0.1) and seeding fraction (0.05, i.e., 7 vertices) is assumed.

4.1.1. Target 1: Male Aged 0–29

In this scenario, the aim of the viral marketing campaign is to reach men aged 0–29, that is, the targets are described by specific values of two criteria: gender (C2) and age (C5). The target group, therefore, consists of 28 nodes (see Figure 2). Apart from the two target-describing attributes, some other criteria are also available: degree (C1), degree male (C3), degree female (C4), degree aged 0–29 (C6), degree aged 30–59 (C7), degree aged 60+ (C8). The decision maker (DM)/analyst, based on their expertise, provide the preference weights for all criteria: C1: 8.20, C2: 25.40, C3: 12.60, C4: 3.80, C5: 28.40, C6: 14, C7: 3.80, C8: 3.80. These weights are provided by the DM as input data to the proposed approach, as the ones which, according to the DM, allow to rank the nodes in order to find the seeds potentially best for maximizing influence in the targeted group. In order to provide such weights, the analyst can refer to archival knowledge and use decision support systems or MCDA methods such as AHP [39].

Once the preference weights are known, the TOPSIS method is used to evaluate all vertices. The top seven (seeding fraction 0.05) are chosen as seeds and the campaign is started.

For this scenario, the simulations (see Figure A1 in Appendix A) have shown the campaign averagely reached 9/28 targeted nodes (32.14%), with global coverage 0.2224. A traditional degree-based approach for the same network results averagely in reaching 7.7/28 targeted nodes (27.5%), with global coverage 0.2881. The multi-criteria approach reached 4.64% more of the targeted nodes with global coverage lower by 0.0657.

4.1.2. Target 2: Female Aged 30–59

In this scenario, the aim of the viral marketing campaign is to reach women aged 30–59. The target group consists of 24 nodes (see Figure 2). Again, apart from the two target-describing attributes, some other criteria are also available: degree (C1), degree male (C3), degree female (C4), degree aged 0–29 (C6), degree aged 30–59 (C7), degree aged 60+ (C8). It is important to note that, contrary to other approaches [4], in the proposed approach the criteria values are reused and only the preference weights are adjusted. This time, the decision maker, based on their expertise, provide the following preference weights for the criteria: C1: 4.4, C2: 30.4, C3: 4, C4: 10.4, C5: 30.40, C6: 5.4, C7: 10.4, C8: 4.4.

Vertex		1	2	3	4	5	6	7	8	9	10	11	12	13	14	15	16	17	18	19	20	21	22	23	24	25	26	27	28	29	30	31	32	33	34	35	36
Attribute	Sex	1	2	1	1	1	1	1	2	1	2	2	1	2	2	1	2	2	2	1	1	1	2	2	2	2	1	2	2	1	1	1	2	2	1	1	2
	Age	2	1	1	1	1	3	2	1	2	2	2	3	1	1	1	3	1	1	1	1	3	3	1	1	1	3	1	2	2	2	2	2	3	2	2	1
Target	1	0	0	1	1	1	0	0	0	0	0	0	0	0	0	1	0	0	0	1	1	0	0	0	0	0	0	0	0	0	0	0	0	0	0	0	0
	2	0	0	0	0	0	0	0	0	0	1	1	0	0	0	0	0	0	0	0	0	0	0	0	0	0	0	0	1	0	0	0	1	0	0	0	0
	Deg.	132	30	33	37	122	66	98	128	34	77	76	91	42	59	139	55	2	48	17	11	90	28	95	72	103	45	47	52	43	105	8	12	120	115	49	89
Ranking	1	94	20	7	6	47	107	89	77	53	118	124	115	43	51	46	134	5	38	3	1	116	112	70	55	73	103	27	100	28	90	13	99	141	96	68	63
	2	102	41	117	125	137	129	92	83	58	13	12	124	44	56	143	53	4	49	110	109	126	40	68	62	65	115	60	14	79	95	39	2	75	98	70	66

Vertex		37	38	39	40	41	42	43	44	45	46	47	48	49	50	51	52	53	54	55	56	57	58	59	60	61	62	63	64	65	66	67	68	69	70	71	72
Attribute	Sex	1	1	1	2	2	2	2	2	1	1	2	1	1	1	2	2	1	2	2	2	2	1	2	2	2	2	2	1	1	1	2	1	1	2	1	2
	Age	2	3	3	1	1	1	3	2	2	2	1	2	2	1	2	1	2	1	2	1	2	3	2	2	2	1	1	2	2	1	2	1	2	2	1	2
Target	1	0	0	0	0	0	0	0	0	0	0	0	0	0	1	0	0	0	0	0	0	0	0	0	0	0	0	0	0	0	1	0	1	0	0	1	0
	2	0	0	0	0	0	0	0	1	0	0	0	0	0	0	1	0	0	0	1	0	1	0	1	1	1	0	0	0	0	0	1	0	0	1	0	1
	Deg.	24	118	67	97	74	141	6	110	106	117	16	4	50	15	46	126	26	79	109	25	84	68	119	27	93	130	140	29	21	41	19	38	18	81	39	13
Ranking	1	62	117	106	71	59	82	102	128	83	91	26	15	60	12	92	80	45	40	129	33	122	108	132	97	126	74	79	44	25	18	52	23	16	119	8	66
	2	37	136	119	63	51	86	27	25	99	100	33	35	67	107	10	82	46	69	22	34	17	118	28	6	19	84	90	64	47	116	7	112	45	21	121	5

Vertex		73	74	75	76	77	78	79	80	81	82	83	84	85	86	87	88	89	90	91	92	93	94	95	96	97	98	99	100	101	102	103	104	105	106	107	108
Attribute	Sex	1	2	2	1	1	2	1	1	2	1	2	2	2	1	2	2	1	2	2	1	1	1	1	1	1	1	2	2	1	1	1	2	2	1	2	2
	Age	2	3	2	1	1	2	1	2	2	2	2	1	1	3	3	2	1	1	1	1	1	2	2	1	2	2	3	1	3	1	2	1	3	2	2	3
Target	1	0	0	0	1	1	0	1	0	0	0	0	0	0	0	0	0	1	0	0	1	1	0	0	1	0	0	0	0	0	1	0	0	0	0	0	0
	2	0	0	1	0	0	1	0	0	1	0	1	0	0	0	0	1	0	0	0	0	0	0	0	0	0	0	0	0	0	0	0	0	0	0	1	0
	Deg.	75	9	22	88	32	83	102	143	134	82	101	104	63	92	121	134	123	61	7	138	124	100	3	124	131	142	71	44	36	57	99	60	1	108	70	112
Ranking	1	75	120	104	30	17	123	32	95	130	76	125	69	48	109	138	130	37	54	21	49	42	84	9	42	98	93	135	39	101	19	86	56	11	88	111	140
	2	81	24	3	130	114	16	134	104	30	91	26	73	54	132	80	30	141	52	31	142	140	94	23	140	101	105	57	43	113	128	93	48	1	96	11	71

Vertex		109	110	111	112	113	114	115	116	117	118	119	120	121	122	123	124	125	126	127	128	129	130	131	132	133	134	135	136	137	138	139	140	141	142	143
Attribute	Sex	1	1	1	2	2	1	2	1	2	2	2	2	1	1	2	2	2	2	2	1	1	1	2	1	2	2	1	1	2	2	1	2	2	1	1
	Age	2	1	1	1	3	1	2	2	1	1	1	3	2	1	3	3	2	1	1	2	1	1	3	1	1	2	3	1	3	3	1	1	2	1	2
Target	1	0	1	1	0	0	1	0	0	0	0	0	0	0	1	0	0	0	0	0	0	1	1	0	1	0	0	0	1	0	0	1	0	0	1	0
	2	0	0	0	0	0	0	1	0	0	0	0	0	0	0	0	0	1	0	0	0	0	0	0	0	0	1	0	0	0	0	0	0	1	0	0
	Deg.	64	94	78	62	136	113	53	108	80	20	73	86	35	23	31	14	51	96	114	116	88	58	111	5	129	85	133	10	54	136	56	127	69	40	65
Ranking	1	64	34	31	61	142	36	110	88	67	35	65	137	50	10	133	127	114	58	72	85	30	22	139	4	78	113	121	2	136	142	24	81	105	14	57
	2	89	133	127	42	88	138	9	96	61	32	50	55	59	111	36	20	8	74	76	103	130	122	72	106	78	18	135	108	38	88	123	77	15	120	85

Figure 2. Visual presentation of two real-life usage scenarios for targeting male aged 0–29 (target 1) or female aged 30–59 (target 2). The table contains: values of the sex and age attributes, information on targeted nodes for both scenarios, and the rankings of nodes for seeding.

Once the preference weights are known, the TOPSIS method is used to evaluate all vertices. The top seven (seeding fraction 0.05) are chosen as seeds, and the campaign is started.

For this scenario, the simulations (see Figure A2 in Appendix A) have shown the campaign on average reached 9.5/24 targeted nodes (39.58%), with global coverage 0.2552. A traditional degree-based approach for the same network results averagely in reaching 6.8/24 targeted nodes (28.33%), with global coverage 0.2881. The multi-criteria approach reached 11.25% more of the targeted nodes with global coverage lower by 0.0329.

4.1.3. Real-Life Example Discussion

In the real-life example, two complete scenarios with two different targets were presented. As expected, in both cases the proposed approach resulted in lowering the global coverage but increasing the influence in the targeted set of nodes. In both cases, it was the decision-maker (DM) who first determined the values for weights. This is a subjective assessment, based on the DM's knowledge, skills and experience. In case the weights would have been estimated improperly, the ranking of the nodes would be ordered differently, and, therefore, different 7 nodes would be selected as seeds (see Section 3.4). This, in turn, could result in reaching fewer targeted nodes in the network (see Section 4.8).

The actual participation of the decision-maker in the process of solving the task is very important in MCDA, and the actual performance of the obtained solution is dependent on both the quality of the attributes and the proper selection of the values of the vector of the relative importance of the decision model criteria. Attempting to obtain the maximum potential to reach through the seeded nodes to the targeted nodes requires searching for the most satisfying values of the vector of the relative importance of the decision model criteria.

4.2. Setup of the Comprehensive Experiment

The basic usage example presented above is followed by a set of three more in-depth analysis scenarios, performed on a larger synthetic network. In order to illustrate the proposed approach, the empirical study was performed on a Barabasi-Albert (BA) synthetic network [55]. The Barabasi-Albert network model was created as an outcome of a research of the structure of the WWW in the 90's. Two complementary mechanisms drive the construction of BA networks: network growth and preferential attachment. In the BA synthetic networks, several selected nodes (hubs) have an unusually high degree compared to the other vertices in the network.

Over the recent years, there has been an abundance of research showing that a vast number of social networks, both virtual and real, are scale-free in their nature [55–58]. Their degree k follows a power law $k^{-\lambda}$ and exponent λ is typically $2 < \lambda < 3$. The sample network was generated with exponent λ with value in the middle of this range $\lambda = 2.5$. Moreover, in order to allow clear visualisation of the network, the vertices count was set to 1000. The resulting network was characterized by the following the average values of its centrality metrics:

- Betweenness—1687.295;
- Degree—3.994;
- Closeness—0.0002310899;
- Eigen Centrality—0.03661858.

Since the proposed approach is intended for networks whose nodes are described with multiple attributes, the subsequent step was to assign a set of attributes to each of the vertices of the obtained network. The most of publicly available network datasets are based mainly on set of nodes and edges, without node attributes. To overcome this problem, we used node attributes following distributions from demographic data. It is similar to approach presented in [16]. The information on sex distribution from demographic data was overlaid on the network to obtain the first attribute [54]. This resulted in 470 network nodes marked as male and 530 marked as female. Subsequently, the age distribution information [54] was used to add to the network the second attribute, with three possible values:

- young, i.e., aged 0–49, 64.62% of the population;
- mid-aged, i.e., aged 50–69, 25.34% of the population;
- elderly, i.e., aged 70 and above, 10.04% of the population.

Finally, the goal of the information spreading campaign was chosen for the empirical research. For illustrative purposes, it was decided that a real-life example of social campaign for a breast cancer prevention program (mammography) would be used [59]. This campaign targets women aged 50–69, which in the case of the network generated for this experiment translated to 130 out of the total of 1000 nodes of the network.

4.3. Criteria for Seed Selection

As was described in Section 3, in the proposed approach the initial seeds were selected from the network based on multiple criteria. In the case of the studied synthetic network, apart from the sex and age attributes, the general degree of each node was also taken into account, as well as the degree measurements based on each value of the two attributes. This resulted in a total of eight evaluation criteria, presented in Table 1.

Table 1. Seed selection criteria.

No	Criterion	Preference
C1	Degree	max
C2	Sex (Match/Mismatch)	min
C3	Degree Male	max
C4	Degree Female	max
C5	Age (Match/Mismatch)	min
C6	Degree Young	max
C7	Degree Mid-Aged	max
C8	Degree Elderly	max

The criterion C1 represents the number of neighbors of each evaluated vertex. Criterion C2 is based on the sex attribute and is equal to 0 if there is a match between the targeted and actual sex or 1 in the case of a mismatch. Criterion C3 represents the count of male neighbors of a vertex, whereas criterion C4 represents female neighbors of a vertex. In turn, criterion C5 indicates the difference between the targeted and actual age group of a vertex. For example, if the targeted age group was young, vertices from age groups young, mid-aged and elderly would obtain the values of 0, 1 and 2 respectively. Since the targeted group in this experiment is in the middle, that is, mid-aged, vertices from this group would obtain value 0 and from other groups would obtain value 1 for criterion C5. Last, but not least, criteria C6, C7 and C8 represent the count of respectively young, mid-aged and elderly neighbors of a vertex. All criteria C1–C8 were then assembled to create a single decision matrix for the TOPSIS method. At this stage, it is important to note that during the research the authors decided to follow the degree-based criteria, as the degree is the most basic measure which can be used for benchmarking of the approach. If other measure, such as closeness, betweenness, eigencentrality, and so forth, was used as criterion C1, also the remaining criteria C3, C4, C6, C7, C8 would need to be modified to use the selected metric.

The last step required for the seed-selection setup was specifying the preference direction of all evaluation criteria C1–C8. Because criteria C2 and C5 represent difference between the targeted and actual values, the lowest possible values were preferred. On the other hand, since the remaining criteria are based on the degree network centrality measure, the preference direction for these criteria was maximum.

After the experiment was set up, three scenarios based on various weights of individual criteria were studied. Their description and results are presented in the following sections.

4.4. Scenario 1: Single Criterion

The first scenario studied was intended to be similar to the approaches that are based solely on a single centrality measure, here—the degree. Therefore, the preference weights for the TOPSIS ranking-generation method were set to a significant value of 100 for C1, and a negligible value of 1 for all other criteria. All vertices were evaluated and ordered by rank. It was decided, that in the simulations the seeding fraction of 0.05 and propagation of 0.3 will be used. Therefore, the 50 vertices with the highest CCi scores were selected as seeds (see Table 2).

The analysis of Table 2 allows us to observe that the best vertex, labelled *3* obtained significantly more score than any other vertex (0.9975 compared to 0.6800 and 0.6000 for vertices *4* and *2* ranked 2 and 3, respectively). It is also noticeable that the score of the best vertex *3* was over two-fold higher than the score of vertices *24* and *1* ranked 6/7, with an equal score of 0.4400. These scores can be confirmed, when the degree measure of each of the nodes is verified. The degree of the leading vertex *3* is equal to 52, followed by 36, 32, 29, 28 for vertices *4*, *2*, *12*, *5* respectively and 24 for vertices *1* and *24*. Last, but not least, it can be observed that because the degree was used as the main criteria for the selection of seeds, multiple of the selected nodes are scored equally, for example all nodes ranked 40–45 are scored 0.1800 and all nodes ranked 46–50 are scored 0.1600.

Table 2. Seeds selected for Scenario 1, ordered by their rank and CCi score obtained in the applied TOPSIS method.

Rank	Vertex	Score	Rank	Vertex	Score	Rank	Vertex	Score	Rank	Vertex	Score	Rank	Vertex	Score
1	3	0.9975	11	49	0.4000	21	29	0.2800	31	18	0.2400	41	151	0.1800
2	4	0.6800	12	6	0.4000	22	170	0.2800	32	153	0.2400	42	97	0.1800
3	2	0.6000	13	11	0.3800	23	47	0.2800	33	57	0.2200	43	65	0.1800
4	12	0.5400	14	16	0.3400	24	21	0.2600	34	10	0.2200	44	59	0.1800
5	5	0.5200	15	26	0.3400	25	14	0.2600	35	40	0.2200	45	101	0.1800
6	24	0.4400	16	7	0.3400	26	45	0.2600	36	238	0.2200	46	36	0.1600
7	1	0.4400	17	113	0.3400	27	103	0.2600	37	56	0.2000	47	116	0.1600
8	30	0.4200	18	135	0.2800	28	82	0.2600	38	172	0.2000	48	37	0.1600
9	185	0.4200	19	17	0.2800	29	9	0.2400	39	20	0.1801	49	93	0.1600
10	19	0.4000	20	53	0.2800	30	42	0.2400	40	143	0.1800	50	55	0.1600

After the seeds were selected, the campaign was simulated over the same network, with the same seeds for 10 consecutive times. In order to allow repeatability of the simulation conditions, a set of 10 pre-drawn weights for each connection (edge) in the network was used. The outcomes of each simulation were stored and presented in the form of a visual graph (see Figure A3 in Appendix A). On average, the simulation took 8.6 iterations and resulted in 433.6 nodes being infected (0.4336 coverage). However, only 50.5 nodes of the 130 targeted nodes were infected (0.3885 target coverage).

4.5. Scenario 2: Two Criteria

In the second scenario, the preference weight of the degree measure was reduced in favor of the more accurate female degree (C4) and mid-aged degree (C7). Therefore the weights of C4 and C7 were set to 100 while the weights of the rest of the criteria was set to 1. All vertices were evaluated again, under the new conditions and their ranking was built. The correlation coefficient between the rankings for both scenarios is equal to 0.9022 for the scores and 0.7510 for the ranks of the vertices. The results of the top 50 vertices, selected as seeds, are presented in Table 3.

Table 3. Seeds selected for Scenario 2, ordered by their rank and CCi score obtained in the applied TOPSIS method.

Rank	Vertex	Score	Rank	Vertex	Score	Rank	Vertex	Score	Rank	Vertex	Score	Rank	Vertex	Score
1	3	0.9980	11	30	0.4075	21	20	0.3645	31	116	0.3073	41	34	0.2560
2	4	0.8142	12	9	0.4048	22	18	0.3606	32	26	0.3045	42	93	0.2476
3	2	0.7554	13	19	0.4036	23	7	0.3482	33	29	0.3045	43	464	0.2476
4	5	0.5836	14	11	0.3936	24	170	0.3482	34	152	0.3044	44	14	0.2445
5	12	0.5392	15	113	0.3857	25	153	0.3442	35	174	0.2913	45	48	0.2445
6	24	0.5178	16	17	0.3857	26	185	0.3260	36	82	0.2900	46	56	0.2354
7	6	0.4741	17	42	0.3856	27	53	0.3260	37	10	0.2840	47	69	0.2341
8	1	0.4452	18	21	0.3708	28	172	0.3250	38	238	0.2839	48	33	0.2341
9	135	0.4296	19	57	0.3658	29	16	0.3135	39	195	0.2839	49	97	0.2325
10	49	0.4164	20	143	0.3658	30	47	0.3135	40	122	0.2589	50	295	0.2325

When Table 3 is analyzed, it is clearly visible that the scores obtained by the best vertices are much more diversified than in case of the first scenario. The three leading vertices are still the ones labelled *3*, *4* and *2*; however, the order of the subsequent two has changed. The vertex *5* is now ranked 4 with the score of 0.5836 (previously 0.5200), followed by the vertex *12* now scored 0.5392 (previously 0.5400). The vertex *24* remained on position 6; however, it is now followed by vertex *6*, scored 0.4741, which in the previous scenario was ranked 12th with the score of 0.4000. A detailed analysis of the differences between ranks obtained by vertices in the rankings for scenarios 1 and 2 is presented on Figure 3A. The horizontal axis presents the consecutive ranks of all 1000 vertices of the studied network in scenario 1, whereas the vertical axis shows how these vertices were then ranked in scenario 2. The closer the point representing a vertex is to the diagonal line on the chart, the smaller the change in the rank occurred. It can be observed, that while in case of the top-ranked vertices only small changes in rank occur, as it can be confirmed in Table 3, in the case of the vertices further down the list, changes of even hundreds of levels in rank can be observed.

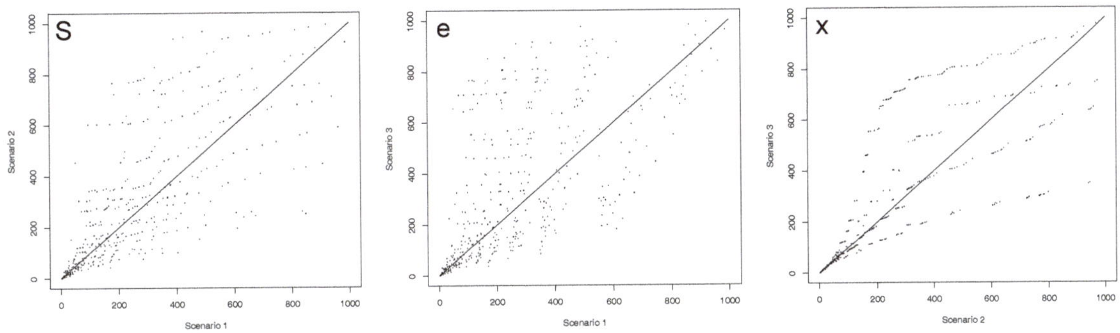

Figure 3. Visual comparison of ranks of nodes obtained in rankings for various scenarios: (**A**) scenarios 1 and 2; (**B**) scenarios 1 and 3; (**C**) scenarios 2 and 3.

Subsequent to the selection of the seeds, ten simulations were performed with the same conditions as in the first scenario. The visual representation of the outcomes of the simulations are presented in Figure A4 in Appendix A. In this scenario, the simulations averagely lasted 9.1 iterations, that is, longer by 0.5 iteration and resulted in 435.6 nodes infected (0.4356 coverage, 0.0020 more). What is interesting, the usage of two criteria allowed us to increase the coverage in the target group. Averagely 52 targeted nodes were infected, that is, 0.4 target coverage, which is 0.0115 more than in the first scenario.

4.6. Scenario 3: Four Criteria

In the third scenario, it was decided to focus on seeding information not only to vertices with high values of female degree (C4) and mid-aged degree (C7), but also to nodes which are already in the target group, that is, the right sex (C2, female) and age (C5, mid-aged). The seeds selected for this scenario are presented in Table 4.

Table 4. Seeds selected for Scenario 3, ordered by their rank and CCi score obtained in the applied TOPSIS method.

Rank	Vertex	Score	Rank	Vertex	Score	Rank	Vertex	Score	Rank	Vertex	Score	Rank	Vertex	Score
1	3	0.9069	11	9	0.4120	21	20	0.3750	31	29	0.3197	41	122	0.2782
2	4	0.7842	12	11	0.4023	22	153	0.3561	32	185	0.3197	42	34	0.2731
3	2	0.7191	13	30	0.3985	23	170	0.3535	33	116	0.3148	43	33	0.2717
4	5	0.5821	14	19	0.3950	24	18	0.3534	34	152	0.3125	44	93	0.2679
5	24	0.5291	15	143	0.3862	25	7	0.3412	35	174	0.3067	45	14	0.2660
6	12	0.5248	16	21	0.3810	26	53	0.3326	36	195	0.2934	46	130	0.2577
7	6	0.4782	17	113	0.3775	27	172	0.3315	37	82	0.2846	47	69	0.2566
8	1	0.4508	18	17	0.3774	28	16	0.3279	38	464	0.2822	48	97	0.2543
9	49	0.4236	19	42	0.3774	29	47	0.3278	39	10	0.2788	49	74	0.2474
10	135	0.4198	20	57	0.3757	30	26	0.3197	40	238	0.2788	50	104	0.2474

The analysis of Table 4 shows that the vertex 3 is still the leading one, however its score is much lower in case of this scenario (0.9069, compared to 0.9975 and 0.9980 in scenarios 1 and 2 respectively). Some minor changes in ranks can also be observed for the remaining seeds. Figure 3B visualizes the comparison of ranks between scenarios 1 and 3, whereas Figure 3C between scenarios 2 and 3. The analysis of these figures allows us to visually observe that the ranking obtained in scenario 3 is more similar to the one obtained in scenario 2 than to the one in scenario 1. This can be confirmed, indeed, by comparing the correlation coefficients between all scenarios (see Table 5).

Table 5. Correlation matrix between the three scenarios' ranks (**A**) and scores (**B**).

(A) RANKS	Scenario 1	Scenario 2	Scenario 3	(B) SCORE	Scenario 1	Scenario 2	Scenario 3
Scenario 1	x	0.7510	0.7099	Scenario 1	x	0.9022	0.8186
Scenario 2	0.7510	x	0.7308	Scenario 2	0.9022	x	0.8933
Scenario 3	0.7099	0.7308	x	Scenario 3	0.8186	0.8933	x

The results of the ten simulations performed for this scenario under the same conditions as used previously, are visually presented in Figure A5 in Appendix A. The average duration of the simulations was 8.7 iterations, which is slightly longer than in scenario 1 but shorter than that in scenario 2. On average, 435 nodes were infected (0.4350 coverage), which, similarly, is better than scenario 1 but worse than scenario 2. Finally, averagely 52.7 targeted nodes were infected, that is, 0.4054 targeted coverage, which is 0.0054 better than in scenario 2 and 0.0169 better than in the traditional approach, mimicked in scenario 1 (see Tables 6 and 7).

Table 6. Average simulation results for scenarios 1–3.

Scenario	Preferences	Avg. Last Iter.	Inf. Nodes	Coverage	Targeted Inf. Nodes	Targeted Coverage
1	100-1-1-1-1-1-1-1	8.60	433.60	0.4336	50.50	0.3885
2	1-1-1-100-1-1-100-1	9.10	435.60	0.4356	52.00	0.4000
3	1-100-1-100-100-1-100-1	8.70	435.00	0.4350	52.70	0.4054

Table 7. Comparison of differences between the average simulation results for scenarios 1–3.

Average Last Iteration				Average Coverage				Average Targeted Coverage			
Δ	**S1**	**S2**	**S3**	**Δ**	**S1**	**S2**	**S3**	**Δ**	**S1**	**S2**	**S3**
S1	x	−0.5	−0.1	**S1**	x	−0.0020	−0.0014	**S1**	x	−0.0115	−0.0169
S2	0.5	x	0.4	**S2**	0.0020	x	0.0006	**S2**	0.0115	x	−0.0054
S3	0.1	−0.4	x	**S3**	0.0014	−0.0006	x	**S3**	0.0169	0.0054	x

4.7. Sensitivity Analysis

As it was observed in Sections 4.4–4.6, depending on the preference weights regarding evaluation criteria, the evaluation score of each vertex varied, resulting in differences in the obtained rankings and diverse sets of initial seeds for performing the information propagation campaign. The MCDA methodological foundations of the proposed approach allow to perform sensitivity analysis of the obtained rankings, and thus recognize how changes in the criteria preference affect the final rankings and, in turn, the selected seeds.

In this section, a sensitivity analysis for the seed selection problem for the studied network is presented. For clarity, the subset of analyzed vertices was limited to the ones which were selected as seeds in any of the scenarios 1–3. This resulted in a subset comprising of a total of 63 vertices: 1, 2, 3, 4, 5, 6, 7, 9, 10, 11, 12, 14, 16, 17, 18, 19, 20, 21, 24, 26, 29, 30, 33, 34, 36, 37, 40, 42, 45, 47, 48, 49, 53, 55, 56, 57, 59, 65, 69, 74, 82, 93, 97, 101, 103, 104, 113, 116, 122, 130, 135, 143, 151, 152, 153, 170, 172, 174, 185, 195, 238, 295, 464.

In order to perform the sensitivity analysis, at first the weights of all criteria were set to 1. Then, the weight of each criterion was gradually changed to 1, 25, 50, 75 and 100, while the rest of criteria remained at an unchanged level. Afterwards, the level of all criteria was increased to 25, and each criterion was tested again with the weight of 1, 25, 50, 75 and 100, while the rest of the criteria remained at an unchanged level. The same was then repeated for the levels of 50 and 75. At each combination of weights, the TOPSIS method was used to compute a ranking. The score and ranks of each of the 63 studied vertices was stored, and plotted afterwards. The plots representing the changes of score of each vertex is presented in Figure 4. The changes of ranks are presented in Figure 5.

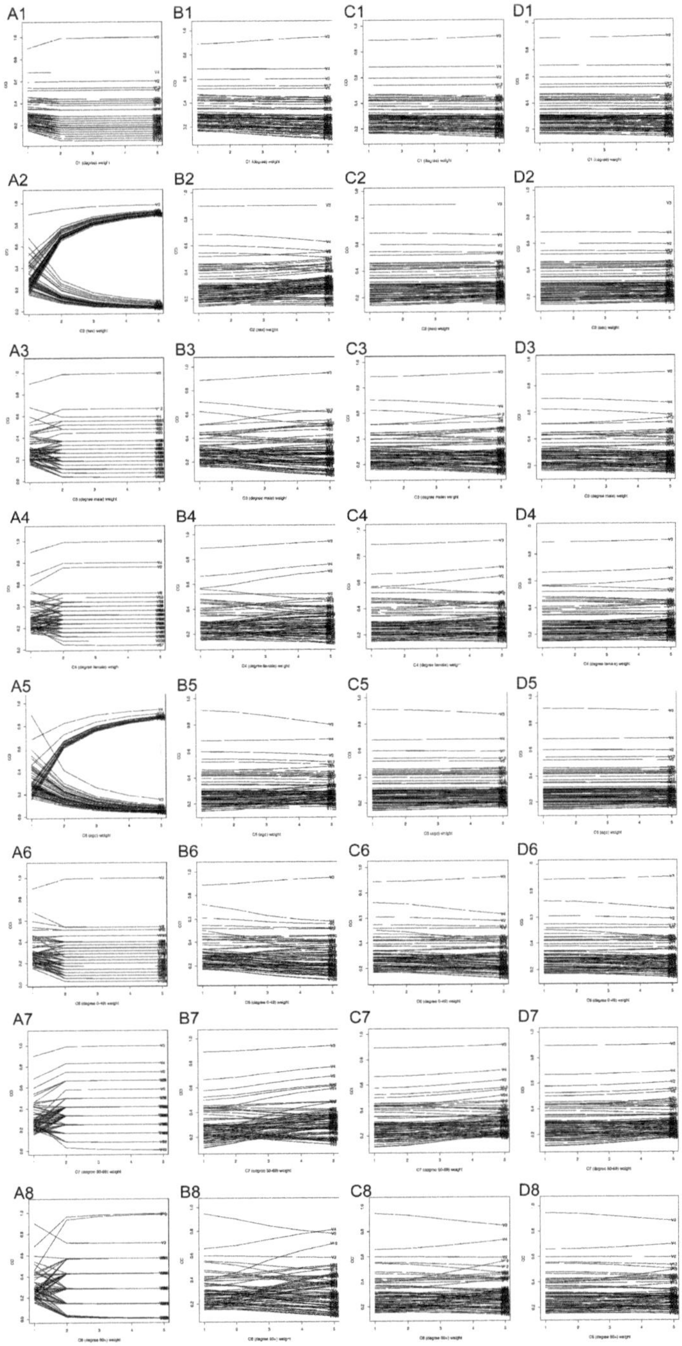

Figure 4. Sensitivity analysis on the subset of 63 network vertices. The charts represent how changes in a single criterion (1–8) affect the score obtained by the analysed vertices, when the weights of the other criteria are set to 1 (**A**), 25 (**B**), 50 (**C**) or 75 (**D**).

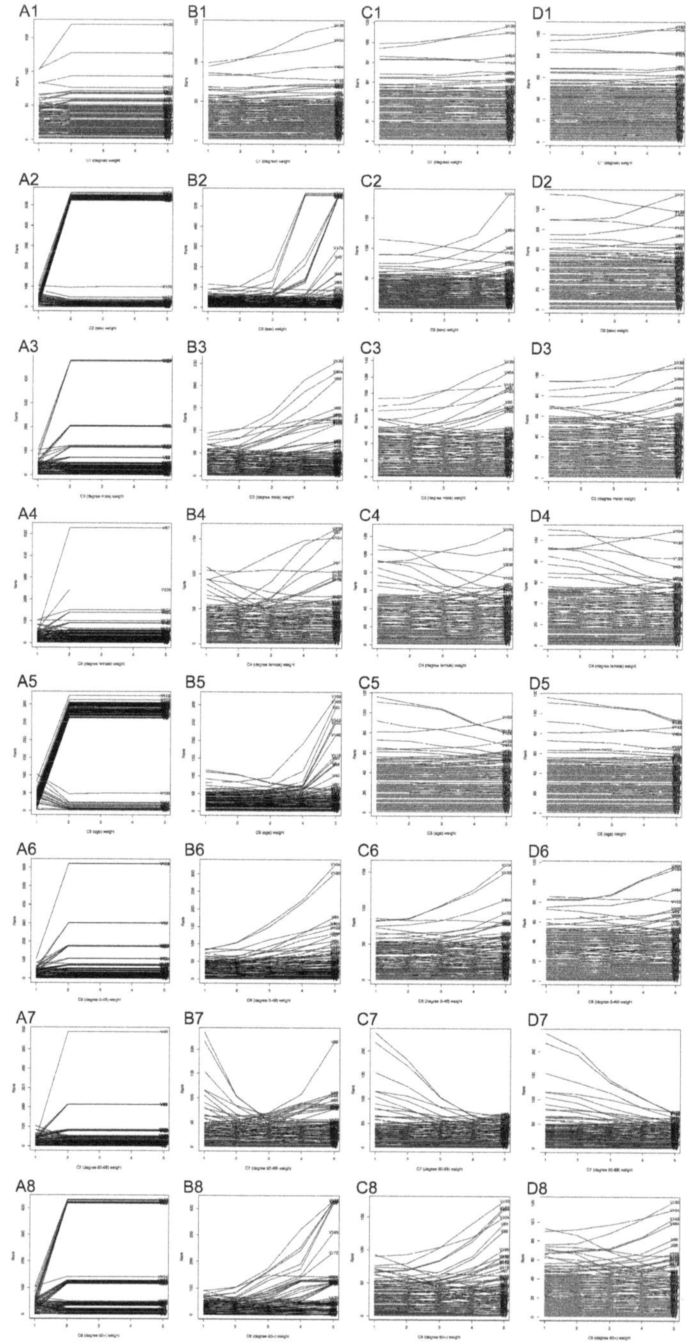

Figure 5. Sensitivity analysis on the subset of 63 network vertices. The charts represent how changes in a single criterion (1–8) affect the ranks obtained by the analysed vertices, when the weights of the other criteria are set to 1 (**A**), 25 (**B**), 50 (**C**) or 75 (**D**).

The analysis of Figure 4A shows how each of the criteria support or conflict with individual vertices. It is particularly clear because, while the weight of each criterion is increased in the range 1–100, the weights of the remaining criteria are locked at the level of 1. The chart A8 demonstrates that, in some cases, the vertex *3*, which was the leading one in all three exemplary scenarios, in some cases can be outran by other vertices. If the weight of criterion C8 (elderly degree) was increased to 25, while the weights of the other criteria remained negligible at the value of 1, the score of vertex *3* would drop below 0.8 and it would be ranked 3rd. However, if the weights of the other criteria were levelled at 25, the vertex would be the leader again, unless the weight of criterion C8 was increased close to 100. Then the vertex *3* would be ranked second.

Similarly, as can be observed in chart A5, if the weight of criterion C5 (age) was increasing, yet the other weights remained at 1, the vertex *3* would lose score very fast, down to a level of approximately 0.2. However, if the weights of the other criteria were increasing, the downfall of the score would be reduced to 0.8 (B5) or even 0.9 (C5, D5).

An interesting observation can be made looking at charts A1–A8. As was seen in Table 2 in Section 4.4, many vertices obtained the same score, and therefore their rank could vary. During the sensitivity analysis, this resulted in plots for multiple vertices being superimposed one on another. For example, on chart A1, only vertices *3*, *4*, *2*, *12* and *5* can be located easily, while the remaining vertices are stacked together on the chart.

Because criterion C1 is based on the degree centrality measure, the vertices' plots cluster in multiple score-groups, based on a plentiful, yet enumerable set of possible degree values, in the case of the studied network. On the other hand, due to the fact that the criteria C7 and C8 are based on the degrees of less numerous social groups (mid-aged and elderly), the possible values of the degree measure are more limited in this case and, therefore, there are less possible score values, which can be observed on the charts A7 and A8. In case of the chart A2, it can be observed that if the vertices are appraised based on the criterion C2 (sex), where only two values are possible, the vertices cluster in two groups. Since both sexes are distributed in the studied network at a roughly even probability level, it can be observed on the chart that both groups of vertices' plots are similar in size. On the other hand, however, in case of criterion C5, also only two values are possible, so the vertices are plotted in two groups too. However, because only about a quarter of the studied network is in the targeted middle-aged group, a clear disproportion between the groups of plots can be observed on the chart A5.

Whilst in the case of Figure 4, the values on the vertical axis were limited to the range from 0 to 1, and multiple vertices were allowed to have the same value, in case of Figure 5 each value can be assigned only to a single vertex at a time. As was mentioned earlier, the set of analyzed vertices is limited to 63 for readability. The charts on Figure 5 are scaled to show ranks from 1 (best) to the worst one obtained by any of the 63 studied vertices. It is important to reiterate, that each of the 63 studied nodes was in the group of 50 best vertices in one of the scenarios described above. Therefore it is very unforeseen to observe that the chart C1 ends at about rank 120, obtained by the worst vertex *130*, and the chart A6 ends around rank 600 for vertices *104* and *130*. These observations emphasize the importance of proper selection of seeds for information spreading campaigns in social networks.

4.8. Full Range Analysis

The empirical study was concluded by performing a comprehensive set of 65,610 simulations based on the full range of the seed selection preference weights. For each of the eight decision criteria, the weights of 1, 50 and 100 were assigned. That resulted in 3^8 possible sets of criteria preference weights and, consequently, 6561 sets of seeds, for each of which ten simulations under invariable conditions were performed. The results of the performed 65,610 simulations were then stored and aggregated for further analysis.

For the studied synthetic network, the highest number of infected vertices was reached for the seeds indicated by rankings based on high weights of the C5 (age) criterion, and negligible weights of the other criteria. It was equal to 459.7 infected nodes, that is, 0.4597 coverage. For such scenarios, averagely 61.3 targeted nodes were infected, that is, 0.4715 coverage of the targets.

On the other hand, the highest coverage within the targeted nodes was achieved in the simulations originating from the rankings produced by the scenarios in which high weight values were assigned to criteria C2 (sex) and C5 (age). On average 75.8 targeted nodes were infected in these simulations, that is, 0.5831 targets' coverage. For these scenarios, on average 458.6 vertices were infected, that is, 0.4586 coverage. This substantial increase in the count of the infected targets might be caused by the fact, that for this scenario, all seeds were part of the target group themselves (resulting in on average 25.8 non-seed targets infected, i.e., 0.1985), whereas in the scenario described in Section 4.6, only 5 of the initial seeds were from the target group (resulting in, on average, 47.7 non-seed targets infected, i.e., 0.3669 of the targets).

All in all, the simulation results have shown that the use of a multi-attribute seed selection approach, proposed in this paper, at the cost of reducing the coverage on the studied network by 0.0011, allowed us to increase the coverage within the targeted nodes by 0.1116 compared to the approach oriented on maximizing the global network coverage.

5. Conclusions

Large-scale networks used daily by billions of users [60] create a medium for transmitting information and content. While most influence maximisation methods focus on increasing coverage, it is also important to reach users interested in content or services to avoid the distribution of unwanted messages, decrease information overload and habituation effect and, as a result, increase campaign performance. Earlier research in the area of information spreading focused mainly on influence maximisation. Only limited number of studies discussed targeting nodes with specific characteristics with main focus on their single attributes.

This paper proposes a novel approach to seeding information in multi-attribute social networks, in order to target multi-attribute groups of nodes. In the proposed approach, the seeds for initializing the campaign are chosen based on the ranking obtained with an MCDA method. During information spreading initialization, it is possible to adjust the weights assigned to each attribute. This, in turn, allows to manipulate the symmetry between the global coverage and coverage within the targeted group of nodes. Particularly, the coverage within the targeted multi-attribute nodes' group can be increased, at the cost of potentially reducing the global coverage. The experimental research has shown a superior performance of the proposed approach, compared to traditional approaches focused on the degree centrality measure.

Although the empirical research has shown that the multi-attribute approach to the seed selection allowed us to significantly increase the coverage within the targeted group of nodes, the full-scope study has shown that even higher increase could be obtained if the higher weights were assigned to the criteria which were not initially selected for research in the empirical study. Therefore, grasping this experimental domain knowledge, especially in form of creation of an ontology for selection of criteria for targeting particular types of targets, is a very promising possible future field of research. Such ontology could provide guidelines for the marketer, for assigning weights to the multi-attribute seed rank generation.

Moreover, during the research, finding a multi-attribute model of a real network proved to be very problematic and it was necessary to perform the empirical study on networks with attributes superimposed artificially, based on the known distributions of these attributes in population. This allowed us to study the efficiency of the proposed approach, but comparing to other similar works in this field was not possible. It would be beneficial to include in future work the collection of knowledge about a real multi-attribute social network, in order to allow benchmarking of the proposed approach on a real model. This, in turn, implies additional methodical challenges, as proper reflecting of the non-deterministic nature of performance data in complex networks requires proper adjusting of the MCDA-based decision models and methods used. In practice, the usage of fuzzy extensions of MCDA methods (which proved to be powerful tools for dealing with data uncertainty) seems to be very promising.

Last, but not least, this research focused only on the multiple values of the network attributes. Future work should include a more profound look into the main aspects of the multi-attributed complex network itself.

Author Contributions: Conceptualization, A.K., J.J. and J.W.; Data curation, A.K. and J.J.; Formal analysis, A.K., J.J. and J.W.; Funding acquisition, J.J. and J.W.; Investigation, J.J.; Methodology, A.K., J.J. and J.W.; Project administration, J.J.; Resources, A.K.; Software, A.K.; Supervision, J.J., J.W.; Validation, J.J.; Visualization, A.K. and J.J.; Writing—original draft, A.K., J.J. and J.W.; Writing—review and editing, J.J. All authors have read and agreed to the published version of the manuscript.

Funding: This work was supported by the National Science Centre of Poland, the decision no. 2017/27/B/HS4/01216 (A.K., J.J.) and within the framework of the program of the Minister of Science and Higher Education under the name "Regional Excellence Initiative" in the years 2019–2022, project number 001/RID/2018/19, the amount of financing PLN 10,684,000.00 (J.W.).

Institutional Review Board Statement: Not applicable.

Informed Consent Statement: Not applicable.

Conflicts of Interest: The authors declare no conflict of interest.

Appendix A

The final steps of each of the 10 simulations from various scenarios are presented below. The blue "s" vertices represent the seeds. The green "i" nodes represent the non-targeted vertices which were infected. The empty vertices with red outline represent the targets of the campaign. The fully-colored red vertices represent the targets which were successfully reached in the campaign.

Figure A1 presents the target 1, and Figure A2 the target 2 of the real-life usage example from Section 4.1. Subsequently, Figures A3–A5 present scenarios on the synthetic network simulations from Sections 4.4–4.6 respectively.

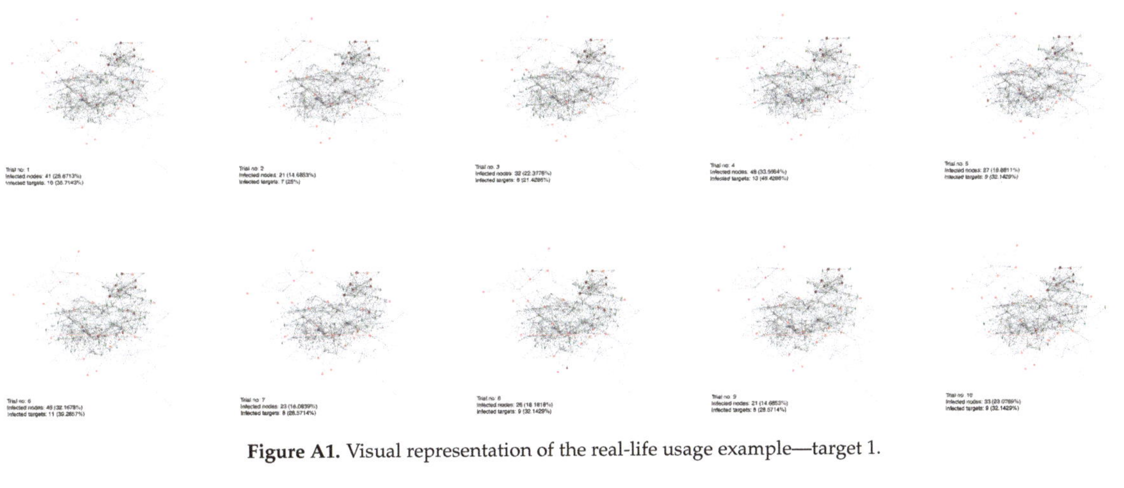

Figure A1. Visual representation of the real-life usage example—target 1.

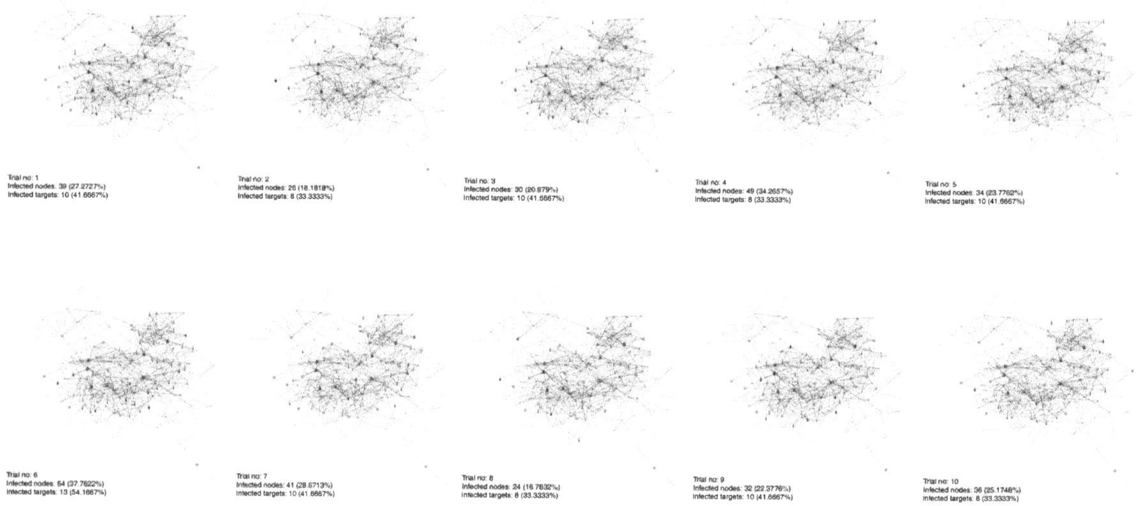

Figure A2. Visual representation of the real-life usage example—target 2.

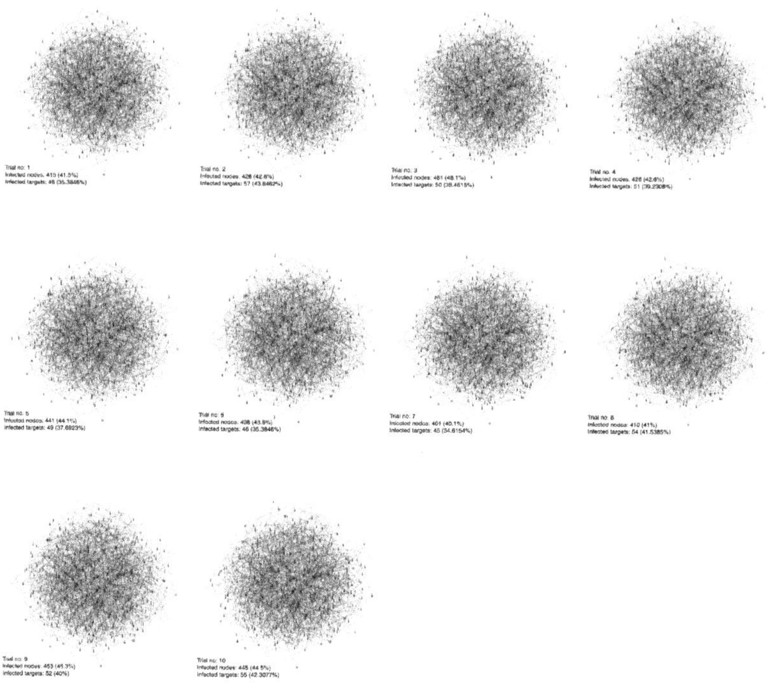

Figure A3. Visual representation of 10 trials for Scenario 1.

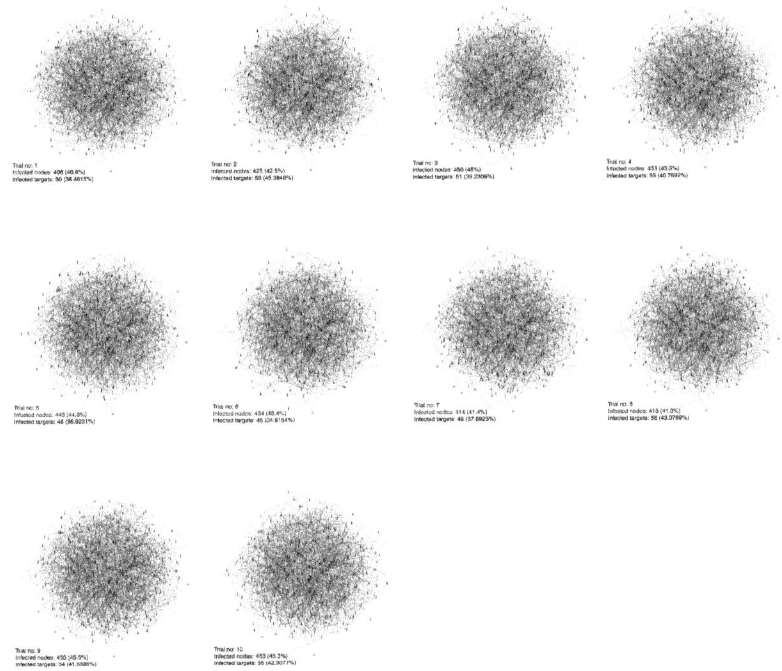

Figure A4. Visual representation of 10 trials for Scenario 2.

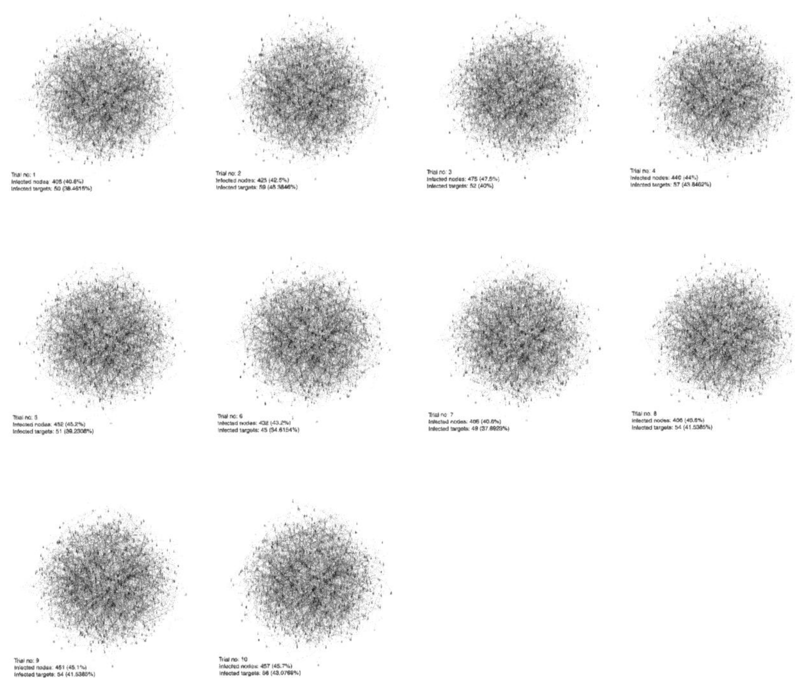

Figure A5. Visual representation of 10 trials for Scenario 3.

References

1. Dunbar, R.I. Do online social media cut through the constraints that limit the size of offline social networks? *R. Soc. Open Sci.* **2016**, *3*, 150292. [CrossRef] [PubMed]
2. Vinerean, S. Importance of strategic social media marketing. *Expert J. Mark.* **2017**, *5*. Available online: http://hdl.handle.net/11159/1381 (accessed on 27 June 2020).
3. Iribarren, J.L.; Moro, E. Impact of Human Activity Patterns on the Dynamics of Information Diffusion. *Phys. Rev. Lett.* **2009**, *103*, 038702. [CrossRef] [PubMed]
4. Nguyen, H.T.; Dinh, T.N.; Thai, M.T. Cost-aware targeted viral marketing in billion-scale networks. In Proceedings of the IEEE INFOCOM 2016—The 35th Annual IEEE International Conference on Computer Communications, San Francisco, CA, USA, 10–15 April 2016; pp. 1–9.
5. Mochalova, A.; Nanopoulos, A. A targeted approach to viral marketing. *Electron. Commer. Res. Appl.* **2014**, *13*, 283–294. [CrossRef]
6. Liu, Q.; Dong, Z.; Liu, C.; Xie, X.; Chen, E.; Xiong, H. Social marketing meets targeted customers: A typical user selection and coverage perspective. In Proceedings of the 2014 IEEE International Conference on Data Mining, Shenzhen, China, 14–17 December 2014; pp. 350–359.
7. Voss, G.; Godfrey, A.; Seiders, K. Do satisfied customers always buy more? The roles of satiation and habituation in customer repurchase. In *Marketing Science Institute Working Paper Series 2010*; Marketing Science Institute: Cambridge, MA, USA, 2010; pp. 10–101.
8. Luo, C.; Lan, Y.; Wang, C.; Ma, L. The Effect of Information Consistency and Information Aggregation on eWOM Readers' Perception of Information Overload. In Proceedings of the PACIS 2013, Jeju Island, Korea, 18–22 June 2013; p. 180.
9. Datta, S.; Majumder, A.; Shrivastava, N. Viral marketing for multiple products. In Proceedings of the 2010 IEEE International Conference on Data Mining, Sydney, Australia, 13–17 December 2010; pp. 118–127.
10. Thakur, N.; Han, C.Y. An approach to analyze the social acceptance of virtual assistants by elderly people. In Proceedings of the 8th International Conference on the Internet of Things, Santa Barbara, CA, USA, 15–18 October 2018; pp. 1–6.
11. Thakur, N.; Han, C.Y. Framework for an intelligent affect aware smart home environment for elderly people. *Int. J. Recent Trends Hum. Comput. Interact. (IJHCI)* **2019**, *9*, 23–43.
12. Pamučar, D.S.; Božanić, D.; Ranđelović, A. Multi-criteria decision making: An example of sensitivity analysis. *Serbian J. Manag.* **2017**, *12*, 1–27. [CrossRef]
13. Mukhametzyanov, I.; Pamucar, D. A sensitivity analysis in MCDM problems: A statistical approach. *Decis. Mak. Appl. Manag. Eng.* **2018**, *1*, 51–80. [CrossRef]
14. Kempe, D.; Kleinberg, J.; Tardos, É. Maximizing the spread of influence through a social network. In Proceedings of the Ninth ACM SIGKDD International Conference on Knowledge Discovery and Data Mining, Washington, DC, USA, 24–27 August 2003; pp. 137–146.
15. Hinz, O.; Skiera, B.; Barrot, C.; Becker, J.U. Seeding strategies for viral marketing: An empirical comparison. *J. Mark.* **2011**, *75*, 55–71. [CrossRef]
16. Zareie, A.; Sheikhahmadi, A.; Jalili, M. Identification of influential users in social networks based on users' interest. *Inf. Sci.* **2019**, *493*, 217–231. [CrossRef]
17. Li, X.; Smith, J.D.; Dinh, T.N.; Thai, M.T. Why approximate when you can get the exact? Optimal targeted viral marketing at scale. In Proceedings of the IEEE INFOCOM 2017—IEEE Conference on Computer Communications, Atlanta, GA, USA, 1–4 May 2017; pp. 1–9.
18. Pasumarthi, R.; Narayanam, R.; Ravindran, B. Near optimal strategies for targeted marketing in social networks. In Proceedings of the 2015 International Conference on Autonomous Agents and Multiagent Systems, Paris, France, 10–15 July 2015; pp. 1679–1680.
19. Zareie, A.; Sheikhahmadi, A.; Khamforoosh, K. Influence maximization in social networks based on TOPSIS. *Expert Syst. Appl.* **2018**, *108*, 96–107. [CrossRef]
20. Yang, P.; Liu, X.; Xu, G. A dynamic weighted TOPSIS method for identifying influential nodes in complex networks. *Mod. Phys. Lett. B* **2018**, *32*, 1850216. [CrossRef]
21. Yang, Y.; Yu, L.; Zhou, Z.; Chen, Y.; Kou, T. Node Importance Ranking in Complex Networks Based on Multicriteria Decision Making. *Math. Probl. Eng.* **2019**, *2019*. [CrossRef]
22. Liu, Z.; Jiang, C.; Wang, J.; Yu, H. The node importance in actual complex networks based on a multi-attribute ranking method. *Knowl. Based Syst.* **2015**, *84*, 56–66. [CrossRef]
23. Robles, J.F.; Chica, M.; Cordon, O. Evolutionary Multiobjective Optimization to Target Social Network Influentials in Viral Marketing. *Expert Syst. Appl.* **2020**, 113183. [CrossRef]
24. Wang, L.; Yu, Z.; Xiong, F.; Yang, D.; Pan, S.; Yan, Z. Influence Spread in Geo-Social Networks: A Multiobjective Optimization Perspective. *IEEE Trans. Cybern.* **2019**. [CrossRef]
25. Gandhi, M.; Muruganantham, A. Potential influencers identification using multi-criteria decision making (MCDM) methods. *Procedia Comput. Sci.* **2015**, *57*, 1179–1188. [CrossRef]

26. Muruganantham, A.; Gandhi, G.M. Framework for Social Media Analytics based on Multi-Criteria Decision Making (MCDM) Model. *Multimed. Tools Appl.* **2020**, *79*, 3913–3927. [CrossRef]
27. Montazerolghaem, M. Effective Factors in Network Marketing Success and Ranking Using Multi-criteria Decision Making Techniques. *Int. J. Appl. Optim. Stud.* **2019**, *2*, 73–89.
28. Karczmarczyk, A.; Jankowski, J.; Wątróbski, J. Multi-criteria decision support for planning and evaluation of performance of viral marketing campaigns in social networks. *PLoS ONE* **2018**, *13*, e0209372. [CrossRef] [PubMed]
29. Cinelli, M.; Kadziński, M.; Gonzalez, M.; Słowiński, R. How to Support the Application of Multiple Criteria Decision Analysis? Let Us Start with a Comprehensive Taxonomy. *Omega* **2020**, 102261. [CrossRef] [PubMed]
30. Pamučar, D.S.; Božanić, D.I.; Kurtov, D.V. Fuzzification of the Saaty's scale and a presentation of the hybrid fuzzy AHP-TOPSIS model: An example of the selection of a brigade artillery group firing position in a defensive operation. *Vojnoteh. Glas.* **2016**, *64*, 966–986. [CrossRef]
31. Chatterjee, P.; Stević, Ž. A two-phase fuzzy AHP-fuzzy TOPSIS model for supplier evaluation in manufacturing environment. *Oper. Res. Eng. Sci. Theory Appl.* **2019**, *2*, 72–90. [CrossRef]
32. Wątróbski, J.; Jankowski, J.; Ziemba, P.; Karczmarczyk, A.; Zioło, M. Generalised framework for multi-criteria method selection. *Omega* **2019**, *86*, 107–124. [CrossRef]
33. Stević, Ž.; Tanackov, I.; Vasiljević, M.; Novarlić, B.; Stojić, G. An integrated fuzzy AHP and TOPSIS model for supplier evaluation. *Serbian J. Manag.* **2016**, *11*, 15–27. [CrossRef]
34. Mardani, A.; Jusoh, A.; Zavadskas, E.K. Fuzzy multiple criteria decision-making techniques and applications—Two decades review from 1994 to 2014. *Expert Syst. Appl.* **2015**, *42*, 4126–4148. [CrossRef]
35. Freeman, L.C. Centrality in social networks conceptual clarification. *Soc. Netw.* **1978**, *1*, 215–239. [CrossRef]
36. Bonacich, P. Technique for analyzing overlapping memberships. *Sociol. Methodol.* **1972**, *4*, 176–185. [CrossRef]
37. Valente, T.W.; Coronges, K.; Lakon, C.; Costenbader, E. How correlated are network centrality measures? *Connections* **2008**, *28*, 16.
38. Likert, R. A technique for the measurement of attitudes. *Arch. Psychol.* **1932**, *22*, 55.
39. Saaty, T.L.; Vargas, L.G. The legitimacy of rank reversal. *Omega* **1984**, *12*, 513–516. [CrossRef]
40. Sabidussi, G. The centrality index of a graph. *Psychometrika* **1966**, *31*, 581–603. [CrossRef]
41. Freeman, L.C. A set of measures of centrality based on betweenness. *Sociometry* **1977**, 35–41. [CrossRef]
42. Roy, B.; Vanderpooten, D. The European school of MCDA: Emergence, basic features and current works. *J. Multi Criteria Decis. Anal.* ***1996***, *5*, 22–38. [CrossRef]
43. Roy, B. Paradigms and challenges. In *Multiple Criteria Decision Analysis: State of the Art Surveys*; Springer: Berlin/Heidelberg, Germany, 2005; pp. 3–24.
44. Guitouni, A.; Martel, J.M. Tentative guidelines to help choosing an appropriate MCDA method. *Eur. J. Oper. Res.* **1998**, *109*, 501–521. [CrossRef]
45. Roy, B.; Słowiński, R. Questions guiding the choice of a multicriteria decision aiding method. *EURO J. Decis. Process.* **2013**, *1*, 69–97. [CrossRef]
46. Vansnick, J.C. On the problem of weights in multiple criteria decision making (the noncompensatory approach). *Eur. J. Oper. Res.* **1986**, *24*, 288–294. [CrossRef]
47. Wątróbski, J.; Jankowski, J.; Ziemba, P.; Karczmarczyk, A.; Zioło, M. Generalised framework for multi-criteria method selection: Rule set database and exemplary decision support system implementation blueprints. *Data Brief* **2019**, *22*, 639. [CrossRef] [PubMed]
48. Stević, Ž.; Alihodžić, A.; Božičković, Z.; Vasiljević, M.; Vasiljević, Đ. Application of combined AHP-TOPSIS model for decision making in management. In Proceedings of the 5th International Conference Economics and Management-Based on New Technologies "EMONT", Vrnjačka Banja, Serbia, 18–21 June 2015; pp. 33–40.
49. Behzadian, M.; Otaghsara, S.K.; Yazdani, M.; Ignatius, J. A state-of-the-art survey of TOPSIS applications. *Expert Syst. Appl.* **2012**, *39*, 13051–13069. [CrossRef]
50. Chen, S.J.; Hwang, C.L. Fuzzy multiple attribute decision making methods. In *Fuzzy Multiple Attribute Decision Making*; Springer: Berlin/Heidelberg, Germany, 1992; pp. 289–486.
51. Yoon, K.P.; Hwang, C.L. *Multiple Attribute Decision Making: An Introduction*; Sage Publications: Thousand Oaks, CA, USA, 1995; Volume 104.
52. Hwang, C.L.; Yoon, K. Multiple criteria decision making. In *Lecture Notes in Economics and Mathematical Systems*; Springer: Berlin/Heidelberg, Germany, 1981; Volume 186, pp. 58–191.
53. Rossi, R.A.; Ahmed, N.K. The Network Data Repository with Interactive Graph Analytics and Visualization. In Proceedings of the AAAI 2015, Austin, TX, USA, 25–30 January 2015.
54. Gus. *Ludność. Stan i Struktura Ludności Oraz Ruch Naturalny w Przekroju Terytorialnym*; Statistics Poland: Warsaw, Poland, 2016.
55. Barabási, A.L.; Bonabeau, E. Scale-free networks. *Sci. Am.* **2003**, *288*, 60–69. [CrossRef] [PubMed]
56. Chiasserini, C.F.; Garetto, M.; Leonardi, E. Social network de-anonymization under scale-free user relations. *IEEE ACM Trans. Netw.* **2016**, *24*, 3756–3769. [CrossRef]
57. Luo, Y.; Ma, J. The influence of positive news on rumor spreading in social networks with scale-free characteristics. *Int. J. Mod. Phys. C* **2018**, *29*, 1850078. [CrossRef]

58. Liu, W.; Li, T.; Liu, X.; Xu, H. Spreading dynamics of a word-of-mouth model on scale-free networks. *IEEE Access* **2018**, *6*, 65563–65572. [CrossRef]
59. Ministerstwo Zdrowia. *Program Profilaktyki Raka Piersi (Mammografia)*; www.gov.pl; Ministerstwo Zdrowia: Warsaw, Poland, 2018.
60. WeAreSocial Digital 2020. Available online: https://wearesocial.com/digital-2020 (accessed on 27 June 2020).

symmetry

MDPI

Article

Cubic M-polar Fuzzy Hybrid Aggregation Operators with Dombi's T-norm and T-conorm with Application

Muhammad Riaz [1], Muhammad Abdullah Khokhar [1], Dragan Pamucar [2,*] and Muhammad Aslam [3]

1 Department of Mathematics, University of the Punjab, Lahore 54590, Pakistan; mriaz.math@pu.edu.pk (M.R.); mabdullahk1394@gmail.com (M.A.K.)
2 Department of Logistics, Military Academy, University of Defence in Belgarde, Belgarde 11000, Serbia
3 Department of Mathematics, College of Sciences, King Khalid University, Abha 61413, Saudi Arabia; muamin@kku.edu.sa
* Correspondence: dragan.pamucar@va.mod.gov.rs

Abstract: A cubic m-polar fuzzy set (CmPFS) is a new hybrid extension of cubic set (CS) and m-polar fuzzy set (mPFS). A CS comprises two parts; one part consists of a fuzzy interval (may sometimes be a fuzzy number) acting as membership grade (MG), and the second part consists of a fuzzy number acting as non-membership grade (NMG). An mPFS assigns m number of MGs against each alternative in the universe of discourse. A CmPFS deals with single as well as multi-polar information in the cubic environment. In this article, we explore some new aspects and consequences of the CmPFS. We define score and accuracy functions to find the priorities of alternatives/objects in multi-criteria decision-making (MCDM). For this objective, some new operations, like addition, scalar/usual multiplication, and power, are defined under Dombi's t-norm and t-conorm. We develop several new aggregation operators (AOs) using cubic m-polar fuzzy Dombi's t-norm and t-conorm. We present certain properties of suggested operators like monotonicity, commutativity, idempotency, and boundedness. Additionally, to discuss the application of these AOs, we present an advanced superiority and inferiority ranking (SIR) technique to deal with the problem of conversion from a linear economy to a circular economy. Moreover, a comparison analysis of proposed methodology with some other existing methods is also given.

Keywords: cubic m-polar fuzzy set; Dombi's operations; cubic m-polar fuzzy aggregation operators with P-order (R-order); SIR technique; multi-criteria group decision making

Citation: Riaz, M.; Khokhar, M.A.; Pamucar, D.; Aslam, M. Cubic M-polar Fuzzy Hybrid Aggregation Operators with Dombi's T-norm and T-conorm with Application. *Symmetry* **2021**, *13*, 646. https://doi.org/10.3390/sym13040646

Academic Editor: José Carlos R. Alcantud

Received: 24 March 2021
Accepted: 6 April 2021
Published: 11 April 2021

1. Introduction

The three core concepts of conventional linear economy (CLE) are assemble, use, and dispose. This illustrates the acquisition of raw materials and their conversion into products that are ultimately discarded as waste. By depleting natural resources and adding toxins to the atmosphere, such waste generation causes environmental degradation. Natural resource extraction is inextricably linked to the so-called CLE [1–4]. The carcinogenic effects of human activities on the environment, such as water scarcity, soil depletion, greenhouse effect, and smog weather, are major global concerns. Climate change is, in reality, the most pressing problem we face. As a result, the United Nations Environment Programme (UNEP) has devised a broad definition of sustainable development, which is a concept that includes not only economic growth and environmental protection, but also social inclusion. Without a doubt, the CLE has aided humanity, but it has also been a big source of concern due to the challenges it poses. We are all aware that our common environment is insecure and unsustainable. We are aware of its complexities, such as waste generation, natural resource use, and biodiversity depletion, among others. Aside from these problems, we want to help our economies and provide opportunities to the world's growing population.

The ecological effects of CLE, while guaranteeing its benefits for humankind, cannot be avoided, but can be minimized to some extent. The minimizing effort of the adversities of CLE is referred as circular economy (CE) [1–4]. A CE is structured to recycle and regenerate goods, parts, and resources, allowing for a considerable difference between technological and biological processes at all periods of the recycling process. CE is not a new concept; rather, it is a modification of CLE, which guarantees a minor net impact on the climate. CE is intended to restore any harm to the resources while guaranteeing as little waste as possible during the entire life cycle of a good. A CE is an adjunct to a CLE, where resources are preserved as long as possible, and the optimum displacement is collected, retained, and regenerated at the end of each access lifespan. Many biochemical and geochemical cycles around the motivated the idea of circular economy. For instance, water evaporates from the earth water bodies, forms rain drops, comes back to the earth and again becomes a part of the rivers, seas, oceans etc. The idea of CE is being actively encouraged by many corporations and governments round the world.

Although businesses are agile and well-equipped, many people worldwide have attended series of conferences on sustainable practices, with discussions how well circular economy guidelines could be coordinated and applied. If we assume that a lack of creative business models would interfere with creating a sustainable future, it appears critical to identify more forward-thinking alternatives. In this regard, we see the circular economy as a modern way to practice sustainability that stems from the need for companies of all sizes to retain flexibility in order to meet these challenges. Despite the growing popularity of CE as a business model, there is still little formal empirical discussion in the literature on enterprise risk management . Financial/sustainable success is also seen as a priority over ecological, social, and ethical values in light of the numerous academic debates on sustainable and environmentally responsible businesses. As a result, the circular economy is a crucial and timely idea to investigate. The circular economy has captured the minds of elected officials and business leaders in order to help meet the overwhelming environmental goals. It is a practical way to improve asset flow efficiency and allocation of current supply and frameworks through material transfer, recycling, and conservation, with a focus on improving the effectiveness of existing performance measurement in businesses. Many scientists have worked tirelessly to develop mathematical models for solving CE decision problems in unpredictable environments. The readers are referred to the following papers for ore information [5–9].

1.1. Literature Review

There is an overwhelming amount of uncertain and vague information in a wide range of real scenarios. While dealing with real-life challenges such as decision-making, medical diagnosis, pattern recognition, sustainability, and many others, uncertainties play a significant role, and it is a challenging task for decision-makers to make sensible decisions while dealing with imperfect, uncertain, or vague data. In fact, the majority of the ideas we come across in our daily lives are ambiguous. In certain contexts, dealing with apprehension or confusion is a significant problem. Vagueness or ambiguity can be evident in a variety of ways, resulting in a wide range of concerns. As a result, there is a need to deal with the uncertainties.

This idea was discussed by Zadeh [10] in 1965, who introduced a revolutionary idea of fuzzy set (FS) as a direct extension of crisp set. Researchers have introduced various theories and models to cope with the uncertainties in the real-life problems. Atanassov [11] introduced the intuitionistic fuzzy set (IFS), Molodtsov [12] originated the notion of a soft set (SS), Zhang [13,14] presented the idea of bipolar fuzzy set (BFS), Smarandache [15,16] proposed neutrosophic set, Cuong [17] introduced picture fuzzy set (PiFS), Yager [18,19] proposed Pythagorean fuzzy set (PyFS), and Yager [20] proposed q-rung orthopair fuzzy set (q-ROFS). These models have strong acceptance for modeling uncertainties in decision-making problems [21–25]. Dombi aggregation operators for information aggregation in the environment of different fuzzy sets have been studied by many researchers [26–32]. Chen et al. [33] introduced the idea of m-polar fuzzy sets to express multi-polarity in the objects/alternatives. Jun et al. [34] introduced cubic sets and their internal and external behaviors. Riaz and Hashmi [35] developed the notion of cubic m-polar fuzzy sets and established cubic m-polar fuzzy averaging aggregation operators for agribusiness MAGDM. Recently, Riaz and Hashmi [36–38] introduced some new extensions of fuzzy sets named as linear Diophantine fuzzy set (LDFS), soft rough linear Diophantine fuzzy set, and spherical linear Diophantine sets. Kamaci [39] introduced algebraic structure to LDFS with an interesting application to coding theory, which is based on LDFS codes.

Innovation of multi-criteria decision-making (MCDM) in fuzzy set theory is still an important topic at present. MCDM is a branch of decision science theory that is considered a cognitive based human behavior for choosing the best option under multiple criteria and has been widely applied across a variety of domains. One of the most difficult issues is to address uncertainties in MCDM by an efficient fuzzy model. Another objective in MCDM is to find ranking of feasible objects and then finally the selection of an optimal object. In actual decision-making, the individual needs to provide the assessment of the choices made by different types of assessment conditions, such as crisp numbers and intervals. However, in many situations, it is difficult for a person to opt for the correct option due to the existence of a variety of data inconsistencies that may occur due to lack of information or human error. Many aggregation operators (AOs) have been defined for information fusion [40–43]. Jain et al. [44] greatly contribution to circular economy by giving a DM solution in green marketing strategy.

1.2. Objectives and Organization of the Paper

The first objective of this paper is to address uncertainties more effectively by using cubic m-polar fuzzy numbers (CmPFNs). The second objective is to extend Dombi's operations to CmPFNs and develop various aggregation operators listed as follows. Cubic m-polar fuzzy Dombi P-averaging operator (*CmPFDPAO*).Cubic m-polar fuzzy Dombi R-averaging operator (*CmPFDRAO*). Cubic m-polar fuzzy Dombi weighted P-averaging operator (*CmPFDWPAO*). Cubic m-polar fuzzy Dombi weighted R-averaging operator (*CmPFDWRAO*). Cubic m-polar fuzzy Dombi ordered weighted P-averaging operator (*CmPFDOWPAO*). Cubic m-polar fuzzy Dombi ordered weighted R-averaging operator (*CmPFDOWRAO*). Cubic m-polar fuzzy Dombi hybrid P-averaging Operator (*CmPFDH-PAO*). Cubic m-polar fuzzy Dombi hybrid R-averaging operator (*CmPFDHRAO*). The third objective is to investigate certain properties of suggested operators like monotonicity, commutativity, idempotency, and boundedness. Additionally, proposed Dombi's AOs are more useful to investigate ranking of objects/alternatives in MCDM with the help of CmPFNs. The fourth objective to develop an advanced superiority and inferiority ranking

(SIR) technique to deal with the problem of conversion from the linear economy to the circular economy.

The remainder of the paper is organized as follows. In Section 2, some basic concepts like fuzzy sets, m-polar fuzzy sets, and cubic sets are reviewed. In Section 3, we discuss some results of cubic m-polar fuzzy sets. In Section 4, we present some Dombi's operations for cubic m-polar fuzzy environment. In Section 5, some cubic m-polar fuzzy Dombi aggregation operators with P-order are defined. In Section 5, some cubic m-polar fuzzy Dombi aggregation operators with R-order are developed. An interesting application to the circular economy using the proposed operators is given in Section 7. An advanced superiority and inferiority ranking (SIR) technique to deal with the problem of conversion from the linear economy to the circular economy is developed in Section 7. Lastly, the conclusion of this research work is given in Section 8.

2. Preliminaries

In this section, we review some basic concepts of fuzzy sets, m-polar fuzzy sets, and cubic sets.

Definition 1 ([10]). *A fuzzy set in the universe of discourse Q is defined as*

$$F = \{(\hbar, \mu_F(\hbar)) : \hbar \in Q\}$$

where the membership function is $\mu_F : Q \rightarrow [0,1]$ and the membership degree (MD) of $\hbar$ is $\mu_F(\hbar)$.

Definition 2 ([34]). *A cubic set $\ddot{\mathbb{C}}$ on a universe Q is an object of the form*

$$\ddot{\mathbb{C}} = \{(\hbar, A(\hbar), B(\hbar)) : \hbar \in Q\}$$

where $A(\hbar)$ is a fuzzy interval and $B(\hbar)$ is a fuzzy number assigned to the alternative $\hbar$ representing the membership and non-membership grades, respectively. For short, the cubic set can be denoted as $\langle A, B\rangle$.

Definition 3. *An m-polar fuzzy set (mPFS) with universe Q is a mapping, $Q \longrightarrow [0,1]^m$, that assigns m-independent fuzzy membership grades to each element of Q. An mPFS can be written as*

$$\mathfrak{M}_{\mathbb{P}} = \{\langle \gamma, (\mu_i(\gamma))_{i=1}^m \rangle : \gamma \in Q\}$$

Definition 4 ([35]). *A cubic m-polar fuzzy set (CmPFS) in a universe W is an object like $C_{cm} = \{(x, [\mu_1^-(x), \mu_1^+(x)], [\mu_2^-(x), \mu_2^+(x)], \cdots, [\mu_m^-(x), \mu_m^+(x)], \mu_1(x), \mu_2(x), \cdots, \mu_m(x)) : x \in W\}$, where $[\mu_j^-(x), \mu_j^+(x)]$ are fuzzy intervals and $\mu_j(x)$ are fuzzy numbers. μ_j^- are called lower fuzzy numbers and μ_j^+ are called upper fuzzy numbers. Briefly, we can write CmPFN as $([\mu_j^-, \mu_j^+], \mu_j)_{j=1}^m$.*

Definition 5 ([34]). *Given two fuzzy intervals $J_a = [\mu_a^-, \mu_a^+]$ and $J_b = [\nu_b^-, \nu_b^+]$, then*

1. $J_a \leq J_b \Leftrightarrow \mu_a^- \leq \nu_b^-$ *and* $\mu_a^+ \leq \nu_b^+$
2. $J_a \geq J_b \Leftrightarrow \mu_a^- \geq \nu_b^-$ *and* $\mu_a^+ \geq \nu_b^+$
3. $J_a = J_b \Leftrightarrow \mu_a^- = \nu_b^-$ *and* $\mu_a^+ = \nu_b^+$

Definition 6 ([35]). *Let $A = ([\mu_j^-, \mu_j^+], \mu_j)_{j=1}^m$ and $B = ([\nu_j^-, \nu_j^+], \nu_j)_{j=1}^m$, be the two CmPFNs.*

1. *(P-Order)* $A \leq_P B \Leftrightarrow [\mu_j^-, \mu_j^+] \leq [\nu_j^-, \nu_j^+]$ *and* $\mu_j \leq \nu_j$.
2. *(R-Order)* $A \leq_R B \Leftrightarrow [\mu_j^-, \mu_j^+] \leq [\nu_j^-, \nu_j^+]$ *and* $\mu_j \geq \nu_j$.

3 *(Equality)* $A = B \Leftrightarrow [\mu_j^-, \mu_j^+] = [\nu_j^-, \nu_j^+]$ *and* $\mu_j = \nu_j$ *for all* $j = 1, 2, \cdots, m$.

2.1. Operations for CmPFNs

In this part we discuss some operations on CmPFNs (see [35]). Let $A_i = ([\mu_{ij}^-, \mu_{ij}^+], \mu_{ij})_{j=1}^m$, $i \in \Omega$, be the collection of CmPFNs. Then

1 (Complement) $A_i^c = ([1 - \mu_{ij}^+, 1 - \mu_{ij}^-], 1 - \mu_{ij})_{j=1}^m$
2 (P-Maximum) $\vee_P A_i = ([\sup_{i \in \Omega} \mu_{ij}^-, \sup_{i \in \Omega} \mu_{ij}^+], \sup_{i \in \Omega} \mu_{ij})_{j=1}^m$
3 (P-Minimum) $\wedge_P A_i = ([\inf_{i \in \Omega} \mu_{ij}^-, \inf_{i \in \Omega} \mu_{ij}^+], \inf_{i \in \Omega} \mu_{ij})_{j=1}^m$
4 (R-Maximum) $\vee_P A_i = ([\sup_{i \in \Omega} \mu_{ij}^-, \sup_{i \in \Omega} \mu_{ij}^+], \inf_{i \in \Omega} \mu_{ij})_{j=1}^m$
5 (R-Minimum) $\wedge_P A_i = ([\inf_{i \in \Omega} \mu_{ij}^-, \inf_{i \in \Omega} \mu_{ij}^+], \sup_{i \in \Omega} \mu_{ij})_{j=1}^m$

3. Some Results on CmPFS

In this section, we give some basic results of CmPFS that will help in the next section to better understanding of the proposed aggregation operators.

Definition 7. *A CmPFS* $\mathfrak{C}_m = \{\langle q, ([\mu_j^-(q), \mu_j^+(q)], \mu_j(q))_{j=1}^m \rangle : q \in Q\}$ *on a discourse* Q *is said to be an Internal Cubic m-Polar Fuzzy Set (ICmPFS) if* $\mu_j^-(q) \leq \mu_j(q) \leq \mu_j^+(q)$, *for all* $q \in Q$ *and* $j = 1, 2, \cdots, m$.

Definition 8. *A CmPFS* $\mathfrak{C}_m = \{\langle q, ([\mu_j^-(q), \mu_j^+(q)], \mu_j(q))_{j=1}^m \rangle : q \in Q\}$ *is referred to as External Cubic m-Polar Fuzzy Set (ECmPFS) if it is not internal, that is, if* $\mu_j^-(q) \nleq \mu_j(q) \nleq \mu_j^+(q)$, *for some* $q \in Q$ *or* $j = 1, 2, \cdots, m$.

Thus, ECmPFS is simply the negation of ICmPFS.

Definition 9. *A CmPFS* $\mathfrak{C}_m = \{\langle q, (A_j(q), \mu_j(q))_{j=1}^m \rangle : q \in Q\}$ *is characterized as a Null Cubic m-Polar Fuzzy Set (NCmPFS) if* $A_j(q) = \mathbf{0}$ *and* $\mu_j(q) = 1$ *for all* $q \in Q$ *and* $j = 1, 2, \cdots, m$.

Definition 10. *If for a CmPFS* $\mathfrak{C}_m = \{\langle q, (A_j(q), \mu_j(q))_{j=1}^m \rangle : q \in Q\}$, $A_j(q) = \mathbf{1}$ *and* $\mu_j(q) = 0$ *for all* $q \in Q$ *and* $j = 1, 2, \cdots, m$, *it is called an Absolute Cubic m-Polar Fuzzy Set (ACmPFS).*

Theorem 1. *The set of all ICmPFSs on a discourse* Q *is closed under the operation of complement; that is,* A *is ICmPFS if and only if* A^c *is ICmPFS.*

Proof. Consider an Internal Cubic m-Polar Fuzzy Set $\mathfrak{C}_m = \{\langle q, ([\mu_j^-(q), \mu_j^+(q)], \mu_j(q))_{j=1}^m \rangle : q \in Q\}$. Then $\mu_j^-(q) \leq \mu_j(q) \leq \mu_j^+(q)$, for all $q \in Q$ and $j = 1, 2, \cdots, m$. This implies that

$$1 - \mu_j^+(q) \leq 1 - \mu_j(q) \leq 1 - \mu_j^-(q),$$

for all $q \in Q$ and $j = 1, 2, \cdots, m$. This shows that $C^c = \{\langle q, ([1 - \mu_j^+(q), 1 - \mu_j^-(q)], 1 - \mu_j(q))_{j=1}^m \rangle : q \in Q\}$ is also an ICmPFS. □

Remark 1. *Since ECmPFS is the negation of ICmPFS, and a certain CmPFS falls in exactly one of the two categories (by definition), the above characterization immediately characterizes the closeness of the set of all ECmPFSs on a certain discourse X.*

Theorem 2. *For a collection of ICmPFNs $A_i = ([\mu_{ij}^-, \mu_{ij}^+], \mu_{ij})_{j=1}^m$, $i \in \Omega$, P-maximum and P-minimum are also ICmPFN.*

Proof. Since $A_i's$ are ICmPFNs, $\mu_{ij}^-(x) \leq \mu_{ij}(x) \leq \mu_{ij}^+(x)$. This implies that

$$\sup_{i\in\Omega} \mu_{ij}^-(x) \leq \sup_{i\in\Omega} \mu_{ij}(x) \leq \sup_{i\in\Omega} \mu_{ij}^+(x),$$

and

$$\inf_{i\in\Omega} \mu_{ij}^-(x) \leq \inf_{i\in\Omega} \mu_{ij}(x) \leq \inf_{i\in\Omega} \mu_{ij}^+(x),\ j = 1, 2, \cdots, m.$$

This shows that $\vee_P A_i = ([\sup_{i\in\Omega} \mu_{ij}^-, \sup_{i\in\Omega} \mu_{ij}^+], \sup_{i\in\Omega} \mu_{ij})_{j=1}^m$ and $\wedge_P A_i = ([\inf_{i\in\Omega} \mu_{ij}^-, \inf_{i\in\Omega} \mu_{ij}^+], \inf_{i\in\Omega} \mu_{ij})_{j=1}^m$ are also ICmPFS. □

Remark 2. *R-minimum and R-maximum of ICmPFNs may not be ICmPFN. Similarly, R-minimum, R-maximum, P-minimum and P-maximum of ECmPFNs may not be ECmPFN. The counter examples are easy to compute.*

In any decision-making process, ranking is a basic tool. Decision makers are required to rank the uncertainties on the basis of which the most favorite alternative is filtered. To help decision makers rank the vagueness in CmPF environment, we define score and accuracy functions for CmPFNs.

Definition 11. *Let $\check{\mathbb{A}} = (\Im_j, \wp_j)_{j=1}^m$ be a CmPFN. The score and accuracy functions are, respectively, defined as*

$$S(\check{\mathbb{A}}) = \frac{\Sigma_{j=1}^m |\ell(\Im_j) - \wp_j|}{m} \tag{1}$$

and

$$\alpha(\check{\mathbb{A}}) = \frac{\Sigma_{j=1}^m (\ell(\Im_j) + \wp_j)}{2m}, \tag{2}$$

where $\ell(\Im_j)$ is the length of the fuzzy interval $\Im_j$. It is clear that $S(\check{\mathbb{A}}) \in [-1, 1]$ and $\alpha(\check{\mathbb{A}}) \in [0, 1]$.

Proposition 1. *The ranking of CmPFNs with the help of the proposed score and accuracy functions is observed as follows.*

If $\mathbb{A}_m$ and $\mathbb{B}_m$ are two CmPFNs. Then

- *$\mathbb{A}_m < \mathbb{B}_m$ if $S(\mathbb{A}_m) < S(\mathbb{B}_m)$,*
- *If $S(\mathbb{A}_m) = S(\mathbb{B}_m)$, then $\mathbb{A}_m < \mathbb{B}_m$ if $\alpha(\mathbb{A}_m) < \alpha(\mathbb{B}_m)$,*
- *If, however, $S(\mathbb{A}_m) = S(\mathbb{B}_m)$ and $\alpha(\mathbb{A}_m) = \alpha(\mathbb{B}_m)$, then $\mathbb{A}_m = \mathbb{B}_m$.*

Definition 12. *Let $\mathbb{A}_m = \langle [\mu_1^-, \mu_1^+], [\mu_2^-, \mu_2^+], \cdots, [\mu_m^-, \mu_m^+], \mu_1, \mu_2, \cdots, \mu_m \rangle = \langle [\mu_j^-, \mu_j^+], \mu_j \rangle_{j=1}^m$ and $\mathbb{B}_m = \langle [\nu_1^-, \nu_1^+], [\nu_2^-, \nu_2^+], \cdots, [\nu_m^-, \nu_m^+], \nu_1, \nu_2, \cdots, \nu_m \rangle = \langle [\nu_j^-, \nu_j^+], \nu_j \rangle_{j=1}^m$ be two cubic m-polar fuzzy sets.*

The distance between the two CmPFSs is defined by

$$d(\mathbb{A}_m, \mathbb{B}_m) = \left[\sum_{j=1}^m \left| \frac{\mu_j^- + \mu_j^+}{2} - \frac{\nu_j^- + \nu_j^+}{2} \right|^m + \sum_{j=1}^m |\mu_j - \nu_j|^m \right]^{1/m}. \tag{3}$$

4. Extension of Dombi's T-norm and T-conorm to CmPFSs

In 1982, Dombi [26] proposed some special kinds of t-conorm and t-norm. These notions laid the foundation of various operations in different uncertainty environments. On the basis of these operations, various kinds of aggregation operators (AOs) were defined, which made the MCDM process very effective. Dombi t-conorm and t-norm are, respectively, defined as follows:

$$Dom^*(k,p) = 1 - \frac{1}{1+\left\{\left(\frac{k}{1-k}\right)^s + \left(\frac{p}{1-p}\right)^s\right\}^{1/s}}$$

$$Dom(k,p) = \frac{1}{1+\left\{\left(\frac{1-k}{k}\right)^s + \left(\frac{1-p}{p}\right)^s\right\}^{1/s}}$$

where $s \geq 1$ and $k, p \in [0,1]$.

4.1. Dombi P-operations for Cubic M-polar Fuzzy Environment

Owing to Dombi t-conorm and t-norm, we define some basic Dombi P-operations for CmPFS. Let $\mathbb{A}_{\mathrm{m}} = \{(x, [\mu_1^-(x), \mu_1^+(x)], [\mu_2^-(x), \mu_2^+(x)], \cdots, [\mu_m^-(x), \mu_m^+(x)], \mu_1(x), \mu_2(x), \cdots, \mu_m(x)) : x \in X\}$ and $\mathbb{B}_{\mathrm{m}} = \{(x, [\nu_1^-(x), \nu_1^+(x)], [\nu_2^-(x), \nu_2^+(x)], \cdots, [\nu_m^-(x), \nu_m^+(x)], \nu_1(x), \nu_2(x), \cdots, \nu_m(x)) : x \in X\}$ be two CmPFSs with underlying set X. Then

- $$\mathbb{A}_{\mathrm{m}} \oplus_P \mathbb{B}_{\mathrm{m}} = \left\{\left(x, \left[1 - \frac{1}{1+\{(\frac{\mu_j^-(x)}{1-\mu_j^-(x)})^s + (\frac{\nu_j^-(x)}{1-\nu_j^-(x)})^s\}^{1/s}}, 1 - \frac{1}{1+\{(\frac{\mu_j^+(x)}{1-\mu_j^+(x)})^s + (\frac{\nu_j^+(x)}{1-\nu_j^+(x)})^s\}^{1/s}}\right], 1 - \frac{1}{1+\{(\frac{\mu_j(x)}{1-\mu_j(x)})^s + (\frac{\nu_j(x)}{1-\nu_j(x)})^s\}^{1/s}}\right)_{j=1}^m\right\}$$
- $$\mathbb{A}_{\mathrm{m}} \otimes_P \mathbb{B}_{\mathrm{m}} = \left\{\left(x, \left[\frac{1}{1+\{(\frac{1-\mu_j^-(x)}{\mu_j^-(x)})^s + (\frac{1-\nu_j^-(x)}{\nu_j^-(x)})^s\}^{1/s}}, \frac{1}{1+\{(\frac{1-\mu_j^+(x)}{\mu_j^+(x)})^s + (\frac{1-\nu_j^+(x)}{\nu_j^+(x)})^s\}^{1/s}}\right], \frac{1}{1+\{(\frac{1-\mu_j(x)}{\mu_j(x)})^s + (\frac{1-\nu_j(x)}{\nu_j(x)})^s\}^{1/s}}\right)_{j=1}^m\right\}$$
- (P-Scalar Multiplication)
  $$\lambda\mathbb{A}_{\mathrm{m}} = \left\{\left(x, \left[1 - \frac{1}{1+\{\lambda(\frac{\mu_j^-(x)}{1-\mu_j^-(x)})^s\}^{1/s}}, 1 - \frac{1}{1+\{\lambda(\frac{\mu_j^+(x)}{1-\mu_j^+(x)})^s\}^{1/s}}\right], 1 - \frac{1}{1+\{\lambda(\frac{\mu_j(x)}{1-\mu_j(x)})^s\}^{1/s}}\right)_{j=1}^m\right\}$$
- (P-Power)
  $$\mathbb{A}_{\mathrm{m}}^{\lambda} = \left\{\left(x, \left[\frac{1}{1+\{\lambda(\frac{1-\mu_j^-(x)}{\mu_j^-(x)})^s\}^{1/s}}, \frac{1}{1+\{\lambda(\frac{1-\mu_j^+(x)}{\mu_j^+(x)})^s\}^{1/s}}\right], \frac{1}{1+\{\lambda(\frac{1-\mu_j(x)}{\mu_j(x)})^s\}^{1/s}}\right)_{j=1}^m\right\}$$

  where $s \geqslant 1$.

Theorem 3. *Let $\mathbb{A}_{\mathrm{m}}$, $\mathbb{B}_{\mathrm{m}}$ and $\mathbb{C}_{\mathrm{m}}$ be the CmPFSs. Then*

1. $\mathbb{A}_{\mathrm{m}} \oplus_P \mathbb{B}_{\mathrm{m}} = \mathbb{B}_{\mathrm{m}} \oplus_P \mathbb{A}_{\mathrm{m}}$
2. $\mathbb{A}_{\mathrm{m}} \otimes_P \mathbb{B}_{\mathrm{m}} = \mathbb{B}_{\mathrm{m}} \otimes_P \mathbb{A}_{\mathrm{m}}$
3. $\mathbb{A}_{\mathrm{m}} \oplus_P (\mathbb{B}_{\mathrm{m}} \oplus_P \mathbb{C}_{\mathrm{m}}) = (\mathbb{A}_{\mathrm{m}} \oplus_P \mathbb{B}_{\mathrm{m}}) \oplus_P \mathbb{C}_{\mathrm{m}} = \mathbb{A}_{\mathrm{m}} \oplus_P \mathbb{B}_{\mathrm{m}} \oplus_P \mathbb{C}_{\mathrm{m}}$
4. $\mathbb{A}_{\mathrm{m}} \otimes_P (\mathbb{B}_{\mathrm{m}} \otimes_P \mathbb{C}_{\mathrm{m}}) = (\mathbb{A}_{\mathrm{m}} \otimes_P \mathbb{B}_{\mathrm{m}}) \otimes_P \mathbb{C}_{\mathrm{m}} = \mathbb{A}_{\mathrm{m}} \otimes_P \mathbb{B}_{\mathrm{m}} \otimes_P \mathbb{C}_{\mathrm{m}}$
5. $\mu(\lambda\mathbb{A}_{\mathrm{m}}) = (\mu\lambda)\mathbb{A}_{\mathrm{m}}$
6. $\lambda(\mathbb{A}_{\mathrm{m}} \oplus_P \mathbb{B}_{\mathrm{m}}) = \lambda\mathbb{A}_{\mathrm{m}} \oplus_P \lambda\mathbb{B}_{\mathrm{m}}$
7. $\lambda(\mathbb{A}_{\mathrm{m}} \otimes_P \mathbb{B}_{\mathrm{m}}) = \lambda\mathbb{A}_{\mathrm{m}} \otimes_P \lambda\mathbb{B}_{\mathrm{m}}$

8. $(\mathbb{A}_m \oplus_P \mathbb{B}_m)^{\lambda} = \mathbb{A}_m^{\lambda} \oplus_P \mathbb{B}_m^{\lambda}$
9. $(\mathbb{A}_m \otimes_P \mathbb{B}_m)^{\lambda} = \mathbb{A}_m^{\lambda} \otimes_P \mathbb{B}_m^{\lambda}$
10. $(\mathbb{A}_m^{\lambda})^{\mu} = \mathbb{A}_m^{\lambda\mu} = \mathbb{A}_m^{\mu\lambda}$

Proof. We prove (without any loss) our claim by considering CmPFNs, $\mathbb{A}_m = ([\mu_j^-, \mu_j^+], \mu_j)_{j=1}^m$, $\mathbb{B}_m = ([\nu_j^-, \nu_j^+], \nu_j)_{j=1}^m$ and $\mathbb{C}_m = ([\omega_j^-, \omega_j^+], \omega_j)_{j=1}^m$, corresponding to the alternative $x \in X$. We only prove the statements for lower fuzzy numbers. The rest of the cases are similar.

1. 2. The proof follows from definition.

3. $(\mathbb{A}_m \oplus_P \mathbb{B}_m) \oplus_P \mathbb{C}_m = 1 - \frac{1}{1+\left\{\left(\frac{\mu_j^-}{1-\mu_j^-}\right)^s + \left(\frac{\nu_j^-}{1-\nu_j^-}\right)^s\right\}^{1/s}} \oplus_P \omega_j^-$

$$= 1 - \frac{1}{1+\left\{\left(\frac{1-\frac{1}{1+\left\{\left(\frac{\mu_j^-}{1-\mu_j^-}\right)^s+\left(\frac{\nu_j^-}{1-\nu_j^-}\right)^s\right\}^{1/s}}}{\frac{1}{1+\left\{\left(\frac{\mu_j^-}{1-\mu_j^-}\right)^s+\left(\frac{\nu_j^-}{1-\nu_j^-}\right)^s\right\}^{1/s}}}\right)^s + \left(\frac{\omega_j^-}{1-\omega_j^-}\right)^s\right\}^{1/s}}$$

$$= 1 - \frac{1}{1+\left\{\left(\frac{\mu_j^-}{1-\mu_j^-}\right)^s + \left(\frac{\nu_j^-}{1-\nu_j^-}\right)^s + \left(\frac{\omega_j^-}{1-\omega_j^-}\right)^s\right\}^{1/s}}$$

$$= 1 - \frac{1}{1+\left\{\left(\frac{\mu_j^-}{1-\mu_j^-}\right)^s + \left(\frac{1-\frac{1}{1+\left\{\left(\frac{\nu_j^-}{1-\nu_j^-}\right)^s+\left(\frac{\omega_j^-}{1-\omega_j^-}\right)^s\right\}^{1/s}}}{\frac{1}{1+\left\{\left(\frac{\nu_j^-}{1-\nu_j^-}\right)^s+\left(\frac{\omega_j^-}{1-\omega_j^-}\right)^s\right\}^{1/s}}}\right)^s\right\}^{1/s}}$$

$$= \mu_j^- \oplus_P 1 - \frac{1}{1+\left\{\left(\frac{\nu_j^-}{1-\nu_j^-}\right)^s + \left(\frac{\omega_j^-}{1-\omega_j^-}\right)^s\right\}^{1/s}}$$

$$= \mathbb{A}_m \oplus_P (\mathbb{B}_m \oplus_P \mathbb{C}_m)$$

4. Similar to 3.

5. $\lambda\mathbb{A}_m = 1 - \frac{1}{1+\{\lambda(\frac{\mu_j^-}{1-\mu_j^-})^s\}^{1/s}}$

$$\Rightarrow \mu(\lambda\mathbb{A}_m) = 1 - \frac{1}{1+\left\{\mu\left(\frac{1-\frac{1}{1+\{\lambda(\frac{\mu_j^-}{1-\mu_j^-})^s\}^{1/s}}}{\frac{1}{1+\{\lambda(\frac{\mu_j^-}{1-\mu_j^-})^s\}^{1/s}}}\right)^s\right\}^{1/s}}$$

$$\Rightarrow \mu(\lambda\mathbb{A}_m) = 1 - \frac{1}{1+\left\{\mu\lambda\left(\frac{\mu_j^-}{1-\mu_j^-}\right)^s\right\}^{1/s}} = (\mu\lambda)\mathbb{A}_m$$

6. $\lambda(\mathbb{A}_m \oplus_P \mathbb{B}_m) = 1 - \frac{1}{1+\left\{\lambda\left(\frac{\mu_j^-}{1-\mu_j^-}\right)^s + \lambda\left(\frac{\nu_j^-}{1-\nu_j^-}\right)^s\right\}^{1/s}}$

$$= 1 - \frac{1}{1+\left\{\left(\frac{1-\frac{1}{1+\left\{\lambda\left(\frac{\mu_j^-}{1-\mu_j^-}\right)^s\right\}^{1/s}}}{\frac{1}{1+\left\{\lambda\left(\frac{\mu_j^-}{1-\mu_j^-}\right)^s\right\}^{1/s}}}\right)^s \left(\frac{1-\frac{1}{1+\left\{\lambda\left(\frac{\nu_j^-}{1-\nu_j^-}\right)^s\right\}^{1/s}}}{\frac{1}{1+\left\{\lambda\left(\frac{\nu_j^-}{1-\nu_j^-}\right)^s\right\}^{1/s}}}\right)^s\right\}^{1/s}}$$

$$= 1 - \frac{1}{1+\left\{\lambda\left(\frac{\mu_j^-}{1-\mu_j^-}\right)^s\right\}^{1/s}} \oplus_P 1 - \frac{1}{1+\left\{\lambda\left(\frac{\nu_j^-}{1-\nu_j^-}\right)^s\right\}^{1/s}}$$
$$= \lambda\mathbb{A}_{\mathrm{m}} \oplus_P \lambda\mathbb{B}_{\mathrm{m}}$$

7. 8. 9. Similar to 6.

10. Follows from definition. □

Theorem 4. *Let $\mathbb{A}_{\mathrm{m}} = ([\mu_j^-, \mu_j^+], \mu_j)_{j=1}^m$ and $\mathbb{B}_{\mathrm{m}} = ([\nu_j^-, \nu_j^+], \nu_j)_{j=1}^m$ be two ICmPFSs (we are referring to CmPFNs as CmPFSs without any loss). Then $\mathbb{A}_{\mathrm{m}} \oplus_P \mathbb{B}_{\mathrm{m}}$, $\mathbb{A}_{\mathrm{m}} \otimes_P \mathbb{B}_{\mathrm{m}}$, $\lambda\mathbb{A}_{\mathrm{m}}$ (P-scalar multiplication) and $\mathbb{A}_{\mathrm{m}}^\lambda$ (P-power) are are also ICmPFS.*

Proof. Since $\mathbb{A}_{\mathrm{m}}$ is ICmPFS, so $\mu_j^- \leq \mu_j \leq \mu_j^+ \Rightarrow 1-\mu_j^+ \leq 1-\mu_j \leq 1-\mu_j^- \Rightarrow \frac{1}{1-\mu_j^-} \leq \frac{1}{1-\mu_j} \leq \frac{1}{1-\mu_j^+} \Rightarrow \frac{\mu_j^-}{1-\mu_j^-} \leq \frac{\mu_j}{1-\mu_j} \leq \frac{\mu_j^+}{1-\mu_j^+} \Rightarrow \left(\frac{\mu_j^-}{1-\mu_j^-}\right)^s \leq \left(\frac{\mu_j}{1-\mu_j}\right)^s \leq \left(\frac{\mu_j^+}{1-\mu_j^+}\right)^s$.

Similarly for ICmPFS $\mathbb{B}_{\mathrm{m}}$, $\left(\frac{\nu_j^-}{1-\nu_j^-}\right)^s \leq \left(\frac{\nu_j}{1-\nu_j}\right)^s \leq \left(\frac{\nu_j^+}{1-\nu_j^+}\right)^s$.

Adding both inequalities, we have

$$\left(\frac{\mu_j^-}{1-\mu_j^-}\right)^s + \left(\frac{\nu_j^-}{1-\nu_j^-}\right)^s \leq \left(\frac{\mu_j}{1-\mu_j}\right)^s + \left(\frac{\nu_j}{1-\nu_j}\right)^s \leq \left(\frac{\mu_j^+}{1-\mu_j^+}\right)^s + \left(\frac{\nu_j^+}{1-\nu_j^+}\right)^s.$$
$$\Rightarrow 1 - \frac{1}{1+\left\{\left(\frac{\mu_j^-}{1-\mu_j^-}\right)^s+\left(\frac{\nu_j^-}{1-\nu_j^-}\right)^s\right\}^{1/s}} \leq 1 - \frac{1}{1+\left\{\left(\frac{\mu_j}{1-\mu_j}\right)^s+\left(\frac{\nu_j}{1-\nu_j}\right)^s\right\}^{1/s}} \leq 1 - \frac{1}{1+\left\{\left(\frac{\mu_j^+}{1-\mu_j^+}\right)^s+\left(\frac{\nu_j^+}{1-\nu_j^+}\right)^s\right\}^{1/s}},$$

for all $j = 1, 2, \cdots, m$. □

Following the same root, it can be easily proved that $\mathbb{A}_{\mathrm{m}} \otimes_P \mathbb{B}_{\mathrm{m}}$, $\lambda\mathbb{A}_{\mathrm{m}}$ and $\mathbb{A}_{\mathrm{m}}^\lambda$ are also ICmPFSs.

Remark 3. *If $\mathbb{A}_{\mathrm{m}}$ and $\mathbb{B}_{\mathrm{m}}$ are ECmPFSs, then $\mathbb{A}_{\mathrm{m}} \oplus_P \mathbb{B}_{\mathrm{m}}$, $\mathbb{A}_{\mathrm{m}} \otimes_P \mathbb{B}_{\mathrm{m}}$, $\lambda\mathbb{A}_{\mathrm{m}}$, and $\mathbb{A}_{\mathrm{m}}^\lambda$ may not be ECmPFSs. Counter examples are easy to compute.*

4.2. Dombi R-operations for Cubic M-polar Fuzzy Sets

Let $\mathbb{A}_{\mathrm{m}}$ and $\mathbb{B}_{\mathrm{m}}$ be the CmPFSs as mentioned in Section 2.1. Then

- $$\mathbb{A}_{\mathrm{m}} \oplus_R \mathbb{B}_{\mathrm{m}} = \left\{\left(x, \left[1 - \frac{1}{1+\{(\frac{\mu_j^-(x)}{1-\mu_j^-(x)})^s+(\frac{\nu_j^-(x)}{1-\nu_j^-(x)})^s\}^{1/s}}, 1 - \frac{1}{1+\{(\frac{\mu_j^+(x)}{1-\mu_j^+(x)})^s+(\frac{\nu_j^+(x)}{1-\nu_j^+(x)})^s\}^{1/s}}\right], \frac{1}{1+\{(\frac{1-\mu_j(x)}{\mu_j(x)})^s+(\frac{1-\nu_j(x)}{\nu_j(x)})^s\}^{1/s}}\right)_{j=1}^m\right\}$$
- $$\mathbb{A}_{\mathrm{m}} \otimes_R \mathbb{B}_{\mathrm{m}} = \left\{\left(x, \left[\frac{1}{1+\{(\frac{1-\mu_j^-(x)}{\mu_j^-(x)})^s+(\frac{1-\nu_j^-(x)}{\nu_j^-(x)})^s\}^{1/s}}, \frac{1}{1+\{(\frac{1-\mu_j^+(x)}{\mu_j^+(x)})^s+(\frac{1-\nu_j^+(x)}{\nu_j^+(x)})^s\}^{1/s}}\right], 1 - \frac{1}{1+\{(\frac{\mu_j(x)}{1-\mu_j(x)})^s+(\frac{\nu_j(x)}{1-\nu_j(x)})^s\}^{1/s}}\right)_{j=1}^m\right\}$$
- (R-Scalar Multiplication)
$$\lambda\mathbb{A}_{\mathrm{m}} = \left\{\left(x, \left[1 - \frac{1}{1+\{\lambda(\frac{\mu_j^-(x)}{1-\mu_j^-(x)})^s\}^{1/s}}, 1 - \frac{1}{1+\{\lambda(\frac{\mu_j^+(x)}{1-\mu_j^+(x)})^s\}^{1/s}}\right], \frac{1}{1+\{\lambda(\frac{1-\mu_j(x)}{\mu_j(x)})^s\}^{1/s}}\right)_{j=1}^m\right\}$$

- (R-Power)

$$\mathbb{A}_{\mathrm{m}}^{\lambda}=\left\{\left(x,\left[\frac{1}{1+\{\lambda(\frac{1-\mu_j^-(x)}{\mu_j^-(x)})^s\}^{1/s}},\frac{1}{1+\{\lambda(\frac{1-\mu_j^+(x)}{\mu_j^+(x)})^s\}^{1/s}}\right],1-\frac{1}{1+\{\lambda(\frac{\mu_j(x)}{1-\mu_j(x)})^s\}^{1/s}}\right)_{j=1}^{m}\right\}$$

where $s\geqslant 1$.

Theorem 5. *Let $\mathbb{A}_{\mathrm{m}}$, $\mathbb{B}_{\mathrm{m}}$ and $\mathbb{C}_{\mathrm{m}}$ be the CmPFSs. Then*

1. $\mathbb{A}_{\mathrm{m}}\oplus_R\mathbb{B}_{\mathrm{m}}=\mathbb{B}_{\mathrm{m}}\oplus_R\mathbb{A}_{\mathrm{m}}$
2. $\mathbb{A}_{\mathrm{m}}\otimes_R\mathbb{B}_{\mathrm{m}}=\mathbb{B}_{\mathrm{m}}\otimes_R\mathbb{A}_{\mathrm{m}}$
3. $\mathbb{A}_{\mathrm{m}}\oplus_R(\mathbb{B}_{\mathrm{m}}\oplus_R\mathbb{C}_{\mathrm{m}})=(\mathbb{A}_{\mathrm{m}}\oplus_R\mathbb{B}_{\mathrm{m}})\oplus_R\mathbb{C}_{\mathrm{m}}=\mathbb{A}_{\mathrm{m}}\oplus_R\mathbb{B}_{\mathrm{m}}\oplus_R\mathbb{C}_{\mathrm{m}}$
4. $\mathbb{A}_{\mathrm{m}}\otimes_R(\mathbb{B}_{\mathrm{m}}\otimes_R\mathbb{C}_{\mathrm{m}})=(\mathbb{A}_{\mathrm{m}}\otimes_R\mathbb{B}_{\mathrm{m}})\otimes_R\mathbb{C}_{\mathrm{m}}=\mathbb{A}_{\mathrm{m}}\otimes_R\mathbb{B}_{\mathrm{m}}\otimes_R\mathbb{C}_{\mathrm{m}}$
5. $\mu(\lambda\mathbb{A}_{\mathrm{m}})=(\mu\lambda)\mathbb{A}_{\mathrm{m}}$
6. $\lambda(\mathbb{A}_{\mathrm{m}}\oplus_R\mathbb{B}_{\mathrm{m}})=\lambda\mathbb{A}_{\mathrm{m}}\oplus_R\lambda\mathbb{B}_{\mathrm{m}}$
7. $\lambda(\mathbb{A}_{\mathrm{m}}\otimes_R\mathbb{B}_{\mathrm{m}})=\lambda\mathbb{A}_{\mathrm{m}}\otimes_R\lambda\mathbb{B}_{\mathrm{m}}$
8. $(\mathbb{A}_{\mathrm{m}}\oplus_R\mathbb{B}_{\mathrm{m}})^{\lambda}=\mathbb{A}_{\mathrm{m}}^{\lambda}\oplus_R\mathbb{B}_{\mathrm{m}}^{\lambda}$
9. $(\mathbb{A}_{\mathrm{m}}\otimes_R\mathbb{B}_{\mathrm{m}})^{\lambda}=\mathbb{A}_{\mathrm{m}}^{\lambda}\otimes_R\mathbb{B}_{\mathrm{m}}^{\lambda}$
10. $(\mathbb{A}_{\mathrm{m}}^{\lambda})^{\mu}=\mathbb{A}_{\mathrm{m}}^{\lambda\mu}=\mathbb{A}_{\mathrm{m}}^{\mu\lambda}$

Proof. Similar to Theorem 3. □

Remark 4. *If $\mathbb{A}_{\mathrm{m}}$ and $\mathbb{B}_{\mathrm{m}}$ are ICmPFNs (or ECmPFNs), then $\mathbb{A}_{\mathrm{m}}\oplus_R\mathbb{B}_{\mathrm{m}}$, $\mathbb{A}_{\mathrm{m}}\otimes_R\mathbb{B}_{\mathrm{m}}$, $\lambda\mathbb{A}_{\mathrm{m}}$ (R-Scalar Multiplication), and $\mathbb{A}_{\mathrm{m}}^{\lambda}$ (R-Power) may not be ICmPFNs (or ECmPFNs). Counter examples can be easily computed.*

5. CmPF Dombi Aggregation Operators with P-order

In this section, we develop Dombi P-aggregation operators in cubic m-polar fuzzy environment and give a brief description with the help of examples. These are cubic m-polar fuzzy Dombi P-averaging operator (*CmPFDPAO*), Cubic m-polar fuzzy Dombi weighted P-averaging operator (*CmPFDWPAO*), and cubic m-polar fuzzy Dombi ordered weighted P-averaging operator (*CmPFDOWPAO*). We will examine some properties of the proposed aggregation operators as well.

Definition 13. *For the family of CmPFNs $\mathbb{A}_{\mathrm{m}_1},\mathbb{A}_{\mathrm{m}_2},\cdots,\mathbb{A}_{\mathrm{m}_n}$, the cubic m-polar fuzzy Dombi P-averaging operator is defined as*

$$CmPFDPAO(\mathbb{A}_{\mathrm{m}_1},\mathbb{A}_{\mathrm{m}_2},\cdots,\mathbb{A}_{\mathrm{m}_n})=\mathbb{A}_{\mathrm{m}_1}\oplus_P\mathbb{A}_{\mathrm{m}_2}\oplus_P\cdots\oplus_P\mathbb{A}_{\mathrm{m}_n}.$$

Theorem 6. *Let $\mathbb{A}_{\mathrm{m}_i}=([\mu_{ij}^-,\mu_{ij}^+],\mu_{ij})_{j=1}^{m}$, $i=1,2,\cdots,n$, be the family of CmPFNs. Then their aggregated value is again a CmPFN and*

$$CmPFDPAO(\mathbb{A}_{\mathrm{m}_1},\mathbb{A}_{\mathrm{m}_2},\cdots,\mathbb{A}_{\mathrm{m}_n})=$$

$$\left(\left[1-\frac{1}{1+\{\Sigma_{i=1}^{n}(\frac{\mu_{ij}^-}{1-\mu_{ij}^-})^s\}^{1/s}},1-\frac{1}{1+\{\Sigma_{i=1}^{n}(\frac{\mu_{ij}^+}{1-\mu_{ij}^+})^s\}^{1/s}}\right],1-\frac{1}{1+\{\Sigma_{i=1}^{n}(\frac{\mu_{ij}}{1-\mu_{ij}})^s\}^{1/s}}\right)_{j=1}^{m}$$

Proof. We can prove it by induction on n.

For $n=2$, we have

$$CmPFDPAO(\mathbb{A}_{\mathrm{m}_1},\mathbb{A}_{\mathrm{m}_2})=$$

$$\left(\left[1-\frac{1}{1+\{(\frac{\mu_{1j}^-}{1-\mu_{1j}^-})^s+(\frac{\mu_{2j}^-}{1-\mu_{2j}^-})^s\}^{1/s}},1-\frac{1}{1+\{(\frac{\mu_{1j}^+}{1-\mu_{1j}^+})^s+(\frac{\mu_{2j}^+}{1-\mu_{2j}^+})^s\}^{1/s}}\right],1-\frac{1}{1+\{(\frac{\mu_{1j}}{1-\mu_{1j}})^s+(\frac{\mu_{2j}}{1-\mu_{2j}})^s\}^{1/s}}\right)_{j=1}^m$$

which is a CmPFN, by definition.

Suppose $n > 2$, and our proposed averaging formula is true for CmPFNs numbered less than n.

Now we see that

$$CmPFDPAO(\mathbb{A}_{m_1},\mathbb{A}_{m_2},\cdots,\mathbb{A}_{m_n}) =$$
$$\left(\left[1-\frac{1}{1+\{\Sigma_{i=1}^n(\frac{\mu_{ij}^-}{1-\mu_{ij}^-})^s\}^{1/s}},1-\frac{1}{1+\{\Sigma_{i=1}^n(\frac{\mu_{ij}^+}{1-\mu_{ij}^+})^s\}^{1/s}}\right],1-\frac{1}{1+\{\Sigma_{i=1}^n(\frac{\mu_{ij}}{1-\mu_{ij}})^s\}^{1/s}}\right)_{j=1}^m$$
$$=\left(\left[1-\frac{1}{1+\{\Sigma_{i=1}^{n-1}(\frac{\mu_{ij}^-}{1-\mu_{ij}^-})^s\}^{1/s}},1-\frac{1}{1+\{\Sigma_{i=1}^{n-1}(\frac{\mu_{ij}^+}{1-\mu_{ij}^+})^s\}^{1/s}}\right],1-\frac{1}{1+\{\Sigma_{i=1}^{n-1}(\frac{\mu_{ij}}{1-\mu_{ij}})^s\}^{1/s}}\right)_{j=1}^m$$
$$\oplus_P\left([\mu_{nj}^-,\mu_{nj}^+],\mu_{nj}\right)$$

which is a CmPFN by induction hypothesis. □

Remark 5. *Theorem 4 implies that the aggregation of ICmPFNs $\mathbb{A}_{m_1},\mathbb{A}_{m_2},\cdots,\mathbb{A}_{m_n}$, under CmPFDPAO is again an ICmPFN. However, there is no assurance about external aggregation.*

Example 1. *Let us consider four C3PFNs*

$\mathbb{A}_{m_1} = ([0.20,0.27],[0.30,0.41],[0.25,0.31],0.25,0.80,0.25)$
$\mathbb{A}_{m_2} = ([0.21,0.29],[0.29,0.40],[0.21,0.33],0.28,0.77,0.27)$
$\mathbb{A}_{m_3} = ([0.19,0.25],[0.32,0.38],[0.23,0.29],0.26,0.82,0.26)$
$\mathbb{A}_{m_4} = ([0.22,0.26],[0.28,0.39],[0.24,0.32],0.29,0.81,0.28)$.

For $s = 4$, the aggregation under C3PFDPAO is given by

$$CmPFDPAO(\mathbb{A}_{m_1},\mathbb{A}_{m_2},\mathbb{A}_{m_3},\mathbb{A}_{m_4}) =$$
$$\left(\left[1-\frac{1}{1+\{\Sigma_{i=1}^4(\frac{\mu_{ij}^-}{1-\mu_{ij}^-})^s\}^{1/s}},1-\frac{1}{1+\{\Sigma_{i=1}^4(\frac{\mu_{ij}^+}{1-\mu_{ij}^+})^s\}^{1/s}}\right],1-\frac{1}{1+\{\Sigma_{i=1}^4(\frac{\mu_{ij}}{1-\mu_{ij}})^s\}^{1/s}}\right)_{j=1}^3$$
$$=\left(\left[1-\frac{1}{1+\left\{\left(\frac{0.2}{1-0.2}\right)^4+\left(\frac{0.21}{1-0.21}\right)^4+\left(\frac{0.19}{1-0.19}\right)^4+\left(\frac{0.22}{1-0.22}\right)^4\right\}^{1/4}},1-\frac{1}{1+\left\{\left(\frac{0.27}{1-0.27}\right)^4+\left(\frac{0.29}{1-0.29}\right)^4+\left(\frac{0.25}{1-0.25}\right)^4+\left(\frac{0.26}{1-0.26}\right)^4\right\}^{1/4}}\right],\right.$$
$$\left[1-\frac{1}{1+\left\{\left(\frac{0.30}{1-0.30}\right)^4+\left(\frac{0.29}{1-0.29}\right)^4+\left(\frac{0.32}{1-0.32}\right)^4+\left(\frac{0.28}{1-0.28}\right)^4\right\}^{1/4}},1-\frac{1}{1+\left\{\left(\frac{0.41}{1-0.41}\right)^4+\left(\frac{0.40}{1-0.40}\right)^4+\left(\frac{0.38}{1-0.38}\right)^4+\left(\frac{0.39}{1-0.39}\right)^4\right\}^{1/4}}\right],$$
$$\left[1-\frac{1}{1+\left\{\left(\frac{0.25}{1-0.25}\right)^4+\left(\frac{0.21}{1-0.21}\right)^4+\left(\frac{0.23}{1-0.23}\right)^4+\left(\frac{0.24}{1-0.24}\right)^4\right\}^{1/4}},1-\frac{1}{1+\left\{\left(\frac{0.31}{1-0.31}\right)^4+\left(\frac{0.33}{1-0.33}\right)^4+\left(\frac{0.29}{1-0.29}\right)^4+\left(\frac{0.32}{1-0.32}\right)^4\right\}^{1/4}}\right],$$
$$1-\frac{1}{1+\left\{\left(\frac{0.25}{1-0.25}\right)^4+\left(\frac{0.28}{1-0.28}\right)^4+\left(\frac{0.26}{1-0.26}\right)^4+\left(\frac{0.29}{1-0.29}\right)^4\right\}^{1/4}},1-\frac{1}{1+\left\{\left(\frac{0.80}{1-0.80}\right)^4+\left(\frac{0.77}{1-0.77}\right)^4+\left(\frac{0.82}{1-0.82}\right)^4+\left(\frac{0.81}{1-0.81}\right)^4\right\}^{1/4}}$$
$$\left.1-\frac{1}{1+\left\{\left(\frac{0.25}{1-0.25}\right)^4+\left(\frac{0.27}{1-0.27}\right)^4+\left(\frac{0.26}{1-0.26}\right)^4+\left(\frac{0.28}{1-0.28}\right)^4\right\}^{1/4}}\right)$$
$$= ([0.27,0.34],[0.35,0.48],[0.30,0.39],0.35,0.85,0.34).$$

In the following, we see that *CmPFDPAO* is commutative.

Theorem 7 (Commutative)**.** *Let $\mathbb{A}_{m_i} = ([\mu_{ij}^-,\mu_{ij}^+],\mu_{ij})_{j=1}^m$, $i = 1,2,\cdots,n$, be the assembly of CmPFNs. Then*

$$CmPFDPAO(\mathbb{A}_{m_1},\mathbb{A}_{m_2},\cdots,\mathbb{A}_{m_n}) = CmPFDPAO(\mathbb{A}'_{m_1},\mathbb{A}'_{m_2},\cdots,\mathbb{A}'_{m_n}),$$

where $(\mathbb{A}'_{m_i})_{i=1}^n$ is a permutation of $(\mathbb{A}_{m_i})_{i=1}^n$.

Definition 14. *For a collection of CmPFNs $A_1, A_2, \cdots, A_n$, the cubic m-polar fuzzy Dombi weighted P-averaging operator is defined as*

$$CmPFDWPAO(A_1, A_2, \cdots, A_n) = w_1 A_1 \oplus_P w_2 A_2 \oplus_P \cdots \oplus_P w_n A_n,$$

where $w = (w_1, w_2, \cdots, w_n)$ is a weight vector with $\Sigma_{j=1}^{n} w_j = 1$ and $w_j > 0$.

Theorem 8. *Let $A_i = ([\mu_{ij}^-, \mu_{ij}^+], \mu_{ij})_{j=1}^m$, $i = 1, 2, \cdots, n$, be the collection of CmPFNs. Then their aggregated value under CmPFDWPAO is again a CmPFN and*
$CmPFDWPAO(A_1, A_2, \cdots, A_n)$
$$= \left(\left[1 - \frac{1}{1+\{\Sigma_{i=1}^n w_i(\frac{\mu_{ij}^-}{1-\mu_{ij}^-})^k\}^{1/k}}, 1 - \frac{1}{1+\{\Sigma_{i=1}^n w_i(\frac{\mu_{ij}^+}{1-\mu_{ij}^+})^k\}^{1/k}}\right], 1 - \frac{1}{1+\{\Sigma_{i=1}^n w_i(\frac{\mu_{ij}}{1-\mu_{ij}})^k\}^{1/k}}\right)_{j=1}^m$$

Proof. We can prove it by induction on n.

For $n = 2$, we have
$CmPFDWPAO(A_1, A_2)$
$$= \left(\left[1 - \frac{1}{1+\{w_1(\frac{\mu_{1j}^-}{1-\mu_{1j}^-})^k + w_2(\frac{\mu_{2j}^-}{1-\mu_{2j}^-})^k\}^{1/k}}, 1 - \frac{1}{1+\{w_1(\frac{\mu_{1j}^+}{1-\mu_{1j}^+})^k + w_2(\frac{\mu_{2j}^+}{1-\mu_{2j}^+})^k\}^{1/k}}\right],\right.$$
$$\left. 1 - \frac{1}{1+\{w_1(\frac{\mu_{1j}}{1-\mu_{1j}})^k + w_2(\frac{\mu_{2j}}{1-\mu_{2j}})^k\}^{1/k}}\right)_{j=1}^m$$
which is a CmPFN, by definition.

Suppose $n > 2$, and our proposed averaging formula is true for CmPFNs numbered less than n.

Now we see that
$CmPFDWPAO(A_1, A_2, \cdots, A_n) = w_1 A_1 \oplus_P w_2 A_2 \oplus_P \cdots \oplus_P w_n A_n$
$$= \left(\left[1 - \frac{1}{1+\{\Sigma_{i=1}^n w_i(\frac{\mu_{ij}^-}{1-\mu_{ij}^-})^k\}^{1/k}}, 1 - \frac{1}{1+\{\Sigma_{i=1}^n w_i(\frac{\mu_{ij}^+}{1-\mu_{ij}^+})^k\}^{1/k}}\right], 1 - \frac{1}{1+\{\Sigma_{i=1}^n w_i(\frac{\mu_{ij}}{1-\mu_{ij}})^k\}^{1/k}}\right)_{j=1}^m$$
$$= \left(\left[1 - \frac{1}{1+\{\Sigma_{i=1}^{n-1} w_i(\frac{\mu_{ij}^-}{1-\mu_{ij}^-})^k\}^{1/k}}, 1 - \frac{1}{1+\{\Sigma_{i=1}^{n-1} w_i(\frac{\mu_{ij}^+}{1-\mu_{ij}^+})^k\}^{1/k}}\right], 1 - \frac{1}{1+\{\Sigma_{i=1}^{n-1} w_i(\frac{\mu_{ij}}{1-\mu_{ij}})^k\}^{1/k}}\right)_{j=1}^m$$
$\oplus_P w_n([\mu_{nj}^-, \mu_{nj}^+], \mu_{nj})$
which is surely a CmPFN by induction hypothesis. □

Theorem 9. *Let $A_i = ([\mu_{ij}^-, \mu_{ij}^+], \mu_{ij})_{j=1}^m$, $i = 1, 2, \cdots, n$ be the collection of ICmPFNs with a weight vector $w = (w_1, w_1, \cdots, w_n)$. Then $CmPFDWPAO(A_1, A_2, \cdots, A_n)$ is also an ICmPFN.*

Proof. Since $A_i's$ are ICmPFNs, so
$$\mu_{ij}^- \leq \mu_{ij} \leq \mu_{ij}^+ \Rightarrow 1 - \mu_{ij}^+ \leq 1 - \mu_{ij} \leq 1 - \mu_{ij}^- \Rightarrow \frac{\mu_{ij}^-}{1-\mu_{ij}^-} \leq \frac{\mu_{ij}}{1-\mu_{ij}} \leq \frac{\mu_{ij}^+}{1-\mu_{ij}^+}$$
$$\Rightarrow \Sigma_{i=1}^n w_i\left(\frac{\mu_{ij}^-}{1-\mu_{ij}^-}\right)^k \leq \Sigma_{i=1}^n w_i\left(\frac{\mu_{ij}}{1-\mu_{ij}}\right)^k \leq \Sigma_{i=1}^n w_i\left(\frac{\mu_{ij}^+}{1-\mu_{ij}^+}\right)^k$$
$$\Rightarrow 1 - \frac{1}{1+\left\{\Sigma_{i=1}^n w_i\left(\frac{\mu_{ij}^-}{1-\mu_{ij}^-}\right)^k\right\}^{1/k}} \leq 1 - \frac{1}{1+\left\{\Sigma_{i=1}^n w_i\left(\frac{\mu_{ij}}{1-\mu_{ij}}\right)^k\right\}^{1/k}} \leq 1 - \frac{1}{1+\left\{\Sigma_{i=1}^n w_i\left(\frac{\mu_{ij}^+}{1-\mu_{ij}^+}\right)^k\right\}^{1/k}},$$
for all $j = 1, 2, \cdots, m$. This proves our claim. □

Example 2. *Consider the data of Example 1 and let the weights assigned to $A_i's$ be $(0.31, 0.42, 0.17, 0.10)^t$. The dictation under CmPFDWPAO ($for k = 4$) is given by*
$CmPFDWPAO(A_1, A_2, A_3, A_4)$

$$= \left(\left[1 - \frac{1}{1+\{\Sigma_{i=1}^4 w_i (\frac{\mu_{ij}^-}{1-\mu_{ij}^-})^k\}^{1/k}}, 1 - \frac{1}{1+\{\Sigma_{i=1}^4 w_i (\frac{\mu_{ij}^+}{1-\mu_{ij}^+})^k\}^{1/k}} \right], 1 - \frac{1}{1+\{\Sigma_{i=1}^4 w_i (\frac{\mu_{ij}}{1-\mu_{ij}})^k\}^{1/k}} \right)_{j=1}^3$$

$$= \left(\left[1 - \frac{1}{1+\left\{0.31\left(\frac{0.2}{1-0.2}\right)^4+0.42\left(\frac{0.21}{1-0.21}\right)^4+0.17\left(\frac{0.19}{1-0.19}\right)^4+0.10\left(\frac{0.22}{1-0.22}\right)^4\right\}^{1/4}}, \right. \right.$$

$$1 - \frac{1}{1+\left\{0.31\left(\frac{0.27}{1-0.27}\right)^4+0.42\left(\frac{0.29}{1-0.29}\right)^4+0.17\left(\frac{0.25}{1-0.25}\right)^4+0.10\left(\frac{0.26}{1-0.26}\right)^4\right\}^{1/4}} \Bigg],$$

$$\Bigg[1 - \frac{1}{1+\left\{0.31\left(\frac{0.30}{1-0.30}\right)^4+0.42\left(\frac{0.29}{1-0.29}\right)^4+0.17\left(\frac{0.32}{1-0.32}\right)^4+0.10\left(\frac{0.28}{1-0.28}\right)^4\right\}^{1/4}},$$

$$1 - \frac{1}{1+\left\{0.31\left(\frac{0.41}{1-0.41}\right)^4+0.42\left(\frac{0.40}{1-0.40}\right)^4+0.17\left(\frac{0.38}{1-0.38}\right)^4+0.10\left(\frac{0.39}{1-0.39}\right)^4\right\}^{1/4}} \Bigg],$$

$$\Bigg[1 - \frac{1}{1+\left\{0.31\left(\frac{0.25}{1-0.25}\right)^4+0.42\left(\frac{0.21}{1-0.21}\right)^4+0.17\left(\frac{0.23}{1-0.23}\right)^4+0.10\left(\frac{0.24}{1-0.24}\right)^4\right\}^{1/4}},$$

$$1 - \frac{1}{1+\left\{0.31\left(\frac{0.31}{1-0.31}\right)^4+0.42\left(\frac{0.33}{1-0.33}\right)^4+0.17\left(\frac{0.29}{1-0.29}\right)^4+0.10\left(\frac{0.32}{1-0.32}\right)^4\right\}^{1/4}} \Bigg],$$

$$1 - \frac{1}{1+\left\{0.31\left(\frac{0.25}{1-0.25}\right)^4+0.42\left(\frac{0.28}{1-0.28}\right)^4+0.17\left(\frac{0.26}{1-0.26}\right)^4+0.10\left(\frac{0.29}{1-0.29}\right)^4\right\}^{1/4}},$$

$$1 - \frac{1}{1+\left\{0.31\left(\frac{0.80}{1-0.80}\right)^4+0.42\left(\frac{0.77}{1-0.77}\right)^4+0.17\left(\frac{0.82}{1-0.82}\right)^4+0.10\left(\frac{0.81}{1-0.81}\right)^4\right\}^{1/4}},$$

$$\left. 1 - \frac{1}{1+\left\{0.31\left(\frac{0.25}{1-0.25}\right)^4+0.42\left(\frac{0.27}{1-0.27}\right)^4+0.17\left(\frac{0.26}{1-0.26}\right)^4+0.10\left(\frac{0.28}{1-0.28}\right)^4\right\}^{1/4}} \right).$$

$$= ([0.21, 0.28], [0.30, 0.40], [0.23, 0.32], 0.27, 0.80, 0.26).$$

The following properties can be easily proved for $CmPFDWPAO$.

Theorem 10 (Idempotency). *Let $A_i = ([\mu_{ij}^-, \mu_{ij}^+], \mu_{ij})_{j=1}^m$, $i = 1, 2, \cdots, n$, be the collection of equal CmPFNs, say $A_i = A = ([\mu_j^-, \mu_j^+], \mu_j)_{j=1}^m$. Then the aggregated value under CmPFDWPAO is again a CmPFN A. Mathematically, $CmPFDWPAO(A_1, A_2, \cdots, A_n) = A$.*

Proof. $CmPFDWPAO(A_1, A_2, \cdots, A_n) = w_1 A_1 \oplus_P w_2 A_2 \oplus_P \cdots \oplus_P w_n A_n = w_1 A \oplus_P w_2 A \oplus_P \cdots \oplus_P w_n A$

$$= \left(\left[1 - \frac{1}{1+\{\Sigma_{i=1}^n w_i (\frac{\mu_j^-}{1-\mu_j^-})^k\}^{1/k}}, 1 - \frac{1}{1+\{\Sigma_{i=1}^n w_i (\frac{\mu_j^+}{1-\mu_j^+})^k\}^{1/k}} \right], 1 - \frac{1}{1+\{\Sigma_{i=1}^n w_i (\frac{\mu_j}{1-\mu_j})^k\}^{1/k}} \right)_{j=1}^m$$

$$= \left(\left[1 - \frac{1}{1+\{(\frac{\mu_j^-}{1-\mu_j^-})^k\}^{1/k}}, 1 - \frac{1}{1+\{(\frac{\mu_j^+}{1-\mu_j^+})^k\}^{1/k}} \right], 1 - \frac{1}{1+\{(\frac{\mu_j}{1-\mu_j})^k\}^{1/k}} \right)_{j=1}^m$$

$$= ([\mu_j^-, \mu_j^+], \mu_j)_{j=1}^m = A \quad \square$$

Theorem 11 (Monotonicity). *Let $A_i = ([\mu_{ij}^-, \mu_{ij}^+], \mu_{ij})_{j=1}^m$ and $B_i = ([\nu_{ij}^-, \nu_{ij}^+], \nu_{ij})_{j=1}^m$, $i = 1, 2, \cdots, n$, be the two collections of CmPFNs such that $A_i \leq_P B_i$ for all i. Then*

$$CmPFDWPAO(A_1, A_2, \cdots, A_n) \leq_P CmPFDWPAO(B_1, B_2, \cdots, B_n).$$

Proof. By our assumption we have

$$\mu_{ij}^- \leq \nu_{ij}^-$$

$$\Rightarrow w_i \left(\frac{\mu_{ij}^-}{1-\mu_{ij}^-} \right)^k \leq w_i \left(\frac{\nu_{ij}^-}{1-\nu_{ij}^-} \right)^k$$

$$\Rightarrow \left\{1+\Sigma_{i=1}^{n} w_i \left(\frac{\mu_{ij}^-}{1-\mu_{ij}^-}\right)^k\right\}^{1/k} \leq \left\{1+\Sigma_{i=1}^{n} w_i \left(\frac{\nu_{ij}^-}{1-\nu_{ij}^-}\right)^k\right\}^{1/k}$$
$$\Rightarrow 1-\frac{1}{\left\{1+\Sigma_{i=1}^{n} w_i \left(\frac{\mu_{ij}^-}{1-\mu_{ij}^-}\right)^k\right\}^{1/k}} \leq 1-\frac{1}{\left\{1+\Sigma_{i=1}^{n} w_i \left(\frac{\nu_{ij}^-}{1-\nu_{ij}^-}\right)^k\right\}^{1/k}}.$$

Using similar observations for $\mu_{ij}^+ \leq \nu_{ij}^+$ and $\mu_{ij} \leq \nu_{ij}$, the result follows. □

Theorem 12 (Boundedness). *Let $A_i = ([\mu_{ij}^-, \mu_{ij}^+], \mu_{ij})_{j=1}^m$, $i = 1, 2, \cdots, n$, be the collection of CmPFNs. We define $\vee_P A_i = A^+$ and $\wedge_P A_i = A^-$. Then*

$$A^- \leq CmPFDWPAO(A_1, A_2, \cdots, A_n) \leq A^+.$$

Proof. The proof is straightforward. □

Definition 15. *Let $A_1, A_2, \cdots, A_n$ be the family of CmPFNs; the cubic m-polar fuzzy Dombi ordered weighted P-averaging operator is defined as*

$$CmPFDOWPAO(A_1, A_2, \cdots, A_n) = w_1 A_{\sigma(1)} \oplus_P w_2 A_{\sigma(2)} \oplus_P \cdots \oplus_P w_n A_{\sigma(n)},$$

where $w = (w_1, w_2, \cdots, w_n)$ is a weight vector with $\Sigma_{j=1}^n w_j = 1$ and $w_j > 0$, and $\sigma(i)$ is a permutation of $(i)_{i=1}^n$ dictating $A_{\sigma(1)} \geq_P A_{\sigma(2)} \geq_P \cdots \geq_P A_{\sigma(n)}$.

Theorem 13. *Let $A_i = ([\mu_{ij}^-, \mu_{ij}^+], \mu_{ij})_{j=1}^m$, $i = 1, 2, \cdots, n$, be the knot of CmPFNs. Then the accumulated/aggregated value under CmPFDOWPAO is a CmPFN and*
$CmPFDOWPAO(A_1, A_2, \cdots, A_n)$
$$= \left(\left[1-\frac{1}{1+\{\Sigma_{i=1}^n w_i(\frac{\mu_{\sigma(i)j}^-}{1-\mu_{\sigma(i)j}^-})^k\}^{1/k}}, 1-\frac{1}{1+\{\Sigma_{i=1}^n w_i(\frac{\mu_{\sigma(i)j}^+}{1-\mu_{\sigma(i)j}^+})^k\}^{1/k}}\right], 1-\frac{1}{1+\{\Sigma_{i=1}^n w_i(\frac{\mu_{\sigma(i)j}}{1-\mu_{\sigma(i)j}})^k\}^{1/k}}\right)_{j=1}^m.$$
The w_i and $\sigma(i)$ have usual meanings.

Proof. We can prove it by induction.

For $n = 2$, we have
$CmPFDOWPAO(A_1, A_2)$
$$= \left(\left[1-\frac{1}{1+\{w_1(\frac{\mu_{\sigma(1)j}^-}{1-\mu_{\sigma(1)j}^-})^k+w_2(\frac{\mu_{\sigma(2)j}^-}{1-\mu_{\sigma(2)j}^-})^k\}^{1/k}}, 1-\frac{1}{1+\{w_1(\frac{\mu_{\sigma(1)j}^+}{1-\mu_{\sigma(1)j}^+})^k+w_2(\frac{\mu_{\sigma(2)j}^+}{1-\mu_{\sigma(2)j}^+})^k\}^{1/k}}\right],\right.$$
$$\left.1-\frac{1}{1+\{w_1(\frac{\mu_{\sigma(1)j}}{1-\mu_{\sigma(1)j}})^k+w_2(\frac{\mu_{\sigma(2)j}}{1-\mu_{\sigma(2)j}})^k\}^{1/k}}\right)_{j=1}^m$$
which is a CmPFN, by definition.

We can grip induction hypothesis. Now we see that
$CmPFDOWPAO(A_1, A_2, \cdots, A_n) = w_1 A_{\sigma(1)} \oplus_P w_2 A_{\sigma(2)} \oplus_P \cdots \oplus_P w_n A_{\sigma(n)}$
$$= \left(\left[1-\frac{1}{1+\{\Sigma_{i=1}^n w_i(\frac{\mu_{\sigma(i)j}^-}{1-\mu_{\sigma(i)j}^-})^k\}^{1/k}}, 1-\frac{1}{1+\{\Sigma_{i=1}^n w_i(\frac{\mu_{\sigma(i)j}^+}{1-\mu_{\sigma(i)j}^+})^k\}^{1/k}}\right], 1-\frac{1}{1+\{\Sigma_{i=1}^n w_i(\frac{\mu_{\sigma(i)j}}{1-\mu_{\sigma(i)j}})^k\}^{1/k}}\right)_{j=1}^m$$
$$= \left(\left[1-\frac{1}{1+\{\Sigma_{i=1}^{n-1} w_i(\frac{\mu_{\sigma(i)j}^-}{1-\mu_{\sigma(i)j}^-})^k\}^{1/k}}, 1-\frac{1}{1+\{\Sigma_{i=1}^{n-1} w_i(\frac{\mu_{\sigma(i)j}^+}{1-\mu_{\sigma(i)j}^+})^k\}^{1/k}}\right], 1-\frac{1}{1+\{\Sigma_{i=1}^{n-1} w_i(\frac{\mu_{\sigma(i)j}}{1-\mu_{\sigma(i)j}})^k\}^{1/k}}\right)_{j=1}^m$$
$\oplus_P w_n([\mu_{\sigma(n)j}^-, \mu_{\sigma(n)j}^+], \mu_{\sigma(n)j})$
which is surely a CmPFN by induction basis/hypothesis.

We can prove the following properties for *CmPFDOWPAO*. □

Theorem 14. *CmPFDOWPAO ensures its compatibility for ICmPFNs. That is, if* $A_1, A_2, \cdots, A_n$ *are ICmPFNs, then* $CmPFDOWPAO(A_1, A_2, \cdots, A_n)$ *is an ICmPFN.*

Proof. The proof is similar to Theorem 9. □

Theorem 15 (Idempotency). *Let* $A_i = ([\mu_{ij}^-, \mu_{ij}^+], \mu_{ij})_{j=1}^m$, $i = 1, 2, \cdots, n$, *be the assemblage of CmPFNs such that* $A_i = A = ([\mu_j^-, \mu_j^+], \mu_j)_{j=1}^m$ *for all i. Then* $CmPFDOWPAO(A_1, A_2, \cdots, A_n) = A$.

Proof. Consider $CmPFDOWPAO(A_1, A_2, \cdots, A_n) = w_1 A_{\sigma(1)} \oplus_P w_2 A_{\sigma(2)} \oplus_P \cdots \oplus_P w_n A_{\sigma(n)}$
$= w_1 A \oplus_P w_2 A \oplus_P \cdots \oplus_P w_n A$

$$= \left(\left[1 - \frac{1}{1+\{\Sigma_{i=1}^n w_i(\frac{\mu_j^-}{1-\mu_j^-})^k\}^{1/k}}, 1 - \frac{1}{1+\{\Sigma_{i=1}^n w_i(\frac{\mu_j^+}{1-\mu_j^+})^k\}^{1/k}}\right], 1 - \frac{1}{1+\{\Sigma_{i=1}^n w_i(\frac{\mu_j}{1-\mu_j})^k\}^{1/k}}\right)_{j=1}^m$$

$$= \left(\left[1 - \frac{1}{1+\{(\frac{\mu_j^-}{1-\mu_j^-})^k\}^{1/k}}, 1 - \frac{1}{1+\{(\frac{\mu_j^+}{1-\mu_j^+})^k\}^{1/k}}\right], 1 - \frac{1}{1+\{(\frac{\mu_j}{1-\mu_j})^k\}^{1/k}}\right)_{j=1}^m$$

$= ([\mu_j^-, \mu_j^+], \mu_j)_{j=1}^m = A,$
$w = (w_i)_{i=1}^n$ being the weight vector. □

Theorem 16 (Monotonicity). *For the two collections of CmPFNs* $A_i = ([\mu_{ij}^-, \mu_{ij}^+], \mu_{ij})_{j=1}^m$ *and* $B_i = ([\nu_{ij}^-, \nu_{ij}^+], \nu_{ij})_{j=1}^m$, $i = 1, 2, \cdots, n$, *with* $A_i \leq_P B_i$ *for all i,* $CmPFDOWPAO(A_1, A_2, \cdots, A_n) \leq_P CmPFDOWPAO(B_1, B_2, \cdots, B_n)$.

Proof. Theorem is the same as Theorem 3. □

Theorem 17 (Boundedness). *Let* $A_i = ([\mu_{ij}^-, \mu_{ij}^+], \mu_{ij})_{j=1}^m$, $i = 1, 2, \cdots, n$, *be the collection of CmPFNs. We define* $\vee_P A_i = A^+$ *and* $\wedge_P A_i = A^-$. *Then*

$$A^- \leq_P CmPFDOWPAO(A_1, A_2, \cdots, A_n) \leq_P A^+$$

Proof. Straightforward. To date, we have discussed *CmPFDPAO*, *CmPFDWPAO*, and *CmPFDOWPAO* and related properties for CmPFEs. These operators have their own advantages. However, they have some limitations as well. *CmPFDPAO* does not work in a weighted environment, *CmPFDWPAO* weights only CmPF values, and only ordered positions are weighted under *CmPFDOWPAO*. To overcome this limitation, we define a new aggregation operator that is a hybrid of *CmPFDWPAO* and *CmPFDOWPAO* and will weight CmPF values as well as their ordered positions. □

Definition 16. *A cubic m-polar fuzzy Dombi hybrid P-averaging operator (CmPFDHPAO) is a function from n-dimensional CmPF space to CmPF space. If we have a collection of CmPFNs* $A_i = ([\mu_{ij}^-, \mu_{ij}^+], \mu_{ij})_{j=1}^m$, $i = 1, 2, \cdots, n$, *then the CmPFDHPAO weighted by* $w = (w_1, w_2, \cdots, w_n)$, $w_i > 0$, $\Sigma_{i=1}^n w_i = 1$ *is defined as*

$$CmPFDHPAO(A_1, A_2, \cdots, A_n) = w_1 A'_{\sigma(1)} \oplus_P w_2 A'_{\sigma(2)} \oplus_P \cdots \oplus_P w_n A'_{\sigma(n)},$$

where $A'_i = n\mho_i A_i$; *n is balancing factor,* $\mho = (\mho_i)_{i=1}^n$ *is weight vector for* $A'_{i=1}$ *with the condition* $\mho_i > 0$ *and* $\Sigma_{i=1}^n \mho_i = 1$. *Here,* σ *has usual meanings as in Definition 3.*

Interestingly, *CmPFDHPAO* becomes *CmPFDWPAO* if we take $w = (1/n, 1/n, \cdots, 1/n)$, and it becomes *CmPFDOWPAO* if we take $\mho = (1/n, 1/n, \cdots, 1/n)$. Therefore,

CmPFDHPAO is the generalized one with *CmPFDWPAO* and *CmPFDOWPAO* as its special cases.

6. CmPF Dombi Averaging Aggregation Operators with R-order

In this section, we introduce some Dombi R-aggregation operators for CmPF information. We will discuss some properties of these AOs.

Definition 17. *For a collection of CmPFNs $A_1, A_2, \cdots, A_n$, the cubic m-polar fuzzy Dombi R-averaging operator is defined as*

$$CmPFDRAO(A_1, A_2, \cdots, A_n) = A_1 \oplus_R A_2 \oplus_R \cdots \oplus_R A_n.$$

Theorem 18. *Let $A_i = ([\mu_{ij}^-, \mu_{ij}^+], \mu_{ij})_{j=1}^m$, $i = 1, 2, \cdots, n$, be the collection of CmPFNs. Then the aggregated value under CmPFDRAO is again a CmPFN and*

$$CmPFDRAO(A_1, A_2, \cdots, A_n) = \left(\left[1 - \frac{1}{1+\{\Sigma_{i=1}^n (\frac{\mu_{ij}^-}{1-\mu_{ij}^-})^k\}^{1/k}}, 1 - \frac{1}{1+\{\Sigma_{i=1}^n (\frac{\mu_{ij}^+}{1-\mu_{ij}^+})^k\}^{1/k}}\right], \frac{1}{1+\{\Sigma_{i=1}^n (\frac{1-\mu_{ij}}{\mu_{ij}})^k\}^{1/k}}\right)_{j=1}^m$$

Proof. Proof is the same as Theorem 6. □

Theorem 19 (Commutative)**.** *For any collection of CmPFNs $A_i = ([\mu_{ij}^-, \mu_{ij}^+], \mu_{ij})_{j=1}^m$, $i = 1, 2, \cdots, n$,*

$CmPFDRAO(A_1, A_2, \cdots, A_n) = CmPFDRAO(\acute{A}_1, \acute{A}_2, \cdots, \acute{A}_n)$, where $(\acute{A}_i)_{i=1}^n$ is a permutation of $(A_i)_{i=1}^n$.

Proof. Follows from definition. □

Definition 18. *For a collection of CmPFNs $A_1, A_2, \cdots, A_n$, the Cubic m-Polar Fuzzy Dombi Weighted R-Averaging Operator is defined as*
$CmPFDWRAO(A_1, A_2, \cdots, A_n) = w_1 A_1 \oplus_R w_2 A_2 \oplus_R \cdots \oplus_R w_n A_n$, where $w = (w_1, w_2, \cdots, w_n)$ is a weight vector with $\Sigma_{j=1}^n w_j = 1$ and $w_j > 0$.

Theorem 20. *Let $A_i = ([\mu_{ij}^-, \mu_{ij}^+], \mu_{ij})_{j=1}^m$, $i = 1, 2, \cdots, n$, be the collection of CmPFNs. Then the aggregated value under CmPFDWRAO is again a CmPFN and*

$$CmPFDWRAO(A_1, A_2, \cdots, A_n) = \left(\left[1 - \frac{1}{1+\{\Sigma_{i=1}^n w_i (\frac{\mu_{ij}^-}{1-\mu_{ij}^-})^k\}^{1/k}}, 1 - \frac{1}{1+\{\Sigma_{i=1}^n w_i (\frac{\mu_{ij}^+}{1-\mu_{ij}^+})^k\}^{1/k}}\right], \frac{1}{1+\{\Sigma_{i=1}^n w_i (\frac{1-\mu_{ij}}{\mu_{ij}})^k\}^{1/k}}\right)_{j=1}^m$$

Proof. The following properties can be easily proved for *CmPFDWRAO*. □

Theorem 21 (Idempotency)**.** *Let $A_i = ([\mu_{ij}^-, \mu_{ij}^+], \mu_{ij})_{j=1}^m$, $i = 1, 2, \cdots, n$, be the assembly of CmPFNs such that $A_i = A = ([\mu_j^-, \mu_j^+], \mu_j)_{j=1}^m$. Then, $CmPFDWRAO(A_1, A_2, \cdots, A_n) = A$.*

Theorem 22 (Monotonicity)**.** *Let $A_i = ([\mu_{ij}^-, \mu_{ij}^+], \mu_{ij})_{j=1}^m$ and $B_i = ([\nu_{ij}^-, \nu_{ij}^+], \nu_{ij})_{j=1}^m$, $i = 1, 2, \cdots, n$, be the two collections of CmPFNs such that $A_i \leq_R B_i$ for all i. Then*
$CmPFDWRAO(A_1, A_2, \cdots, A_n) \leq_R CmPFDWRAO(B_1, B_2, \cdots, B_n)$.

Theorem 23 (Boundedness). *Let* $A_i = ([\mu_{ij}^-, \mu_{ij}^+], \mu_{ij})_{j=1}^m$, $i = 1, 2, \cdots, n$, *be the collection of CmPFNs. We define* $\vee_R A_i = A^+$ *and* $\wedge_R A_i = A^-$. *Then*

$$A^- \leq_R CmPFDWRAO(A_1, A_2, \cdots, A_n) \leq_R A^+$$

Definition 19. *Let* $A_1, A_2, \cdots, A_n$ *be the fabrication of CmPFNs, the Cubic m-Polar Fuzzy Dombi Ordered Weighted R-Averaging Operator is defined as* $CmPFDOWRAO(A_1, A_2, \cdots, A_n) = w_1 A_{\sigma(1)} \oplus_R w_2 A_{\sigma(2)} \oplus_R \cdots \oplus_R w_n A_{\sigma(n)}$, *where* $w = (w_1, w_2, \cdots, w_n)$ *is a weight vector with* $\Sigma_{j=1}^n w_j = 1$ *and* $w_j > 0$, *and* $\sigma(i)$ *is a permutation of* $(i)_{i=1}^n$ *dictating* $A_{\sigma(1)} \geq_R A_{\sigma(2)} \geq_R \cdots \geq_R A_{\sigma(n)}$.

Theorem 24. *Let* $A_i = ([\mu_{ij}^-, \mu_{ij}^+], \mu_{ij})_{j=1}^m$, $i = 1, 2, \cdots, n$, *be the knot of CmPFNs. Then, the accumulated value under CmPFDOWRAO is a CmPFN and*

$$CmPFDOWRAO(A_1, A_2, \cdots, A_n)$$
$$= \left(\left[1 - \frac{1}{1 + \{\Sigma_{i=1}^n w_i (\frac{\mu_{\sigma(i)j}^-}{1 - \mu_{\sigma(i)j}^-})^k\}^{1/k}}, 1 - \frac{1}{1 + \{\Sigma_{i=1}^n w_i (\frac{\mu_{\sigma(i)j}^+}{1 - \mu_{\sigma(i)j}^+})^k\}^{1/k}} \right], \frac{1}{1 + \{\Sigma_{i=1}^n w_i (\frac{1 - \mu_{\sigma(i)j}}{\mu_{\sigma(i)j}})^k\}^{1/k}} \right)_{j=1}^m.$$

The w_i *and* $\sigma(i)$ *have usual meanings.*

We can prove the following properties for *CmPFDOWRAO*.

Theorem 25 (Idempotency). *Let* $A_i = ([\mu_{ij}^-, \mu_{ij}^+], \mu_{ij})_{j=1}^m$, $i = 1, 2, \cdots, n$, *be the assemblage of CmPFNs such that* $A_i = A = ([\mu_j^-, \mu_j^+], \mu_j)_{j=1}^m$, *say, for all i. Then,* $CmPFDOWRAO(A_1, A_2, \cdots, A_n) = A$.

Theorem 26 (Monotonicity). *For any two collections of CmPFNs* $A_i = ([\mu_{ij}^-, \mu_{ij}^+], \mu_{ij})_{j=1}^m$ *and* $B_i = ([\nu_{ij}^-, \nu_{ij}^+], \nu_{ij})_{j=1}^m$, $i = 1, 2, \cdots, n$, *with* $A_i \leq_R B_i$ *for all i,* $CmPFDOWRAO(A_1, A_2, \cdots, A_n) \leq_R CmPFDOWRAO(B_1, B_2, \cdots, B_n)$.

Theorem 27 (Boundedness). *Let* $A_i = ([\mu_{ij}^-, \mu_{ij}^+], \mu_{ij})_{j=1}^m$, $i = 1, 2, \cdots, n$, *be the collection of CmPFNs. We define* $\vee_R A_i = A^+$ *and* $\wedge_R A_i = A^-$. *Then,*

$$A^- \leq_R CmPFDOWRAO(A_1, A_2, \cdots, A_n) \leq_R A^+.$$

We have discussed *CmPFDRAO*, *CmPFDWRAO*, and *CmPFDOWRAO* and related properties for CmPFEs. These operators have some limitations already mentioned in Section 3. Therefore, hybridization of *CmPFDWRAO* and *CmPFDOWRAO* is mandatory.

Definition 20. *A cubic m-polar fuzzy Dombi hybrid R-averaging operator (CmPFDHRAO) is a function* $CmPFDHRAO : A^n \to A$. *For CmPFNs* $A_i = ([\mu_{ij}^-, \mu_{ij}^+], \mu_{ij})_{j=1}^m$, $i = 1, 2, \cdots, n$, *the CmPFDHRAO weighted by* $w = (w_1, w_2, \cdots, w_n)$, $w_i > 0$, $\Sigma_{i=1}^n w_i = 1$ *is defined as*

$$CmPFDHRAO(A_1, A_2, \cdots, A_n) = w_1 A'_{\sigma(1)} \oplus_R w_2 A'_{\sigma(2)} \oplus_R \cdots \oplus_R w_n A'_{\sigma(n)},$$

where $A'_i = n\mho_i A_i$, *n is balancing factor,* $\mho = (\mho_i)_{i=1}^n$ *is weight vector for* $A'_{i=1}$ *with the condition* $\mho_i > 0$ *and* $\Sigma_{i=1}^n \mho_i = 1$. *Here,* σ *is a permutation on* $\{1, 2, \cdots, n\}$ *which dictates* A'_i*s in descending order. CmPFDWRAO and CmPFDOWRAO can be observed as special cases of CmPFDHRAO by taking* $w = (1/n, 1/n, \cdots, 1/n)$ *and* $\mho = (1/n, 1/n, \cdots, 1/n)$, *respectively.*

7. MCDM towards the Circular Economy

In this section, we develop a multi-criteria decision-making (MCDM) technique under cubic m-polar fuzzy information and its application to circular economy (CE). The circular economy (CE) is currently a common concept advocated by many white collar countries and many businesses around the world. However, the science and research fabric of the CE theory is simplistic and unfocused. CE, no doubt, is the best alternative of the linear economy, but its applicability is reduced until its complexities are alleviated.
The word "circular economy" has both a descriptive and linguistic sense. In latter sense, it is opposite to CLE, which is characterized as the conversion of natural resources into waste through processing. Such waste generation leads to environmental destruction by depleting natural resources and increasing pollution. The word "linear economy" has been extensively used since the birth of "circular economy", which is an economy with a minor or no net impact on the climate. It is intended to restore any harm to the resources while guaranteeing little waste during the entire manufacturing period. There are many biochemical and geochemical cycles on the earth that inspired the idea of CE. For instance, water evaporates from the earth water bodies, forms rain drops, comes back to the earth and again becomes a part of the rivers, seas, oceans etc. Similar biogeochemical cycles can be observed on the earth. Each cycle has its own time perio, e.g., water cycle takes about 9 to 10 days, carbon dioxide takes 4.5 years, oxygen in the atmosphere takes 3.8 years to complete. Such biogeochemical cycles in nature are the reason of the existence of humankind on the earth. The water cycle is shown in the Figure 1.

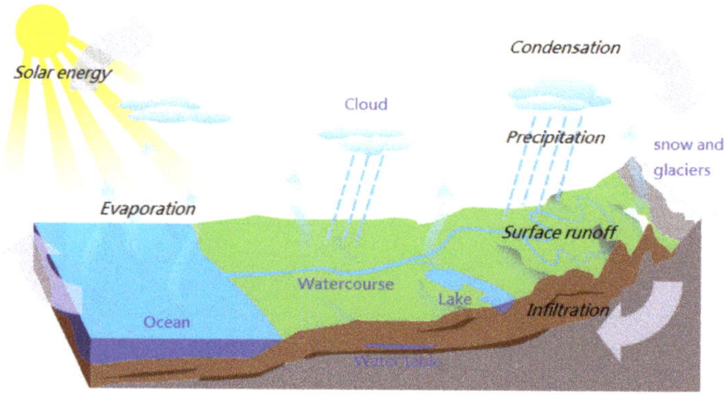

Figure 1. Water cycle.

The practice of CLE has altered almost every cycle. In order to safeguard the existing cycles in nature, it is advisable to promote CE. What makes CE implementable are recycling, repairing, recovering, regenerating etc. The most important and achievable of these is recycling. Recycling refers to the process of transferring sludge into new materials and products. This definition also includes energy recovery from waste materials. The ability of a material to reclaim the properties it had in its pure state determines its renewability. Recycling can help to reduce waste from genuinely useful products while also lowering the cost of new raw materials. Recycling is a central facet of current waste diversion and is the third level of the "Reduce, Reuse, and Recycle" hierarchy. The materials that can be recycled include glass, cardboard, plastic, paper, tires, textiles, metals, and electronics. Each of these are recycled in a unique way. For example, if we focus on recycling plastic materials, three major processes are frankly useful depending on the type of the plastic under consideration.

- Chemical recycling
- Heat compression
- Mechanical recycling

Chemical recycling.

Polymers are a special type of plastic manufactured chemically. These are basically complex chemical combinations of monomers. A wide range of polymers may be converted back into monomers. PET, for example, is a well-known polymer. It is converted to dialkyl terephthalate if treated with alcohol and an appropriate catalyst. The terephthalate diester is then treated with ethylene glycol, yielding a pure form of a new polymer known as polyester polymer. As a result, various types of plastics can be effectively recycled using chemical methods.

Heat compression.

In heat compression, plastics of all sorts are mixed together, compressed, and rolled in a large heated and rolling tumbler. This is a beneficial way to recycle the plastic. However, the tumblers involved render this process uneconomical because it again involves the usage of natural resources like coal, oil, gas etc. to rotate the tumbler and for compression purpose. Therefore, this process bears some criticism.

Mechanical recycling.

Some plastics are melted down to shape new objects. For example, PET plastic can be processed into polyester, which is intended for clothes. A downside of this recycling method is that the polymer's molecular mass can alter with each remelt, and the amounts of fish waste in the plastic can increase.

Plastic recycling process can be categorized into three steps: Collection, Reprocessing, and Production. The main contribution to these three steps mainly comes from collectors, suppliers, sorters, and recyclers.

Collection.

Recycling operation starts with the contribution of garbage pickers and dealers. A recycling organization involves a network of formal collectors participating in collecting and sorting of recyclable plastic materials. Garbage pickers include two categories: those who work legally with a company and those who are not bound to any specific organization. The second type of picker is critical to the industry. They work independently, inconsistently, and they do not bother the liability of the industry. However, the plastic recycling industry relies on them, to some extent, indirectly. Due to their informal and erratic work hours, recyclables are not routinely supplied to recyclers, and hence it is not beneficial to the industry. Therefore, to secure a reliable position in the market, a recycler must minimize its dependance on critical pickers.

Reprocessing.

After the waste plastic is collected, it is supplied to the recycling plants by the dealers, where it undergoes one of the above mentioned recycling process followed by resorting. Resorting is indispensable for the circular economy. Some plastic materials are economically recycled under heat compression, some using chemical and some mechanical methods according to their resin type. This categorization is accomplished in reprocessing.

Production.

When sorted, plastic recyclables are eviscerated for mechanical, chemical, or heated recycling. The pieces are shredded and treated in order to extract impurities such as paper annotations. The material is melted or chemically treated to produce other items.

In order to make unanimous, clever and well-suited decisions in cubic m-polar premises, we propose an extended SIR method that is based on coding superiority index/flow and inferiority index/flow and that dictates the affirmation of the most desired/ideal option in contrast. We first give an algorithm/technique and then apply it to deal with the problem of selecting the most effective recycling plant that can help transform a CLE into a CE in an ideal way. An extended superiority and inferiority ranking (SIR) technique under CmPFSs is developed in the following Algorithm 1.

Algorithm 1: (SIR method)

Consider a set of alternatives $X = \{x_1, x_2, \cdots, x_m\}$, a group of decision makers $E = \{e_1, e_2, \cdots, e_l\}$, fuzzy weights $W = \{W_1, W_2, \cdots, W_l\}$, and a set of criterion $C = \{c_1, c_2, \cdots, c_n\}$. Let p_{ij}^k be the cubic m-polar fuzzy number assigned to i^{th} alternative, with respect to the jth criteria, by the kth expert. Construct the cubic m-polar fuzzy decision matrices $P(k) = (p_{ij}^k)_{m\times n}, k = 1, 2, \cdots, l$. Assume that w_j^k is the cubic m-polar fuzzy wight value of the criteria c_j given by the expert e_k, and construct the criteria decision matrix $w = (w_j^k)_{l\times n}$. The most suited alternative is filtered by the technique proposed below.

Step 1: Determine the relative proximity coefficient by the formula

$$\xi_k = \frac{d(W_k, W^-)}{d(W_k, W^-) + d(W_k, W^+)}, \tag{4}$$

where W^- and W^+ denote, respectively, the P-minimum and P-maximum. It immediately follows from the formula that if $W_k \to W^+$, then $\xi_k \to 1$. Similarly, if $W_k \to W^-$, then $\xi_k \to 0$. Furthermore, $0 \le \xi_k \le 1$.

Step 2: If the ξ_k are in normal form, that is, if they sum up to unity, name them as ζ_k. Otherwise, normalize them by the formula

$$\zeta_k = \frac{\xi_k}{\sum_{k=1}^{l} \xi_k}. \tag{5}$$

In this way, we obtain normalized estimation degrees $\zeta = (\zeta_1, \zeta_2, \cdots, \zeta_l)$.

Step 3: Obtain the combined cubic m-polar decision matrix $p = (\bar{p}_{ij})_{m\times n}$ and the weight vector $\varpi = (\varpi_j)_{j=1}^n$ using one of the proposed operators, where

$$\bar{p}_{ij} = CmPFDWPAO(p_{ij}^1, p_{ij}^2, \cdots, p_{ij}^l) = CmPFDWPAO(p_{ij}^k)_{k=1}^l, \tag{6}$$

$$\varpi_j = CmPFDWPAO(w_j^1, w_j^2, \cdots, w_j^l) = CmPFDWPAO(w_j^k)_{k=1}^l. \tag{7}$$

(In the end, we give a comparison analysis of *CmPFDWPAO* with the other proposed operators.)

Step 4: Construct the relative performance relation

$$f_{ij} = \frac{d(\bar{p}_{ij}, \bar{p}^-)}{d(\bar{p}_{ij}, \bar{p}^-) + d(\bar{p}_{ij}, \bar{p}^+)}, \tag{8}$$

where $\bar{p}^+ = \max_i \bar{p}_{ij}$ and $\bar{p}^- = \min_i \bar{p}_{ij}$. Clearly, if $\bar{p}_{ij} \to \bar{p}^-$, then $f_{ij} \to 0$ and if $\bar{p}_{ij} \to \bar{p}^+$, then $f_{ij} \to 1$. Furthermore, $0 \leq f_{ij} \leq 1$.

After this, construct superiority matrix $S = (S_{ij})_{m\times n}$ and inferiority matrix $I = (I_{ij})_{m\times n}$, where

$$S_{ij} = \sum_{t=1}^{m} \phi(f_{ij} - f_{tj}); \tag{9}$$

and

$$I_{ij} = \sum_{t=1}^{m} \phi(f_{tj} - f_{ij}). \tag{10}$$

$\phi(x)$ being the threshold function given by

$$\phi(x) = \begin{cases} 0.01 & 0 < x < 1 \\ 0.00 & x \leq 0 \; or \; x \geq 1. \end{cases}$$

Step 5: The superiority index and inferiority index can be calculated, respectively, as follows.

$$\phi^{>}(x_i) = CmPFDWPAO_{S_{ij}}(\varpi_j)_{j=1}^{n} = (S_{i1}\varpi_1 \oplus_P S_{i2}\varpi_2 \oplus_P \cdots \oplus_P S_{in}\varpi_n), \tag{11}$$

and

$$\phi^{<}(x_i) = CmPFDWPAO_{I_{ij}}(\varpi_j)_{j=1}^{n} = (I_{i1}\varpi_1 \oplus_P I_{i2}\varpi_2 \oplus_P \cdots \oplus_P I_{in}\varpi_n). \tag{12}$$

Step 6: Calculate the score functions of $\phi^{<}(x_i)$ and $\phi^{>}(x_i)$, for all $i = 1, 2, \cdots, m$, using the Formula (1).

Step 7: Find the superiority flow and inferiority flow according to the following rules.

Superiority Flow Rules (SFRs)

- $x_i > x_t$ if $S(\phi^{>}(x_i)) > S(\phi^{>}(x_t))$ and $S(\phi^{<}(x_i)) < S(\phi^{<}(x_t))$,
- $x_i > x_t$ if $S(\phi^{>}(x_i)) > S(\phi^{>}(x_t))$ and $S(\phi^{<}(x_i)) = S(\phi^{<}(x_t))$,
- $x_i > x_t$ if $S(\phi^{>}(x_i)) = S(\phi^{>}(x_t))$ and $S(\phi^{<}(x_i)) < S(\phi^{<}(x_t))$,

Inferiority Flow Rules (SFRs)

- $x_i < x_t$ if $S(\phi^{>}(x_i)) < S(\phi^{>}(x_t))$ and $S(\phi^{<}(x_i)) > S(\phi^{<}(x_t))$,
- $x_i < x_t$ if $S(\phi^{>}(x_i)) < S(\phi^{>}(x_t))$ and $S(\phi^{<}(x_i)) = S(\phi^{<}(x_t))$,
- $x_i < x_t$ if $S(\phi^{>}(x_i)) = S(\phi^{>}(x_t))$ and $S(\phi^{<}(x_i)) > S(\phi^{<}(x_t))$.

Step 8: SF rules coupled with IF rules can filter the optimal alternative.

7.1. Numerical Example

The evidence gained in tandem with the circular recycling curriculum is used for the purpose of elucidating model implementation in response to mutually beneficial channels of the program and the towns where it functions and identifies compassionate economic policies for foragers for recyclable materials. A city mayor plans to initiate the practice of CE in their city. The first step for this purpose is to install a recycling plant. The mayor hires three economists e_1, e_2, e_3 and assigns them the credibility weights W_1, W_2, W_3 (shown in Table 1). They chose three companies/recycling plants x_1, x_2 *and* x_3, which are currently contributing to CE in certain areas. (Note: We are restricting ourselves to three alternatives and three criteria because our intention is to propose a mathematical model for selecting an optimal recycling plant. The same model is efficient for a big data). Each of the three companies claims that it is the best option for recycling plastic materials, rubber wastes,

glass wastes, etc. These companies recycle the things in three steps "collection, reprocessing and production". The main problem is to filter the best plant to be installed in the city. The efficiency of each plant is observed on the basis of three criteria shown in Table 2. Their individual assessment turn out to be cubic m-polar fuzzy matrices (shown in Tables 3–5).
Step 1: Find $W^- = \langle [0.10, 0.30], [0.20, 0.70], [0.30, 0.80], 0.12, 0.11, 0.50 \rangle$ and $W^+ = \langle [0.80, 0.90], [0.83, 0.91], [0.85, 0.93], 0.90, 0.81, 0.76 \rangle$. Utilize the Formula (3) to calculate
$d(W_1, W^-) = 0.49852; d(W_2, W^-) = 0.727081; d(W_3, W^-) = 0.947559;$
$d(W_1, W^+) = 0.856648; d(W_2, W^+) = 0.847022; d(W_3, W^+) = 0.539338.$
Calculate the relative proximity coefficients (using Formula (4))

$$\xi = (0.3679, 0.4619, 0.6373).$$

Step 2: Normalize the estimated proximity degree (using the Formula (5))

$$\zeta = (0.2508, 0.3148, 0.4344).$$

Step 3: Aggregate the cubic m-polar fuzzy decision information (for k = 4), provided by the three economists, to figure out the joint information (given in Table 6). The identified criterions are given in Table 7.

Furthermore, obtain the unanimous criteria weights using Equation (7),

$$\bar{\varpi}_1 = \langle [0.28, 0.589], [0.32, 0.717], [0.329, 0.821], 0.346, 0.749, 0.208 \rangle$$

$$\bar{\varpi}_2 = \langle [0.161, 0.72], [0.255, 0.711], [0.436, 0.47], 0.159, 0.649, 0.325 \rangle$$

$$\bar{\varpi}_3 = \langle [0.143, 0.532], [0.448, 0.77], [0.85, 0.976], 0.13, 0.145, 0.878 \rangle.$$

Step 4: The relative performance matrix (using the Formula (8)) is given by

$$(f_{ij}) = \begin{pmatrix} 0.604 & 0.289 & 0.300 \\ 0.311 & 0.615 & 0.796 \\ 0.608 & 0.456 & 0.106 \end{pmatrix}.$$

Construct the superiority and inferiority decision matrices using the Equations (9) and (10), respectively.

$$S = \begin{pmatrix} 0.01 & 0.00 & 0.01 \\ 0.00 & 0.02 & 0.02 \\ 0.02 & 0.01 & 0.00 \end{pmatrix}$$

and

$$I = \begin{pmatrix} 0.01 & 0.02 & 0.01 \\ 0.02 & 0.00 & 0.00 \\ 0.00 & 0.01 & 0.02 \end{pmatrix}.$$

Steps 5, 6: The superiority and inferiority indices of the alternatives and their respective score functions are given in Tables 8 and 9.
Step 7: The superiority flow is given by

$$x_2 > x_1 > x_3,$$

and the inferiority flow is given by

$$x_2 > x_1 > x_3.$$

Step 8: Both the superiority and inferiority flow agree at the optimal alternative x_2.

Table 1. Credibility weights.

Economists	Weights
e_1	$W_1 = \langle[0.20, 0.30], [0.50, 0.70], [0.45, 0.93], 0.61, 0.11, 0.50\rangle$
e_2	$W_2 = \langle[0.80, 0.90], [0.83, 0.91], [0.85, 0.80], 0.12, 0.30, 0.70\rangle$
e_3	$W_3 = \langle[0.10, 0.80], [0.20, 0.75], [0.30, 0.85], 0.90, 0.81, 0.76\rangle$

Table 2. Criteria weights assigned by the economists.

	c_1	c_2	c_3
e_1	$\langle[0.27,0.57],[0.30,0.75],[0.32,0.80],0.30,0.70,0.19\rangle$	$\langle[0.14,0.70],[0.24,0.67],[0.40,0.45],0.14,0.67,0.31\rangle$	$\langle[0.11,0.55],[0.44,0.79],[0.87,0.95],0.10,0.10,0.90\rangle$
e_2	$\langle[0.29,0.60],[0.32,0.72],[0.29,0.78],0.33,0.73,0.17\rangle$	$\langle[0.16,0.74],[0.27,0.70],[0.46,0.49],0.17,0.62,0.34\rangle$	$\langle[0.13,0.54],[0.47,0.77],[0.85,0.93],0.13,0.14,0.83\rangle$
e_3	$\langle[0.28,0.59],[0.33,0.67],[0.35,0.84],0.37,0.77,0.23\rangle$	$\langle[0.17,0.71],[0.25,0.73],[0.43,0.47],0.16,0.65,0.32\rangle$	$\langle[0.16,0.51],[0.43,0.75],[0.83,0.98],0.14,0.16,0.87\rangle$

Table 3. Decision matrix by e_1.

e_1	c_1	c_2	c_3
x_1	$\langle[0.60,0.70],[0.50,0.80],[0.40,0.90],0.40,0.90,0.10\rangle$	$\langle[0.70,0.90],[0.40,0.70],[0.50,0.80],0.10,0.20,0.30\rangle$	$\langle[0.45,0.55],[0.55,0.75],[0.75,0.85],0.90,0.10,0.70\rangle$
x_2	$\langle[0.60,0.80],[0.50,0.70],[0.30,0.60],0.45,0.85,0.15\rangle$	$\langle[0.60,0.84],[0.43,0.74],[0.55,0.83],0.12,0.23,0.34\rangle$	$\langle[0.43,0.54],[0.54,0.77],[0.85,0.93],0.88,0.13,0.73\rangle$
x_3	$\langle[0.55,0.70],[0.60,0.75],[0.35,0.80],0.43,0.83,0.25\rangle$	$\langle[0.66,0.88],[0.39,0.79],[0.60,0.87],0.16,0.28,0.32\rangle$	$\langle[0.41,0.55],[0.57,0.75],[0.78,0.81],0.87,0.14,0.71\rangle$

Table 4. Decision matrix by e_2.

e_2	c_1	c_2	c_3
x_1	$\langle[0.59,0.71],[0.49,0.81],[0.39,0.91],0.37,0.87,0.08\rangle$	$\langle[0.69,0.91],[0.39,0.71],[0.49,0.81],0.07,0.17,0.27\rangle$	$\langle[0.44,0.56],[0.54,0.76],[0.74,0.86],0.87,0.13,0.67\rangle$
x_2	$\langle[0.59,0.81],[0.49,0.71],[0.29,0.61],0.42,0.83,0.13\rangle$	$\langle[0.59,0.85],[0.42,0.75],[0.54,0.84],0.09,0.21,0.32\rangle$	$\langle[0.42,0.55],[0.53,0.78],[0.84,0.94],0.88,0.13,0.73\rangle$
x_3	$\langle[0.53,0.72],[0.58,0.77],[0.33,0.82],0.38,0.80,0.22\rangle$	$\langle[0.64,0.90],[0.37,0.81],[0.59,0.89],0.13,0.25,0.29\rangle$	$\langle[0.39,0.57],[0.55,0.77],[0.76,0.83],0.84,0.11,0.68\rangle$

Table 5. Decision matrix by e_3.

e_3	c_1	c_2	c_3
x_1	$\langle[0.64,0.66],[0.54,0.76],[0.44,0.86],0.38,0.89,0.13\rangle$	$\langle[0.73,0.87],[0.43,0.66],[0.53,0.78],0.12,0.21,0.30\rangle$	$\langle[0.49,0.52],[0.59,0.71],[0.79,0.82],0.92,0.17,0.70\rangle$
x_2	$\langle[0.64,0.77],[0.55,0.65],[0.33,0.57],0.47,0.85,0.17\rangle$	$\langle[0.65,0.82],[0.47,0.70],[0.50,0.80],0.14,0.25,0.35\rangle$	$\langle[0.40,0.51],[0.58,0.73],[0.89,1.00],0.90,0.17,0.73\rangle$
x_3	$\langle[0.58,0.68],[0.63,0.73],[0.38,0.79],0.43,0.83,0.24\rangle$	$\langle[0.68,0.86],[0.42,0.76],[0.65,0.83],0.17,0.29,0.33\rangle$	$\langle[0.44,0.53],[0.59,0.73],[0.75,0.80],0.87,0.18,0.70\rangle$

Table 6. Combined/Aggregated decision matrix.

	c_1	c_2	c_3
x_1	$\langle[0.62,0.69],[0.52,0.79],[0.42,0.9],0.38,0.89,0.11\rangle$	$\langle[0.71,0.90],[0.41,0.69],[0.51,0.80],0.11,0.20,0.29\rangle$	$\langle[0.47,0.54],[0.57,0.74],[0.77,0.85],0.91,0.15,0.69\rangle$
x_2	$\langle[0.62,0.79],[0.52,0.69],[0.31,0.59],0.45,0.84,0.16\rangle$	$\langle[0.63,0.84],[0.45,0.73],[0.53,0.82],0.13,0.24,0.44\rangle$	$\langle[0.42,0.53],[0.56,0.76],[0.87,1.00],0.89,0.15,0.73\rangle$
x_3	$\langle[0.56,0.70],[0.61,0.75],[0.36,0.80],0.42,0.82,0.24\rangle$	$\langle[0.67,0.88],[0.40,0.80],[0.63,0.87],0.16,0.27,0.31\rangle$	$\langle[0.42,0.55],[0.58,0.75],[0.76,0.82],0.86,0.16,0.69\rangle$

Table 7. Identified criterions.

c_1	**Global Warming Mitigation**
c_2	Friendly to the environment
c_3	Low energy consumption

Table 8. CmPF-SI with their scores.

Alternatives	Superiority Indices	Scores
x_1	$\langle[0.11, 0.33], [0.209, 0.532], [0.642, 0.928], 0.144, 0.486, 0.695\rangle$	0.216
x_2	$\langle[0.075, 0.494], [0.235, 0.573], [0.681, 0.939], 0.072, 0.410, 0.730\rangle$	0.297
x_3	$\langle[0.128, 0.459], [0.155, 0.511], [0.208, 0.633], 0.166, 0.533, 0.137\rangle$	0.210

Table 9. CmPF-II with their scores.

Alternatives	Superiority Indices	Scores
x_1	$\langle[0.113, 0.496], [0.211, 0.555], [0.642, 0.928], 0.145, 0.502, 0.695\rangle$	0.268
x_2	$\langle[0.128, 0.35], [0.15, 0.489], [0.156, 0.633], 0.166, 0.529, 0.09\rangle$	0.211
x_3	$\langle[0.068, 0.453], [0.234, 0.566], [0.681, 0.939], 0.064, 0.369, 0.73\rangle$	0.277

7.2. Comparison Analysis

In Table 10, we compare suggested aggregation operators with some existing operators to examine the harmony of the proposed model with previous existing operators. The analysis provided therein demonstrates that our proposed model is compatible with those already in the literature. The proposed operators make a credible and legitimate contribution to dealing with uncertainties by utilizing cubic m-polar fuzzy information.

Table 10. Comparative analysis of the proposed operators and existing ones.

Method	Ranking of Alternatives	The Optimal Alternative
PFDOWA (Jana [30])	$x_2 \succ x_3 \succ x_4$	x_2
PFDHWA (Jana [30])	$x_2 \succ x_3 \succ x_1$	x_2
PFOWA (Garg [24])	$x_2 \succ x_1 \succ x_3$	x_2
PFHA (Garg [24])	$x_2 \succ x_1 \succ x_3$	x_2
CqROFBM (Liu et al. [41])	$x_2 \succ x_3 \succ x_4$	x_2
IFEIO (Liu and Wang [42])	$x_2 \succ x_4 \succ x_1$	x_2
CMPFWAO (Riaz and Hashmi [35])	$x_2 \succ x_1 \succ x_4$	x_2
CMPFOWAO (Riaz and Hashmi [35])	$x_2 \succ x_1 \succ x_4$	x_2
CMPFHAO (Riaz and Hashmi [35])	$x_2 \succ x_1 \succ x_4$	x_2
CmPFDPAO (Proposed)	$x_2 \succ x_1 \succ x_4$	x_2
CmPFDRAO (Proposed)	$x_2 \succ x_1 \succ x_4$	x_2
CmPFDWRAO (Proposed)	$x_2 \succ x_1 \succ x_4$	x_2
CmPFDOWPAO (Proposed)	$x_2 \succ x_1 \succ x_4$	x_2
CmPFDOWRAO (Proposed)	$x_2 \succ x_1 \succ x_4$	x_2
CmPFDHPAO (Proposed)	$x_2 \succ x_1 \succ x_4$	x_2
CmPFDHRAO (Proposed)	$x_2 \succ x_1 \succ x_4$	x_2

8. Conclusions

A cubic m-polar fuzzy set (CmPFS) is a powerful model for dealing with various uncertainties in multi-criteria decision making (MCDM) problems. A cubic set (CS) can express vague information using two components: one is a fuzzy interval and the other is a fuzzy number. While an m-polar fuzzy set (mPFS) assigns m degrees to each alternative in the discourse universe. We focus on CmPFS, which is more efficient to address uncertainties in the multi polar information with a group of m fuzzy intervals and m fuzzy numbers. We investigate some new aspects and consequences of CmPFSs. We define score and accuracy functions to find the ranking of alternatives/objects in MCDM. Additionally, we introduced some new operations, like addition, scalar/usual multiplication and power, under Dombi's t-conorm and t-norm. We developed several new aggregation operators (AOs) named cubic m-polar fuzzy Dombi P-averaging operator (*CmPFDPAO*), cubic m-polar fuzzy Dombi R-averaging operator (*CmPFDRAO*), cubic m-polar fuzzy Dombi weighted P-averaging operator (*CmPFDWPAO*), cubic m-polar fuzzy Dombi weighted R-averaging operator (*CmPFDWRAO*), cubic m-polar fuzzy Dombi ordered weighted P-averaging operator (*CmPFDOWPAO*), cubic m-polar fuzzy Dombi ordered weighted R-averaging operator (*CmPFDOWRAO*), cubic m-polar fuzzy Dombi hybrid P-averaging Operator (*CmPFDHPAO*) and cubic m-polar fuzzy Dombi hybrid R-averaging operator (*CmPFDHRAO*). Certain properties, like, monotonicity, commutativity, idempotency, and boundedness are explored. An advanced superiority and inferiority ranking (SIR) technique is developed to deal with the problem of conversion from linear economy to circular economy. Lastly, a comparison analysis of proposed methodology with some other existing methods is also given.

Author Contributions: M.R., D.P., and M.A.K., conceived and worked together to achieve this manuscript, D.P., and M.A. construct the ideas and algorithms for data analysis and design the model of the manuscript, M.R., M.A.K., and M.A. processed the data collection and wrote the paper. All authors have read and agreed to the published version of the manuscript.

Funding: Abha 61413, Saudi Arabia, research groups program under grant number R.G. P-2/29/42.

Institutional Review Board Statement: Not applicable.

Informed Consent Statement: Not applicable.

Data Availability Statement: Not applicable.

Acknowledgments: The authors extend their appreciation to the Deanship of Scientific Research at King Khalid University, Abha 61413, Saudi Arabia for funding this work through research groups program under grant number R.G. P-2/29/42.

Conflicts of Interest: The authors declare no conflict of interest.

References

1. Korhonen, J.; Honkasalo, A.; Seppala, J. Circular Economy: The Concept and its Limitations. *Ecol. Econ.* **2018**, *143*, 37–46. [CrossRef]
2. Morseletto, P. Targets for a circular economy. *Resour. Conserv. Recycl.* **2019**, *153*, 1–12. [CrossRef]
3. Saidani, M.; Yannou, B.; Leroy, Y.; Cluzel, F.; Kendall, A. A taxonomy of circular economy indicators. *J. Clean. Prod.* **2019**, *207*, 542–559. [CrossRef]
4. Ghosh, S.K. Introduction to circular economy and summary analysis of chapters. In *Circular Economy: Global Perspective*; Springer: Berlin/Heidelberg, Germany, 2019; pp. 1–23. [CrossRef]
5. Zhao, H.; Guo, S.; Zhao, H. Comprehensive benefit evaluation of eco-industrial parks by employing the best-worst method based on circular economy and sustainability. *Environ. Dev. Sustain.* **2018**, *20*, 1229–1253. [CrossRef]
6. Sanchez, F.A.C.; Boudaoud, H.; Camargo, M.; Pearce, J.M. Plastic recycling in additive manufacturing: A systematic literature review and opportunities for the circular economy. *J. Clean. Prod.* **2020**, *264*, 121602. [CrossRef]
7. Yang, X.; Niu, D.; Chen, M.; Wang, K.; Wang, Q.; Xu, X. An operation benefit analysis and decision model of thermal power enterprises in china against the background of large-scale new energy consumption. *Sustainability* **2020**, *12*, 4642. [CrossRef]
8. Bacher, J.; Pihkola, H.; Kujanpaa, L.; Mroueh, U. Advancing the circular economy through group decision-making and stakeholder involvement. *Detritus* **2018**, *4*, 22–35. [CrossRef]

9. Fidelis, R.; Ferreira, M.A.; Colmenero, J.C. Selecting a location to install a plastic processing center: Network of recycling cooperatives. *Resour. Conserv. Recycl.* **2015**, *103*, 1–8. [CrossRef]
10. Zadeh, L.A. Fuzzy sets. *Inf. Control.* **1965**, *8*, 338–353. [CrossRef]
11. Atanassov, K.T. Intuitionistic fuzzy sets. *Fuzzy Sets Syst.* **1986**, *20*, 87–96. [CrossRef]
12. Molodtsov, D. Soft set theory-first results. *Comput. Math. Appl.* **1999**, *37*, 19–31. [CrossRef]
13. Zhang, W.R. Bipolar fuzzy sets and relations: a computational framework for cognitive modeling and multiagent decision analysis, NAFIPS/IFIS/NASA94. In Proceedings of the First International Joint Conference of The North American Fuzzy Information Processing Society Biannual Conference. The Industrial Fuzzy Control and Intellige, San Antonio, TX, USA, 18–21 December 1994 ; pp. 305–309.
14. Zhang, W.R. Bipolar fuzzy sets. In Proceedings of the IEEE Inrenational Conference on Fuzzy Systems, Anchorage, AK, USA, 4–9 May 1998; pp. 835–840.
15. Smarandache, F. *A Unifying Field in Logics. Neutrosophy: Neutrosophic Probability, Set and Logic*; American Research Press: Rehoboth, DE, USA, 1999.
16. Smarandache F. Neutrosophic set-a generalization of the intuitionistic fuzzy set. *Int. J. Pure Appl. Math.* **2005**, *24*, 287–297.
17. Cuong, B.C. Picture fuzzy sets. *Comput. Sci. Cybern.* **2014**, *30*, 409–420.
18. Yager, R.R. Pythagorean fuzzy subsets. In Proceedings of the Joint IFSA World Congress and NAFIPS Annual Meeting, Edmonton, AB, Canada, 24–28 June 2013; pp. 57–61.
19. Yager, R.R. Pythagorean membership grades in multi-criteria decision making. *IEEE Trans. Fuzzy Syst.* **2014**, *22*, 958–965. [CrossRef]
20. Yager, R.R. Generalized Orthopair Fuzzy sets. *IEEE Trans. Fuzzy Syst.* **2017**, *25*, 1220–1230. [CrossRef]
21. Yager, R.R. On ordered weighted averaging aggregation operators in multicriteria decisionmaking. *IEEE Trans. Syst. Man, Cybern.* **1988**, *18*, 183–190. [CrossRef]
22. Xu, Z.S. Intuitionistic fuzzy aggregation operators. *IEEE Trans Fuzzy Syst.* **2007**, *15*,1179–1187.
23. Zhang, X.L.; Xu, Z.S. Extension of TOPSIS to multi-criteria decision making with Pythagorean fuzzy sets. *Int. J. Intell. Syst.* **2014**, *29*, 1061–1078. [CrossRef]
24. Garg, H.; Arora, R. A nonlinear-programming methodology for multi-attribute decision-making problem with interval-valued intuitionistic fuzzy soft sets information. *Appl. Intell.* **2018**, *48*, 2031–2046. [CrossRef]
25. Nancy, G.H. Linguistic single-valued neutrosophic prioritized aggregation operators and their applications to multiple-attribute group decision-making. *J. Ambient. Intell. Humaniz. Comput.* **2018**, *9*, 1975–1997.
26. Dombi, J. A general class of fuzzy operators, the DeMorgan class of fuzzy operators and fuzziness measures induced by fuzzy operators. *Fuzzy Sets Syst.* **1982**, *8*, 149–163. [CrossRef]
27. Ashraf, S.; Abdullah, S.; Mahmood, T. Spherical fuzzy Dombi aggregation operators and their application in group decision making problems. *J. Ambient. Intell. Humaniz. Comput.* **2019**, *11*, 2731–2749. [CrossRef]
28. Akram, M.; Yaqoob, N.; Ali, G.; Chammam, W. Extensions of Dombi Aggregation Operators for Decision Making under m-Polar Fuzzy Information. *J. Math.* **2020**, *6*, 1–20. [CrossRef]
29. Du, W.S. More on Dombi operations and Dombi aggregation operators for q-rung orthopair fuzzy values. *J. Intell. Fuzzy Syst.* **2020**, *39*, 3715–3735. [CrossRef]
30. Jana, C.; Senapati, T.; Pal, M.; Yager, R.R. Picture fuzzy Dombi aggregation operators: Application to MADM process. *Appl. Soft Comput. J.* **2019**, *74*, 99–109. [CrossRef]
31. Lu, X.; Ye, J. Dombi aggregation operators of linguistic cubic variables for multiple attribute decision making. *Information (Switzerland)* **2018**, *9*. [CrossRef]
32. Shi, L.; Ye, J. Dombi aggregation operators of neutrosophic cubic sets for multiple attribute decision-making. *Algorithms* **2018**, *11*, 1–15.
33. Chen, J.; Li, S.; Ma, S.; Wang, X. m-Polar Fuzzy Sets: An Extension of Bipolar Fuzzy Sets. *Sci. World J.* **2014**. [CrossRef]
34. Jun, Y.B.; Kim, C.S.; Yang, K.O. Cubic Sets. *Ann. Fuzzy Math. Informatics* **2012**, *4*, 83–98.
35. Riaz, M.; Hashmi, M.R. MAGDM for agribusiness in the environment of various cubic m-polar fuzzy averaging aggregation operators. *J. Intell. Fuzzy Syst.* **2019**, *37*, 3671–3691. [CrossRef]
36. Riaz, M.; Hashmi, M.R. Linear Diophantine fuzzy set and its applications towards multi-attribute decision making problems. *J. Intell. Fuzzy Syst.* **2019**, *37*, 5417–5439. [CrossRef]
37. Riaz, M.; Kalsoom, M.R.H.H.; Pamucar, D.; Chu, Y. Linear Diophantine fuzzy soft rough sets for the selection of sustainable material handling equipment. *Symmetry* **2020**, *12*, 1–39. [CrossRef]

38. Riaz, M.; Hashmi, M.R.; Pamucar, D.; Chu, Y.M. Spherical linear Diophantine fuzzy sets with modeling uncertainties in MCDM. *Comput. Model. Eng. Sci.* **2021**, *126*, 1125–1164.
39. Kamaci, H. Linear Diophantine fuzzy algebraic structures. *J. Ambient. Intell. Humaniz. Comput.* **2021**. [CrossRef]
40. Karaaslan, F. Neutrosophic soft set with applications in decision making. *Int. J. Inf. Sci. Intell. Syst.* **2015**, *4*, 1–20.
41. Liu, P.; Ali, Z.; Mahmood, T.; Hassan, N. Group decision-making using complex q-rung orthopair fuzzy Bonferroni mean. *Int. J. Comput. Intell. Syst.* **2020**, *13*, 822–851. [CrossRef]
42. Liu, P.; Wang, P. Multiple attribute group decision making method based on intuitionistic fuzzy Einstein interactive operations. *Int. J. Fuzzy Syst.* **2020**, *22*, 790–809. [CrossRef]
43. Liu, X.; Ju, Y.; Yang, S. Hesitant intuitionistic fuzzy linguistic aggregation operators and their applications to multi-attribute decision making. *J. Intell. Fuzzy Syst.* **2014**, *26*, 1187–1201. [CrossRef]
44. Jain, A.; Darbari, J.; Kaul, A.; Jha, P.C. Selection of a green marketing strategy using MCDM under fuzzy environment. In *Soft Computing for Problem Solving*; Springer: Berlin/Heidelberg, Germany, 2020; doi:10.1007/978-981-15-0184-5_43. [CrossRef]

symmetry

MDPI

Article

On the Analytic Hierarchy Process Structure in Group Decision-Making Using Incomplete Fuzzy Information with Applications

Atiq ur Rehman [1], Andrii Shekhovtsov [2], Nighat Rehman [3], Shahzad Faizi [4] and Wojciech Sałabun [2,*]

1 Department of Mathematics, COMSATS University Islamabad, Lahore Campus, Punjab 53710, Pakistan; atiqurehman@cuilahore.edu.pk
2 Research Team on Intelligent Decision Support Systems, Department of Artificial Intelligence and Applied Mathematics, Faculty of Computer Science and Information Technology, West Pomeranian University of Technology in Szczecin, ul. Żołnierska 49, 71-210 Szczecin, Poland; andrii-shekhovtsov@zut.edu.pl
3 Department of Mathematics, University of Lahore, Lahore 53710, Pakistan; nighat.rehman@math.uol.edu.pk
4 Department of Mathematics, Virtual University of Pakistan, Lahore 54000, Pakistan; shahzadfaizi@vu.edu.pk
* Correspondence: wojciech.salabun@zut.edu.pl; Tel.: +48-91-449-5580

Abstract: The multi-criteria decision-making (MCDM) problem has a solution whose quality can be affected by the experts' inclinations. Under essential conditions, the fuzzy MCDM method can provide more acceptable and efficient outcomes to select the best alternatives. This work consists of a consensus-based technique for selecting and evaluating suppliers in an incomplete fuzzy preference relations (IFPRs) environment utilizing T_L-transitivity (Lukasiewicz transitivity). The suggested method is developed based on the criteria of the Analytical Hierarchy Process (AHP) Fframework, and the decision matrix is construtced using consistent fuzzy preference relations (FPRs). We use the symmetrical decisional matrix approach. A variety of numerical explanations and an analysis of quantitative results illustrate the suggested methodology's logic and effectiveness.

Keywords: multiplicative preference relation (MPR); fuzzy preference relation (FPR); group decision-making (GDM); incomplete fuzzy preference relation (IFPR); T_L-consistency; AHP

Citation: Rehman, A.u.; Shekhovtsov, A.; Rehman, N.; Faizi, S.; Sałabun, W. On the Analytic Hierarchy Process Structure in Group Decision-Making Using Incomplete Fuzzy Information with Applications. *Symmetry* **2021**, *13*, 609. https://doi.org/10.3390/sym13040609

Academic Editor: José Carlos R. Alcantud

Received: 23 March 2021
Accepted: 5 April 2021
Published: 6 April 2021

1. Introduction

The supply chain includes divisions responsible for developing new services and products, acquiring raw substances, transforming them into a finished form and delivering them to target consumers. The process of evaluating and selecting appropriate vendors appears to play an important role in the long-term performance and effectiveness of supply networks throughout business corporations. Consequently, a systematic and efficient strategy/method for choosing the most appropriate supplier ultimately reduces the risk of procurement, which tends to increase the number of in-time suppliers available and enhance manufacturing quality [1–4]. Swaminathan and Tayur [5] identified significant problems in conventional supply chain management (SCM) and obtained an insight into the related theoretical frameworks for use during e-business and supply chain sectors. Subsequently, works can be found involving the selection of an effective and appropriate approach for evaluating potential suppliers [6–10].

A well-established manufacturing company puts together a team of specialists to obtain suitable vendors to procure raw materials and important components to manufacture new products. The team of specialists consider a set of factors to evaluate the best alternatives and may change the criteria and philosophy related to different products and services. It is critical which criteria are considered to be sufficient to assess vendors in the context of decision-making problems. A review of the literature regarding the criteria used to select the best alternatives takes us back to Dickson [11], who analyzed and identified 23 criteria for selecting a supplier in 1966, including price, distribution and success experience as the most important considerations, and [12–15] contributed a great deal to strengthening this area. Different organizations that have different corporate and social histories may influence the procurement process for suppliers.

Fundamentally, the multi-criteria decision-making (MCDM) problem is associated with the supplier preference challenge in the group decision-making (GDM) framework [10,16]. The MCDM problem carries a solution whose quality can be affected by the inclinations of the experts. Under essential conditions, the fuzzy MCDM method can provide more acceptable and efficient outcomes to select the best alternatives [17,18]. Numerous methodologies have been proposed to address fuzzy MCDM [19–25]. All of these methods are based on comprehensive information on preferences.

Besides this, in some instances [26,27], experts can have only partial recommendation data for various factors, such as time constraints, a lack of experience or evidence or limited abilities in the problem area. In [27,28], Gong and Xu presented the least square procedure and two-goal-programming models based on incomplete fuzzy preference relations (IFPRs) to evaluate priority weights in GDM. Herrera-Viedma et al. [29] suggested an additive consistency-based recursive method to assess all unknown elements in IFPR. Then, the authors adopted a fuzzy consensus-based procedure to choose the best alternative. In [30], Alonso et al. borrowed the optimization technique given by [29] to propose the framework for estimating unknown values in various formats, including multiplicative, fuzzy, linguistic and interval valued preference relations. Furthermore, Xu deliberated on GDM with four templates of flawed pairwise comparisons [31] to produce a reliable vector of priority weights; first, related optimization techniques to translate various preference formats to FPRs were constructed by the author, and afterwards, the model parameters were obtained by addressing the defined optimization technique. The key concern with this approach is that it does not consider consensus or examine consistency. Encouraged by [29], Lee [32] developed a new GDM methodology based on additive and order consistencies using IFPRs. Later on, Chen et al. [33], presented an improved version of this method. In [34], Rehman et al. proposed a T-transitivity and order consistency-based technique to evaluate the GDM problem. Kerre et al. [35] proposed the GDM model based on multiplicative consistency using incomplete reciprocal fuzzy preference relations.

As mentioned above, several procedures to handle MCDM situations have been proposed in the literature under the condition of complete information. This inspired us to establish a multi-criteria group decision-making (MCGDM) procedure that uses the Analytical Hierarchy Process (AHP) model [36,37], which has already provided significant outcomes in a variety of domains with limited information [38–40]. The use of a consensus-based method consisting of several consensus stages is the best way to address GDM problems. Experts agree that several views are exchanged at a reasonable point; however, an unquestionable or full consensus is not conceivable in reality. The research presented above on GDM in an incomplete environment did not use the AHP model with consensus measure. The consensus-based MCGDM approach using the AHP model in an incomplete environment is the main novelty of this work.

This paper provides a framework for building consensus in MCGDM based on T_L-consistency in the IFPR context. Since consistency has been a crucial problem to be addressed once information from experts is presented, the developed model will approximate relatively rational and consistent values for IFPRs. Transitivity is synonymous with consistency, and therefore a variety of useful types of transitivity is proposed in the FPR literature [41]. T_L-transitivity—i.e., $r_{ik} \geq \max(r_{ij} + r_{jk} - 1, 0)$—is the most suitable and weakest type of transitivity used for fuzzy ordering [42]. In the first step, the missing IFPRs' preferences are evaluated using the T_L-transitivity property. The customized T_L-consistent relations are constructed and maintain the degree of consistency. The degrees of importance are allocated to experts based on the weights of consistency. The suggested approach provides us with a powerful way to achieve consensus in MCGDM using T_L-transitivity with IFPRs.

This paper is structured as follows. In Section 2, some of the preliminary findings used during the paper are mentioned. The recommended MCGDM process is detailed in Section 3. Numerical examples and a comparative analysis are provided in Sections 4 and 5, respectively, to highlight the rationality and feasibility of the proposed technique. Section 6 presents some conclusions.

2. Preliminaries

In 1965, Zadeh developed the concept of fuzzy set theory [43], which shows how an entity is more or less linked with a specific group to which we want to adjust.

Definition 1 ([36]). *A relation H with a finite set A of alternatives characterized by function* $H : A \times A \longrightarrow [1/9, 9]$, $H(h_i, h_j) = h_{ij}$, *satisfying* $h_{ij} \cdot h_{ji} = 1$ *for* $i, j \in \{1, 2, \ldots, m\}$ *is called MPR.*

Definition 2 ([44]). *A relation R with a finite set* $A = \{a_1, a_2, \ldots, a_m\}$ *of alternatives characterized by mapping* $R : A \times A \longrightarrow [0, 1]$, *satisfying:* $r_{ij} + r_{ji} = 1$ *(additive reciprocity) for* $1 \leq i \leq m$ *and* $1 \leq j \leq m$, $r_{ij} \in [0, 1]$ *shows preference degree of alternative* a_i *over* $a_j yba$

Remark 1 ([45]). *For* $H = (h_{ij})_{m \times m}$, *a related FPR* $R = (r_{ij})_{m \times m}$ *is constructed as follows:*

$$r_{ij} = f(h_{ij}) = \frac{1}{2}(1 + \log_9 h_{ij}) \tag{1}$$

Function (1), as bijective mapping, allows the notions defined for the FPR to be transferred to the MPR and vice versa.

Definition 3 ([29]). *If FPR* $R = (r_{ij})_{m \times m}$ *carries at least one missing pairwise comparison* r_{ij} *of alternative* a_i *over* a_j, *then it is an IFPR.*

Definition 4. *If* $r_{ij} \geq \max(r_{ik} + r_{kj} - 1, 0)$ *(T_L-transitivity),* $i \neq j \neq k \in \{1, 2, \ldots, m\}$, *is satisfied; then, R is the T_L-consistent symbolized by* $\widetilde{R} = (\widetilde{r}_{ij})_{m \times m}$.

Definition 5. *The ranking values* $v(a_i)$ *of alternatives* a_i, $i = 1, 2, .., n$, *for* $\widetilde{R} = (\widetilde{r}_{ij})_{n \times n}$ *are determined as*

$$v(a_i) = \frac{2}{n(n-1)} \sum_{j=1,\, j \neq i}^{m} \widetilde{r}_{ij}$$

with $\sum_{i=1}^{m} v(a_i) = 1$.

3. Proposed Procedure for the MCGDM Problem

The proposed procedure for the MCGDM problem consists of various phases. The problem is first put to a group of experts $E = \{E_1, E_2, \ldots, E_l\}$, with given sets of alternatives $A = \{a_1, a_2, \ldots, a_m\}$ and criteria $C = \{c_1, c_2, \ldots, c_n\}$. The experts measure their own preferences $\{R^1, R^2, \ldots, R^l\}$ regarding the criteria and $\{_C R^1, _C R^2, \ldots, _C R^l\}$ of alternatives for each criterion using FPRs based on their evaluation of an issue. A few of the values for preferences in FPRs might be missing, considering the time pressure and lack of information. Following this, the Łukasiewicz transitivity property (T_L-transitivity) with max aggregated operator is used to fill the missing places. Once the FPRs have been completed, the transitive closure formula plays a significant role in building entirely consistent FPRs. A consistency study is conducted to compute consistency-based indices of preference matrices to make the final result more trustworthy. The consensus level among the experts is estimated based on the set preferences: if a sufficient level is reached, the entire decision process undergoes the selection phase; otherwise, experts will be asked to revise existing values. Several levels are discussed in detail below.

3.1. Estimating Missing Values

Here, the subsection includes a method for estimating missed preferences inside an IFPR to build an FPR with full understanding that relies on T_L-consistency. It should always be observed that each IFPR can only be completed based on the T_L consistency when every alternative has a comparison among the known values of preferences values, at least once. Therefore, the system encourages an expert to define a sufficient number of parameters, where every alternative is evaluated at least once to allow the IFPR to become a complete FPR. Additionally, the order of measurement of the missing preference values affects the final result. To evaluate missing values of preferences in $R = (r_{ij})_{m\times m}$, the following sets of known and unknown preference values to identify pairs of alternatives are defined:

$$K = \{(i,j) \mid r_{ij} \text{ is known}\}, \tag{2}$$

$$U = \{(i,j) \mid r_{ij} \text{ is unknown}\}, \tag{3}$$

where $r_{ij} \in [0,1]$ and represents the degree of preference for alternative a_i to a_j. Based on the T_L-transitivity $r_{ij} \geq T_L(r_{ik}, r_{kj})$, the following set can then be established for estimating a missing value r_{ij} of the preference for alternative a_i over a_j.

$$Q_{ij} = \{k \neq i,j \mid (i,k) \in K, (k,j) \in K \text{ and } (i,j) \in U\}, \tag{4}$$

where $i,j,k \in \{1,2,\ldots,m\}$. Therefore, based on the set defined in (4), r_{ij} is estimated using

$$r_{ij} = \begin{cases} \max\limits_{k\in Q_{ij}}(T_L(r_{ik}, r_{kj})), & \text{if } |Q_{ij}| \neq 0 \\ 0.5, & \text{otherwise} \end{cases}, \tag{5}$$

$$r_{ji} = 1 - r_{ij}, \tag{6}$$

where $|Q_{ij}|$ shows the number of elements in set Q_{ij}. Now, we present the following newer sets K' and U'

$$K' = K \cup \{(i,j)\}, \text{ and } U' = U - \{(i,j)\}. \tag{7}$$

Once FPR $R = (r_{ij})_{m\times m}$ has been completed, we can construct a T_L-consistent FPR $\widetilde{R} = (\widetilde{r}_{ij})_{m\times m}$ using the following expression:

$$\widetilde{r}_{ij} = \max_{k\neq i,j}(r_{ij}, T_L(r_{ik}, r_{kj})) \text{ with } \widetilde{r}_{ij} + \widetilde{r}_{ji} = 1. \tag{8}$$

There are many decision-making procedures in the real world that take place in a multi-person framework, since the increasing difficulty and volatility of the socio-economic setting makes it less feasible for an individual to understand all the aspects of a decision-making problem.

3.2. Consistency Measures

In this subsection, some consistency measures are defined: the consistency index of a pair of alternatives, the consistency index of alternatives and the consistency index of FPRs. The term consistency index (CI) stands for a consistency degree whose value lies within the ragne $[0,1]$.

Let R^p be an IFPR given by expert E_p $(1 \leq p \leq l)$; then, after evaluating the missing preferences, (8) helps us to construct T_L-consistent FPRs $\widetilde{R}^p$. It is then possible to estimate the consistency level for the FPR R^p on the basis of its likeness to the correlating relation $\widetilde{R}^p$ by measuring their distances [46].

1. The T_L-consistency Index (T_LCI) of each pair of alternatives is computed using the following expression:

$$T_LCI(r^p_{ij}) = 1 - d(r^p_{ij}, \widetilde{r}^p_{ij}), \tag{9}$$

where $d(r^p_{ij}, \tilde{r}^p_{ij}) = \left|r^p_{ij} - \tilde{r}^p_{ij}\right|$. Obviously, the greater the value of $T_L CI(r^p_{ij})$, the more acceptable r^p_{ij} is with respect to the remaining preference values of a_i and a_j.

2. $T_L CI$ values for the alternatives a_i and $1 \leq i \leq n$ are determined using

$$T_L CI(a_i) = \frac{1}{2(m-1)} \sum_{j=1}^{m} (T_L CI(r^p_{ij}) + T_L CI(r^p_{ji})). \tag{10}$$

3. $T_L CI$ for an FPR R^p is therefore evaluated by calculating the mean of $T_L CI$ against all alternatives a_i:

$$T_L CI(R^p) = \frac{1}{m} \sum_{i=1}^{m} T_L CI(a_i). \tag{11}$$

4. After evaluating $T_L CI$ in three stages (9)–(11), higher weights are assigned rationally to the experts with higher consistency degrees. Consistency weights may therefore be allocated to experts in the sense of the following relation:

$$w_p = \frac{T_L CI(R^p)}{\sum_{p=1}^{l} T_L CI(R^p)}. \tag{12}$$

3.3. Consensus Measures

The subsection includes several measures to assess a global consensus of experts to decide whether the decision process should be moved into the selection phase or not.

When the FPRs carry complete information, it us quite important to calculate the level of consensus among experts. In this context, the similarity relations $S^{qr} = (s^{qr}_{ij})_{m \times m}$ with each pair of experts (E_q, E_r), $1 \leq q \leq l-1$ and $q+1 \leq r \leq l$, need to be established. A similarity matrix, also known as a distance matrix, helps us to understand how close or far apart a pair of factors is from the participants' perspective. Therefore, we define s^{qr}_{ij} by

$$s^{qr}_{ij} = 1 - \left|r^q_{ij} - r^r_{ij}\right|. \tag{13}$$

The aggregation of all similarity matrices results in a cumulative similarity matrix $S = (s_{ij})_{m \times m}$ as follows:

$$s_{ij} = \frac{2}{l(l-1)} \sum_{q=1}^{l-1} \sum_{r=q+1}^{l} s^{qr}_{ij}. \tag{14}$$

The degree of consensus among experts is the result of the following three phases of the process [46]:

1. First, the degree of consensus for every pair (a_i, a_j) of alternatives, referred to as cod_{ij}, is determined:

$$cod_{ij} = s_{ij}. \tag{15}$$

2. At level 2, the degree of consensus among the experts on each alternative a_i, referred to as CoD_i for $1 \leq i \leq m$, is established as

$$CoD_i = \frac{1}{2(m-1)} \sum_{j=1, j \neq i}^{m} (s_{ij} + s_{ji}). \tag{16}$$

3. The third level includes the global consensus degree, symbolized by CoD, among all experts on their observations:

$$CoD = \frac{1}{m} \sum_{i=1}^{m} CoD_i. \tag{17}$$

Once a global level of consensus has been reached among all experts, it is necessary to compare this with a threshold degree of consensus η, usually pre-determined based on the problem at hand. If $CoD \geq \eta$, it indicates that a sufficient degree of consensus is achieved, and so the decision-making process begins. However, if the degree of consensus is not secure, experts may be asked to update their priorities. When the consensus is not sufficiently strong, the input process provides the experts with ample knowledge to adjust their views and increase the degree of consensus. The following identifier is therefore defined in order to recognize the preference values that need to be modified:

$$I^p = \left\{(i,j) \mid cod_{ij} < CoD \text{ and } r_{ij}^p \text{ is known}\right\}.$$

The corresponding experts are then advised to increase the value if it is lower than the average value of the other experts' valuations and to reduce it if it is higher than the average.

For the hierarchical problem on the basis of GDM, consider a set $\{a_1,a_2,..,a_m\}$ of m alternatives; a set $\{c_1, c_2, \ldots, c_n\}$ of n criteria and a team $\{E_1, E_2, \ldots, E_l\}$ of l experts with priority weights $\lambda = (\lambda_1, \lambda_2, \lambda_3, \ldots, \lambda_l)^T$, so that $\sum_{p=1}^{l} \lambda_p = 1$. The MCGDM procedure using the AHP structure is described as follows:

3.4. Final Priority Weights of the Experts

The final priority weights of the experts are measured by considering the consistency weights and predefined weights, respectively, as

$$\beta_p = \frac{\lambda_p \times w_p}{\sum_{p=1}^{l} \lambda_p \times w_p}$$

where λ_p and $1 \leq p \leq l$ are the predetermined priority weights of the experts and $\sum_{p=1}^{l} \beta_p = 1$. In the absence of a predetermined priority weight vector, the consistency weights are taken as final weights for the experts.

3.5. Ranking of Criteria

In this subsection, priority weights of criteria are evaluated and ranked according to their importance under the following steps.

In step 1, the experts E_p $(p = 1, 2, 3, \ldots, l)$ make pairwise comparisons of the criteria and may provide their evaluations in the form of the following IFPRs, $R^{(p)} = [r_{ij}^{(p)}]_{m \times m}$:

$$R^{(p)} = [r_{ij}^{(p)}]_{m\times m} = \begin{array}{c} \\ c_1 \\ c_2 \\ \cdot \\ \cdot \\ c_n \end{array} \begin{array}{c} \begin{array}{ccccc} c_1 & c_2 & \cdot & \cdot & c_n \end{array} \\ \begin{bmatrix} 0.5 & r_{12}^{(p)} & \cdot & \cdot & r_{1n}^{(p)} \\ r_{21}^{(p)} & 0.5 & \cdot & \cdot & r_{2n}^{(p)} \\ \cdot & \cdot & \cdot & & \cdot \\ \cdot & \cdot & & \cdot & \cdot \\ r_{n1}^{(p)} & r_{n2}^{(p)} & \cdot & \cdot & 0.5 \end{bmatrix} \end{array},$$

and $r_{ij}^{(p)} \in [0,1]$ shows the degree of preference of criterion c_i compared to criterion c_j, evaluated by expert E_p, $r_{ij}^{(p)} + r_{ji}^{(p)} = 1, 1 \leq i,j \leq n, 1 \leq p \leq l$.

In step 2, (4)–(8) allow the estimation of all missing preference degrees for $R^{(p)}$, and T_L-consistent $\widetilde{R}^{(p)} = [\widetilde{r}_{ij}^{(p)}]_{n\times n}, 1 \leq p \leq l$ values are constructed.

In step 3, since consistent FPRs have been constructed, the consistency degree for each FPR of the criteria are calculated using (9)–(11). Usually, an FPR is called consistent to some extent if the level of consistency is higher than 0.5, while it is fully consistent when that level is 1. The degree of consensus regarding the criteria by all experts is measured with the use of (13)–(17).

In step 4, we construct the aggregated relation R^c as follows:

$$R^c = \left[r^c_{ij}\right]_{n\times n} = \left[\sum_{p=1}^{l} \beta_p \widetilde{r}^{(p)}_{ij}\right]_{n\times n}, \tag{18}$$

where $1 \le i \le n, 1 \le j \le n$ and $1 \le p \le l$.

In step 5, using definition 6, we evaluate the ranking values of criteria as follows:

$$v(c_i) = \frac{2}{n(n-1)} \sum_{i=1, i\neq j}^{n} r^c_{ij}, \tag{19}$$

for $\sum_{i=1}^{n} v(c_i) = 1$.

3.6. Ranking of Alternatives Regarding Each Criterion

In this subsection, priority weights of alternatives regarding each criterion are evaluated to rank them according to their importance in the following steps.

In step 1, experts E_p $(p = 1,2,3,\ldots,l)$ make pairwise comparisons of the alternatives regarding each criterion q $(q = 1,2,3\ldots,n)$ and may provide their evaluations in the form of IFPRs ${}_qR^{(p)} = [{}_qr^{(p)}_{uv}]_{m\times m}$.

In step 2, (4)–(8) are used to estimate all missing preference degrees for ${}_qR^{(p)}$, and T_L-consistent ${}_q\widetilde{R}^{(p)} = [{}_q\widetilde{r}^{(p)}_{uv}]_{m\times m}$ values are constructed.

In step 3, since consistent FPRs have been constructed, the consistency degree for each FPR for each criterion is calculated using (9)–(11). The degree of consensus among all experts is measured with the use of (13)–(17).

In step 4, we construct the aggregated relation ${}_qR^c$ as follows:

$${}_qR^c = [{}_qr^c_{ij}]_{m\times m} = \left[\sum_{p=1}^{l} \beta_p \left({}_q\widetilde{r}^{(p)}_{uv}\right)\right]_{m\times m}, \tag{20}$$

where $1 \le u \le m, 1 \le v \le m$ and $1 \le p \le l$.

In step 5, using definition 6, we evaluate the ranking values of alternatives regarding each criterion as follows:

$${}_qv(a_u) = \frac{2}{m(m-1)} \sum_{v=1, v\neq u}^{m} \left({}_qr^c_{uv}\right), \tag{21}$$

where $1 \le u \le m$ and $\sum_{u=1}^{m} \left({}_qv(a_u)\right) = 1$.

3.7. Final Ranking of Alternatives

In order to evaluate the final ranking order of alternatives, we have to perform a simple matrix multiplication of the matrix of the priority scores of alternatives corresponding to each criterion and the column matrix for the priority weights of criteria. Suppose the score matrix of alternatives regarding each criterion is symbolized by A and the column matrix for the priority weights of criteria is denoted by w_c; then, the priority weight vector w_x of alternatives is determined using

$$w_x = A \cdot w_c. \tag{22}$$

In order to better understand the proposed technique, we therefore take the following fuzzy MCDM problem within the IFPR setting.

4. Example

In order to procure important components for new brands, a high-tech manufacturing corporation chooses an appropriate material supplier. After the initial selection, four candidates (a_1, a_2, a_3, a_4) proceed to some final analysis. In order to find the most appropriate supplier, a group including experts (E_1, E_2, E_3) is established, with the priority weights $\lambda = (1/3, 1/3, 1/3)^T$. Five benefit criteria are considered: (1) technical abilities and leadership (c_1); (2) social responsibility (c_2); (3) competitive pricing (c_3); (4) quality and safety (c_4); (5) delivery (c_5). The pre-established threshold level η of consensus to the set of criteria is 0.75.

The hierarchical structure for this decision problem can be seen in Figure 1 below.

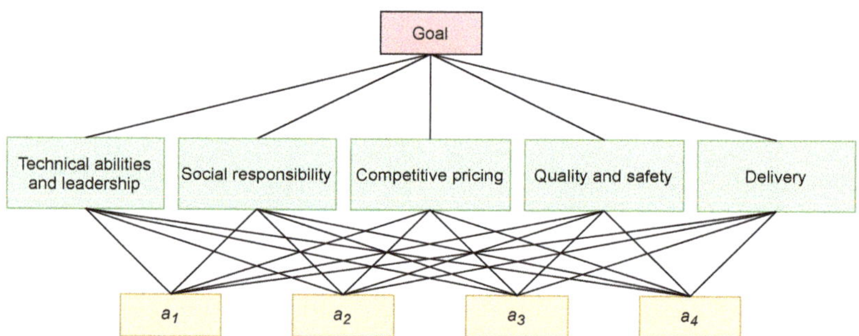

Figure 1. Hierarchical structure of the decision problem.

After the pairwise comparison of the five criteria, the experts provide the following IFPRs:

$$R^{(1)} = \begin{bmatrix} 0.5 & 0.6 & r_{13}^1 & 0.4 & 0.7 \\ 0.4 & 0.5 & r_{23}^1 & 0.6 & 0.7 \\ r_{31}^1 & r_{32}^1 & 0.5 & 0.3 & 0.4 \\ 0.6 & 0.4 & 0.7 & 0.5 & r_{45}^1 \\ 0.3 & 0.3 & 0.6 & r_{54}^1 & 0.5 \end{bmatrix}; R^{(2)} = \begin{bmatrix} 0.5 & 0.4 & r_{13}^2 & 0.6 & r_{15}^2 \\ 0.6 & 0.5 & 0.6 & 0.5 & r_{25}^2 \\ r_{31}^2 & 0.4 & 0.5 & 0.3 & 0.7 \\ 0.4 & 0.5 & 0.7 & 0.5 & 0.2 \\ r_{51}^2 & r_{52}^2 & 0.3 & 0.8 & 0.5 \end{bmatrix}; R^{(3)} = \begin{bmatrix} 0.5 & 0.3 & 0.4 & 0.7 & 0.7 \\ 0.7 & 0.5 & r_{23}^3 & r_{24}^3 & r_{25}^3 \\ 0.6 & r_{32}^3 & 0.5 & 0.2 & 0.8 \\ 0.3 & r_{42}^3 & 0.8 & 0.5 & 0.3 \\ 0.3 & r_{52}^3 & 0.2 & 0.7 & 0.5 \end{bmatrix}.$$

After the pairwise comparison of the four alternatives for each criterion, the experts provide the following IFPRs:

Technical abilities and leadership:

$${}_1R^{(1)} = \begin{bmatrix} 0.5 & 0.8 & {}_1r_{13}^1 & {}_1r_{14}^1 \\ 0.2 & 0.5 & 0.4 & 0.6 \\ {}_1r_{31}^1 & 0.6 & 0.5 & 0.7 \\ {}_1r_{41}^1 & 0.4 & 0.3 & 0.5 \end{bmatrix}; {}_1R^{(2)} = \begin{bmatrix} 0.5 & 0.7 & 1r_{13}^2 & 0.6 \\ 0.3 & 0.5 & 0.5 & 0.7 \\ 1r_{31}^2 & 0.5 & 0.5 & {}_1r_{34}^2 \\ 0.4 & 0.3 & {}_1r_{43}^2 & 0.5 \end{bmatrix}; {}_1R^{(3)} = \begin{bmatrix} 0.5 & {}_1r_{12}^3 & 0.7 & {}_1r_{14}^3 \\ {}_1r_{21}^3 & 0.5 & {}_1r_{23}^3 & 0.6 \\ 0.3 & {}_1r_{32}^3 & 0.5 & 0.5 \\ {}_1r_{41}^3 & 0.4 & 0.5 & 0.5 \end{bmatrix}.$$

Social responsibility:

$${}_2R^{(1)} = \begin{bmatrix} 0.5 & 0.7 & 0.5 & {}_2r_{14}^1 \\ 0.3 & 0.5 & 0.4 & 0.6 \\ 0.5 & 0.6 & 0.5 & 0.8 \\ {}_2r_{41}^1 & 0.4 & 0.2 & 0.5 \end{bmatrix}; {}_2R^{(2)} = \begin{bmatrix} 0.5 & 0.8 & {}_2r_{13}^2 & {}_2r_{14}^2 \\ 0.2 & 0.5 & 0.3 & 0.5 \\ {}_2r_{31}^2 & 0.7 & 0.5 & 0.3 \\ {}_2r_{41}^2 & 0.5 & 0.7 & 0.5 \end{bmatrix}; {}_2R^{(3)} = \begin{bmatrix} 0.5 & 0.9 & {}_2r_{13}^3 & 0.6 \\ 0.1 & 0.5 & 0.4 & 0.4 \\ {}_2r_{31}^3 & 0.6 & 0.5 & {}_2r_{34}^3 \\ 0.4 & 0.6 & {}_2r_{43}^3 & 0.5 \end{bmatrix}.$$

Competitive pricing:

$${}_3R^{(1)} = \begin{bmatrix} 0.5 & 0.6 & {}_3r_{13}^1 & 0.7 \\ 0.4 & 0.5 & 0.3 & {}_3r_{24}^1 \\ {}_3r_{31}^1 & 0.7 & 0.5 & 0.4 \\ 0.3 & {}_3r_{42}^1 & 0.6 & 0.5 \end{bmatrix}; {}_3R^{(2)} = \begin{bmatrix} 0.5 & {}_3r_{12}^2 & {}_3r_{13}^2 & 0.6 \\ {}_3r_{21}^2 & 0.5 & {}_3r_{23}^2 & 0.2 \\ {}_3r_{31}^2 & {}_3r_{32}^2 & 0.5 & 0.4 \\ 0.4 & 0.8 & 0.6 & 0.5 \end{bmatrix}; {}_3R^{(3)} = \begin{bmatrix} 0.5 & {}_3r_{12}^3 & 0.3 & 0.5 \\ {}_3r_{21}^3 & 0.5 & {}_3r_{23}^3 & 0.3 \\ 0.7 & {}_3r_{32}^3 & 0.5 & {}_3r_{34}^3 \\ 0.5 & 0.7 & {}_3r_{43}^3 & 0.5 \end{bmatrix}.$$

Quality and safety:

$$ {}_4R^{(1)} = \begin{bmatrix} 0.5 & 0.2 & {}_4r^1_{13} & 0.7 \\ 0.8 & 0.5 & {}_4r^1_{23} & {}_4r^1_{24} \\ {}_4r^1_{31} & {}_4r^1_{32} & 0.5 & {}_4r^1_{34} \\ 0.3 & {}_4r^1_{42} & {}_4r^1_{43} & 0.5 \end{bmatrix}; {}_4R^{(2)} = \begin{bmatrix} 0.5 & 0.4 & 0.7 & {}_4r^2_{14} \\ 0.6 & 0.5 & 0.7 & {}_4r^2_{24} \\ 0.3 & 0.3 & 0.5 & 0.6 \\ {}_4r^2_{41} & {}_4r^2_{42} & 0.4 & 0.5 \end{bmatrix}; {}_4R^{(3)} = \begin{bmatrix} 0.5 & {}_4r^3_{12} & 0.3 & 0.4 \\ {}_4r^3_{21} & 0.5 & 0.2 & 0.6 \\ 0.7 & 0.8 & 0.5 & {}_4r^3_{34} \\ 0.6 & 0.4 & {}_4r^3_{43} & 0.5 \end{bmatrix}. $$

Delivery:

$$ {}_5R^{(1)} = \begin{bmatrix} 0.5 & {}_5r^1_{12} & {}_5r^1_{13} & 0.1 \\ {}_5r^1_{21} & 0.5 & 0.4 & {}_5r^1_{24} \\ {}_5r^1_{31} & 0.6 & 0.5 & 0.7 \\ 0.9 & {}_5r^1_{42} & 0.3 & 0.5 \end{bmatrix}; {}_5R^{(2)} = \begin{bmatrix} 0.5 & 0.2 & {}_5r^2_{13} & 0.4 \\ 0.8 & 0.5 & {}_5r^2_{23} & 0.3 \\ {}_5r^2_{31} & {}_5r^2_{32} & 0.5 & 0.3 \\ {}_5r^2_{41} & 0.7 & 0.7 & 0.5 \end{bmatrix}; {}_5R^{(3)} = \begin{bmatrix} 0.5 & 0.3 & 0.4 & {}_5r^3_{14} \\ 0.7 & 0.5 & 0.6 & {}_5r^3_{24} \\ 0.6 & 0.4 & 0.5 & {}_5r^3_{34} \\ {}_5r^3_{41} & {}_5r^3_{42} & {}_5r^3_{43} & 0.5 \end{bmatrix}. $$

The use of the suggested method results in the cumulative FPR for five criteria and the corresponding priority weights, as seen in Table 1, whereas the level of consistency and the degree of consensus for the experts are as follows:

$$ T_LCI(R^1) = 1;\ T_LCI(R^2) = 0.98;\ T_LCI(R^3) = 0.95, \text{ and } CoD = 0.7933. $$

Table 1. Accumulated fuzzy preference relation (FPR) of criteria and ranking values.

	c_1	c_2	c_3	c_4	c_5	**Priority Weights**
c_1	0.50000	0.4358	0.3648	0.5642	0.4658	0.1830
c_2	0.5642	0.5000	0.3679	0.5017	0.4689	0.1903
c_3	0.6352	0.6321	0.5000	0.4317	0.6300	0.2329
c_4	0.4358	0.4983	0.5683	0.5000	0.2666	0.1769
c_5	0.5342	0.5311	0.3700	0.7334	0.5000	0.2169

The aggregated FPRs for the four suppliers corresponding to the criteria and the priority scores can be seen in Table 2, and the consistency as well as consensus levels for each criterion are calculated as follows:

Technical abilities and leadership:

$$ T_LCI({}_1R^1) = 1;\ T_LCI({}_1R^2) = 1;\ T_LCI({}_1R^3) = 1, \text{ and } CoD = 0.8189. $$

Social responsibility:

$$ T_LCI({}_2R^1) = 1;\ T_LCI({}_2R^2) = 1;\ T_LCI({}_2R^3) = 1, \text{ and } CoD = 0.8111. $$

Competitive pricing:

$$ T_LCI({}_3R^1) = 1;\ T_LCI({}_3R^2) = 1;\ T_LCI({}_3R^3) = 1, \text{ and } CoD = 0.8445. $$

Quality and safety:

$$ T_LCI({}_4R^1) = 1;\ T_LCI({}_4R^2) = 1;\ T_LCI({}_4R^3) = 1, \text{ and } CoD = 0.7933. $$

Delivery:

$$ T_LCI({}_5R^1) = 1;\ T_LCI({}_5R^2) = 1;\ T_LCI({}_5R^3) = 1, \text{ and } CoD = 0.7877. $$

Table 2. Accumulated FPRs for suppliers in relation to each criterion and ranking values.

	a_1	a_2	a_3	a_4	**Priority Ratings**
c_1					
a_1	0.5000	0.6667	0.3667	0.4000	0.2389
a_2	0.3333	0.5000	0.3667	0.6333	0.2222
a_3	0.6333	0.6333	0.5000	0.4333	0.2833
a_4	0.6000	0.3667	0.5667	0.5000	0.2556
c_2					
a_1	0.5000	0.8000	0.3000	0.4000	0.2500
a_2	0.2000	0.5000	0.3667	0.5000	0.1778
a_3	0.7000	0.6333	0.5000	0.4667	0.3000
a_4	0.6000	0.5000	0.5333	0.5000	0.2722
c_3					
a_1	0.5000	0.4000	0.2667	0.6000	0.2111
a_2	0.6000	0.5000	0.1333	0.2000	0.1556
a_3	0.7333	0.8667	0.5000	0.3333	0.3222
a_4	0.4000	0.8000	0.6667	0.5000	0.3111
c_4					
a_1	0.5000	0.2333	0.5000	0.4667	0.2000
a_2	0.7667	0.5000	0.4000	0.4667	0.2722
a_3	0.5000	0.6000	0.5000	0.4000	0.2500
a_4	0.5333	0.5333	0.6000	0.5000	0.2778
c_5					
a_1	0.5000	0.3333	0.1667	0.3333	0.1389
a_2	0.6667	0.5000	0.5000	0.1667	0.2222
a_3	0.8333	0.5000	0.5000	0.3667	0.2833
a_4	0.6667	0.8333	0.6333	0.5000	0.3556

The last column of Table 3 is used to show the final ranking values of the four suppliers, which are $w_{a_1} = 0.2060$, $w_{a_2} = 0.2071$, $w_{a_3} = 0.2896$ and $w_{a_4} = 0.2973$. As $w_{a_4} > w_{a_3} > w_{a_2} > w_{a_1}$; therefore, the ranking order of the four suppliers a_1, a_2, a_3 and a_4 is $a_4 > a_3 > a_2 > a_1$.

Table 3. Final priority weights of the four suppliers.

	c_1	c_2	c_3	c_4	c_5	**Priority Weights**
Criteria weights	0.1830	0.1903	0.2329	0.1769	0.2169	
a_1	0.2389	0.2500	0.2111	0.2000	0.1389	0.2060
a_2	0.2222	0.1778	0.1556	0.2722	0.2222	0.2071
a_3	0.2833	0.3000	0.3222	0.2500	0.2833	0.2896
a_4	0.2556	0.2722	0.3111	0.2778	0.3556	0.2973

5. Comparison

To validate the productivity of the proposed scheme, we compare the results after concluding the problem taken from [22] with our proposed technique.

Problem Statement

A funds, and five potential candidates (loan users) are in competition for the remaining funds. The problem is to rank the applicants and allocate the loan following the principle of loan allocation until the funds are completely used. A team of five decision makers (DMs) participate in the ranking: the President of the Fund Council (DM1), a senior advisor to the Fund (DM2), the fund manager (DM3), an external expert advisor (DM4) and an expert representative of the Ministry. Three criteria are considered by the team: (1) Service, (2) Loan History (LOANH) and (3) Insurance. After pairwise comparison, the MPRs provided by the DMs are given as presented in Tables 4–8.

Table 4. Comparison matrices provided by President of the Fund Council (DM1) [22].

Criteria	Service	LOANH	Insurance
Service		2	9
LOANH			5
Insurance			

	Service					LOANH					Insurance				
	U_1	U_2	U_3	U_4	U_5	U_1	U_2	U_3	U_4	U_5	U_1	U_2	U_3	U_4	U_5
U_1		3	1/2	8	4		1/9	1/9	1/4	1/6		2	5	1/2	1/6
U_2			1/3	7	3			1	3	2			5	1/3	1/8
U_3				9	6				3	2				1/7	1/9
U_4					1/4					1/2					1/3
U_5															

Table 5. Comparison matrices provided by Senior advisor of the Fund (DM2) [22].

Criteria	Service	LOANH	Insurance
Service		5	9
LOANH			6
Insurance			

	Service					LOANH					Insurance				
	U_1	U_2	U_3	U_4	U_5	U_1	U_2	U_3	U_4	U_5	U_1	U_2	U_3	U_4	U_5
U_1		4	1/3	6	5		1/6	1/6	1/3	1/3		2	4	1/2	1/4
U_2			1/4	5	3			1	2	2			4	1/4	1/6
U_3				9	8				2	2				1/8	1/9
U_4					1/3					1/2					1/2
U_5															

Table 6. Comparison matrices provided by Fund manager (DM3) [22].

Criteria	Service	LOANH	Insurance
Service		1/5	1/3
LOANH			6
Insurance			

	Service					LOANH					Insurance				
	U_1	U_2	U_3	U_4	U_5	U_1	U_2	U_3	U_4	U_5	U_1	U_2	U_3	U_4	U_5
U_1		2	1/3	7	6		1/5	1/5	1/2	1/4		3	6	1/2	1/7
U_2			1/5	5	3			1	2	2			2	1/4	1/7
U_3				9	7				2	2				1/6	1/9
U_4					1/4					1/2					1/5
U_5															

Table 7. Comparison matrices provided by External expert advisor (DM4) [22].

Criteria	Service	LOANH	Insurance
Service		3	7
LOANH			5
Insurance			

	Service					LOANH					Insurance				
	U_1	U_2	U_3	U_4	U_5	U_1	U_2	U_3	U_4	U_5	U_1	U_2	U_3	U_4	U_5
U_1		3	1/3	8	5		1/8	1/8	1/5	1/6		4	6	1/3	1/5
U_2			1/4	6	3			1	3	2			2	1/4	1/7
U_3				9	5				3	2				1/6	1/9
U_4					1/4					1/3					1/4
U_5															

Table 8. Comparison matrices provided by Expert representative of the Ministry (DM5) [22].

Criteria	Service	LOANH	Insurance
Service		7	9
LOANH			5
Insurance			

	Service					LOANH					Insurance				
	U_1	U_2	U_3	U_4	U_5	U_1	U_2	U_3	U_4	U_5	U_1	U_2	U_3	U_4	U_5
U_1		3	1/5	7	5		1/9	1/9	1/5	1/7		3	6	1/3	1/5
U_2			1/6	6	5			1	7	5			4	1/5	1/7
U_3				9	7				7	5				1/7	1/9
U_4					1/3					1/4					1/4
U_5															

Srdevic et al. [22] determined the ranking oder of five applicants as $U_3 > U_2 > U_1 > U_5 > U_4$. However, the priority weights of applicants obtained by the proposed model after transforming the above problem in a fuzzy environment, with the help of Remark 1, are U_1 = 0.17781, U_2 = 0.23454, U_3 = 0.29778, U_4 = 0.10693, U_5 = 0.18294, which lead to a ranking order of

$$U_3 > U_2 > U_5 > U_1 > U_4$$

The result shows that the ranking positions for applicants U_2, U_3 and U_4 are the same as in [22], while the order of applicants U_1 and U_5 are interchanged, but applicant U_3 is the first preference in both models to get the desired loan. The similarities of these two rankings are very high, where the r_w and WS coefficients of the both rankings are equal 0.9167 [47]. There may be two factors that resulted in a different ranking order in few places: (i) different techniques were used to determine the ranking order, and (ii) the corresponding parameters regarding different models could have been evaluated in various ways, and the results may be affected. We think that the proposed model can equally handle complete and incomplete information and provides better results.

6. Conclusions

This paper provides a clear and effective methodology for selecting and ranking suppliers based on a consensus-derived and consistent model for MCGDM in an incomplete AHP environment. The T_L-transitivity property plays a main role in evaluating unknown preference values, as it symbolizes one of the most suitable means to model consistent FPRs. T_LCI was defined to determine the consistency level of the information provided by each expert. The proposed method was used in three steps: firstly, we evaluated the priority weight vector of criteria; secondly, we estimated the priority ratings of each alternative against each criterion; finally, we determined the priority weight vector for alternatives, which allowed us to obtain the best alternative. At the end of this study, we successfully applied the proposed procedure to select a suitable supplier in SCM by illustrating a numerical example to highlight the practicability and efficacy of the method.

In summary, the proposed method has the following major advantages: (i) in this manuscript, T_L-transitivity was considered to measure the FPRs' unspecified preference values. T_L-transitivity is more suitable to model consistent FPRs compared with other consistency-based techniques; (ii) the consistency degrees of experts' opinions were measured to strengthen the final decision; (iii) after reaching the required level of consensus among the experts, first, a ranking of the criteria was established, and then alternatives were prioritized under each criterion based on the consistent information.

To the best of our knowledge, a similar method to deal with MCGDM problems using the AHP model has not previously been proposed. From our perspective, this procedure is an efficient and reliable way to gain a greater insight to solve MCGDM problems in the current environment. This study suffers from limitations that should be addressed in future work: (i) experts might exhibit a degree of hesitancy while providing their preferences—it will be interesting to develop procedures to deal with MCGDM in AHP under hesitant fuzzy preference relations; (ii) the threshold consensus degree η has a direct influence on the consensus round but is typically evaluated in advance—it will be interesting to observe how this parameter can be estimated based on different factors; (iii) there are some risks that some experts may provide their information dishonestly or refuse to make changes with the preferences. Thus, some mechanism may be introduced to handle non-cooperative activities in consensus-building. We will try to work in the above-mentioned directions to face future challenges; these will contribute to the acceptance of this research area.

Author Contributions: Conceptualization, A.u.R., A.S., N.R., S.F. and W.S.; methodology, A.u.R., A.S., N.R., S.F. and W.S.; software, A.u.R., A.S., N.R. and S.F.; validation, F.S. and W.S.; formal analysis, A.u.R. and N.R.; investigation, A.u.R., A.S., N.R., S.F. and W.S.; resources, A.S. and F.S.; data curation, A.u.R., N.R. and W.S.; writing—original draft preparation, A.R., A.S., N.R. and S.F.; writing—review and editing, A.S. and W.S.; visualization, S.F.; supervision, W.S.; project administration, W.S.; funding acquisition, W.S. All authors have read and agreed to the published version of the manuscript.

Funding: The work was supported by the National Science Centre, Decision number UMO-2018/29/B/HS4/02725 and by statutory funds from the Research Team on Intelligent Decision Support Systems, Department of Artificial Intelligence and Applied Mathematics, Faculty of Computer Science and Information Technology, West Pomeranian University of Technology in Szczecin.

Institutional Review Board Statement: Not applicable.

Informed Consent Statement: Not applicable.

Data Availability Statement: Not applicable.

Acknowledgments: The authors would like to thank the editor and the anonymous reviewers, whose insightful comments and constructive suggestions helped us to significantly improve the quality of this paper.

Conflicts of Interest: The authors declare no conflict of interest.

Abbreviations

The following abbreviations are used in this manuscript:

AHP	Analytical Hierarchy Process
FPR	Fuzzy preference relation
IFPR	Incomplete fuzzy preference relation
MPR	Multiplicative preference relation
SCM	Supply chain management
GDM	Group decision-making
MCDM	Multi-criteria decision-making
MCGDM	Multi-criteria group decision-making

References

1. Durmić, E.; Stević, Ž.; Chatterjee, P.; Vasiljević, M.; Tomašević, M. Sustainable supplier selection using combined FUCOM—Rough SAW model. *Rep. Mech. Eng.* **2020**, *1*, 34–43. [CrossRef]
2. Sałabun, W.; Ziemba, P. Application of the Characteristic Objects Method in Supply Chain Management and Logistics. In *Recent Developments in Intelligent Information and Database Systems*; Springer: Berlin/Heidelberg, Germany, 2016; pp. 445–453.
3. Badi, I.; Pamucar, D. Supplier selection for steelmaking company by using combined Grey-MARCOS methods. *Decis. Mak. Appl. Manag. Eng.* **2020**, *3*, 37–48. [CrossRef]
4. Chakraborty, S.; Chattopadhyay, R.; Chakraborty, S. An integrated D-MARCOS method for supplier selection in an iron and steel industry. *Decis. Mak. Appl. Manag. Eng.* **2020**, *3*, 49–69.
5. Swaminathan, J.M.; Tayur, S.R. Models for supply chains in e-business. *Manage. Sci.* **2003**, *49*, 1387–1406. [CrossRef]
6. Chen, C.T.; Lin, C.T.; Huang, S.F. A fuzzy approach for supplier evaluation & selection in supply chain management. *Int. J. Prod. Econ.* **2006**, *102*, 289–301.
7. De Boer, L.; Labro, E.; Morlacchi, P. A review of methods supporting supplier selection. *Eur. J. Purch. Supply Manag.* **2001**, *7*, 75–89. [CrossRef]
8. Demirtas, E.; Üstün, Ö. An integrated multiobjective decision making process for supplier selection and order allocation. *Omega* **2008**, *36*, 76–90. [CrossRef]
9. Hwang, C.L.; Yoon, K. *Multiple Attributes Decision Making Methods & Applications*; Springer: New York, NY, USA, 1981.
10. Ng, W.L. An efficient & simple model for multiple criteria supplier selection problem. *Eur. J. Oper. Res.* **2008**, *186*, 1059–1067.
11. Dickson, G.W. A analysis of vender selection systems & decisions. *J. Suppl. Chain Manag.* **1966**, *2*, 5–17.
12. Barbarosoglu, G.; Yazgaç, T. An application of the analytic hierarchy process to the supplier selection problem. *Prod. Inventory Manag. J.* **1997**, *38*, 14–21.
13. Goffin, K.; Szwejczewski, M.; New, C. Managing suppliers when fewer can mean more, *Int. J. Phys. Distrib. Logist. Manag.* **1997**, *27*, 422–436. [CrossRef]
14. Swift, C.O. Preference for single sourcing & supplier selection criteria. *J. Bus. Res.* **1995**, *32*, 105–111.
15. Weber, C.A.; Current, J.R.; Benton, W.C. Vender selection criteria & method. *Eur. J. Oper. Res.* **1991**, *50*, 2–18.
16. Chai, J.; Liu, J.N.K.; Ngai, E.W.T. Application of decision-making techniques in supplier selection: A systematic review of literature. *Expert Syst. Appl.* **2013**, *40*, 3872–3885. [CrossRef]
17. Faizi, S.; Sałabun, W.; Rashid, T.; Wątróbski, J.; Zafar, S. Group decision-making for hesitant fuzzy sets based on characteristic objects method. *Symmetry* **2017**, *9*, 136. [CrossRef]
18. Faizi, S.; Sałabun, W.; Rashid, T.; Zafar, S.; Wątróbski, J. Intuitionistic fuzzy sets in multi-criteria group decision making problems using the characteristic objects method. *Symmetry* **2020**, *12*, 1382. [CrossRef]
19. Chen, P.C. A fuzzy multiple criteria decision making model in employee recruitment. *Int. J. Comput. Sci. Net. Secur.* **2009**, *9*, 113–117.
20. Hadi-Vencheh, A.; Mokhtarian, M.N. A new fuzzy MCDM approach based on centroid of fuzzy numbers. *Expert Syst. Appl.* **2011**, *38*, 5226–5230. [CrossRef]
21. Önüt, S.; Efendigil, T.; Kara, S.S. A combined fuzzy MCDM approach for selecting shopping center site: An example from Istanbul, Turkey. *Expert Syst. Appl.* **2010**, *37*, 1973–1980. [CrossRef]
22. Srdevic, Z.; Blagojevic, B.; Srdevic, B. AHP based group decision making in ranking loan applicants for purchasing irrigation equipment: A case study. *Bulg. J. Agric. Sci.* **2011**, *17*, 531–543.
23. Sun, C.C.; Lin, G.T.R.; Tzeng, G.H. The evaluation of cluster policy by fuzzy MCDM: Empirical evidence from Hsin Chu Science Park. *Expert Syst. Appl.* **2009**, *36*, 11895–11906. [CrossRef]
24. Wu, H.Y.; Tzeng, G.H.; Chen, Y.H. A fuzzy MCDM approach for evaluating banking performance based on balanced scorecard. *Expert Syst. Appl.* **2009**, *36*, 10135–10147. [CrossRef]
25. Bashir, Z.; Rashid, T.; Wątróbski, J. Sałabun, W.; Malik, A. Hesitant probabilistic multiplicative preference relations in group decision making. *Appl. Sci.* **2018**, *8*, 398. [CrossRef]
26. Kim, S.H.; Ahn, B.S. Interactive group decision making procedure under incomplete information. *Eur. J. Oper. Res.* **1999**, *116*, 498–507. [CrossRef]
27. Xu, Z.S. Goal programming models for obtaining the priority vector of incomplete fuzzy preference relation. *Int. J. Approx. Reason.* **2004**, *36*, 261–270. [CrossRef]
28. Gong, Z.W. Least-square method to priority of the fuzzy preference relations with incomplete information. *Int. J. Approx. Reason.* **2008**, *47*, 258–264. [CrossRef]
29. Herrera-Viedma, E.; Chiclana, F.; Herrera, F.; Alonso, S. Group decision-making model with incomplete fuzzy preference relations based on additive consistency. *IEEE Trans. Syst. Man Cybern. Part B Cybern.* **2007**, *37*, 176–189. [CrossRef]
30. Alonso, S.; Chiclana, F.; Herrera, F.; Herrera-Viedma, E. A consistency based procedure to estimate missing pairwise preference values. *Int. J. Intell. Syst.* **2008**, *23*, 155–175. [CrossRef]
31. Xu, Y.J. On group decision making with four formats of incomplete preference relations. *Comput. Ind. Eng.* **2011**, *61*, 48–54. [CrossRef]
32. Lee, L.W. Group decision making with incomplete fuzzy preference relations based on the additive consistency and the order consistency. *Expert Syst. Appl.* **2012**, *39*, 11666–11676. [CrossRef]

33. Chen, S.M.; Lin, T.E.; Lee, L.W. Group decision making using incomplete fuzzy preference relations based on the additive consistency and the order consistency. *Inf. Sci.* **2014**, *259*, 1–15. [CrossRef]
34. Rehman, A.; Kerre, E.E.; Ashraf, S. Group decision making by using incomplete fuzzy preference relations based on *T*-Consistency Order Consistency. *Int. J. Intell. Syst.* **2015**, *30*, 120–143. [CrossRef]
35. Kerre, E.E.; Rehman, A.U.; Ashraf, S. Group decision making with incomplete reciprocal preference relations based on multiplicative consistency. *Int. J. Comput. Intell. Syst.* **2018**, *11*, 1030–1040. [CrossRef]
36. Saaty, T.L. *The Analytic Hierarchy Process: Planning, Priority Setting & Resource Allocation*; McGraw-Hill: New York, NY, USA, 1980.
37. Saaty, T.L. How to make a decision: The analytic hierarchy process. *Eur. J. Oper. Res.* **1990**, *48*, 9–26. [CrossRef]
38. Lin, C.T.; Hsu, P.F. Adopting an analytic hierarchy process to select internet advertising networks. *Mark. Intell. Plan.* **2003**, *21*, 183–191. [CrossRef]
39. Omasa, T.; Kisshimoto, M.; Kawase, M.; Yagi, K. An attempt at decision making in tissue engineering: Reactor evaluation using the analytic hierarchy process (AHP). *Biochem. Eng. J.* **2004**, *20*, 173–179. [CrossRef]
40. Wei, C.C.; Chien, C.F.; Wang, M.J. An AHP-based approach to ERP system selection. *Int. J. Prod. Econ.* **2005**, *96*, 47–62. [CrossRef]
41. Tanino, T. Fuzzy preference relations in group decision making. In *Non-Conventional Preference Relations in Decision Making*; Lecture Notes in Economics and Mathematical Systems; Springer: Berlin/Heidelberg, Germany, 1988; Volume 301, pp. 54–71.
42. Venugopalan, P. Fuzzy ordered sets. *Fuzzy Sets Syst.* **1992**, *46*, 221–226. [CrossRef]
43. Zadeh, L.A. Fuzzy sets. *Inf. Control* **1965**, *8*, 338–353. [CrossRef]
44. Tanino, T. Fuzzy preference orderings in group decision making. *Fuzzy Sets Syst.* **1984**, *12*, 117–131. [CrossRef]
45. Ureña, R.; Chiclana, F.; Alonso, S.; Morente-Molinera, J.A.; Herrera-Viedma, E. On incomplete fuzzy and multiplicative preference relations in multi-person decision making. *Procedia Comput. Sci.* **2014**, *31*, 793–801. [CrossRef]
46. Zhang, X.; Ge, B.; Jiang, J.; Tan, Y. Consensus building in group decision making based on multiplicative consistency with incomplete reciprocal preference relations. *Knowl.-Based Syst.* **2016**, *106*, 96–104. [CrossRef]
47. Sałabun, W.; Urbaniak, K. A new coefficient of rankings similarity in decision-making problems. In *International Conference on Computational Science*; Springer: Cham, Switzerland, 2020; pp. 632–645.

symmetry

MDPI

Article

Representations of a Comparison Measure between Two Fuzzy Sets

Juin-Han Chen [1] and Hui-Chin Tang [2,*]

[1] Department of Industrial Engineering and Management, Cheng Shiu University, Kaohsiung 83347, Taiwan; K0411@gcloud.csu.edu.tw
[2] Department of Industrial Engineering and Management, National Kaohsiung University of Science and Technology, Kaohsiung 80778, Taiwan
* Correspondence: tang@nkust.edu.tw

Received: 24 October 2020; Accepted: 3 December 2020; Published: 5 December 2020

Abstract: This paper analyzes the representation behaviors of a comparison measure between two compared fuzzy sets. Three types of restrictions on two fuzzy sets are considered in this paper: two disjoint union fuzzy sets, two disjoint fuzzy sets and two general fuzzy sets. Differences exist among the numbers of possible representations of a comparison measure for the three types of fuzzy sets restrictions. The value of comparison measure is constant for two disjoint union fuzzy sets. There are 49 candidate representations of a comparison measure for two disjoint fuzzy sets, of which 13 candidate representations with one or two terms are obtained. For each candidate representation, a variant of the general axiomatic definition for a comparison measure is presented. Choosing the right candidate representation for a given application, we can easily and efficiently calculate and compare a comparison measure.

Keywords: fuzzy set; comparison measure; representation; disjoint

---

1. Introduction

The concept of fuzzy sets (FSs), proposed by Zadeh [1], is characterized by a membership function and has successfully been applied in various fields. This paper deals with the well-known notions of comparison measures between two compared FSs. A comparison measure calculates the degree of equality or inequality between two compared FSs. Some related definitions such as similarity, similitude, proximity or resemblance were proposed for the equality measures [2–18], as well as some other dual definitions such as dissimilarity, dissimilitude, divergence or distance for the inequality measures [6,9,13,18–23]. The inequality measures have received much less attention in the literature. The degree of comparison measure is an important tool for cluster analysis [8], decision-making [7,14,21,22], e-waste [2,17,20], image processing [10], medical diagnosis [13], pattern recognition [3,4,9,12] and service quality [11,18]. Recently, many papers [5,9,10,12,15,16,18,20–22] have been dedicated to the comparison measures, and research on this area is still carried out in the literature.

Couso et al. [6] surveyed a large collection of axiomatic definitions from the literature regarding the notions of comparison measures between two compared FSs. Three separate lists of properties are provided: general axioms, axioms for the equality measures and axioms for the inequality measures. One of the general axioms of a comparison measure is as follows. For two disjoint FSs, A and B, if both comparison measures between A and empty set and that of B and empty set are less, then the degree of a comparison measure $m(A,B)$ between A and B is less. More precisely, if $A \cap B = \varnothing$, $A' \cap B' = \varnothing$, $m(A,\varnothing) \leq m(A',\varnothing)$ and $m(B,\varnothing) \leq m(B',\varnothing)$, then $m(A,B) \leq m(A',B')$, for all FSs A, B, A', B'. From this axiomatic definition, we analyze the comparison measure behaviors of two FSs, A and B, in terms of the other simple comparison measures, especially for the intersection and the union of A and B, the empty set and the universal set. This general axiomatic definition has received much less attention in the literature. Consider a local divergence $d(A,\ B)$ for two disjoint FSs A and B, proposed by Montes et al. [19]. Couso et al. [6] showed that $d(A,\ B) = d(A,\ \varnothing) + d(B,\ \varnothing)$, which satisfies this general axiomatic definition. This paper adopts the representations of a comparison measure to generalize this axiomatic definition and to efficiently compare the comparison measure between two FSs. The representations of a comparison measure between two FSs can not only present the important components of a comparison measure but also analyze the comparison measure behaviors of two FSs in terms of other simple comparison measures. The representative equivalence between two representations indicates that these representations fulfill symmetric property.

To analyze the representation behaviors of a comparison measure between two FSs, three kinds of two FSs are considered in this paper: two disjoint union FSs, two disjoint FSs and two general FSs. The two disjoint union FSs is a special case of two disjoint FSs, and the latter is a special case of two general FSs. Both special cases derive some interesting results, especially for the case of two disjoint FSs. For two FSs A and B, this paper deals with the representations of a comparison measure for the case that $A \cap B = \varnothing$ and $A \cup B = U$, the case that $A \cap B = \varnothing$ and the general FSs A and B.

The organization of this paper is as follows. Section 2 briefly reviews the FSs and the comparison measures between two compared FSs. We present representations of a comparison measure for two disjoint union FSs in Section 3, two disjoint FSs in Section 4 and two general FSs in Section 5. Finally, some concluding remarks and future research are presented.

2. Fuzzy Sets and Comparison Measures

We firstly review the basic notations of FSs. Let U be a non-empty universal set or referential set.

Definition 1. *A FS A over U is defined as*

$$A = \{(x,\ \mu_A(x))|x \in U\}$$

where the membership function $\mu_A(x) : U \to [0,1]$. *We denote by* $\mathcal{F}(U)$ *the set of all FSs over U.*

Definition 2. *For two FSs* $A, B \in \mathcal{F}(U)$, *define the membership functions of* $A \cap B$, $A \cup B$ *and* $A \backslash B$ *as follows:*

1. $\mu_{A\cap B}(x) = min\{\mu_A(x), \mu_B(x)\}$.
2. $\mu_{A\cup B}(x) = max\{\mu_A(x), \mu_B(x)\}$.
3. $\mu_{A\backslash B}(x) = min\{\mu_A(x), 1 - \mu_B(x)\}$.

We now recall the definition of comparison measures between two FSs. The following properties are general axioms that may be required in equality measure and inequality measure between two FSs [6].

Definition 3. *A comparison measure* $m : \mathcal{F}(U)^2 \to \mathcal{R}$ *should satisfy the following properties:*

- *G1:* $0 \le m(A,B) \le 1, \forall\, A, B \in \mathcal{F}(U)$.
- *G1*:* $0 \le m(A,B) \le 1, \forall\, A, B \in \mathcal{F}(U)$ *and there exists two FSs* $C, D \in \mathcal{F}(U)$ *such that* $m(C,D) = 1$.
- *G2:* $m(A,B) = m(B,A), \forall\, A, B \in \mathcal{F}(U)$.
- *G3: Let* $\rho : U \to U$ *be a permutation for finite U. Define* $A^\rho \in \mathcal{F}(U)$ *with membership function* $\mu_{A^\rho}(x) = \mu_A(\rho(x))$ *for* $A \in \mathcal{F}(U)$. *Then* $m(A,B) = m(A^\rho, B^\rho)$.
- *G3*: For finite set U, there exists a function* $h : [0,1] \times [0,1] \to \mathcal{R}$ *such that* $m(A,B) = \sum_{x\in U} h(\mu_A(x), \mu_B(x)), \forall\, A, B \in \mathcal{F}(U)$.
- *G4: There exists a function* $f : \mathcal{F}(U)^3 \to \mathcal{R}$ *such that* $m(A,B) = f(A \cap B, A\backslash B, B\backslash A), \forall\, A, B \in \mathcal{F}(U)$.
- *G4*: There exists a function* $F : \mathcal{R}^3 \to \mathcal{R}$ *and a fuzzy measure* $M : \mathcal{F}(U) \to \mathcal{R}$ *such that* $m(A,B) = F(M(A \cap B), M(A\backslash B), M(B\backslash A)), \forall\, A, B \in \mathcal{F}(U)$.

- *G5: If $A \cap B = \varnothing$, $A' \cap B' = \varnothing$, $m(A,\varnothing) \leq m(A',\varnothing)$ and $m(B,\varnothing) \leq m(B',\varnothing)$, then $m(A,B) \leq m(A',B')$, $\forall\, A,B,A',B' \in \mathcal{F}(U)$.*

Couso et al. [6] showed that the asterisk will be understood as stronger than. More precisely, if a comparison measure satisfies Gi*, then it fulfills Gi, for $i = 1, 3, 4$.

Consider a fuzzy measure $M: \mathcal{F}(U) \to \mathcal{R}$ with $M(A \cap B) = c$, $M(A\backslash B) = a$ and $M(B\backslash A) = b$, $a,\ b,\ c \in [0,\ 1]$. Define a comparison measure as follows:

$$m(A,B) = F(M(A \cap B), M(A\backslash B), M(B\backslash A)) = F(c,a,b) = \frac{c+1-a+1-b}{3}.$$

For two disjoint FSs A and B, we have

$$m(A,B) = F(0,a,b) = \frac{2-a-b}{3},$$

$$m(A,\varnothing) = F(0,\ a,\ 0) = \frac{2-a}{3}$$

and

$$m(B,\varnothing) = F(0,\ b,\ 0) = \frac{2-b}{3},$$

it implies that

$$m(A,\ B) = -\frac{2}{3} + m(A,\ \varnothing) + m(B,\varnothing).$$

If $A \cap B = \varnothing$, $A' \cap B' = \varnothing$, $m(A,\varnothing) \leq m(A',\varnothing)$ and $m(B,\varnothing) \leq m(B',\varnothing)$, we obtain

$$m(A,B) = -\frac{2}{3} + m(A,\ \varnothing) + m(B,\varnothing) \leq -\frac{2}{3} + m(A',\ \varnothing) + m(B',\varnothing) = m(A',B')$$

which coincides with the result of G5. The representation of $m(A,\ B)$ can not only present its important ingredients but also compare $m(A,\ B)$ in terms of other measures $m(A,\ \varnothing)$ and $m(B,\varnothing)$. On the other hand, we have

$$m(A,U) = F(a,\ 0,\ 1-a) = \frac{1+2a}{3},$$

$$m(B,U) = F(b,\ 0,\ 1-b) = \frac{1+2b}{3}$$

and

$$m(A,\ B) = 1 - \frac{1}{2}m(A,U) - \frac{1}{2}m(B,U).$$

The general axiomatic definition G5 can be written as follows.

If $A \cap B = \varnothing$, $A' \cap B' = \varnothing$, $m(A,U) \geq m(A',U)$ and $m(B,U) \geq m(B',U)$, then $m(A,B) \leq m(A',B')$, $\forall\, A,B,A',B' \in \mathcal{F}(U)$.

Applying different representations of $m(A,B)$, the alternative expressions of the general axiom G5 are presented. For two FSs, A and B, the adopted components of a comparison measure are A, B, the intersection and the union of A and B, the empty set and the universal set. To represent a comparison measure $m(A,\ B)$, the adopted comparison measures other than $m(A,\ B)$ are $m(X,Y)$ for different FSs, X and Y, $(X,Y) \neq (A,\ B)$, $X,Y \in \{\varnothing,\ A,\ B,\ A\cap B,\ A\cup B,\ U\}$.

The following sections list the representations of a comparison measure $m(A,\ B)$ for two disjoint union FSs A and B, two disjoint FSs A and B and two general FSs A and B. More precisely, we consider the case that $A \cap B = \varnothing$ and $A \cup B = U$ for Section 3, $A \cap B = \varnothing$ for Section 4 and the general FSs A and B for Section 5. Sections 3 and 4 are special cases of Section 5. Some interesting conclusions can be drawn from these special cases.

3. Representations of a Comparison Measure for Two Disjoint Union Fuzzy Sets

This section will present the representations of a comparison measure $m(A,\ B)$ for two disjoint union FSs A and B. For $A \cap B = \varnothing$ and $A \cup B = U$, we have that $M(A \cap B) = 0$, $M(A \cup B) = 1$, $M(A \backslash B) = a$, $M(B \backslash A) = b$, $a + b = 1$, $a,\ b \in [0,\ 1]$ and

$$m(A,B) = F(M(A \cap B), M(A \backslash B), M(B \backslash A)) = F(0,a,b) = \frac{2-a-b}{3} = \frac{1}{3}.$$

Since $A \cap B = \varnothing$ and $A \cup B = U$, the adopted components of a comparison measure are $\{\varnothing,\ A,\ B,\ U\}$. For two different FSs, X and Y, $X, Y \in \{\varnothing,\ A,\ B,\ U\}$, the number of the possible forms of $m(X,Y)$ is six described as follows:

$$m(A,B) = F(0,a,b) = \frac{1}{3},$$

$$m(A,\varnothing) = F(0,\ a,\ 0) = \frac{2-a}{3},$$

$$m(B,\varnothing) = F(0,\ b,\ 0) = \frac{2-b}{3},$$

$$m(A,U) = F(a,\ 0,\ 1-a) = \frac{1+2a}{3},$$

$$m(B,U) = F(b,\ 0,\ 1-b) = \frac{1+2b}{3}$$

and

$$m(\varnothing,U) = F(0,0,1) = \frac{1}{3}.$$

From these six measures $m(X,Y)$, we obtain six equations for the representations of $\frac{a}{3}$ and six equations for those of $\frac{b}{3}$ presented as follows:

$$\begin{aligned} \tfrac{a}{3} &= \tfrac{1}{2}(m(A,\ U) - m(A,\ B)) = m(B,\ \varnothing) - m(A,\ B) \\ &= \tfrac{1}{2}\big(\tfrac{4}{3} - m(A,\ B) - m(B,\ U)\big) = \tfrac{4}{3} - m(B,\ U) - m(B,\ \varnothing) \\ &= m(A,\ U) - m(B,\varnothing) = \tfrac{1}{2}(1 - m(B,\ U)) \end{aligned}$$

and

$$\begin{aligned} \tfrac{b}{3} &= \tfrac{1}{2}(m(B,\ U) - m(A,\ B)) = m(A,\ \varnothing) - m(A,\ B) \\ &= \tfrac{1}{2}\big(\tfrac{4}{3} - m(A,\ B) - m(A,U)\big) = \tfrac{4}{3} - m(A,\ U) - m(A,\ \varnothing) \\ &= m(B,U) - m(A,\varnothing) = \tfrac{1}{2}(1 - m(A,\ U)). \end{aligned}$$

Since the constant value of

$$m(A,B) = \frac{1}{3}$$

for $A \cap B = \varnothing$ and $A \cup B = U$, we cannot compare the degree of $m(A,B)$ for two disjoint union FSs A and B.

4. Representations of a Comparison Measure for Two Disjoint Fuzzy Sets

For two disjoint FSs A and B, $A \cap B = \varnothing$, we denote $M(A \cap B) = 0$, $M(A \backslash B) = a$, $M(B \backslash A) = b$, $a,\ b \in [0,\ 1]$ and

$$m(A,B) = F(M(A \cap B), M(A \backslash B), M(B \backslash A)) = F(0,a,b) = \frac{2-a-b}{3}.$$

The number of total combinations $m(X,Y)$ for two different FSs, X and Y, $X,Y \in \{\varnothing,\ A,\ B,\ A\cup B,\ U\}$, is 10 presented as follows:

$$m(A,B) = F(0,a,b) = \frac{2-a-b}{3},$$

$$m(A,\varnothing) = F(0,\ a,\ 0) = \frac{2-a}{3},$$

$$m(B,\varnothing) = F(0,\ b,\ 0) = \frac{2-b}{3},$$

$$m(A,A\cup B) = F(a,\ 0,\ b) = \frac{2+a-b}{3},$$

$$m(B,A\cup B) = F(b,\ 0,\ a) = \frac{2-a+b}{3},$$

$$m(A,U) = F(a,\ 0,\ 1-a) = \frac{1+2a}{3},$$

$$m(B,U) = F(b,\ 0,\ 1-b) = \frac{1+2b}{3},$$

$$m(A\cup B,\varnothing) = F(0,\ a+b,\ 0) = \frac{2-a-b}{3},$$

$$m(A\cup B,U) = F(a+b,0,1-a-b) = \frac{1+2a+2b}{3}$$

and

$$m(\varnothing,U) = F(0,0,1) = \frac{1}{3}.$$

To represent $m(A,B) = \frac{2-a-b}{3}$, from above ten measures $m(X,Y)$, we obtain nine equations for the representations of $\frac{a}{3}$ and nine equations for those of $\frac{b}{3}$ described as follows:

$$\frac{a}{3}$$

$$
\begin{aligned}
&[1]= \tfrac{1}{2}(m(A,\ A\cup B) - m(A,\ B))\\
&[2]= m(B,\ \varnothing) - m(A,\ B)\\
&[3]= \tfrac{1}{2}\left(\tfrac{4}{3} - m(A,\ B) - m(B,\ A\cup B)\right)\\
&[4]= \tfrac{1}{2}\left(\tfrac{5}{3} - 2m(A,\ B) - m(B,\ U)\right)\\
&[5]= \tfrac{4}{3} - m(B,\ A\cup B) - m(B,\ \varnothing)\\
&[6]= m(A,\ A\cup B) - m(B,\varnothing)\\
&[7]= \tfrac{1}{2}\left(-\tfrac{5}{3} + m(A\cup B,U) + 2m(B,\ \varnothing)\right)\\
&[8]= \tfrac{1}{4}(1 + m(A\cup B,U) - 2m(B,\ A\cup B))\\
&[9]= \tfrac{1}{2}(m(A\cup B,U) - m(B,\ U))
\end{aligned}
$$

and

$$\frac{b}{3}$$

$$\begin{aligned}
[1] &= \tfrac{1}{2}(m(B,\ A\cup B) - m(A,\ B)) \\
[2] &= m(A,\ \varnothing) - m(A,\ B) \\
[3] &= \tfrac{1}{2}\left(\tfrac{4}{3} - m(A,\ B) - m(A,\ A\cup B)\right) \\
[4] &= \tfrac{1}{2}\left(\tfrac{5}{3} - 2m(A,\ B) - m(A,\ U)\right) \\
[5] &= \tfrac{4}{3} - m(A,\ A\cup B) - m(A,\ \varnothing) \\
[6] &= m(B,\ A\cup B) - m(A,\varnothing) \\
[7] &= \tfrac{1}{2}\left(-\tfrac{5}{3} + m(A\cup B, U) + 2m(A,\ \varnothing)\right) \\
[8] &= \tfrac{1}{4}(1 + m(A\cup B, U) - 2m(A,\ A\cup B)) \\
[9] &= \tfrac{1}{2}(m(A\cup B, U) - m(A,\ U)).
\end{aligned}$$

The number of the total combinations of forms of $\frac{a}{3}$ and $\frac{b}{3}$ to represent a comparison measure $m(A,\ B)$ is $9\times 9 = 81$. We will denote by [i]-[j], the combination of ith form of $\frac{a}{3}$ and jth form of $\frac{b}{3}$ to represent $m(A,\ B)$. We classify these 81 combinations into four types (I, II, III, IV). The first type I is the candidate representation of a comparison measure $m(A,\ B)$. For example, the combination [1]-[2], the 1st form of $\frac{a}{3}$ and the 2nd form of $\frac{b}{3}$ are adopted. Applying $\frac{a}{3} = \frac{1}{2}(m(A,\ A\cup B) - m(A,\ B))$ and $\frac{b}{3} = m(A,\ \varnothing) - m(A,\ B)$ to $m(A,B) = \frac{2-a-b}{3}$, we obtain

$$m(A,B) = \frac{2}{3} - \frac{1}{2}(m(A,\ A\cup B) - m(A,\ B)) - (m(A,\ \varnothing) - m(A,\ B)) = -\frac{4}{3} + m(A,\ A\cup B) + 2m(A,\ \varnothing).$$

Among these 81 combinations, there are 49 candidate representations of $m(A,\ B)$ for type I. The number of terms $m(X,Y)$, $X,Y \in \{\varnothing,\ A,\ B,\ A\cup B,\ U\}$ of a candidate representation of $m(A,\ B)$ is 1, 2, 3 and 4, except for the constant term. There are 1, 12, 27 and 9 candidate representations of $m(A,\ B)$ for the number of terms being 1, 2, 3 and 4, respectively. The combination [1]-[8] is the one term $m(X,Y)$ of a candidate representation of $m(A,\ B)$ as follows.

$$[1]\text{-}[8] : m(A,B) = \frac{5}{6} - \frac{1}{2}m(A\cup B, U).$$

Using this candidate representation, a variant of general axiom G5 is described as follows. If $A\cap B = \varnothing$, $A'\cap B' = \varnothing$ and $m(A\cup B, U) \geq m(A'\cup B', U)$, then $m(A,B) \leq m(A',B')$. The two terms $m(X,Y)$, $X,Y \in \{\varnothing,\ A,\ B,\ A\cup B,\ U\}$ of candidate representations of $m(A,\ B)$ are as follows.

$$[1]\text{-}[2] : m(A,\ B) = -\frac{4}{3} + m(A,\ A\cup B) + 2m(A,\ \varnothing)$$

$$[2]\text{-}[1] : m(A,B) = -\frac{4}{3} + m(B,\ A\cup B) + 2m(B,\ \varnothing)$$

$$[2]\text{-}[2] : m(A,\ B) = -\frac{2}{3} + m(A,\ \varnothing) + m(B,\varnothing)$$

$$[2]\text{-}[3] : m(A,B) = -\,m(A,\ A\cup B) + 2m(B,\ \varnothing)$$

$$[3]\text{-}[2] : m(A,\ B) = -m(B,\ A\cup B) + 2m(A,\ \varnothing)$$

$$[2]\text{-}[4] : m(A,\ B) = \frac{1}{6} - \frac{1}{2}m(A,U) + m(B,\ \varnothing)$$

$$[4]\text{-}[2] : m(A,\ B) = \frac{1}{6} - \frac{1}{2}m(B,U) + m(A,\ \varnothing)$$

$$[1]\text{-}[4] : m(A,\ B) = \frac{1}{3} + m(A,\ A\cup B) - m(A,U)$$

$$[4]\text{-}[1] : m(A,B) = \frac{1}{3} + m(B,\ A\cup B) - m(B,U)$$

$$[4]\text{-}[4]:\ m(A,\ B) = 1 - \frac{1}{2}m(A, U) - \frac{1}{2}m(B, U)$$

$$[3]\text{-}[4]:\ m(A,\ B) = \frac{5}{3} - m(B,\ A \cup B) - m(A, U)$$

and

$$[4]\text{-}[3]:\ m(A, B) = \frac{5}{3} - m(A,\ A \cup B) - m(B,\ U).$$

If FSs A and B are interchanged, the representation of combination [1]-[2] becomes

$$m(B, A) = -\frac{4}{3} + m(B,\ A \cup B) + 2m(B,\ \varnothing)$$

which is equal to the representation of combination [2]-[1]. This symmetric property is also satisfied for combinations [2]-[3] and [3]-[2], combinations [2]-[4] and [4]-[2], combinations [1]-[4] and [4]-[1], combinations [3]-[4] and [4]-[3]. While combinations [2]-[2] and [4]-[4] derive the same representation when FSs A and B are interchanged. Therefore, if combination [i]-[j]: $m(A,\ B)$ is a candidate representation, then both combination [i]-[j]: $m(B, A)$ and combination [j]-[i]: $m(A,\ B)$ are equal and are also candidate representations.

The second type II is the relationship between different terms of $m(X, Y)$, $X, Y \in \{\varnothing,\ A,\ B,\ A \cup B,\ U\}$ other than $m(A,\ B)$. For example, the combination [1]-[1], $\frac{a}{3} = \frac{1}{2}(m(A,\ A \cup B) - m(A,\ B))$ and $\frac{b}{3} = \frac{1}{2}(m(B,\ A \cup B) - m(A,\ B))$, we get that

$$m(A, B) = \frac{2}{3} - \frac{1}{2}(m(A,\ A \cup B) - m(A,\ B)) - \frac{1}{2}(m(B,\ A \cup B) - m(A,\ B))$$

so

$$m(A,\ A \cup B) + m(B,\ A \cup B) = \frac{4}{3}.$$

The combinations [1]-[1], [2]-[5], [2]-[6], [2]-[7], [2]-[8], [2]-[9], [3]-[3], [4]-[5], [4]-[6], [4]-[7], [4]-[8], [4]-[9], [5]-[2], [5]-[4], [6]-[2], [6]-[4], [7]-[2], [7]-[4], [8]-[2], [8]-[4] and [9]-[2] are included in type II. Among these 21 combinations, the number of different relationships between different terms of $m(X, Y)$, $X, Y \in \{\varnothing,\ A,\ B,\ A \cup B,\ U\}$ other than $m(A,\ B)$ is 16.

The third type III is the identical equation 0=0. For example, for the combination [1]-[3], we obtain

$$m(A, B) = \frac{2}{3} - \frac{1}{2}(m(A,\ A \cup B) - m(A,\ B)) - \frac{1}{2}\left(\frac{4}{3} - m(A,\ B) - m(A,\ A \cup B)\right)$$

so

$$0 = 0.$$

The combinations [1]-[3], [3]-[1] and [9]-[4] are listed in the type III.

The fourth type IV is the duplicate representations of a comparison measure $m(A,\ B)$ which appear in type I. For example, for the combination [1]-[5], we obtain that

$$m(A, B) = \frac{2}{3} - \frac{1}{2}(m(A,\ A \cup B) - m(A,\ B)) - \left(\frac{4}{3} - m(A,\ A \cup B) - m(A,\ \varnothing)\right)$$

$$m(A, B) = -\frac{4}{3} + m(A,\ A \cup B) + 2m(A,\ \varnothing)$$

which is the same as that of combination [1]-[2]. For simplicity, we adopt the notation [1]-[2] ≡ [1]-[5] to denote the representative equivalence between [1]-[2] and [1]-[5]. There are eight combinations in type IV described as follows:

[2]-[2] ≡[5]-[6] ≡[6]-[5] ≡ [7]-[6],

[1]-[2] ≡[[8]-[1], [2]-[1] ≡[[6]-[3] and [3]-[2] ≡ [3]-[6].

The largest number of duplicate representations is three with the associated combination [2]-[2]

$$m(A,\ B) = -\frac{2}{3} + m(A,\ \varnothing) + m(B, \varnothing).$$

Therefore, there are 81 combinations of a comparison measure $m(A,\ B)$ for $A \cap B = \varnothing$. Among these 81 combinations, we obtain 49 candidate representations of $m(A,\ B)$, 8 duplicate representations of $m(A,\ B)$, 21 relationships between different terms of $m(X, Y)$, $X, Y \in \{\varnothing,\ A,\ B,\ A \cup B,\ U\}$ other than $m(A,\ B)$ and 3 identical equations. There are one and 12 candidate representations of $m(A,\ B)$ for one and two terms $m(X, Y)$, $X, Y \in \{\varnothing,\ A,\ B,\ A \cup B,\ U\}$, respectively. These 13 candidate representations can be used to easily compare $m(A,\ B)$ with $A \cap B = \varnothing$.

5. Representations of a Comparison Measure for Two General Fuzzy Sets

This section lists the representations of a comparison measure $m(A,\ B)$ for two general FSs, A and B. Let $M(A \cap B) = c$, $M(A \backslash B) = a$, $M(B \backslash A) = b$, $a,\ b,\ c \in [0,\ 1]$ and

$$m(A, B) = F(M(A \cap B), M(A \backslash B), M(B \backslash A)) = F(c, a, b) = \frac{c + 1 - a + 1 - b}{3}.$$

The adopted components of a comparison measure are $\{\varnothing,\ A,\ B,\ A \cap B,\ A \cup B,\ U\}$. There are 15 combinations $m(X, Y)$ of different FSs, X and Y, $X, Y \in \{\varnothing,\ A,\ B,\ A \cap B,\ A \cup B,\ U\}$ as follows.

$$m(A, B) = F(c, a, b) = \frac{2 - a - b + c}{3},$$

$$m(A, \varnothing) = F(0,\ a + c,\ 0) = \frac{2 - a - c}{3},$$

$$m(B, \varnothing) = F(0,\ b + c,\ 0) = \frac{2 - b - c}{3},$$

$$m(A, A \cap B) = F(c,\ a,\ 0) = \frac{2 - a + c}{3},$$

$$m(B, A \cap B) = F(c,\ b,\ 0) = \frac{2 - b + c}{3},$$

$$m(A, A \cup B) = F(a + c,\ 0,\ b) = \frac{2 + a - b + c}{3},$$

$$m(B, A \cup B) = F(b + c,\ 0,\ a) = \frac{2 - a + b + c}{3},$$

$$m(A, U) = F(a + c,\ 0,\ 1 - a - c) = \frac{1 + 2a + 2c}{3},$$

$$m(B, U) = F(b + c,\ 0,\ 1 - b - c) = \frac{1 + 2b + 2c}{3},$$

$$m(A \cap B, \varnothing) = F(0,\ c,\ 0) = \frac{2 - c}{3},$$

$$m(A \cup B, \varnothing) = F(0,\ a + b + c,\ 0) = \frac{2 - a - b - c}{3},$$

$$m(A \cap B, \mathrm{A} \cup B) = F(c, a + b, 0) = \frac{2 - a - b + c}{3},$$

$$m(A \cap B, U) = F(c, 0, 1 - c) = \frac{1 + 2c}{3},$$

$$m(A \cup B, U) = F(a + b + c, 0, 1 - a - b - c) = \frac{1 + 2a + 2b + 2c}{3}$$

and

$$m(\varnothing, U) = F(0,0,1) = \frac{1}{3}.$$

One can make several notable observations. Firstly, we have that

$$m(A \cap B, A \cup B) = \frac{2-a-b+c}{3} = m(A, B).$$

So, to calculate the degree of a comparison measure $m(A,B)$ is equivalent to calculate that of $m(A \cap B, A \cup B)$.

Secondly, we have 33 different relationships between different terms of $m(X,Y)$, $X,Y \in \{\varnothing,\ A,\ B,\ A\cap B,\ A\cup B,\ U\}$. Since $m(A,B) = \frac{2-a-b+c}{3}$, from these 33 relationships, we obtain 12 equations for the representations of $\frac{a}{3}$, 12 equations for those of $\frac{b}{3}$ and 3 equations for those of $\frac{c}{3}$ presented as follows:

$$\begin{aligned}\tfrac{a}{3} &= \tfrac{1}{2}(m(A,\ A\cup B) - m(A,\ B)) = m(B,\ A\cap B) - m(A,\ B) = m(A\cap B, \varnothing) - m(A, \varnothing)\\ &= \tfrac{1}{2}\big(\tfrac{4}{3} - m(A,\ A\cap B) - m(A,\ \varnothing)\big) = \tfrac{4}{3} - m(B,\ A\cup B) - m(B,\ \varnothing) = m(A,\ A\cup B) - m(B,\ A\cap B)\\ &= m(B,\ \varnothing) - m(A\cup B,\ \varnothing) = \tfrac{1}{2}\big(\tfrac{4}{3} - m(A\cup B,\ \varnothing) - m(B,\ A\cup B)\big) = \tfrac{1}{2}\big(\tfrac{5}{3} - 2m(A\cup B,\ \varnothing) - m(B,\ U)\big)\\ &= \tfrac{1}{2}\big(-\tfrac{5}{3} + m(A\cup B, U) + 2m(B,\ \varnothing)\big) = \tfrac{1}{4}(1 + m(A\cup B, U) - 2m(B,\ A\cup B)) = \tfrac{1}{2}(m(A\cup B, U) - m(B,\ U)),\end{aligned}$$

$$\begin{aligned}\tfrac{b}{3} &= \tfrac{1}{2}(m(B,\ A\cup B) - m(A,\ B)) = m(A,\ A\cap B) - m(A,\ B) = m(A\cap B, \varnothing) - m(B, \varnothing)\\ &= \tfrac{1}{2}\big(\tfrac{4}{3} - m(B,\ A\cap B) - m(B,\ \varnothing)\big) = \tfrac{4}{3} - m(A,\ A\cup B) - m(A,\ \varnothing) = m(B,\ A\cup B) - m(A,\ A\cap B)\\ &= m(A,\ \varnothing) - m(A\cup B,\ \varnothing) = \tfrac{1}{2}\big(\tfrac{4}{3} - m(A\cup B,\ \varnothing) - m(A,\ A\cup B)\big) = \tfrac{1}{2}\big(\tfrac{5}{3} - 2m(A\cup B,\ \varnothing) - m(A,\ U)\big)\\ &= \tfrac{1}{2}\big(-\tfrac{5}{3} + m(A\cup B, U) + 2m(A,\ \varnothing)\big) = \tfrac{1}{4}(1 + m(A\cup B, U) - 2m(A,\ A\cup B)) = \tfrac{1}{2}(m(A\cup B, U) - m(A,\ U))\end{aligned}$$

and

$$\frac{c}{3} = \frac{1}{2}\Big[m(A,\ A\cap B) - m(A,\ \varnothing)] = \frac{1}{2}[m(B,\ A\cap B) - m(B,\ \varnothing)\Big] = \frac{1}{2}\Big(-\frac{4}{3} + m(A,\ A\cup B) + m(B,\ A\cup B)\Big).$$

The number of total combinations $m(A,B)$ of forms of $\frac{a}{3}$, $\frac{b}{3}$ and $\frac{c}{3}$ is $12\times 12\times 3 = 432$. The number of combinations is large. Detailed representations of a comparison measure $m(A,\ B)$ are available from authors.

From $\frac{a}{3} = m(B,\ A\cap B) - m(A,\ B)$, $\frac{b}{3} = m(A,\ A\cap B) - m(A,\ B)$ and $\frac{c}{3} = \frac{1}{2}[m(A,\ A\cap B) - m(A,\ \varnothing)]$, it implies that

$$m(A,B) = \frac{2}{3} - m(B,\ A\cap B) + m(A,\ B) - m(A,\ A\cap B) + m(A,\ B) + \frac{1}{2}[m(A,\ A\cap B) - m(A,\ \varnothing)]$$

$$m(A,B) = -\frac{2}{3} + \frac{1}{2}m(A,\ A\cap B) + m(B,\ A\cap B) + \frac{1}{2}m(A,\ \varnothing).$$

Similarly, we have that

$$m(A,B) = -\frac{2}{3} + m(A,\ A\cap B) + \frac{1}{2}m(B,\ A\cap B) + \frac{1}{2}m(B,\ \varnothing),$$

$$m(A,B) = \frac{2}{3} - 2m(A\cap B,\ \varnothing) + \frac{1}{2}m(A,\ A\cap B) + \frac{1}{2}m(A,\ \varnothing) + m(B,\ \varnothing)$$

and

$$m(A,B) = \frac{2}{3} - 2m(A\cap B,\ \varnothing) + \frac{1}{2}m(B,\ A\cap B) + m(A,\ \varnothing) + \frac{1}{2}m(B,\ \varnothing).$$

If $A\cap B = \varnothing$, the above four representations of a comparison measure $m(A,\ B)$ reduce to

$$m(A,B) = -\frac{2}{3} + m(A,\ \varnothing) + m(B,\ \varnothing)$$

which is the representation [2]-[2] of a comparison measure $m(A,\ B)$ with $A \cap B = \varnothing$ appearing in Section 4. Therefore, for two disjoint FSs, A and B, the representation of a comparison measure $m(A, B)$ with general FSs can be reduced to that of $m(A, B)$ with $A \cap B = \varnothing$.

6. Conclusions and Future Research

For two FSs, A and B, this paper presents the representations of a comparison measure $m(A, B)$ for two disjoint union FSs, two disjoint FSs and two general FSs. The numbers of total combinations $m(A, B)$ are 36, 81 and 432 for two disjoint union FSs, two disjoint FSs and two general FSs, respectively. The smaller the number of restrictions placed on two FSs, the greater the number of possible representations of a comparison measure. For two disjoint union FSs, the constant value of $m(A, B) = \frac{1}{3}$ implies that we cannot compare the comparison behaviors of two disjoint union FSs A and B. Among the 81 combinations of two disjoint FSs A and B, there are 49 candidate representations of $m(A,\ B)$, 8 duplicate representations of $m(A,\ B)$, 21 relationships between different $m(X, Y)$, $X, Y \in \{\varnothing,\ A,\ B,\ A \cup B,\ U\}$ other than $m(A,\ B)$ and 3 identical equations. There are one and 12 candidate representations of $m(A,\ B)$ for one and two terms $m(X, Y)$, $X, Y \in \{\varnothing,\ A,\ B,\ A \cup B,\ U\}$, respectively. For each candidate representation, if combination [i]-[j]: $m(A,\ B)$ is a candidate representation, then both combination [i]-[j]: $m(B, A)$ and combination [j]-[i]: $m(A,\ B)$ are also candidate representations. The representative equivalence between combination [i]-[j]: $m(B, A)$ and combination [j]-[i]: $m(A,\ B)$ indicates that the candidate representation fulfills symmetric property. Applying these 13 candidate representations, the alternative expressions of the general axiom G5 are presented. Choosing the right general axiom G5 for a given application, we can easily and efficiently calculate and compare the degree of a comparison measure $m(A,\ B)$ with $A \cap B = \varnothing$.

In the future, we will analyze the representation behaviors of comparison measures for the generalization of FSs and the general forms of a comparison measure. In particular, the analysis can be extended to the intuitionistic fuzzy sets, hesitant fuzzy sets and neutrosophic sets. Thus, the representation analysis of comparison measures for the intuitionistic fuzzy sets is a subject of considerable ongoing research.

Author Contributions: Both J.-H.C. and H.-C.T. contributed equally towards the accomplishment of this research. All authors have read and agreed to the published version of the manuscript.

Funding: This research received no external funding.

Conflicts of Interest: The authors declare that they have no competing interests.

References

1. Zadeh, L.A. Fuzzy sets. *Inf. Control* **1965**, *8*, 338–356. [CrossRef]
2. Awasthi, A.K.; Cucchiella, F.; D'Adamo, I.; Li, J.; Rosa, P.; Terzi, S.; Wei, G.; Zeng, X. Modelling the correlations of e-waste quantity with economic increase. *Sci. Total Environ.* **2018**, *613*, 46–53. [CrossRef]
3. Boran, F.E.; Akay, D. A biparametric similarity measure on intuitionistic fuzzy sets with applications to pattern recognition. *Inf. Sci.* **2014**, *255*, 45–57. [CrossRef]
4. Chen, S.M.; Cheng, S.H.; Lan, T.C. A novel similarity measure between intuitionistic fuzzy sets based on the centroid points of transformed fuzzy numbers with applications to pattern recognition. *Inf. Sci.* **2016**, *343–344*, 15–40. [CrossRef]
5. Chu, C.H.; Yen, C.P.; Lin, Y.F. The fourth axiom of similarity measures. *Symmetry* **2020**, *12*, 1735. [CrossRef]
6. Couso, I.; Garrido, L.; Sánchez, L. Similarity and dissimilarity measures between fuzzy sets: A formal relational study. *Inf. Sci.* **2013**, *229*, 122–141. [CrossRef]
7. Garg, H.; Kumar, K. An advanced study on the similarity measures of intuitionistic fuzzy sets based on the set pair analysis theory and their application in decision making. *Soft Comput.* **2018**, *22*, 4959–4970. [CrossRef]
8. Hwang, C.M.; Yang, M.S.; Hung, W.L. New similarity measures of intuitionistic fuzzy sets based on the Jaccard index with its application to clustering. *Int. J. Intell. Syst.* **2018**, *33*, 1672–1688. [CrossRef]

9. Jiang, Q.; Jin, X.; Lee, S.J.; Yao, S. A new similarity/distance measure between intuitionistic fuzzy sets based on the transformed isosceles triangles and its applications to pattern recognition. *Expert Syst. Appl.* **2019**, *116*, 439–453. [CrossRef]
10. Lee, S.H.; Park, C.M.; Choi, U.J. A new measure to characterize the degree of self-similarity of a shape and its applicability. *Entropy* **2020**, *22*, 1061. [CrossRef]
11. Mishra, A.R.; Jain, D.; Hooda, D.S. Exponential intuitionistic fuzzy information measure with assessment of service quality. *Int. J. Fuzzy Syst.* **2017**, *19*, 788–798. [CrossRef]
12. Naeem, M.; Qiyas, M.; Al-Shomrani, M.M.; Abdullah, S. Similarity measures for fractional orthotriple fuzzy sets using cosine and cotangent functions and their application in accident emergency response. *Mathematics* **2020**, *8*, 1653. [CrossRef]
13. Papacostas, G.A.; Hatzimichaillidis, A.G.; Kaburlasos, V.G. Distance and similarity measures between intuitionistic fuzzy sets: A comparative analysis from a pattern recognition point view. *Pattern Recognit. Lett.* **2013**, *34*, 1609–1622. [CrossRef]
14. Pedrycz, W.; Chen, S.M. *Granular Computing and Decision-Making: Interactive and Iterative Approaches*; Springer: Berlin/Heidelberg, Germany, 2015.
15. Tang, H.C.; Cheng, K.S. Counterintuitive test problems for transformed fuzzy numbers based similarity measures between intuitionistic fuzzy sets. *Symmetry* **2019**, *11*, 612. [CrossRef]
16. Tang, H.C.; Yang, S.T. Counterintuitive test problems for distance based similarity measures between intuitionistic fuzzy sets. *Mathematics* **2019**, *7*, 437. [CrossRef]
17. Xu, Y.; Yeh, C.-H. Sustainability-based selection decisions for e-waste recycling operations. *Ann. Oper. Res.* **2017**, *248*, 531–552. [CrossRef]
18. Mishra, A.R.; Rani, P.; Mardani, A.; Kumari, R.; Zavadskas, E.K.; Sharma, D.K. An extended shapley todim approach using novel exponential fuzzy divergence measures for multi-criteria service quality in vehicle insurance firms. *Symmetry* **2020**, *12*, 1452. [CrossRef]
19. Montes, S.; Couso, I.; Gil, P.; Bertoluzza, C. Divergence measure between fuzzy sets. *Int. J. Approx. Reason.* **2002**, *30*, 91–105. [CrossRef]
20. Rani, P.; Govindan, K.; Mishra, A.R.; Mardani, A.; Alrasheedi, M.; Hooda, D.S. Unified fuzzy divergence measures with multi-criteria decision making problems for sustainable planning of an e-waste recycling job selection. *Symmetry* **2020**, *12*, 90. [CrossRef]
21. Şenel, G.; Lee, J.G.; Hur, K. Distance and similarity measures for octahedron sets and their application to MCGDM problems. *Mathematics* **2020**, *8*, 1690. [CrossRef]
22. Zeng, S.; Asharf, S.; Arif, M.; Abdullah, S. Application of exponential jensen picture fuzzy divergence measure in multi-criteria group decision making. *Mathematics* **2019**, *7*, 191. [CrossRef]
23. Zhang, H.; Zhang, W.; Mei, C. Entropy of interval-valued fuzzy sets based on distance and its relationship with similarity measure. *Knowl.-Based Syst.* **2009**, *22*, 449–454. [CrossRef]

Publisher's Note: MDPI stays neutral with regard to jurisdictional claims in published maps and institutional affiliations.

symmetry

MDPI

Article

A Hybrid MCDM Model to Evaluate and Classify Outsourcing Providers in Manufacturing

Ching-Fang Liaw [1], Wan-Chi Jackie Hsu [2,3] and Huai-Wei Lo [1,*]

1 Department of Industrial Engineering and Management, Chaoyang University of Technology, 168, Jifeng E. Rd., Wufeng District, Taichung 413310, Taiwan; cfliaw@cyut.edu.tw
2 Graduate Institute of Cultural and Educational Management, Central Taiwan University of Sciences and Technology, 666, Buzih R., Beitun District, Taichung 40601, Taiwan; 108281@ctust.edu.tw
3 College of Management, National Taipei University of Technology, 1, Sec. 3, Zhongxiao E. Rd., Taipei 10608, Taiwan
* Correspondence: w110168888@gmail.com or t105749006@ntut.org.tw

Received: 5 November 2020; Accepted: 25 November 2020; Published: 27 November 2020

Abstract: It is a common practice for enterprises to use outsourcing strategies to reduce operating costs and improve product competitiveness. Outsourcing providers or operators need to be aware of environmental protection and make products comply with the restrictions of international environmental regulations. Therefore, this study proposes a set of multiple criteria decision-making (MCDM) approaches for systematic green outsourcing evaluation. First, a team of experts is established to discuss mutually dependent relationships among criteria, and the decision-making trial and evaluation laboratory (DEMATEL) technique is applied to generate subjective influential weights. Then, a large amount of data from outsourcing providers is collected, and the criteria importance through the intercriteria correlation (CRITIC) method is used to obtain the objective influential weights. Finally, a novel classifiable technique for ordering preference based on similarity to ideal solutions (classifiable TOPSIS) is proposed to integrate the performance of green outsourcing providers and classify them into four levels. The classifiable TOPSIS improves the shortcomings of conventional TOPSIS and establishes a visual rating diagram to help decision-makers to distinguish the performance of outsourcing providers more clearly. Taking a Taiwanese multinational machine tool manufacturer as an example, the performance of outsourcing providers related to manufacturing activities was investigated to demonstrate the effectiveness and applicability of this proposed model.

Keywords: multiple criteria decision-making (MCDM); outsourcing provider; DEMATEL; CRITIC; TOPSIS

---

1. Introduction

Outsourcing has become one of the most important strategies in business operations. Through outsourcing operations, manpower and equipment investment can be greatly reduced, thereby operating costs can be effectively controlled. The range covered by outsourcing is very wide, including component production, financial planning, accounting, logistics management, legal consulting, marketing, after-sales service, etc. [1]. In 2018, the total amount of global companies signing outsourcing services contracts is estimated to be as high as US $85.6 billion [2]. This phenomenon shows that outsourcing activities have been widespread in all walks of life. An effective outsourcing evaluation system can maximize the benefits of outsourcing activities [3,4]. Improper selection of outsourcing providers can easily lead to the failure of outsourcing strategies, causing a decline in corporate competitiveness, and even financial risks or corporate failures [5,6].

The application of outsourcing strategy brings out diversified decision issues. In general, different business process owners should define not only the most appropriate conditions to gain a full compliance between in-house processes and outsourcing activities, but also require them harmonically converge towards the guidelines at the roots of decision-making [1,3]. However, the rise of environmental awareness has changed the concept of decision-making. It is no longer only cost-effectiveness as the ultimate consideration, but must be incorporated into green criteria to facilitate environmental protection [7,8]. The evaluation and selection of green outsourcing providers is an important task in supply chain management. Especially in the manufacturing industry, for highly complex products such as machine tools or ships, the number of outsourcers they have is very considerable. When an enterprise has many outsourcers, it must have a complete and systematic model to determine the weight of the evaluation criteria and the priority of outsourcing providers, otherwise the management of providers will appear very messy and difficult. [1,3–6].

Many scholars have made significant contributions to the evaluation and selection of outsourcing providers. Some studies have pointed out that the selection of outsourcing providers can be categorized as a multiple criteria decision-making (MCDM) problem [3–5,9–11]. The MCDM method has excellent evaluation performance under many mutually constrained conditions. Its computing concept is different from statistics. MCDM can process expert interview data with a small sample, and can also analyze large sample data from the database. The goal of MCDM is to integrate both objective quantitative data and subjective expert judgment, and provide effective management suggestions to support decision-makers in formulating optimal strategies [12–14]. It is suitable to establish a complete evaluation framework based on the expertise of researchers or experts and the extensive experience of practitioners [15–17]. The evaluation and selection of MCDM projects can usually be divided into three execution stages, namely the identification of evaluation criteria, the calculation of criteria weights, and the performance analysis of alternatives [18].

In the past, research on selecting outsourcing providers has laid the foundation for industry and academia; however, there are still some research gaps and practical application restrictions.

(i) Some evaluation models do not take into account criteria related to environmental protection.

Many manufacturing activities have caused various environmental pollution and destruction. Operators need to be aware of environmental protection and make products comply with the restrictions of international environmental regulations. Therefore, whether outsourcing providers have environmental awareness and green manufacturing capabilities deserves our consideration [7].

(ii) Many weight-setting methods assume that the criteria are independent.

Past studies on outsourcing provider selection have often overlooked the mutually dependent relationships among criteria. For example, the analytic hierarchy process (AHP) and the best-worst method (BWM) are used to obtain criteria weights. In fact, the root causes of problems are composed of many interrelated factors [19–21]. The decision-making trial and evaluation laboratory (DEMATEL) can overcome the assumption of independence of the criteria and determine the interdependence among the criteria [6,9].

(iii) Few studies consider both subjectivity and objectivity.

The methods of determining the importance of the criteria can be divided into two categories. Experts conduct pairwise comparisons of the criteria to evaluate their importance and call them subjective weights. Common methods are AHP, BWM, analytic network process (ANP), and DEMATEL. The other type is based on a large amount of data to estimate a set of criteria weights, called objective weights. Entropy and criteria importance through intercriteria correlation (CRITIC) belong to this type of method. If both perspectives can be included in the evaluation model, the results will be comprehensive and complete [22].

(iv) When an enterprise has a large number of outsourcing providers, the ranking of outsourcing providers can no longer meet the needs of decision-makers.

For industries with a wide variety and a small amount of production (such as machinery), there would be a lot of outsourcing providers needed. However, even though the ranking of outsourcing providers is determined, it is impossible to give each outsourcing provider practical suggestions for improvement. If all outsourcing providers can be classified into different levels and given appropriate management suggestions for each level, the management efficiency of the managers can be improved. It is a good practice to classify outsourcing providers through the closeness coefficient of technique for ordering preference based on similarity to ideal solutions (TOPSIS) [8].

Therefore, in order to tackle the aforementioned problems, this study proposes a MCDM model with a systematic green outsourcing evaluation. First, based on the existing evaluation criteria of the case company and the documentation, a complete evaluation framework for green outsourcing providers was established. The proposed framework can be divided into four main dimensions: capacity of operation, capacity of professional skills, capacity of service, and environment management. These dimensions can be divided into 15 evaluation criteria. Here, the dimension of environmental management was added to conform to the development trend of environmental awareness. Next, the DEMATEL technique was used to explore the mutually dependent relationship among the criteria, and a set of subjective weights was obtained. The DEMATEL questionnaires were obtained by interviewing eight senior managers of the case company. Furthermore, the external auditors surveyed the performance data of 165 outsourcing providers, and applied CRITIC's algorithm to generate a set of objective weights. The proposed DEMATEL–CRITIC method can reflect the importance of mutually dependent relationships among the criteria. Finally, this study develops a classifiable TOPSIS technique, which not only introduces the concept of aspiration level, but also divides the performance of outsourcing providers into four levels. Appropriate management suggestions are given for the four levels to support outsourcing providers in formulating improvement strategies to enhance their business performance. The DEMATEL, CRITIC, and TOPSIS used in this model are all breakthrough improvements, which make the analysis ability improved and more in line with the actual needs of the industry.

To demonstrate the effectiveness of the proposed model, a Taiwanese multinational machine tool manufacturer is used as an example. Sensitivity analysis and model comparisons are also conducted in this study to demonstrate the robustness of this methodology. The proposed hybrid model is not limited to the amount of data in use. The data can be a small sample or a big data. In addition, when new outsourcing providers join, their performance levels can be quickly classified. Based on the results obtained, the decision-makers can decide whether to cooperate with a new outsourcing provider or not. In summary, the advantages and contribution of our study are described below.

(i) Integrating environmental protection criteria in the framework of green outsourcing providers.
(ii) Using the DEMATEL–CRITIC method which considers both subjectivity and objectivity. And, this method can identify the mutual influence of the criteria.
(iii) Proposing a classifiable TOPSIS to classify a large number of green outsourcing providers, and give appropriate suggestions for improvement according to their levels.
(iv) The effective and robustness of the proposed model being confirmed through the model comparisons and sensitivity analysis.

The rest of the paper is organized as follows. Section 2 reviews the research on using MCDM to evaluate outsourcing providers. Section 3 introduces the proposed novel model. Moreover, we improved the DEMATEL, CRITIC, and TOPSIS methods and introduced the calculation process and execution steps in detail. Section 4 uses a real case to demonstrate the applicability of the proposed model. Section 5 discusses management implication issues, sensitivity analysis and model comparisons. Finally, conclusions and future research directions are given in Section 6.

2. A Brief Review of the Evaluation of Applying MCDM to Outsourcing Providers

At present, compared with the articles of suppliers, there are relatively few studies on evaluation and selection of outsourcing providers. With the rapid development of outsourcing strategies, the issue of evaluation of outsourcing providers has become increasingly important [3,4]. When enterprises face shortages of technology and manpower, they often increase their operational capabilities through outsourcing. From the process of finding outsourced objects to the willingness of cooperation between both parties, many details need to be coordinated and improved.

The success of the outsourcing strategies will create a lot of added values, including saving setup costs, reducing operational risks, and focusing more on core business. However, outsourcing activities will produce a certain degree of two-way information exchange and communication, and the success or failure of cooperation will involve many complicated factors [23]. Therefore, the evaluation of outsourcing providers is a difficult and complex MCDM problem. Previous studies have used various MCDM methods to explore this issue. Research based on linear programming, for example, Li and Wan [24] developed a method of fuzzy linear programming to address the issue of outsourcing provider selection. This method is implemented in the largest light-emitting diode (LED) production company in China. The results show that both positive and negative ideal solutions should be considered when evaluating outsourcing providers, to overcome the shortcoming that the linear programming technique for multidimensional analysis of preference (LINMAP) can only obtain local optimal solutions. In the same year, Li and Wan [25] extended Li and Wan [24] research and applied to a well-known information technology company in Jiangxi, China. The study shows that it is feasible to determine the weights of attributes through linear programming. In order to consider the importance of experts, Wan et al. [8] optimized the linear programming method of Li and Wan [25], combined with intuitionistic fuzzy preference relations (IFPRs) to determine the weights of experts to effectively integrate the group decision-making judgment.

In addition, Ji et al. [3] proposed a comprehensive MCDM framework to solve the problem of non-compensatory criteria. The modified multi-attributive border approximation area comparison (MABAC) method is a novel weight determination method, which can explore the non-compensatory structure of the criteria. Next, the elimination et choice translating reality (ELECTRE) technique was used to rank the outsourcing providers. The study used data from Li and Wan [24] to analyze and compare TOPSIS, weighted bonferrroni mean, and traditional MABAC methods, to explain the advantages of the proposed method. In recent years, several novel MCDM models have extended the research on outsourcing providers evaluation. Zarbakhshnia et al. [26] combined fuzzy AHP (FAHP) and gray multi-objective optimization by ratio analysis (MOORA-G) methods to select the third-party reverse logistics providers for a car parts manufacturing company. Their research shows that the combined model can effectively deal with uncertain qualitative data. A hybrid framework was proposed by Prajapati et al. [27], who integrated fuzzy Delphi, FAHP, and fuzzy additive ratio assessment (F-ARAS) methods to prioritize alternative outsourcing providers in energy industry. However, these studies all consider the criteria to be independent, which violates the situation in which the existing social factors depend on one another.

Taking into account factor-dependent research, for example, Liou and Chuang [9] proposed a hybrid MCDM model to evaluate more than 50 outsourcing providers of Taiwan Airlines. The study used DEMATEL and ANP to discuss the influential relationships and influential weights of the criteria, and applied the visekriterijumska optimizacija i kompromisno resenje (VIKOR) to obtain the gap between each alternative and the ideal level. Hsu et al. [6] improved the methodology of Liou and Chuang [9] and integrated DEMATEL-based ANP (DANP) and modified grey relation analysis (GRA), where the DANP method puts the output values of DEMATEL into ANP to generate a set of dependent weight values. Next, modified GRA is used to determine and rank the grey correlation coefficient of each outsourcing provider. Uygun et al. [11] combined fuzzy theory with the ANP method to evaluate the competitiveness of a Turkish communications company's outsourcing providers. Their research focuses on the processing of uncertain information.

Table 1 summarizes the existing studies applying MCDM model to evaluate and select outsourcing providers. The studies mentioned above have made significant contributions to this topic. Unfortunately, no research has simultaneously discussed and solved the four research gaps mentioned in Section 1.

Table 1. Literature review of the evaluation of applying multiple criteria decision-making (MCDM) to outsourcing providers.

Author	Research Methodology	Application Field	Green Criteria Included	Consideration of Criteria Dependence
Li and Wan [24]	Fuzzy inhomogenous multi-attribute group decision making approach	Light-emitting diode (LED) production company	No	No
Li and Wan [25]	Fuzzy heterogeneous multi-attribute decision making method	Information technology company	No	No
Wan et al. [10]	An intuitionistic fuzzy linear programming method	Logistics industry	No	No
Ji et al. [3]	Combined MABAC and ELECTRE techniques.	Information technology company	No	No
Zarbakhshnia et al. [26]	Combined FAHP and MOORA-G methods.	Car parts manufacturing company	Yes	No
Prajapati et al. [27]	Integrated fuzzy Delphi, FAHP, and F-ARAS methods.	Energy industry	No	No
Liou and Chuang [9]	Integrated DEMATEL, ANP, and VIKOR methods.	Airlines	No	Yes
Hsu et al. [6]	Integrated DANP and modified GRA approaches.	Airlines	No	Yes
Uygun et al. [11]	Combined DEMATEL and fuzzy ANP methods.	GSM (global system for mobile) communication company	No	Yes

DEMATEL, decision-making trial and evaluation laboratory; MABAC, multi-attributive border approximation area comparison; AHP, analytic hierarchy process; MOORA-G, multi-objective optimization by ratio analysis; F-ARAS, fuzzy additive ratio assessment; ANP, analytic network process; VIKOR, visekriterijumska optimizacija i kompromisno resenje; DANP, DEMATEL-based ANP; GRA, grey relation analysis.

3. The Proposed Classifiable MCDM Model

This section introduces the proposed classifiable MCDM model. First, the influential weights of the criteria for evaluating outsourcing providers are obtained through the DEMATEL–CRITIC model. Next, these weights are used by the classifiable TOPSIS algorithm to evaluate the performance of outsourcing providers. The proposed model converts the performance of each outsourcing provider into a score between 0 to 1, which is further divided into four levels. Appropriate suggestions for improvement strategies for outsourcing providers in each level are given. Past research has focused on the selection of outsourcing providers, often only able to determine the ranking of outsourcing providers. However, in the face of a large number of outsourcing providers, ranking can no longer meet the requirement of the enterprise. Figure 1 presents the analysis flow of this study. The detailed implementation steps of this study are described below.

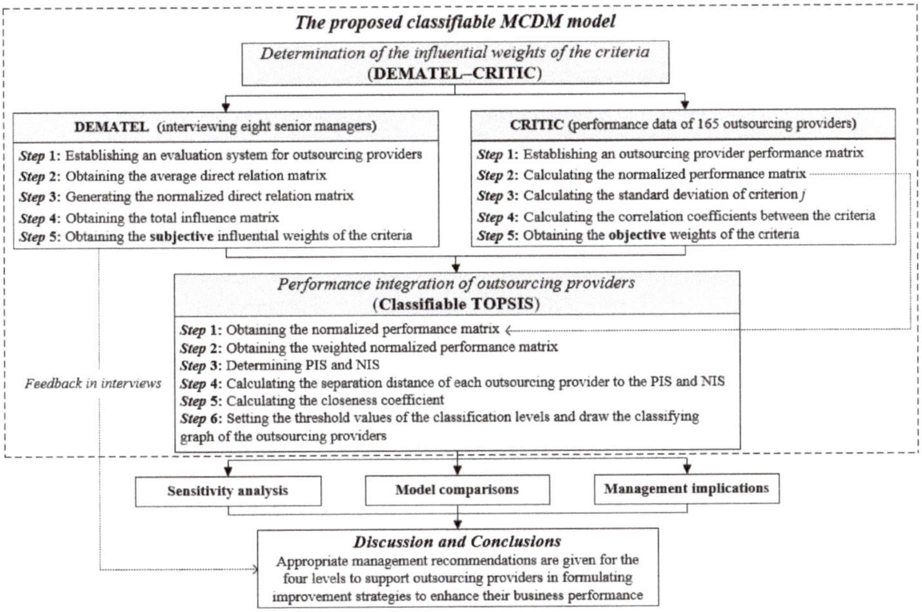

Figure 1. The analysis flow of this study. CRITIC, criteria importance through intercriteria correlation; TOPSIS, technique for ordering preference based on similarity to ideal solutions.

3.1. Determination of the Influential Weights of the Criteria (DEMATEL–CRITIC)

In the past, most academic articles used a single MCDM method to obtain the subjective weights of criteria (e.g., AHP, ANP, BWM, DEMATEL, and DANP). Unfortunately, few studies have discussed the subjective and objective weights of criteria at the same time. This study proposes the DEMATEL–CRITIC method to construct a reliable set of criteria weights and takes into account the dependency of the criteria. This method can quickly process the big data of multiple criteria, construct the dependency relationships of the criteria through correlation coefficients and standard deviations, and extract the information on the influence degrees of the criteria in the complex systems.

3.1.1. DEMATEL (Subjective Weights)

DEMATEL is a technique that effectively explores the mutual influence among criteria. This technique can identify the influential relationships and strength among the criteria, and then help decision-makers to find the key causes in a complex evaluation system. DEMATEL is widely used in various industries, including disaster prevention science [20], e-commerce [28], advertising design [29], transportation [19], and green building [30]. The issue of evaluation of outsourcing providers involves factors such as government regulations, company policies, and process requirements. How to generate a reasonable set of weights from these factors is the purpose of DEMATEL. DEMATEL conducts interviews through experts or inspectors to give back quantifiable linguistics to reflect their true feelings. The calculation steps of the DEMATEL technique are described below.

Step 1. Establishing an evaluation system for outsourcing providers

In reality, every company has an evaluation system for outsourcing providers. The evaluation period of outsourcing providers may last half a year or once a year. We define the evaluation criterion as $c_i,\ i = 1,\ 2, \ldots,\ n$.

Step 2. Obtaining the average direct relation matrix A

Experts are required to evaluate the mutual influence of n criteria. Each expert evaluates the direct influence of criterion i on criterion j through linguistic variables (Table 2) to obtain the direct relation matrix.

Table 2. Linguistic variables for the influence evaluation.

Linguistic Variable (Code)	Crisp
No influence (N)	0
Low influence (L)	1
Medium influence (M)	2
High influence (H)	3
Very high influence (VH)	4

In this study, the arithmetic mean is used to integrate the opinions of multiple experts, and an average direct relation matrix A is formed, as shown in Equation (1).

$$A = \left[a_{ij}\right]_{n\times n} = \begin{bmatrix} 0 & a_{12} & \cdots & a_{1j} & \cdots & a_{1n} \\ a_{21} & 0 & \cdots & a_{2j} & \cdots & a_{2n} \\ \vdots & \vdots & \ddots & \vdots & \ddots & \vdots \\ a_{i1} & a_{i2} & \cdots & 0 & \cdots & a_{in} \\ \vdots & \vdots & \ddots & \vdots & \ddots & \vdots \\ a_{n1} & a_{n2} & \cdots & a_{nj} & \cdots & 0 \end{bmatrix}_{n\times n},i,j = 1,\ 2, \ldots,\ n. \tag{1}$$

In the operation rules of DEMATEL, the criteria have no self-influential relationship, indicating that the diagonal elements in the matrix are 0, i.e., $a_{ii} = 0,\ i = 1,\ 2, \ldots,\ n$.

Step 3. Generating the normalized direct relation matrix $\boldsymbol{X}$

The normalization formulas (Equations (2) and (3)) are used to convert the range of elements in the matrix to be between 0 and 1.

$$\boldsymbol{X} = \left[x_{ij}\right]_{n\times n} = \begin{bmatrix} 0 & \varepsilon\cdot a_{12} & \cdots & \varepsilon\cdot a_{1j} & \cdots & \varepsilon\cdot a_{1n} \\ \varepsilon\cdot a_{21} & 0 & \cdots & \varepsilon\cdot a_{2j} & \cdots & \varepsilon\cdot a_{2n} \\ \vdots & \vdots & \ddots & \vdots & \ddots & \vdots \\ \varepsilon\cdot a_{i1} & \varepsilon\cdot a_{i2} & \cdots & 0 & \cdots & \varepsilon\cdot a_{in} \\ \vdots & \vdots & \ddots & \vdots & \ddots & \vdots \\ \varepsilon\cdot a_{n1} & \varepsilon\cdot a_{n2} & \cdots & \varepsilon\cdot a_{nj} & \cdots & 0 \end{bmatrix}_{n\times n},i,j = 1,\ 2, \ldots,\ n. \tag{2}$$

$$\varepsilon = \min\left\{\frac{1}{\max_i \sum_{j=1}^{n} a_{ij}}, \frac{1}{\max_j \sum_{i=1}^{n} a_{ij}}\right\} \tag{3}$$

Step 4. Obtaining the total influence matrix T

Here, the total direct and indirect influential relationships of all the criteria are considered. Therefore, the total influence matrix T is obtained by summing up all the powers of the matrix X, such as Equation (4). Equation (4) can be converted to Equation (5), to simplify the calculation of the total influence matrix T.

$$T = X + X^2 + \cdots + X^{\infty} \tag{4}$$

$$\begin{aligned} T &= X + X^2 + \cdots + X^{\infty} = X\left(I + X + X^2 + \cdots + X^{\infty-1}\right) \\ &= X(I - X^{\infty})(I - X)^{-1} = X(I - X)^{-1} \end{aligned} \tag{5}$$

where $X^{\infty} = [0]_{n\times n}$, I is the identity matrix, and the superscript symbol "−1" indicates the inverse matrix.

$$T = \left[t_{ij}\right]_{n\times n} = \begin{bmatrix} t_{11} & t_{12} & \cdots & t_{1j} & \cdots & t_{1n} \\ t_{21} & t_{22} & \cdots & t_{2j} & \cdots & t_{2n} \\ \vdots & \vdots & \ddots & \vdots & \ddots & \vdots \\ t_{i1} & t_{i2} & \cdots & t_{ij} & \cdots & t_{in} \\ \vdots & \vdots & \ddots & \vdots & \ddots & \vdots \\ t_{n1} & t_{n2} & \cdots & t_{nj} & \cdots & t_{nn} \end{bmatrix}_{n\times n}, i, j = 1,\ 2, \ldots,\ n. \tag{6}$$

Step 5. Obtaining the subjective influential weights of the criteria

The elements of the total influence matrix are summed horizontally to obtain a vector r, such as Equation (7). Similarly, using Equation (8), the elements of the matrix T are summed vertically to obtain the vector s.

$$r = (r_1, r_2, \ldots, r_i, \ldots, r_n) \tag{7}$$

$$s = \left(s_1, s_2, \ldots, s_j, \ldots, s_n\right) \tag{8}$$

where $r_i = \sum_{j=1}^{n} t_{ij}$ and $s_j = \sum_{i=1}^{n} t_{ij}$, $i, j = 1,\ 2, \ldots,\ n$.

r_i represents the extent of criterion i affecting other criteria, and s_i represents the extent of criterion i affected by other criteria. Therefore, we can define $r_i + s_i$ as the total influence and $r_i - s_i$ as the net influence for each criterion i. If $r_i - s_i$ is positive, it means that the effect of criterion i affecting other criteria is more significant, which is called a causal factor; otherwise, if $r_i - s_i$ is negative, it means that criterion i is greatly affected by other criteria, which is called an affected factor. Moreover, according to the study of Lo et al. [21], $r_i + s_i$ can reflect the total influence of criterion i on the overall evaluation system. Therefore, Equation (9) can generate the subjective influential weight of criterion i, namely $w_i^{subjective}$, $i = 1,\ 2, \ldots,\ n$. It can be seen that $w_i^{subjective} \geq 0$ and $\sum_{i=1}^{n} w_i^{subjective} = 1$.

$$w_i^{subjective} = \frac{r_i + s_i}{\sum_{i=1}^{n} (r_i + s_i)} \tag{9}$$

3.1.2. CRITIC (Objective Weights)

CRITIC is a type of objective weights based on performance data (the performance scores of all outsourcing providers under each criterion). This method is measured by the linear correlation coefficient among the criteria, so it contains information about the degree of correlation. CRITIC mainly constructs the dependent weights of the criteria from the "standard deviation of the criteria" and the "correlation coefficient among the criteria". The conflict among criteria is measured through the relevance of criteria to echo the core concepts of MCDM. The detailed steps of the CRITIC method are as follows:

Step 1. Establishing an outsourcing provider performance matrix $\boldsymbol{D}$

There are m outsourcing providers A_h, $h = 1, 2, \ldots, m$ and n criteria c_j, $j = 1, 2, \ldots, n$. In the construction of the performance matrix, the rows of the matrix correspond to the outsourcing providers and the columns of the matrix correspond to the criteria. The element d_{hj} of matrix $\boldsymbol{D}$ represents the evaluation performance of outsourcing provider h under criterion j, as shown in Equation (10).

$$\boldsymbol{D} = \left[d_{hj}\right]_{m \times n} = \begin{bmatrix} d_{11} & d_{12} & \cdots & d_{1j} & \cdots & d_{1n} \\ d_{21} & d_{22} & \cdots & d_{2j} & \cdots & d_{2n} \\ \vdots & \vdots & \ddots & \vdots & \ddots & \vdots \\ d_{h1} & d_{h2} & \cdots & d_{hj} & \cdots & d_{hn} \\ \vdots & \vdots & \ddots & \vdots & \ddots & \vdots \\ d_{m1} & t_{m2} & \cdots & d_{mj} & \cdots & d_{mn} \end{bmatrix}_{m \times n}, \quad h = 1, 2, \ldots, m; j = 1, 2, \ldots, n. \tag{10}$$

where the rating score d_{hj}, ranging from 0 to 100, is developed by the case company's rating system.

Step 2. Calculating the normalized performance matrix $\boldsymbol{D}^*$

The matrix $\boldsymbol{D}^*$ can be obtained through normalization (Equation (11)). The conventional normalization method is to take the best performance of the alternatives under each criterion as the denominator, which will result in the situation of "pick the best apple from a bucket of rotten apples". Therefore, this article introduces the concept of aspiration level to modify the normalization scheme, such as Equation (12).

$$\boldsymbol{D}^* = \left[d^*_{hj}\right]_{m \times n} \tag{11}$$

where

$$d^*_{hj} = \frac{d_{hj}}{\max\limits_{1 \le i \le n} d_{ij}}. \qquad d^*_{hj} = \frac{d_{hj}}{d_j^{aspire}} \tag{12}$$

where d_j^{aspire} represents the highest rating score (the aspiration level is 100) of criterion j.

Step 3. Calculating the standard deviation of criterion j

Matrix $\boldsymbol{D}^*$ presents the performance of each outsourcing provider under various criteria. Through the standard deviation σ_j, the degree of variation of outsourcing providers under criterion j can be known.

$$\sigma_j = \sqrt{\frac{\sum_{h=1}^{m}\left(d_{hj} - \bar{d}_j\right)^2}{m-1}} \tag{13}$$

where $\bar{d}_j = \frac{\sum_{h=1}^{m} d_{hj}}{m}$.

Step 4. Calculating the correlation coefficients between the criteria

Considering the correlation among the criteria, a linear correlation coefficient is used to measure the correlation between every two criteria, such as Equation (14). These coefficients are used to construct the correlation matrix $\boldsymbol{R}$ of the criteria, such as Equation (15).

$$r_{jj'} = \frac{\sum_{h=1}^{m}\left(d_{hj} - \bar{d}_j\right)\left(d_{hj'} - \bar{d}_{j'}\right)}{\sqrt{\sum_{h=1}^{m}\left(d_{hj} - \bar{d}_j\right)^2} \cdot \sqrt{\sum_{h=1}^{m}\left(d_{hj'} - \bar{d}_{j'}\right)^2}} \tag{14}$$

$$\boldsymbol{R} = \left[r_{jj'}\right]_{n \times n} = \begin{bmatrix} 1 & r_{12} & \cdots & r_{1n} \\ r_{12} & 1 & \cdots & r_{2n} \\ \vdots & \vdots & \ddots & \vdots \\ r_{1n} & r_{2n} & \cdots & 1 \end{bmatrix}_{n \times n}, \; j, j' = 1, 2, \ldots, n \tag{15}$$

Step 5. Obtaining the objective weights of the criteria

Through Equation (16), the "standard deviation" and "correlation coefficient between every two criteria" are integrated to generate an overall evaluation value. Next, the objective weights of the criteria are computed through normalization (Equation (17)). Thus, the sum of the weights is 1, and all the weights are greater than or equal to 0.

$$\varphi_j = \sigma_j \sum_{j'=1}^{n} \left(1 - r_{jj'}\right) \tag{16}$$

$$w_j^{objective} = \frac{\varphi_j}{\sum_{i=1}^{n} \varphi_i} \tag{17}$$

3.2. *Performance Integration of Outsourcing Providers (Classifiable TOPSIS)*

TOPSIS technique is one of the effective MCDM methods for integrating performance values. This method determines the relative position of each outsourcing provider by calculating the distance between each outsourcing provider and the positive and negative ideal solutions (PIS and NIS). The best outsourcing provider is the one closest to the positive ideal solution and farthest from the negative ideal solution. The solution time and quality of TOPSIS will not be affected by the numbers of outsourcing providers or criteria. By improving the conventional TOPSIS, this study proposes a classifiable TOPSIS technique which can generate more reliable performance scores. In this technique, all outsourcing providers are classified into four levels. When a new outsourcing provider is included, this technique can be used to quickly classify it. The detailed steps of the classifiable TOPSIS technique are explained as follows:

Step 1. Obtaining the normalized performance matrix $\boldsymbol{D}^*$

The input data of TOPSIS and CRITIC are the same. Therefore, the normalized performance matrix $\boldsymbol{D}^*$ can be obtained through Steps 1 and 2 of the CRITIC.

Step 2. Obtaining the weighted normalized performance matrix $\boldsymbol{D}^{**}$

We consider the importance of the criteria to be different and multiply the weights obtained by DEMATEL and CRITIC with the normalized performance matrix to obtain a weighted normalized performance matrix, such as Equation (18). Since both subjective (DEMATEL) and objective (CRITIC) influential weights are considered, here, parameter α is used to express preference between subjective and objective weights, and the final weights are shown as in Equation (19).

$$\boldsymbol{D}^{**} = \left[d_{hj}^{**}\right]_{m \times n} \tag{18}$$

where $d_{hj}^{**} = w_j^* \cdot d_{hj}^*$.

$$w_j^* = \alpha w_j^{subjective} + (1 - \alpha) w_j^{objective} \tag{19}$$

where $w_j^{subjective}$ is the subjective weight of criterion j generated by DEMATEL (Equation (9)), and $w_j^{objective}$ is the objective weight of criterion j obtained by CRITIC (Equation (17)).

Step 3. Determining PIS and NIS

After normalization, the value of aspiration (positive) and worst (negative) level should be 1 and 0, respectively. Therefore, after considering the criteria weights, the PIS (z_j^+) and NIS (z_j^-) of the system can be obtained, as shown in Equations (20) and (21).

$$\text{PIS} = \left(z_1^+,\ z_2^+, \ldots,\ z_j^+, \ldots,\ z_n^+\right) = \left(1 \cdot w_1^*,\ 1 \cdot w_2^*, \ldots,\ 1 \cdot w_j^*, \ldots,\ 1 \cdot w_n^*\right) \quad (20)$$

$$\text{NIS} = \left(z_1^-,\ z_2^-, \ldots,\ z_j^-, \ldots,\ z_n^-\right) = \left(0 \cdot w_1^*,\ 0 \cdot w_2^*, \ldots,\ 0 \cdot w_j^*, \ldots,\ 0 \cdot w_n^*\right) \quad (21)$$

Step 4. Calculating the separation distance of each outsourcing provider to the PIS and NIS

This article uses the Euclidean distance to measure the degree of separation of outsourcing provider h from PIS and NIS, as shown in Equations (22) and (23).

$$S_h^+ = \sqrt{\sum_{j=1}^{n}\left(z_j^+ - d_{hj}^{**}\right)^2} \quad (22)$$

$$S_h^- = \sqrt{\sum_{j=1}^{n}\left(d_{hj}^{**} - z_j^-\right)^2} \quad (23)$$

Step 5. Calculating the closeness coefficient

The closeness coefficient (CC_h) was proposed by Kuo [31]. This index improves many disadvantages of conventional TOPSIS to obtain more reliable ranking results, as shown in Equation (24). The new ranking index has an excellent basis for judgment. The range of CC_h is from −1 to 1 for each outsourcing provider h, and the total of CC_h for all outsourcing providers is 0.

$$CC_h = \frac{w^+ S_h^-}{\sum_{h=1}^{m} S_h^-} - \frac{w^- S_h^+}{\sum_{h=1}^{m} S_h^+},\ -1 \le CC_h \le 1. \quad (24)$$

where w^+ and w^- represents the relative importance of PIS and NIS, respectively. Since $w^+ + w^- = 1$, the settings of w^+ and w^- will affect each other. Generally, both w^+ and w^- are set to be 0.5.

However, the ranking index proposed by Kuo [31] has a disadvantage that when the number of outsourcing providers increases, CC_h will also decrease, making it difficult to interpret this value. Therefore, in this study, CC_h is further normalized to obtain a new ranking index CC_h^*, as shown in Equation (25).

$$CC_h^* = \frac{CC_h - CC^{worst}}{CC^{aspire} - CC^{worst}},\ 0 \le CC_h^* \le 1 \quad (25)$$

Step 6. Setting the threshold values of the classification levels and draw the classifying graph of the outsourcing providers

The closer the value of CC_h^* is to 1, outsourcing provider h is more preferred. On the other hand, when the value of CC_h^* is close to 0, outsourcing provider h should be eliminated. Here, according to the nature of CC_h^*, the threshold values are set by the decision-making team, and then the outsourcing providers are classified into four levels. We set the horizontal axis to be the indices of outsourcing providers, and the vertical axis to be the values of CC_h^*. According to the classification in Table 3, we can construct an outsourcing provider classification graph.

Table 3. Classification levels of outsourcing providers.

CC_h	Evaluation Level	Description
$0.9 \leq CC^*_h \leq 1$	A^+	Level A^+ outsourcing providers have performance close to the aspiration level and are excellent outsourcing providers.
$0.75 \leq CC^*_h < 0.9$	A	Level A outsourcing providers perform well, but they still need to strengthen some of their capabilities.
$0.5 \leq CC^*_h < 0.75$	B	The performance of Level B outsourcing providers is average, and it needs to be greatly improved to meet the requirements of enterprises.
$0 \leq CC^*_h < 0.5$	C	The performance of Level C outsourcing providers is close to the worst level, hardly meets the requirements of enterprises, and should be eliminated.

4. Illustration of a Real Case

This section uses a real case to illustrate the calculation procedure in Section 3.

4.1. Problem Description

The case company is a multinational machine tool manufacturing company in Taiwan, dedicated to the manufacture of cutting processing equipment and laser processing equipment. The company already has a number of intellectual property rights and invention patents related to machine tools. The accuracy and stability of the products are comparable to those of well-known equipment manufacturers in Europe and America. The products have been successfully sold to electronics, machinery, shipbuilding, aerospace, and other industries around the world. In recent years, the development trend of intelligent machinery has brought about many markets and opportunities. The case company actively expanded its sales channels (finding agents and distributors), and signed a joint cooperation with government agencies or labor union organizations, hoping to bring more profit to the enterprise. Due to the expansion of the company's business territory (the global dealers have exceeded 80 cities), coupled with factors such as global competition and high investment costs, the case company has implemented outsourcing policies for many years.

At present, the case company has an evaluation system for outsourcing providers, which mainly focuses on the business conditions and cooperation capabilities of its partners. Unfortunately, the weights of the evaluation criteria are only given directly from senior managers, and the method of performance integration of outsourcing providers is the simple additive weighting (SAW) method. The existing weight determination method is easily affected by the personal preferences of senior executives. In addition, although the SAW calculation process is simple, it does not take into account the comprehensiveness of the evaluation system. Therefore, it is obvious that a scientific and systematic analysis model is needed to support decision makers in formulating business policies.

Through literature review and the existing company outsourcing provider evaluation system, after discussion with the company's decision-making team, four dimensions, 15 criteria and 165 outsourcing providers were identified. The outsourcing providers evaluated in this case were all related to manufacturing. The decision-making team was composed of eight senior executives of the case company, including the chairman, the general manager, and six department managers. The six managers are from the business, manufacturing, purchasing, logistics, quality control, and marketing departments. Each expert had at least fifteen years of professional work experience in manufacturing industry and was specifically selected for their expertise in the evaluation process. In terms of academic qualifications, this team has three PhDs and five masters degrees. In addition, all experts have experience in the business activities of outsourcing strategies. They mainly assisted in drafting outsourcing provider evaluation framework (Table 4) and filling out the DEMATEL questionnaire.

Table 4. Outsourcing provider evaluation criteria and descriptions.

Dimension	Criterion	Description
Capacity of operation (D_1)	Enterprise size and financial capabilities (C_{11})	The criterion includes evaluating the capital, turnover, number of employees, market share, and organizational structure of the outsourcing providers. Moreover, information such as the company's solvency, the company's internal control, board functions, and business status are all very important basis for financial capability.
	Project management capabilities (C_{12})	The success factors of outsourcing providers working with the enterprise to promote projects include experience and technology. The outsourcing providers should have the experience of undertaking outsourcing, focusing on shortening the completion time and the ability of quality assurance.
	Supply chain audit planning (C_{13})	The outsourcing provider's ability to integrate the supply chain includes the process of inspecting the incoming, production, inventory, and sales of all products of the provider. Maintaining the stability of overall supply chain activities is a must for outsourcing providers.
	Maintenance of corporate confidentiality (C_{14})	All gold flow, information flow, and logistics of enterprises and outsourcing providers must be strictly controlled and kept secret.
Capacity of professional skills (D_2)	R&D and design capabilities (C_{21})	Whether the outsourcing provider has mastered leading technology and knowledge during the R&D and design stage, clearly understands the needs of the market, and can innovate products.
	Process quality control (C_{22})	Whether the outsourcing provider's manufacturing process is stable and whether the product meets the quality required by the customer.
	Key component inventory control (C_{23})	Whether the inventory of key components and their procurement channels are stable.
	Management information system integration (C_{24})	Outsourcing information should be published on a common information platform immediately and correctly, including all cash flows, information flows, and logistics.
	Finished product quality assurance and reliability (C_{25})	The outsourcing provider's ability to analyze the reliability of the product includes the formulation of the product's life, usage specifications, and maintenance methods.
Capacity of service (D_3)	After-sales service and improvement capabilities (C_{31})	Products should be continuously tracked and evaluated during the stages of design, manufacturing, and after-sale use. Outsourcing providers should take the initiative to actively optimize products to effectively reduce costs and improve quality.
	Customer relationship management and loyalty (C_{32})	Outsourcing providers use effective information technology to collect data and analyze customer needs and quickly process customer orders. In addition, the loyalty of outsourcing providers will affect the tacit understanding of long-term cooperation.
	Communication channels and message sharing (C_{33})	A good communication channel is a basis for stable cooperation. Enterprises and outsourcing providers must trust each other and open up more information conducive to cooperation.
Environment management (D_4)	Green resource integration (C_{41})	Outsourcing providers must respect the surrounding environment and protect the natural ecology in the production process, and create a green supply chain system. Outsourcing providers' emphasis on environmental protection can effectively enhance their corporate image.
	Environmental certification (C_{42})	Outsourcing providers must abide by the local government's environmental regulations and obtain relevant environmental certifications and certificates.
	Pollution emission treatment (C_{43})	Evaluate whether outsourcing providers are actively implementing pollutant emission reduction policies. Moreover, the utilization rate of renewable energy is also one of the evaluation projects.

4.2. Using DEMATEL–CRITIC to Calculate the Influential Weights of the Criteria

According to the implementation process of DEMATEL in Section 3.1.1, the eight experts used linguistic variables (Table 2) to evaluate the influence among the criteria. Table 5 presents the results of the DEMATEL questionnaire filled by the first expert. In order to check the consensus level (consistency) of the eight experts, the average sample gap (ASG) index can be calculated through Equation (26) [19,21].

$$ASG = (n(n-1)(p-1))^{-1} \times \sum_{k=2}^{p} \sum_{i=1}^{n} \sum_{j=1}^{n} \left(\frac{\left| a_{ij}^{(k)} - a_{ij}^{(k-1)} \right|}{a_{ij}^{(k)}} \right) \times 100\% \tag{26}$$

where n is the number of criteria (15), and $a_{ij}^{(k)}$ is the evaluation value of the kth expert, $k = 1, 2, \ldots, p$. According to the index, the average gap of the eight experts is 3.8%, indicating that there is 96.2% of the confidence level that these experts have achieved a consensus.

Table 5. The direct relation matrix of the first expert.

	C_{11}	C_{12}	C_{13}	C_{14}	C_{21}	C_{22}	C_{23}	C_{24}	C_{25}	C_{31}	C_{32}	C_{33}	C_{41}	C_{42}	C_{43}
C_{11}	0	3	3	3	3	3	2	2	2	3	3	4	2	0	1
C_{12}	1	0	3	2	3	0	1	3	2	1	3	4	4	3	3
C_{13}	2	3	0	1	2	2	2	4	4	2	2	3	3	2	3
C_{14}	1	4	3	0	4	2	2	4	2	2	3	4	0	0	0
C_{21}	1	2	2	3	0	4	2	3	4	2	2	4	4	2	4
C_{22}	0	2	1	2	1	0	3	2	3	4	2	2	4	3	4
C_{23}	1	2	3	1	1	4	0	4	2	4	3	1	1	1	1
C_{24}	1	4	4	4	2	2	4	0	2	2	4	4	2	2	2
C_{25}	1	2	2	4	1	4	2	1	0	4	3	3	3	3	2
C_{31}	1	4	3	2	4	1	1	1	4	0	2	2	2	1	2
C_{32}	4	4	4	4	4	1	1	3	2	1	0	4	3	3	3
C_{33}	1	4	4	4	4	0	4	4	2	1	4	0	4	2	2
C_{41}	2	2	3	0	4	2	1	4	1	3	3	1	0	4	4
C_{42}	3	3	3	2	3	2	2	4	1	1	1	1	4	0	4
C_{43}	2	2	3	1	0	2	1	0	0	3	1	1	4	4	0

Table 6 shows the total influence ($r_i + s_i$) and net influence ($r_i - s_i$) of all criteria. Enterprise size and financial capabilities (C_{11}) has the largest net influence (0.838), indicating that many criteria are affected by this criterion. Moreover, green resource integration (C_{41}) has the highest total influence ($r_{41} + s_{41} = 8.886$) in the overall evaluation system, and its influential weight is 0.076. DEMATEL's results not only facilitate decision-makers to quickly understand which criteria are the main causes or consequences, but also generate a set of subjective influential weights. Next, we adopt the CRITIC method, using the performance matrix as input data to derive a set of objective influential weights.

Table 6. DEMATEL calculation results and subjective influential weights.

	r	s	$r+s$	$r-s$	DEMATEL Weight
C_{11}	3.437	2.599	6.037	0.838	0.052
C_{12}	3.934	4.195	8.130	−0.261	0.069
C_{13}	4.004	4.477	8.481	−0.473	0.072
C_{14}	3.454	3.745	7.198	−0.291	0.062
C_{21}	4.442	4.049	8.491	0.393	0.073
C_{22}	3.654	3.128	6.782	0.526	0.058
C_{23}	4.208	3.554	7.762	0.654	0.066
C_{24}	4.079	3.968	8.047	0.111	0.069
C_{25}	4.243	3.407	7.650	0.836	0.065
C_{31}	3.952	3.442	7.394	0.509	0.063
C_{32}	4.308	4.204	8.511	0.104	0.073
C_{33}	4.092	4.121	8.212	−0.029	0.070
C_{41}	4.000	4.886	8.886	−0.886	0.076
C_{42}	3.867	4.276	8.142	−0.409	0.070
C_{43}	2.831	4.453	7.284	−1.621	0.062

The off-site auditors of the case company surveyed a total of 165 manufacturing-related outsourcing providers, and each outsourcing provider was summed up with 15 performance scores, with a maximum score of 100 points and a minimum score of 0 points. The performance matrix of outsourcing providers is 165 × 15 and there is no missing value for the data in this matrix. Table 7 presents the first 10 data of outsourcing providers. The calculation is performed through the steps in Section 3.1.2. The standard deviation (σ), influence degree (φ), and objective influential weights are presented in Table 8.

Table 7. Performance matrix of the first 10 data of the outsourcing providers.

	C_{11}	C_{12}	C_{13}	C_{14}	C_{21}	C_{22}	C_{23}	C_{24}	C_{25}	C_{31}	C_{32}	C_{33}	C_{41}	C_{42}	C_{43}
A_1	77	87	82	77	69	84	80	76	87	60	80	82	95	80	93
A_2	71	80	91	77	85	56	73	76	87	67	67	82	98	80	67
A_3	83	80	100	77	90	72	73	76	100	73	73	87	95	90	60
A_4	89	80	96	71	88	80	73	68	80	40	80	39	90	85	100
A_5	71	73	87	77	88	64	80	80	73	67	73	73	94	80	93
A_6	83	80	100	77	90	64	73	76	100	73	80	82	88	100	33
A_7	60	80	73	71	88	56	60	72	67	35	60	31	81	40	80
A_8	89	80	100	83	98	72	80	80	100	87	100	91	95	100	67
A_9	83	93	91	66	93	84	60	80	93	73	67	64	87	65	93
A_{10}	77	53	87	54	81	56	67	64	87	60	67	69	85	85	93

Table 8. CRITIC calculation results and final weights.

	σ	φ	CRITIC Weight	DEMATEL Weight	Final Weight	Ranking
C_{11}	0.152	1.082	0.063	0.052	0.057	14
C_{12}	0.145	1.067	0.062	0.069	0.066	8
C_{13}	0.106	0.687	0.040	0.072	0.056	15
C_{14}	0.141	0.916	0.053	0.062	0.057	13
C_{21}	0.104	0.857	0.050	0.073	0.061	10
C_{22}	0.151	1.027	0.060	0.058	0.059	11
C_{23}	0.182	1.352	0.078	0.066	0.072	5
C_{24}	0.155	1.121	0.065	0.069	0.067	6
C_{25}	0.160	1.110	0.064	0.065	0.065	9
C_{31}	0.190	1.544	0.090	0.063	0.076	4
C_{32}	0.168	1.437	0.083	0.073	0.078	2
C_{33}	0.160	1.479	0.086	0.070	0.078	3
C_{41}	0.097	0.676	0.039	0.076	0.058	12
C_{42}	0.156	1.078	0.063	0.070	0.066	7
C_{43}	0.184	1.807	0.105	0.062	0.084	1

DEMATEL–CRITIC overcomes the traditional problem of considering only subjective or objective perspectives, and generates a final influential weight with a more comprehensive perspective. The top five criteria with the highest weights are pollution emission treatment (C_{43}), customer relationship management and loyalty (C_{32}), communication and information sharing (C_{33}), after-sales service and improvement capabilities (C_{31}), and key component inventory control capabilities (C_{23}).

4.3. Using a Classifiable TOPSIS Rating for the Performance of Outsourcing Providers

The process of evaluation and classification of green outsourcing providers is complex and difficult. It is one of the purposes of this study to use simple and clear reports or diagrams to help operators understand the performance of outsourcing providers. The proposed classifiable TOPSIS technique introduces the concept of aspiration level and avoids considering only the relative preference solution of the current scheme. Therefore, the first 10 outsourcing provider performance data are taken as an example (Table 7), and all scores are divided by 100 (the aspiration level) to convert the value range from 0 to 1 to form a normalized performance matrix, as shown in Table 9. Here, the aspiration level and the worst level are considered as alternatives, so their scores are 1 and 0, respectively. Table 10 presents the weighted normalized performance matrix.

Table 9. Normalized performance matrix of the first 10 data of outsourcing providers.

	C_{11}	C_{12}	C_{13}	C_{14}	C_{21}	C_{22}	C_{23}	C_{24}	C_{25}	C_{31}	C_{32}	C_{33}	C_{41}	C_{42}	C_{43}
A_1	0.772	0.866	0.823	0.772	0.685	0.840	0.800	0.760	0.866	0.600	0.800	0.823	0.952	0.800	0.933
A_2	0.714	0.800	0.911	0.772	0.855	0.560	0.734	0.760	0.866	0.666	0.666	0.823	0.976	0.800	0.667
A_3	0.828	0.800	1.000	0.772	0.903	0.720	0.734	0.760	1.000	0.734	0.734	0.867	0.952	0.900	0.600
A_4	0.886	0.800	0.956	0.714	0.879	0.800	0.734	0.680	0.800	0.400	0.800	0.389	0.903	0.850	1.000
A_5	0.714	0.734	0.867	0.772	0.879	0.640	0.800	0.800	0.734	0.666	0.734	0.733	0.940	0.800	0.933
A_6	0.828	0.800	1.000	0.772	0.903	0.640	0.734	0.760	1.000	0.734	0.800	0.823	0.879	1.000	0.333
A_7	0.600	0.800	0.733	0.714	0.879	0.560	0.600	0.720	0.666	0.350	0.600	0.305	0.807	0.400	0.800
A_8	0.886	0.800	1.000	0.828	0.976	0.720	0.800	0.800	1.000	0.866	1.000	0.911	0.952	1.000	0.667
A_9	0.828	0.934	0.911	0.658	0.927	0.840	0.600	0.800	0.934	0.734	0.666	0.644	0.867	0.650	0.933
A_{10}	0.772	0.534	0.867	0.542	0.807	0.560	0.666	0.640	0.866	0.600	0.666	0.689	0.855	0.850	0.933
A^{aspire}	1	1	1	1	1	1	1	1	1	1	1	1	1	1	1
A^{worst}	0	0	0	0	0	0	0	0	0	0	0	0	0	0	0

Table 10. Weighted normalized performance matrix of the first 10 data of outsourcing providers.

	C_{11}	C_{12}	C_{13}	C_{14}	C_{21}	C_{22}	C_{23}	C_{24}	C_{25}	C_{31}	C_{32}	C_{33}	C_{41}	C_{42}	C_{43}
A_1	0.044	0.057	0.046	0.044	0.042	0.049	0.058	0.051	0.056	0.046	0.062	0.064	0.055	0.053	0.078
A_2	0.041	0.053	0.051	0.044	0.052	0.033	0.053	0.051	0.056	0.051	0.052	0.064	0.056	0.053	0.056
A_3	0.047	0.053	0.056	0.044	0.055	0.042	0.053	0.051	0.065	0.056	0.057	0.068	0.055	0.059	0.050
A_4	0.051	0.053	0.054	0.041	0.054	0.047	0.053	0.045	0.052	0.031	0.062	0.030	0.052	0.056	0.084
A_5	0.041	0.048	0.049	0.044	0.054	0.038	0.058	0.054	0.048	0.051	0.057	0.057	0.054	0.053	0.078
A_6	0.047	0.053	0.056	0.044	0.055	0.038	0.053	0.051	0.065	0.056	0.062	0.064	0.051	0.066	0.028
A_7	0.034	0.053	0.041	0.041	0.054	0.033	0.043	0.048	0.043	0.027	0.047	0.024	0.046	0.026	0.067
A_8	0.051	0.053	0.056	0.047	0.060	0.042	0.058	0.054	0.065	0.066	0.078	0.071	0.055	0.066	0.056
A_9	0.047	0.061	0.051	0.038	0.057	0.049	0.043	0.054	0.061	0.056	0.052	0.050	0.050	0.043	0.078
A_{10}	0.044	0.035	0.049	0.031	0.049	0.033	0.048	0.043	0.056	0.046	0.052	0.054	0.049	0.056	0.078
A^{aspire} (z^+)	0.057	0.066	0.056	0.057	0.061	0.059	0.072	0.067	0.065	0.076	0.078	0.078	0.058	0.066	0.084
A^{worst} (z^-)	0	0	0	0	0	0	0	0	0	0	0	0	0	0	0

According to the calculation steps in Section 3.2, the analysis results can be summarized in Table 11. The degrees of separation of outsourcing provider A_h from PIS and NIS (S^+ and S^-) can be determined. In particular, the degree of separation between the aspiration level and PIS must be 0 (the aspiration level is PIS). Conversely, the degree of separation between the worst level and the negative ideal solution is also 0 (the worst level is NIS). The degree of separation between the aspiration level and the worst level is 0.260 (the Euclidean distance between PIS and NIS is 0.260).

Table 11. Calculation results of the classifiable TOPSIS and the rating scale of the first 10 data of outsourcing providers.

	S^+	S^-	*CC* (Equation (24))	*CC** (Equation (25))	*Gap*	*Rating*
A_1	0.056	0.211	0.0003	0.792	0.208	A
A_2	0.068	0.200	−0.0005	0.746	0.254	B
A_3	0.059	0.211	0.0001	0.782	0.218	A
A_4	0.080	0.203	−0.0011	0.712	0.288	B
A_5	0.061	0.205	−0.0001	0.771	0.229	A
A_6	0.074	0.207	−0.0007	0.732	0.268	B
A_7	0.109	0.168	−0.0030	0.595	0.405	B
A_8	0.044	0.229	0.0011	0.843	0.157	A
A_9	0.064	0.207	−0.0002	0.762	0.238	A
A_{10}	0.079	0.192	−0.0012	0.704	0.296	B
A^{aspire}	0.000	0.260	0.0037	1		
A^{worst}	0.260	0.000	−0.0128	0		

The case company uses the values of 0.5, 0.75, and 0.9 as the classification thresholds. All outsourcing providers are then classified into four levels, including A$^+$, A, B, and C. Furthermore, the gap between each outsourcing provider and the aspiration level has also been determined. The larger the gap, the greater the room for improvement is for the corresponding outsourcing provider. For example, although outsourcing provider A_1 is rated as a Level A outsourcing provider, its overall evaluation performance is still 0.208 units away from the aspiration level. The proposed model has many potential management implications, as detailed in Section 4.3.

5. Management Implications and Discussion

Due to the development trend of artificial intelligence, many machine tool equipment companies have created customized machines for customers. This also increases the research and development and manufacturing costs for the companies. Therefore, co-production through outsourcing providers becomes a good strategy. Under the Taiwan government's "5 + 2 Industry Innovation Program" policy, the machinery industry has become one of the emerging high-tech industries, and many organizations have invested huge amounts of money to promote the industry. In order to improve the level of machine intelligence, machine tools related to smart machines have been continuously developed. Compared with other manufacturing industries, the manufacturing technology threshold for smart machinery is relatively high, and most companies will use outsourcing strategies to reduce research and development (R&D) and production costs.

According to DEMATEL–CRITIC analysis, pollution emission treatment (C_{43}) is the most important criterion, with a weight of 0.084. The waste reduction and carbon reduction are among the most critical evaluation indicators for manufacturing. Facing the rise of environmental awareness, many international environmental protection and trade organizations have formulated many environmental protection regulations to require companies to pay attention to environmental issues. Customer relationship management and loyalty (C_{32}) is the second most important criterion. The customer relationship management capabilities of an outsourcing provider will directly affect the willingness of the company to sign a contract, especially the coordination of design changes and the enthusiasm of after-sales service. In addition, the loyalty of outsourcing companies is particularly valued by the company's senior management, which involves a long-term willingness to sign a contract. The weights of communication and message sharing (C_{33}) and C_{32} are very close, indicating that the degree of information sharing by outsourcing providers is also highly valued. The remaining criteria can also give outsourcing providers suggestions for improvement through the weight values.

The proposed model establishes a visual rating diagram to help decision-makers to judge the performance of outsourcing providers more clearly, as shown in Figure 2. The diagram clearly classifies all outsourcing providers into four levels, including 11 in Level A$^+$, 100 in Level A, 50 in Level B, and 4 in Level C. The thresholds for these classifications are determined by the decision-making team established by the company. The analysis results are verified by the case company to be both reasonable and helpful. Most of the outsourcing companies in Level A have cooperated with the company for more than 10 years, and their performance in all aspects has met the requirements of the senior management. Although the outsourcing providers of Level A have a good rating score, there are still some gaps from the aspiration level. Outsourcing companies at this level can focus on improving the criteria with greater weights first, including C_{43}, C_{32}, C_{33}, C_{31}, and C_{23}. Level B outsourcing providers should conduct a comprehensive review of the company's current operating conditions and provide complete improvement measures in four major directions: operation (D_1), professional skills, (D_2), service (D_3), and environment management (D_4) to move toward Level A. Otherwise, they will face elimination in the future. Finally, the performance of the outsourcing providers at Level C does not meet the expectations of the case company at all, so the partnership of outsourcing providers at this level should be dissolved.

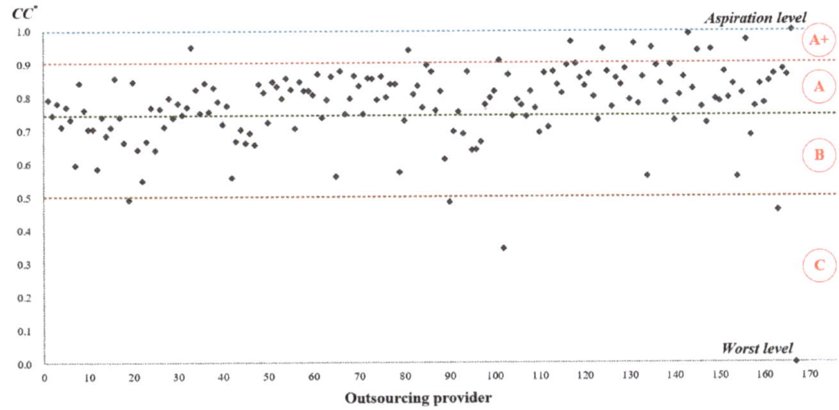

Figure 2. One hundred and sixty-five outsourcing providers' CC^* and their classification levels.

Next, we discuss whether the proposed DEMATEL–CRITIC method will affect the results of the classifiable TOPSIS because of the change in the ratio of subjectivity and objectivity. Therefore, the sensitivity analysis was performed nine times to test whether the priorities of outsourcing providers have changed significantly. By changing the parameters of Equation (19) from 0.1 to 0.9, all the criteria weights are changed, as shown in Table 12.

Table 12. Weight configuration of sensitivity analysis performed nine times.

	Run 1	Run 2	Run 3	Run 4	Run 5	Run 6	Run 7	Run 8	Run 9
	$\alpha = 0.1$	$\alpha = 0.2$	$\alpha = 0.3$	$\alpha = 0.4$	$\alpha = 0.5$	$\alpha = 0.6$	$\alpha = 0.7$	$\alpha = 0.8$	$\alpha = 0.9$
C_{11}	0.062	0.061	0.059	0.058	0.057	0.056	0.055	0.054	0.053
C_{12}	0.063	0.063	0.064	0.065	0.066	0.066	0.067	0.068	0.069
C_{13}	0.043	0.046	0.050	0.053	0.056	0.059	0.063	0.066	0.069
C_{14}	0.054	0.055	0.056	0.057	0.057	0.058	0.059	0.060	0.061
C_{21}	0.052	0.054	0.057	0.059	0.061	0.063	0.066	0.068	0.070
C_{22}	0.059	0.059	0.059	0.059	0.059	0.059	0.058	0.058	0.058
C_{23}	0.077	0.076	0.075	0.074	0.072	0.071	0.070	0.069	0.068
C_{24}	0.065	0.066	0.066	0.067	0.067	0.067	0.068	0.068	0.068
C_{25}	0.064	0.065	0.065	0.065	0.065	0.065	0.065	0.065	0.065
C_{31}	0.087	0.084	0.082	0.079	0.076	0.074	0.071	0.068	0.066
C_{32}	0.082	0.081	0.080	0.079	0.078	0.077	0.076	0.075	0.074
C_{33}	0.084	0.083	0.081	0.080	0.078	0.076	0.075	0.073	0.072
C_{41}	0.043	0.047	0.050	0.054	0.058	0.061	0.065	0.069	0.072
C_{42}	0.063	0.064	0.065	0.065	0.066	0.067	0.067	0.068	0.069
C_{43}	0.101	0.096	0.092	0.088	0.084	0.079	0.075	0.071	0.067

Figure 3 shows the ranking results after the nine times of sensitivity analysis performed. Obviously, the ranking of outsourcing providers will not be changed significantly because of the excessive emphasis on the weight of subjectivity or objectivity. The sensitivity analysis shows that the proposed model is robust.

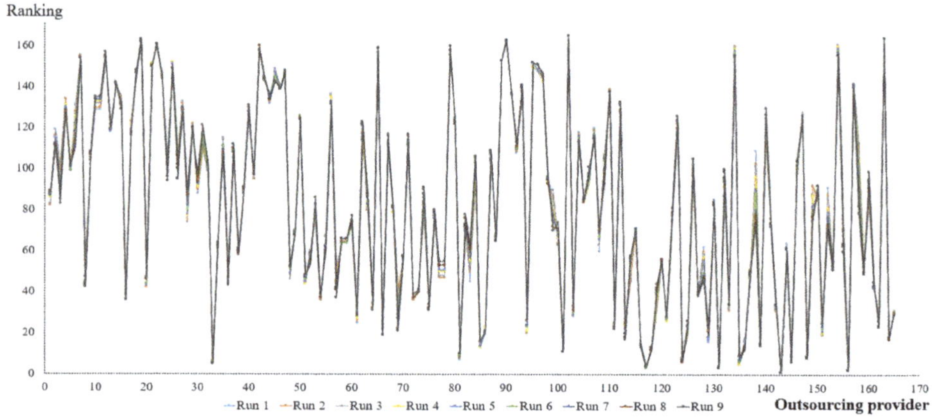

Figure 3. Results of the sensitivity analysis performed nine times.

In addition, we conducted model comparisons to demonstrate the differences between this study and previous studies. Model 1 is the original SAW analysis method of the case company, and the criteria weights are directly given by the senior executives. Model 2 uses the weights of DEMATEL–CRITIC and uses SAW for performance integration. Model 3 is the proposed model. Figure 4 shows the ranking results of all the outsourcing providers in the three models. It can be found that the ranking results of Models 1 and 2 are almost the same. There are 14 outsourcing providers in the first place in these two models. In this case, the company cannot distinguish the pros and cons of these 14 outsourcing providers. Moreover, each outsourcing provider will not be able to know what the gap is from the aspiration level. Although the SAW method is simple, it has not considered the comprehensiveness of the evaluation system, only the scores are multiplied by the weight values. The ranking result of the proposed model (Model 3) is significantly different from the other models. We determine the whole range of performance by formulating PIS and NIS, and use the concept of distance to define the relative position of each outsourcing provider. Moreover, the new index proposed by the model clearly points out the gap between the outsourcing provider and the aspiration level.

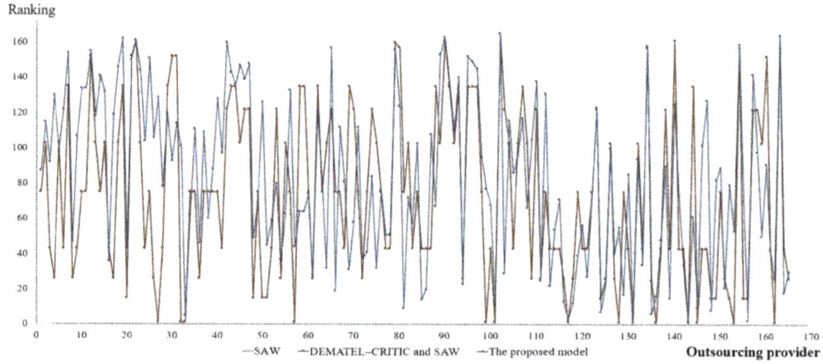

Figure 4. Comparisons of the proposed model with other methods.

6. Conclusions

This study contributes to the research of green outsourcing evaluation. The contribution and advantages of this research include four aspects: (i) integrating environmental protection criteria in the evaluation framework of outsourcing providers, to reflect the awareness that enterprises should pay attention to environmental protection. (ii) By considering the mutual influence of the criteria, it overcomes the shortcomings of the previous studies that need to assume the criteria to be independent. (iii) Aspect three involves using the DEMATEL–CRITIC method, which considers both subjectivity and objectivity; the impact of the criteria on the evaluation system is also explored. (iv) Aspect four involves proposing a classifiable TOPSIS to classify a large number of outsourcing providers, and give appropriate suggestions for improvement according to their levels. In addition to the above contributions, our research has also discovered some findings, including the robustness of the proposed model being confirmed through the sensitivity analysis, which means that the analysis results will not be significantly affected by the changes in weights. Moreover, the model comparisons confirmed that our model is more practical and effective. In short, the research method in this paper can be copied to other MCDM evaluation and selection topics, especially the classification of information with big data.

The analysis process of this study is highly dependent on the judgment of experts, so there are several limitations on its use, including the following: (i) the selected experts are sufficiently representative; (ii) the evaluation criteria need to be repeatedly confirmed, whether it is appropriate or not; and (iii) the analysts must be able to interpret the results of each method. Moreover, the classification of TOPSIS in terms of setting the classification thresholds can be further determined by more scientific methods.

Since the methodology proposed in this study is novel, there are some suggestions for further studies in the future. The proposed model has not yet taken into consideration the uncertainty of the information and evaluation environment. Future research can combine fuzzy or grey or Z-number or neutrosophic logic theories to enhance the adaptability of the model. Finally, the proposed model can be coded and incorporated into business software to facilitate the convenient use in industry.

Author Contributions: C.-F.L. designed the research and wrote the paper. W.-C.J.H. collected the data and verified the model. H.-W.L. co-wrote, administered the project, and made revisions to the paper. All authors have read and agreed to the published version of the manuscript.

Funding: This research received no external funding.

Conflicts of Interest: The authors declare no conflict of interest.

References

1. Ciasullo, M.V.; Fenza, G.; Loia, V.; Orciuoli, F.; Troisi, O.; Herrera-Viedma, E. Business process outsourcing enhanced by fuzzy linguistic consensus model. *Appl. Soft. Comput.* **2018**, *64*, 436–444. [CrossRef]
2. Awasthy, P.; Hazra, J. Collaboration under outcome-based contracts for information technology services. *Eur. J. Oper. Res.* **2020**, *286*, 350–359. [CrossRef]
3. Ji, P.; Zhang, H.Y.; Wang, J.Q. Selecting an outsourcing provider based on the combined MABAC–ELECTRE method using single-valued neutrosophic linguistic sets. *Comput. Ind. Eng.* **2018**, *120*, 429–441. [CrossRef]
4. Perçin, S. An integrated fuzzy SWARA and fuzzy AD approach for outsourcing provider selection. *J. Manuf. Technol. Manag.* **2019**, *30*, 531–552. [CrossRef]
5. Wang, J.J.; Yang, D.L. Using a hybrid multi-criteria decision aid method for information systems outsourcing. *Comput. Oper. Res.* **2007**, *34*, 3691–3700. [CrossRef]
6. Hsu, C.C.; Liou, J.J.; Chuang, Y.C. Integrating DANP and modified grey relation theory for the selection of an outsourcing provider. *Expert Syst. Appl.* **2013**, *40*, 2297–2304. [CrossRef]
7. Vazifehdan, M.N.; Darestani, S.A. Green Logistics Outsourcing Employing Multi Criteria Decision Making and Quality Function Deployment in the Petrochemical Industry. *Asian J. Shipp. Logist.* **2019**, *35*, 243–254. [CrossRef]

8. Chang, M.H.; Liou, J.J.; Lo, H.W. A Hybrid MCDM Model for Evaluating Strategic Alliance Partners in the Green Biopharmaceutical Industry. *Sustainability* **2019**, *11*, 4065. [CrossRef]
9. Liou, J.J.; Chuang, Y.T. Developing a hybrid multi-criteria model for selection of outsourcing providers. *Expert Syst. Appl.* **2010**, *37*, 3755–3761. [CrossRef]
10. Wan, S.P.; Wang, F.; Lin, L.L.; Dong, J.Y. An intuitionistic fuzzy linear programming method for logistics outsourcing provider selection. *Knowl. Based Syst.* **2015**, *82*, 80–94. [CrossRef]
11. Uygun, Ö.; Kaçamak, H.; Kahraman, Ü.A. An integrated DEMATEL and Fuzzy ANP techniques for evaluation and selection of outsourcing provider for a telecommunication company. *Comput. Ind. Eng.* **2015**, *86*, 137–146. [CrossRef]
12. Stojčić, M.; Zavadskas, E.K.; Pamučar, D.; Stević, Ž.; Mardani, A. Application of MCDM methods in sustainability engineering: A literature review 2008–2018. *Symmetry* **2019**, *11*, 350. [CrossRef]
13. Yazdani, M.; Chatterjee, P.; Pamucar, D.; Chakraborty, S. Development of an integrated decision making model for location selection of logistics centers in the Spanish autonomous communities. *Expert Syst. Appl.* **2020**, *148*, 113208. [CrossRef]
14. Pamučar, D.; Janković, A. The application of the hybrid interval rough weighted Power-Heronian operator in multi-criteria decision making. *Oper. Res. Eng. Sci. Theory Appl.* **2020**, *3*, 54–73. [CrossRef]
15. Türk, S.; Deveci, M.; Özcan, E.; Canıtez, F.; John, R. Interval type-2 fuzzy sets improved by Simulated Annealing for locating the electric charging stations. *Inf. Sci.* **2021**, *547*, 641–666. [CrossRef]
16. Pamucar, D.; Deveci, M.; Canıtez, F.; Lukovac, V. Selecting an airport ground access mode using novel fuzzy LBWA-WASPAS-H decision making model. *Eng. Appl. Artif. Intell.* **2020**, *93*, 103703. [CrossRef]
17. Hsu, W.C.J.; Liou, J.J.; Lo, H.W. A group decision-making approach for exploring trends in the development of the healthcare industry in Taiwan. *Decis. Support Syst.* **2020**, 113447. [CrossRef]
18. Matić, B.; Jovanović, S.; Das, D.K.; Zavadskas, E.K.; Stević, Ž.; Sremac, S.; Marinković, M. A new hybrid MCDM model: Sustainable supplier selection in a construction company. *Symmetry* **2019**, *11*, 353. [CrossRef]
19. Hsu, C.C.; Liou, J.J.; Lo, H.W.; Wang, Y.C. Using a hybrid method for evaluating and improving the service quality of public bike-sharing systems. *J. Clean Prod.* **2018**, *202*, 1131–1144. [CrossRef]
20. Lo, H.W.; Liou, J.J.; Huang, C.N.; Chuang, Y.C.; Tzeng, G.H. A new soft computing approach for analyzing the influential relationships of critical infrastructures. *Int. J. Crit. Infrastruct. Prot.* **2020**, *28*, 100336. [CrossRef]
21. Lo, H.W.; Shiue, W.; Liou, J.J.; Tzeng, G.H. A hybrid MCDM-based FMEA model for identification of critical failure modes in manufacturing. *Soft Comput.* **2020**, *24*, 15733–15745. [CrossRef]
22. Du, Y.; Zheng, Y.; Wu, G.; Tang, Y. Decision-making method of heavy-duty machine tool remanufacturing based on AHP-entropy weight and extension theory. *J. Clean Prod.* **2020**, *252*, 119607. [CrossRef]
23. Heydari, J.; Govindan, K.; Nasab, H.R.E.; Taleizadeh, A.A. Coordination by quantity flexibility contract in a two-echelon supply chain system: Effect of outsourcing decisions. *Int. J. Prod. Econ.* **2020**, *225*, 107586. [CrossRef]
24. Li, D.F.; Wan, S.P. A fuzzy inhomogenous multiattribute group decision making approach to solve outsourcing provider selection problems. *Knowl. Based Syst.* **2014**, *67*, 71–89. [CrossRef]
25. Li, D.F.; Wan, S.P. Fuzzy heterogeneous multiattribute decision making method for outsourcing provider selection. *Expert Syst. Appl.* **2014**, *41*, 3047–3059. [CrossRef]
26. Zarbakhshnia, N.; Wu, Y.; Govindan, K.; Soleimani, H. A novel hybrid multiple attribute decision-making approach for outsourcing sustainable reverse logistics. *J. Clean Prod.* **2020**, *242*, 118461. [CrossRef]
27. Prajapati, H.; Kant, R.; Tripathi, S.M. An integrated framework for prioritizing the outsourcing performance outcomes. *J. Glob. Oper. Strateg. Sourc.* **2020**. [CrossRef]
28. Song, W.; Zhu, Y.; Zhao, Q. Analyzing barriers for adopting sustainable online consumption: A rough hierarchical DEMATEL method. *Comput. Ind. Eng.* **2020**, *140*, 106279. [CrossRef]
29. Zhang, X.; Su, J. A combined fuzzy DEMATEL and TOPSIS approach for estimating participants in knowledge-intensive crowdsourcing. *Comput. Ind. Eng.* **2019**, *137*, 106085. [CrossRef]
30. Liu, P.C.; Lo, H.W.; Liou, J.J. A Combination of DEMATEL and BWM-Based ANP Methods for Exploring the Green Building Rating System in Taiwan. *Sustainability* **2020**, *12*, 3216. [CrossRef]

31. Kuo, T. A modified TOPSIS with a different ranking index. *Eur. J. Oper. Res.* **2017**, *260*, 152–160. [CrossRef]

symmetry

MDPI

Article

Sustainable Decision Making Using a Consensus Model for Consistent Hesitant Fuzzy Preference Relations—Water Allocation Management Case Study

Atiq-ur Rehman [1], Jarosław Wątróbski [2,*], Shahzad Faizi [3], Tabasam Rashid [4] and Małgorzata Tarczyńska-Łuniewska [5]

1 Department of Mathematics, COMSATS University Islamabad at Lahore, Lahore 5400, Pakistan; atiqurehman@cuilahore.edu.pk
2 Institute of Management, University of Szczecin, Cukrowa 6, 71-104 Szczecin, Poland
3 Department of Mathematics, Virtual University of Pakistan, Lahore 54000, Pakistan; shahzadfaizi@vu.edu.pk
4 Department of Mathematics, University of Management and Technology, Lahore 54770, Pakistan; tabasam.rashid@umt.edu.pk
5 Institute of Economic and Finance, University of Szczecin, Mickiewicza 64, 71-101 Szczecin, Poland; malgorzata.tarczynska@usz.edu.pl
* Correspondence: jaroslaw.watrobski@usz.edu.pl; Tel.: +48-91-444-1996

Received: 21 October 2020; Accepted: 24 November 2020; Published: 26 November 2020

Abstract: This paper presents an improved consensus-based procedure to handle multi-person decision making (MPDM) using hesitant fuzzy preference relations (HFPRs) which are not in normal format. At the first level, we proposed a Łukasiewicz transitivity (T_L-transitivity) based scheme to get normalized hesitant fuzzy preference relations (NHFPRs), subject to which, a consensus-based model is established. Then, a transitive closure formula is defined to construct T_L-consistent HFPRs and creates symmetrical matrices. Following this, consistency analysis is made to estimate the consistency degrees of the information provided by the decision-makers (DMs), and consequently, to assign the consistency weights to them. The final priority weights vector of DMs is calculated after the combination of consistency weights and predefined priority weights (if any). The consensus process concludes whether the aggregation of data and selection of the best alternative should be originated or not. The enhancement mechanism is indulged in improving the consensus measure among the DMs, after introducing an identifier used to locate the weak positions, in case of the poor consensus reached. In the end, a comparative example reflects the applicability and the efficiency of proposed scheme. The results show that the proposed method can offer useful comprehension into the MPDM process.

Keywords: consistency weights; fuzzy preference relation (FPR); hesitant fuzzy preference relation (HFPR); Łukasiewicz consistency; normal hesitant fuzzy preference relation (NHFPR)

1. Introduction

Making decisions is an integral part of human life. Many of them require "rational" or "good" decisions to be sought from decision makers (DMs), taking into account different criteria for evaluating individual decision options [1,2]. A typical practical area where the choice of a decision option requires consideration of a set of conflicting criteria is the domain of sustainability [3,4]. In such situations, the evaluation of decision alternatives with consideration of ecological, economic and social perspectives is carried out using multi-criteria decision support methods [5,6].

In modern society, multi-person decision making (MPDM) is an important process of getting optimal decision results [7]. In any case, the evaluation contributed by DMs might well fluctuate depending on different interpretation skills, experience and judgments of the DMs [8,9]. Therefore, it is difficult to achieve a unified consensus under this condition [10]. This is a significant issue for the assessment of the outcomes of decisions that are generally appropriate to most DMs when the decision-making process originates. However, a great challenge for the researchers is to achieve unanimous and acceptable decision results and approach a strong consensus level [11]. Therefore, different algorithms to reach a strong consensus level in a GDM process have been thoroughly studied. For instance, Zhang et al. [12] established a maximum support degree consensus model under hesitant information and linguistic assessments. Li et al. [13] introduced an interactive process of reaching the consensus level at uncertain and minimum cost. Li and Wang [14] proposed an automatic iterative algorithm to reach a consensus level in the context of probabilistic hesitant fuzzy preference relations. Tian and Wang et al. [15] established signed distance-based consensus measures on three levels with multi-granular hesitant unbalanced linguistic assessments to find the consensus degree. Zhang et al. [16] developed a consensus model with heterogeneous large-scale GDM with satisfaction and individual concerns. Furthermore, Herrera-Viedma et al. [17] studied analysis of consensus-reaching models in fuzzy environments.

In MPDM processes, the consensus-building mechanism is commonly used as a tool based on preference relations. The definition of hesitant fuzzy preference relation (HFPR) developed by Xia and Xu [18], which is now being used as an efficient and easy method for communicating alternative data for a group of DMs, e.g., while providing the decision degree to which an alternative x_1 is preferable to another alternative x_2 for a group of three DMs. Suppose three DMs provide 0.3, 0.4 and 0.5, respectively. If all the DMs cannot establish a consensus to accept their assessment, then a set comprising their combined decisions in the form of the hesitant fuzzy element (HFE) {0.3, 0.4, 0.5} can be considered as the preference degree of x_1 to x_2. The HFPR proposed in [18] has been studied by many researchers in the perspective of GDM [19–21] but despite all these extensive studies and developments, certain disputes remain. The immediate benefit of the HFPR is that the DMs may have a set of values that display the consequences of the assessment. However, the HFEs in the HFPR will provide a specific number of elements that can cause difficulties in creating a consensus in the decision-making process. For instance, most consensus models are focused on distance calculation between two HFPRs, and it is very difficult to determine an effective distance between two unequal HFEs [22]. As a result, DMs are confused in deriving the priority weight vectors from the HFPR having unequal HFEs [23]. Based on this discussion, it raises a query that either a normalization-based method is rational after reviewing all these controversies. However, some researchers focused on using the normalization-based method, and others denied this idea [24].

The normalization-based method required any two HFEs to have an equal number of elements. Various scholars in the decision-making process have greatly appreciated this method. In the case of those HFEs having an unequal number of elements, the HFEs having an equal number of elements can be obtained by inserting various elements to the shorter one or removing several elements in the longer HFE. Zhu et al. [23] initially introduced α and β normalization methods. Based on these two methods, many researchers have developed different methods of the extraction of priority weight vector as well as the consensus reaching models [25,26]. Zhang and Wu [26] designed goal programming models for incomplete hesitant multiplicative preference relation and determine the priority weight vectors by using α and β normalization methods. Meng et al. [27] proposed a new consistency concept for hesitant multiplicative preference relations and then derive the hesitant fuzzy priority weight vector. Furthermore, Zhang [28] developed a goal-programming model for an incomplete HFPR and derive priority weight vectors based on α and β normalization methods respectively. Zhang et al. and Li et al. [29,30] defined some preference relations based on q-rung orthopair fuzzy sets and investigated a technique to obtain the priority weights from individual or group q-rung orthopair fuzzy preference relations. Since various scholars have continuously forced on using these two methods, therefore, various new normalization methods have been constructed, for example, Xu et al. [31] introduced an additive consistency-based normalization method and developed a consensus model for solving water allocation management problems.

Due to the limited expertise and experience of DMs, it can be difficult for them to establish complete preference relations during pairwise decisions on alternatives [32,33]. Therefore, there is a need for the development of some approaches which help to manage HFPRs with incomplete information. Based on the additive consistency of HFPR, Zhang et al. [34] proposed a method to guess missing elements of an incomplete HFPR. Zhang [28] further defined the multiplicative consistency of an HFPR, and by using a normalization method, the missing elements of HFPR were estimated based on the multiplicative consistency. Based on the additive consistency and multiplicative consistency of incomplete HFPRs in local and group decision-making settings, Xu et al. [21] designed mixed 0–1 programming models to find a priority weight vector from incomplete HFPRs. To estimate the missing elements for an incomplete HFPR, Khalid and Beg [35] proposed an algorithm by utilizing hesitant upper bound condition for the DMs.

The stability of preference relations plays a critical role in the decision-making phase in the pairwise assessments of DM's preferences [36]. The idea of the consistency of fuzzy preference relation was extended to establish the concept of consistency of HFPR. It is very important to measure the consistency of fuzzy preference relations to get consistent results from a decision making process. By using the α-normalization method, Zhu [37] introduced a regression method and established a methodology to transform HFPR into a fuzzy preference relation having the highest level of consistency measure. To measure the consistency level of HFPR, the distance measure between normalized HFPR and consistent HFPR plays an important role. By using this idea, Zhang et al. [38] constructed a consistent HFPR based on the concept of additive consistency and multiplicative consistency of HFPR. Some feedback and automatic optimization algorithms were developed in the same study to improve the consistency level of those HFPRs which are not of acceptable consistency [39]. Liu et al. [40] derived some operational laws for fuzzy preference relations with self-confidence. They presented an additive consistency index that reflects both the fuzzy preference values and self-confidence to include their consistency levels.

A concise literature review shows that the consensus reaching process must be considered in MPDM problems. As discussed in our previous works, while outstanding achievements in this field have been made, very little work has been centered on consensus and consistency measures and, therefore, the novelty of our paper is to establish a consensus model in the context of HFPRs, based on another effective consistency measure approach called the T_L-consistency. This research study is based on two research questions. The first one is to propose a consensus-based method to handle MPDM problem using consistent HFPRs, and the second one is to incorporate an enhancement mechanism to accelerate the execution of a higher consensus level on an easy path. In this paper, the authors present an improved technique for consensus proposing in group decision making based on T_L-consistency in HFPRs environment. As consistency is an important issue to accept when the experts provide data, the proposed method can estimate more reasonable and consistent values when an FPR carries missing preferences. Consistency is associated with the transitivity property for which several useful forms or conditions have been suggested in the literature of FPRs [41]. The weakest of them is T_L-transitivity, i.e., $r_{ik} \geq \max(r_{ij} + r_{jk} - 1, 0)$, and it is the most appropriate notion of transitivity for fuzzy ordering [42]. Therefore, the individual and collective FPRs obtained by this method are fully consistent under the use of t-norm. At the first step, we evaluate the missing preferences of IFPRs using T_L-transitivity property. Then, we propose the changed consistency matrices of experts, which have to satisfy the T_L-consistency, and measure the level of consistency. The degree of significance is given to the experts based on accuracy weights aggregated with confidence weights. The proposed approach provides us with a powerful way to create consensus in group decision-making based on T_L-transitivity with IFPRs.

This manuscript is organized as follows: in Section 2, some basic definitions are provided to facilitate the paper understanding. In Section 3, a new procedure to normalize the HFPRs is proposed and further extended to the MPDM problem using consistency and consensus measures, respectively. Section 4 is comprised of a comparative example to examine the efficiency of the proposed method.

Section 5 provides a comparison of the results obtained, using our proposed technique, with the ones in the literature. The last section includes some conclusions.

2. Preliminaries

In this section, some basic information is given in order to better understand the article. L. A. Zadeh introduced the notion of a fuzzy set [43] in 1965 and used it to illustrate how an entity is more or less connected to a particular category that we want to conform to.

Definition 1. *Fuzzy Set [43]: A set A on universe X associated with a mapping from X to* $[0,1]$ *is called fuzzy set, symbolizes as* $A = \{(x, A(x))\}$. *The output* $A(x)$ *for all* $x \in X$ *is known as the degree to which x belongs to A i.e.,* $A(x)$ *=Degree*$(x \in A)$ *under the membership function* $A : X \rightarrow [0,1]$.

Definition 2. *Hesitant Fuzzy Set [44]: A hesitant fuzzy set A on a fixed finite set X is associated with a function* $h_A(x)$ *from X to a finite subset of* $[0,1]$.

To have been properly described, Xia and Xu [45] articulate the HFS with following mathematical symbol:

$$E = \{< x, h_E(x) > \ | x \in X\},$$

where $h_E(x)$ *is a set of some values in* $[0,1]$, *denoting the possible membership degrees of the element* $x \in X$ *to the set E. For convenience, Xia and Xu [45] named* $h_E(x)$ *a hesitant fuzzy element (HFE).*

Definition 3. *Fuzzy Preference Relation [46]: A relation R on a finite set* $X = \{x_1, x_2, x_3, \ldots, x_n\}$ *of alternatives characterized by law* $R : X \times X \rightarrow [0,1]$, *satisfying:* $r_{ij} + r_{ji} = 1$ *(additive reciprocity) for* $1 \leq i \leq n$ *and* $1 \leq j \leq n$, *is called a fuzzy preference relation where* r_{ij} *denotes the degree of preference of alternative* x_i *to the alternative* x_j *with* $R(x_i, x_j) = r_{ij} \in [0,1]$. *If* $r_{ij} = 0.5$, *then there is no difference between the alternatives* x_i *and* x_j. *If* $r_{ij} > 0.5$, *then alternative* x_i *is preferred over the alternative* x_j, *if* $r_{ij} = 1$, *then the alternative* x_i *is definitely preferred over the alternative* x_j.

Definition 4. *Hesitant Fuzzy Preference Relation [31]: Let* $X = \{x_1, x_2, \ldots, x_n\}$ *be a fixed set, and then the HFPR on X is expressed by a matrix* $H = (h_{ij})_{n \times n} \subset X \times X$, *where* $h_{ij} = \{h_{ij}^{\beta} \mid \beta = 1, 2, \ldots, \#h_{ij}\}$ *is hesitant fuzzy preference value (HFPV) that indicates all the possible preference degrees of alternative* x_i *over* x_j. *Moreover,* h_{ij} *must satisfy the following conditions:*

$$\begin{cases} h_{ij}^{\beta} + h_{ji}^{\beta} = 1, \ i, j = 1, 2, \ldots, n \\ h_{ii} = \{0.5\}, \ i = 1, 2, \ldots, n \\ \#h_{ij} = \#h_{ji}, \ i, j = 1, 2, \ldots, n \end{cases},$$

where $\#h_{ij}$ *is the number of values in* h_{ij}, *and* h_{ij}^{β} *is the* β*th element in* h_{ij}.

Definition 5. *Incomplete Fuzzy Preference Relation [47]: A FPR* $R = (r_{ij})n \times n$ *is considered to be incomplete if it includes at least one uncertain value of preference* r_{ij} *for which the expert has no idea of the degree of preference of alternative* x_i *over* x_j.

Definition 6. *Consistent Fuzzy Preference Relation: A FPR R is said to be* T_L*-consistent, if for* $i, k \neq j \in \{1, 2, 3, \ldots, n\} : r_{ik} \geq \max(r_{ij} + r_{jk} - 1, 0)$ *(*T_L*-transitivity) is satisfied.*

3. Proposed Procedure

In this section, the authors presented an improved procedure to handle MPDM problems using HFPRs, and comprising of: normalization process; consistency measures; consensus measures; consensus improving process; assigning priority weights to decision makers and selection process (aggregation and ranking process).

3.1. Normalization Process

In this subsection, a new procedure to normalize HFPRs is proposed, because in most of the cases for any two hesitant fuzzy preference values (HFPVs) h_{ij} and h_{lm}, $|h_{ij}| \neq |h_{lm}|$ for $i,j,l,m \in \{1,2,3,\ldots,n\}$ where $|h_{ij}|$ and $|h_{lm}|$ represent the cardinalities of sets of pairwise comparisons at ijth and lmth positions. In order to operate smoothly, Zhu et al. [23] presented a procedure known as β-normalization to construct HFPRs with preference values having same cardinalities. This study includes that if $h_{ij} = \left\{h_{ij}^{\beta} \mid \beta = 1,2,\ldots,|h_{ij}|\right\}$ is a HFPV with h_{ij}^{+} and h_{ij}^{-} as maximum and minimum elements in h_{ij}, respectively, and let ξ $(0 \leq \xi \leq 1)$ be a parameter, then the element $\overline{h}_{ij}$ to be added can be estimated using $\overline{h}_{ij} = \xi h_{ij}^{+} + (1-\xi)h_{ij}^{-}$. In particular sense, $\xi = 1$ implies that $\overline{h}_{ij} = h_{ij}^{+}$, and $\overline{h}_{ij} = h_{ij}^{-}$ when $\xi = 0$, which are known as optimism and pessimism rules in Xu and Xia [48]'s approach, respectively.

There are some restrictions that exist in both the techniques described above. In Zhu et al. [23]'s technique, various possibilities exist to normalize the HFPVs, it is due to the different values of parameter ξ. In Xu and Xia [48]'s approach, the estimated element is only the maximum or minimum entry of HFPV and other intermediate values cannot be taken as an added element. Due to these restrictions, Xu et al. [31] presented another scheme to normalize the given HFPRs based on additive transitivity.

After getting motivation from Xu et al. [31]'s work, we put forward a new scheme to estimate the elements to be added in HFPVs regarding the normalization of the given HFPRs. The proposed scheme is based on T_L-consistency in which we take the elements to be added as unknown preference values, and construct the incomplete fuzzy preference relation(s) (IFPR(s)). It is to be noted that an IFPR can only be completed based on the T_L-consistency if each one of the alternatives is compared at least once among the known preference values. Thus, the system needs to ask the expert to form an adequate number of preferences in which each one of the alternatives is compared at least once to let the IFPR become a complete FPR. The order of measuring the missing preference values affects the final result. In order to determine the unknown preference values in an IFPR $R = (r_{ij})_{n\times n}$, the following sets can be defined to represent the pairs of alternatives for known and unknown preference values:

$$K_e = \{(i,j) \mid r_{ij} \text{ is known}\}, \tag{1}$$

$$U_e = \{(i,j) \mid r_{ij} \text{ is unknown}\}, \tag{2}$$

where $r_{ij} \in [0,1]$ shows the preference values of alternative a_i over the alternative a_j, $r_{ij} + r_{ji} = 1 \implies r_{ii} = 0.5\ \forall i \in \{1,2,\ldots,n\}$. Therefore, the following set can be defined to estimate the unknown preference value r_{ij} of alternative a_i over alternative a_j based on T_L-transitivity $r_{ik} \geq \max(r_{ik} + r_{kj} - 1, 0)$:

$$E_{ij} = \{k \neq i,j \mid (i,k) \in K_e, (k,j) \in K_e \text{ and } (i,j) \in U_e\}, \tag{3}$$

for $i,j,k \in \{1,2,3,\ldots,n\}$. Based on Equation (3), final value of r_{ij} is estimated using:

$$r_{ij} = \begin{cases} \underset{k\in E_{ij}}{ave}\left(\max(r_{ik} + r_{kj} - 1, 0)\right), & \text{if } |E_{ij}| \neq 0 \\ 0.5, & \text{otherwise} \end{cases}. \tag{4}$$

To get satisfy the additive reciprocity ($r_{ij} + r_{ji} = 1$) of constructed complete preference relation R in case of $r_{ij} + r_{ji} > 1$ or $r_{ij} + r_{ji} < 1$, following scaling condition helps us:

$$(r_{ij} - g) + (r_{ji} - g) = 1 \text{ such that } g = \frac{r_{ij} + r_{ji} - 1}{2}. \tag{5}$$

Finally, a complete FPR $R^* = (r^*_{ij})_{n\times n}$ is obtained, where $r^*_{ij} = r_{ij} - g$ such that $r^*_{ij} + r^*_{ji} = 1$. Now, two new sets K'_e and U'_e of known and unknown elements are defined as follows:

$$K'_e = K_e \cup \{(i,j)\}, \text{ and } U'_e = U_e - \{(i,j)\}. \tag{6}$$

Consequently, a normalized hesitant fuzzy preference relation (NHFPR) $H^* = (h^*_{ij})_{n\times n}$ with $h^{*\beta}_{ij} + h^{*\beta}_{ji} = 1$, $h^*_{ij} = \{h^{*\beta}_{ij} \mid \beta = 1,2,\ldots,\left|h^*_{ij}\right|\}$ for $\left|h^*_{ij}\right| = \left|h^*_{ji}\right|$, is constructed. In real world, there are many decision-making processes which take place in multi-person settings because the increase of complexity and uncertainty of the socio-economic environment makes it less possible for a single decision maker to consider all related traits of a decision-making problem.

Example 1. *Let H be the following HFPR:*

$$H = \begin{bmatrix} \{0.5\} & \{0.3\} & \{0.5,0.7\} & \{0.4\} \\ \{0.7\} & \{0.5\} & \{0.7,0.9\} & \{0.8\} \\ \{0.5,0.3\} & \{0.3,0.1\} & \{0.5\} & \{0.6,0.7\} \\ \{0.6\} & \{0.2\} & \{0.4,0.3\} & \{0.5\} \end{bmatrix}.$$

To normalize H, first, we have to transform it into two FPRs as follows:

$$R_1 = \begin{bmatrix} 0.5 & 0.3 & 0.5 & 0.4 \\ 0.7 & 0.5 & 0.7 & 0.8 \\ 0.5 & 0.3 & 0.5 & 0.6 \\ 0.6 & 0.2 & 0.4 & 0.5 \end{bmatrix}, R_2 = \begin{bmatrix} 0.5 & r_{12} & 0.7 & r_{14} \\ r_{21} & 0.5 & 0.9 & r_{24} \\ 0.3 & 0.1 & 0.5 & 0.7 \\ r_{41} & r_{42} & 0.3 & 0.5 \end{bmatrix}.$$

Clearly, R_2 is an IFPR. Now, we estimate the unknown preference values using T_L-consistency based procedure as follows:
(Round-i) The sets of pairs of alternatives for known and unknown preference values, respectively, are:

$$K_e = \{(1,3),(2,3),(3,1),(3,2),(3,4),(4,3)\},$$

$$U_e = \{(1,2),(1,4),(2,1),(2,4),(4,1),(4,2)\}.$$

Here, we neglect the diagonal entries. To find the value of r_{12}, the set E_{12} of intermediate alternatives a_k is defined such that $(1,k),(k,2) \in K_e$, as:

$$E_{12} = \{3\}.$$

Now, the value of r_{12} is estimated based on E_{12} as:

$$r_{12} = max(r_{13} + r_{32} - 1, 0) = max(0.7 + 0.1 - 1, 0) = 0.$$

The new sets of known and unknown preference values are:

$$K'_e = \{(1,2),(1,3),(2,3),(3,1),(3,2),(3,4),(4,3)\},$$

$$U'_e = \{(1,4),(2,1),(2,4),(4,1),(4,2)\}.$$

After repeating the process as in Round-i, we can easily estimate the remaining values $r_{14}, r_{21}, r_{24}, r_{41}$ and r_{42}. After evaluating all the missing values, we get:

$$R_2 = \begin{bmatrix} 0.5 & 0 & 0.7 & 0.4 \\ 0.2 & 0.5 & 0.9 & 0.3 \\ 0.3 & 0.1 & 0.5 & 0.7 \\ 0 & 0 & 0.3 & 0.5 \end{bmatrix}.$$

The scaling condition (5) helps us to construct the following FPR R_2 after getting the complete form:

$$R_2 = \begin{bmatrix} 0.5 & 0.4 & 0.7 & 0.7 \\ 0.6 & 0.5 & 0.9 & 0.65 \\ 0.3 & 0.1 & 0.5 & 0.7 \\ 0.3 & 0.35 & 0.3 & 0.5 \end{bmatrix}.$$

Hence, the NHFPR H^* is constructed as:

$$H = \begin{bmatrix} \{0.5, 0.5\} & \{0.3, 0.4\} & \{0.5, 0.7\} & \{0.4, 0.7\} \\ \{0.7, 0.6\} & \{0.5, 0.5\} & \{0.7, 0.9\} & \{0.8, 0.65\} \\ \{0.5, 0.3\} & \{0.3, 0.1\} & \{0.5, 0.5\} & \{0.6, 0.7\} \\ \{0.6, 0.3\} & \{0.2, 0.35\} & \{0.4, 0.3\} & \{0.5, 0.5\} \end{bmatrix}.$$

3.2. Consistency Analysis

In this subsection, some consistency measures, such as consistency level of pair of alternatives, consistency level of alternatives and the consistency level of HFPR, are defined. The term consistency index (CI) stands for consistency degree whose value lies in $[0, 1]$.

Let H^q be the HFPR associated to the decision maker D_q $(1 \leq q \leq l)$, then after getting NHFPR H^{*q}, T_L-consistent HFPR $\widetilde{H^{*q}}$ can be obtained with the help of following transitive closure formula:

$$\widetilde{h_{ij}^{*q\beta}} = \max_{k \neq i,j}(h_{ij}^{*q\beta}, \max(h_{ik}^{*q\beta} + h_{kj}^{*q\beta} - 1, 0)), \; \widetilde{h_{ij}^{*q\beta}} + \widetilde{h_{ji}^{*q\beta}} = 1 \tag{7}$$

where $h_{ij}^{*q} = \{h_{ij}^{*q\beta} \mid \beta = 1, 2, \ldots, \left|h_{ij}^{q*}\right|\}$. Now, we can estimate the consistency level of HFPR H^{*q} based on its similarity with the corresponding T_L-consistency $\widetilde{H^{*q}}$ after evaluating distance between them in the following manner.

1. T_L consistency index (T_LCI) for a pair of alternatives evaluated as:

$$T_LCI(h_{ij}^{*q}) = 1 - \frac{1}{\left|h_{ij}^*\right|} \sum_{\beta=1}^{\left|h_{ij}^*\right|} d\left(h_{ij}^{*q\beta}, \widetilde{h_{ij}^{*q\beta}}\right) \tag{8}$$

   where $d(h_{ij}^{*q\beta}, \widetilde{h_{ij}^{*q\beta}})$ represents the distance obtained by $d\left(h_{ij}^{*q\beta}, \widetilde{h_{ij}^{*q\beta}}\right) = \left|h_{ij}^{*q\beta} - \widetilde{h_{ij}^{*q\beta}}\right|$. Usually, the higher the level of $T_LCI(h_{ij}^{*q})$, the more consistent h_{ij}^{*q} is as compared to the rest of HFPVs regarding alternatives a_i and a_j.
2. T_LCI for alternatives $a_i, 1 \leq i \leq n$, is determined as:

$$T_LCI(a_i) = \frac{1}{2(n-1)} \sum_{j=1, j \neq i}^{n} (T_LCI(h_{ij}^{*q}) + T_LCI(h_{ji}^{*q})) \tag{9}$$

with $T_LCI(a_i) \in [0,1]$. If $T_LCI(a_i) = 1$, then the preference values concerning alternative a_i are fully consistent, else the smaller $T_LCI(a_i)$ the more inconsistent these preference values are.

3. At the end, T_LCI against NHFPR H^{*q} is evaluated using average operator:

$$T_LCI(H^{*q}) = \frac{1}{n}\sum_{i=1}^{n} T_LCI(a_i) \tag{10}$$

with $T_LCI(H^{*q}) \in [0,1]$. If $T_LCI(H^{*q}) = 1$, then NHFPR H^{*q} is fully consistent, else the smaller $T_LCI(H^{*q})$ the more inconsistent H^{*q} is.

The consistency index evaluated by Equation (10) is associated with DM D_q, while the global consistency index CI can be measured using average operator and given as:

$$CI = \frac{1}{l}\sum_{q=1}^{l} T_LCI(H^{*q}) \tag{11}$$

with $CI \in [0,1]$. Once, the T_LCI is measured in three stages involving Equations (8)–(10), it is expressible to assign higher weights to the experts which provided the HFPR with larger consistency indices respectively. Therefore, consistency weights can be allocated to the experts using following relation:

$$Cw(Dq) = \frac{T_LCI(H^{*q})}{\sum\limits_{q=1}^{l} T_LCI(H^{*q})} \tag{12}$$

with $Cw(Dq) \in [0,1]$ and $\sum\limits_{q=1}^{l} Cw(Dq) = 1$.

3.3. Consensus Analysis

In this subsection, some levels to estimate global consensus degree amongst decision makers are defined. After evaluating NHFPRs H^{*q}, $q = 1,2,\ldots,l$, it is essential to estimate the consensus level amongst the decision makers. In relation to this, a collective similarity matrix $S = (s_{ij})_{n\times n}$ can be obtained, after aggregating the similarity matrices $S^{qr} = (s_{ij}^{qr})_{n\times n}$ for every pair of decision makers (D_q, D_r) $(q = 1,2,\ldots,l-1; r = q+1,\ldots,l)$, as follows:

$$S = (s_{ij})_{n\times n} = \left(\frac{2}{l(l-1)}\sum_{q=1}^{l-1}\sum_{r=q+1}^{l}\left(1 - \frac{1}{|h_{ij}^*|}\sum_{\beta=1}^{|h_{ij}^*|} d\left(h_{ij}^{*q\beta}, h_{ij}^{*r\beta}\right)\right)\right)_{n\times n} \tag{13}$$

where $1 - \frac{1}{|h_{ij}^*|}\sum\limits_{\beta=1}^{|h_{ij}^*|} d\left(h_{ij}^{*q\beta}, h_{ij}^{*r\beta}\right) = s_{ij}^{qr}$ and $d\left(h_{ij}^{*q\beta}, h_{ij}^{*r\beta}\right) = \left|h_{ij}^{*q\beta} - h_{ij}^{*r\beta}\right|$, $\beta = \{1,2,\ldots,|h_{ij}^*|\}$.

The following levels involve to estimate the global consensus degree amongst the decision makers:

1. At the first level, the consensus degree on a pair of alternatives (a_i, a_j), denoted by cd_{ij} is defined to estimate the degree of consensus amongst all experts on that pair of alternatives:

$$cd_{ij} = s_{ij} \tag{14}$$

2. At the second level, the consensus degree on alternatives a_i denoted by CD_i, is defined to determine the consensus degree amongst all the experts on that alternative:

$$CD_i = \frac{1}{2(n-1)} \sum_{j=1, j\neq i}^{n} (s_{ij} + s_{ji}) \tag{15}$$

3. At the third level, the consensus degree on the relation denoted by CR, is defined to calculate the global degree of consensus amongst all DMs:

$$CR = \frac{1}{n} \sum_{i=1}^{n} CD_i \tag{16}$$

If the global consensus level of all experts is reached, it needs a comparison with the threshold consensus degree η, usually pre-determined based on the nature of the issue. If $CR \geq \eta$ is obtained, this indicates that a sufficient degree of consensus has been achieved and the decision-making process starts. Otherwise, the consensus degree is not stable, and experts are asked to revise their preferences.

3.4. Enhancement Mechanism

The enhancement mechanism plays the role of a moderator in the consensus-reaching process and provides comprehensive information to decision makers in order to enhance their findings. In case of insufficient consensus level, we have to identify the positions at which preference values are to be modified, so as to reach the acceptable consensus degree amongst the decision makers. In this regard, an identifier is defined as follow:

$$I^q = \{(i,j) \mid cd_{ij} < CR \text{ and } h_{ij}^{q\beta} \text{ is a known value}\} \tag{17}$$

As soon as an identifier has determined the positions, the enhancement mechanism suggests the respective DM D_q to increase the element $h_{ij}^{q\beta}$ of HFPV h_{ij}^{q}, if it is smaller than the mean value $h_{ij,\ ave}^{*q\beta}$ of the opinions by the participants, or to decrease in case of higher than the mean, and remains the same in case of equal to mean.

The advice made above only provides the direction to DMs for updating their preferences, but is unable to suggest the values. In order to update the element(s) of HFPV, the DMs are suggested to choose the new element $h_{ij,\ new}^{q\beta}$ from the interval $[min(h_{ij}^{q\beta}, h_{ij,\ ave}^{*q\beta}), max(h_{ij}^{q\beta}, h_{ij,\ ave}^{*q\beta})]$.

In order to enhance the consensus automatically, the DMs would not have to provide their updated elements in automatic mechanism. In such a situation, the following expression could be used to evaluate the new element $h_{ij,\ new}^{q\beta}$ for $cd_{ij} < CR$:

$$h_{ij,\ new}^{q\beta} = \lambda h_{ij}^{q\beta} + (1-\lambda) h_{ij,\ ave}^{*q\beta}, \tag{18}$$

where $\lambda \in [0,1]$ is known as the optimization parameter. It is obvious that the new evaluated values will be closer to mean values as compare to old ones, and hence the consensus degree enhances.

3.5. Rating of Decision Makers

The final priority rating of decision makers is evaluated by emerging consistency weights and predefined priority weights as:

$$w(D_q) = \frac{\omega_q \times Cw(Dq)}{\sum_{q=1}^{l} \omega_q \times Cw(Dq)} \tag{19}$$

where $\omega_q, 1 \le q \le l$, represent the predefined priority weights of decision makers, while $\sum_{q=1}^{l} w(D_q) = 1$. If the decision makers do not carry a predefined priority weights, then their consistency weights will be considered as the final priority rating.

3.6. Aggregated NHFPR

It may habitually occurs that the preference level associated to each DM is weighted differently. After evaluating the priority rating of decision makers, their opinions are to be aggregated into global one. We construct the collective consistent NHFPR H^{*c} using weighted average operator as:

$$H^{*c} = (h_{ij}^{*c})_{n\times n} = \left(\sum_{q=1}^{l} w(D_q) \times \widetilde{h_{ij}^{*q}}\right)_{n\times n} \tag{20}$$

for $1 \le i \le n,\ 1 \le j \le n$.

3.7. Ranking of Alternatives

As soon as the consensus amongst the decision makers is reached at an acceptable level, the process to rank the alternatives initiates and chooses the best one. In this regard, we define the ranking value $v(a_i)$ of alternative $a_i, i = 1, 2, \ldots n$, as follows:

$$v(a_i) = \frac{2}{n(n-1)} \sum_{\substack{j=1 \\ j \ne i}}^{n} \left(\frac{1}{\left|h_{ij}^{*c}\right|} \sum_{\beta=1}^{\left|h_{ij}^{*c}\right|} h_{ij}^{*c\beta} \right) \tag{21}$$

with $\sum_{i=1}^{n} v(a_i) = 1$.

4. Comparative Example

In this section, we apply the proposed consensus-based procedure on a case study attempted by Xu et al. [31] to allocate water in the Jiangxi Province, China.

The following four alternatives with specific traits are considered as water allocation alternatives: (i) The first alternative a_1 is associated to social factor. (ii) The economic factor is considered by second alternative a_2. (iii) The third alternative a_3 considers the ecological factors to protect the local ecological environment. (iv) The final alternative a_4 thinks of the final output and return the local important scare resources.

A team of four decision makers $D_q, q = 1, 2, 3, 4$, from different departments is organized to provide assessments on the four alternatives $a_i, i = 1, 2, 3, 4$. After pairwise comparisons, following HFPRs $H^q, q = 1, 2, 3, 4$, are provided by the decision makers $D_q, q = 1, 2, 3, 4$, respectively.

$$H^1 = \begin{bmatrix} \{0.5\} & \{0.3\} & \{0.5, 0.7\} & \{0.4\} \\ \{0.7\} & \{0.5\} & \{0.7, 0.9\} & \{0.8\} \\ \{0.5, 0.3\} & \{0.3, 0.1\} & \{0.5\} & \{0.6, 0.7\} \\ \{0.6\} & \{0.2\} & \{0.4, 0.3\} & \{0.5\} \end{bmatrix},$$

$$H^2 = \begin{bmatrix} \{0.5\} & \{0.3, 0.5\} & \{0.1, 0.2\} & \{0.6\} \\ \{0.7, 0.5\} & \{0.5\} & \{0.7, 0.8\} & \{0.1, 0.3, 0.5\} \\ \{0.9, 0.8\} & \{0.3, 0.2\} & \{0.5\} & \{0.5, 0.6, 0.7\} \\ \{0.4\} & \{0.9, 0.7, 0.5\} & \{0.5, 0.4, 0.3\} & \{0.5\} \end{bmatrix},$$

$$H^3 = \begin{bmatrix} \{0.5\} & \{0.3, 0.5\} & \{0.7\} & \{0.7, 0.8\} \\ \{0.7, 0.5\} & \{0.5\} & \{0.2, 0.3, 0.4\} & \{0.5, 0.6\} \\ \{0.3\} & \{0.8, 0.7, 0.6\} & \{0.5\} & \{0.7, 0.8, 0.9\} \\ \{0.3, 0.2\} & \{0.5, 0.4\} & \{0.3, 0.2, 0.1\} & \{0.5\} \end{bmatrix}$$

$$H^4 = \begin{bmatrix} \{0.5\} & \{0.4, 0.5, 0.6\} & \{0.3, 0.4\} & \{0.5, 0.7\} \\ \{0.6, 0.5, 0.4\} & \{0.5\} & \{0.3\} & \{0.6, 0.7, 0.8\} \\ \{0.7, 0.6\} & \{0.7\} & \{0.5\} & \{0.8, 0.9\} \\ \{0.5, 0.3\} & \{0.4, 0.3, 0.2\} & \{0.2, 0.1\} & \{0.5\} \end{bmatrix}$$

Normalization:

In order to normalize the given information, expressions (1)–(6) were used to construct NHFPRs as (22)–(25).

$$H^{*1} = \begin{bmatrix} \{0.5, 0.5, 0.5\} & \{0.3, 0.4, 0.3\} & \{0.5, 0.7, 0.7\} & \{0.4, 0.7, 0.55\} \\ \{0.7, 0.6, 0.7\} & \{0.5, 0.5, 0.5\} & \{0.7, 0.9, 0.9\} & \{0.8, 0.65, 0.8\} \\ \{0.5, 0.3, 0.3\} & \{0.3, 0.1, 0.9\} & \{0.5, 0.5, 0.5\} & \{0.6, 0.7, 0.475\} \\ \{0.6, 0.3, 0.45\} & \{0.2, 0.35, 0.2\} & \{0.4, 0.3, 0.525\} & \{0.5, 0.5, 0.5\} \end{bmatrix} \tag{22}$$

$$H^{*2} = \begin{bmatrix} \{0.5, 0.5, 0.5\} & \{0.3, 0.5, 0.55\} & \{0.1, 0.2, 0.45\} & \{0.6, 0.4, 0.6\} \\ \{0.7, 0.5, 0.45\} & \{0.5, 0.5, 0.5\} & \{0.7, 0.8, 0.45\} & \{0.1, 0.3, 0.5\} \\ \{0.9, 0.8, 0.55\} & \{0.3, 0.2, 0.55\} & \{0.5, 0.5, 0.5\} & \{0.5, 0.6, 0.7\} \\ \{0.4, 0.6, 0.4\} & \{0.9, 0.7, 0.5\} & \{0.5, 0.4, 0.3\} & \{0.5, 0.5, 0.5\} \end{bmatrix} \tag{23}$$

$$H^{*3} = \begin{bmatrix} \{0.5, 0.5, 0.5\} & \{0.3, 0.5, 0.65\} & \{0.7, 0.45, 0.7\} & \{0.7, 0.8, 0.8\} \\ \{0.7, 0.5, 0.35\} & \{0.5, 0.5, 0.5\} & \{0.2, 0.3, 0.4\} & \{0.5, 0.6, 0.575\} \\ \{0.3, 0.55, 0.3\} & \{0.8, 0.7, 0.6\} & \{0.5, 0.5, 0.5\} & \{0.7, 0.8, 0.9\} \\ \{0.3, 0.2, 0.2\} & \{0.5, 0.4, 0.425\} & \{0.3, 0.2, 0.1\} & \{0.5, 0.5, 0.5\} \end{bmatrix} \tag{24}$$

$$H^{*4} = \begin{bmatrix} \{0.5, 0.5, 0.5\} & \{0.4, 0.5, 0.6\} & \{0.3, 0.4, 0.4\} & \{0.5, 0.7, 0.7\} \\ \{0.6, 0.5, 0.4\} & \{0.5, 0.5, 0.5\} & \{0.3, 0.425, 0.3\} & \{0.6, 0.7, 0.8\} \\ \{0.7, 0.6, 0.6\} & \{0.7, 0.575, 0.7\} & \{0.5, 0.5, 0.5\} & \{0.8, 0.9, 0.625\} \\ \{0.5, 0.3, 0.3\} & \{0.4, 0.3, 0.2\} & \{0.2, 0.1, 0.375\} & \{0.5, 0.5, 0.5\} \end{bmatrix} \tag{25}$$

Consistency measures:

Expressions (7)–(12) helped us to measure the consistency levels of the HFPRs provided by the decision makers as (26)–(29).

$$\widetilde{H^{*1}} = \begin{bmatrix} \{0.5, 0.5, 0.5\} & \{0.3, 0.4, 0.3\} & \{0.5, 0.7, 0.7\} & \{0.4, 0.7, 0.55\} \\ \{0.7, 0.6, 0.7\} & \{0.5, 0.5, 0.5\} & \{0.7, 0.9, 0.9\} & \{0.8, 0.65, 0.8\} \\ \{0.5, 0.3, 0.3\} & \{0.3, 0.1, 0.9\} & \{0.5, 0.5, 0.5\} & \{0.6, 0.7, 0.475\} \\ \{0.6, 0.3, 0.45\} & \{0.2, 0.35, 0.2\} & \{0.4, 0.3, 0.525\} & \{0.5, 0.5, 0.5\} \end{bmatrix} \tag{26}$$

$$\widetilde{H^{*2}} = \begin{bmatrix} \{0.5,0.5,0.5\} & \{0.4,0.45,0.55\} & \{0.15,0.25,0.45\} & \{0.5,0.4,0.6\} \\ \{0.6,0.55,0.45\} & \{0.5,0.5,0.5\} & \{0.65,0.75,0.45\} & \{0.2,0.35,0.5\} \\ \{0.85,0.75,0.55\} & \{0.35,0.25,0.55\} & \{0.5,0.5,0.5\} & \{0.45,0.55,0.7\} \\ \{0.4,0.6,0.4\} & \{0.8,0.65,0.5\} & \{0.55,0.45,0.3\} & \{0.5,0.5,0.5\} \end{bmatrix} \tag{27}$$

$$\widetilde{H^{*3}} = \begin{bmatrix} \{0.5,0.5,0.5\} & \{0.4,0.5,0.65\} & \{0.6,0.45,0.7\} & \{0.7,0.8,0.8\} \\ \{0.6,0.5,0.35\} & \{0.5,0.5,0.5\} & \{0.3,0.3,0.4\} & \{0.5,0.6,0.575\} \\ \{0.4,0.55,0.3\} & \{0.7,0.7,0.6\} & \{0.5,0.5,0.5\} & \{0.7,0.8,0.9\} \\ \{0.3,0.2,0.2\} & \{0.5,0.4,0.425\} & \{0.3,0.2,0.1\} & \{0.5,0.5,0.5\} \end{bmatrix} \tag{28}$$

$$\widetilde{H^{*4}} = \begin{bmatrix} \{0.5,0.5,0.5\} & \{0.4,0.5,0.6\} & \{0.3,0.4,0.4\} & \{0.5,0.7,0.7\} \\ \{0.6,0.5,0.4\} & \{0.5,0.5,0.5\} & \{0.3,0.425,0.3\} & \{0.6,0.7,0.8\} \\ \{0.7,0.6,0.6\} & \{0.7,0.575,0.7\} & \{0.5,0.5,0.5\} & \{0.8,0.9,0.625\} \\ \{0.5,0.3,0.3\} & \{0.4,0.3,0.2\} & \{0.2,0.1,0.375\} & \{0.5,0.5,0.5\} \end{bmatrix} \tag{29}$$

(i). The consistency measures of pairs of alternatives in NHFPRs H^{*q}, $q = 1,2,3,4$, are:

$$T_L CI(h_{ij}^{*1}) = \begin{bmatrix} 1 & 1 & 1 & 1 \\ 1 & 1 & 1 & 1 \\ 1 & 1 & 1 & 1 \\ 1 & 1 & 1 & 1 \end{bmatrix}, \; T_L CI(h_{ij}^{*2}) = \begin{bmatrix} 1 & 0.9500 & 0.9667 & 0.9667 \\ 0.9500 & 1 & 0.9667 & 0.9500 \\ 0.9667 & 0.9667 & 1 & 0.9667 \\ 0.9667 & 0.9500 & 0.9667 & 1 \end{bmatrix},$$

$$T_L CI(h_{ij}^{*3}) = \begin{bmatrix} 1 & 0.9667 & 0.9667 & 1 \\ 0.9667 & 1 & 0.9667 & 1 \\ 0.9667 & 0.9667 & 1 & 1 \\ 1 & 1 & 1 & 1 \end{bmatrix}, \; T_L CI(h_{ij}^{*4}) = \begin{bmatrix} 1 & 0.9500 & 0.9667 & 0.9667 \\ 0.9500 & 1 & 0.9667 & 0.9500 \\ 0.9667 & 0.9667 & 1 & 0.9667 \\ 0.9667 & 0.9500 & 0.9667 & 1 \end{bmatrix}.$$

(ii). The consistency measures of alternatives a_1, a_2, a_3 and a_4 are:

$$T_L CI(a_1) = (1,\ 0.9611,\ 0.9778,\ 1), \qquad T_L CI(a_2) = (1,\ 0.9556,\ 0.9778,\ 1),$$
$$T_L CI(a_3) = (1,\ 0.9667,\ 0.9778,\ 1), \qquad T_L CI(a_4) = (1,\ 0.9611,\ 1,\ 1).$$

(iii). The consistency measures of NHFPRs are:

$$T_L CI(H^{*1}) = 1,\ T_L CI(H^{*2}) = 0.961125,$$
$$T_L CI(H^{*3}) = 0.98335,\ T_L CI(H^{*4}) = 1.$$

The global consistency index under the use of (11) is obtained as:

$$CI = 0.9861.$$

Now, the consistency weights of the decision makers D_1, D_2, D_3 and D_4 are estimated using (12) as:

$$Cw(D_1) = 0.2535,\ Cw(D_2) = 0.2437,$$
$$Cw(D_3) = 0.2493,\ Cw(D_4) = 0.2535.$$

Consensus measures:

(i). The consensus measures on each pair of alternatives are shown in the following, collectively aggregated, similarity matrix using (13):

$$S = \begin{bmatrix} 1 & 0.9000 & 0.7500 & 0.8361 \\ 0.9000 & 1 & 0.6486 & 0.7736 \\ 0.7500 & 0.6486 & 1 & 0.8083 \\ 0.8361 & 0.7736 & 0.8083 & 1 \end{bmatrix}.$$

(ii). Based on similarity matrix S, the consensus measures on the alternatives a_1, a_2, a_3 and a_4, applying (14) are:

$$CD_1 = 0.8287,\ CD_2 = 0.7708,$$
$$CD_3 = 0.7356,\ CD_4 = 0.8060.$$

(iii). The consensus measure on the information provided by the decision makers is:

$$CR = 0.7853.$$

Final weights of decision makers:

The final weights of decision makers can be evaluated by using (19), but in this case the consistency weights $Cw(D_q), q = 1,2,3,4,$ will be used as the final weights of the decision maker, because the predefined weights are not involved. Therefore, we have

$$w(D_1) = 0.2535,\ w(D_2) = 0.2437,$$
$$w(D_3) = 0.2493,\ w(D_4) = 0.2535.$$

Construction of collective NHFPR:

The collective NHFPR H^{*c} is constructed after applying (20) and we get (30).

$$H^{*c} = \begin{bmatrix} \{0.5, 0.5, 0.5\} & \{0.3746, 0.4625, 0.5242\} & \{0.3889, 0.4520, 0.5630\} & \{0.5245, 0.6518, 0.6625\} \\ \{0.6254, 0.5375, 0.4758\} & \{0.5, 0.5, 0.5\} & \{0.4867, 0.5935, 0.5136\} & \{0.5283, 0.5771, 0.6708\} \\ \{0.6111, 0.5480, 0.4370\} & \{0.5133, 0.4065, 0.4864\} & \{0.5, 0.5, 0.5\} & \{0.6391, 0.7391, 0.6738\} \\ \{0.4755, 0.3482, 0.3375\} & \{0.4717, 0.4229, 0.3292\} & \{0.3609, 0.2609, 0.3262\} & \{0.5, 0.5, 0.5\} \end{bmatrix} \quad (30)$$

The final ranking of alternatives:

The expression (21) is used to get the final ranking order of the alternatives after evaluating the ranking values as: $v(a_1) = 0.2558$, $v(a_2) = 0.27825$, $v(a_3) = 0.2808$ and $v(a_4) = 0.18515$. Hence, the preference order of alternatives is

$$a_3 \succ a_2 \succ a_1 \succ a_4,$$

which leads us to the best alternative a_3, ecological factor, and suggests that the ecosystem must be protected primarily to ensure a healthy environment. While the economic factor is the second feasible choice, and the social factor carries third place in the ranking. The least important factor in the ranking order is the output and return.

The enhancement mechanism:

In order to incorporate the enhancement mechanism, we consider the threshold consensus level η in the above example as 0.80, while, the obtained value is $CR = 0.7853$. Therefore, DMs have to change their preferences using (17), based on the mean values of the preferences provided by the expert shown as follows:

$$H_{ave} = \begin{bmatrix} \{0.5,0.5,0.5\} & \{0.325,0.475,0.525\} & \{0.4,0.4375,0.5625\} & \{0.55,0.65,0.6625\} \\ \{0.675,0.525,0.475\} & \{0.5,0.5,0.5\} & \{0.475,0.6062,0.5125\} & \{0.5,0.5625,0.6687\} \\ \{0.6,0.5625,0.4375\} & \{0.525,0.3938,0.4875\} & \{0.5,0.5,0.5\} & \{0.65,0.75,0.675\} \\ \{0.45,0.35,0.3375\} & \{0.5,0.4375,0.3312\} & \{0.35,0.25,0.325\} & \{0.5,0.5,0.5\} \end{bmatrix}.$$

Now the identifier (17) provides the following set of positions to enhance the respective preference values

$$I = \{(1,3),(2,3),(2,4),(3,1),(3,2),(4,2)\}.$$

Suppose that the DMs welcomed the recommendations and improved their preference relations appropriately, given as

$$H^1_{new} = \begin{bmatrix} \{0.5\} & \{0.3\} & \{0.45,0.5\} & \{0.4\} \\ \{0.7\} & \{0.5\} & \{0.48,0.62\} & \{0.5\} \\ \{0.55,0.5\} & \{0.52,0.38\} & \{0.5\} & \{0.6,0.7\} \\ \{0.6\} & \{0.5\} & \{0.4,0.3\} & \{0.5\} \end{bmatrix},$$

$$H^2_{new} = \begin{bmatrix} \{0.5\} & \{0.3,0.5\} & \{0.38,0.41\} & \{0.6\} \\ \{0.7,0.5\} & \{0.5\} & \{0.48,0.63\} & \{0.45,0.55,0.65\} \\ \{0.62,0.59\} & \{0.52,0.37\} & \{0.5\} & \{0.5,0.6,0.7\} \\ \{0.4\} & \{0.55,0.45,0.35\} & \{0.5,0.4,0.3\} & \{0.5\} \end{bmatrix},$$

$$H^3_{new} = \begin{bmatrix} \{0.5\} & \{0.3,0.5\} & \{0.45\} & \{0.7,0.8\} \\ \{0.7,0.5\} & \{0.5\} & \{0.38,0.58,0.5\} & \{0.5,0.57\} \\ \{0.55\} & \{0.62,0.42,0.5\} & \{0.5\} & \{0.7,0.8,0.9\} \\ \{0.3,0.2\} & \{0.5,0.43\} & \{0.3,0.2,0.1\} & \{0.5\} \end{bmatrix},$$

$$H^4_{new} = \begin{bmatrix} \{0.5\} & \{0.4,0.5,0.6\} & \{0.38,0.55\} & \{0.5,0.7\} \\ \{0.6,0.5,0.4\} & \{0.5\} & \{0.45\} & \{0.55,0.57,0.68\} \\ \{0.62,0.45\} & \{0.55\} & \{0.5\} & \{0.8,0.9\} \\ \{0.5,0.3\} & \{0.45,0.43,0.32\} & \{0.2,0.1\} & \{0.5\} \end{bmatrix}.$$

After normalizing these HFPRs using (1)–(6), and constructing consistent HFPRs using (7), the consistency indices of new NHFPRs can be evaluated as:

$$T_L CI(H^{*1}_{new}) = 1,\ T_L CI(H^{*2}_{new}) = 1,$$
$$T_L CI(H^{*3}_{new}) = 1,\ T_L CI(H^{*4}_{new}) = 1.$$

We developed the collective similarity matrix S_{new} with (13), and is given as follows:

$$S_{new} = \begin{bmatrix} 1.0000 & 0.9233 & 0.9406 & 0.8433 \\ 0.9233 & 1.0000 & 0.9374 & 0.9456 \\ 0.9406 & 0.9374 & 1.0000 & 0.8151 \\ 0.8433 & 0.9456 & 0.8151 & 1.0000 \end{bmatrix}.$$

The consensus measures on the alternatives a_1, a_2, a_3 and a_4 are estimated after applying (14) on similarity matrix S_{new} as:

$$CD_{1new} = 0.9024,\ CD_{2new} = 0.9354,$$
$$CD_{3new} = 0.8977,\ CD_{4new} = 0.8680.$$

Hence, the consensus measure on the information provided by the decision makers is evaluated by (16):

$$CR_{new} = 0.9009.$$

This shows that the enhancement mechanism clearly improves the consensus level amongst DMs from $CR = 0.7853$ to $CR_{new} = 0.9009$ which is higher than the threshold level $\eta = 0.80$ i.e., $CR_{new} > \eta$. Now, the collective NHFPR H^{*c}_{new} can be constructed using (19) and (20), given as below: The expression (21) is used to get the final ranking order of the alternatives after evaluating the ranking values as: $v(a_1) = 0.2473$, $v(a_2) = 0.2719$, $v(a_3) = 0.2876$ and $v(a_4) = 0.1932$. Therefore, the preference order of alternatives is $a_3 \succ a_2 \succ a_1 \succ a_4$, and is same as before the application of enhancement mechanism.

$$H^{*c}_{new} = \begin{bmatrix} \{0.5000, 0.5000, 0.5000\} & \{0.3250, 0.4850, 0.4625\} & \{0.4150, 0.4950, 0.4875\} & \{0.5500, 0.6538, 0.5787\} \\ \{0.6750, 0.5150, 0.5375\} & \{0.5000, 0.5000, 0.5000\} & \{0.4475, 0.5650, 0.4794\} & \{0.5000, 0.5675, 0.6075\} \\ \{0.5850, 0.5050, 0.5125\} & \{0.5525, 0.4350, 0.5206\} & \{0.5000, 0.5000, 0.5000\} & \{0.6500, 0.7500, 0.6656\} \\ \{0.4500, 0.3463, 0.4213\} & \{0.5000, 0.4325, 0.3925\} & \{0.3500, 0.2500, 0.3344\} & \{0.5000, 0.5000, 0.5000\} \end{bmatrix} \quad (31)$$

5. Comparison

To clearly validate the proposed procedure, we compare our results to findings of Xu et al. [31] based on consistency measure, consensus measure and the final ranking. The initial consistency levels, consensus level and the final ranking of alternatives in Xu et al. [31]'s sense based on additive transitivity are: $cl^1 = 0.9750$, $cl^2 = 0.8833$, $cl^3 = 0.9389$, $cl^4 = 0.9847$; $CR = 0.7653$ and $a_3 \succ a_2 \succ a_1 \succ a_4$, respectively.

In our proposed scheme, T_L-transitivity is introduced to evaluate the unknown elements of HFPVs in the normalization process and construct the consistent HFPRs, accordingly. Consequently, the initial consistency indices, consensus level amongst DMs and final ranking order of alternatives are: $T_LCI(H^{*1}) = 1$, $T_LCI(H^{*2}) = 0.961125$, $T_LCI(H^{*3}) = 0.98335$, $T_LCI(H^{*4}) = 1$; $CR = 0.7853$ and $a_3 \succ a_2 \succ a_1 \succ a_4$, respectively. Evidently, the consistency and consensus levels estimated by the proposed method are higher than the levels obtained by Xu et al. [31]'s procedure, but the final ranking order of both the methods are identical. This shows that T_L-transitive property is much useful to strengthen the consistency of data, and consensus amongst DMs, as well. To incorporate the enhancement mechanism to improve the consensus level amongst DMs, we considered the case with threshold consensus level $\eta = 0.80$ and estimated the new global consensus level. After applying simple steps of enhancement mechanism, we evaluated the global consensus level $CR_{new} = 0.9009$ which shows a significant improvement when comparing to the threshold level. Most interestingly, we obtained the same ranking order $a_3 \succ a_2 \succ a_1 \succ a_4$ of alternatives before the application of the enhancement mechanism. Thus, it validates and strengthens the proposed scheme. In an easy manner, the following Table 1 provides the information to observe and compare the values obtained in [31] and proposed schemes:

Table 1. Comparison of reference results and the proposed approach.

Methods	Consistency Levels of				Consensus Level	Ranking
	H^1	H^2	H^3	H^4	(CR)	Order
Xu et al. [31]	0.9750	0.8833	0.9389	0.9847	0.7653	$a_3 \succ a_2 \succ a_1 \succ a_4$
Proposed (Round 1)	1	0.9611	0.9834	1	0.7853	$a_3 \succ a_2 \succ a_1 \succ a_4$
Proposed (Round 2)	1	1	1	1	0.9009	$a_3 \succ a_2 \succ a_1 \succ a_4$

Here, Rounds 1 and 2 represent the evaluations before and after application of the enhancement mechanism, respectively.

6. Conclusions

In this manuscript, a consensus-based method to handle the MPDM problem using consistent HFPRs is proposed. In this regard, the definition of HFPRs has been borrowed from Xu et al. [31]'s work, and an efficient T_L-consistency-based procedure to normalize HFPRs is presented. A step by step procedure to normalize the HFPR is shown in Example 1. The consistency weights have been assigned to DMs after the consistency analysis made, it is rational to allocate higher weights to DMs with a high level of consistency in order to carry more importance in the aggregation process. Furthermore, an enhancement mechanism is incorporated to accelerate the execution of a higher consensus level on an easy path. After reaching an acceptable consensus level amongst DMs, the entire process moves to the selection phase, comprising of aggregation and ranking processes, to select the best alternative. A comparative example is elaborated to highlight the practicality with the efficiency of the proposed method. The results help us to have greater insight into the MPDM process.

A few of the main advantages of the setting method are: (1) In this article, Łukasiewicz transitivity is used to determine the unspecified preference values in order to normalize the HFPRs. Compared to some other approaches focused on consistency measures, Łukasiewicz transitivity generates better values and consistency as well. (2) The priority weights are assigned to DMs after merging the consistency weights, based on the information provided, and the predefined weights (if any) that play a significant role in assessing the consistency indices of the DM opinions. (3) The enhancement mechanism helps DMs to think in various directions in order to reach a consensus among them. We believe that there are only a few techniques of this kind presented in the literature to deal with MPDM in HFPRs' setting. (4) There is no need to simulate proximity measures in the proposed method, which decreases the computing workload while accelerating the speed at which consensus is achieved. (5) The proposed method resulted in highly consistent NHFPRs as compare to the model given in [31]. (6) In the end, consistent NHFPRs are aggregated into collective consistent NHFPR in order to achieve the ranking order of alternatives. Because it is quite often that the preference values provided by DMs are weighted differently, if the DMs' weights have been calculated, their views are to be aggregated into a global one.

At the same time, there are certain limitations to be discussed in future study: (1) The GDM could contain too many parameters in the decision-making process, including cognitive science, political culture, people's risk attitudes, etc., that certain variables need to be taken into account. (2) When voicing their preferential relationships, experts can show some degree of reluctance. Thus in the case of type-2 fuzzy preference relations, it would be interesting to establish processes to deal with GDM. (3) The threshold consensus measure directly affects the consensus round but is normally decided in advance. How this criterion will be calculated on the basis of multiple parameters, e.g., the number of experts, the number of requirements, or alternatives, may be fascinating to see.

The traditional approach of consensus building fails to consider more uncertain factors and limitations of the language scale. Therefore, it would be interesting to propose another approach for consensus building in group decision making based on T_L-consistency in clustering analysis and medical diagnosis in the framework of various linguistic settings like hesitant fuzzy linguistic preference relation, hesitant intuitionistic fuzzy linguistic preference relation, etc. as future research. The consensus-reaching process for complex linguistic information [49] is another interesting research area for a future study.

Author Contributions: Conceptualization, A.-u.R., J.W., S.F., T.R., and M.T.-Ł.; methodology, A.-u.R., J.W., S.F., T.R., and M.T.-Ł.; software, A.-u.R., J.W., S.F., T.R., and M.T.-Ł.; validation, A.-u.R., J.W., S.F., T.R., and M.T.-Ł.; formal analysis, A.-u.R., J.W., S.F., T.R., and M.T.-Ł.; investigation, A.-u.R., J.W., S.F., T.R., and M.T.-Ł.; resources, A.-u.R., J.W., S.F., T.R., and M.T.-Ł.; data curation, A.-u.R., J.W., S.F., T.R., and M.T.-Ł.; writing–original draft preparation, A.-u.R., J.W., S.F., T.R., and M.T.-Ł.; writing–review and editing, A.-u.R., J.W., S.F., T.R., and M.T.-Ł.; visualization, A.-u.R., J.W., S.F., T.R., and M.T.-Ł.; supervision, A.-u.R., J.W., S.F., T.R., and M.T.-Ł.; project administration, S.F., J.W.; funding acquisition, J.W. and M.T.-Ł. All authors have read and agreed to the published version of the manuscript.

Funding: The work was supported by the project financed within the framework of the program of the Minister of Science and Higher Education under the name "Regional Excellence Initiative" in the years 2019–2022, Project Number 001/RID/2018/19; the amount of financing: PLN 10.684.000,00 (J.W.; M.T.-Ł.-Ł.).

Acknowledgments: The authors would like to thank the editor and the anonymous reviewers, whose insightful comments and constructive suggestions helped us to significantly improve the quality of this paper.

Conflicts of Interest: The authors declare no conflict of interest.

References

1. Wątróbski, J.; Jankowski, J.; Ziemba, P.; Karczmarczyk, A.; Zioło, M. Generalised framework for multi-criteria method selection. *Omega* **2019**, *86*, 107–124. [CrossRef]
2. Shekhovtsov, A.; Kołodziejczyk, J.; Sałabun, W. Fuzzy Model Identification Using Monolithic and Structured Approaches in Decision Problems with Partially Incomplete Data. *Symmetry* **2020**, *12*, 1541. [CrossRef]
3. Stojčić, M.; Zavadskas, E.K.; Pamučar, D.; Stević, Ž.; Mardani, A. Application of MCDM methods in sustainability engineering: A literature review 2008–2018. *Symmetry* **2019**, *11*, 350. [CrossRef]
4. Shekhovtsov, A.; Kozlov, V.; Nosov, V.; Sałabun, W. Efficiency of Methods for Determining the Relevance of Criteria in Sustainable Transport Problems: A Comparative Case Study. *Sustainability* **2020**, *12*, 7915. [CrossRef]
5. Chatterjee, K.; Pamucar, D.; Zavadskas, E.K. Evaluating the performance of suppliers based on using the R'AMATEL-MAIRCA method for green supply chain implementation in electronics industry. *J. Clean. Prod.* **2018**, *184*, 101–129. [CrossRef]
6. Pamučar, D.; Mihajlović, M.; Obradović, R.; Atanasković, P. Novel approach to group multi-criteria decision making based on interval rough numbers: Hybrid DEMATEL-ANP-MAIRCA model. *Expert Syst. Appl.* **2017**, *88*, 58–80. [CrossRef]
7. Sałabun, W.; Wątróbski, J.; Shekhovtsov, A. Are MCDA Methods Benchmarkable? A Comparative Study of TOPSIS, VIKOR, COPRAS, and PROMETHEE II Methods. *Symmetry* **2020**, *12*, 1549. [CrossRef]
8. Dong, Y.; Zhang, H. Multiperson decision making with different preference representation structures: A direct consensus framework and its properties. *Knowl. Based Syst.* **2014**, *58*, 45–57. [CrossRef]
9. Xu, Y.; Wen, X.; Zhang, W. A two-stage consensus method for large-scale multi-attribute group decision making with an application to earthquake shelter selection. *Comput. Ind. Eng.* **2018**, *116*, 113–129. [CrossRef]
10. Pamučar, D.; Petrović, I.; Ćirović, G. Modification of the Best–Worst and MABAC methods: A novel approach based on interval-valued fuzzy-rough numbers. *Expert Syst. Appl.* **2018**, *91*, 89–106. [CrossRef]
11. Wu, J.; Dai, L.; Chiclana, F.; Fujita, H.; Herrera-Viedma, E. A minimum adjustment cost feedback mechanism based consensus model for group decision making under social network with distributed linguistic trust. *Inf. Fusion* **2018**, *41*, 232–242. [CrossRef]
12. Zhang, C.; Zhang, H.; Wang, J. Personalized restaurant recommendation method combining group correlations and customer preferences. *Inf. Sci.* **2018**, *454*, 128–143. [CrossRef]
13. Li, Y.; Zhang, H.; Dong, Y. The interactive consensus reaching process with the minimum and uncertain cost in group decision making. *Appl. Soft Comput.* **2017**, *60*, 202–212. [CrossRef]
14. Li, J.; Wang, Z.X. Consensus building for probabilistic hesitant fuzzy preference relations with expected additive consistency. *Int. J. Fuzzy Syst.* **2018**, *20*, 1495–1510. [CrossRef]

15. Tian, Z.P.; Wang, J.Q.; Zhang, H.Y.; Wang, T.L. Signed distance-based consensus in multi-criteria group decision-making with multi-granular hesitant unbalanced linguistic information. *Comput. Ind. Eng.* **2018**, *124*, 125–138. [CrossRef]
16. Zhang, H.; Dong, Y.; Herrera-Viedma, E. Consensus building for the heterogeneous large-scale GDM with the individual concerns and satisfactions. *IEEE Trans. Fuzzy Syst.* **2017**, *26*, 884–898. [CrossRef]
17. Herrera-Viedma, E.; Cabrerizo, F.J.; Kacprzyk, J.; Pedrycz, W. A review of soft consensus models in a fuzzy environment. *Inf. Fusion* **2014**, *17*, 4–13. [CrossRef]
18. Xia, M.; Xu, Z. Managing hesitant information in GDM problems under fuzzy and multiplicative preference relations. *Int. J. Uncertainty Fuzziness Knowl. Based Syst.* **2013**, *21*, 865–897. [CrossRef]
19. He, Y.; Xu, Z. A consensus reaching model for hesitant information with different preference structures. *Knowl. Based Syst.* **2017**, *135*, 99–112. [CrossRef]
20. Wu, Z.; Jin, B.; Xu, J. Local feedback strategy for consensus building with probability-hesitant fuzzy preference relations. *Appl. Soft Comput.* **2018**, *67*, 691–705. [CrossRef]
21. Xu, Y.; Chen, L.; Rodríguez, R.M.; Herrera, F.; Wang, H. Deriving the priority weights from incomplete hesitant fuzzy preference relations in group decision making. *Knowl. Based Syst.* **2016**, *99*, 71–78. [CrossRef]
22. Meng, F.; An, Q. A new approach for group decision making method with hesitant fuzzy preference relations. *Knowl. Based Syst.* **2017**, *127*, 1–15. [CrossRef]
23. Zhu, B.; Xu, Z.; Xu, J. Deriving a ranking from hesitant fuzzy preference relations under group decision making. *IEEE Trans. Cybern.* **2013**, *44*, 1328–1337. [CrossRef] [PubMed]
24. Faizi, S.; Sałabun, W.; Rashid, T.; Wątróbski, J.; Zafar, S. Group decision-making for hesitant fuzzy sets based on characteristic objects method. *Symmetry* **2017**, *9*, 136. [CrossRef]
25. Ali, A.; Rashid, T. Hesitant fuzzy best-worst multi-criteria decision-making method and its applications. *Int. J. Intell. Syst.* **2019**, *34*, 1953–1967. [CrossRef]
26. Zhang, Z.; Wu, C. A decision support model for group decision making with hesitant multiplicative preference relations. *Inf. Sci.* **2014**, *282*, 136–166. [CrossRef]
27. Meng, F.; Tang, J.; An, Q.; Chen, X. A new procedure for hesitant multiplicative preference relations. *Int. J. Intell. Syst.* **2019**, *34*, 819–857. [CrossRef]
28. Zhang, Z. Deriving the priority weights from incomplete hesitant fuzzy preference relations based on multiplicative consistency. *Appl. Soft Comput.* **2016**, *46*, 37–59. [CrossRef]
29. Li, H.; Yin, S.; Yang, Y. Some preference relations based on q-rung orthopair fuzzy sets. *Int. J. Intell. Syst.* **2019**, *34*, 2920–2936. [CrossRef]
30. Zhang, C.; Liao, H.; Luo, L. Additive consistency-based priority-generating method of q-rung orthopair fuzzy preference relation. *Int. J. Intell. Syst.* **2019**, *34*, 2151–2176. [CrossRef]
31. Xu, Y.; Cabrerizo, F.J.; Herrera-Viedma, E. A consensus model for hesitant fuzzy preference relations and its application in water allocation management. *Appl. Soft Comput.* **2017**, *58*, 265–284. [CrossRef]
32. Ureña, R.; Chiclana, F.; Morente-Molinera, J.A.; Herrera-Viedma, E. Managing incomplete preference relations in decision making: a review and future trends. *Inf. Sci.* **2015**, *302*, 14–32. [CrossRef]
33. Zhang, Z.; Guo, C. An approach to group decision making with heterogeneous incomplete uncertain preference relations. *Comput. Ind. Eng.* **2014**, *71*, 27–36. [CrossRef]
34. Zhang, Z.; Wang, C.; Tian, X. Multi-criteria group decision making with incomplete hesitant fuzzy preference relations. *Appl. Soft Comput.* **2015**, *36*, 1–23. [CrossRef]
35. Khalid, A.; Beg, I. Incomplete hesitant fuzzy preference relations in group decision making. *Int. J. Fuzzy Syst.* **2017**, *19*, 637–645. [CrossRef]
36. Wind, Y.; Saaty, T.L. Marketing applications of the analytic hierarchy process. *Manag. Sci.* **1980**, *26*, 641–658. [CrossRef]
37. Zhu, B. Studies on consistency measure of hesitant fuzzy preference relations. *Procedia Comput. Sci.* **2013**, *17*, 457–464. [CrossRef]
38. Zhang, Z. A framework of group decision making with hesitant fuzzy preference relations based on multiplicative consistency. *Int. J. Fuzzy Syst.* **2017**, *19*, 982–996. [CrossRef]
39. Kizielewicz, B.; Sałabun, W. A New Approach to Identifying a Multi-Criteria Decision Model Based on Stochastic Optimization Techniques. *Symmetry* **2020**, *12*, 1551. [CrossRef]

40. Liu, X.; Xu, Y.; Montes, R.; Dong, Y.; Herrera, F. Analysis of self-confidence indices-based additive consistency for fuzzy preference relations with self-confidence and its application in group decision making. *Int. J. Intell. Syst.* **2019**, *34*, 920–946. [CrossRef]
41. Tanino, T. Fuzzy preference relations in group decision making. In *Non-Conventional Preference Relations in Decision Making*; Springer: Berlin/Heidelberg, Germany, 1988; pp. 54–71.
42. Venugopalan, P. Fuzzy ordered sets. *Fuzzy Sets Syst.* **1992**, *46*, 221–226. [CrossRef]
43. Zadeh, L.A. Fuzzy sets. *Inf. Control.* **1965**, *8*, 338–353. [CrossRef]
44. Torra, V. Hesitant fuzzy sets. *Int. J. Intell. Syst.* **2010**, *25*, 529–539. [CrossRef]
45. Xia, M.; Xu, Z. Hesitant fuzzy information aggregation in decision making. *Int. J. Approx. Reason.* **2011**, *52*, 395–407. [CrossRef]
46. Tanino, T. Fuzzy preference orderings in group decision making. *Fuzzy Sets Syst.* **1984**, *12*, 117–131. [CrossRef]
47. Herrera-Viedma, E.; Chiclana, F.; Herrera, F.; Alonso, S. Group decision-making model with incomplete fuzzy preference relations based on additive consistency. *IEEE Trans. Syst. Man Cybern. Part B (Cybern.)* **2007**, *37*, 176–189. [CrossRef] [PubMed]
48. Xu, Z.; Xia, M. Distance and similarity measures for hesitant fuzzy sets. *Inf. Sci.* **2011**, *181*, 2128–2138. [CrossRef]
49. Wu, X.L.; Liao, H.C. A consensus-based probabilistic linguistic gained and lost dominance score method. *Eur. J. Oper. Res.* **2019**, *272*, 1017–1027. [CrossRef]

symmetry

MDPI

Article

Are MCDA Methods Benchmarkable? A Comparative Study of TOPSIS, VIKOR, COPRAS, and PROMETHEE II Methods

Wojciech Sałabun [1,*], Jarosław Wątróbski [2] and Andrii Shekhovtsov [1,*]

1 Research Team on Intelligent Decision Support Systems, Department of Artificial Intelligence Methods and Applied Mathematics, Faculty of Computer Science and Information Technology, West Pomeranian University of Technology, Szczecin ul. Żołnierska 49, 71-210 Szczecin, Poland

2 Department of Information Systems Engineering, Faculty of Economics and Management, University of Szczecin, Mickiewicza 64, 71-101 Szczecin, Poland; jaroslaw.watrobski@usz.edu.pl

* Correspondence: wojciech.salabun@zut.edu.pl (W.S.); andrii-shekhovtsov@zut.edu.pl (A.S.); Tel.: +48-91-449-5580 (W.S.)

Received: 23 August 2020; Accepted: 14 September 2020; Published: 20 September 2020

Abstract: Multi-Criteria Decision-Analysis (MCDA) methods are successfully applied in different fields and disciplines. However, in many studies, the problem of selecting the proper methods and parameters for the decision problems is raised. The paper undertakes an attempt to benchmark selected Multi-Criteria Decision Analysis (MCDA) methods. To achieve that, a set of feasible MCDA methods was identified. Based on reference literature guidelines, a simulation experiment was planned. The formal foundations of the authors' approach provide a reference set of MCDA methods (Technique for Order Preference by Similarity to Ideal Solution (TOPSIS), VlseKriterijumska Optimizacija I Kompromisno Resenje (VIKOR), Complex Proportional Assessment (COPRAS), and PROMETHEE II: Preference Ranking Organization Method for Enrichment of Evaluations) along with their similarity coefficients (Spearman correlation coefficients and WS coefficient). This allowed the generation of a set of models differentiated by the number of attributes and decision variants, as well as similarity research for the obtained rankings sets. As the authors aim to build a complex benchmarking model, additional dimensions were taken into account during the simulation experiments. The aspects of the performed analysis and benchmarking methods include various weighing methods (results obtained using entropy and standard deviation methods) and varied techniques of normalization of MCDA model input data. Comparative analyses showed the detailed influence of values of particular parameters on the final form and a similarity of the final rankings obtained by different MCDA methods.

Keywords: optimization; multi-criteria decision-analysis; MCDA benchmark; normalization; entropy; decision-making methods

1. Introduction

Making decisions is an integral part of human life. All such decisions are made based on the assessment of individual decision options, usually based on preferences, experience, and other data available to the decision maker. Formally, a decision can be defined as a choice made based on the available information, or a method of action aimed at solving a specific decision problem [1]. Taking into account the systematics of the decision problem itself and the classical paradigm of single criterion optimization, it should be noted that it is now widely accepted to extend the process of decision support beyond the classical model of single goal optimization described on the set of acceptable solutions [2]. This extension allows one to tackle multi-criteria problems with a focus on obtaining a solution that meets enough many, often contradictory, goals [3–7].

The concept of rational decisions is, at the same time, a paradigm of multi-criteria decision support and is the basis of the whole family of Multi-Criteria Decision-Analysis (MCDA) methods [8]. These methods aim to support the decision maker in the process of finding a solution that best suits their preferences. Such an approach is widely discussed in the literature. In the course of the research, whole groups of MCDA methods and even "schools" of multi-criteria decision support have developed. There are also many different individual MCDA methods and their modifications developed so far. The common MCDA methods belonging to the American school include Technique for Order Preference by Similarity to Ideal Solution (TOPSIS) [9–11], VlseKriterijumska Optimizacija I Kompromisno Resenje (VIKOR) [12], Analytic Hierarchy Process (AHP) [13,14], and Complex Proportional Assessment (COPRAS) [15]. Examples of the most popular methods belonging to the European school are the ELECTRE [16,17] and Preference Ranking Organization Method for Enrichment of Evaluations (PROMETHEE) [18] method families. The third best-known group of methods are mixed approaches, based on the decision-making rules of [19–21]. The result of the research is also a dynamic development of new MCDA methods and extensions of existing methods [22].

Despite the large number of MCDA methods, it should be remembered that no method is perfect and cannot be considered suitable for use in every decision-making situation or for solving every decision problem [23]. Therefore, using different multi-criteria methods may lead to different decision recommendations [24]. It should be noted, however, that if different multi-criteria methods achieve contradictory results, then the correctness of the choice of each of them is questioned [25]. In such a situation, the choice of a decision support method appropriate to the given problem [22] becomes an important research issue, as only an adequately chosen method allows one to obtain a correct solution reflecting the preferences of the decision maker [2,26]. The importance of this problem is raised by Roy, who points out that in stage IV of the decision-making model defined by him, the choice of the calculation procedure should be made in particular [2]. This is also confirmed by Hanne [27], Cinelli et al. [26].

It should be noted that it is difficult to answer the question of which method is the most suitable to solve a specific type of problem [24]. This is related to the apparent universality of MCDA methods, because many methods meet the formal requirements of a given decision-making problem so that they can be selected independently of the specificity of a particular problem (e.g., the existence of a finite set of alternatives may be a determinant for the decision-maker when choosing a method) [27]. Therefore, Guitouni et al. recommend to study different methods and determine their areas of application by identifying their limitations and conditions of applicability [23]. This is very important because different methods can provide different solutions to the same problem [28]. Differences in results using different calculation procedures can be influenced by, for example, the following factors: Individual techniques use different weights of criteria in calculations, the algorithms of methods themselves differ significantly, and many algorithms try to scale the targets [24].

Many methodologies, frameworks, and formal approaches to identify a subset of MCDA methods suitable for the given problem have been developed in prior works [20,22]. The synthesis of available terms is presented later in the article. It should be noted that the assessment of accuracy and reliability of results obtained using various MCDA methods remains a separate research problem. The examples of work on the accuracy assessment and more broadly benchmarking of MCDA methods include Zanakis et al. [24], Chang et al. [29], Hajkowicz and Higgins [30], Żak [31], and others. Their broader discussion is also conducted later in the paper. The authors, focusing their research on selected MCDA methods, effectively use a simulation environment (e.g., Monte Carlo simulation) to generate a set of ranks. The authors most often use Spearman's rank correlation coefficient to assess and analyze the similarity of the rankings. However, the shortcomings of the indicated approaches should be indicated. In the vast majority of the available literature, the approaches are focused on a given domain of the MCDA method (or a subset of methods) application. Thus, despite the use of a simulation environment, the studies are not comprehensive, limiting the range of obtained results. Most of the papers are focused on the assessment of only selected aspects of the accuracy of single MCDA methods or contain narrow comparative studies of selected MCDA methods. Another important challenge related to multi-criteria decision-making problems that are not included in the works mentioned above is the proper determination of weights [32]. It seems to be an investigation into how various methods to determine criteria weights (subjective weighting methods and objective weighting methods) affect final ranking [33]. In our research, we attempt a complex benchmarking for a subset of carefully selected MCDA methods. Taking care of the correctness and comprehensiveness of the conducted research and at the same time following the guidelines of the authors of publications in this area, we use a simulation environment and apply multiple model input parameters (see Figure 1). The aspects of the conducted analysis and benchmarking of methods include not only the generation of final rankings for a variable number of decision-making options, but also take into account different weighing methods (results obtained using entropy and standard deviation methods) and different techniques of normalizing input data of the MCDA model. The analysis of rank similarities obtained under different conditions and using different MCDA methods was carried out based on reference publications and using Spearman's ranking correlation coefficient and *WS* coefficients.

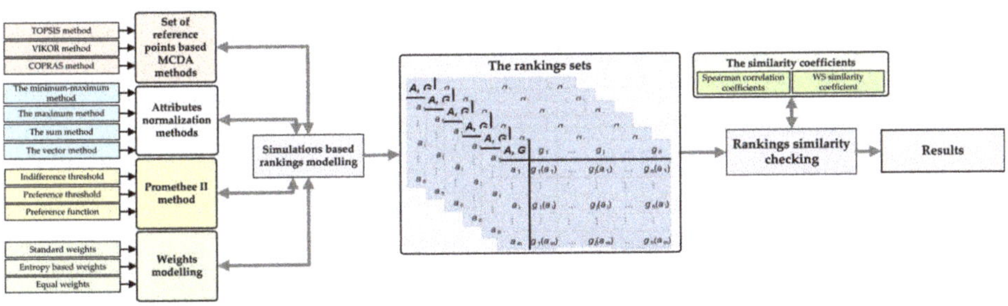

Figure 1. Methodical framework.

The study aims to analyze the similarity of rankings obtained using the selected four MCDA methods. It should be noted that in research, we analyze this problem only from the technical (algorithmic) point of view, leaving in the background the conceptual aspects of the method and the systemic assumptions of obtaining model input data. For each of these methods using a simulation environment, several rankings were calculated. The simulation itself was divided into two parts. The first part refers to a comparison of the similarity of the results separately for TOPSIS, VIKOR, COPRAS, and PROMETHEE II. In the second part, these methods were compared with each other. As illustrated in Figure 1), the calculation procedure took into account different normalization methods, weighting methods, preference thresholds, and preference functions. Thus, in the case of the TOPSIS method for each decision matrix, 12 separate rankings were created, where each of them is a different combination of a standardization method and a weighing method. Then, for the same matrix, a set of rankings using other MCDA methods (VIKOR, COPRAS, and PROMETHEE II) was created respectively. This procedure was repeated for different parameters of the decision matrix (in terms of the number of analyzed alternatives and number of criteria). In this way, the simulation provides a complex dataset in which similarities were analyzed using the Spearman and WS coefficients.

In this paper, we used several MCDA methods (TOPSIS, VIKOR, COPRAS, and PROMETHEE II) to make comparative tests. The choice of this set was dictated by the properties and popularity of these methods. These methods and their modifications found an application in many different domains such as sustainability assessment [34–36], logistics [37–39], supplier selection [7,40,41], manufacturing [42–44], environment management [45–47], waste management [48,49], energy management [50–55], chemical engineering [56–58], and many more [59,60]. The choice of a group of TOPSIS, VIKOR, and COPRAS methods is justified, as they form a coherent group of methods of the American MCDA school and are based on the same principles, using the concepts of the so-called reference points. At the same time, unlike other methods of the American school, they are not merely trivial (in the algorithmic sense) elaborations of the simple additional or multiplicative weighted aggregation. The choice of the PROMETHEE II method was dictated by the fact that this method belongs to the European school and that the PROMETHEE II algorithm implements the properties of other European school-based MCDA methods (outranking relations, thresholds, and different preference functions). It should be noted that for benchmarking purposes, the choice of this method has one more justification—unlike other methods of this school, the method provides a full, quantitative final ranking of decision-making options.

The rest of the article is structured as follows. Section 2.1.1 present the most important MCDA foundations. Operational point of view and preference aggregation techniques are presented in Section 2.1.2. Sections 2.1.3 and 2.1.4 describe respectively American and European-based MCDA methods. Mixed and rule-based methods are shown in Section 2.1.5. Section 2.2 presents the MCDA method selection and benchmarking problem. Section 3.1.1 contains a description of the TOPSIS method and Section 3.1.2 describes the VIKOR method. A description of the COPRAS method can be found in Section 3.1.3 and a description of the PROMETHEE II method is in Section 3.1.4. Section 3.2 describes the normalization methods, which could be applied to data before executing any MCDA methods. Section 3.3 contains a description of weighting methods, which would be used in article. Section 3.4 describes the correlation coefficients that will be used to compare results. The research experiment and the numerical example are presented in Section 4. Section 5 provides the most relevant results and their discussion. Finally, the conclusions are formulated in Section 6.

2. Literature Review

2.1. MCDA State of the Art

In this section, we introduce the methodological assumptions of MCDA, taking into account the operational point of view and available data aggregation techniques. At the same time, we provide an outline of existing methods and decision-making schools.

2.1.1. MCDA Foundations

Almost in every case, the nature of the decision problem makes it a multi-criteria problem. This means that making a "good" decision requires considering many decision options, where each option should be considered in terms of many factors (criteria) that characterize its acceptability. The values of these factors may limit the number of variants in case their values exceed the assumed framework. They can also serve for grading the admissibility of variants in the situation when each of them is admissible, and the multi-criteria problem consists in choosing subjectively the best of them. For different decision makers, different criteria may have a different relevance, so in no case can a multi-criteria decision be considered as completely objective. Only the ranking of individual variants with given weights of individual criteria is objective here, as this ranking is usually generated using a specific multi-criteria method. Therefore, concerning recommended multi-criteria decisions, the term "optimal" is not used but "most satisfactory decision-maker" [23] which means optimum in the sense of Pareto [2]. In conclusion, it can be concluded that multi-criteria models should take into account elements that can be described as a multi-criteria paradigm: The existence of multiple criteria, the existence of conflicts between criteria, and the complex, subjective, and poorly structured nature of the decision-making problem [61].

The MCDA methods are used to solve decision problems where there are many criteria. The literature provides various models of the decision-making process, e.g., Roy, Guitouni, and Keeney. For example, Guitouni's model distinguishes five stages: Decision problem structuring, articulating and modeling preferences, preference aggregation, exploitation of aggregation, and obtaining a solution recommendation [62]. The essential elements of a multi-criteria decision problem are formed by a triangle (A, C, and E), where A defines a set of alternative decision options, C is a set of criteria, while E represents the criteria performance of the options [62]. Modeling of the decision maker's preferences can be done in two ways, i.e., directly or indirectly, using the so-called disaggregation procedures [63]. The decision maker's preferences are expressed using binary relations. When comparing decision options, two fundamental indifference relations (a_i I a_j) and strict preference (a_i P a_j) may occur. Moreover, the set of basic preferential relations may be extended by the relations of a weak preference of one of the variants to another and their incomparability (variants) [64], creating together with the basic relations the so-called outranking relation.

2.1.2. Operational Point of View and Preference Aggregation Techniques

The structured decision problem, for which the modeling of the decision maker's preferences was carried out, is an input for the multi-criteria preference aggregation procedure (MCDA methods). This procedure should take into account the preferences of the decision-maker, modeled using the weighting of criteria, and preference thresholds. This procedure is responsible for aggregating the performance of the criteria of individual variants to obtain a global result of comparing the variants consistent with one of the multi-criteria issues. The individual aggregation procedures can be divided according to their operational approach. In the literature three main approaches exist [63]:

- The use of a single synthesized criterion: In this approach, the result of the variants' comparisons is determined for each criterion separately. Then the results are synthesized into a global assessment. The full order of variants is obtained here [65];
- The synthesis of the criteria based on the relation of outranking: Due to the occurrence of incomparability relations, this approach allows for obtaining the partial order of variants [65];
- Aggregation based on decision rules [63]: This approach is based on the rough sets set theory [66]. It uses cases and reference ranking from which decision rules are generated [67].

The difference between the use of a single synthesized criterion and the synthesis based on the relation of exceedance is that in methods using synthesis to one criterion there is a compensation, while methods using the relation of exceedance by many researchers are considered uncompensated [68,69].

Research on multi-criteria decision support has developed two main groups of methods. These groups can be distinguished due to the operational approach used in them. These are the methods of the so-called American school of decision support and the methods of the European school [70,71]. There is also a group of so-called basic methods, most of which are similar in terms of the operational approach to the American school methods. Examples of basic methods are the lexicographic method, the ejection method for the minimum attribute value, the maximum method, or the additive weighting method. Besides, there is a group of methods combining elements of the American and European approaches, as well as methods based on the previously mentioned rule approach.

2.1.3. American School-Based MCDA Methods

The methods of the American school of decision support are based on a functional approach [63], namely, the use of value or usability. These methods usually do not take into account the uncertainty, inaccuracy, and uncertainty that can occur in data or decision-maker preferences [1]. This group of methods is strongly connected with the operational approach using a single synthesized criterion. The basic methods of the American school are MAUT, AHP, ANP, SMART, UTA, MACBETH (Measuring Attractiveness by a Categorical Based Evaluation Technique), or TOPSIS.

In the MAUT method, the most critical assumption is that the preferences of the decision-maker can be expressed using a global usability function, taking into account all the criteria taken into account. The AHP method is the best known and most commonly used functional method. This method allows one to prioritize the decision-making problem. The ANP method is a generalization of AHP. Instead of prioritizing the decision problem, it allows the building of a network model in which there may be links between criteria and variants and their feedback. In the SMART method, the criteria values of variants are converted to a common internal scale. This is done mathematically by the decision-maker, and the value function is used [72]. In the UTA method, the decision maker's preferences are extracted from the reference set of variants [73]. The MACBETH method (Measuring Attractiveness by a Categorical Based Evaluation Technique) is based on qualitative evaluations. The individual variants are compared here in a comparison matrix in pairs. The criterion preferences of the variants are aggregated as a weighted average [74,75]. In the TOPSIS (Technique for Order Preference by Similarity to Ideal Solution) method, the decision options considered are compared for the ideal and the anti-ideal solution [76–79].

2.1.4. European School-Based MCDA Methods

The methods of the European School use a relational model. Thus, they use a synthesis of criteria based on the relation of outranking. This relation is characterized by transgression between pairs of decision options. Among the methods of the European School of Decision Support, the groups of ELECTRE and PROMETHEE methods should be mentioned above all [1].

ELECTRE I and ELECTRE Is methods are used to solve the selection problem. In the ELECTRE I method there is a true criterion (there are no indifference and preference thresholds), while in ELECTRE Is, pseudo-criteria have been introduced including thresholds. It should be noted here that indifference and preference thresholds can be expressed directly as fixed quantities for a given criterion or as functions, which would allow distinguishing the relation of weak and strong preferences. The relations of the excess occurring between the variants are presented on the graph and the best variants are those which are not exceeded by any other [80,81]. The ELECTRE II method is similar to the ELECTRE I since no indifference and preference thresholds are defined here as well, i.e., the true criteria are also present here. Furthermore, the calculation algorithm is the same almost throughout the procedure. However, the ELECTRE II method distinguishes weak and strong preference [82]. The ELECTRE III method is one of the most frequently used methods of multi-criteria decision support and it deals with the ranking problem. The ELECTRE IV method is similar to ELECTRE III in terms of using pseudo-criteria. Similarly, the final ranking of variants is also determined here. The ELECTRE IV method determines two orders (ascending and descending) from which the final ranking of variants is generated. However, the ELECTRE IV method does not define the weights of criteria, so all criteria are equal [83]. ELECTRE Tri is the last of the discussed ELECTRE family methods. It deals with the classification problem and uses pseudo-criteria. This method is very similar to ELECTRE III in procedural terms. However, in the ELECTRE Tri method, the decisional variants are compared with so-called variants' profiles, i.e., "artificial variants" limiting particular quality classes [84].

PROMETHEE methods are used to determine a synthetic ranking of alternatives. Depending on the implementation, they operate on true or pseudo-criteria. The methods of this family combine most of the ELECTRE methods as they allow one to apply one of the six preference functions, reflecting, among others, the true criterion and pseudo-criteria. Moreover, they enrich the ELECTRE methodology at the stage of object ranking. These methods determine the input and output preference flows, based on which we can create a partial ranking in the PROMETHEE I method [85]. In contrast, in the PROMETHEE II method, the net preference flow values for individual variants are calculated based on input and output preference flows. Based on net values, a complete ranking of variants is determined [86,87].

NAIADE (Novel Approach to Imprecise Assessment and Decision Environment) methods are similar to PROMETHEE in terms of calculation because the ranking of variants is determined based on input and output preference flows [88]. However, when comparing the variants, six preferential relations defined based on trapezoidal fuzzy numbers are used (apart from indistinguishability of variants, weak, and strong preference is distinguished). The methods of this family do not define the weights of criteria [89].

Other examples of methods from the European MCDA field are ORESTE, REGIME, ARGUS, TACTIC, MELCHIOR, or PAMSSEM. The ORESTE method requires the presentation of variant evaluations and a ranking of criteria on an ordinal scale [90]. Then, using the distance function, the total order of variants is determined concerning the subsequent criteria [91]. The REGIME method is based on the analysis of variants' compatibility. The probability of dominance for each pair of variants being compared is determined and on this basis the order of variants is determined [92]. In the ARGUS method for the representation of preferences on the order scale, qualitative measures are used [93]. The TACTIC method (Treatment of the Alternatives According To the Importance of Criteria) is based on quantitative assessments of alternatives and weights of criteria. Furthermore, it allows the use of true criteria and quasi-criteria, thus using the indistinguishability threshold as well as the veto. Similarly to ELECTRE I, TACTIC and ARGUS methods use preference aggregation based on compliance and non-compliance analysis [94]. In the MELCHIOR method pseudo-criteria are used, the calculation is similar to ELECTRE IV, while in the MELCHIOR method the order relationship between the criteria is established [93]. The PAMSSEM I and II methods are a combination of ELECTRE III, NAIADE, and Promethee and implement the computational procedure used in these methods [95,96].

2.1.5. Mixed and Rule-Based Methods

Many multi-criteria methods combine the approaches of the American and European decision support school. An example is the EVAMIX method [23], which allows taking into account both quantitative and qualitative criteria, using two separate measures of domination [97]. Another mishandled method is the QUALIFLEX method [98], which allows for the use of qualitative evaluations of variants and both quantitative and qualitative criteria weights [99]. PCCA (Pairwise Criterion Comparison Approach) methods can be treated as a separate group of multi-criteria methods. They focus on the comparison of variants concerning different pairs of criteria considered instead of single criteria. The partial results obtained in this way are then aggregated into the evaluation and final ranking [100]. The methods are based on the PCCA approach: MAPPAC, PRAGMA, PACMAN, and IDRA [101].

The last group of methods are methods based strictly on decision rules [102]. These are methods using fuzzy sets theory (COMET: Characteristic Objects Method) [22] and rough sets theory (DRSA: (Dominance-based Rough Set Approach) [103]. In the methods belonging to this group, the decision rules are initially built. Then, based on these rules, variants are compared and evaluated, and a ranking is generated.

The COMET (Characteristic Objects Method) requires giving fuzzy triangular numbers for each criterion [104], determining the degree of belonging of variants to particular linguistic values describing the criteria [105]. Then, from the values of vertices of particular fuzzy numbers, the characteristic variants are generated. These variants are compared in pairs by the decision-maker, and their model ranking is generated. These variants, together with their aggregated ranking values, create a fuzzy rule database [21]. After the decision system of the considered variants is given to the decision system, each of the considered variants activates appropriate rules and its aggregated rating is determined as the sum of the products of the degrees in which the variants activate individual rules [106,107].

The DRSA method (Dominance-based Rough Set Approach) is based on the rough set theory and requires the definition of a decision table taking into account the values of criteria and consequences of previous decisions (in other words, the table contains historical decision options together with their criteria assessments as well as their aggregated global assessments) [108]. The decision defines the relation of exceedance. The final assessment of a variant is determined as the number of variants which, based on the rules, the considered variant exceeds or is not exceeded by. Moreover, the number of variants that are exceeded or not exceeded by the considered variant is deducted from the assessment [109,110].

2.2. MCDA Methods Selection and Benchmarking Problem

The complexity of the problem of choosing the right multi-criteria method to solve a specific decision problem results in numerous works in the literature where this issue is addressed. These works can be divided according to their approach to method selection. Their authors apply approaches based on benchmarks, multi-criteria analysis, and informal and formal structuring of the problem or decision-making situation. An attempt at a short synthesis of available approaches to the selection of MCDA methods to a decision-making problem is presented below.

The selection of a method based on multi-criteria analysis requires defining criteria against which individual methods will be evaluated. This makes it necessary to determine the structure of the decision problem at least partially [111]. Moreover, it should be noted that treating the MCDA method selection based on the multi-criteria approach causes a looping of the problem, because for this selection problem, the appropriate multi-criteria method should also be chosen [112]. Nevertheless, the multi-criteria approach to MCDA method selection is used in the literature. Examples include works by Gershon [113], Al-Shemmeri et al. [111], and Celik and Deha Er [114].

The informal approach to method selection consists of selecting the method for a given decision problem based on heuristic analysis performed by the analyst/decision-maker [115]. This analysis is usually based on the author's thoughts and unstructured description of the decision problem and the characteristics of particular methods. The methodological approach is similar to the semi-formal one, with the difference that the characteristics of individual MCDA methods are to some extent formalized here (e.g., table describing the methods). The informal approach was used in Adil et al. [115] and Bagheri Moghaddam et al. [116]. The semi-formal approach has been used in the works of Salinesi and Kornyshov [117], De Montis et al. [118], and Cinelli et al. [119].

In the formal approach to the selection of the MCDA method, the description of individual methods is fully structured (e.g., taxonomy or a table of features of individual MCDA methods) [120,121]. The decision problem and the method of selecting a single or group of MCDA methods from among those considered are formally defined (e.g., based on decision rules [122], artificial neural networks [123], or decision trees [23,124]). These are frameworks, which enable a selection of MCDA method based on the formal description of methods and decision problem. Such an approach is proposed, among others, in works: Hwang and Yoon [125], Moffett and Sarkar [124], Guitouni and Martel [23], Guitouni et al. [62], Wątróbski [120], Wątróbski and Jankowski [122], Celik and Topcu [126], Cicek et al. [127], and Ulengin et al. [123].

The benchmarking approach seems particularly important. It focuses on a comparison of the results obtained by individual methods. The main problem of applying this approach is to find a reference point against which the results of the examined multi-criteria methods would be compared. Some authors take the expert ranking as a point of reference whilst others compare the results to the performance of one selected method or examine the compliance of individual rankings obtained using particular MCDA methods. Examples of benchmark-based approach to selection/comparison of MCDA methods are works: Zanakisa et al. [24], Chang et al. [29] Hajkowicz and Higgins [30], and Żak [31].

The publication of Zanakis et al. [29] presents results of benchmarks for eight MCDA methods (Simple Additive Weighting, Multiplicative Exponential Weighting, TOPSIS, ELECTRE, and four AHP variants). In the simulation test scenario, randomly generated decision problems were assumed in which the number of variants was equal: 3, 5, 7, and 9; the number of criteria were: 5, 10, 15, and 20; and the weights of the criteria could be equal, have a uniform distribution in the range <0; 1> with a standard deviation of 1/12, or a beta U-shaped distribution in the range <0; 1> with a standard deviation of 1/24. Moreover, the assessments of alternatives were randomly generated according to a uniform distribution in the range <0; 1>. The number of repetitions was 100 for each combination of criteria, variants, and weights. Therefore, 4800 decision problems were considered in the benchmark (4 number of criteria × 4 number of variants × 3 weightings types × 100 repetitions) and 38,400 solutions were obtained in total (4800 problems × 8 MCDA methods). Within the tests, the average results of all rankings generated by each method were compared with the average results of rankings generated by the SAW method, which was the reference point. Comparisons were made using, among others, Spearman's rank correlation coefficient for rankings.

Benchmark also examined the phenomenon of ranking reversal after introducing an additional non-dominant variant to the evaluation. The research on the problem of ranking reversal was carried out based on similar measures, with the basic ranking generated by a given MCDA method being the point of reference in this case. The authors of the study stated that the AHP method gives the rankings closest to the SAW method, while in terms of ranking reversal, the TOPSIS method turned out to be the best.

Chang et al. [29] took up a slightly different problem. They presented the procedure of selecting a group fuzzy multi-criteria method generating the most preferred group ranking for a given problem. The authors defined 18 fuzzy methods, which are combinations of two methods of group rating averaging (arithmetic and geometric mean), three multi-criteria methods (Simple Additive Weighting, Weighted Product, and TOPSIS), and three methods of results defuzzification (Center-of-area, graded mean integration, and metric distance). The best group ranking was selected by comparing each of the 18 rankings with nine individual rankings of each decision maker created using methods that are a combination of multi-criteria procedures and defuzzification methods. Spearman's correlation was used to compare group and individual rankings.

In the work of Hajkowicz and Higgins [30] rankings were compared using five methods (Simple Additive Weighting, Range of Value Method, PROMETHEE II, Evamix, and Compromise programming). To compare the rankings, we used Spearman's and Kendall's correlations for full rankings and a coefficient that directly determines the compliance on the first three positions of each of the compared rankings. The study considered six decision-making problems, in the field of water resources management, undertaken in the scientific literature. Nevertheless, it should be noted that this statement is based on the analysis of features and possibilities offered by individual MCDA methods. However, it does not result from the conducted benchmark.

Another publication cited in which the benchmark was applied to the work of Żak [31]. The author considered five multi-criteria methods (ELECTRE, AHP, UTA, MAPPAC, and ORESTE). The study was based on the examination of the indicated methods concerning three decision-making problems related to transport, i.e., (I) evaluation of the public transportation system development scenarios, (II) ranking of maintenance and repair contractors in the public transportation system, and (III) selection of the means of transport used in the public transportation system. The benchmark uses expert evaluations for each of the methods in terms of versatility and relevance to the problem, computational performance, modeling capabilities for decision-makers, reliability, and usefulness of the ranking.

The problem of MCDA methods benchmarking is also addressed in many up-to-date studies. Thus in the paper [128] using building performance simulation reliability of rankings generated using AHP, TOPSIS, ELECTRE III, and PROMETHEE II methods was evaluated. In the paper [129] using Monte Carlo simulation, Weighted Sum, and Weighted Product Methods (WSM/WPM), TOPSIS, AHP, PROMETHEE I, and ELECTRE I were compared. The next study [130] adopted the same benchmarking environment as in the study [24]. The authors empirically compare the rankings produced by multi-MOORA, TOPSIS, and VIKOR methods. In the paper [131] another benchmark of selected MCDA methods was presented. AHP, Fuzzy AHP, TOPSIS, Fuzzy TOPSIS, and PROMETHEE I methods were used here. The similarity of rankings was evaluated using Spearman's rank correlation coefficient. In the next paper [132], the impact of different uncertainty sources on the rankings of MCDA problems in the context of food safety was analyzed. In this study, MMOORA, TOPSIS, VIKOR, WASPAS, and ELECTRE II were compared. In the last example work [133], using a simulation environment, the impact of different standardization techniques in the TOPSIS method on the final form of final rankings was examined. The above literature analysis unambiguously shows the effectiveness of the simulation environment in benchmarking methods from the MCDA family. However, at the same time, it constitutes a justification for the authors of this article for the research methods used.

3. Preliminaries

3.1. MCDA Methods

In this section, we introduced formal foundations of MCDA methods used during the simulation. We selected three methods belonging to the American school (TOPSIS, VIKOR, and COPRAS) and one popular method of the European school called PROMETHEE II.

3.1.1. TOPSIS

The first one is Technique of Order Preference Similarity (TOPSIS). In this approach, we measure the distance of alternatives from the reference elements, which are respectively positive and negative ideal solution. This method was widely presented in [9,134]. The TOPSIS method is a simple MCDA technique used in many practical problems. Thanks to its simplicity of use, it is widely used in solving multi-criteria problems. Below we present its algorithm [9]. We assume that we have a decision matrix with m alternatives and n criteria is represented as $X = (x_{ij})_{m \times n}$.

Step 1. Calculate the normalized decision matrix. The normalized values r_{ij} calculated according to Equation (1) for profit criteria and (2) for cost criteria. We use this normalization method, because [11] shows that it performs better than classical vector normalization. Although, we can also use any other normalization method.

$$r_{ij} = \frac{x_{ij} - min_j(x_{ij})}{max_j(x_{ij}) - min_j(x_{ij})} \tag{1}$$

$$r_{ij} = \frac{max_j(x_{ij}) - x_{ij}}{max_j(x_{ij}) - min_j(x_{ij})} \tag{2}$$

Step 2. Calculate the weighted normalized decision matrix v_{ij} according to Equation (3).

$$v_{ij} = w_i r_{ij} \tag{3}$$

Step 3. Calculate Positive Ideal Solution (PIS) and Negative Ideal Solution (NIS) vectors. PIS is defined as maximum values for each criteria (4) and NIS as minimum values (5). We do not need to split criteria into profit and cost here, because in step 1 we use normalization which turns cost criteria into profit criteria.

$$v_j^+ = \{v_1^+, v_2^+, \cdots, v_n^+\} = \{max_j(v_{ij})\} \tag{4}$$

$$v_j^- = \{v_1^-, v_2^-, \cdots, v_n^-\} = \{min_j(v_{ij})\} \tag{5}$$

Step 4. Calculate distance from PIS and NIS for each alternative. As shown in Equations (6) and (7).

$$D_i^+ = \sqrt{\sum_{j=1}^{n} (v_{ij} - v_j^+)^2} \tag{6}$$

$$D_i^- = \sqrt{\sum_{j=1}^{n} (v_{ij} - v_j^-)^2} \tag{7}$$

Step 5. Calculate each alternative's score according to Equation (8). This value is always between 0 and 1, and the alternatives which have values closer to 1 are better.

$$C_i = \frac{D_i^-}{D_i^- + D_i^+} \tag{8}$$

3.1.2. VIKOR

VIKOR is an acronym in Serbian that stands for VlseKriterijumska Optimizacija I Kompromisno Resenje. The decision maker chooses an alternative that is the closest to the ideal and the solutions are assessed according to all considered criteria. The VIKOR method was originally introduced by Opricovic [135] and the whole algorithm is presented in [134]. These both methods are based on closeness to the ideal objects [136]. However, they differ in their operational approach and how these methods consider the concept of proximity to the ideal solutions.

The VIKOR method, similarly to the TOPSIS method, is based on distance measurements. In this approach a compromise solution is sought. The description of the method will be quoted according to [135,136]. Let us say that we have a decision matrix with m alternatives and n criteria is represented as $X = f_{ij}(A_i)_{m\times n}$. Before actually applying this method, the decision matrix can be normalized with one of the methods described in Section 3.2.

Step 1. Determine the best f_i^* and the worth f_i^- values for each criteria functions. Use (9) for profit criteria and (10) for cost criteria.

$$f_j^* = \max_i f_{ij}, \quad f_j^- = \min_i f_{ij} \tag{9}$$

$$f_j^* = \min_i f_{ij}, \quad f_j^- = \max_i f_{ij} \tag{10}$$

Step 2. Calculate the S_i and R_i values by Equations (11) and (12).

$$S_i = \sum_{j=1}^{n} w_j \left(f_j^* - f_{ij}\right) / \left(f_j^* - f_j^-\right) \tag{11}$$

$$R_i = \max_j \left[w_j \left(f_j^* - f_{ij}\right) / \left(f_j^* - f_j^-\right)\right] \tag{12}$$

Step 3. Compute the Q_i values using Equation (13).

$$Q_i = v\left(S_i - S^*\right) / \left(S^- - S^*\right) + (1 - v)\left(R_i - R^*\right) / \left(R^- - R^*\right) \tag{13}$$

where
$S^* = \min_i S_i, \quad S^* = \min_i S_i$
$R^* = \min_i R_i, \quad R^* = \max_i R_i$
and v is introduced as a weigh for the strategy "majority of criteria". We use $v = 0.5$ here.

Step 4. Rank alternatives, sorting by the values S, R, and Q in ascending order. Result is three ranking lists.

Step 5. Normally, we should use S, R, and Q ranking lists to propose the compromise solution or set of compromise solutions, as shown in [134,136]. However, in this paper would use only the Q ranking list.

3.1.3. COPRAS

Third used method is a COPRAS (Complex Proportional Assessment), introduced by Zavadskas [137,138]. This approach assumes a direct and proportional relationship of the importance of investigated variants on a system of criteria adequately describing the decision variants and on values and weights of the criteria [139]. This method ranks alternatives based on their relative importance (weight). Final ranking is creating using the positive and negative ideal solutions [138,140]. Assuming, that we have a decision matrix with m alternatives and n criteria is represented as $X = f_{ij}(A_i)_{m\times n}$, the COPRAS method is defined in five steps:

Step 1. Calculate the normalized decision matrix using Equation (14).

$$r_{ij} = \frac{x_{ij}}{\sum_{i=1}^{m} x_{ij}} \tag{14}$$

Step 2. Calculate the difficult normalized decision matrix, which represents a multiplication of the normalized decision matrix elements with the appropriate weight coefficients using Equation (15).

$$v_{ij} = r_{ij} \cdot w_j \tag{15}$$

Step 3. Determine the sums of difficult normalized values, which was calculated previously. Equation (16) should be used for profit criteria and Equation (17) for cost criteria.

$$S_{+i} = \sum_{j=1}^{k} v_{ij} \tag{16}$$

$$S_{-i} = \sum_{j=k+1}^{n} v_{ij} \tag{17}$$

where k is the number of attributes that must be maximized. The rest of attributes from $k+1$ to n prefer lower values. The S_{+i} and S_{-i} values show the level of the goal achievement for alternatives. A higher value of S_{+i} means that this alternative is better and the lower value of S_{-i} also points to better alternative.

Step 4. Calculate the relative significance of alternatives using Equation (18).

$$Q_i = S_{+i} + \frac{S_{-\min} \cdot \sum_{i=1}^{m} S_{-i}}{S_{-i} \cdot \sum_{i=1}^{m} \left(\frac{S_{-\min}}{S_{-i}} \right)} \tag{18}$$

Step 5. Final ranking is performed according U_i values (19).

$$U_i = \frac{Q_i}{Q_i^{max}} \cdot 100\% \tag{19}$$

where Q_i^{max} stands for the maximum value of the utility function. Better alternatives have a higher U_i value, e.g., the best alternative would have $U_i = 100$.

3.1.4. PROMETHEE II

The Preference Ranking Organization Method for Enrichment of Evaluations (PROMETHEE) is a family of MCDA methods developed by Brans [18,141]. It is similar to other methods input data, but it optionally requires to choose preference function and some other variables. In this article we use PROMETHEE II method, because the output of this method has a full ranking of the alternatives. It is the approach where a complete ranking of the actions is based on the multi-criteria net flow. It includes preferences and indifferences (preorder) [142]. According to [134,141], PROMETHEE II is designed to solve the following multicriteria problems:

$$max\{g_1(a), g_2(a), \dots g_n(a) | a \in A\} \tag{20}$$

where A is a finite set of alternatives and $g_i(\cdot)$ is a set of evaluation criteria either to be maximized or minimized. In other words, $g_i(a_j)$ is a value of criteria i for alternative a_j. With these values and weights we can define evaluation table (see Table 1).

Table 1. Evaluation table.

a	$g_1(\cdot)$	$g_2(\cdot)$	$\cdots$	$g_n(\cdot)$
	w_1	w_2	$\cdots$	w_n
a_1	$g_1(a_1)$	$g_2(a_1)$	$\cdots$	$g_n(a_1)$
a_1	$g_1(a_2)$	$g_2(a_2)$	$\cdots$	$g_n(a_2)$
$\vdots$	$\vdots$	$\vdots$	$\ddots$	$\vdots$
a_m	$g_1(a_m)$	$g_2(a_m)$	$\cdots$	$g_n(a_m)$

Step 1. After defining the problem as described above, calculate the preference function values. It is defined as (21) for profit criteria.

$$P(a,b) = F\left[d(a,b)\right], \quad \forall a,b \in A \tag{21}$$

where $d(a,b)$ is the difference between two actions (pairwise comparison):

$$d(a,b) = g(a) - g(b) \tag{22}$$

and the value of the preference function P is always between 0 and 1 and it is calculating for each criterion. The Table 2 presents possible preference functions.

This preference functions and variables such as p and q allows one to customize the PROMETHEE model. For our experiment these variables are calculated according to Equations (23) and (24):

$$q = \bar{D} - k \cdot \sigma_D \tag{23}$$

$$p = \bar{D} + k \cdot \sigma_D, \tag{24}$$

where D is a positive value of the d values (22) for each criterion and k is a modifier. In our experiments $k \in \{0.25, 0.5, 1.0\}$.

Step 2. Calculate the aggregated preference indices (25).

$$\begin{cases} \pi(a,b) = \sum_{j=1}^{n} P_j(a,b)w_j \\ \pi(b,a) = \sum_{j=1}^{n} P_j(b,a)w_j \end{cases} \tag{25}$$

where a and b are alternatives and $\pi(a,b)$ shows how much alternative a is preferred to b over all of the criteria. There are some properties (26) which must be true for all alternatives set A.

$$\begin{cases} \pi(a,a) = 0 \\ 0 \leq \pi(a,b) \leq 1 \\ 0 \leq \pi(b,a) \leq 1 \\ 0 \leq \pi(a,b) + \pi(b,a) \leq 1 \end{cases} \tag{26}$$

Step 3. Next, calculate positive (27) and negative (28) outranking flows.

$$\phi^{+}(a) = \frac{1}{m-1} \sum_{x \in A} \pi(a,x) \tag{27}$$

$$\phi^{-}(a) = \frac{1}{m-1} \sum_{x \in A} \pi(x,a) \tag{28}$$

Step 4. In this article we will use only PROMETHEE II, which results in a complete ranking of alternatives. Ranking is based on the net flow Φ (29).

$$\Phi(a) = \Phi^{+}(a) - \Phi^{-}(a) \tag{29}$$

Larger value of $\Phi(a)$ means better alternative.

Table 2. PROMETHEE (Preference Ranking Organization Method for Enrichment of Evaluations) preference functions.

Generalized Criterion	Definition	Parameters to Fix
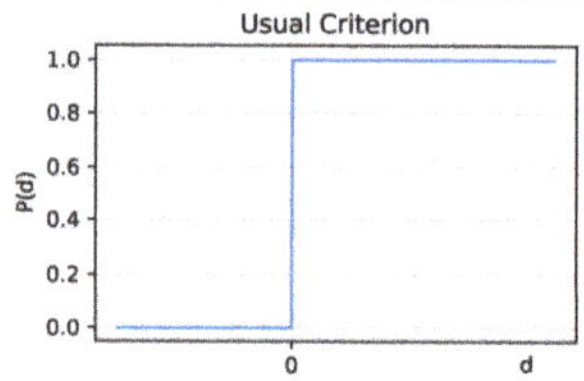	$P(d) = \begin{cases} 0 & d \leq 0 \\ 1 & d > 0 \end{cases}$	–
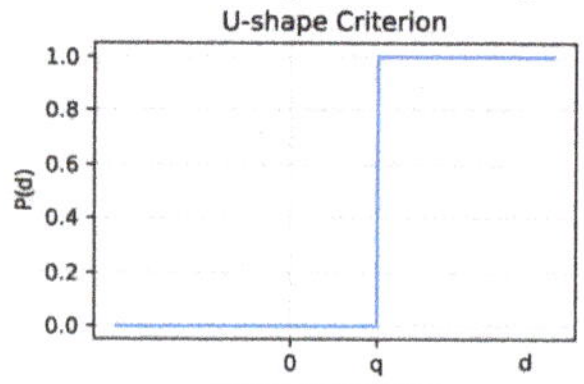	$P(d) = \begin{cases} 0 & d \leq q \\ 1 & d > q \end{cases}$	q
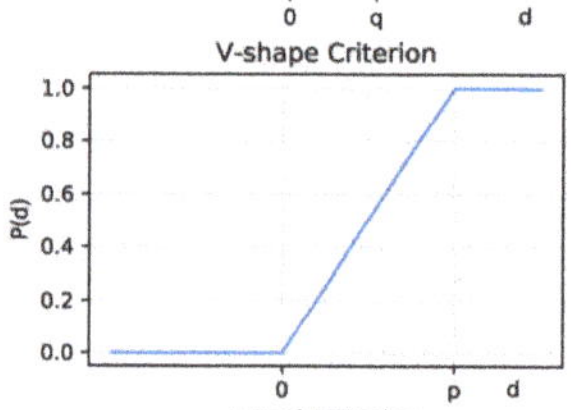	$\mathrm{P(d)} = \begin{cases} 0 & d \leq 0 \\ \frac{d}{p} & 0 < d \leq p \\ 1 & d > p \end{cases}$	p
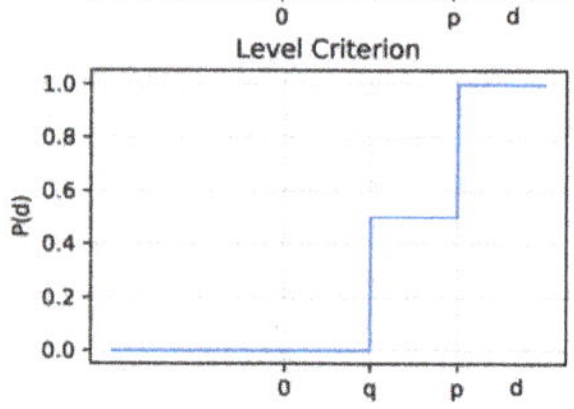	$\mathrm{P(d)} = \begin{cases} 0 & d \leq q \\ \frac{1}{2} & q < d \leq p \\ 1 & d > p \end{cases}$	p, q
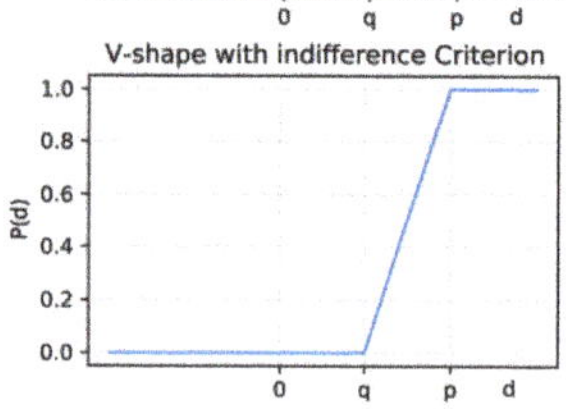	$\mathrm{P(d)} = \begin{cases} 0 & d \leq q \\ \frac{d-q}{p-q} & q < d \leq p \\ 1 & d > p \end{cases}$	p, q

3.2. Normalization Methods

In the literature, there is no clear assignment to which decision-makers' methods of data normalization are used. This situation poses a problem, as it is necessary to consider the influence of a particular normalization on the result. The most common normalization methods in MCDA methods can be divided into two groups [143], i.e., methods designed to profit (30), (32), (34) and (36) and cost criteria (31), (33), (35), and (37).

The minimum-maximum method: In this approach, the greatest and the least values in the considered set are used. The formulas are described as follows (30) and (31):

$$r_{ij} = \frac{x_{ij} - min_j(x_{ij})}{max_j(x_{ij}) - X_{min}} \tag{30}$$

$$r_{ij} = \frac{max_j(x_{ij}) - x_{ij}}{max_j(x_{ij}) - min_j(x_{ij})} \tag{31}$$

The maximum method: In this technique, only the greatest value in the considered set is used. The formulas are described as follows (32) and (33):

$$r_{ij} = \frac{x_{ij}}{max_j(x_{ij})} \tag{32}$$

$$r_{ij} = 1 - \frac{x_{ij}}{max_j(x_{ij})} \tag{33}$$

The sum method: In this method, the sum of all values in the considered set is used. The formulas are described as follows (34) and (35):

$$r_{ij} = \frac{x_{ij}}{\sum_{i=1}^{m} x_{ij}} \tag{34}$$

$$r_{ij} = \frac{\frac{1}{x_{ij}}}{\sum_{i=1}^{m} \frac{1}{x_{ij}}} \tag{35}$$

The vector method: In this method, the square root of the sum of all values. The formulas are described as follows (36) and (37):

$$r_{ij} = \frac{x_{ij}}{\sqrt{\sum_{i=1}^{m} x_{ij}^2}} \tag{36}$$

$$r_{ij} = 1 - \frac{x_{ij}}{\sqrt{\sum_{i=1}^{m} x_{ij}^2}} \tag{37}$$

3.3. *Weighting Methods*

In this section, we present three popular methods related to objective criteria weighting. These are the most popular methods currently found in the literature. In the future, this set should be extended to other methods.

3.3.1. Equal Weights

The first and least effective weighted method is the equal weight method. All criteria's weights are equal and calculated by Equation (38), where n is the number of criteria.

$$w_j = 1/n \tag{38}$$

3.3.2. Entropy Method

According to [33], the entropy method is based on a measure of uncertainty in the information. It is calculated using Equations (39)–(41) below.

$$p_{ij} = \frac{x_{ij}}{\sum_{i=1}^{m} x_{ij}} \quad i = 1, \ldots, m; j = 1, \ldots, n \tag{39}$$

$$E_j = -\frac{\sum_{i=1}^{m} p_{ij} ln(p_{ij})}{ln(m)} \quad j = 1, \ldots, n \tag{40}$$

$$w_j = \frac{1 - E_j}{\sum_{i=1}^{n}(1 - E_i)} \quad j = 1, \ldots, n \tag{41}$$

3.3.3. Standard Deviation Method

This method is similar to entropy at some point and assigns small weights to an attribute which has similar values across alternatives. The SD method is defined with Equations (42) and (43), where w_j is the weight of criteria and σ_j is the standard deviation [33].

$$\sigma_j = \sqrt{\frac{\sum_{i=1}^{m}\left(x_{ij} - \overline{x_j}\right)^2}{m}} j = 1, \ldots, n \tag{42}$$

$$w_j = \sigma_j / \sum_{j=1}^{n} \sigma_j \quad j = 1, \ldots, n \tag{43}$$

3.4. Correlation Coefficients

Correlation coefficients make it possible to compare obtained results and determine how similar they are. In this paper we compare ranking lists obtained by several MCDA methods using Spearman rank correlation coefficient (44), weighted Spearman correlation coefficient (46), and rank similarity coefficient (47).

3.4.1. Spearman's Rank Correlation Coefficient

Rank values rg_X and rg_Y are defined as (44). However, if we are dealing with rankings where the values of preferences are unique and do not repeat themselves, each variant has a different position in the ranking, the formula (45) can be used.

$$r_s = \frac{cov(rg_X, rg_Y)}{\sigma_{rg_X}\sigma_{rg_Y}} \tag{44}$$

$$r_s = 1 - \frac{6 \cdot \sum_{i=1}^{N}(rg_{X_i} - rg_{Y_i})}{N(N^2 - 1} \tag{45}$$

3.4.2. Weighted Spearman's Rank Correlation Coefficient

For a sample of size N, rank values x_i and y_i are defined as (46). In this approach, the positions at the top of both rankings are more important. The weight of significance is calculated for each comparison. It is the element that determines the main difference to the Spearman's rank correlation coefficient, which examines whether the differences appeared and not where they appeared.

$$r_w = 1 - \frac{6\sum_{i=1}^{N}(x_i - y_i)^2((N - x_i + 1) + (N - y_i + 1))}{N^4 + N^3 - N^2 - N} \tag{46}$$

3.4.3. Rank Similarity Coefficient

For a samples of size N, the rank values x_i and y_i is defined as (47) [144]. It is an asymmetric measure. The weight of a given comparison is determined based on the significance of the position in the first ranking, which is used as a reference ranking during the calculation.

$$WS = 1 - \sum_{i=1}^{N} 2^{-x_i} \frac{|x_i - y_i|}{max(|x_i - 1|, |x_i - N|)} \tag{47}$$

4. Study Case and Numerical Examples

The main goal of the experiments is to test if the MCDA method or weight calculation method has an impact on the final ranking and how significant this impact is. For this purpose, we applied four commonly used classical MCDA methods, which are listed in Section 3.1. In the case of TOPSIS and

VIKOR methods, we would use different normalization methods, and for the PROMETHEE method, we use various preference function and use different p and q values. The primary way to analyze the results obtained from numerical experiments is to use selected correlation coefficients, described in Section 3.4.

Algorithm 1 presents the simplified pseudo-code of the experiment, where we process matrices with different number of criteria and alternatives. The number of criteria changed from 2 to 5 and the number of the alternatives belongs to the set $\{3, 5, 10, 50, 100\}$. For each of the 20 combinations, the number of alternatives and criteria was generated after 1000 random decision matrices. They contain attribute values for all analyzed alternatives for all analyzed criteria. The preference values of the drawn alternatives are not known, but three different vectors of criteria weights are derived from this data. Rankings are then calculated using these different methods with different settings. This way, we obtain research material in the form of rankings calculated using different approaches. Analyzing the results using similarity coefficients, we try to determine the similarity of the obtained results. For each matrix we perform the following steps:

Step 1. Calculate 3 vectors of weights, using equations described in Section 3.3;

Step 2. Split criteria into profit and cost criteria: Assuming we have n criteria, first $\lceil n/2 \rceil$ are considered to be profit criteria and the rest ones are considered to be cost;

Step 3. Compute 3 rankings using MCDA methods listed in Section 3.1 and three different weighting vectors.

Algorithm 1 Research algorithm

```
N ← 1000
for num_of_crit = 2 to 5 do
    types ← generate_crit_types(num_of_crit)
    equal_weights ← generate_equal_weights(num_of_crit)
    for num_of_alts in [3, 5, 10, 50, 100] do
        for i = 1 to N do
            matrix ← generate_random_matrix(num_of_alts, num_of_crit)
            entropy_weights ← entropy_weights(matrix)
            std_weights ← std_weights(matrix)
            result ← Result()
            for method in methods do
                result.add(method(matrix, equal_weights, types))
                result.add(method(matrix, entropy_weights, types))
                result.add(method(matrix, std_weights, types))
            end for
            save_result(result)
        end for
    end for
end for
```

The further part of this section presents two examples that are intended to explain our simulation study better. The sample data and how it is handled in the following section will be reviewed. Due to the vast number of generated results, some figures have been placed in the Appendix A for clarity.

4.1. Decision Matrices

We have chosen two random matrices with three criteria and five alternatives to show how exactly these matrices are processed during the experiment. These matrices were chosen to demonstrate how many different or similar the rankings obtained with different MCDA methods in particular cases could be. Tables 3 and A1 contain chosen matrices and their weights which was calculated with three different methods described in Section 3.3. In the following sections, the example from Table 3 will be discussed separately for clarity. The results for the second example (Table A1) will be shown in the Appendix B.

Table 3. The first numerical example of a decision matrix with three different criteria weighting vectors.

	C_1	C_2	C_3
A_1	0.619	0.449	0.447
A_2	0.862	0.466	0.006
A_3	0.458	0.698	0.771
A_4	0.777	0.631	0.491
A_5	0.567	0.992	0.968
w_{equal}	0.333	0.333	0.333
$w_{entropy}$	0.075	0.134	0.791
w_{std}	0.217	0.294	0.488

4.2. TOPSIS

Processing a matrix with the TOPSIS method, using four different normalization methods and three different weighting methods gives us 12 rankings. Table 4 presents all rankings for the analyzed example showed in Table 4, and rankings for the second example are shown in Table A2. The orders in both cases are not identical and we can observe that the impact of different parameters varies for almost every case in the first example (Table 3). It depends mainly on the applied normalization method and selected weight vector. However, we need to determine exactly the similarity of considered rankings. Therefore, we use coefficients similarity, which are presented in heat maps in Figures 2 and 3. The results for the second numerical example is presented in Figures A1 and A2. These figures show exactly how different these rankings are using the r_w and WS coefficients described in Section 3.4. Each figure shows three heat maps corresponding to three weighting methods.

Table 4. TOPSIS (Technique for Order Preference by Similarity to Ideal Solution) rankings for matrix 1: **(a)** Equal weights, **(b)** entropy method, and **(c)** std method.

	Minmax			Max			Sum			Vector		
	(a)	(b)	(c)	(a)	(b)	(c)	(a)	(b)	(c)	(a)	(b)	(c)
A_1	4	2	3	3	2	3	5	5	5	3	2	2
A_2	1	1	1	1	1	1	1	1	1	1	1	1
A_3	5	4	5	5	4	5	4	4	4	5	4	5
A_4	2	3	2	2	3	2	3	3	3	2	3	3
A_5	3	5	4	4	5	4	2	2	2	4	5	4

Figures 2 and 3 presents r_w and WS correlations between rankings obtained using different normalization methods with TOPSIS method. The most significant difference is obtained for the ranking calculated using the entropy method and sum-based normalization. Only a single discrepancy appears for the alternatives A_1 and A_5 while comparing this ranking with the rest of the rankings. There is a change in the ranking on positions 2 and 5. These figures also show that the WS coefficient is asymmetrical as opposed to r_w. Therefore both coefficients will also be used in further analyses.

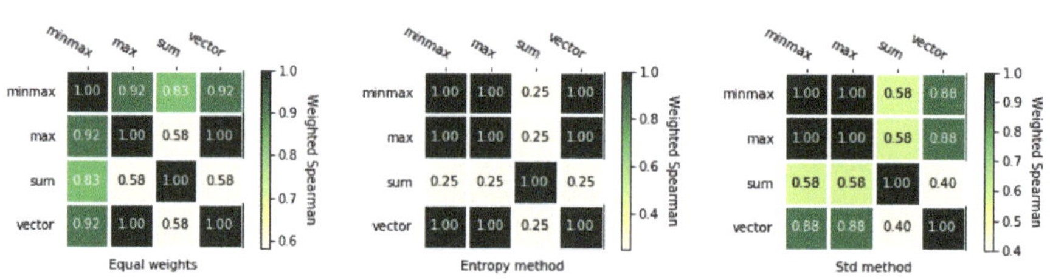

Figure 2. r_w correlations heat map for TOPSIS with different normalization methods (matrix 1).

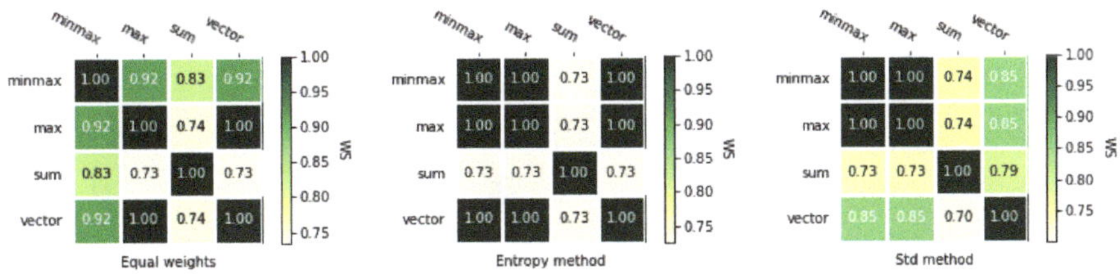

Figure 3. *WS* correlations heat map for TOPSIS with different normalization methods (matrix 1).

Next, Figures A1 and A2 show r_w and WS correlations for the second matrix. Rankings obtained using different normalization methods with TOPSIS are far more correlated than for the first matrix. The entropy methods weights gave as equal rankings and the ranking for the minmax normalization method is slightly different for equal weights and standard deviation weighting method.

4.3. VIKOR

Next, we calculate rankings for both matrices using the VIKOR method in combination with four different normalization methods and three weighting methods. Besides, we also use VIKOR without normalization (represented by "none" in the tables and on the figures). Rankings are shown in Tables 5 and A3. These rankings have more differences between themselves than the rankings obtained using TOPSIS method with different normalization methods.

Table 5. VIKOR (VlseKriterijumska Optimizacija I Kompromisno Resenje) rankings for matrix 1: **(a)** Equal weights, **(b)** entropy method, and **(c)** std method.

	None			Minmax			Max			Sum			Vector		
	(a)	**(b)**	**(c)**	**(a)**	**(b)**	**(c)**	**(a)**	**(b)**	**(c)**	**(a)**	**(b)**	**(c)**	**(a)**	**(b)**	**(c)**
A_1	5	4	4	4	2	3	4	2	3	5	5	5	4	2	3
A_2	4	5	5	2	1	1	2	1	1	1	1	1	2	1	1
A_3	3	2	2	5	4	4	5	4	4	4	4	4	5	4	4
A_4	2	3	3	1	3	2	1	3	2	2	3	3	1	3	2
A_5	1	1	1	3	5	5	3	5	5	3	2	2	3	5	5

Figures 4 and 5 with r_w and WS correlation coefficients show us that in this case the entropy weighting method performed worse than the other two weighting methods. In addition, it is noticeable how small size of the correlation between VIKOR without normalization. For the entropy weighting method, the r_w value is -1.0 which means that rankings obtained with VIKOR without normalization are reversed to VIKOR with any other normalization methods.

The rankings calculated for the second matrix are more correlated between themselves, which is presented on heat maps Figures A2 and A3. Similarly to TOPSIS, the entropy weighted method gives perfectly correlated rankings and the other two weighting method gives us fewer correlated rankings. Moreover, it is noticeable that the ranking obtained using VIKOR without normalization is less correlated to VIKOR with normalization methods.

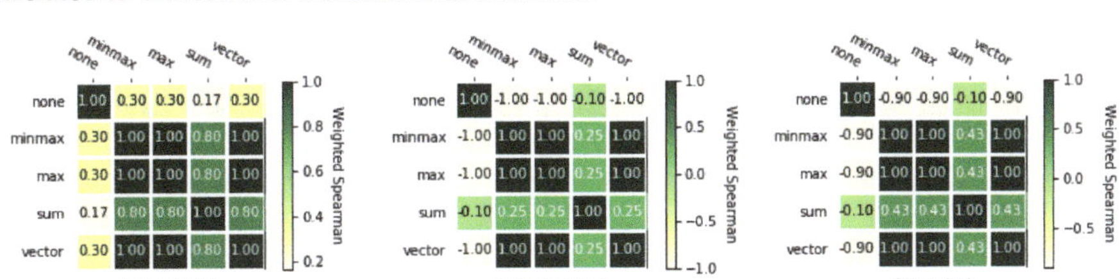

Figure 4. r_w correlations heat map for VIKOR with different normalization methods (matrix 1).

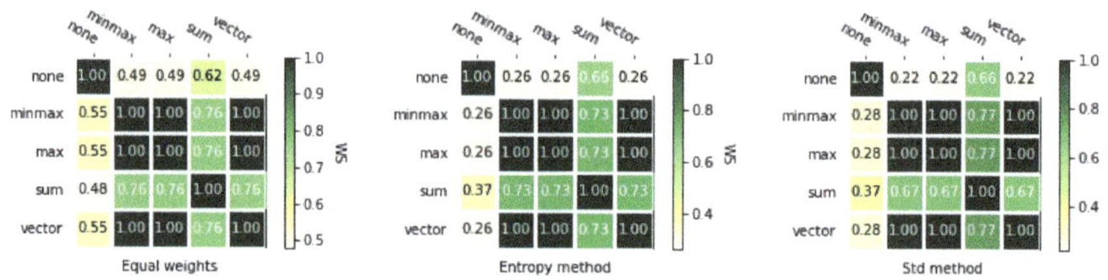

Figure 5. *WS* correlations heat map for VIKOR with different normalization methods (matrix 1).

4.4. PROMETHEE II

For exemplary purposes, we use the PROMETHEE II method with five different preference functions, and the q and p values for them are calculated as follows:

$$q = \bar{D} - (0.25 \cdot \sigma_D), \tag{48}$$

$$p = \bar{D} - (0.25 \cdot \sigma_D), \tag{49}$$

where D stands for positive values of the differences (see Section 3.1.4 for a more detailed explanation). As previously mentioned, Tables 6 and A4 contains rankings obtained using different preference functions and different weighting methods.

Table 6. PROMETHEE II rankings for matrix 1: **(a)** Equal weights, **(b)** entropy method, and **(c)** std method.

	Usual			**U-Shape**			**V-Shape**			**Level**			**V-Shape 2**		
	(a)	**(b)**	**(c)**	**(a)**	**(b)**	**(c)**	**(a)**	**(b)**	**(c)**	**(a)**	**(b)**	**(c)**	**(a)**	**(b)**	**(c)**
A_1	4	2	3	5	3	5	4	3	3	4	2	3	4	2	3
A_2	1	1	1	1	1	1	1	1	1	1	1	1	1	1	1
A_3	5	4	5	4	4	3	5	4	5	5	4	5	5	4	5
A_4	2	3	2	2	2	2	2	2	2	2	3	2	2	3	2
A_5	3	5	4	3	5	4	3	5	4	3	5	4	3	5	4

According to Figures 6 and 7, entropy weighting methods give slightly less correlated rankings than the two other methods. It is noticeable that for equal weights and for std-based method ranking obtained using U-shape preference function was not the same as for other rankings.

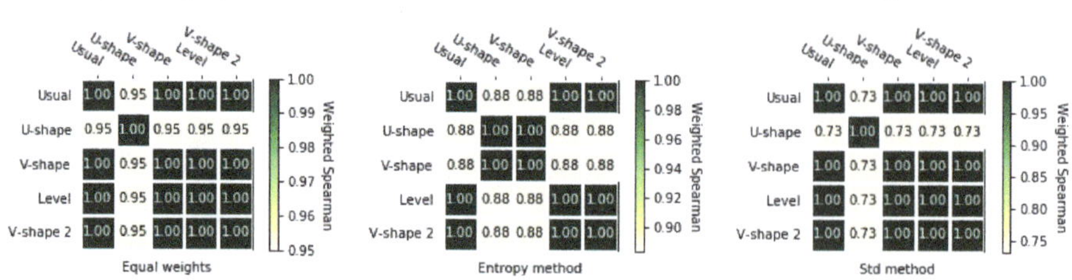

Figure 6. r_w correlations heat map for PROMETHEE II with different preference functions (matrix 1).

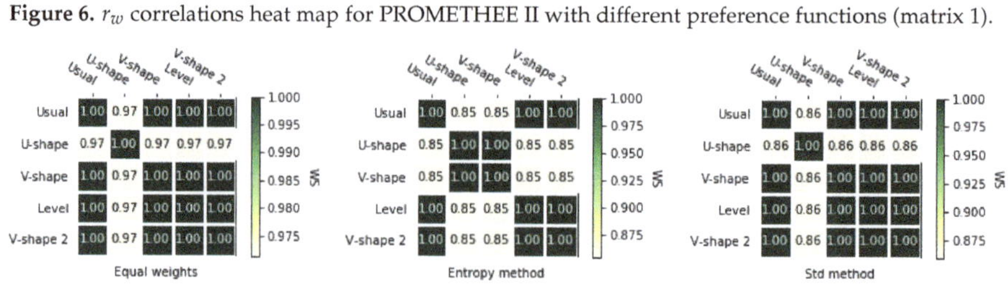

Figure 7. *WS* correlations heat map for PROMETHEE II with different preference functions (matrix 1).

For the second matrix, rankings obtained with the usual preference function and equal weights is quite different than other rankings which is shown in Figures A5 and A6. For the entropy weighting method, we could see that the rankings obtained with the usual preference function and the v-shape 2 preference function are equal, but applying other preference functions gave us slightly different rankings. In the case of the standard weighting methods, preference functions usual, level, and v-shape 2 have equal rankings, but, as previously mentioned, they are different from the rankings obtained by other preference functions.

4.5. Different Methods

In this part, we show how different rankings could be obtained by different methods. We compare rankings obtained by TOPSIS with minmax-based normalization, VIKOR without normalization, PROMETHEE II with the usual preference function, and COPRAS. Obtained rankings for first and second matrices are shown in Tables 7 and A5 accordingly.

Table 7. Rankings obtained with different Multi-Criteria Decision-Analysis (MCDA) methods for matrix 1: **(a)** Equal weights, **(b)** entropy method, and **(c)** std method.

	TOPSIS			**VIKOR**			**PROM. II**			**COPRAS**		
	(a)	**(b)**	**(c)**	**(a)**	**(b)**	**(c)**	**(a)**	**(b)**	**(c)**	**(a)**	**(b)**	**(c)**
A_1	4	2	3	5	4	4	4	2	3	5	5	5
A_2	1	1	1	4	5	5	1	1	1	1	1	1
A_3	5	4	5	3	2	2	5	4	5	4	4	4
A_4	2	3	2	2	3	3	2	3	2	3	3	3
A_5	3	5	4	1	1	1	3	5	4	2	2	2

Correlation heat maps are shown in Figures 8 and 9. The differences between rankings in the case of the first example are the smallest. It can be seen that the ranking obtained using VIKOR and entropy weighting method is reversed to rankings obtained using TOPSIS minmax and PROMETHEE II methods. It also poorly correlated with the ranking obtained with the COPRAS method. This is also noticeable that for other two weighting methods, with the VIKOR ranking being much less correlated with other rankings.

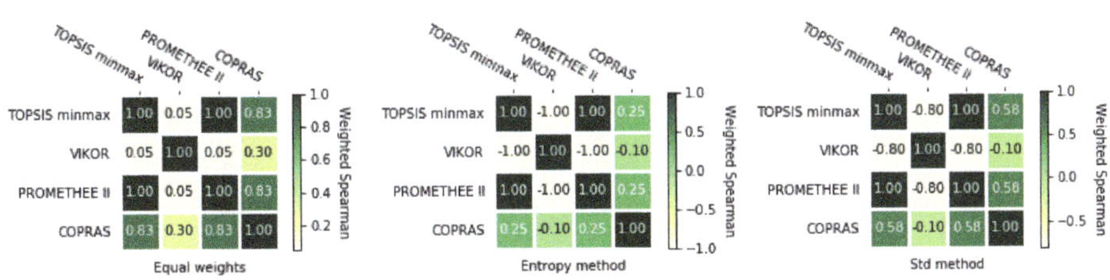

Figure 8. r_w correlations heat map for PROMETHEE II with different preference functions (matrix 1).

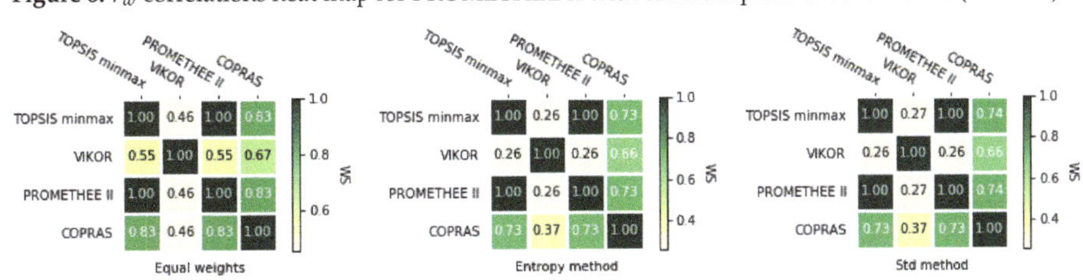

Figure 9. *WS* correlations heat map for PROMETHEE II with different preference functions (matrix 1).

The second matrix situation is opposite. As shown in Figures A7 and A8, rankings obtained using entropy methods are equal. For other two weighting methods we notice that rankings obtained by VIKOR are less correlated with other rankings.

4.6. Summary

Based on the results of the two numerical examples presented in Sections 4.1–4.5, it can be seen that the selection of the MCDA method is important for the results in the final ranking. Both numerical examples were presented to show positive and negative cases. In both samples, it can be seen that once a given method is selected, the weighing method and the normalization used in this method play a key role. The impact of parameters in the decision-making process in the discussed examples was different. Therefore, simulations should be performed in order to examine the typical similarity between the received rankings concerning a different number of alternatives. In Section 4.5, comparisons are made between methods using the most common configuration, where each of the analyzed scenarios has a huge impact on the final ranking. Therefore, simulation studies will be conducted to show the similarity of the rankings examined in the next section.

5. Results and Discussion

5.1. TOPSIS

In this section, we compare TOPSIS between different normalization methods. Figures 10–12 contain results of simulations. Each dot represents the correlation between two rankings for certain random matrix. The color of the dot shows which weighting method it is. For TOPSIS we compare rankings with three correlation coefficients described in Section 3.4, but other methods would be compared only using the r_w and WS correlation coefficients because the Spearman correlation has some limitations. At first, we could not use the r_s correlation for rankings where standard deviations are 0. It is frequent occurrences for the VIKOR method for decision matrices with a small number of alternatives. The second reason is that the cardinality of the Spearman correlation coefficient values set is strictly less than the cardinality of possible values sets of other two correlation coefficients. It is perfectly seen in Figure 10 for five alternative.

Figure 11 shows the r_w correlation between rankings obtained using the TOPSIS method with different normalization methods. We have some reversed rankings for matrices with three alternatives but with a greater number of alternatives, rankings become increasingly similar. It is noticeable that for a big number of alternatives, such as 50 or 100, rankings obtained using minmax vs. max normalization, minmax vs. vector normalization, and max vs. vector normalization methods are almost perfectly correlated. It is clearly seen in Table A6, which contains mean values of this correlations. The table gives details of the average correlation values for the number of alternatives (3, 5, 10, 50, or 100) and the number of criteria (2, 3, 4, and 5). Overall, the value of r_w reaches the lowest values for five criteria and three alternatives. The closest results are obtained for the max and minmax normalizations, but when not applying an equal distribution of criteria weights. Then, in the worst case, we get the value of the coefficient 0.897, where for the method of equal distribution of weights we get the result 0.735. Other pairs of normalizations reach, in the worst case, the r_w correlation of 0.571. It is also visible that rankings obtained using the sum normalization method are less correlated to rankings obtained with other normalization methods. Herein we can conclude that sum normalization is performing poorly with TOPSIS compared to other normalization methods.

On Figure 12, we see similar results to r_w. Rankings obtained using sum normalization are less correlated with other rankings. It is noticeable that according to the WS similarity coefficient, there are more poorly correlated rankings for the sum vs. vector normalization methods case than for r_w correlation. A problem of interpretation may be that both coefficients have a different domain. Nevertheless, this is the only case where the number of alternatives is increasing and there is no improvement in the similarity of the rankings obtained. The detailed data in Table A7 also confirm this. It may also come as a big surprise that the choice of the weighting method is not so important. Relatively similar results are obtained regardless of the method used.

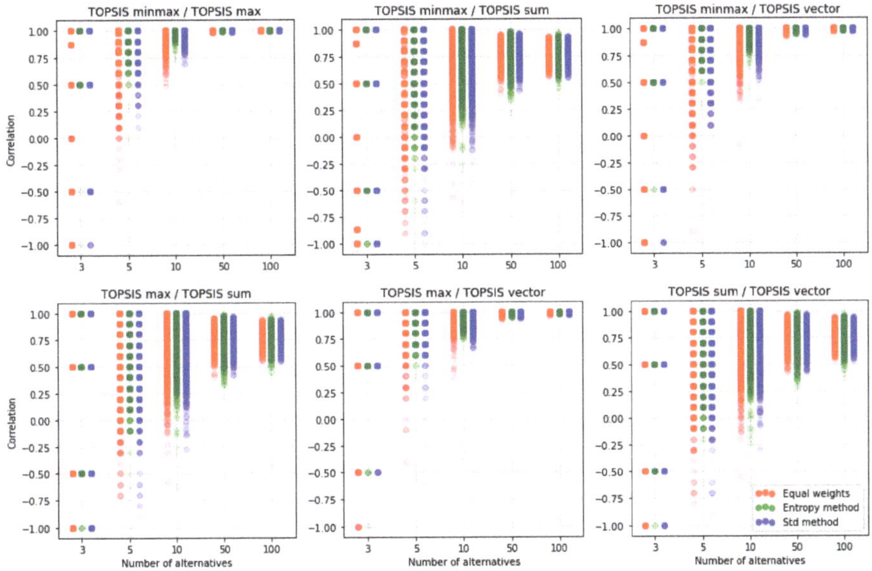

Figure 10. Comparison of the r_s similarity coefficient for the TOPSIS method with different normalization methods.

In general, it follows that with a small number of alternatives that do not exceed 10 decision-making options, the rankings may vary considerably depending on the normalization chosen. Thus, this shows that a problem as important as the choice of the method of weighting is the choice of the method used to normalize the input data. For larger groups of alternatives, the differences are also significant, although a smaller difference can be expected. The analysis of the data in Tables A6 and A7 shows that the increase in the complexity of the problem, understood as an increase in the number of criteria, practically always results in the decrease in similarity between the results obtained as a result of different normalizations applied.

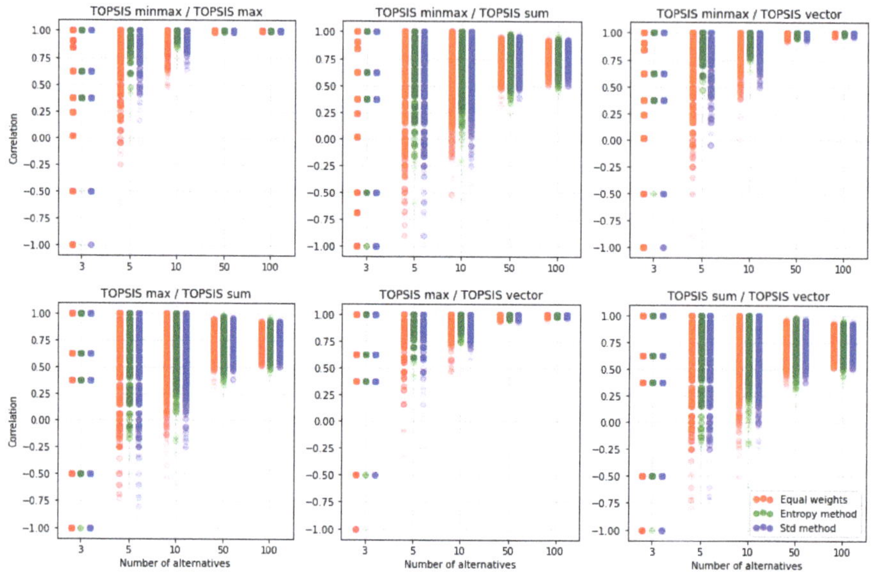

Figure 11. Comparison of the r_w similarity coefficient for the TOPSIS method with different normalization methods.

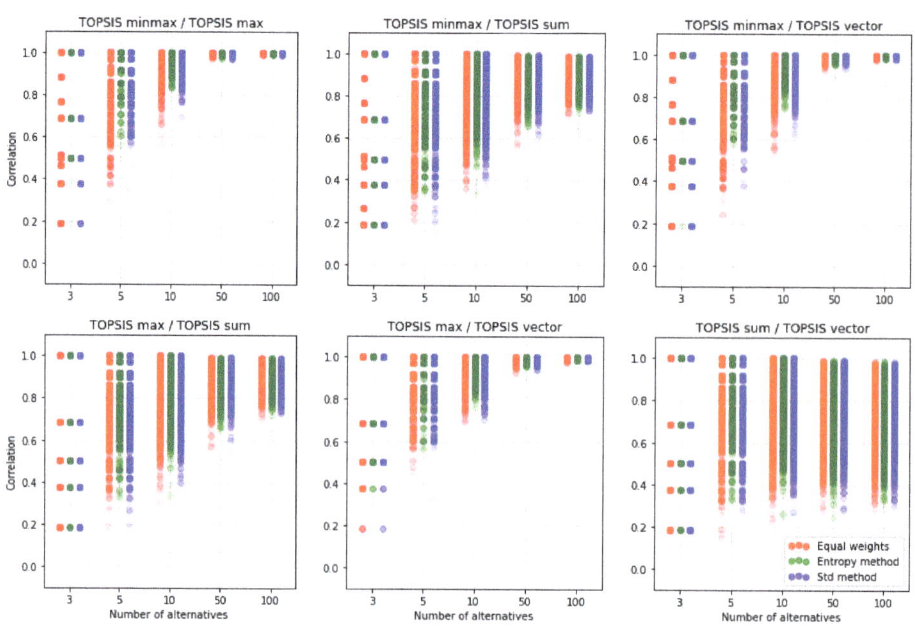

Figure 12. Comparison of the WS similarity coefficient for the TOPSIS method with different normalization methods.

5.2. VIKOR

As mentioned previously, we would use only r_w and WS correlation coefficients for the following comparisons. Figure 13 shows correlation between rankings obtained using VIKOR with different normalization and without normalization. It is clearly seen that VIKOR without normalization is poorly correlated to VIKOR when normalization is applied. In Table A8, we could see that mean values of the correlation values for VIKOR without normalization with cases where normalization was applied is around 0. It is also noticeable that VIKOR with minmax, max, and vector normalization gives very similar rankings.

This is similar to the TOPSIS method, where sum normalization has less similar rankings than other methods. Interestingly, correlations of rankings in the case of VIKOR without normalization vs. VIKOR with any normalization have a mean around zero, but rankings obtained with equal weight have less variance. In this case, less variability may be of concern, as it means that it is not possible to get rankings that are compatible. In addition to the three exceptions mentioned earlier, it should be noted that the choice of normalization has a significantly stronger impact on the similarity of rankings than in the TOPSIS method.

We can observe a similar situation on Figure 14, where WS similar coefficient values are presented. It confirms the results obtained using r_w correlation coefficient: Rankings obtained using VIKOR without normalization is less correlated with rankings obtained using VIKOR with normalization than other rankings correlated between themselves. It is also noticeable that in the sum vs. vector normalization methods case, the WS similarity coefficient values are also visibly smaller, as it was for TOPSIS. Therefore, we can conclude that rankings obtained using the sum and vector normalization method usually should be quite different.

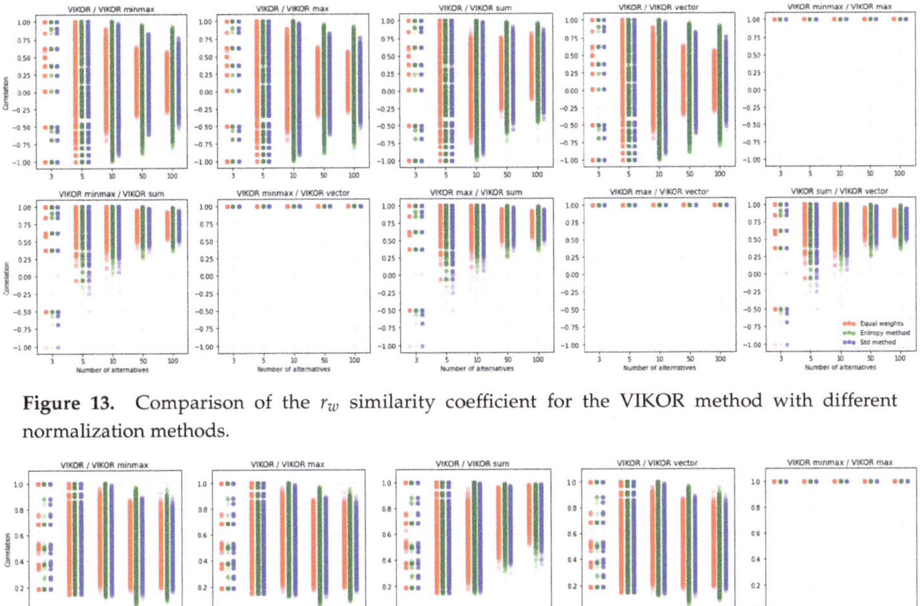

Figure 13. Comparison of the r_w similarity coefficient for the VIKOR method with different normalization methods.

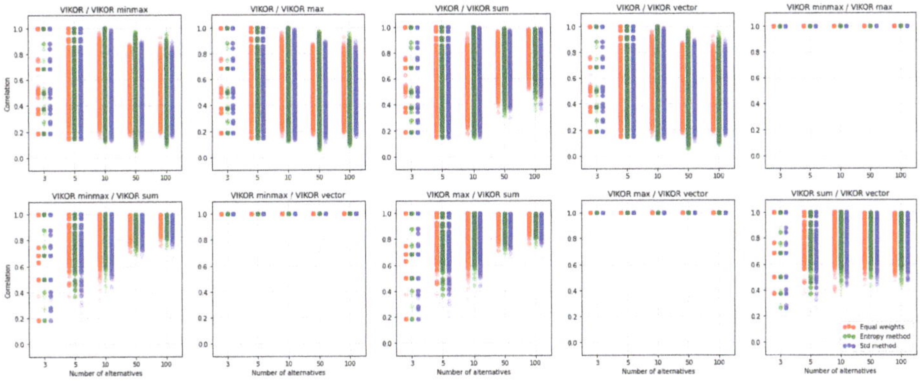

Figure 14. Comparison of the WS similarity coefficient for the VIKOR method with different normalization methods.

A detailed analysis of the results of mean values of r_W (Table A8) and mean WS (Table A9) show that the mean significance of similarities is significantly lower than in the TOPSIS method. Besides, the dependence of the change in the values of both coefficients in the tables is more random and more challenging to predict. Nevertheless, it means that the final result of the ranking is significant whether or not we apply the method with or without normalization, and which normalization we apply. Again, the influence of the selection of the method of criteria weighting was not as significant as one might expect. Generally, the proof is shown here that standardization can have a considerable impact on the final result.

5.3. PROMETHEE II

For PROMETHEE II, the normalization of the decision matrix does not apply. That is why this section will analyze receiving the rankings with different values of parameters p, q, and preference function. Figure 15 shows the results of the r_w factor for the U-shape preference function concerning different techniques of criteria weighting. The values p and q are calculated automatically and we only scale them. The differences between the individual rankings are very similar. If we analyze up to 10 alternatives, using any scaling value, we get significantly different results. As the number of alternatives increases, the spread of possible correlation values decreases. However, when analyzing the values contained in Tables A10 and A11 we see that the average values indicate a much smaller impact than in the case of the selection of standardization methods in the two previous MCDA methods.

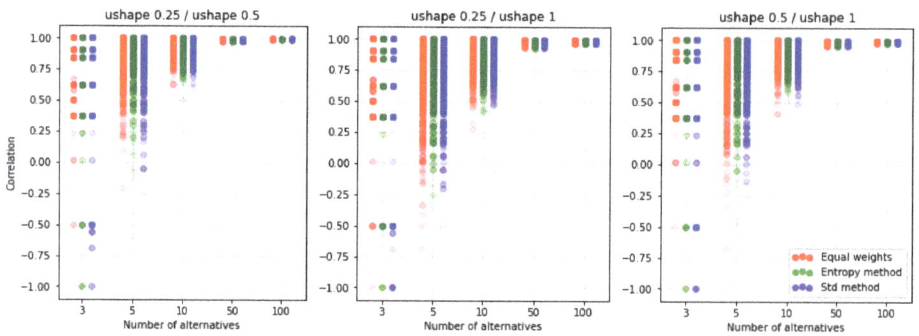

Figure 15. Comparison of the r_w similarity coefficient for the PROMETHEE II method with U-shape preference function and different k values.

For comparison, we present Figure 16 where another preference function is shown but also for the r_w ratio. It turns out that by choosing the V-shape preference function instead of the U-shape we get more of a similarity of results. Again, it turns out that the methods of weighting do not have such a significant impact on the similarity results obtained.

An important observation is that despite the lack of possibilities to normalize input data, there are still differences depending on the selected parameters and functions of preferences. The other two preference functions for the r_w ratio are shown in Figures A9 and A10. The results also indicate a similar level of similarity between the rankings. The WS coefficient for the corresponding cases is shown in Figures A11–A14. Both coefficients indicate the same nature of the influence of the applied parameters on the similarity of rankings. To sum up, in all the discussed cases, we see significant differences between the rankings obtained. Thus, not only normalization but other parameters are important for the results obtained and it is always necessary to make an in-depth analysis by selecting a specific method and assumptions, i.e., such as normalization, etc.

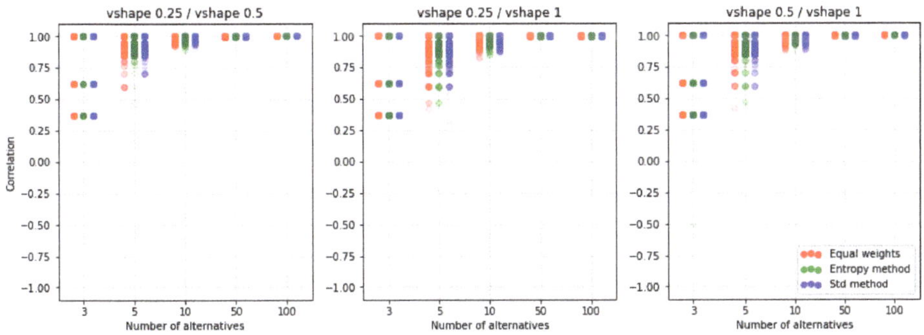

Figure 16. Comparison of the r_w similarity coefficient for the PROMETHEE II method with V-shape preference function and different k values.

5.4. Comparison of the MCDA Methods

Figure 17 shows how much correlated rankings obtained by four different methods could be: TOPSIS with minmax normalization, VIKOR without normalization, PROMETHEE II with usual preference function, and COPRAS. We can see that VIKOR has quite different rankings in comparison to other methods.

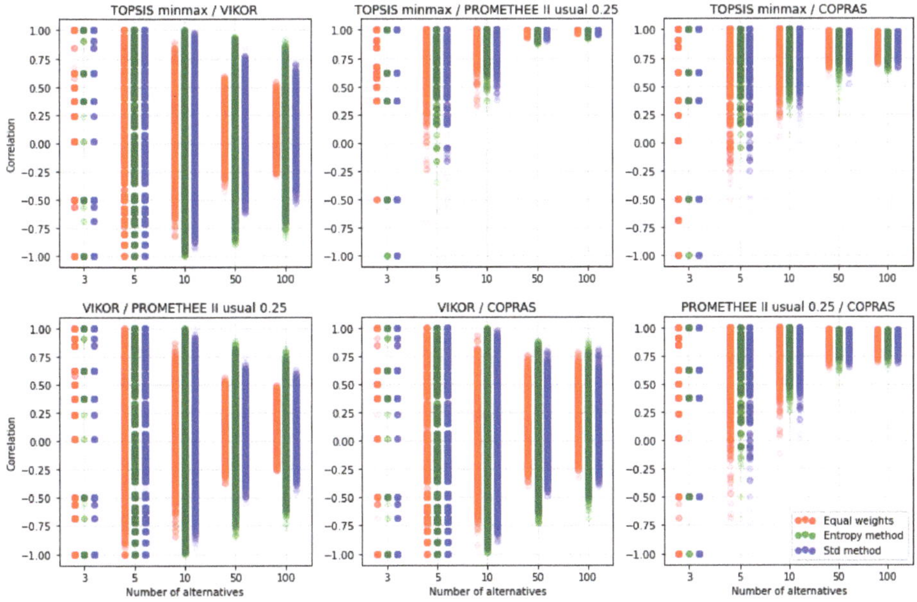

Figure 17. Comparison of the r_w similarity coefficient for the different MCDA methods.

Table A12 shows that the mean values of the correlation between VIKOR rankings and other methods' rankings are around zero. It is also noticeable that for cases VIKOR vs. other method correlation for rankings obtained using equal weights has a smaller variance in comparison to the other two weighting methods. Next, we could see that mostly correlated rankings could be obtained with TOPSIS minmax and PROMETHEE II usual methods. The comparisons between TOPSIS minmax vs. COPRAS and PROMETHEE II usual vs. COPRAS look quite similar and this methods' rankings are less correlated between themselves than TOPSIS minmax and PROMETHEE II usual methods' rankings.

The general situation is quite similar for WS correlation coefficient, as it shows Figure 18. The rankings obtained by VIKOR are far less correlated to rankings obtained using the other three methods than these rankings between themselves. Similarly to r_w, WS points that rankings obtained using TOPSIS minmax and PROMETHEE II usual methods have a strong correlation between themselves. Rankings obtained by TOPSIS minmax, COPRAS, and PROMETHEE II with the usual preference function are slightly less correlated. However, correlations between them are stronger than in the case of VIKOR vs. other methods.

5.5. Dependence of Ranking Similarity Coefficients on the Distance between Weight Vectors

The last section is devoted to a short presentation of distance distributions between weight vectors and similarity coefficients. All these distributions are asymmetric and will be briefly discussed for each of the four methods used. Thus, Figure 19 shows the relations between rw coefficient and TOPSIS method. The smallest difference in the distance between the vectors of weights is between the equal weights and those obtained by the std method. These values refer to all simulations that have been performed and cannot be generalized to the whole space. In Figure A15, there is a distribution for the WS coefficient, which confirms that there is a moderate relation between the distance of weight vectors and the similarity coefficient of obtained rankings.

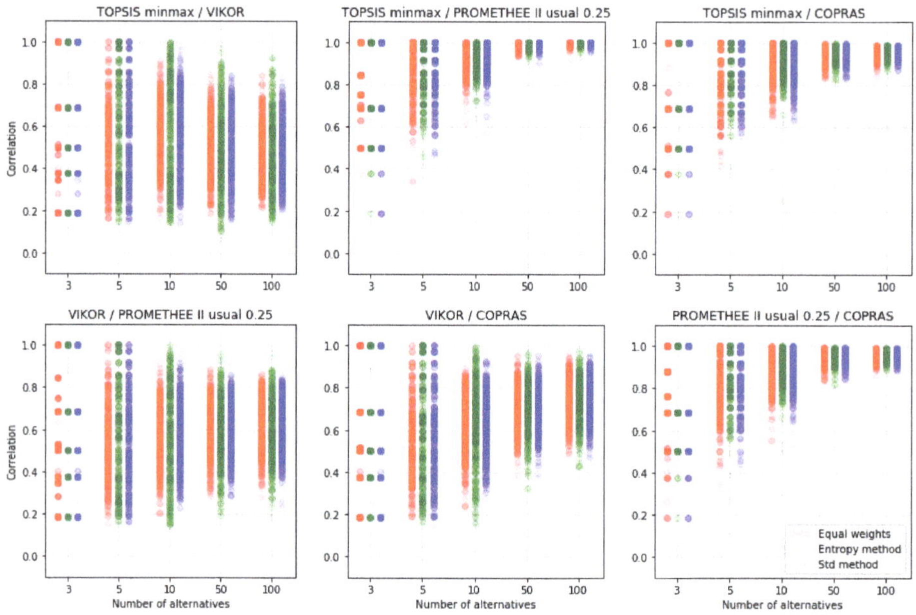

Figure 18. Comparison of the WS similarity coefficient for the different MCDA methods.

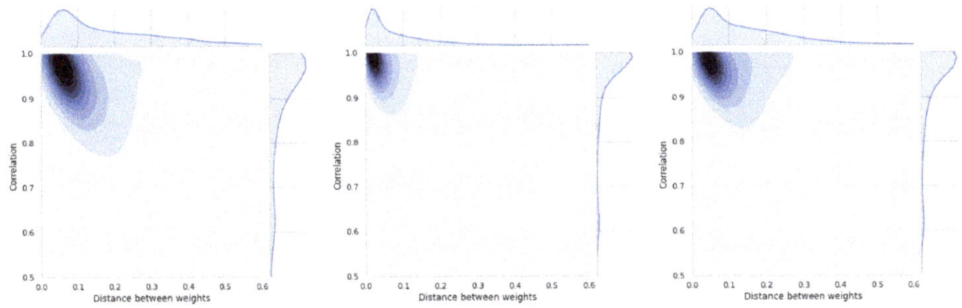

Figure 19. Relationship between the euclidean distance of weights and r_w similarity coefficient for rankings obtained by the TOPSIS method with different weighting methods, where (**left**) equal/entropy, (**center**) equal/std, and (**right**) std/entropy.

In Figure 20, the results of the VIKOR method are presented. The distribution of similarity coefficient rw is very similar to the distribution obtained for the TOPSIS method. Distance distributions between vectors of respective methods are the same for all presented graphs. Figure A16 shows the relationships for the VIKOR method and WS coefficient.

Using the PROMETHEE II method (usual), we can observe changes in the relation which is presented in Figures 21 and A17. This means that the use of different weights in the presented simulation was less important in the PROMETHEE II method than in the TOPSIS or VIKOR method. The distance between the scale vectors was the least important in the COPRAS method, the results of which are presented in Figures 22 and A18.

These results are important preliminary research on whether the weights and their differences always have a important influence on the compliance of the obtained rankings. TOPSIS and VIKOR have the highest sensitivity in the presented experiment, and COPRAS has the lowest sensitivity.

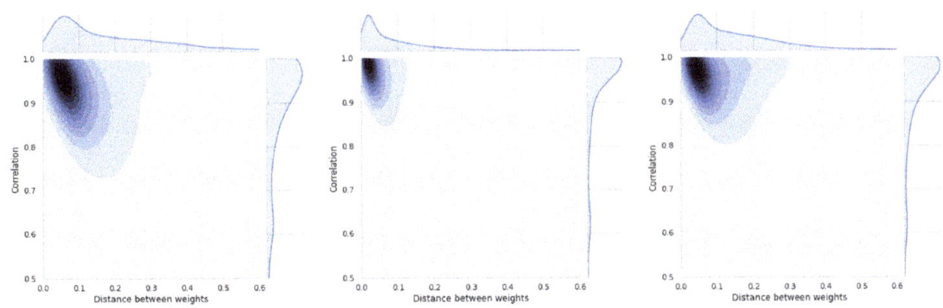

Figure 20. Relationship between the euclidean distance of weights and r_w similarity coefficient for rankings obtained by the VIKOR method with different weighting methods, where (**left**) equal/entropy, (**center**) equal/std, and (**right**) std/entropy.

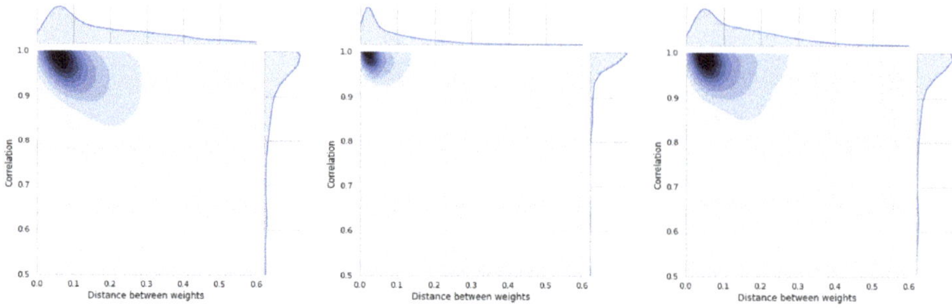

Figure 21. Relationship between the euclidean distance of weights and r_w similarity coefficient for rankings obtained by the PROMETHEE II (usual) method with different weighting methods, where (**left**) equal/entropy, (**center**) equal/std, and (**right**) std/entropy.

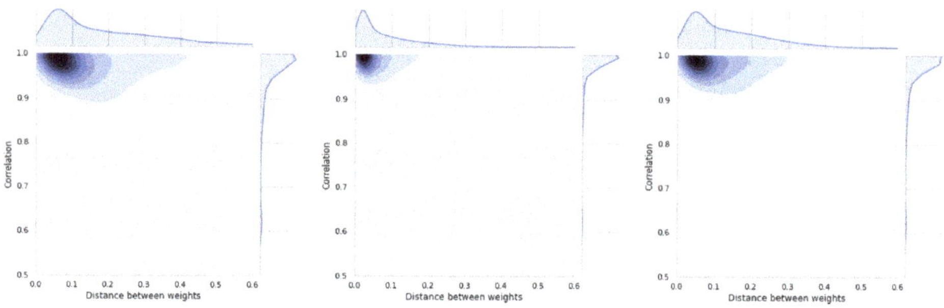

Figure 22. Relationship between the euclidean distance of weights and r_w similarity coefficient for rankings obtained by the COPRAS method with different weighting methods, where (**left**) equal/entropy, (**center**) equal/std, and (**right**) std/entropy.

6. Conclusions

The results of the conducted research indicate that when choosing the MCDA method, not only the method itself but also the method of normalization and other parameters should be carefully selected. Almost every combination of the method and its parameters may bring us different results. In our study, we have checked how much influence these decisions can have on the ranking of the decision problem. As it turns out, it may weigh not only the correct identification of the best alternative but also the whole ranking.

For the TOPSIS method, rankings obtained using minmax, max, and vector normalization method could be quite similar, especially for the big number of alternatives. In this case, equal weights performed worse than entropy or standard deviation method. Furthermore, with these normalization methods, correlation of rankings had a smaller variance when the entropy weighting method was used. For VIKOR, rankings obtained using any normalization methods could be even reversed in comparison to rankings obtained using VIKOR without normalization. Thus, although it was not necessary to apply normalization when using VIKOR, applying one could be noticeable to improve rankings and the overall performance of the method. Equal weights performed better with VIKOR. The PROMETHEE II method, despite the lack of use of normalization, returned quite different results depending on the set of parameters used and it clearly showed that the choice of the method and its configuration for the decision-making problem was important and should be the subject of further benchmarking. In four different method comparison, rankings obtained using VIKOR without normalization were very different from rankings obtained by other methods. Some equal rankings for the small number of alternatives was achieved. However, for a greater number of alternatives, correlations between

VIKOR's rankings and other methods rankings had oscillated around zero, which means that there was no correlation between these rankings. Most similar rankings were obtained using TOPSIS minmax and PROMETHEE II usual methods. In this case, equal weighting methods performed slightly better. This proves that it is worthwhile to research in order to develop reliable and generalized benchmarks.

The direction of future work should be focused on the development of an algorithm for estimation of accuracy for multi-criteria decision analysis method and estimating the accuracy of selected multi-criteria decision-making methods. However, special attention should be paid to the family of fuzzy set-based MCDA methods and group decision making methods as well. Another challenge is to create a method that, based on the results of the benchmarks, will be able to recommend a proper solution.

Author Contributions: Conceptualization, A.S. and W.S.; methodology, A.S. and W.S.; software, A.S.; validation, A.S., J.W., and W.S.; formal analysis, A.S., J.W., and W.S.; investigation, A.S. and W.S.; resources, A.S.; data curation, A.S.; writing—original draft preparation, A.S. and W.S.; writing—review and editing, A.S., J.W., and W.S.; visualization, A.S. and W.S.; supervision, W.S.; project administration, W.S.; funding acquisition, W.S. All authors have read and agreed to the published version of the manuscript.

Funding: The work was supported by the National Science Centre, Decision number UMO-2018/29/B/HS4/02725.

Acknowledgments: The authors would like to thank the editor and the anonymous reviewers, whose insightful comments and constructive suggestions helped us to significantly improve the quality of this paper.

Conflicts of Interest: The authors declare no conflict of interest.

Abbreviations

The following abbreviations are used in this manuscript:

TOPSIS — Technique for Order of Preference by Similarity to Ideal Solution
VIKOR — VlseKriterijumska Optimizacija I Kompromisno Resenje (Serbian)
COPRAS — Complex Proportional Assessment
PROMETHEE — Preference Ranking Organization Method for Enrichment of Evaluation
MCDA — Multi Criteria Decision Analysis
MCDM — Multi Criteria Decision Making
PIS — Positive Ideal Solution
NIS — Negative ideal Solution
SD — Standard Deviation

Appendix A. Figures

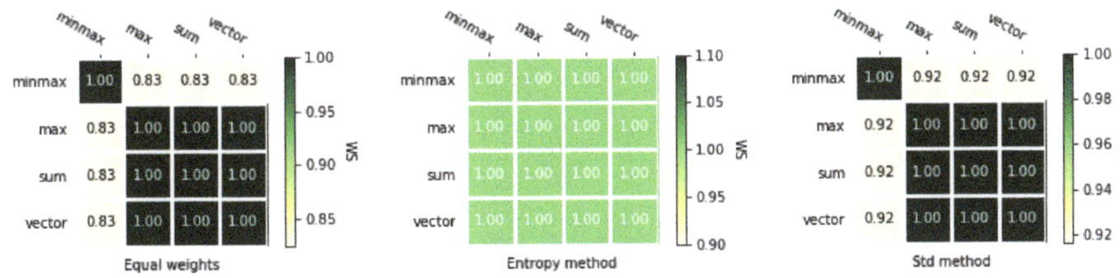

Figure A1. *WS* correlations heat map for TOPSIS with different normalization methods (matrix 2).

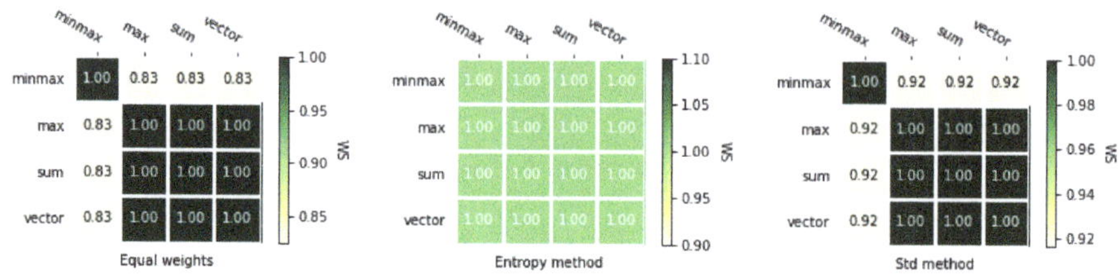

Figure A2. *WS* correlations heat map for TOPSIS with different normalization methods (matrix 2).

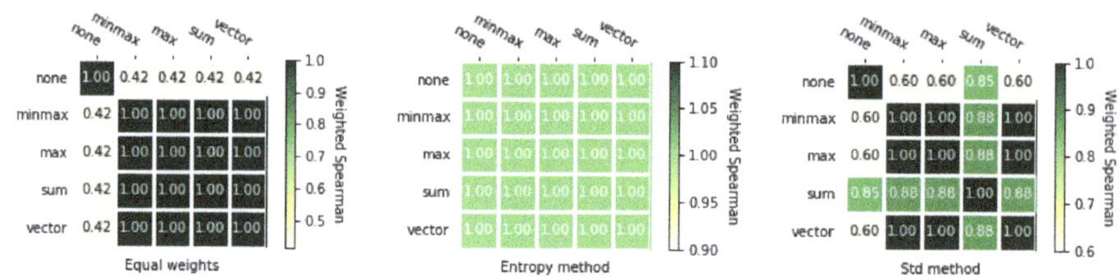

Figure A3. r_w correlations heat map for VIKOR with different normalization methods (matrix 2).

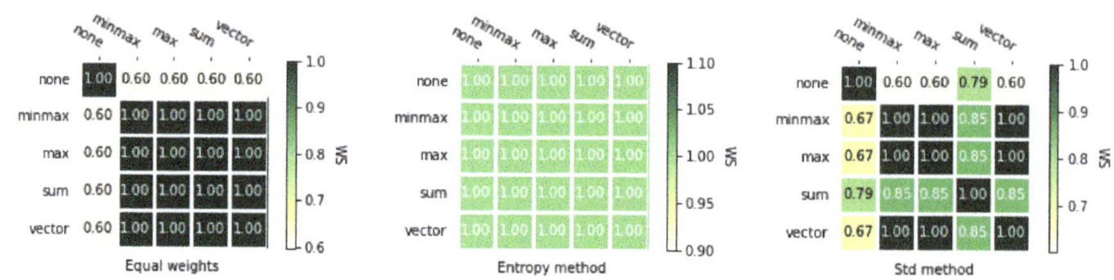

Figure A4. *WS* correlations heat map for VIKOR with different normalization methods (matrix 2).

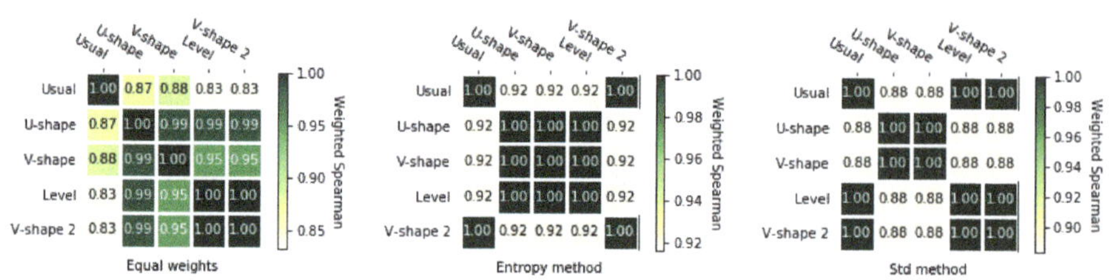

Figure A5. r_w correlations heat map for PROMETHEE II with different preference functions (matrix 2).

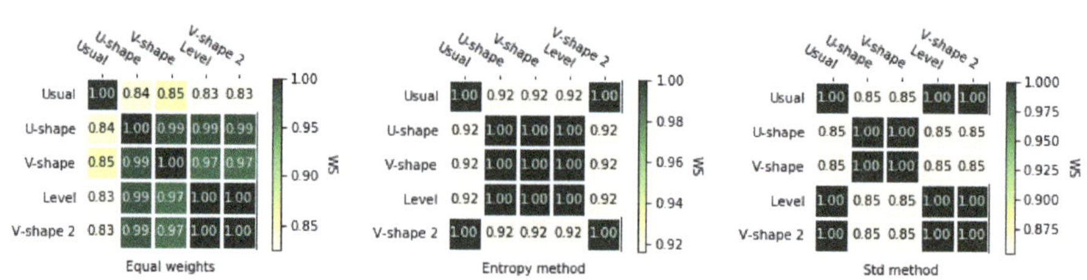

Figure A6. *WS* correlations heat map for PROMETHEE II with different preference functions (matrix 2).

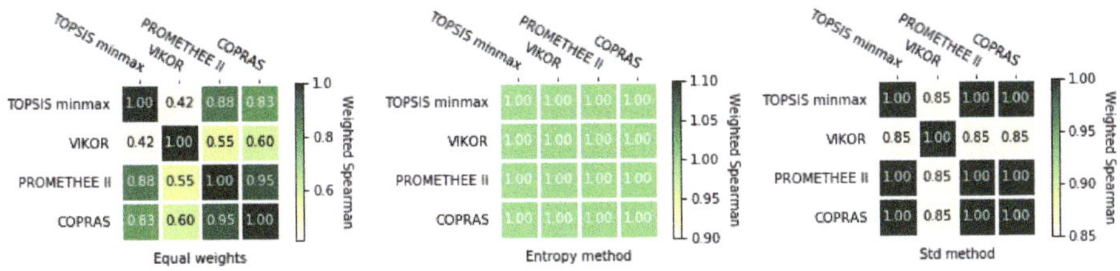

Figure A7. r_w correlations heat map for PROMETHEE II with different preference functions (matrix 2).

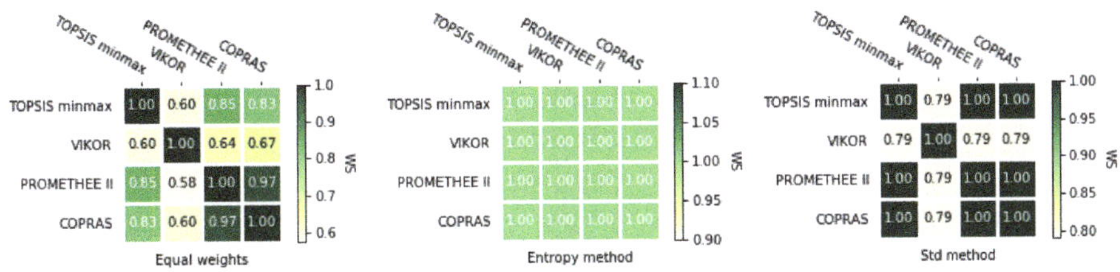

Figure A8. WS correlations heat map for PROMETHEE II with different preference functions (matrix 2).

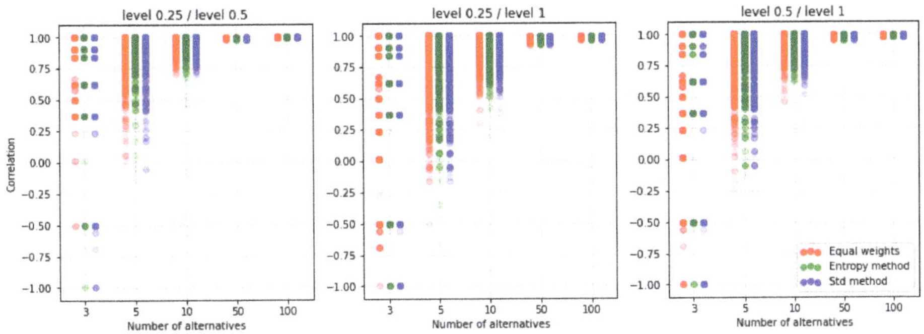

Figure A9. Comparison of the r_w similarity coefficient for the PROMETHEE II method with level preference function and different k values.

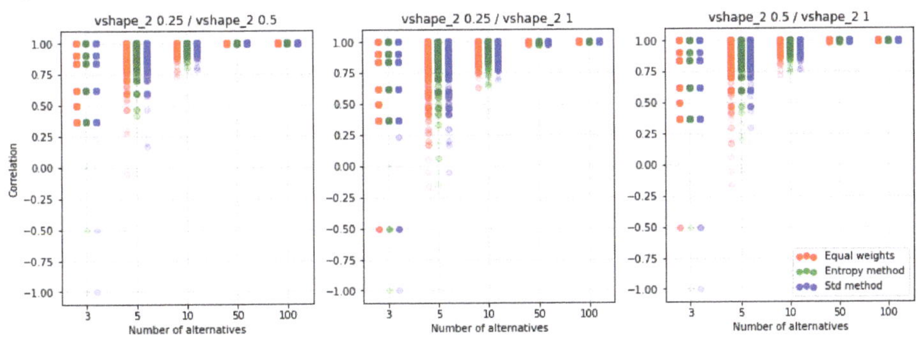

Figure A10. Comparison of the r_w similarity coefficient for the PROMETHEE II method with V-shape 2 preference function and different k values.

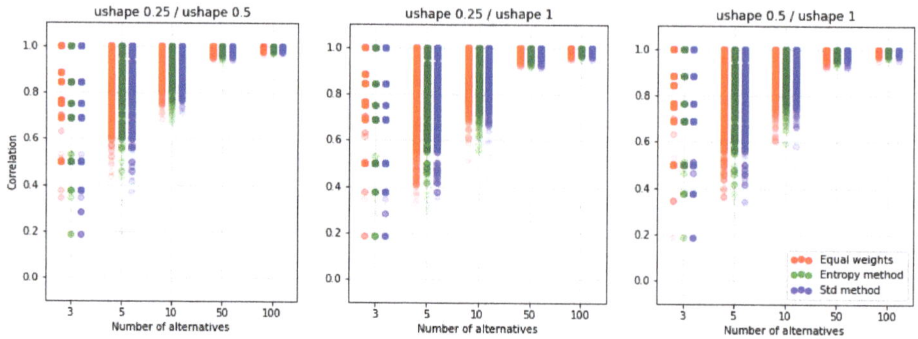

Figure A11. Comparison of the *WS* similarity coefficient for the PROMETHEE II method with U-shape preference function and different k values.

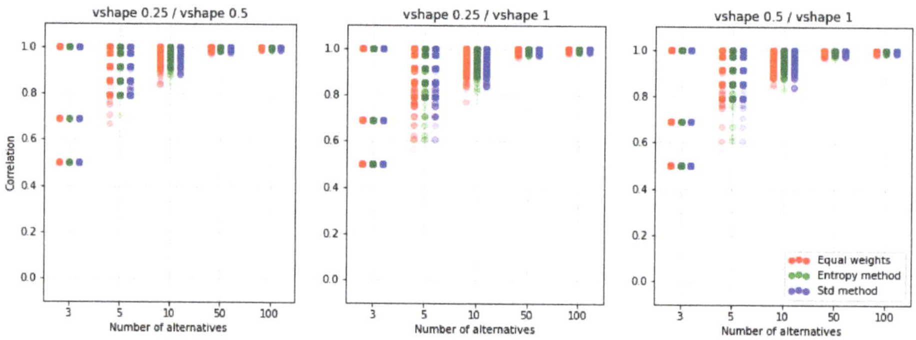

Figure A12. Comparison of the *WS* similarity coefficient for the PROMETHEE II method with V-shape preference function and different k values.

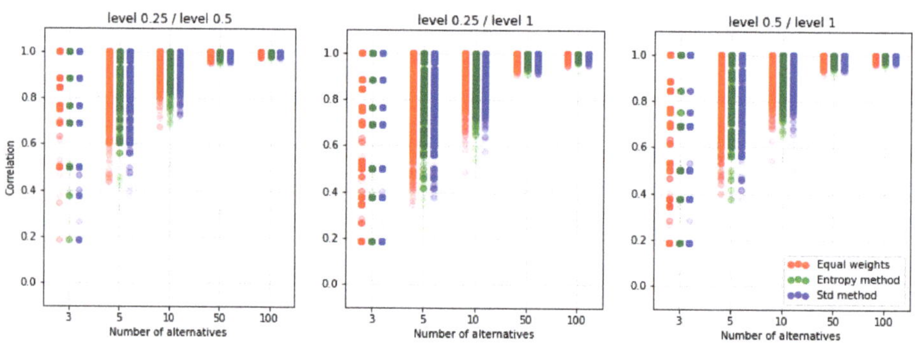

Figure A13. Comparison of the *WS* similarity coefficient for the PROMETHEE II method with level preference function and different k values.

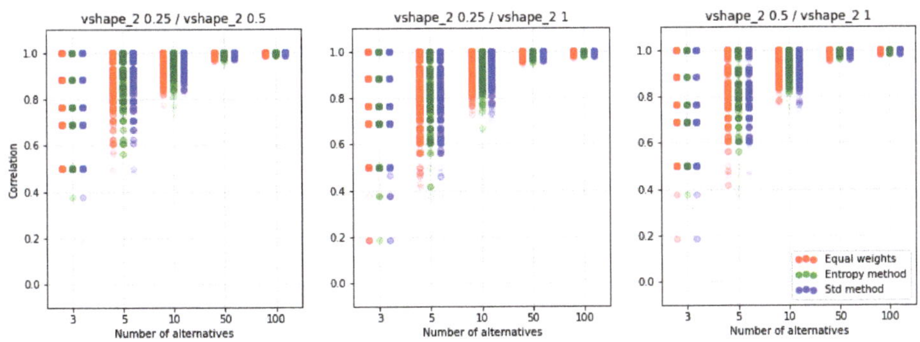

Figure A14. Comparison of the *WS* similarity coefficient for the PROMETHEE II method with V-shape 2 preference function and different *k* values.

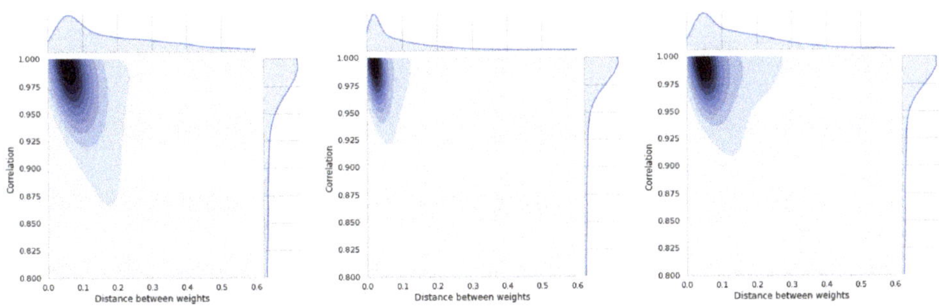

Figure A15. Relationship between the euclidean distance of weights and *WS* similarity coefficient for rankings obtained by the TOPSIS method with different weighting methods, where (**left**) equal/entropy, (**center**) equal/std, and (**right**) std/entropy.

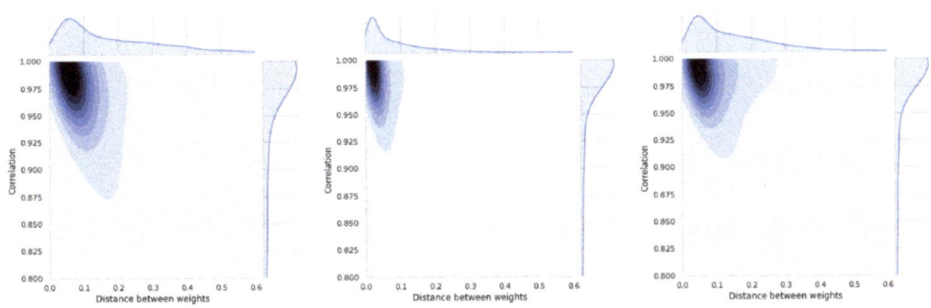

Figure A16. Relationship between the euclidean distance of weights and *WS* similarity coefficient for rankings obtained by the VIKOR method with different weighting methods, where (**left**) equal/entropy, (**center**) equal/std, and (**right**) std/entropy.

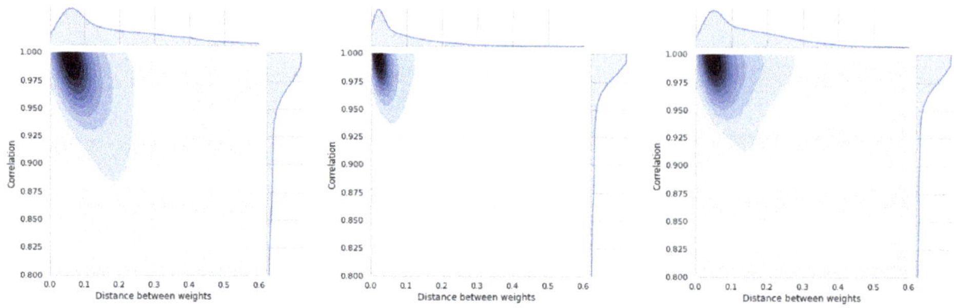

Figure A17. Relationship between the euclidean distance of weights and *WS* similarity coefficient for rankings obtained by the PROMETHEE II (usual) method with different weighting methods, where (**left**) equal/entropy, (**center**) equal/std, and (**right**) std/entropy.

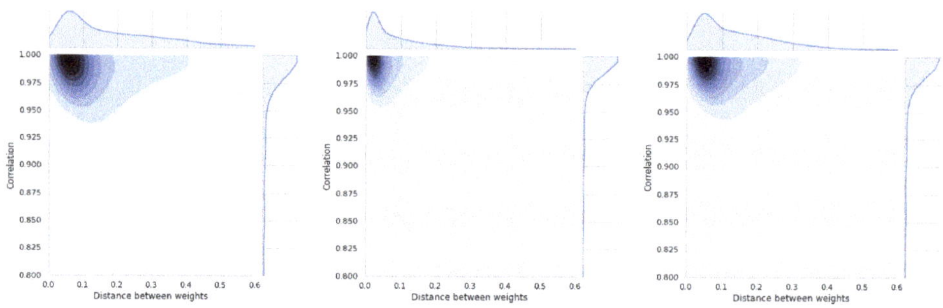

Figure A18. Relationship between the euclidean distance of weights and *WS* similarity coefficient for rankings obtained by the COPRAS method with different weighting methods, where (**left**) equal/entropy, (**center**) equal/std, and (**right**) std/entropy.

Appendix B. Tables

Table A1. The second example decision matrix with three different criteria weighting vectors.

	C_1	C_2	C_3
A_1	0.947	0.957	0.275
A_2	0.018	0.631	0.581
A_3	0.565	0.295	0.701
A_4	0.423	0.602	0.509
A_5	0.664	0.637	0.786
w_{equal}	0.333	0.333	0.333
$w_{entropy}$	0.678	0.172	0.151
w_{std}	0.442	0.303	0.255

Table A2. TOPSIS rankings for matrix 2: **(a)** Equal weights, **(b)** entropy method, and **(c)** std method.

	Minmax			**Max**			**Sum**			**Vector**		
	(a)	**(b)**	**(c)**	**(a)**	**(b)**	**(c)**	**(a)**	**(b)**	**(c)**	**(a)**	**(b)**	**(c)**
A_1	1	1	1	1	1	1	1	1	1	1	1	1
A_2	4	5	5	5	5	5	5	5	5	5	5	5
A_3	5	3	4	4	3	3	4	3	3	4	3	3
A_4	2	4	3	3	4	4	3	4	4	3	4	4
A_5	3	2	2	2	2	2	2	2	2	2	2	2

Table A3. VIKOR rankings for matrix 2: **(a)** Equal weights, **(b)** entropy method, and **(c)** std method.

	None			Minmax			Max			Sum			Vector		
	(a)	(b)	(c)	(a)	(b)	(c)	(a)	(b)	(c)	(a)	(b)	(c)	(a)	(b)	(c)
A_1	3	1	2	1	1	1	1	1	1	1	1	1	1	1	1
A_2	5	5	5	4	5	5	4	5	5	4	5	5	4	5	5
A_3	4	3	4	5	3	4	5	3	4	5	3	4	5	3	4
A_4	2	4	3	2	4	2	2	4	2	2	4	3	2	4	2
A_5	1	2	1	3	2	3	3	2	3	3	2	2	3	2	3

Table A4. PROMETHEE II rankings for matrix 2: **(a)** Equal weights, **(b)** entropy method, and **(c)** std method.

	Usual			U-Shape			V-Shape			Level			V-Shape 2		
	(a)	(b)	(c)	(a)	(b)	(c)	(a)	(b)	(c)	(a)	(b)	(c)	(a)	(b)	(c)
A_1	1	1	1	1	1	1	1	1	1	1	1	1	1	1	1
A_2	4	5	5	4	5	5	4	5	5	5	5	5	5	5	5
A_3	5	3	4	4	4	4	5	4	4	4	4	4	4	3	4
A_4	3	4	3	2	3	2	2	3	2	2	3	3	2	4	3
A_5	2	2	2	3	2	3	3	2	3	3	2	2	3	2	2

Table A5. Rankings obtained with different MCDA methods for matrix 2: **(a)** Equal weights, **(b)** entropy method, and **(c)** std method.

	TOPSIS			VIKOR			PROM. II			COPRAS		
	(a)	(b)	(c)	(a)	(b)	(c)	(a)	(b)	(c)	(a)	(b)	(c)
A_1	1	1	1	3	1	2	1	1	1	1	1	1
A_2	4	5	5	5	5	5	4	5	5	5	5	5
A_3	5	3	4	4	3	4	5	3	4	4	3	4
A_4	2	4	3	2	4	3	3	4	3	3	4	3
A_5	3	2	2	1	2	1	2	2	2	2	2	2

Table A6. Mean values of the r_w correlation coefficient for the TOPSIS method with different normalization methods: **(a)** Minmax/max, **(b)** minmax/sum, **(c)** minmax/vector, **(d)** max/sum, **(e)** max/vector, and **(f)** sum/vector.

Norm	Weighting Method	2 Criteria					3 Criteria					4 Criteria					5 Criteria				
		Alternatives					Alternatives					Alternatives					Alternatives				
		3	5	10	50	100	3	5	10	50	100	3	5	10	50	100	3	5	10	50	100
(a)	equal	0.828	0.923	0.977	0.999	1.000	0.755	0.897	0.966	0.999	1.000	0.744	0.887	0.966	0.998	1.000	0.735	0.871	0.964	0.998	1.000
	entropy	0.979	0.986	0.991	0.999	1.000	0.973	0.980	0.989	0.999	1.000	0.977	0.974	0.989	0.999	1.000	0.973	0.973	0.988	0.999	1.000
	std	0.916	0.960	0.985	0.999	1.000	0.913	0.949	0.977	0.999	1.000	0.904	0.938	0.976	0.998	1.000	0.897	0.933	0.974	0.998	1.000
(b)	equal	0.740	0.808	0.821	0.815	0.807	0.651	0.754	0.805	0.825	0.821	0.596	0.679	0.714	0.733	0.735	0.571	0.658	0.702	0.742	0.748
	entropy	0.916	0.895	0.851	0.812	0.804	0.905	0.878	0.847	0.826	0.820	0.878	0.796	0.755	0.731	0.733	0.865	0.796	0.766	0.742	0.745
	std	0.836	0.844	0.832	0.813	0.805	0.823	0.815	0.819	0.824	0.820	0.783	0.735	0.727	0.732	0.734	0.762	0.722	0.720	0.741	0.747
(c)	equal	0.803	0.900	0.957	0.994	0.997	0.703	0.856	0.934	0.991	0.996	0.696	0.839	0.929	0.989	0.995	0.701	0.818	0.922	0.989	0.995
	entropy	0.972	0.977	0.984	0.996	0.998	0.961	0.969	0.976	0.993	0.997	0.963	0.959	0.973	0.992	0.996	0.960	0.958	0.967	0.991	0.996
	std	0.899	0.942	0.970	0.994	0.997	0.890	0.921	0.951	0.991	0.996	0.875	0.903	0.947	0.990	0.996	0.874	0.893	0.938	0.989	0.995
(d)	equal	0.870	0.849	0.827	0.813	0.806	0.842	0.829	0.821	0.824	0.821	0.785	0.747	0.732	0.732	0.733	0.782	0.741	0.723	0.741	0.747
	entropy	0.925	0.895	0.850	0.810	0.802	0.913	0.882	0.847	0.824	0.819	0.883	0.802	0.756	0.729	0.732	0.873	0.802	0.769	0.740	0.744
	std	0.895	0.864	0.833	0.811	0.804	0.880	0.850	0.827	0.822	0.819	0.833	0.763	0.734	0.731	0.733	0.839	0.763	0.731	0.739	0.746
(e)	equal	0.966	0.971	0.980	0.995	0.998	0.926	0.950	0.965	0.992	0.996	0.917	0.941	0.960	0.991	0.996	0.923	0.934	0.956	0.990	0.995
	entropy	0.986	0.986	0.989	0.996	0.998	0.976	0.980	0.983	0.994	0.997	0.974	0.972	0.977	0.993	0.996	0.970	0.964	0.972	0.992	0.996
	std	0.975	0.979	0.983	0.995	0.998	0.970	0.963	0.971	0.992	0.996	0.954	0.952	0.966	0.991	0.996	0.947	0.943	0.960	0.990	0.996
(f)	equal	0.868	0.850	0.829	0.812	0.806	0.861	0.846	0.833	0.826	0.822	0.788	0.750	0.729	0.732	0.733	0.795	0.751	0.731	0.742	0.748
	entropy	0.922	0.897	0.849	0.808	0.801	0.925	0.890	0.852	0.824	0.819	0.886	0.803	0.755	0.727	0.730	0.874	0.808	0.771	0.740	0.744
	std	0.899	0.870	0.835	0.811	0.804	0.888	0.859	0.837	0.825	0.821	0.830	0.767	0.734	0.731	0.733	0.848	0.764	0.736	0.741	0.747

Table A7. Mean values of the *WS* correlation coefficient for the TOPSIS method with different normalization methods: **(a)** Minmax/max, **(b)** minmax/sum, **(c)** minmax/vector, **(d)** max/sum, **(e)** max/vector, and **(f)** sum/vector.

Norm	Weighting Method	2 Criteria					3 Criteria					4 Criteria					5 Criteria				
		Alternatives					Alternatives					Alternatives					Alternatives				
		3	5	10	50	100	3	5	10	50	100	3	5	10	50	100	3	5	10	50	100
(a)	equal	0.864	0.931	0.980	0.999	1.000	0.837	0.910	0.967	0.999	1.000	0.826	0.900	0.966	0.999	1.000	0.821	0.886	0.962	0.998	1.000
	entropy	0.983	0.986	0.988	0.999	1.000	0.978	0.979	0.987	0.999	1.000	0.982	0.973	0.985	0.999	1.000	0.979	0.972	0.984	0.999	1.000
	std	0.939	0.961	0.985	0.999	1.000	0.934	0.946	0.974	0.999	1.000	0.925	0.940	0.974	0.999	1.000	0.921	0.936	0.971	0.999	1.000
(b)	equal	0.812	0.842	0.865	0.926	0.944	0.774	0.813	0.857	0.915	0.932	0.748	0.776	0.810	0.868	0.885	0.740	0.767	0.809	0.869	0.886
	entropy	0.936	0.908	0.889	0.927	0.945	0.928	0.898	0.887	0.917	0.932	0.908	0.843	0.836	0.873	0.887	0.897	0.841	0.838	0.873	0.889
	std	0.889	0.871	0.874	0.926	0.944	0.878	0.852	0.865	0.916	0.932	0.852	0.805	0.816	0.869	0.886	0.840	0.801	0.815	0.870	0.886
(c)	equal	0.847	0.912	0.964	0.998	0.999	0.805	0.881	0.945	0.996	0.999	0.800	0.868	0.939	0.995	0.998	0.803	0.852	0.932	0.993	0.998
	entropy	0.977	0.976	0.981	0.998	0.999	0.969	0.969	0.975	0.996	0.999	0.970	0.957	0.970	0.995	0.998	0.968	0.957	0.965	0.995	0.998
	std	0.927	0.946	0.972	0.998	0.999	0.919	0.923	0.955	0.996	0.999	0.906	0.910	0.949	0.995	0.998	0.909	0.905	0.944	0.994	0.998
(d)	equal	0.909	0.871	0.868	0.925	0.944	0.889	0.865	0.865	0.915	0.932	0.853	0.809	0.818	0.867	0.885	0.852	0.812	0.816	0.869	0.886
	entropy	0.943	0.909	0.891	0.927	0.945	0.936	0.902	0.890	0.917	0.932	0.913	0.847	0.839	0.873	0.887	0.906	0.844	0.840	0.873	0.889
	std	0.924	0.884	0.875	0.926	0.944	0.914	0.878	0.871	0.916	0.932	0.883	0.823	0.821	0.868	0.886	0.890	0.824	0.821	0.869	0.886
(e)	equal	0.972	0.969	0.980	0.998	0.999	0.945	0.951	0.967	0.997	0.999	0.939	0.943	0.960	0.995	0.998	0.943	0.937	0.956	0.994	0.998
	entropy	0.989	0.984	0.987	0.998	0.999	0.983	0.979	0.981	0.997	0.999	0.979	0.969	0.976	0.996	0.998	0.978	0.963	0.971	0.995	0.998
	std	0.980	0.978	0.983	0.998	0.999	0.977	0.963	0.971	0.996	0.999	0.964	0.950	0.963	0.996	0.999	0.960	0.945	0.960	0.994	0.998
(f)	equal	0.906	0.870	0.848	0.825	0.821	0.897	0.866	0.839	0.791	0.773	0.857	0.800	0.774	0.745	0.734	0.852	0.801	0.770	0.730	0.724
	entropy	0.942	0.909	0.872	0.821	0.816	0.942	0.904	0.865	0.781	0.769	0.913	0.841	0.802	0.740	0.731	0.905	0.843	0.802	0.725	0.721
	std	0.926	0.885	0.854	0.823	0.821	0.917	0.879	0.846	0.788	0.774	0.881	0.817	0.782	0.744	0.733	0.891	0.813	0.774	0.730	0.722

Table A8. Mean values of the r_w correlation coefficient for the VIKOR method with different normalization methods, **(a)** none/minmax, **(b)** none/max, **(c)** none/sum, **(d)** none/vector, **(e)** minmax/max, **(f)** minmax/sum, **(g)** minmax/vector, **(h)** max/sum, **(i)** max/vector, and **(j)** sum/vector.

Norm	Weighting Method	2 Criteria					3 Criteria					4 Criteria					5 Criteria				
		Alternatives					Alternatives					Alternatives					Alternatives				
		3	5	10	50	100	3	5	10	50	100	3	5	10	50	100	3	5	10	50	100
(a)	equal	0.083	−0.003	−0.029	−0.028	−0.030	0.237	0.317	0.313	0.344	0.338	0.043	0.058	0.066	0.067	0.069	0.162	0.223	0.238	0.255	0.255
	entropy	0.010	−0.030	−0.036	−0.016	−0.026	0.310	0.345	0.336	0.361	0.330	0.031	0.006	0.037	0.053	0.066	0.211	0.192	0.260	0.236	0.233
	std	0.022	−0.033	−0.040	−0.027	−0.032	0.270	0.329	0.304	0.345	0.329	0.038	0.014	0.033	0.057	0.065	0.199	0.175	0.226	0.237	0.246
(b)	equal	0.083	−0.003	−0.029	−0.028	−0.030	0.237	0.317	0.313	0.344	0.338	0.043	0.058	0.066	0.067	0.069	0.162	0.223	0.238	0.255	0.255
	entropy	0.010	−0.030	−0.036	−0.016	−0.026	0.310	0.345	0.336	0.361	0.330	0.031	0.006	0.037	0.053	0.066	0.211	0.192	0.260	0.236	0.233
	std	0.022	−0.033	−0.040	−0.027	−0.032	0.270	0.329	0.304	0.345	0.329	0.038	0.014	0.033	0.057	0.065	0.199	0.175	0.226	0.237	0.246
(c)	equal	0.088	−0.033	−0.020	0.222	0.358	0.250	0.265	0.231	0.377	0.468	0.055	0.018	−0.029	0.121	0.235	0.159	0.210	0.129	0.237	0.335
	entropy	0.022	0.003	0.046	0.277	0.386	0.315	0.356	0.370	0.499	0.532	0.026	−0.006	0.048	0.173	0.248	0.194	0.181	0.240	0.305	0.356
	std	0.017	−0.014	0.014	0.242	0.367	0.266	0.305	0.290	0.426	0.487	−0.002	−0.044	−0.025	0.094	0.186	0.164	0.108	0.141	0.220	0.290
(d)	equal	0.083	−0.003	−0.029	−0.028	−0.030	0.237	0.317	0.313	0.344	0.338	0.043	0.058	0.066	0.067	0.069	0.162	0.223	0.238	0.255	0.255
	entropy	0.010	−0.030	−0.036	−0.016	−0.026	0.310	0.345	0.336	0.361	0.330	0.031	0.006	0.037	0.053	0.066	0.211	0.192	0.260	0.236	0.233
	std	0.022	−0.033	−0.040	−0.027	−0.032	0.270	0.329	0.304	0.345	0.329	0.038	0.014	0.033	0.057	0.065	0.199	0.175	0.226	0.237	0.246
(e)	equal	1.000	1.000	1.000	1.000	1.000	1.000	1.000	1.000	1.000	1.000	1.000	1.000	1.000	1.000	1.000	1.000	1.000	1.000	1.000	1.000
	entropy	1.000	1.000	1.000	1.000	1.000	1.000	1.000	1.000	1.000	1.000	1.000	1.000	1.000	1.000	1.000	1.000	1.000	1.000	1.000	1.000
	std	1.000	1.000	1.000	1.000	1.000	1.000	1.000	1.000	1.000	1.000	1.000	1.000	1.000	1.000	1.000	1.000	1.000	1.000	1.000	1.000
(f)	equal	0.950	0.889	0.851	0.791	0.760	0.964	0.915	0.865	0.826	0.812	0.925	0.903	0.843	0.793	0.778	0.925	0.918	0.852	0.805	0.795
	entropy	0.938	0.901	0.865	0.795	0.759	0.937	0.909	0.884	0.846	0.821	0.892	0.846	0.813	0.767	0.748	0.909	0.857	0.849	0.793	0.772
	std	0.917	0.880	0.847	0.791	0.758	0.922	0.901	0.867	0.833	0.814	0.873	0.839	0.806	0.765	0.749	0.896	0.849	0.836	0.784	0.769

Table A8. *Cont.*

Norm	Weighting Method	2 Criteria					3 Criteria					4 Criteria					5 Criteria				
		Alternatives					Alternatives					Alternatives					Alternatives				
		3	5	10	50	100	3	5	10	50	100	3	5	10	50	100	3	5	10	50	100
(g)	equal	1.000	1.000	1.000	1.000	1.000	1.000	1.000	1.000	1.000	1.000	1.000	1.000	1.000	1.000	1.000	1.000	1.000	1.000	1.000	1.000
	entropy	1.000	1.000	1.000	1.000	1.000	1.000	1.000	1.000	1.000	1.000	1.000	1.000	1.000	1.000	1.000	1.000	1.000	1.000	1.000	1.000
	std	1.000	1.000	1.000	1.000	1.000	1.000	1.000	1.000	1.000	1.000	1.000	1.000	1.000	1.000	1.000	1.000	1.000	1.000	1.000	1.000
(h)	equal	0.950	0.889	0.851	0.791	0.760	0.964	0.915	0.865	0.826	0.812	0.925	0.903	0.843	0.793	0.778	0.925	0.918	0.852	0.805	0.795
	entropy	0.938	0.901	0.865	0.795	0.759	0.937	0.909	0.884	0.846	0.821	0.892	0.846	0.813	0.767	0.748	0.909	0.857	0.849	0.793	0.772
	std	0.917	0.880	0.847	0.791	0.758	0.922	0.901	0.867	0.833	0.814	0.873	0.839	0.806	0.765	0.749	0.896	0.849	0.836	0.784	0.769
(i)	equal	1.000	1.000	1.000	1.000	1.000	1.000	1.000	1.000	1.000	1.000	1.000	1.000	1.000	1.000	1.000	1.000	1.000	1.000	1.000	1.000
	entropy	1.000	1.000	1.000	1.000	1.000	1.000	1.000	1.000	1.000	1.000	1.000	1.000	1.000	1.000	1.000	1.000	1.000	1.000	1.000	1.000
	std	1.000	1.000	1.000	1.000	1.000	1.000	1.000	1.000	1.000	1.000	1.000	1.000	1.000	1.000	1.000	1.000	1.000	1.000	1.000	1.000
(j)	equal	0.950	0.889	0.851	0.791	0.760	0.964	0.915	0.865	0.826	0.812	0.925	0.903	0.843	0.793	0.778	0.925	0.918	0.852	0.805	0.795
	entropy	0.938	0.901	0.865	0.795	0.759	0.937	0.909	0.884	0.846	0.821	0.892	0.846	0.813	0.767	0.748	0.909	0.857	0.849	0.793	0.772
	std	0.917	0.880	0.847	0.791	0.758	0.922	0.901	0.867	0.833	0.814	0.873	0.839	0.806	0.765	0.749	0.896	0.849	0.836	0.784	0.769

Table A9. Mean values of the *WS* correlation coefficient for the VIKOR method with different normalization methods, **(a)** none/minmax, **(b)** none/max, **(c)** none/sum, **(d)** none/vector, **(e)** minmax/max, **(f)** minmax/sum, **(g)** minmax/vector, **(h)** max/sum, **(i)** max/vector, and **(j)** sum/vector.

Norm	Weighting Method	2 Criteria					3 Criteria					4 Criteria					5 Criteria				
		Alternatives					Alternatives					Alternatives					Alternatives				
		3	5	10	50	100	3	5	10	50	100	3	5	10	50	100	3	5	10	50	100
(a)	equal	0.458	0.487	0.475	0.369	0.340	0.570	0.596	0.621	0.601	0.567	0.537	0.521	0.533	0.468	0.441	0.570	0.582	0.610	0.592	0.575
	entropy	0.599	0.526	0.489	0.392	0.355	0.686	0.662	0.643	0.613	0.570	0.570	0.528	0.519	0.457	0.435	0.623	0.590	0.613	0.570	0.554
	std	0.549	0.493	0.474	0.374	0.343	0.622	0.624	0.621	0.605	0.567	0.540	0.511	0.520	0.463	0.441	0.593	0.571	0.599	0.584	0.571
(b)	equal	0.458	0.487	0.475	0.369	0.340	0.570	0.596	0.621	0.601	0.567	0.537	0.521	0.533	0.468	0.441	0.570	0.582	0.610	0.592	0.575
	entropy	0.599	0.526	0.489	0.392	0.355	0.686	0.662	0.643	0.613	0.570	0.570	0.528	0.519	0.457	0.435	0.623	0.590	0.613	0.570	0.554
	std	0.549	0.493	0.474	0.374	0.343	0.622	0.624	0.621	0.605	0.567	0.540	0.511	0.520	0.463	0.441	0.593	0.571	0.599	0.584	0.571
(c)	equal	0.470	0.507	0.564	0.747	0.829	0.571	0.588	0.644	0.814	0.878	0.540	0.514	0.542	0.700	0.790	0.566	0.580	0.595	0.746	0.823
	entropy	0.607	0.560	0.593	0.763	0.836	0.691	0.686	0.712	0.844	0.891	0.580	0.550	0.580	0.710	0.780	0.628	0.614	0.650	0.761	0.818
	std	0.558	0.531	0.580	0.754	0.832	0.627	0.639	0.675	0.828	0.883	0.533	0.515	0.549	0.675	0.755	0.588	0.564	0.606	0.726	0.789
(d)	equal	0.458	0.487	0.475	0.369	0.340	0.570	0.596	0.621	0.601	0.567	0.537	0.521	0.533	0.468	0.441	0.570	0.582	0.610	0.592	0.575
	entropy	0.599	0.526	0.489	0.392	0.355	0.686	0.662	0.643	0.613	0.570	0.570	0.528	0.519	0.457	0.435	0.623	0.590	0.613	0.570	0.554
	std	0.549	0.493	0.474	0.374	0.343	0.622	0.624	0.621	0.605	0.567	0.540	0.511	0.520	0.463	0.441	0.593	0.571	0.599	0.584	0.571
(e)	equal	1.000	1.000	1.000	1.000	1.000	1.000	1.000	1.000	1.000	1.000	1.000	1.000	1.000	1.000	1.000	1.000	1.000	1.000	1.000	1.000
	entropy	1.000	1.000	1.000	1.000	1.000	1.000	1.000	1.000	1.000	1.000	1.000	1.000	1.000	1.000	1.000	1.000	1.000	1.000	1.000	1.000
	std	1.000	1.000	1.000	1.000	1.000	1.000	1.000	1.000	1.000	1.000	1.000	1.000	1.000	1.000	1.000	1.000	1.000	1.000	1.000	1.000
(f)	equal	0.959	0.897	0.890	0.946	0.962	0.970	0.916	0.884	0.937	0.957	0.942	0.909	0.874	0.931	0.952	0.944	0.923	0.876	0.923	0.949
	entropy	0.950	0.914	0.903	0.948	0.963	0.951	0.924	0.909	0.945	0.960	0.917	0.875	0.868	0.911	0.930	0.929	0.882	0.883	0.915	0.933
	std	0.933	0.896	0.889	0.946	0.962	0.944	0.909	0.890	0.940	0.958	0.907	0.863	0.858	0.914	0.935	0.926	0.871	0.867	0.912	0.933

Table A9. *Cont.*

Norm	Weighting Method	2 Criteria					3 Criteria					4 Criteria					5 Criteria				
		Alternatives					Alternatives					Alternatives					Alternatives				
		3	5	10	50	100	3	5	10	50	100	3	5	10	50	100	3	5	10	50	100
(g)	equal	1.000	1.000	1.000	1.000	1.000	1.000	1.000	1.000	1.000	1.000	1.000	1.000	1.000	1.000	1.000	1.000	1.000	1.000	1.000	1.000
	entropy	1.000	1.000	1.000	1.000	1.000	1.000	1.000	1.000	1.000	1.000	1.000	1.000	1.000	1.000	1.000	1.000	1.000	1.000	1.000	1.000
	std	1.000	1.000	1.000	1.000	1.000	1.000	1.000	1.000	1.000	1.000	1.000	1.000	1.000	1.000	1.000	1.000	1.000	1.000	1.000	1.000
(h)	equal	0.959	0.897	0.890	0.946	0.962	0.970	0.916	0.884	0.937	0.957	0.942	0.909	0.874	0.931	0.952	0.944	0.923	0.876	0.923	0.949
	entropy	0.950	0.914	0.903	0.948	0.963	0.951	0.924	0.909	0.945	0.960	0.917	0.875	0.868	0.911	0.930	0.929	0.882	0.883	0.915	0.933
	std	0.933	0.896	0.889	0.946	0.962	0.944	0.909	0.890	0.940	0.958	0.907	0.863	0.858	0.914	0.935	0.926	0.871	0.867	0.912	0.933
(i)	equal	1.000	1.000	1.000	1.000	1.000	1.000	1.000	1.000	1.000	1.000	1.000	1.000	1.000	1.000	1.000	1.000	1.000	1.000	1.000	1.000
	entropy	1.000	1.000	1.000	1.000	1.000	1.000	1.000	1.000	1.000	1.000	1.000	1.000	1.000	1.000	1.000	1.000	1.000	1.000	1.000	1.000
	std	1.000	1.000	1.000	1.000	1.000	1.000	1.000	1.000	1.000	1.000	1.000	1.000	1.000	1.000	1.000	1.000	1.000	1.000	1.000	1.000
(j)	equal	0.954	0.897	0.874	0.874	0.876	0.971	0.917	0.878	0.870	0.869	0.943	0.910	0.869	0.873	0.876	0.945	0.922	0.873	0.865	0.869
	entropy	0.950	0.913	0.889	0.885	0.884	0.950	0.922	0.900	0.892	0.885	0.919	0.872	0.858	0.856	0.853	0.930	0.881	0.873	0.866	0.866
	std	0.934	0.894	0.872	0.877	0.878	0.944	0.908	0.882	0.879	0.875	0.906	0.863	0.849	0.862	0.865	0.928	0.869	0.865	0.866	0.865

Table A10. Mean values of the *WS* correlation coefficient for the PROMETHEE II method with different *k* value and different preference functions: **(a)** U-shape; **(b)** V-shape **(c)** Level; and **(d)** V-shape2.

Type	k	Weighting Method	2 Criteria					3 Criteria					4 Criteria					5 Criteria				
			Alternatives					Alternatives					Alternatives					Alternatives				
			3	5	10	50	100	3	5	10	50	100	3	5	10	50	100	3	5	10	50	100
(a)	0.25/0.5	equal	0.967	0.930	0.959	0.992	0.996	0.951	0.929	0.956	0.994	0.997	0.952	0.929	0.957	0.994	0.997	0.944	0.923	0.958	0.993	0.997
		entropy	0.971	0.937	0.955	0.992	0.996	0.965	0.932	0.958	0.993	0.997	0.958	0.926	0.954	0.993	0.997	0.968	0.927	0.956	0.993	0.997
		std	0.967	0.933	0.957	0.992	0.996	0.956	0.928	0.954	0.993	0.997	0.952	0.919	0.956	0.993	0.997	0.957	0.924	0.958	0.993	0.997
	0.25/1	equal	0.946	0.885	0.938	0.990	0.995	0.934	0.875	0.928	0.989	0.995	0.931	0.874	0.928	0.988	0.995	0.931	0.860	0.925	0.988	0.994
		entropy	0.969	0.898	0.931	0.989	0.995	0.945	0.877	0.927	0.988	0.995	0.948	0.874	0.924	0.988	0.994	0.952	0.873	0.924	0.988	0.994
		std	0.951	0.887	0.934	0.990	0.995	0.932	0.870	0.926	0.989	0.995	0.929	0.865	0.925	0.988	0.994	0.931	0.862	0.926	0.988	0.994
	0.5/1	equal	0.958	0.906	0.946	0.991	0.995	0.950	0.897	0.941	0.991	0.996	0.944	0.900	0.940	0.990	0.996	0.944	0.888	0.939	0.990	0.995
		entropy	0.973	0.915	0.943	0.991	0.995	0.952	0.902	0.941	0.990	0.996	0.956	0.899	0.935	0.990	0.995	0.961	0.894	0.939	0.990	0.995
		std	0.964	0.906	0.945	0.991	0.995	0.944	0.892	0.941	0.991	0.996	0.949	0.889	0.937	0.990	0.996	0.946	0.889	0.939	0.991	0.995
(b)	0.25/0.5	equal	1.000	0.991	0.994	0.999	1.000	0.996	0.990	0.994	0.999	1.000	0.997	0.992	0.994	0.999	1.000	0.993	0.985	0.994	0.999	1.000
		entropy	0.996	0.993	0.995	0.999	1.000	0.997	0.992	0.995	0.999	1.000	0.997	0.992	0.994	0.999	1.000	0.994	0.991	0.994	0.999	1.000
		std	0.995	0.991	0.995	0.999	1.000	0.996	0.991	0.994	0.999	1.000	0.994	0.990	0.994	0.999	1.000	0.995	0.990	0.994	0.999	1.000
	0.25/1	equal	1.000	0.980	0.989	0.998	0.999	0.995	0.980	0.984	0.998	0.999	0.992	0.980	0.985	0.998	0.999	0.987	0.977	0.986	0.998	0.999
		entropy	0.992	0.985	0.989	0.998	0.999	0.986	0.982	0.988	0.998	0.999	0.990	0.982	0.986	0.998	0.999	0.986	0.980	0.986	0.998	0.999
		std	0.995	0.982	0.989	0.998	0.999	0.984	0.982	0.987	0.998	0.999	0.990	0.980	0.986	0.998	0.999	0.985	0.978	0.986	0.998	0.999
	0.5/1	equal	1.000	0.987	0.993	0.999	0.999	0.993	0.988	0.989	0.998	0.999	0.991	0.985	0.990	0.998	0.999	0.987	0.986	0.990	0.999	0.999
		entropy	0.992	0.989	0.992	0.999	0.999	0.986	0.988	0.992	0.999	0.999	0.991	0.987	0.991	0.999	0.999	0.987	0.986	0.990	0.999	0.999
		std	0.994	0.986	0.993	0.999	1.000	0.986	0.987	0.992	0.999	0.999	0.990	0.988	0.990	0.999	0.999	0.983	0.985	0.990	0.998	0.999

Table A10. *Cont.*

Type	k	Weighting Method	2 Criteria					3 Criteria					4 Criteria					5 Criteria				
			Alternatives					Alternatives					Alternatives					Alternatives				
			3	5	10	50	100	3	5	10	50	100	3	5	10	50	100	3	5	10	50	100
(c)	0.25/0.5	equal	0.936	0.930	0.967	0.994	0.997	0.930	0.935	0.964	0.995	0.998	0.940	0.935	0.962	0.995	0.998	0.929	0.929	0.962	0.995	0.998
		entropy	0.954	0.938	0.962	0.993	0.997	0.949	0.934	0.964	0.994	0.998	0.947	0.937	0.960	0.994	0.997	0.944	0.935	0.960	0.994	0.997
		std	0.948	0.937	0.965	0.994	0.997	0.943	0.937	0.963	0.995	0.997	0.944	0.935	0.962	0.994	0.998	0.930	0.932	0.964	0.995	0.998
	0.25/1	equal	0.854	0.888	0.943	0.992	0.996	0.858	0.876	0.934	0.988	0.995	0.870	0.880	0.930	0.987	0.994	0.859	0.864	0.928	0.988	0.993
		entropy	0.942	0.898	0.935	0.991	0.996	0.917	0.886	0.931	0.988	0.996	0.901	0.878	0.924	0.987	0.993	0.900	0.873	0.926	0.987	0.993
		std	0.904	0.889	0.939	0.991	0.996	0.871	0.877	0.930	0.988	0.995	0.873	0.876	0.929	0.987	0.994	0.867	0.868	0.928	0.987	0.993
	0.5/1	equal	0.862	0.909	0.952	0.993	0.996	0.876	0.899	0.946	0.991	0.996	0.879	0.903	0.945	0.990	0.995	0.874	0.891	0.941	0.990	0.995
		entropy	0.941	0.917	0.948	0.993	0.996	0.922	0.909	0.944	0.990	0.996	0.912	0.899	0.940	0.990	0.995	0.907	0.902	0.939	0.990	0.995
		std	0.913	0.911	0.950	0.993	0.996	0.884	0.900	0.945	0.990	0.996	0.883	0.896	0.944	0.990	0.995	0.885	0.894	0.940	0.990	0.995
(d)	0.25/0.5	equal	0.962	0.965	0.986	0.997	0.999	0.970	0.970	0.985	0.998	0.999	0.974	0.975	0.985	0.998	0.999	0.972	0.973	0.984	0.998	0.999
		entropy	0.969	0.970	0.983	0.997	0.999	0.976	0.970	0.985	0.998	0.999	0.977	0.975	0.983	0.998	0.999	0.980	0.973	0.985	0.998	0.999
		std	0.973	0.971	0.986	0.997	0.999	0.979	0.974	0.986	0.998	0.999	0.974	0.979	0.986	0.998	0.999	0.973	0.973	0.987	0.998	0.999
	0.25/1	equal	0.922	0.933	0.973	0.995	0.998	0.932	0.937	0.968	0.995	0.998	0.948	0.941	0.967	0.995	0.997	0.936	0.938	0.965	0.995	0.997
		entropy	0.939	0.942	0.966	0.995	0.998	0.946	0.935	0.968	0.995	0.998	0.943	0.944	0.964	0.994	0.997	0.951	0.940	0.966	0.994	0.997
		std	0.940	0.940	0.972	0.995	0.998	0.946	0.936	0.968	0.995	0.998	0.942	0.945	0.966	0.995	0.997	0.946	0.938	0.966	0.995	0.997
	0.5/1	equal	0.937	0.957	0.983	0.997	0.999	0.948	0.958	0.978	0.997	0.999	0.960	0.959	0.978	0.996	0.998	0.956	0.953	0.977	0.996	0.998
		entropy	0.963	0.964	0.978	0.997	0.999	0.964	0.956	0.978	0.997	0.999	0.962	0.959	0.976	0.996	0.998	0.968	0.960	0.976	0.996	0.998
		std	0.961	0.961	0.980	0.997	0.999	0.960	0.956	0.977	0.997	0.998	0.961	0.960	0.977	0.996	0.998	0.964	0.958	0.976	0.996	0.998

Table A11. Mean values of the r_w correlation coefficient for the PROMETHEE II method with different k value and different preference functions: **(a)** U-shape; **(b)** V-shape **(c)** Level; and **(d)** V-shape2.

Type	k	Weighting Method	2 Criteria					3 Criteria					4 Criteria					5 Criteria				
			Alternatives					Alternatives					Alternatives					Alternatives				
			3	5	10	50	100	3	5	10	50	100	3	5	10	50	100	3	5	10	50	100
(a)	0.25/0.5	equal	0.969	0.942	0.967	0.994	0.997	0.952	0.940	0.965	0.993	0.997	0.961	0.940	0.965	0.993	0.997	0.944	0.928	0.962	0.993	0.996
		entropy	0.970	0.940	0.963	0.993	0.997	0.955	0.929	0.961	0.993	0.996	0.944	0.923	0.958	0.993	0.996	0.957	0.923	0.957	0.993	0.996
		std	0.958	0.934	0.961	0.994	0.997	0.942	0.927	0.957	0.993	0.997	0.935	0.915	0.958	0.993	0.996	0.942	0.916	0.959	0.993	0.996
	0.25/1	equal	0.939	0.892	0.937	0.986	0.992	0.924	0.871	0.923	0.982	0.990	0.926	0.871	0.925	0.982	0.989	0.924	0.842	0.919	0.982	0.989
		entropy	0.965	0.895	0.929	0.985	0.991	0.925	0.864	0.918	0.982	0.989	0.929	0.852	0.915	0.981	0.989	0.938	0.849	0.909	0.981	0.989
		std	0.940	0.881	0.930	0.985	0.991	0.907	0.852	0.917	0.982	0.990	0.900	0.842	0.917	0.981	0.989	0.905	0.833	0.914	0.981	0.989
	0.5/1	equal	0.954	0.916	0.952	0.989	0.994	0.945	0.902	0.943	0.988	0.993	0.943	0.902	0.943	0.987	0.993	0.939	0.885	0.942	0.987	0.993
		entropy	0.968	0.918	0.946	0.989	0.994	0.938	0.899	0.938	0.987	0.993	0.941	0.884	0.935	0.987	0.993	0.947	0.879	0.933	0.987	0.993
		std	0.955	0.906	0.946	0.989	0.994	0.925	0.883	0.939	0.987	0.993	0.928	0.876	0.937	0.987	0.993	0.927	0.875	0.936	0.987	0.993
(b)	0.25/0.5	equal	1.000	0.992	0.996	1.000	1.000	0.995	0.991	0.996	1.000	1.000	0.997	0.993	0.996	0.999	1.000	0.992	0.987	0.996	0.999	1.000
		entropy	0.995	0.994	0.997	1.000	1.000	0.996	0.993	0.996	0.999	1.000	0.997	0.993	0.996	0.999	1.000	0.993	0.992	0.996	0.999	1.000
		std	0.994	0.992	0.996	1.000	1.000	0.995	0.992	0.996	0.999	1.000	0.993	0.991	0.996	1.000	1.000	0.994	0.991	0.996	0.999	1.000
	0.25/1	equal	1.000	0.982	0.991	0.999	1.000	0.994	0.982	0.989	0.999	0.999	0.990	0.981	0.990	0.999	0.999	0.984	0.979	0.989	0.999	0.999
		entropy	0.991	0.987	0.993	0.999	1.000	0.983	0.983	0.991	0.999	0.999	0.988	0.983	0.990	0.999	0.999	0.983	0.981	0.989	0.999	0.999
		std	0.994	0.984	0.991	0.999	1.000	0.981	0.984	0.991	0.999	0.999	0.988	0.981	0.990	0.999	0.999	0.981	0.981	0.990	0.999	0.999
	0.5/1	equal	1.000	0.989	0.995	0.999	1.000	0.992	0.989	0.993	0.999	1.000	0.990	0.987	0.994	0.999	1.000	0.984	0.987	0.993	0.999	1.000
		entropy	0.990	0.990	0.995	0.999	1.000	0.983	0.989	0.994	0.999	1.000	0.989	0.988	0.994	0.999	1.000	0.983	0.988	0.993	0.999	1.000
		std	0.992	0.988	0.995	0.999	1.000	0.982	0.989	0.994	0.999	1.000	0.987	0.989	0.993	0.999	1.000	0.979	0.987	0.993	0.999	1.000

Table A11. *Cont.*

Type	k	Weighting Method	2 Criteria					3 Criteria					4 Criteria					5 Criteria				
			Alternatives					Alternatives					Alternatives					Alternatives				
			3	5	10	50	100	3	5	10	50	100	3	5	10	50	100	3	5	10	50	100
(c)	0.25/0.5	equal	0.940	0.941	0.974	0.995	0.998	0.930	0.943	0.971	0.995	0.997	0.944	0.945	0.970	0.995	0.997	0.926	0.935	0.968	0.995	0.997
		entropy	0.947	0.941	0.969	0.995	0.997	0.932	0.936	0.968	0.995	0.997	0.932	0.935	0.965	0.994	0.997	0.926	0.932	0.965	0.994	0.997
		std	0.933	0.940	0.969	0.995	0.998	0.926	0.937	0.967	0.995	0.997	0.926	0.935	0.966	0.994	0.997	0.902	0.927	0.967	0.994	0.997
	0.25/1	equal	0.802	0.893	0.944	0.985	0.990	0.827	0.867	0.930	0.981	0.987	0.841	0.874	0.929	0.980	0.986	0.812	0.848	0.924	0.980	0.986
		entropy	0.924	0.894	0.935	0.983	0.989	0.884	0.871	0.923	0.979	0.986	0.856	0.859	0.919	0.979	0.986	0.858	0.849	0.914	0.979	0.985
		std	0.865	0.882	0.937	0.984	0.989	0.815	0.860	0.924	0.980	0.987	0.815	0.858	0.923	0.979	0.986	0.806	0.841	0.920	0.979	0.986
	0.5/1	equal	0.807	0.918	0.958	0.989	0.993	0.854	0.902	0.948	0.987	0.992	0.855	0.904	0.948	0.987	0.991	0.844	0.888	0.943	0.987	0.991
		entropy	0.921	0.918	0.951	0.988	0.993	0.893	0.902	0.944	0.986	0.991	0.877	0.888	0.940	0.986	0.991	0.873	0.889	0.937	0.986	0.991
		std	0.876	0.908	0.952	0.988	0.993	0.834	0.895	0.945	0.987	0.991	0.831	0.887	0.944	0.986	0.991	0.830	0.881	0.940	0.986	0.991
(d)	0.25/0.5	equal	0.966	0.970	0.988	0.999	0.999	0.971	0.973	0.988	0.998	0.999	0.973	0.978	0.988	0.998	0.999	0.968	0.976	0.988	0.998	0.999
		entropy	0.965	0.974	0.988	0.999	0.999	0.970	0.973	0.989	0.998	0.999	0.972	0.977	0.988	0.998	0.999	0.975	0.976	0.989	0.998	0.999
		std	0.972	0.974	0.989	0.999	0.999	0.975	0.976	0.989	0.999	0.999	0.967	0.981	0.988	0.998	0.999	0.966	0.975	0.990	0.998	0.999
	0.25/1	equal	0.924	0.935	0.976	0.996	0.998	0.924	0.937	0.972	0.995	0.997	0.941	0.942	0.970	0.995	0.997	0.921	0.938	0.970	0.995	0.997
		entropy	0.933	0.946	0.973	0.995	0.997	0.932	0.935	0.972	0.995	0.997	0.929	0.945	0.968	0.994	0.997	0.936	0.939	0.970	0.994	0.997
		std	0.934	0.943	0.975	0.996	0.998	0.935	0.936	0.972	0.995	0.997	0.927	0.946	0.970	0.994	0.997	0.928	0.937	0.971	0.995	0.997
	0.5/1	equal	0.929	0.958	0.985	0.998	0.999	0.936	0.959	0.983	0.997	0.998	0.950	0.961	0.982	0.997	0.998	0.945	0.955	0.982	0.997	0.998
		entropy	0.958	0.967	0.984	0.997	0.999	0.954	0.959	0.982	0.997	0.998	0.953	0.960	0.981	0.997	0.998	0.960	0.960	0.980	0.997	0.998
		std	0.956	0.965	0.984	0.997	0.999	0.950	0.958	0.982	0.997	0.998	0.952	0.962	0.981	0.997	0.998	0.953	0.960	0.981	0.997	0.998

Table A12. Mean values of the r_w correlation coefficient for different MCDA methods: **(a)** TOPSIS minmax/VIKOR, **(b)** TOPSIS minmax/PROMETHEE II usual, **(c)** TOPSIS minmax/COPRAS, **(d)** VIKOR/PROMETHEE II usual, **(e)** VIKOR/COPRAS, and **(f)** PROMETHEE II usual/COPRAS.

Method	Weighting Method	2 Criteria					3 Criteria					4 Criteria					5 Criteria				
		Alternatives					Alternatives					Alternatives					Alternatives				
		3	5	10	50	100	3	5	10	50	100	3	5	10	50	100	3	5	10	50	100
(a)	equal	0.060	−0.009	−0.024	−0.025	−0.029	0.181	0.261	0.272	0.300	0.296	0.030	−0.019	−0.003	−0.014	−0.011	0.135	0.133	0.148	0.165	0.170
	entropy	0.018	−0.024	−0.033	−0.010	−0.023	0.307	0.330	0.317	0.326	0.294	0.011	−0.025	−0.002	−0.014	−0.004	0.182	0.156	0.207	0.159	0.157
	std	0.024	−0.034	−0.032	−0.021	−0.030	0.246	0.304	0.277	0.307	0.290	0.011	−0.028	−0.013	−0.015	−0.008	0.166	0.128	0.167	0.158	0.167
(b)	equal	0.891	0.889	0.934	0.985	0.992	0.896	0.879	0.919	0.982	0.990	0.881	0.876	0.925	0.983	0.990	0.860	0.872	0.922	0.983	0.991
	entropy	0.900	0.898	0.936	0.980	0.988	0.850	0.866	0.913	0.969	0.983	0.837	0.848	0.899	0.967	0.980	0.790	0.831	0.883	0.965	0.980
	std	0.848	0.865	0.925	0.983	0.990	0.789	0.852	0.907	0.977	0.988	0.798	0.836	0.904	0.977	0.987	0.771	0.821	0.903	0.978	0.988
(c)	equal	0.754	0.832	0.853	0.873	0.872	0.735	0.803	0.852	0.884	0.885	0.751	0.851	0.906	0.944	0.948	0.760	0.835	0.905	0.941	0.946
	entropy	0.919	0.900	0.874	0.869	0.868	0.914	0.880	0.867	0.877	0.880	0.912	0.889	0.910	0.938	0.944	0.900	0.884	0.903	0.934	0.941
	std	0.839	0.860	0.859	0.871	0.870	0.847	0.840	0.855	0.881	0.884	0.854	0.875	0.909	0.942	0.947	0.855	0.860	0.909	0.939	0.944
(d)	equal	0.173	0.044	−0.011	−0.028	−0.029	0.209	0.259	0.266	0.293	0.292	0.084	0.004	−0.003	−0.018	−0.017	0.169	0.150	0.149	0.159	0.164
	entropy	0.019	−0.019	−0.031	−0.016	−0.025	0.269	0.310	0.298	0.313	0.288	0.010	−0.039	−0.004	−0.017	−0.012	0.167	0.127	0.180	0.150	0.152
	std	0.004	−0.017	−0.026	−0.025	−0.030	0.197	0.271	0.264	0.298	0.287	−0.006	−0.021	−0.020	−0.017	−0.014	0.144	0.110	0.155	0.153	0.162
(e)	equal	0.014	−0.018	0.002	0.085	0.124	0.113	0.171	0.218	0.305	0.324	−0.003	−0.039	−0.005	−0.009	−0.003	0.115	0.080	0.113	0.138	0.142
	entropy	0.005	−0.010	0.014	0.098	0.130	0.289	0.305	0.306	0.345	0.337	0.002	−0.040	0.002	−0.007	0.003	0.181	0.127	0.177	0.138	0.139
	std	0.006	−0.021	0.003	0.089	0.125	0.233	0.247	0.248	0.317	0.325	−0.022	−0.041	−0.011	−0.007	0.000	0.133	0.098	0.133	0.135	0.142
(f)	equal	0.776	0.820	0.853	0.882	0.883	0.742	0.778	0.832	0.883	0.889	0.764	0.818	0.879	0.940	0.949	0.741	0.793	0.871	0.935	0.945
	entropy	0.895	0.877	0.877	0.885	0.884	0.857	0.836	0.859	0.887	0.890	0.855	0.847	0.890	0.942	0.950	0.811	0.838	0.883	0.938	0.946
	std	0.811	0.826	0.854	0.882	0.883	0.767	0.793	0.836	0.884	0.889	0.774	0.826	0.878	0.940	0.949	0.758	0.799	0.871	0.936	0.945

Table A13. Mean values of the *WS* correlation coefficient for different MCDA methods: **(a)** TOPSIS minmax/VIKOR, **(b)** TOPSIS minmax/PROMETHEE II usual, **(c)** TOPSIS minmax/COPRAS, **(d)** VIKOR/PROMETHEE II usual, **(e)** VIKOR/COPRAS, and **(f)** PROMETHEE II usual/COPRAS.

Method	Weighting Method	2 Criteria					3 Criteria					4 Criteria					5 Criteria				
		Alternatives					Alternatives					Alternatives					Alternatives				
		3	5	10	50	100	3	5	10	50	100	3	5	10	50	100	3	5	10	50	100
(a)	equal	0.463	0.465	0.464	0.374	0.339	0.561	0.569	0.592	0.590	0.561	0.528	0.489	0.495	0.442	0.420	0.562	0.546	0.563	0.566	0.558
	entropy	0.596	0.520	0.490	0.403	0.357	0.672	0.652	0.638	0.614	0.569	0.569	0.527	0.512	0.452	0.424	0.611	0.588	0.611	0.560	0.542
	std	0.540	0.477	0.466	0.380	0.342	0.611	0.604	0.598	0.596	0.561	0.519	0.494	0.490	0.443	0.423	0.573	0.544	0.571	0.559	0.555
(b)	equal	0.873	0.876	0.933	0.990	0.995	0.903	0.878	0.924	0.988	0.994	0.884	0.876	0.924	0.986	0.993	0.875	0.879	0.926	0.985	0.992
	entropy	0.919	0.905	0.933	0.990	0.995	0.885	0.881	0.924	0.987	0.994	0.880	0.872	0.914	0.985	0.993	0.851	0.857	0.906	0.983	0.992
	std	0.876	0.879	0.932	0.990	0.995	0.847	0.873	0.923	0.988	0.994	0.859	0.860	0.916	0.986	0.993	0.842	0.854	0.916	0.985	0.992
(c)	equal	0.822	0.857	0.881	0.941	0.955	0.821	0.840	0.879	0.935	0.947	0.830	0.873	0.912	0.958	0.965	0.836	0.861	0.911	0.954	0.962
	entropy	0.938	0.910	0.900	0.942	0.955	0.935	0.898	0.897	0.937	0.948	0.933	0.903	0.918	0.958	0.966	0.922	0.896	0.914	0.955	0.963
	std	0.890	0.879	0.887	0.941	0.955	0.891	0.867	0.882	0.935	0.947	0.891	0.890	0.915	0.957	0.965	0.891	0.877	0.914	0.955	0.963
(d)	equal	0.492	0.505	0.523	0.510	0.507	0.567	0.586	0.642	0.730	0.745	0.532	0.500	0.522	0.506	0.508	0.556	0.549	0.586	0.632	0.644
	entropy	0.626	0.544	0.520	0.512	0.506	0.674	0.639	0.651	0.725	0.737	0.570	0.515	0.525	0.508	0.508	0.601	0.564	0.601	0.624	0.635
	std	0.578	0.506	0.519	0.511	0.507	0.595	0.609	0.642	0.730	0.744	0.521	0.508	0.520	0.507	0.509	0.567	0.549	0.590	0.630	0.643
(e)	equal	0.481	0.545	0.604	0.701	0.741	0.547	0.595	0.682	0.806	0.838	0.518	0.516	0.570	0.627	0.657	0.562	0.553	0.612	0.703	0.730
	entropy	0.604	0.564	0.598	0.700	0.740	0.676	0.670	0.706	0.809	0.836	0.573	0.540	0.575	0.625	0.653	0.619	0.594	0.642	0.701	0.728
	std	0.562	0.547	0.600	0.702	0.741	0.617	0.634	0.690	0.808	0.838	0.531	0.520	0.570	0.627	0.658	0.579	0.566	0.622	0.703	0.730
(f)	equal	0.777	0.831	0.882	0.945	0.958	0.804	0.824	0.875	0.940	0.951	0.811	0.845	0.898	0.959	0.967	0.807	0.836	0.894	0.956	0.965
	entropy	0.919	0.893	0.898	0.945	0.958	0.893	0.864	0.892	0.942	0.952	0.890	0.870	0.905	0.960	0.967	0.861	0.861	0.899	0.957	0.966
	std	0.870	0.850	0.880	0.944	0.958	0.837	0.836	0.877	0.940	0.951	0.840	0.854	0.898	0.958	0.967	0.834	0.843	0.893	0.957	0.965

References

1. Greco, S.; Figueira, J.; Ehrgott, M. *Multiple Criteria Decision Analysis*; Springer: Berlin/Heidelberg, Germany, 2016.
2. Roy, B. *Multicriteria Methodology for Decision Aiding*; Springer Science & Business Media: Berlin/Heidelberg, Germany, 2013; Volume 12.
3. Kodikara, P.N. Multi-Objective Optimal Operation of Urban Water Supply Systems. Ph.D. Thesis, Victoria University, Footscray, Australia, 2008.
4. Mulliner, E.; Malys, N.; Maliene, V. Comparative analysis of MCDM methods for the assessment of sustainable housing affordability. *Omega* **2016**, *59*, 146–156. [CrossRef]
5. Tzeng, G.H.; Chiang, C.H.; Li, C.W. Evaluating intertwined effects in e-learning programs: A novel hybrid MCDM model based on factor analysis and DEMATEL. *Expert Syst. Appl.* **2007**, *32*, 1028–1044. [CrossRef]
6. Deveci, M.; Özcan, E.; John, R.; Covrig, C.F.; Pamucar, D. A study on offshore wind farm siting criteria using a novel interval-valued fuzzy-rough based Delphi method. *J. Environ. Manag.* **2020**, *270*, 110916. [CrossRef] [PubMed]
7. Chatterjee, K.; Pamucar, D.; Zavadskas, E.K. Evaluating the performance of suppliers based on using the R'AMATEL-MAIRCA method for green supply chain implementation in electronics industry. *J. Clean. Prod.* **2018**, *184*, 101–129. [CrossRef]
8. Zopounidis, C.; Doumpos, M. Multicriteria classification and sorting methods: A literature review. *Eur. J. Oper. Res.* **2002**, *138*, 229–246. [CrossRef]
9. Behzadian, M.; Otaghsara, S.K.; Yazdani, M.; Ignatius, J. A state-of the-art survey of TOPSIS applications. *Expert Syst. Appl.* **2012**, *39*, 13051–13069. [CrossRef]
10. Palczewski, K.; Sałabun, W. The fuzzy TOPSIS applications in the last decade. *Procedia Comput. Sci.* **2019**, *159*, 2294–2303. [CrossRef]
11. Sałabun, W. The mean error estimation of TOPSIS method using a fuzzy reference models. *J. Theor. Appl. Comput. Sci.* **2013**, *7*, 40–50.
12. Opricovic, S.; Tzeng, G.H. Extended VIKOR method in comparison with outranking methods. *Eur. J. Oper. Res.* **2007**, *178*, 514–529. [CrossRef]
13. Saaty, T. *The Analytic Hierarchy Process*; Mcgraw Hill: New York, NY, USA, 1980.
14. Saaty, T.L. A scaling method for priorities in hierarchical structures. *J. Math. Psychol.* **1977**, *15*, 234–281. [CrossRef]
15. Zavadskas, E.K.; Kaklauskas, A.; Peldschus, F.; Turskis, Z. Multi-attribute assessment of road design solutions by using the COPRAS method. *Balt. J. Road Bridge Eng.* **2007**, *2*, 195–203.
16. Govindan, K.; Jepsen, M.B. ELECTRE: A comprehensive literature review on methodologies and applications. *Eur. J. Oper. Res.* **2016**, *250*, 1–29. [CrossRef]
17. Hashemi, S.S.; Hajiagha, S.H.R.; Zavadskas, E.K.; Mahdiraji, H.A. Multicriteria group decision making with ELECTRE III method based on interval-valued intuitionistic fuzzy information. *Appl. Math. Model.* **2016**, *40*, 1554–1564. [CrossRef]
18. Brans, J.P.; Vincke, P.; Mareschal, B. How to select and how to rank projects: The PROMETHEE method. *Eur. J. Oper. Res.* **1986**, *24*, 228–238. [CrossRef]
19. Uhde, B.; Hahn, W.A.; Griess, V.C.; Knoke, T. Hybrid MCDA methods to integrate multiple ecosystem services in forest management planning: A critical review. *Environ. Manag.* **2015**, *56*, 373–388. [CrossRef] [PubMed]
20. Wątróbski, J.; Jankowski, J.; Ziemba, P.; Karczmarczyk, A.; Zioło, M. Generalised framework for multi-criteria method selection: Rule set database and exemplary decision support system implementation blueprints. *Data Brief* **2019**, *22*, 639. [CrossRef]
21. Więckowski, J.; Kizielewicz, B.; Kołodziejczyk, J. Application of Hill Climbing Algorithm in Determining the Characteristic Objects Preferences Based on the Reference Set of Alternatives. In *Proceedings of the International Conference on Intelligent Decision Technologies*; Springer: Berlin/Heidelberg, Germany, 2020; pp. 341–351.
22. Wątróbski, J.; Jankowski, J.; Ziemba, P.; Karczmarczyk, A.; Zioło, M. Generalised framework for multi-criteria method selection. *Omega* **2019**, *86*, 107–124. [CrossRef]

23. Guitouni, A.; Martel, J.M. Tentative guidelines to help choosing an appropriate MCDA method. *Eur. J. Oper. Res.* **1998**, *109*, 501–521. [CrossRef]
24. Zanakis, S.H.; Solomon, A.; Wishart, N.; Dublish, S. Multi-attribute decision making: A simulation comparison of select methods. *Eur. J. Oper. Res.* **1998**, *107*, 507–529. [CrossRef]
25. Gershon, M. The role of weights and scales in the application of multiobjective decision making. *Eur. J. Oper. Res.* **1984**, *15*, 244–250. [CrossRef]
26. Cinelli, M.; Kadziński, M.; Gonzalez, M.; Słowiński, R. How to Support the Application of Multiple Criteria Decision Analysis? Let Us Start with a Comprehensive Taxonomy. *Omega* **2020**, *96*, 102261. [CrossRef]
27. Hanne, T. Meta decision problems in multiple criteria decision making. In *Multicriteria Decision Making*; Springer: Berlin/Heidelberg, Germany, 1999; pp. 147–171.
28. Wang, X.; Triantaphyllou, E. Ranking irregularities when evaluating alternatives by using some ELECTRE methods. *Omega* **2008**, *36*, 45–63. [CrossRef]
29. Chang, Y.H.; Yeh, C.H.; Chang, Y.W. A new method selection approach for fuzzy group multicriteria decision making. *Appl. Soft Comput.* **2013**, *13*, 2179–2187. [CrossRef]
30. Hajkowicz, S.; Higgins, A. A comparison of multiple criteria analysis techniques for water resource management. *Eur. J. Oper. Res.* **2008**, *184*, 255–265. [CrossRef]
31. Zak, J. The comparison of multiobjective ranking methods applied to solve the mass transit systems' decision problems. In Proceedings of the 10th Jubilee Meeting of the EURO Working Group on Transportation, Poznan, Poland, 13–16 September 2005; pp. 13–16.
32. Pamučar, D.; Stević, Ž.; Sremac, S. A new model for determining weight coefficients of criteria in mcdm models: Full consistency method (fucom). *Symmetry* **2018**, *10*, 393. [CrossRef]
33. Zardari, N.H.; Ahmed, K.; Shirazi, S.M.; Yusop, Z.B. *Weighting Methods and Their Effects on Multi-Criteria Decision Making Model Outcomes in Water Resources Management*; Springer: Berlin/Heidelberg, Germany, 2015.
34. Wątróbski, J.; Ziemba, E.; Karczmarczyk, A.; Jankowski, J. An index to measure the sustainable information society: The Polish households case. *Sustainability* **2018**, *10*, 3223. [CrossRef]
35. Sałabun, W.; Palczewski, K.; Wątróbski, J. Multicriteria approach to sustainable transport evaluation under incomplete knowledge: Electric bikes case study. *Sustainability* **2019**, *11*, 3314. [CrossRef]
36. Wątróbski, J.; Sałabun, W. Green supplier selection framework based on multi-criteria decision-analysis approach. In *Proceedings of the International Conference on Sustainable Design and Manufacturing*; Springer: Berlin/Heidelberg, Germany, 2016; pp. 361–371.
37. Alimardani, M.; Hashemkhani Zolfani, S.; Aghdaie, M.H.; Tamošaitienė, J. A novel hybrid SWARA and VIKOR methodology for supplier selection in an agile environment. *Technol. Econ. Dev. Econ.* **2013**, *19*, 533–548. [CrossRef]
38. Chu, T.C. Selecting plant location via a fuzzy TOPSIS approach. *Int. J. Adv. Manuf. Technol.* **2002**, *20*, 859–864. [CrossRef]
39. Madić, M.; Marković, D.; Petrović, G.; Radovanović, M. Application of COPRAS method for supplier selection. In *The Fifth International Conference Transport and Logistics-TIL 2014*; Proceedings: Niš, Serbia, 2014; pp. 47–50.
40. Elevli, B. Logistics freight center locations decision by using Fuzzy-PROMETHEE. *Transport* **2014**, *29*, 412–418. [CrossRef]
41. Stević, Ž.; Pamučar, D.; Puška, A.; Chatterjee, P. Sustainable supplier selection in healthcare industries using a new MCDM method: Measurement of alternatives and ranking according to COmpromise solution (MARCOS). *Comput. Ind. Eng.* **2020**, *140*, 106231. [CrossRef]
42. Ahmadi, A.; Gupta, S.; Karim, R.; Kumar, U. Selection of maintenance strategy for aircraft systems using multi-criteria decision making methodologies. *Int. J. Reliab. Qual. Saf. Eng.* **2010**, *17*, 223–243. [CrossRef]
43. Venkata Rao, R. Evaluating flexible manufacturing systems using a combined multiple attribute decision making method. *Int. J. Prod. Res.* **2008**, *46*, 1975–1989. [CrossRef]
44. Aghdaie, M.H.; Zolfani, S.H.; Zavadskas, E.K. Decision making in machine tool selection: An integrated approach with SWARA and COPRAS-G methods. *Eng. Econ.* **2013**, *24*, 5–17.
45. Hashemi, H.; Bazargan, J.; Mousavi, S.M. A compromise ratio method with an application to water resources management: An intuitionistic fuzzy set. *Water Resour. Manag.* **2013**, *27*, 2029–2051. [CrossRef]

46. Liu, C.; Frazier, P.; Kumar, L.; Macgregor, C.; Blake, N. Catchment-wide wetland assessment and prioritization using the multi-criteria decision-making method TOPSIS. *Environ. Manag.* **2006**, *38*, 316–326. [CrossRef] [PubMed]
47. Roozbahani, A.; Ghased, H.; Hashemy Shahedany, M. Inter-basin water transfer planning with grey COPRAS and fuzzy COPRAS techniques: A case study in Iranian Central Plateau. *Sci. Total Environ.* **2020**, *726*, 138499. [CrossRef]
48. Kapepula, K.M.; Colson, G.; Sabri, K.; Thonart, P. A multiple criteria analysis for household solid waste management in the urban community of Dakar. *Waste Manag.* **2007**, *27*, 1690–1705. [CrossRef]
49. Carnero, M.C. Waste Segregation FMEA Model Integrating Intuitionistic Fuzzy Set and the PAPRIKA Method. *Mathematics* **2020**, *8*, 1375. [CrossRef]
50. Boran, F.; Boran, K.; Menlik, T. The evaluation of renewable energy technologies for electricity generation in Turkey using intuitionistic fuzzy TOPSIS. *Energy Sources Part B Econ. Plan. Policy* **2012**, *7*, 81–90. [CrossRef]
51. Kaya, T.; Kahraman, C. Multicriteria renewable energy planning using an integrated fuzzy VIKOR & AHP methodology: The case of Istanbul. *Energy* **2010**, *35*, 2517–2527.
52. Krishankumar, R.; Ravichandran, K.; Kar, S.; Cavallaro, F.; Zavadskas, E.K.; Mardani, A. Scientific decision framework for evaluation of renewable energy sources under q-rung orthopair fuzzy set with partially known weight information. *Sustainability* **2019**, *11*, 4202. [CrossRef]
53. Rehman, A.U.; Abidi, M.H.; Umer, U.; Usmani, Y.S. Multi-Criteria Decision-Making Approach for Selecting Wind Energy Power Plant Locations. *Sustainability* **2019**, *11*, 6112. [CrossRef]
54. Wątróbski, J.; Ziemba, P.; Wolski, W. Methodological aspects of decision support system for the location of renewable energy sources. In 2015 Federated Conference on Computer Science and Information Systems (FedCSIS), Lodz, Poland, 13–16 September 2015; pp. 1451–1459.
55. Riaz, M.; Sałabun, W.; Farid, H.M.A.; Ali, N.; Wątróbski, J. A Robust q-Rung Orthopair Fuzzy Information Aggregation Using Einstein Operations with Application to Sustainable Energy Planning Decision Management. *Energies* **2020**, *13*, 2155. [CrossRef]
56. Tong, L.I.; Chen, C.C.; Wang, C.H. Optimization of multi-response processes using the VIKOR method. *Int. J. Adv. Manuf. Technol.* **2007**, *31*, 1049–1057. [CrossRef]
57. Tong, L.I.; Wang, C.H.; Chen, H.C. Optimization of multiple responses using principal component analysis and technique for order preference by similarity to ideal solution. *Int. J. Adv. Manuf. Technol.* **2005**, *27*, 407–414. [CrossRef]
58. Mlela, M.K.; Xu, H.; Sun, F.; Wang, H.; Madenge, G.D. Material Analysis and Molecular Dynamics Simulation for Cavitation Erosion and Corrosion Suppression in Water Hydraulic Valves. *Materials* **2020**, *13*, 453. [CrossRef]
59. Yazdani, M.; Graeml, F.R. VIKOR and its applications: A state-of-the-art survey. *Int. J. Strateg. Decis. Sci. (IJSDS)* **2014**, *5*, 56–83. [CrossRef]
60. Behzadian, M.; Kazemzadeh, R.; Albadvi, A.; Aghdasi, M. PROMETHEE: A comprehensive literature review on methodologies and applications. *Eur. J. Oper. Res.* **2010**, *200*, 198–215. [CrossRef]
61. Zavadskas, E.K.; Turskis, Z. Multiple criteria decision making (MCDM) methods in economics: An overview. *Technol. Econ. Dev. Econ.* **2011**, *17*, 397–427. [CrossRef]
62. Guitouni, A.; Martel, J.M.; Vincke, P.; North, P. *A Framework to Choose a Discrete Multicriterion Aggregation Procedure*; Defence Research Establishment Valcatier (DREV): Ottawa, ON, Canada, 1998. Available online: https://pdfs.semanticscholar.org/27d5/9c846657268bc840c4df8df98e85de66c562.pdf (accessed on 28 June 2020).
63. Spronk, J.; Steuer, R.E.; Zopounidis, C. Multicriteria decision aid/analysis in finance. In *Multiple Criteria Decision Analysis: State of the Art Surveys*; Springer: Berlin/Heidelberg, Germany, 2005; pp. 799–848.
64. Roy, B. The outranking approach and the foundations of ELECTRE methods. In *Readings in Multiple Criteria Decision Aid*; Springer: Berlin/Heidelberg, Germany, 1990; pp. 155–183.
65. Ishizaka, A.; Nemery, P. *Multi-Criteria Decision Analysis: Methods and Software*; John Wiley & Sons: Hoboken, NJ, USA, 2013.
66. Stević, Ž.; Pamučar, D.; Subotić, M.; Antuchevičiene, J.; Zavadskas, E.K. The location selection for roundabout construction using Rough BWM-Rough WASPAS approach based on a new Rough Hamy aggregator. *Sustainability* **2018**, *10*, 2817. [CrossRef]

67. Fortemps, P.; Greco, S.; Słowiński, R. Multicriteria choice and ranking using decision rules induced from rough approximation of graded preference relations. In *Proceedings of the International Conference on Rough Sets and Current Trends in Computing*; Springer: Berlin/Heidelberg, Germany, 2004; pp. 510–522.
68. e Costa, C.A.B.; Vincke, P. Multiple criteria decision aid: An overview. In *Readings in Multiple Criteria Decision Aid*; Springer: Berlin/Heidelberg, Germany, 1990; pp. 3–14.
69. Wang, J.J.; Yang, D.L. Using a hybrid multi-criteria decision aid method for information systems outsourcing. *Comput. Oper. Res.* **2007**, *34*, 3691–3700. [CrossRef]
70. Figueira, J.; Mousseau, V.; Roy, B. ELECTRE methods. In *Multiple Criteria Decision Analysis: State of the Art Surveys*; Springer: Berlin/Heidelberg, Germany, 2005; pp. 133–153.
71. Blin, M.J.; Tsoukiàs, A. Multi-criteria methodology contribution to the software quality evaluation. *Softw. Qual. J.* **2001**, *9*, 113–132. [CrossRef]
72. Edwards, W.; Newman, J.R.; Snapper, K.; Seaver, D. *Multiattribute Evaluation*; Number 26; Chronicle Books; SAGE Publications: London, UK, 1982.
73. Jacquet-Lagreze, E.; Siskos, J. Assessing a set of additive utility functions for multicriteria decision-making, the UTA method. *Eur. J. Oper. Res.* **1982**, *10*, 151–164. [CrossRef]
74. e Costa, C.A.B.; Vansnick, J.C. MACBETH—An interactive path towards the construction of cardinal value functions. *Int. Trans. Oper. Res.* **1994**, *1*, 489–500. [CrossRef]
75. Bana E Costa, C.A.; Vansnick, J.C. Applications of the MACBETH approach in the framework of an additive aggregation model. *J. Multi-Criteria Decis. Anal.* **1997**, *6*, 107–114. [CrossRef]
76. Chen, C.T.; Lin, C.T.; Huang, S.F. A fuzzy approach for supplier evaluation and selection in supply chain management. *Int. J. Prod. Econ.* **2006**, *102*, 289–301. [CrossRef]
77. Vahdani, B.; Mousavi, S.M.; Tavakkoli-Moghaddam, R. Group decision making based on novel fuzzy modified TOPSIS method. *Appl. Math. Model.* **2011**, *35*, 4257–4269. [CrossRef]
78. Rashid, T.; Beg, I.; Husnine, S.M. Robot selection by using generalized interval-valued fuzzy numbers with TOPSIS. *Appl. Soft Comput.* **2014**, *21*, 462–468. [CrossRef]
79. Krohling, R.A.; Campanharo, V.C. Fuzzy TOPSIS for group decision making: A case study for accidents with oil spill in the sea. *Expert Syst. Appl.* **2011**, *38*, 4190–4197. [CrossRef]
80. Roy, B. Classement et choix en présence de points de vue multiples. *Rev. Française Inform. Rech. Oper.* **1968**, *2*, 57–75. [CrossRef]
81. Roy, B.; Skalka, J.M. *ELECTRE IS: Aspects Méthodologiques et Guide D'utilisation*; LAMSADE, Unité Associée au CNRS no 825; Université de Paris Dauphine: Paris, France, 1987.
82. Roy, B.; Bertier, P.; La méthode ELECTRE, I. *Une Application au Media Planning*; North Holland: Amsterdam, The Netherlands, 1973.
83. Roy, B.; Hugonnard, J.C. Ranking of suburban line extension projects on the Paris metro system by a multicriteria method. *Transp. Res. Part A Gen.* **1982**, *16*, 301–312. [CrossRef]
84. Roy, B.; Bouyssou, D. *Aide Multicritère à la Décision: Méthodes et Cas*; Economica Paris: Paris, France, 1993.
85. Mareschal, B.; Brans, J.P.; Vincke, P. *PROMETHEE: A New Family of Outranking Methods in Multicriteria Analysis*; Technical Report; ULB—Universite Libre de: Bruxelles, Belgium, 1984.
86. Janssens, G.K.; Pangilinan, J.M. Multiple criteria performance analysis of non-dominated sets obtained by multi-objective evolutionary algorithms for optimisation. In Proceedings of the IFIP International Conference on Artificial Intelligence Applications and Innovations, Larnaca, Cyprus, 6–7 October 2010; Springer: Berlin/Heidelberg, Germany, 2010; pp. 94–103.
87. Chen, T.Y. A PROMETHEE-based outranking method for multiple criteria decision analysis with interval type-2 fuzzy sets. *Soft Comput.* **2014**, *18*, 923–940. [CrossRef]
88. Martinez-Alier, J.; Munda, G.; O'Neill, J. Weak comparability of values as a foundation for ecological economics. *Ecol. Econ.* **1998**, *26*, 277–286. [CrossRef]
89. Munda, G. Cost-benefit analysis in integrated environmental assessment: Some methodological issues. *Ecol. Econ.* **1996**, *19*, 157–168. [CrossRef]
90. Ana, E., Jr.; Bauwens, W.; Broers, O. Quantifying uncertainty using robustness analysis in the application of ORESTE to sewer rehabilitation projects prioritization—Brussels case study. *J. Multi-Criteria Decis. Anal.* **2009**, *16*, 111–124. [CrossRef]
91. Roubens, M. Preference relations on actions and criteria in multicriteria decision making. *Eur. J. Oper. Res.* **1982**, *10*, 51–55. [CrossRef]

92. Hinloopen, E.; Nijkamp, P. Qualitative multiple criteria choice analysis. *Qual. Quant.* **1990**, *24*, 37–56. [CrossRef]
93. Martel, J.M.; Matarazzo, B. Other outranking approaches. In *Multiple Criteria Decision Analysis: State of the Art Surveys*; Springer: Berlin/Heidelberg, Germany, 2005; pp. 197–259.
94. Marchant, T. An axiomatic characterization of different majority concepts. *Eur. J. Oper. Res.* **2007**, *179*, 160–173. [CrossRef]
95. Bélanger, M.; Martel, J.M. An Automated Explanation Approach for a Decision Support System based on MCDA. *ExaCt* **2005**, *5*, 4.
96. Guitouni, A.; Martel, J.; Bélanger, M.; Hunter, C. *Managing a Decision-Making Situation in the Context of the Canadian Airspace Protection*; Faculté des Sciences de L'administration de L'Université Laval, Direction de la Recherche: Quebec City, QC, Canada, 1999.
97. Nijkamp, P.; Rietveld, P.; Voogd, H. *Multicriteria Evaluation in Physical Planning*; Elsevier: Amsterdam, The Netherlands, 2013.
98. Vincke, P. Outranking approach. In *Multicriteria Decision Making*; Springer: Berlin/Heidelberg, Germany, 1999; pp. 305–333.
99. Paelinck, J.H. Qualitative multiple criteria analysis, environmental protection and multiregional development. In *Papers of the Regional Science Association*; Springer: Berlin/Heidelberg, Germany, 1976; Volume 36, pp. 59–74.
100. Matarazzo, B. MAPPAC as a compromise between outranking methods and MAUT. *Eur. J. Oper. Res.* **1991**, *54*, 48–65. [CrossRef]
101. Greco, S. A new pcca method: Idra. *Eur. J. Oper. Res.* **1997**, *98*, 587–601. [CrossRef]
102. Sałabun, W. The Characteristic Objects Method: A New Distance-based Approach to Multicriteria Decision-making Problems. *J. Multi-Criteria Decis. Anal.* **2015**, *22*, 37–50. [CrossRef]
103. Kujawińska, A.; Rogalewicz, M.; Diering, M.; Piłacińska, M.; Hamrol, A.; Kochańskib, A. Assessment of ductile iron casting process with the use of the DRSA method. *J. Min. Metall. Sect. B Metall.* **2016**, *52*, 25–34. [CrossRef]
104. Więckowski, J.; Kizielewicz, B.; Kołodziejczyk, J. Finding an Approximate Global Optimum of Characteristic Objects Preferences by Using Simulated Annealing. In Proceedings of the International Conference on Intelligent Decision Technologies, Split, Croatia, 17–19 June 2020; Springer: Berlin/Heidelberg, Germany, 2020; pp. 365–375.
105. Sałabun, W.; Wątróbski, J.; Piegat, A. Identification of a multi-criteria model of location assessment for renewable energy sources. In Proceedings of the International Conference on Artificial Intelligence and Soft Computing, Split, Croatia, 17–19 June 2020; Springer: Berlin/Heidelberg, Germany, 2016; pp. 321–332.
106. Sałabun, W.; Karczmarczyk, A.; Wątróbski, J.; Jankowski, J. Handling data uncertainty in decision making with COMET. In Proceedings of the 2018 IEEE Symposium Series on Computational Intelligence (SSCI), Bangalore, India, 18–21 November 2018; pp. 1478–1484.
107. Więckowski, J.; Kizielewicz, B.; Kołodziejczyk, J. The Search of the Optimal Preference Values of the Characteristic Objects by Using Particle Swarm Optimization in the Uncertain Environment. In *Proceedings of the International Conference on Intelligent Decision Technologies*; Springer: Berlin/Heidelberg, Germany, 2020; pp. 353–363.
108. Inuiguchi, M.; Yoshioka, Y.; Kusunoki, Y. Variable-precision dominance-based rough set approach and attribute reduction. *Int. J. Approx. Reason.* **2009**, *50*, 1199–1214. [CrossRef]
109. Greco, S.; Matarazzo, B.; Slowinski, R. Rough approximation by dominance relations. *Int. J. Intell. Syst.* **2002**, *17*, 153–171. [CrossRef]
110. Słowiński, R.; Greco, S.; Matarazzo, B. Rough-set-based decision support. In *Search Methodologies*; Springer: Berlin/Heidelberg, Germany, 2014; pp. 557–609.
111. Al-Shemmeri, T.; Al-Kloub, B.; Pearman, A. Model choice in multicriteria decision aid. *Eur. J. Oper. Res.* **1997**, *97*, 550–560. [CrossRef]
112. Kornyshova, E.; Salinesi, C. MCDM techniques selection approaches: State of the art. In Proceedings of the 2007 IEEE Symposium on Computational Intelligence in Multi-Criteria Decision-Making, Honolulu, HI, USA, 1–5 April 2007; pp. 22–29.
113. Gershon, M.; Duckstein, L. An algorithm for choosing of a multiobjective technique. In *Essays and Surveys on Multiple Criteria Decision Making*; Springer: Berlin/Heidelberg, Germany, 1983; pp. 53–62.

114. Celik, M.; Cicek, K.; Cebi, S. Establishing an international MBA program for shipping executives: Managing OR/MS foundation towards a unique curriculum design. In Proceedings of the 2009 International Conference on Computers & Industrial Engineering, Troyes, France, 6–9 July 2009; pp. 459–463.
115. Adil, M.; Nunes, M.B.; Peng, G.C. Identifying operational requirements to select suitable decision models for a public sector e-procurement decision support system. *JISTEM J. Inf. Syst. Technol. Manag.* **2014**, *11*, 211–228. [CrossRef]
116. Moghaddam, N.B.; Nasiri, M.; Mousavi, S. An appropriate multiple criteria decision making method for solving electricity planning problems, addressing sustainability issue. *Int. J. Environ. Sci. Technol.* **2011**, *8*, 605–620. [CrossRef]
117. Salinesi, C.; Kornyshova, E. Choosing a Prioritization Method-Case of IS Security Improvement. In *CAiSE Forum*; 2006. Available online: https://pdfs.semanticscholar.org/ef7b/3d0658d0176aee128562b8a9a4c0bb278354.pdf (accessed on 10 July 2020) .
118. De Montis, A.; De Toro, P.; Droste-Franke, B.; Omann, I.; Stagl, S. Assessing the quality of different MCDA methods. *Altern. Environ. Valuat.* **2004**, *4*, 99–133.
119. Cinelli, M.; Coles, S.R.; Kirwan, K. Analysis of the potentials of multi criteria decision analysis methods to conduct sustainability assessment. *Ecol. Indic.* **2014**, *46*, 138–148. [CrossRef]
120. Wątróbski, J. Outline of multicriteria decision-making in green logistics. *Transp. Res. Procedia* **2016**, *16*, 537–552. [CrossRef]
121. Wątróbski, J.; Jankowski, J. Knowledge management in MCDA domain. In Proceedings of the 2015 Federated Conference on Computer Science and Information Systems (FedCSIS), Lodz, Poland, 13–16 September 2015; pp. 1445–1450.
122. Wątróbski, J.; Jankowski, J. Guideline for MCDA method selection in production management area. In *New Frontiers in Information and Production Systems Modelling and Analysis*; Springer: Berlin/Heidelberg, Germany, 2016; pp. 119–138.
123. Ulengin, F.; Topcu, Y.I.; Sahin, S.O. An artificial neural network approach to multicriteria model selection. In *Multiple Criteria Decision Making in the New Millennium*; Springer: Berlin/Heidelberg, Germany, 2001; pp. 101–110.
124. Moffett, A.; Sarkar, S. Incorporating multiple criteria into the design of conservation area networks: A minireview with recommendations. *Divers. Distrib.* **2006**, *12*, 125–137. [CrossRef]
125. Hwang, C.L.; Yoon, K. Methods for multiple attribute decision making. In *Multiple Attribute Decision Making*; Springer: Berlin/Heidelberg, Germany, 1981; pp. 58–191.
126. Celik, M.; Topcu, Y.I. Analytical modelling of shipping business processes based on MCDM methods. *Marit. Policy Manag.* **2009**, *36*, 469–479. [CrossRef]
127. Cicek, K.; Celik, M.; Topcu, Y.I. An integrated decision aid extension to material selection problem. *Mater. Des.* **2010**, *31*, 4398–4402. [CrossRef]
128. Kokaraki, N.; Hopfe, C.J.; Robinson, E.; Nikolaidou, E. Testing the reliability of deterministic multi-criteria decision-making methods using building performance simulation. *Renew. Sustain. Energy Rev.* **2019**, *112*, 991–1007. [CrossRef]
129. Kolios, A.; Mytilinou, V.; Lozano-Minguez, E.; Salonitis, K. A comparative study of multiple-criteria decision-making methods under stochastic inputs. *Energies* **2016**, *9*, 566. [CrossRef]
130. Ceballos, B.; Lamata, M.T.; Pelta, D.A. A comparative analysis of multi-criteria decision-making methods. *Prog. Artif. Intell.* **2016**, *5*, 315–322. [CrossRef]
131. Sarraf, R.; McGuire, M.P. Integration and comparison of multi-criteria decision making methods in safe route planner. *Expert Syst. Appl.* **2020**, 154, 113399. [CrossRef]
132. Garre, A.; Boué, G.; Fernández, P.S.; Membré, J.M.; Egea, J.A. Evaluation of Multicriteria Decision Analysis Algorithms in Food Safety: A Case Study on Emerging Zoonoses Prioritization. *Risk Anal.* **2020**, *40*, 336–351. [CrossRef]
133. Chakraborty, S.; Yeh, C.H. A simulation comparison of normalization procedures for TOPSIS. In Proceedings of the 2009 International Conference on Computers & Industrial Engineering, Troyes, France, 6–9 July 2009; pp. 1815–1820.
134. Papathanasiou, J.; Ploskas, N. *Multiple Criteria Decision Aid*; Springer: Berlin/Heidelberg, Germany, 2018.
135. Opricovic, S. Multicriteria optimization of civil engineering systems. *Fac. Civ. Eng. Belgrade* **1998**, *2*, 5–21.

136. Opricovic, S.; Tzeng, G.H. Compromise solution by MCDM methods: A comparative analysis of VIKOR and TOPSIS. *Eur. J. Oper. Res.* **2004**, *156*, 445–455. [CrossRef]
137. Zavadskas, E.; Kaklauskas, A. Determination of an efficient contractor by using the new method of multicriteria assessment. In Proceedings of the International Symposium for "The Organization and Management of Construction". Shaping Theory and Practice, Glasgow, UK, 28 August–3 September 1996; Taylor & Francis: Oxfordshire, UK, 1996; Volume 2, pp. 94–104.
138. Zavadskas, E.K.; Kaklauskas, A.; Sarka, V. The new method of multicriteria complex proportional assessment of projects. *Technol. Econ. Dev. Econ.* **1994**, *1*, 131–139.
139. Pamučar, D.; Božanić, D.; Lukovac, V.; Komazec, N. Normalized weighted geometric bonferroni mean operator of interval rough numbers—Application in interval rough dematel-copras model. *Facta Univ. Ser. Mech. Eng.* **2018**, *16*, 171–191.
140. Stanojković, J.; Radovanović, M. Selection of drill for drilling with high pressure coolant using entropy and copras MCDM method. *UPB Sci. Bull. Ser. D Mech. Eng.* **2017**, *79*, 199–204.
141. Brans, J.P.; De Smet, Y. PROMETHEE methods. In *Multiple Criteria Decision Analysis*; Springer: Berlin/Heidelberg, Germany, 2016; pp. 187–219.
142. Ranjan, R.; Chatterjee, P.; Panchal, D.; Pamucar, D. Performance Evaluation of Sustainable Smart Cities in India: An Adaptation of Cartography in PROMETHEE-GIS Approach. In *Advanced Multi-Criteria Decision Making for Addressing Complex Sustainability Issues*; IGI Global: Hershey, PA, USA, 2019; pp. 14–40.
143. Podviezko, A. Distortions introduced by normalisation of values of criteria in multiple criteria methods of evaluation. *LMD Darb* **2014**, *55*, 51–56. [CrossRef]
144. Sałabun, W.; Urbaniak, K. A new coefficient of rankings similarity in decision-making problems. In Proceedings of the International Conference on Computational Science, Amsterdam, The Netherlands, 3–5 June 2020; Springer: Cham, Switzerland, 2020.

symmetry

Article

A New Approach to Identifying a Multi-Criteria Decision Model Based on Stochastic Optimization Techniques

Bartłomiej Kizielewicz and Wojciech Sałabun *

Research Team on Intelligent Decision Support Systems, Department of Artificial Intelligence and Applied Mathematics, Faculty of Computer Science and Information Technology, West Pomeranian University of Technology in Szczecin, ul. Żołnierska 49, 71-210 Szczecin, Poland; bartlomiej-kizielewicz@zut.edu.pl

* Correspondence: wojciech.salabun@zut.edu.pl; Tel.: +48-91-449-5580

Received: 17 August 2020; Accepted: 15 September 2020; Published: 20 September 2020

Abstract: Many scientific papers are devoted to solving multi-criteria problems. Researchers solve these problems, usually using methods that find discrete solutions and with the collaboration of domain experts. In both symmetrical and asymmetrical problems, the challenge is when new decision-making variants emerge. Unfortunately, discreet identification of preferences makes it impossible to determine the preferences for new alternatives. In this work, we propose a new approach to identifying a multi-criteria decision model to address this challenge. Our proposal is based on stochastic optimization techniques and the characteristic objects method (COMET). An extensive work comparing the use of hill-climbing, simulated annealing, and particle swarm optimization algorithms are presented in this paper. The paper also contains preliminary studies on initial conditions. Finally, our approach has been demonstrated using a simple numerical example.

Keywords: optimization; multi-criteria problems; evolutionary algorithms; MCDA; multi-criteria decision-analysis; machine learning; fuzzy logic; uncertain data

1. Introduction

Optimization is one of the instruments used to solve various types of decision-making problems [1,2]. Formally, optimization is a method of determining the best solution from a defined quality criterion [3–5]. Moreover, optimization is also a part of operational research, which focuses on determining the method and solving defined problems connected to making the right decisions. In optimization, one can identify single and multi-criteria optimizations [6–8]. Multi-criteria optimizations exist where optimal decisions must be made in the presence of compromises between conflicting objectives [9,10].

Deterministic and stochastic methods are the main groups of optimization techniques used in decision-making problems. In the optimization process, deterministic methods use mathematical formulas, while stochastic methods also use random processes for this purpose [11]. The deterministic techniques find local extremes more frequently, which often makes it impossible to find global extremes. On the other hand, the stochastic methods have techniques to avoid falling into local extremes [12,13]. In the deterministic approach, fewer objective function evaluations are needed to reach a solution than in the stochastic approach. Deterministic methods can find global extremes through a close search and have no stochastic elements [14]. There are two approaches in stochastic methods: the global approach and the local approach [15]. The global approach is based on evaluating functions at several random points [16]. In the local approach, the selection of points is directed to get a candidate for the global extremity using local searches.

Solving decision-making problems using stochastic methods does not guarantee success, but they can solve severe and different problems [17,18]. Furthermore, stochastic techniques are easy to implement for problems complex to evaluate the "black box" function [19]. The mathematical structure of the problem under investigation is more important in understanding the deterministic approach than the stochastic approach. However, deterministic methods are effective in local search.

Random global search algorithms are methods that take into account randomly selected neighboring states. Simple structure and little resistance to the irregularity of the objective function behavior make the global random search algorithms very attractive. Global random search algorithms can also be associated with the metaheuristic term, because they do not directly solve any problem, but provide a way to create a suitable algorithm for it [20].

The algorithm that moves between possible solutions in search of the right solution is called the metaheuristics algorithm [19,21]. Metaheuristic algorithms, such as evolutionary algorithms (EA) or genetic algorithm (GA), can be adapted to meet the most realistic optimization problems in terms of expected solution quality and calculation time [22].

The examples of global random search algorithms are the hill-climbing algorithm, simulated annealing, and particle swarm optimization [23]. The hill-climbing algorithm works by selecting a random state from the neighborhood and comparing it with the current state [24,25]. If the state from the neighborhood turns out to be better, it becomes the current state. This step is performed in a loop until the stop condition is reached.

The simulated annealing is a method based on simulated annealing of solids [26,27]. It uses the Boltzmann coefficient, which during the optimization process can assume a worse state than the current one, in order not to fall into local extremes if the value of a random variable from a uniform distribution [0, 1] is smaller than it [28,29]. Updating the current state is the same as in the hill-climbing algorithm.

Particle swarm optimization is based on finding a solution using unique points in spaces, described through feature vectors [17,30]. Particles have parameters such as position, velocity, and direction of movement. The particles also remember their best solution found, which is known as a local solution. The best solution from the whole swarm is a global solution [31,32].

The stochastic methods, such as hill-climbing algorithm, simulated annealing and particle swarm optimization can be used in continuous and discrete space. However, they are not able to provide a global solution. Unlike simulated annealing and particle swarm optimization, the hill-climbing algorithm has no mechanisms to protect it from falling into local extremes. However, in contrast, it is characterized by lower memory requirements and more frequent acceptance of solutions. The PSO method is more probable and useful in finding global extremes compared to the hill-climbing algorithm. Also, particle swarm optimization is capable of performing parallel calculations, but setting PSO parameters is a big challenge [33]. The simulated annealing method works very well in discrete spaces, while the iteration time it takes to find an extremity is extensive compared to other stochastic methods.

The methods mentioned above will be used in the problem of searching for optimal values of preferences of objects characteristic for given sets of decision variants, i.e., those for which the objective function will reach the lowest value. The characteristic objects are defined in Section 2.2. This problem occurs when we want to calculate the preference of decision-making variants, with unknown preferences of characteristic objects and known calculated by the model preferences of decision-making variants [34–36]. The objective function in this problem is defined as the absolute difference of the sums of the preferences of the reference decision variants with the calculated ones. The preference of decision variants is calculated using the COMET method. Although the RAFSI method is also resistant to rank reversal, our study was conducted based on COMET modeling, which seems to be more proper according to the identification of the continuous space of the problem [37].

The COMET method is a new method designed to solve decision-making problems. Among the methods of multi-criteria decision making, the characteristic object technique has a unique property, i.e., resistance to the paradox of reversal of ranking order [38,39]. This property results from the fact that the assessment of decision variants is based on characteristic object assessments, which are independent of the set of assessed alternatives. The advantage of the COMET method is also the ease of identification of linear and non-linear decision-making functions.

The novelties and contributions are presented as follows. The paper presents an innovative approach, which consists of building a decision-making model based on already evaluated alternatives and stochastic optimization techniques. Multi-Criteria Decision-Analysis (MCDA) methods use an approach in which an expert in a given field defines the model, and then the decision variants are evaluated [40–42]. The method proposed in the paper allows building a proper decision-making model without the need to interfere with the process. With this approach, we can assess a set of alternatives with the help of already assessed alternatives. The alternatives we have in our possession enable us to estimate the expert's model. Additionally, the model built with such an approach can be further exploited. The suggested method can be useful when an expert in a given field is not available.

For this purpose, stochastic methods have been used, which allow one to approximate the evaluation of the expert model. The defined model, with the help of stochastic techniques, can evaluate the given alternatives similar to the unknown decision model. Additionally, stochastic algorithms are easy to implement and adapt, so the proposed approach can be tested on more metaheuristic methods. The paper uses such methods as the hill-climbing algorithm, simulated annealing method, and particle swarm optimization. The effectiveness of stochastic techniques has been compared to estimate which one works best with different input data.

The rest of the paper is organized as follows. In Section 2 there are definitions. Section 2.2 presents the COMET method. The selected stochastic methods, i.e., the climbing algorithm, the simulated annealing method, and optimization by means of a particle swarm are presented in Sections 2.3–2.5. The selected similarity coefficients are presented in Section 2.6. Section 3 shows the research carried out. It consists of Section 3.1 on the effects of the initial conditions, Section 3.2 showing the distribution of fitness functions, and Section 3.3 which presents the application of the proposed approach. Section 4 contains conclusions.

2. Preliminaries

2.1. Fuzzy Set Theory

Fuzzy Set Theory is used in many scientific fields and could be especially useful for solving MCDA problems [43–45]. Here we present some definitions and basic concepts of the Fuzzy Set Theory which are necessary to understand the COMET method [46,47].

Definition 1. *The fuzzy set A in a certain non-empty space of solutions X is defined as follows in Equation (1).*

$$A = \{(x, \mu_A(x)) ; x \in X\}, \tag{1}$$

where

$$\mu_A(x) : X \to [0,1], \tag{2}$$

is a membership function of the fuzzy set A. This function indicates the degree of the membership of the element in the set A. $\mu_A(x) = 1$ *means full membership,* $0 < \mu_A(x) < 1$ *means partial membership and* $\mu_A(x) = 0$ *means no membership at all.*

Definition 2. *The triangular fuzzy number* $A(a, m, b)$ *is a fuzzy set whose membership function is defined as Equation (3):*

$$\mu_A(x,a,m,b) = \begin{cases} 0 & x \leq a \\ \frac{x-a}{m-a} & a \leq x \leq m \\ 1 & x = m \\ \frac{b-x}{b-m} & m \leq x \leq b \\ 0 & x \geq b \end{cases} \tag{3}$$

and the following conditions Equations (4) and (5):

$$x_1, x_2 \in [a, m] \wedge x_2 > x_1 \Rightarrow \mu_A(x_2) > \mu_A(x_1) \tag{4}$$

$$x_1, x_2 \in [m, b] \wedge x_2 > x_1 \Rightarrow \mu_A(x_2) < \mu_A(x_1) \tag{5}$$

Definition 3. *The support of a TFN—subset of the A set in which all elements have a non-zero membership value in the A set of Equation (6).*

$$S(\tilde{A}) = x : \mu_{\tilde{A}}(x) > 0 = [a, b] \tag{6}$$

Definition 4. *The core of a TFN is a singleton with membership value* 1 *shown in Equation (7).*

$$C(\tilde{A}) = x : \mu_{\tilde{A}}(x) = 1 = m \tag{7}$$

Definition 5. *The fuzzy rule—it is based on the $IF - THEN$, OR, and AND logical connectives, which are used in the reasoning process.*

Definition 6. *The rule base—it includes logical rules defining the relations in the system.*

Definition 7. *The intersection operator (T-norm)—it is a function modeling the AND operation. This operator is described by using properties: boundary Equation (8), monotonicity Equation (9), commutativity Equation (10), associativity Equation (11), for any $a, b, c, d \in [0, 1]$.*

$$T(0,0) = 0, T(a,1) = T(1,a) = a \tag{8}$$

$$T(a,b) < T(c,d) \Leftrightarrow \text{ if } a < c \text{ and } b < d \tag{9}$$

$$T(a,b) = T(b,a) \tag{10}$$

$$T(a, T(b,c)) = T(T(a,b),c) \tag{11}$$

Definition 8. *The S-norm operator or T-conorm is a function modeling the OR operator. It should fulfill the following properties: boundary Equation (12), monotonicity Equation (13), commutativity Equation (14), associativity Equation (15), for any $a, b, c, d \in [0, 1]$.*

$$S(1,1) = 1, S(a,0) = S(0,a) = a \tag{12}$$

$$S(a,b) < S(c,d) \Leftrightarrow \text{ if } \quad a < c \quad \text{ and } \quad b < d \tag{13}$$

$$S(a,b) = S(b,a) \tag{14}$$

$$S(a, S(b,c)) = S(S(a,b),c) \tag{15}$$

2.2. The Comet Method

Many MCDM methods exhibit the rank reversal phenomenon. To see the above point more clearly, suppose that we have set of three alternatives A, B, and C. Suppose that the best variant is A, followed by B, which is followed by C. Next, we suppose that an even worse element replace B, say alternative D. When the new set of variants are ranked collectively and by considering that the criteria have equal weights as before. Sometimes, it turns out that under some decision-making techniques, the best choice may be changed now, and this is known as a rank reversal. It is only of the types of rank reversals. However, the Characteristic Objects Method (COMET) is completely free of this problem [48]. In previous works, the accuracy of the COMET method was verified [43]. The formal notation of the COMET method should be briefly recalled [46,47,49]:

Step 1. The expert defines the dimensionality of the problem by choosing r criteria, $C_1, C_2, \ldots, C_r$. Then, a set of fuzzy numbers is selected for each criterion C_i, e.g., $\{\tilde{C}_{i1}, \tilde{C}_{i2}, \ldots, \tilde{C}_{ic_i}\}$ Equation (16):

$$\begin{array}{c} C_1 = \left\{\tilde{C}_{11}, \tilde{C}_{12}, \ldots, \tilde{C}_{1c_1}\right\} \\ C_2 = \left\{\tilde{C}_{21}, \tilde{C}_{22}, \ldots, \tilde{C}_{2c_1}\right\} \\ \cdots \\ C_r = \left\{\tilde{C}_{r1}, \tilde{C}_{r2}, \ldots, \tilde{C}_{rc_r}\right\} \end{array} \tag{16}$$

where $C_1, C_2, \ldots, C_r$ are the ordinals of the fuzzy numbers for all criteria.

Step 2. The characteristic objects (CO) are determined with the method of the Cartesian product of the triangular fuzzy numbers' cores of all the criteria Equation (17):

$$CO = \langle C(C_1) \times C(C_2) \times \cdots \times C(C_r) \rangle \tag{17}$$

As a result, an ordered set of all CO is obtained Equation (18):

$$\begin{array}{c} CO_1 = \langle C(\tilde{C}_{11}), C(\tilde{C}_{21}), \ldots, C(\tilde{C}_{r1}) \rangle \\ CO_2 = \langle C(\tilde{C}_{11}), C(\tilde{C}_{21}), \ldots, C(\tilde{C}_{r1}) \rangle \\ \cdots \\ CO_t = \langle C(\tilde{C}_{1c_1}), C(\tilde{C}_{2c_2}), \ldots, C(\tilde{C}_{rc_r}) \rangle \end{array} \tag{18}$$

where t is the count of COs and is equal to Equation (19):

$$t = \prod_{i=1}^{r} c_i \tag{19}$$

Step 3. The expert identifies the Matrix of Expert Judgment (MEJ) by pairwise comparison of the COs. The MEJ matrix is shown as Equation (20):

$$MEJ = \begin{pmatrix} \alpha_{11} & \alpha_{12} & \cdots & \alpha_{1t} \\ \alpha_{21} & \alpha_{22} & \cdots & \alpha_{2t} \\ \cdots & \cdots & \cdots & \cdots \\ \alpha_{t1} & \alpha_{t2} & \cdots & \alpha_{tt} \end{pmatrix} \tag{20}$$

where α_{ij} is the result of comparing CO_i and CO_j by the expert. The function f_{exp} denotes the subjective judgment of the selected expert. It depends entirely on the knowledge and experience of the expert. The expert's preferences are presented in the following Equation (21):

$$\alpha_{ij} = \begin{cases} 0.0, f_{exp}(CO_i) < f_{exp}(CO_j) \\ 0.5, f_{exp}(CO_i) = f_{exp}(CO_j) \\ 1.0, f_{exp}(CO_i) > f_{exp}(CO_j) \end{cases} \tag{21}$$

After the MEJ matrix is prepared, a vertical vector of the Summed Judgments (SJ) is obtained as follows Equation (22):

$$SJ_i = \sum_{j=1}^{t} \alpha_{ij} \quad (22)$$

Finally, the values of preference are estimated for each CO. As a result, a vector P is determined, where the i-th row contains the approximate value of preference for CO_i.

Step 4. Each CO and its preference value is changed to a fuzzy rule by using the following Equation (23):

$$IF\ C\left(\tilde{C}_{1i}\right)\ AND\ C\left(\tilde{C}_{2i}\right)\ AND\ \ldots\ THEN\ P_i \quad (23)$$

In this way, a complete fuzzy rule base is obtained.

Step 5. Each decision variant is shown as a set of crisp numbers, e.g., $A_i = \{a_{i1}, a_{i2}, a_{ri}\}$. This set corresponds to the criteria $C_1, C_2, \ldots, C_r$. The preference of the i-th alternative is calculated by using Mamdani's fuzzy inference method. The constant rule base guarantees that the received results are unambiguous. The whole process of the COMET method is presented in Figure 1.

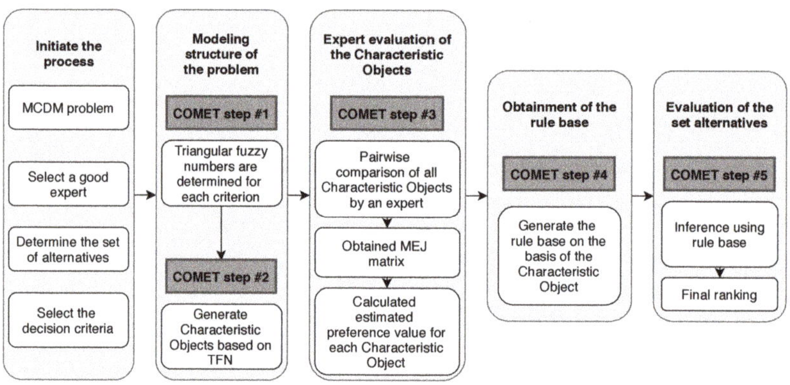

Figure 1. The flow chart of the COMET procedure [44].

2.3. Hill-Climbing

Hill-Climbing (HC) is a mathematical method used for optimization purposes, which belongs to the field of local search methods. HC technique starts with generating an initial state, i.e., an initial solution. Local ekstremum is searched in the neighborhood of the current state, where the first accepted value of the current state is the initial state value. Solution c is called local optimization, where the N(c) neighborhood does not have a better solution, and it is not the best solution in the whole set of solutions [50]. In optimizing with a hill-climbing algorithm it is not possible to determine whether the local extreme found is a global one. The process of optimization using a hill-climbing algorithm can be presented as follows:

Step 1. *Initialization of the hill-climbing algorithm.* Randomly create one candidate solution $\vec{c_0}$, depending on the length $\vec{c}$.

Step 2. *Evaluation.* Create a fitness function $f(\vec{c_0})$ to evaluate the current solution. The first generation is as follows:

$$\begin{gathered} \vec{c}_* = \vec{c}_0 \\ f_{\max} = f\left(\vec{c}_*\right) \end{gathered} \quad (24)$$

Step 3. *Mutation.* Mutate the current solution $\vec{c}_*$ one by one and evaluate the new solution $\vec{c}_i$.

Step 4. *Selection.* If the value of the fitness function for the new solution is better than for the current solution, replace as follows:

$$f(\bar{c}_i) > f(\bar{c}_*) \iff \vec{c}_* = \vec{c}_i \tag{25}$$

Step 5. *Termination.* When there is no improvement in fitness function after a few generations The pseudocode of the hill-climbing method is presented by using the Algorithm 1.

Algorithm 1: Hill-climbing [51].

Result: Find the optimum function
i = initial solution;
while $f(s) \leq f(i)$ *for all* $s \in Neighbours(i)$ **do**
  $Generatesans \in Neighbours(i)$
  if $fitness(s) > fitness(i)$ **then**
    Replace s with the i;
end

2.4. Simulated Annealing

Simulated annealing is a stochastic method that has a mechanism to avoid getting stuck in local extremes. The mechanism for further searching the global extremes allows you to accept a worse solution to get out of the local extremes and explore the entire problem area [52]. The simulated annealing method is presented as Algorithm 2 and may look like this:

Step 1. *Initialization of the simulated annealing method.* Select the initial temperature value T_0 and randomly create one feasible candidate solution $\vec{c_0}$. Select a parameter $r < 1$ and the maximum number of iterations L. Let the iteration counter be initiated as $K = 0$ and a further counter $k = 1$.

Step 2. *Evaluation.* Create a fitness function $f(\vec{c_0})$ to evaluate the current solution. The first generation is as follows:

$$\begin{aligned} \vec{c}_* &= \vec{c}_0 \\ f_{\max} &= f(\vec{c}_*) \end{aligned} \tag{26}$$

Step 3. *Mutation.* Randomly choose a new solution $\vec{c_i}$ in the neighborhood of the current solution $\vec{c_*}$

Step 4. *Selection.* If the value of the fitness function for the new solution is better than for the current solution, replace as follows:

$$f(\bar{c}_i) > f(\bar{c}_*) \Rightarrow \bar{c}_* = \bar{c}_i \tag{27}$$

Otherwise, calculate the difference between the value of the fitness function of the new solution ΔE and the current solution, followed by the probability density function $P(\Delta E)$ as follows:

$$\begin{aligned} \Delta E &= f(\vec{c_i}) - f(\vec{c_*}) \\ P(\Delta E) &= \frac{1}{1 + \exp(\frac{\Delta E}{T_k})} \end{aligned} \tag{28}$$

Generate a random number z uniformly distributed in [0,1]. If $z < P(\Delta E)$, then the new solution $\vec{c_i}$ becomes the current solution $\vec{c_*}$.

Step 5. *Increasing the temperature* If $k = L$, the iteration counter is increased $K = K + 1$ and the counter is reset $k = 1$. A new temperature T_K value is calculated following the Equation (29).

$$T_K = rT_{K-1} \tag{29}$$

Otherwise $k = k + 1$ and return to the mutation.

Step 6. *Termination* If $k > L$ and one of the stop criteria is satisfied, terminate the algorithm and return the current solution $\vec{c_*}$.

Algorithm 2: Simulated annealing.

```
Result: Find the optimum function
i = initial solution;
k = 0;
while k < k_max do
    T ← temperature((k + 1)/k_max)
    Choose a random neighbor, s ← neighbour(i);
    if P(E(i), E(s), T) ≥ random(0, 1) then
        i ← s;
    k++;
end
```

2.5. Particle Swarm Optimization

Particle swarm optimization is a metaheuristic technique that was designed in 1995 by Kennedy and Eberhart [53]. The original idea of PSO was to simulate a simplified social system. PSO is a population-based method in which individuals are called particles and a population is called a swarm. Each particle in the swarm is a possible solution to a given optimization problem. All individuals in the swarm move towards their own best solution and towards the best global solution in the swarm [54,55]. The overall performance of the particle swarm optimization can be presented as follows:

Step 1. *Initialization of the PSO method.* Set population size S. Choose cognitive ϕ_p and social ϕ_g coefficients. Then initiate the swarm and randomly select the position x_i and velocity v_i for each particle in the swarm. Set the maximum number of iterations k_{max} and initialize the iteration counter $k = 0$.

Step 2. *Evaluation.* In the first generation, for each particle from the swarm, the position x_i becomes its best position p_i. Select the particle that has the best position in the swarm from the whole population and assigns it the best position in the swarm $g \leftarrow p_i$.

Step 3. *Mutation.* For each particle, some vectors are randomized from a uniform distribution as follows:

$$\vec{r}_p, \vec{r}_g \in U[0, 1] \tag{30}$$

The particle velocity $\vec{v}_i$ and the position $\vec{x}_i$ of the particle are then updated. This is explained by Equation (31).

$$\begin{gathered} \vec{v}_i = \omega \vec{v}_i + \phi_p \vec{r}_p \left(\vec{p}_i - \vec{x}_i\right) + \phi_g \vec{r}_g \left(\vec{g}_d - \vec{x}_i\right) \\ \vec{x}_i = \vec{x}_i + \vec{v}_i \end{gathered} \tag{31}$$

Step 4. *Selection.* Compare the evaluation of the position of the particle and the evaluation of its best position. The evaluation is provided by the fitness function. If it is better, the position of the particle becomes the best position of the particle. Compare it with an evaluation of the best position in the swarm. Replace the best position in the swarm when the evaluation of the best position of the particle is better.

Step 5. *Termination* The algorithm terminates when the iteration counter reaches a higher value than the number of maximum iterations. One iteration cycle starts from mutation to selection.

The pseudocode of the particle swarm optimization is presented by using the Algorithm 3.

Algorithm 3: Particle swarm optimization.

Result: Find the optimum function
foreach *particle* $i = 1, \cdots, S$ **do**
  Initialize the particle's position with a uniformly distributed random vector: $x_i = U(b_{lo}, b_{up})$
  Initialize the particle's best known position to its initial position: $p_i \leftarrow x_i$
  if $f(p_i) < f(g)$ **then**
    Update the swarm's best known position: $g \leftarrow p_i$
  Initialize the particle's velocity: $v_i = U(-|b_{up} - b_{lo}|, |b_{up} - b_{lo}|)$
end
while $k < k_{max}$ **do**
  foreach *particle* $i = 1, \cdots, S$ **do**
    foreach *dimension* $d = 1, \cdots, n$ **do**
      Select random numbers: $r_p, r_g = U(0,1)$
      Update the particle's velocity: $v_{i,d} \leftarrow \omega v_{i,d} + \phi_p r_p (p_{i,d} - x_{i,d}) + \phi_g r_g (g_d - x_{i,d})$
    end
    Update the particle's position: $x_i \leftarrow x_i + v_i$
    if $f(x_i) < f(p_i)$ **then**
      Update the particle's position: $p_i \leftarrow x_i$
      if $f(p_i) < f(g)$ **then**
        Update the swarm's best known position: $g \leftarrow p_i$
  end
  k++;
end

2.6. Similarity Coefficient

The similarity coefficients of the rankings allow us to compare the two indicated order. It is important to choose such coefficients that work well in the decision-making field. The paper uses three such coefficients, i.e., Spearman correlation coefficient Equation (32), Spearman weighted correlation coefficient Equation (33) and WS similarity coefficients Equation (34) [56].

$$r_s = 1 - \frac{6 \cdot \sum_{i=1}^{n} d_i^2}{n \cdot (n^2 - 1)} \tag{32}$$

$$r_w = 1 - \frac{6 \cdot \sum_{i=1}^{n} (x_i - y_i)^2 ((N - x_i + 1) + (N - y_i + 1))}{n \cdot (n^3 + n^2 - n - 1)} \tag{33}$$

$$WS = 1 - \sum_{i=1}^{n} \left(2^{-x_i} \frac{|x_i - y_i|}{max\{|x_i - 1|, |x_i - N|\}} \right) \tag{34}$$

3. Results and Discussion of The Research

The goal of the experiment is to compare the quality of three stochastic methods in searching for optimal preference values of characteristic objects at different initial states. The initial state in the study determines the initial preference values of characteristic objects. The selected methods for the experiment are the hill-climbing algorithm, the simulated annealing method, and particle swarm optimization. Several particles in the PSO method have been set to 20, while parameters ϕ_p, ϕ_g, ω have been given values of 0.5, 0.3, and 0.9, respectively. The maximum number of iterations in each method has been set to 1000. Preference of characteristic objects has been determined using a set of alternatives. A set of alternatives determined the preference of characteristic objects.

The optimization process consisted in obtaining the smallest difference in the absolute value of the sum of alternatives preferences calculated with reference alternatives. The calculated alternatives are those whose preference values were calculated using a model defined using characteristic objects whose preference is a candidate for the solution. For this purpose, the objective function has been defined by Equation (35).

$$f(x) = \sum_{i=1}^{N} |P(A_i) - \hat{P}(A_i)| \tag{35}$$

where $P(A_i)$ means calculated alternatives and $\hat{P}(A_i)$ means reference alternatives.

The experiment was conducted for 200 sets of decision variants consisting of 5, 10, 15, 20, 25 alternatives. The preference of decision variants forming the set intended for the optimization process was selected randomly or calculated using a generated random SJ vector. The criteria by which characteristic objects were defined took static values [0, 0.5, 1] and dynamic values depending on the set of alternatives. In Equation (36) this is given.

$$\begin{aligned} C_1 &= \{\min_i\{a_{i1}\}, \frac{\sum_{i=1}^{N} a_{i1}}{N}, \max_i\{a_{i1}\}\} \\ C_2 &= \{\min_i\{a_{i2}\}, \frac{\sum_{i=1}^{N} a_{i2}}{N}, \max_i\{a_{i2}\}\} \end{aligned} \tag{36}$$

The study was conducted with four initial state variants. The characteristic objects assumed a preference value equal to 0, 0.5, 1, or a random value.

3.1. Impact of the Initial Conditions

Figure 2 presents heat maps with nuclear density estimators for a hill-climbing algorithm for a static variant of criteria with a non-existent model, i.e., one in which the preferences of the alternatives were selected randomly. The charts show the solutions found about the number of iterations for the given number of alternatives in the set and the initial state variants.

For an increasing number of alternatives for characteristic objects assuming the value of preference 0 at the beginning, one can see an increase in the value of found solutions. The accuracy of the five alternatives in the set is high because the concentration of the smallest found values of the fitness function is close to the value of 0. The largest number of solutions found was between 300 and 500 iterations. With more alternatives, the number of iterations in which solutions have been found slightly increases. However, the values of the solutions were found to increase significantly. For the ten alternatives, the highest concentration of the smallest found fitness values oscillates between [1, 1.5]. For fifteen alternatives [2, 2.35], twenty alternatives [2.9, 3.1], and for twenty five alternatives [4.5, 5].

The initial state in which the preference of characteristic objects is set to 0.5 does not reach as large values in the range of the number of iterations needed to find a solution as in the initial state for the value 0. This range is [175, 280]. The clusters of solutions found about their costs are slightly different from the initial state for the value 0.

In the initial state, where characteristic objects take preference values equal to 1, the distribution of found solutions is much larger than in the case where the initial state value is 0.5. The most massive clusters of found solutions occur between iterations 390 and 500.

For a randomly selected preference value of the characteristic objects, the number of iterations needed to find a solution is much smaller than when the initial state takes a preference value of 0 or 1. However, compared with the initial state where the characteristic objects take a preference value of 0.5, the initial state with a random value is worse due to the density nuclear estimator. It shows that the method needed more iteration when estimating some of the smallest fitness function values.

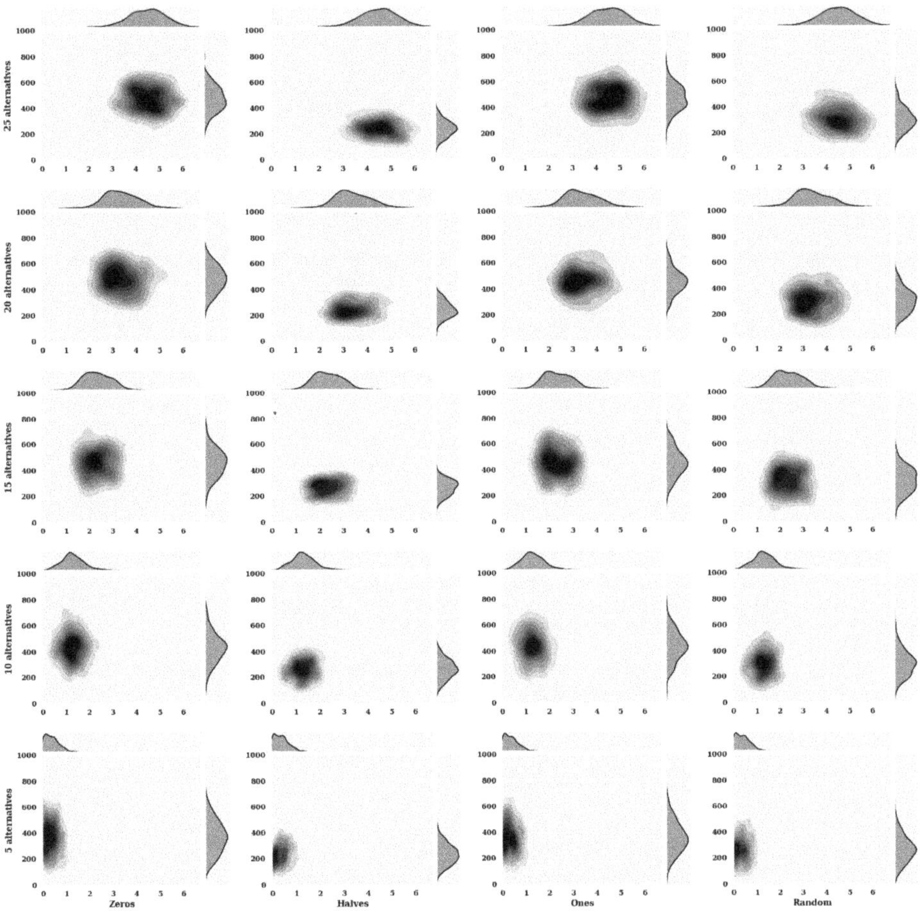

Figure 2. The value of the target function depending on the number of iterations, the number of alternatives, and initial conditions (method: HC; criteria variant: static; model: not existing).

Thermal maps, together with nuclear density estimators for a hill-climbing algorithm for a dynamic variant of criteria with a non-existent model, are presented using Figure 3. Solutions found about the number of iterations for the given number of alternatives in the set and variants of the initial state are presented in the charts.

For characteristic objects taking at the beginning the value of preference 0 for an increasing number of alternatives, you can see an increase in the value of found solutions. For a set consisting of five alternatives, the concentration of the smallest found values of the fitness function is close to 0, which means that the accuracy is high. However, as the number of alternatives increases, the accuracy decreases. For the ten alternatives, the highest concentration of the smallest found fitness values is in the range [1.5, 1.6]. For fifteen alternatives [1.9, 2.2], twenty alternatives [3.1] and for twenty five alternatives [4.1, 4.9]. Most of the solutions found for 10, 15, 20, 25 alternatives were between 400 and 500 iterations. The exception is a set consisting of five alternatives in which most of the solutions were found before the 400 iterations. With more alternatives, the number of iterations in which solutions were found slightly increases. The value of the solutions found increases significantly.

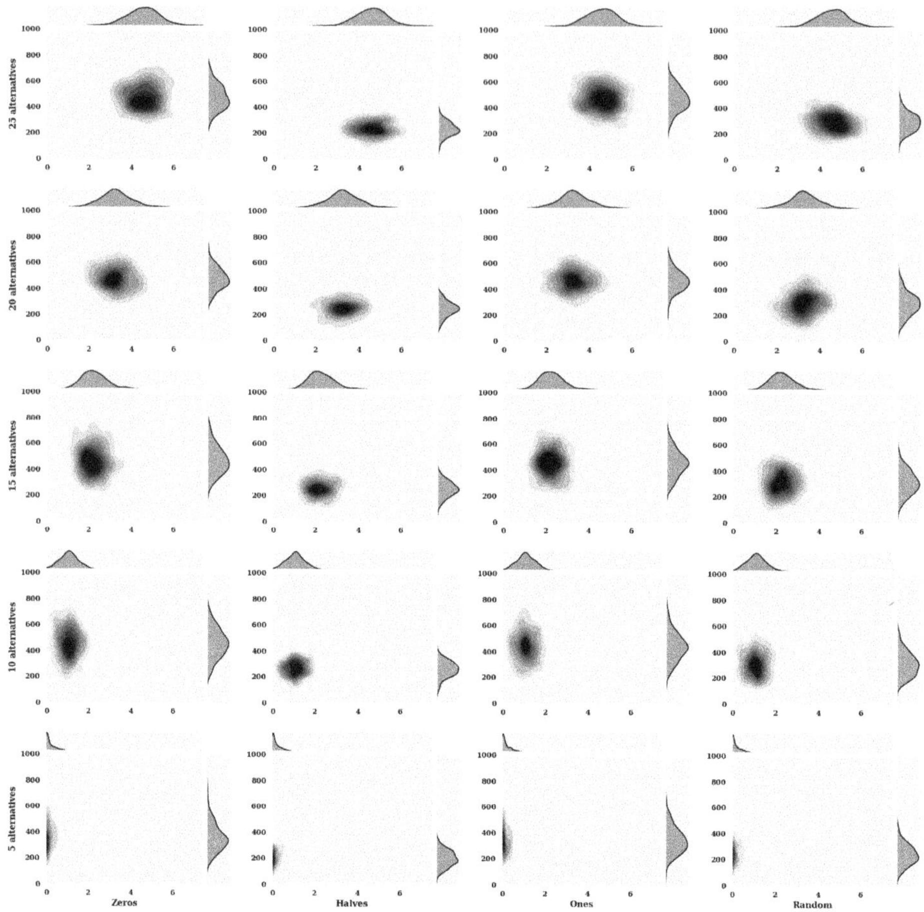

Figure 3. The value of the target function depending on the number of iterations, the number of alternatives, and initial conditions (method: HC; criteria variant: dynamic; model: not existing).

The initial state where the preference of the characteristic objects is set to 0.5 does not reach as high values in the range of the number of iterations needed to find a solution as the preference of the characteristic objects is 0. This range is approximately [190, 280]. The clusters of solutions found about their values differ slightly from the initial state for 0.

In the initial state where the characteristic objects take values of 1, the distribution of solutions found is higher than for the initial state value of 0.5. The most significant clusters of solutions found occur between iterations 400 and 500. Compared with the initial state where the characteristic objects take a preference value of 0, the differences are slight.

The number of iterations needed to find a solution for a randomly selected preference value of the characteristic objects is much smaller than when the initial state takes a preference value of 0 or 1. However, compared with the initial state where the characteristic objects take a preference value of 0.5, the initial state with a random value is worse due to the nuclear density estimator. It shows that the method needed more iteration when estimating some of the smallest fitness function values.

Figure 4 shows thermal maps together with nuclear density estimators for a hill-climbing algorithm for a static variant of criteria with an existing model. A current model means a model in which the preferences of alternatives have been calculated using a randomly selected vector SJ. The individual charts show the solutions found concerning iteration numbers for the given alternatives and initial state variants.

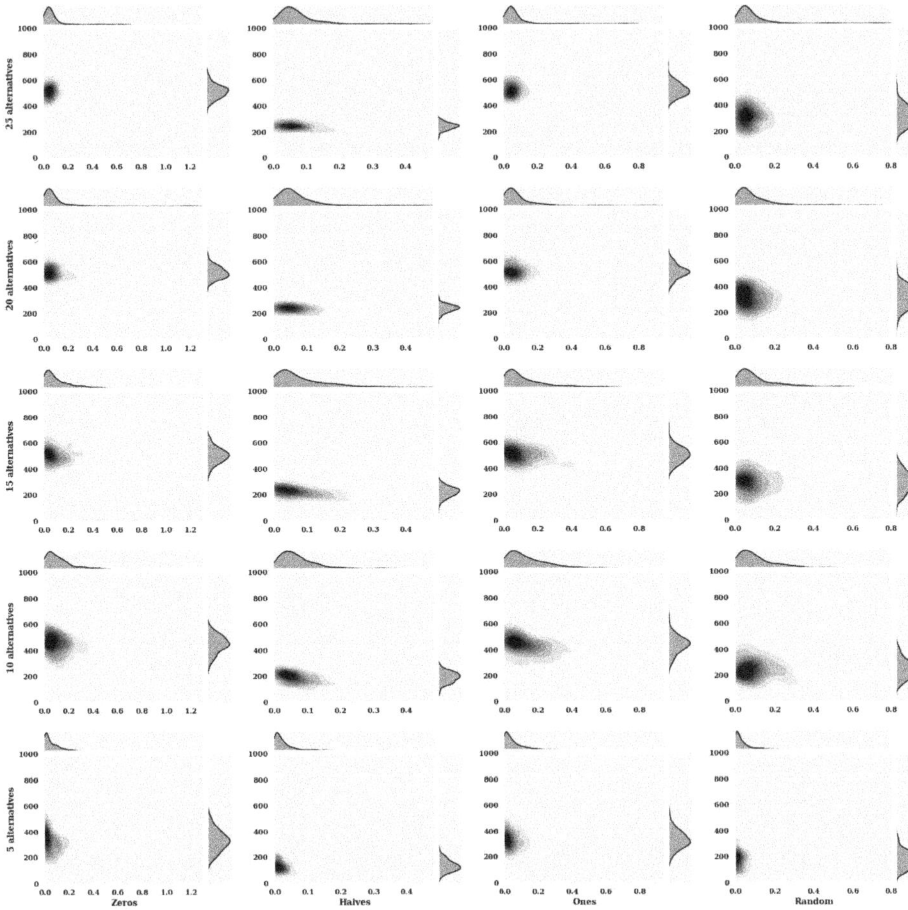

Figure 4. The value of the target function depending on the number of iterations, the number of alternatives, and initial conditions (method: HC; criteria variant: static; model: existing).

For a start preference of characteristic objects of 0, the change in the value of found solutions with an increase in the number of alternatives is not substantial. The hill-climbing algorithm usually finds a solution between 400 and 600 iterations. However, the solutions found are in the range [0, 0.2], which indicates very high accuracy.

However, a better solution seems to be the starting value of the preference of characteristic objects of 0.5. This variant needs less iteration than finding solutions, and their cost is lower.

However, this cannot be said about the variant where the characteristic objects take a preference value of 1. The distribution of the values of the solutions found is much greater than in the case of the start preference value of 0. An example of this is ten alternatives where the cloud is more extensive when the start state has a value of 1 than when it takes the amount of 0.

In the initial state, where characteristic objects take random preference values, the number of iterations needed to find a solution is much smaller than for the initial state values of 0 and 1. However, the costs of solutions are much higher than for the initial state with a value of 0.5. The increase in the number of iterations compared to the number of alternatives is not so large.

Figure 5 shows thermal maps together with nuclear density estimators for a hill-climbing algorithm for a dynamic variant of criteria with an existing model. The individual charts show the solutions found concerning iteration numbers for the given alternatives and initial state variants.

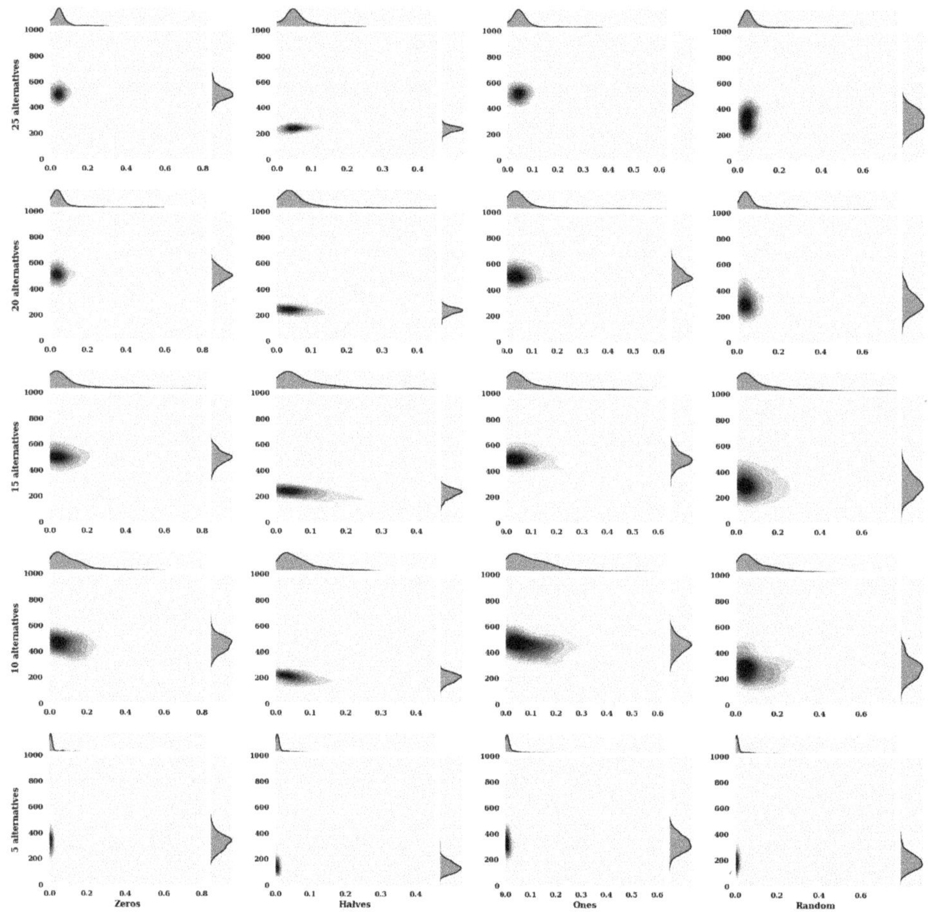

Figure 5. The value of the target function depending on the number of iterations, the number of alternatives, and initial conditions (method: HC; criteria variant: dynamic; model: existing).

In the case of a starting preference of characteristic objects of 0, the change in the value of found solutions decreases with the number of alternatives. The hill-climbing algorithm usually finds a solution between 400 and 600 iterations. Solutions found for five alternatives are in the range [0, 0.05], for ten and fifteen [0, 0.2], for twenty and twenty-five [0, 0.1], which indicates very high accuracy.

However, the starting value of the characteristic object preference of 0.5 seems to be a better solution. This option needs less iteration than finding solutions, and its cost is lower.

The variant in which the characteristic objects take the initial preference value of 1 needs more iterations to find solutions than for the start value of 0.5. The distribution of found solutions is much higher than for the start value of 0. An example is ten alternatives where the cloud is more extensive when the start state has the benefit of 1 than when it takes the amount of 0.

In the initial state where the characteristic objects take random preference values, the number of iterations needed to find a solution is much smaller than for the initial state values of 0 and 1. However, the costs of solutions are much higher than for the initial state with a value of 0.5. The increase in the number of iterations compared to the number of alternatives is not so large.

Figure 6 presents thermal maps with density nuclear estimators for simulated annealing method for a static variant of criteria with a non-existent model. The charts show the solutions found about the number of iterations for the given number of alternatives in the set and the initial state variants.

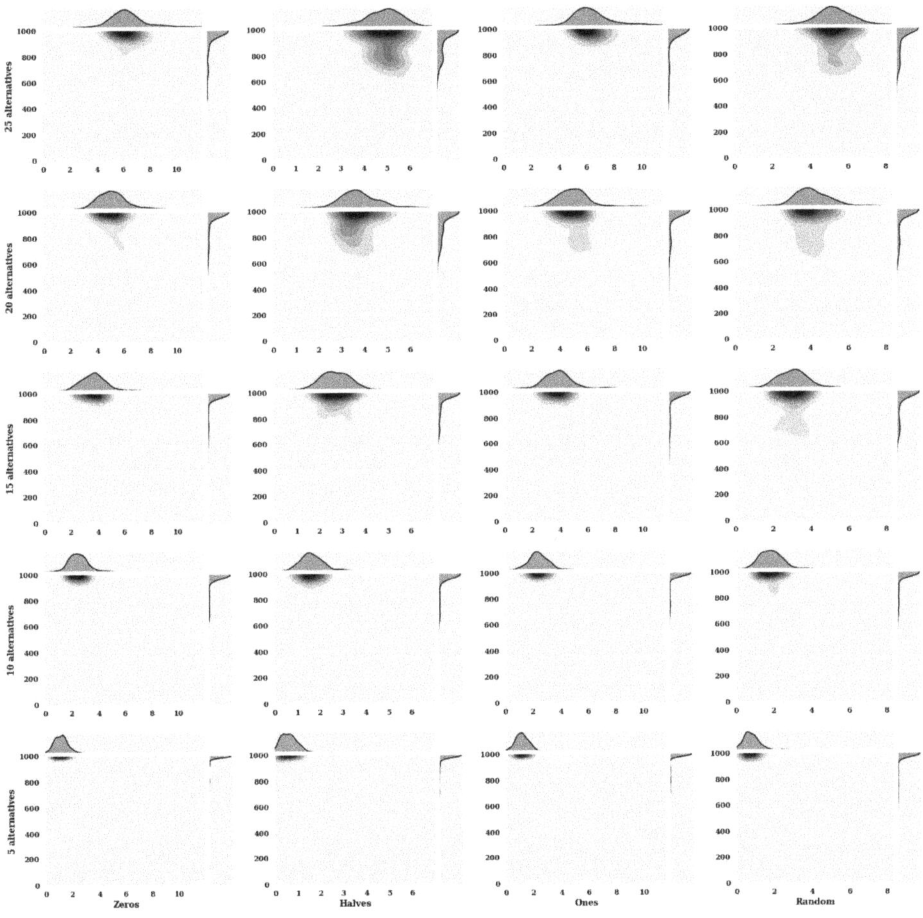

Figure 6. The value of the target function depending on the number of iterations, the number of alternatives, and initial conditions (method: SA; criteria variant: static; model: not existing).

For an increasing number of alternatives for characteristic objects assuming the value of preference 0 at the beginning, one can see an increase in the value of found solutions. The accuracy of the five alternatives in the set is high because the concentration of the smallest found values of the fitness function is close to 0. Most of the solutions were found in 1000 iterations. With more alternatives, the number of iterations in which solutions were found slightly decreases. However, the values of the solutions were found to increase significantly. For the ten alternatives, the largest concentration of the smallest found fitness values is in the range [2, 3.1]. For fifteen alternatives [3, 4.1], twenty alternatives [4.05, 5.9], and for twenty-five alternatives [5.8, 6.2].

The initial state where the preference of the characteristic objects is set to 0.5 reaches as high values in the range of the number of iterations needed to find a solution as for the initial state for value 0. The clusters of found solution values differ significantly from the initial state for value 0 because they are smaller.

In the initial state, where characteristic objects take preference values equal to 1, the distribution of solutions found is much larger than in the case where the initial state value is 0.5. However, the number of iterations needed to find an answer is the same.

For a randomly selected preference value of the characteristic objects, the values of the solutions found are much smaller than when the initial state takes the value 0 or 1. However, compared with the initial state where the characteristic objects take the preference value 0.5, the initial state with a random value is worse due to the nuclear density estimator. It shows that the method has found smaller fitness function values.

Thermal maps, together with nuclear density estimators for the simulated annealing method for a dynamic variant of criteria with a non-existent model, are presented using Figure 7. The solutions found about the number of iterations for the given number of alternatives in the set and variants of the initial state are presented in the charts.

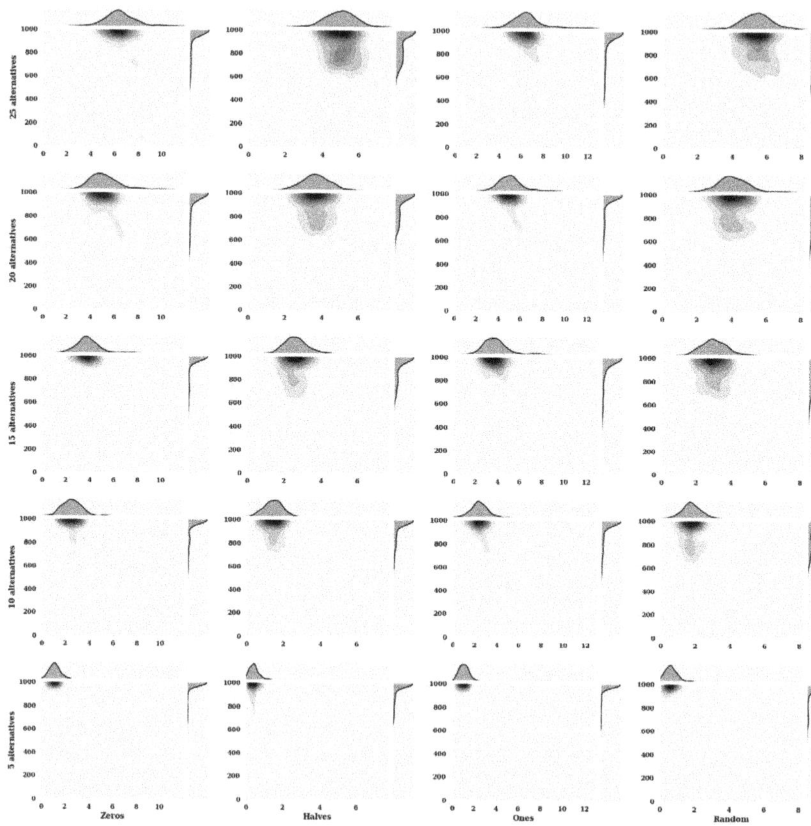

Figure 7. The value of the target function depending on the number of iterations, the number of alternatives, and initial conditions (method: SA; criteria variant: dynamic; model: not existing).

For characteristic objects assuming at the beginning, the value of preference 0 for an increasing number of alternatives, an increase in the amount of found solutions can be observed. For a set consisting of five choices, the concentration of the smallest found importance of the fitness function is close to 0, which means that the accuracy is high. However, as the number of alternatives increases, the efficiency decreases. For the ten alternatives, the highest concentration of the smallest found fitness values is in the range [2, 3], for the fifteen options [3.8, 4], for twenty alternatives [4.1, 5.8], and the twenty-five alternatives [5.95, 6.8]. The most significant number of solutions found for all the considered number of other options was between 980 and 1000 iterations. With a more substantial amount of alternatives, the number of iterations in which solutions were found slightly decreases.

The initial state in which the preference of characteristic objects is set to 0.5 does not need as large numbers of iterations to find a solution as in the case of the preference of characteristic objects of 0. The values of found solutions for a given amount of alternatives are increasing, but they are not as large as for the initial state with value 0.

In the initial state, where characteristic objects take preference values equal to 1, the distribution of found solutions is higher than in the case where the value of the initial state is 0.5. A large concentration of found solutions occurs between the iteration 985 and 1000. Compared to the initial state where characteristic objects take preference values equal to 0, the differences are insignificant.

The iteration numbers needed to find a solution for a randomly selected preference value of the characteristic objects are approximately the same as when the initial state takes the value 0, 0.5, or 1. However, the values of the solutions found are much smaller than when the initial state takes the value 0 or 1. Compared to the initial state where the characteristic objects take the preference value 0.5, the initial state with a random value is worse due to the nuclear density estimator. It shows that the method has found smaller fitness function values.

Figure 8 shows thermal maps together with nuclear density estimators for the simulated annealing method for a static variant of criteria with an existing model. Individual charts show solutions found against iteration numbers for given alternatives and initial state variants.

For a starting preference of characteristic objects of 0, the value of found solutions increases with the number of alternatives. The simulated annealing method usually finds solutions between 990 and 1000 iterations. The accuracy is high for five alternatives because the solution values found are less than 1. However, the efficiency decreases as the number of alternatives increases, e.g., for 25 alternatives numbers, several solutions reach amounts greater than 4.

A better solution seems to be the starting value of the characteristic object preference of 0.5. The increase of the smallest found values of the fitness function is not as big as in the case of a starting state with a value of 0. The accuracy is also very high because, for all considered numbers of alternatives, most of the solution values are in the range [0, 1].

This cannot be said about the variant, where the characteristic objects take the preference value of 1. The distribution of the found solution values is much larger than in the case of the starter preference value of 0.5. An example is the 25 alternatives, where the solution values are in the range [2.1, 4] in case the starter state takes the amount of 1, while for the starter state with the cost of 0.5 they are in the range [0, 1].

The number of iterations needed to find a solution for a randomly selected preference value of the characteristic objects is approximately the same as when the initial state takes the amount 0, 0.5, or 1. However, the amounts of solutions found are much smaller than when the initial state takes the value 0 or 1. Compared to the initial state where the characteristic objects take the preference value 0.5, the initial state with a random value is worse due to the nuclear density estimator. It shows that the method has found smaller fitness function values.

Figure 9 shows thermal maps together with nuclear density estimators for the simulated annealing method for a dynamic variant of criteria with an existing model. Individual charts show solutions for a given number of alternatives and initial parameters.

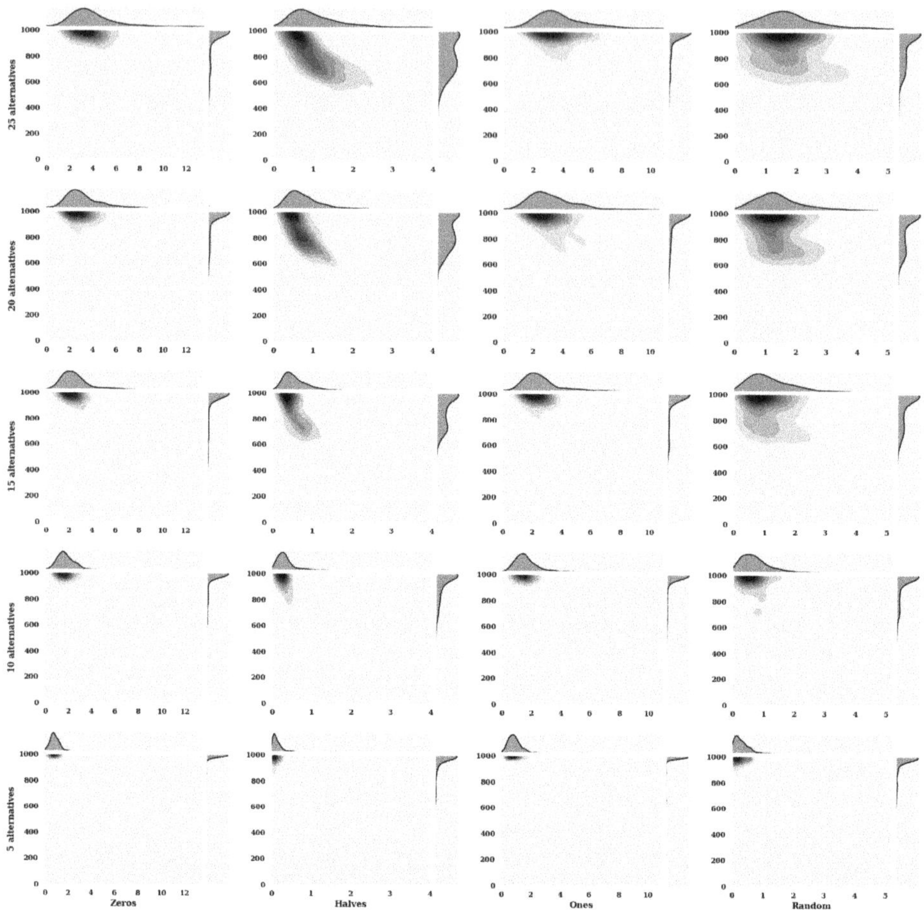

Figure 8. The value of the target function depending on the number of iterations, the number of alternatives, and initial conditions (method: SA; criteria variant: static; model: existing).

For a starting preference of characteristic objects of 0, the values of found solutions increase with the number of alternatives. The simulated annealing method usually gets final solutions between 900 and 1000 iterations. Solutions found for five alternatives are in the range [0.2, 1.4], for ten [0.8, 2.1], for fifteen [1.85, 2.8], for twenty and twenty-five [2.2, 3.4]. This indicates a decrease in accuracy as the number of alternatives increases.

A better solution seems to be the starting value of characteristic objects' preferences amounting to 0.5. This variant, with the increase in the number of alternatives, needs less iteration to find solutions, and its value is lower compared to the initial state with the amount of 0. A variant in which the characteristic objects take an initial preference value of 1 needs more iterations to find solutions than for a start value of 0.5. The distribution of the costs of solutions found is the same as for a start value of 0.

In the initial state where the characteristic objects take random preference values, the number of iterations needed to find a solution is much smaller than for the initial state values of 0 and 1. However, the costs of solutions are much higher than for the initial state of 0.5. The increase of iterations compared to the number of alternatives is not significant.

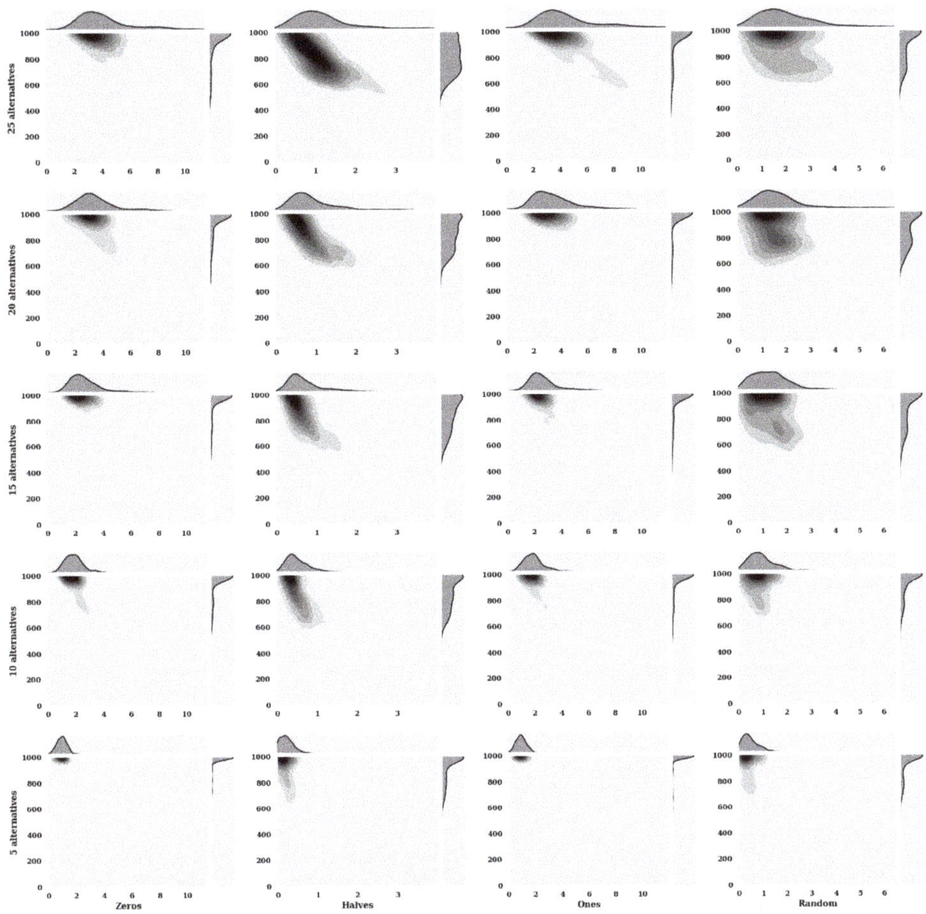

Figure 9. The value of the target function depending on the number of iterations, the number of alternatives, and initial conditions (method: SA; criteria variant: dynamic; model: existing).

Figure 10 shows thermal maps with nuclear density estimators for particle swarm optimization for the static variant of criteria with the non-existent model. The charts show the solutions found about the number of iterations for the given number of alternatives in the set and the initial state variants.

For the increasing number of alternatives for characteristic objects assuming the value of preference 0 at the beginning, one can see an increase in the value of found solutions. The accuracy of the five alternatives in the set is high because the concentration of the smallest found values of the fitness function is in the range [0, 1]. The number of iterations increases with the number of alternatives in the set and the value of the solutions found. For the ten alternatives, the largest concentration of the smallest found fitness values is in the range [1, 1.9]. For fifteen alternatives [2, 3.15], twenty alternatives [2.95, 4], and for twenty five alternatives [4, 5.4].

The initial state where the preference of the characteristic objects is set to 0.5 reaches as high values in the range of the number of iterations needed to find a solution as for the initial state for value 0. The clusters of found solution values differ significantly from the initial state for value 0 because the solution values are smaller.

In the initial state, where characteristic objects take preference values equal to 1, the distribution of solutions found is slightly different from the case where the initial state value is 0.5. However, the number of iterations needed to find a solution, as the number of alternatives increases is smaller.

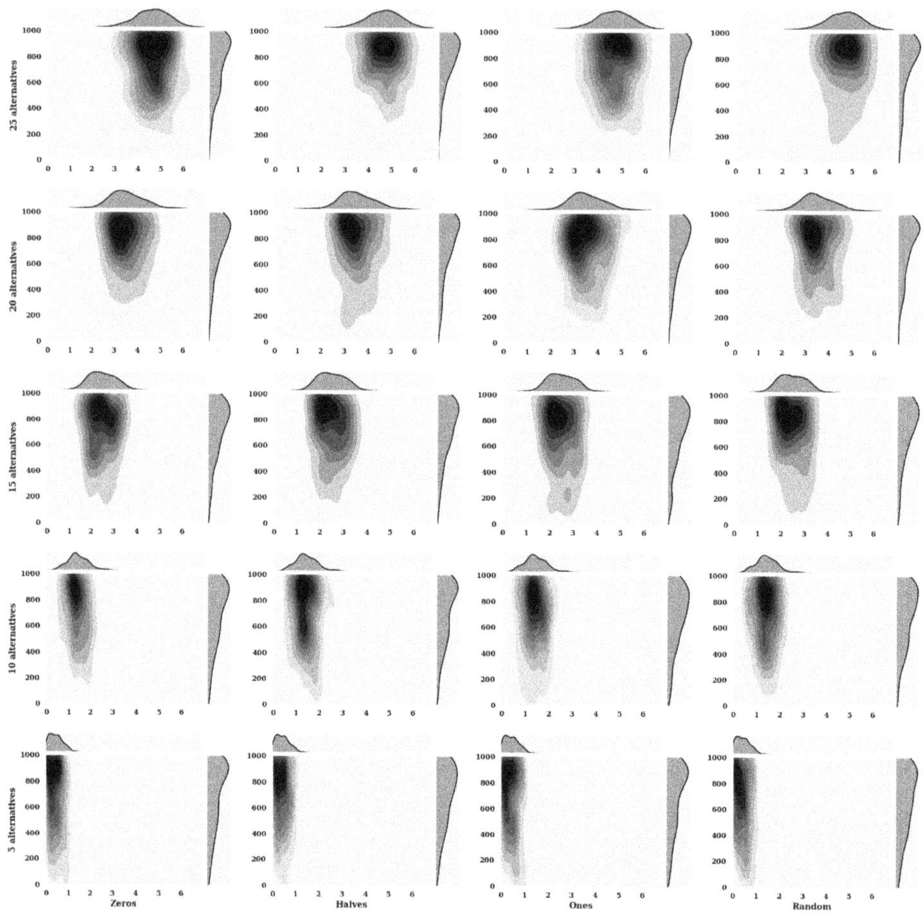

Figure 10. The value of the target function depending on the number of iterations, the number of alternatives, and initial conditions (method: PSO; criteria variant: static; model: not existing).

For a randomly selected preference value of characteristic objects, the number of iterations needed to find solutions and the costs of solutions increase with the number of alternatives. An example is a graph for twenty-five alternatives where a minority of solutions were found in 400 iterations, which cannot be said about the chart for five alternatives.

Thermal maps, together with nuclear density estimators for particle swarm optimization for a dynamic variant of criteria with a non-existent model, are presented in Figure 11. Solutions found about the number of iterations for the given number of alternatives in the set and variants of the initial state are presented on the charts.

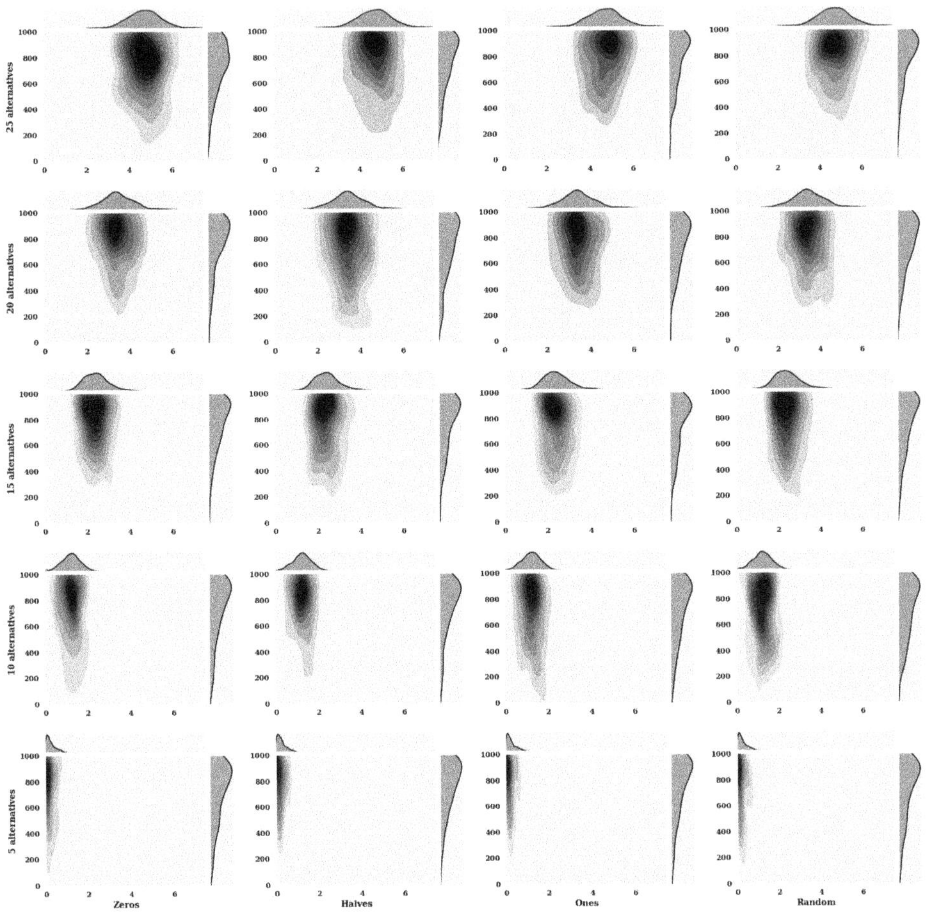

Figure 11. The value of the target function depending on the number of iterations, the number of alternatives, and initial conditions (method: PSO; criteria variant: dynamic; model: not existing).

For characteristic objects assuming at the beginning, the value of preference 0 for an increasing number of alternatives, an increase in the value of found solutions can be observed. For a set consisting of five alternatives, the concentration of the smallest found values of the fitness function is close to 0, which means that the accuracy is high. However, as the number of alternatives increases, the accuracy decreases. For the ten alternatives, the highest concentration of the smallest fitness values found is in the range [1, 1.4].For the fifteen alternatives [1.9, 2.9], twenty alternatives [3.1, 3.85] and for the twenty-five alternatives [4.05, 5.1]. The largest number of solutions found for all the considered number of alternatives was between 800 and 1000 iterations. With a larger number of alternatives, the number of iterations in which solutions have been found increases.

The initial state in which the preference of characteristic objects is set to 0.5 for ten alternatives needs smaller numbers of iterations to find a solution than the initial state of 0.

In other cases, there are no statistically significant differences.

Figure 12 shows thermal maps together with nuclear density estimators for particle swarm optimization for a static variant of criteria with an existing model. The individual charts show the solutions found for iteration numbers for the given alternatives and initial state variants.

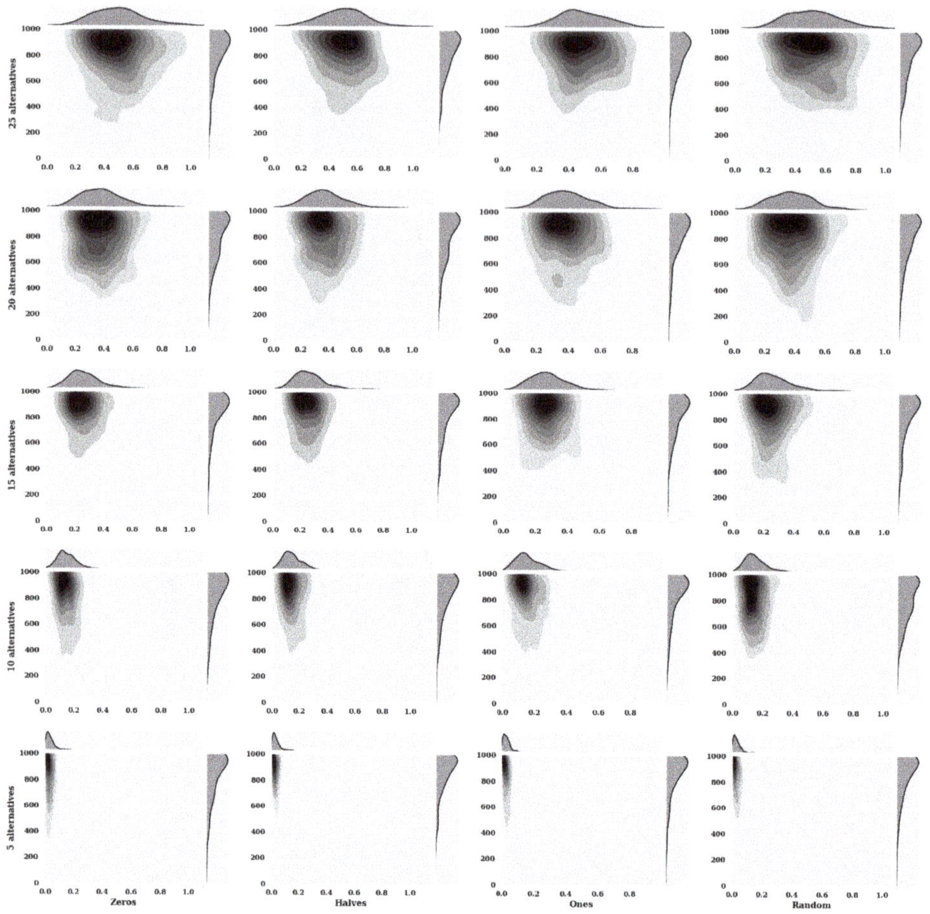

Figure 12. The value of the target function depending on the number of iterations, the number of alternatives, and initial conditions (method: PSO; criteria variant: static; model: existing).

For a starting preference of characteristic objects of 0, the values of found solutions increase with the number of alternatives. Particle swarm optimization usually finds solutions between 600 and 1000 iterations. The accuracy is very high for all considered alternatives numbers because all solution values are less than 1.

A variant where the start value of the characteristic object preference is 0.5 performs worse for five alternatives than the start value of 0. The number of iterations that this variant achieves for the solution values found is much higher.

The variants in which the characteristic objects take the initial preference value of 1 and random are missing statistically significant differences.

Figure 13 shows thermal maps together with nuclear density estimators for particle swarm optimization for a dynamic variant of criteria with an existing model. The individual charts show the solutions found for iteration numbers for the given alternatives and initial state variants.

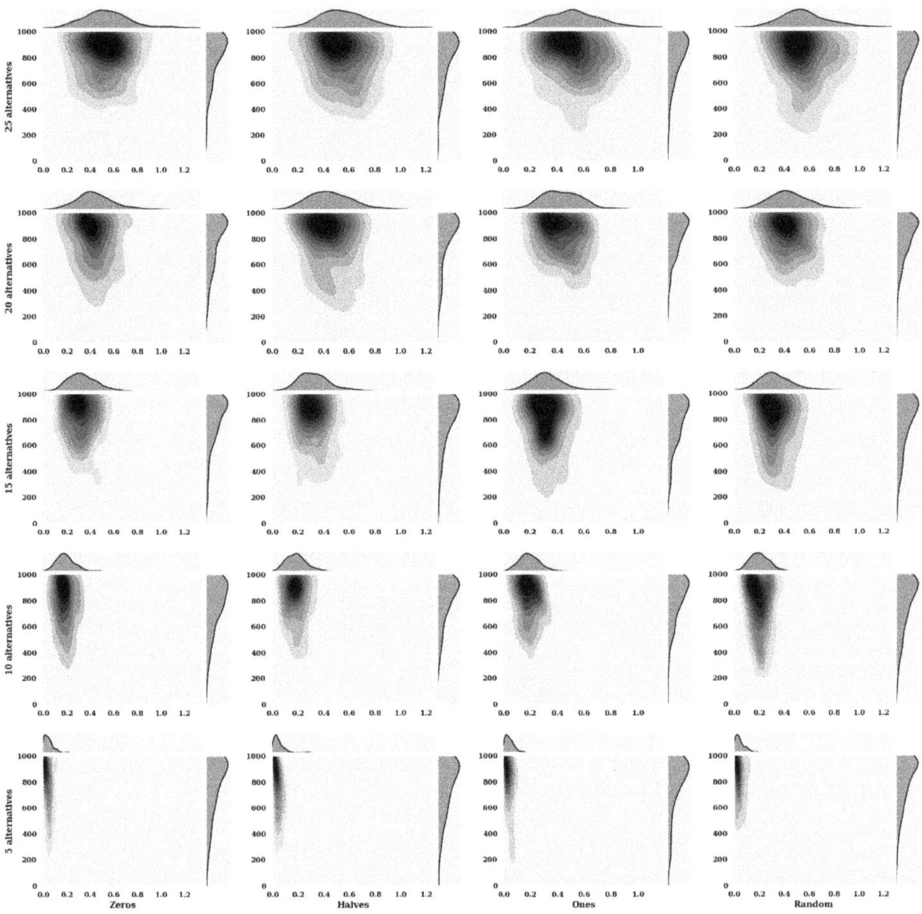

Figure 13. The value of the target function depending on the number of iterations, number of alternatives and initial conditions (method: PSO; criteria variant: dynamic; model: existing).

For a starting preference of characteristic objects of 0, the values of found solutions increase with the number of alternatives. Particle swarm optimization usually finds solutions between 600 and 1000 iterations. Solutions found for five alternatives are in the range [0, 0.05], for ten [0.15, 0.21], for fifteen [0.22, 0.38], for twenty [0.33, 0.42] and twenty-five [0.4, 0.6]. This indicates a small decrease in accuracy as the number of alternatives increases.

A better solution seems to be the starting value of characteristic objects' preferences amounting to 0.5. In the case of sets consisting of 5 and 20 alternatives, the distribution of the found smallest values of the fitness function indicates lower values obtained than in the case of the initial state in which the characteristic objects' preferences are 0. The variant that obtained the lowest values of solutions for 25 alternatives is the initial state with a value of 1. The highest concentration of solutions is close to 0.4, where for the initial state with a value of 0 and 0.5, the highest level was with an amount of solution 0.5.

For the initial state in which characteristic objects take a random preference value, there are no differences that would be statistically significant.

3.2. Fitness Function Distribution

Figure 14 shows violin charts for a hill-climbing algorithm for a non-existent model. The graphs show variants of criteria and variants of initial states.

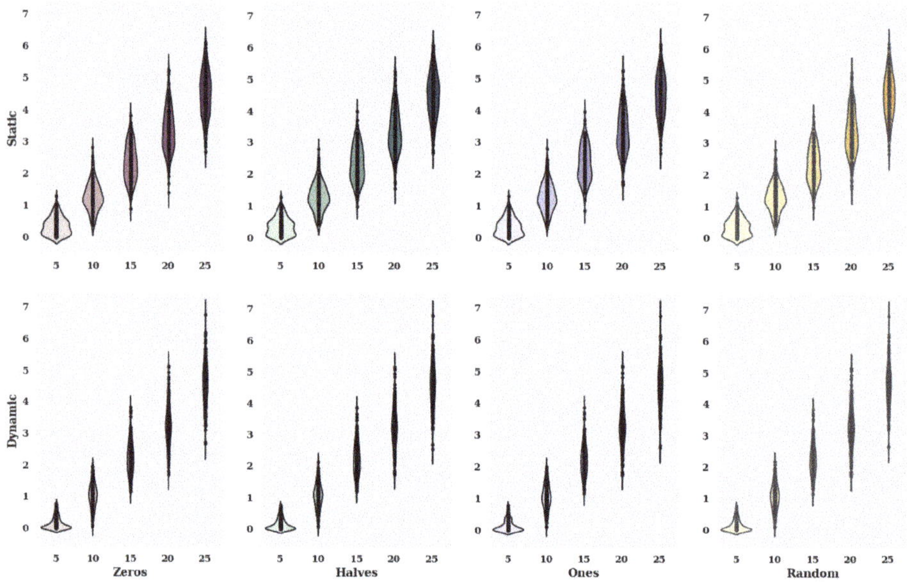

Figure 14. Visualization of the value of solutions in relation to the number of alternatives to criteria and initial state variants (method: HC; model: not existing).

In the case of the charts for the initial state, in which the preferences of characteristic objects took the value of 0, the static value of criteria has smaller values of solutions than the dynamic value. Therefore, the size of the violin for a static case is much larger with small values of solutions. It is worth mentioning, however, that the data distribution for the five alternatives in the set for the dynamic case indicates that most of the smallest values of the fitness function obtained take values smaller than 0.2, which is a much better result than for the static variant.

For the initial state, where the preference of the characteristic objects took the value 0.5, 1, and random, the same relationship between the static values of the criteria and the dynamic values of the criteria occurs as for the initial state with the value 0.

Figure 15 shows fiddle charts for the hill-climbing algorithm for an existing model. The charts show variants of criteria and variants of initial states.

In the case of the charts for the initial state, in which the preferences of characteristic objects took the value of 0, the static value of criteria has smaller values of solutions than the dynamic value. Therefore, the size of the violin for a static case is much larger with small values of solutions. It is worth mentioning, however, that the data distribution for the five alternatives in the set for the dynamic case indicates that most of the smallest values of the fitness function obtained take values smaller than 0.1, which is a much better result than for the static variant. However, the static variant has higher maximum found values for twenty and twenty-five alternatives than the dynamic variant.

For the initial state, where the preference of the characteristic objects takes the value of 0.5, the values of the solutions are lower than for the initial state, where the criteria are chosen statically, the accuracy is very high. In contrast, for the dynamic criteria variant, it is much lower. Many solutions in the static variant were found in the range [0, 0.1], which cannot be said for the dynamic variant.

On the other hand, the static variant of criteria has much higher maximum values of solutions found for all the considered number of alternatives than the dynamic variant.

For initial state values equal to 1, the static variant of criteria takes smaller values of solutions than the static variant. The distribution of solutions found is similar for the distribution of the initial state variant with a value of 0. However, the found values of solutions are more significant than for the initial state in which the characteristic objects take preference values of 0.5.

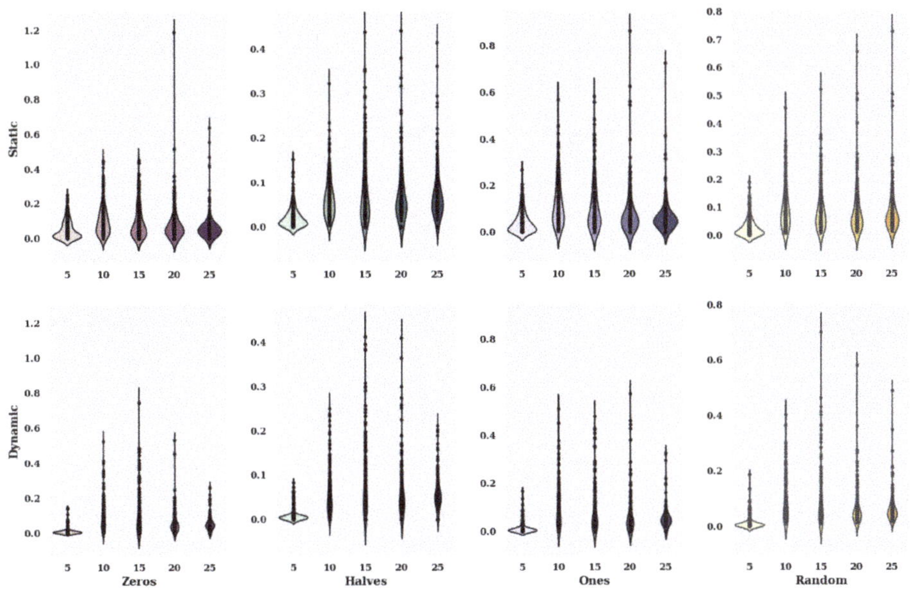

Figure 15. Visualization of the value of solutions in relation to the number of alternatives to criteria and initial state variants (method: HC; model: existing).

In the case of graphs for the initial state where the preference of the characteristic objects took a random value, the static value of the criteria has smaller values of solutions than the dynamic value. The accuracy decreases with the increase of the number of alternatives in the set in the case of the static criteria variant.

Figure 16 shows violin charts for the simulated annealing method for a non-existent model. The charts show variants of criteria and variants of initial states.

In the case of charts for the initial state, in which the preferences of characteristic objects took the value of 0, the static value of criteria has smaller values of solutions than the dynamic value. Therefore, the size of the violin for a static case is much larger with small values of solutions.

For the initial state, where the preference of the characteristic objects has taken the value of 0.5, the values of the solutions are smaller than when the initial state takes the value of 0. When the criteria are chosen statically, the accuracy is very high, while for the dynamic criteria variant, it is much lower. Moreover, the dynamic criteria variant has much higher maximum solution values found for 5, 15, and 25 alternatives than the static variant. For an initial state value of 1, the static variant of criteria has similar distributions of solution values as the dynamic variant due to its violin appearance. However, the most significant solution values found vary considerably.

In the case of the graphs for the initial state, in which the preferences of characteristic objects took a random value, there are no statistically significant differences between the static variant and the dynamic variant of the criteria.

Figure 17 shows violin charts for the simulated annealing method for an existing model. The graphs show variants of criteria and options of initial states.

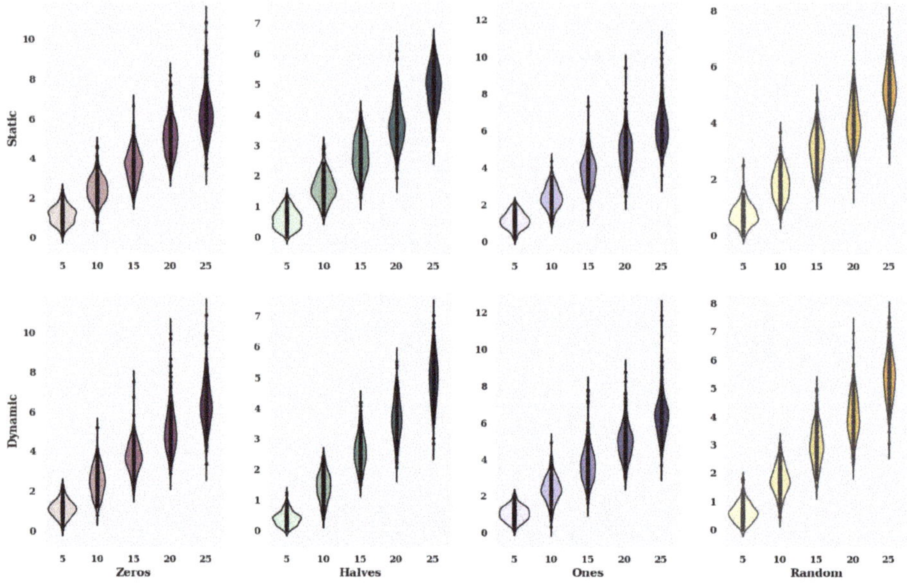

Figure 16. Visualization of the value of solutions in relation to the number of alternatives to criteria and initial state variants (method: SA; model: not existing).

In the case of the charts for the initial state, in which the preferences of characteristic objects took the value 0, the static value of criteria has similar amounts of solutions as the dynamic value. The accuracy in both variants of criteria selection decreases with the increase in the number of alternatives.

For the initial state where the preference of the characteristic objects has assumed the value of 0.5, the amounts of the solutions are smaller than when the initial state assumes the cost of 0. This is indicated by the size of the violin, which is significantly higher when the initial value of the preference of the characteristic objects is 0.5. When criteria are selected dynamically, the accuracy is very high, while for the variant of static criteria, it is significantly lower. However, the dynamic criteria option has much higher maximum solution values found for 5, 10, 15, and 25 alternatives than the static variant.

For an initial state value of 1, the static variant of criteria has similar distributions of solution values as the dynamic variant due to its violin appearance. However, the most significant solution values found vary considerably.

In the case of the graphs for the initial state, in which the preference of characteristic objects took a random value, the static variant of the criteria is characterized by small benefits of solutions. Higher amounts of solutions assume the dynamic variant. The static variant is more accurate than the dynamic option.

Figure 18 shows violin charts for particle swarm optimization for a non-existent model. The graphs show variants of criteria and options of initial states.

In the case of charts for the initial state, in which the preference of characteristic objects took the value 0, the static value of criteria has smaller amounts of solutions than the dynamic value. Therefore, the size of the violin for a static case is much larger with small values of solutions.

For the initial state, where the preference of the characteristic objects has assumed the value of 0.5, the costs of solutions are similar to those of 0. When criteria are chosen statically, the accuracy decreases as the number of alternatives increases. In addition, the dynamic variant of criteria has much higher maximum solution values found for 15 and 25 alternatives than the static option.

For an initial state value of 1 fiddle size for solutions found are similar to those where the initial state is 0.5. The accuracy for static criteria is higher than for dynamic criteria. The smallest and largest solution values found are significantly different for dynamic and static criteria.

For a random initial state value, the distribution of solutions found is similar to when the initial state is 0.5 and 1. For five alternatives, the static variant has significantly higher amounts of solutions than the dynamic option. For ten, fifteen, twenty, and twenty-five choices, the static variant has higher accuracy than the static variant.

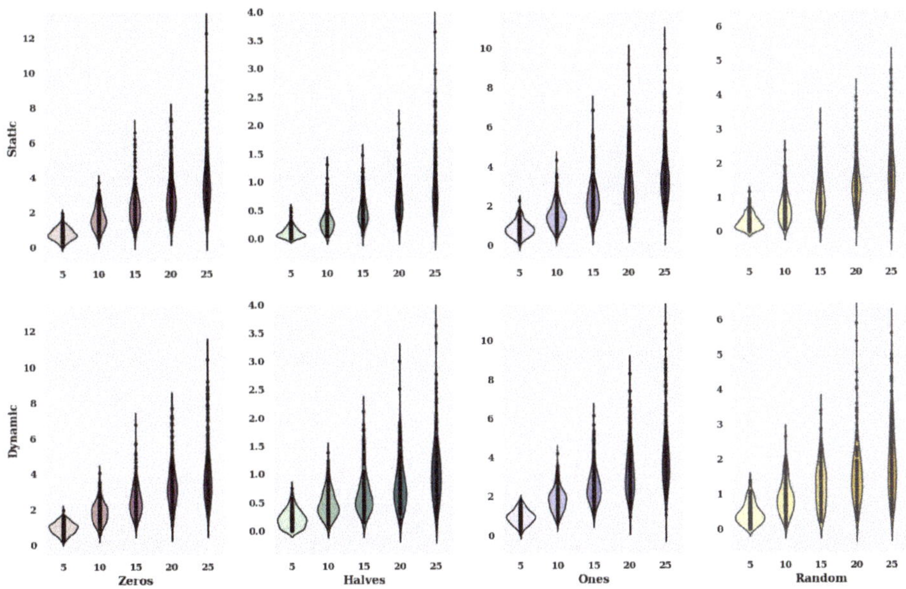

Figure 17. Visualization of the value of solutions in relation to the number of alternatives to criteria and initial state variants (method: SA; model: existing).

Figure 19 shows violin charts for particle swarm optimization for the existing model. The graphs show variants of criteria and options of initial states.

In the case of diagrams for the initial state, where the preference of characteristic objects took the value 0, the static value of criteria has smaller amounts of solutions than the dynamic value. For 5 and 10 alternatives, the accuracy of static criteria is higher than for dynamic criteria. However, where there are 15, 20 and 25 alternatives in a set, the accuracy for static criteria is lower than for dynamic criteria.

For an initial state where the preference of the characteristic objects has taken the value 0.5, the benefits of the solutions are more significant than when the initial state takes the amount 0. The accuracy decreases as the number of alternatives for each criterion selection variant increases. The dynamic variant of criteria has significantly higher maximum solution values found for 15, 20, and 25 options than the static option.

For an initial state value of 1, the static values of the criteria have smaller solution values than the static variant of the criteria. The accuracy for static criteria is higher than for dynamic criteria. The smallest and largest solution values found are significantly different for dynamic and static criteria.

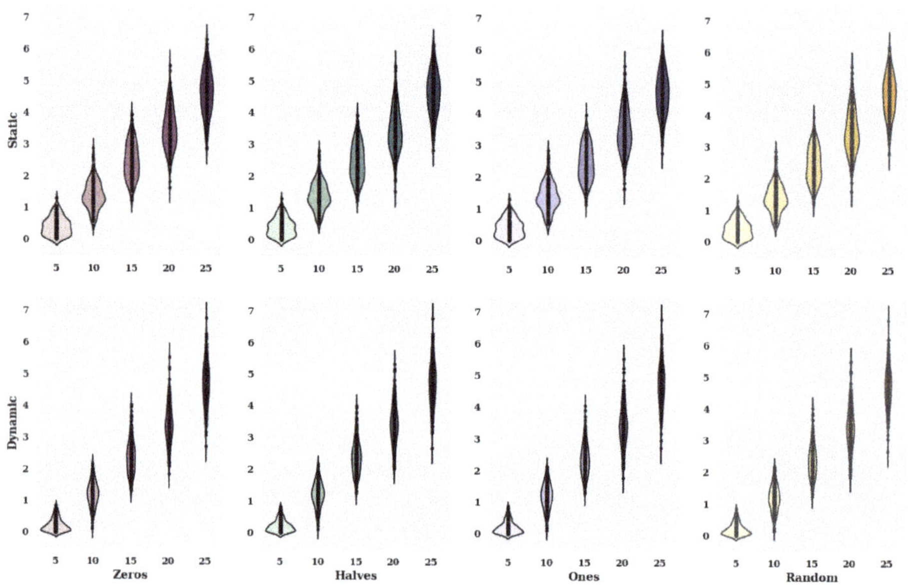

Figure 18. Visualization of the value of solutions in relation to the number of alternatives to criteria and initial state variants (method: PSO; model: nonexistent).

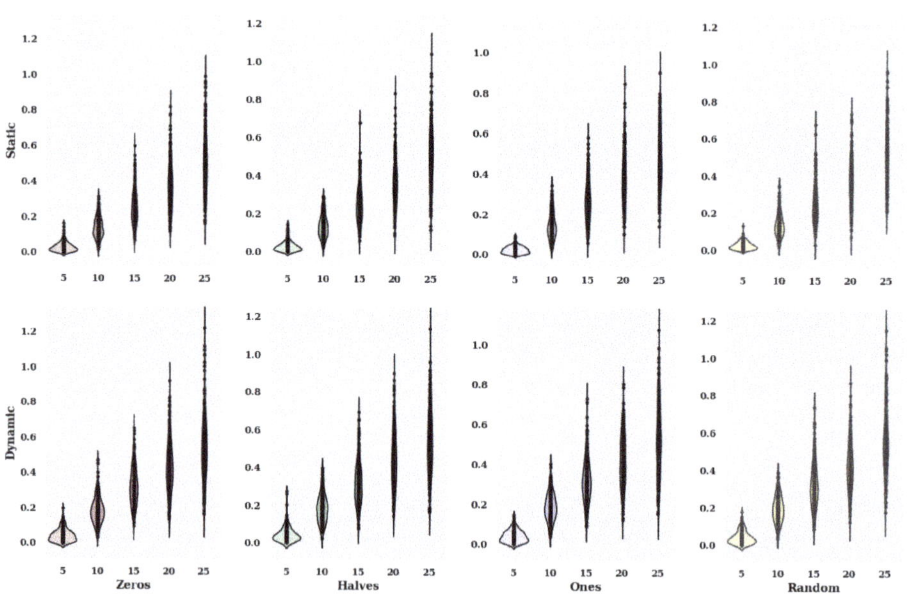

Figure 19. Visualization of the value of solutions in relation to the number of alternatives to criteria and initial state variants (method: PSO; model: existing).

For a random initial state value, the distribution of solutions found differs slightly from a 0 initial state. For all alternatives considered, the dynamic variant has significantly higher amounts of solutions than the static option. The accuracy of the static variant is much higher than for the dynamic variant.

3.3. Use of the Proposed Approach

A study was carried out to demonstrate the operation of the proposed approach. For dynamic and static criteria with an existing model, twenty alternatives were drawn. The preference for characteristic objects was set to 0.5 as the initial state, as this approach is more productive according to the previously presented surveys.

To calculate the similarity coefficient of final rankings between the reference ranking and the one obtained using stochastic methods, the alternatives were divided into a training set and a test set. The division of the set of alternatives was partial, i.e., the first half was a teaching set and the second a test set.

The static criteria were set to [0, 0.5, 0], while the dynamic ones were calculated with the use of the teaching set according to the Formula (36). A randomly generated SJ vector evaluated the alternatives constituting the teaching and test set.

Then, the teaching set was used to determine the preferences of characteristic objects using selected stochastic methods. The defined model evaluated the alternatives from the test set using the calculated preferences of characteristic objects.

Training set of 10 alternatives for a static variant of the criteria are presented in Table 1. The preference was calculated using a randomly generated SJ vector. The generated points served as input for HC, SA and PSO techniques. On their basis, decision models were identified using each method.

Table 1. Summary of ten alternatives from the training set (criteria variant: static; model: existing; start state: 0.5).

A_i	C_1	C_2	P_{ref}
A_1	0.5818	0.7693	0.5585
A_2	0.7422	0.2597	0.5509
A_3	0.9056	0.3015	0.5747
A_4	0.7582	0.6266	0.7337
A_5	0.1834	0.0011	0.1842
A_6	0.7756	0.8393	0.7193
A_7	0.9367	0.2326	0.4896
A_8	0.0895	0.8439	0.3946
A_9	0.7983	0.5505	0.7625
A_{10}	0.7378	0.5845	0.7297

Table 2 presents alternatives included in the test set and their preferences as well as rankings for a static variant of the criteria. The simulated annealing method performed slightly worse than the hill-climbing algorithm and particle swarm optimization. The lowest value of fitness function obtained by it is much higher than the other two methods. The particle swarm optimization method did very well because the ranking of the assessed alternatives is approximate to a reference ranking. The same is true for the hill-climbing algorithm, whose preferences are very similar to those of the reference model.

Spearman's correlation coefficients for a static variant of the criteria between the reference ranking and calculated by stochastic methods are 0.9879 (HC), 0.9152 (SA), 0.9636 (PSO). The high accuracy of the methods used can be seen here, however, the simulated annealing method differs significantly from the PSO and HC methods. The strongest correlation between the reference ranking and the calculated one has a hill-climbing algorithm.

Spearman's weighted correlation coefficients for a static variant of the criteria for stochastic methods are as follows: 0.9835 (HC), 0.9096 (SA), 0.9736 (PSO). Similarly to Spearman's correlation coefficients, the weighted coefficients show that the strongest correlation is with the hill-climbing algorithm and the weakest with the simulated overhang method. However, the difference between the coefficient for PSO and HC methods is much smaller than for Spearman's correlation coefficient.

Table 2. Summary of ten alternatives from the test set for selected stochastic methods (criteria variant: static; model: existing; start state: 0.5).

A_i	C_1	C_2	P_{ref}	P_{HC}	P_{SA}	P_{PSO}	R_{ref}	R_{HC}	R_{SA}	R_{PSO}
A_1	0.0466	0.6193	0.4720	0.4849	0.4095	0.5102	7	7	9	8
A_2	0.3480	0.4003	0.5626	0.5873	0.5703	0.5646	5	5	5	5
A_3	0.5312	0.1669	0.5452	0.5347	0.5153	0.5456	6	6	6	7
A_4	0.6623	0.5324	0.7096	0.7250	0.7430	0.7120	4	3	2	4
A_5	0.9999	0.1820	0.4094	0.4211	0.4130	0.4337	9	9	8	9
A_6	0.5734	0.9810	0.4411	0.4749	0.4503	0.5631	8	8	7	6
A_7	0.8184	0.9220	0.7602	0.7512	0.6585	0.7584	2	2	4	2
A_8	0.3801	0.2630	0.2877	0.3065	0.3083	0.2917	10	10	10	10
A_9	0.8305	0.5536	0.7765	0.7629	0.7739	0.7659	1	1	1	1
A_{10}	0.9236	0.4421	0.7395	0.7165	0.7380	0.7306	3	4	3	3

WS correlation coefficients calculated for the preference of a reference testing set and the preference calculated using stochastic methods for a static variant of the criteria are as follows: 0.9717 (HC), 0.9143 (SA), 0.9919 (PSO). The most substantial relation between the reference ranking and the calculated one is particle swarm optimization. In the case of rs and rw coefficient, the most correlated method was the HC method. Moreover, a much higher difference in the ws factor between the PSO method and the hill-climbing algorithm can be seen here than in the case of the Spearman weighted factor. On the other hand, the correlation of the simulated annealing method, as in the case of the rest of correlation coefficients, is the weakest of the methods considered.

Table 3 shows a training set of 10 alternatives and their preference for a dynamic variant of criteria. The preference was calculated using a randomly generated SJ vector. The generated points served as input for HC, SA, and PSO techniques. On their basis, decision models were identified using each method.

Table 4 shows the alternatives included in the test set and their preferences, as well as rankings for the dynamic variant of criteria. The simulated annealing method has fared worse than the hill-climbing algorithm and particle swarm optimization. The lowest value of fitness function obtained by it is much higher than the other two methods. The particle swarm optimization method did very well because the ranking of the assessed alternatives is the same as the reference ranking. The same is true for the hill-climbing algorithm, whose preferences are very similar to those of the reference model.

Table 3. Summary of ten alternatives from the training set (criteria variant: dynamic; model: existing; start state: 0.5).

A_i	C_1	C_2	P_{ref}
A_1	0.5521	0.4725	0.5542
A_2	0.0451	0.9382	0.3333
A_3	0.3959	0.3165	0.4985
A_4	0.0908	0.9099	0.3243
A_5	0.9733	0.1467	0.6688
A_6	0.9828	0.7295	0.7900
A_7	0.6073	0.9875	0.2435
A_8	0.4992	0.0279	0.7220
A_9	0.8436	0.5352	0.6192
A_{10}	0.7014	0.7132	0.5135

Table 4. Summary of ten alternatives from the test set for selected stochastic methods (criteria variant: dynamic; model: existing; start state: 0.5).

A_i	C_1	C_2	P_{ref}	P_{HC}	P_{SA}	P_{PSO}	R_{ref}	R_{HC}	R_{SA}	R_{PSO}
A_1	0.9660	0.6767	0.7338	0.7416	0.7343	0.7649	2	2	2	2
A_2	0.6514	0.1735	0.7294	0.7277	0.6935	0.6827	3	3	3	3
A_3	0.8497	0.7176	0.6536	0.6551	0.6379	0.6716	4	4	4	4
A_4	0.3286	0.9875	0.2431	0.2388	0.2696	0.2317	10	10	10	10
A_5	0.3945	0.3619	0.4880	0.4986	0.5044	0.4935	5	5	5	5
A_6	0.2104	0.0834	0.2751	0.2781	0.4683	0.2985	9	9	6	9
A_7	0.4468	0.5993	0.4476	0.4601	0.4354	0.4679	6	6	7	6
A_8	0.1510	0.4498	0.3208	0.3553	0.3440	0.3611	8	8	9	8
A_9	0.9775	0.9581	0.9660	0.9310	0.7610	0.9497	1	1	1	1
A_{10}	0.6122	0.7942	0.3778	0.3784	0.3893	0.3763	7	7	8	7

The obtained Spearman correlation coefficients between the reference ranking and the one calculated by stochastic methods for the dynamic variant of criteria are 1.0 (HC), 0.9273 (SA), 1.0 (PSO). The accuracy of HC and PSO methods is very high, whereas the simulated expression method has much lower accuracy.

Spearman's weighted correlation coefficients for stochastic methods for the dynamic variant of criteria are as follows: 1.0 (HC), 0.9537 (SA), 1.0 (PSO). As with Spearman's correlation coefficients, the weighted coefficients show that the strongest correlation occurs with the hill-climbing algorithm and particle swarm optimization, and the weakest with the simulated overhang method.

WS correlation coefficients calculated for the preference of the reference testing set and the preference calculated using stochastic methods for the dynamic variant of the criteria are as follows: 1.0 (HC), 0.9885(SA), 1.0 (PSO). The PSO and HC methods have the most substantial relationship between the reference ranking and the calculated one. However, the correlation of the simulated annealing method, as in the case of the rest of the correlation coefficients, is the weakest of the methods considered.

4. Conclusions and Future Research Directions

In this paper, we consider a new approach to the identification of a multi-criteria decision-making model, based on the stochastic optimization technologies. The research carried out has shown that the proposed approach has a very high accuracy for an initial state of 0.5 and the models existing for the two criterion variants under consideration, i.e., static and dynamic. The novelties and contributions are presented as follows. The paper presents an innovative approach, which consists of building a decision-making model based on already evaluated alternatives and stochastic optimization techniques.

The hill-climbing algorithm is best suited for an initial state with a value of 0.5, which is the most accurate for all the tested variants of criteria with existing and non-existent models. The state with a random value is slightly worse and has lower accuracy. On the other hand, the initial states with a value of 0 and 1 have the lowest accuracy of the tested states. Moreover, the state with a value of 0.5 and random needs fewer iterations than the initial state with 0 and 1.

The simulated annealing method is best suited for finding solutions when the start state is 0.5. At this state, the method finds the smallest values of solutions. Initial states with a value of 0 and 1, which are less accurate than those for 0.5 and random states, are much worse. The random value of the starting preference of characteristic objects is characterized by a quite high accuracy, but not higher than when the starting preference is 0.5. It is worth mentioning that with the increase in the number of alternatives to the SA method, the number of iterations needed to find a solution at a random initial state and equal to 0.5 for the existing model decreases. However, solutions found with fewer iterations have a much higher value than those found with more iterations.

Particle swarm optimization with an existing model for dynamic and static criteria values is best performed when the initial state is 1. It has higher accuracy than a random initial state value, 0 or 0.5. Also, it does not need as many iterations as the rest of the initial state values. For a model that does not exist for dynamic criterion values, the starting value of the preference of characteristic objects equal to 0.5 works best. The accuracy of the rest of the initial states is lower than that of the model, but for the number of iterations, the initial states differ slightly. With static values of criteria and a non-existent model, the starting states of 0 and 1 perform best. Their accuracy is slightly higher than when the start preference of the characteristic objects takes a random value or equal to 0.5.

Compared to the HC technique, the SA technique needs more iteration to find a solution, and the solutions found have much more value. On the other hand, in the hill-climbing algorithm, the decrease in the number of iterations with an increase in the number of alternatives does not occur as in the case of the simulated annealing method.

The PSO method, unlike the SA method, needs much smaller numbers of iterations to find a solution, whilst the PSO method needs more iterations compared to the HC method. The number of iterations in particle swarm optimization relative to an increase in the number of alternatives is increasing as in the case of a hill-climbing algorithm.

The correlation coefficients used in the example show that the HC and PSO methods are best suited for identifying a multi-criteria model. On the other hand, the SA method has a worse correlation than them, so that the obtained rankings are far from the ranking of the reference model. The main limitations are that we have researched only the simple case where characteristic objects are constant. We should determine the algorithm of obtained optimal characteristic values. Additionally, empirical case studies should be continued.

The directions for further research should focus on the parameters of the stochastic methods considered to obtain the best possible value of solutions and the smallest possible number of iterations. The issue of iteration numbers in the simulated annealing method should also be looked at because it obtained very high values compared to the hill-climbing algorithm and particle swarm optimization. Furthermore, some tests should be carried out for a more significant number of criteria and their values. The number of sets of decision variants tested should also be more significant to make the results more accurate. Other stochastic methods should also be tested for smaller solution values and fewer iterations.

Author Contributions: Conceptualization, W.S.; methodology, B.K. and W.S.; software, B.K.; validation, B.K. and W.S.; formal analysis, W.S.; investigation, B.K.; resources, B.K.; data curation, B.K.; writing—original draft preparation, B.K. and W.S.; writing—review and editing, B.K. and W.S.; visualization, B.K. and W.S.; supervision, W.S.; project administration, W.S.; funding acquisition, W.S. All authors have read and agreed to the published version of the manuscript.

Funding: The work was supported by the National Science Centre, Decision No. UMO-2016/23/N/HS4/01931.

Acknowledgments: The authors would like to thank the editor and the anonymous reviewers, whose insightful comments and constructive suggestions helped us to significantly improve the quality of this paper.

Conflicts of Interest: The authors declare no conflict of interest.

Abbreviations

The following abbreviations are used in this manuscript:

EA	Evolutionary Algorithms
GA	Genetic Algorithm
HC	Hill-Climbing
SA	Simulated Annealing
PSO	Particle Swarm Optimization

MCDA	Multi-Criteria Decision-Analysis
COMET	Characteristic Objects METhod
MEJ	Matrix of Expert Judgment
SJ	vector of the Summed Judgments

References

1. Stojčić, M.; Pamučar, D.; Mahmutagić, E.; Stević, Ž. Development of an ANFIS Model for the Optimization of a Queuing System in Warehouses. *Information* **2018**, *9*, 240. [CrossRef]
2. Jovanović, A.D.; Pamučar, D.S.; Pejčić-Tarle, S. Green vehicle routing in urban zones—A neuro-fuzzy approach. *Expert Syst. Appl.* **2014**, *41*, 3189–3203. [CrossRef]
3. Nocedal, J.; Wright, S. *Numerical Optimization*; Springer Science & Business Media: Berlin/Heidelberg, Germany, 2006.
4. Törn, A.; Žilinskas, A. *Global Optimization*; Springer: Berlin/Heidelberg, Germany, 1989; Volume 350.
5. Sauer, M. *Operations Research Kompakt*; De Gruyter: Berlin, Germany, 2020.
6. Ehrgott, M. *Multicriteria Optimization*; Springer Science & Business Media: Berlin/Heidelberg, Germany, 2005; Volume 491.
7. Miettinen, K. *Nonlinear Multiobjective Optimization*; Springer Science & Business Media: Berlin/Heidelberg, Germany, 2012; Volume 12.
8. Ćirović, G.; Pamučar, D.; Božanić, D. Green logistic vehicle routing problem: Routing light delivery vehicles in urban areas using a neuro-fuzzy model. *Expert Syst. Appl.* **2014**, *41*, 4245–4258. [CrossRef]
9. Muravev, D.; Hu, H.; Zhou, H.; Pamucar, D. Location Optimization of CR Express International Logistics Centers. *Symmetry* **2020**, *12*, 143. [CrossRef]
10. Softić, E.; Radičević, V.; Subotić, M.; Stević, Ž.; Talić, Z.; Pamučar, D. Sustainability of the Optimum Pavement Model of Reclaimed Asphalt from a Used Pavement Structure. *Sustainability* **2020**, *12*, 1912. [CrossRef]
11. Horst, R.; Pardalos, P.M. *Handbook of Global Optimization*; Springer Science & Business Media: Berlin/Heidelberg, Germany, 2013; Volume 2.
12. Floudas, C.A. *Deterministic Global Optimization: Theory, Methods and Applications*; Springer Science & Business Media: Berlin/Heidelberg, Germany, 2013; Volume 37.
13. Leyffer, S. Deterministic Methods for Mixed Integer Nonlinear Programming. Ph.D. Thesis, University of Dundee, Dundee, Scotland, 1993.
14. Lin, M.H.; Tsai, J.F.; Yu, C.S. A review of deterministic optimization methods in engineering and management. *Math. Probl. Eng.* **2012**, *2012*. [CrossRef]
15. Boender, C.G.E.; Romeijn, H.E. Stochastic methods. In *Handbook of Global Optimization*; Springer: Berlin/Heidelberg, Germany, 1995; pp. 829–869.
16. Kan, A.R.; Timmer, G. Stochastic methods for global optimization. *Am. J. Math. Manag. Sci.* **1984**, *4*, 7–40. [CrossRef]
17. Yang, X.S.; Deb, S.; Fong, S.; He, X.; Zhao, Y.X. From swarm intelligence to metaheuristics: Nature-inspired optimization algorithms. *Computer* **2016**, *49*, 52–59. [CrossRef]
18. Erten, H.I.; Deveci, H.; Artem, H.S. Stochastic Optimization Methods. In *Designing Engineering Structures Using Stochastic Optimization Methods*; CRC Press: Boca Raton, FL, USA, 2020.
19. Zabinsky, Z.B. Random search algorithms. *Wiley Encyclopedia of Operations Research and Management Science*; John Wiley and Sons Ltd.: Hoboken, NJ, USA, 2010.
20. Zhigljavsky, A.; Zilinskas, A. *Stochastic Global Optimization*; Springer Science & Business Media: Berlin/Heidelberg, Germany, 2007; Volume 9.
21. Kaveh, A. *Advances in Metaheuristic Algorithms for Optimal Design of Structures*; Springer: Berlin/Heidelberg, Germany, 2014.
22. Sörensen, K.; Glover, F. Metaheuristics. *Encycl. Oper. Res. Manag. Sci.* **2013**, *62*, 960–970.
23. Lones, M.A. Metaheuristics in nature-inspired algorithms. In Proceedings of the Companion Publication of the 2014 Annual Conference on Genetic and Evolutionary Computation, Vancouver, BC, Canada, 12–16 July 2014; pp. 1419–1422.
24. Selman, B.; Gomes, C.P. Hill-climbing search. *Encycl. Cogn. Sci.* **2006**, *81*, 82.

25. Kvasnicka, V.; Pelikán, M.; Pospichal, J. Hill climbing with learning (an abstraction of genetic algorithm). In *Neural Network World, 6*; Citeseer: Slovak Technical University, Bratislava, Slovakia, 1995.
26. Van Laarhoven, P.J.; Aarts, E.H. Simulated annealing. In *Simulated Annealing: Theory and Applications*; Springer: Berlin/Heidelberg, Germany, 1987; pp. 7–15.
27. Lukovac, V.; Pamučar, D.; Popović, M.; Đorović, B. Portfolio model for analyzing human resources: An approach based on neuro-fuzzy modeling and the simulated annealing algorithm. *Expert Syst. Appl.* **2017**, *90*, 318–331. [CrossRef]
28. Dowsland, K.A.; Thompson, J. Simulated annealing. In *Handbook of Natural Computing*; Springer: Berlin/Heidelberg, Germany, 2012; pp. 1623–1655.
29. Bertsimas, D.; Tsitsiklis, J. Simulated annealing. *Stat. Sci.* **1993**, *8*, 10–15. [CrossRef]
30. Sahoo, R.K.; Ojha, D.; Dash, S. Nature Inspired Metaheuristic Algorithms—A Comparative Review. *Int. J. Dev. Res.* **2016**, *6*, 8427–8432.
31. Yang, X.S. *Nature-Inspired Metaheuristic Algorithms*; Luniver Press: London, UK, 2010.
32. Kennedy, J.; Eberhart, R. Particle swarm optimization. In Proceedings of the ICNN'95-International Conference on Neural Networks, Perth, WA, Australia, 27 November–1 December 1995; IEEE: Piscataway, NJ, USA, 1995; Volume 4, pp. 1942–1948.
33. Abdmouleh, Z.; Gastli, A.; Ben-Brahim, L.; Haouari, M.; Al-Emadi, N.A. Review of optimization techniques applied for the integration of distributed generation from renewable energy sources. *Renew. Energy* **2017**, *113*, 266–280. [CrossRef]
34. Więckowski, J.; Kizielewicz, B.; Kołodziejczyk, J. Application of Hill Climbing Algorithm in Determining the Characteristic Objects Preferences Based on the Reference Set of Alternatives. In Proceedings of the International Conference on Intelligent Decision Technologies, Split, Croatia, 17–19 June 2020; Springer: Berlin/Heidelberg, Germany, 2020; pp. 341–351.
35. Więckowski, J.; Kizielewicz, B.; Kołodziejczyk, J. The Search of the Optimal Preference Values of the Characteristic Objects by Using Particle Swarm Optimization in the Uncertain Environment. In Proceedings of the International Conference on Intelligent Decision Technologies, Split, Croatia, 17–19 June 2020; Springer: Berlin/Heidelberg, Germany, 2020; pp. 353–363.
36. Więckowski, J.; Kizielewicz, B.; Kołodziejczyk, J. Finding an Approximate Global Optimum of Characteristic Objects Preferences by Using Simulated Annealing. In Proceedings of the International Conference on Intelligent Decision Technologies, Split, Croatia, 17–19 June 2020; Springer: Berlin/Heidelberg, Germany, 2020; pp. 365–375.
37. Žižović, M.; Pamučar, D.; Albijanić, M.; Chatterjee, P.; Pribićević, I. Eliminating Rank Reversal Problem Using a New Multi-Attribute Model—The RAFSI Method. *Mathematics* **2020**, *8*, 1015. [CrossRef]
38. Faizi, S.; Sałabun, W.; Ullah, S.; Rashid, T.; Więckowski, J. A New Method to Support Decision-Making in an Uncertain Environment Based on Normalized Interval-Valued Triangular Fuzzy Numbers and COMET Technique. *Symmetry* **2020**, *12*, 516. [CrossRef]
39. Palczewski, K.; Sałabun, W. Identification of the football teams assessment model using the COMET method. *Procedia Comput. Sci.* **2019**, *159*, 2491–2501. [CrossRef]
40. Podvezko, V. The comparative analysis of MCDA methods SAW and COPRAS. *Eng. Econ.* **2011**, *22*, 134–146. [CrossRef]
41. Zavadskas, E.K.; Turskis, Z. Multiple criteria decision making (MCDM) methods in economics: An overview. *Technol. Econ. Dev. Econ.* **2011**, *17*, 397–427. [CrossRef]
42. Wątróbski, J.; Jankowski, J.; Ziemba, P.; Karczmarczyk, A.; Zioło, M. Generalised framework for multi-criteria method selection. *Omega* **2019**, *86*, 107–124. [CrossRef]
43. Sałabun, W.; Piegat, A. Comparative analysis of MCDM methods for the assessment of mortality in patients with acute coronary syndrome. *Artif. Intell. Rev.* **2017**, *48*, 557–571. [CrossRef]
44. Sałabun, W.; Palczewski, K.; Wątróbski, J. Multicriteria approach to sustainable transport evaluation under incomplete knowledge: Electric Bikes Case Study. *Sustainability* **2019**, *11*, 3314. [CrossRef]
45. Si, A.; Das, S.; Kar, S. An approach to rank picture fuzzy numbers for decision making problems. *Decis. Mak. Appl. Manag. Eng.* **2019**, *2*, 54–64. [CrossRef]
46. Faizi, S.; Sałabun, W.; Rashid, T.; Wątróbski, J.; Zafar, S. Group decision-making for hesitant fuzzy sets based on characteristic objects method. *Symmetry* **2017**, *9*, 136. [CrossRef]

47. Faizi, S.; Rashid, T.; Sałabun, W.; Zafar, S.; Wątróbski, J. Decision making with uncertainty using hesitant fuzzy sets. *Int. J. Fuzzy Syst.* **2018**, *20*, 93–103. [CrossRef]
48. Jankowski, J.; Sałabun, W.; Wątróbski, J. Identification of a multi-criteria assessment model of relation between editorial and commercial content in web systems. In *Multimedia and Network Information Systems*; Springer: Berlin/Heidelberg, Germany, 2017; pp. 295–305.
49. Piegat, A.; Sałabun, W. Identification of a multicriteria decision-making model using the characteristic objects method. *Appl. Comput. Intell. Soft Comput.* **2014**, *2014*. [CrossRef]
50. Sha, Z.C.; Huang, Z.T.; Zhou, Y.Y.; Wang, F.H. Blind spreading sequence estimation based on hill-climbing algorithm. In Proceedings of the 2012 IEEE 11th International Conference on Signal Processing, Beijing, China, 21–25 October 2012; IEEE: Piscataway, NJ, USA, 2012; Volume 2, pp. 1299–1302.
51. Shehab, M.; Khader, A.T.; Al-Betar, M.A.; Abualigah, L.M. Hybridizing cuckoo search algorithm with hill climbing for numerical optimization problems. In Proceedings of the 2017 8th International Conference on Information Technology (ICIT), Amman, Jordan, 17 May 2017; IEEE: Piscataway, NJ, USA, 2017; pp. 36–43.
52. Arora, J.S. 15—Discrete Variable Optimum Design Concepts and Methods. In *Introduction to Optimum Design*, 2nd ed.; Arora, J.S., Ed.; Academic Press: San Diego, CA, USA, 2004; pp. 513–530. [CrossRef]
53. Trelea, I.C. The particle swarm optimization algorithm: Convergence analysis and parameter selection. *Inf. Process. Lett.* **2003**, *85*, 317–325. [CrossRef]
54. Van den Bergh, F.; Engelbrecht, A.P. A cooperative approach to particle swarm optimization. *IEEE Trans. Evol. Comput.* **2004**, *8*, 225–239. [CrossRef]
55. Ganguly, S. Multi-objective distributed generation penetration planning with load model using particle swarm optimization. *Decis. Mak. Appl. Manag. Eng.* **2020**, *3*, 30–42. [CrossRef]
56. Sałabun, W.; Urbaniak, K. A new coefficient of rankings similarity in decision-making problems. In *International Conference on Computational Science*; Springer: Cham, Switzerland, 2020.

symmetry

MDPI

Article

A Distributionally Robust Chance-Constrained Approach for Modeling Demand Uncertainty in Green Port-Hinterland Transportation Network Optimization

Qian Dai * and Jiaqi Yang

School of Transportation, Wuhan University of Technology, Wuhan 430063, China; styjq@whut.edu.cn
* Correspondence: daiqianxixi@163.com or daiqian@whut.edu.cn

Received: 13 August 2020; Accepted: 7 September 2020; Published: 10 September 2020

Abstract: This paper discusses a bi-objective programming of the port-hinterland freight transportation system based on intermodal transportation with the consideration of uncertain transportation demand for green concern. Economic and environmental aspects are integrated in order to obtain green flow distribution solutions for the proposed port-hinterland network. A distributionally robust chance constraint optimization model is then established for the uncertainty of transportation demand, in which the chance constraint is described such that transportation demand is satisfied under the worst-case distribution based on the partial information of the mean and variance. The trade-offs among different objectives and the uncertainty theory applied in the modeling both involve the notion of symmetry. Taking the actual port-hinterland transportation network of the Yangtze River Economic Belt as an example, the results reveal that the railway-road intermodal transport is promoted and the change in total network CO_2 emissions is contrary to that in total network costs. Additionally, both network costs and network emissions increase significantly with the growth of the lower bound of probability for chance constraint. The higher the probability level grows, the greater the trade-offs between two objectives are influenced, which indicates that the operation capacity of inland intermodal terminals should be increased to meet the high probability level. These findings can help provide decision supports for the green development strategy of the port-hinterland container transportation network, which meanwhile faces a dynamic planning problem caused by stochastic demands in real life.

Keywords: port-hinterland transportation system; bi-objective programming; intermodal transportation; carbon emissions; uncertain demand; distributionally robust; chance constraint; Yangtze River Economic Belt

1. Introduction

Port-hinterland container transportation, as an extension of maritime shipping in inland areas, is an indispensable part of the whole container supply chain in order to obtain "door-to-door" service. The efficiency of port-hinterland connection influences not only the service quality of entire container transportation chain, but also the port competitions [1,2].The optimization of the transportation system in the port-hinterland part is facing complicated and comprehensive challenges in achieving cost-saving, fast, safe, and environmentally friendly movement of goods. Intermodal transport, which is a combination of at least two transportation modes without changing a loading unit in the haul, emerges and is promoted as it presents the advantage of offering greener or more sustainable transportation compared with the mode of road. Generally, the main long haulage is undertaken by the railway or waterway, while the road transport is only applied in the pre-haulage or post-haulage of the entire route. Although there have been a number of academic articles dealing with planning problem of intermodal transport [3–6], the road–rail intermodal transport is the major issue, while road–waterway intermodal transport or other intermodal forms are rarely discussed. Thus, the network design problem in the port-hinterland transportation system based on intermodal freight transportation, in which the modes of road, railway, and waterway are all modeled, is the research focus of this paper.

The greenness issue in the port-hinterland container transportation system is one of the research focuses in this paper. The optimization of the hinterland transportation network needs to consider not only cost savings, but also environmental protection. Owing to the high carbon emissions by road transportation, intermodal transportation has been highly encouraged in transportation activities because of the advantage of low carbon [7–11]. So far, there have been a number of studies handling the green port-hinterland transportation network design problem through monetary measures, in which carbon emissions impact is internalized by policy intervention. For example, Iannone [12] assessed the impact of a set of policy instruments and operational measures on the sustainability of hinterland container logistics in Campania, Southern Italy. Santos et al. [13] investigated the impact of a set of transport policies likely subsidizing intermodal transport operations, internalizing external costs, and optimizing the location of inland terminals from a system perspective on a railroad intermodal freight system in Belgium, aiming to reduce external effects. Zhang et al. [14] incorporated measures of CO_2 pricing, terminal network configuration, and hub-service networks in freight transport optimization model and used the case of hinterland container transport in the Netherlands to calibrate and validate the model. On top of that, there were also a few articles analyzing the trade-off relationship between multiple objectives (such as cost, time, emissions, and so on) in the port-hinterland freight logistics field. Lam and Gu [15] analyzed the trade-offs between cost and time in multimodal transport network optimization under different limitations on total network emission. Demir et al. [16] discussed the modeling of transportation planning incorporating environment criteria and present a bi-objective hinterland intermodal transportation model. However, the trade-offs analysis has been insufficient and can be further explored.

The aforementioned studies generally trade input parameters, such as transport demands, as deterministic factors. In the real-world hinterland transportation system, the generation of transport demand is fluctuating and uncertain. This might result in dynamic transportation planning, which increases the difficulty of decision making in hinterland transportation system optimization. The performances of cost, time, and emissions of the transportation network are all influenced as well. How to efficiently deal with uncertainty in the green optimization problem for port-hinterland transportation system is another research focus in this paper.

Methodologies to logistics network optimization considering uncertainty generally fall into stochastic programming and robust optimization. The former has been a leading method in dealing with the problem of uncertainty in recent years, where the key assumption is that the complete information non probability distribution of the stochastic factor can be obtained through either empirical data or subjective judgment. Contreras et al. [17] studied stochastic incapacitated hub location problems with uncertain demands and uncertain transportation costs, where the equivalent associated deterministic expected value problem was obtained by replacing stochastic variables with their expectations. Ardjmand et al. [18] introduced the genetic algorithm to a bi-objective stochastic model for transportation, location, and allocation of hazardous materials, where the transportation cost was considered to be stochastic. Wang [19] developed a constrained stochastic programming model for resource allocation of containerized cargo transportation networks with uncertain capacities, in which an approximation model was built and a sampling-based algorithm was proposed to solve the approximation model. Zhao et al. [20] developed a two-stage chance constrained programming model for a sea–rail intermodal service network design problem with the consideration of stochastic travel time, stochastic transfer time, and stochastic container demand. Then, a hybrid heuristic algorithm incorporating sample average approximation and ant colony optimization was proposed to solve the model. Specifically, the distribution function employed in these studies was generally not able to represent the true distribution of variables accurately, which might result in the lack of robustness on the optimal solution.

As a follow-up, robust optimization develops as another reasonable alternative method for uncertainty optimization, which aims to find a robust solution that is feasible for any realization value of uncertain parameters in an uncertainty set under certain constraints. The early robust optimization research generally did not assume that the uncertain parameters obeyed any distribution, but assumed that they took values in a certain interval. Karoonsoontawong and Waller [21] developed a robust optimization model for dynamic traffic assignment-based continuous network design problem. The robust model provided the optimal solution that was least sensitive to the variation of travel demand, given the degree of robustness by transportation planners. Sun [22] proposed a min-max model for urban traffic network design under user equilibrium with robust optimization, where uncertain demand belonged to a bounded interval. Ng and Lo [23] discussed two robust models for transportation service network design and applied them in the ferry service in Hong Kong. Owing to the insufficiency distribution information of uncertainty, the solution of robust optimization is likely to be conservative. In view of this, distributionally robust optimization was developed to address the issue of distributional uncertainty using available distribution information (likely moment) of uncertain factors [24] and has been studied over the past few decades. It assumes that the probability distribution of uncertainty belongs to a certain distribution set rather than a determined probability distribution, and makes an optimal decision on the basis of the worst distribution from the set. Yin et al. [25] discussed the p-hub median problem with uncertain carbon emissions under the carbon cap-and-trade policy and proposed a novel distributionally robust optimization model with the ambiguous chance constraint. Gourtani et al. [26] developed a two-stage facility location problem with stochastic customer demand and proposed a distributinally robust optimization framework to hedge risks that arose from incomplete information on the distribution of the uncertainty.

In this paper, we focus on the uncertainty in green port-hinterland intermodal transportation network optimization with uncertain demand. This paper differs from the aforementioned literature in two aspects. Firstly, a distributionally robust chance constrained approach is introduced with the distributional information of mean and variance for the uncertain demand, and a tractable approximation of the chance constrained problem is developed to reformulate the model as a deterministic linear programming. Secondly, hybrid intermodal transportation alternatives are encompassed to help analyze the greenness of hinterland transportation network and trade-offs between economic and environmental goals are investigated by incorporating the variation in the lower bound of probability for chance constraint.

The reminder of this paper is organized as follows. Section 2 presents the problem statement and model formulation of the distributionally robust chance constrained bi-objective optimization problem. The proposed model is applied in the case of the port-hinterland container intermodal transportation network in the Yangtze River Economic Belt in China and the numerical experiments are reported in Section 3. Finally, Section 4 discusses the results and Section 5 concludes the paper and outlines future research directions.

2. The Distributionally Robust Chance Constrained Bi-Objective Modeling

2.1. ProblemStatement

In order to describe the actual port-hinterland container transportation system, this study intends to design the network based on the intermodal transportation. The majority of studies about intermodal transportation network optimization are mainly aimed at a combination of road transport and the railway or the waterway, while few articles consider the combination of rail and barge, barge and barge or rail and rail, especially in some inland areas where inland waterway and railway can both be employed by transport users, such as the hinterlands in the Yangtze River Economic Belt of China.

For the network architecture in this study, the nodes of gateway seaports (GPs), inland intermodal terminals (IITs), and inland cities (ICs) are identified and transportations modes of road, rail, and waterway can be available. Specially, inland intermodal terminals in this study contain two types of terminals: inland river ports (IRPs) and freight rail stations (FRSs). Both of them could undertake the transshipments of containerized freight and connections of transportation modes. However, the former supports barge intermodal transport and the latter promotes railway intermodal transport. The proposed port-hinterland transportation network is depicted in Figure 1. As shown, the transportation demands of goods that are generated in inland cities can be transported to the gateway seaports through direct transportation links by road, visiting one inland intermodal terminal (road–rail intermodal or road-waterway intermodal option)as well as routing through at most two connected terminals of different types or the same type (inter-terminal intermodal options).

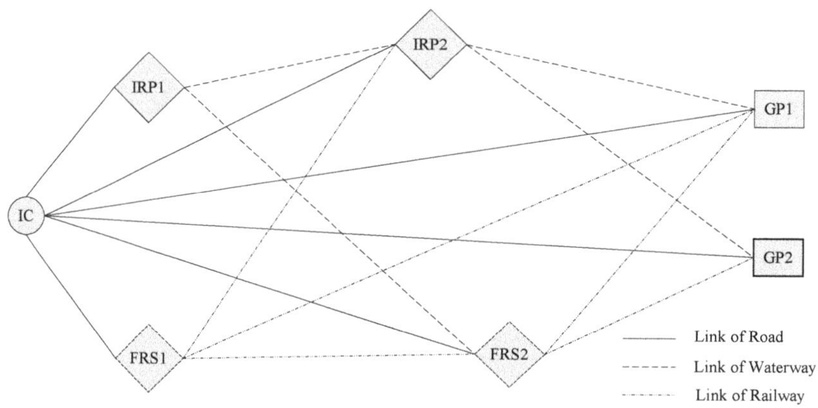

Figure 1. The proposed port-hinterland intermodal transportation network. FRS, freight rail station; IRP, inland river port; IC, inland city; GP, gateway seaport.

With the concern for the greenness, the economic objective and environmental goal are the main focuses and they are integrated for the purpose of trade-off relationship analysis and then finding green network distribution solutions. With regards to the symmetry, the economic and environmental objectives might come to a compromise in these solutions. Thus, the optimization problem in this study is to obtain green freight distribution solutions through the proposed network under the given transportation demands in inland cities and some capacity restrictions, in which the choice of transport routes, the selection of gateway ports, and network flow distribution are determined by the competition in economic and environmental objectives.

This is not a standard hub-spoke network design problem, as it is assumed that there could be direct links from inland city origin to gateway seaport destination and the inland city nodes also can be assigned to more than one inland intermodal terminal. On top of that, it is also assumed that the transshipments and connections of transportation modes only occur at inland intermodal terminals. The number, type, and maximum container handling capacity of inland intermodal nodes are known. Thus, these assumptions increase the number of possible routes from origin to destination, and thus better reflect reality as they allow hybrid inter-terminal connections by rail–barge, barge–rail, barge–barge, and rail–rail intermodal options, especially for the case of long-range freight transportation.

Moreover, in the actual port-hinterland container transportation system, the transportation demand for each inland city is uncertain, and it is also difficult to determine the accurate probability distribution of demand through historical data. Therefore, this study additionally assumes that the specific probability distribution of transportation demand is unknown and only some distribution information such as the mean and variance of demand parameter is given. Although there are different categories of goods for foreign trade and different types of loading containers, the freight unit of TEU (twenty-foot equivalent unit) is applied for the consideration of unification and the freight export direction is mainly focused on in this study. In view of this, a distributionally robust optimization approach with chance constraint, which ensures that the uncertain transportation demand can be satisfied under the worse-case distribution condition, is applied to address the uncertainty. It could help analyze the performance of the port-hinterland transportation network on economic and environmental objectives and their trade-off relationships under different lower bounds of the probability for the chance constraint. The impacts of uncertain transportation demands on the green port-hinterland freight distribution network optimization can also be further explored.

2.2. Notations

The set of index, decision variables and input parameters for the model are listed in Tables 1–3 respectively.

Table 1. The list of index set.

	Description
I	Set of inland cities, indexed by i
S	Set of gateway seaports, indexed by s
H	Set of inland intermodal terminals, indexed by j, k, $H = H_W \cup H_R$
H_W	Set of inland river ports, indexed by j, k
H_R	Set of dry ports, indexed by j, k
M	Set of transportation modes, indexed by m, $m' \in \{1,2,3\}$, {1} = truck, {2} = barge, {3} = rail

Table 2. The list of decision variables.

	Description
Q_{is}	TEU flows from inland city i to gateway seaport s directly by road, $\forall i \in I$, $\forall s \in S$
Q_{ijs}	TEU flows from inland city i to gateway seaport s, only transshipping at inland intermodal terminal j with the long-haul travel by barge or rail, $\forall i \in I$, $\forall s \in S$, $\forall j \in H$
Q_{ijks}	TEU flows from inland city i, firstly collected to inland intermodal terminal j and then routed through terminal k, and finally arrived at gateway seaport s, $\forall i \in I$, $\forall s \in S$, $\forall j,k \in H$

Table 3. The list of input parameters.

	Description
D_i	Transportation demand of city i
μ_i	The mean of transportation demand for city i
σ_i^2	The variance of transportation demand forcity i
p	A probability distribution ofparameter of transportation demand
Γ	Set of probability distributions p
α	The lower bound of probability for chance constraint
X_{ij}	Total TEU volume of goods from city i to the assigned intermodalterminal j
Y_{ks}	Total TEU volume of goods from the final intermodalterminal k to gateway seaport s
$C_{is}{}^m$, $d_{is}{}^m$	Unit transport cost, transport distance from inland city i to gateway seaport s by transportation mode m
$C_{ij}{}^m$, $d_{ij}{}^m$	Unit transport cost, transport distance from inland city i to inland intermodal terminal j by transportation mode m
$C_{jk}{}^m$, $d_{jk}{}^m$	Unit transport cost, transport distance between inland intermodal terminal j and k by transportation mode m
$C_{ks}{}^m$, $d_{ks}{}^m$	Unit transport cost, transport distance from inland intermodal terminal k to gateway seaport s by transportation mode m
$HC_j^{mm'}$	Unit container handling cost at inland intermodal terminal j, for transshipment between mode m and mode m'
SC_j	Unit container storage cost at inland intermodal terminal j
U_k	Container handling capacity of inland intermodal terminal k
U_s	Container handling capacity of gateway seaport s
e^m	CO_2 emission rate of transportation mode m
$e_j^{mm'}$	CO_2 emission rate of handling a TEU at inland intermodal terminal j for transshipment between mode m and mode m'
ε	Limitation on network carbon emissions

As for the mathematical expression, $Tr(A, B)$ refers to the trace of matrix A and B, which is denoted by $\langle A, B\rangle$. $A - B \succcurlyeq 0$ implies that $(A - B)$ is positive semi-definite. Given the mean and variance of uncertain demand, the matrix of second-order moment can be expressed as $\sum_i = E\begin{bmatrix} D_i \\ 1 \end{bmatrix}\begin{bmatrix} D_i \\ 1 \end{bmatrix}^T = \begin{bmatrix} s_i & \mu_i \\ \mu_i & 1 \end{bmatrix}$, in which s_i is the second-order moment and is the sum of the squares of the mean and variance ($s_i = \delta_i^2 + \mu_i^2$). When $\delta_i^2 > 0$, $\sum_i$ is positive definite ($\sum_i \succ 0$).

2.3. Model Formulation

The economic objective and environmental objective of proposed transportation network are measured by the total logistics costs and the total CO_2 emissions of the network, respectively. The former includes the transportation costs on the transportation routes and the handling as well as storage costs at the inland intermodal terminals. The latter consists of the corresponding route emissions and terminal handling CO_2 emissions. A bi-objective optimization model for the port-hinterland container intermodal transportation network with chance constraint can be constructed as follows:

$$\begin{aligned} \min C_{TSP} = & \sum_{i\in I}\sum_{s\in S} C_{is}^1 \cdot Q_{is} + \sum_{i\in I}\sum_{j\in H}\sum_{m\in(2,3)} \left(C_{ij}^1 + HC_j^{1m} + SC_j\right) \cdot X_{ij} + \sum_{i\in I}\sum_{s\in S}\sum_{j\in H}\sum_{k\neq j\in H}\sum_{m,m'\in(2,3)} \left(C_{jk}^m + HC_k^{mm'} + SC_k\right) \cdot Q_{ijks} \\ & + \sum_{k\in H_w}\sum_{s\in S}\sum_{m\in(2,3)} C_{ks}^m \cdot Y_{ks} \end{aligned} \tag{1}$$

$$\begin{aligned} \min EM = & \sum_{i\in I}\sum_{s\in S} e^1 \cdot d_{is}^1 \cdot Q_{is} + \sum_{i\in I}\sum_{j\in H}\sum_{m\in(2,3)} \left(e^1 \cdot d_{ij}^1 + e_j^{1m}\right) \cdot X_{ij} + \sum_{i\in I}\sum_{s\in S}\sum_{j\in H}\sum_{k\neq j\in H}\sum_{m,m'\in(2,3)} \left(e^m \cdot d_{jk}^m + e_k^{mm'}\right) \cdot Q_{ijks} \\ & + \sum_{k\in H}\sum_{s\in S}\sum_{m\in(2,3)} e^m \cdot d_{ks}^m \cdot Y_{ks} \end{aligned} \tag{2}$$

$$\min_{P\in\Gamma} \Pr\left\{\sum_{s\in S} Q_{is} + \sum_{j\in H}\sum_{s\in S} Q_{ijs} + \sum_{j\in H}\sum_{k\neq j\in H}\sum_{s\in S} Q_{ijks} \geq D_i\right\} \geq \alpha,\ \forall i \in I \tag{3}$$

$$\sum_{s\in S} Q_{ijs} + \sum_{k\neq j\in H}\sum_{s\in S} Q_{ijks} = X_{ij},\ \forall i \in I, \forall j \in H \tag{4}$$

$$\sum_{i\in I} Q_{iks} + \sum_{i\in I}\sum_{j\neq k\in H} Q_{ijks} = Y_{ks},\ \forall k \in H, \forall s \in S \tag{5}$$

$$\sum_{s\in S} Y_{ks} \leq U_k,\ \forall k \in H \tag{6}$$

$$\sum_{i\in I} Q_{is} + \sum_{i\in I}\sum_{j\in H} Q_{ijs} + \sum_{i\in I}\sum_{j\in H}\sum_{k\neq j\in H} Q_{ijks} \leq U_s,\ \forall s \in S \tag{7}$$

$$Q_{is} \in \mathbf{N},\ \forall i, s \tag{8}$$

$$Q_{ijs} \in \mathbf{N},\ \forall i, j, s \tag{9}$$

$$Q_{ijks} \in \mathbf{N},\ \forall i, j, k, s \tag{10}$$

Equations (1) and (2) are objective functions representing the minimum total logistics costs of the network and the minimum total CO_2 emissions of the network, respectively. Constraint (3) is the chance constraint, which ensures that the total amount of goods transported from inland city to all seaports meets the worst distribution of the transportation demand of each city. Constraint (4) indicates that the quantity of containers routed from the city to the assigned intermodal terminal is the sum of the volume through road–rail or road–waterway intermodal transportation and the volume through inter-terminal transportation. Constraint (5) ensures the balance of goods entering and leaving the inland intermodal terminals. Constraints (6) and (7) are the container handling capacity limitations of inland intermodal terminals and gateway seaports, respectively. Constraints (8)–(10) are non-negative integer constraints of decision variables.

2.4. Model Transformation

As the model contains the distributionally chance constraint, which is difficult to solve, we can first transform it into the corresponding Lagrange equivalent problem. Then, it is further transformed into a semi-definite programming problem through classified discussion. Finally, it can be transformed into a mixed integer linear optimization equivalent problem, which is easy to solve.

For distributionally robust chance Constraint (3), because $\Pr\left\{\sum\limits_{s\in S} Q_{is} + \sum\limits_{j\in H}\sum\limits_{s\in S} Q_{ijs} + \sum\limits_{j\in H}\sum\limits_{k\neq j\in H}\sum\limits_{s\in S} Q_{ijks} \geq D_i\right\} \geq \alpha,\ \forall i \in I,$ so $\Pr\left\{\sum\limits_{s\in S} Q_{is} + \sum\limits_{j\in H}\sum\limits_{s\in S} Q_{ijs} + \sum\limits_{j\in H}\sum\limits_{k\neq j\in H}\sum\limits_{s\in S} Q_{ijks} \leq D_i\right\} \leq 1-\alpha,\ \forall i \in I$ and Constraint (3) is equivalent to Equation (11).

$$\max_{P\in\Gamma}\Pr\left\{\sum_{s\in S} Q_{is} + \sum_{j\in H}\sum_{s\in S} Q_{ijs} + \sum_{j\in H}\sum_{k\neq j\in H}\sum_{s\in S} Q_{ijks} \leq D_i\right\} \leq 1-\alpha,\ \forall i \in I \tag{11}$$

Lemma 1. *The following problem (12) is equivalent to Equation (11)*

$$\begin{gathered}\langle M_i, \Sigma_i\rangle \leq 1-\alpha,\\ \lambda_i \geq 0,\\ M_i \succcurlyeq 0,\\ M_i + \begin{bmatrix} 0 & -\lambda_i \\ -\lambda_i & 2\lambda_i\left(\sum\limits_{s\in S} Q_{is} + \sum\limits_{j\in H}\sum\limits_{s\in S} Q_{ijs} + \sum\limits_{j\in H}\sum\limits_{k\neq j\in H}\sum\limits_{s\in S} Q_{ijks}\right) - 1 \end{bmatrix} \succcurlyeq 0.\end{gathered} \tag{12}$$

Proof. An indicative function [27] is defined as follows:

$$\prod(D_i) = \begin{cases} 1, & \text{if} \sum\limits_{s\in S} Q_{is} + \sum\limits_{j\in H}\sum\limits_{s\in S} Q_{ijs} + \sum\limits_{j\in H}\sum\limits_{k\neq j\in H}\sum\limits_{s\in S} Q_{ijks} \leq D_i, \\ 0, & \text{otherwise}. \end{cases} \tag{13}$$

Introducing the indicative function into Equation (11), $\max\limits_{P\in\Gamma}\Pr\left\{\sum\limits_{s\in S} Q_{is} + \sum\limits_{j\in H}\sum\limits_{s\in S} Q_{ijs} + \sum\limits_{j\in H}\sum\limits_{k\neq j\in H}\sum\limits_{s\in S} Q_{ijks} \leq D_i\right\}$ can be expressed as follows:

$$\begin{gathered}\max \int \prod(D_i)\mathrm{d}P \\ \text{s.t.} \\ \int \begin{bmatrix} D_i \\ 1 \end{bmatrix}\begin{bmatrix} D_i \\ 1 \end{bmatrix}^{\mathrm{T}} \mathrm{d}P = \Sigma_i .\end{gathered} \tag{14}$$

The Lagrange function is defined as follows:

$$L(P, M_i) = \int \prod(D_i)\mathrm{d}P + \langle M_i, \Sigma_i - \int \begin{bmatrix} D_i \\ 1 \end{bmatrix}\begin{bmatrix} D_i \\ 1 \end{bmatrix}^{\mathrm{T}} \mathrm{d}P\rangle = \langle M_i, \Sigma_i\rangle + \int (\prod(D_i) - \begin{bmatrix} D_i \\ 1 \end{bmatrix}^{\mathrm{T}} M_i \begin{bmatrix} D_i \\ 1 \end{bmatrix})\mathrm{d}P, \tag{15}$$

where M_i is the variable matrix of Lagrange product term. Because $\sum_i \succ 0$, the strong duality holds.

Let $f(D_i) = \begin{bmatrix} D_i \\ 1 \end{bmatrix}^{\mathrm{T}} M_i \begin{bmatrix} D_i \\ 1 \end{bmatrix}$, the problem (14) is then equivalent to (16):

$$g(Q) = \min_{M_i = M_i^T} \max_P \langle M_i, \sum_i \rangle + \int (\prod (D_i) - f(D_i)) \mathrm{d}P, \tag{16}$$

where

$$\max_P \langle M_i, \sum_i \rangle + \int (\prod (D_i) - f(D_i)) \mathrm{d}P = \begin{cases} \langle M_i, \Sigma_i \rangle, & \text{if } \Pi(D_i) - f(D_i) \leq 0, \\ +\infty, & \text{otherwise.} \end{cases} \tag{17}$$

In other words, only if $\prod (D_i) - f(D_i) \leq 0$, $g(Q)$ is finite.

As for $f(D_i)$, there are two situations:

(1) $f(D_i) \geq 0$, for any D_i;
(2) $f(D_i) \geq 1$, for any D_i, which satisfies $\sum\limits_{s \in S} Q_{is} + \sum\limits_{j \in H} \sum\limits_{s \in S} Q_{ijs} + \sum\limits_{j \in H} \sum\limits_{k \neq j \in H} \sum\limits_{s \in S} Q_{ijks} \geq D_i$.

Situation 1 is equivalent to $M_i \succcurlyeq 0$; situation2 is valid only if there exists $\lambda_i \geq 0$, which makes $f(D_i) \geq 1 - 2\lambda_i (\sum\limits_{s \in S} Q_{is} + \sum\limits_{j \in H} \sum\limits_{s \in S} Q_{ijs} + \sum\limits_{j \in H} \sum\limits_{k \neq j \in H} \sum\limits_{s \in S} Q_{ijks} - D_i)$ and

$$M_i + \begin{bmatrix} 0 & -\lambda_i \\ -\lambda_i & 2\lambda_i \left(\sum\limits_{s \in S} Q_{is} + \sum\limits_{j \in H} \sum\limits_{s \in S} Q_{ijs} + \sum\limits_{j \in H} \sum\limits_{k \neq j \in H} \sum\limits_{s \in S} Q_{ijks} \right) - 1 \end{bmatrix} \succcurlyeq 0$$

Therefore, problem (14) is equivalent to (18):

$$\begin{gathered} \min \langle M_i, \Sigma_i \rangle \\ \text{s.t.} \\ \lambda_i \geq 0, \\ M_i \succcurlyeq 0, \\ M_i + \begin{bmatrix} 0 & -\lambda_i \\ -\lambda_i & 2\lambda_i \left(\sum\limits_{s \in S} Q_{is} + \sum\limits_{j \in H} \sum\limits_{s \in S} Q_{ijs} + \sum\limits_{j \in H} \sum\limits_{k \neq j \in H} \sum\limits_{s \in S} Q_{ijks} \right) - 1 \end{bmatrix} \succcurlyeq 0. \end{gathered} \tag{18}$$

In other words, Equation (11) is equivalent to the problem (12). □

Theorem 1. *Constraint (3) with worst-case probability can be approximated from the following constraint:*

$$\sqrt{\frac{\alpha}{1-\alpha}} \sqrt{\delta_i^2} + u_i \leq \sum_{s \in S} Q_{is} + \sum_{j \in H} \sum_{s \in S} Q_{ijs} + \sum_{j \in H} \sum_{k \neq j \in H} \sum_{s \in S} Q_{ijks}, \forall i \in I. \tag{19}$$

Proof. It can be seen from problem (18) that the optimal value is available when $\lambda_i > 0$. We divide (12) by λ_i at both sides of the formula and then replace $\frac{M_i}{\lambda_i}$ and $\frac{1}{\lambda_i}$ with a new M_i and new λ_i, respectively. Then, (12) can be represented by (20):

$$\begin{gathered} \langle M_i, \Sigma_i \rangle \leq \lambda_i (1 - \alpha), \\ \lambda_i \geq 0, \\ M_i \succcurlyeq 0, \\ M_i + \begin{bmatrix} 0 & -1 \\ -1 & 2 \left(\sum\limits_{s \in S} Q_{is} + \sum\limits_{j \in H} \sum\limits_{s \in S} Q_{ijs} + \sum\limits_{j \in H} \sum\limits_{k \neq j \in H} \sum\limits_{s \in S} Q_{ijks} \right) - \lambda_i \end{bmatrix} \succcurlyeq 0. \end{gathered} \tag{20}$$

Owing to the equivalent relationship between the following formulas according to [27],

(1) $\sqrt{\frac{1-\beta}{\beta}}\sqrt{x^{T}\Gamma_{i}x}-u^{T}x\leq\gamma;$

(2) there is asymmetric matrix M and $\tau\in\mathbb{R}^{+}$, which means that

$$\begin{aligned}\langle M,\textstyle\sum\rangle&\leq\tau\beta,\\ \tau&\geq 0,\\ M&\succcurlyeq 0,\\ M+\begin{bmatrix}0 & x\\ x & 2\gamma-\tau\end{bmatrix}&\succcurlyeq 0,\end{aligned}$$

Thus, we can obtain that distributionally robust chance Constraint (3) is equivalent to (19). □

To solve the bi-objective model, the ε-constraint method is adopted by selecting one of objectives as the main goal and converting another objective into an additional constraint. In this paper, costs minimization is selected as the main goal and network emissions formula is added as additional constraint. Therefore, after the transformation approach on the chance constraint above, the bi-objective optimization problem can be then reformulated as following:

$$\begin{aligned}\min C_{TSP}=&\sum_{i\in I}\sum_{s\in S}C_{is}^{1}\cdot Q_{is}+\sum_{i\in I}\sum_{j\in H}\sum_{m\in(2,3)}\left(C_{ij}^{1}+HC_{j}^{1m}+SC_{j}\right)\cdot X_{ij}+\sum_{i\in I}\sum_{s\in S}\sum_{j\in H}\sum_{k\neq j\in H}\sum_{m,m'\in(2,3)}\left(C_{jk}^{m}+HC_{k}^{mm'}+SC_{k}\right)\cdot Q_{ijks}\\&+\sum_{k\in H_{w}}\sum_{s\in S}\sum_{m\in(2,3)}C_{ks}^{m}\cdot Y_{ks}\end{aligned}\tag{21}$$

s.t.

$$\sqrt{\frac{\alpha}{1-\alpha}}\sqrt{\delta_{i}^{2}}+u_{i}\leq\sum_{s\in S}Q_{is}+\sum_{j\in H}\sum_{s\in S}Q_{ijs}+\sum_{j\in H}\sum_{k\neq j\in H}\sum_{s\in S}Q_{ijks},\forall i\in I\tag{22}$$

$$\begin{aligned}&\sum_{i\in I}\sum_{s\in S}e^{1}\cdot d_{is}^{1}\cdot Q_{is}+\sum_{i\in I}\sum_{j\in H}\sum_{m\in(2,3)}\left(e^{1}\cdot d_{ij}^{1}+e_{j}^{1m}\right)\cdot X_{ij}+\sum_{i\in I}\sum_{s\in S}\sum_{j\in H}\sum_{k\neq j\in H}\sum_{m,m'\in(2,3)}\left(e^{m}\cdot d_{jk}^{m}+e_{k}^{mm'}\right)\cdot Q_{ijks}\\&+\sum_{k\in H}\sum_{s\in S}\sum_{m\in(2,3)}e^{m}\cdot d_{ks}^{m}\cdot Y_{ks}\leq\varepsilon\end{aligned}\tag{23}$$

$$\sum_{s\in S}Q_{ijs}+\sum_{k\neq j\in H}\sum_{s\in S}Q_{ijks}=X_{ij},\ \forall i\in I,\forall j\in H\tag{24}$$

$$\sum_{i\in I}Q_{iks}+\sum_{i\in I}\sum_{j\neq k\in H}Q_{ijks}=Y_{ks},\ \forall k\in H,\forall s\in S\tag{25}$$

$$\sum_{s\in S}Y_{ks}\leq U_{k},\ \forall k\in H\tag{26}$$

$$\sum_{i\in I}Q_{is}+\sum_{i\in I}\sum_{j\in H}Q_{ijs}+\sum_{i\in I}\sum_{j\in H}\sum_{k\neq j\in H}Q_{ijks}\leq U_{s},\ \forall s\in S\tag{27}$$

$$Q_{is}\in\mathbf{N},\ \forall i,s\tag{28}$$

$$Q_{ijs}\in\mathbf{N},\ \forall i,j,s\tag{29}$$

$$Q_{ijks}\in\mathbf{N},\ \forall i,j,k,s\tag{30}$$

2.5. Model Solution

The trade-off relationships between total cost and total emissions as well as the Pareto frontier under a certain probability level of chance constraint can be obtained by applying the ε-constraint method, in which a range of network emissions limitations (ε) according to different emissions reduction percentages is set, while minimizing the total costs of the transportation network is selected as the main objective. The model in each ε setting is solved with the software of CPLEX solver to obtain the numerical results of network cost, network emissions, and modal split. After that, various probability levels are proposed in the model and the above-mentioned process is repeated.

3. Case Study

3.1. CaseDescription and Data Collection

The Yangtze River Economic Belt in China is known worldwide because of the Yangtze River golden waterway. It is the longest inland river in Asia and connects the eastern, central, and western parts of China. The port-hinterland container intermodal transportation system of the Yangtze River Economic Belt completes most of the foreign containerized cargo transportation through Shanghai Port and Ningbo-Zhoushan Port. They rank first and fourth in container traffic, respectively [28], and increasing container volume worldwide is forcing them to improve hinterland connections. In this paper, they are recognized as gateway seaports for the proposed port-hinterland intermodal transportation network and 72 inland cities are selected as the freight transportation demand generation nodes according to their importance in the aspects of population scale, economic scale, and foreign volume. As for inland intermodal terminals in the Yangtze River Economic Belt, several river ports that can process substantial containers have developed well in the past decades, while the container railway stations only witnessed growth in volume in the past years. As for the data source, Table 4 gives the mean and standard deviation of transportation demand of each inland city, which are estimated by the authors. The container handling capacity of inland intermodal terminals and gateway seaports are shown in Table 5. Transportation costs per TEU from node to node are gathered from third logistics firms, China Railway Service Center website, and Changjiang Waterway Bureau website. CO_2 emissions rate varies from country to country and the work of Die Zhang [29], which reflects the emissions situation of inland transportation activities in China, is referred in this paper. The carbon emissions factor of each transportation mode is shown in Table 6. The carbon emissions factor for transshipment at inland intermodal terminals is estimated as 5.8 kg/TEU, according to China Port Yearbook.

Table 4. The mean and standard deviation of transportation demand of inland cities (unit: twenty-foot equivalent unit (TEU)).

City No.	Mean	Standard Deviation	City No.	Mean	Standard Deviation	City No.	Mean	Standard Deviation	City No.	Mean	Standard Deviation	City No.	Mean	Standard Deviation
1	1,817,448	56,795	16	597,304	26,132	31	9335	584	46	6586	494	61	1027	52
2	410,016	12,813	17	255,286	11,168	32	21,575	1348	47	5458	409	62	1398	70
3	97,103	3035	18	222,058	11,103	33	23,724	1483	48	4870	366	63	1054	53
4	71,051	2220	19	26,332	1316	34	272,821	20,461	49	9308	698	64	1324	66
5	9482	297	20	89,750	4488	35	30,337	2275	50	285,409	21,406	65	1810	90
6	35,681	1115	21	35,255	1762	36	48,450	3634	51	161,931	12,144	66	63,857	3193
7	16,311	509	22	26,737	1337	37	38,854	2914	52	16,103	1208	67	3674	183
8	54,174	1693	23	23,352	1167	38	15,862	1190	53	12,975	973	68	17,183	859
9	891,286	38,994	24	28,405	1420	39	17,518	1314	54	7389	554	69	47	2
10	1,134,601	49,639	25	10,737	537	40	19,103	1433	55	4296	322	70	2918	146
11	83,857	3669	26	48,063	3004	41	21,209	1591	56	2925	220	71	12,509	625
12	209,270	9155	27	14,802	925	42	82,092	6157	57	4640	348	72	4249	213
13	172,693	7555	28	27,896	1743	43	10,752	806	58	1918	144			
14	120,057	5252	29	19,144	1197	44	7105	533	59	54,022	2701			
15	554,651	24,266	30	13,564	848	45	12,747	956	60	5910	295			

Table 5. Container handling capacity at terminals and seaports (10^3 TEUs).

Inland River Port	Capacity	Inland Railway Container Station	Capacity	Gateway Seaport	Capacity
Suzhou port	400	Yiwu	650	Shanghai	5000
Nanjing port	500	Hefei	260	Ningbo-Zhoushan	5000
Wuhu port	420	Bengbu	50		
Jiujiang port	200	Nanchang	130		
Wuhan port	500	Wuhan	200		
Yueyang port	200	Xiangyang	50		
Chongqing port	400	Changsha	150		
Luzhou port	100	Chongqing	50		
Yibin port	350	Chengdu	200		
		Guiyang	60		
		Kunming	150		

Table 6. Carbon emissions factors of transportation modes (Unit: kg/(TEU·km)).

	Road	Waterway	Railway
Carbon emissions factor	2.189	0.423	0.094

3.2. Experimental Results

3.2.1. Results in Different Objective Optimization and Trade-Off Relationship Analysis ($\alpha = 0.90$)

The model is firstly computed and runs with different optimization goals (costs minimization only, emissions minimization only and bi-objective optimization) by inputting parameters mentioned in Section 3.1 under the probability level of chance constraint with 0.90. Table 7 gives the model outputs on total network costs, network emissions, and flow distribution of the port-hinterland intermodal transportation network in the Yangtze River Economic Belt under three optimization objectives. In the costs minimization model, the lowest network cost that the transportation network of the Yangtze River Economic Belt could achieve is 3255.6 million dollars and the corresponding network emissions is 4.448 million tons. When the optimization objective is network emissions, the minimumCO_2 emissions that the transportation network could achieve is 3.238 million tons, which is approximately 27.2% lower than the network emissions in the lowest cost model, and the corresponding total network cost is 3511.2 million dollars.

When it comes to the bi-objective optimization model, Figure 2 depicts the Pareto frontier of cost goal and emissions goal in detail, which shows the trade-off relationship between total costs and total emissions. As shown in Figure 2, after the limitation percentage of 85.0% on network emissions, maintaining the same percentage of emissions reduction requires a greater network cost increase. It indicates that the 85.0% limitation level would be a watershed between the cost target and emissions target. The numerical results at this level are also listed in Table 7. At this point, the network costs and network emissions reach a compromise in the trade-off relationships. In other words, the transportation network not only could achieve considerable emissions reduction at this emission limitation level, but also could avoid the substantial increase in total logistics costs through the network.

It can also be found that the cost goal and emissions reduction present opposite trends for the case in the Yangtze River Economic Belt. With the decrease of the limitation on network emissions (ε), the emissions reduction percentage increases, while the total network cost trend keeps growing.

Through careful examination, it can be noticed that, in the three optimization models, the proportion of direct road transportation is always the highest, while the usage rates of intermodal transportation alternatives are relatively low. This also can be found from the difference in flow distribution in Table 7. This is because, in the actual case of the Yangtze River Economic Belt, many inland cities have road links to gateway seaports, while they do not have barge shipping lines or railway trains to seaports. With the tightening of the emissions limitation, the flow market of rail intermodal transportation increases obviously while that of barge intermodal and inter-terminal transportation decrease. This implies that the choice of intermodal transport alternatives in the Yangtze River Economic Belt is restricted by the trade-offs between costs and emissions.

Table 7. Results of total costs, total emissions, and flow distribution with different optimization objectives ($\alpha = 0.90$).

	Total Costs/Million US$	Total Emissions/Million Tons	Flow Distribution			
			Direct Road	Waterway/Road Transshipment	Rail/Road Transshipment	Inter-Terminal Transshipment
Cost minimization	3255.6	4.448	61.0%	23.8%	9.3%	5.9%
Bi-objective optimization	3320.7	3.781 (−15.0%) [1]	60.8%	21.3%	15.2%	2.7%
CO_2 emissions minimization	3511.2	3.238 (−27.2%) [1]	60.6%	20.1%	19.30%	0.0%

[1] The value in bracket indicates the percentage of emissions reduction compared to cost minimization model.

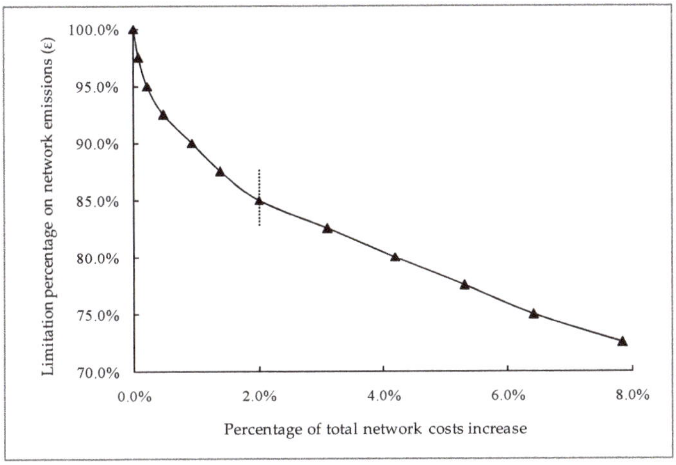

Figure 2. Pareto Frontier between total costs and total emissions ($\alpha = 0.90$).

3.2.2. Sensitivity Analysis of Probability Levels of Chance Constraint

In order to investigate the effects of different probability levels of chance constraint on the bi-objective optimization decision of port-hinterland transportation network, the model results under the lower bounds of the probability of 0.8, 0.85, 0.9, 0.95, and 0.98 for the chance constraint of transportation demand are all calculated and their Pareto frontier graphs are depicted in Figure 3. It can be found that the model obtains different Pareto optimal solutions under various probability levels of chance constraint for transportation demand, as shown in Figure 3. With the increase of the lower bound of probability for chance constraint, the Pareto frontier moves forward and total costs and total emissions are both on the rise. This indicates that the performance of network costs and network emissions of the transportation network can be influenced by the lower bound of probability. In addition, the higher the required lower bound of probability for chance constraint, the greater the impact brought about.

As for the trade-offs between two targets under different probability levels of chance constraint, the Pareto frontier also varies remarkably. When higher requirements for the lower bound of probability are put forward, the trend of Pareto frontier tends to be gentler, as shown in Figure 3. Especially at the probability level of 0.95 and 0.98, the slope of the Pareto frontier drops more prominently than that at lower probability levels (0.80, 0.85, and 0.90). This means that the cost to achieve emission reduction targets for the case in Yangtze River Economic Belt becomes higher and the compromise solution between two objectives is also more difficult to obtain. Therefore, when the required lower bound of probability for chance constraint of transportation demand is high, there exists a great impact on the trade-off relationship between network costs and network emissions.

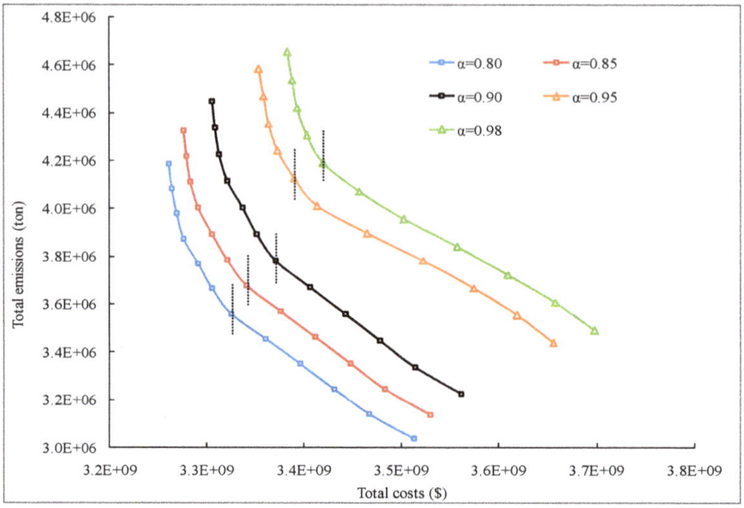

Figure 3. Trends of Pareto frontier between total costs and total emissions under different settings on α.

Further, Figure 4 investigates the comparison of flow distribution of each compromise solution in bi-objective optimization under different probability levels of chance constraint. It is also the reason why the trade-offs between cost target and emissions target change, as depicted in Figure 3. As shown, there is nearly no difference in flow distribution at low probability levels of 0.8, 0.85, and 0.9. However, when the high lower bound of probability for chance constraint is required, such as 0.95 and 0.98, flows on direct road climb up, while intermodal flows decrease to different degrees. This is because the inland terminal capacity of handling container transshipment has become saturated. Thus, if the high lower bound of probability for chance constraint is required for the port-hinterland transportation network in the Yangtze River Economic Belt, it would be better to expand the handling capacity of inland intermodal terminals.

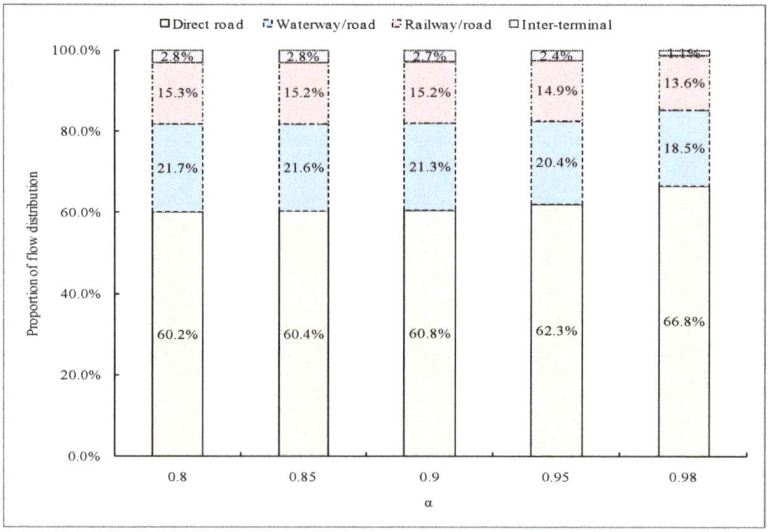

Figure 4. The comparison of network flow distribution under different settings on α.

4. Discussion

This paper differs from the previous literature in two aspects. Firstly, hybrid intermodal transportation alternatives are encompassed to help analyze the greenness of hinterland transportation network. Secondly, a distributionally robust chance constrained approach is introduced with the partial distributional information of mean and variance for the uncertain demand, and then trade-offs between economic and environmental goals are investigated by incorporating the variation in lower bound of probability for chance constraint.

The flow distribution results indicate that railway–road intermodal transport can be promoted with the greenness requirement on the proposed port-hinterland transportation network. In other words, more flows are absorbed to the railway–road intermodal routes when the optimization objective is the bi-objective case or the CO_2 minimum emissions case. It is an interesting finding for intermodal freight transport, because it implies that there is competition in hybrid intermodal transportation alternatives, rather than the only competition in unimodal and single intermodal options in most intermodal transport research articles (such as the works of Crainic et al. [5], Santoset al. [13], and Bouchery and Fransoo [30]). This finding might provide a different perspective for the port-hinterland intermodal transportation network optimization with the greenness consideration.

As for the uncertainty of transportation demand in port-hinterland freight network optimization, this study considers the situation that the accurate distribution formation of stochastic variation is usually difficult to obtain in reality. In recent literature, most studies on hinterland freight transportation network planning traded the transportation demand as the determined parameter or stochastic parameter with the known distribution (such as the works of Dai et al. [31], Liu et al. [32], and Chen and Wang [33]. For this case, a distributionally robust chance constrained approach is introduced and a tractable approximation of the chance constrained problem is then developed to reformulate the model as a deterministic linear programming. The results indicate that the green solution under bi-objective optimization model for the port-hinterland transportation system is more difficult to obtain with the higher requirement of lower bound of probability for chance constraint of transportation demand. It also offers a different perspective for the green port-hinterland intermodal transportation network optimization with the uncertainty of transportation demand.

5. Conclusions

This paper models the uncertainty in green port-hinterland intermodal transportation network optimization through a distributionally robust chance constrained method and a bi-objective approach. The chance constraint that transportation demand is satisfied under the worst-case distribution situation is proposed based on the mean and variance of probability distribution for uncertain demand. The approaches of equivalent transformation on chance constraint and ε-constraint method are employed to help reformulate the model.

The trade-offs between network costs and network emissions are analyzed and the sensitivity of probability levels for chance constraint on Pareto frontier is followed by an application of the port-hinterland intermodal transportation network in the Yangtze River Economic Belt in China. The results show that network costs and network emissions both increase significantly with the increase of the lower bound of probability for chance constraint. When the probability level climbs to some high values, the movement of Pareto frontier changes a lot, which indicates that the probability level has a great impact on the trade-offs between network costs and network emissions. This also implies that it is better to expand the handling capacity of inland intermodal terminals at high probability levels for chance constraint. Overall, the approach of distributionally robust chance constraint in the model provides a novel insight to solve the dynamic planning problem caused by the fluctuation of demands in real life. The decision makers can also choose an appropriate solution according to their preference for economic and environmental aspects.

Although the study of this paper provides some decision supports for the green port-hinterland container transportation network with uncertain demand, it also has a lack of consideration of more uncertain parameters in the model. For example, transportation cost, carbon emissions, and terminal handling capacity may all face uncertainty in the real-world case. Thus, further research might extend uncertain programming in the green logistics network in a more comprehensive direction.

Author Contributions: Conceptualization, Q.D.; Investigation, Q.D.; Methodology, Q.D.; Resources, J.Y.; Software, Q.D.; Supervision, J.Y.; Writing—original draft, Q.D.; Writing—review & editing, J.Y. All authors have read and agreed to the published version of the manuscript.

Funding: The authors would like to thank the financial supports from Jilin Province Transportation Science and Technology Plan Project (46160101).

Acknowledgments: The first author is grateful to the support of China Scholarship Council for the joint Doctoral Program with one-year period in University of Liverpool of UK.

Conflicts of Interest: The authors declare no conflict of interest.

References

1. Notteboom, T. The relationship between seaports and the intermodal hinterland in light of global supply chains: European challenges. In *Port Competition and Hinterland Connections*; Round Table 143; OECD Publishing: Paris, France, 2009; p. 30.
2. OECD/ITF. *Port Competition and Hinterland Connections*; OECD Publishing: Paris, France, 2009; ISBN 9789282102244.
3. Woxenius, J. Generic framework for transport network designs: Applications and treatment in intermodal freight transport literature. *Transp. Rev.* **2007**, *27*, 733–749. [CrossRef]
4. Frémont, A.; Franc, P. Hinterland transportation in Europe: Combined transport versus road transport. *J. Transp. Geogr.* **2010**, *18*, 548–556. [CrossRef]
5. Crainic, T.G.; Dell'Olmo, P.; Ricciardi, N.; Sgalambro, A. Modeling dry-port-based freight distribution planning. *Transp. Res. Part C Emerg. Technol.* **2015**, *55*, 518–534. [CrossRef]
6. Caris, A.; Limbourg, S.; Macharis, C.; Van Lier, T.; Cools, M. Integration of inland waterway transport in the intermodal supply chain: A taxonomy of research challenges. *J. Transp. Geogr.* **2014**, *41*, 126–136. [CrossRef]
7. European Commission White Paper. Roadmap to a Single European Transport Area—Towards a Competitive and Resource Efficient Transport System.2011. Available online: https://eur-lex.europa.eu/legal-content/EN/ALL/?uri=CELEX:52011DC0144 (accessed on 12 October 2017).
8. Caris, A.; Macharis, C.; Janssens, G.K. Decision support in intermodal transport: A new research agenda. *Comput. Ind.* **2013**, *64*, 105–112. [CrossRef]
9. Macharis, C.; Van Hoeck, E.; Pekin, E.; Van Lier, T. A decision analysis framework for intermodal transport: Comparing fuel price increases and the internalisation of external costs. *Transp. Res. Part. A Policy Pract.* **2010**, *44*, 550–561. [CrossRef]
10. Macharis, C.; Caris, A.; Jourquin, B.; Pekin, E. A decision support framework for intermodal transport policy. *Eur. Transp. Res. Rev.* **2011**, *3*, 167–178. [CrossRef]
11. Mostert, M.; Caris, A.; Limbourg, S. Road and intermodal transport performance: The impact of operational costs and air pollution external costs. *Res. Transp. Bus. Manag.* **2017**, *23*, 75–85. [CrossRef]
12. Iannone, F. The private and social cost efficiency of port hinterland container distribution through a regional logistics system. *Transp. Res. Part. A Policy Pract.* **2012**, *46*, 1424–1448. [CrossRef]
13. Santos, B.; Limbourg, S.; Carreira, J.S. The impact of transport policies on railroad intermodal freight competitiveness—The case of Belgium. *Transp. Res. Part D: Transp. Environ.* **2015**, *34*, 230–244. [CrossRef]
14. Zhang, M.; Janic, M.; Tavasszy, L. A freight transport optimization model for integrated network, service, and policy design. *Transp. Res. Part. E Logist. Transp. Rev.* **2015**, *77*, 61–76. [CrossRef]
15. Lam, J.S.L.; Gu, Y. A market-oriented approach for intermodal network optimisation meeting cost, time and environmental requirements. *Int. J. Prod. Econ.* **2016**, *171*, 266–274. [CrossRef]
16. Demir, E.; Hrušovský, M.; Jammernegg, W.; Van Woensel, T. Green intermodal freight transportation: Bi-objective modelling and analysis. *Int. J. Prod. Res.* **2019**, *57*, 6162–6180. [CrossRef]
17. Contreras, I.; Cordeau, J.; Laporte, G. Stochastic uncapacitated hub location. *Eur. J. Oper. Res.* **2011**, *212*, 518–528. [CrossRef]

18. Ardjmand, E.; Young, W.A.; Weckman, G.R.; Bajgiran, O.S.; Aminipour, B.; Park, N.; Ii, W.A.Y. Applying genetic algorithm to a new bi-objective stochastic model for transportation, location, and allocation of hazardous materials. *Expert Syst. Appl.* **2016**, *51*, 49–58. [CrossRef]
19. Wang, X. Stochastic resource allocation for containerized cargo transportation networks when capacities are uncertain. *Transp. Res. Part. E Logist. Transp. Rev.* **2016**, *93*, 334–357. [CrossRef]
20. Zhao, Y.; Xue, Q.; Cao, Z.C.; Zhang, X. A Two-stage chance constrained approach with application to stochastic intermodal service network design problems. *J. Adv. Transp.* **2018**, *2018*, 1–18. [CrossRef]
21. Karoonsoontawong, A.; Waller, S.T. Robust dynamic continuous network design problem. *Transp. Res. Rec.* **2007**, *2029*, 58–71. [CrossRef]
22. Sun, H.; Gao, Z.; Long, J.C. The robust model of continuous transportation network design problem with demand uncertainty. *J. Transp. Syst. Eng. Inf. Technol.* **2011**, *11*, 70–76. [CrossRef]
23. Ng, M.; Lo, H.K. Robust models for transportation service network design. *Transp. Res. Part. B Methodol.* **2016**, *94*, 378–386. [CrossRef]
24. Scarf, H.E. A min-max solution of an inventory problem. Herbert Scarf's contributions to economics. *Int. J. Game Theory Res.* **1958**, *6*, 19–27.
25. Yin, F.; Chen, Y.; Song, F.; Liu, Y. A new distributionally robust p-hub median problem with uncertain carbon emissions and its tractable approximation method. *Appl. Math. Model.* **2019**, *74*, 668–693. [CrossRef]
26. Gourtani, A.; Nguyen, T.D.; Xu, H. A distributionally robust optimization approach for two-stage facility location problems. *EURO J. Comput. Optim.* **2020**, *8*, 141–172. [CrossRef]
27. El Ghaoui, L.; Oks, M.; Oustry, F. Worst-case value-at-risk and robust portfolio optimization: A conic programming approach. *Oper. Res.* **2003**, *51*, 543–556. [CrossRef]
28. World Shipping Council. Top 50 World Container Ports. Available online: http://www.worldshipping.org/about-the-industry/global-trade/top-50-world-container-ports (accessed on 2 May 2018).
29. Zhang, D. Study on the Container Port Inland Transportation System's Network Optimization with Low Carbon Theory. Dalian Maritime University, 2015. Available online: http://kns.cnki.net/KCMS/detail/.detail.aspx?dbcode=CMFD&dbname=CMFD201601&filename=1015656920.nh&v=MTM3NjNMdXhZUzdEaDFUM3FUcldNMUZyQ1VSTEtmYitSbkZ5L2dXNy9OVkYyNkc3VzlHTmpPcjVFYlBJUjhlWDE= (accessed on 23 October 2018).
30. Bouchery, Y.; Fransoo, J. Cost, carbon emissions and modal shift in intermodal network design decisions. *Int. J. Prod. Econ.* **2015**, *164*, 388–399. [CrossRef]
31. Dai, Q.; Yang, J.; Li, D. Modeling a three-mode hybrid port-hinterland freight intermodal distribution network with environmental consideration: The case of the yangtze river economic belt in China. *Sustainability* **2018**, *10*, 3081. [CrossRef]
32. Liu, K.; Li, Q.; Zhang, Z.H. Distributionally robust optimization of an emergency medical service station location and sizing problem with joint chance constraints. *Transp. Res. Part. B Methodol.* **2019**, *119*, 79–101. [CrossRef]
33. Chen, X.; Wang, X. Effects of carbon emission reduction policies on transportation mode selections with stochastic demand. *Transp. Res. E Logist. Transp. Rev.* **2015**, *90*, 196–205. [CrossRef]

symmetry

MDPI

Article

An Extended Shapley TODIM Approach Using Novel Exponential Fuzzy Divergence Measures for Multi-Criteria Service Quality in Vehicle Insurance Firms

Arunodaya Raj Mishra [1], Pratibha Rani [2], Abbas Mardani [3,4,*], Reetu Kumari [5], Edmundas Kazimieras Zavadskas [6] and Dilip Kumar Sharma [5]

1 Department of Mathematics, Govt College, Jaitwara 485221, MP, India; arunodaya87@outlook.com
2 Department of Mathematics, NIT, Warangal 506004, Telangana, India; pratibha138@gmail.com
3 Informetrics Research Group, Ton Duc Thang University, Ho Chi Minh City 758307, Vietnam
4 Faculty of Business Administration, Ton Duc Thang University, Ho Chi Minh City 758307, Vietnam
5 Department of Mathematics, Jaypee University of Engineering & Technology, Guna 473226, MP, India; tomarritu1987@gmail.com (R.K.); dilipsharmajiet@rediffmail.com (D.K.S.)
6 Institute of Sustainable Construction, Vilnius Gediminas Technical University, Sauletekio Ave. 11, LT-10223 Vilnius, Lithuania; edmundas.zavadskas@vgtu.lt
* Correspondence: abbas.mardani@tdtu.edu.vn

Received: 9 June 2020; Accepted: 26 August 2020; Published: 3 September 2020

Abstract: Classification of the divergence measure for fuzzy sets (FSs) has been a successful approach since it has been utilized in several disciplines, e.g., image segmentation, pattern recognition, decision making, etc. The objective of the manuscript is to show the advantage of the combined methodology. A comparison clearly shows the usefulness of the proposed technique over the existing ones under the fuzzy environment. This study presents novel exponential-type divergence measures with some elegant features, which can be applied to FSs. Next, a TODIM (an acronym in Portuguese for Interactive Multicriteria Decision Making) approach derived from prospect theory, Shapley function, and divergence measure for multi-criteria decision-making (MCDM) is proposed. Besides, for the reason of evaluating the dominance degree of the option, and the weights of the criteria, proposed divergence measures are implemented. Evaluating and selecting the service quality is the most important issue in management; it has a direct influence on the way the manufacturer performs its tasks. Selecting the service quality can be thought of as a problem of MCDM involving numerous contradictory criteria (whether of a quantitative or qualitative nature) for the evaluation processes. In recent years, the service quality assessment is becoming increasingly complex and uncertain; as a result, some criteria assessment processes cannot be efficiently done by numerical assessments. In addition, decision experts (DEs) may not always show full rationality in different real-life situations that need decision making. Here, a real service quality evaluation problem is considered to discuss the efficacy of the developed methods. The algorithm (TODIM based on the Shapley function and divergence measures) has a unique procedure among MCDM approaches, which is demonstrated for the first time in this paper.

Keywords: service quality; fuzzy set; Jensen–Shannon divergence; shapley function; MCDM; TODIM

1. Introduction

Shannon entropy [1] and Kullback–Leibler (K-L) [2] divergences are two critical measures in the information theory. On account of their accomplishment, there are several efforts to extend these notions. In the literature, the author(s) have achieved various information measures. K-L [2] pioneered the concept of divergence, which measures the discrimination level among probability distributions. Later on, numerous researchers developed several generalized divergence measures and described their behaviors and applications [3,4]. A novel measure called the Jensen–Shannon (J-S) divergence, which was introduced by Lin [5], which has received interest from researchers and been effectively implemented in various constraints [6,7].

Analogous to the idea of probability doctrine, Zadeh [8] initiated the conception of fuzzy sets (FSs) to handle the ambiguity that arises in daily life problems. The concept of fuzzy entropy measures refers to the amount of fuzziness that arises due to the ambiguity of being or not being a member of the set. Based on Shannon entropy, De Luca and Termini [9] pioneered the axiomatic definition of fuzzy entropy. Pal and Pal [10] decisively investigated Shannon's function to propose novel entropy based on the exponential function. Hooda [11] developed two generalized measures based on fuzzy entropy. Based on exponential function, Verma and Sharma [12] studied a new generalized parametric fuzzy entropy. Mishra et al. [13] established logarithmic-fuzzy entropy with the applications in pattern recognition and medical diagnosis. Aside from these articles, copious numbers of fuzzy entropy have been developed by numerous authors [14–17].

Moreover, Bhandari and Pal [18] established the notion of the measure of divergence for FSs, which describes the measure of discrimination between FSs. Next, the exponential divergence measure for FSs was introduced by Fan and Xie [19] and deliberated its properties. An automated leukocyte recognition application of the divergence measure for FSs was discussed by Ghosh et al. [6]. Mishra et al. [12,15] proposed a discrimination measure for FSs and applied these measures to medical and crop diagnosis. Rani et al. [20] studied unified fuzzy divergence measures with an application in the e-waste recycling selection problem. Arora and Dhiman [21] presented a novel measure of fuzzy directed divergence with an application in decision making. Divergence measures for FSs and their extensions have ample applications in various disciplines viz. pattern recognition, signal and image processing, medical diagnosis, and so on [22–25].

Multi-criteria decision making (MCDM) has been proven as an important research discipline of decision science and is currently broadly applied in business and management [26,27], engineering [20,28], economy [29,30], and so on. In real-life applications, it is quite a challenging issue to find the solution of MCDM problems. Over the last few decades, several new MCDM methods have been introduced. By increasing the difficulty and the extensive changes in today's environment, the classical MCDM methods were not adequate to deal with the practical MCDM problems. Nowadays, various procedures have been developed to tackle the MCDM problems, viz. the technique for order of preference by similarity to ideal solution (TOPSIS) [31,32], weighted aggregated sum product assessment (WASPAS) [33,34], multi-attributive border approximation area comparison (MABAC) [35,36], Vlse Kriterijumska Optimizacija Kompromisno Resenje (VIKOR) [37,38], ELimination and Choice Expressing REality (ELECTRE) [39,40], Preference Ranking Organization METHod for Enrichment of Evaluations (PROMETHEE) [41,42], TODIM (which is the acronym in Portuguese language for Interactive MCDM) [43,44] and so on.

The prospect doctrine is a descriptive doctrine that can be implemented in the process of making decisions under risk [45]. An MCDM technique named TODIM was introduced by Gomes and Lima [46] initially. The base of this technique was the prospect theory, and it was used to explain the MCDM problem in cases where the psychological behaviors of decision experts (DEs) are considered. Next, TODIM has also been widely employed in a variety of fields with decision-making problems, e.g., portfolio allocation and selection [43], internet banking website quality [47], and sustainability perspective [48]. In another study, Gomes et al. [49] considered the fact that relationships amongst different criteria are sometimes interdependent; thus, they introduced a method integrating TODIM and Choquet integral for the purpose of handling the MCDM problems using criteria interactions. TODIM was expanded by Qin et al. [50] using the interval-valued type-2 fuzzy sets to solve the green supplier selection problem. Mishra and Rani [51] presented the interval-valued intuitionistic fuzzy TODIM procedure based on bi-parametric information measures to evaluate the plant location selection problem. On the other hand, Hesitant-TODIM was introduced by Fan et al. [52] to handle the hybrid MCDM problems using interval, crisp, and fuzzy numbers. Liu and Shen [53] suggested the Choquet-TODIM method within a linguistic intuitionistic fuzzy set environment. Further, Zhang et al. [54] studied the TODIM approach for IFSs to rank the products with online reviews. Though TODIM was capable of effectively solving the decision-making problems using crisp numbers, in a variety of conditions, crisp data is not sufficient for modeling the decision-making issues in real-life problems. Moreover, the fuzzy set and their extended forms have been found to be more effective in modeling human judgments. It has encouraged lots of scholars to design extended forms of TODIM as this method efficiently solves the MCDM problems in a variety of fuzzy settings.

As we recognize, any MCDM problem aims to deal with two major concerns: (1) The weights of criteria (and experts), and (2) aggregation operators. Many scholars have taken into account the divergence measure because of its effectiveness in the evaluation of uncertain information. In such conditions, this is generally applied to acquiring the criteria weights for MCDM in uncertain environments [55,56]. Nevertheless, experts' weights, criteria, and aggregation operators for FSs are all on the basis of the assumption indicating the significance of experts and criteria are considered only in their additive weights. Although, in several practical MCDM problems, the independent features between the experts and the criteria are generally violated. Therefore, numerous researchers have studied the fuzzy measure [57], which is an efficient tool for modeling the interactions between elements that exist within a set. In the case of the additive measures, such measures only make the monotonicity instead of additively. They can be used in numerous fields, especially in decision making and game theory.

Motivated by the above-mentioned works, the present paper proposes the new Jensen–Shannon exponential divergence (JSED) measures are applied to FSs and discusses some elegant properties, which are useful in improving the usefulness of the proposed measure. Next, a fuzzy TODIM technique for MCDM is proposed. To extend the F-TODIM method, the concepts of the Shapley function and divergence measure are used. In the course of calculating the criteria weight and the proposed method's dominance degree, some modifications are done when necessary. Such integration is able to result in more realistic criteria weights for decision-making as well as higher stability in the various weights of criteria. We make use of an instance of the service quality selection problem in a way to show more clearly the process and to demonstrate how the proposed method performs its defined tasks when faced with real-world decision-making problems. At the final step, the proposed F-TODIM method is compared with some currently used methods, aiming at illustrating the obtained results' validity.

The arrangement of this article is provided in the given sections. The preliminaries and the divergence measure for FSs are provided in Section 2. Section 3 introduces the novel Jensen–Shannon exponential divergence measures for FSs. Section 4 provides the integrated TODIM approach based on the Shapley function and divergence measure. In Section 5, the application of service quality as a case study and comparative analysis is provided. The conclusion of this study is provided in Section 6.

2. Preliminaries

For the probability distribution, $Q = (q_1, q_2, \ldots, q_n) \in \Delta_n$, Shannon's entropy [1] is described by

$$H(Q) = -\sum_{i=1}^{n} q_i \log q_i, \tag{1}$$

Additionally, Renyi entropy [3] is given as

$$H_R(Q) = \frac{1}{\alpha - 1} \ln\left(\sum_{i=1}^{n} q_i^{\alpha}\right), \text{ where } \alpha > 0, \ \alpha \neq 1. \tag{2}$$

The exponential entropy was suggested by Pal and Pal [10] as another measure as expressed below:

$$H_{Pal}(Q) = \sum_{i=1}^{n} q_i e^{(1-q_i)} - 1. \tag{3}$$

According to Pal and Pal [10], from a certain perspective, the exponential entropy is better than Shannon's entropy [1]. In the uniform distribution $Q = \left(\frac{1}{n}, \frac{1}{n}, \cdots, \frac{1}{n}\right)$, the measure (3) is fixed as the upper-bound $\lim_{n\to\infty} H\left(\frac{1}{n}, \frac{1}{n}, \cdots, \frac{1}{n}\right) = e - 1$, which is not possible for (1).

Later on, Kullback and Leibler (K-L) [2] introduced a divergence measure among the probability distributions Q and S, given as:

$$C_{KL}(Q||S) = \sum_{i=1}^{n} q_i \log \frac{q_i}{s_i},. \tag{4}$$

Its symmetric version, i.e., Jeffrey's invariant, is given by

$$J(Q||S) = C_{KL}(Q||S) + C_{KL}(S||Q). \tag{5}$$

Renyi divergence is associated with entropy (2) by various settings as follows:

$$C_R(Q||S) = \frac{1}{\alpha - 1} \ln\left(\sum_{i=1}^{n} q_i^{\alpha} s_i^{1-\alpha}\right), \ \alpha > 0, \ \alpha \neq 1. \tag{6}$$

Lin [5] proposed the Jensen–Shannon divergence measure between two probability distributions Q and S, given as

$$C_{JS}(Q||S) = H\left(\frac{Q+S}{2}\right) - \frac{H(Q) + H(S)}{2}, \tag{7}$$

which $H(.)$ stands for the Shannon entropy expressed earlier in (1).

For simplicity, Jensen–Shannon divergence (7) can be demonstrated regarding the K-L divergence as follows:

$$C_{JK}(Q||S) = \frac{1}{2}\left[C_{JS}\left(Q||\frac{Q+S}{2}\right) + C_{JS}\left(S||\frac{Q+S}{2}\right)\right]. \tag{8}$$

2.1. Fuzzy Sets (FSs)

Definition 1. *(Zadeh [8]). A fuzzy set P on finite discourse set $V = \{v_1, \ v_2, \ \ldots, \ v_n\}$ is given by:*

$$P = \{(v_i, \mu_P(v_i)) : \mu_P(v_i) \in [0, 1]; \forall\, v_i \in V\},$$

where the function $\mu_P(v_i)(0 \leq \mu_P(v_i) \leq 1)$ is the membership degree of v_i to P in V.

For $P \in FS(V)$, we utilize P^c to find the complement of P, i.e., $\mu_{P^c}(v_i) = 1 - \mu_P(v_i), \ \forall\, v_i \in V$. For $P, \ E \in FSs(V)$, $P \cup E$ is given as $\mu_{P\cup E}(v_i) = \max\{\mu_P(v_i), \ \mu_E(v_i)\}$. $P \cap E$ is defined as $\mu_{P\cap E}(v_i) = \min\{\mu_P(v_i), \ \mu_E(v_i)\}$ and $P \subseteq E$ iff $\mu_P(v_i) \leq \mu_E(v_i)$.

De Luca and Termini [9], for the first time, presented the definition of entropy for FSs.

Definition 2. *(De Luca and Termini [9]). A real-valued mapping $H : FS(V) \to R^+$ is called an entropy on FS(V) if H satisfies the axioms:*

(A1). $H(D) = 0, \ \ \forall\, D \in P(V)$ = Set of all crisp sets in V;
(A2). $H\left(\left[\frac{1}{2}\right]\right) = \max_{P\in FS(V)} H(P)$;
(A3). $H(P^*) \leq H(P)$, P^* is the sharper version of P; and
(A4). $H(P) = H(P^c), \ \ \forall\, P \in FS(V)$.

Analogous to (1), De Luca and Termini [9] pioneered the constructive measure as:

$$H_D(P) = -\frac{1}{n}\sum_{i=1}^{n}[\mu_P(v_i)\ln\mu_P(v_i) + (1-\mu_P(v_i))\ln(1-\mu_P(v_i))]. \tag{9}$$

Pal and Pal [20] firstly introduced the exponential fuzzy entropy corresponding to (2), which is:

$$H_P(P) = \frac{1}{n\left(\sqrt{e}-1\right)}\sum_{i=1}^{n}\left[\mu_P(v_i)e^{(1-\mu_P(v_i))} + (1-\mu_P(v_i))e^{\mu_P(v_i)} - 1\right]. \tag{10}$$

Further, Mishra et al. [15] studied an exponential fuzzy entropy measure as:

$$H_A(P) = \frac{1}{n\sqrt{e}\left(\sqrt{e}-1\right)}\sum_{i=1}^{n}\left[e - \mu_P(v_i)e^{\mu_P(v_i)} - (1-\mu_P(v_i))e^{(1-\mu_P(v_i))}\right]. \tag{11}$$

2.2. Divergence Measure for FSs

Indeed, the divergence measure is employed for the purpose of measuring the discrimination information. Montes et al. [58] constructed the definition of F-divergence measure based on axioms.

Definition 3. *(Montes et al. [58]). Let $P,\ E \in FSs(V)$, then $J : FSs(V) \times FSs(V) \to \mathbb{R}$ is an F-divergence measure if it fulfills the given postulates:*

(P1). $J(P,\ E) = J(E,\ P)$;
(P2). $J(P,\ E) = 0$ iff $P = E$;
(P3). $J(P \cap T,\ E \cap T) \leq J(P,\ E),\ \forall T \in FS(V)$; and
(P4). $J(P \cup T,\ E \cup T) \leq J(P,\ E),\ T \in FS(V)$.

The simplest divergence measure for FSs, as suggested by Bhandari and Pal [18], is given as:

$$C(P||E) = \sum_{i=1}^{n}\left[\mu_P(v_i)\ \log\ \frac{\mu_P(v_i)}{\mu_E(v_i)} + (1-\mu_P(v_i))\log\ \frac{(1-\mu_P(v_i))}{(1-\mu_E(v_i))}\right]. \tag{12}$$

Fan and Xie [19] founded a new measure for FSs as:

$$C_{FX}(P||E) = \sum_{i=1}^{n}\left[\left\{1 - (1-\mu_P(v_i))e^{(\mu_P(v_i)-\mu_E(v_i))} + (1-\mu_P(v_i))e^{(\mu_E(v_i)-\mu_P(v_i))}\right\}\right]. \tag{13}$$

The distance measure depicts the difference between the two fuzzy sets. Fan and Xie [19] defined the distance measure for FSs as follows:

Definition 4. *(Fan and Xie [19]). A real-valued function $d : FSs(V) \times FSs(V) \to [0,1]$ is a distance measure for FSs if d fulfills the given postulates:*

(D1). $d(P,\ E) = d(E,\ P);\ \ \forall\ P, E \in FSs(V)$;
(D2). $d(P,\ P) = 0,\ \ \forall P \in FS(V)$;
(D3). $d(P,\ P^c) = 1,\ \ \forall\ P \in FS(V)$; and
(D4). $\forall P,\ E,\ T \in FSs(V)$, if $P \subset E \subset T$, then $d(P,T) \geq d(P,E)$ and $d(P,T) \geq d(E,\ T)$.

3. New Divergence Measure for FSs

Here, we proposed the Jensen–Shannon divergence measure for FSs corresponding to Shannon entropy concepts and Jensen's inequality. A key feature of the Jensen–Shannon divergence is the fact that to each probability distribution, a different weight can be allocated. Such a characteristic has made it appropriate for studying the decision problems in cases in which weights can be prior probabilities. The majority of divergence measures have been created for two probability distributions. In the case of some particular applications, e.g., taxonomy studies in biology and genetics, one is needed for measuring the overall difference of more than two distributions. It is completely possible to generalize the Jensen–Shannon divergence in order to arrange such a measure for any finite number of distributions. In addition, it can be effectively applied to multiclass decision making.

Jensen–Shannon Exponential Divergence Measures for FSs

The idea of the Jensen–Shannon divergence promoted the authors to introduce an innovative divergence measure to describe the distinction between two fuzzy FSs and demonstrate various elegant properties.

Definition 5. *Let $P,\ E \in FSs(V)$. Based on Mishra et al. [15], an exponential Jensen–Shannon divergence measure for P and E is described as follows:*

$$\begin{aligned} C_e(P\|E) &= H_A\left(\tfrac{P+E}{2}\right) - \left(\tfrac{H_A(P)+H_A(E)}{2}\right) \\ &= \frac{-1}{n\sqrt{e}(\sqrt{e}-1)} \sum_{i=1}^{n} \left[\begin{array}{c} \left(\frac{\mu_P(v_i)+\mu_E(v_i)}{2}\right)\exp\left(\frac{\mu_P(v_i)+\mu_E(v_i)}{2}\right) \\ +\left(\frac{2-\mu_P(v_i)-\mu_E(v_i)}{2}\right)\exp\left(\frac{2-\mu_P(v_i)-\mu_E(v_i)}{2}\right) \end{array} \right. \\ &\quad \left. -\frac{1}{2}\left(\begin{array}{c} \mu_P(v_i)\exp(\mu_P(v_i)) + (1-\mu_P(v_i))\exp(1-\mu_P(v_i)) \\ +\mu_E(v_i)\exp(\mu_E(v_i)) + (1-\mu_E(v_i)) + \exp(1-\mu_E(v_i)) \end{array} \right) \right]. \end{aligned} \tag{14}$$

Next, to test the validity of measure (14), we established the given theorem.

Theorem 1. *For $P,\ E,\ T \in FSs(V)$, the measure (14) holds the following postulates:*

(a) $C_e(P\|\ E) \geq 0$ and $0 \leq C_e(P\|\ E) \leq 1$,
(b) $C_e(P\|\ E) = 0$ if and only if $P = E$,
(c) $C_e(P\|\ E) = C_e(E\|P)$,
(d) $C_e(P\|P^c) = 1$, if and only if $P \in P(V)$,
(e) $C_e(P\|E) = C_e(P^c\|E^c)$ and $C_e(P\|E^c) = C_e(P^c\|E)$, and
(f) $C_e(P\|E) \leq C_e(P\|T)$ and $C_e(E\|T) \leq C_e(P\|T)$, for $P \subseteq E \subseteq T$.

Proof. The proof of the theorem is given in Appendix A.1. □

Proposition 1. *If $E = P^c$, then the relation between $C_e(P\|E)$ and $H_A(P)$:*

$$H_A(P) = 1 - C_e(P\|E), \tag{15}$$

where $H_A(P)$ is entropy for *FSs*(V).

Proof. The proof is given in Appendix A.2. □

Corollary 1. *The measure $C_e(P\|E)$ is the distance measure on FSs(V).*

Proof. From Theorem 1, $C_e(P\|E)$ fulfills all the essential postulates of the distance measure (Definition 6). Hence, $C_e(P\|E)$ is also a distance measure for *FSs*(V). □

Proposition 2. *For all* $P,\ E \in FSs(V)$,

$$\begin{aligned}
&(a)\ C_e(P||P \cup E) = C_e(E||P \cap E),\\
&(b)\ C_e(P||P \cap E) = C_e(E||P \cup E),\\
&(c)\ C_e(P \cup E||P \cap E) = C_e(P||E),\\
&(d)\ C_e(P||P \cup E) + C_e(P||P \cap E) = C_e(P||E), \text{ and}\\
&(e)\ C_e(E||P \cup E) + C_e(E||P \cap E) = C_e(P||E).
\end{aligned}$$

Proof. The proof is given in Appendix A.3. □

Next, Jain and Chhabra [59] develop the exponential divergence measure for FSs as follows:

$$C_{JC}(P,\ E) = \sum_{i=1}^{n}\left[(\mu_P(v_i) - \mu_E(v_i))\exp\left(\frac{\mu_P(v_i)}{\mu_E(v_i)}\right) + (\mu_E(v_i) - \mu_P(v_i))\exp\left(\frac{1-\mu_P(v_i)}{1-\mu_E(v_i)}\right)\right]. \tag{16}$$

Moreover, the symmetric divergence measure for FSs P and E is defined as:

$$C_{JC}(P||E) = \sum_{i=1}^{n}\left[\left(\mu_p(v_i) - \mu_E(v_i)\right)\left\{\exp\left(\frac{\mu_P(v_i)}{\mu_E(v_i)}\right) - \exp\left(\frac{1-\mu_P(v_i)}{1-\mu_E(v_i)}\right)\right\}\right]. \tag{17}$$

There is not any need for non-negativity of the divergence in the previous axioms, but this is too insignificant to deduce it from Definition 2. Now, suppose $\mu_E(v_i) = 0$. Then, from (16) and (17), $C_{JC}(P,E)$ and $C_{JC}(P||E)$ are undefined. To overcome this drawback, based on Jain and Chhabra [59], we develop a new modified exponential divergence measure for FSs as follows:

$$\begin{aligned}
C_2(P||E) = \frac{1}{n(\exp(2)-1)}\sum_{i=1}^{n}\Bigg[&(\mu_P(v_i) - \mu_E(v_i))\exp\left(\frac{\mu_P(v_i)}{\frac{1}{2}(\mu_P(v_i)+\mu_E(v_i))}\right)\\
&+(\mu_E(v_i) - \mu_P(v_i))\exp\left(\frac{1-\mu_P(v_i)}{1-\frac{1}{2}(\mu_P(v_i)+\mu_E(v_i))}\right)\Bigg].
\end{aligned} \tag{18}$$

Theorem 2. *For all* $P, E,\ T \in FSs(V)$, *then the measure* $C_2(P||E)$ *given by (18) holds the postulates given in Theorem 1.*

Proof. Proof is the same as Theorem 1. □

Corollary 2. *The mapping* $C_2(P||E)$ *is the distance measure on FSs(V).*

Proof. Proof is obvious. □

4. An Integrated TODIM Approach Using the Shapley Function and Divergence Measure

Here, the conventional TODIM method is extended according to the Shapley function and divergence measure under the FSs context.

4.1. Shapley Function

Historically, the concept of fuzzy measures was pioneered in 1974 by Sugeno [60], and it would become well-known as an efficient instrument for modeling the interaction phenomena and addressing the decision-making problems [61–63].

Definition 6. *(Sugeno [60]). A mapping* $g : P(V) \to [0,\ 1]$ *is recognized as a fuzzy measure (F-measure) on* $V = \{v_j :\ j = 1\ (1)\ n\}$*, if it fulfills the given requirements:*

$$\begin{aligned}&(a)\ g(\varnothing) = 0,\ \ g(V) = 1; \text{ and}\\ &(b)\ \text{If } E \subseteq F, \text{ then } g(E) \le g(F),\ \ \forall\, E,\ F \in V.\end{aligned}$$

In MCDM procedures, $g(E)$ can be represented by the consequence of criteria E. As a result, the typical weights upon the criteria are taken in an independent way, and also the weights upon any set of criteria are suggested. Subsequently, the interactions that exist amongst the criteria are characterized. If $\sum_{v_j \in E} g(v_j)$ for any $E \in P(V)$, then the fuzzy measure g deteriorates as an additive measure.

Lots of studies have been carried out onthe Shapley function [64] as a key interaction index; it is articulated as follows:

$$\phi_j(g,\ V) = \sum_{K \subseteq V \backslash v_j} \frac{(n-k-1)!\ k!}{n!}\left[g\left(K \cup \{v_j\}\right) - g(K)\right],\ \ \forall\, v_j \in V, \tag{19}$$

where g is a F-measure on V.

Here, the set K is characterized as an association that is generated by the game theory players, and it is perceived as a criterion set in the MCDM topic. The Shapley value ϕ_j assumes as a category the mean value of the input of the object v_j in any associations $K \backslash v_j$. Furthermore, $\phi_j(g,\ V) = g(v_j)$, when there is no connection.

Property 1. *If* $g : P(V) \to [0,\ 1]$ *is an F-measure, then* $\phi_j(g,\ V) \ge 0,\ \ \forall\, v_j \in V;\ \ j = 1(1)n.$

Property 2. *If* $g : P(V) \to [0,\ 1]$ *is an F-measure, then* $\sum_{j=1}^{n} \phi_j(g,\ V) = g(V) = 1.$

Thus, $\{\phi_i(g,\ V) :\ \ i = 1(1)n\}$ is a weight value.

4.2. Models for Criteria Weight Based on the Optimal Additive Measure

The entropy of criteria values needs to be taken into account; then, in case the information in regard with the criteria weights is partly unknown, or if it is completely unidentified, the amount of entropy for criteria $v_i (i = 1(1)n)$ is suggested as $\sum_{i=1}^{n} H(\varepsilon_{ij})$, where ε_{ij} signifies a fuzzy number (FNs) of the option S_i concerning the criterion E_j. In accordance with the entropy rule, if the entropy of an object is small, it would deliver valued information to the DEs. As a result, the criterion needs to be consigned with a greater weight; unless, the criterion would be considered insignificant by most DEs. In addition, this criterion needs to be estimated as a smaller weight. Hence, the optimal F-measure will form a greater inclusive value for each alternative that is preferable.

Remember that in this system, no option is inferior, and information associated to the criteria weights is completely unknown; therefore, to have the best fuzzy measure, the linear programming model on criteria E is formed by:

$$\begin{aligned}&\min \sum_{j=1}^{n} \sum_{i=1}^{m} H_\alpha(\varepsilon_{ij})\phi_j(g,\ E)\\ &s.t. \begin{cases} g(\varnothing) = 0,\ \ g(E) = 1, \\ g(K) \le g(L) \quad \forall\, K,\ \ L \subseteq E,\ K \subseteq L, \end{cases}\end{aligned} \tag{20}$$

while information associated with the criteria weights are partially known, then, for the optimal F-measure, the linear programming model on criteria E is assembled:

$$\min \sum_{j=1}^{n} \sum_{i=1}^{m} H_\alpha(\varepsilon_{ij})\, \phi_j(g,\ E)$$
$$s.t. \begin{cases} g(\varnothing) = 0,\ \ g(E) = 1, \\ g(E_j) \in T_j,\ \ j = 1(1)n, \\ g(K) \le g(L)\ \forall\, K,\ L \subseteq E,\ K \subseteq L, \end{cases} \tag{21}$$

where $\phi_j(g,\ E)$ is the Shapley degree of criteria $E_j(j = 1(1)n)$ and $T_j = \left[t_j^-,\ t_j^+\right]$ is its range.

4.3. Shapley Function-Based TODIM Technique for MCDM

TODIM [46] was initially introduced to carefully take into consideration the psychological behaviors of decision making (DM). This tool is also capable of handling the MCDM problems efficiently. According to the prospect theory, through the use of this approach, the user can determine the dominance of each option over the different ones by creating a multi-values function [65].

Let $S_i(i = 1(1)m)$ be the options on criteria $E_j(j = 1(1)n)$, then the procedure for the Shapley function-based TODIM technique is as follows (see Figure 1).

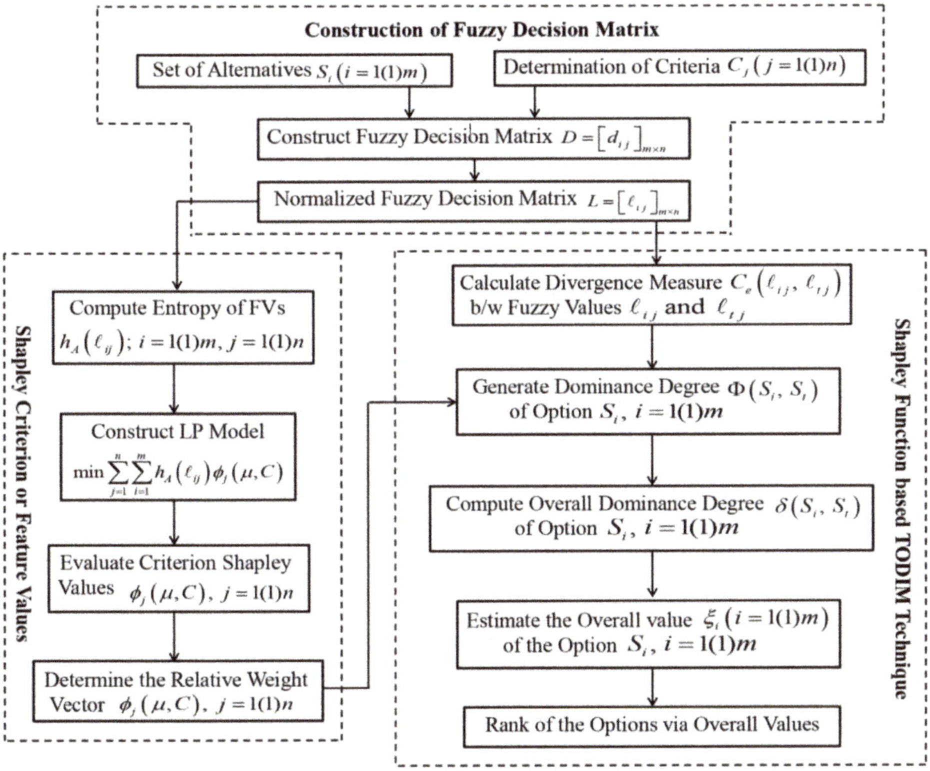

Figure 1. Graphical implementation of the proposed approach.

Step I: Construct a decision matrix $D = (d_{ij})_{m\times n}$, in which d_{ij} presents an assessment value of an option S_i concerning the criterion E_j. Initially, the information should be normalized. A larger value shows a higher quality assessment of benefit criteria, but the same condition reveals the poorer quality performance of a cost criterion. As a result, for the purpose of guaranteeing all criteria to be with complete compatibility, the cost criteria were transformed into benefit one using the formula below: $\ell_{ij} = \begin{cases} d_{ij}, & \text{for benefit criterion } E_j \\ (d_{ij})^c, & \text{for cost criterion } E_j \end{cases}$, where $(d_{ij})^c$ denotes the complement of d_{ij}, through this procedure, and it is possible to attain the normalized fuzzy decision matrix $L = (\ell_{ij})_{m \times n}$.

Step II: For a better judgment, we need to identify the significance of the judgment of each DE. Therefore, each criterion weight needs to be determined. If the characteristics among the criteria are interdependent, the weight vector of the criteria is calculated in forms of Shapley values. Employ (19), and model (20) and (21) with respect to (11), to find the criteria weight.

Step III: Calculate the criteria's relative weight vector using the formula $\varphi_{jr}(g,\ V) = \frac{\varphi_j(g,\ V)}{\varphi_r(g,\ V)}$, where $\varphi_r(g,\ V) = \max\{\varphi_j(g,\ V)\}$ and $\varphi_j(g,\ V)$ is the criteria weight E_j.

Step IV: Determine the degree of dominance of an option S_i over each option S_t by:

$$\Phi_j(S_i,\ S_t) = \begin{cases} \sqrt{\dfrac{\varphi_{jr}(g,\ V)\ C_e(\ell_{ij},\ \ell_{tj})}{\sum_{j=1}^{n} \varphi_{jr}(g,\ V)}}, & if\ \ell_{ij} > \ell_{tj} \\ 0, & if\ \ell_{ij} = \ell_{tj} \\ -\frac{1}{\theta}\sqrt{\dfrac{\sum_{j=1}^{n} \varphi_{jr}(g,\ V)\ C_e(\ell_{ij},\ \ell_{tj})}{\varphi_{jr}(g,\ V)}}, & if\ \ell_{ij} < \ell_{tj} \end{cases}, \tag{22}$$

measure between the fuzzy numbers ℓ_{ij} and ℓ_{tj} by using formula (14), and factor θ denotes the attenuation degree of the losses. If $\ell_{ij} > \ell_{tj}$, then $\Phi_j(S_i,\ S_t)$ characterizes again and if $\ell_{ij} < \ell_{tj}$, then $\Phi_j(S_i,\ S_t)$ denotes a loss.

Step V: Evaluate the overall dominance value of an option S_i over each option S_t by:

$$\delta(S_i,\ S_t) = \sum_{j=1}^{n} \Phi_j(S_i,\ S_t),\ (i,\ t = 1,\ 2, \ldots, m). \tag{23}$$

Step VI: Determine the overall value of each option S_i using the expression:

$$\xi_i = \frac{\sum_{t=1}^{m} \delta(S_i,\ S_t) - \min_i\left\{\sum_{j=1}^{n} \delta(S_i,\ S_t)\right\}}{\max_i\left\{\sum_{j=1}^{n} \delta(S_i,\ S_t)\right\} - \min_i\left\{\sum_{j=1}^{n} \delta(S_i,\ S_t)\right\}},\ i = 1,\ 2,\ \ldots, m. \tag{24}$$

Step VII: Determine the rank of options based on the overall values.

5. Case Study of the Proposed Method

Typically, in the evaluating process of the service quality, a set of m options S_i $(i = 1, 2, \ldots, m)$ is involved. In this case, options refer to vehicle insurance firms. The service quality of these firms delivered to their customers is evaluated by the customers, which is denoted by a set of n criteria E_j $(j = 1, 2, \ldots, n)$. Toloie et al. [66] suggested a modified survey questionnaire for the purpose of estimating the customer-perceived quality of services. Four vehicle insurance firms that were chosen for this study are Oriental Insurance (S_1), National Insurance (S_2), Bajaj Insurance (S_3), and New India Insurance (S_4). The questionnaires indices contain four evaluation criteria, i.e., confidence (E_1), responsiveness (E_2), reliability (E_3), and tangibles (E_4).

Step I: Through the integration of the preference value results obtained from the four above-noted firms based on four evaluation criteria, the decision matrix of options is attained, as presented in Table 1. The importance of criteria is given by [0.15, 0.4], [0.25, 0.5], [0.25, 0.6], and [0.2, 0.3].

Table 1. Fuzzy decision matrix.

Option	E_1	E_2	E_3	E_4
S_1	0.5395	0.7655	0.6770	0.5915
S_2	0.7015	0.6990	0.7725	0.7650
S_3	0.7365	0.5350	0.6595	0.6340
S_4	0.7800	0.6985	0.5995	0.7455

Step II: By using (11), the entropy measure of the option S_i $(i = 1, \ldots, 4)$, considering the criteria $E_j;\ j = 1(1)4$, is listed in Table 2.

Table 2. Entropy values w. r. t. S.

Entropy	E_1	E_2	E_3	E_4
$H(S_1)$	0.6029	0.4400	0.5329	0.5869
$H(S_2)$	0.5111	0.5134	0.4310	0.4406
$H(S_3)$	0.4747	0.6037	0.5468	0.5644
$H(S_4)$	0.4211	0.5139	0.5834	0.4644

From Table 2, the next LP-model is constructed:

$$\begin{aligned}&\min\,[-0.0160\,\{\mu(E_1)-\mu(E_2,\,E_3,\,E_4)\}\,+0.0044\,\{\mu(E_2)-\mu(E_1,\,E_3,\,E_4)\}+\,0.0121\,\{\mu(E_3)-\mu(E_1,\,E_2,E_4)\}\\&-0.0005\,\{\mu(E_4)-\mu(E_1,\,E_2,\,E_3)\}-0.0058\,\{\mu(E_1,\,E_2)-\mu(E_3,\,E_4)\}-0.0019\,\{\mu(E_1,\,E_3)-\mu(E_2,\,E_4)\}\\&-0.0083\,\{\mu(E_1,\,E_4)-\mu(E_2,\,E_3)\}+\,2.0578]\end{aligned}$$

such that

$$\left\{\begin{array}{l}\mu(E_1)\le\mu(E_1,\,E_2),\ \mu(E_1)\le\mu(E_1,\,E_3),\ \mu(E_1)\le\mu(E_1,\,E_4),\ \mu(E_2)\le\mu(E_1,\,E_2),\\ \mu(E_2)\le\mu(E_2,\,E_3),\ \mu(E_2)\le\mu(E_2,\,E_4),\mu(E_3)\le\mu(E_1,\,E_3),\ \mu(E_3)\le\mu(E_2,\,E_3),\\ \mu(E_3)\le\mu(E_3,\,E_4),\ \mu(E_4)\le\mu(E_1,\,E_4),\ \mu(E_4)\le\mu(E_2,\,E_4),\ \mu(E_4)\le\mu(E_3,\,E_4),\\ \mu(E_1,\,E_2)\le\mu(E_1,\,E_2,\,E_3),\ \mu(E_1,\,E_3)\le\mu(E_1,\,E_2,\,E_3),\ \mu(E_2,\,E_3)\le\mu(E_1,\,E_2,\,E_3),\\ \mu(E_1,\,E_4)\le\mu(E_1,\,E_2,\,E_4),\ \mu(E_2,\,E_4)\le\mu(E_1,\,E_2,\,E_4),\mu(E_1,\,E_2)\le\mu(E_1,\,E_2,\,E_4),\\ \mu(E_1,\,E_3)\le\mu(E_1,\,E_3,\,E_4),\ \mu(E_1,\,E_4)\le\mu(E_1,\,E_3,\,E_4),\ \mu(E_3,\,E_4)\le\mu(E_1,\,E_3,\,E_4),\\ \mu(E_1,\,E_2,\,E_3)\le\mu(E_2,\,E_3,\,E_4),\ \mu(E_3,\,E_4)\le\mu(E_2,\,E_3,\,E_4),\mu(E_2,\,E_4)\le\mu(E_2,\,E_3,\,E_4),\\ \mu(E_1,\,E_2,\,E_3)\le 1,\ \mu(E_1,\,E_3,\,E_4)\le 1,\ \mu(E_1,\,E_2,\,E_4)\le 1,\ \mu(E_2,\,E_3,\,E_4)\le 1,\\ \mu(E_1)\in[0.15,\,0.4],\ \mu(E_2)\in[0.25,\,0.5],\ \mu(E_3)\in[0.25,\,0.6],\ \mu(E_4)\in[0.2,\,0.3]\end{array}\right.. \quad (25)$$

Solving (25) using MATHEMATICA, the F-measures on the criteria E_j are as follows:

$$\begin{gathered}\mu(E_1)=0.4,\ \mu(E_2)=0.25=\mu(E_3),\ \mu(E_4)=0.25,\ \mu(E_2,\,E_3)=0.25=\mu(E_2,\,E_4)=\mu(E_3,\,E_4),\\ \mu(E_1,\,E_2,\,E_3)=1=\mu(E_1,\,E_2,\,E_4)=\mu(E_1,\,E_3,\,E_4),\ \mu(E_1,\,E_2)=1=\mu(E_1,\,E_3)=\mu(E_1,\,E_4),\\ \mu(E_2,\,E_3,\,E_4)=0.25,\ \mu(E_1,\,E_2,\,E_3,\,E_4)=1.\end{gathered}$$

The calculated Shapley values are

$$\varphi_{E_1}^{HA}(g,\,V)=0.6625,\ \varphi_{E_2}^{HA}(g,\,V)=0.1125,\ \varphi_{E_3}^{HA}(g,\,V)=0.1125,\ \varphi_{E_4}^{HA}(g,\,V)=0.1125\,.$$

As a result, the Shapley degrees of the criteria are attained as follows:

$$W=\left(\varphi_{E_1}^{HA}(g,\,V)\,,\,\varphi_{E_2}^{HA}(g,\,V)\,,\,\varphi_{E_3}^{HA}(g,\,V),\,\varphi_{E_4}^{HA}(g,\,V)\right)^T=(0.6625,\,0.1125,\,0.1125,\,0.1125)^T.$$

Step III: The relative weights of the given criteria $E_j;\ j = 1(1)4$ are $\varphi_{1r}(g,\,V) = 1$, $\varphi_{2r}(g,\,V) = 0.1698$, $\varphi_{3r}(g,\,V) = 0.1698$, and $\varphi_{4r}(g,\,V) = 0.1698$.

Step IV: The dominance degree matrices of the options over the criteria E_j; $j = 1(1)4$ are as follows:

$$\Phi_1 = \begin{bmatrix} 0 & -0.1966 & -0.2398 & -0.2928 \\ 0.1302 & 0 & -0.0426 & -0.0967 \\ 0.1589 & 0.0282 & 0 & -0.0521 \\ 0.1940 & 0.0641 & 0.0345 & 0 \end{bmatrix}, \Phi_2 = \begin{bmatrix} 0 & 0.0225 & 0.0769 & 0.0225 \\ -0.2000 & 0 & 0.0543 & 0.0052 \\ -0.6838 & -0.4826 & 0 & -0.4808 \\ -0.2000 & -0.0459 & 0.0541 & 0 \end{bmatrix},$$
$$\Phi_3 = \begin{bmatrix} 0 & -0.4971 & 0.0049 & 0.0258 \\ 0.0559 & 0 & 0.0379 & 0.0578 \\ -0.0439 & -0.3373 & 0 & 0.0201 \\ -0.2290 & -0.5138 & -0.1789 & 0 \end{bmatrix}, \Phi_4 = \begin{bmatrix} 0 & -0.5147 & -0.1155 & -0.4571 \\ 0.0579 & 0 & 0.0439 & 0.0084 \\ 0.0130 & -0.3899 & 0 & -0.3307 \\ 0.0514 & -0.0744 & 0.0372 & 0 \end{bmatrix}.$$

Step V: The total dominance degree matrix of option S_i over each option S_t is evaluated as:

$$\delta = \begin{bmatrix} 0 & -1.1859 & -0.2735 & -0.7016 \\ 0.0440 & 0 & 0.0935 & -0.0253 \\ -0.5558 & -1.1816 & 0 & -0.8435 \\ -0.1836 & -0.5700 & -0.0531 & 0 \end{bmatrix}.$$

Step VI: Now, the calculated overall values are as follows:

$$\xi_1 = 0.1559, \xi_2 = 1.0000, \xi_3 = 0.0000, \xi_4 = 0.6588.$$

Step VII: Finally, the ranking of the alternatives is $S_2 \succ S_4 \succ S_1 \succ S_3$ and thus, S_2 is the optimal choice.

It is mentioned that any conflict does not exist in the preference ordering of all the options via the proposed technique and Mishra [67] technique. There is only one distinction between the proposed, and Mishra et al.'s [68] technique is obtained in deciding the preference ordering of S_1 and S_4. Additionally, the ranking obtained via the proposed technique is totally different from the Krohling, and de Souza [69] and Fan et al. [52] techniques (see Table 3).

Table 3. Comparisons with different existing techniques.

Techniques	Ranking	Optimal Choice
Krohling and de Souza [69] technique	$S_1 \succ S_2 \succ S_4 \succ S_3$	S_1
Fan et al. [52] technique	$S_1 \succ S_4 \succ S_2 \succ S_3$	S_1
Mishra et al. [68] technique	$S_2 \succ S_4 \succ S_1 \succ S_3$	S_2
Mishra [67] technique	$S_2 \succ S_1 \succ S_4 \succ S_3$	S_2
Proposed technique	$S_2 \succ S_4 \succ S_1 \succ S_3$	S_2

Comparative Analysis

Here, the comparison of methods is based on a set of characteristics to adequately deal with the problem of service selection as follows:

In Mishra [67], the TOPSIS method is presented to find the solution of the MCDM problem, which is not capable of demonstrating the DMs behaviors. While, in this study, the TODIM approach is used to find the accurate solution of the MCDM problem, which assumes the psychological attitudes on DEs under risk. In the proposed method, we applied a fuzzy measure-based Shapley function to calculate the weight vector, which relaxes the additive condition of the conventional measure to the monotonicity condition. The fuzzy measure is a very important tool to deal with the criteria interaction. In Mishra [67], the entropy approach is used for the determination of the criteria weight. In the entropy method, in case the entropy value of each of the existing criteria is smaller than that of the available alternatives, a greater weight needs to be allocated to the criterion; otherwise, the criterion needs to be evaluated with a smaller weight. The authors in Mishra et al. [68] attempted to find out the criteria weight vector using the ordered weighted operator. The aggregation arguments need to be ordered before being aggregated. In Fan et al. [52] and Krohling, and de Souza [69], the criteria weights are assumed by the DMs.

The proposed method makes a ranking system for the available options through the measurement of their values of loss and gain and provides a significant total value for each one of the options; whereas, in Mishra [36], the authors made use of the positive-ideal value (PIV) and negative-ideal value (NIV) as benchmarks, which may be unrealistic to be the attained practically. By calculating the overall values in the developed method, we found that the related performance of all options with respect to each other on the considered factors or criteria. On the other hand, the score function applied in Mishra et al. [68] does not consider the related performance of all options with regards to each other, thereby it loses some valuable information, which can be helpful in the determination of the alternatives' rank. The developed method is applied to deal with both independent and interdependent sets of criteria. However, the approach developed in Fan et al. [52], Krohling and de Souza [69], Mishra et al. [68], and Mishra [67] is only applicable for an independent set of criteria. Thus, the developed approach is more effective and reliable than the existing ones.

6. Conclusions

TODIM was found to be efficient in the solution of the MCDM-related problems, especially in the conditions in which the behaviors of DMs are taken into consideration, although the approach fails to solve the MCDM procedures directly under the FSs. In the present study, we proposed new exponential-type divergence measures for FSs and demonstrated many elegant properties, which were found to be capable of enhancing the usefulness of the proposed measure. Next, a TODIM method for MCDM based on the prospect theory, Shapley function, and divergence measure was developed. Models for optimal F-measures on the criteria or experts set via the Shapley function are, respectively, constructed, where the weights information of the DEs and the criteria are partly or fully unknown. A real service quality selection problem was used to express the effectiveness of the considered approach. The comparative discussion was demonstrated to exemplify the advantages of the proposed technique over the existing techniques for MCDM problems under the fuzzy environment.

Meanwhile, we will integrate the TODIM approach with various conventional MCDM methods like Preference PROMETHEE, stepwise weight assessment ratio analysis (SWARA), and analytic hierarchy process (AHP) methods. The method introduced in this study has the potential to be generalized to the MCDM procedures with interdependent criteria on PFSs and HFSs; in addition, it can be applied to comparable MCDM problems, e.g., risk investment, healthcare waste management, and performance evaluation.

Author Contributions: Conceptualization, A.R.M. and P.R.; methodology, A.R.M. and P.R.; software, P.R. and R.K.; validation, A.M., A.R.M. and P.R.; formal analysis, A.R.M. and D.K.S.; investigation, A.M.; resources, D.K.S.; data curation, R.K.; writing—original draft preparation, A.R.M. and P.R.; writing—review and editing, A.M. and E.K.Z.; visualization, A.M.; supervision, E.K.Z.; All authors have read and agreed to the published version of the manuscript.

Funding: This research received no external funding.

Conflicts of Interest: The authors declare no conflict of interest.

Appendix A

Appendix A.1 Proof of Theorem 1

(a) & (b). Let:

$$C_e(P\|E) = \frac{1}{n}\sum_{i=1}^{n} \xi(\mu_P(v_i), \mu_E(v_i)), \ \forall\, v_i \in V,$$
$$\text{where } \xi(\mu_P(v_i), \mu_E(v_i)) = \frac{-1}{\sqrt{e}(\sqrt{e}-1)}\left[\begin{array}{c} \left(\frac{\mu_P(v_i)+\mu_E(v_i)}{2}\right)\exp\left(\frac{\mu_P(v_i)+\mu_E(v_i)}{2}\right) \\ +\left(\frac{2-\mu_P(v_i)-\mu_E(v_i)}{2}\right)\exp\left(\frac{2-\mu_P(v_i)-\mu_E(v_i)}{2}\right) \end{array}\right. \tag{A1}$$
$$\left. -\frac{1}{2}\left(\begin{array}{c} \mu_P(v_i)\exp(\mu_P(v_i)) + (1-\mu_P(v_i))\exp(1-\mu_P(v_i)) \\ +\mu_E(v_i)\exp(\mu_E(v_i)) + (1-\mu_E(v_i))\exp(1-\mu_E(v_i)) \end{array}\right)\right].$$

Since $f = v_i \exp(v_i)$ and $0 \le v_i \le 1$, then $f' = (1+ v_i)\exp(v_i) \ge 0$ and $f'' = (2+ v_i)\exp(v_i) > 0$,; thus, f is a concave up mapping of v_i and $C_e(P\|E)$ is a convex function. Therefore, $\xi(\mu_P(v_i), \mu_E(v_i))$ increases as $\|P-E\|_\gamma$ increases such that $\|P-E\|_\gamma = |\mu_P - \mu_E|$, and attains its maximum at $P = \{1\}$, $E = \{0\}$(or $P = \{0\}$, $E = \{1\}$), i.e., $P,\ E \in P(V)$ and attains its minimum $P = E$. Hence, $0 \le C_e(P\|E) \le 1$ and $C_e(P\|E) = 0$ if $P = E$.

(c). It is evident from (14), we obtain:

$$C_e(P\|E) = C_e(E\|P).$$

(d) & (e). Both are obvious; therefore, the proofs are omitted.

(f). Let $P \subseteq E \subseteq T$, i.e., $\mu_P \le \mu_E \le \mu_T$, then $\|E-T\|_\gamma \le \|P- E\|_\gamma$ and $\|P-E\|_\gamma \le \|P- T\|_\gamma$. Therefore, $C_e(P\|E) \le C_e(P\|T)$ and $C_e(E\|T) \le C_e(P\|T)$, for $P \subseteq E \subseteq T$.

Appendix A.2 Proof of Proposition 1

$$C_e(P\|P^c) = \frac{-1}{n\sqrt{e}(\sqrt{e}-1)} \times \sum_{i=1}^{n}\left[\begin{array}{c} \left(\frac{\mu_P(v_i)+\mu_{P^c}(v_i)}{2}\right)\exp\left(\frac{\mu_P(v_i)+\mu_{P^c}(v_i)}{2}\right) \\ \left(\frac{2-\mu_P(v_i)-\mu_{P^c}(v_i)}{2}\right)\exp\left(\frac{2-\mu_P(v_i)-\mu_{P^c}(v_i)}{2}\right) \end{array}\right. \tag{A2}$$
$$\left. -\frac{1}{2}\left(\begin{array}{c} \mu_P(v_i)\exp(\mu_P(v_i)) + (1-\mu_P(v_i))\exp(1-\mu_P(v_i)) \\ +\mu_{P^c}(v_i)\exp(\mu_{P^c}(v_i)) + (1-\mu_{P^c}(v_i))\exp(1-\mu_{P^c}(v_i)) \end{array}\right)\right].$$

It implies:

$$1 - C_e(P\|P^c) = 1 + \frac{1}{n\sqrt{e}(\sqrt{e}-1)} \times \sum_{i=1}^{n}\left[\sqrt{e} - \left(\begin{array}{c} \mu_P(v_i)\exp(\mu_P(v_i)) \\ +(1-\mu_P(v_i))\exp(1-\mu_P(v_i)) \end{array}\right)\right]$$
$$= \frac{1}{n\sqrt{e}(\sqrt{e}-1)}\sum_{i=1}^{n}\left[e - \mu_P(v_i)e^{\mu_P(v_i)} - (1-\mu_P(v_i))e^{(1-\mu_P(v_i))}\right] = H_A(P).$$

Hence:

$$1 - C_e(P\|E) = H_A(P).$$

Appendix A.3 Proof of Proposition 2

To prove the (i)–(v), we consider that the finite discourse set V is divided into two disjoint sets V_1 and V_2 as:

$$V_1 = \{v_i | v_i \in V,\ \mu_P(v_i) \ge \mu_E(v_i)\} \ \text{ and } \ V_2 = \{v_i | v_i \in V,\ \mu_P(v_i) < \mu_E(v_i)\}.$$

(a). From (14), we have:

$$
\begin{aligned}
C_e(P\|P\cup E) = {} & \frac{-1}{n\sqrt{e}(\sqrt{e}-1)}\sum_{i=1}^{n}\left[\begin{array}{c} \left(\frac{\mu_P(v_i)+\mu_{P\cup E}(v_i)}{2}\right)\exp\left(\frac{\mu_P(v_i)+\mu_{P\cup E}(v_i)}{2}\right) \\ \left(\frac{2-\mu_P(v_i)-\mu_{P\cup E}(v_i)}{2}\right)\exp\left(\frac{2-\mu_P(v_i)-\mu_{P\cup E}(v_i)}{2}\right) \end{array}\right. \\
& \left.-\frac{1}{2}\left(\begin{array}{c} \mu_P(v_i)\exp(\mu_P(v_i))+(1-\mu_P(v_i))\exp(1-\mu_P(v_i)) \\ +\mu_{P\cup E}(v_i)\exp(\mu_{P\cup E}(v_i))+(1-\mu_{P\cup E}(v_i))\exp(1-\mu_{P\cup E}(v_i)) \end{array}\right)\right] \\
= {} & \frac{-1}{n\sqrt{e}(\sqrt{e}-1)}\left[\sum_{v_i\in V_1}\left\{\begin{array}{c} \left(\frac{\mu_P(v_i)+\mu_P(v_i)}{2}\right)\exp\left(\frac{\mu_P(v_i)+\mu_P(v_i)}{2}\right) \\ \left(\frac{2-\mu_P(v_i)-\mu_P(v_i)}{2}\right)\exp\left(\frac{2-\mu_P(v_i)-\mu_P(v_i)}{2}\right) \end{array}\right.\right. \\
& \left.-\frac{1}{2}\left(\begin{array}{c} \mu_P(v_i)\exp(\mu_P(v_i))+(1-\mu_P(v_i))\exp(1-\mu_P(v_i)) \\ +\mu_P(v_i)\exp(\mu_P(v_i))+(1-\mu_P(v_i))\exp(1-\mu_P(v_i)) \end{array}\right)\right\} \\
& +\sum_{v_i\in V_2}\left\{\begin{array}{c} \left(\frac{\mu_P(v_i)+\mu_E(v_i)}{2}\right)\exp\left(\frac{\mu_P(v_i)+\mu_E(v_i)}{2}\right) \\ \left(\frac{2-\mu_P(v_i)-\mu_E(v_i)}{2}\right)\exp\left(\frac{2-\mu_P(v_i)-\mu_E(v_i)}{2}\right) \end{array}\right. \\
& \left.\left.-\frac{1}{2}\left(\begin{array}{c} \mu_P(v_i)\exp(\mu_P(v_i))+(1-\mu_P(v_i))\exp(1-\mu_P(v_i)) \\ +\mu_E(v_i)\exp(\mu_E(v_i))+(1-\mu_E(v_i))\exp(1-\mu_E(v_i)) \end{array}\right)\right\}\right].
\end{aligned}
$$

Hence:

$$
\begin{aligned}
C_e(P\|P\cup E) = {} & \frac{-1}{n\sqrt{e}(\sqrt{e}-1)}\left[\sum_{v_i\in V_2}\left\{\begin{array}{c} \left(\frac{\mu_P(v_i)+\mu_E(v_i)}{2}\right)\exp\left(\frac{\mu_P(v_i)+\mu_E(v_i)}{2}\right) \\ \left(\frac{2-\mu_P(v_i)-\mu_E(v_i)}{2}\right)\exp\left(\frac{2-\mu_P(v_i)-\mu_E(v_i)}{2}\right) \end{array}\right.\right. \\
& \left.\left.-\frac{1}{2}\left(\begin{array}{c} \mu_P(v_i)\exp(\mu_P(v_i))+(1-\mu_P(v_i))\exp(1-\mu_P(v_i)) \\ +\mu_E(v_i)\exp(\mu_E(v_i))+(1-\mu_E(v_i))\exp(1-\mu_E(v_i)) \end{array}\right)\right\}\right].
\end{aligned}
\tag{A3}
$$

Again:

$$
\begin{aligned}
C_e(P\|P\cap E) = {} & \frac{-1}{n\sqrt{e}(\sqrt{e}-1)}\sum_{i=1}^{n}\left[\begin{array}{c} \left(\frac{\mu_E(v_i)+\mu_{P\cap E}(v_i)}{2}\right)\exp\left(\frac{\mu_E(v_i)+\mu_{P\cap E}(v_i)}{2}\right) \\ \left(\frac{2-\mu_E(v_i)-\mu_{P\cap E}(v_i)}{2}\right)\exp\left(\frac{2-\mu_E(v_i)-\mu_{P\cap E}(v_i)}{2}\right) \end{array}\right. \\
& \left.-\frac{1}{2}\left(\begin{array}{c} \mu_E(v_i)\exp(\mu_E(v_i))+(1-\mu_E(v_i))\exp(1-\mu_E(v_i)) \\ +\mu_{P\cap E}(v_i)\exp(\mu_{P\cap E}(v_i))+(1-\mu_{P\cap E}(v_i))\exp(1-\mu_{P\cap E}(v_i)) \end{array}\right)\right] \\
= {} & \frac{-1}{n\sqrt{e}(\sqrt{e}-1)}\left[\sum_{v_i\in V_1}\left\{\begin{array}{c} \left(\frac{\mu_P(v_i)+\mu_P(v_i)}{2}\right)\exp\left(\frac{\mu_P(v_i)+\mu_P(v_i)}{2}\right) \\ \left(\frac{2-\mu_P(v_i)-\mu_P(v_i)}{2}\right)\exp\left(\frac{2-\mu_P(v_i)-\mu_P(v_i)}{2}\right) \end{array}\right.\right. \\
& \left.-\frac{1}{2}\left(\begin{array}{c} \mu_P(v_i)\exp(\mu_P(v_i))+(1-\mu_P(v_i))\exp(1-\mu_P(v_i)) \\ +\mu_P(v_i)\exp(\mu_P(v_i))+(1-\mu_P(v_i))\exp(1-\mu_P(v_i)) \end{array}\right)\right\} \\
& +\sum_{v_i\in V_2}\left\{\begin{array}{c} \left(\frac{\mu_E(v_i)+\mu_P(v_i)}{2}\right)\exp\left(\frac{\mu_E(v_i)+\mu_P(v_i)}{2}\right) \\ \left(\frac{2-\mu_E(v_i)-\mu_P(v_i)}{2}\right)\exp\left(\frac{2-\mu_E(v_i)-\mu_P(v_i)}{2}\right) \end{array}\right. \\
& \left.\left.-\frac{1}{2}\left(\begin{array}{c} \mu_E(v_i)\exp(\mu_E(v_i))+(1-\mu_E(v_i))\exp(1-\mu_E(v_i)) \\ +\mu_P(v_i)\exp(\mu_P(v_i))+(1-\mu_P(v_i))\exp(1-\mu_P(v_i)) \end{array}\right)\right\}\right].
\end{aligned}
$$

Hence:

$$
\begin{aligned}
C_e(E\|P\cap E) = {} & \frac{-1}{n\sqrt{e}(\sqrt{e}-1)}\left[\sum_{v_i\in V_2}\left\{\begin{array}{c} \left(\frac{\mu_P(v_i)+\mu_E(v_i))}{2}\right)\exp\left(\frac{\mu_P(v_i)+\mu_E(v_i))}{2}\right) \\ \left(\frac{2-\mu_P(v_i)-\mu_E(v_i)}{2}\right)\exp\left(\frac{2-\mu_P(v_i)-\mu_E(v_i)}{2}\right) \end{array}\right.\right. \\
& \left.\left.-\frac{1}{2}\left(\begin{array}{c} \mu_P(v_i)\exp(\mu_P(v_i))+(1-\mu_P(v_i))\exp(1-\mu_P(v_i)) \\ +\mu_E(v_i)\exp(\mu_E(v_i))+(1-\mu_E(v_i))\exp(1-\mu_E(v_i)) \end{array}\right)\right\}\right].
\end{aligned}
\tag{A4}
$$

From (A3) and (A4), we obtain $C_e(P||P\cup E) = C_e(E||P\cap E)$.

(b) & (c). The proofs are similar to (a).

(d). From (A3), we get:

$$C_e(P||P\cup E) = \frac{-1}{n\sqrt{e}(\sqrt{e}-1)}\left[\sum_{v_i\in V_2}\left\{\begin{array}{c}\left(\frac{\mu_P(v_i)+\mu_E(v_i)}{2}\right)\exp\left(\frac{\mu_P(v_i)+\mu_E(v_i)}{2}\right)\\ \left(\frac{2-\mu_P(v_i)-\mu_E(v_i)}{2}\right)\exp\left(\frac{2-\mu_P(v_i)-\mu_E(v_i)}{2}\right)\end{array}\right.\right.$$
$$\left.\left.-\frac{1}{2}\left(\begin{array}{c}\mu_P(v_i)\exp(\mu_P(v_i))+(1-\mu_P(v_i))\exp(1-\mu_P(v_i))\\ +\mu_E(v_i)\exp(\mu_E(v_i))+(1-\mu_E(v_i))\exp(1-\mu_E(v_i))\end{array}\right)\right\}\right]. \tag{A5}$$

$$C_e(P||P\cap E) = \frac{-1}{n\sqrt{e}(\sqrt{e}-1)}\sum_{i=1}^{n}\left[\begin{array}{c}\left(\frac{\mu_P(v_i)+\mu_{P\cap E}(v_i)}{2}\right)\exp\left(\frac{\mu_P(v_i)+\mu_{P\cap E}(v_i)}{2}\right)\\ \left(\frac{2-\mu_P(v_i)-\mu_{P\cap E}(v_i)}{2}\right)\exp\left(\frac{2-\mu_P(v_i)-\mu_{P\cap E}(v_i)}{2}\right)\end{array}\right.$$
$$\left.-\frac{1}{2}\left(\begin{array}{c}\mu_P(v_i)\exp(\mu_P(v_i))+(1-\mu_P(v_i))\exp(1-\mu_P(v_i))\\ +\mu_{P\cap E}(v_i)\exp(\mu_{P\cap E}(v_i))+(1-\mu_{P\cap E}(v_i))\exp(1-\mu_{P\cap E}(v_i))\end{array}\right)\right],$$
$$= \frac{-1}{n\sqrt{e}(\sqrt{e}-1)}\left[\sum_{v_i\in V_1}\left\{\begin{array}{c}\left(\frac{\mu_P(v_i)+\mu_E(v_i)}{2}\right)\exp\left(\frac{\mu_P(v_i)+\mu_E(v_i)}{2}\right)\\ \left(\frac{2-\mu_P(v_i)-\mu_E(v_i)}{2}\right)\exp\left(\frac{2-\mu_P(v_i)-\mu_E(v_i)}{2}\right)\end{array}\right.\right.$$
$$\left.-\frac{1}{2}\left(\begin{array}{c}\mu_P(v_i)\exp(\mu_P(v_i))+(1-\mu_P(v_i))\exp(1-\mu_P(v_i))\\ +\mu_E(v_i)\exp(\mu_E(v_i))+(1-\mu_E(v_i))\exp(1-\mu_E(v_i))\end{array}\right)\right\}$$
$$+\sum_{v_i\in V_2}\left\{\begin{array}{c}\left(\frac{\mu_P(v_i)+\mu_P(v_i)}{2}\right)\exp\left(\frac{\mu_P(v_i)+\mu_P(v_i)}{2}\right)\\ \left(\frac{2-\mu_P(v_i)-\mu_P(v_i)}{2}\right)\exp\left(\frac{2-\mu_P(v_i)-\mu_P(v_i)}{2}\right)\end{array}\right.$$
$$\left.\left.-\frac{1}{2}\left(\begin{array}{c}\mu_P(v_i)\exp(\mu_P(v_i))+(1-\mu_P(v_i))\exp(1-\mu_P(v_i))\\ +\mu_P(v_i)\exp(\mu_P(v_i))+(1-\mu_P(v_i))\exp(1-\mu_P(v_i))\end{array}\right)\right\}\right].$$

Hence:

$$C_e(M||M\cap N) = \frac{-1}{n\sqrt{e}(\sqrt{e}-1)}\left[\sum_{v_i\in V_1}\left\{\begin{array}{c}\left(\frac{\mu_P(v_i)+\mu_E(v_i)}{2}\right)\exp\left(\frac{\mu_P(v_i)+\mu_E(v_i)}{2}\right)\\ \left(\frac{2-\mu_P(v_i)-\mu_E(v_i)}{2}\right)\exp\left(\frac{2-\mu_P(v_i)-\mu_E(v_i)}{2}\right)\end{array}\right.\right.$$
$$\left.\left.-\frac{1}{2}\left(\begin{array}{c}\mu_P(v_i)\exp(\mu_P(v_i))+(1-\mu_P(v_i))\exp(1-\mu_P(v_i))\\ +\mu_E(v_i)\exp(\mu_E(v_i))+(1-\mu_E(v_i))\exp(1-\mu_E(v_i))\end{array}\right)\right\}\right]. \tag{A6}$$

Adding (A5) and (A6), we have:

$$C_e(P||P\cup E)+C_e(P||P\cap E) = \frac{-1}{n\sqrt{e}(\sqrt{e}-1)}\left[\sum_{v_i\in V_2}\left\{\begin{array}{c}\left(\frac{\mu_P(v_i)+\mu_E(v_i)}{2}\right)\exp\left(\frac{\mu_P(v_i)+\mu_E(v_i)}{2}\right)\\ \left(\frac{2-\mu_P(v_i)-\mu_V(v_i)}{2}\right)\exp\left(\frac{2-\mu_P(v_i)-\mu_E(v_i)}{2}\right)\end{array}\right.\right.$$
$$\left.-\frac{1}{2}\left(\begin{array}{c}\mu_P(v_i)\exp(\mu_P(v_i))+(1-\mu_P(v_i))\exp(1-\mu_P(v_i))\\ +\mu_E(v_i)\exp(\mu_E(v_i))+(1-\mu_E(v_i))\exp(1-\mu_E(v_i))\end{array}\right)\right\}$$
$$+\sum_{v_i\in V_1}\left\{\begin{array}{c}\left(\frac{\mu_P(v_i)+\mu_E(v_i)}{2}\right)\exp\left(\frac{\mu_P(v_i)+\mu_E(v_i)}{2}\right)\\ \left(\frac{2-\mu_P(v_i)-\mu_E(v_i)}{2}\right)\exp\left(\frac{2-\mu_P(v_i)-\mu_E(v_i)}{2}\right)\end{array}\right. \tag{A7}$$
$$\left.\left.-\frac{1}{2}\left(\begin{array}{c}\mu_P(v_i)\exp(\mu_P(v_i))+(1-\mu_P(v_i))\exp(1-\mu_P(v_i))\\ +\mu_E(v_i)\exp(\mu_E(v_i))+(1-\mu_E(v_i))\exp(1-\mu_E(v_i))\end{array}\right)\right\}\right].$$
$$= \left[\sum_{i=1}^{n}\left\{\begin{array}{c}\left(\frac{\mu_P(v_i)+\mu_E(v_i)}{2}\right)\exp\left(\frac{\mu_P(v_i)+\mu_E(v_i)}{2}\right)\\ \left(\frac{2-\mu_P(v_i)-\mu_E(v_i)}{2}\right)\exp\left(\frac{2-\mu_P(v_i)-\mu_E(v_i)}{2}\right)\end{array}\right.\right.$$
$$\left.\left.-\frac{1}{2}\left(\begin{array}{c}\mu_P(v_i)\exp(\mu_P(v_i))+(1-\mu_P(v_i))\exp(1-\mu_P(v_i))\\ +\mu_E(v_i)\exp(\mu_E(v_i))+(1-\mu_E(v_i))\exp(1-\mu_E(v_i))\end{array}\right)\right\}\right] = C_e(P||E).$$

Hence, $C_e(E||P \cup E) + C_e(E||P \cap E) = C_e(P||E)$.

(e). The proof is similar to (d).

References

1. Shannon, C.E. A mathematical theory of communication. *Bell Syst. Tech. J.* **1948**, *27*, 379–423. [CrossRef]
2. Kullback, S.; Leibler, R.A. On information and sufficiency. *Ann. Math. Stat.* **1951**, *22*, 79–86. [CrossRef]
3. Rényi, A. On measures of entropy and information. In *Proceedings of the Fourth Berkeley Symposium on Mathematical Statistics and Probability, Contributions to the Theory of Statistics*; The Regents of the University of California: Berkeley, CA, USA, 1961; Volume 1.
4. Sharma, B.; Mittal, D. New non-additive measures of relative information. *J. Comb. Inf. Syst. Sci.* **1977**, *2*, 122–132.
5. Lin, J. Divergence measures based on the Shannon entropy. *IEEE Trans. Inf. Theory* **1991**, *37*, 145–151. [CrossRef]
6. Ghosh, M.; Das, D.; Chakraborty, C.; Ray, A.K. Automated leukocyte recognition using fuzzy divergence. *Micron* **2010**, *41*, 840–846. [CrossRef] [PubMed]
7. Neagoe, I.M.; Popescu, D.; Niculescu, V. Applications of entropic divergence measures for DNA segmentation into high variable regions of cryptosporidium spp. gp60 gene. *Rom. Rep. Phys.* **2014**, *66*, 1078–1087.
8. Zadeh, L.A. Fuzzy sets. *Inf. Control.* **1965**, *8*, 338–353. [CrossRef]
9. De Luca, A.; Termini, S. A definition of a nonprobabilistic entropy in the setting of fuzzy sets theory. *Inf. Control* **1972**, *20*, 301–312. [CrossRef]
10. Pal, N.R.; Pal, S.K. Object-background segmentation using new definitions of entropy. *IEE Proc. E Comput. Digit. Tech.* **1989**, *136*, 284–295. [CrossRef]
11. Hooda, D.S. On generalized measures of fuzzy entropy. *Math. Slovaca* **2004**, *54*, 315–325.
12. Verma, R.K.; Sharma, B.D. On generalized exponential fuzzy entropy. *World Acad. Sci. Eng. Technol.* **2011**, *60*, 1402–1405.
13. Mishra, A.R.; Jain, D.; Hooda, D.S. On logarithmic fuzzy measures of information and discrimination. *J. Inf. Optim. Sci.* **2016**, *37*, 213–231. [CrossRef]
14. Kvalseth, T.O. On exponential entropies. *IEEE Int. Conf. Syst. Man Cybern.* **2000**, *4*, 2822–2826.
15. Mishra, A.R.; Hooda, D.S.; Jain, D. On exponential fuzzy measures of information and discrimination. *Int. J. Comput. Appl.* **2015**, *119*, 1–7.
16. Montes, I.; Pal, N.R.; Montes, S. Entropy measures for Atanassov intuitionistic fuzzy sets based on divergence. *Soft Comput.* **2018**, *22*, 5051–5071. [CrossRef]
17. Mishra, A.R.; Jain, D.; Hooda, D.S. On fuzzy distance and induced fuzzy information measures. *J. Inf. Optim. Sci.* **2016**, *37*, 193–211. [CrossRef]
18. Bhandari, D.; Pal, N.R. Some new information measures for fuzzy sets. *Inf. Sci.* **1993**, *67*, 209–228. [CrossRef]
19. Fan, J.; Xie, W. Distance measure and induced fuzzy entropy. *Fuzzy Sets Syst.* **1999**, *104*, 305–314. [CrossRef]
20. Rani, P.; Kannan, G.; Mishra, A.R.; Mardani, A.; Alrasheedi, M.; Hooda, D.S. Unified fuzzy divergence measures with multi-criteria decision making problems for sustainable planning of an e-waste recycling job selection. *Symmetry* **2020**, *12*, 90. [CrossRef]
21. Arora, H.D.; Dhiman, A. On some generalised information measure of fuzzy directed divergence and decision making. *Int. J. Comput. Sci. Math.* **2016**, *7*, 263–273. [CrossRef]
22. Xiao, F.; Ding, W. Divergence measure of Pythagorean fuzzy sets and its application in medical diagnosis. *Appl. Soft Comput.* **2019**, *79*, 254–267. [CrossRef]
23. Thao, N.X.; Smarandache, F. Divergence measure of neutrosophic sets and applications. *Neutrosophic Sets Syst.* **2018**, *21*, 142–152.
24. Ju, F.; Yuan, Y.; Yuan, Y.; Quan, W. A divergence-based distance measure for intuitionistic fuzzy sets and its application in the decision-making of innovation management. *IEEE Access* **2019**, *8*, 1105–1117. [CrossRef]
25. Joshi, R.; Kumar, S. An exponential Jensen fuzzy divergence measure with applications in multiple attribute decision-making. *Math. Probl. Eng.* **2018**, *2018*, 4342098. [CrossRef]

26. Dahooie, J.H.; Zavadskas, E.K.; Firoozfar, H.R.; Vanaki, A.S.; Mohammadi, N.; Brauers, W.K.M. An improved fuzzy MULTIMOORA approach for multi-criteria decision making based on objective weighting method (CCSD) and its application to technological forecasting method selection. *Eng. Appl. Artif. Intell.* **2019**, *79*, 114–128. [CrossRef]
27. Keshavarz Ghorabaee, M.; Amiri, M.; Zavadskas, E.K.; Turskis, Z.; Antucheviciene, J. A new hybrid simulation-based assignment approach for evaluating airlines with multiple service quality criteria. *J. Air Transp. Manag.* **2017**, *63*, 45–60. [CrossRef]
28. Mardani, A.; Jusoh, A.; Zavadskas, E.K.; Khalifah, Z.; Nor, K.M.D. Application of multiple-criteria decision-making techniques and approaches to evaluating of service quality: A systematic review of the literature. *J. Bus. Econ. Manag.* **2015**, *16*, 1034–1068. [CrossRef]
29. Calabrese, A.; Costa, R.; Levialdi, N.; Menichini, T. Integrating sustainability into strategic decision-making: A fuzzy AHP method for the selection of relevant sustainability issues. *Technol. Forecast. Soc. Chang.* **2019**, *139*, 155–168. [CrossRef]
30. Cavallaro, F.; Zavadskas, E.K.; Streimikiene, D.; Mardani, A. Assessment of concentrated solar power (CSP) technologies based on a modified intuitionistic fuzzy topsis and trigonometric entropy weights. *Technol. Forecast. Soc. Chang.* **2019**, *140*, 258–270. [CrossRef]
31. Akram, M.; Adeel, A. Novel TOPSIS method for group decision-making based on hesitant m−polar fuzzy model. *J. Intell. Fuzzy Syst.* **2019**. [CrossRef]
32. Han, Q.; Li, W.; Lu, Y.; Zheng, M.; Quan, W.; Song, Y. TOPSIS method based on novel entropy and distance measure for linguistic Pythagorean fuzzy sets with their application in multiple attribute decision making. *IEEE Access* **2019**, *8*, 14401–14412. [CrossRef]
33. Deveci, M.; Canitez, F.; Gökaşar, I. WASPAS and TOPSIS based interval type-2 fuzzy MCDM method for a selection of a car sharing station. *Sustain. Cities Soc.* **2018**, *41*, 777–791. [CrossRef]
34. Badalpur, M.; Nurbakhsh, E. An application of WASPAS method in risk qualitative analysis: A case study of a road construction project in Iran. *Int. J. Constr. Manag.* **2019**. [CrossRef]
35. Pamučar, D.; Božanić, D. Selection of a location for the development of multimodal logistics center: Application of single-valued neutrosophic MABAC model. *Oper. Res. Eng. Sci. Theory Appl.* **2019**, *2*, 55–71. [CrossRef]
36. Mishra, A.R.; Chandel, A.; Motwani, D. Extended MABAC method based on divergence measures for multi-criteria assessment of programming language with interval-valued intuitionistic fuzzy sets. *Granul. Comput.* **2020**, *5*, 97–117. [CrossRef]
37. Chatterjee, K.; Kar, S. Unified Granular-number-based AHP-VIKOR multi-criteria decision framework. *Granul. Comput.* **2017**, *2*, 199–221. [CrossRef]
38. Chen, T.-Y. A novel VIKOR method with an application to multiple criteria decision analysis for hospital-based post-acute care within a highly complex uncertain environment. *Neural Comput. Appl.* **2019**, *31*, 3969–3999. [CrossRef]
39. Fei, L.; Xia, J.; Feng, Y.; Liu, L. An ELECTRE-based multiple criteria decision making method for supplier selection using dempster-Shafer theory. *IEEE Access* **2019**, *7*, 84701–84716. [CrossRef]
40. Liao, H.; Jiang, L.; Lev, B.; Fujita, H. Novel operations of PLTSs based on the disparity degrees of linguistic terms and their use in designing the probabilistic linguistic ELECTRE III method. *Appl. Soft Comput.* **2019**, *80*, 450–464. [CrossRef]
41. Rani, P.; Jain, D. Intuitionistic fuzzy PROMETHEE technique for multi-criteria decision making problems based on entropy measure. In *Proceedings of Communications in Computer and Information Science (CCIS)*; Springer: Singapore, 2017; Volume 721, pp. 290–301.
42. Wu, X.; Zhang, C.; Jiang, L.; Liao, H. An integrated method with PROMETHEE and conflict analysis for qualitative and quantitative decision-making: Case study of site selection for wind power plants. *Cogn. Comput.* **2019**, in press. [CrossRef]
43. Alali, F.; Tolga, A.C. Portfolio allocation with the TODIM method. *Expert Syst. Appl.* **2019**, *124*, 341–348. [CrossRef]
44. Wang, L.; Wang, Y.-M.; Martínez, L. Fuzzy TODIM method based on alpha-level sets. *Expert Syst. Appl.* **2019**, 112899. [CrossRef]
45. Kai-Ineman, D.; Tversky, A. Prospect theory: An analysis of decision under risk. *Econometrica* **1979**, *47*, 363–391.

46. Gomes, L.; Lima, M. TODIM: Basics and application to multicriteria ranking of projects with environmental impacts. *Found. Comput. Decis. Sci.* **1992**, *16*, 113–127.
47. Liang, D.; Zhang, Y.; Xu, Z.; Jamaldeen, A. Pythagorean fuzzy VIKOR approaches based on TODIM for evaluating internet banking website quality of Ghanaian banking industry. *Appl. Soft Comput.* **2019**, *78*, 583–594. [CrossRef]
48. Wu, Y.; Wang, J.; Hu, Y.; Ke, Y.; Li, L. An extended TODIM-PROMETHEE method for waste-to-energy plant site selection based on sustainability perspective. *Energy* **2018**, *156*, 1–16. [CrossRef]
49. Gomes, L.F.A.M.; Machado, M.A.S.; da Costa, F.F.; Rangel, L.A.D. Criteria interactions in multiple criteria decision aiding: A choquet formulation for the TODIM method. *Procedia Comput. Sci.* **2013**, *17*, 324–331. [CrossRef]
50. Qin, J.; Liu, X.; Pedrycz, W. An extended TODIM multi-criteria group decision making method for green supplier selection in interval type-2 fuzzy environment. *Eur. J. Oper. Res.* **2017**, *258*, 626–638. [CrossRef]
51. Mishra, A.R.; Rani, P. Biparametric information measures-based TODIM technique for interval-valued intuitionistic fuzzy environment. *Arab. J. Sci. Eng.* **2018**, *43*, 3291–3309. [CrossRef]
52. Fan, Z.P.; Zhang, X.; Chen, F.D.; Liu, Y. Extended TODIM method for hybrid multiple attribute decision making problems. *Knowl. Based Syst.* **2013**, *42*, 40–48. [CrossRef]
53. Liu, P.; Shen, M. An extended C-TODIM method with linguistic intuitionistic fuzzy numbers. *J. Intell. Fuzzy Syst.* **2019**, *37*, 3615–3627. [CrossRef]
54. Zhang, D.; Li, Y.; Wu, C. An extended TODIM method to rank products with online reviews under intuitionistic fuzzy environment. *J. Oper. Res. Soc.* **2020**, *71*, 322–334. [CrossRef]
55. Wang, J.Q.; Li, J.J. Multi-criteria fuzzy decision-making method based on cross entropy and score functions. *Expert Syst. Appl.* **2011**, *38*, 1032–1038. [CrossRef]
56. Xia, M.; Xu, Z. Entropy/cross entropy-based group decision making under intuitionistic fuzzy environment. *Inf. Fusion* **2012**, *13*, 31–47. [CrossRef]
57. Shao, Y.; Mou, Q.; Gong, Z. On retarded fuzzy functional differential equations and nonabsolute fuzzy integrals. *Fuzzy Sets Syst.* **2019**, *375*, 121–140. [CrossRef]
58. Montes, S.; Couso, I.; Gil, P.; Bertoluzza, C. Divergence measure between fuzzy sets. *Int. J. Approx. Reason.* **2002**, *30*, 91–105. [CrossRef]
59. Jain, K.; Chhabra, P. A new exponential directed divergence information measure. *J. Appl. Math. Inform.* **2016**, *34*, 295–308. [CrossRef]
60. Sugeno, M. *Theory of Fuzzy Integral and its Application*; Tokyo Institute of Technology: Tokyo, Japan, 1974.
61. Rani, P.; Jain, D.; Hooda, D.S. Shapley function based interval-valued intuitionistic fuzzy VIKOR technique for correlative multi-criteria decision making problems. *Iran. J. Fuzzy Syst.* **2018**, *15*, 25–54.
62. Kumari, R.; Mishra, A.R.; Sharma, D.K. Intuitionistic fuzzy Shapley-TOPSIS method for multi-criteria decision making problems based on information measures. *Recent Adv. Comput. Sci. Commun.* **2020**. [CrossRef]
63. Meng, F.; Wang, C.; Chen, X.; Zhang, Q. Correlation coefficients of interval-valued hesitant fuzzy sets and their application based on the Shapley function. *Int. J. Intell. Syst.* **2016**, *31*, 17–43. [CrossRef]
64. Shapley, L.S. A value for n-person games. *Contrib. Theory Games* **1953**, *2*, 307–317.
65. Kahneman, D.; Tversky, A. Prospect theory: An analysis of decision under risk. In *Handbook of the Fundamentals of Financial Decision Making: Part I. World Scientific*; World Scientific: Singapore, 2013; pp. 99–127.
66. Toloie, A.; Nasimi, M.; Poorebrahimi, A. Assessing quality of insurance companies using multiple criteria decision making. *Eur. J. Sci. Res.* **2011**, *54*, 448–457.
67. Mishra, A.R. Intuitionistic fuzzy information measures with application in rating of township development. *Iran. J. Fuzzy Syst.* **2016**, *13*, 49–70.
68. Mishra, A.R.; Jain, D.; Hooda, D.S. Exponential intuitionistic fuzzy information measure with assessment of service quality. *Int. J. Fuzzy Syst.* **2017**, *19*, 788–798. [CrossRef]
69. Krohling, R.A.; de Souza, T.T.M. Combining prospect theory and fuzzy numbers to multi-criteria decision making. *Expert Syst. Appl.* **2012**, *39*, 11487–11493. [CrossRef]

symmetry

MDPI

Article

Intuitionistic Fuzzy Sets in Multi-Criteria Group Decision Making Problems Using the Characteristic Objects Method

Shahzad Faizi [1], Wojciech Sałabun [2,*], Tabasam Rashid [3], Sohail Zafar [3] and Jarosław Wątróbski [4]

1 Department of Mathematics, Virtual University of Pakistan, Lahore 54000, Pakistan; shahzadfaizi@vu.edu.pk
2 Research Team on Intelligent Decision Support Systems, Department of Artificial Intelligence Methods and Applied Mathematics, Faculty of Computer Science and Information Technology, West Pomeranian University of Technology in Szczecin ul. Żołnierska 49, 71-210 Szczecin, Poland
3 Department of Mathematics, University of Management and Technology, Lahore 54770, Pakistan; tabasam.rashid@umt.edu.pk (T.R.); sohail.zafar@umt.edu.pk (S.Z.)
4 The Faculty of Economics, Finance and Management of the University of Szczecin, Mickiewicza 64, 71-101 Szczecin, Poland; jaroslaw.watrobski@usz.edu.pl
* Correspondence: wojciech.salabun@zut.edu.pl; Tel.: +48-91-449-5580

Received: 1 August 2020; Accepted: 14 August 2020; Published: 19 August 2020

Abstract: Over the past few decades, several researchers and professionals have focused on the development and application of multi-criteria group decision making (MCGDM) methods under a fuzzy environment in different areas and disciplines. This complex research area has become one of the more popular topics, and it seems that this trend will be increasing. In this paper, we propose a new MCGDM approach combining intuitionistic fuzzy sets (IFSs) and the Characteristic Object Method (COMET) for solving the group decision making (GDM) problems. The COMET method is resistant to the rank reversal phenomenon, and at the same time it remains relatively simple and intuitive in practical problems. This method can be used for both symmetric and asymmetric information. The Triangular Intuitionistic Fuzzy Numbers (TIFNs) have been used to handle uncertain data. This concept can ensure the preference information about an alternative under specific criteria more comprehensively and allows for easy modelling of symmetrical or asymmetrical linguistic values. Each expert provides the membership and non-membership degree values of intuitionistic fuzzy numbers (IFNs). So this approach deals with a different kind of uncertainty than with hesitant fuzzy sets (HFSs). The proposed combination of COMET and IFSs required an adaptation of the matrix of expert judgment (MEJ) and allowed to capture the behaviour aspects of the decision makers (DMs). Therefore, we get more reliable solutions while solving MCGDM problems. Finally, the proposed method is presented in a simple academic example.

Keywords: intuitionistic fuzzy sets; multi-criteria group decision making; the COMET method

---

1. Introduction

During the process of MCGDM, DMs usually use qualitative or quantitative measures or both to assess the performance of different alternatives under certain criteria concerning the overall objective. Individually DMs express their assessments based on the quality of the features representing the given set of alternatives as well as their expertise. On the other hand, sometimes, it is difficult to get exact assessment values under many real decision situations due to the presence of implicit vagueness and uncertainty in human judgments [1,2]. Atanassov [3] extended the fuzzy sets [4] to develop the concept of IFSs as an important extension, including non-membership function, to express this type of vagueness and uncertainty more accurately as compared to fuzzy sets [5]. The IFS describes the fuzzy characteristics of things more comprehensibly. IFS has been extensively used and widely applied to decision making problems [2,6–12]. In recent years, most of the researchers have used the IFSs to complicated real-life MCDM problems. For example, Xu [10] investigated fuzzy multiple attribute GDM problems where the attribute values are represented in IFNs with the information on attribute weights provided by DMs according to one or some of the different preference structures. Xu et al. [11] introduced a new outranking choice method to solve MCGDM problems under interval-valued intuitionistic fuzzy conditions. Chen [6] created an inclusion-based TOPSIS method in the interval-valued IFS framework to address MCGDM medical problems. Next, Xu and Liao [13] presented a new way to check the consistency of an IPR and then introduced an automatic procedure to repair the inconsistent one without the participation of the DMs, Park et al. [7] extended the GDM VIKOR method in the presence of partially known attribute weight information under the interval-valued intuitionistic fuzzy environment while Shena et al. [14] proposed an outranking sorting method to solve MCGDM problems using IFSs.

The consistency level of the preference relations has a vital role in decision making during the pairwise judgments to depict DM's preferences [15]. Different consistency definitions have been proposed in the context of IPRs [16,17]. For instance, Xu [18,19] proposed multiplicative consistent IPRs with known weights of the DMs. He has also introduced an intuitionistic fuzzy weighted averaging operator to construct a method to solve MCGDM problems. Xu et al. [19,20] have identified the deficiency of the multiplicative transitivity condition and proposed a new definition of the multiplicative consistency for IPRs. Besides, Gong et al. [21] presented the consistent additive requirements of the IPR according to that of IFN preference relation. Wang [22] confirmed that the additive consistency defined indirectly in [21] and proved that the consistency transformation equations matrix may not always be an IPR. Wang [23] suggested linear goal programming models for determining intuitionistic fuzzy weights from IPRs and put forward the new definitions of additive consistency and weak transitivity for IPRs.

The triangular IFS, as an important extension of the IFS, can represent decision information from different dimensions [24] and allows for easy modelling of symmetrical or asymmetrical linguistic values. The triangular IFS extends the nature of the discourse of the IFS from a discrete set of points to a continuous set [22]. The TFN and the traditional IFN can be considered as particular types of TIFN. By adding the TFN to the IFN, TIFN makes the information given by DMs not only relevant to a fuzzy concept of "excellent" or "good", but also expressed more accurately [25,26]. Recently, the research on MCDM problems in the context of TIFNs is developing. For example, Otay [27] introduced a multi-expert fuzzy approach combining intuitionistic fuzzy data envelopment analysis and IF-AHP (Analytic Hierarchy Process) for solving the performance evaluation problem of health care organizations. Qin et al. [28] proposed the extended TODIM method to handle the MCGDM problems with TIFNs. In contrast, Sainia et al. [29] proposed the triangular intuitionistic fuzzy MCDM problem for finding the best option when the phonetic factors for the given criteria are pre-characterized. Mishra et al. have proposed new divergence measures using interval-valued IF-TODIM method [30].

The COMET method is effective in dealing with MCDM problems [31–35] and has been widely studied and refined since then in practical decision situations [36,37]. It is an innovative idea for handling the solved problems of rational decision making in the presence of vagueness and uncertainty, which always avoids the rank reversal phenomenon paradox. When the complexity of the process is completely independent of the number of alternatives, this method is effective. It helps the DMs to make analyses, assessments, and ranking of the alternatives in real decision-making problems. Moreover, it is much easier for a DM to make pairwise comparisons of characteristic objects (COs) than directly the comparison between the alternatives. Finally, the overall ranking of alternatives is formulated on the basis of these pairwise comparisons of COs. Another advantage of the COMET method is that, unlike methods such as MIVES [38,39], AHP [1], TOPSIS [6], DEMATEL–MAIRCA [40] or ELECTRE [41], it does not require explicit determination of the criteria, which will significantly facilitate the decision-making process.

In this paper, we propose a new MCGDM metho by combining the COMET method and TIFNs. The primary motivation for this approach is the advantages of the COMET method and IFSs. In this approach, we use TIFNs to get the degree of membership and non-membership values in the form of IFN for an alternative under particular criteria. It is an entirely different approach to dealing with uncertain data than for hesitant fuzzy sets (HFSs) [42]. This change is due to the focus on another type of possible data uncertainty. An additional methodical contribution is the possibility to task the logical consistency of the MEJ matrix. This is a complete novelty in decision making using the COMET method while performing pairwise judgments of all the COs by the DMs, and the MEJ obtained as a result, which is a preference relation, can be an inconsistent matrix. To resolve this issue, MEJ is improved to an additive consistent matrix in this paper to avoid any inconsistency in the solution to MCGDM problems.

The rest part of the paper can be summarized as follows: Some basic concepts related to IFS, TIFN, IPR and the additive consistency measure for IPR are introduced in Section 2. An approach based on the COMET method is constructed in Section 3 to handle the intuitionistic fuzzy MCGDM problems in which the assessment values of alternatives under certain criteria take the form of IFNs. A practical example is given to make out the practicality and effectiveness of the proposed method in Section 4. We wind up the paper with a useful comparison and some final remarks in Section 5.

2. Basic Concepts

Basic definitions of IFS, IPR and comparison method for two IFNs based on the score and accuracy functions have to be recalled. The additive consistency measure for IPR and the concept of TIFN are also discussed in this section.

Definition 1. *An IFS $\tilde{A}$ in X is given by $\tilde{A} = \{(x, \mu_{\tilde{A}}(x), \nu_{\tilde{A}}(x)) | x \in X\}$ where $\mu_{\tilde{A}} : X \to [0,1]$ and $\nu_{\tilde{A}} : X \to [0,1]$ with the condition that $0 \leq \mu_{\tilde{A}} + \nu_{\tilde{A}} \leq 1$ for every $x \in X$. The numbers $\mu_{\tilde{A}}(x)$, $\nu_{\tilde{A}}(x) \in [0,1]$ denote, respectively, the degree of membership and non-membership of the element $x \in X$ to the set $\tilde{A}$. For convenience, in this paper, $\tilde{A} = (\mu_{\tilde{A}}, \nu_{\tilde{A}})$ is called the intuitionistic fuzzy number (IFN) [3,43].*

To develop a mechanism to compare two IFNs, Chen and Tan [44] defined score function for an IFN as follows:

$$Sc(\tilde{A}) = \mu_{\tilde{A}} - \nu_{\tilde{A}} \tag{1}$$

Afterwards, Hong and Choi [45] defined an accuracy function as

$$H(\tilde{A}) = \mu_{\tilde{A}} + \nu_{\tilde{A}} \tag{2}$$

It can be easily observed that $Sc(\tilde{A}) \in [-1,1]$ and $H(\tilde{A}) \in [0,1]$. The hesitancy degree of $\tilde{A}$ can be further calculated as

$$\pi(\tilde{A}) = 1 - H(\tilde{A}). \tag{3}$$

It can be easily observed that as higher the value of $H(\tilde{A})$, the lower the value of $\pi(\tilde{A})$. Furthermore, when $\pi(\tilde{A}) = 0$, the IFN $\tilde{A}$ is reduced to a fuzzy number $\mu_{\tilde{A}}$.

For any two IFNs $\tilde{A} = (\mu_{\tilde{A}}, \nu_{\tilde{A}})$ and $\tilde{B} = (\mu_{\tilde{B}}, \nu_{\tilde{B}})$, Xu and Yager [46] proposed a prioritized comparison method for two IFNs on the basis of the aforementioned $Sc(\tilde{A})$ and $H(\tilde{A})$ as follows:

1. if $Sc(\tilde{A}) < Sc(\tilde{B})$, then $\tilde{A} < \tilde{B}$;
2. if $Sc(\tilde{A}) = Sc(\tilde{B})$, and

(i) $H(\tilde{A}) < H(\tilde{B})$, then $\tilde{A} < \tilde{B}$;
(ii) $H(\tilde{A}) = H(\tilde{B})$, then $\tilde{A} = \tilde{B}$.

Xu [18] introduced the following operations on IFSs:

Definition 2. *Let two IFNs A and B in X be* $\tilde{A} = (\mu_{\tilde{A}}, \nu_{\tilde{A}})$ *and* $\tilde{B} = (\mu_{\tilde{B}}, \nu_{\tilde{B}})$. *Then*

1. $k\tilde{A} = (1 - (1 - \mu_{\tilde{A}})^k, (\nu_{\tilde{A}})^k), k \in [0,1]$;
2. $\tilde{A} \oplus \tilde{B} = (\mu_{\tilde{A}} + \mu_{\tilde{B}} - \mu_{\tilde{A}}\mu_{\tilde{B}}, \nu_{\tilde{A}}\nu_{\tilde{B}})$;
3. $\tilde{A} \otimes \tilde{B} = (\nu_{\tilde{A}}\nu_{\tilde{B}}, \mu_{\tilde{A}} + \mu_{\tilde{B}} - \mu_{\tilde{A}}\mu_{\tilde{B}})$.

The IPR is an effective tool that can describe the fuzzy characteristics of things more delightedly and comprehensively, and is very helpful in dealing with vagueness and uncertainty of actual decision making problems. Xu [19] introduced the concept of IPR which can express the hesitancy and uncertainty more effectively in pairwise comparisons of the DMs as follows:

Definition 3. *An IPR R on* $X = \{x_1, x_2, ..., x_n\}$ *is represented by a matrix* $R = (r_{ij})_{n\times n}$ *where* $r_{ij} = (\mu(x_i, x_j), \nu(x_i, x_j))$ *for all* $i, j = 1, 2, ..., n$ *[19]. For convenience, let* r_{ij} *be shortly written as* (μ_{ij}, ν_{ij}), *where* μ_{ij} *indicates the degree to which* x_i *is preferred to* x_j, ν_{ij} *indicates the degree to which* x_i *is not preferred to* x_j, *and* $\pi(x_i, x_j) = 1 - \mu_{ij} - \nu_{ij}$ *is denoted as an indeterminacy degree or a hesitancy degree with the conditions* $\mu_{ij}, \nu_{ij} \in [0,1]$, $\mu_{ij} + \nu_{ij} \leq 1$, $\mu_{ij} = \nu_{ji}$, $\mu_{ji} = \nu_{ij}$, $\mu_{ii} = \nu_{ii} = 0.5$, $\pi_{ij} = 1 - \mu_{ij} - \nu_{ij}$ *for all* $i, j = 1, 2, ..., n$.

A significant property of preference relations is additive consistency. Wang [23] directly used the membership degrees in the pairwise judgment matrix and proposed the additive consistent IPRs as follows:

Definition 4. *An IPR* $R = (r_{ik})_{n\times n}$ *where* $r_{ik} = (\mu(x_i, x_k), \nu(x_i, x_k))$ *for all* $i, k = 1, 2, ..., n$ *is additive consistent if for all* $i, j, k = 1, 2, ..., n$, *the following condition is satisfied.*

$$\mu_{ij} + \mu_{jk} + \mu_{ki} = \mu_{kj} + \mu_{ji} + \mu_{ik}$$

Since $\mu_{ij} = \nu_{ji}$, $\nu_{ij} = \mu_{ji}$ *for all* $i, j = 1, 2, ..., n$. *Therefore for all* $i, j, k = 1, 2, ..., n$, *it follows from the above equation that*

$$\nu_{ij} + \nu_{jk} + \nu_{ki} = \nu_{kj} + \nu_{ji} + \nu_{ik}$$

Based on above definition, and the score function, Wang [23] established a result to check the additive consistency of an IPR as

Definition 5. *An IPR* $R = (r_{ik})_{n\times n}$ *is additive consistent if*

$$S(r_{ij}) = S(r_{ik}) - S(r_{jk}) \text{ for all } i, j, k = 1, 2, ..., n. \tag{4}$$

To derive a consistent IPR from an inconsistent one, Tong and Wang [47] first introduced the rectified inconsistence IPR $\tilde{R} = (\tilde{r}_{ik})_{n\times n}$, $\tilde{r}_{ik} = (\tilde{\mu}(x_i, x_k), \tilde{\nu}(x_i, x_k))$ for all $i, k = 1, 2, ..., n$ where

$$\tilde{\mu}_{ij} = \frac{1}{2n}\left(\sum_{l=1}^{n} Sc(\tilde{r}_{il}) - \sum_{l=1}^{n} Sc(\tilde{r}_{jl})\right) + 0.5(1 - \pi(\tilde{r}_{ij})), \tag{5}$$

$$\tilde{\nu}_{ij} = \frac{1}{2n}\left(\sum_{l=1}^{n} Sc(\tilde{r}_{jl}) - \sum_{l=1}^{n} Sc(\tilde{r}_{il})\right) + 0.5(1 - \pi(\tilde{r}_{ij})), \tag{6}$$

for all $i, j = 1, 2, ..., n$.

If $\tilde{\mu}_{ij} \geq 0$ and $\tilde{\nu}_{ij} \geq 0$ by using Formulae (5) and (6), then $\tilde{R}$ is a consistent IPR. Each IFN in $\tilde{R}$, in this case, has the same hesitancy degree as that of the corresponding element in $\tilde{R}$. However, when Equations (5) and (6) provide any one of the result $\tilde{\mu}_{ij} < 1$, $\tilde{\mu}_{ij} > 0$, $\tilde{\nu}_{ij} < 1$ or $\tilde{\nu}_{ij} > 0$, then $\tilde{R}$ will not be a consistent IPR. In order to derive a consistent one from IPR $\tilde{R}$, Tong and Wang [47] proposed a transformation function as follows:

$$d = \begin{cases} 0, & \text{if } \tilde{\mu}_{ij} \geq 0, \text{ for all } i,j = 1,2,...,n \\ \max\{|\tilde{\mu}_{ij}|, \tilde{\mu}_{ij} < 0, i,j = 1,2,...,n\}, & \text{otherwise} \end{cases} \quad (7)$$

Tong and Wang [47] further converted the IPR $\tilde{R}$ to $\widetilde{\tilde{R}} = (\widetilde{\tilde{r}}_{ij})_{n\times n}$ by applying the above transformation function, where

$$\widetilde{\tilde{r}}_{ij} = (\hat{\mu}_{ij}, \hat{v}_{ij}) = \left(\frac{\hat{\mu}_{ij} + d}{1+2d}, \frac{\hat{v}_{ij} + d}{1+2d}\right) \quad (8)$$

for all $i, k = 1,2,...,n$.

If $\widetilde{\tilde{R}} = (\widetilde{\tilde{r}}_{ij})_{n\times n}$ is additive consistent IPR, then the additive consistency rectification process will stop otherwise it will continue until the desired result is obtained.

Dubois and Prade [48] introduced the concept of a triangular fuzzy number. In a similar way, the concept of a TIFN is defined as follows.

Definition 6. *A TIFN $\tilde{T}$ is an intuitionistic fuzzy subset with the following membership function and non-membership function:*

$$\mu_{\tilde{T}}(x) = \begin{cases} \frac{x-\tilde{t}^L}{\tilde{t}^M-\tilde{t}^L}, & \tilde{t}^L \leq x \leq \tilde{t}^M \\ \frac{\tilde{t}^U-x}{\tilde{t}^U-\tilde{t}^M} & \tilde{t}^M \leq x \leq \tilde{t}^U \\ 0, & \text{Otherwise} \end{cases}$$

and

$$\nu_{\tilde{T}}(x) = \begin{cases} \frac{\tilde{t}^M-x}{\tilde{t}^M-\tilde{t}'^L}, & \tilde{t}'^L \leq x \leq \tilde{t}^M \\ \frac{x-\tilde{t}^M}{\tilde{t}'^U-\tilde{t}^M} & \tilde{t}^M \leq x \leq \tilde{t}'^U \\ 0, & \text{Otherwise} \end{cases}$$

where, $\tilde{t}'^L \leq \tilde{t}^L \leq \tilde{t}^M \leq \tilde{t}^U \leq \tilde{t}'^U$, $0 \leq \mu_{\tilde{T}}(x) + \nu_{\tilde{T}}(x) \leq 1$ and TIFN is denoted by $\tilde{T} = (\tilde{t}^L, \tilde{t}^M, \tilde{t}^U; \tilde{t}'^L, \tilde{t}^M, \tilde{t}'^U)$.

Definition 7. *For a TIFN $\tilde{A}$, we define the support of $\tilde{A}$ as the set of all elements of X with nonzero membership and non-membership values in $\tilde{A}$, or symbolically the support of $\tilde{A}$ is defined as*

$$S(\tilde{A}) = \{x : \mu_{\tilde{A}}(x) > 0 \text{ and } \nu_{\tilde{A}}(x) > 0\}$$

Definition 8. *For a TIFN $\tilde{A}$, we define the core of $\tilde{A}$ as the set of all elements of X with membership value one and non-membership value zero in $\tilde{A}$, or symbolically the core of $\tilde{A}$ is defined as*

$$C(\tilde{A}) = \{x : \mu_{\tilde{A}}(x) = 1 \text{ and } \nu_{\tilde{A}}(x) = 0\}$$

3. MCDM with COMET Method Using IFSs

The COMET method is proposed to handle MCGDM problems under IFS environment which can be described as follows. Assume that A_j $(j = 1,2,...,m)$ is a discrete set of alternatives and $D = \{d_1, d_2, ..., d_k\}$ is a set of DMs who are requested to provide their opinion about the given alternatives under the criteria C_i $(i = 1,2,...,n)$. The proposed approach can be described in five following steps:

Step 1: Define the space of the problem as follows:

Let $\tilde{T}_i^{\delta}(1 \leq i \leq n)$ be different subsets of a family $\mathscr{F}$ of all TIFNs selected by a DM d_δ $(\delta = 1,2,...,k)$ for each criteria C_i $(i = 1,2,...,n)$ where $\tilde{T}_i^{\delta} = \{\tilde{T}_{i1}^{\delta}, \tilde{T}_{i2}^{\delta}, ..., \tilde{T}_{ic_i}^{\delta}\}$. In this way, the following families of TIFNs for each criterion are obtained:

$\tilde{T}_1^{\delta} = \{\tilde{T}_{11}^{\delta}, \tilde{T}_{12}^{\delta}, ..., \tilde{T}_{1c_1}^{\delta}\}$ for criteria C_1;

$\tilde{T}_2^{\delta} = \{\tilde{T}_{21}^{\delta}, \tilde{T}_{22}^{\delta}, ..., \tilde{T}_{2c_2}^{\delta}\}$ for criteria C_2;

$\vdots$

$\tilde{T}_n^{\delta} = \{\tilde{T}_{n1}^{\delta}, \tilde{T}_{n2}^{\delta}, ..., \tilde{T}_{nc_n}^{\delta}\}$ for criteria C_n.

where $c_1, c_2, ..., c_n$ are numbers of TIFNs in each family $\tilde{T}_i^{\delta}(1 \leq i \leq n)$ for all criteria.

The core corresponding to each criterion is defined as the core of each member of the family $\tilde{T}_i^{\delta}(1 \leq i \leq n)$, i.e.,

$$C(C_1) = \left\{C(\tilde{T}_{11}^{\delta}), C(\tilde{T}_{12}^{\delta}), ..., C(\tilde{T}_{1c_1}^{\delta})\right\};$$
$$C(C_2) = \left\{C(\tilde{T}_{21}^{\delta}), C(\tilde{T}_{22}^{\delta}), ..., C(\tilde{T}_{2c_2}^{\delta})\right\};$$
$$\vdots$$
$$C(C_n) = \left\{C(\tilde{T}_{n1}^{\delta}), C(\tilde{T}_{n2}^{\delta}), ..., C(\tilde{T}_{nc_n}^{\delta})\right\}.$$

Step 2: Generate the COs:

By using the Cartesian product of all TIFNs cores, all COs can be obtained as follows:

$CO = C(C_1) \times C(C_2) \times ... \times C(C_n)$

As the result of this, the ordered set of all COs is obtained:

$$CO_1 = \{C(\tilde{T}_{11}^{\delta}), C(\tilde{T}_{21}^{\delta}), ..., C(\tilde{T}_{n1}^{\delta})\};$$
$$CO_2 = \{C(\tilde{T}_{11}^{\delta}), C(\tilde{T}_{21}^{\delta}), ..., C(\tilde{T}_{n2}^{\delta})\};$$
$$\vdots$$
$$CO_s = \left\{C(\tilde{T}_{1c_1}^{\delta}), C(\tilde{T}_{2c_2}^{\delta}), ..., C(\tilde{T}_{nc_n}^{\delta})\right\}.$$

where s is total number of COs which can be computed by the formula $s = \prod_{i=1}^{n} c_i$.

Step 3: Rank and evaluate the COs:

A pairwise comparison of all the COs can be achieved by inserting the opinion each DM in the form of IFNs. Hereafter, the MEJ is determined as follows:

$$MEJ^{\delta} = \begin{array}{c} \\ CO_1 \\ CO_2 \\ \vdots \\ CO_s \end{array} \begin{array}{c} \begin{array}{cccc} CO_1 & CO_2 & \cdots & CO_s \end{array} \\ \begin{bmatrix} \tilde{A}_{11}^{\delta} & \tilde{A}_{12}^{\delta} & \cdots & \tilde{A}_{1s}^{\delta} \\ \tilde{A}_{21}^{\delta} & \tilde{A}_{22}^{\delta} & \cdots & \tilde{A}_{2s}^{\delta} \\ \vdots & \vdots & \ddots & \vdots \\ \tilde{A}_{s1}^{\delta} & \tilde{A}_{s2}^{\delta} & \cdots & \tilde{A}_{ss}^{\delta} \end{bmatrix} \end{array},$$

where $\tilde{A}_{\alpha\beta}^{\delta}(\alpha, \beta = 1,2,...,s$ and $\delta = 1,2,...,k)$ is an IFN selected by each DM in pairwise comparison of CO_α and CO_β, $\alpha, \beta = 1,2,...,s$ and preferred the IFN $(0.5, 0.5)$ to those when $\alpha = \beta$. The selection of $\tilde{A}_{\alpha\beta}^{\delta}(\alpha, \beta = 1,2,...,s)$ depends entirely on the expertise and judgment of the DMs.

The aggregated $MEJ = (\tilde{A}_{\alpha\beta})_{s \times s}$ of expert judgment can be obtained by using Definition 2 where $\tilde{A}_{\alpha\beta} = \oplus_{\delta=1}^{k} \tilde{A}_{\alpha\beta}^{\delta}$, where $\alpha, \beta = 1,2,...,s$.

Step 4: Consistency measure:

A consistency check is fundamentally required in order to avoid inconsistent solutions. Extensive studies have been done to estimate the level of the inconsistency of numerical preference relations [20,49,50]. Saaty [51] developed a concept of the consistency ratio (CR) to measure the inconsistency degree of numerical preference relations. He proposed that the preference relation is like acceptable consistency if $CR < 0.1$; otherwise, it is inconsistent and required to return it to the DMs again for the improvement of their preferences until acceptable. Xu and Liao [13] introduced a method to check the consistency of an IPR and proposed an interesting procedure to improve the inconsistent

IPR without the support of the DM. Tong and Wang [47] discussed the additive consistency criteria for IPR. In this paper, we improve the consistency level of an inconsistent aggregated MEJ based on the idea of additive consistency measure for IPR proposed by Tong and Wang in [47].

Now, if $MEJ{=}(\tilde{A}_{\alpha\beta})_{s\times s}$ is not additive consistent based on Definition 5, then rectification process as discussed in Section 2 has to be carried out. Let $MEJ^c{=}(\widetilde{\bar{A}}_{\alpha\beta})_{s\times s}$ is an additive consistent matrix as obtained in the rectification process. To get the vertical vector SJ of the Summed Judgments, we use the following formula:

$$SJ = [\frac{1}{s}\sum_{\beta=1}^{s} Sc(\widetilde{\bar{A}}_{\alpha\beta})\ |\alpha,\beta = 1,2,...,s]^T \tag{9}$$

Finally, to assign each CO the approximate value of preference, we find a vertical vector P whose α^{th} component represents the approximate preference value of CO_α. The vector P can be obtained by using the following MATLAB code:

```
k=length(unique(SJ));
P=zeros(t,1);
for i=1:k
    ind=find(SJ == max(SJ))
    P(ind)=(k-i)/(k-1);
    SJ(ind)= min(SJ)-1;
end
```

It is noted here that the Matlab code presented by Sałabun in [33] can work only for positive real numbers. However, this Matlab code work for all real numbers.

Step 5: Inference in a fuzzy model and final ranking:

It can be easily observed that $A_j = \{a_{1j}, a_{2j}, ..., a_{nj}\}, j = 1,2,...,m$ is a set of crisp number with respect to criteria $C_1, C_2, ..., C_n$ which fulfills the following conditions:

$a_{1j} \in [C(\tilde{T}^{\delta}_{11}), C(\tilde{T}^{\delta}_{1c_1})]$;
$a_{2j} \in [C(\tilde{T}^{\delta}_{21}), C(\tilde{T}^{\delta}_{2c_2})]$;
$\vdots$
$a_{nj} \in [C(\tilde{T}^{\delta}_{n1}), C(\tilde{T}^{\delta}_{nc_n})]$.

In order to get the final ranking of alternatives, we proceed further as follows:
For each $j = 1,2,...,m$,
$a_{1j} \in [C(\tilde{T}^{\delta}_{1k_1}), C(\tilde{T}^{\delta}_{1(k_1+1)})]$;
$a_{2j} \in [C(\tilde{T}^{\delta}_{2k_2}), C(\tilde{T}^{\delta}_{2(k_2+1)})]$;
$\vdots$
$a_{nj} \in [C(\tilde{T}^{\delta}_{nk_n}), C(\tilde{T}^{\delta}_{n(k_n+1)})]$.
where $k_i = 1,2,...,(c_i - 1)$, $(1 \leq i \leq n)$. The group of the activated rules can be selected as:
$\left(C(\tilde{T}^{\delta}_{1k_1}), C(\tilde{T}^{\delta}_{2k_2}), ..., C(\tilde{T}^{\delta}_{nk_n})\right)$;
$\left(C(\tilde{T}^{\delta}_{1k_1}), C(\tilde{T}^{\delta}_{2k_2}), ..., C(\tilde{T}^{\delta}_{n(k_n+1)})\right)$;
$\vdots$
$\left(C(\tilde{T}^{\delta}_{1(k_1+1)}), C(\tilde{T}^{\delta}_{2(k_2+1)}), ..., C(\tilde{T}^{\delta}_{n(k_n+1)})\right)$.

Here, the total number of COs is 2^n where $1 \leq 2^n \leq s$. Note that the group of activated rules is the collection of all those COs where the membership and non-membership values of all the IFNs corresponding to each element of alternative A_j $(1 \leq j \leq m)$ are non-zero.

Let the approximate preference values of the activated rules (COs) be $p_1, p_2, ..., p_{2^n}$ which are actually some values in P_α's $(1 \le \alpha \le s)$. Suppose TIFN value at $x \in A_j$ $(1 \le j \le m)$ provided by each DM d_δ $(\delta = 1, 2, ..., k)$ for each criterion C_i $(i = 1, 2, .., n)$ are represented by the IFN as

$$\tilde{T}_{ij}^{\delta}(x) = (\mu_{\tilde{T},ij}^{\delta}(x),\ \nu_{\tilde{T},ij}^{\delta}(x))$$

Corresponding to each $a_{ij} \in A_j$ $(1 \le i \le n, 1 \le j \le m)$, suppose $\tilde{T}_{ij}(x)$ is an IFN achieved by aggregating all the IFNs $\tilde{T}_{ij}^{\delta}(x)$ using Definition 2 where

$$\tilde{T}_{ij}(x) = (\oplus_{\delta=1}^{k}\mu_{\tilde{T},ij}^{\delta}(x),\ \oplus_{\delta=1}^{k}\nu_{\tilde{T},ij}^{\delta}(x)).$$

Let $\tilde{A}_j$ be IFN which is calculated as the sum of the product of fulfillment degrees of all the activated rules and their preference values, i.e.,

$$\begin{aligned} \tilde{A}_j = p_1(\tilde{T}_{1k_1}(a_{1j}) \otimes \tilde{T}_{2k_2}(a_{2j}) \otimes \dots \\ \tilde{T}_{nk_n}(a_{nj})) \oplus p_2(\tilde{T}_{1k_1}(a_{1j}) \otimes \tilde{T}_{2k_2}(a_{2j}) \otimes \dots \\ \tilde{T}_{n(k_n+1)}(a_{nj})) \oplus \dots \\ p_{2^n}(\tilde{T}_{1(k_1+1)}(a_{1j}) \otimes \tilde{T}_{2(k_2+1)}(a_{2j}) \otimes \dots \\ \tilde{T}_{n(k_n+1)}(a_{nj})). \end{aligned} \quad (10)$$

The final preference value of each alternative A_j $(1 \le j \le m)$ is computed by as

$$A_j = Sc(\tilde{A}_j),\ 1 \le j \le m.$$

where $Sc(\tilde{A}_j)$ $(1 \le j \le m)$ represents the score value of each A_j $(1 \le j \le m)$ obtained by using the Formula (1). Finally, the final ranking order of the alternatives is obtained by sorting these preference values. The larger the preference value, the superior the alternative A_j $(1 \le j \le m)$. The whole procedure is presented as the flowchart in Figure 1.

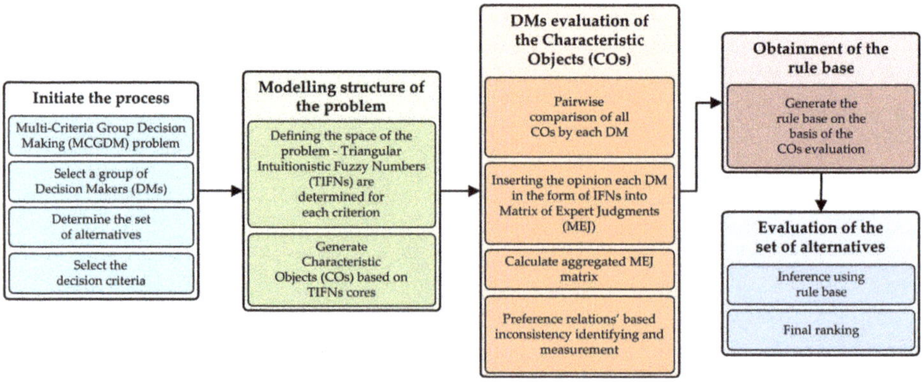

Figure 1. The flowchart of the proposed approach combining the advantages of the Characteristic Object Method (COMET) and Triangular Intuitionistic Fuzzy Numbers (TIFNs).

4. Illustrative Example

In this section, we show the same problem as presented by Faizi et al. in [52] but with another type of uncertainity which provide membership and non-membership values. The decision problem is defined as the selection of the best mobile company for a factory.

Let us consider a company whose supreme capability of using mobile units is a quantity of 1000 per month expects to select a new mobile partnership. Four firms A_1, A_2, A_3 and A_4 are possible, and three DMs are suggested to consider two criteria C_1 (fixed line rent) and C_2 (rates per unit) to decide which mobile company should be chosen. The original ranking order of the mobile companies along with fixed line rent and rates per unit can be shown in Table 1.

Table 1. The original ranking order of the alternatives.

Alternatives	C_1 (LR)	C_2 (R/U)	Bill Amount	Original Rank
A_1	150	1.5	1650	2
A_2	50	2	2050	3
A_3	250	1.25	1500	1
A_4	30	2.15	2180	4

A set of TIFNs for both criteria C_1 and C_2 set by all the DMs are shown as in Tables 2 and 3 respectively.

Table 2. Different families of TIFNs chosen by the decision makers (DMs) for criteria C_1.

DM1	$\{(0,0,180;0,0,190),(0,200,350;0,200,360),(200,300,380;200,300,400)\}$
DM2	$\{(0,0,190;0,0,250),(0,200,380;0,200,390),(200,300,400;200,300,400)\}$
DM3	$\{(0,0,170;0,0,210),(0,200,370;0,200,380),(200,300,340;200,300,390)\}$

Table 3. Different families of TIFNs chosen by the DMs for criteria C_2.

DM1	$\{(1100,1200,1600;1000,1200,1700),(1200,1800,2500;1100,1800,2600),$ $(1800,2500,2800;1700,2500,3000)\}$
DM2	$\{(1050,1200,1500;1000,1200,1600),(1100,1800,2700;1000,1800,2900),$ $(1800,2500,3000;1800,2500,3000)\}$
DM3	$\{(1150,1200,1400;1000,1200,1600),(1300,1800,2900;1100,1800,3000),$ $(1800,2500,2850;1800,2500,2900)\}$

The graphical representations of TIFNs chosen by the DMs for both the criteria C_1 and C_2 are shown in Figures 2 and 3, respectively.

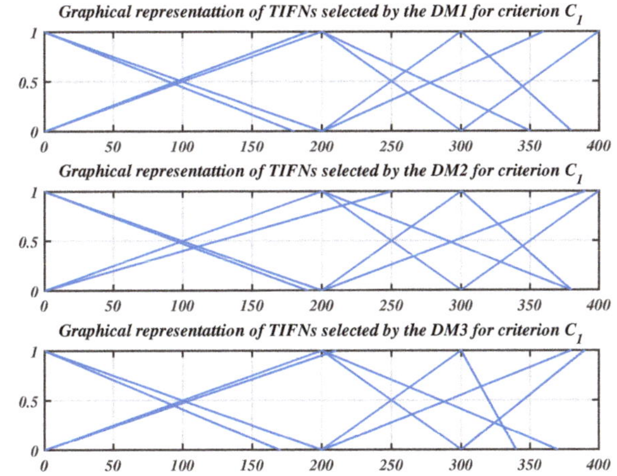

Figure 2. Graphs of asymmetrical TIFNs chosen by the DMs for criteria C_1.

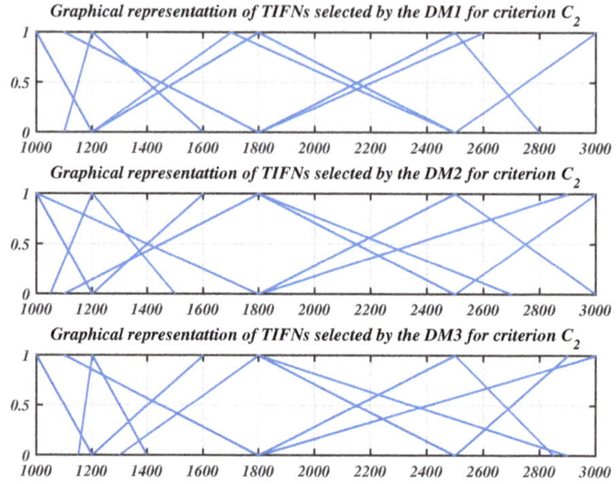

Figure 3. Graphs of asymmetrical TIFNs chosen by the DMs for criteria C_2.

The sets of cores of a given family of TIFNs are $\{30, 200, 300\}$ and $\{1200, 1800, 2500\}$ for both the criteria C_1 and C_2 respectively. The optimal solution of the given MCGDM problem by using the COMET method can be determined by taking different number of COs. Here, in this paper, we find the optimal solution to this problem with the use of following nine COs.

$$\begin{aligned}
&CO_1 = \{30, 1200\},\ CO_2 = \{30, 1800\},\\
&CO_3 = \{30, 2500\},\ CO_4 = \{200, 1200\},\\
&CO_5 = \{200, 1800\},\ CO_6 = \{200, 2500\},\\
&CO_7 = \{300, 1200\},\ CO_8 = \{300, 1800\},\\
&CO_9 = \{300, 2500\}.
\end{aligned}$$

During the pairwise comparison of all the COs, suppose the three DMs agreed to provide their joint assessment values in the form of IFNs that are unified in the matrix MEJ. Then, the unified MEJ can be shown as below.

$$MEJ = \begin{bmatrix}
(0.5,0.5) & (0.8,0.1) & (0.9,0.1) & (0.7,0.2) & (0.8,0.1) & (0.8,0.2) & (0.6,0.2) & (0.7,0.1) & (0.2,0.6)\\
(0.1,0.8) & (0.5,0.5) & (0.8,0.1) & (0.2,0.6) & (0.6,0.2) & (0.8,0.1) & (0,0.8) & (0.7,0.2) & (0.9,0.1)\\
(0.1,0.9) & (0.1,0.8) & (0.5,0.5) & (0.2,0.7) & (0.1,0.7) & (0.9,0.1) & (0,0.8) & (0.3,0.6) & (0.7,0.3)\\
(0.2,0.7) & (0.6,0.2) & (0.7,0.2) & (0.5,0.5) & (0.9,0.1) & (0.8,0.2) & (0.8,0.2) & (0.7,0.1) & (0.8,0.1)\\
(0.1,0.8) & (0.2,0.6) & (0.7,0.1) & (0.1,0.9) & (0.5,0.5) & (0.9,0.1) & (0.1,0.6) & (0.8,0.1) & (0.7,0.2)\\
(0.2,0.8) & (0.1,0.8) & (0.1,0.9) & (0.2,0.8) & (0.1,0.9) & (0.5,0.5) & (0.3,0.6) & (0.2,0.7) & (0.6,0.2)\\
(0.2,0.6) & (0.8,0) & (0.8,0) & (0.2,0.8) & (0.6,0.1) & (0.6,0.3) & (0.5,0.5) & (0.8,0.2) & (0.9,0.1)\\
(0.1,0.7) & (0.2,0.7) & (0.6,0.3) & (0.1,0.7) & (0.1,0.8) & (0.7,0.2) & (0.2,0.8) & (0.5,0.5) & (0.7,0.1)\\
(0.6,0.2) & (0.1,0.9) & (0.3,0.7) & (0.1,0.8) & (0.2,0.7) & (0.2,0.6) & (0.1,0.9) & (0.1,0.7) & (0.5,0.5)
\end{bmatrix}$$

It is easy to verify that the above MEJ which is infact an IPR is not additive consistent based on Definition 5. Therefore, the rectification process as mentioned in Section 2 has to be performed for this MEJ. By using Equations (5) and (6), the transformation matrix MEJ^t can be computed as above.

$$MEJ^t = \begin{bmatrix}
(0.5,0.5) & (0.600,0.300) & (0.856,0.144) & (0.461,0.439) & (0.656,0.244) & (0.933,0.067) & (0.461,0.339) & (0.706,0.094) & (0.828,-0.028) \\
(0.300,0.600) & (0.5,0.5) & (0.656,0.244) & (0.261,0.539) & (0.456,0.344) & (0.733,0.167) & (0.311,0.489) & (0.606,0.294) & (0.778,0.222) \\
(0.144,0.856) & (0.244,0.656) & (0.5,0.5) & (0.106,0.794) & (0.250,0.550) & (0.578,0.422) & (0.106,0.694) & (0.400,0.500) & (0.572,0.428) \\
(0.439,0.461) & (0.539,0.261) & (0.794,0.106) & (0.5,0.5) & (0.694,0.306) & (0.922,0.078) & (0.550,0.450) & (0.694,0.106) & (0.867,0.033) \\
(0.244,0.656) & (0.344,0.456) & (0.550,0.250) & (0.306,0.694) & (0.5,0.5) & (0.728,0.272) & (0.206,0.494) & (0.550,0.350) & (0.672,0.228) \\
(0.067,0.933) & (0.167,0.733) & (0.422,0.578) & (0.078,0.922) & (0.272,0.728) & (0.5,0.5) & (0.078,0.822) & (0.322,0.578) & (0.394,0.406) \\
(0.339,0.461) & (0.489,0.311) & (0.694,0.106) & (0.450,0.550) & (0.494,0.206) & (0.822,0.078) & (0.5,0.5) & (0.744,0.256) & (0.867,0.133) \\
(0.094,0.706) & (0.294,0.606) & (0.500,0.400) & (0.106,0.694) & (0.350,0.550) & (0.578,0.322) & (0.256,0.744) & (0.5,0.5) & (0.522,0.278) \\
(-0.028,0.828) & (0.222,0.778) & (0.428,0.572) & (0.033,0.867) & (0.228,0.672) & (0.406,0.394) & (0.133,0.867) & (0.278,0.522) & (0.5,0.5)
\end{bmatrix}$$

In transformed IPR, $\mu_{91} < 0$ (correspondingly, $\nu_{19} < 0$). The d value for the transformed IPR can be obtained as 0.0278 using Formula (7). According to Equation (8), we obtain the additively consistent IPR MEJ^c as shown below.

$$MEJ^c = \begin{bmatrix}
(0.5,0.5) & (0.595,0.311) & (0.837,0.163) & (0.463,0.442) & (0.647,0.258) & (0.911,0.090) & (0.463,0.347) & (0.695,0.116) & (0.811,0.000) \\
(0.311,0.595) & (0.5,0.5) & (0.647,0.258) & (0.274,0.537) & (0.458,0.353) & (0.721,0.184) & (0.321,0.490) & (0.600,0.305) & (0.763,0.237) \\
(0.163,0.837) & (0.258,0.648) & (0.5,0.5) & (0.126,0.779) & (0.263,0.547) & (0.574,0.426) & (0.126,0.684) & (0.405,0.500) & (0.568,0.432) \\
(0.442,0.463) & (0.537,0.274) & (0.779,0.126) & (0.5,0.5) & (0.684,0.316) & (0.900,0.100) & (0.547,0.453) & (0.684,0.126) & (0.847,0.058) \\
(0.258,0.648) & (0.353,0.458) & (0.547,0.263) & (0.316,0.684) & (0.5,0.5) & (0.716,0.284) & (0.221,0.495) & (0.547,0.358) & (0.663,0.242) \\
(0.900,0.911) & (0.184,0.721) & (0.426,0.574) & (0.100,0.900) & (0.284,0.716) & (0.5,0.5) & (0.100,0.805) & (0.332,0.574) & (0.400,0.411) \\
(0.347,0.463) & (0.490,0.321) & (0.684,0.126) & (0.453,0.548) & (0.495,0.221) & (0.805,0.100) & (0.5,0.5) & (0.732,0.268) & (0.847,0.153) \\
(0.116,0.695) & (0.305,0.600) & (0.500,0.405) & (0.126,0.684) & (0.358,0.547) & (0.574,0.332) & (0.268,0.737) & (0.5,0.5) & (0.521,0.290) \\
(0.000,0.811) & (0.237,0.763) & (0.432,0.568) & (0.058,0.848) & (0.242,0.663) & (0.411,0.400) & (0.153,0.847) & (0.290,0.521) & (0.5,0.5)
\end{bmatrix}$$

The vector SJ is obtained by using Formula (9) as follows:

$$SJ = [0.4105, 0.1263, -0.2631, 0.3895, 0.0211, \\ -0.4105, 0.2947, -0.1684, -0.4000]^T$$

The corresponding vector P by using the Matlab code as mentioned in Section 3 is determined as:

$$P = [1, 0.6250, 0.25, 0.8750, 0.50, 0.75, 0.3750, 0.125]^T$$

The P vector actually provides the approximate preference values of all the nine COs as mentioned above. Now, in order to calculate the preference value of first alternative A_1, we proceed as follows:

There are 9 rules (COs) for the alternative $A_1 = \{150, 1500\}$, but the activated rules are CO_1, CO_2, CO_4, CO_5. The approximate preference values of corresponding COs are $p_1 \sim 1$, $p_2 \sim 0.6250$, $p_3 \sim 0.8750$, $p_4 \sim 0.5$. The IFN $\tilde{A}_1$ corresponding to the alternative A_1 is computed by using Formula (10) as follows:

$$\tilde{A}_1 = p_1\tilde{T}_{11}(150) \otimes \tilde{T}_{21}(1500) \oplus p_2\tilde{T}_{11}(150) \otimes \tilde{T}_{22}(1500) \oplus p_3\tilde{T}_{12}(150) \otimes \tilde{T}_{21}(1500) \oplus p_4\tilde{T}_{12}(150) \otimes \tilde{T}_{22}(1500) = (0.8625, 0.0122)$$

The preference value of the alternative A_1 can be determined by computing the score value of $\tilde{A}_1$ by using Formula (1). i.e., $A_1 = Sc(\tilde{A}_1) = 0.8502$.

Similarly the preference values of the remaining alternatives can be found in the same way by following the five steps. A sharp comparison of the ranking order of alternatives using the proposed COMET method with the original ranking as well as the ranking obtained in [52] can be seen in Table 4.

Table 4. Comparison of the ranking obtained using intuitionistic fuzzy sets (IFSs) and hesitant fuzzy sets (HFSs) with the original ranking.

Alternatives	C_1 (LR)	C_2 (R/U)	Original Ranking	Ranking Using HFSs	Preference Values Using IFSs	Ranking Using IFSs
A_1	150	1.5	2	3	0.8502	3
A_2	50	2	3	2	0.9069	2
A_3	250	1.25	1	1	0.9849	1
A_4	30	2.15	4	4	0.8479	4

From Table 4, A_3 is the best alternative, followed by A_2, A_1, and A_4, in this order. It can be easily observed that this ranking order of the alternatives is reasonably matched with the original ranking of alternatives as mentioned in the same table.

5. Conclusions

The uncertainty and diversity of assessment information provided by the DMs can be well reflected and modeled using IFSs. The symmetrical and asymmetrical IFSs are very useful to express vagueness and uncertainty more accurately as compared to fuzzy sets. Therefore, we extend the COMET method to develope a useful technique for solving MCGDM problems with IFSs. To illustrate the effectiveness of the COMET method using IFSs, we presented a simple numerical example and analyzed the academic problem of selection of the best mobile company. This problem has already been solved in [52] by using HFSs. In the problem discussed in [52], the L-R type generalized fuzzy numbers are preferred by the DMs to get the hesitance degree values for the given set of alternatives. Table 4 exhibits the ranking results of all the alternatives as derived by the COMET method using IFSs and HFSs. It can be observed that the ranking orders of the alternatives obtained by the COMET method using IFSs are exactly matched with those derived by the same method using HFSs. Therefore, the present method is also validated. By using the COMET method with IFSs and HFSs, the ranking of the alternatives is obtained as $A_3 \succ A_1 \succ A_2 \succ A_4$, which adequately matches as those with the original ranking as shown in Table 4. The accuracy in the results appeared only due to the inclusion of the idea of an additive consistent MEJ. However, some differences are also observed in the ranking order of the alternatives A_1 and A_2. This is due to the increase of uncertainty level for both membership and non-membership values given by TIFNs during computations, e.g., for alternatives A_1 and A_2, the aggregated IFNs obtained as a result of aggregating all the IFNs for both criteria were equal to $(0.4195, 0.3383)$ and $(0.5781, 0.4219)$, respectively. This fact may represent the observed difference in the ranking order of both alternatives. However, it is quite reasonable that the optimal ranking is difficult to find by increasing the level of uncertainty. From the above investigation, it can be assumed that the order of the alternatives given by the proposed method is also stable and accurate. The main feature of the COMET method is that it always ignores the issue of rank reversal paradox, i.e., it delivers accurate evaluations of objects that are not subject to change by the introduction of new objects to the original object set. For example, by inserting 5th alternative $A_5 = \{225, 1750\}$ in the given decision problem, then, the original ranking of five alternatives is obtained as $A_3 \succ A_1 \succ A_5 \succ A_2 \succ A_4$. The preference value of A_5 using the proposed method is obtained as 0.9271, which makes the new ranking order as $A_3 \succ A_2 \succ A_5 \succ A_1 \succ A_4$. From both ranking orders as calculated above, it can be easily observed that the inclusion of the new alternative A_5 does not affect the ranking order of the remaining alternatives. This observation justifies the basis of our claim. The prominent characteristic of the proposed approach is to provide a valuable and flexible way to efficiently assist the DMs under an uncertain environment. Furthermore, the proposed approach can be applied for both TIFNs and IFNs, which reflects the uncertainty appropriately. In the future, we hope that the COMET method can be applied to MCDM/MCGDM problems under more uncertain environments such as interval-valued fuzzy sets, interval-valued intuitionistic fuzzy sets, hesitant fuzzy linguistic term sets, and so on.

Author Contributions: Conceptualization, S.F., W.S., T.R., S.Z. and J.W.; methodology, S.F., W.S., T.R., S.Z. and J.W.; software, S.F., W.S., T.R., S.Z. and J.W.; validation, S.F., W.S., T.R., S.Z. and J.W.; formal analysis, S.F., W.S., T.R., S.Z. and J.W.; investigation, S.F., W.S., T.R., S.Z. and J.W.; resources, S.F., W.S., T.R., S.Z. and J.W.; data curation, S.F., W.S., T.R., S.Z. and J.W.; writing—original draft preparation, S.F., W.S., J.W.; writing—review and editing, S.F., W.S., T.R., S.Z. and J.W.; visualization, S.F., W.S., T.R., S.Z. and J.W.; supervision, S.F., W.S., T.R., S.Z. and J.W.; project administration, S.F., W.S., T.R., S.Z. and J.W.; funding acquisition, W.S. All authors have read and agreed to the published version of the manuscript.

Funding: The work was supported by the National Science Centre, Decision No. DEC-2016/23/N/HS4/01931, and by the Faculty of Computer Science and Information Technology, West Pomeranian University of Technology, Szczecin statutory funds.

Acknowledgments: The authors would like to thank the editor and the anonymous reviewers, whose insightful comments and constructive suggestions helped us to significantly improve the quality of this paper.

Conflicts of Interest: The authors declare no conflict of interest.

Abbreviations

The following abbreviations are used in this manuscript:

MCGDM	Multi-Criteria Group Decision Making
MCDM	Multi-Criteria Decision Making
GDM	Group Decision Making
DM	Decision Maker
IF	Intuitionistic Fuzzy
IFS	Intuitionistic Fuzzy Set
IFN	Intuitionistic Fuzzy Number
TIFN	Triangular Intuitionistic Fuzzy Number
IPR	Intuitionistic Preference Relations
HFS	Hesitant Fuzzy Set
COMET	Characteristic Objects METhod
MEJ	Matrix of Expert Judgments

References

1. Božanić, D.; Pamučar, D.; Bojanić, D. Modification of the analytic hierarchy process (AHP) method using fuzzy logic: Fuzzy AHP approach as a support to the decision making process concerning engagement of the group for additional hindering. *Serbian J. Manag.* **2015**, *10*, 151–171. [CrossRef]
2. Xu, J.; Wu, Z. A discrete consensus support model for multiple attribute group decision making. *Knowl.-Based Syst.* **2011**, *24*, 1196–1202. [CrossRef]
3. Atanassov, K.T. New operations defined over the intuitionistic fuzzy sets. *Fuzzy Sets Syst.* **1994**, *61*, 137–142. [CrossRef]
4. Zadeh, L.A. Fuzzy sets. *Inf. Control* **1965**, *8*, 338–353. [CrossRef]
5. Roy, J.; Das, S.; Kar, S.; Pamučar, D. An extension of the CODAS approach using interval-valued intuitionistic fuzzy set for sustainable material selection in construction projects with incomplete weight information. *Symmetry* **2019**, *11*, 393. [CrossRef]
6. Chen, T.Y. The inclusion-based TOPSIS method with interval-valued intuitionistic fuzzy sets for multiple criteria group decision making. *Appl. Soft Comput.* **2015**, *26*, 57–73. [CrossRef]

7. Park, J.H.; Cho, H.J.; Kwun, Y.C. Extension of the VIKOR method for group decision making with interval-valued intuitionistic fuzzy information. *Fuzzy Optim. Decis. Mak.* **2011**, *10*, 233–253. [CrossRef]
8. Wu, J.; Chiclana, F. A social network analysis trust–consensus based approach to group decision-making problems with interval-valued fuzzy reciprocal preference relations. *Knowl.-Based Syst.* **2014**, *59*, 97–107. [CrossRef]
9. Wu, J.; Chiclana, F. A risk attitudinal ranking method for interval-valued intuitionistic fuzzy numbers based on novel attitudinal expected score and accuracy functions. *Appl. Soft Comput.* **2014**, *22*, 272–286. [CrossRef]
10. Xu, Z. An integrated model-based interactive approach to FMAGDM with incomplete preference information. *Fuzzy Optim. Decis. Mak.* **2010**, *9*, 333–357. [CrossRef]
11. Xu, J.; Shen, F. A new outranking choice method for group decision making under Atanassov's interval-valued intuitionistic fuzzy environment. *Knowl.-Based Syst.* **2014**, *70*, 177–188. [CrossRef]
12. Faizi, S.; Sałabun, W.; Ullah, S.; Rashid, T.; Więckowski, J. A New Method to Support Decision-Making in an Uncertain Environment Based on Normalized Interval-Valued Triangular Fuzzy Numbers and COMET Technique. *Symmetry* **2020**, *12*, 516. [CrossRef]
13. Xu, Z.; Liao, H. Intuitionistic fuzzy analytic hierarchy process. *IEEE Trans. Fuzzy Syst.* **2013**, *22*, 749–761. [CrossRef]
14. Shen, F.; Xu, J.; Xu, Z. An outranking sorting method for multi-criteria group decision making using intuitionistic fuzzy sets. *Inf. Sci.* **2016**, *334*, 338–353. [CrossRef]
15. Saaty, T.L. Decision making with the analytic hierarchy process. *Int. J. Serv. Sci.* **2008**, *1*, 83–98. [CrossRef]
16. Wang, Z.J. Geometric consistency based interval weight elicitation from intuitionistic preference relations using logarithmic least square optimization. *Fuzzy Optim. Decis. Mak.* **2015**, *14*, 289–310. [CrossRef]
17. Xu, Z.; Liao, H. A survey of approaches to decision making with intuitionistic fuzzy preference relations. *Knowl.-Based Syst.* **2015**, *80*, 131–142. [CrossRef]
18. Xu, Z. Intuitionistic fuzzy aggregation operators. *IEEE Trans. Fuzzy Syst.* **2007**, *15*, 1179–1187.
19. Xu, Z. Intuitionistic preference relations and their application in group decision making. *Inf. Sci.* **2007**, *177*, 2363–2379. [CrossRef]
20. Xu, Z.; Cai, X.; Szmidt, E. Algorithms for estimating missing elements of incomplete intuitionistic preference relations. *Int. J. Intell. Syst.* **2011**, *26*, 787–813. [CrossRef]
21. Gong, Z.W.; Li, L.S.; Forrest, J.; Zhao, Y. The optimal priority models of the intuitionistic fuzzy preference relation and their application in selecting industries with higher meteorological sensitivity. *Expert Syst. Appl.* **2011**, *38*, 4394–4402. [CrossRef]
22. Wan, S.P.; Wang, Q.Y.; Dong, J.Y. The extended VIKOR method for multi-attribute group decision making with triangular intuitionistic fuzzy numbers. *Knowl.-Based Syst.* **2013**, *52*, 65–77. [CrossRef]
23. Wang, Z.J. Derivation of intuitionistic fuzzy weights based on intuitionistic fuzzy preference relations. *Appl. Math. Model.* **2013**, *37*, 6377–6388. [CrossRef]
24. Shu, M.H.; Cheng, C.H.; Chang, J.R. Using intuitionistic fuzzy sets for fault-tree analysis on printed circuit board assembly. *Microelectron. Reliab.* **2006**, *46*, 2139–2148. [CrossRef]
25. Li, D.F. A ratio ranking method of triangular intuitionistic fuzzy numbers and its application to MADM problems. *Comput. Math. Appl.* **2010**, *60*, 1557–1570.
26. Yu, D. Prioritized information fusion method for triangular intuitionistic fuzzy set and its application to teaching quality evaluation. *Int. J. Intell. Syst.* **2013**, *28*, 411–435. [CrossRef]
27. Otay, İ.; Oztaysi, B.; Onar, S.C.; Kahraman, C. Multi-expert performance evaluation of healthcare institutions using an integrated intuitionistic fuzzy AHP&DEA methodology. *Knowl.-Based Syst.* **2017**, *133*, 90–106.
28. Qin, Q.; Liang, F.; Li, L.; Chen, Y.W.; Yu, G.F. A TODIM-based multi-criteria group decision making with triangular intuitionistic fuzzy numbers. *Appl. Soft Comput.* **2017**, *55*, 93–107. [CrossRef]
29. Saini, N.; Bajaj, R.K.; Gandotra, N.; Dwivedi, R.P. Multi-criteria decision making with triangular intuitionistic fuzzy number based on distance measure & parametric entropy approach. *Procedia Comput. Sci.* **2018**, *125*, 34–41.
30. Mishra, A.R.; Rani, P.; Pardasani, K.R.; Mardani, A.; Stević, Ž.; Pamučar, D. A novel entropy and divergence measures with multi-criteria service quality assessment using interval-valued intuitionistic fuzzy TODIM method. *Soft Comput.* **2020**, *24*, 11641–11661. [CrossRef]
31. Faizi, S.; Rashid, T.; Sałabun, W.; Zafar, S.; Wątróbski, J. Decision making with uncertainty using hesitant fuzzy sets. *Int. J. Fuzzy Syst.* **2018**, *20*, 93–103. [CrossRef]

32. Watróbski, J.; Sałabun, W. The characteristic objects method: A new intelligent decision support tool for sustainable manufacturing. In Proceedings of the International Conference on Sustainable Design and Manufacturing, Chania, Greece, 5–6 April 2016; Springer: Berlin/Heidelberg, Germany, 2016; pp. 349–359.
33. Sałabun, W. The Characteristic Objects Method: A New Distance-based Approach to Multicriteria Decision-making Problems. *J. Multi-Criteria Decis. Anal.* **2015**, *22*, 37–50. [CrossRef]
34. Sałabun, W.; Ziemba, P.; Wątróbski, J. The rank reversals paradox in management decisions: The comparison of the ahp and comet methods. In Proceedings of the International Conference on Intelligent Decision Technologies, Puerto de la Cruz, Spain, 15–17 June 2016; Springer: Berlin/Heidelberg, Germany, 2016; pp. 181–191.
35. Sałabun, W.; Karczmarczyk, A.; Wątróbski, J.; Jankowski, J. Handling data uncertainty in decision making with COMET. In Proceedings of the 2018 IEEE Symposium Series on Computational Intelligence (SSCI), Bengaluru, India, 18–21 November 2018; pp. 1478–1484.
36. Wątróbski, J.; Sałabun, W.; Karczmarczyk, A.; Wolski, W. Sustainable decision-making using the COMET method: An empirical study of the ammonium nitrate transport management. In Proceedings of the 2017 Federated Conference on Computer Science and Information Systems (FedCSIS), Prague, Czech Republic, 3–6 September 2017; pp. 949–958.
37. Wątróbski, J.; Sałabun, W. Green supplier selection framework based on multi-criteria decision-analysis approach. In Proceedings of the International Conference on Sustainable Design and Manufacturing, Chania, Greece, 5–6 April 2016; Springer: Berlin/Heidelberg, Germany, 2016; pp. 361–371.
38. Pujadas, P.; Pardo-Bosch, F.; Aguado-Renter, A.; Aguado, A. MIVES multi-criteria approach for the evaluation, prioritization, and selection of public investment projects. A case study in the city of Barcelona. *Land Use Policy* **2017**, *64*, 29–37. [CrossRef]
39. Roigé Montornés, N.; Pujadas Álvarez, P.; Cardús González, J.; Aguado de Cea, A. Water network renewal strategy: A case study of Aigües de Barcelona. In *Water Management*; ICE: London, UK, 2019.
40. Pamucar, D.S.; Pejcic Tarle, S.; Parezanovic, T. New hybrid multi-criteria decision-making DEMATELMAIRCA model: sustainable selection of a location for the development of multimodal logistics centre. *Econ. Res.-Ekon. Istraživanja* **2018**, *31*, 1641–1665. [CrossRef]
41. Wątróbski, J.; Jankowski, J.; Ziemba, P.; Karczmarczyk, A.; Zioło, M. Generalised framework for multi-criteria method selection. *Omega* **2019**, *86*, 107–124. [CrossRef]
42. Bashir, Z.; Rashid, T.; Wątróbski, J.; Sałabun, W.; Malik, A. Hesitant probabilistic multiplicative preference relations in group decision making. *Appl. Sci.* **2018**, *8*, 398. [CrossRef]
43. Atanassov, K.T. Interval valued intuitionistic fuzzy sets. In *Intuitionistic Fuzzy Sets*; Springer: Berlin/Heidelberg, Germany, 1999; pp. 139–177.
44. Chen, S.M.; Tan, J.M. Handling multicriteria fuzzy decision-making problems based on vague set theory. *Fuzzy Sets Syst.* **1994**, *67*, 163–172. [CrossRef]
45. Hong, D.H.; Choi, C.H. Multicriteria fuzzy decision-making problems based on vague set theory. *Fuzzy Sets Syst.* **2000**, *114*, 103–113. [CrossRef]
46. Xu, Z.; Yager, R.R. Some geometric aggregation operators based on intuitionistic fuzzy sets. *Int. J. Gen. Syst.* **2006**, *35*, 417–433. [CrossRef]
47. Tong, X.; Wang, Z.J. A group decision framework with intuitionistic preference relations and its application to low carbon supplier selection. *Int. J. Environ. Res. Public Health* **2016**, *13*, 923. [CrossRef]
48. Piegat, A. *Fuzzy Modeling and Control*; Springer: Berlin/Heidelberg, Germany, 2013; Volume 69.
49. Cutello, V.; Montero, J. Fuzzy rationality measures. *Fuzzy Sets Syst.* **1994**, *62*, 39–54. [CrossRef]
50. Herrera-Viedma, E.; Herrera, F.; Chiclana, F.; Luque, M. Some issues on consistency of fuzzy preference relations. *Eur. J. Oper. Res.* **2004**, *154*, 98–109. [CrossRef]
51. Saaty, T.L. A scaling method for priorities in hierarchical structures. *J. Math. Psychol.* **1977**, *15*, 234–281. [CrossRef]
52. Faizi, S.; Sałabun, W.; Rashid, T.; Wątróbski, J.; Zafar, S. Group decision-making for hesitant fuzzy sets based on characteristic objects method. *Symmetry* **2017**, *9*, 136. [CrossRef]

symmetry

MDPI

Article

q-Rung Orthopair Fuzzy Geometric Aggregation Operators Based on Generalized and Group-Generalized Parameters with Application to Water Loss Management

Muhammad Riaz [1], Ayesha Razzaq [1], Humaira Kalsoom [2], Dragan Pamučar [3], Hafiz Muhammad Athar Farid [1] and Yu-Ming Chu [4,5,*]

1 Department of Mathematics, University of the Punjab, Lahore 54590, Pakistan; mriaz.math@pu.edu.pk (M.R.); ayesharazzaq061@gmail.com (A.R.); hmatharfarid@gmail.com (H.M.A.F.)
2 School of Mathematical Sciences, Zhejiang University, Hangzhou 310027, China; humaira87@zju.edu.cn
3 Department of Logistics, University of Defence, 11000 Belgrade, Serbia; dragan.pamucar@va.mod.gov.rs
4 Department of Mathematics, Huzhou University, Huzhou 313000, China
5 Hunan Provincial Key Laboratory of Mathematical Modeling and Analysis in Engineering, Changsha University of Science and Technology, Changsha 410114, China
* Correspondence: chuyuming@zjhu.edu.cn

Received: 5 July 2020; Accepted: 23 July 2020; Published: 27 July 2020

Abstract: The notions of fuzzy set (FS) and intuitionistic fuzzy set (IFS) make a major contribution to dealing with practical situations in an indeterminate and imprecise framework, but there are some limitations. Pythagorean fuzzy set (PFS) is an extended form of the IFS, in which degree of truthness and degree of falsity meet the condition $0 \leq \ddot{\Theta}^2(x) + \mathfrak{K}^2(x) \leq 1$. Another extension of PFS is a ɋ-rung orthopair fuzzy set (ɋ-ROFS), in which truthness degree and falsity degree meet the condition $0 \leq \ddot{\Theta}^{ɋ}(x) + \mathfrak{K}^{ɋ}(x) \leq 1, (ɋ \geq 1)$, so they can characterize the scope of imprecise information in more comprehensive way. ɋ-ROFS theory is superior to FS, IFS, and PFS theory with distinguished characteristics. This study develops a few aggregation operators (AOs) for the fusion of ɋ-ROF information and introduces a new approach to decision-making based on the proposed operators. In the framework of this investigation, the idea of a generalized parameter is integrated into the ɋ-ROFS theory and different generalized ɋ-ROF geometric aggregation operators are presented. Subsequently, the AOs are extended to a "group-based generalized parameter", with the perception of different specialists/decision makers. We developed ɋ-ROF geometric aggregation operator under generalized parameter and ɋ-ROF geometric aggregation operator under group-based generalized parameter. Increased water requirements, in parallel with water scarcity, force water utilities in developing countries to follow complex operating techniques for the distribution of the available amounts of water. Reducing water losses from water supply systems can help to bridge the gap between supply and demand. Finally, a decision-making approach based on the proposed operator is being built to solve the problems under the ɋ-ROF environment. An illustrative example related to water loss management has been given to show the validity of the developed method. Comparison analysis between the proposed and the existing operators have been performed in term of counter-intuitive cases for showing the liability and dominance of proposed techniques to the existing one is also considered.

Keywords: q-Rung orthopair fuzzy sets; geometric aggregation operators based on generalized and group-generalized parameters; water loss management; decision making

1. Introduction

For many years, the issue of vague and imperfect information has been at the forefront. Information aggregation is the key factor for the decision management in the areas of business, management, engineering, psychology, social sciences, medical sciences, and artificial intelligence. Various problems in different areas aligned with vague and imprecise information. Modeling obscurities and data accumulation are most important components for the decision management in many areas comprising artificial intelligence, medical diagnosis, image processing i.e., it is extremely difficult challenge for experts to acquire precise decision without dealing with indeterminate and ambiguous data. Due to the critical, complex, subjective, and poorly structured nature of the issues themselves, many of the scientists contributions are directed to the area of building objective models of decision support. The reason for this phenomenon should be sought in the fact that modeling this class of problems requires correct mapping not only of the assessed alternatives/variants or scenarios. In such a case, experts must also consider the consequences of analyzing the decision problem from different perspectives and points of view taking into account several conflicting criteria. Water services, particularly in developing countries, continue to operate with considerable inefficiencies in terms of water and revenue losses. With increasing demand for water and scarcity, utilities require effective strategies to make optimum use of the available water resources. There are various options for reducing water loss. Deciding on which option to choose between conflicting multiple criteria and different stakeholder interests is a challenging task. One of the main challenges facing water utilities worldwide is the high levels of water losses in the distribution networks. According to the World Bank [1] study, approximately 32 billion m^3 of treated water is lost yearly as leakage from urban water distribution systems around the world, while 16 billion m^3 is lost but not paid for. They also guesstimate that these losses cost water utilities as much as US 14 billion $ per year, with one-third occurring in developing countries. In the light of global pressure (climate change, urbanization, demand, scarcity, etc.) water utilities, particularly in developing countries, need to operate more effectively to provide sustainable water services. Water loss management (WLM) has become an important decision issue in meeting utilityŠs strategic goals. Whereas strategic planning (SP) has proven to be a valuable tool for sustainable urban water management [2], water utilities in developing countries often lack the necessary capabilities to carryout SP [3].

Water losses from water distribution systems (WDSs) have a major effect on the economic viability of urban water supplies and are perhaps the most important measure of their inefficiency. Its control encourages the efficient use of water as a valuable natural resource by allowing less water to be collected from the environment [4]. There is a broad variety of choices for handling and reducing.

Water losses, including the use of advanced techniques such as online monitoring, multi- parameter sensors, pressure control, and asset management. The entire method is complex. Costly, it needs trained personnel, requires various levels of collaboration and includes different stakeholder interests. Multi-criteria decision making (MCDM) methods are suggested to reduce the difficulty of this multi-criteria task [5]. A number of researchers have recently addressed water resource management and planning issues by applying various MCDM strategies, such as PROMETHEE (preference ranking organization method for enrichment evaluations) [6,7], ELECTRE II (elimination et choix traduisant la realite) [8], fuzzy TOPSIS (technique for the order preference by similarity to ideal solution) [9], and fuzzy AHP (analytic hierarchy process) [10].

Addressing this problem, the idea of the generalized q́-rung orthopair fuzzy set (q́-ROFS) is presented in this study.

To facilitate our debate, the paper is categorized as follows: in Section 2, we provided some literature review about uncertain data modeling. In Section 3, some basis concepts including fuzzy set (FS), intuitionistic fuzzy set (IFS), Pythagorean fuzzy set (PFS), and q́-ROFS are presented. Moreover, some operational laws of q́-ROFSs and q́-ROFNs, accuracy function, score function of q́-ROFNs and aggregation operators are also provided. In Section 4, we introduce generalized q́-rung orthopair fuzzy set (GQROFS). In Section 5, some q́-ROF geometric aggregation operator based on a generalized parameter are presented. Section 6 consists of some ǭ-ROF geometric aggregation operators based on a group-generalized parameter. In Section 6, we established an MCDM approach and presented a numerical example of the proposed method for water loss management. In Section 6, we compared the proposed operators with existing ones.

1.1. Literature Review

Traditionally, the information about an alternative has been believed to be a crisp number or linguistic number. Nevertheless, information can not be aggregated in a simple form due to its uncertainty. MCDM is a critical framework for decision making science, the purpose of which is to identify the most exceptional goals among the most feasible ones. The person needs to assess the choices made by different types of assessment criteria, such as crisp numbers and intervals, in the actual decision-making process. However, in many cases, due to the presence of a number of data anomalies that may arise due to lack of knowledge or human error, it is difficult for a person to choose the correct choice. Consequently, in order to measure these inconsistencies and to analyze the mechanism, a large number of theories have been suggested. To cope up with such situations, fuzzy set, which is an extended form of classical set, innovated by Zadeh [11] entrained a insurgence in mathematics. FS is a substantial model to make a distinction and assembling of the various challenges with ambiguous boundary. A FS is a collection of object, explicated by a truthness function which allocates a degree of truthness, whose range lies between 0 and 1 to each element. IFS, innovated by Atanassov [12] as an extended form of FS. Yager [13–15] established PFS, which is an extended form of IFS [12]. Ali et al. [16] provided certain characteristics of soft sets (SSs), rough sets(RSs), and fuzzy soft sets(FSSs). Wang et al. [17] introduced spatial multi-criteria approach for flood risk management in the Dongting Lake Region. Wang et al. [18] introduced Single valued neutrosophic sets. Cubic IF aggregation operators are established by Kaur and Garg [19]. TOPSIS technique on the basis of connection number under interval-valued IFS environment, presented by Kumar and Garg [20]. The notion of Pythagorean fuzzy number presented by Peng and Yang [21] and examined certain results for PFSs. Different PF-information measures and their enrollments are innovated by Peng et al. [22].

The concept of linear Diophantine fuzzy set (LDFS) and its enrollments in MCDMs was innovated by Riaz and Hashmi [23]. LDFS with indicative attributes improves the existing approaches and the decision experts (DEs) can select the grading values without any restriction. Riaz and Tehrim [24] introduced cubic bipolar fuzzy set with application to multi-criteria group decision making using geometric aggregation operators. Riaz and Tehrim [25] used a robust extension of VIKOR method for bipolar fuzzy sets using connection numbers of SPA theory based metric spaces. Sharma H. K. et al. [26] introduced a rough set approach for forecasting models. Petrovic and Kankaras [27] introduced a hybridized multi-criteria decision making approach for the selection and evaluation of criteria for determination of air traffic control radar position. Yager [28] established an idea of ǭ-ROFS which is extended form of PFS, in which the degree of truthness $\breve{\Theta}_A(x)$ and degree of falsity $\mathfrak{K}_A(x)$ satisfy the condition $0 \leq \breve{\Theta}_A(x)^{ǭ} + \mathfrak{K}_A(x)^{ǭ} \leq 1, (ǭ \geq 1)$ and degree of indefiniteness is given by $\pi_A(x) = (\breve{\Theta}_A(x)^{ǭ} + \mathfrak{K}_A(x)^{ǭ} - \breve{\Theta}_A(x)^{ǭ}\mathfrak{K}_A(x)^{ǭ})^{1/ǭ}$.

Multi-criteria decision making (MCDM) with various fuzzy sets have been studied by; Peng et al. [29], Ali [30], Chen et al. [31], Chi and Lui [32], Feng et al. [33–36], Garg [37], Garg and Arora [38–41], Jose and Kuriaskose [42], Joshi [43], Karaaslan [44], Liu and Wang [45], Liu et al. [46], and Peng and Dai [47].

Riaz et al. [48–51] introduced the concepts of q-rung orthopair fuzzy prioritized aggregation operators, q-rung orthopair fuzzy hybrid aggregation operators, q-rung orthopair fuzzy information aggregation using Einstein operations, q-rung orthopair fuzzy Einstein prioritized aggregation operators with application towards multi-criteria group decision making (MCGDM). Aggregation operators and MCDM methods have been studied by; Xu [52], Xu and Cai [53], Xu [54], Yager [55], Ye [56,57], Zhan et al. [58,59], Zhang and Zhan [60,61], Zhang et al. [62], and Harrison et al. [5].

In realistic situations, different kinds of conditions are not completely fulfilled, as in MCDM issues, a preference of experts throughout the decision-making process is done entirely by his opinions and may result in the wrong decisions. In addition, the decision maker's priority is a characteristic of his own understanding and should be verified by some other senior specialist/decision maker. There are number of circumstances when the original data should be verified by some other specialist/decision expert.

(1) A patient can explain the symptoms to a doctor in accordance with his/her observations and circumstances. The actual details may not be authentic, in denouncing the symptoms. Otherwise this distortion factorized by a doctor, this would be conducive to an incorrect diagnosis. Respect of this, it might be most cautious to seek advice of another doctor to temperate the intensity of a patient's symptoms through a generalized parameter, which signifying the reliability of the provided data.

(2) For the selection of a manager for a firm, an unfair decision can be done by the individual's judgment, it must be confirmed by some other observer/decision maker by a general attribute corresponding to the situation.

(3) In every MCDM method, it is necessary to demonstrate prior evaluation by another specialist/decision expert in terms of generalized parameter to minimize the indeterminacy in the provided data and produce an indeterminate comportment more precise.

In such situations, the chances of mistakes in decision of the expert's field cannot be excluded. Consequently in these circumstances, there is a requirement of a generalize parameter, signifying an specialist's degree of confidence in the reliability of presented data to make the method very close to realistic circumstances substantially.

2. Preliminaries

In the presented section, we concisely review certain fundamentals of different sets which have been very helpful in understanding the contributions in the paper.

Definition 1 ([11]). *Let $\check{Y}$ be a set of elements of universe and $\breve{\Theta}_F : \check{Y} \to [0,1]$ is a truthness mapping. The fuzzy set (FS) $\mathcal{F}$ is defined as,*

$$\mathcal{F} = \left\{ (\breve{\mathbb{U}}, \breve{\Theta}_{\mathcal{F}}(\breve{\mathbb{U}})) : \breve{\mathbb{U}} \in \check{Y} \right\}$$

where, $\breve{\Theta}_{\mathcal{F}}(\breve{\mathbb{U}})$ is a truthness degree of $\breve{\mathbb{U}}$. The accumulation of all FSs defined on $\check{Y}$ is represented as $\mathbf{F}(\check{Y})$.

Definition 2 ([12]). *An intuitionistic fuzzy set (IFS) $\mathcal{I}$ defined on the universe $\check{Y}$ is the set of ordered triplets ,*

$$\mathcal{I} = \left\{ (\breve{\mathbb{U}}, \breve{\Theta}_{\mathcal{I}}(\breve{\mathbb{U}}), \mathfrak{K}_{\mathcal{I}}(\breve{\mathbb{U}})) : \breve{\mathbb{U}} \in \check{Y} \right\}$$

with the condition that $0 \leq \breve{\Theta}_{\mathcal{I}}(\breve{\mathbb{U}}) + \mathfrak{K}_{\mathcal{I}}(\breve{\mathbb{U}}) \leq 1$, where $\breve{\Theta}_{\mathcal{I}}(\breve{\mathbb{U}})$ is the truthness degree and $\mathfrak{K}_{\mathcal{I}}(\breve{\mathbb{U}})$ is a degree of falsity of an alternative $\breve{\mathbb{U}}$ to $\mathcal{I}$.

Definition 3. *Let $\check{Y}$ be a collection of universal elements. The Pythagorean fuzzy set (PFS) $\widetilde{\mathcal{P}}$ on $\check{Y}$ is defined as,*

$$\widetilde{\mathcal{P}} = \left\{ (\breve{\mathbb{U}}, \breve{\Theta}_{\widetilde{\mathcal{P}}}(\breve{\mathbb{U}}), \mathfrak{K}_{\widetilde{\mathcal{P}}}(\breve{\mathbb{U}})) : \breve{\mathbb{U}} \in \check{Y} \right\}$$

with the condition that $0 \leq \breve{\Theta}^2_{\widetilde{\mathcal{P}}}(\breve{\mathbb{U}}) + \mathfrak{K}^2_{\widetilde{\mathcal{P}}}(\breve{\mathbb{U}}) \leq 1$ where $\breve{\Theta}_{\widetilde{\mathcal{P}}}(\breve{\mathbb{U}}) : \check{Y} \to [0,1]$ is an indication of truthness degree and $\mathfrak{K}_{\widetilde{\mathcal{P}}}(\breve{\mathbb{U}}) : \check{Y} \to [0,1]$ indicates the degree of falsity of an universal element $\breve{\mathbb{U}} \in \check{Y}$. The degree of indeterminacy is given as $\pi_{\widetilde{\mathcal{P}}}(\breve{\mathbb{U}}) = \left(\breve{\Theta}^2_{\widetilde{\mathcal{P}}}(\breve{\mathbb{U}}) + \mathfrak{K}^2_{\widetilde{\mathcal{P}}}(\breve{\mathbb{U}}) - \breve{\Theta}^2_{\widetilde{\mathcal{P}}}(\breve{\mathbb{U}})\mathfrak{K}^2_{\widetilde{\mathcal{P}}}(\breve{\mathbb{U}})\right)^{1/2}$. For assistance, a fundamental component $\langle \breve{\Theta}_{\widetilde{\mathcal{P}}}, \mathfrak{K}_{\widetilde{\mathcal{P}}} \rangle$ in a PFS is called a PF-Number (PFN).

Definition 4 ([28]). *Let $\check{Y}$ be a collection of universal elements. A $\acute{\mathfrak{q}}$-rung orthopair fuzzy set ($\acute{\mathfrak{q}}$-ROFS) $\mathfrak{P}$, is characterized as*

$$\mathfrak{P} = \left\{ (\breve{\mathbb{U}}, \breve{\Theta}_{\mathfrak{P}}(\breve{\mathbb{U}}), \mathfrak{K}_{\mathfrak{P}}(\breve{\mathbb{U}})) : \breve{\mathbb{U}} \in \check{Y} \right\}$$

with the condition that $0 \leq \breve{\Theta}^{\acute{q}}_{\mathfrak{P}}(\mathbb{U}) + \mathfrak{K}^{\acute{q}}_{\mathfrak{P}}(\mathbb{U}) \leq 1, (\acute{q} \geq 1)$, *where* $\breve{\Theta}_{\mathfrak{P}}(\mathbb{U}) : \check{Y} \to [0,1]$ *indicates the truthness degree and* $\mathfrak{K}_{\mathfrak{P}}(\mathbb{U}) : \check{Y} \to [0,1]$ *indicates the degree of falsity of an alternative* $\mathbb{U} \in \check{Y}$. *The degree of indeterminacy is given as* $\pi_{\mathfrak{P}}(\mathbb{U}) = \left(\breve{\Theta}^{\acute{q}}_{\mathfrak{P}}(\mathbb{U}) + \mathfrak{K}^{\acute{q}}_{\mathfrak{P}}(\mathbb{U}) - \breve{\Theta}^{\acute{q}}_{\mathfrak{P}}(\mathbb{U})\mathfrak{K}^{\acute{q}}_{\mathfrak{P}}(\mathbb{U})\right)^{1/\acute{q}}$.
For convenience, a basic element $\langle \breve{\Theta}_{\mathfrak{P}}(\mathbb{U}), \mathfrak{K}_{\mathfrak{P}}(\mathbb{U}) \rangle$ *in a* $\acute{q}$*-ROF is denoted by* $\widetilde{\Xi} = \langle \breve{\Theta}_{\mathfrak{P}}, \mathfrak{K}_{\mathfrak{P}} \rangle$ *for short, which is called (*$\acute{q}$*-ROFN).*

The proposed models of aggregated operators are credible, valid, versatile, and superior to others since they are based on the generalized q-ROFN structure. Whether the proposed operators are used in the sense of IFNs or PFNs, the results may be imprecise due to the lack of information in the input data. This loss is due to limitations on membership and non-membership of IFNs and PFNs (see Figure 1). IFNs and PFNs are special cases of q-ROFNs where q = 1 and q = 2 , respectively.

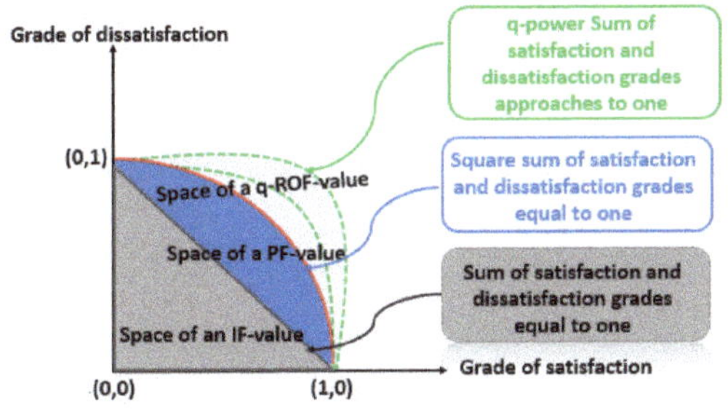

Figure 1. Graphical comparison between the IF-value, PF-value, and q-ROF-value.

2.1. Operational Laws of $\hat{\acute{q}}$-ROFS

Let $\hat{\beth}_1 = \langle \breve{\Theta}_{\hat{\beth}_1}(\mathbb{U}), \mathfrak{K}_{\hat{\beth}_1}(\mathbb{U}) \rangle$ and $\hat{\beth}_2 = \langle \breve{\Theta}_{\hat{\beth}_2}(\mathbb{U}), \mathfrak{K}_{\hat{\beth}_2}(\mathbb{U}) \rangle$ be $\acute{q}$-ROFSs on $\check{Y}$. Then,

(1) $\overline{\hat{\beth}_1} = \langle \mathfrak{K}_{\hat{\beth}_1}(\mathbb{U}), \breve{\Theta}_{\hat{\beth}_1}(\mathbb{U}) \rangle$.

(2) $\hat{\beth}_1 \widetilde{\subseteq} \hat{\beth}_2 \Leftrightarrow \breve{\Theta}_{\hat{\beth}_1}(\mathbb{U}) \leqslant \breve{\Theta}_{\hat{\beth}_2}(\mathbb{U})$ and $\mathfrak{K}_{\hat{\beth}_2}(\mathbb{U}) \leqslant \mathfrak{K}_{\hat{\beth}_1}(\mathbb{U})$.

(3) $\hat{\beth}_1 = \hat{\beth}_2 \Leftrightarrow \hat{\beth}_1 \widetilde{\subseteq} \hat{\beth}_2$ and $\hat{\beth}_2 \widetilde{\subseteq} \hat{\beth}_1$.

(4) $\hat{\beth}_1 \widetilde{\sqcup} \hat{\beth}_2 = \left\{ \langle \mathbb{U}, max\{\breve{\Theta}_{\hat{\beth}_1}(\mathbb{U}), \breve{\Theta}_{\hat{\beth}_2}(\mathbb{U})\}, \ min\{\mathfrak{K}_{\hat{\beth}_1}(\mathbb{U}), \mathfrak{K}_{\hat{\beth}_2}(\mathbb{U})\} \rangle : \mathbb{U} \in \check{Y} \right\}$.

(5) $\hat{\beth}_1 \widetilde{\sqcap} \hat{\beth}_2 = \left\{ \langle \mathbb{U}, min\{\breve{\Theta}_{\hat{\beth}_1}(\mathbb{U}), \breve{\Theta}_{\hat{\beth}_2}(\mathbb{U})\}, \ max\{\mathfrak{K}_{\hat{\beth}_1}(\mathbb{U}), \mathfrak{K}_{\hat{\beth}_2}(\mathbb{U})\} \rangle : \mathbb{U} \in \check{Y} \right\}$.

(6) $\hat{\beth}_1 + \hat{\beth}_2 = \left\{ \langle \mathbb{U}, (\breve{\Theta}^{\acute{q}}_{\hat{\beth}_1}(\mathbb{U}) + \breve{\Theta}^{\acute{q}}_{\hat{\beth}_2}(\mathbb{U}) - \breve{\Theta}^{\acute{q}}_{\hat{\beth}_1}(\mathbb{U})\breve{\Theta}^{\acute{q}}_{\hat{\beth}_2}(\mathbb{U}))^{1/\acute{q}}, \ \mathfrak{K}_{\hat{\beth}_1}(\mathbb{U})\mathfrak{K}_{\hat{\beth}_2}(\mathbb{U}) \rangle : \mathbb{U} \in \check{Y} \right\}$.

(7) $\hat{\beth}_1 . \hat{\beth}_2 = \left\{ \langle \mathbb{U}, (\breve{\Theta}_{\hat{\beth}_1}(\mathbb{U})\breve{\Theta}_{\hat{\beth}_2}(\mathbb{U}), \ \mathfrak{K}^{\acute{q}}_{\hat{\beth}_1}(\mathbb{U}) + \mathfrak{K}^{\acute{q}}_{\hat{\beth}_2}(\mathbb{U}) - \mathfrak{K}^{\acute{q}}_{\hat{\beth}_1}(\mathbb{U})\breve{\Theta}^{\acute{q}}_{\hat{\beth}_2}(\mathbb{U}))^{1/\acute{q}} \rangle : \mathbb{U} \in \check{Y} \right\}$.

(8) $\alpha \hat{\beth}_1 = \left\{ \langle \mathbb{U}, (1 - (1 - \breve{\Theta}_{\hat{\beth}_1}(\mathbb{U})^{\acute{q}})^{\alpha})^{1/\acute{q}}, \ \mathfrak{K}_{\hat{\beth}_1}(\mathbb{U})^{\alpha} \rangle \right\}$.

(9) $\hat{\beth}_1^{\alpha} = \left\{ \langle \mathbb{U}, \breve{\Theta}_{\hat{\beth}_1}(\mathbb{U})^{\alpha}, \ (1 - (1 - \mathfrak{K}^{\acute{q}}_{\hat{\beth}_1}(\mathbb{U}))^{\alpha})^{1/\acute{q}} \rangle \right\}$.

2.2. Operational Laws of $\acute{q}$-ROFNs

Let $\widetilde{\Xi}_1 = \langle \breve{\Theta}_1, \mathfrak{K}_1 \rangle$ and $\widetilde{\Xi}_2 = \langle \breve{\Theta}_2, \mathfrak{K}_2 \rangle$ be $\acute{q}$-ROFNs on a $\check{Y}$ [45]. Then

(1) $\overline{\widetilde{\Xi}_1} = \langle \mathfrak{K}_1, \breve{\Theta}_1 \rangle$

(2) $\widetilde{\Xi}_1 \vee \widetilde{\Xi}_2 = \left\langle max\{\breve{\Theta}_1, \breve{\Theta}_2\}, \ min\{\mathfrak{K}_1, \mathfrak{K}_2\} \right\rangle$

(3) $\widetilde{\Xi}_1 \wedge \widetilde{\Xi}_2 = \left\langle min\{\breve{\Theta}_1, \breve{\Theta}_2\}, \ max\{\mathfrak{K}_1, \mathfrak{K}_2\} \right\rangle$

(4) $\widetilde{\Xi}_1 \oplus \widetilde{\Xi}_2 = \left\langle (\breve{\Theta}_1^{\acute{q}} + \breve{\Theta}_2^{\acute{q}} - \breve{\Theta}_1^{\acute{q}}\breve{\Theta}_2^{\acute{q}})^{1/\acute{q}}, \ \mathfrak{K}_1\mathfrak{K}_2 \right\rangle$

(5) $\widetilde{\Xi}_1 \otimes \widetilde{\Xi}_2 = \left\langle (\breve{\Theta}_1\breve{\Theta}_2, \ (\mathfrak{K}_1^{\acute{q}} + \mathfrak{K}_2^{\acute{q}} - \mathfrak{K}_1^{\acute{q}}\mathfrak{K}_2^{\acute{q}})^{1/\acute{q}} \right\rangle$

(6) $\alpha\widetilde{\Xi}_1 = \left\langle \left(1 - (1 - \breve{\Theta}_1^{\mathfrak{q}})^{\alpha}\right)^{1/\mathfrak{q}}, \mathfrak{K}_1^{\alpha} \right\rangle$

(7) $\widetilde{\Xi}_1^{\alpha} = \left\langle \breve{\Theta}_1^{\alpha}, 1 - \left((1 - \mathfrak{K}_1^{\mathfrak{q}})^{\alpha}\right)^{1/\mathfrak{q}} \right\rangle$

Definition 5 ([45]). *Let $\widetilde{\Xi}_i = \langle \breve{\Theta}_i, \mathfrak{K}_i \rangle, i = (1, \ldots, n)$ is a set of $\mathfrak{q}$-ROFNs with weight vector $\hat{\omega} = (\hat{\omega}_1, \hat{\omega}_2, \ldots, \hat{\omega}_n)$ such that $\hat{\omega}_i \in [0,1]$ and $\sum_{i=1}^{n} \hat{\omega}_i = 1$. The ($\mathfrak{q}$-ROFWG) operator is*

$$\mathfrak{q}\text{-}ROFWG(\widetilde{\Xi}_1, \widetilde{\Xi}_2, \ldots, \widetilde{\Xi}_n) = \left(\widetilde{\prod}_{\mathfrak{k}=1}^{n} \breve{\Theta}_{\mathfrak{k}}^{\hat{\omega}_{\mathfrak{k}}}, \sqrt[\mathfrak{q}]{1 - \widetilde{\prod}_{\mathfrak{k}=1}^{n} (1 - \mathfrak{K}_{\mathfrak{k}}^{\mathfrak{q}})^{\hat{\omega}_{\mathfrak{k}}}} \right)$$

Definition 6 ([28]). *Suppose $\widetilde{\Xi} = \langle \breve{\Theta}, \mathfrak{K} \rangle$ is a $\mathfrak{q}$-ROFN. The score function $\daleth$ of $\widetilde{\Xi}$ is determined as,*

$$\daleth(\widetilde{\Xi}) = \breve{\Theta}^{q} - \mathfrak{K}^{q}$$

$\daleth(\widetilde{\Xi}) \in [-1, 1]$. The ranking of $\mathfrak{q}$-ROFNs is described by score function. Large value of score function specifies high preference of $\mathfrak{q}$-ROFN. Although, score function is not efficient in several instances of $\mathfrak{q}$-ROFN. As for example, suppose $\widetilde{\Xi}_1 = \langle 0.6138, 0.2534 \rangle$ and $\widetilde{\Xi}_2 = \langle 0.7147, 0.4453 \rangle$ are two $\mathfrak{q}$-ROFNs. Consider $q = 2$, then $\daleth(\widetilde{\Xi}_1) = 0.3125 = \daleth(\widetilde{\Xi}_2)$ i.e., score functions of $\widetilde{\Xi}_1$ and $\widetilde{\Xi}_2$ are same. While comparing the $\mathfrak{q}$-ROFNs, there is no need to only depend on the score function. To solve this problem, there is another approach, the accuracy function.

Definition 7 ([28]). *Suppose $\widetilde{\Xi} = \langle \breve{\Theta}, \mathfrak{K} \rangle$ is a $\mathfrak{q}$-ROFN. An accuracy function $\mathfrak{S}$ of $\widetilde{\Xi}$ is determined as*

$$\mathfrak{S}(\widetilde{\Xi}) = \breve{\Theta}^{\mathfrak{q}} + \mathfrak{K}^{\mathfrak{q}}$$

$\mathfrak{S}(\widetilde{\Xi}) \in [0, 1]$. The large value of accuracy function $\mathfrak{S}(\widetilde{\Xi})$, determines high priorities of $\mathfrak{q}$-ROFN. For the above example, their accuracy functions are $\mathfrak{S}(\widetilde{\Xi}_1) = 0.4409$ and $\mathfrak{S}(\widetilde{\Xi}_2) = 0.7090$, so by the accuracy function we have $\widetilde{\Xi}_1 < \widetilde{\Xi}_2$.

Definition 8. *Let $\widetilde{\Xi}_1 = \langle \breve{\Theta}_1, \mathfrak{K}_1 \rangle$ and $\widetilde{\Xi}_2 = \langle \breve{\Theta}_2, \mathfrak{K}_2 \rangle$ are any two $\mathfrak{q}$-ROFNs, $\daleth(\widetilde{\Xi}_1), \daleth(\widetilde{\Xi}_2)$ are the score function of $\widetilde{\Xi}_1$ and $\widetilde{\Xi}_2$ and $\mathfrak{S}(\widetilde{\Xi}_1), \mathfrak{S}(\widetilde{\Xi}_2)$ are the accuracy functions of $\widetilde{\Xi}_1$ and $\widetilde{\Xi}_2$, respectively. Then*

(1) If $\daleth(\widetilde{\Xi}_1) > \daleth(\widetilde{\Xi}_2)$, then $\widetilde{\Xi}_1 > \widetilde{\Xi}_2$.
(2) If $\daleth(\widetilde{\Xi}_1) = \daleth(\widetilde{\Xi}_2)$, then

(1) If $\mathfrak{S}(\widetilde{\Xi}_1) > \mathfrak{S}(\widetilde{\Xi}_2)$ then $\widetilde{\Xi}_1 > \widetilde{\Xi}_2$.
(2) If $\mathfrak{S}(\widetilde{\Xi}_1) = \mathfrak{S}(\widetilde{\Xi}_2)$, then $\widetilde{\Xi}_1 = \widetilde{\Xi}_2$.

3. $\mathfrak{q}$-ROF Information Under Generalized Parameter

Suppose in a medical diagnosis, a patient is suffering an anonymous disease and provide his/her inclinations as $\mathfrak{q}$-ROFNs regarding symptoms $\mathfrak{E} = \{\mathfrak{h}_1, \mathfrak{h}_2, \mathfrak{h}_3\}$, where

(1) $\mathfrak{h}_1$= Dry Cough (DC);
(2) $\mathfrak{h}_2$= High Fever (HF);
(3) $\mathfrak{h}_3$= Sore Throat (ST).

Let the $\mathfrak{q}$-ROFS, $\mathfrak{P} = \{(0.23, 0.67)_{DC}, (0.42, 0.77)_{HF}, (0.78, 0.55)_{ST}\}$ ($\mathfrak{q} = 3$) represents the preferences of the patient. The collected information is entirely based on his/her understanding, physical conditions and awareness in reporting the symptoms. Thereby, doctors treat the patient as a result of his presentation of symptoms, this may cause an imprecise outcome and patient might not be recovered according to data presented by a patient is not confirmed by one more doctor. Therefore, it is necessary to demonstrate the presented data to make the method quite similar to the situation of a patient. It can be obtained by introducing the idea of general parameter in the initial information, which indicates the confidence of an expert in conviction of the presented data to make the method very close to the actual circumstances. When a patient provided his/her preferences and is additionally evaluated by a physician/senior doctor who presents his/her data as $h = (0.5, 0.4)$, ꞯ-ROFS under generalized parameter (GP) is a

$$\mathfrak{P}^G = \{(0.23, 0.67)_{DC}, (0.42, 0.77)_{HF}, (0.78, 0.55)_{ST}(\mathbf{0.41, 0.84})\} \quad (\acute{q} = 3)$$

Here, the indication of GP in bold is a ꞯ-ROFN which diminish the inaccurate demonstration of imprecise data across the system of knowledge representation. The GP value capable of providing optimum solution of upgrading existing systems of decision experts, making sure a better accuracy in crucial decisions. The prior evaluation remains imprecise without the GP, which demonstrates that effectiveness of evaluation is uncertain. Whereby, in the information mapping system, the chances of substantial deformations of vague information can be discarded on the basis of judgment of a particular observer through another expert's opinion (in form of GP) in implementing the original ꞯ-ROPFNs. Consequently, the generalized ꞯ-rung orthopair FS (GQROFS) is defined as

Definition 9. *Let $\check{Y}$ be a set of universal elements, a generalized ꞯ-rung orthopair FS (GQROFS) is of the form*

$$\mathfrak{G} = \left\{ \left(\langle \mathbb{U}, \breve{\Theta}_{\mathfrak{G}}(\mathbb{U}), \mathfrak{K}_{\mathfrak{G}}(\mathbb{U}) \rangle (\breve{\Theta}_{\breve{\mathfrak{g}}}, \mathfrak{K}_{\breve{\mathfrak{g}}}) \right) : \mathbb{U} \in \check{Y} \right\}$$

with the condition that $0 \leq \breve{\Theta}^{\acute{q}}_{\mathfrak{G}}(\mathbb{U}) + \mathfrak{K}^{\acute{q}}_{\mathfrak{G}}(\mathbb{U}) \leq 1, (\acute{q} \geq 1)$ where, $\breve{\Theta}_{\mathfrak{G}}(\mathbb{U}) : \check{Y} \to [0,1]$ indicates the degree of truthness and $\mathfrak{K}_{\mathfrak{G}}(\mathbb{U}) : \check{Y} \to [0,1]$ indicates the degree of falsity of an alternative $\mathbb{U} \in \check{Y}$. Here $(\breve{\Theta}_{\breve{\mathfrak{g}}}, \mathfrak{K}_{\breve{\mathfrak{g}}})$ is said to be GP which is a ꞯ-ROFN indicated by other observer/decision maker signifying the preferable evaluation.

4. ꞯ-ROF Geometric Aggregation Operator Under Generalized Parameter

In the presented section we introduce some geometric aggregation operators under generalized parameter, including the generalized ꞯ-rung orthopair fuzzy weighted geometric (GQROFWG) operator, generalized ꞯ-rung orthopair fuzzy ordered weighted geometric (GQROFOWG) operator, and generalized ꞯ-rung orthopair fuzzy hybrid geometric aggregation (GQROFHG) operator.

4.1. The Generalized ꞯ-ROF Weighted Geometric Operator

Definition 10. *Let $\breve{\mathfrak{g}} = (\breve{\Theta}_{\breve{\mathfrak{g}}}, \mathfrak{K}_{\breve{\mathfrak{g}}})$ be the GP for the ꞯ-ROFNs $\widetilde{\Xi}_i = (\breve{\Theta}_i, \mathfrak{K}_i)(i = 1, 2, \ldots, n)$, then the GQROFWG-operator is determined as,*

$$GQROFWG((\widetilde{\Xi}_1, \widetilde{\Xi}_2, \ldots, \widetilde{\Xi}_n, \breve{\mathfrak{g}})) = \breve{\mathfrak{g}} \otimes \acute{q}\text{-}ROFWG(\widetilde{\Xi}_1, \widetilde{\Xi}_2, \ldots, \widetilde{\Xi}_n)$$

Theorem 11. *Let $\widetilde{\Xi}_i = (\breve{\Theta}_i, \mathfrak{K}_i)(i = 1, 2, \ldots, n)$ be a set of ꞯ-ROFNs and $\hat{\omega} = (\hat{\omega}_1, \hat{\omega}_2, \ldots, \hat{\omega}_n)^T$ is a weight vector of $\widetilde{\Xi}_i$ such that $\hat{\omega}_i \in [0,1]$ and $\sum_{i=1}^{n} \hat{\omega}_i = 1$. The GP is $\breve{\mathfrak{g}} = (\breve{\Theta}_{\breve{\mathfrak{g}}}, \mathfrak{K}_{\breve{\mathfrak{g}}})$, then the GQROFWG-operator is determined as*

$$\begin{aligned} GQROFWG((\widetilde{\Xi}_1, \widetilde{\Xi}_2, \ldots, \widetilde{\Xi}_n), \breve{\mathfrak{g}}) &= \breve{\mathfrak{g}} \otimes \acute{q}\text{-}ROFWG(\widetilde{\Xi}_1, \widetilde{\Xi}_2, \ldots, \widetilde{\Xi}_n) \\ &= \left(\sqrt[\acute{q}]{(\breve{\Theta}_{\breve{\mathfrak{g}}})^{\acute{q}} + (1 - (\breve{\Theta}_{\breve{\mathfrak{g}}})^{\acute{q}}) \widetilde{\prod}_{i=1}^{n} (\breve{\Theta}_i^{\hat{\omega}_i})^{\acute{q}}},\ \mathfrak{K}_{\breve{\mathfrak{g}}} . \sqrt[\acute{q}]{1 - \prod_{i=1}^{n} (1 - (\mathfrak{K}_i)^{\acute{q}})^{\hat{\omega}_i}} \right) \end{aligned}$$

Proof. We use mathematical induction.

For $n = 2$,

$$GQROFWG((\widetilde{\Xi}_1, \widetilde{\Xi}_2), \breve{\mathfrak{g}}) = \breve{\mathfrak{g}} \otimes (\widetilde{\Xi}_1^{\hat{\omega}_1} \otimes \widetilde{\Xi}_2^{\hat{\omega}_2})$$

First we solve $(\widetilde{\Xi}_1^{\acute{\omega}_1} \otimes \widetilde{\Xi}_2^{\acute{\omega}_2})$, by using the operational law of $\acute{q}$-ROFS, we have

$$\begin{aligned}\widetilde{\Xi}_1^{\acute{\omega}_1} \otimes \widetilde{\Xi}_2^{\acute{\omega}_2} &= (\breve{\Theta}_1, \mathfrak{K}_1)^{\acute{\omega}_1} \otimes (\breve{\Theta}_2, \mathfrak{K}_2)^{\acute{\omega}_2} \\ &= \left(\breve{\Theta}_1^{\acute{\omega}_1}, \sqrt[\acute{q}]{1-(1-\mathfrak{K}_1^{\acute{q}})^{\acute{\omega}_1}} \otimes \breve{\Theta}_2^{\acute{\omega}_2}, \sqrt[\acute{q}]{1-(1-\mathfrak{K}_2^{\acute{q}})^{\acute{\omega}_2}}\right) \\ &= \left(\breve{\Theta}_1^{\acute{\omega}_1}.\breve{\Theta}_2^{\acute{\omega}_2}, \sqrt[\acute{q}]{1-(1-\mathfrak{K}_1^{\acute{q}})^{\acute{\omega}_1}.(1-\mathfrak{K}_2^{\acute{q}})^{\acute{\omega}_2}}\right)\end{aligned}$$

Now,

$$\breve{g} \otimes (\widetilde{\Xi}_1^{\acute{\omega}_1} \otimes \widetilde{\Xi}_2^{\acute{\omega}_2}) = (\breve{\Theta}_{\breve{g}}, \mathfrak{K}_{\breve{g}}) \otimes \left(\breve{\Theta}_1^{\acute{\omega}_1}.\breve{\Theta}_2^{\acute{\omega}_2}, \sqrt[\acute{q}]{1-(1-\mathfrak{K}_1^{\acute{q}})^{\acute{\omega}_1}.(1-\mathfrak{K}_2^{\acute{q}})^{\acute{\omega}_2}}\right)$$

$$= \left(\sqrt[\acute{q}]{(\breve{\Theta}_{\breve{g}})^{\acute{q}} + (\breve{\Theta}_1^{\acute{\omega}_1}.\breve{\Theta}_2^{\acute{\omega}_2})^{\acute{q}} - (\breve{\Theta}_{\breve{g}})^{\acute{q}}.(\breve{\Theta}_1^{\acute{\omega}_1}.\breve{\Theta}_2^{\acute{\omega}_2})^{\acute{q}}}, \mathfrak{K}_{\breve{g}}.\sqrt[\acute{q}]{1-(1-\mathfrak{K}_1^{\acute{q}})^{\acute{\omega}_1}.(1-\mathfrak{K}_2^{\acute{q}})^{\acute{\omega}_2}}\right)$$

$$= \left(\sqrt[\acute{q}]{(\breve{\Theta}_{\breve{g}})^{\acute{q}} + (1-(\breve{\Theta}_{\breve{g}})^{\acute{q}}).((\breve{\Theta}_1^{\acute{\omega}_1})^{\acute{q}}((\breve{\Theta}_2^{\acute{\omega}_2})^{\acute{q}}}, \mathfrak{K}_{\breve{g}}.\sqrt[\acute{q}]{1-(1-\mathfrak{K}_1^{\acute{q}})^{\acute{\omega}_1}.(1-\mathfrak{K}_2^{\acute{q}})^{\acute{\omega}_2}}\right)$$

$$GQROFWG((\widetilde{\Xi}_1, \widetilde{\Xi}_2), g) = \left(\sqrt[\acute{q}]{(\breve{\Theta}_{\breve{g}})^{\acute{q}} + (1-(\breve{\Theta}_{\breve{g}})^{\acute{q}}).\widetilde{\prod}_{i=1}^{2}((\breve{\Theta}_i^{\acute{\omega}_i})^{\acute{q}}}, \mathfrak{K}_{\breve{g}}.\sqrt[\acute{q}]{1-\widetilde{\prod}_{i=1}^{2}(1-\mathfrak{K}_i^{\acute{q}})^{\acute{\omega}_i}}\right)$$

For $\mathfrak{n} = 2$, result is true.
Suppose that result satisfied for $\mathfrak{n} = \mathfrak{k}$,

$$\begin{aligned}GQROFWG((\widetilde{\Xi}_1, \widetilde{\Xi}_2, \ldots, \widetilde{\Xi}_\mathfrak{n}), \breve{g}) &= \breve{g} \otimes \acute{q}\text{-ROFWG}(\widetilde{\Xi}_1, \widetilde{\Xi}_2, \ldots, \widetilde{\Xi}_\mathfrak{n}) \\ &= \left(\sqrt[\acute{q}]{(\breve{\Theta}_{\breve{g}})^{\acute{q}} + (1-(\breve{\Theta}_{\breve{g}})^{\acute{q}})\widetilde{\prod}_{i=1}^{\mathfrak{k}}(\breve{\Theta}_i^{\acute{\omega}_i})^{\acute{q}}}, \mathfrak{K}_{\breve{g}}.\sqrt[\acute{q}]{1-\widetilde{\prod}_{i=1}^{\mathfrak{k}}(1-(\mathfrak{K}_i)^{\acute{q}})^{\acute{\omega}_i}}\right)\end{aligned}$$

Now we will prove for $\mathfrak{n} = \mathfrak{k}+1$,

$$\begin{aligned}GQROFWG((\widetilde{\Xi}_1, \widetilde{\Xi}_2, \ldots, \widetilde{\Xi}_\mathfrak{k}, \widetilde{\Xi}_{\mathfrak{k}+1}), \breve{g}) &= \breve{g} \otimes (\widetilde{\Xi}_1^{\acute{\omega}_1} \otimes \ldots, \otimes \widetilde{\Xi}_\mathfrak{k}^{\acute{\omega}_\mathfrak{k}} \otimes \widetilde{\Xi}_{\mathfrak{k}+1}^{\acute{\omega}_{\mathfrak{k}+1}}) \\ &= \left(\sqrt[\acute{q}]{(\breve{\Theta}_{\breve{g}})^{\acute{q}} + (1-(\breve{\Theta}_{\breve{g}})^{\acute{q}})((\breve{\Theta}_{\mathfrak{k}+1})^{\acute{\omega}_{\mathfrak{k}+1}})^{\acute{q}}\widetilde{\prod}_{i=1}^{\mathfrak{k}}(\breve{\Theta}_i^{\acute{\omega}_i})^{\acute{q}}},\right. \\ &\left.\mathfrak{K}_{\breve{g}}.\sqrt[\acute{q}]{1-(1-(\mathfrak{K}_{\mathfrak{k}+1})^{\acute{q}})^{\acute{\omega}_{\mathfrak{k}+1}}\widetilde{\prod}_{i=1}^{\mathfrak{k}}(1-(\mathfrak{K}_i)^{\acute{q}})^{\acute{\omega}_i}}\right) \\ &= \left(\sqrt[\acute{q}]{(\breve{\Theta}_{\breve{g}})^{\acute{q}} + (1-(\breve{\Theta}_{\breve{g}})^{\acute{q}})\widetilde{\prod}_{i=1}^{\mathfrak{k}+1}(\breve{\Theta}_i^{\acute{\omega}_i})^{\acute{q}}}, \mathfrak{K}_{\breve{g}}.\sqrt[\acute{q}]{1-\widetilde{\prod}_{i=1}^{\mathfrak{k}+1}(1-(\mathfrak{K}_i)^{\acute{q}})^{\acute{\omega}_i}}\right)\end{aligned}$$

The result is true for $\mathfrak{n} = \mathfrak{k}+1$. Consequently, the result holds, under generalized parameter for any number. □

Theorem 12. *By using GQROFWG-operator, the aggregated value is also a* $\acute{q}$*-ROPFN.*

Proof. For every $i = 1, 2, \ldots, \mathfrak{n}$, we have $0 \le \breve{\Theta}_i, \mathfrak{K}_i \le 1$ and $0 \le \breve{\Theta}_i^{\acute{q}} + \mathfrak{K}_i^{\acute{q}} \le 1, (\acute{q} \ge 1)$ implies that $0 \le 1 - \mathfrak{K}_i^{\acute{q}} \le 1$. Therefore,

$$\begin{aligned}&0 \le \widetilde{\prod}_{i=1}^{\mathfrak{n}}(1-\mathfrak{K}_i^{\acute{q}})^{\acute{\omega}_i} \le 1 \\ &0 \le \mathfrak{K}_g.\sqrt[\acute{q}]{1-\widetilde{\prod}_{i=1}^{\mathfrak{n}}(1-\mathfrak{K}_i^{\acute{q}})^{\acute{\omega}_i}} \le 1 \quad \text{for} \quad 0 \le \mathfrak{K}_{\breve{g}} \le 1.\end{aligned}$$

In addition, for $0 \le \breve{\Theta}_{\breve{g}} \le 1$, one can write, $0 \le \sqrt[\acute{q}]{(\breve{\Theta}_{\breve{g}})^{\acute{q}} + (1-(\breve{\Theta}_{\breve{g}})^{\acute{q}})\widetilde{\prod}_{i=1}^{\mathfrak{n}}(\breve{\Theta}_i^{\acute{\omega}_i})^{\acute{q}}} \le 1$.

Now,

$$= \left(\sqrt[\mathfrak{q}]{(\breve{\Theta}_{\breve{\mathfrak{g}}})^{\mathfrak{q}} + (1-(\breve{\Theta}_{\breve{\mathfrak{g}}})^{\mathfrak{q}})\widetilde{\prod}_{i=1}^{n}(\breve{\Theta}_i^{\hat{\omega}_i})^{\mathfrak{q}}} \right)^{\mathfrak{q}} + \left(\mathfrak{K}_{\breve{\mathfrak{g}}} \cdot \sqrt[\mathfrak{q}]{1-\widetilde{\prod}_{i=1}^{n}(1-(\mathfrak{K}_i)^{\mathfrak{q}})^{\hat{\omega}_i}} \right)^{\mathfrak{q}}$$
$$= \left((\breve{\Theta}_{\breve{\mathfrak{g}}})^{\mathfrak{q}} + (1-(\breve{\Theta}_{\breve{\mathfrak{g}}})^{\mathfrak{q}})\widetilde{\prod}_{i=1}^{n}(\breve{\Theta}_i^{\hat{\omega}_i})^{\mathfrak{q}} \right) + (\mathfrak{K}_{\breve{\mathfrak{g}}})^{\mathfrak{q}} \left(1-\widetilde{\prod}_{i=1}^{n}(1-(\mathfrak{K}_i)^{\mathfrak{q}})^{\hat{\omega}_i} \right)$$
$$= ((\mathfrak{K}_{\breve{\mathfrak{g}}})^{\mathfrak{q}} + (\breve{\Theta}_{\breve{\mathfrak{g}}})^{\mathfrak{q}}) + \widetilde{\prod}_{i=1}^{n}(\breve{\Theta}_i^{\hat{\omega}_i})^{\mathfrak{q}} - (\mathfrak{K}_{\breve{\mathfrak{g}}})^{\mathfrak{q}}\widetilde{\prod}_{i=1}^{n}(1-(\mathfrak{K}_i)^{\mathfrak{q}})^{\hat{\omega}_i} - (\breve{\Theta}_{\breve{\mathfrak{g}}})^{\mathfrak{q}}\widetilde{\prod}_{i=1}^{n}(\breve{\Theta}_i^{\hat{\omega}_i})^{\mathfrak{q}}$$
$$\leq ((\mathfrak{K}_{\breve{\mathfrak{g}}})^{\mathfrak{q}} + (\breve{\Theta}_{\breve{\mathfrak{g}}})^{\mathfrak{q}}) + \widetilde{\prod}_{i=1}^{n}(\breve{\Theta}_i^{\hat{\omega}_i})^{\mathfrak{q}} - (\mathfrak{K}_{\breve{\mathfrak{g}}})^{\mathfrak{q}}\widetilde{\prod}_{i=1}^{n}(\breve{\Theta}_i^{\hat{\omega}_i})^{\mathfrak{q}} - (\breve{\Theta}_{\breve{\mathfrak{g}}})^{\mathfrak{q}}\widetilde{\prod}_{i=1}^{n}(\breve{\Theta}_i^{\hat{\omega}_i})^{\mathfrak{q}} \quad \text{as} \quad \breve{\Theta}_i^{\mathfrak{q}} \leq 1-\mathfrak{K}_i^{\mathfrak{q}}$$
$$\leq ((\mathfrak{K}_{\breve{\mathfrak{g}}})^{\mathfrak{q}} + (\breve{\Theta}_{\breve{\mathfrak{g}}})^{\mathfrak{q}}) + \widetilde{\prod}_{i=1}^{n}(\breve{\Theta}_i^{\hat{\omega}_i})^{\mathfrak{q}} - ((\mathfrak{K}_{\breve{\mathfrak{g}}})^{\mathfrak{q}} + (\breve{\Theta}_{\breve{\mathfrak{g}}})^{\mathfrak{q}})\widetilde{\prod}_{i=1}^{n}(\breve{\Theta}_i^{\hat{\omega}_i})^{\mathfrak{q}}$$
$$\leq ((\mathfrak{K}_{\breve{\mathfrak{g}}})^{\mathfrak{q}} + (\breve{\Theta}_{\breve{\mathfrak{g}}})^{\mathfrak{q}}) \left(1-\widetilde{\prod}_{i=1}^{n}(\breve{\Theta}_i^{\hat{\omega}_i})^{\mathfrak{q}}\right) + \widetilde{\prod}_{i=1}^{n}(\breve{\Theta}_i^{\hat{\omega}_i})^{\mathfrak{q}}$$
$$\leq 1-\widetilde{\prod}_{i=1}^{n}(\breve{\Theta}_i^{\hat{\omega}_i})^{\mathfrak{q}} + \widetilde{\prod}_{i=1}^{n}(\breve{\Theta}_i^{\hat{\omega}_i})^{\mathfrak{q}} \leq 1$$

Hence, the aggregated value obtained by the GQROFWG-operator is a $\mathfrak{q}$-ROPFN. □

Example 13. *Consider* $\breve{\mathfrak{g}} = (0.5, 0.7)$ *is a GP of four* $\mathfrak{q}$*-ROPFNs.* $\widetilde{\Xi}_1 = (0.23, 0.67)$, $\widetilde{\Xi}_2 = (0.42, 0.77)$, $\widetilde{\Xi}_3 = (0.78, 0.55)$ *and* $\widetilde{\Xi}_4 = (0.41, 0.84)$ *with a weight vector* $\hat{\omega} = (0.1, 0.2, 0.3, 0.4)$, *here* $\mathfrak{q} = 3$, *then*

$$\sqrt[\mathfrak{q}]{(\breve{\Theta}_{\breve{\mathfrak{g}}})^{\mathfrak{q}} + (1-(\breve{\Theta}_{\breve{\mathfrak{g}}})^{\mathfrak{q}})\widetilde{\prod}_{i=1}^{n}(\breve{\Theta}_i^{\hat{\omega}_i})^{\mathfrak{q}}} = 0.60071$$

In addition,

$$\mathfrak{K}_{\breve{\mathfrak{g}}} \cdot \sqrt[\mathfrak{q}]{1-\widetilde{\prod}_{i=1}^{n}(1-(\mathfrak{K}_i)^{\mathfrak{q}})^{\hat{\omega}_i}} = 0.53054$$

By Theorem 3.2, we have

$$\begin{aligned} GQROFWG((\widetilde{\Xi}_1, \widetilde{\Xi}_2, \widetilde{\Xi}_3, \widetilde{\Xi}_4), \mathfrak{g}) &= \breve{\mathfrak{g}} \otimes \mathfrak{q}\text{-}ROFWG(\widetilde{\Xi}_1, \widetilde{\Xi}_2, \ldots, \widetilde{\Xi}_n) \\ &= \left(\sqrt[\mathfrak{q}]{(\breve{\Theta}_{\breve{\mathfrak{g}}})^{\mathfrak{q}} + (1-(\breve{\Theta}_{\breve{\mathfrak{g}}})^{\mathfrak{q}})\widetilde{\prod}_{i=1}^{\mathfrak{k}}(\breve{\Theta}_i^{\hat{\omega}_i})^{\mathfrak{q}}},\ \mathfrak{K}_{\breve{\mathfrak{g}}} \cdot \sqrt[\mathfrak{q}]{1-\widetilde{\prod}_{i=1}^{\mathfrak{k}}(1-(\mathfrak{K}_i)^{\mathfrak{q}})^{\hat{\omega}_i}} \right) \\ &= (0.60071, 0.53054) \end{aligned}$$

Proposition 14. *Let* $\widetilde{\Xi}_i = (\breve{\Theta}_i, \mathfrak{K}_i)(i = 1, 2, \ldots, n)$ *be a set of* $\mathfrak{q}$*-ROFNs and* $\hat{\omega} = (\hat{\omega}_1, \hat{\omega}_2, \ldots, \hat{\omega}_n)^T$ *is a weight vector of* $\widetilde{\Xi}_i$ *such that* $\hat{\omega}_i \in [0, 1]$ *and* $\sum_{i=1}^{n} \hat{\omega}_i = 1$. *Generalized parameter is* $\breve{\mathfrak{g}} = (\breve{\Theta}_{\breve{\mathfrak{g}}}, \mathfrak{K}_{\breve{\mathfrak{g}}})$, *then the GQROFWG-operator has the following properties:*
1. *(Idempotency)* *If* $\widetilde{\Xi}_i = \widetilde{\Xi}$ $(\forall i = 1, 2, \ldots, n)$, *then*

$$GQROFWG((\widetilde{\Xi}_1, \widetilde{\Xi}_2, \ldots, \widetilde{\Xi}_n), \mathfrak{g}) = \breve{\mathfrak{g}} \otimes \widetilde{\Xi}$$

2. *(Boundary condition)* *if* $\widetilde{\Xi}_i^- = (\breve{\Theta}^{min}_{\breve{\mathfrak{g}} \otimes \widetilde{\Xi}_i}, \mathfrak{K}^{max}_{\breve{\mathfrak{g}} \otimes \widetilde{\Xi}_i})$ *and* $\widetilde{\Xi}_i^+ = (\breve{\Theta}^{max}_{\breve{\mathfrak{g}} \otimes \widetilde{\Xi}_i}, \mathfrak{K}^{min}_{\breve{\mathfrak{g}} \otimes \widetilde{\Xi}_i})$, *then for every* $\hat{\omega}_i$,

$$\widetilde{\Xi}_i^- \leq GQROFWG((\widetilde{\Xi}_1, \widetilde{\Xi}_2, \ldots, \widetilde{\Xi}_n), \breve{\mathfrak{g}}) \leq \widetilde{\Xi}_i^+$$

3. *(Monotonicity)* *Let* $\widetilde{\Xi}_i^\star = (\breve{\Theta}_i^\star, \mathfrak{K}_i^\star)(i = 1, 2, \ldots, n)$ *be a set of* $\mathfrak{q}$*-ROFNs such that* $\breve{\Theta}_i \leq \breve{\Theta}_i^\star$ *and* $\mathfrak{K}_i \geq \mathfrak{K}_i^\star$ *for all* i, *then for every* $\hat{\omega}_i$,

$$GQROFWG((\widetilde{\Xi}_1, \widetilde{\Xi}_2, \ldots, \widetilde{\Xi}_n), \mathfrak{g}) \leq GQROFWG((\widetilde{\Xi}_1^\star, \widetilde{\Xi}_2^\star, \ldots, \widetilde{\Xi}_n^\star), \breve{\mathfrak{g}})$$

4. (Commutativity) *Let* $\widetilde{\Xi}_i = (\breve{\Theta}_i, \mathfrak{K}_i)(i = 1, 2, \ldots, n)$ *and* $\widetilde{\Xi}_i^* = (\breve{\Theta}_i^*, \mathfrak{K}_i^*)(i = 1, 2, \ldots, n)$ *be two sets of* n *q-ROFNs such that* $\widetilde{\Xi}_i^*$ *is any permutation of* $\widetilde{\Xi}_i$*, then*

$$GQROFWG((\widetilde{\Xi}_1, \widetilde{\Xi}_2, \ldots, \widetilde{\Xi}_n), \mathfrak{g}) = GQROFWG((\widetilde{\Xi}_1^*, \widetilde{\Xi}_2^*, \ldots, \widetilde{\Xi}_n^*), \mathfrak{g})$$

Proof. 1. if $\widetilde{\Xi}_i = \widetilde{\Xi}$ $(\forall i = 1, 2, \ldots, n)$, then by GQROFWG-operator,

$$\begin{aligned} GQROFWG((\widetilde{\Xi}_1, \widetilde{\Xi}_2, \ldots, \widetilde{\Xi}_n), \mathfrak{g}) &= \left(\sqrt[q]{(\breve{\Theta}_{\breve{g}})^q + (1 - (\breve{\Theta}_{\breve{g}})^q)\widetilde{\prod}_{i=1}^n (\breve{\Theta}_i^{\hat{\omega}_i})^q},\ \mathfrak{K}_{\breve{g}} \cdot \sqrt[q]{1 - \widetilde{\prod}_{i=1}^n (1 - (\mathfrak{K}_i)^q)^{\hat{\omega}_i}} \right) \\ &= \left(\sqrt[q]{(\breve{\Theta}_{\breve{g}})^q + (1 - (\breve{\Theta}_{\breve{g}})^q)\left(\breve{\Theta}^{\Sigma_{i=1}^n \hat{\omega}_i}\right)^q},\ \mathfrak{K}_{\breve{g}} \cdot \sqrt[q]{1 - (1 - (\mathfrak{K})^q)^{\Sigma_{i=1}^n \hat{\omega}_i}} \right) \\ &= \left(\sqrt[q]{(\breve{\Theta}_{\breve{g}})^q + (1 - (\breve{\Theta}_{\breve{g}})^q)(\breve{\Theta})^q},\ \mathfrak{K}_{\breve{g}} \cdot \sqrt[q]{1 - (1 - (\mathfrak{K})^q)} \right) \\ &= \left(\sqrt[q]{(\breve{\Theta}_{\breve{g}})^q + \breve{\Theta}^q - (\breve{\Theta}_{\breve{g}})^q(\breve{\Theta})^q},\ \mathfrak{K}_{\breve{g}} . \mathfrak{K} \right) \\ &= \breve{g} \otimes \widetilde{\Xi} \end{aligned}$$

2. Let $\widetilde{\Xi}_i^- = (\breve{\Theta}^{min}_{\breve{g}\otimes\widetilde{\Xi}_i}, \mathfrak{K}^{max}_{\breve{g}\otimes\widetilde{\Xi}_i})$ and $\widetilde{\Xi}_i^+ = (\breve{\Theta}^{max}_{g\otimes\widetilde{\Xi}_i}, \mathfrak{K}^{min}_{g\otimes\widetilde{\Xi}_i})$, where $\mathfrak{K}^{min}_{\breve{g}\otimes\widetilde{\Xi}_i} = \mathfrak{K}_{\breve{g}}(min\mathfrak{K}_i)$, $\mathfrak{K}^{max}_{\breve{g}\otimes\widetilde{\Xi}_i} = \mathfrak{K}_{\breve{g}}(max\mathfrak{K}_i)$, $\mathfrak{K}^{min}_{\breve{g}\otimes\widetilde{\Xi}_i} = \sqrt[q]{\breve{\Theta}_{\breve{g}}^q + (1 - \breve{\Theta}_{\breve{g}}^q)(min(\breve{\Theta}_i))^q}$, and $\mathfrak{K}^{max}_{g\otimes\widetilde{\Xi}_i} = \sqrt[q]{\breve{\Theta}_{\breve{g}}^q + (1 - \breve{\Theta}_{\breve{g}}^q)(max(\breve{\Theta}_i))^q}$ for all i, it is clear that $min(\mathfrak{K}_i) \leq \mathfrak{K}_i \leq max(\mathfrak{K}_i) \Rightarrow max(1 - \mathfrak{K}_i^q) \leq (1 - \mathfrak{K}_i^q) \leq min(1 - \mathfrak{K}_i^q)$, for each $\hat{\omega}$,

$$\Rightarrow \widetilde{\prod}_{i=1}^n (1 - max(\mathfrak{K}_i)^q)^{\hat{\omega}_i} \leq \widetilde{\prod}_{i=1}^n (1 - \mathfrak{K}_i^q)^{\hat{\omega}_i} \leq \widetilde{\prod}_{i=1}^n (1 - min(\mathfrak{K}_i)^q)^{\hat{\omega}_i}$$

$$\Rightarrow (1 - max(\mathfrak{K}_i)^q)^{\Sigma_{i=1}^n \hat{\omega}_i} \leq \widetilde{\prod}_{i=1}^n (1 - \mathfrak{K}_i^q)^{\hat{\omega}_i} \leq (1 - min(\mathfrak{K}_i)^q)^{\Sigma_{i=1}^n \hat{\omega}_i}$$

$$\Rightarrow 1 - ((1 - min(\mathfrak{K}_i)^q)) \leq \widetilde{\prod}_{i=1}^n (1 - \mathfrak{K}_i^q)^{\hat{\omega}_i} \leq 1 - ((1 - max(\mathfrak{K}_i)^q))$$

$$\Rightarrow \sqrt[q]{1 - ((1 - min(\mathfrak{K}_i)^q))} \leq \sqrt[q]{\widetilde{\prod}_{i=1}^n (1 - \mathfrak{K}_i^q)^{\omega_i}} \leq \sqrt[q]{1 - ((1 - max(\mathfrak{K}_i)^q))}$$

$$\Rightarrow min(\mathfrak{K}_i) \leq \sqrt[q]{\widetilde{\prod}_{i=1}^n (1 - \mathfrak{K}_i^q)^{\hat{\omega}_i}} \leq max(\mathfrak{K}_i)$$

As we know, $0 \leq \mathfrak{K}_g$
$leq1$, we can write

$$\mathfrak{K}_{\breve{g}}.min(\mathfrak{K}_i) \leq \mathfrak{K}_{\breve{g}} \cdot \sqrt[q]{\widetilde{\prod}_{i=1}^n (1 - \mathfrak{K}_i^q)^{\hat{\omega}_i}} \leq \mathfrak{K}_{\breve{g}}.max(\mathfrak{K}_i)$$

$$\mathfrak{K}^{min}_{\breve{g}\otimes\widetilde{\Xi}_i} \leq \mathfrak{K}_{\breve{g}} \cdot \sqrt[q]{\widetilde{\prod}_{i=1}^n (1 - \mathfrak{K}_i^q)^{\hat{\omega}_i}} \leq \mathfrak{K}^{max}_{\breve{g}\otimes\widetilde{\Xi}_i}.$$

Furthermore, $min(\breve{\Theta}_i) \leq \breve{\Theta}_i \leq max(\breve{\Theta}_i) \iff (min(\breve{\Theta}_i))^q \leq \widetilde{\prod}_{i=1}^n (\breve{\Theta}_i^{\hat{\omega}_i})^q \leq (max(\breve{\Theta}_i))^q$. In addition, for $0 \leq \breve{\Theta}_{\breve{g}} \leq 1$, we can write

$$\Longrightarrow (1 - \breve{\Theta}_{\breve{g}}^q)(min(\breve{\Theta}_i))^q \leq (1 - \breve{\Theta}_{\breve{g}}^q)\widetilde{\prod}_{i=1}^n (\breve{\Theta}_i^{\hat{\omega}_i})^q \leq (1 - \breve{\Theta}_{\breve{g}}^q)(max(\breve{\Theta}_i))^q$$

$$\Longrightarrow \breve{\Theta}_{\breve{g}}^q + (1 - \breve{\Theta}_{\breve{g}}^q)(min(\breve{\Theta}_i))^q \leq \breve{\Theta}_{\breve{g}}^q + (1 - \breve{\Theta}_{\breve{g}}^q)\widetilde{\prod}_{i=1}^n (\breve{\Theta}_i^{\hat{\omega}_i})^q \leq \breve{\Theta}_{\breve{g}}^q + (1 - \breve{\Theta}_{\breve{g}}^q)(max(\breve{\Theta}_i))^q$$

$$\Longrightarrow \sqrt[q]{\breve{\Theta}_{\breve{g}}^q + (1 - \breve{\Theta}_{\breve{g}}^q)(min(\breve{\Theta}_i))^q} \leq \sqrt[q]{\breve{\Theta}_{\breve{g}}^q + (1 - \breve{\Theta}_{\breve{g}}^q)\widetilde{\prod}_{i=1}^n (\breve{\Theta}_i^{\hat{\omega}_i})^q} \leq \sqrt[q]{\breve{\Theta}_{\breve{g}}^q + (1 - \breve{\Theta}_{\breve{g}}^q)(max(\breve{\Theta}_i))^q}$$

$$\Longrightarrow \breve{\Theta}^{max}_{\breve{g}\otimes\widetilde{\Xi}_i} \leq \sqrt[q]{\breve{\Theta}_{\breve{g}}^q + (1 - \breve{\Theta}_{\breve{g}}^q)\widetilde{\prod}_{i=1}^n (\breve{\Theta}_i^{\hat{\omega}_i})^q} \leq \breve{\Theta}^{min}_{\breve{g}\otimes\widetilde{\Xi}_i}$$

$GQROFWG((\widetilde{\Xi}_1, \widetilde{\Xi}_2, \ldots, \widetilde{\Xi}_n), \breve{\mathfrak{g}}) = \widetilde{\Xi} = (\breve{\Theta}_{\breve{\mathfrak{g}}\otimes\widetilde{\Xi}_i}, \mathfrak{K}_{\breve{\mathfrak{g}}\otimes\widetilde{\Xi}_i})$, then we have $\mathfrak{K}^{min}_{\breve{\mathfrak{g}}\otimes\widetilde{\Xi}_i} \leq \mathfrak{K}_{\breve{\mathfrak{g}}\otimes\widetilde{\Xi}_i} \leq \mathfrak{K}^{max}_{\breve{\mathfrak{g}}\otimes\widetilde{\Xi}_i}$ and $\breve{\Theta}^{min}_{\breve{\mathfrak{g}}\otimes\widetilde{\Xi}_i} \leq \breve{\Theta}_{\breve{\mathfrak{g}}\otimes\widetilde{\Xi}_i} \leq \breve{\Theta}^{max}_{\breve{\mathfrak{g}}\otimes\widetilde{\Xi}_i}$. Thus, by definition of score function, we get

$$\widetilde{\Xi}_i^- \leq GQROFWG((\widetilde{\Xi}_1, \widetilde{\Xi}_2, \ldots, \widetilde{\Xi}_n), \breve{\mathfrak{g}}) \leq \widetilde{\Xi}_i^+$$

3. It can be easily done by the above proof.
4. It follows trivially from definition.

□

Proposition 15. *If the first priority of a another decision expert to the assessed object is considered to be $\breve{\mathfrak{g}} = (0, 1)$, then the GQROFWG-operator minimizes in the the ά-ROFWG-operator.*

Proof. If we take $\breve{\mathfrak{g}} = (0, 1)$ as given then by Theorem 3.2, we have

$$\begin{aligned} GQROFWG((\widetilde{\Xi}_1, \widetilde{\Xi}_2, \ldots, \widetilde{\Xi}_n), \breve{\mathfrak{g}}) &= \left(\sqrt[\acute{q}]{(\breve{\Theta}_{\breve{\mathfrak{g}}})^{\acute{q}} + (1 - (\breve{\Theta}_{\breve{\mathfrak{g}}})^{\acute{q}}) \widetilde{\prod}_{i=1}^{n} (\breve{\Theta}_i^{\hat{\omega}_i})^{\acute{q}}},\ \mathfrak{K}_{\breve{\mathfrak{g}}} \cdot \sqrt[\acute{q}]{1 - \widetilde{\prod}_{i=1}^{n} (1 - (\mathfrak{K}_i)^{\acute{q}})^{\hat{\omega}_i}} \right) \\ &= \left(\sqrt[\acute{q}]{\widetilde{\prod}_{i=1}^{n} (\breve{\Theta}_i^{\hat{\omega}_i})^{\acute{q}}},\ \sqrt[\acute{q}]{1 - \widetilde{\prod}_{i=1}^{n} (1 - (\mathfrak{K}_i)^{\acute{q}})^{\hat{\omega}_i}} \right) \\ &= \left(\widetilde{\prod}_{i=1}^{n} (\breve{\Theta}_i^{\hat{\omega}_i})^{\acute{q}},\ \sqrt[\acute{q}]{1 - \widetilde{\prod}_{i=1}^{n} (1 - (\mathfrak{K}_i)^{\acute{q}})^{\hat{\omega}_i}} \right) \\ &= \acute{q}\text{-ROFWG}(\widetilde{\Xi}_1, \widetilde{\Xi}_2, \ldots, \widetilde{\Xi}_n). \end{aligned}$$

□

Proposition 16. *If the first priority of another decision maker to the assessed object is considered to be $\breve{\mathfrak{g}} = (1, 0)$, then the GQROFWG-operator provides the value $(1, 0)$.*

Proof. If we take $\breve{\mathfrak{g}} = (1, 0)$ as given then by Theorem 3.2, we have

$$\begin{aligned} GQROFWG((\widetilde{\Xi}_1, \widetilde{\Xi}_2, \ldots, \widetilde{\Xi}_n), \breve{\mathfrak{g}}) &= \left(\sqrt[\acute{q}]{(\breve{\Theta}_{\breve{\mathfrak{g}}})^{\acute{q}} + (1 - (\breve{\Theta}_{\breve{\mathfrak{g}}})^{\acute{q}}) \widetilde{\prod}_{i=1}^{n} (\breve{\Theta}_i^{\hat{\omega}_i})^{\acute{q}}},\ \mathfrak{K}_{\breve{\mathfrak{g}}} \cdot \sqrt[\acute{q}]{1 - \widetilde{\prod}_{i=1}^{n} (1 - (\mathfrak{K}_i)^{\acute{q}})^{\hat{\omega}_i}} \right) \\ &= \left(\sqrt[\acute{q}]{1 + (1 - 1) \widetilde{\prod}_{i=1}^{n} (\breve{\Theta}_i^{\hat{\omega}_i})^{\acute{q}}},\ 0 \right) \\ &= (1,\ 0). \end{aligned}$$

□

4.2. The Generalized ά-ROF Ordered Weighted Geometric Operator

Definition 17. *Let $\breve{\mathfrak{g}} = (\breve{\Theta}_{\breve{\mathfrak{g}}}, \mathfrak{K}_{\breve{\mathfrak{g}}})$ be a GP for the ά-ROFNs $\widetilde{\Xi}_i = (\breve{\Theta}_i, \mathfrak{K}_i)(i = 1, 2, \ldots, n)$, then the GQROFOWG-operator is characterized as,*

$$GQROFWG((\widetilde{\Xi}_1, \widetilde{\Xi}_2, \ldots, \widetilde{\Xi}_n, \breve{\mathfrak{g}})) = \breve{\mathfrak{g}} \otimes \acute{q}\text{-}ROFOWG(\widetilde{\Xi}_1, \widetilde{\Xi}_2, \ldots, \widetilde{\Xi}_n)$$

Theorem 18. *Let $\widetilde{\Xi}_i = (\breve{\Theta}_i, \mathfrak{K}_i)(i = 1, 2, \ldots, n)$ be a set of ά-ROFNs and $\hat{\omega} = (\hat{\omega}_1, \hat{\omega}_2, \ldots, \hat{\omega}_n)^T$ is the weight vector of $\widetilde{\Xi}_i$ such that $\hat{\omega}_i \in [0, 1]$ and $\sum_{i=1}^{n}$. GP is $\breve{\mathfrak{g}} = (\breve{\Theta}_{\breve{\mathfrak{g}}}, \mathfrak{K}_{\breve{\mathfrak{g}}})$, then the GQROFOWG-operator is defined as*

$$\begin{aligned} GQROFWG((\widetilde{\Xi}_1, \widetilde{\Xi}_2, \ldots, \widetilde{\Xi}_n), \breve{\mathfrak{g}}) &= \mathfrak{g} \otimes \acute{q}\text{-}ROFOWG(\widetilde{\Xi}_1, \widetilde{\Xi}_2, \ldots, \widetilde{\Xi}_n) \\ &= \left(\sqrt[\acute{q}]{(\breve{\Theta}_{\breve{\mathfrak{g}}})^{\acute{q}} + (1 - (\breve{\Theta}_{\breve{\mathfrak{g}}})^{\acute{q}}) \widetilde{\prod}_{i=1}^{n} (\breve{\Theta}_{\sigma(i)}^{\hat{\omega}_i})^{\acute{q}}},\ \mathfrak{K}_{\breve{\mathfrak{g}}} \cdot \sqrt[\acute{q}]{1 - \widetilde{\prod}_{i=1}^{n} (1 - (\mathfrak{K}_{\sigma(i)})^{\acute{q}})^{\hat{\omega}_i}} \right) \end{aligned}$$

$(\sigma(1), \sigma(2), \ldots, \sigma(\mathfrak{n}))$ is a permutation of $(1, 2, \ldots, \mathfrak{n})$, such that $\widetilde{\Xi}_{\sigma(\mathfrak{i}-1)} \geq \widetilde{\Xi}_{\sigma(\mathfrak{i})}$ for any $\mathfrak{i}$.

Proof. The proof can be done as Theorem 3.2. □

Example 19. *Let $\breve{\mathfrak{g}} = (0.5, 0.7)$ be the GP of four q-ROPFNs. $\widetilde{\Xi}_1 = (0.23, 0.67)$, $\widetilde{\Xi}_2 = (0.42, 0.77)$, $\widetilde{\Xi}_3 = (0.78, 0.55)$ and $\widetilde{\Xi}_4 = (0.41, 0.84)$ with a weight vector $\hat{\omega} = (0.1, 0.2, 0.3, 0.4)$, here $\acute{q} = 3$, then first we find score functions of all $\widetilde{\Xi}_\mathfrak{i}$.*

$$\widetilde{\daleth}(\widetilde{\Xi}_1) = -0.2885$$
$$\widetilde{\daleth}(\widetilde{\Xi}_2) = -0.3824$$
$$\widetilde{\daleth}(\widetilde{\Xi}_3) = 0.3081$$
$$\widetilde{\daleth}(\widetilde{\Xi}_4) = -0.5237$$

On the behalf of score functions, $\widetilde{\Xi}_{\sigma(1)} = \widetilde{\Xi}_3$, $\widetilde{\Xi}_{\sigma(2)} = \widetilde{\Xi}_1$, $\widetilde{\Xi}_{\sigma(3)} = \widetilde{\Xi}_2$, and $\widetilde{\Xi}_{\sigma(4)} = \widetilde{\Xi}_4$

$$\sqrt[\acute{q}]{(\breve{\Theta}_{\breve{\mathfrak{g}}})^{\acute{q}} + (1 - (\breve{\Theta}_{\breve{\mathfrak{g}}})^{\acute{q}}) \widetilde{\prod}_{\mathfrak{i}=1}^{\mathfrak{n}} (\breve{\Theta}_{\sigma(\mathfrak{i})}^{\hat{\omega}_\mathfrak{i}})^{\acute{q}}} = 0.5623$$

In addition,

$$\mathfrak{K}_{\breve{\mathfrak{g}}} \cdot \sqrt[\acute{q}]{1 - \widetilde{\prod}_{\mathfrak{i}=1}^{\mathfrak{n}} (1 - (\mathfrak{K}_{\sigma(\mathfrak{i})})^{\acute{q}})^{\hat{\omega}_\mathfrak{i}}} = 0.5436$$

By Theorem 3.9, we have

$$\begin{aligned} GQROFOWG((\widetilde{\Xi}_1, \widetilde{\Xi}_2, \widetilde{\Xi}_3, \widetilde{\Xi}_4), \breve{\mathfrak{g}}) &= \breve{\mathfrak{g}} \otimes \acute{q}\text{-}ROFOWG(\widetilde{\Xi}_1, \widetilde{\Xi}_2, \ldots, \widetilde{\Xi}_\mathfrak{n}) \\ &= \left(\sqrt[\acute{q}]{(\breve{\Theta}_{\breve{\mathfrak{g}}})^{\acute{q}} + (1 - (\breve{\Theta}_{\breve{\mathfrak{g}}})^{\acute{q}}) \widetilde{\prod}_{\mathfrak{i}=1}^{\mathfrak{k}} (\breve{\Theta}_\mathfrak{i}^{\hat{\omega}_\mathfrak{i}})^{\acute{q}}},\ \mathfrak{K}_{\breve{\mathfrak{g}}} \cdot \sqrt[\acute{q}]{1 - \widetilde{\prod}_{\mathfrak{i}=1}^{\mathfrak{k}} (1 - (\mathfrak{K}_\mathfrak{i})^{\acute{q}})^{\hat{\omega}_\mathfrak{i}}} \right) \\ &= (0.5623,\ 0.5436) \end{aligned}$$

Proposition 20. *Let $\widetilde{\Xi}_\mathfrak{i} = (\breve{\Theta}_\mathfrak{i}, \mathfrak{K}_\mathfrak{i})(\mathfrak{i} = 1, 2, \ldots \mathfrak{n})$ be a set of q-ROFNs and $\hat{\omega} = (\hat{\omega}_1, \hat{\omega}_2, \ldots, \hat{\omega}_\mathfrak{n})^T$ is the weight vector of $\widetilde{\Xi}_\mathfrak{i}$ such that $\hat{\omega}_\mathfrak{i} \in [0, 1]$ and $\sum_{\mathfrak{i}=1}^{\mathfrak{n}}$. Generalized parameter is $\breve{\mathfrak{g}} = (\breve{\Theta}_{\breve{\mathfrak{g}}}, \mathfrak{K}_{\breve{\mathfrak{g}}})$, the GQROFOWG-operator has the following properties:*

1. *(Idempotency)* *If $\widetilde{\Xi}_\mathfrak{i} = \widetilde{\Xi}$ $(\forall \mathfrak{i} = 1, 2, \ldots, \mathfrak{n})$, then*

$$GQROFOWG((\widetilde{\Xi}_1, \widetilde{\Xi}_2, \ldots, \widetilde{\Xi}_\mathfrak{n}), \breve{\mathfrak{g}}) = \breve{\mathfrak{g}} \otimes \widetilde{\Xi}$$

2. *(Boundary condition)* *If $\widetilde{\Xi}_\mathfrak{i}^- = (\breve{\Theta}_{\breve{\mathfrak{g}} \otimes \widetilde{\Xi}_\mathfrak{i}}^{min}, \mathfrak{K}_{\breve{\mathfrak{g}} \otimes \widetilde{\Xi}_\mathfrak{i}}^{max})$ and $\widetilde{\Xi}_\mathfrak{i}^+ = (\breve{\Theta}_{\breve{\mathfrak{g}} \otimes \widetilde{\Xi}_\mathfrak{i}}^{max}, \mathfrak{K}_{\breve{\mathfrak{g}} \otimes \widetilde{\Xi}_\mathfrak{i}}^{min})$, then for every $\hat{\omega}_\mathfrak{i}$,*

$$\widetilde{\Xi}_\mathfrak{i}^- \leq GQROFOWG((\widetilde{\Xi}_1, \widetilde{\Xi}_2, \ldots, \widetilde{\Xi}_\mathfrak{n}), \mathfrak{g}) \leq \widetilde{\Xi}_\mathfrak{i}^+$$

3. *(Monotonicity)* *Let $\widetilde{\Xi}_\mathfrak{i}^\star = (\breve{\Theta}_\mathfrak{i}^\star, \mathfrak{K}_\mathfrak{i}^\star)(\mathfrak{i} = 1, 2, \ldots, \mathfrak{n})$ be a set of q-ROFNs such that $\mathfrak{K}_\mathfrak{i}^\star \leq \mathfrak{K}_\mathfrak{i}$ and $\breve{\Theta}_\mathfrak{i} \leq \breve{\Theta}_\mathfrak{i}^\star$ for all $\mathfrak{i}$, then for every $\hat{\omega}_\mathfrak{i}$,*

$$GQROFOWG((\widetilde{\Xi}_1, \widetilde{\Xi}_2, \ldots,, \widetilde{\Xi}_\mathfrak{n}), \breve{\mathfrak{g}}) \leq GQROFOWG((\widetilde{\Xi}_1^\star, \widetilde{\Xi}_2^\star, \ldots, \widetilde{\Xi}_\mathfrak{n}^\star), \breve{\mathfrak{g}})$$

4. *(Commutativity)* *Let $\widetilde{\Xi}_\mathfrak{i} = (\breve{\Theta}_\mathfrak{i}, \mathfrak{K}_\mathfrak{i})(\mathfrak{i} = 1, 2, \ldots, \mathfrak{n})$ and $\widetilde{\Xi}_\mathfrak{i}^* = (\breve{\Theta}_\mathfrak{i}^*, \mathfrak{K}_\mathfrak{i}{}^*)(\mathfrak{i} = 1, 2, \ldots, \mathfrak{n})$ be a two collection of $\mathfrak{n}$ q-ROFNs such that $\widetilde{\Xi}_\mathfrak{i}^*$ is any permutation of $\widetilde{\Xi}_\mathfrak{i}$, then*

$$GQROFOWG((\widetilde{\Xi}_1, \widetilde{\Xi}_2, \ldots, \widetilde{\Xi}_\mathfrak{n}), \breve{\mathfrak{g}}) = GQROFOWG((\widetilde{\Xi}_1^*, \widetilde{\Xi}_2^*, \ldots, \widetilde{\Xi}_\mathfrak{n}^*), \mathfrak{g})$$

5. *If the preference of another decision maker to the assessed object is considered to be* $\breve{\mathfrak{g}} = (0,1)$*, then the GQROFOWG-operator becomes the* $\acute{\mathfrak{q}}$*-ROFOWG-operator.*
6. *If the preference of another decision maker to the assessed object is considered to be* $\breve{\mathfrak{g}} = (1,0)$*, then the GQROFOWG-operator provides the value* $(1,0)$*.*

Proof. Here we leave proof. □

4.3. The Generalized $\acute{\mathfrak{q}}$*-ROF Hybrid Geometric Operator*

Definition 21. *Suppose* $\breve{\mathfrak{g}} = (\breve{\Theta}_{\breve{\mathfrak{g}}}, \mathfrak{K}_{\breve{\mathfrak{g}}})$ *be the generalized parameter for the* $\acute{\mathfrak{q}}$*-ROFNs* $\widetilde{\Xi}_i = (\breve{\Theta}_i, \mathfrak{K}_i)$ $(i = 1,2,\ldots,n)$*, then the GQROFHG-operator is determined as,*

$$GQROFHG((\widetilde{\Xi}_1,\widetilde{\Xi}_2,\ldots,\widetilde{\Xi}_n,\mathfrak{g})) = \breve{\mathfrak{g}} \otimes \acute{\mathfrak{q}}\text{-}ROFHG(\widetilde{\Xi}_1,\widetilde{\Xi}_2,\ldots,\widetilde{\Xi}_n)$$

Theorem 22. *Let* $\widetilde{\Xi}_i = (\breve{\Theta}_i, \mathfrak{K}_i)(i = 1,2,\ldots,n)$ *be a set of* $\acute{\mathfrak{q}}$*-ROFNs and* $\hat{\varpi} = (\hat{\varpi}_1, \hat{\varpi}_2, \ldots, \hat{\varpi}_n)^T$ *be a weight vector of* $\widetilde{\Xi}_i$ *such that* $\hat{\varpi}_i \in [0,1]$ *and* $\sum_{i=1}^{n} \hat{\varpi}_i = 1$*. The GP is* $\breve{\mathfrak{g}} = (\breve{\Theta}_{\breve{\mathfrak{g}}}, \mathfrak{K}_{\breve{\mathfrak{g}}})$ *and the standard vector is* $\xi = (\xi_1, \xi_2, \ldots, \xi_n)^T$ *such that* $\xi_i \in [0,1]$ *and* $\sum_{i=1}^{n} \xi_i = 1$*. The GQROFHG-operator is determined as,*

$$\begin{aligned} GQROFHG((\widetilde{\Xi}_1,\widetilde{\Xi}_2,\ldots,\widetilde{\Xi}_n),\breve{\mathfrak{g}}) &= \breve{\mathfrak{g}} \otimes \acute{\mathfrak{q}}\text{-}ROFHG(\widetilde{\Xi}_1,\widetilde{\Xi}_2,\ldots,\widetilde{\Xi}_n) \\ &= \left(\sqrt[\acute{\mathfrak{q}}]{(\breve{\Theta}_{\breve{\mathfrak{g}}})^{\acute{\mathfrak{q}}} + (1-(\breve{\Theta}_{\breve{\mathfrak{g}}})^{\acute{\mathfrak{q}}}) \widetilde{\prod}_{i=1}^{n} (\breve{\breve{\Theta}}_{\sigma(i)}^{\hat{\varpi}_i})^{\acute{\mathfrak{q}}}},\ \mathfrak{K}_{\breve{\mathfrak{g}}}.\sqrt[\acute{\mathfrak{q}}]{1-\widetilde{\prod}_{i=1}^{n}(1-(\breve{\breve{\mathfrak{K}}}_{\sigma(i)})^{\acute{\mathfrak{q}}})^{\hat{\varpi}_i}} \right) \end{aligned}$$

here $\breve{\widetilde{\Xi}}_i = n\xi_i\widetilde{\Xi}_i$*,* n *is the number of* $\acute{\mathfrak{q}}$*-ROFNs,* ξ_i *is a standard weight vector of* $\widetilde{\Xi}_i$*, and* $(\sigma(1), \sigma(2), \ldots, \sigma(n))$ *is a permutation of* $(1,2,\ldots,n)$*, such that* $\breve{\widetilde{\Xi}}_{\sigma(i-1)} \geq \breve{\widetilde{\Xi}}_{\sigma(i)}$ *for any* i*.*

Proof. The proof can be done same as Theorem 3.2. □

Example 23. *Let* $\breve{\mathfrak{g}} = (0.5, 0.7)$ *be the GP of four* $\acute{\mathfrak{q}}$*-rung orthopair fuzzy numbers.* $\widetilde{\Xi}_1 = (0.23, 0.67)$*,* $\widetilde{\Xi}_2 = (0.42, 0.77)$*,* $\widetilde{\Xi}_3 = (0.78, 0.55)$*, and* $\widetilde{\Xi}_3 = (0.41, 0.84)$ *with a weight vector* $\varpi = (0.1, 0.2, 0.3, 0.4)$*, here* $\acute{\mathfrak{q}} = 4$*. Standard weight vector will be* $\xi_i = (0.4, 0.3, 0.2, 0.1)$*. First we find* $\breve{\widetilde{\Xi}}_i = n\xi_i\widetilde{\Xi}_i$ *for each* $\widetilde{\Xi}_i$*, then we find score functions of each* $\breve{\widetilde{\Xi}}_i$*.*

$$\breve{\widetilde{\Xi}}_1 = (0.258622, 0.526889)$$
$$\breve{\widetilde{\Xi}}_2 = (0.439241, 0.730783)$$
$$\breve{\widetilde{\Xi}}_3 = (0.745657, 0.619855)$$
$$\breve{\widetilde{\Xi}}_4 = (0.326760, 0.932635)$$

The score functions will be,

$$\widetilde{\urcorner}(\breve{\widetilde{\Xi}}_1) = -0.072594$$
$$\widetilde{\urcorner}(\breve{\widetilde{\Xi}}_2) = -0.247979$$
$$\widetilde{\urcorner}(\breve{\widetilde{\Xi}}_3) = 0.161515$$
$$\widetilde{\urcorner}(\breve{\widetilde{\Xi}}_3) = -0.745165$$

On the behalf of score functions, $\widetilde{\Xi}_{\sigma(1)} = \breve{\widetilde{\Xi}}_3$*,* $\widetilde{\Xi}_{\sigma(2)} = \breve{\widetilde{\Xi}}_1$*,* $\widetilde{\Xi}_{\sigma(3)} = \breve{\widetilde{\Xi}}_2$*, and* $\widetilde{\Xi}_{\sigma(4)} = \breve{\widetilde{\Xi}}_4$

$$\sqrt[\acute{\mathfrak{q}}]{(\breve{\Theta}_{\breve{\mathfrak{g}}})^{\acute{\mathfrak{q}}} + (1-(\breve{\Theta}_{\breve{\mathfrak{g}}})^{\acute{\mathfrak{q}}}) \widetilde{\prod}_{i=1}^{n} (\breve{\breve{\Theta}}_{\sigma(i)}^{\hat{\varpi}_i})^{\acute{\mathfrak{q}}}} = 0.531970$$

In addition,

$$\mathfrak{K}_{\breve{\mathfrak{g}}}.\sqrt[\mathfrak{q}]{1-\widetilde{\prod}_{i=1}^{n}(1-(\breve{\mathfrak{K}}_{\sigma(i)})^{\mathfrak{q}})^{\hat{\omega}_i}}=0.589324$$

By Theorem 3.13, we have

$$GQROFHG((\widetilde{\Xi}_1,\widetilde{\Xi}_2,\widetilde{\Xi}_3),\breve{\mathfrak{g}})=\left(\sqrt[\mathfrak{q}]{(\breve{\Theta}_{\breve{\mathfrak{g}}})^{\mathfrak{q}}+(1-(\breve{\Theta}_{\breve{\mathfrak{g}}})^{\mathfrak{q}})\widetilde{\prod}_{i=1}^{\mathfrak{k}}(\breve{\Theta}_i^{\hat{\omega}_i})^{\mathfrak{q}}},\ \mathfrak{K}_{\breve{\mathfrak{g}}}.\sqrt[\mathfrak{q}]{1-\widetilde{\prod}_{i=1}^{\mathfrak{k}}(1-(\mathfrak{K}_i)^{\mathfrak{q}})^{\hat{\omega}_i}},\right)$$
$$=(0.531970,0.589324)$$

The following observation are derived from definition of GQROFHG-operator:

1. If the preference of another decision maker to the assessed object is considered to be $\breve{\mathfrak{g}}=(0,1)$, then the GQROFHG-operator becomes the ɋ-ROFHG-operator.
2. If the preference of another decision maker to the assessed object is considered to be $\breve{\mathfrak{g}}=(1,0)$, then the GQROFHG-operator provides the value $(1,0)$.
3. If $\xi=(\frac{1}{n},\frac{1}{n},\ldots,\frac{1}{n})^T$, then the GQROFHG-operator reduces to GQROFWG-operator.
4. If $\hat{\omega}=(\frac{1}{n},\frac{1}{n},\ldots,\frac{1}{n})^T$, then the GQROFHG-operator reduces to GQROFOWG-operator.

5. ɋ-ROF Geometric Aggregation Operator Based On Group-Generalized Parameter

The presented section is dedicated to extending collaborators above geometric aggregation operators by taking the conceptions of different specialists/decision experts on the preliminary information to better integrate different preferences of decision makers. This can be obtained by providing a group-generalized ɋ-rung orthopair fuzzy weighted geometric(GGQROFWG-operator), group-generalized ɋ-rung orthopair fuzzy ordered weighted geometric(GGQROFOWG-operator) and group-generalized ɋ-rung orthopair fuzzy hybrid geometric(GGQROFHG-operator).

5.1. Group-Generalized ɋ-ROF Weighted Geometric Operator

Definition 24. *Suppose there are ɋ specialists/decision experts to verify the ɋ-ROF information. Let $\mathfrak{g}_z=(\breve{\Theta}_{\breve{\mathfrak{g}}_z},\mathfrak{K}_{\breve{\mathfrak{g}}_z})$ be the specialists/decision experts for the ɋ-ROFNs $\widetilde{\Xi}_i=(\breve{\Theta}_i,\mathfrak{K}_i)(i=1,2,\ldots,n)$, then GGQROFWG-operator is determined as,*

$$GGQROFWG((\widetilde{\Xi}_1,\widetilde{\Xi}_2,\ldots,\widetilde{\Xi}_n),(\breve{\mathfrak{g}}_1,\breve{\mathfrak{g}}_2,\ldots,\breve{\mathfrak{g}}_{\mathfrak{q}}))=\mathfrak{q}\text{-}ROFWG(\breve{\mathfrak{g}}_1,\breve{\mathfrak{g}}_2,\ldots,\breve{\mathfrak{g}}_{\mathfrak{q}})\otimes\mathfrak{q}\text{-}ROFWG(\widetilde{\Xi}_1,\widetilde{\Xi}_2,\ldots,\widetilde{\Xi}_n)$$

Theorem 25. *Let there be ɋ specialists/decision experts to verify the ɋ-ROF information. Let $\breve{\mathfrak{g}}_z=(\breve{\Theta}_{\breve{\mathfrak{g}}_z},\mathfrak{K}_{\breve{\mathfrak{g}}_z})$ $(i=1,2,\ldots,\mathfrak{q})$ be the specialists/decision experts for the ɋ-ROFNs $\widetilde{\Xi}_i=(\breve{\Theta}_i,\mathfrak{K}_i)(i=1,2,\ldots,n)$. $\hat{\omega}'=(\hat{\omega}'_1,\hat{\omega}'_2,\ldots,\hat{\omega}'_{\mathfrak{q}})^T$ and $\hat{\omega}=(\hat{\omega}_1,\omega_2,\ldots,\hat{\omega}_n)^T$ are the weight vectors of specialists/decision experts and $\widetilde{\Xi}_i$, respectively and $\hat{\omega}'_i\in[0,1]$, $\sum_{i=1}^{\mathfrak{q}}\hat{\omega}'_i=1$, $\hat{\omega}_i\in[0,1]$, and $\sum_{i=1}^{n}\hat{\omega}_i=1$, then the GGQROFWG-operator is determined as,*

$$GGQROFWG((\widetilde{\Xi}_1,\widetilde{\Xi}_2,\ldots,\widetilde{\Xi}_n),(\mathfrak{g}_1,\breve{\mathfrak{g}}_2,\ldots,\breve{\mathfrak{g}}_{\mathfrak{q}}))=\mathfrak{q}\text{-}ROFWG(\breve{\mathfrak{g}}_1,\breve{\mathfrak{g}}_2,\ldots,\breve{\mathfrak{g}}_{\mathfrak{q}})\otimes\mathfrak{q}\text{-}ROFWG(\widetilde{\Xi}_1,\widetilde{\Xi}_2,\ldots,\widetilde{\Xi}_n)$$
$$=\left(\sqrt[\mathfrak{q}]{\widetilde{\prod}_{z=1}^{\mathfrak{q}}(\breve{\Theta}_{\breve{\mathfrak{g}}_z}^{\hat{\omega}'_z})^{\mathfrak{q}}+\widetilde{\prod}_{i=1}^{n}(\breve{\Theta}_i^{\hat{\omega}_i})^{\mathfrak{q}}-\widetilde{\prod}_{z=1}^{\mathfrak{q}}(\breve{\Theta}_{\breve{\mathfrak{g}}_z}^{\omega'_z})^{\mathfrak{q}}.\widetilde{\prod}_{i=1}^{n}(\breve{\Theta}_i^{\hat{\omega}_i})^{\mathfrak{q}}},\right.$$
$$\left.\sqrt[\mathfrak{q}]{1-\widetilde{\prod}_{z=1}^{\mathfrak{q}}(1-(\mathfrak{K}_{\breve{\mathfrak{g}}_z})^{\mathfrak{q}})^{\hat{\omega}'_z}}.\sqrt[\mathfrak{q}]{1-\widetilde{\prod}_{i=1}^{n}(1-(\mathfrak{K}_i)^{\mathfrak{q}})^{\hat{\omega}_i}}\right)$$

Proof. We will use mathematical induction.

For $\mathfrak{n} = 2$,

$$GGQROFWG((\widetilde{\Xi}_1, \widetilde{\Xi}_2), (\breve{\mathfrak{g}}_1, \mathfrak{g}_2, \ldots, \breve{\mathfrak{g}}_{\mathfrak{q}})) = \mathfrak{q}\text{-ROFWG}(\breve{\mathfrak{g}}_1, \breve{\mathfrak{g}}_2, \ldots, \breve{\mathfrak{g}}_{\mathfrak{q}}) \otimes \mathfrak{q}\text{-ROFWG}(\widetilde{\Xi}_1, \widetilde{\Xi}_2)$$

$$= \left(\widetilde{\prod}_{k=1}^{\mathfrak{n}} \breve{\Theta}_{\breve{\mathfrak{g}}_z}^{\hat{\omega}'_z}, \sqrt[\mathfrak{q}]{1 - \widetilde{\prod}_{z=1}^{\mathfrak{q}} (1 - (\mathfrak{K}_{\breve{\mathfrak{g}}_z})^{\mathfrak{q}})^{\hat{\omega}'_z}}\right) \otimes (\widetilde{\Xi}_1^{\hat{\omega}_1} \otimes \widetilde{\Xi}_2^{\hat{\omega}_2})$$

$$= \left(\widetilde{\prod}_{k=1}^{\mathfrak{n}} \breve{\Theta}_{\breve{\mathfrak{g}}_z}^{\hat{\omega}'_z}, \sqrt[\mathfrak{q}]{1 - \widetilde{\prod}_{z=1}^{\mathfrak{q}} (1 - (\mathfrak{K}_{\breve{\mathfrak{g}}_z})^{\mathfrak{q}})^{\hat{\omega}'_z}}\right)$$

$$\otimes \left(\breve{\Theta}_1^{\hat{\omega}_1}.\breve{\Theta}_2^{\hat{\omega}_2}, \sqrt[\mathfrak{q}]{1 - (1 - \mathfrak{K}_1^{\mathfrak{q}})^{\hat{\omega}_1}.(1 - \mathfrak{K}_2^{\mathfrak{q}})^{\hat{\omega}_2}}\right)$$

$$= \left(\sqrt[\mathfrak{q}]{\widetilde{\prod}_{k=1}^{\mathfrak{n}} (\breve{\Theta}_{\breve{\mathfrak{g}}_z}^{\hat{\omega}'_z})^{\mathfrak{q}} + (\breve{\Theta}_1^{\hat{\omega}_1}.\breve{\Theta}_2^{\hat{\omega}_2})^{\mathfrak{q}} - \widetilde{\prod}_{k=1}^{\mathfrak{n}} (\breve{\Theta}_{\breve{\mathfrak{g}}_z}^{\hat{\omega}'_z})^{\mathfrak{q}}.(\breve{\Theta}_1^{\hat{\omega}_1}.\breve{\Theta}_2^{\hat{\omega}_2})^{\mathfrak{q}}},\right.$$

$$\left.\sqrt[\mathfrak{q}]{1 - \widetilde{\prod}_{z=1}^{\mathfrak{q}} (1 - (\mathfrak{K}_{\breve{\mathfrak{g}}_z})^{\mathfrak{q}})^{\hat{\omega}'_z}}. \sqrt[\mathfrak{q}]{1 - (1 - \mathfrak{K}_1^{\mathfrak{q}})^{\hat{\omega}_1}.(1 - \mathfrak{K}_2^{\mathfrak{q}})^{\hat{\omega}_2}}\right)$$

$$= \left(\sqrt[\mathfrak{q}]{\widetilde{\prod}_{z=1}^{\mathfrak{q}} (\breve{\Theta}_{\breve{\mathfrak{g}}_z}^{\hat{\omega}'_z})^{\mathfrak{q}} + \widetilde{\prod}_{i=1}^{2} (\breve{\Theta}_i^{\hat{\omega}_i})^{\mathfrak{q}} - \widetilde{\prod}_{z=1}^{\mathfrak{q}} (\breve{\Theta}_{\breve{\mathfrak{g}}_z}^{\hat{\omega}'_z})^{\mathfrak{q}}.\widetilde{\prod}_{i=1}^{2} (\breve{\Theta}_i^{\hat{\omega}_i})^{\mathfrak{q}}},\right.$$

$$\left.\sqrt[\mathfrak{q}]{1 - \widetilde{\prod}_{z=1}^{\mathfrak{q}} (1 - (\mathfrak{K}_{\breve{\mathfrak{g}}_z})^{\mathfrak{q}})^{\hat{\omega}'_z}}. \sqrt[\mathfrak{q}]{1 - \widetilde{\prod}_{i=1}^{2} (1 - (\mathfrak{K}_i)^{\mathfrak{q}})^{\hat{\omega}_i}}\right)$$

For $\mathfrak{n} = 2$, result is satisfied.
Suppose result is true for $\mathfrak{n} = \mathfrak{k}$,

$$GGQROFWG((\widetilde{\Xi}_1, \widetilde{\Xi}_2, \ldots, \widetilde{\Xi}_k), (\breve{\mathfrak{g}}_1, \breve{\mathfrak{g}}_2, \ldots, \breve{\mathfrak{g}}_{\mathfrak{q}})) = \mathfrak{q}\text{-ROFWG}(\breve{\mathfrak{g}}_1, \breve{\mathfrak{g}}_2, \ldots, \breve{\mathfrak{g}}_{\mathfrak{q}}) \otimes \mathfrak{q}\text{-ROFWG}(\widetilde{\Xi}_1, \widetilde{\Xi}_2, \ldots, \widetilde{\Xi}_k)$$

$$= \left(\sqrt[\mathfrak{q}]{\widetilde{\prod}_{z=1}^{\mathfrak{q}} (\breve{\Theta}_{\breve{\mathfrak{g}}_z}^{\hat{\omega}'_z})^{\mathfrak{q}} + \widetilde{\prod}_{i=1}^{\mathfrak{k}} (\breve{\Theta}_i^{\hat{\omega}_i})^{\mathfrak{q}} - \widetilde{\prod}_{z=1}^{\mathfrak{q}} (\breve{\Theta}_{\breve{\mathfrak{g}}_z}^{\hat{\omega}'_z})^{\mathfrak{q}}.\widetilde{\prod}_{i=1}^{\mathfrak{k}} (\breve{\Theta}_i^{\hat{\omega}_i})^{\mathfrak{q}}},\right.$$

$$\left.\sqrt[\mathfrak{q}]{1 - \widetilde{\prod}_{z=1}^{\mathfrak{q}} (1 - (\mathfrak{K}_{\breve{\mathfrak{g}}_z})^{\mathfrak{q}})^{\hat{\omega}'_z}}. \sqrt[\mathfrak{q}]{1 - \widetilde{\prod}_{i=1}^{\mathfrak{k}} (1 - (\mathfrak{K}_i)^{\mathfrak{q}})^{\hat{\omega}_i}},\right)$$

For $\mathfrak{n} = \mathfrak{k} + 1$, we will prove

$$GGQROFWG((\widetilde{\Xi}_1, \widetilde{\Xi}_2, \ldots, \widetilde{\Xi}_{k+1}), (\breve{\mathfrak{g}}_1, \breve{\mathfrak{g}}_2, \ldots, \breve{\mathfrak{g}}_{\mathfrak{q}})) = \mathfrak{q}\text{-ROFWG}(\breve{\mathfrak{g}}_1, \breve{\mathfrak{g}}_2, \ldots, \breve{\mathfrak{g}}_{\mathfrak{q}}) \otimes \mathfrak{q}\text{-ROFWG}(\widetilde{\Xi}_1, \widetilde{\Xi}_2, \ldots, \widetilde{\Xi}_{k+1})$$

$$= \left(\sqrt[\mathfrak{q}]{\widetilde{\prod}_{z=1}^{\mathfrak{q}} (\breve{\Theta}_{\breve{\mathfrak{g}}_z}^{\hat{\omega}'_z})^{\mathfrak{q}} + \widetilde{\prod}_{i=1}^{\mathfrak{k}+1} (\breve{\Theta}_i^{\hat{\omega}_i})^{\mathfrak{q}} - \widetilde{\prod}_{z=1}^{\mathfrak{q}} (\breve{\Theta}_{\breve{\mathfrak{g}}_z}^{\hat{\omega}'_z})^{\mathfrak{q}}.\widetilde{\prod}_{i=1}^{\mathfrak{k}+1} (\breve{\Theta}_i^{\hat{\omega}_i})^{\mathfrak{q}}},\right.$$

$$\left.\sqrt[\mathfrak{q}]{1 - \widetilde{\prod}_{z=1}^{\mathfrak{q}} (1 - (\mathfrak{K}_{\breve{\mathfrak{g}}_z})^{\mathfrak{q}})^{\hat{\omega}'_z}}. \sqrt[\mathfrak{q}]{1 - \widetilde{\prod}_{i=1}^{\mathfrak{k}+1} (1 - (\mathfrak{K}_i)^{\mathfrak{q}})^{\hat{\omega}_i}}\right)$$

Therefore, the result satisfied for $\mathfrak{n} = \mathfrak{k} + 1$, under more than one specialist's/decision expert's preference. □

Example 26. *Let $\breve{\mathfrak{g}}_z = \{\breve{\mathfrak{g}}_1, \breve{\mathfrak{g}}_2, \breve{\mathfrak{g}}_3, \breve{\mathfrak{g}}_4\}$ be the group of four senior specialists/decision experts with weight vector $\hat{\omega}' = (0.1, 0.2, 0.3, 0.4)$, where $\breve{\mathfrak{g}}_1 = (0.7, 0.1)$, $\breve{\mathfrak{g}}_2 = (0.5, 0.7)$, $\mathfrak{g}_3 = (0.8, 0.4)$ and $\breve{\mathfrak{g}}_4 = (0.2, 0.3)$. Here we have four $\mathfrak{q}$-rung orthopair fuzzy numbers, $\widetilde{\Xi}_1 = (0.78, 0.45)$, $\widetilde{\Xi}_2 = (0.32, 0.56)$, $\widetilde{\Xi}_3 = (0.67, 0.33)$, and $\widetilde{\Xi}_4 = (0.87, 0.21)$ with associated weight vector $\hat{\omega} = (0.4, 0.3, 0.2, 0.1)$, here $\mathfrak{q} = 4$, then*

$$\sqrt[\mathfrak{q}]{\widetilde{\prod}_{z=1}^{\mathfrak{q}} (\breve{\Theta}_{\mathfrak{g}_z}^{\hat{\omega}'_z})^{\mathfrak{q}} + \widetilde{\prod}_{i=1}^{\mathfrak{n}} (\breve{\Theta}_i^{\hat{\omega}_i})^{\mathfrak{q}} - \widetilde{\prod}_{z=1}^{\mathfrak{q}} (\breve{\Theta}_{\breve{\mathfrak{g}}_z}^{\hat{\omega}'_z})^{\mathfrak{q}}.\widetilde{\prod}_{i=1}^{\mathfrak{n}} (\breve{\Theta}_i^{\hat{\omega}_i})^{\mathfrak{q}}} = 0.615040$$

In addition,

$$\sqrt[\mathfrak{q}]{1 - \widetilde{\prod}_{z=1}^{\mathfrak{q}} (1 - (\mathfrak{K}_{\breve{\mathfrak{g}}_z})^{\mathfrak{q}})^{\hat{\omega}'_z}}. \sqrt[\mathfrak{q}]{1 - \widetilde{\prod}_{i=1}^{\mathfrak{n}} (1 - (\mathfrak{K}_i)^{\mathfrak{q}})^{\hat{\omega}_i}} = 0.236624$$

By Theorem 4.2, we have

$$GGQROFWG((\widetilde{\Xi}_1,\widetilde{\Xi}_2,\widetilde{\Xi}_3,\widetilde{\Xi}_4),(\breve{g}_1,\breve{g}_2,\breve{g}_3,\breve{g}_4)) = \acute{q}\text{-}ROFWG(\breve{g}_1,\breve{g}_2,\breve{g}_3,\breve{g}_4)\otimes\acute{q}\text{-}ROFWG(\widetilde{\Xi}_1,\widetilde{\Xi}_2,\widetilde{\Xi}_3,\widetilde{\Xi}_4)$$
$$=\left(\sqrt[\acute{q}]{\widetilde{\prod}_{z=1}^{\acute{q}}(\breve{\Theta}_{\breve{g}_z}^{\acute{\omega}'_z})^{\acute{q}}+\widetilde{\prod}_{i=1}^{n}(\breve{\Theta}_i^{\acute{\omega}_i})^{\acute{q}}-\widetilde{\prod}_{z=1}^{\acute{q}}(\breve{\Theta}_{\breve{g}_z}^{\acute{\omega}'_z})^{\acute{q}}.\widetilde{\prod}_{i=1}^{n}(\breve{\Theta}_i^{\acute{\omega}_i})^{\acute{q}}},\right.$$
$$\left.\sqrt[\acute{q}]{1-\widetilde{\prod}_{z=1}^{\acute{q}}(1-(\mathfrak{K}_{\breve{g}_z})^{\acute{q}})^{\acute{\omega}'_z}}.\sqrt[\acute{q}]{1-\widetilde{\prod}_{i=1}^{n}(1-(\mathfrak{K}_i)^{\acute{q}})^{\acute{\omega}_i}}\right)$$
$$=(0.615040, 0.236624)$$

Proposition 27. *Let $\widetilde{\Xi}_i = (\breve{\Theta}_i,\mathfrak{K}_i)(i = 1,2,\ldots,n)$ be a set of ḉ-ROFNs, there are $\acute{q}$ specialists/decision experts to verify the ḉ-ROF information. If $\breve{g}_z = (\breve{\Theta}_{g_z},\mathfrak{K}_{\breve{g}_z})$ $(i = 1,2,\ldots,\acute{q})$ be the specialists/decision experts for the ḉ-ROFNs $\widetilde{\Xi}_i$, then the GGQROFWG-operator has the given characteristics:*
1. (Idempotency) *If $\widetilde{\Xi}_i = \widetilde{\Xi}$ and $\breve{g}_z = \breve{g}$, for all i and z, then*

$$GGQROFWG((\widetilde{\Xi}_1,\widetilde{\Xi}_2,\ldots,\widetilde{\Xi}_n),(\breve{g}_1,\breve{g}_2,\ldots,\breve{g}_{\acute{q}})) = \breve{g}\otimes\widetilde{\Xi}$$

2. (Monotonicity) *Let $\widetilde{\Xi}_i^* = (\breve{\Theta}_i^*,\mathfrak{K}_i^*)(i = 1,2,\ldots,n)$ be a set of ḉ-ROFNs such that $\mathfrak{K}_i^* \le \mathfrak{K}_i$ and $\breve{\Theta}_i \le \breve{\Theta}_i^*$ for all i, then*

$$GGQROFWG((\widetilde{\Xi}_1,\widetilde{\Xi}_2,\ldots,\widetilde{\Xi}_n),(\breve{g}_1,\breve{g}_2,\ldots,\breve{g}_{\acute{q}})) \le GGQROFWG((\widetilde{\Xi}_1^*,\widetilde{\Xi}_2^*,\ldots,\widetilde{\Xi}_n^*),(\breve{g}_1,\breve{g}_2,\ldots,\breve{g}_{\acute{q}}))$$

3. (Commutativity) *Let $\widetilde{\Xi}_i = (\breve{\Theta}_i,\mathfrak{K}_i)$ and $\widetilde{\Xi}_i^* = (\mathfrak{K}_i{}^*,\breve{\Theta}_i^*)(i = 1,2,\ldots,n)$ be two sets of n ḉ-ROFNs such that $\widetilde{\Xi}_i^*$ is any permutation of $\widetilde{\Xi}_i$, then*

$$GGQROFWG((\widetilde{\Xi}_1,\widetilde{\Xi}_2,\ldots,\widetilde{\Xi}_n),(\breve{g}_1,\breve{g}_2,\ldots,\breve{g}_{\acute{q}})) = GGQROFWG((\widetilde{\Xi}_1^*,\widetilde{\Xi}_2^*,\ldots,\widetilde{\Xi}_n^*),(\breve{g}_1,\breve{g}_2,\ldots,\breve{g}_{\acute{q}}))$$

4. *If the preference of another decision maker to the assessed object is considered to be $\breve{g}_z = (0,1)$ for all z, then the GGQROFWG operator becomes the ḉ-ROFWG-operator.*
5. *If the preference of another decision maker to the assessed object is considered to be $\breve{g}_z = (1,0)$ for all z, then the GGQROFWG operator provides the value (1,0).*

Proof. Here we leave proof. □

5.2. Group-Generalized ḉ-ROF Ordered Weighted Geometric Operator

Definition 28. *Suppose there are $\acute{q}$ specialists/decision experts to verify the ḉ-ROF information. Let $\breve{g}_z = (\breve{\Theta}_{\breve{g}_z},\mathfrak{K}_{\breve{g}_z})$ $(i = 1,2,\ldots,\acute{q})$ be the specialists/decision experts for the ḉ-ROFNs $\widetilde{\Xi}_i = (\breve{\Theta}_i,\mathfrak{K}_i)$ $(i = 1,2,\ldots,n)$, then the GGQROFOWG-operator is described as,*

$$GGQROFOWG((\widetilde{\Xi}_1,\widetilde{\Xi}_2,\ldots,\widetilde{\Xi}_n),(\breve{g}_1,\breve{g}_2,\ldots,\breve{g}_{\acute{q}})) = \acute{q}\text{-}ROFWG(\breve{g}_1,\breve{g}_2,\ldots,\breve{g}_{\acute{q}})\otimes\acute{q}\text{-}ROFOWG(\widetilde{\Xi}_1,\widetilde{\Xi}_2,\ldots,\widetilde{\Xi}_n)$$

Theorem 29. *Let $\acute{q}$ be the number of specialists/decision experts to verify the ḉ-ROF information. Let $\breve{g}_z = (\breve{\Theta}_{\breve{g}_z},\mathfrak{K}_{\breve{g}_z})$ $(i = 1,2,\ldots,\acute{q})$ be the specialists/decision experts for the ḉ-ROFNs $\widetilde{\Xi}_i = (\breve{\Theta}_i,\mathfrak{K}_i)$ $(i = 1,2,\ldots,n)$. $\omega' = (\acute{\omega}'_1,\acute{\omega}'_2,\ldots,\acute{\omega}'_{\acute{q}})^T$, $\acute{\omega} = (\acute{\omega}_1,\acute{\omega}_2,\ldots,\omega_n)^T$ are the weight vectors of specialists/decision makers and $\widetilde{\Xi}_i$ respectively and $\acute{\omega}'_i \in [0,1]$, $\sum_{i=1}^{\acute{q}}\acute{\omega}'_i = 1$, $\acute{\omega}_i \in [0,1]$, $\sum_{i=1}^{n}\acute{\omega}_i = 1$, then the GGQROFOWG-operator is described as*

$$GGQROFOWG((\widetilde{\Xi}_1,\widetilde{\Xi}_2,\ldots,\widetilde{\Xi}_n),(\breve{g}_1,\breve{g}_2,\ldots,\breve{g}_{\acute{q}})) = \acute{q}\text{-}ROFWG(\breve{g}_1,\breve{g}_2,\ldots,\breve{g}_{\acute{q}})\otimes\acute{q}\text{-}ROFOWG(\widetilde{\Xi}_1,\widetilde{\Xi}_2,\ldots,\widetilde{\Xi}_n)$$
$$=\left(\sqrt[\acute{q}]{\widetilde{\prod}_{z=1}^{\acute{q}}(\breve{\Theta}_{\breve{g}_z}^{\omega'_z})^{\acute{q}}+\widetilde{\prod}_{i=1}^{n}(\breve{\Theta}_{\sigma(i)}^{\acute{\omega}_i})^{\acute{q}}-\widetilde{\prod}_{z=1}^{\acute{q}}(\breve{\Theta}_{\breve{g}_z}^{\acute{\omega}'_z})^{\acute{q}}.\widetilde{\prod}_{i=1}^{n}(\breve{\Theta}_{\sigma(i)}^{\acute{\omega}_i})^{\acute{q}}},\right.$$
$$\left.\sqrt[\acute{q}]{1-\widetilde{\prod}_{z=1}^{\acute{q}}(1-(\mathfrak{K}_{\breve{g}_z})^{\acute{q}})^{\acute{\omega}'_z}}.\sqrt[\acute{q}]{1-\widetilde{\prod}_{i=1}^{n}(1-(\mathfrak{K}_{\sigma(i)})^{\acute{q}})^{\acute{\omega}_i}}\right)$$

$(\sigma(1), \sigma(2), \ldots, \sigma(\mathfrak{n}))$ is a permutation of $(1, 2, \ldots, \mathfrak{n})$, such that $\widetilde{\Xi}_{\sigma(i-1)} \geq \widetilde{\Xi}_{\sigma(i)}$ for any i.

Proof. Proof is same as Theorem 4.2. □

Example 30. *Let $\breve{\mathfrak{g}}_z = \{\breve{\mathfrak{g}}_1, \mathfrak{g}_2, \breve{\mathfrak{g}}_3, \breve{\mathfrak{g}}_4\}$ be the group of four senior specialists/decision experts with weight vector $\hat{\omega}' = (0.1, 0.2, 0.3, 0.4)$, where $\breve{\mathfrak{g}}_1 = (0.7, 0.1)$, $\mathfrak{g}_2 = (0.5, 0.7)$, $\breve{\mathfrak{g}}_3 = (0.8, 0.4)$ and $\breve{\mathfrak{g}}_4 = (0.2, 0.3)$. Here we have four $\acute{\mathfrak{q}}$-rung orthopair fuzzy numbers. $\widetilde{\Xi}_1 = (0.78, 0.45)$, $\widetilde{\Xi}_2 = (0.32, 0.56)$, $\widetilde{\Xi}_3 = (0.67, 0.33)$, and $\widetilde{\Xi}_4 = (0.87, 0.21)$ with associated weight vector $\omega = (0.4, 0.3, 0.2, 0.1)$. Here $\acute{\mathfrak{q}} = 4$, first we find score functions of all $\widetilde{\Xi}_i$.*

$$\widetilde{\daleth}(\widetilde{\Xi}_1) = 0.329144$$
$$\widetilde{\daleth}(\widetilde{\Xi}_2) = -0.087859$$
$$\widetilde{\daleth}(\widetilde{\Xi}_3) = 0.189652$$
$$\widetilde{\daleth}(\widetilde{\Xi}_4) = 0.570952$$

On the behalf of score functions, $\widetilde{\Xi}_{\sigma(1)} = \widetilde{\Xi}_4, \widetilde{\Xi}_{\sigma(2)} = \widetilde{\Xi}_1, \widetilde{\Xi}_{\sigma(3)} = \widetilde{\Xi}_3$, and $\widetilde{\Xi}_{\sigma(4)} = \widetilde{\Xi}_2$, then

$$\sqrt[\acute{\mathfrak{q}}]{\widetilde{\prod}_{z=1}^{\acute{\mathfrak{q}}} (\breve{\Theta}_{\breve{\mathfrak{g}}_z}^{\hat{\omega}'_z})^{\acute{\mathfrak{q}}} + \widetilde{\prod}_{i=1}^{n} (\breve{\Theta}_{\sigma(i)}^{\omega_i})^{\acute{\mathfrak{q}}} - \widetilde{\prod}_{z=1}^{\acute{\mathfrak{q}}} (\breve{\Theta}_{\breve{\mathfrak{g}}_z}^{\hat{\omega}'_z})^{\acute{\mathfrak{q}}} . \widetilde{\prod}_{i=1}^{n} (\breve{\Theta}_{\sigma(i)}^{\hat{\omega}_i})^{\acute{\mathfrak{q}}}} = 0.424947$$

In addition,

$$\sqrt[\acute{\mathfrak{q}}]{1 - \widetilde{\prod}_{z=1}^{\acute{\mathfrak{q}}} (1 - (\mathfrak{K}_{\breve{\mathfrak{g}}_z})^{\acute{\mathfrak{q}}})^{\hat{\omega}'_z}} . \sqrt[\acute{\mathfrak{q}}]{1 - \widetilde{\prod}_{i=1}^{n} (1 - (\mathfrak{K}_{\sigma(i)})^{\acute{\mathfrak{q}}})^{\hat{\omega}_i}} = 0.201330$$

By Theorem 4.6, we have

$$\begin{aligned} &GGQROFOWG((\widetilde{\Xi}_1, \widetilde{\Xi}_2, \widetilde{\Xi}_3, \widetilde{\Xi}_4), (\breve{\mathfrak{g}}_1, \breve{\mathfrak{g}}_2, \breve{\mathfrak{g}}_3, \breve{\mathfrak{g}}_4)) = \acute{\mathfrak{q}}\text{-}ROFWG(\mathfrak{g}_1, \breve{\mathfrak{g}}_2, \breve{\mathfrak{g}}_3, \breve{\mathfrak{g}}_4) \otimes \acute{\mathfrak{q}}\text{-}ROFOWG(\widetilde{\Xi}_1, \widetilde{\Xi}_2, \widetilde{\Xi}_3, \widetilde{\Xi}_4) \\ &= \Bigg(\sqrt[\acute{\mathfrak{q}}]{\widetilde{\prod}_{z=1}^{\acute{\mathfrak{q}}} (\breve{\Theta}_{\breve{\mathfrak{g}}_z}^{\hat{\omega}'_z})^{\acute{\mathfrak{q}}} + \widetilde{\prod}_{i=1}^{n} (\breve{\Theta}_{\sigma(i)}^{\hat{\omega}_i})^{\acute{\mathfrak{q}}} - \widetilde{\prod}_{z=1}^{\acute{\mathfrak{q}}} (\breve{\Theta}_{\breve{\mathfrak{g}}_z}^{\hat{\omega}'_z})^{\acute{\mathfrak{q}}} . \widetilde{\prod}_{i=1}^{n} (\breve{\Theta}_{\sigma(i)}^{\hat{\omega}_i})^{\acute{\mathfrak{q}}}}, \\ &\sqrt[\acute{\mathfrak{q}}]{1 - \widetilde{\prod}_{z=1}^{\acute{\mathfrak{q}}} (1 - (\mathfrak{K}_{\breve{\mathfrak{g}}_z})^{\acute{\mathfrak{q}}})^{\hat{\omega}'_z}} . \sqrt[\acute{\mathfrak{q}}]{1 - \widetilde{\prod}_{i=1}^{n} (1 - (\mathfrak{K}_{\sigma(i)})^{\acute{\mathfrak{q}}})^{\hat{\omega}_i}} \Bigg) \\ &= (0.424947, 0.201330) \end{aligned}$$

Proposition 31. *Let $\widetilde{\Xi}_i = (\breve{\Theta}_i, \mathfrak{K}_i)(i = 1, 2, \ldots, n)$ be a set of $\acute{\mathfrak{q}}$-ROFNs, there are $\acute{\mathfrak{q}}$ specialists/decision to verify the $\acute{\mathfrak{q}}$-ROF information. Let $\breve{\mathfrak{g}}_z = (\breve{\Theta}_{\mathfrak{g}_z}, \mathfrak{K}_{\breve{\mathfrak{g}}_z})$ $(i = 1, 2, \ldots, \acute{\mathfrak{q}})$ be the specialists/decision for the $\acute{\mathfrak{q}}$-ROFNs $\widetilde{\Xi}_i$, then the GGQROFOWG-operator has the given characteristics:*

1. *(Idempotency)* *If $\widetilde{\Xi}_i = \widetilde{\breve{\Xi}}$ and $\breve{\mathfrak{g}}_z = \breve{\mathfrak{g}}$, for all i and z then*

$$GGQROFOWG((\widetilde{\Xi}_1, \widetilde{\Xi}_2, \ldots, \widetilde{\Xi}_n), (\breve{\mathfrak{g}}_1, \breve{\mathfrak{g}}_2, \ldots, \breve{\mathfrak{g}}_{\acute{\mathfrak{q}}})) = \breve{\mathfrak{g}} \otimes \widetilde{\Xi}$$

2. *(Monotonicity)* *Let $\widetilde{\Xi}_i^{\star} = (\breve{\Theta}_i^{\star}, \mathfrak{K}_i^{\star})(i = 1, 2, \ldots, n)$ be a set of $\acute{\mathfrak{q}}$-ROFNs such that $\mathfrak{K}_i^{\star} \leq \mathfrak{K}_i$ and $\breve{\Theta}_i \leq \breve{\Theta}_i^{\star}$ for all i, then*

$$GGQROFOWG((\widetilde{\Xi}_1, \widetilde{\Xi}_2, \ldots,, \widetilde{\Xi}_n), (\breve{\mathfrak{g}}_1, \breve{\mathfrak{g}}_2, \ldots, \breve{\mathfrak{g}}_{\acute{\mathfrak{q}}})) \leq GGQROFOWG((\widetilde{\Xi}_1^{\star}, \widetilde{\Xi}_2^{\star}, \ldots, \widetilde{\Xi}_n^{\star}), (\breve{\mathfrak{g}}_1, \breve{\mathfrak{g}}_2, \ldots, \breve{\mathfrak{g}}_{\acute{\mathfrak{q}}}))$$

3. *(Commutativity)* *Let $\widetilde{\Xi}_i = (\breve{\Theta}_i, \mathfrak{K}_i)(i = 1, 2, \ldots, n)$ and $\widetilde{\Xi}_i^{*} = (\breve{\Theta}_i^{*}, \mathfrak{K}_i^{*})(i = 1, 2, \ldots, n)$ be a two collection of n $\acute{\mathfrak{q}}$-ROFNs such that $\widetilde{\Xi}_i^{*}$ is any permutation of $\widetilde{\Xi}_i$, then*

$$GGQROFOWG((\widetilde{\Xi}_1, \widetilde{\Xi}_2, \ldots, \widetilde{\Xi}_n), (\breve{\mathfrak{g}}_1, \breve{\mathfrak{g}}_2, \ldots, \breve{\mathfrak{g}}_{\acute{\mathfrak{q}}})) = GGQROFOWG((\widetilde{\Xi}_1^{*}, \widetilde{\Xi}_2^{*}, \ldots, \widetilde{\Xi}_n^{*}), (\breve{\mathfrak{g}}_1, \breve{\mathfrak{g}}_2, \ldots, \breve{\mathfrak{g}}_{\acute{\mathfrak{q}}}))$$

4. *If the preference of the specialists/decision experts to the assessed object is considered to be* $\breve{\mathfrak{g}}_z = (0,1)$ *for all z, then the GGQROFOWG-operator becomes the* $\acute{\mathfrak{q}}$*-ROFOWG-operator.*
5. *If the preference of another decision maker to the assessed object is considered to be* $\breve{\mathfrak{g}}_z = (1,0)$ *for all z, then the GGQROFOWG-operator provides the value* $(1,0)$.

Proof. Here we leave the proof. □

5.3. Group-Generalized $\acute{\mathfrak{q}}$*-ROF Hybrid Geometric Operator*

Definition 32. *Suppose there are* $\acute{\mathfrak{q}}$ *specialists/decision experts to verify the* $\acute{\mathfrak{q}}$*-ROF information. Let* $\breve{\mathfrak{g}}_z = (\breve{\Theta}_{\breve{\mathfrak{g}}_z}, \mathfrak{K}_{\breve{\mathfrak{g}}_z})$ $(i = 1, 2, \ldots, \acute{\mathfrak{q}})$ *be the specialists/decision experts for the* $\acute{\mathfrak{q}}$*-ROFNs* $\widetilde{\Xi}_i = (\breve{\Theta}_i, \mathfrak{K}_i)(i = 1, 2, \ldots, \mathfrak{n})$*, then the GGQROFHG-operator is described as,*

$$GGQROFHG((\widetilde{\Xi}_1, \widetilde{\Xi}_2, \ldots, \widetilde{\Xi}_\mathfrak{n}), (\breve{\mathfrak{g}}_1, \breve{\mathfrak{g}}_2, \ldots, \breve{\mathfrak{g}}_{\acute{\mathfrak{q}}})) = \acute{\mathfrak{q}}\text{-}ROFWG(\breve{\mathfrak{g}}_1, \breve{\mathfrak{g}}_2, \ldots, \mathfrak{g}_{\acute{\mathfrak{q}}}) \otimes \acute{\mathfrak{q}}\text{-}ROFHG(\widetilde{\Xi}_1, \widetilde{\Xi}_2, \ldots, \widetilde{\Xi}_\mathfrak{n})$$

Theorem 33. *Let there be* $\acute{\mathfrak{q}}$ *specialists/decision experts to verify the* $\acute{\mathfrak{q}}$*-ROF information. Let* $\mathfrak{g}_z = (\breve{\Theta}_{\breve{\mathfrak{g}}_z}, \mathfrak{K}_{\breve{\mathfrak{g}}_z})$ $(i = 1, 2, \ldots, \acute{\mathfrak{q}})$ *be the specialists/decision experts for the* $\acute{\mathfrak{q}}$*-ROFNs* $\widetilde{\Xi}_i = (\breve{\Theta}_i, \mathfrak{K}_i)(i = 1, 2, \ldots, \mathfrak{n})$*,* $\hat{\omega}' = (\hat{\omega}'_1, \hat{\omega}'_2, \ldots, , \hat{\omega}'_{\acute{\mathfrak{q}}})^T$*, and* $\hat{\omega} = (\hat{\omega}_1, \hat{\omega}_2, \ldots, \omega_\mathfrak{n})^T$ *are the weight vectors of specialists/observers and* $\widetilde{\Xi}_i$*, respectively and* $\hat{\omega}'_i \in [0,1]$*,* $\sum_{i=1}^{\acute{\mathfrak{q}}} \omega'_i = 1$*,* $\hat{\omega}_i \in [0,1]$*, and* $\sum_{i=1}^{\mathfrak{n}} \hat{\omega}_i = 1$*, then GGQROFHG-operator is described as*

$$\begin{aligned}
GGQROFHG((\widetilde{\Xi}_1, \widetilde{\Xi}_2, \ldots, \widetilde{\Xi}_\mathfrak{n}), (\mathfrak{g}_1, \breve{\mathfrak{g}}_2, \ldots, aa\breve{\mathfrak{g}}_{\acute{\mathfrak{q}}})) &= \acute{\mathfrak{q}}\text{-}ROFWG(\breve{\mathfrak{g}}_1, \breve{\mathfrak{g}}_2, \ldots, \breve{\mathfrak{g}}_{\acute{\mathfrak{q}}}) \otimes \acute{\mathfrak{q}}\text{-}ROFHG(\widetilde{\Xi}_1, \widetilde{\Xi}_2, \ldots, \widetilde{\Xi}_\mathfrak{n}) \\
&= \Bigg(\sqrt[\acute{\mathfrak{q}}]{\widetilde{\prod}_{z=1}^{\acute{\mathfrak{q}}} (\breve{\Theta}_{\breve{\mathfrak{g}}_z}^{\hat{\omega}'_z})^{\acute{\mathfrak{q}}} + \prod_{i=1}^{\mathfrak{n}} (\breve{\Theta}_{\sigma(i)}^{\hat{\omega}_i})^{\acute{\mathfrak{q}}} - \widetilde{\prod}_{z=1}^{\acute{\mathfrak{q}}} (\breve{\Theta}_{\breve{\mathfrak{g}}_z}^{\hat{\omega}'_z})^{\acute{\mathfrak{q}}} . \widetilde{\prod}_{i=1}^{\mathfrak{n}} (\breve{\Theta}_{\sigma(i)}^{\hat{\omega}_i})^{\acute{\mathfrak{q}}}}, \\
&\quad \sqrt[\acute{\mathfrak{q}}]{1 - \widetilde{\prod}_{z=1}^{\acute{\mathfrak{q}}} (1 - (\mathfrak{K}_{\breve{\mathfrak{g}}_z})^{\acute{\mathfrak{q}}})^{\hat{\omega}'_z}} . \sqrt[\acute{\mathfrak{q}}]{1 - \widetilde{\prod}_{i=1}^{\mathfrak{n}} (1 - (\breve{\mathfrak{K}}_{\sigma(i)})^{\acute{\mathfrak{q}}})^{\hat{\omega}_i}} \Bigg)
\end{aligned}$$

Here $\breve{\widetilde{\Xi}}_i = \mathfrak{n}\xi_i\widetilde{\Xi}_i$*, n is the number of* $\acute{\mathfrak{q}}$*-ROFNs,* ξ_i *is a standard weight vector of* $\widetilde{\Xi}_i$*, and* $(\sigma(1), \sigma(2), \ldots, \sigma(\mathfrak{n}))$ *is a permutation of* $(1, 2, \ldots, \mathfrak{n})$*, such that* $\breve{\widetilde{\Xi}}_{\sigma(i-1)} \geq \breve{\widetilde{\Xi}}_{\sigma(i)}$ *for any* i.

Proof. Proof is the same as Theorem 4.2. □

Example 34. *Let* $\breve{\mathfrak{g}}_z = \{\breve{\mathfrak{g}}_1, \breve{\mathfrak{g}}_2, \mathfrak{g}_3, \breve{\mathfrak{g}}_4\}$ *be the group of four senior specialists/decision experts with weight vector* $\hat{\omega}' = (0.1, 0.2, 0.3, 0.4)$*, where* $\breve{\mathfrak{g}}_1 = (0.7, 0.1)$*,* $\mathfrak{g}_2 = (0.5, 0.7)$*,* $\breve{\mathfrak{g}}_3 = (0.8, 0.4)$*, and* $\breve{\mathfrak{g}}_4 = (0.2, 0.3)$*. Here we have four* $\acute{\mathfrak{q}}$*-rung orthopair fuzzy numbers.* $\widetilde{\Xi}_1 = (0.78, 0.45)$*,* $\widetilde{\Xi}_2 = (0.32, 0.56)$*,* $\widetilde{\Xi}_3 = (0.67, 0.33)$*, and* $\widetilde{\Xi}_3 = (0.67, 0.33)$ *with associated weight vector* $\hat{\omega} = (0.4, 0.3, 0.2, 0.1)$*. Here* $\acute{\mathfrak{q}} = 4$ *and a standard weight vector will be* $\xi_i = (0.2, 0.2, 0.3, 0.3)$*. First we find* $\breve{\widetilde{\Xi}}_i = n\xi_i\widetilde{\Xi}_i$ *for each* $\widetilde{\Xi}_i$*, then we find score functions of each* $\breve{\widetilde{\Xi}}_i$*.*

$$\breve{\widetilde{\Xi}}_1 = (0.745657, 0.527922)$$

$$\breve{\widetilde{\Xi}}_2 = (0.302716, 0.628854)$$

$$\breve{\widetilde{\Xi}}_3 = (0.697473, 0.264372)$$

$$\breve{\widetilde{\Xi}}_4 = (0.894329, 0.153696)$$

The score function will be,

$$\widetilde{\daleth}(\breve{\widetilde{\Xi}}_1) = 0.231466$$

$$\widetilde{\daleth}(\breve{\widetilde{\Xi}}_2) = -0.147989$$

$$\widetilde{\daleth}(\breve{\widetilde{\Xi}}_3) = -0.231766$$

$$\widetilde{\daleth}(\check{\widetilde{\Xi}}_3) = 0.639160$$

On the behalf of score functions, $\widetilde{\Xi}_{\sigma(1)} = \check{\widetilde{\Xi}}_4, \widetilde{\Xi}_{\sigma(2)} = \check{\widetilde{\Xi}}_3, \widetilde{\Xi}_{\sigma(3)} = \check{\widetilde{\Xi}}_1$, *and* $\widetilde{\Xi}_{\sigma(4)} = \check{\widetilde{\Xi}}_2$

$$\sqrt[\mathfrak{q}]{\widetilde{\prod}_{z=1}^{\mathfrak{q}} (\breve{\Theta}_{\breve{\mathfrak{g}}_z}^{\varpi'_z})^{\mathfrak{q}} + \widetilde{\prod}_{\mathfrak{i}=1}^{\mathfrak{n}} (\breve{\Theta}_{\sigma(\mathfrak{i})}^{\hat{\varpi}_{\mathfrak{i}}})^{\mathfrak{q}} - \widetilde{\prod}_{z=1}^{\mathfrak{q}} (\breve{\Theta}_{\breve{\mathfrak{g}}_z}^{\hat{\varpi}_z})^{\mathfrak{q}} \widetilde{\prod}_{\mathfrak{i}=1}^{n} (\breve{\Theta}_{\sigma(\mathfrak{i})}^{\hat{\varpi}_{\mathfrak{i}}})^{\mathfrak{q}}} = 0.287407$$

In addition,

$$\sqrt[\mathfrak{q}]{1 - \widetilde{\prod}_{z=1}^{\mathfrak{q}} (1 - (\mathfrak{K}_{\mathfrak{g}_z})^{\mathfrak{q}})^{\hat{\varpi}'_z}} . \sqrt[\mathfrak{q}]{1 - \widetilde{\prod}_{\mathfrak{i}=1}^{\mathfrak{n}} (1 - (\mathfrak{K}_{\sigma(\mathfrak{i})})^{\mathfrak{q}})^{\hat{\varpi}_{\mathfrak{i}}}} = 0.216261$$

By Theorem 4.10, we have

$$\begin{aligned} GGQROFHG((\widetilde{\Xi}_1, \widetilde{\Xi}_2, \widetilde{\Xi}_3, \widetilde{\Xi}_4), (\breve{\mathfrak{g}}_1, \breve{\mathfrak{g}}_2, \breve{\mathfrak{g}}_3, \breve{\mathfrak{g}}_4)) &= \mathfrak{q}\text{-}ROFWG(\breve{\mathfrak{g}}_1, \breve{\mathfrak{g}}_2, \breve{\mathfrak{g}}_3, \breve{\mathfrak{g}}_4) \otimes \mathfrak{q}\text{-}ROFHG(\widetilde{\Xi}_1, \widetilde{\Xi}_2, \widetilde{\Xi}_3, \widetilde{\Xi}_4) \\ &= \Bigg(\sqrt[\mathfrak{q}]{\widetilde{\prod}_{z=1}^{\mathfrak{q}} (\breve{\Theta}_{\breve{\mathfrak{g}}_z}^{\hat{\varpi}'_z})^{\mathfrak{q}} + \widetilde{\prod}_{\mathfrak{i}=1}^{\mathfrak{n}} (\breve{\Theta}_{\sigma(\mathfrak{i})}^{\hat{\varpi}_{\mathfrak{i}}})^{\mathfrak{q}} - \widetilde{\prod}_{z=1}^{\mathfrak{q}} (\breve{\Theta}_{\breve{\mathfrak{g}}_z}^{\hat{\varpi}'_z})^{\mathfrak{q}} . \widetilde{\prod}_{\mathfrak{i}=1}^{\mathfrak{n}} (\breve{\Theta}_{\sigma(\mathfrak{i})}^{\hat{\varpi}_{\mathfrak{i}}})^{\mathfrak{q}}}, \\ &\quad \sqrt[\mathfrak{q}]{1 - \widetilde{\prod}_{z=1}^{\mathfrak{q}} (1 - (\mathfrak{K}_{\breve{\mathfrak{g}}_z})^{\mathfrak{q}})^{\hat{\varpi}'_z}} . \sqrt[\mathfrak{q}]{1 - \widetilde{\prod}_{\mathfrak{i}=1}^{\mathfrak{n}} (1 - (\mathfrak{K}_{\sigma(\mathfrak{i})})^{\mathfrak{q}})^{\hat{\varpi}_{\mathfrak{i}}}} \Bigg) \\ &= (0.287407, 0.216261) \end{aligned}$$

The following observation are taken from the definition of GGQROFHG-operator:

1. If the priorities of the specialists/decision experts to the assessed object are considered to be $\breve{\mathfrak{g}}_z = (0, 1)$ for all z, then the GGQROFHG-operator becomes the $\mathfrak{q}$-ROFHG-operator.
2. If the priorities of the specialists/decision to the assessed object is considered to be $\breve{\mathfrak{g}}_z = (1, 0)$ for all z, then the GQROFHG-operator provides the value $(1, 0)$.
3. If $\zeta = (\frac{1}{n}, \frac{1}{n}, \ldots, \frac{1}{n})^T$, then the GGQROFHG-operator reduces to GQROFWG-operator.
4. If $\hat{\varpi} = (\frac{1}{n}, \frac{1}{n}, \ldots, \frac{1}{n})^T$, then the GGQROFHG-operator reduces to GQROFOWG-operator.

6. Multi-Attribute Decision-Making Method With Application Based On Group-Generalized Parameter

In this section, the provided method examines MADM challenges, in accordance with proposed aggregation operators. To illustrate the MADM technique efficiently, a numerical demonstration is also discussed in Algorithm 1.

6.1. Methodology

Suppose $\Omega = \{\breve{\mathbb{U}}_1, \breve{\mathbb{U}}_2, \ldots, \breve{\mathbb{U}}_m\}$ is a collection of universal elements, $\mathcal{C} = \{\lambda_1, \lambda_2, \ldots, \lambda_n\}$ be a collection of evaluation criteria/attributes and $\hat{\varpi} = \{\varpi_1, \hat{\varpi}_2, \ldots, \hat{\varpi}_n\}$ is the weight vector, in a such way that $\hat{\varpi}_j \in [0, 1]$ and $\sum_{j=1}^{n} \hat{\varpi}_j = 1$, $(j = 1, 2, \ldots, n)$. A universal element on the evaluation attribute is assessed by the specialist and the assessment values should be in $\mathfrak{q}$-ROFNs. Suppose that $(\Omega_{ij})_{m \times n} = (\breve{\Theta}_{ij}, \mathfrak{K}_{ij})_{m \times n}$ is a matrix characterized by decision makers. Here $\breve{\Theta}_{ij}$ and $\mathfrak{K}_{ij}$ demonstrates the degree of appreciation and non-appreciation corresponding to alternatives $\breve{\mathbb{U}}_{\mathfrak{i}}$ to the evaluation attribute λ_j respectively. To make the situation more credible, consider a group of different specialists/decision experts $\eth = \{\breve{\mathfrak{g}}_1, \breve{\mathfrak{g}}_2, \ldots, \breve{\mathfrak{g}}_{\mathfrak{l}}\}$ with weight vector $w' = \{w'_1, w'_2, \ldots, w'_{\mathfrak{l}}\}$ satisfying $w'_k > 0$, $k = (1, 2, \ldots \mathfrak{l})$ and $\sum\limits_{k=1}^{n} w'_{\mathfrak{i}} = 1$. These decision experts provide their evaluation regarding the priority for each alternative in the terms of $\mathfrak{q}$-ROFNs indicated by $\mathfrak{g}_k = (\breve{\Theta}_{\breve{\mathfrak{g}}_k}, \mathfrak{K}_{\breve{\mathfrak{g}}_k})$ $(k = 1, 2, \ldots, \mathfrak{l})$. To solve the MADM problems, the steps of the algorithm are in the following manner.

Algorithm 1:

Step 1: Take the experts point of view corresponding to each alternative over specific evaluation attribute in terms of ɋ́-ROFNs and then produce a decision matrix $[\pounds]_{m\times n} = (\breve{\Theta}_{ij}, \mathfrak{K}_{ij})_{m\times n}$.
If normalization of decision matrix is necessary then normalize the decision matrix.
If evaluation attributes are of different categories like cost and benefit, then we normalize the decision matrix. By normalizing the decision matrix we handle all evaluation attributes in a similar manner. Apart from that, distinct evaluation attributes need to be aggregate in distinct manners.

Step 2: According to the idea of generalized parameter, collect the priorities of the group of other specialists/decision experts for every alternative and then acquire a GP matrix $[\mho]_{m\times l} = (\breve{\Theta}_{\breve{\mathfrak{g}}_{ik}}, \mathfrak{K}_{\breve{\mathfrak{g}}_{ik}})_{m\times l}$ $(k = 1, 2, \ldots, l)$.

Step 3: Add the matrices derived in the first two steps to design a new structure $[\beta]_{m\times(n+k)}$ row-wise, which provides the decision makers evaluation for each universal element over the evaluation attribute under GPs.

Step 4: By using GGQROFWG-operator, we aggregate the efficiency of each universal element of the matrix $[\beta]_{m\times(n+k)}$ row-wise to achieve entire execution and it is represented by $\aleph_i$.
Here, we can also use GGQROFOWG-operator and GGQROFHG-operator.

Step 5: Compute the score functions of all aggregated values, denoted by $\aleph_i$.

Step 6: According to the score values, give the order of priority to all $\aleph_i$ $(i = 1, 2, \ldots, m)$ in descending order and choose an universal element with the high score value, calculated by proposed aggregation operators.

The flow chart of proposed Algorithm is given by Figure 2.

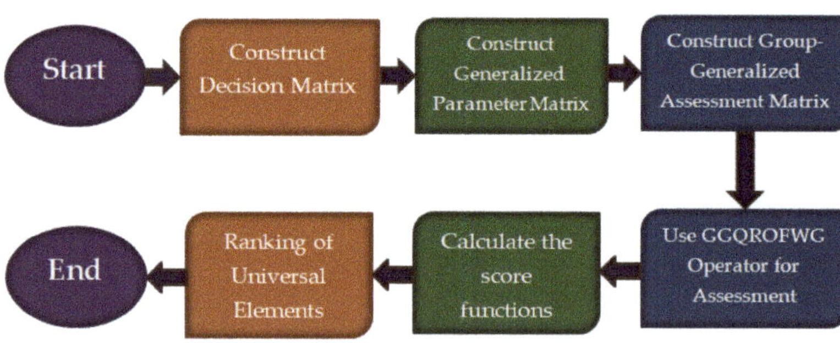

Figure 2. Flow chart of Algorithm.

6.2. Case Study

Water is classified among the fundamental life-sustaining needs. If there is no water on the planet earth then life is impossible. However, it is a sad fact that we are not taking appropriate actions for preservation and protection of our natural endowments. Even among the other natural endowments we have, water has the most significance. Currently, Pakistan is facing several problems but possibly the most challenging is the water scarcity. As reported by International Monetary Fund (IMF), Pakistan has 3rd position confronting serious deficiency of water. The requirement of water is escalating, as population of Pakistan is rapidly growing. Therefore, we need more water for agricultural and domestic use. The historical water demands by sector are given in Figure 3. Currently, about 40 percent of Pakistanis do not have availability of fresh water and are influenced by contaminated water mainly polluted by sewerage, pesticides, by fertilizer, and industrial waste water (source: jworldtimes.com). It should be pointed out that while in the 1950s the accessibility of water was nearly 5000 m^3 per year, it is now reduced to below 1000 m^3, that is worldwide limit of shortage of water. From 2009, per annum water reduction is 1500 cubic meters per capita to only 1017 cubic meters (source: tribune.com.pk). The comparison of population and water availability in Pakistan is shown in Figure 4.

One of the main causes of this problem is the lack of actions in water loss management. Due to bad administration and mismanagement, about 30 million acre feet (MAF) of water is wasted. Owing to the fact that, the water accessibility in Pakistan is uniformly decreasing. In May 2018, the "Pakistan Council of Research in water Resources" (PCRWR) declared that, there will be short or no availability of clean water in the country in 2025 (source: jworldtimes.com). The situation of water losses in irrigation systems in Pakistan is shown in Figure 5.

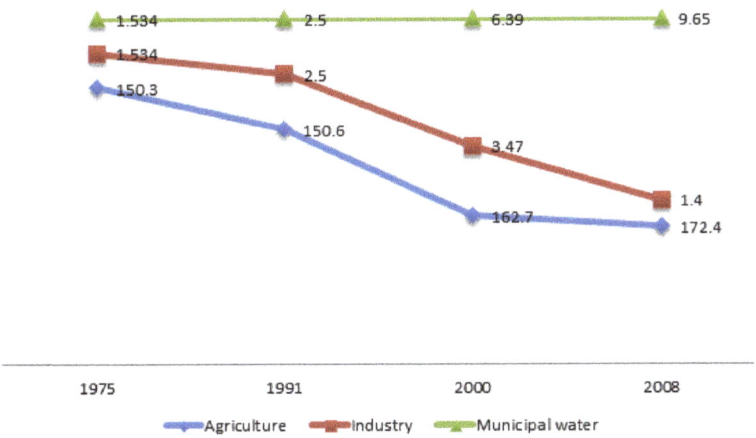

Figure 3. Historical water demands (source: www.undp.org).

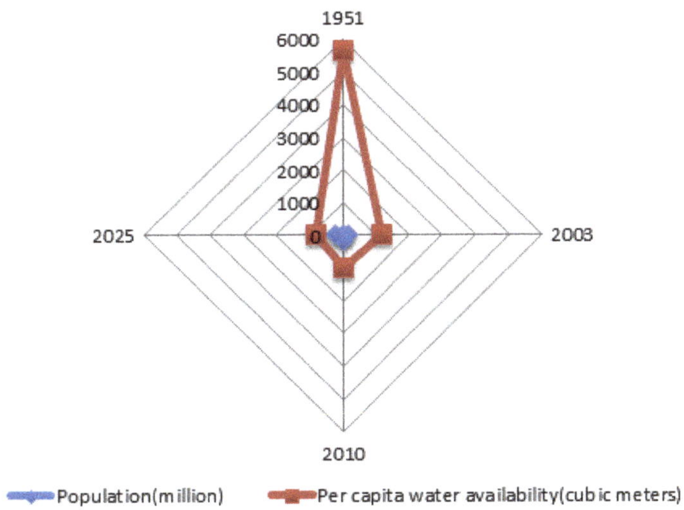

Figure 4. Population vs. water availability in Pakistan (source: pcwr.gov.pk).

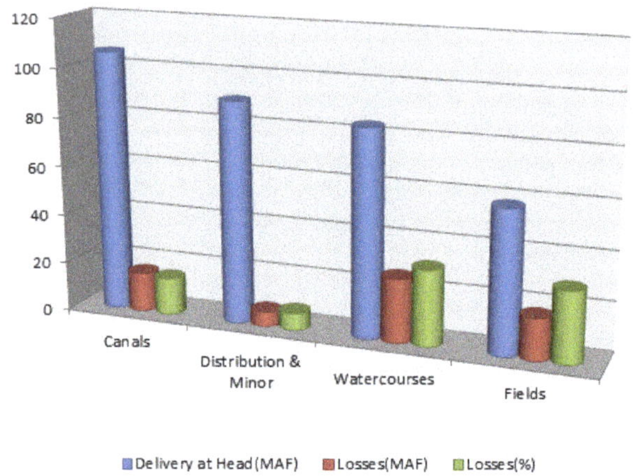

Figure 5. Water losses in an irrigation system (Source: Final PAS water 2019 (pcrwr.gov.pk)).

An adequate and efficient water loss management needs to be considered as a primary objective in improvement of drinkable supply of water. Across the board, policy makers/decision experts need to be aware that any strategy to control water loss in order to be effective must be a continuous activity based on a long term strategy. The success of the strategy will necessarily rely upon the engagement and devotion at every stage throughout the service and obviously the acceptance of suitable policies and methods. The advantages of strategy to control the loss of water could be summarized as follows:

(1) Rescuing an affected and precious expedient.
(2) Growing the effectiveness of available systems.
(3) Retarding enormous financial assets of infrastructure.
(4) Increasing the average life span of the systems.
(5) Increasing the earnings for the service of water.
(6) Reduction of energy demands.
(7) Improvement in Carbon Footprint of the service.

The fundamental goal of this investigation is to construct a comprehensive structure of strategies to recognize and emphasize the suitable strategy to overcome the water loss problem. The selected strategy needs to be able to meet the goals and has compatibility with general policy of water sector particularly ensure the maximum supply, enhancing the water quality, preserving the accessible supply of water. Whereas the administration of losses of water is usually a complicated process of making decisions including various goals and potentials, the concerns of different involved persons as well as the demands of the amendable authorities must take into account to establish a well-organized scheme explicated by efficiently and with clarity. Current situation encompasses the participation of policy makers/decision experts who have a profound knowledge of the decision problem. The preferred strategies were originated from review of the literature on water loss management with specialists and policy makers and on the basis of domestic circumstances of region of interest, as given in Table 1. The considered strategies are established for water loss management in water distribution network. Particular provisions are usually established in persistent water distribution network, like leakage control. Some of the strategies are closely linked to the situation of recurring supply. To evaluate the efficiency of each strategy, the evaluation attributes (EA) are used. The significance of evaluation attributes need to be clear to recognize the most convenient strategy. The evaluation attributes are derived from review of literature [5,10], as given in Table 2.

Table 1. Explanation of strategies.

Code	Strategies	Explanation
$\mathbb{U}_1$	Pressure management	Managing pressure of system to the highest grade of service, guarantee the adequate and effective supply, while reducing useless or excessive pressures
$\mathbb{U}_2$	Management of assets for service lines	Replacement of mains and affected service lines
$\mathbb{U}_3$	Enhancing the repairing quality	To prevent repetition of explosions, and to minimize the harmful effects of breakdown of the service
$\mathbb{U}_4$	Monitoring of inefficient use of water service	Raising awareness of people through beneficial supervision and campaigning, to eradicate the improper utilization of water
$\mathbb{U}_5$	Leakage control	Adopt measures for identification and repair of leaks that have not indicated
$\mathbb{U}_6$	Water meters replacements	Installation of automatic water meters to eliminate water meters uncertainty

Table 2. Explanation of evaluation attributes.

Code	Evaluation Attributes	Explanation
$人_1$	Cost Figure	Related expenses for execution of alternatives
$人_2$	Benefit Period	Measurement of useful life expectancy of alternative
$人_3$	Energy Saved	If the alternative has ability to reduce the utilization of energy and discharges of green house gas
$人_4$	Supply Reliability	If the alternative has ability to save a sustained service and reduce supply hindrances
$人_5$	Flexibility	If the alternative has capacity of being adjusted to fulfill different requirements and imprecisions

6.3. Numerical Example

The demonstrative example of water loss management is presented to demonstrate the method. Let $\Omega = \{\mathbb{U}_1, \mathbb{U}_2, \mathbb{U}_3, \mathbb{U}_4, \mathbb{U}_5, \mathbb{U}_6\}$ be the collection of alternative, $\mathcal{C} = \{人_1, 人_2, 人_3, 人_4, 人_5\}$ be the collection of evaluation attributes as given in Table 1, Table 2, respectively, $\varpi = (0.1, 0.1, 0.2, 0.2, 0.4)^T$ are the associated weights assigned by different policy makers/decision experts from Pakistan Water and Power Development Authority (WAPDA) and take $\acute{q} = 3$. The policy makers/decision makers are asked to give their evaluation in terms of $\acute{q}$-ROFNs for each strategy against each evaluation criteria.

Step 1: According to the preferences of policy makers/decision experts for each alternative against the distinct evaluation attribute, construct the decision matrix $[\pounds]_{6\times5} = (\check{\Theta}_{ij}, \mathfrak{K}_{ij})_{6\times5}$, as given in Table 3.

Table 3. $\acute{q}$-rung orthopair fuzzy decision expert assessment matrix $[\pounds]_{6\times5}$.

$\Omega/\mathcal{C}$	$人_1$	$人_2$	$人_3$	$人_4$	$人_5$
$\mathbb{U}_1$	(0.67, 0.21)	(0.57, 0.11)	(0.86, 0.14)	(0.72, 0.21)	(0.62, 0.21)
$\mathbb{U}_2$	(0.35, 0.38)	(0.21, 0.68)	(0.51, 0.66)	(0.27, 0.38)	(0.72, 0.23)
$\mathbb{U}_3$	(0.41, 0.17)	(0.35, 0.45)	(0.67, 0.51)	(0.28, 0.78)	(0.72, 0.21)
$\mathbb{U}_4$	(0.13, 0.66)	(0.32, 0.31)	(0.35, 0.61)	(0.31, 0.52)	(0.81, 0.24)
$\mathbb{U}_5$	(0.67, 0.21)	(0.57, 0.32)	(0.86, 0.14)	(0.70, 0.20)	(0.72, 0.20)
$\mathbb{U}_6$	(0.46, 0.38)	(0.32, 0.68)	(0.62, 0.66)	(0.38, 0.28)	(0.81, 0.31)

Step 2: On each strategy, collect the preferences of group of three other specialists/experts of different environmental groups of Pakistan like, Pakistan Environmentalists Association (PEA), Society for conservation and protection of Environment (SCOPE), i.e., with a weight vector $(0.2, 0.3, 0.5)^T$ according to their experiences, that would be helpful in aggregation information. The corresponding generalized parameter matrix $[\mho]_{6\times3} = (\check{\Theta}_{\breve{g}_{ik}}, \mathfrak{K}_{\breve{g}_{ik}})_{6\times3}$. $(k = 1, 2, \ldots, l)$ is given in Table 4.

Table 4. ɋ-rung orthopair fuzzy generalized parameter preference matrix $[℧]_{6\times3}$.

Ω/℧	$\mathfrak{g}_1$	$\mathfrak{g}_2$	$\mathfrak{g}_3$
$\mathbb{U}_1$	(0.72, 0.25)	(0.68, 0.12)	(0.58, 0.22)
$\mathbb{U}_2$	(0.21, 0.35)	(0.35, 0.63)	(0.82, 0.26)
$\mathbb{U}_3$	(0.45, 0.26)	(0.35, 0.71)	(0.67, 0.52)
$\mathbb{U}_4$	(0.14, 0.62)	(0.25, 0.14)	(0.38, 0.27)
$\mathbb{U}_5$	(0.20, 0.17)	(0.31, 0.23)	(0.26, 0.25)
$\mathbb{U}_6$	(0.24, 0.13)	(0.32, 0.20)	(0.27, 0.13)

Step 3: By combining the evaluations of all specialists/policy makers, construct the matrix $[\beta]_{6\times(5+3)}$. (see Table 5)

Table 5. Group generalized ɋ-rung orthopair fuzzy assessment matrix $[\beta]_{6\times8}$.

	⅄$_1$	⅄$_2$	⅄$_3$	⅄$_4$
$\mathbb{U}_1$	(0.67, 0.21)	(0.57, 0.11)	(0.86, 0.14)	(0.72, 0.21)
$\mathbb{U}_2$	(0.35, 0.38)	(0.21, 0.68)	(0.51, 0.66)	(0.27, 0.38)
$\mathbb{U}_3$	(0.41, 0.17)	(0.35, 0.45)	(0.67, 0.51)	(0.28, 0.78)
$\mathbb{U}_4$	(0.13, 0.66)	(0.32, 0.31)	(0.35, 0.61)	(0.31, 0.52)
$\mathbb{U}_5$	(0.67, 0.21)	(0.57, 0.32)	(0.86, 0.14)	(0.70, 0.20)
$\mathbb{U}_6$	(0.46, 0.38)	(0.32, 0.68)	(0.62, 0.66)	(0.38, 0.28)
	⅄$_5$	$\mathfrak{g}_1$	$\mathfrak{g}_2$	$\mathfrak{g}_3$
$\mathbb{U}_1$	(0.62, 0.21)	(0.72, 0.25)	(0.68, 0.12)	(0.58, 0.22)
$\mathbb{U}_2$	(0.72, 0.23)	(0.21, 0.35)	(0.35, 0.63)	(0.82, 0.26)
$\mathbb{U}_3$	(0.34, 0.21)	(0.45, 0.26)	(0.35, 0.71)	(0.67, 0.52)
$\mathbb{U}_4$	(0.81, 0.24)	(0.14, 0.62)	(0.25, 0.14)	(0.38, 0.27)
$\mathbb{U}_5$	(0.72, 0.20)	(0.20, 0.17)	(0.31, 0.23)	(0.26, 0.25)
$\mathbb{U}_6$	(0.81, 0.31)	(0.24, 0.13)	(0.32, 0.20)	(0.27, 0.13)

Step 4: Calculate $\aleph_i$ for all ɋ-ROFNs using GGQROWG-operator. The results obtained by GGQROFOWG-operator and GGQROFHG-operator are also mentioned in Table 6. For GGQROFHG-operator, policy makers/decision experts will determine a standard weight vector $(0.4, 0.2, 0.2, 0.1, 0.1)$ in accordance with evaluation attributes to hybridize the specified information. The hybridization is slightly different method to choose the suitable strategy and very useful to identify the precise conclusions. Ranking can be obtained by using one of three given operators.

Table 6. Aggregated matrix by using aggregation operators.

	GGQROFWG	GGQROFOWG	GGQROFHG
$\mathbb{U}_1$	(0.789337, 0.040080)	(0.766308, 0.036567)	(0.740615, 0.079633)
$\mathbb{U}_2$	(0.581194, 0.227714)	(0.519988, 0.271544)	(0.382272, 0.357161)
$\mathbb{U}_3$	(0.565361, 0.310873)	(0.551443, 0.364875)	(0.539303, 0.239981)
$\mathbb{U}_4$	(0.460982, 0.194678)	(0.328874, 0.232439)	(0.343440, 0.246197)
$\mathbb{U}_5$	(0.383551, 0.049236)	(0.690241, 0.054126)	(0.629404, 0.090020)
$\mathbb{U}_6$	(0.585816, 0.077892)	(0.463008, 0.093438)	(0.447749, 0.097445)

Step 5: Calculate the score values for each $\aleph_i$, as given in Table 7.

Table 7. Score values of $\aleph_i$.

	GGQROFWG	GGQROFOWG	GGQROFHG
$\tilde{ℸ}(\aleph_1)$	0.491734	0.449948	0.405730
$\tilde{ℸ}(\aleph_2)$	0.184511	0.119768	0.010301
$\tilde{ℸ}(\aleph_3)$	0.150664	0.119110	0.143034
$\tilde{ℸ}(\aleph_4)$	0.090582	0.023012	0.025586
$\tilde{ℸ}(\aleph_5)$	0.056305	0.328694	0.248608
$\tilde{ℸ}(\aleph_6)$	0.200567	0.098442	0.088839

Step 6: The order of preferences of the alternatives by using GGQROPFWG-operaor, GGQROPFOWG-operator, and GGQROPFHG-operator are given in Table 8 and the graphical representations are given in Figures 6–8 respectively.

Table 8. Final ranking of alternatives.

Method	Ranking of Alternatives
GGQROFWG-operator	$\mathbb{U}_1 \succ \mathbb{U}_6 \succ \mathbb{U}_2 \succ \mathbb{U}_3 \succ \mathbb{U}_4 \succ \mathbb{U}_5$
GGQROFOWG-operator	$\mathbb{U}_1 \succ \mathbb{U}_5 \succ \mathbb{U}_2 \succ \mathbb{U}_3 \succ \mathbb{U}_6 \succ \mathbb{U}_4$
GGQROFHG-operator	$\mathbb{U}_1 \succ \mathbb{U}_5 \succ \mathbb{U}_3 \succ \mathbb{U}_6 \succ \mathbb{U}_4 \succ \mathbb{U}_2$

The final ranking shows that $\ddot{\alpha}_1$ is the best strategy to control the water loss. It should be emphasized that all aggregation operators provides nearby similar outcomes. By the reason of different techniques of provided aggregation operators, the little difference in the ranking of strategies can be observed but the optimal outcomes acquired from all proposed aggregation operators are precise and provide appropriate order of priority regarding the choice of suitable strategy. The highly preferred option is pressure management that is focused by policy makers/decision experts. The execution of this strategy comprises the formation of pressure zones to sustain the pressure range and the pressure would have to be restricted as required, by the use of pressure reducers. The main objective of this provided strategy is the inadequate explanation of pressure zones related with subsequent components: big difference in elevations which leads high level water pressure, leading finally to physical losses of water with breakage of pipes and irregular water supply, which is connected with highly esteemed pumping equipment, which leads to pressure relief and subsequently gives rise to the pipe bursts. The pressure management strategy is applied by many developed countries to control their water loss.

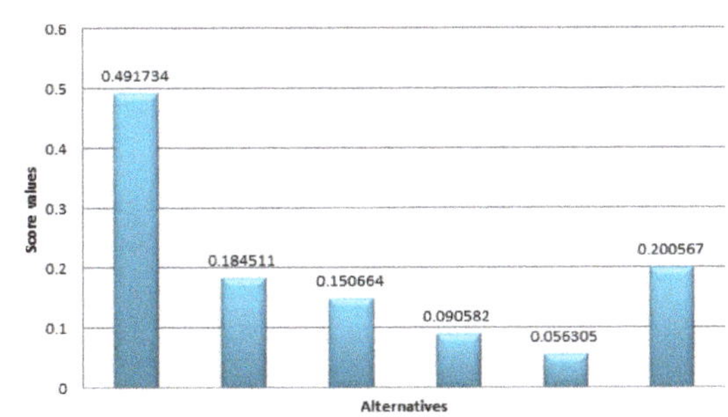

Figure 6. Score values obtained by GGQROFWG-operator.

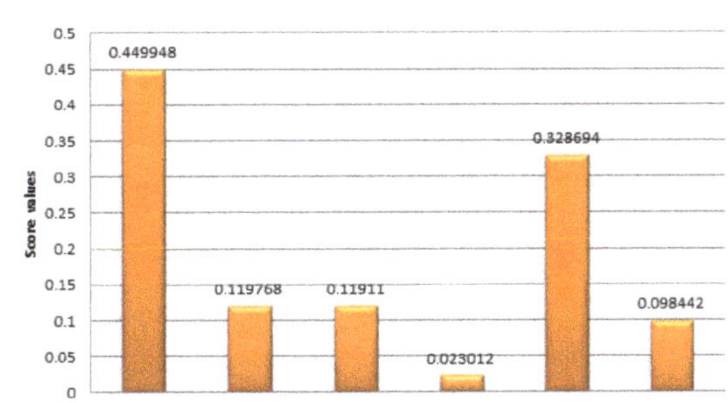

Figure 7. Score values obtained by GGQROFOWG-operator.

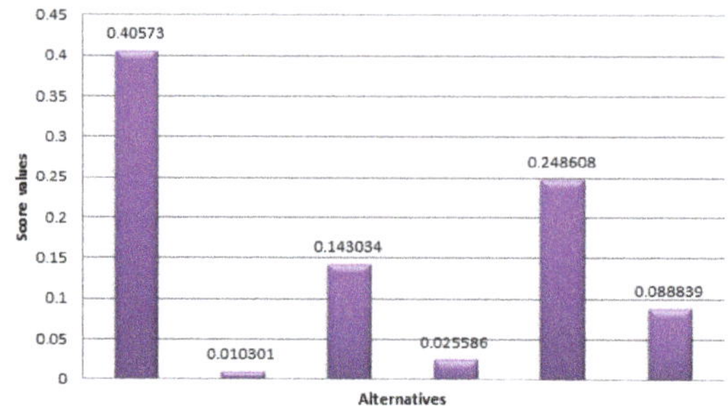

Figure 8. Score values obtained by GGQROFHG-operator.

6.4. Sensitive Analysis

In the presented section, we investigate the impact, by considering only one specialist/decision expert on decision analysis. If the analysis done on the recommendation of one specialist/decision expert regarding authenticity of the provided information, then we have the following conclusions:

(1) If only $\mathfrak{g}_1$ is to be considered, then by the above analysis we get the ranking $\breve{\mathbb{U}}_1 \succ \breve{\mathbb{U}}_5 \succ \breve{\mathbb{U}}_6 \succ \breve{\mathbb{U}}_3 \succ \breve{\mathbb{U}}_2 \succ \breve{\mathbb{U}}_4$. The score values are given in Figure 9.

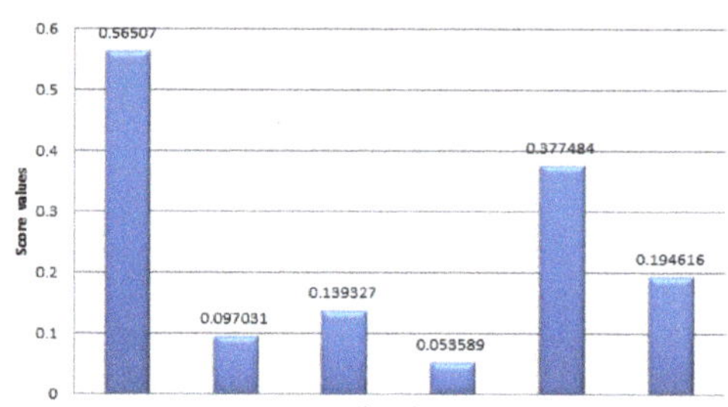

Figure 9. Score values when only $\breve{\mathfrak{g}}_1$ is considered.

(2) If only $\mathfrak{g}_2$ is to be considered, then by the above analysis, we get the ranking $\breve{\mathbb{U}}_1 \succ \breve{\mathbb{U}}_5 \succ \breve{\mathbb{U}}_6 \succ \breve{\mathbb{U}}_2 \succ \breve{\mathbb{U}}_4 \succ \breve{\mathbb{U}}_3$. The score values are given in Figure 10.

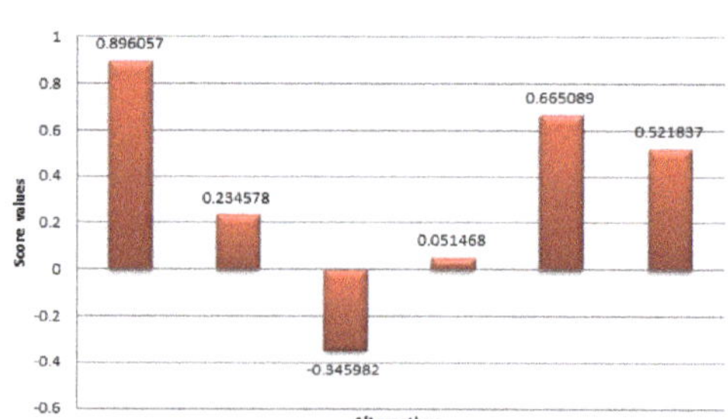

Figure 10. Score values when only $\breve{\mathfrak{g}}_2$ is considered.

(3) If only $\mathfrak{g}_3$ is to be considered, then by the above analysis we get the ranking $\breve{\mathbb{U}}_1 \succ \breve{\mathbb{U}}_6 \succ \breve{\mathbb{U}}_5 \succ \breve{\mathbb{U}}_4 \succ \breve{\mathbb{U}}_3 \succ \breve{\mathbb{U}}_2$. The score values are given in Figure 11.

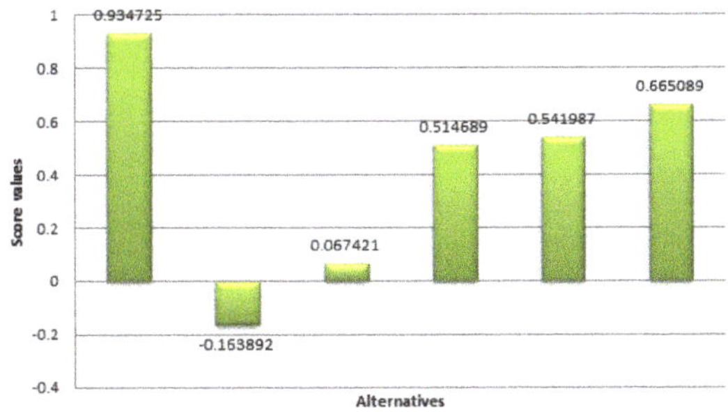

Figure 11. Score values when only $\breve{g}_3$ is considered.

The final ranking achieved by taking into account only a single policy maker/decision expert, is changed but the suitable universal element remained same, which is signifying and demonstrating that each policy maker/specialist has own priorities and values of evaluation attributes, due to his/her own awareness, confessions, knowledge, and personal experiences.

6.5. Comparison Analysis

To demonstrate the productiveness and eminent benefits of the established aggregation operators, the same numerical example is solved by utilizing other aggregation operators including GPFEWG-operator, QROFWA-operator, QROFWG-operator, QROFEWG-operator, QROFEOWG-operator by ignoring the additional preference matrix in some existing operators. Different aggregation operators have distinct classification of strategies so they are able to sustain a little difference in accordance with their consultation. It can be noted in comparison, the suitable choice developed by any aggregation operator, is significant and acknowledges the viability and efficiency of the proposed aggregation operators. The comparison analysis of final rankings of all aggregation operators is given in Table 9.

Table 9. Comparison analysis of final ranking with existing aggregation operators.

Method	Ranking of Alternatives	Optimal Alternative
GGQROFWG operator (Proposed)	$\breve{\mathbb{U}}_1 \succ \breve{\mathbb{U}}_6 \succ \breve{\mathbb{U}}_2 \succ \breve{\mathbb{U}}_3 \succ \breve{\mathbb{U}}_4 \succ \breve{\mathbb{U}}_5$	$\breve{\mathbb{U}}_1$
GGQROFOWG operator (Proposed)	$\breve{\mathbb{U}}_1 \succ \breve{\mathbb{U}}_5 \succ \breve{\mathbb{U}}_2 \succ \breve{\mathbb{U}}_3 \succ \breve{\mathbb{U}}_6 \succ \breve{\mathbb{U}}_4$	$\breve{\mathbb{U}}_1$
GGQROFHG operator (Proposed)	$\breve{\mathbb{U}}_1 \succ \breve{\mathbb{U}}_5 \succ \breve{\mathbb{U}}_3 \succ \breve{\mathbb{U}}_6 \succ \breve{\mathbb{U}}_4 \succ \breve{\mathbb{U}}_2$	$\breve{\mathbb{U}}_1$
ʠ-ROFEPWA operator (Riaz et al. [51])	$\breve{\mathbb{U}}_1 \succ \breve{\mathbb{U}}_3 \succ \breve{\mathbb{U}}_5 \succ \breve{\mathbb{U}}_6 \succ \breve{\mathbb{U}}_4 \succ \breve{\mathbb{U}}_2$	$\breve{\mathbb{U}}_1$
ʠ-ROFEPWG operator (Riaz et al. [51])	$\breve{\mathbb{U}}_1 \succ \breve{\mathbb{U}}_3 \succ \breve{\mathbb{U}}_5 \succ \breve{\mathbb{U}}_6 \succ \breve{\mathbb{U}}_4 \succ \breve{\mathbb{U}}_2$	$\breve{\mathbb{U}}_1$
ʠ-ROFWG operator (Liu and Wang [45])	$\breve{\mathbb{U}}_1 \succ \breve{\mathbb{U}}_2 \succ \breve{\mathbb{U}}_3 \succ \breve{\mathbb{U}}_6 \succ \breve{\mathbb{U}}_4 \succ \breve{\mathbb{U}}_5$	$\breve{\mathbb{U}}_1$
ʠ-ROFOWG operator (Liu and Wang [45])	$\breve{\mathbb{U}}_1 \succ \breve{\mathbb{U}}_2 \succ \breve{\mathbb{U}}_6 \succ \breve{\mathbb{U}}_3 \succ \breve{\mathbb{U}}_4 \succ \breve{\mathbb{U}}_5$	$\breve{\mathbb{U}}_1$
ʠ-ROFWA operator (Liu and Wang [45])	$\breve{\mathbb{U}}_1 \succ \breve{\mathbb{U}}_6 \succ \breve{\mathbb{U}}_2 \succ \breve{\mathbb{U}}_3 \succ \breve{\mathbb{U}}_4 \succ \breve{\mathbb{U}}_5$	$\breve{\mathbb{U}}_1$
ʠ-ROFOWA operator (Liu and Wang [45])	$\breve{\mathbb{U}}_1 \succ \breve{\mathbb{U}}_6 \succ \breve{\mathbb{U}}_2 \succ \breve{\mathbb{U}}_3 \succ \breve{\mathbb{U}}_4 \succ \breve{\mathbb{U}}_5$	$\breve{\mathbb{U}}_1$
ʠ-ROFEWG operator(Riaz et al. [48])	$\breve{\mathbb{U}}_1 \succ \breve{\mathbb{U}}_5 \succ \breve{\mathbb{U}}_3 \succ \breve{\mathbb{U}}_4 \succ \breve{\mathbb{U}}_2 \succ \breve{\mathbb{U}}_6$	$\breve{\mathbb{U}}_1$
ʠ-ROFEOWG operator(Riaz et al. [48])	$\breve{\mathbb{U}}_1 \succ \breve{\mathbb{U}}_3 \succ \breve{\mathbb{U}}_5 \succ \breve{\mathbb{U}}_6 \succ \breve{\mathbb{U}}_4 \succ \breve{\mathbb{U}}_2$	$\breve{\mathbb{U}}_1$
ʠ-ROFPWA operator (Riaz et al. [49])	$\breve{\mathbb{U}}_1 \succ \breve{\mathbb{U}}_3 \succ \breve{\mathbb{U}}_5 \succ \breve{\mathbb{U}}_6 \succ \breve{\mathbb{U}}_4 \succ \breve{\mathbb{U}}_2$	$\breve{\mathbb{U}}_1$
ʠ-ROFPWG operator (Riaz et al. [49])	$\breve{\mathbb{U}}_1 \succ \breve{\mathbb{U}}_3 \succ \breve{\mathbb{U}}_5 \succ \breve{\mathbb{U}}_6 \succ \breve{\mathbb{U}}_4 \succ \breve{\mathbb{U}}_2$	$\breve{\mathbb{U}}_1$
ʠ-ROFHWAGA operator (Riaz et al. [50])	$\breve{\mathbb{U}}_1 \succ \breve{\mathbb{U}}_3 \succ \breve{\mathbb{U}}_5 \succ \breve{\mathbb{U}}_6 \succ \breve{\mathbb{U}}_4 \succ \breve{\mathbb{U}}_2$	$\breve{\mathbb{U}}_1$
ʠ-ROFHOWAGA operator (Riaz et al. [50])	$\breve{\mathbb{U}}_1 \succ \breve{\mathbb{U}}_3 \succ \breve{\mathbb{U}}_5 \succ \breve{\mathbb{U}}_6 \succ \breve{\mathbb{U}}_2 \succ \breve{\mathbb{U}}_4$	$\breve{\mathbb{U}}_1$

Consequently the provided method establish the similar alternative as achieved by different aggregation operators which states that the provided method is beneficial and conceivable.

7. Conclusions

A variety of methods have been suggested to incorporate ʠ-ROF values. Even though prevailing ʠ-ROF aggregation operators were established under the presumption that decision experts have a profound knowledge, these kinds of circumstances were not met while handling the realistic issues, as the policy maker/decision experts priorities regarding alternatives are characteristic of one's own apprehension. Consequently it is required to establish a few different and modern approaches. To deal with this problem, the idea of GQROFS is established by integrating the concept of GP of the other specialist/experts and provides the structure for evaluating the morality of the provided data in initial q́-ROFS to eliminate any distortion in the preferences of senior expert. The most important advantage of addition of generalized parameter is to overcome the chances of mistakes resulting from inaccurate information. This theory is extended to group generalized parameter by integrating the evaluation of different specialists/decision makers which will decrease the influence of single decision expert's choices and will approximate the far more realistic condition under q́-ROF environment. In this paper, we developed q́-ROF geometric aggregation operator under generalized parameter and q́-ROF geometric aggregation operator under group-based generalized parameter. The viability and effectiveness of the proposed aggregation operators are demonstrated by a numerical example. This examination is favorable to utilities of water in respect of achievement a clear idea and evaluation of elements of water loss management strategies, their collaborations and proportions which are not restricted to economic zone, but are expanded to cover environmental, potentially health, and security concerns. The outcomes deliberate the policy maker's concerns in considering the most efficient strategies to reduce the shortages in the water supply system connected with the adoption of unsystematic supply scheme. For further studies, taking into account the advanced simulation capabilities of q-ROFSs, in the q-ROF context we may further examine different kinds of AOs and apply them to realistic decision-making situations. Moreover, the methodological advances for many fields like machine learning, robotics, green supply chain management (GSCM), medical diagnosis, weather forecasting, intelligence, informatics, and sustainable energy planning decision making are promising areas for future studies.

Author Contributions: M.R., A.R., H.K., D.P., and Y.-M.C. conceived of and worked together to achieve this manuscript; M.R., H.M.A.F., D.P., and Y.-M.C. constructed the ideas and algorithms for data analysis and designed the model of the manuscript; A.R., H.K., H.M.A.F., and M.R. processed the data collection and wrote the paper. All authors read and agreed to the published version of the manuscript.

Funding: This research received no external funding.

Acknowledgments: The authors are highly thankful to the Editor-in-Chief and referees for their valuable comments and suggestions for the improvement of our manuscript.

Conflicts of Interest: The authors declare that they have no conflict of interest.

References

1. Kingdom, B.; Liemberger, R.; Marin, P. *The Challenge of Reducing Non-revenue Water (NRW) in Developing Countries*; The World Bank: Washington, DC, USA, 2006.
2. Malmqvist, P.A.; Heinicke, G.; Karrman, E.; Stenstrom, T.A.; Svensson, G. Urban water in context. In *Strategic Planning of Sustainable Urban Water Management*; Malmqvist, P.A., Heinecke, G., Karrman, E., Stenstrom, T.A., Eds.; IWA Publishing: London, UK, 2006.
3. Mugabi, J.; Kayaga, S.; Njiru, C. Strategic planning for water utilities in developing countries. *Util. Policy* **2007**, *15*, 1–8. [CrossRef]
4. Loureiro, D.; Amado, C.; Martins, A.; Vitorino, D.; Mamade, A.; Coelho, S.T. Water distribution systems flow monitoring and anomalous event detection: A practical approach. *Urban Water J.* **2016**, *13*, 1–11. [CrossRef]
5. Mutikanga, H.E.; Sharma, S.K.; Vairavamoorthy, K. Multicriteria decision analysis: A strategic planning tool for water loss management. *Water Resour. Manag.* **2011**, *25*, 3947–3969. [CrossRef]
6. Morais, D.C.; Almeida, A.T. Group decision making for leakage management strategy of water network. *Resour. Conserv. Recycl.* **2007**, *52*, 441–458. [CrossRef]
7. Silva, V.B.S.; Morais, D.C.; Almeida, A.T. A multicriteria group decision model to support watershed committees in Brazil. *Water Resour. Manag.* **2010**, *24*, 4075–4091. [CrossRef]
8. Bouchard, C.; Abi-zeid, I.; Beauchamp, N.; Lamontagne, L.; Desrosiers, J. Multicriteria decision analysis for the selection of a small drinking water system. *Water Suppl. Res. Technol. AQUA* **2010**, *59*, 230–242. [CrossRef]

9. Afshar, A.; Marino, M.A.; Afshar, S.M. Fuzzy TOPSIS multicriteria decision analysis applied to Karun reservoir system. *Water Resour. Manag.* **2011**, *25*, 545–563. [CrossRef]
10. Shaher, H.Z.; Shaheen, H.; Samhan, S.; Rabi, A.; Al-Wadi, F.; Fuchs-Hanusch, D. Utilizing analytic hierarchy process (AHP) for decision making in water loss management of intermittent water supply systems. *J. Water Sanit. Hyg. Dev.* **2016**, *6*, 534–546.
11. Zadeh, L.A. Fuzzy sets. *Inf. Control.* **1965**, *8*, 338–353. [CrossRef]
12. Atanassov, K.T. Intuitionistic fuzzy sets. *Fuzzy Sets Syst.* **1986**, *20*, 87–96. [CrossRef]
13. Yager, R.R. Pythagorean fuzzy subsets. In Prcoceedings of the 2013 Joint IFSA World Congress and NAFIPS Annual Meeting (IFSA/NAFIPS), Edmonton, AB, Canada, 24–28 June 2013; pp. 57–61.
14. Yager, R.R.; Abbasov, A.M. Pythagorean membership grades, complex numbers, and decision making. *Int. J. Intell. Syst.* **2013**, *28*, 436–452. [CrossRef]
15. Yager, R.R. Pythagorean membership grades in multi-criteria decision making. *IEEE Trans. Fuzzy Syst.* **2014**, *22*, 958–965. [CrossRef]
16. Ali, M.I. A note on soft sets, rough soft sets and fuzzy soft sets. *Appl. Soft Comput.* **2011**, *11*, 3329–3332.
17. Wang, Y.; Li, Z.; Tang, Z.; Zeng, G. A GIS-based spatial multi-criteria approach for flood risk management in the Dongting Lake Region, Hunan, Central China. *Water Resour. Manag.* **2011**, *25*, 3465–3484. [CrossRef]
18. Wang, H.; Smarandache, F.; Zhang, Y.Q.; Sunderraman, R. Single valued neutrosophic sets. *Multispace Multistruct.* **2010**, *4*, 410–413.
19. Kaur, G.; Garg, H. Cubic intuitionistic fuzzy aggregation operators. *Int. J. Uncertain. Quantif.* **2018**, *8*, 405–427. [CrossRef]
20. Kumar, K.; Garg, H. TOPSIS method based on the connection number of set pair analysis under interval-valued intuitionistic fuzzy set environment. *Comput. Appl. Math.* **2018**, *37*, 1319–1329. [CrossRef]
21. Peng, X.D.; Yang, Y. Some results for Pythagorean fuzzy sets. *Int. J. Intell. Syst.* **2015**, *30*, 1133–1160. [CrossRef]
22. Peng, X.D.; Yang, Y.Y.; Song, J.; Jiang, Y. Pythagorean Fuzzy Soft Set and Its Application. *Comput. Eng.* **2015**, *41*, 224–229.
23. Riaz, M.; Hashmi, M.R. Linear Diophantine fuzzy set and its applications towards multi-attribute decision making problems. *J. Intell. Fuzzy Syst.* **2019**, *37*, 5417–5439. [CrossRef]
24. Riaz, M.; Tehrim, S.T. Cubic bipolar fuzzy set with application to multi-criteria group decision making using geometric aggregation operators. *Soft Comput.* **2020**. [CrossRef]
25. Riaz, M.; Tehrim, S.T. A Robust Extension of VIKOR Method for Bipolar Fuzzy Sets using Connection Numbers of SPA Theory Based Metric Spaces. *Artif. Intell. Rev.* **2020**. [CrossRef]
26. Sharma, H.K.; Kumari, K.; Kar, S. A rough set approach for forecasting models. *Decis. Mak. Appl. Manag. Eng.* **2020**, *3*, 1–21. [CrossRef]
27. Petrovic, I.; Kankaras, M. A hybridized IT2FS-DEMATEL-AHP-TOPSIS multicriteria decision making approach: Case study of selection and evaluation of criteria for determination of air traffic control radar position. *Decis. Mak. Appl. Manag. Eng.* **2020**, *3*, 146–164. [CrossRef]
28. Yager, R.R. Generalized Orthopair Fuzzy sets. *IEEE Trans. Fuzzy Syst.* **2017**, *25*, 1220–1230. [CrossRef]
29. Peng, X.D.; Yuan, H.Y.; Yang, Y. Pythagorean fuzzy information measures and their applications. *Int. J. Intell. Syst.* **2017**, *32*, 991–1029. [CrossRef]
30. Ali, M.I. Another view on q́-Rung orthopair fuzzy sets. *Int. J. Intell. Syst.* **2018**, *33*, 2139–2153. [CrossRef]
31. Chen, J.; Li, S.; Ma, S.; Wang, X. m-Polar Fuzzy Sets: An Extension of Bipolar Fuzzy Sets. *Sci. World J.* **2014**. [CrossRef]
32. Chi, P.P.; Lui, P.D. An extended TOPSIS method for the multiple ttribute decision making problems based on interval neutrosophic set. *Neutrosophic Sets Syst.* **2013**, *1*, 63–70.
33. Feng, F.; Jun, Y.B.; Liu, X.; Li, L. An adjustable approach to fuzzy soft set based decision making. *J. Comput. Appl. Math.* **2010**, *234*, 10–20. [CrossRef]
34. Feng, F.; Li, C.; Davvaz, B.; Ali, M.I. Soft sets combined with fuzzy sets and rough sets; A tentative approach. *Soft Comput.* **2010**, *14*, 899–911. [CrossRef]
35. Feng, F.; Liu, X.Y.; Leoreanu-Fotea, V.; Jun, Y.B. Soft sets and soft rough sets. *Inf. Sci.* **2011**, *181*, 1125–1137. [CrossRef]

36. Feng, F.; Fujita, H.; Ali, M.I.; Yager, R.R.; Liu, X. Another view on generalized intuitionistic fuzzy soft sets and related multi-attribute decision making methods. *IEEE Trans. Fuzzy Syst.* **2019**, *27*, 474–488. [CrossRef]
37. Garg, H. Generalized pythagorean fuzzy geometric aggregation operator using Einstein t-norm and t-conorm for Multi-criteria decision making process. *Int. J. Intell. Syst.* **2017**, *32*, 597–630. [CrossRef]
38. Garg, H.; Arora, R. Generalized intuitionistic fuzzy soft power aggregation operator based on t-norm and their application in multicriteria decision-making. *Int. J. Intell. Syst.* **2019**, *34*, 215–246. [CrossRef]
39. Garg, H.; Arora, R. Dual hesitant fuzzy soft aggregation operators and their applicatio in decision-making. *Cogn. Comput.* **2018**, *10*, 769–789. [CrossRef]
40. Garg, H.; Arora, R. A nonlinear-programming methodology for multi-attribute decision-making problem with interval-valued intuitionistic fuzzy soft sets information. *Appl. Intell.* **2018**, *48*, 2031–2046. [CrossRef]
41. Garg, H.; Arora, R. Novel scaled prioritized intuitionistic fuzzy soft interaction averaging aggregation operators and their application to multi criteria decision-making. *Eng. Appl. Artif. Intell. EAAI* **2018**, *71*, 100–112. [CrossRef]
42. Jose, S.; Kuriaskose, S. Aggregation operators, score function and accuracy function for multi criteria decision making in intuitionistic fuzzy context. *Notes Intuit. Fuzzy Sets* **2014**, *20*, 40–44.
43. Joshi, B.P. Pythagorean fuzzy average aggregation operators based on generalized and group-generalized parameter with application in MCDM problems. *Int. J. Intell. Syst.* **2019**, *34*, 895–919. [CrossRef]
44. Karaaslan, F. Neutrosophic Soft Set with Applications in Decision Making. *Int. J. Inf. Sci. Intell. Syst.* **2015**, *4*, 1–20.
45. Liu, P.; Wang, P. Some q-rung orthopair fuzzy aggregation operator and their application to multi-attribute decision making. *Int. J. Intell. Syst.* **2018**, *33*, 2259–2280.
46. Liu, Y.; Zhang, H.; Wu, Y.; Dong, Y. Ranking range based approach to MADM under incomplete context and its application in venture investment evaluation. *Technol. Econ. Dev. Econ.* **2019**, in press. [CrossRef]
47. Peng, X.D.; Dai, J. Approaches to single-valued neutrosophic MADM based on MABAC, TOPSIS and new similarity measure with score function. *Neural Comput. Appl.* **2018**, *29*, 939–954. [CrossRef]
48. Riaz, M.; Salabun, W.; Farid, H.M.A.; Ali, N.; Watróbski, J. A robust q-rung orthopair fuzzy information aggregation using Einstein operations with application to sustainable energy planning decision management. *Energies* **2020**, *13*, 2155. [CrossRef]
49. Riaz, M.; Pamucar, D.; Farid, H.M.A.; Hashmi, M.R. q-Rung Orthopair Fuzzy Prioritized Aggregation Operators and Their Application Towards Green Supplier Chain Management. *Symmetry* **2020**, *12*, 976. [CrossRef]
50. Riaz, M.; Karaaslan, F.; Farid, H.M.A.; Hashmi, M.R. Some q-rung orthopair fuzzy hybrid aggregation operators and TOPSIS method for multi-attribute decision-making. *J. Intell. Fuzzy Syst.* **2020**. JIFS-192114. [CrossRef]
51. Riaz, M.; Farid, H.M.A.; Kalsoom, H.; Pamucar, D.; Chu, Y.M. A Robust q-rung orthopair fuzzy Einstein prioritized aggregation operators with application towards MCGDM. *Symmetry* **2020**, *12*, 1058. [CrossRef]
52. Xu, Z.S. Intuitionistic fuzzy aggregation operators. *IEEE Trans. Fuzzy Syst.* **2007**, *15*, 1179–1187.
53. Xu, Z.S.; Cai, X.Q. *Intuitionistic Fuzzy Information Aggregation: Theory and Applications*; Science Press: Beijing, China; Springer: Berlin/Heidelberg, Germany, 2012.
54. Xu, Z.S. *Studies in Fuzziness and Soft Computing: Hesitant Fuzzy Sets Theory*; Springer International Publishing: Cham, Switzerland, 2014.
55. Yager, R.R. On ordered weighted averaging aggregation operators in multi-criteria decision making. *IEEE Trans. Syst. Man Cybern.* **1988**, *18*, 183–190. [CrossRef]
56. Ye, J. Interval-valued hesitant fuzzy prioritized weighted aggregation operators for multi attribute decision-making. *J. Algorithms Comput. Technol.* **2013**, *8*, 179–192. [CrossRef]
57. Ye, J. Linguistic neutrosophic cubic numbers and their multiple attribute decision-making method. *Information* **2017**, *8*, 1–11. [CrossRef]
58. Zhan, J.; Liu, Q.; Davvaz, B. A new rough set theory: Rough soft hemirings. *J. Intell. Fuzzy Syst.* **2015**, *28*, 1687–1697. [CrossRef]
59. Zhan, J.; Alcantud, J.C.R. A novel type of soft rough covering and its application to multi-criteria group decision-making. *Artif. Intell. Rev.* **2018**. [CrossRef]

60. Zhang, L.; Zhan, J. Fuzzy soft β-covering based fuzzy rough sets and corresponding decision-making applications. *Int. J. Mach. Learn. Cybern.* **2018**, *10*, 1487–1502. [CrossRef]
61. Zhang, L.; Zhan, J. Novel classes of fuzzy soft β-coverings-based fuzzy rough sets with applications to multi-criteria fuzzy group decision-making. *Soft Comput.* **2018**, *23*, 5327–5351. [CrossRef]
62. Zhang, L.; Zhan, J.; Xu, Z.S. Covering-based generalized IF rough sets with applications to multi-attribute decision-making. *Inf. Sci.* **2019**, *478*, 275–302. [CrossRef]

symmetry

MDPI

Article

Linear Diophantine Fuzzy Soft Rough Sets for the Selection of Sustainable Material Handling Equipment

Muhammad Riaz [1], Masooma Raza Hashmi [1,2], Humaira Kalsoom [3], Dragan Pamucar [4] and Yu-Ming Chu [5,6,*]

1 Department of Mathematics, University of the Punjab, Lahore 54590, Pakistan; mriaz.math@pu.edu.pk (M.R.); masoomaraza@kfueit.edu.pk (M.R.H.)
2 Department of Mathematics, Khawaja Fareed University of Engineering and Information Technology (KFUEIT), Rahim Yar Khan 64200, Pakistan
3 School of Mathematical Sciences, Zhejiang University, Hangzhou 310027, China; humaira87@zju.edu.cn
4 Department of Logistics, University of Defence, 11000 Belgrade, Serbia; dragan.pamucar@va.mod.gov.rs
5 Department of Mathematics, Huzhou University, Huzhou 313000, China
6 Hunan Provincial Key Laboratory of Mathematical Modeling and Analysis in Engineering, Changsha University of Science & Technology, Changsha 410114, China
* Correspondence: chuyuming@zjhu.edu.cn

Received: 25 June 2020; Accepted: 22 July 2020; Published: 24 July 2020

Abstract: The concept of linear Diophantine fuzzy sets (LDFSs) is a new approach for modeling uncertainties in decision analysis. Due to the addition of reference or control parameters with membership and non-membership grades, LDFS is more flexible and reliable than existing concepts of intuitionistic fuzzy sets (IFSs), Pythagorean fuzzy sets (PFSs), and q-rung orthopair fuzzy sets (q-ROFSs). In this paper, the notions of linear Diophantine fuzzy soft rough sets (LDFSRSs) and soft rough linear Diophantine fuzzy sets (SRLDFSs) are proposed as new hybrid models of soft sets, rough sets, and LDFS. The suggested models of LDFSRSs and SRLDFSs are more flexible to discuss fuzziness and roughness in terms of upper and lower approximation operators. Certain operations on LDFSRSs and SRLDFSs have been established to discuss robust multi-criteria decision making (MCDM) for the selection of sustainable material handling equipment. For these objectives, some algorithms are developed for the ranking of feasible alternatives and deriving an optimal decision. Meanwhile, the ideas of the upper reduct, lower reduct, and core set are defined as key factors in the proposed MCDM technique. An application of MCDM is illustrated by a numerical example, and the final ranking in the selection of sustainable material handling equipment is computed by the proposed algorithms. Finally, a comparison analysis is given to justify the feasibility, reliability, and superiority of the proposed models.

Keywords: linear Diophantine fuzzy set; linear Diophantine fuzzy soft rough set; soft rough linear Diophantine fuzzy set; upper reduct and lower reduct; core set; multi-criteria decision making

1. Introduction

The multi-criteria decision making (MCDM) techniques have been rigorously investigated by many researchers around the real world. Due to uncertain and vague information, the complexity of human's decision making has grown broadly in the present era. This pursuit gave rise to many resourceful techniques to deal with real-world problems. The methodologies developed for this objective essentially rely on the description of the problem under contemplation. The problem of imperfect, uncertain, and vague information has been focused on by many researchers in the last few decades.

Zadeh (1965) developed the notion of fuzzy sets, fuzzy numbers, and linguistic variables to describe hidden uncertain information in the objects by using membership grades. Researchers found that membership/affiliation grades alone are not enough to express some real-life situations such as: benefit and loss claims, positive results and side effects of drugs, inferiority and superiority, perfection and imperfection, affiliation and non-affiliation, etc. In order to cope with these challenges, Atanassov (1983) proposed the idea of intuitionistic fuzzy sets (IFSs) with the inclusion of satisfaction or membership grade (MG) and dissatisfaction or non-membership grade (NMG). Yager (2014, 2017) extended IFSs to Pythagorean fuzzy sets (PFSs) and q-rung orthopair fuzzy sets (q-ROFSs).

In inadequate information data, the vagueness caused by the indiscernibility can be manipulated by utilizing the rough set techniques. This is an individualistic generalization of crisp set theory and was first originated by Pawlak (1982). This hypothesis acts as a tool for investigating and implementing solutions for various decision making difficulties found in the fields of computer intelligence, image processing, data analysis, medical sciences, and many more. It eliminates vagueness by using upper and lower approximation operators of a collection by assembling the equivalence relation. The above-listed theories do not deal with the parameterizations of the input information set. For this purpose, Molodtsov (1999) proposed soft set theory to deal with the uncertainties in parametric behavior.

Sustainability is the ability to exist constantly. The main components of sustainability are society, the economy, and the environment. The equilibrium of local and global efforts for sustainability is necessary to meet elementary human needs without destroying the environment. The ability to finance all capital projects is essential for the sustainability of the economy. The environmental concerns while retaining sustainable growth for the environment are becoming increasingly relevant to decision analysis around the world. Sustainability is regarded as a task, process, activity, and exercise through which humankind avoids the destruction of natural resources. The selection of sustainable material handling equipment is essential for the development of infrastructure.

Multi-criteria decision making (MCDM) is a branch of operations research that explicitly evaluates multiple conflicting criteria in decision making. The purpose of MCDM is to support decision makers (DMs) facing problems in ranking feasible alternatives/objects. There are different types of criteria for determining weights for the alternatives/objects. The subjective criteria weights depend on the DM and can change if another DM computes them. On the opposite side, there is the idea of objective weights, which are different because they have the capacity to evaluate alternatives. For determining subjective and objective weights, there are different fuzzy and crisp methods like SWARA (step-wise weight assessment ratio analysis), WASPAS (weighted aggregated sum product assessment), ARAS (additive ratio assessment), AHP (analytic hierarchy process), PIPRECIA (pivot pairwise relative criteria importance assessment), and CRITIC (criteria importance through inter-criteria correlation). Some integrated MCDM methods studied by researchers are TOPSIS (technique for the order preference by similarity to ideal solution), VIKOR (vlse kriterijumska optimizacija kompromisno resenje), PROMETHEE (preference ranking organization method for enrichment evaluations), COPRAS (complex proportional assessment), MOORA (multi-objective optimization by ratio analysis), GRA (grey relational analysis), ANP (analytic network process), BWM (best worst method), and aggregation operators.

1.1. Literature Review

Bellman and Zadeh [1] proposed the MCDM technique based on fuzzy sets for the first time in 1970. Akram et al. [2] introduced the m-polar fuzzy soft rough sets and presented their applications in multi-attribute decision making (MADM) difficulties. Ali et al. [3] established certain properties of rough sets, soft sets, and fuzzy soft sets. Chen and Tan [4] established the concept of the score function, which was presented by Tversky and Kahneman [5] earlier. Feng et al. [6–9] proposed the idea of soft rough sets. Garg [10] investigated Einstein operators and established the Pythagorean operators to solve decision making obstacles. Hashmi et al. [11] invented the hybrid structure of m-polar neutrosophic set (MPNS) as an abstraction of the bipolar neutrosophic set by combining MPFSsand neutrosophic sets. They developed innovative algorithms to deal with the difficulties in medical sciences and for the clustering of information data. Hashmi and Riaz [12] introduced Pythagorean m-polar fuzzy Dombi operators and proposed a novel technique to the censuses process.

Jose and Kuriaskose [13] proposed the MCDM model for intuitionistic fuzzy numbers (IFNs) by using operators. Naeem et al. [14] introduced multi-criteria group decision making (MCGDM) methods based on TOPSIS and VIKOR using Pythagorean fuzzy soft sets. Pawlak and Skowron [15] presented certain extensions of rough sets.

Riaz and Hashmi [16,17] invented the notions of cubic m-polar fuzzy sets and Pythagorean m-polar fuzzy soft rough sets with applications to decision making difficulties. They established novel structures of soft rough Pythagorean m-polar fuzzy sets and Pythagorean m-polar fuzzy soft rough sets with their applications. Riaz et al. [18,19] introduced the soft rough topology including its applications to group decision making. Riaz and Tehrim [20–22] originated the notions of the bipolar fuzzy soft topology, cubic bipolar fuzzy sets, and operators. By using diverse algorithms, they solved some new and challenging decision making applications. Roy et al. [23] introduced a rough strength relational decision making trial and evaluation laboratory (DEMATEL) model for analyzing the key success factors of hospital service quality. Sharma et al. [24] introduced a rough set theory application in forecasting models.

Wei et al. [25] proposed aggregation operators based on hesitant triangular fuzzy information to determine MADM obstacles. Zhang et al. [26] established the concept of intuitionistic fuzzy soft rough sets and presented its applications.

Zhao [27] et al. discovered novel algorithms based on generalized intuitionistic fuzzy aggregation operators. Xu and Chen [28] practiced distance and similarity measures on IFSs. Kulak et al. [29] and Karande et al. [30] prepared some techniques for the assortment of material handling equipment using the information axiom and weighted utility additive theory. Zubair et al. [31] presented the optimization of a material handling system. Vashist [32] presented an algorithm for finding the reduct and core of the information dataset. Zhang et al. [33–35] discovered different covering based rough sets, fuzzy rough sets, and intuitionistic fuzzy rough sets with their applications to MADM obstacles. Wang and Triantaphyllou [36] identified irregularities in the ranking when evaluating alternatives using certain elimination et choix traduisant la realite (ELECTRE) methods. In order to evaluate green suppliers, Búyúkózkan and Çifçi [37] presented a novel hybrid MCDM approach based on fuzzy DEMATEL, fuzzy ANP, and fuzzy TOPSIS.

Govindan et al. [38] developed a DEMATEL approach focused on experience to establish sustainability strategies and efficiency in a green supply chain. Via flipped e-learning, Jeong and González-Gómez [39] built a system adjusting to the pedagogical changes in sustainable mathematics education through pre-service teachers (PSTs) : rating the requirements with MCDA/F -DEMATEL. Under a q-rung orthopair fuzzy set, Wang and Li [40] established a novel approach for green supplier selection. Xu et al. [41] presented some q-rung dual hesitant Heronian mean operators with their application to multiple group decision making attributes. Soft rough fuzzy sets were developed by Sun and Ma [42] with their applications in strategic decision making. Including its various results and illustrations, Meng et al. [43] introduced the structures of soft rough fuzzy sets and soft fuzzy rough sets. Hussain et al. [44] invented Pythagorean fuzzy soft-rough set models and presented their applications in decision making. Zadeh [45] introduced the concept of a linguistic variable and its application to approximate reasoning.

1.2. Motivation and Objectives

A q-ROFS is the generalization of both IFS and PFS. The main feature of q-ROFS is that the uncertain space for MG and NMG is boarder. Each IFS is a PFS, and each PFS is a q-ROFS, but not conversely. A q-ROFS is more powerful in growing the freedom between MG and NMG. However, there are some situations when these theories are unable to deal with uncertain information. In order to relax existing constraints on MG and NMG, Riaz and Hashmi (2019) introduced the innovative idea of linear Diophantine fuzzy sets (LDFSs). The use of reference or control parameters in LDFS give freedom to DMs in choosing MG and NMG. Moreover, IFSs, PFSs, and q-ROFSs can be considered as specific cases of LDFSs with some limitations (see Figure 1). The semantic comparison of suggested technique with some existing structures is given in Table 1.

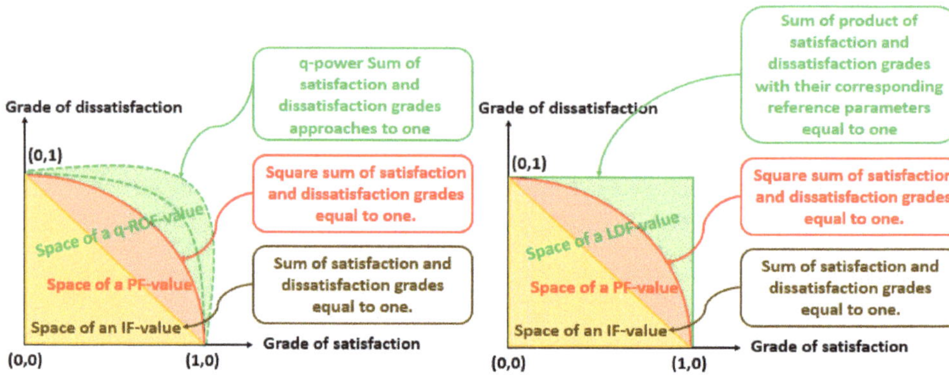

Figure 1. Graphical comparison among IFNs, PFFNs, q-ROFNs, and LDFNs.

The goal of this paper is to develop strong models for MCDM that have less limitations than other models. Table 1 shows the advantages and drawbacks of some set theoretical models. The notions of linear Diophantine fuzzy soft rough sets (LDFSRSs) and soft rough linear Diophantine fuzzy sets (SRLDFSs) are established as new hybrid models of soft sets, rough sets, and LDFSs. The suggested models of LDFSRSs and SRLDFSs are more flexible to discuss fuzziness and roughness in terms of upper and lower approximation operators. Certain operations on LDFSRSs and SRLDFSs have been established to discuss a robust multi-criteria decision making (MCDM) for the selection of sustainable material handling equipment. We present four new algorithms based on LDFS, crisp soft approximation spaces, core sets, and reducts.

The organization of this article is provided as follows. Section 2 implies certain fundamental notions of fuzzy sets, IFSs, PFSs, q-ROFSs, and LDFSs. We investigate fascinating operations and score functions of LDFSs. In Section 3, we invent the notions of LDFSRSs and SRLDFSs by applying the LDFS approximation space and crisp soft approximation space. We establish multiple results based on intended structures with the help of illustrations. In Section 4, we present four novel algorithms to determine the material handling equipment selection obstacle. These algorithms are based on the approximation spaces, score functions, upper and lower reducts, and core set. We examine and compare our suggested structures and their results with certain existing notions. Section 5 provides the conclusion of this manuscript.

Table 1. Semantic comparison of the suggested technique with some existing models.

Set Theories	Advantages	Semantic Disadvantages
Fuzzy sets [46]	Contribute knowledge about specific property	Dose not give information about the falsity and roughness of information system
Intuitionistic fuzzy sets [47,48]	Detect vagueness with agree and disagree criteria	Restricted valuation space and does not deal with roughness
Pythagorean fuzzy sets [49–51]	Detect vagueness with larger valuation space than IFSs	Cannot handle the roughness of the data and dependency between the grades
q-rung orthopair fuzzy sets [52,53]	Increase the valuation space of grades to deal with real-life situations	For smaller values of q, creates dependency in grades and cannot handle roughness
Linear Diophantine fuzzy sets [54]	Create independency between the degrees and increase their valuation space under the effect of control parameterizations	Does not give information about the roughness of information data and cannot deal with multi-valued parameterizations
Rough sets [55]	Contain upper and lower approximations of information dataset to handle roughness	Does not characterize the agree and disagree degrees with parameterizations
Soft sets [56]	Produce multi-valued mapping based parameterizations under different criteria	Does not contain fuzziness and roughness in optimization
Linear Diophantine fuzzy soft sets (proposed)	Produce multi-valued mapping based on the LDF value information system	Does not characterize the roughness of real-life dataset
Linear Diophantine fuzzy soft rough sets (proposed)	Contain upper and lower approximations with LDF degrees under double parameterizations (soft and reference) and collect data without any loss of information	Due to the use of LDFS approximation space for evaluations, it contains heavy calculations, but easy to handle
Soft rough linear Diophantine fuzzy sets (proposed)	Use crisp soft approximation space to evaluate upper and lower approximations with LDF degrees and collect data without any loss of information	Easy calculations as compared to LDFSRS, but heavy as compared to others (easy to handle)

2. Some Basic Concepts

First, we assemble fascinating fundamental ideas of LDFSs, rough sets, soft sets, and soft rough sets.

Definition 1 ([54]). *A linear Diophantine fuzzy set $\mathscr{D}$ in $\ddot{\mathcal{Q}}$ is defined as:*

$$\mathscr{D} = \{(\mathfrak{G}, \langle \ddot{\mathscr{T}}_{\mathscr{D}}(\mathfrak{G}), \ddot{\mathfrak{S}}_{\mathscr{D}}(\mathfrak{G})\rangle, \langle \alpha_{\mathscr{D}}(\mathfrak{G}), \beta_{\mathscr{D}}(\mathfrak{G})\rangle) : \mathfrak{G} \in \ddot{\mathcal{Q}}\},$$

where $\ddot{\mathscr{T}}_{\mathscr{D}}(\mathfrak{G}), \ddot{\mathfrak{S}}_{\mathscr{D}}(\mathfrak{G}), \alpha_{\mathscr{D}}(\mathfrak{G}), \beta_{\mathscr{D}}(\mathfrak{G}) \in [0,1]$ are the satisfaction grade, the dissatisfaction grade, and the corresponding reference parameters, respectively. Moreover, it is required that:

$$0 \leq \alpha_{\mathscr{D}}(\mathfrak{G}) + \beta_{\mathscr{D}}(\mathfrak{G}) \leq 1,$$

and:

$$0 \leq \alpha_{\mathscr{D}}(\mathfrak{G})\ddot{\mathscr{T}}_{\mathscr{D}}(\mathfrak{G}) + \beta_{\mathscr{D}}(\mathfrak{G})\ddot{\mathfrak{S}}_{\mathscr{D}}(\mathfrak{G}) \leq 1$$

for all $\mathfrak{G} \in \ddot{\mathcal{Q}}$. The LDFS:

$$\mathscr{D}_{\ddot{\mathcal{Q}}} = \{(\mathfrak{G}, \langle 1,0\rangle, \langle 1,0\rangle) : \mathfrak{G} \in \ddot{\mathcal{Q}}\}$$

is called the absolute LDFS in $\ddot{\mathcal{Q}}$. The LDFS:

$$\mathscr{D}_{\phi} = \{(\mathfrak{G}, \langle 0,1\rangle, \langle 0,1\rangle) : \mathfrak{G} \in \ddot{\mathcal{Q}}\}$$

is called the null LDFS in $\ddot{\mathcal{Q}}$.

The reference parameters are useful for describing objective weights for each pair of MG and NMG. These parameters can be used for multiple objectives to express the physical interpretation of a dynamical system. In addition, $\gamma_{\mathscr{D}}(\mathfrak{G})\dot{\pi}_{\mathscr{D}}(\mathfrak{G}) = 1 - (\alpha_{\mathscr{D}}(\mathfrak{G})\ddot{\mathscr{T}}_{\mathscr{D}}(\mathfrak{G}) + \beta_{\mathscr{D}}(\mathfrak{G})\ddot{\mathfrak{S}}_{\mathscr{D}}(\mathfrak{G}))$, where $\dot{\pi}_{\mathscr{D}}(\mathfrak{G})$ is called the indeterminacy degree of $\mathfrak{G}$ to $\mathscr{D}$ and $\gamma_{\mathscr{D}}(\mathfrak{G})$ is the reference parameter related to the indeterminacy part. It can be seen that the tuples $(\langle \ddot{\mathscr{T}}_{\mathscr{D}}(\mathfrak{G}), \ddot{\mathfrak{S}}_{\mathscr{D}}(\mathfrak{G})\rangle, \langle \alpha_{\mathscr{D}}(\mathfrak{G}), \beta_{\mathscr{D}}(\mathfrak{G})\rangle)$ with $\mathfrak{G} \in \ddot{\mathcal{Q}}$ are crucial for specifying the LDFS $\mathscr{D}$. Due to this fact, we introduce the new notion of the linear Diophantine fuzzy number (LDFN) denoted as $\ddot{A}_{\mathscr{D}} = (\langle \dot{t}_{\mathscr{D}}, \dot{f}_{\mathscr{D}}\rangle, \langle \alpha_{\mathscr{D}}, \beta_{\mathscr{D}}\rangle)$ satisfying all the constraints listed above for LDFSs. The collection of all LDFSs in $\ddot{\mathcal{Q}}$ is denoted as $\mathscr{D}(\ddot{\mathcal{Q}})$.

Example 1 (Combination of drugs in medicine for better treatment.). *Medicines are chemicals or compounds used to cure, halt, or prevent disease, ease symptoms, or help in the diagnosis of illnesses. Advances in medicines have enabled doctors to cure many diseases and save lives. A combination drug or a fixed-dose combination (FDC) is a medicine that includes two or more active ingredients combined in a single dosage form. For example: aspirin/paracetamol and caffeine is a combination drug for the treatment of pain, especially tension headaches and migraines. Let $\ddot{\mathcal{Q}} = \{\mathcal{G}_1, \mathcal{G}_2, \mathcal{G}_3, \mathcal{G}_4, \mathcal{G}_5\}$ be the collection of some life-saving drugs. In order to gain a high impact of medicine, two or more drugs can be combined in the preparation of a medicine. If the reference or control parameter is considered as:*

$$\alpha = \text{excellent impact against infection produced during surgeries}$$
$$\beta = \text{no high impact against infection produced during surgeries}$$

then its LDFS is given in Table 2.

Table 2. LDFS for medication.

Alternatives	LDFNs
$\mathcal{G}_1$	$(\langle 00.963, 00.472\rangle, \langle 00.731, 00.121\rangle)$
$\mathcal{G}_2$	$(\langle 00862, 00.576\rangle, \langle 00.631, 00.222\rangle)$
$\mathcal{G}_3$	$(\langle 00.665, 00.874\rangle, \langle 00.332, 00.123\rangle)$
$\mathcal{G}_4$	$(\langle 00.664, 00.773\rangle, \langle 00.234, 00.225\rangle)$
$\mathcal{G}_5$	$(\langle 00.867, 00.776\rangle, \langle 00.435, 00.225\rangle)$

According to the quality, variety, and severity of the disease, a physician provides medicine to the subject. The information data can be classified using control parameters. These parameters represent how much that portion is necessary for the treatment, and their grade values describe how much that factor is present in that medicine. If we change the parameter as:

$$\alpha = \text{"Excellent impact against ear infection"}$$
$$\beta = \text{"Not highly affective for ear infection"}$$
$$\text{OR}$$
$$\alpha = \text{"Fewer side effects"}$$
$$\beta = \text{"More side effects"},$$

then we can establish various LDFSs that are suitable in other situations. This model helps a pharmacist/doctor/consultant prescribe the most reliable and suitable medicine to the patient for his/her disease. Moreover, reference or control parameters can be used for the purpose of various alternatives in medicine.

Theorem 1 ([54])**.** *LDFSs have a larger valuation space than IFSs and PFSs.*

Definition 2 ([54])**.** *Let $\ddot{A}_{\mathscr{D}} = (\langle \dot{t}_{\mathscr{D}}, \dot{f}_{\mathscr{D}}\rangle, \langle \alpha_{\mathscr{D}}, \beta_{\mathscr{D}}\rangle)$ be an LDFN and $\mathcal{X} > 0$. Then:*

- $\ddot{A}^c_{\mathscr{D}} = (\langle \dot{f}_{\mathscr{D}}, \dot{t}_{\mathscr{D}}\rangle, \langle \beta_{\mathscr{D}}, \alpha_{\mathscr{D}}\rangle)$;
- $\mathcal{X}\ddot{A}_{\mathscr{D}} = (\langle 1-(1-\dot{t}_{\mathscr{D}})^{\mathcal{X}}, \dot{f}^{\mathcal{X}}_{\mathscr{D}}\rangle, \langle 1-(1-\alpha_{\mathscr{D}})^{\mathcal{X}}, \beta^{\mathcal{X}}_{\mathscr{D}}\rangle)$;
- $\ddot{A}^{\mathcal{X}}_{\mathscr{D}} = (\langle \dot{t}^{\mathcal{X}}_{\mathscr{D}}, 1-(1-\dot{f}_{\mathscr{D}})^{\mathcal{X}}\rangle, \langle \alpha^{\mathcal{X}}_{\mathscr{D}}, 1-(1-\beta_{\mathscr{D}})^{\mathcal{X}}\rangle)$.

Definition 3 ([54])**.** *Let $\ddot{A}_i = (\langle \dot{t}_{\mathscr{D}_i}, \dot{f}_{\mathscr{D}_i}\rangle, \langle \alpha_{\mathscr{D}}, \beta_{\mathscr{D}}\rangle)$ be two LDFNs with $i = 1, 2$. Then:*

- $\ddot{A}_{\mathscr{D}_1} \subseteq \ddot{A}_{\mathscr{D}_2} \Leftrightarrow \dot{t}_{\mathscr{D}_1} \le \dot{t}_{\mathscr{D}_2}, \dot{f}_{\mathscr{D}_2} \le \dot{f}_{\mathscr{D}_1}, \alpha_{\mathscr{D}_1} \le \alpha_{\mathscr{D}_2}, \beta_{\mathscr{D}_2} \le \beta_{\mathscr{D}_1}$;
- $\ddot{A}_{\mathscr{D}_1} = \ddot{A}_{\mathscr{D}_2} \Leftrightarrow \dot{t}_{\mathscr{D}_1} = \dot{t}_{\mathscr{D}_2}, \dot{f}_{\mathscr{D}_1} = \dot{f}_{\mathscr{D}_2}, \alpha_{\mathscr{D}_1} = \alpha_{\mathscr{D}_2}, \beta_{\mathscr{D}_1} = \beta_{\mathscr{D}_2}$;
- $\ddot{A}_{\mathscr{D}_1} \oplus \ddot{A}_{\mathscr{D}_2} = (\langle \dot{t}_{\mathscr{D}_1} + \dot{t}_{\mathscr{D}_2} - \dot{t}_{\mathscr{D}_1}\dot{t}_{\mathscr{D}_2}, \dot{f}_{\mathscr{D}_1}\dot{f}_{\mathscr{D}_2}\rangle, \langle \alpha_{\mathscr{D}_1} + \alpha_{\mathscr{D}_2} - \alpha_{\mathscr{D}_1}\alpha_{\mathscr{D}_2}, \beta_{\mathscr{D}_1}\beta_{\mathscr{D}_2}\rangle)$;
- $\ddot{A}_{\mathscr{D}_1} \otimes \ddot{A}_2 = (\langle \dot{t}_{\mathscr{D}_1}\dot{t}_{\mathscr{D}_2}, \dot{f}_{\mathscr{D}_1} + \dot{f}_{\mathscr{D}_2} - \dot{f}_{\mathscr{D}_1}\dot{f}_{\mathscr{D}_2}\rangle, \langle \alpha_{\mathscr{D}_1}\alpha_{\mathscr{D}_2}, \beta_{\mathscr{D}_1} + \beta_{\mathscr{D}_2} - \beta_{\mathscr{D}_1}\beta_{\mathscr{D}_2}\rangle)$.

Definition 4 ([54])**.** *Let $\ddot{A}_{\mathscr{D}_i} = (\langle \dot{t}_{\mathscr{D}_i}, \dot{f}_{\mathscr{D}_i}\rangle, \langle \alpha_{\mathscr{D}_i}, \beta_{\mathscr{D}_i}\rangle)$ be a collection of LDFNs with $i \in \Delta$. Then:*

- $\bigcup_{i\in\Delta} \ddot{A}_{\mathscr{D}_i} = \left(\langle \sup_{i\in\Delta} \dot{t}_{\mathscr{D}_i}, \inf_{i\in\Delta} \dot{f}_{\mathscr{D}_i}\rangle, \langle \sup_{i\in\Delta} \alpha_{\mathscr{D}_i}, \inf_{i\in\Delta} \beta_{\mathscr{D}_i}\rangle\right)$;
- $\bigcap_{i\in\Delta} \ddot{A}_{\mathscr{D}_i} = \left(\langle \inf_{i\in\Delta} \dot{t}_{\mathscr{D}_i}, \sup_{i\in\Delta} \dot{f}_{\mathscr{D}_i}\rangle, \langle \inf_{i\in\Delta} \alpha_{\mathscr{D}_i}, \sup_{i\in\Delta} \beta_{\mathscr{D}_i}\rangle\right)$.

Definition 5 ([56])**.** *For the non-empty collection of alternatives $\ddot{\mathcal{Q}}$ and the collection of attributes $\dot{\mathcal{G}}$, the soft set is evaluated by the mapping $\dot{\Omega} : \dot{\mathcal{G}} \to \widetilde{\mathscr{P}}(\ddot{\mathcal{Q}})$. Alternatively, it can be represented as:*

$$(\dot{\Omega}, \dot{\mathcal{G}}) = \{(\wp, \dot{\Omega}(\wp)) : \dot{\Omega}(\wp) \in \widetilde{\mathscr{P}}(\ddot{\mathcal{Q}}), \wp \in \dot{\mathcal{G}}\}$$

The collection of all subsets of $\ddot{\mathcal{Q}}$ is denoted as $\widetilde{\mathscr{P}}(\ddot{\mathcal{Q}})$.

Definition 6 ([55]). *Suppose the indiscernibility relation on $\ddot{\mathcal{Q}}$ is denoted as $\mathcal{R}$. We assume arbitrarily that $\mathcal{R}$ is an equivalence relation. Moreover, $Neg_{\mathcal{R}}\mathcal{K} = \ddot{\mathcal{Q}} - \mathcal{K}^*$, $Pos_{\mathcal{R}}\mathcal{K} = \mathcal{K}_{\circledast}$, and $Bnd_{\mathcal{R}}\mathcal{K} = \mathcal{K}^* - \mathcal{K}_{\circledast}$ are said to be negative, positive, and boundary regions of $\mathcal{K} \subseteq \ddot{\mathcal{Q}}$. The characteristics of these regions are given as follows:*

(1) $\mathcal{G} \in Pos_{\mathcal{R}}\mathcal{K}$ *implies that $\mathcal{K}$ certainly contains the elements $\mathcal{G}$ of $\ddot{\mathcal{Q}}$.*
(2) $\mathcal{G} \in Neg_{\mathcal{R}}\mathcal{K}$ *implies that $\mathcal{K}$ does not contains the elements $\mathcal{G}$ of $\ddot{\mathcal{Q}}$.*
(3) $\mathcal{G} \in Bnd_{\mathcal{R}}\mathcal{K}$ *implies that $\mathcal{K}$ may or may not contain the elements $\mathcal{G}$ of $\ddot{\mathcal{Q}}$.*

The equivalence class of object $\mathcal{G}$ under the relation $\mathcal{R}$ is represented as $[\mathcal{G}]_{\mathcal{R}}$. The pair $(\ddot{\mathcal{Q}}, \mathcal{R})$ is said to be a "Pawlak approximation space", and $\mathcal{R}$ will generate the partition $\ddot{\mathcal{Q}}/\mathcal{R} = \{[\mathcal{G}]_{\mathcal{R}} : \mathcal{G} \in \ddot{\mathcal{Q}}\}$. Then, pair $(\mathcal{R}^*(\mathcal{K}), \mathcal{R}_{\circledast}(\mathcal{K}))$ is called the rough set of crisp set $\mathcal{K}$, where:

$$\mathcal{R}_{\circledast}(\mathcal{K}) = \{\mathcal{G} \in \ddot{\mathcal{Q}} : [\mathcal{G}]_{\mathcal{R}} \subseteq \mathcal{K}\}$$

$$\mathcal{R}^*(\mathcal{K}) = \{\mathcal{G} \in \ddot{\mathcal{Q}} : [\mathcal{G}]_{\mathcal{R}} \cap \mathcal{K} \neq \phi\}$$

are called "lower and upper approximations" of $\mathcal{K}$ with respect to $(\ddot{\mathcal{Q}}, \mathcal{R})$. If $\mathcal{R}_{\circledast}(\mathcal{K}) = \mathcal{R}^*(\mathcal{K})$, then $\mathcal{K}$ is said to be definable; otherwise, it is called a rough set.

Remark 1. *The concepts of the core and reduct in rough set theory are very significant tools in the decision making methods. We can deduce the reduct from the reference set $\ddot{\mathcal{Q}}$. It is used to reduce the unimportant information in the input data. The core is the intersection of all reducts and provides the final optimal decision about the decision making problem (see [3,32]).*

Definition 7 ([26]). *For a non-empty collection of alternatives $\ddot{\mathcal{Q}}$ and the collection of attributes $\dot{\mathcal{G}}$, the crisp soft relation $\mathcal{R} \subseteq \ddot{\mathcal{Q}} \times \dot{\mathcal{G}}$ is written as:*

$$\mathcal{R} = \{\langle(\mathcal{G}, \wp), \psi_{\mathcal{R}}(\mathcal{G}, \wp)\rangle : (\mathcal{G}, \wp) \in \ddot{\mathcal{Q}} \times \dot{\mathcal{G}}\}$$

where $\psi_{\mathcal{R}} : \ddot{\mathcal{Q}} \times \dot{\mathcal{G}} \to \{0, 1\}$ and:

$$\psi_{\mathcal{R}}(\mathcal{G}, \wp) = \begin{cases} 1 & \text{if } (\mathcal{G}, \wp) \in \mathcal{R} \\ 0 & ;\text{otherwise} \end{cases}$$

Definition 8 ([26]). *For a non-empty collection of alternatives $\ddot{\mathcal{Q}}$ and the collection of attributes $\dot{\mathcal{G}}$, we have a crisp soft relation $\tilde{\mathscr{A}} \subseteq \ddot{\mathcal{Q}} \times \dot{\mathcal{G}}$. A mapping $\tilde{\mathscr{A}}_s : \ddot{\mathcal{Q}} \to P(\dot{\mathcal{G}})$ is written as:*

$$\tilde{\mathscr{A}}_s(\mathcal{G}) = \{\wp \in \dot{\mathcal{G}} : (\mathcal{G}, \wp) \in \tilde{\mathscr{A}}; \mathcal{G} \in \ddot{\mathcal{Q}}\}$$

$\tilde{\mathscr{A}}$ is called serial if $\forall \mathcal{G} \in \ddot{\mathcal{Q}}, \tilde{\mathscr{A}}_s(\mathcal{G}) \neq \phi$. The "crisp soft approximation space" is represented by this triplet $(\ddot{\mathcal{Q}}, \dot{\mathcal{G}}, \tilde{\mathscr{A}})$. For arbitrary $\mathcal{H} \subseteq \dot{\mathcal{G}}$, $\tilde{\mathscr{A}}_{\circledast}(\mathcal{H})$ and $\tilde{\mathscr{A}}^*(\mathcal{H})$ are called the "lower and upper approximations", respectively, defined as:

$$\tilde{\mathscr{A}}_{\circledast}(\mathcal{H}) = \{\mathcal{G} \in \ddot{\mathcal{Q}} : \tilde{\mathscr{A}}_s(\mathcal{G}) \cap \mathcal{H} \neq \phi\}$$

$$\tilde{\mathscr{A}}^*(\mathcal{H}) = \{\mathcal{G} \in \ddot{\mathcal{Q}} : \tilde{\mathscr{A}}_s(\mathcal{G}) \subseteq \ddot{\mathcal{Q}}\}$$

The pair $(\tilde{\mathscr{A}}_{\circledast}(\mathcal{H}), \tilde{\mathscr{A}}^*(\mathcal{H}))$ is called the crisp soft rough set, and $\tilde{\mathscr{A}}_{\circledast}, \tilde{\mathscr{A}}^* : \widetilde{\mathscr{P}}(\dot{\mathcal{G}}) \to \widetilde{\mathscr{P}}(\ddot{\mathcal{Q}})$ are called "lower and upper approximation operators". $\widetilde{\mathscr{P}}(\dot{\mathcal{G}})$ and $\widetilde{\mathscr{P}}(\ddot{\mathcal{Q}})$ are an assembly of all subsets of $\dot{\mathcal{G}}$ and $\ddot{\mathcal{Q}}$, respectively. If $\tilde{\mathscr{A}}_{\circledast}(\mathcal{H}) = \tilde{\mathscr{A}}^*(\mathcal{H})$, then $\ddot{\mathcal{Q}}$ is called definable.

3. Construction of SRLDFSs and LDFSRSs

In this part, we organize the innovative hybrid structures of soft rough linear Diophantine fuzzy sets (SRLDFSs) and linear Diophantine fuzzy soft rough sets (LDFSRSs) by merging the fundamental compositions of LDFSs, soft sets, and rough sets. In decision making obstacles, we deal with the ambiguities and vagueness in the initial input information. Due to these circumstances, we cannot manage these inputs by utilizing simplistic models. In fuzzy sets, IFSs, PFSs, and q-ROFSs, the opportunities for the assortment of satisfaction and dissatisfaction degrees are restricted due to constraints $0 \leq \dddot{\mathscr{T}} \leq 1$, $0 \leq \dddot{\mathscr{T}} + \ddot{\mathscr{S}} \leq 1$, $0 \leq \dddot{\mathscr{T}}^2 + \ddot{\mathscr{S}}^2 \leq 1$, and $0 \leq \dddot{\mathscr{T}}^q + \ddot{\mathscr{S}}^q \leq 1$. However, in the LDFS, we can comfortably choose the degrees from $[0,1]$, due to the reference or control parameters. However, this set does not deal with the vagueness or roughness. We cannot handle uncertainties and parameterizations if we deal only with the roughness of a set. The soft set only works for parameterizations. Therefore, to eliminate these ambiguities and to fill in the research gap, we assemble SRLDFSs and LDFSRSs. These models dispense with the fuzzy degrees, parameterizations, and roughness of the data in the decision making difficulties. The significance of these generalized and authentic notions can be examined in the entire article. Table 3 represents the notations used in the whole manuscript.

Table 3. Description of the notations used in the whole manuscript.

Notation	Explanation
$\ddot{\mathcal{Q}}$	Universal set
$\dot{\mathcal{G}}$	Set of decision variables
$\mathcal{G}$	Elements of set $\ddot{\mathcal{Q}}$
$\dot{\wp}$	Elements of set $\dot{\mathcal{G}}$
$\tilde{\mathscr{A}}_{*}$	Lower approximation operator for SRLDFSs
$\tilde{\mathscr{A}}^{*}$	Upper approximation operator for SRLDFSs
$\tilde{\eth}_{*}$	Lower approximation operator for LDFSRSs
$\tilde{\eth}^{*}$	Upper approximation operator for LDFSRSs
$\dddot{\mathscr{T}}$	Satisfaction grade
$\ddot{\mathscr{S}}$	Dissatisfaction grade
$\mathscr{D}(\dot{\mathcal{G}})$	Collection of all LDFSs over $\dot{\mathcal{G}}$
$\mathscr{D}(\ddot{\mathcal{Q}})$	Collection of all LDFSs over $\ddot{\mathcal{Q}}$

3.1. Soft Rough Linear Diophantine Fuzzy Sets

Definition 9. *For the reference set $\ddot{\mathcal{Q}}$ and set of decision variables $\dot{\mathcal{G}}$, if we define a crisp soft relation $\tilde{\mathscr{A}}$ over $\ddot{\mathcal{Q}} \times \dot{\mathcal{G}}$, then $(\ddot{\mathcal{Q}}, \dot{\mathcal{G}}, \tilde{\mathscr{A}})$ is called a "crisp soft approximation space". If $\mathscr{Y}_{\mathscr{D}} \in \mathscr{D}(\dot{\mathcal{G}})$, then $\tilde{\mathscr{A}}^{*}(\mathscr{Y}_{\mathscr{D}})$ and $\tilde{\mathscr{A}}_{*}(\mathscr{Y}_{\mathscr{D}})$ are called "upper and lower approximations" of $\mathscr{Y}_{\mathscr{D}}$ about $(\ddot{\mathcal{Q}}, \dot{\mathcal{G}}, \tilde{\mathscr{A}})$ respectively and written as:*

$$\tilde{\mathscr{A}}_{*}(\mathscr{Y}_{\mathscr{D}}) = \{(\mathcal{G}, \langle \dddot{\mathscr{T}}_{\tilde{\mathscr{A}}_{*}(\mathscr{Y}_{\mathscr{D}})}(\mathcal{G}), \ddot{\mathscr{S}}_{\tilde{\mathscr{A}}_{*}(\mathscr{Y}_{\mathscr{D}})}(\mathcal{G})\rangle, \langle \alpha_{\tilde{\mathscr{A}}_{*}(\mathscr{Y}_{\mathscr{D}})}(\mathcal{G}), \beta_{\tilde{\mathscr{A}}_{*}(\mathscr{Y}_{\mathscr{D}})}(\mathcal{G})\rangle) : \mathcal{G} \in \ddot{\mathcal{Q}}\}$$

$$\tilde{\mathscr{A}}^{*}(\mathscr{Y}_{\mathscr{D}}) = \{(\mathcal{G}, \langle \dddot{\mathscr{T}}_{\tilde{\mathscr{A}}^{*}(\mathscr{Y}_{\mathscr{D}})}(\mathcal{G}), \ddot{\mathscr{S}}_{\tilde{\mathscr{A}}^{*}(\mathscr{Y}_{\mathscr{D}})}(\mathcal{G})\rangle, \langle \alpha_{\tilde{\mathscr{A}}^{*}(\mathscr{Y}_{\mathscr{D}})}(\mathcal{G}), \beta_{\tilde{\mathscr{A}}^{*}(\mathscr{Y}_{\mathscr{D}})}(\mathcal{G})\rangle) : \mathcal{G} \in \ddot{\mathcal{Q}}\}$$

where the degrees can be calculated as given in Table 4.

Table 4. Formulation of SRLDFSs.

Notation	Formulation	Notation	Formulation
$\ddot{\mathcal{T}}_{\tilde{\mathscr{A}}^*(\mathscr{Y}_{\mathscr{D}})}(\mathcal{G})$	$\max_{\dot{\wp}\in\tilde{\mathscr{A}}_s(\mathcal{G})} (\ddot{\mathcal{T}}_{\mathscr{Y}_{\mathscr{D}}}(\dot{\wp}))$	$\ddot{\mathcal{S}}_{\tilde{\mathscr{A}}^*(\mathscr{Y}_{\mathscr{D}})}(\mathcal{G})$	$\min_{\dot{\wp}\in\tilde{\mathscr{A}}_s(\mathcal{G})} (\ddot{\mathcal{S}}_{\mathscr{Y}_{\mathscr{D}}}(\dot{\wp}))$
$\ddot{\mathcal{T}}_{\tilde{\mathscr{A}}_*(\mathscr{Y}_{\mathscr{D}})}(\mathcal{G})$	$\min_{\dot{\wp}\in\tilde{\mathscr{A}}_s(\mathcal{G})} (\ddot{\mathcal{T}}_{\mathscr{Y}_{\mathscr{D}}}(\dot{\wp}))$	$\ddot{\mathcal{S}}_{\tilde{\mathscr{A}}_*(\mathscr{Y}_{\mathscr{D}})}(\mathcal{G})$	$\max_{\dot{\wp}\in\tilde{\mathscr{A}}_s(\mathcal{G})} (\ddot{\mathcal{S}}_{\mathscr{Y}_{\mathscr{D}}}(\dot{\wp}))$
$\alpha_{\tilde{\mathscr{A}}^*(\mathscr{Y}_{\mathscr{D}})}(\mathcal{G})$	$\max_{\dot{\wp}\in\tilde{\mathscr{A}}_s(\mathcal{G})} (\alpha_{\mathscr{Y}_{\mathscr{D}}}(\dot{\wp}))$	$\beta_{\tilde{\mathscr{A}}^*(\mathscr{Y}_{\mathscr{D}})}(\mathcal{G})$	$\min_{\dot{\wp}\in\tilde{\mathscr{A}}_s(\mathcal{G})} (\beta_{\mathscr{Y}_{\mathscr{D}}}(\dot{\wp}))$
$\alpha_{\tilde{\mathscr{A}}_*(\mathscr{Y}_{\mathscr{D}})}(\mathcal{G})$	$\min_{\dot{\wp}\in\tilde{\mathscr{A}}_s(\mathcal{G})} (\alpha_{\mathscr{Y}_{\mathscr{D}}}(\dot{\wp}))$	$\beta_{\tilde{\mathscr{A}}_*(\mathscr{Y}_{\mathscr{D}})}(\mathcal{G})$	$\max_{\dot{\wp}\in\tilde{\mathscr{A}}_s(\mathcal{G})} (\beta_{\mathscr{Y}_{\mathscr{D}}}(\dot{\wp}))$

The notions given in Table 4 satisfy the following constraints::

$$0 \leq \alpha_{\tilde{\mathscr{A}}^*(\mathscr{Y}_{\mathscr{D}})}(\mathcal{G})\ddot{\mathcal{T}}_{\tilde{\mathscr{A}}^*(\mathscr{Y}_{\mathscr{D}})}(\mathcal{G}) + \beta_{\tilde{\mathscr{A}}^*(\mathscr{Y}_{\mathscr{D}})}(\mathcal{G})\ddot{\mathcal{S}}_{\tilde{\mathscr{A}}^*(\mathscr{Y}_{\mathscr{D}})}(\mathcal{G}) \leq 1$$

$$0 \leq \alpha_{\tilde{\mathscr{A}}_*(\mathscr{Y}_{\mathscr{D}})}(\mathcal{G})\ddot{\mathcal{T}}_{\tilde{\mathscr{A}}_*(\mathscr{Y}_{\mathscr{D}})}(\mathcal{G}) + \beta_{\tilde{\mathscr{A}}_*(\mathscr{Y}_{\mathscr{D}})}(\mathcal{G})\ddot{\mathcal{S}}_{\tilde{\mathscr{A}}_*(\mathscr{Y}_{\mathscr{D}})}(\mathcal{G}) \leq 1$$

$$0 \leq \alpha_{\tilde{\mathscr{A}}^*(\mathscr{Y}_{\mathscr{D}})}(\mathcal{G}) + \beta_{\tilde{\mathscr{A}}^*(\mathscr{Y}_{\mathscr{D}})}(\mathcal{G}) \leq 1 \quad \textit{and}$$

$$0 \leq \alpha_{\tilde{\mathscr{A}}_*(\mathscr{Y}_{\mathscr{D}})}(\mathcal{G}) + \beta_{\tilde{\mathscr{A}}_*(\mathscr{Y}_{\mathscr{D}})}(\mathcal{G}) \leq 1$$

$\mathscr{D}(\dot{\mathcal{G}})$ is an assembly of LDFSs over $\dot{\mathcal{G}}$. $\tilde{\mathscr{A}}_*(\mathscr{Y}_{\mathscr{D}})$ and $\tilde{\mathscr{A}}^*(\mathscr{Y}_{\mathscr{D}})$ are LDFSs over $\ddot{\mathcal{Q}}$. Thus, the pair $(\tilde{\mathscr{A}}_*(\mathscr{Y}_{\mathscr{D}}), \tilde{\mathscr{A}}^*(\mathscr{Y}_{\mathscr{D}}))$ is called the soft rough linear Diophantine fuzzy set (SRLDFS) about $(\ddot{\mathcal{Q}}, \dot{\mathcal{G}}, \tilde{\mathscr{A}})$, and $\tilde{\mathscr{A}}^*, \tilde{\mathscr{A}}_* : \mathscr{D}(\dot{\mathcal{G}}) \to \mathscr{D}(\ddot{\mathcal{Q}})$ are called upper and lower SRLDF approximation operators. If $\tilde{\mathscr{A}}_*(\mathscr{Y}_{\mathscr{D}}) = \tilde{\mathscr{A}}^*(\mathscr{Y}_{\mathscr{D}})$, then $\mathscr{Y}_{\mathscr{D}}$ is called definable.

Example 2. *We consider the collection of well known cars given as $\ddot{\mathcal{Q}} = \{\mathcal{G}_1, \mathcal{G}_2, \mathcal{G}_3, \mathcal{G}_4\}$ and the assembly of suitable attributes $\dot{\mathcal{G}} = \{\dot{\wp}_1, \dot{\wp}_2, \dot{\wp}_3, \dot{\wp}_4\}$. The attributes are given as "comfortable and reliable", "good safety", "good maintenance", and "affordable". Let $(\eta, \dot{\mathcal{G}})$ be the soft set in $\ddot{\mathcal{Q}}$ given as:*

$$\eta(\dot{\wp}_1) = \{\mathcal{G}_1, \mathcal{G}_2, \mathcal{G}_3\}, \qquad \eta(\dot{\wp}_2) = \{\mathcal{G}_2, \mathcal{G}_4\}$$
$$\eta(\dot{\wp}_3) = \{\mathcal{G}_1, \mathcal{G}_2, \mathcal{G}_3, \mathcal{G}_4\}, \qquad \eta(\dot{\wp}_4) = \{\mathcal{G}_1, \mathcal{G}_4\}$$

A crisp relation over $\ddot{\mathcal{Q}} \times \dot{\mathcal{G}}$ is given as
$\tilde{\mathscr{A}} = \{(\mathcal{G}_1, \dot{\wp}_1), (\mathcal{G}_2, \dot{\wp}_1), (\mathcal{G}_3, \dot{\wp}_1), (\mathcal{G}_2, \dot{\wp}_2), (\mathcal{G}_4, \dot{\wp}_2), (\mathcal{G}_1, \dot{\wp}_3), (\mathcal{G}_2, \dot{\wp}_3), (\mathcal{G}_3, \dot{\wp}_3), (\mathcal{G}_4, \dot{\wp}_3), (\mathcal{G}_1, \dot{\wp}_4), (\mathcal{G}_4, \dot{\wp}_4)\}$.
By definition, we have:

$$\tilde{\mathscr{A}}_s(\mathcal{G}_1) = \{\dot{\wp}_1, \dot{\wp}_3, \dot{\wp}_4\}$$
$$\tilde{\mathscr{A}}_s(\mathcal{G}_2) = \{\dot{\wp}_1, \dot{\wp}_2, \dot{\wp}_3\}$$
$$\tilde{\mathscr{A}}_s(\mathcal{G}_3) = \{\dot{\wp}_1, \dot{\wp}_3\}$$
$$\tilde{\mathscr{A}}_s(\mathcal{G}_4) = \{\dot{\wp}_2, \dot{\wp}_3, \dot{\wp}_4\}$$

We consider LDFS, $\mathscr{Y}_{\mathscr{D}} \in \mathscr{D}(\dot{\mathcal{G}})$, given as:

$$\mathscr{Y}_{\mathscr{D}} = \{(\dot{\wp}_1, \langle 0.786, 0.765\rangle, \langle 0.234, 0.123\rangle), (\dot{\wp}_2, \langle 0.987, 0.574\rangle, \langle 0.232, 0.423\rangle),$$
$$(\dot{\wp}_3, \langle 0.912, 0.536\rangle, \langle 0.235, 0.635\rangle), (\dot{\wp}_4, \langle 0.726, 0.825\rangle, \langle 0.765, 0.122\rangle)\}$$

The "upper and lower approximations" can be computed by using Definition 9. Upper approximations are given as:

$$\ddot{\mathcal{T}}_{\tilde{\mathscr{A}}^*(\mathscr{Y}_{\mathscr{D}})}(\mathcal{G}_1) = 0.912, \ddot{\mathcal{S}}_{\tilde{\mathscr{A}}^*(\mathscr{Y}_{\mathscr{D}})}(\mathcal{G}_1) = 0.536, \alpha_{\tilde{\mathscr{A}}^*(\mathscr{Y}_{\mathscr{D}})}(\mathcal{G}_1) = 0.765, \beta_{\tilde{\mathscr{A}}^*(\mathscr{Y}_{\mathscr{D}})}(\mathcal{G}_1) = 0.122$$
$$\ddot{\mathcal{T}}_{\tilde{\mathscr{A}}^*(\mathscr{Y}_{\mathscr{D}})}(\mathcal{G}_2) = 0.987, \ddot{\mathcal{S}}_{\tilde{\mathscr{A}}^*(\mathscr{Y}_{\mathscr{D}})}(\mathcal{G}_2) = 0.574, \alpha_{\tilde{\mathscr{A}}^*(\mathscr{Y}_{\mathscr{D}})}(\mathcal{G}_2) = 0.765, \beta_{\tilde{\mathscr{A}}^*(\mathscr{Y}_{\mathscr{D}})}(\mathcal{G}_2) = 0.122$$
$$\ddot{\mathcal{T}}_{\tilde{\mathscr{A}}^*(\mathscr{Y}_{\mathscr{D}})}(\mathcal{G}_3) = 0.912, \ddot{\mathcal{S}}_{\tilde{\mathscr{A}}^*(\mathscr{Y}_{\mathscr{D}})}(\mathcal{G}_3) = 0.536, \alpha_{\tilde{\mathscr{A}}^*(\mathscr{Y}_{\mathscr{D}})}(\mathcal{G}_3) = 0.235, \beta_{\tilde{\mathscr{A}}^*(\mathscr{Y}_{\mathscr{D}})}(\mathcal{G}_3) = 0.123$$
$$\ddot{\mathcal{T}}_{\tilde{\mathscr{A}}^*(\mathscr{Y}_{\mathscr{D}})}(\mathcal{G}_4) = 0.987, \ddot{\mathcal{S}}_{\tilde{\mathscr{A}}^*(\mathscr{Y}_{\mathscr{D}})}(\mathcal{G}_4) = 0.536, \alpha_{\tilde{\mathscr{A}}^*(\mathscr{Y}_{\mathscr{D}})}(\mathcal{G}_4) = 0.765, \beta_{\tilde{\mathscr{A}}^*(\mathscr{Y}_{\mathscr{D}})}(\mathcal{G}_4) = 0.122$$

Lower approximations are evaluated as:

$$\ddot{\mathcal{T}}_{\tilde{\mathscr{A}}_*(\mathscr{Y}_{\mathscr{D}})}(\mathcal{G}_1) = 0.726, \ddot{\mathcal{S}}_{\tilde{\mathscr{A}}_*(\mathscr{Y}_{\mathscr{D}})}(\mathcal{G}_1) = 0.825, \alpha_{\tilde{\mathscr{A}}_*(\mathscr{Y}_{\mathscr{D}})}(\mathcal{G}_1) = 0.234, \beta_{\tilde{\mathscr{A}}_*(\mathscr{Y}_{\mathscr{D}})}(\mathcal{G}_1) = 0.635$$
$$\ddot{\mathcal{T}}_{\tilde{\mathscr{A}}_*(\mathscr{Y}_{\mathscr{D}})}(\mathcal{G}_2) = 0.786, \ddot{\mathcal{S}}_{\tilde{\mathscr{A}}_*(\mathscr{Y}_{\mathscr{D}})}(\mathcal{G}_2) = 0.765, \alpha_{\tilde{\mathscr{A}}_*(\mathscr{Y}_{\mathscr{D}})}(\mathcal{G}_2) = 0.232, \beta_{\tilde{\mathscr{A}}_*(\mathscr{Y}_{\mathscr{D}})}(\mathcal{G}_2) = 0.635$$
$$\ddot{\mathcal{T}}_{\tilde{\mathscr{A}}_*(\mathscr{Y}_{\mathscr{D}})}(\mathcal{G}_3) = 0.786, \ddot{\mathcal{S}}_{\tilde{\mathscr{A}}_*(\mathscr{Y}_{\mathscr{D}})}(\mathcal{G}_3) = 0.765, \alpha_{\tilde{\mathscr{A}}_*(\mathscr{Y}_{\mathscr{D}})}(\mathcal{G}_3) = 0.234, \beta_{\tilde{\mathscr{A}}_*(\mathscr{Y}_{\mathscr{D}})}(\mathcal{G}_3) = 0.635$$
$$\ddot{\mathcal{T}}_{\tilde{\mathscr{A}}_*(\mathscr{Y}_{\mathscr{D}})}(\mathcal{G}_4) = 0.726, \ddot{\mathcal{S}}_{\tilde{\mathscr{A}}_*(\mathscr{Y}_{\mathscr{D}})}(\mathcal{G}_4) = 0.825, \alpha_{\tilde{\mathscr{A}}_*(\mathscr{Y}_{\mathscr{D}})}(\mathcal{G}_4) = 0.232, \beta_{\tilde{\mathscr{A}}_*(\mathscr{Y}_{\mathscr{D}})}(\mathcal{G}_4) = 0.635$$

Thus:

$$\begin{aligned}\tilde{\mathscr{A}}^*(\mathscr{Y}_{\mathscr{D}}) = \{&(\mathcal{G}_1, \langle 00.912, 00.536\rangle, \langle 00.765, 00.122\rangle), (\mathcal{G}_2, \langle 00.987, 00.574\rangle, \langle 00.765, 00.122\rangle),\\ &(\mathcal{G}_3, \langle 00.912, 00.536\rangle, \langle 00.235, 00.123\rangle)\}, (\mathcal{G}_4, \langle 00.987, 00.536\rangle, \langle 00.765, 00.122\rangle)\}\\ \tilde{\mathscr{A}}_*(\mathscr{Y}_{\mathscr{D}}) = \{&(\mathcal{G}_1, \langle 00.726, 00.825\rangle, \langle 00.234, 00.635\rangle), (\mathcal{G}_2, \langle 00.786, 00.765\rangle, \langle 00.232, 00.635\rangle),\\ &(\mathcal{G}_3, \langle 00.786, 00.765\rangle, \langle 00.234, 00.635\rangle)\}, (\mathcal{G}_4, \langle 00.726, 00.825\rangle, \langle 00.232, 00.635\rangle)\}\end{aligned}$$

Therefore, $(\tilde{\mathscr{A}}_*(\mathscr{Y}_{\mathscr{D}}), \tilde{\mathscr{A}}^*(\mathscr{Y}_{\mathscr{D}}))$ is said to be SRLDFS.

Remark 2. *For the "crisp soft approximation space" $(\ddot{\mathcal{Q}}, \dot{\mathcal{G}}, \tilde{\mathscr{A}})$, if we take the upper and lower approximations of the following sets listed in Table 5, then we can observe the degeneration of SRLDF approximation operators into different structures based on rough sets.*

It is evident from Table 5 that our proposed model is superior and powerful in contrast with other existing structures. However, we cannot decompose the described theories into the SRLDFSs and their respective approximation operators. In simple terms, SRLDFS is the generalization of "soft rough sets, soft rough fuzzy sets, soft rough intuitionistic fuzzy sets, soft rough Pythagorean fuzzy sets, and soft rough q-rung orthopair fuzzy sets".

Theorem 2. *Let $\mathscr{Y}_{\mathscr{D}}, \mathscr{B}_{\mathscr{D}} \in \mathscr{D}(\mathcal{G})$ and $\tilde{\mathscr{A}}^*(\mathscr{Y}_{\mathscr{D}})$, $\tilde{\mathscr{A}}^*(\mathscr{Y}_{\mathscr{D}})$ be "upper and lower approximation operators" over the approximation space $(\ddot{\mathcal{Q}}, \dot{\mathcal{G}}, \tilde{\mathscr{A}})$, then the following axioms are true:*

(1) $\tilde{\mathscr{A}}_*(\mathscr{Y}_{\mathscr{D}}) = \sim \tilde{\mathscr{A}}^*(\sim \mathscr{Y}_{\mathscr{D}})$,
(2) $\mathscr{Y}_{\mathscr{D}} \subseteq \mathscr{B}_{\mathscr{D}} \Rightarrow \tilde{\mathscr{A}}_*(\mathscr{Y}_{\mathscr{D}}) \subseteq \tilde{\mathscr{A}}_*(\mathscr{B}_{\mathscr{D}})$,
(3) $\tilde{\mathscr{A}}_*(\mathscr{Y}_{\mathscr{D}} \cap \mathscr{B}_{\mathscr{D}}) = \tilde{\mathscr{A}}_*(\mathscr{Y}_{\mathscr{D}}) \cap \tilde{\mathscr{A}}_*(\mathscr{B}_{\mathscr{D}})$,
(4) $\tilde{\mathscr{A}}_*(\mathscr{Y}_{\mathscr{D}} \cup \mathscr{B}_{\mathscr{D}}) \supseteq \tilde{\mathscr{A}}_*(\mathscr{Y}_{\mathscr{D}}) \cup \tilde{\mathscr{A}}_*(\mathscr{B}_{\mathscr{D}})$,
(5) $\tilde{\mathscr{A}}^*(\mathscr{Y}_{\mathscr{D}}) = \sim \tilde{\mathscr{A}}_*(\sim \mathscr{Y}_{\mathscr{D}})$,
(6) $\mathscr{Y}_{\mathscr{D}} \subseteq \mathscr{B}_{\mathscr{D}} \Rightarrow \tilde{\mathscr{A}}^*(\mathscr{Y}_{\mathscr{D}}) \subseteq \tilde{\mathscr{A}}^*(\mathscr{B}_{\mathscr{D}})$,
(7) $\tilde{\mathscr{A}}^*(\mathscr{Y}_{\mathscr{D}} \cup \mathscr{B}_{\mathscr{D}}) = \tilde{\mathscr{A}}^*(\mathscr{Y}_{\mathscr{D}}) \cup \tilde{\mathscr{A}}^*(\mathscr{B}_{\mathscr{D}})$,
(8) $\tilde{\mathscr{A}}^*(\mathscr{Y}_{\mathscr{D}} \cap \mathscr{B}_{\mathscr{D}}) \subseteq \tilde{\mathscr{A}}^*(\mathscr{Y}_{\mathscr{D}}) \cap \tilde{\mathscr{A}}^*(\mathscr{B}_{\mathscr{D}})$.

The complement of $\mathscr{Y}_{\mathscr{D}}$ is represented by $\sim \mathscr{Y}_{\mathscr{D}}$.

Proof. See Appendix A. □

Now, we provide a counter example to prove that equality does not exist in Parts (4) and (8) of Theorem 2.

Table 5. Degeneration of SRLDF approximation operators into different rough set models.

Approximation Space	Set Theories	Family of Sets	Degeneration of SRLDF Approximation Operators	After Degeneration of the Constructed Model
Crisp soft $(\ddot{\mathcal{Q}}, \dot{\mathcal{G}}, \ddot{\mathscr{A}})$	$\mathscr{Y}_{\mathscr{D}}$=crisp set$\in P(\dot{\mathcal{G}})$	$P(\dot{\mathcal{G}})$ collection of all crisp subsets of $\dot{\mathcal{G}}$	Yes	Soft rough sets [26]
Crisp soft $(\ddot{\mathcal{Q}}, \dot{\mathcal{G}}, \ddot{\mathscr{A}})$	$\mathscr{Y}_{\mathscr{D}} = \{\langle \dot{\wp}, \ddot{\mathscr{T}}(\dot{\wp})\rangle : \dot{\wp} \in \dot{\mathcal{G}}\} \in \mathcal{F}(\dot{\mathcal{G}})$	$\mathcal{F}(\dot{\mathcal{G}})$ collection of all fuzzy subsets of $\dot{\mathcal{G}}$	Yes	Soft rough fuzzy sets [42,43]
Crisp soft $(\ddot{\mathcal{Q}}, \dot{\mathcal{G}}, \ddot{\mathscr{A}})$	$\mathscr{Y}_{\mathscr{D}} = \{\langle \dot{\wp}, \ddot{\mathscr{T}}(\dot{\wp}), \ddot{\mathcal{S}}(\dot{\wp})\rangle : \dot{\wp} \in \dot{\mathcal{G}}\} \in \mathcal{I}(\dot{\mathcal{G}})$	$\mathcal{I}(\dot{\mathcal{G}})$ collection of all IF-subsets of $\dot{\mathcal{G}}$	Yes	Soft rough intuitionistic fuzzy sets [26]
Crisp soft $(\ddot{\mathcal{Q}}, \dot{\mathcal{G}}, \ddot{\mathscr{A}})$	$\mathscr{Y}_{\mathscr{D}} = \{\langle \dot{\wp}, \ddot{\mathscr{T}}(\dot{\wp}), \ddot{\mathcal{S}}(\dot{\wp})\rangle : \dot{\wp} \in \dot{\mathcal{G}}\} \in \mathcal{P}(\dot{\mathcal{G}})$	$\mathcal{P}(\dot{\mathcal{G}})$ collection of all PF-subsets of $\dot{\mathcal{G}}$	Yes	Soft rough Pythagorean fuzzy sets [44]
Crisp soft $(\ddot{\mathcal{Q}}, \dot{\mathcal{G}}, \ddot{\mathscr{A}})$	$\mathscr{Y}_{\mathscr{D}} = \{\langle \dot{\wp}, \ddot{\mathscr{T}}(\dot{\wp}), \ddot{\mathcal{S}}(\dot{\wp})\rangle : \dot{\wp} \in \dot{\mathcal{G}}\} \in \mathcal{R}(\dot{\mathcal{G}})$	$\mathcal{R}(\dot{\mathcal{G}})$ collection of all PF-subsets of $\dot{\mathcal{G}}$	Yes	Soft rough q-rung orthopair fuzzy sets

Example 3. *For the reference set* $\ddot{\mathcal{Q}} = \{\mathcal{G}_1, \mathcal{G}_2, \mathcal{G}_3, \mathcal{G}_4\}$ *and assembly of decision variables* $\dot{\mathcal{G}} = \{\dot{\wp}_1, \dot{\wp}_2, \dot{\wp}_3\}$, *we define a soft set* $(\eta, \dot{\mathcal{G}})$ *in* $\ddot{\mathcal{Q}}$ *written as:*

$$\beta(\dot{\wp}_1) = \{\mathcal{G}_1, \mathcal{G}_4\}, \beta(\dot{\wp}_2) = \{\mathcal{G}_1, \mathcal{G}_2, \mathcal{G}_4\}, \beta(\dot{\wp}_3) = \{\mathcal{G}_2, \mathcal{G}_3\}$$

The crisp soft relation $\tilde{\mathscr{A}}$ *in* $\ddot{\mathcal{Q}} \times \dot{\mathcal{G}}$ *is given as* $\tilde{\mathscr{A}} = \{(\mathcal{G}_1, \dot{\wp}_1), (\mathcal{G}_4, \dot{\wp}_1), (\mathcal{G}_1, \dot{\wp}_2), (\mathcal{G}_2, \dot{\wp}_2), (\mathcal{G}_4, \dot{\wp}_2), (\mathcal{G}_2, \dot{\wp}_3), (\mathcal{G}_3, \dot{\wp}_3)\}$. *We can write it as:*

$$\tilde{\mathscr{A}}_s(\mathcal{G}_1) = \{\dot{\wp}_1, \dot{\wp}_2\}, \tilde{\mathscr{A}}_s(\mathcal{G}_2) = \{\dot{\wp}_2, \dot{\wp}_3\}, \tilde{\mathscr{A}}_s(\mathcal{G}_3) = \{\dot{\wp}_3\}, \tilde{\mathscr{A}}_s(\mathcal{G}_4) = \{\dot{\wp}_1, \dot{\wp}_2\}$$

Let $\mathscr{Y}_{\mathscr{D}}, \mathscr{B}_{\mathscr{D}} \in \mathscr{D}(\mathcal{G})$ *be given as follows:*

$$\begin{aligned}\mathscr{Y}_{\mathscr{D}} = \{&(\dot{\wp}_1, \langle 0.573, 0.273\rangle, \langle 0.271, 0.531\rangle),\\ &(\dot{\wp}_2, \langle 0.378, 0.177\rangle, \langle 0.291, 0.532\rangle),\\ &(\dot{\wp}_3, \langle 0.678, 0.178\rangle, \langle 0.271, 0.521\rangle)\}\end{aligned} \qquad \begin{aligned}\mathscr{B}_{\mathscr{D}} = \{&(\dot{\wp}_1, \langle 0.773, 0.273\rangle, \langle 0.281, 0.523\rangle),\\ &(\dot{\wp}_2, \langle 0.778, 0.371\rangle, \langle 0.283, 0.521\rangle),\\ &(\dot{\wp}_3, \langle 0.873, 0.371\rangle, \langle 0.261, 0.532\rangle)\}\end{aligned}$$

The "upper approximations" are given as:

$$\begin{aligned}\tilde{\mathscr{A}}^*(\mathscr{Y}_{\mathscr{D}}) &= \{(\mathcal{G}_1, \langle 00.573, 00.177\rangle, \langle 00.291, 00.531\rangle), (\mathcal{G}_2, \langle 00.678, 00.177\rangle, \langle 00.291, 00.521\rangle),\\ &\quad(\mathcal{G}_3, \langle 00.678, 00.178\rangle, \langle 00.271, 00.521\rangle), (\mathcal{G}_4, \langle 00.573, 00.177\rangle, \langle 00.291, 00.531\rangle)\}\\ \tilde{\mathscr{A}}^*(\mathscr{B}_{\mathscr{D}}) &= \{(\mathcal{G}_1, \langle 00.778, 00.273\rangle, \langle 00.283, 00.521\rangle), (\mathcal{G}_2, \langle 00.873, 00.371\rangle, \langle 00.261, 00.521\rangle),\\ &\quad(\mathcal{G}_3, \langle 00.873, 00.371\rangle, \langle 00.261, 00.532\rangle), (\mathcal{G}_4, \langle 00.778, 00.273\rangle, \langle 00.283, 00.521\rangle)\}\\ \tilde{\mathscr{A}}^*(\mathscr{Y}_{\mathscr{D}} \cap \mathscr{B}_{\mathscr{D}}) &= \{(\mathcal{G}_1, \langle 00.573, 00.273\rangle, \langle 00.283, 00.531\rangle), (\mathcal{G}_2, \langle 00.678, 00.371\rangle, \langle 00.261, 00.532\rangle),\\ &\quad(\mathcal{G}_3, \langle 00.678, 00.371\rangle, \langle 00.261, 00.532\rangle), (\mathcal{G}_4, \langle 00.573, 00.273\rangle, \langle 00.283, 00.531\rangle)\}\\ \tilde{\mathscr{A}}^*(\mathscr{Y}_{\mathscr{D}}) \cap \tilde{\mathscr{A}}^*(\mathscr{B}_{\mathscr{D}}) &= \{(\mathcal{G}_1, \langle 00.573, 00.273\rangle, \langle 00.283, 00.531\rangle), (\mathcal{G}_2, \langle 00.678, 00.371\rangle, \langle 00.261, 00.521\rangle),\\ &\quad(\mathcal{G}_3, \langle 00.678, 00.371\rangle, \langle 00.261, 00.532\rangle), (\mathcal{G}_4, \langle 00.573, 00.273\rangle, \langle 00.283, 00.531\rangle)\}\end{aligned}$$

From the above calculations, it is clear that $\tilde{\mathscr{A}}^*(\mathscr{Y}_{\mathscr{D}}) \cap \tilde{\mathscr{A}}^*(\mathscr{B}_{\mathscr{D}}) \nsubseteq \tilde{\mathscr{A}}^*(\mathscr{Y}_{\mathscr{D}} \cap \mathscr{B}_{\mathscr{D}})$ *as for alternative* $\mathcal{G}_2$, *the degrees of reference parameter* $\beta_{\tilde{\mathscr{A}}^*(\mathscr{Y}_{\mathscr{D}}) \cap \tilde{\mathscr{A}}^*(\mathscr{B}_{\mathscr{D}})}(\mathcal{G}_2) \ngeq \beta_{\tilde{\mathscr{A}}^*(\mathscr{Y}_{\mathscr{D}} \cap \mathscr{B}_{\mathscr{D}})}(\mathcal{G}_2)$, *i.e.*, $00.521 \ngeq 00.532$. *Similarly, we can check that* $\tilde{\mathscr{A}}_*(\mathscr{Y}_{\mathscr{D}} \cup \mathscr{B}_{\mathscr{D}}) \nsubseteq \tilde{\mathscr{A}}_*(\mathscr{Y}_{\mathscr{D}}) \cup \tilde{\mathscr{A}}_*(\mathscr{B}_{\mathscr{D}})$.

Proposition 1. *If* $\mathscr{Y}_{\mathscr{D}}, \mathscr{B}_{\mathscr{D}} \in \mathscr{D}(\mathcal{G})$, *then* $\tilde{\mathscr{A}}_*(\mathscr{Y}_{\mathscr{D}}), \tilde{\mathscr{A}}_*(\mathscr{B}_{\mathscr{D}}), \tilde{\mathscr{A}}^*(\mathscr{Y}_{\mathscr{D}})$ *and* $\tilde{\mathscr{A}}^*(\mathscr{B}_{\mathscr{D}})$ *are "lower and upper approximations" of LDFSs over the "crisp soft approximation space"* $(\ddot{\mathcal{Q}}, \dot{\mathcal{G}}, \tilde{\mathscr{A}})$ *satisfying the following axioms:*

(1) $\sim(\tilde{\mathscr{A}}_*(\mathscr{Y}_{\mathscr{D}}) \cup \tilde{\mathscr{A}}_*(\mathscr{B}_{\mathscr{D}})) = \tilde{\mathscr{A}}^*(\sim\mathscr{Y}_{\mathscr{D}}) \cap \tilde{\mathscr{A}}^*(\sim\mathscr{B}_{\mathscr{D}})$,
(2) $\sim(\tilde{\mathscr{A}}_*(\mathscr{Y}_{\mathscr{D}}) \cup \tilde{\mathscr{A}}^*(\mathscr{B}_{\mathscr{D}})) = \tilde{\mathscr{A}}^*(\sim\mathscr{Y}_{\mathscr{D}}) \cap \tilde{\mathscr{A}}_*(\sim\mathscr{B}_{\mathscr{D}})$,
(3) $\sim(\tilde{\mathscr{A}}^*(\mathscr{Y}_{\mathscr{D}}) \cup \tilde{\mathscr{A}}_*(\mathscr{B}_{\mathscr{D}})) = \tilde{\mathscr{A}}_*(\sim\mathscr{Y}_{\mathscr{D}}) \cap \tilde{\mathscr{A}}^*(\sim\mathscr{B}_{\mathscr{D}})$,
(4) $\sim(\tilde{\mathscr{A}}^*(\mathscr{Y}_{\mathscr{D}}) \cup \tilde{\mathscr{A}}^*(\mathscr{B}_{\mathscr{D}})) = \tilde{\mathscr{A}}_*(\sim\mathscr{Y}_{\mathscr{D}}) \cap \tilde{\mathscr{A}}_*(\sim\mathscr{B}_{\mathscr{D}})$,
(5) $\sim(\tilde{\mathscr{A}}_*(\mathscr{Y}_{\mathscr{D}}) \cap \tilde{\mathscr{A}}_*(\mathscr{B}_{\mathscr{D}})) = \tilde{\mathscr{A}}^*(\sim\mathscr{Y}_{\mathscr{D}}) \cup \tilde{\mathscr{A}}^*(\sim\mathscr{B}_{\mathscr{D}})$,
(6) $\sim(\tilde{\mathscr{A}}_*(\mathscr{Y}_{\mathscr{D}}) \cap \tilde{\mathscr{A}}^*(\mathscr{B}_{\mathscr{D}})) = \tilde{\mathscr{A}}^*(\sim\mathscr{Y}_{\mathscr{D}}) \cup \tilde{\mathscr{A}}_*(\sim\mathscr{B}_{\mathscr{D}})$,
(7) $\sim(\tilde{\mathscr{A}}^*(\mathscr{Y}_{\mathscr{D}}) \cap \tilde{\mathscr{A}}_*(\mathscr{B}_{\mathscr{D}})) = \tilde{\mathscr{A}}_*(\sim\mathscr{Y}_{\mathscr{D}}) \cup \tilde{\mathscr{A}}^*(\sim\mathscr{B}_{\mathscr{D}})$,
(8) $\sim(\tilde{\mathscr{A}}^*(\mathscr{Y}_{\mathscr{D}}) \cap \tilde{\mathscr{A}}^*(\mathscr{B}_{\mathscr{D}})) = \tilde{\mathscr{A}}_*(\sim\mathscr{Y}_{\mathscr{D}}) \cup \tilde{\mathscr{A}}_*(\sim\mathscr{B}_{\mathscr{D}})$.

Proof. The proof is obvious. □

3.2. Linear Diophantine Fuzzy Soft Rough Sets

Definition 10. *For the non-empty set of alternatives $\ddot{\mathcal{Q}}$ and the collection of attributes $\dot{\mathcal{G}}$, we consider a subset $\dot{\mathcal{O}} \subseteq \dot{\mathcal{G}}$. Then, we define linear Diophantine fuzzy soft set (LDFSS), $(\ddot{\delta}, \dot{\mathcal{O}})$ represented by the mapping:*

$$\ddot{\delta} : \dot{\mathcal{O}} \to \mathscr{D}(\ddot{\mathcal{Q}})$$

where $\mathscr{D}(\ddot{\mathcal{Q}})$ is an assembly of all LDF-subsets of $\ddot{\mathcal{Q}}$. Alternatively, it can be written as:

$$(\ddot{\delta}, \dot{\mathcal{O}}) = \{(\dot{\wp}, \ddot{\delta}(\dot{\wp})) : \dot{\wp} \in \dot{\mathcal{O}}, \ddot{\delta}(\dot{\wp}) \in \mathscr{D}(\ddot{\mathcal{Q}})\}$$

Definition 11. *Let $(\ddot{\delta}, \dot{\mathcal{O}})$ be an LDFSS in $\ddot{\mathcal{Q}}$. Then, an LDF-subset $\tilde{\mathfrak{F}}$ of $\ddot{\mathcal{Q}} \times \dot{\mathcal{G}}$ is called a linear Diophantine fuzzy soft relation (LDFSR) from $\ddot{\mathcal{Q}}$ to $\dot{\mathcal{G}}$ written as:*

$$\tilde{\mathfrak{F}} = \{((\mathcal{G}, \dot{\wp}), \langle \ddot{\mathscr{T}}_{\mathfrak{F}}(\mathcal{G}, \dot{\wp}), \ddot{\mathcal{S}}_{\mathfrak{F}}(\mathcal{G}, \dot{\wp})\rangle, \langle \alpha_{\mathfrak{F}}(\mathcal{G}, \dot{\wp}), \beta_{\mathfrak{F}}(\mathcal{G}, \dot{\wp})\rangle) : (\mathcal{G}, \dot{\wp}) \in \ddot{\mathcal{Q}} \times \dot{\mathcal{G}}\}$$

where ${}^{\alpha}\ddot{\mathscr{T}}_{\mathfrak{F}}(\mathcal{G}, \dot{\wp}), {}^{\alpha}\ddot{\mathcal{S}}_{\mathfrak{F}}(\mathcal{G}, \dot{\wp}) \in [0,1]$ are truth and falsity grades, respectively, with the corresponding reference parameters $\alpha_{\mathfrak{F}}(\mathcal{G}, \dot{\wp}), \beta_{\mathfrak{F}}(\mathcal{G}, \dot{\wp}) \in [0,1]$ satisfying the constraints:

$$0 \leq \alpha_{\mathfrak{F}}(\mathcal{G}, \dot{\wp})^{\alpha} \ddot{\mathscr{T}}^2_{\mathfrak{F}}(\mathcal{G}, \dot{\wp}) + \beta_{\mathfrak{F}}(\mathcal{G}, \dot{\wp})^{\alpha} \ddot{\mathcal{S}}^2_{\mathfrak{F}}(\mathcal{G}, \dot{\wp}) \leq 1$$

$$0 \leq \alpha_{\mathfrak{F}}(\mathcal{G}, \dot{\wp}) + \beta_{\mathfrak{F}}(\mathcal{G}, \dot{\wp}) \leq 1$$

If $\ddot{\mathcal{Q}} = \{\mathcal{G}_1, \mathcal{G}_2, ..., \mathcal{G}_n\}$ and $\dot{\mathcal{G}} = \{\dot{\wp}_1, \dot{\wp}_2, ..., \dot{\wp}_m\}$, then LDFSR $\tilde{\mathfrak{F}}$ on $\ddot{\mathcal{Q}} \times \dot{\mathcal{G}}$ can be represented in tabular form as Table 6.

Table 6. LDFSR.

$\tilde{\mathfrak{F}}$	$\dot{\wp}_1$	...	$\dot{\wp}_m$
$\mathcal{G}_1$	$\langle \ddot{\mathscr{T}}_{\mathfrak{F}}(\mathcal{G}_1, \dot{\wp}_1), \ddot{\mathcal{S}}_{\mathfrak{F}}(\mathcal{G}_1, \dot{\wp}_1)\rangle, \langle \alpha_{\mathfrak{F}}(\mathcal{G}_1, \dot{\wp}_1), \beta_{\mathfrak{F}}(\mathcal{G}_1, \dot{\wp}_1)\rangle$	...	$\langle \ddot{\mathscr{T}}_{\mathfrak{F}}(\mathcal{G}_1, \dot{\wp}_m), \ddot{\mathcal{S}}_{\mathfrak{F}}(\mathcal{G}_1, \dot{\wp}_m)\rangle, \langle \alpha_{\mathfrak{F}}(\mathcal{G}_1, \dot{\wp}_m), \beta_{\mathfrak{F}}(\mathcal{G}_1, \dot{\wp}_m)\rangle$
$\mathcal{G}_2$	$\langle \ddot{\mathscr{T}}_{\mathfrak{F}}(\mathcal{G}_2, \dot{\wp}_1), \ddot{\mathcal{S}}_{\mathfrak{F}}(\mathcal{G}_2, \dot{\wp}_1)\rangle, \langle \alpha_{\mathfrak{F}}(\mathcal{G}_2, \dot{\wp}_1), \beta_{\mathfrak{F}}(\mathcal{G}_2, \dot{\wp}_1)\rangle$	...	$\langle \ddot{\mathscr{T}}_{\mathfrak{F}}(\mathcal{G}_2, \dot{\wp}_m), \ddot{\mathcal{S}}_{\mathfrak{F}}(\mathcal{G}_2, \dot{\wp}_m)\rangle, \langle \alpha_{\mathfrak{F}}(\mathcal{G}_2, \dot{\wp}_m), \beta_{\mathfrak{F}}(\mathcal{G}_2, \dot{\wp}_m)\rangle$
...	...	...	...
$\mathcal{G}_n$	$\langle \ddot{\mathscr{T}}_{\mathfrak{F}}(\mathcal{G}_n, \dot{\wp}_1), \ddot{\mathcal{S}}_{\mathfrak{F}}(\mathcal{G}_n, \dot{\wp}_1)\rangle, \langle \alpha_{\mathfrak{F}}(\mathcal{G}_n, \dot{\wp}_1), \beta_{\mathfrak{F}}(\mathcal{G}_n, \dot{\wp}_1)\rangle$	...	$\langle \ddot{\mathscr{T}}_{\mathfrak{F}}(\mathcal{G}_n, \dot{\wp}_m), \ddot{\mathcal{S}}_{\mathfrak{F}}(\mathcal{G}_n, \dot{\wp}_m)\rangle, \langle \alpha_{\mathfrak{F}}(\mathcal{G}_n, \dot{\wp}_m), \beta_{\mathfrak{F}}(\mathcal{G}_n, \dot{\wp}_m)\rangle$

Definition 12. *For the reference set $\ddot{\mathcal{Q}}$ and set of decision variables $\dot{\mathcal{G}}$, if we define an LDFSR $\tilde{\mathfrak{F}}$ over $\ddot{\mathcal{Q}} \times \dot{\mathcal{G}}$, then $(\ddot{\mathcal{Q}}, \dot{\mathcal{G}}, \tilde{\mathfrak{F}})$ is called an "LDFS approximation space". If $\mathscr{Y}_{\mathscr{D}} \in \mathscr{D}(\dot{\mathcal{G}})$, then $\tilde{\mathfrak{F}}^*(\mathscr{Y}_{\mathscr{D}})$ and $\tilde{\mathfrak{F}}_*(\mathscr{Y}_{\mathscr{D}})$ are "upper and lower approximations" of $\mathscr{Y}_{\mathscr{D}}$ about $(\ddot{\mathcal{Q}}, \dot{\mathcal{G}}, \tilde{\mathfrak{F}})$ respectively and written as:*

$$\tilde{\mathfrak{F}}^*(\mathscr{Y}_{\mathscr{D}}) = \{(\mathcal{G}, \langle \ddot{\mathscr{T}}_{\tilde{\mathfrak{F}}^*(\mathscr{Y}_{\mathscr{D}})}(\mathcal{G}), \ddot{\mathcal{S}}_{\tilde{\mathfrak{F}}^*(\mathscr{Y}_{\mathscr{D}})}(\mathcal{G})\rangle, \langle \alpha_{\tilde{\mathfrak{F}}^*(\mathscr{Y}_{\mathscr{D}})}(\mathcal{G}), \beta_{\tilde{\mathfrak{F}}^*(\mathscr{Y}_{\mathscr{D}})}(\mathcal{G})\rangle) : \mathcal{G} \in \ddot{\mathcal{Q}}\}$$

$$\tilde{\mathfrak{F}}_*(\mathscr{Y}_{\mathscr{D}}) = \{(\mathcal{G}, \langle \ddot{\mathscr{T}}_{\tilde{\mathfrak{F}}_*(\mathscr{Y}_{\mathscr{D}})}(\mathcal{G}), \ddot{\mathcal{S}}_{\tilde{\mathfrak{F}}_*(\mathscr{Y}_{\mathscr{D}})}(\mathcal{G})\rangle, \langle \alpha_{\tilde{\mathfrak{F}}_*(\mathscr{Y}_{\mathscr{D}})}(\mathcal{G}), \beta_{\tilde{\mathfrak{F}}_*(\mathscr{Y}_{\mathscr{D}})}(\mathcal{G})\rangle) : \mathcal{G} \in \ddot{\mathcal{Q}}\}$$

where the degrees can be calculated as given in Table 7.

Table 7. Formulation of LDFSRSs.

Notation	Formulation	Notation	Formulation
$\ddot{\mathscr{T}}_{\tilde{\mathfrak{F}}^*(\mathscr{Y}_{\mathscr{D}})}(\mathcal{G})$	$\max_{\dot{\wp} \in \dot{\mathcal{G}}}[\ddot{\mathscr{T}}_{\mathfrak{F}}(\mathcal{G}, \dot{\wp}) \wedge \ddot{\mathscr{T}}_{\mathscr{Y}_{\mathscr{D}}}(\dot{\wp})]$	$\ddot{\mathcal{S}}_{\tilde{\mathfrak{F}}^*(\mathscr{Y}_{\mathscr{D}})}(\mathcal{G})$	$\min_{\dot{\wp} \in \dot{\mathcal{G}}}[(1 - \ddot{\mathcal{S}}_{\mathfrak{F}}(\mathcal{G}, \dot{\wp})) \vee \ddot{\mathcal{S}}_{\mathscr{Y}_{\mathscr{D}}}(\dot{\wp})]$
$\alpha_{\tilde{\mathfrak{F}}^*(\mathscr{Y}_{\mathscr{D}})}(\mathcal{G})$	$\max_{\dot{\wp} \in \dot{\mathcal{G}}}[\alpha_{\mathfrak{F}}(\mathcal{G}, \dot{\wp}) \wedge \alpha_{\mathscr{Y}_{\mathscr{D}}}(\dot{\wp})]$	$\beta_{\tilde{\mathfrak{F}}^*(\mathscr{Y}_{\mathscr{D}})}(\mathcal{G})$	$\min_{\dot{\wp} \in \dot{\mathcal{G}}}[(1 - \beta_{\mathfrak{F}}(\mathcal{G}, \dot{\wp})) \vee \beta_{\mathscr{Y}_{\mathscr{D}}}(\dot{\wp})]$
$\ddot{\mathscr{T}}_{\tilde{\mathfrak{F}}_*(\mathscr{Y}_{\mathscr{D}})}(\mathcal{G})$	$\min_{\dot{\wp} \in \dot{\mathcal{G}}}[(1 - \ddot{\mathscr{T}}_{\mathfrak{F}}(\mathcal{G}, \dot{\wp})) \vee \ddot{\mathscr{T}}_{\mathscr{Y}_{\mathscr{D}}}(\dot{\wp})]$	$\ddot{\mathcal{S}}_{\tilde{\mathfrak{F}}_*(\mathscr{Y}_{\mathscr{D}})}(\mathcal{G})$	$\max_{\dot{\wp} \in \dot{\mathcal{G}}}[\ddot{\mathcal{S}}_{\mathfrak{F}}(\mathcal{G}, \dot{\wp}) \wedge \ddot{\mathcal{S}}_{\mathscr{Y}_{\mathscr{D}}}(\dot{\wp})]$
$\alpha_{\tilde{\mathfrak{F}}_*(\mathscr{Y}_{\mathscr{D}})}(\mathcal{G})$	$\min_{\dot{\wp} \in \dot{\mathcal{G}}}[(1 - \alpha_{\mathfrak{F}}(\mathcal{G}, \dot{\wp})) \vee \alpha_{\mathscr{Y}_{\mathscr{D}}}(\dot{\wp})]$	$\beta_{\tilde{\mathfrak{F}}_*(\mathscr{Y}_{\mathscr{D}})}(\mathcal{G})$	$\max_{\dot{\wp} \in \dot{\mathcal{G}}}[\beta_{\mathfrak{F}}(\mathcal{G}, \dot{\wp}) \wedge \beta_{\mathscr{Y}_{\mathscr{D}}}(\dot{\wp})]$

The pair $(\tilde{\eth}_{\ast}(\mathscr{Y}_{\mathscr{D}}), \tilde{\eth}^{\ast}(\mathscr{Y}_{\mathscr{D}}))$ *is a called linear Diophantine fuzzy soft rough set (LDFSRS) in* $(\ddot{\mathcal{Q}}, \dot{\mathcal{G}}, \tilde{\eth})$. *The "lower and upper approximation operators" are represented as* $\tilde{\eth}_{\ast}(\mathscr{Y}_{\mathscr{D}})$ *and* $\tilde{\eth}^{\ast}(\mathscr{Y}_{\mathscr{D}})$*, respectively. If* $\tilde{\eth}_{\ast}(\mathscr{Y}_{\mathscr{D}}) = \tilde{\eth}^{\ast}(\mathscr{Y}_{\mathscr{D}})$*, then* $\mathscr{Y}_{\mathscr{D}}$ *is said to be definable.*

Example 4. *Let* $\ddot{\mathcal{Q}} = \{\mathcal{G}_1, \mathcal{G}_2\}$ *be the collection of certain cloth brands and* $\dot{\mathcal{G}} = \{\dot{\wp}_1, \dot{\wp}_2, \dot{\wp}_3\}$ *be the set of attributes, where:*

$$\dot{\wp}_1 = \textit{Product quality},$$
$$\dot{\wp}_2 = \textit{Affordable},$$
$$\dot{\wp}_3 = \textit{Recovery service}.$$

We construct the LDFSR, $\tilde{\eth} : \ddot{\mathcal{Q}} \to \dot{\mathcal{G}}$*, represented in Table 8.*

Table 8. LDFSR.

$\tilde{\eth}$	Numeric Values of LDFNs
$\mathcal{G}_1$	$\dot{\wp}_1$:$(\langle 0.684, 0.355\rangle, \langle 0.221, 0.325\rangle)$ $\dot{\wp}_2$:$(\langle 0.825, 0.836\rangle, \langle 0.226, 0.123\rangle)$ $\dot{\wp}_3$:$(\langle 0.826, 0.265\rangle, \langle 0.122, 0.323\rangle)$
$\mathcal{G}_2$	$\dot{\wp}_1$:$(\langle 0.973, 0.543\rangle, \langle 0.246, 0.652\rangle)$ $\dot{\wp}_2$:$(\langle 0.822, 0.642\rangle, \langle 0.223, 0.524\rangle)$ $\dot{\wp}_3$:$(\langle 0.752, 0.275\rangle, \langle 0.122, 0.233\rangle)$

Consider a linear Diophantine fuzzy soft subset $\mathscr{Y}_{\mathscr{D}}$ *of* $\dot{\mathcal{G}}$ *given as:*

$$\mathscr{Y}_{\mathscr{D}} = \{(\dot{\wp}_1, \langle 0.837, 0.535\rangle, \langle 0.242, 0.242\rangle), (\dot{\wp}_2, \langle 0.833, 0.635\rangle, \langle 0.634, 0.142\rangle), (\dot{\wp}_3, \langle 0.725, 0.526\rangle, \langle 0.625, 0.211\rangle)\}$$

By using Definition 12, we find the "upper and lower approximations" of $\mathscr{Y}_{\mathscr{D}}$ *given by:*

$$\ddot{\mathscr{T}}_{\tilde{\eth}^{\ast}(\mathscr{Y}_{\mathscr{D}})}(\mathcal{G}_1) = \bigvee_{\dot{\wp}}[0.684, 0.825, 0.725] = 0.825, \quad \ddot{\mathcal{S}}_{\tilde{\eth}^{\ast}(\mathscr{Y}_{\mathscr{D}})}(\mathcal{G}_1) = \max_{\dot{\wp}}[0.645, 0.635, 0.735] = 0.635,$$

$$\alpha_{\tilde{\eth}^{\ast}(\mathscr{Y}_{\mathscr{D}})}(\mathcal{G}_1) = \max_{\dot{\wp}}[0.221, 0.226, 0.122] = 0.226, \quad \beta_{\tilde{\eth}^{\ast}(\mathscr{Y}_{\mathscr{D}})}(\mathcal{G}_1) = \min_{\dot{\wp}}[0.675, 0.877, 0.677] = 0.675$$

Similarly, we find all other values for the "upper and lower approximation" of $\mathscr{Y}_{\mathscr{D}}$*. This implies that:*

$$\tilde{\eth}^{\ast}(\mathscr{Y}_{\mathscr{D}}) = \{(\mathcal{G}_1, \langle 0.825, 0.635\rangle, \langle 0.226, 0.675\rangle), (\mathcal{G}_2, \langle 0.837, 0.535\rangle, \langle 0.242, 0.348\rangle)\}$$
$$\tilde{\eth}_{\ast}(\mathscr{Y}_{\mathscr{D}}) = \{(\mathcal{G}_1, \langle 0.725, 0.635\rangle, \langle 0.774, 0.242\rangle), (\mathcal{G}_2, \langle 0.752, 0.635\rangle, \langle 0.754, 0.242\rangle)\}$$

Thus, $(\tilde{\eth}_{\ast}(\mathscr{Y}_{\mathscr{D}}), \tilde{\eth}^{\ast}(\mathscr{Y}_{\mathscr{D}}))$ *is called LDFSRS.*

Remark 3. *For the "linear Diophantine fuzzy soft approximation space (LDFS approximation space)"* $(\ddot{\mathcal{Q}}, \dot{\mathcal{G}}, \tilde{\eth})$*, if we take the upper and lower approximations of the following sets listed in Table 9, then we can observe the degeneration of LDFSR approximation operators into different structures based on rough sets.*

Table 9. Degeneration of LDFSR approximation operators into different rough set models.

Approximation Space	Set Theories	Family of Sets	Degeneration of LDFSR Approximation Operators	After Degeneration of the Constructed Model
LDFS $(\ddot{\mathcal{Q}}, \dot{\mathcal{G}}, \tilde{\eth})$	$\mathscr{Y}_{\mathscr{D}} = \{\langle \dot{\wp}, \ddot{\mathscr{T}}(\dot{\wp}) \rangle : \dot{\wp} \in \dot{\mathcal{G}}\} \in \mathcal{F}(\dot{\mathcal{G}})$	$\mathcal{F}(\dot{\mathcal{G}})$ collection of all fuzzy subsets of $\dot{\mathcal{G}}$	Yes	Soft fuzzy rough sets [42,43]
LDFS $(\ddot{\mathcal{Q}}, \dot{\mathcal{G}}, \tilde{\eth})$	$\mathscr{Y}_{\mathscr{D}} = \{\langle \dot{\wp}, \ddot{\mathscr{T}}(\dot{\wp}), \ddot{\mathcal{S}}(\dot{\wp}) \rangle : \dot{\wp} \in \dot{\mathcal{G}}\} \in \mathcal{I}(\dot{\mathcal{G}})$	$\mathcal{I}(\dot{\mathcal{G}})$ collection of all IF-subsets of $\dot{\mathcal{G}}$	Yes	Intuitionistic fuzzy soft rough sets [26]
LDFS $(\ddot{\mathcal{Q}}, \dot{\mathcal{G}}, \tilde{\eth})$	$\mathscr{Y}_{\mathscr{D}} = \{\langle \dot{\wp}, \ddot{\mathscr{T}}(\dot{\wp}), \ddot{\mathcal{S}}(\dot{\wp}) \rangle : \dot{\wp} \in \dot{\mathcal{G}}\} \in \mathcal{P}(\dot{\mathcal{G}})$	$\mathcal{P}(\dot{\mathcal{G}})$ collection of all PF-subsets of $\dot{\mathcal{G}}$	Yes	Pythagorean fuzzy soft rough sets [44]
LDFS $(\ddot{\mathcal{Q}}, \dot{\mathcal{G}}, \tilde{\eth})$	$\mathscr{Y}_{\mathscr{D}} = \{\langle \dot{\wp}, \ddot{\mathscr{T}}(\dot{\wp}), \ddot{\mathcal{S}}(\dot{\wp}) \rangle : \dot{\wp} \in \dot{\mathcal{G}}\} \in \mathcal{R}(\dot{\mathcal{G}})$	$\mathcal{R}(\dot{\mathcal{G}})$ collection of all PF-subsets of $\dot{\mathcal{G}}$	Yes	q-rung orthopair fuzzy soft rough sets
Crisp soft $(\ddot{\mathcal{Q}}, \dot{\mathcal{G}}, \mathscr{A})$	$\mathscr{Y}_{\mathscr{D}} = \{\langle \dot{\wp}, \ddot{\mathscr{T}}(\dot{\wp}), \ddot{\mathcal{S}}(\dot{\wp}), \alpha(\dot{\wp}), \beta(\dot{\wp}) \rangle : \dot{\wp} \in \dot{\mathcal{G}}\} \in \mathscr{D}(\dot{\mathcal{G}})$	$\mathscr{D}(\dot{\mathcal{G}})$ collection of all LDF-subsets of $\dot{\mathcal{G}}$	Yes	Soft rough linear Diophantine fuzzy sets

It is evident from Table 9 that our proposed model is superior and powerful in contrast with other existing structures. However, we cannot decompose the described theories into the LDFSRSs and their respective approximation operators. The beauty of this structure is that if we select the "crisp soft approximation space" for LDFSR approximation operators, then it will be degenerated into the proposed SRLDFSs. This generalization provides us a strong relation between both proposed rough set models. In simple terms, LDFSRS is the generalization of "soft fuzzy rough sets, intuitionistic fuzzy soft rough sets, Pythagorean fuzzy soft rough sets, q-rung orthopair fuzzy soft rough sets, and soft rough linear Diophantine fuzzy sets".

Theorem 3. *For arbitrary $\mathscr{Y}_{\mathscr{D}}, \mathscr{B}_{\mathscr{D}} \in \mathscr{D}(\mathcal{G})$, the "upper and lower approximation operators" $\tilde{\eth}_{*}(\mathscr{Y}_{\mathscr{D}}), \tilde{\eth}_{*}(\mathscr{B}_{\mathscr{D}}), \tilde{\eth}^{*}(\mathscr{Y}_{\mathscr{D}})$ and $\tilde{\eth}^{*}(\mathscr{B}_{\mathscr{D}})$ on the "LDFS approximation space" $(\ddot{\mathcal{Q}}, \dot{\mathcal{G}}, \tilde{\eth})$ satisfy the following axioms:*

(1) $\tilde{\eth}_{*}(\mathscr{Y}_{\mathscr{D}}) = \sim \tilde{\eth}^{*}(\sim \mathscr{Y}_{\mathscr{D}})$,
(2) $\mathscr{Y}_{\mathscr{D}} \subseteq \mathscr{B}_{\mathscr{D}} \Rightarrow \tilde{\eth}_{*}(\mathscr{Y}_{\mathscr{D}}) \subseteq \tilde{\eth}_{*}(\mathscr{B}_{\mathscr{D}})$,
(3) $\tilde{\eth}_{*}(\mathscr{Y}_{\mathscr{D}} \cap \mathscr{B}_{\mathscr{D}}) = \tilde{\eth}_{*}(\mathscr{Y}_{\mathscr{D}}) \cap \tilde{\eth}_{*}(\mathscr{B}_{\mathscr{D}})$,
(4) $\tilde{\eth}_{*}(\mathscr{Y}_{\mathscr{D}} \cup \mathscr{B}_{\mathscr{D}}) \supseteq \tilde{\eth}_{*}(\mathscr{Y}_{\mathscr{D}}) \cup \tilde{\eth}_{*}(\mathscr{B}_{\mathscr{D}})$,
(5) $\tilde{\eth}^{*}(\mathscr{Y}_{\mathscr{D}}) = \sim \tilde{\eth}_{*}(\sim \mathscr{Y}_{\mathscr{D}})$,
(6) $\mathscr{Y}_{\mathscr{D}} \subseteq \mathscr{B}_{\mathscr{D}} \Rightarrow \tilde{\eth}^{*}(\mathscr{Y}_{\mathscr{D}}) \subseteq \tilde{\eth}^{*}(\mathscr{B}_{\mathscr{D}})$,
(7) $\tilde{\eth}^{*}(\mathscr{Y}_{\mathscr{D}} \cup \mathscr{B}_{\mathscr{D}}) = \tilde{\eth}^{*}(\mathscr{Y}_{\mathscr{D}}) \cup \tilde{\eth}^{*}(\mathscr{B}_{\mathscr{D}})$,
(8) $\tilde{\eth}^{*}(\mathscr{Y}_{\mathscr{D}} \cap \mathscr{B}_{\mathscr{D}}) \subseteq \tilde{\eth}^{*}(\mathscr{Y}_{\mathscr{D}}) \cap \tilde{\eth}^{*}(\mathscr{B}_{\mathscr{D}})$.

The complement of $\mathscr{Y}_{\mathscr{D}}$ is represented by $\sim \mathscr{Y}_{\mathscr{D}}$.

Proof. The proof is similar to the proof given in Appendix A. □

Proposition 2. *For arbitrary $\mathscr{Y}_{\mathscr{D}}, \mathscr{B}_{\mathscr{D}} \in \mathscr{D}(\mathcal{G})$, the "upper and lower approximation operators" $\tilde{\eth}_{*}(\mathscr{Y}_{\mathscr{D}}), \tilde{\eth}_{*}(\mathscr{B}_{\mathscr{D}}), \tilde{\eth}^{*}(\mathscr{Y}_{\mathscr{D}})$ and $\tilde{\eth}^{*}(\mathscr{B}_{\mathscr{D}})$ on the "LDFS approximation space" $(\ddot{\mathcal{Q}}, \dot{\mathcal{G}}, \tilde{\eth})$ satisfy the following axioms:*

(1) $\sim (\tilde{\eth}_{*}(\mathscr{Y}_{\mathscr{D}}) \cup \tilde{\eth}_{*}(\mathscr{B}_{\mathscr{D}})) = \tilde{\eth}^{*}(\sim \mathscr{Y}_{\mathscr{D}}) \cap \tilde{\eth}^{*}(\sim \mathscr{B}_{\mathscr{D}})$,
(2) $\sim (\tilde{\eth}_{*}(\mathscr{Y}_{\mathscr{D}}) \cup \tilde{\eth}^{*}(\mathscr{B}_{\mathscr{D}})) = \tilde{\eth}^{*}(\sim \mathscr{Y}_{\mathscr{D}}) \cap \tilde{\eth}_{*}(\sim \mathscr{B}_{\mathscr{D}})$,
(3) $\sim (\tilde{\eth}^{*}(\mathscr{Y}_{\mathscr{D}}) \cup \tilde{\eth}_{*}(\mathscr{B}_{\mathscr{D}})) = \tilde{\eth}_{*}(\sim \mathscr{Y}_{\mathscr{D}}) \cap \tilde{\eth}^{*}(\sim \mathscr{B}_{\mathscr{D}})$,
(4) $\sim (\tilde{\eth}^{*}(\mathscr{Y}_{\mathscr{D}}) \cup \tilde{\eth}^{*}(\mathscr{B}_{\mathscr{D}})) = \tilde{\eth}_{*}(\sim \mathscr{Y}_{\mathscr{D}}) \cap \tilde{\eth}_{*}(\sim \mathscr{B}_{\mathscr{D}})$,
(5) $\sim (\tilde{\eth}_{*}(\mathscr{Y}_{\mathscr{D}}) \cap \tilde{\eth}_{*}(\mathscr{B}_{\mathscr{D}})) = \tilde{\eth}^{*}(\sim \mathscr{Y}_{\mathscr{D}}) \cup \tilde{\eth}^{*}(\sim \mathscr{B}_{\mathscr{D}})$,
(6) $\sim (\tilde{\eth}_{*}(\mathscr{Y}_{\mathscr{D}}) \cap \tilde{\eth}^{*}(\mathscr{B}_{\mathscr{D}})) = \tilde{\eth}^{*}(\sim \mathscr{Y}_{\mathscr{D}}) \cup \tilde{\eth}_{*}(\sim \mathscr{B}_{\mathscr{D}})$,
(7) $\sim (\tilde{\eth}^{*}(\mathscr{Y}_{\mathscr{D}}) \cap \tilde{\eth}_{*}(\mathscr{B}_{\mathscr{D}})) = \tilde{\eth}_{*}(\sim \mathscr{Y}_{\mathscr{D}}) \cup \tilde{\eth}^{*}(\sim \mathscr{B}_{\mathscr{D}})$,
(8) $\sim (\tilde{\eth}^{*}(\mathscr{Y}_{\mathscr{D}}) \cap \tilde{\eth}^{*}(\mathscr{B}_{\mathscr{D}})) = \tilde{\eth}_{*}(\sim \mathscr{Y}_{\mathscr{D}}) \cup \tilde{\eth}_{*}(\sim \mathscr{B}_{\mathscr{D}})$.

Proof. The proof is obvious. □

Theorem 4. *For "LDFS approximation space" $(\ddot{\mathcal{Q}}, \dot{\mathcal{G}}, \tilde{\eth})$, if $\tilde{\eth}$ is serial, then $\tilde{\eth}_{*}(\mathscr{Y}_{\mathscr{D}})$ and $\tilde{\eth}^{*}(\mathscr{Y}_{\mathscr{D}})$ satisfy the following:*
(1) $\tilde{\eth}_{*}(\varnothing) = \varnothing, \tilde{\eth}^{*}(\dot{\mathcal{G}}) = \dot{\mathcal{G}}$,
(2) $\tilde{\eth}_{*}(\mathscr{Y}_{\mathscr{D}}) \subseteq \tilde{\eth}^{*}(\mathscr{Y}_{\mathscr{D}}), \ \forall \ \mathscr{Y}_{\mathscr{D}}\mathscr{Y}_{\mathscr{D}} \in \mathscr{D}(\mathcal{G})$.

Proof. The proof is obvious by following Definition 12. □

Definition 13. *Let $\mathscr{Y}_{\mathscr{D}} \in \mathscr{D}(\ddot{\mathcal{Q}})$, and let $\tilde{\eth}_{*}(\mathscr{Y}_{\mathscr{D}}), \tilde{\eth}^{*}(\mathscr{Y}_{\mathscr{D}})$ be lower and upper "LDFSR approximation operators". Then, the ring sum operation of $\tilde{\eth}_{*}(\mathscr{Y}_{\mathscr{D}})$ and $\tilde{\eth}^{*}(\mathscr{Y}_{\mathscr{D}})$ is written as:*

$$\begin{aligned}\tilde{\eth}_{*}(\mathscr{Y}_{\mathscr{D}}) \oplus \tilde{\eth}^{*}(\mathscr{Y}_{\mathscr{D}}) = \{(\mathcal{G}, \langle \ddot{\mathscr{T}}_{\tilde{\eth}_{*}(\mathscr{Y}_{\mathscr{D}})}(\mathcal{G}) + \ddot{\mathscr{T}}_{\tilde{\eth}^{*}(\mathscr{Y}_{\mathscr{D}})}(\mathcal{G}) - (\ddot{\mathscr{T}}_{\tilde{\eth}_{*}(\mathscr{Y}_{\mathscr{D}})}(\mathcal{G}) \times \ddot{\mathscr{T}}_{\tilde{\eth}^{*}(\mathscr{Y}_{\mathscr{D}})}(\mathcal{G})),\\ \ddot{\mathcal{S}}_{\tilde{\eth}_{*}(\mathscr{Y}_{\mathscr{D}})}(\mathcal{G}) \times \ddot{\mathcal{S}}_{\tilde{\eth}^{*}(\mathscr{Y}_{\mathscr{D}})}(\mathcal{G})\rangle, \langle \alpha_{\tilde{\eth}_{*}(\mathscr{Y}_{\mathscr{D}})}(\mathcal{G}) + \alpha_{\tilde{\eth}^{*}(\mathscr{Y}_{\mathscr{D}})}(\mathcal{G}) - (\alpha_{\tilde{\eth}_{*}(\mathscr{Y}_{\mathscr{D}})}(\mathcal{G}) \times \alpha_{\tilde{\eth}^{*}(\mathscr{Y}_{\mathscr{D}})}(\mathcal{G})),\\ \beta_{\tilde{\eth}_{*}(\mathscr{Y}_{\mathscr{D}})}(\mathcal{G}) \times \beta_{\tilde{\eth}^{*}(\mathscr{Y}_{\mathscr{D}})}(\mathcal{G})\rangle) : \mathcal{G} \in \ddot{\mathcal{Q}}\}\end{aligned}$$

Definition 14. *Let $\mathscr{D} = \{(\mathcal{G}, \langle \ddot{\mathscr{T}}_{\mathscr{D}}(\mathcal{G}), \ddot{\mathcal{S}}_{\mathscr{D}}(\mathcal{G})\rangle, \langle \alpha_{\mathscr{D}}(\mathcal{G}), \beta_{\mathscr{D}}(\mathcal{G})\rangle) : \mathcal{G} \in \ddot{\mathcal{Q}}\}$ be an LDFS and the constants $(\langle \eta, \theta\rangle, \langle \zeta, \psi\rangle)$, where $\eta, \theta, \zeta, \psi \in [0,1]$ satisfying the constraints $0 \le \eta\theta + \zeta\psi \le 1$ and $0 \le \theta + \psi \le 1$. Then, the $(\langle \eta, \theta\rangle, \langle \zeta, \psi\rangle)$-level cut set of $\mathscr{D}$ is written as:*

$$\mathscr{D}_{\langle \eta,\theta\rangle}^{\langle \zeta,\psi\rangle} = \{\mathcal{G} \in \ddot{\mathcal{Q}} : \ddot{\mathscr{T}}_{\mathscr{D}}(\mathcal{G}) \ge \eta, \alpha_{\mathscr{D}}(\mathcal{G}) \ge \theta, \ddot{\mathcal{S}}_{\mathscr{D}}(\mathcal{G}) \le \zeta, \beta_{\mathscr{D}}(\mathcal{G}) \le \psi\}.$$

The $\langle \eta, \theta\rangle$-level cut of $\mathscr{D}$ is written as $\mathscr{D}_{\langle \eta,\theta\rangle} = \{\mathcal{G} \in \ddot{\mathcal{Q}} : \ddot{\mathscr{T}}_{\mathscr{D}}(\mathcal{G}) \ge \eta, \alpha_{\mathscr{D}}(\mathcal{G}) \ge \theta\}$.
The strong $\langle \eta, \theta\rangle$-level cut of $\mathscr{D}$ is written as $\mathscr{D}_{\langle \eta,\theta\rangle^{+}} = \{\mathcal{G} \in \ddot{\mathcal{Q}} : \ddot{\mathscr{T}}_{\mathscr{D}}(\mathcal{G}) > \eta, \alpha_{\mathscr{D}}(\mathcal{G}) > \theta\}$.
The $\langle \zeta, \psi\rangle$-level cut of $\mathscr{D}$ is written as $\mathscr{D}^{\langle \zeta,\psi\rangle} = \{\mathcal{G} \in \ddot{\mathcal{Q}} : \ddot{\mathcal{S}}_{\mathscr{D}}(\mathcal{G}) \le \zeta, \beta_{\mathscr{D}}(\mathcal{G}) \le \psi\}$.
The strong $\langle \zeta, \psi\rangle$-level cut of $\mathscr{D}$ is written as $\mathscr{D}^{\langle \zeta,\psi\rangle^{+}} = \{\mathcal{G} \in \ddot{\mathcal{Q}} : \ddot{\mathcal{S}}_{\mathscr{D}}(\mathcal{G}) < \zeta, \beta_{\mathscr{D}}(\mathcal{G}) < \psi\}$.
The other cut sets of an LDFS are analogously described as:

$$\mathscr{D}_{\langle \eta,\theta\rangle^{+}}^{\langle \zeta,\psi\rangle} = \{\mathcal{G} \in \ddot{\mathcal{Q}} : \ddot{\mathscr{T}}_{\mathscr{D}}(\mathcal{G}) > \eta, \alpha_{\mathscr{D}}(\mathcal{G}) > \theta, \ddot{\mathcal{S}}_{\mathscr{D}}(\mathcal{G}) \le \zeta, \beta_{\mathscr{D}}(\mathcal{G}) \le \psi\}.$$

$$\mathscr{D}_{\langle \eta,\theta\rangle}^{\langle \zeta,\psi\rangle^{+}} = \{\mathcal{G} \in \ddot{\mathcal{Q}} : \ddot{\mathscr{T}}_{\mathscr{D}}(\mathcal{G}) \ge \eta, \alpha_{\mathscr{D}}(\mathcal{G}) \ge \theta, \ddot{\mathcal{S}}_{\mathscr{D}}(\mathcal{G}) < \zeta, \beta_{\mathscr{D}}(\mathcal{G}) < \psi\}.$$

$$\mathscr{D}_{\langle \eta,\theta\rangle^{+}}^{\langle \zeta,\psi\rangle^{+}} = \{\mathcal{G} \in \ddot{\mathcal{Q}} : \ddot{\mathscr{T}}_{\mathscr{D}}(\mathcal{G}) > \eta, \alpha_{\mathscr{D}}(\mathcal{G}) > \theta, \ddot{\mathcal{S}}_{\mathscr{D}}(\mathcal{G}) < \zeta, \beta_{\mathscr{D}}(\mathcal{G}) < \psi\}.$$

Theorem 5. *Let $\mathscr{D}, {}^{1}\mathscr{D}, {}^{2}\mathscr{D} \in \mathscr{D}(\ddot{\mathcal{Q}})$ and $\eta, \theta, \zeta, \psi \in [0,1]$ satisfy the constraints $0 \le \eta\theta + \zeta\psi \le 1$ and $0 \le \theta + \psi \le 1$. Then, the cut sets of LDFSs satisfy the following axioms:*

1. $\mathscr{D}_{\langle \eta,\theta\rangle}^{\langle \zeta,\psi\rangle} = \mathscr{D}_{\langle \eta,\theta\rangle} \cap \mathscr{D}^{\langle \zeta,\psi\rangle}$,
2. $(\sim \mathscr{D})_{\langle \eta,\theta\rangle} = \sim \mathscr{D}_{\langle \eta,\theta\rangle^{+}}, (\sim \mathscr{D})^{\langle \zeta,\psi\rangle} = \sim \mathscr{D}^{\langle \zeta,\psi\rangle^{+}}$,
3. ${}^{1}\mathscr{D} \subseteq {}^{2}\mathscr{D} = {}^{1}\mathscr{D}_{\langle \eta,\theta\rangle}^{\langle \zeta,\psi\rangle} \subseteq {}^{2}\mathscr{D}_{\langle \eta,\theta\rangle}^{\langle \zeta,\psi\rangle}$,
4. $({}^{1}\mathscr{D} \cap {}^{2}\mathscr{D})_{\langle \eta,\theta\rangle} = {}^{1}\mathscr{D}_{\langle \eta,\theta\rangle} \cap {}^{2}\mathscr{D}_{\langle \eta,\theta\rangle}, ({}^{1}\mathscr{D} \cap {}^{2}\mathscr{D})^{\langle \zeta,\psi\rangle} = {}^{1}\mathscr{D}^{\langle \zeta,\psi\rangle} \cap {}^{2}\mathscr{D}^{\langle \zeta,\psi\rangle}$,
   $({}^{1}\mathscr{D} \cap {}^{2}\mathscr{D})_{\langle \eta,\theta\rangle}^{\langle \zeta,\psi\rangle} = {}^{1}\mathscr{D}_{\langle \eta,\theta\rangle}^{\langle \zeta,\psi\rangle} \cap {}^{2}\mathscr{D}_{\langle \eta,\theta\rangle}^{\langle \zeta,\psi\rangle}$,
5. $({}^{1}\mathscr{D} \cup {}^{2}\mathscr{D})_{\langle \eta,\theta\rangle} = {}^{1}\mathscr{D}_{\langle \eta,\theta\rangle} \cup {}^{2}\mathscr{D}_{\langle \eta,\theta\rangle}, ({}^{1}\mathscr{D} \cup {}^{2}\mathscr{D})^{\langle \zeta,\psi\rangle} = {}^{1}\mathscr{D}^{\langle \zeta,\psi\rangle} \cup {}^{2}\mathscr{D}^{\langle \zeta,\psi\rangle}$,
   $({}^{1}\mathscr{D} \cup {}^{2}\mathscr{D})_{\langle \eta,\theta\rangle}^{\langle \zeta,\psi\rangle} = {}^{1}\mathscr{D}_{\langle \eta,\theta\rangle}^{\langle \zeta,\psi\rangle} \supseteq {}^{2}\mathscr{D}_{\langle \eta,\theta\rangle}^{\langle \zeta,\psi\rangle}$
6. *If $\eta_1 \ge \eta_2, \theta_1 \ge \theta_2$ and $\zeta_1 \le \zeta_2, \psi_1 \le \psi_2$, then*
   $\mathscr{D}_{\langle \eta_1,\theta_1\rangle} \subseteq \mathscr{D}_{\langle \eta_2,\theta_2\rangle}, \mathscr{D}^{\langle \zeta_1,\psi_1\rangle} \subseteq \mathscr{D}^{\langle \zeta_2,\psi_2\rangle}$ *and* $\mathscr{D}_{\langle \eta_1,\theta_1\rangle}^{\langle \zeta_1,\psi_1\rangle} \subseteq \mathscr{D}_{\langle \eta_1,\theta_1\rangle}^{\langle \zeta_2,\psi_2\rangle}$.

Proof. This proof is inferred explicitly by Definition 14. □

By using the defined idea of cut sets on LDFSs, we can find the cut sets of LDFSR:

$$\tilde{\eth} = \{((\mathcal{G}, \wp), \langle \ddot{\mathscr{T}}_{\tilde{\eth}}(\mathcal{G}, \wp), \ddot{\mathcal{S}}_{\tilde{\eth}}(\mathcal{G}, \wp)\rangle, \langle \alpha_{\tilde{\eth}}(\mathcal{G}, \wp), \beta_{\tilde{\eth}}(\mathcal{G}, \wp)\rangle) : (\mathcal{G}, \wp) \in \ddot{\mathcal{Q}} \times \dot{\mathcal{G}}\}$$

given as:

$$\tilde{\eth}_{\langle \eta,\theta\rangle} = \{((\mathcal{G}, \wp) \in \ddot{\mathcal{Q}} \times \dot{\mathcal{G}} : \ddot{\mathscr{T}}_{\tilde{\eth}}(\mathcal{G}, \wp) \ge \eta, \alpha_{\tilde{\eth}}(\mathcal{G}, \wp) \ge \theta\}$$

$$\tilde{\eth}_{\langle \eta,\theta\rangle}(\mathcal{G}) = \{\wp \in \dot{\mathcal{G}} : \ddot{\mathscr{T}}_{\tilde{\eth}}(\mathcal{G}, \wp) \ge \eta, \alpha_{\tilde{\eth}}(\mathcal{G}, \wp) \ge \theta\} \text{ for } \eta, \theta \in [0,1]$$

$$\tilde{\eth}_{\langle\eta,\theta\rangle^+} = \{((\mathcal{G},\wp) \in \ddot{\mathcal{Q}} \times \dot{\mathcal{G}} : \ddot{\mathcal{T}}_{\tilde{\eth}}(\mathcal{G},\wp) > \eta, \alpha_{\tilde{\eth}}(\mathcal{G},\wp) > \theta\}$$
$$\tilde{\eth}_{\langle\eta,\theta\rangle^+}(\mathcal{G}) = \{\wp \in \dot{\mathcal{G}} : \ddot{\mathcal{T}}_{\tilde{\eth}}(\mathcal{G},\wp) > \eta, \alpha_{\tilde{\eth}}(\mathcal{G},\wp) > \theta\} \text{ for } \eta,\theta \in [0,1)$$

$$\tilde{\eth}^{\langle\eta,\theta\rangle} = \{((\mathcal{G},\wp) \in \ddot{\mathcal{Q}} \times \dot{\mathcal{G}} : \ddot{\mathcal{S}}_{\tilde{\eth}}(\mathcal{G},\wp) \leq \eta, \beta_{\tilde{\eth}}(\mathcal{G},\wp) \leq \theta\}$$
$$\tilde{\eth}^{\langle\eta,\theta\rangle}(\mathcal{G}) = \{\wp \in \dot{\mathcal{G}} : \ddot{\mathcal{S}}_{\tilde{\eth}}(\mathcal{G},\wp) \leq \eta, \beta_{\tilde{\eth}}(\mathcal{G},\wp) \leq \theta\} \text{ for } \eta,\theta \in [0,1]$$
$$\tilde{\eth}^{\langle\eta,\theta\rangle^+} = \{((\mathcal{G},\wp) \in \ddot{\mathcal{Q}} \times \dot{\mathcal{G}} : \ddot{\mathcal{S}}_{\tilde{\eth}}(\mathcal{G},\wp) < \eta, \beta_{\tilde{\eth}}(\mathcal{G},\wp) < \theta\}$$
$$\tilde{\eth}^{\langle\eta,\theta\rangle^+}(\mathcal{G}) = \{\wp \in \dot{\mathcal{G}} : \ddot{\mathcal{S}}_{\tilde{\eth}}(\mathcal{G},\wp) < \eta, \beta_{\tilde{\eth}}(\mathcal{G},\wp) < \theta\} \text{ for } \eta,\theta \in (0,1]$$

where all the calculated cuts are crisp soft relations. Now, we present a result to show that LDFSR approximation operators can be written as crisp soft rough approximation operators.

Theorem 6. *Consider that for LDFSR approximation space $(\ddot{\mathcal{Q}},\dot{\mathcal{G}},\tilde{\eth})$ and $\mathscr{D} \in \mathscr{D}(\ddot{\mathcal{Q}})$, the upper approximation operators can be represented as:*

1.

$$\begin{aligned}
\langle \ddot{\mathcal{T}}_{\tilde{\eth}^*(\mathscr{D})}(\mathcal{G}), \alpha_{\tilde{\eth}^*(\mathscr{D})}(\mathcal{G})\rangle &= \bigvee_{\eta,\theta\in[0,1]} [\langle\eta,\theta\rangle \wedge \tilde{\eth}^*_{\langle\eta,\theta\rangle}(\mathscr{D}_{\langle\eta,\theta\rangle})(\mathcal{G})] \\
&= \bigvee_{\eta,\theta\in[0,1]} [\langle\eta,\theta\rangle \wedge \tilde{\eth}^*_{\langle\eta,\theta\rangle}(\mathscr{D}_{\langle\eta,\theta\rangle^+})(\mathcal{G})] \\
&= \bigvee_{\eta,\theta\in[0,1]} [\langle\eta,\theta\rangle \wedge \tilde{\eth}^*_{\langle\eta,\theta\rangle^+}(\mathscr{D}_{\langle\eta,\theta\rangle})(\mathcal{G})] \\
&= \bigvee_{\eta,\theta\in[0,1]} [\langle\eta,\theta\rangle \wedge \tilde{\eth}^*_{\langle\eta,\theta\rangle^+}(\mathscr{D}_{\langle\eta,\theta\rangle^+})(\mathcal{G})]
\end{aligned}$$

2.

$$\begin{aligned}
\langle \ddot{\mathcal{S}}_{\tilde{\eth}^*(\mathscr{D})}(\mathcal{G}), \beta_{\tilde{\eth}^*(\mathscr{D})}(\mathcal{G})\rangle &= \bigwedge_{\eta,\theta\in[0,1]} [\langle\eta,\theta\rangle \vee (1 - \tilde{\eth}^*_{\langle 1-\eta,1-\theta\rangle}(\mathscr{D}^{\langle\eta,\theta\rangle})(\mathcal{G}))] \\
&= \bigwedge_{\eta,\theta\in[0,1]} [\langle\eta,\theta\rangle \vee \tilde{\eth}^*_{\langle 1-\eta,1-\theta\rangle}(\mathscr{D}^{\langle\eta,\theta\rangle^+})(\mathcal{G})] \\
&= \bigwedge_{\eta,\theta\in[0,1]} [\langle\eta,\theta\rangle \vee \tilde{\eth}^*_{\langle 1-\eta,1-\theta\rangle^+}(\mathscr{D}^{\langle\eta,\theta\rangle})(\mathcal{G})] \\
&= \bigwedge_{\eta,\theta\in[0,1]} [\langle\eta,\theta\rangle \vee \tilde{\eth}^*_{\langle 1-\eta,1-\theta\rangle^+}(\mathscr{D}\langle\eta,\theta\rangle^+)(\mathcal{G})]
\end{aligned}$$

and for arbitrary $\langle\eta,\theta\rangle \in [0,1]$, we have:

3. $[\tilde{\eth}^*(\mathscr{D})]_{\langle\eta,\theta\rangle^+} \subseteq \tilde{\eth}^*_{\langle\eta,\theta\rangle^+}(\mathscr{D}_{\langle\eta,\theta\rangle^+}) \subseteq \tilde{\eth}^*_{\langle\eta,\theta\rangle^+}(\mathscr{D}_{\langle\eta,\theta\rangle}) \subseteq \tilde{\eth}^*_{\langle\eta,\theta\rangle}(\mathscr{D}_{\langle\eta,\theta\rangle}) \subseteq [\tilde{\eth}^*(\mathscr{D})]_{\langle\eta,\theta\rangle}$.
4. $[\tilde{\eth}^*(\mathscr{D})]^{\langle\eta,\theta\rangle^+} \subseteq \tilde{\eth}^*_{\langle 1-\eta,1-\theta\rangle^+}(\mathscr{D}^{\langle\eta,\theta\rangle^+}) \subseteq \tilde{\eth}^*_{\langle 1-\eta,1-\theta\rangle^+}(\mathscr{D}^{\langle\eta,\theta\rangle}) \subseteq \tilde{\eth}^*_{\langle 1-\eta,1-\theta\rangle}(\mathscr{D}^{\langle\eta,\theta\rangle}) \subseteq [\tilde{\eth}^*(\mathscr{D})]^{\langle\eta,\theta\rangle}$.

Proof. One can conclude the proof of this theorem directly by using Definitions 12 and 14. □

Theorem 7. *Consider that for LDFSR approximation space $(\ddot{\mathcal{Q}},\dot{\mathcal{G}},\tilde{\eth})$ and $\mathscr{D} \in \mathscr{D}(\ddot{\mathcal{Q}})$, the upper approximation operators can be represented as:*

1.

$$\langle \ddot{\mathscr{T}}_{\tilde{\eth}_{*}(\mathscr{D})}(\mathcal{G}), \alpha_{\tilde{\eth}_{*}(\mathscr{D})}(\mathcal{G})\rangle = \bigwedge_{\eta,\theta\in[0,1]} [\langle \eta,\theta\rangle \vee \tilde{\eth}_{\langle 1-\eta,1-\theta\rangle_{*}}(\mathscr{D}_{\langle \eta,\theta\rangle^{+}})(\mathcal{G})]$$
$$= \bigwedge_{\eta,\theta\in[0,1]} [\langle \eta,\theta\rangle \vee \tilde{\eth}_{\langle 1-\eta,1-\theta\rangle_{*}^{+}}(\mathscr{D}_{\langle \eta,\theta\rangle})(\mathcal{G})]$$
$$= \bigwedge_{\eta,\theta\in[0,1]} [\langle \eta,\theta\rangle \vee \tilde{\eth}_{\langle 1-\eta,1-\theta\rangle_{*}^{+}}(\mathscr{D}_{\langle \eta,\theta\rangle^{+}})(\mathcal{G})]$$
$$= \bigwedge_{\eta,\theta\in[0,1]} [\langle \eta,\theta\rangle \vee \tilde{\eth}_{\langle 1-\eta,1-\theta\rangle_{*}}(\mathscr{D}_{\langle \eta,\theta\rangle})(\mathcal{G})]$$

2.

$$\langle \ddot{\mathcal{S}}_{\tilde{\eth}_{*}(\mathscr{D})}(\mathcal{G}), \beta_{\tilde{\eth}_{*}(\mathscr{D})}(\mathcal{G})\rangle = \bigvee_{\eta,\theta\in[0,1]} [\langle \eta,\theta\rangle \wedge (1-\tilde{\eth}_{\langle \eta,\theta\rangle_{*}}(\mathscr{D}^{\langle \eta,\theta\rangle})(\mathcal{G}))]$$
$$= \bigvee_{\eta,\theta\in[0,1]} [\langle \eta,\theta\rangle \wedge (1-\tilde{\eth}_{\langle \eta,\theta\rangle_{*}^{+}}(\mathscr{D}^{\langle \eta,\theta\rangle})(\mathcal{G}))]$$
$$= \bigvee_{\eta,\theta\in[0,1]} [\langle \eta,\theta\rangle \wedge (1-\tilde{\eth}_{\langle \eta,\theta\rangle_{*}^{+}}(\mathscr{D}^{\langle \eta,\theta\rangle^{+}})(\mathcal{G}))]$$
$$= \bigvee_{\eta,\theta\in[0,1]} [\langle \eta,\theta\rangle \wedge (1-\tilde{\eth}_{\langle \eta,\theta\rangle_{*}}(\mathscr{D}^{\langle \eta,\theta\rangle^{+}})(\mathcal{G}))]$$

and for arbitrary $\langle \eta,\theta\rangle \in [0,1]$, we have:

3. $[\tilde{\eth}_{*}(\mathscr{D})]_{\langle \eta,\theta\rangle^{+}} \subseteq \tilde{\eth}_{\langle 1-\eta,1-\theta\rangle_{*}}(\mathscr{D}_{\langle \eta,\theta\rangle^{+}}) \subseteq \tilde{\eth}_{\langle 1-\eta,1-\theta\rangle_{*}^{+}}(\mathscr{D}_{\langle \eta,\theta\rangle^{+}}) \subseteq \tilde{\eth}_{\langle 1-\eta,1-\theta\rangle_{*}}(\mathscr{D}_{\langle \eta,\theta\rangle}) \subseteq [\tilde{\eth}_{*}(\mathscr{D})]_{\langle \eta,\theta\rangle}$.
4. $[\tilde{\eth}_{*}(\mathscr{D})]^{\langle \eta,\theta\rangle^{+}} \subseteq \tilde{\eth}_{\langle 1-\eta,1-\theta\rangle_{*}^{+}}(\mathscr{D}^{\langle \eta,\theta\rangle^{+}}) \subseteq \tilde{\eth}_{\langle 1-\eta,1-\theta\rangle_{*}^{+}}(\mathscr{D}^{\langle \eta,\theta\rangle}) \subseteq \tilde{\eth}_{\langle 1-\eta,1-\theta\rangle_{*}}(\mathscr{D}^{\langle \eta,\theta\rangle}) \subseteq [\tilde{\eth}_{*}(\mathscr{D})]^{\langle \eta,\theta\rangle}$.

Proof. The proof of this theorem can be obtained directly by using Definitions 12 and 14. □

4. MCDM for Sustainable Material Handling Equipment

The determination of material handling equipment is extremely substantial in the project of an operative industrial system. The efficiency of material flow depends on the selection of appropriate material handling equipment. It promotes capability utilization and increases productivity. Decision support systems and various programs have been developed by various researchers for the selection of the best material handling equipment. In this section, we establish the novel methodologies for the selection of the appropriate and most reliable material handling equipment by using the LDFSRSs and SRLDFSs. The intelligent system, which consists of both technical and economical criteria in the material handling equipment selection process, is presented in Figure 2.

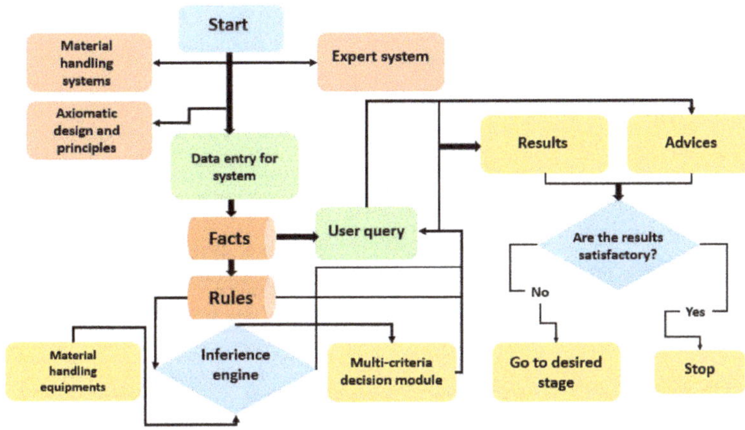

Figure 2. Configuration of modules in the material handling equipment selection process.

4.1. Selection of a Sustainable Material Handling Equipment by Using LDFSRSs

We suppose that a manufacturing company wants to increase efficiency and needs to deal with the materials professionally. The company wants to select that alternative that decreases the lead times and increases productivity. After some basic assessment, the board of the company constructs the set of suitable alternatives given as $\dot{\mathcal{Q}} = \{\mathcal{G}_1, \mathcal{G}_2, \mathcal{G}_3, \mathcal{G}_4, \mathcal{G}_5, \mathcal{G}_6, \mathcal{G}_7\}$. To measure the appropriate alternative, several decision makers from the company's technical board are organized. They choose some significant decision variables according to their requirements, given as set $\dot{\mathcal{G}} = \{\dot{\wp}_1, \dot{\wp}_2, \dot{\wp}_3, \dot{\wp}_4\}$, where:

$\dot{\wp}_1 =$ "Technical: convenience, maintainability, safety required",

$\dot{\wp}_2 =$ "Monetary: setting up and operational cost, maintenance cost, purchasing cost",

$\dot{\wp}_3 =$ "Operational: fuel consumption, moving speed, capacity",

$\dot{\wp}_4 =$ "Strategic: flexibility, level of training required, guarantee".

We divide the attributes into sub-criteria under the effect of parameterizations. This categorizes the data and gives us a wide domain for the selection of truth and falsity grades for the alternatives to the corresponding decision variables. The categorization is given as follows:

- "Technical: convenience, maintainability, safety required" means that the alternative is "highly technical" or may be "low".
- "Monetary: setting up and operational cost, maintenance cost, purchasing cost" means that the alternative may be "expansive" or "inexpensive".
- "Operational: fuel consumption, moving speed, capacity" means that the alternative is "highly operational" or may be "low".
- "Strategic: flexibility, level of training required, guarantee" means that the alternative is "highly strategic" or may be "low".

Table 10 represents the sub-attributes of the listed criteria.

Table 10. Properties of selected attributes.

Attributes	Characteristics for LDFSR
"Technical: convenience, maintainability, safety required"	$(\langle\text{membership, non-membership}\rangle, \langle\text{high, low}\rangle)$
"Monetary: operational cost, maintenance cost, purchasing cost"	$(\langle\text{membership, non-membership}\rangle, \langle\text{expansive, cheap}\rangle)$
"Operational: fuel consumption, moving speed, capacity"	$(\langle\text{membership, non-membership}\rangle, \langle\text{high, low}\rangle)$
"Strategic: flexibility, level of training required, guarantee"	$(\langle\text{membership, non-membership}\rangle, \langle\text{high, low}\rangle)$

We developed two novel algorithms (Algorithms 1 and 2) for the selection of best material handling equipment by using LDFSRSs. The flowchart diagram of both algorithms is given in Figure 3.

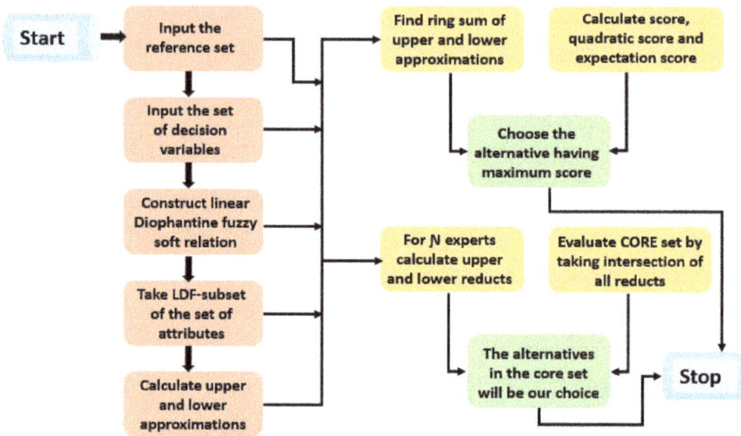

Figure 3. Flowchart diagram of Algorithms 1 and 2.

Algorithm 1: Selection of a best material handling equipment by using LDFSRSs.

Input:

1. Input the reference set $\ddot{\mathcal{Q}}$.
2. Input the assembling of attributes $\dot{\mathcal{G}}$.

Construction:

3. According to the necessity of the DM, build an LDFSR $\tilde{\eth} : \ddot{\mathcal{Q}} \to \dot{\mathcal{G}}$.
4. Based on the needs of the decision maker, construct LDF-subset $\mathscr{B}_{\mathscr{D}}$ of $\dot{\mathcal{G}}$ as an optimal normal decision set.

Calculation:

5. Calculate the "LDFSR approximation operators" $\tilde{\eth}_{*}(\mathscr{B}_{\mathscr{D}})$ and $\tilde{\eth}^{*}(\mathscr{B}_{\mathscr{D}})$ as lower and upper using Definition 12.
6. By using Definition 13 of the ring sum operation, find the choice of LDFS $\tilde{\eth}_{*}(\mathscr{B}_{\mathscr{D}}) \oplus \tilde{\eth}^{*}(\mathscr{B}_{\mathscr{D}})$.

Output:

7. We use the definitions of score, quadratic score, and expectation score functions for LDFNs $\ddot{A}_{\mathscr{D}} = (\langle \dot{t}_{\mathscr{D}}, \dot{f}_{\mathscr{D}} \rangle, \langle \alpha_{\mathscr{D}}, \beta_{\mathscr{D}} \rangle)$ given in [54] and written respectively as:

$$\mathscr{L}_1(\ddot{A}_{\mathscr{D}}) = \frac{1}{2}[(\dot{t}_{\mathscr{D}} - \dot{f}_{\mathscr{D}}) + (\alpha_{\mathscr{D}} - \beta_{\mathscr{D}})]$$

$$\mathscr{L}_2(\ddot{A}_{\mathscr{D}}) = \frac{1}{2}[(\dot{t}^2_{\mathscr{D}} - \dot{f}^2_{\mathscr{D}}) + (\alpha^2_{\mathscr{D}} - \beta^2_{\mathscr{D}})]$$

$$\mathscr{L}_3(\ddot{A}_{\mathscr{D}}) = \frac{1}{2}[\frac{(\dot{t}_{\mathscr{D}} - \dot{f}_{\mathscr{D}} + 1)}{2} + \frac{(\alpha_{\mathscr{D}} - \beta_{\mathscr{D}} + 1)}{2}]$$

of every alternative in $\tilde{\eth}_{*}(\mathscr{B}_{\mathscr{D}}) \oplus \tilde{\eth}^{*}(\mathscr{B}_{\mathscr{D}})$.

8. Rank the alternatives by using calculated score values.

Final decision:

9. Choose the alternative having the maximum score value.

Algorithm 2: Selection of the best material handling equipment by using LDFSRSs.

Input:
1. Input the reference set $\ddot{\mathcal{Q}}$.
2. Input the assembling of attributes $\dot{\mathcal{G}}$.

Construction:
3. According to the necessity of the DM, build an LDFSR $\tilde{\eth} : \ddot{\mathcal{Q}} \to \dot{\mathcal{G}}$.
4. Based on the needs of the decision maker, construct LDF-subset $\mathscr{B}_{\mathscr{D}}$ of $\dot{\mathcal{G}}$ as an optimal normal decision set.

Calculation:
5. Calculate the "LDFSR approximation operators" $\tilde{\eth}_{*}(\mathscr{B}_{\mathscr{D}})$ and $\tilde{\eth}^{*}(\mathscr{B}_{\mathscr{D}})$ as lower and upper using Definition 12.
6. For "$\mathscr{N}$" number of experts, calculate upper and lower reducts from the calculated "upper and lower approximation operators", respectively.

Output:
7. From the calculated "$2.\mathscr{N}$" reducts, we get "$2.\mathscr{N}$" crisp subsets of the reference set $\ddot{\mathcal{Q}}$. The subsets can be constructed by using the "YES" and "NO" logic. The only alternatives in the reduct having final decision "YES" will become the object of the crisp subset.
8. Calculate the core set by taking the intersection of all crisp subsets obtained from the calculated reducts.

Final decision:
9. The alternatives in the core will be our choice for the final decision.

4.1.1. Calculations by Using Algorithm 1

The indiscernibility relation is "the selection of best material handling equipment". This relation can be observed by LDFSR, $\tilde{\eth} : \ddot{\mathcal{Q}} \to \dot{\mathcal{G}}$ given as Table 11.

Table 11. LDFSR.

$\tilde{\eth}$	$\dot{\wp}_1$	$\dot{\wp}_2$	$\dot{\wp}_3$	$\dot{\wp}_4$
$\mathcal{G}_1$	$(\langle 0.73, 0.41\rangle, \langle 0.31, 0.13\rangle)$	$(\langle 0.63, 0.53\rangle, \langle 0.13, 0.23\rangle)$	$(\langle 0.73, 0.41\rangle, \langle 0.23, 0.15\rangle)$	$(\langle 0.63, 0.53\rangle, \langle 0.31, 0.36\rangle)$
$\mathcal{G}_2$	$(\langle 0.63, 0.43\rangle, \langle 0.41, 0.42\rangle)$	$(\langle 0.74, 0.32\rangle, \langle 0.63, 0.21\rangle)$	$(\langle 0.68, 0.41\rangle, \langle 0.53, 0.21\rangle)$	$(\langle 0.71, 0.41\rangle, \langle 0.43, 0.28\rangle)$
$\mathcal{G}_3$	$(\langle 0.71, 0.34\rangle, \langle 0.51, 0.31\rangle)$	$(\langle 0.63, 0.51\rangle, \langle 0.43, 0.39\rangle)$	$(\langle 0.71, 0.41\rangle, \langle 0.31, 0.41\rangle)$	$(\langle 0.69, 0.38\rangle, \langle 0.41, 0.31\rangle)$
$\mathcal{G}_4$	$(\langle 0.69, 0.59\rangle, \langle 0.61, 0.21\rangle)$	$(\langle 0.81, 0.51\rangle, \langle 0.31, 0.42\rangle)$	$(\langle 0.83, 0.41\rangle, \langle 0.32, 0.41\rangle)$	$(\langle 0.73, 0.49\rangle, \langle 0.41, 0.21\rangle)$
$\mathcal{G}_5$	$(\langle 0.72, 0.41\rangle, \langle 0.51, 0.21\rangle)$	$(\langle 0.83, 0.41\rangle, \langle 0.42, 0.31\rangle)$	$(\langle 0.73, 0.41\rangle, \langle 0.31, 0.42\rangle)$	$(\langle 0.83, 0.49\rangle, \langle 0.28, 0.41\rangle)$
$\mathcal{G}_6$	$(\langle 0.63, 0.59\rangle, \langle 0.41, 0.31\rangle)$	$(\langle 0.78, 0.43\rangle, \langle 0.38, 0.41\rangle)$	$(\langle 0.63, 0.48\rangle, \langle 0.28, 0.17\rangle)$	$(\langle 0.58, 0.49\rangle, \langle 0.31, 0.42\rangle)$
$\mathcal{G}_7$	$(\langle 0.81, 0.58\rangle, \langle 0.49, 0.31\rangle)$	$(\langle 0.73, 0.68\rangle, \langle 0.43, 0.49\rangle)$	$(\langle 0.69, 0.73\rangle, \langle 0.31, 0.31\rangle)$	$(\langle 0.68, 0.51\rangle, \langle 0.43, 0.21\rangle)$

Thus, $\tilde{\eth}$ is an LDFSR on $\ddot{\mathcal{Q}} \times \dot{\mathcal{G}}$. This relation gives us the numeric values in the form of LDFNs of each alternative corresponding to every decision variable. For example, for the alternative $\mathcal{G}_1$, the decision variable $\dot{\wp}_1$ ("Technical: convenience, maintainability, safety required") has numeric value $(\langle 0.73, 0.41\rangle, \langle 0.31, 0.13\rangle)$. This value shows that the alternative $\mathcal{G}_1$ is 73% technical and 41% has a falsity value for technicality. The pair $\langle 0.31, 0.13\rangle$ represents the reference parameters for the truth and falsity grades, where we can observe that alternative $\mathcal{G}_1$ is 31% highly technical and it has 13% low technicality. These sub-criteria for the alternatives can be observed from Table 10. All the remaining values can be constructed according to a similar pattern. We consider that experts give some opinion about the attributes and rank them according to their requirement. We convert the verbal description into the LDFS numeric values in the form of LDFS $\mathscr{B}_{\mathscr{D}}$. The set $\mathscr{B}_{\mathscr{D}}$ is the LDF-subset of $\dot{\mathcal{G}}$ and written as follows:

$$\mathscr{B}_{\mathscr{D}} = \{(\wp_1, \langle 00.63, 00.41\rangle, \langle 00.31, 00.33\rangle), (\wp_2, \langle 00.71, 00.51\rangle, \langle 00.41, 00.38\rangle),$$
$$(\wp_3, \langle 00.75, 00.63\rangle, \langle 00.51, 00.32\rangle), (\wp_4, \langle 00.83, 00.51\rangle, \langle 00.41, 00.21\rangle)\}.$$

We evaluate the "lower and upper approximations" of LDFS $\mathscr{B}_{\mathscr{D}}$ on LDFSR $\tilde{\mathfrak{d}}$.

$$\tilde{\mathfrak{d}}^*(\mathscr{B}_{\mathscr{D}}) = \{(\mathcal{G}_1, \langle 00.73, 00.51\rangle, \langle 00.31, 00.64\rangle), (\mathcal{G}_2, \langle 00.71, 00.57\rangle, \langle 00.51, 00.58\rangle), (\mathcal{G}_3, \langle 00.71, 00.51\rangle, \langle 00.41, 00.59\rangle),$$
$$(\mathcal{G}_4, \langle 00.75, 00.41\rangle, \langle 00.41, 00.58\rangle), (\mathcal{G}_5, \langle 00.83, 00.51\rangle, \langle 00.41, 00.58\rangle, (\mathcal{G}_6, \langle 00.71, 00.41\rangle, \langle 00.38, 00.58\rangle,$$
$$(\mathcal{G}_7, \langle 00.71, 00.42\rangle, \langle 00.41, 00.51\rangle)\}$$
$$\tilde{\mathfrak{d}}_*(\mathscr{B}_{\mathscr{D}}) = \{(\mathcal{G}_1, \langle 00.63, 00.51\rangle, \langle 00.69, 00.23\rangle), (\mathcal{G}_2, \langle 00.63, 00.41\rangle, \langle 00.41, 00.33\rangle), (\mathcal{G}_3, \langle 00.63, 00.51\rangle, \langle 00.49, 00.38\rangle),$$
$$(\mathcal{G}_4, \langle 00.63, 00.51\rangle, \langle 00.39, 00.38\rangle), (\mathcal{G}_5, \langle 00.63, 00.49\rangle, \langle 00.49, 00.32\rangle, (\mathcal{G}_6, \langle 00.63, 00.49\rangle, \langle 00.59, 00.38\rangle,$$
$$(\mathcal{G}_7, \langle 00.63, 00.63\rangle, \langle 00.51, 00.38\rangle)\}$$

$$\tilde{\mathfrak{d}}_*(\mathscr{B}_{\mathscr{D}}) \oplus \tilde{\mathfrak{d}}^*(\mathscr{B}_{\mathscr{D}}) = \{(\mathcal{G}_1, \langle 0.900, 0.260\rangle, \langle 0.780, 0.140\rangle), (\mathcal{G}_2, \langle 0.890, 0.230\rangle, \langle 0.710, 0.190\rangle),$$
$$(\mathcal{G}_3, \langle 0.890, 0.260\rangle, \langle 0.690, 0.220\rangle), (\mathcal{G}_4, \langle 0.900, 0.200\rangle, \langle 0.640, 0.220\rangle),$$
$$(\mathcal{G}_5, \langle 0.937, 0.249\rangle, \langle 0.699, 0.185\rangle, (\mathcal{G}_6, \langle 0.892, 0.200\rangle, \langle 0.745, 0.220\rangle,$$
$$(\mathcal{G}_7, \langle 0.890, 0.260\rangle, \langle 0.710, 0.190\rangle)\}$$

Now, we calculate the score values, quadratic score values, and expectation score values of the alternatives in $\tilde{\mathfrak{d}}_*(\mathscr{B}_{\mathscr{D}}) \oplus \tilde{\mathfrak{d}}^*(\mathscr{B}_{\mathscr{D}})$. The final ranking is given in Table 12.

Table 12. Ranking of alternatives for different score values.

LDFS	$\mathcal{G}_1$	$\mathcal{G}_2$	$\mathcal{G}_3$	$\mathcal{G}_4$	$\mathcal{G}_5$	$\mathcal{G}_6$	$\mathcal{G}_7$	Ranking	Final Decision
$\mathscr{L}_1$ (SF)	0.640	0.590	0.550	0.560	0.601	0.608	0.575	$\mathcal{G}_1 \succ \mathcal{G}_6 \succ \mathcal{G}_5 \succ \mathcal{G}_2 \succ \mathcal{G}_7 \succ \mathcal{G}_4 \succ \mathcal{G}_3$	$\mathcal{G}_1$
$\mathscr{L}_2$ (QSF)	0.665	0.603	0.576	0.565	0.635	0.631	0.596	$\mathcal{G}_1 \succ \mathcal{G}_5 \succ \mathcal{G}_6 \succ \mathcal{G}_2 \succ \mathcal{G}_7 \succ \mathcal{G}_3 \succ \mathcal{G}_4$	$\mathcal{G}_1$
$\mathscr{L}_3$ (ESF)	0.820	0.795	0.775	0.780	0.800	0.804	0.787	$\mathcal{G}_1 \succ \mathcal{G}_6 \succ \mathcal{G}_5 \succ \mathcal{G}_2 \succ \mathcal{G}_7 \succ \mathcal{G}_4 \succ \mathcal{G}_3$	$\mathcal{G}_1$

From Table 12, we can observe that the alternative $\mathcal{G}_1$ is most suitable for the final decision. The bar chart of the ranking results for alternatives is given in Figure 4.

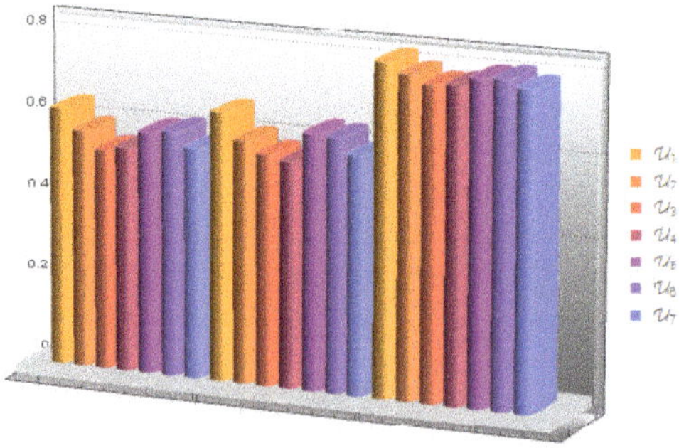

Figure 4. Bar chart of alternatives under LDFSRS for SF $\mathscr{L}_1$, QSF $\mathscr{L}_2$, and ESF $\mathscr{L}_3$.

4.1.2. Calculations by Using Algorithm 2

In Algorithm 1, we use the input data in the form of linguistic terms as LDFNs. We only deal with the truth and falsity grades with their reference parameters, and we have no idea about the expert's opinion. Due to the lack of information, we have some uncertainty in our decision. This uncertainty can be removed by giving some weight to the expert's opinion. Therefore, we establish upper and lower reducts for all the experts one by one. The initial five steps of Algorithm 2 are the same as Algorithm 1. We will proceed next by constructing the upper and lower reducts from "upper and lower approximations" of LDFS for all the experts. Suppose that we have three experts from the company's technical committee given as:

Expert X

Expert Y

Expert Z

The reducts from approximations can be constructed by using the following terms.

$\ddot{\mathscr{T}}_{\mathscr{D}}$ = Truth membership grade,

$\ddot{\mathcal{S}}_{\mathscr{D}}$ = Falsity membership grade,

$\alpha_{\mathscr{D}}$ = Reference parameter corresponding to truth membership grade,

$\beta_{\mathscr{D}}$ = Reference parameter corresponding to falsity membership grade,

$\mathscr{L}_3$ = Expectation score function value of LDFN,

$\widehat{\mathscr{L}}$ = Ranking given by experts to the alternatives from crisp set {0,1},

$\mathscr{L}^*$ = Selection of alternative by using "YES" or "NO", i.e., take average of scores $\mathscr{L}_3$ for all the alternatives. The alternatives that have a greater or equal score $\mathscr{L}_3$ than/to the average can be selected as "YES"; those who have a lesser score than the average value can be neglected as "NO",

$F.D$ = Final decision

The final decision is based on $\widehat{\mathscr{L}}$ and $\mathscr{L}^*$ given in Table 13.

Table 13. The criteria for the final decision (F.D).

$\widehat{\mathscr{L}}$	$\mathscr{L}^*$	F.D
0	NO	NO
1	YES	YES
0	YES	NO
1	NO	NO

For expert-X, the upper reduct of upper approximation $\mathfrak{F}^*(\mathscr{B}_{\mathscr{D}})$ (calculated in Algorithm 1) of LDFS $\mathscr{B}_{\mathscr{D}}$ is given as Table 14. The average of the score values of all the alternatives for $\mathfrak{F}^*(\mathscr{B}_{\mathscr{D}})$ is 0.520.

Table 14. Upper reduct for expert-X (U_X) from $\tilde{\eth}^*(\mathscr{B}_{\mathscr{D}})$.

(U_X)	$\check{\mathscr{T}}_{\mathscr{D}}$	$\check{S}_{\mathscr{D}}$	$\alpha_{\mathscr{D}}$	$\beta_{\mathscr{D}}$	$\mathscr{L}_3$	$\widehat{\mathscr{L}}$	$\mathscr{L}^*$	F.D
$\mathcal{G}_1$	0.73	0.51	0.31	0.64	0.472	1	$\mathscr{L}_3 < 0.520 \rightarrow$ NO	NO
$\mathcal{G}_2$	0.71	0.57	0.51	0.58	0.517	0	$\mathscr{L}_3 < 0.520 \rightarrow$ NO	NO
$\mathcal{G}_3$	0.71	0.51	0.41	0.59	0.505	1	$\mathscr{L}_3 < 0.520 \rightarrow$ NO	NO
$\mathcal{G}_4$	0.75	0.41	0.41	0.58	0.542	0	$\mathscr{L}_3 > 0.520 \rightarrow$ YES	NO
$\mathcal{G}_5$	0.83	0.51	0.41	0.58	0.537	1	$\mathscr{L}_3 > 0.520 \rightarrow$ YES	YES
$\mathcal{G}_6$	0.71	0.41	0.38	0.58	0.525	1	$\mathscr{L}_3 > 0.520 \rightarrow$ YES	YES
$\mathcal{G}_7$	0.71	0.42	0.41	0.51	0.547	1	$\mathscr{L}_3 > 0.520 \rightarrow$ YES	YES

This implies that $U_X = \{\mathcal{G}_5, \mathcal{G}_6, \mathcal{G}_7\}$. For expert-X, the lower reduct of lower approximation $\tilde{\eth}_*(\mathscr{B}_{\mathscr{D}})$ (calculated in Algorithm 1) of LDFS $\mathscr{B}_{\mathscr{D}}$ is given as Table 15. The average of the score values of all the alternatives for $\tilde{\eth}_*(\mathscr{B}_{\mathscr{D}})$ is 0.572.

Table 15. Lower reduct for expert-X (L_X) from $\tilde{\eth}^*(\mathscr{B}_{\mathscr{D}})$.

(L_X)	$\check{\mathscr{T}}_{\mathscr{D}}$	$\check{S}_{\mathscr{D}}$	$\alpha_{\mathscr{D}}$	$\beta_{\mathscr{D}}$	$\mathscr{L}_3$	$\widehat{\mathscr{L}}$	$\mathscr{L}^*$	F.D
$\mathcal{G}_1$	0.63	0.51	0.69	0.23	0.645	1	$\mathscr{L}_3 > 0.572 \rightarrow$ YES	YES
$\mathcal{G}_2$	0.63	0.41	0.41	0.33	0.575	0	$\mathscr{L}_3 > 0.572 \rightarrow$ YES	NO
$\mathcal{G}_3$	0.63	0.51	0.49	0.38	0.557	1	$\mathscr{L}_3 < 0.572 \rightarrow$ NO	NO
$\mathcal{G}_4$	0.63	0.51	0.39	0.38	0.532	0	$\mathscr{L}_3 < 0.572 \rightarrow$ NO	NO
$\mathcal{G}_5$	0.63	0.49	0.49	0.32	0.577	1	$\mathscr{L}_3 > 0.572 \rightarrow$ YES	YES
$\mathcal{G}_6$	0.63	0.49	0.59	0.38	0.587	1	$\mathscr{L}_3 > 0.572 \rightarrow$ YES	YES
$\mathcal{G}_7$	0.63	0.63	0.51	0.38	0.532	1	$\mathscr{L}_3 < 0.572 \rightarrow$ NO	NO

This implies that $L_X = \{\mathcal{G}_1, \mathcal{G}_5, \mathcal{G}_6\}$. For expert-Y, the upper reduct of upper approximation $\tilde{\eth}^*(\mathscr{B}_{\mathscr{D}})$ (calculated in Algorithm 1) of LDFS $\mathscr{B}_{\mathscr{D}}$ is given as Table 16. The average of the score values of all the alternatives for $\tilde{\eth}^*(\mathscr{B}_{\mathscr{D}})$ is 0.520.

Table 16. Upper reduct for expert-Y (U_Y) from $\tilde{\eth}^*(\mathscr{B}_{\mathscr{D}})$.

(U_Y)	$\check{\mathscr{T}}_{\mathscr{D}}$	$\check{S}_{\mathscr{D}}$	$\alpha_{\mathscr{D}}$	$\beta_{\mathscr{D}}$	$\mathscr{L}_3$	$\widehat{\mathscr{L}}$	$\mathscr{L}^*$	F.D
$\mathcal{G}_1$	0.73	0.51	0.31	0.64	0.472	0	$\mathscr{L}_3 < 0.520 \rightarrow$ NO	NO
$\mathcal{G}_2$	0.71	0.57	0.51	0.58	0.517	1	$\mathscr{L}_3 < 0.520 \rightarrow$ NO	NO
$\mathcal{G}_3$	0.71	0.51	0.41	0.59	0.505	0	$\mathscr{L}_3 < 0.520 \rightarrow$ NO	NO
$\mathcal{G}_4$	0.75	0.41	0.41	0.58	0.542	1	$\mathscr{L}_3 > 0.520 \rightarrow$ YES	YES
$\mathcal{G}_5$	0.83	0.51	0.41	0.58	0.537	1	$\mathscr{L}_3 > 0.520 \rightarrow$ YES	YES
$\mathcal{G}_6$	0.71	0.41	0.38	0.58	0.525	1	$\mathscr{L}_3 > 0.520 \rightarrow$ YES	YES
$\mathcal{G}_7$	0.71	0.42	0.41	0.51	0.547	0	$\mathscr{L}_3 > 0.520 \rightarrow$ YES	NO

This implies that $U_Y = \{\mathcal{G}_4, \mathcal{G}_5, \mathcal{G}_6\}$. For expert-Y, the lower reduct of lower approximation $\tilde{\eth}_*(\mathscr{B}_{\mathscr{D}})$ (calculated in Algorithm 1) of LDFS $\mathscr{B}_{\mathscr{D}}$ is given as Table 17. The average of the score values of all the alternatives for $\tilde{\eth}_*(\mathscr{B}_{\mathscr{D}})$ is 0.572.

Table 17. Lower reduct for expert-Y (L_Y) from $\tilde{\mathfrak{d}}^*(\mathscr{B}_{\mathscr{D}})$.

(L_Y)	$\check{\mathscr{F}}_{\mathscr{D}}$	$\check{\mathcal{S}}_{\mathscr{D}}$	$\alpha_{\mathscr{D}}$	$\beta_{\mathscr{D}}$	$\mathscr{L}_3$	$\widehat{\mathscr{L}}$	$\mathscr{L}^*$	F.D
$\mathcal{G}_1$	0.63	0.51	0.69	0.23	0.645	0	$\mathscr{L}_3 > 0.572 \rightarrow$ YES	NO
$\mathcal{G}_2$	0.63	0.41	0.41	0.33	0.575	1	$\mathscr{L}_3 > 0.572 \rightarrow$ YES	YES
$\mathcal{G}_3$	0.63	0.51	0.49	0.38	0.557	0	$\mathscr{L}_3 < 0.572 \rightarrow$ NO	NO
$\mathcal{G}_4$	0.63	0.51	0.39	0.38	0.532	1	$\mathscr{L}_3 < 0.572 \rightarrow$ NO	NO
$\mathcal{G}_5$	0.63	0.49	0.49	0.32	0.577	1	$\mathscr{L}_3 > 0.572 \rightarrow$ YES	YES
$\mathcal{G}_6$	0.63	0.49	0.59	0.38	0.587	1	$\mathscr{L}_3 > 0.572 \rightarrow$ YES	YES
$\mathcal{G}_7$	0.63	0.63	0.51	0.38	0.532	0	$\mathscr{L}_3 < 0.572 \rightarrow$ NO	NO

This implies that $L_Y = \{\mathcal{G}_2, \mathcal{G}_5, \mathcal{G}_6\}$. For expert-Z, the upper reduct of upper approximation $\tilde{\mathfrak{d}}^*(\mathscr{B}_{\mathscr{D}})$ (calculated in Algorithm 1) of LDFS $\mathscr{B}_{\mathscr{D}}$ is given as Table 18. The average of the score values of all the alternatives for $\tilde{\mathfrak{d}}^*(\mathscr{B}_{\mathscr{D}})$ is 0.520.

Table 18. Upper reduct for expert-Z (U_Z) from $\tilde{\mathfrak{d}}^*(\mathscr{B}_{\mathscr{D}})$.

(U_Y)	$\check{\mathscr{F}}_{\mathscr{D}}$	$\check{\mathcal{S}}_{\mathscr{D}}$	$\alpha_{\mathscr{D}}$	$\beta_{\mathscr{D}}$	$\mathscr{L}_3$	$\widehat{\mathscr{L}}$	$\mathscr{L}^*$	F.D
$\mathcal{G}_1$	0.73	0.51	0.31	0.64	0.472	1	$\mathscr{L}_3 < 0.520 \rightarrow$ NO	NO
$\mathcal{G}_2$	0.71	0.57	0.51	0.58	0.517	1	$\mathscr{L}_3 < 0.520 \rightarrow$ NO	NO
$\mathcal{G}_3$	0.71	0.51	0.41	0.59	0.505	0	$\mathscr{L}_3 < 0.520 \rightarrow$ NO	NO
$\mathcal{G}_4$	0.75	0.41	0.41	0.58	0.542	0	$\mathscr{L}_3 > 0.520 \rightarrow$ YES	NO
$\mathcal{G}_5$	0.83	0.51	0.41	0.58	0.537	1	$\mathscr{L}_3 > 0.520 \rightarrow$ YES	YES
$\mathcal{G}_6$	0.71	0.41	0.38	0.58	0.525	0	$\mathscr{L}_3 > 0.520 \rightarrow$ YES	NO
$\mathcal{G}_7$	0.71	0.42	0.41	0.51	0.547	1	$\mathscr{L}_3 > 0.520 \rightarrow$ YES	YES

This implies that $U_Z = \{\mathcal{G}_5, \mathcal{G}_7\}$. For expert-Z, the lower reduct of lower approximation $\tilde{\mathfrak{d}}_*(\mathscr{B}_{\mathscr{D}})$ (calculated in Algorithm 1) of LDFS $\mathscr{B}_{\mathscr{D}}$ is given as Table 19. The average of the score values of all the alternatives for $\tilde{\mathfrak{d}}_*(\mathscr{B}_{\mathscr{D}})$ is 0.572.

Table 19. Lower reduct for expert-Z (L_Z) from $\tilde{\mathfrak{d}}^*(\mathscr{B}_{\mathscr{D}})$.

(L_Z)	$\check{\mathscr{F}}_{\mathscr{D}}$	$\check{\mathcal{S}}_{\mathscr{D}}$	$\alpha_{\mathscr{D}}$	$\beta_{\mathscr{D}}$	$\mathscr{L}_3$	$\widehat{\mathscr{L}}$	$\mathscr{L}^*$	F.D
$\mathcal{G}_1$	0.63	0.51	0.69	0.23	0.645	1	$\mathscr{L}_3 > 0.572 \rightarrow$ YES	YES
$\mathcal{G}_2$	0.63	0.41	0.41	0.33	0.575	1	$\mathscr{L}_3 > 0.572 \rightarrow$ YES	YES
$\mathcal{G}_3$	0.63	0.51	0.49	0.38	0.557	0	$\mathscr{L}_3 < 0.572 \rightarrow$ NO	NO
$\mathcal{G}_4$	0.63	0.51	0.39	0.38	0.532	0	$\mathscr{L}_3 < 0.572 \rightarrow$ NO	NO
$\mathcal{G}_5$	0.63	0.49	0.49	0.32	0.577	1	$\mathscr{L}_3 > 0.572 \rightarrow$ YES	YES
$\mathcal{G}_6$	0.63	0.49	0.59	0.38	0.587	0	$\mathscr{L}_3 > 0.572 \rightarrow$ YES	NO
$\mathcal{G}_7$	0.63	0.63	0.51	0.38	0.532	1	$\mathscr{L}_3 < 0.572 \rightarrow$ NO	NO

This implies that $L_Z = \{\mathcal{G}_1, \mathcal{G}_2, \mathcal{G}_5\}$. Now, we calculate the core set by taking the intersection of all upper and lower reducts for all three experts.

$$\text{core} = U_X \cap L_X \cap U_Y \cap L_Y \cap U_Z \cap L_Z = \{\mathcal{G}_5\}$$

This means that "$\mathcal{G}_5$" is the most suitable alternative for the final decision.

4.2. Selection of the Most Appropriate Material Handling Equipment by Using SRLDFSs

Now, we use our second novel structure of SRLDFS and "crisp soft approximation space" for the selection of the most appropriate material handling equipment. We construct two novel algorithms (Algorithms 3 and 4) for the selection. The flowchart diagram of both algorithms is given in Figure 5.

Algorithm 3: Selection of the best material handling equipment by using SRLDFSs.

Input:

1. Input the reference set $\ddot{\mathcal{Q}}$.
2. Input the assembling of attributes $\dot{\mathcal{G}}$.

Construction:

3. According to the necessity of the DM, build a crisp soft relation $\mathscr{A}$ over $\ddot{\mathcal{Q}} \times \dot{\mathcal{G}}$.
4. Based on the needs of the decision maker, construct LDF-subset $\mathcal{H}$ of $\dot{\mathcal{G}}$ as an optimal normal decision set.

Calculation:

5. Calculate the "SRLDF approximation operators" $\mathscr{A}_*(\mathcal{H})$ and $\mathscr{A}^*(\mathcal{H})$ as "lower and upper approximations" by using Definition 9.
6. By using Definition 13 of the ring sum operation, find the choice of LDFS $\mathscr{A}_*(\mathcal{H}) \oplus \mathscr{A}^*(\mathcal{H})$.

Output:

7. We use the definitions of the score, quadratic score, and expectation score functions for LDFNs $\ddot{A}_{\mathscr{D}} = (\langle \dot{t}_{\mathscr{D}}, \dot{f}_{\mathscr{D}} \rangle, \langle \alpha_{\mathscr{D}}, \beta_{\mathscr{D}} \rangle)$ given in [54] and written respectively as:

$$\mathscr{L}_1(\ddot{A}_{\mathscr{D}}) = \frac{1}{2}[(\dot{t}_{\mathscr{D}} - \dot{f}_{\mathscr{D}}) + (\alpha_{\mathscr{D}} - \beta_{\mathscr{D}})]$$

$$\mathscr{L}_2(\ddot{A}_{\mathscr{D}}) = \frac{1}{2}[(\dot{t}^2_{\mathscr{D}} - \dot{f}^2_{\mathscr{D}}) + (\alpha^2_{\mathscr{D}} - \beta^2_{\mathscr{D}})]$$

$$\mathscr{L}_3(\ddot{A}_{\mathscr{D}}) = \frac{1}{2}[\frac{(\dot{t}_{\mathscr{D}} - \dot{f}_{\mathscr{D}} + 1)}{2} + \frac{(\alpha_{\mathscr{D}} - \beta_{\mathscr{D}} + 1)}{2}]$$

of every alternative in $\mathscr{A}_*(\mathcal{H}) \oplus \mathscr{A}^*(\mathcal{H})$.

8. Rank the alternatives by using calculated score values.

Final decision:

9. Select the object having the highest score value.

Algorithm 4: Selection of the best material handling equipment by using SRLDFSs.

Input:

1. Input the reference set $\ddot{\mathcal{Q}}$.
2. Input the assembling of attributes $\dot{\mathcal{G}}$.

Construction:

3. According to the necessity of the DM, build a crisp soft relation $\mathscr{A}$ over $\ddot{\mathcal{Q}} \times \dot{\mathcal{G}}$.
4. Based on the needs of the decision maker, construct LDF-subset $\mathcal{H}$ of $\dot{\mathcal{G}}$ as an optimal normal decision set.

Calculation:

5. Calculate the "SRLDF approximation operators" $\mathscr{A}_*(\mathcal{H})$ and $\mathscr{A}^*(\mathcal{H})$ as "lower and upper approximations" by using Definition 9.
6. For "$\mathscr{N}$" number of experts, calculate upper and lower reducts from the calculated "upper and lower approximation operators", respectively.

Output:

7. From calculated "$2\mathscr{N}$" reducts, we get "$2\mathscr{N}$" crisp subsets of the reference set $\ddot{\mathcal{Q}}$. The subsets can be constructed by using the "YES" and "NO" logic. The only alternatives in the reduct having final decision "YES" will become the object of the crisp subset.
8. Calculate the core set by taking the intersection of all crisp subsets obtained from the calculated reducts.

Final decision:

9. The alternatives in the core will be our choice for the final decision.

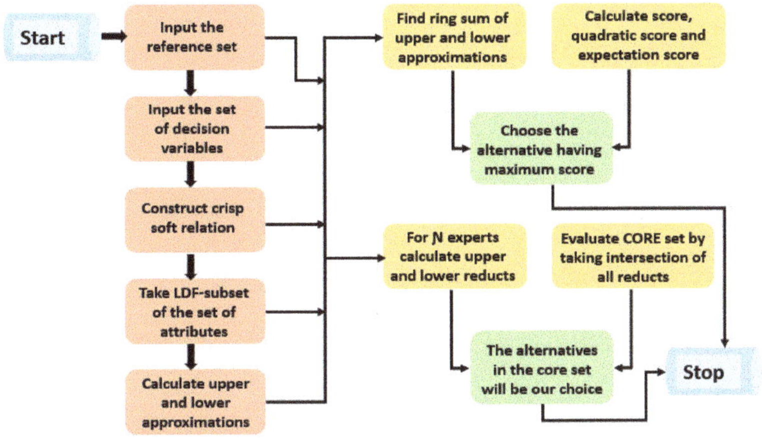

Figure 5. Flowchart diagram of Algorithms 3 and 4.

4.2.1. Calculations by Using Algorithm 3

We consider the indiscernibility relation "selection of best material handling equipment". This relation is represented as a crisp soft relation $\tilde{\mathscr{A}}$ over $\dot{\mathcal{Q}} \times \dot{\mathcal{G}}$ given as Table 20.

Table 20. Crisp soft relation $\tilde{\mathscr{A}}$.

$\tilde{\mathscr{A}}$	$\dot{\wp}_1$	$\dot{\wp}_2$	$\dot{\wp}_3$	$\dot{\wp}_4$
$\mathcal{G}_1$	0	0	1	1
$\mathcal{G}_2$	0	1	1	0
$\mathcal{G}_3$	1	1	0	0
$\mathcal{G}_4$	1	1	1	0
$\mathcal{G}_5$	1	1	0	1
$\mathcal{G}_6$	1	0	0	1
$\mathcal{G}_7$	0	1	1	0

Thus, $\tilde{\mathscr{A}}$ over $\dot{\mathcal{Q}} \times \dot{\mathcal{G}}$ is a crisp soft relation. Table 20 shows that we have:

$$\tilde{\mathscr{A}}_s(\mathcal{G}_1) = \{\dot{\wp}_3, \dot{\wp}_4\}$$
$$\tilde{\mathscr{A}}_s(\mathcal{G}_2) = \{\dot{\wp}_2, \dot{\wp}_3\}$$
$$\tilde{\mathscr{A}}_s(\mathcal{G}_3) = \{\dot{\wp}_1, \dot{\wp}_2\}$$
$$\tilde{\mathscr{A}}_s(\mathcal{G}_4) = \{\dot{\wp}_1, \dot{\wp}_2, \dot{\wp}_3\}$$
$$\tilde{\mathscr{A}}_s(\mathcal{G}_5) = \{\dot{\wp}_1, \dot{\wp}_2, \dot{\wp}_4\}$$
$$\tilde{\mathscr{A}}_s(\mathcal{G}_6) = \{\dot{\wp}_1, \dot{\wp}_4\}$$
$$\tilde{\mathscr{A}}_s(\mathcal{G}_7) = \{\dot{\wp}_2, \dot{\wp}_3\}$$

We consider that experts give some opinion about the attributes and rank them according to their requirements. We convert the verbal description into the LDFS numeric values in the form of LDFS $\mathcal{H}$. The set $\mathcal{H}$ is the LDF-subset of $\dot{\mathcal{G}}$ and written as follows:

$$\mathcal{H} = \{(\dot{\wp}_1, \langle 0.63, 0.41\rangle, \langle 0.31, 0.33\rangle), (\dot{\wp}_2, \langle 0.71, 0.51\rangle, \langle 0.41, 0.38\rangle),$$
$$(\dot{\wp}_3, \langle 0.75, 0.63\rangle, \langle 0.51, 0.32\rangle), (\dot{\wp}_4, \langle 0.83, 0.51\rangle, \langle 0.41, 0.21\rangle)\}.$$

Now, we find "upper and lower approximations" of set $\mathcal{H}$ over the relation $\mathscr{A}$ by using Definition 9 given as:

$$\overline{\mathscr{A}}^*(\mathcal{H}) = \{(\mathcal{G}_1, \langle 00.83, 00.51\rangle, \langle 00.51, 00.21\rangle), (\mathcal{G}_2, \langle 00.75, 00.51\rangle, \langle 00.51, 00.32\rangle), (\mathcal{G}_3, \langle 00.71, 00.41\rangle, \langle 00.41, 00.33\rangle), (\mathcal{G}_4, \langle 00.75, 00.41\rangle, \langle 00.51, 00.32\rangle), (\mathcal{G}_5, \langle 00.83, 00.41\rangle, \langle 00.41, 00.21\rangle, (\mathcal{G}_6, \langle 00.83, 00.41\rangle, \langle 00.41, 00.21\rangle, (\mathcal{G}_7, \langle 00.75, 00.51\rangle, \langle 00.51, 00.32\rangle)\}$$

$$\underline{\mathscr{A}}_*(\mathcal{H}) = \{(\mathcal{G}_1, \langle 00.75, 00.63\rangle, \langle 00.41, 00.32\rangle), (\mathcal{G}_2, \langle 00.71, 00.63\rangle, \langle 00.41, 00.38\rangle), (\mathcal{G}_3, \langle 00.63, 00.51\rangle, \langle 00.31, 00.38\rangle), (\mathcal{G}_4, \langle 00.63, 00.63\rangle, \langle 00.31, 00.38\rangle), (\mathcal{G}_5, \langle 00.63, 00.51\rangle, \langle 00.31, 00.38\rangle, (\mathcal{G}_6, \langle 00.63, 00.51\rangle, \langle 00.31, 00.33\rangle, (\mathcal{G}_7, \langle 00.71, 00.63\rangle, \langle 00.41, 00.38\rangle)\}$$

$$\underline{\mathscr{A}}_*(\mathcal{H}) \oplus \overline{\mathscr{A}}^*(\mathcal{H}) = \{(\mathcal{G}_1, \langle 0.957, 0.321\rangle, \langle 0.710, 0.067\rangle), (\mathcal{G}_2, \langle 0.927, 0.321\rangle, \langle 0.710, 0.121\rangle), (\mathcal{G}_3, \langle 0.892, 0.209\rangle, \langle 0.592, 0.125\rangle), (\mathcal{G}_4, \langle 0.907, 0.258\rangle, \langle 0.661, 0.121\rangle), (\mathcal{G}_5, \langle 0.937, 0.209\rangle, \langle 0.592, 0.079\rangle, (\mathcal{G}_6, \langle 0.937, 0.209\rangle, \langle 0.592, 0.069\rangle, (\mathcal{G}_7, \langle 0.927, 0.321\rangle, \langle 0.710, 0.121\rangle)\}$$

Now, we calculate the score values, quadratic score values, and expectation score values of alternatives in $\underline{\mathscr{A}}_*(\mathcal{H}) \oplus \overline{\mathscr{A}}^*(\mathcal{H})$. The calculated data with the final ranking is given in Table 21.

Table 21. Ranking of alternatives for different score values.

LDFS	$\mathcal{G}_1$	$\mathcal{G}_2$	$\mathcal{G}_3$	$\mathcal{G}_4$	$\mathcal{G}_5$	$\mathcal{G}_6$	$\mathcal{G}_7$	Ranking	Final Decision
$\mathscr{L}_1$ (SF)	0.639	0.597	0.575	0.594	0.620	0.625	0.597	$\mathcal{G}_1 \succ \mathcal{G}_6 \succ \mathcal{G}_5 \succ \mathcal{G}_2 = \mathcal{G}_7 \succ \mathcal{G}_4 \succ \mathcal{G}_3$	$\mathcal{G}_1$
$\mathscr{L}_2$ (QSF)	0.656	0.622	0.543	0.589	0.589	0.589	0.622	$\mathcal{G}_1 \succ \mathcal{G}_2 = \mathcal{G}_7 \succ \mathcal{G}_5 = \mathcal{G}_6 = \mathcal{G}_4 \succ \mathcal{G}_3$	$\mathcal{G}_1$
$\mathscr{L}_3$ (ESF)	0.819	0.798	0.787	0.797	0.810	0.812	0.798	$\mathcal{G}_1 \succ \mathcal{G}_6 \succ \mathcal{G}_5 \succ \mathcal{G}_2 = \mathcal{G}_7 \succ \mathcal{G}_4 \succ \mathcal{G}_3$	$\mathcal{G}_1$

From Table 21, we can observe that the alternative $\mathcal{G}_1$ is most suitable for the final decision. The bar chart of the ranking results for alternatives is given in Figure 6.

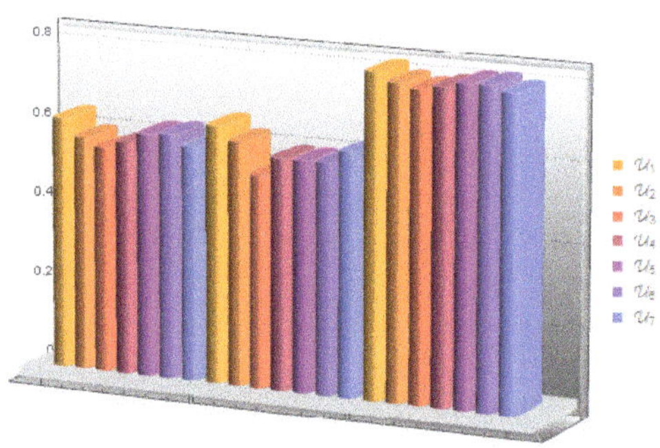

Figure 6. Bar chart of alternatives under SRLDFS for SF $\mathscr{L}_1$, QSF $\mathscr{L}_2$, and ESF $\mathscr{L}_3$.

4.2.2. Calculations by Using Algorithm 4

In this part, we establish upper and lower reducts for all the experts one by one. The initial five steps of Algorithm 4 are the same as Algorithm 3. We will proceed next by constructing the upper and lower reducts from the "upper and lower approximations" of LDFS for all the experts under "crisp soft approximation space". Suppose that we have three experts from the company's technical committee given as:

Expert $\dot{X}$

Expert $\dot{Y}$

Expert $\dot{Z}$

The characteristics and terms for finding the upper and lower reducts are the same as we used in Algorithm 2. Therefore, we directly calculate the reducts for experts.

For expert-$\dot{X}$, the upper reduct of upper approximation $\mathscr{A}^*(\mathcal{H})$ (calculated in Algorithm 3) of LDFS $\mathcal{H}$ is given as Table 22. The average of the score values of all the alternatives for $\mathscr{A}^*(\mathcal{H})$ is 0.629.

Table 22. Upper reduct for expert-$\dot{X}$, $(U_{\dot{X}})$ from $\mathscr{A}^*(\mathcal{H})$.

$(U_{\dot{X}})$	$\mathfrak{F}_{\mathscr{D}}$	$\check{S}_{\mathscr{D}}$	$\alpha_{\mathscr{D}}$	$\beta_{\mathscr{D}}$	$\mathscr{L}_3$	$\widehat{\mathscr{L}}$	$\mathscr{L}^*$	F.D
$\mathcal{G}_1$	0.83	0.51	0.51	0.21	0.655	1	$\mathscr{L}_3 > 0.629 \to$ YES	NO
$\mathcal{G}_2$	0.75	0.51	0.51	0.32	0.607	1	$\mathscr{L}_3 < 0.629 \to$ NO	NO
$\mathcal{G}_3$	0.71	0.41	0.41	0.33	0.595	0	$\mathscr{L}_3 < 0.629 \to$ NO	NO
$\mathcal{G}_4$	0.75	0.41	0.51	0.32	0.632	0	$\mathscr{L}_3 > 0.629 \to$ YES	NO
$\mathcal{G}_5$	0.83	0.41	0.41	0.21	0.655	1	$\mathscr{L}_3 > 0.629 \to$ YES	YES
$\mathcal{G}_6$	0.83	0.41	0.41	0.21	0.655	1	$\mathscr{L}_3 > 0.629 \to$ YES	YES
$\mathcal{G}_7$	0.75	0.51	0.51	0.32	0.607	0	$\mathscr{L}_3 < 0.629 \to$ NO	NO

This implies that $(U_{\dot{X}}) = \{\mathcal{G}_1, \mathcal{G}_5, \mathcal{G}_6\}$. For expert-$\dot{X}$, the lower reduct of lower approximation $\mathscr{A}_*(\mathcal{H})$ (calculated in Algorithm 3) of LDFS $\mathcal{H}$ is given as Table 23. The average of the score values of all the alternatives for $\mathscr{A}_*(\mathcal{H})$ is 0.519.

Table 23. Lower reduct for expert-$\dot{X}$ $(L_{\dot{X}})$ from $\mathscr{A}^*(\mathcal{H})$.

$(L_{\dot{X}})$	$\mathfrak{F}_{\mathscr{D}}$	$\check{S}_{\mathscr{D}}$	$\alpha_{\mathscr{D}}$	$\beta_{\mathscr{D}}$	$\mathscr{L}_3$	$\widehat{\mathscr{L}}$	$\mathscr{L}^*$	F.D
$\mathcal{G}_1$	0.75	0.63	0.41	0.32	0.552	1	$\mathscr{L}_3 > 0.519 \to$ YES	YES
$\mathcal{G}_2$	0.71	0.63	0.41	0.38	0.527	1	$\mathscr{L}_3 > 0.519 \to$ YES	YES
$\mathcal{G}_3$	0.63	0.51	0.31	0.38	0.512	1	$\mathscr{L}_3 < 0.519 \to$ NO	NO
$\mathcal{G}_4$	0.63	0.63	0.31	0.38	0.482	0	$\mathscr{L}_3 < 0.519 \to$ NO	NO
$\mathcal{G}_5$	0.63	0.51	0.31	0.38	0.512	1	$\mathscr{L}_3 < 0.519 \to$ NO	NO
$\mathcal{G}_6$	0.63	0.51	0.31	0.33	0.525	1	$\mathscr{L}_3 > 0.519 \to$ YES	YES
$\mathcal{G}_7$	0.71	0.63	0.41	0.38	0.527	0	$\mathscr{L}_3 > 0.519 \to$ YES	NO

This implies that $L_{\dot{X}} = \{\mathcal{G}_1, \mathcal{G}_2, \mathcal{G}_6\}$. For expert-$\dot{Y}$, the upper reduct of upper approximation $\mathscr{A}^*(\mathcal{H})$ (calculated in Algorithm 3) of LDFS $\mathcal{H}$ is given as Table 24. The average of the score values of all the alternatives for $\mathscr{A}^*(\mathcal{H})$ is 0.629.

Table 24. Upper reduct for expert-$\dot{Y}$, $(U_{\dot{Y}})$ from $\mathscr{A}^*(\mathcal{H})$.

$(U_{\dot{Y}})$	$\mathfrak{F}_{\mathscr{D}}$	$\check{S}_{\mathscr{D}}$	$\alpha_{\mathscr{D}}$	$\beta_{\mathscr{D}}$	$\mathscr{L}_3$	$\widehat{\mathscr{L}}$	$\mathscr{L}^*$	F.D
$\mathcal{G}_1$	0.83	0.51	0.51	0.21	0.655	1	$\mathscr{L}_3 > 0.629 \to$ YES	YES
$\mathcal{G}_2$	0.75	0.51	0.51	0.32	0.607	0	$\mathscr{L}_3 < 0.629 \to$ NO	NO
$\mathcal{G}_3$	0.71	0.41	0.41	0.33	0.595	0	$\mathscr{L}_3 < 0.629 \to$ NO	NO
$\mathcal{G}_4$	0.75	0.41	0.51	0.32	0.632	1	$\mathscr{L}_3 > 0.629 \to$ YES	YES
$\mathcal{G}_5$	0.83	0.41	0.41	0.21	0.655	1	$\mathscr{L}_3 > 0.629 \to$ YES	YES
$\mathcal{G}_6$	0.83	0.41	0.41	0.21	0.655	0	$\mathscr{L}_3 > 0.629 \to$ YES	NO
$\mathcal{G}_7$	0.75	0.51	0.51	0.32	0.607	1	$\mathscr{L}_3 < 0.629 \to$ NO	NO

This implies that $(U_{\dot{Y}}) = \{\mathcal{G}_1, \mathcal{G}_4, \mathcal{G}_5\}$. For expert-$\dot{Y}$, the lower reduct of lower approximation $\mathscr{A}_*(\mathcal{H})$ (calculated in Algorithm 3) of LDFS $\mathcal{H}$ is given as Table 25. The average of the score values of all the alternatives for $\mathscr{A}_*(\mathcal{H})$ is 0.519.

Table 25. Lower reduct for expert-$\dot{Y}$ $(L_{\dot{Y}})$ from $\mathscr{A}^*(\mathcal{H})$.

$(L_{\dot{Y}})$	$\mathfrak{F}_{\mathscr{D}}$	$\check{S}_{\mathscr{D}}$	$\alpha_{\mathscr{D}}$	$\beta_{\mathscr{D}}$	$\mathscr{L}_3$	$\widehat{\mathscr{L}}$	$\mathscr{L}^*$	F.D
$\mathcal{G}_1$	0.75	0.63	0.41	0.32	0.552	1	$\mathscr{L}_3 > 0.519 \rightarrow$ YES	YES
$\mathcal{G}_2$	0.71	0.63	0.41	0.38	0.527	0	$\mathscr{L}_3 > 0.519 \rightarrow$ YES	NO
$\mathcal{G}_3$	0.63	0.51	0.31	0.38	0.512	0	$\mathscr{L}_3 < 0.519 \rightarrow$ NO	NO
$\mathcal{G}_4$	0.63	0.63	0.31	0.38	0.482	1	$\mathscr{L}_3 < 0.519 \rightarrow$ NO	NO
$\mathcal{G}_5$	0.63	0.51	0.31	0.38	0.512	1	$\mathscr{L}_3 < 0.519 \rightarrow$ NO	NO
$\mathcal{G}_6$	0.63	0.51	0.31	0.33	0.525	0	$\mathscr{L}_3 > 0.519 \rightarrow$ YES	NO
$\mathcal{G}_7$	0.71	0.63	0.41	0.38	0.527	1	$\mathscr{L}_3 > 0.519 \rightarrow$ YES	YES

This implies that $L_{\dot{Y}} = \{\mathcal{G}_1, \mathcal{G}_7\}$. For expert-$\dot{Z}$, the upper reduct of upper approximation $\mathscr{A}^*(\mathcal{H})$ (calculated in Algorithm 3) of LDFS $\mathcal{H}$ is given as Table 26. The average of the score values of all the alternatives for $\mathscr{A}^*(\mathcal{H})$ is 0.629.

Table 26. Upper reduct for expert-$\dot{Z}$, $(U_{\dot{Z}})$ from $\mathscr{A}^*(\mathcal{H})$.

$(U_{\dot{Z}})$	$\mathfrak{F}_{\mathscr{D}}$	$\check{S}_{\mathscr{D}}$	$\alpha_{\mathscr{D}}$	$\beta_{\mathscr{D}}$	$\mathscr{L}_3$	$\widehat{\mathscr{L}}$	$\mathscr{L}^*$	F.D
$\mathcal{G}_1$	0.83	0.51	0.51	0.21	0.655	1	$\mathscr{L}_3 > 0.629 \rightarrow$ YES	YES
$\mathcal{G}_2$	0.75	0.51	0.51	0.32	0.607	1	$\mathscr{L}_3 < 0.629 \rightarrow$ NO	NO
$\mathcal{G}_3$	0.71	0.41	0.41	0.33	0.595	0	$\mathscr{L}_3 < 0.629 \rightarrow$ NO	NO
$\mathcal{G}_4$	0.75	0.41	0.51	0.32	0.632	1	$\mathscr{L}_3 > 0.629 \rightarrow$ YES	YES
$\mathcal{G}_5$	0.83	0.41	0.41	0.21	0.655	0	$\mathscr{L}_3 > 0.629 \rightarrow$ YES	NO
$\mathcal{G}_6$	0.83	0.41	0.41	0.21	0.655	1	$\mathscr{L}_3 > 0.629 \rightarrow$ YES	YES
$\mathcal{G}_7$	0.75	0.51	0.51	0.32	0.607	1	$\mathscr{L}_3 < 0.629 \rightarrow$ NO	NO

This implies that $(U_{\dot{Z}}) = \{\mathcal{G}_1, \mathcal{G}_4, \mathcal{G}_6\}$. For expert-$\dot{Z}$, the lower reduct of lower approximation $\mathscr{A}_*(\mathcal{H})$ (calculated in Algorithm 3) of LDFS $\mathcal{H}$ is given as Table 27. The average of the score values of all the alternatives for $\mathscr{A}_*(\mathcal{H})$ is 0.519.

Table 27. Lower reduct for expert-$\dot{Z}$ $(L_{\dot{Z}})$ from $\mathscr{A}^*(\mathcal{H})$.

$(L_{\dot{Z}})$	$\mathfrak{F}_{\mathscr{D}}$	$\check{S}_{\mathscr{D}}$	$\alpha_{\mathscr{D}}$	$\beta_{\mathscr{D}}$	$\mathscr{L}_3$	$\widehat{\mathscr{L}}$	$\mathscr{L}^*$	F.D
$\mathcal{G}_1$	0.75	0.63	0.41	0.32	0.552	1	$\mathscr{L}_3 > 0.519 \rightarrow$ YES	YES
$\mathcal{G}_2$	0.71	0.63	0.41	0.38	0.527	1	$\mathscr{L}_3 > 0.519 \rightarrow$ YES	YES
$\mathcal{G}_3$	0.63	0.51	0.31	0.38	0.512	0	$\mathscr{L}_3 < 0.519 \rightarrow$ NO	NO
$\mathcal{G}_4$	0.63	0.63	0.31	0.38	0.482	1	$\mathscr{L}_3 < 0.519 \rightarrow$ NO	NO
$\mathcal{G}_5$	0.63	0.51	0.31	0.38	0.512	0	$\mathscr{L}_3 < 0.519 \rightarrow$ NO	NO
$\mathcal{G}_6$	0.63	0.51	0.31	0.33	0.525	1	$\mathscr{L}_3 > 0.519 \rightarrow$ YES	YES
$\mathcal{G}_7$	0.71	0.63	0.41	0.38	0.527	1	$\mathscr{L}_3 > 0.519 \rightarrow$ YES	YES

This implies that $L_{\dot{Z}} = \{\mathcal{G}_1, \mathcal{G}_2, \mathcal{G}_6, \mathcal{G}_7\}$.

Now, we calculate the core set by taking the intersection of all upper and lower reducts for all three experts.

$$\text{core} = U_{\dot{X}} \cap L_{\dot{X}} \cap U_{\dot{Y}} \cap L_{\dot{Y}} \cap U_{\dot{Z}} \cap L_{\dot{Z}} = \{\mathcal{G}_1\}$$

This means that "$\mathcal{G}_1$" is the most suitable alternative for the final decision.

4.3. Discussion, Comparison, and Symmetrical Analysis

In this part, we compare our models to the existing approaches and discuss the superiority, authenticity, symmetry, and validity of our proposed structures. The comparison of the proposed structures with existing models is shown in Tables 28 and 29. Such tables reflect the characteristics and limitations of certain current hypotheses. We will observe that our presented models are superior and handle the MCDM techniques efficiently.

Table 28. Comparison of LDFSRS and SRLDFS with the existing concepts.

Concepts	**Satisfaction Degree**	**Dissatisfaction Degree**	**Reference Parameterizations**
Fuzzy set [46]	✓	×	×
Rough set [55]	×	×	×
Soft set [56]	×	×	×
Intuitionistic fuzzy set [47,48]	✓	✓	×
Pythagorean fuzzy set [49–51]	✓	✓	×
q-rung orthopair fuzzy set [52,53]	✓	✓	×
LDFS [54]	✓	✓	✓
LDFSS (proposed)	✓	✓	✓
LDFSRS (proposed)	✓	✓	✓
SRLDFS (proposed)	✓	✓	✓
Concepts	Upper and lower approximations	Boundary region	multi-valued parameterizations
Fuzzy set [46]	×	×	×
Rough set [55]	✓	✓	×
Soft set [56]	×	×	✓
Intuitionistic fuzzy set [47,48]	×	×	×
Pythagorean fuzzy set [49–51]	×	×	×
q-rung orthopair fuzzy set [52,53]	×	×	×
LDFS [54]	×	×	×
LDFSS (proposed)	×	×	✓
LDFSRS (proposed)	✓	✓	✓
SRLDFS (proposed)	✓	✓	✓

Table 29. Comparison of LDFSRS and SRLDFS with the existing concepts.

Concepts	Remarks
Fuzzy set [46]	It only deals with the truth values of objects.
Rough set [55]	It only deal with the vagueness of input data.
Soft set [56]	It only deal with the uncertainties under parameterizations.
Intuitionistic fuzzy set [47]	It cannot be applied if $1 < \mathscr{F}_{\mathcal{I}}(\mathcal{G}) + \mathscr{S}_{\mathcal{I}}(\mathcal{G}) \leq 2$ for some $\mathcal{G}$.
Pythagorean fuzzy set [49–51]	It cannot be applied if $1 < \mathscr{F}^2_{\mathcal{I}}(\mathcal{G}) + \mathscr{S}^2_{\mathcal{I}}(\mathcal{G}) \leq 2$ for some $\mathcal{G}$.
q-rung orthopair fuzzy set [52,53]	It cannot be applied for smaller values of "q" with $1 < \mathscr{F}^q_{\mathcal{O}}(\mathcal{G}) + \mathscr{S}^q_{\mathcal{O}}(\mathcal{G}) \leq 2$ or if $\mathscr{F}_{\mathcal{O}}(\mathcal{G}) = \mathscr{S}_{\mathcal{O}}(\mathcal{G}) = 1$ for some $\mathcal{G}$.
LDFS [54]	(1) It can deal with all the cases in which FS, IFS, PFS, and q-ROFS cannot be applied; (2) it involves a parameterization perspective and works under the influence of reference or control parameters; (3) satisfaction and dissatisfaction degrees can be chosen freely from $[0,1]$.
LDFSS (proposed)	It contains all the properties of LDFS with the addition of multi-valued parameterizations to deal with the uncertainties in a parametric manner.
LDFSRS (proposed)	It contains all the properties of LDFSS with the addition of upper and lower approximations to deal with the roughness of input data under the effect of "LDFS approximation space".
SRLDFS (proposed)	It contains all the properties of LDFSS with the addition of upper and lower approximations to deal with the roughness of input data under the effect of "crisp soft approximation space".

We constructed four algorithms based on LDFSRSs, SRLDFSs, and their corresponding approximation spaces. The final results for the decision making problem of material handling equipment selection obtained from these algorithms are given in Table 30.

Table 30. Comparison of the results obtained from the proposed algorithms.

Proposed Algorithm	Score Function	Core Set	Final Decision
Algorithm 1	$\mathscr{L}_1$	×	$\mathcal{G}_1$
Algorithm 1	$\mathscr{L}_2$	×	$\mathcal{G}_1$
Algorithm 1	$\mathscr{L}_3$	×	$\mathcal{G}_1$
Algorithm 2	×	✓	$\mathcal{G}_5$
Algorithm 3	$\mathscr{L}_1$	×	$\mathcal{G}_1$
Algorithm 3	$\mathscr{L}_2$	×	$\mathcal{G}_1$
Algorithm 3	$\mathscr{L}_3$	×	$\mathcal{G}_1$
Algorithm 4	×	✓	$\mathcal{G}_1$

In existing work, the superiority of the proposed model was discussed by examining its degeneration towards some existing rough set models (see Tables 5 and 9). The proposed algorithms are based on the SRLDFSs and LDFSRSs and their approximation operators. Algorithms 1 and 3 are based on the structures with LDFN score values. These algorithms provide us with information about the best and worst alternative. Algorithms 2 and 4 are focused on the core and reducts of the suggested structures. This also involves expert opinion and produces an outcome only for the essential alternative. This does not offer any comparison of the alternatives. Depending on the situation, each algorithm is essential and useful for real-life issues (see Tables 12 and 21).

By using different score functions and evaluating the reducts and core set, we check the behavior of "upper and lower approximations". The final results of Algorithms 1, 3, and 4 are exactly the same. The result of Algorithm 2 is different from the others. This difference is due to the different formulae and different ordering strategies used in the proposed algorithms. As we can see, the three algorithms produce the same decision, so we will go with the alternative $\mathcal{G}_1$ for the final decision. Such structures demonstrate the symmetry in the findings and provide us with an appropriate, ideal approach for the problem of decision making.

Validity test:

To demonstrate the validity and symmetry of the results, Wang and Triantaphyllou [36] constructed the following test criteria.

Test Criterion 1:

"If we replace non-optimal alternative rating values with the worst alternative then the best alternative should not change, provided the relative weighted criteria remain unchanged".

Test Criterion 2:

"Process should have transitive nature".

Test Criterion 3:

"When a given problem is decomposed into smaller ones and the same MCDM method has been applied, then the combined ranking of alternatives should be identical to the ranking of un-decomposed one".

Via these parameters, when we test our results, we see that our findings are correct and reliable and provide us a satisfactory solution to the MCDM problem. Various researchers used numerous techniques based on rough set theory and its hybrid structures to solve decision making difficulties (see [2,3,7,8,17–19,23,24,26,33–35]). Comparing these hypotheses, we found that our proposed models are reliable, efficient, superior, symmetrical, and valid in comparison with those current models.

5. Conclusions

There are two viewpoints in rough set theory knowledge: positive and axiomatic methods, and it is the same for LDFSRSs and SRLDFSs. This manuscript is a crystal reflection of both aspects of it. We have practiced fundamental ingredients of rough sets, soft sets, and LDFSs and established the proposed structures. With their accompanying illustrations, we provided some findings of such models. Many of the barriers to decision making in the input dataset include unclear, ambiguous, and imprecise details. These models can control these ambiguities better than the fuzzy sets, IFSs, PFSs, q-ROFSs, and LDFSs due to their mathematical formulation, variations, symmetry, and novelty. We introduced several level cut sets of LDFSs and related the recommended approximation operators with these level cut relations. We established various illustrations and results based on LDFSRSs and SRLDFSs approximation operators and corresponding approximations based on level cut sets. We utilized two different approximation spaces to produce variety in the decision making results. We listed the results of the degeneration of the proposed operators and found that our proposed models are generalizations of various existing rough set models. By using approximation spaces, score functions, upper and lower reductions, and core series, we introduced four novel algorithms for the assortment of sustainable material handling equipment. Depending on the situation, each algorithm is essential and useful for solving real-life problems. We discussed the advantages and limitations of the proposed structures with some existing models briefly (see Table 1). In the future, we will expand this research for topological spaces and solve MCDM problems based on the TOPSIS, VIKOR, and AHP families.

Author Contributions: M.R., M.R.H., H.K., D.P., and Y.-M.C. conceived of and worked together to achieve this manuscript; M.R., M.R.H., and D.P. constructed the ideas and algorithms for data analysis and designed the model of the manuscript; M.R.H., H.K., and Y.-M.C. processed the data collection and wrote the paper. All authors read and agreed to the published version of the manuscript.

Funding: This research received no external funding.

Acknowledgments: The authors are highly thankful to the Editor-in-Chief and referees for their valuable comments and suggestions for the improvement of our manuscript.

Conflicts of Interest: The authors declare that they have no conflict of interest.

Abbreviations

FSs	Fuzzy sets
IFSs	Intuitionistic fuzzy sets
PFSs	Pythagorean fuzzy sets
q-ROFSs	q-rung orthopair fuzzy sets
LDFSs	Linear Diophantine fuzzy sets
LDFNs	Linear Diophantine fuzzy numbers
LDFSSs	Linear Diophantine fuzzy soft sets
LDFSRSs	Linear Diophantine fuzzy soft rough sets
SRLDFSs	Soft rough linear Diophantine fuzzy sets
MCDM	Multi-criteria decision making

Appendix A

(1) From Definition 9, we can write that:

$$\begin{aligned}
\sim \mathscr{A}^{*}(\sim \mathscr{Y}_{\mathscr{D}}) &= \{(\mathcal{G}, \langle \ddot{S}_{\mathscr{A}^{*}(\sim\mathscr{Y}_{\mathscr{D}})}(\mathcal{G}), \ddot{\mathcal{T}}_{\mathscr{A}^{*}(\sim\mathscr{Y}_{\mathscr{D}})}(\mathcal{G})\rangle, \langle \beta_{\mathscr{A}^{*}(\sim\mathscr{Y}_{\mathscr{D}})}(\mathcal{G}), \alpha_{\mathscr{A}^{*}(\sim\mathscr{Y}_{\mathscr{D}})}(\mathcal{G})\rangle) : \mathcal{G} \in \ddot{\mathcal{Q}}\} \\
&= \{(\mathcal{G}, \langle \min_{\dot{\wp}\in\mathscr{A}_s(\mathcal{G})} (\ddot{S}_{(\sim\mathscr{Y}_{\mathscr{D}})}(\dot{\wp})), \max_{\dot{\wp}\in\mathscr{A}_s(\mathcal{G})} (\ddot{\mathcal{T}}_{(\sim\mathscr{Y}_{\mathscr{D}})}(\dot{\wp}))\rangle, \\
&\langle \min_{\dot{\wp}\in\mathscr{A}_s(\mathcal{G})} (\beta_{(\sim\mathscr{Y}_{\mathscr{D}})}(\dot{\wp})), \max_{\dot{\wp}\in\mathscr{A}_s(\mathcal{G})} (\alpha_{(\sim\mathscr{Y}_{\mathscr{D}})}(\dot{\wp}))\rangle) : \mathcal{G} \in \ddot{\mathcal{Q}}\} \\
&= \{(\mathcal{G}, \langle \min_{\dot{\wp}\in\mathscr{A}_s(\mathcal{G})} (\ddot{\mathcal{T}}_{\mathscr{Y}_{\mathscr{D}}}(\dot{\wp})), \max_{\dot{\wp}\in\mathscr{A}_s(\mathcal{G})} (\ddot{S}_{\mathscr{Y}_{\mathscr{D}}}(\dot{\wp}))\rangle, \langle \min_{\dot{\wp}\in\mathscr{A}_s(\mathcal{G})} (\alpha_{\mathscr{Y}_{\mathscr{D}}}(\dot{\wp})), \max_{\dot{\wp}\in\mathscr{A}_s(\mathcal{G})} (\beta_{\mathscr{Y}_{\mathscr{D}}}(\dot{\wp}))\rangle) : \mathcal{G} \in \ddot{\mathcal{Q}}\} \\
&= \{(\mathcal{G}, \langle \ddot{\mathcal{T}}_{\mathscr{A}_{*}(\mathscr{Y}_{\mathscr{D}})}(\mathcal{G}), \ddot{S}_{\mathscr{A}_{*}(\mathscr{Y}_{\mathscr{D}})}(\mathcal{G})\rangle, \langle \alpha_{\mathscr{A}_{*}(\mathscr{Y}_{\mathscr{D}})}(\mathcal{G}), \beta_{\mathscr{A}_{*}(\mathscr{Y}_{\mathscr{D}})}(\mathcal{G})\rangle) : \mathcal{G} \in \ddot{\mathcal{Q}}\} \\
&= \mathscr{A}_{*}(\mathscr{Y}_{\mathscr{D}})
\end{aligned}$$

(2) It can be easily proven from Definition 9.

(3) We consider that:

$$\begin{aligned}
\mathscr{A}_{*}(\mathscr{Y}_{\mathscr{D}} \cap \mathscr{B}_{\mathscr{D}}) &= \{(\mathcal{G}, \langle \ddot{\mathcal{T}}_{\mathscr{A}_{*}(\mathscr{Y}_{\mathscr{D}}\cap\mathscr{B}_{\mathscr{D}})}(\mathcal{G}), \ddot{S}_{\mathscr{A}_{*}(\mathscr{Y}_{\mathscr{D}}\cap\mathscr{B}_{\mathscr{D}})}(\mathcal{G})\rangle, \langle \alpha_{\mathscr{A}_{*}(\mathscr{Y}_{\mathscr{D}}\cap\mathscr{B}_{\mathscr{D}})}(\mathcal{G}), \beta_{\mathscr{A}_{*}(\mathscr{Y}_{\mathscr{D}}\cap\mathscr{B}_{\mathscr{D}})}(\mathcal{G})\rangle) : \mathcal{G} \in \ddot{\mathcal{Q}}\} \\
&= \{(\mathcal{G}, \langle \min_{\dot{\wp}\in\mathscr{A}_s(\mathcal{G})} \ddot{\mathcal{T}}_{(\mathscr{Y}_{\mathscr{D}}\cap\mathscr{B}_{\mathscr{D}})}(\dot{\wp}), \max_{\dot{\wp}\in\mathscr{A}_s(\mathcal{G})} \ddot{S}_{(\mathscr{Y}_{\mathscr{D}}\cap\mathscr{B}_{\mathscr{D}})}(\dot{\wp})\rangle, \\
&\langle \min_{\dot{\wp}\in\mathscr{A}_s(\mathcal{G})} \alpha_{(\mathscr{Y}_{\mathscr{D}}\cap\mathscr{B}_{\mathscr{D}})}(\dot{\wp}), \max_{\dot{\wp}\in\mathscr{A}_s(\mathcal{G})} \beta_{(\mathscr{Y}_{\mathscr{D}}\cap\mathscr{B}_{\mathscr{D}})}(\dot{\wp})\rangle) : \mathcal{G} \in \ddot{\mathcal{Q}}\} \\
&= \{(\mathcal{G}, \langle \min_{\dot{\wp}\in\mathscr{A}_s(\mathcal{G})} (\ddot{\mathcal{T}}_{\mathscr{Y}_{\mathscr{D}}}(\dot{\wp}) \wedge {}^{\alpha}\ddot{\mathcal{T}}_{\mathscr{B}_{\mathscr{D}}}(\dot{\wp})), \max_{\dot{\wp}\in\mathscr{A}_s(\mathcal{G})} (\ddot{S}_{\mathscr{Y}_{\mathscr{D}}}(\dot{\wp}) \vee {}^{\alpha}\ddot{S}_{\mathscr{B}_{\mathscr{D}}}(\dot{\wp}))\rangle, \\
&\langle \min_{\dot{\wp}\in\mathscr{A}_s(\mathcal{G})} (\alpha_{\mathscr{Y}_{\mathscr{D}}}(\dot{\wp}) \wedge {}^{\alpha}\ddot{\mathcal{T}}_{\mathscr{B}_{\mathscr{D}}}(\dot{\wp})), \max_{\dot{\wp}\in\mathscr{A}_s(\mathcal{G})} (\beta_{\mathscr{Y}_{\mathscr{D}}}(\dot{\wp}) \vee {}^{\alpha}\ddot{S}_{\mathscr{B}_{\mathscr{D}}}(\dot{\wp}))\rangle)\} \\
&= \{(\mathcal{G}, \langle \min_{\dot{\wp}\in\mathscr{A}_s(\mathcal{G})} (\ddot{\mathcal{T}}_{\mathscr{Y}_{\mathscr{D}}}(\dot{\wp})) \wedge \min_{\dot{\wp}\in\mathscr{A}_s(\mathcal{G})} (\ddot{\mathcal{T}}_{\mathscr{B}_{\mathscr{D}}}(\dot{\wp})), \max_{\dot{\wp}\in\mathscr{A}_s(\mathcal{G})} (\ddot{S}_{\mathscr{Y}_{\mathscr{D}}}(\dot{\wp})) \vee \max_{\dot{\wp}\in\mathscr{A}_s(\mathcal{G})} (\ddot{S}_{\mathscr{B}_{\mathscr{D}}}(\dot{\wp}))\rangle, \\
&\langle \min_{\dot{\wp}\in\mathscr{A}_s(\mathcal{G})} (\alpha_{\mathscr{Y}_{\mathscr{D}}}(\dot{\wp})) \wedge \min_{\dot{\wp}\in\mathscr{A}_s(\mathcal{G})} (\alpha_{\mathscr{B}_{\mathscr{D}}}(\dot{\wp})), \max_{\dot{\wp}\in\mathscr{A}_s(\mathcal{G})} (\beta_{\mathscr{Y}_{\mathscr{D}}}(\dot{\wp})) \vee \max_{\dot{\wp}\in\mathscr{A}_s(\mathcal{G})} (\beta_{\mathscr{B}_{\mathscr{D}}}(\dot{\wp}))\rangle)\} \\
&= \{(\mathcal{G}, \langle \ddot{\mathcal{T}}_{\mathscr{A}_{*}(\mathscr{Y}_{\mathscr{D}})}(\mathcal{G}) \wedge \ddot{\mathcal{T}}_{\mathscr{A}_{*}(\mathscr{B}_{\mathscr{D}})}(\mathcal{G}), \ddot{S}_{\mathscr{A}_{*}(\mathscr{Y}_{\mathscr{D}})}(\mathcal{G}) \vee \ddot{S}_{\mathscr{A}_{*}(\mathscr{B}_{\mathscr{D}})}(\mathcal{G})\rangle, \\
&\langle \alpha_{\mathscr{A}_{*}(\mathscr{Y}_{\mathscr{D}})}(\mathcal{G}) \wedge \alpha_{\mathscr{A}_{*}(\mathscr{B}_{\mathscr{D}})}(\mathcal{G}), \beta_{\mathscr{A}_{*}(\mathscr{Y}_{\mathscr{D}})}(\mathcal{G}) \vee \beta_{\mathscr{A}_{*}(\mathscr{B}_{\mathscr{D}})}(\mathcal{G})\rangle) : \mathcal{G} \in \ddot{\mathcal{Q}}\} \\
&= \mathscr{A}_{*}(\mathscr{Y}_{\mathscr{D}}) \cap \mathscr{A}_{*}(\mathscr{B}_{\mathscr{D}})
\end{aligned}$$

(4) From Definition 9, we can write that:

$$
\begin{aligned}
\tilde{\mathscr{A}}_{*}(\mathscr{Y}_{\mathscr{D}} \cap \mathscr{B}_{\mathscr{D}}) &= \{(\mathcal{G}, \langle \ddot{\mathscr{T}}_{\tilde{\mathscr{A}}_{*}(\mathscr{Y}_{\mathscr{D}} \cup \mathscr{B}_{\mathscr{D}})}(\mathcal{G}), \ddot{S}_{\tilde{\mathscr{A}}_{*}(\mathscr{Y}_{\mathscr{D}} \cup \mathscr{B}_{\mathscr{D}})}(\mathcal{G})\rangle, \langle \alpha_{\tilde{\mathscr{A}}_{*}(\mathscr{Y}_{\mathscr{D}} \cup \mathscr{B}_{\mathscr{D}})}(\mathcal{G}), \beta_{\tilde{\mathscr{A}}_{*}(\mathscr{Y}_{\mathscr{D}} \cup \mathscr{B}_{\mathscr{D}})}(\mathcal{G})\rangle) : \mathcal{G} \in \ddot{\mathscr{Q}}\} \\
&= \{(\mathcal{G}, \langle \min_{\dot{\wp} \in \tilde{\mathscr{A}}_{s}(\mathcal{G})} \ddot{\mathscr{T}}_{(\mathscr{Y}_{\mathscr{D}} \cup \mathscr{B}_{\mathscr{D}})}(\dot{\wp}), \max_{\dot{\wp} \in \tilde{\mathscr{A}}_{s}(\mathcal{G})} \ddot{S}_{(\mathscr{Y}_{\mathscr{D}} \cup \mathscr{B}_{\mathscr{D}})}(\dot{\wp})\rangle, \\
&\langle \min_{\dot{\wp} \in \tilde{\mathscr{A}}_{s}(\mathcal{G})} \alpha_{(\mathscr{Y}_{\mathscr{D}} \cup \mathscr{B}_{\mathscr{D}})}(\dot{\wp}), \max_{\dot{\wp} \in \tilde{\mathscr{A}}_{s}(\mathcal{G})} \beta_{(\mathscr{Y}_{\mathscr{D}} \cup \mathscr{B}_{\mathscr{D}})}(\dot{\wp})\rangle) : \mathcal{G} \in \ddot{\mathscr{Q}}\} \\
&= \{(\mathcal{G}, \langle \min_{\dot{\wp} \in \tilde{\mathscr{A}}_{s}(\mathcal{G})} (\ddot{\mathscr{T}}_{\mathscr{Y}_{\mathscr{D}}}(\dot{\wp}) \vee^{\alpha} \ddot{\mathscr{T}}_{\mathscr{B}_{\mathscr{D}}}(\dot{\wp})), \max_{\dot{\wp} \in \tilde{\mathscr{A}}_{s}(\mathcal{G})} (\ddot{S}_{\mathscr{Y}_{\mathscr{D}}}(\dot{\wp}) \wedge \ddot{S}_{\mathscr{B}_{\mathscr{D}}}(\dot{\wp}))\rangle, \\
&\langle \min_{\dot{\wp} \in \tilde{\mathscr{A}}_{s}(\mathcal{G})} (\alpha_{\mathscr{Y}_{\mathscr{D}}}(\dot{\wp}) \vee^{\alpha} \ddot{\mathscr{T}}_{\mathscr{B}_{\mathscr{D}}}(\dot{\wp})), \max_{\dot{\wp} \in \tilde{\mathscr{A}}_{s}(\mathcal{G})} (\beta_{\mathscr{Y}_{\mathscr{D}}}(\dot{\wp}) \wedge \ddot{S}_{\mathscr{B}_{\mathscr{D}}}(\dot{\wp}))\rangle)\} \\
&\supseteq \{(\mathcal{G}, \langle \min_{\dot{\wp} \in \tilde{\mathscr{A}}_{s}(\mathcal{G})} (\ddot{\mathscr{T}}_{\mathscr{Y}_{\mathscr{D}}}(\dot{\wp})) \vee \min_{\dot{\wp} \in \tilde{\mathscr{A}}_{s}(\mathcal{G})} (\ddot{\mathscr{T}}_{\mathscr{B}_{\mathscr{D}}}(\dot{\wp})), \bigvee_{\dot{\wp} \in \tilde{\mathscr{A}}_{s}(\mathcal{G})} (\ddot{S}_{\mathscr{Y}_{\mathscr{D}}}(\dot{\wp})) \wedge \max_{\dot{\wp} \in \tilde{\mathscr{A}}_{s}(\mathcal{G})} (\ddot{S}_{\mathscr{B}_{\mathscr{D}}}(\dot{\wp}))\rangle, \\
&\langle \min_{\dot{\wp} \in \tilde{\mathscr{A}}_{s}(\mathcal{G})} (\alpha_{\mathscr{Y}_{\mathscr{D}}}(\dot{\wp})) \vee \min_{\dot{\wp} \in \tilde{\mathscr{A}}_{s}(\mathcal{G})} (\alpha_{\mathscr{B}_{\mathscr{D}}}(\dot{\wp})), \max_{\dot{\wp} \in \tilde{\mathscr{A}}_{s}(\mathcal{G})} (\beta_{\mathscr{Y}_{\mathscr{D}}}(\dot{\wp})) \wedge \max_{\dot{\wp} \in \tilde{\mathscr{A}}_{s}(\mathcal{G})} (\beta_{\mathscr{B}_{\mathscr{D}}}(\dot{\wp}))\rangle)\} \\
&= \{(\mathcal{G}, \langle \ddot{\mathscr{T}}_{\tilde{\mathscr{A}}_{*}(\mathscr{Y}_{\mathscr{D}})}(\mathcal{G}) \vee \ddot{\mathscr{T}}_{\tilde{\mathscr{A}}_{*}(\mathscr{B}_{\mathscr{D}})}(\mathcal{G}), \ddot{S}_{\tilde{\mathscr{A}}_{*}(\mathscr{Y}_{\mathscr{D}})}(\mathcal{G}) \wedge \ddot{S}_{\tilde{\mathscr{A}}_{*}(\mathscr{B}_{\mathscr{D}})}(\mathcal{G})\rangle, \\
&\langle \alpha_{\tilde{\mathscr{A}}_{*}(\mathscr{Y}_{\mathscr{D}})}(\mathcal{G}) \vee \alpha_{\tilde{\mathscr{A}}_{*}(\mathscr{B}_{\mathscr{D}})}(\mathcal{G}), \beta_{\tilde{\mathscr{A}}_{*}(\mathscr{Y}_{\mathscr{D}})}(\mathcal{G}) \wedge \beta_{\tilde{\mathscr{A}}_{*}(\mathscr{B}_{\mathscr{D}})}(\mathcal{G})\rangle) : \mathcal{G} \in \ddot{\mathscr{Q}}\} \\
&= \tilde{\mathscr{A}}_{*}(\mathscr{Y}_{\mathscr{D}}) \cup \tilde{\mathscr{A}}_{*}(\mathscr{B}_{\mathscr{D}})
\end{aligned}
$$

Thus, $\tilde{\mathscr{A}}_{*}(\mathscr{Y}_{\mathscr{D}} \cup \mathscr{B}_{\mathscr{D}}) \supseteq \tilde{\mathscr{A}}_{*}(\mathscr{Y}_{\mathscr{D}}) \cup \tilde{\mathscr{A}}_{*}(\mathscr{B}_{\mathscr{D}})$.
Similarly, we can prove the remaining axioms by following these arguments.

References

1. Bellman, R.E.; Zadeh, L.A. Decision-making in a fuzzy environment. *Manag. Sci.* **1970**, *4*, 141–164. [CrossRef]
2. Akram, M.; Ali, G.; Alshehri, N.O. A new multi-attribute decision making method based on m-polar fuzzy soft rough sets. *Symmetry* **2017**, *9*, 271. [CrossRef]
3. Ali, M.I. A note on soft sets, rough soft sets and fuzzy soft sets. *Appl. Soft Comput.* **2011**, *11*, 3329–3332.
4. Chen, S.M.; Tan, J.M. Handling multi-criteria fuzzy decision-makling problems based on vague set theory. *Fuzzy Sets Syst.* **1994**, *67*, 163–172. [CrossRef]
5. Tversky, A.; Kahneman, D. Advances in prospect theory: cumulative representation of uncertainity. *J. Risk Uncertain.* **1992**, *5*, 297–323. [CrossRef]
6. Feng, F.; Jun, Y.B.; Liu, X.; Li, L. An adjustable approach to fuzzy soft set based decision making. *J. Comput. Appl. Math.* **2010**, *234*, 10–20. [CrossRef]
7. Feng, F.; Li, C.; Davvaz, B.; Ali, M.I. Soft sets combined with fuzzy sets and rough sets; A tentative approach. *Soft Comput.* **2010**, *14*, 899–911. [CrossRef]
8. Feng, F.; Liu, X.Y.; Leoreanu-Fotea, V.; Jun, Y.B. Soft sets and soft rough sets. *Inf. Sci.* **2011**, *181*, 1125–1137. [CrossRef]
9. Feng, F.; Fujita, H.; Ali, M.I.; Yager, R.R.; Liu, X. Another view on generalized intuitionistic fuzzy soft sets and related multiattribute decision making methods. *IEEE Trans. Fuzzy Syst.* **2019**, *27*, 474–488. [CrossRef]
10. Garg, H. A new generalized Pythagorean fuzzy information aggregation using Einstein operations and its application to decision making. *Int. J. Intell. Syst.* **2016**, *31*, 886–920. [CrossRef]
11. Hashmi, M.R.; Riaz, M.; Smarandache, F. *m*-polar Neutrosophic Topology with Applications to Multi-Criteria Decision-Making in Medical Diagnosis and Clustering Analysis. *Int. J. Fuzzy Syst.* **2020**, *22*, 273–292. [CrossRef]
12. Hashmi, M.R.; Riaz, M. A Novel Approach to Censuses Process by using Pythagorean *m*-polar Fuzzy Dombi's Aggregation Operators. *J. Intell. Fuzzy Syst.* **2020**, *38*, 1977–1995. [CrossRef]
13. Jose, S.; Kuriaskose, S. Aggregation operators, score function and accuracy function for multi criteria decision making in intuitionistic fuzzy context. *Notes Intuitionistic Fuzzy Sets* **2014**, *20*, 40–44.
14. Naeem, K.; Riaz, M.; Peng, X.; Afzal, D. Pythagorean fuzzy soft MCGDM methods based on TOPSIS, VIKOR and aggregation operators. *J. Intell. Fuzzy Syst.* **2019**, *37*, 6937–6757. [CrossRef]
15. Pawlak, Z.; Skowron, A. Rough sets: Some extensions. *Inf. Sci.* **2007**, *177*, 28–40. [CrossRef]

16. Riaz, M.; Hashmi, M.R. MAGDM for agribusiness in the environment of various cubic m-polar fuzzy averaging aggregation operators. *J. Intell. Fuzzy Syst.* **2019**, *37*, 3671–3691. [CrossRef]
17. Riaz, M.; Hashmi, M.R. Soft Rough Pythagorean m-Polar Fuzzy Sets and Pythagorean m-Polar Fuzzy Soft Rough Sets with Application to Decision-Making. *Comput. Appl. Math.* **2020**, *39*, 16. [CrossRef]
18. Riaz, M.; Davvaz, B.; Firdous, A.; Fakhar, A. Novel Concepts of Soft Rough Set Topology with Applications. *J. Intell. Fuzzy Syst.* **2019**, *36*, 3579–3590. [CrossRef]
19. Riaz, M.; Samrandache, F.; Firdous, A.; Fakhar, A. On Soft Rough Topology with Multi-Attribute Group Decision Making. *Mathematics* **2019**, *7*, 67. [CrossRef]
20. Riaz, M.; Tehrim, S.T. Certain properties of bipolar fuzzy soft topology via Q-neighborhood. *Punjab Univ. J. Math.* **2019**, *51*, 113–131.
21. Riaz, M.; Tehrim, S.T. Cubic bipolar fuzzy ordered weighted geometric aggregation operators and their application using internal and external cubic bipolar fuzzy data. *Comput. Appl. Math.* **2019**, *38*, 87. [CrossRef]
22. Riaz, M.; Tehrim, S.T. Multi-attribute group decision making based cubic bipolar fuzzy information using averaging aggregation operators. *J. Intell. Fuzzy Syst.* **2019**, *37*, 2473–2494. [CrossRef]
23. Roy, J.; Adhikary, K.; Kar, S.; Pamucar, D. A rough strength relational DEMATEL model for analysing the key success factors ofhospital service quality. *Decis. Mak. Appl. Manag. Eng.* **2018**, *1*, 121–142. [CrossRef]
24. Sharma, H.K.; Kumari, K.; Kar, S. A rough set theory application in forecasting models. *Decis. Mak. Appl. Manag. Eng.* **2020**, *3*, 1–21. [CrossRef]
25. Wei, G.; Wang, H.; Zhao, X.; Lin, R. Hesitant triangular fuzzy information aggregation in multiple attribute decision making. *J. Intell. Fuzzy Syst.* **2014**, *26*, 1201–1209. [CrossRef]
26. Zhang, H.; Shu, L.; Liao, S. Intuitionistic fuzzy soft rough set and its applications in decision making. *Abstr. Appl. Anal.* **2014**, 1–13. [CrossRef]
27. Zhao, H.; Xu, Z.S.; Ni, M.F.; Lui, S.S. Generalized aggregation operators for intuitionistic fuzzy sets. *Int. J. Intell. Syst.* **2010**, *25*, 1–30. [CrossRef]
28. Xu, Z.S.; Chen, J. An overview on distance and similarity measures on intuitionistic fuzzy sets. *Int. J. Uncertain. Fuzziness Knowl. Based Syst.* **2008**, *16*, 529–555. [CrossRef]
29. Kulak, O.; Satoglu, S.I.; Durmusoglu, M.B. Multi-attribute material handling equipment selection using information axiom. In Proceedings of the ICAD2004, The third international conferenec on Axiomatic Design, Seoul, Korea, 21–24 June 2004; pp. 1–9.
30. Karande. P.; Chakraborty, S. Material handling equipment selection using weighted utility additive theory. *J. Ind. Eng.* **2013**. [CrossRef]
31. Zubair, M.; Mahmood, S.; Omair, M.; Noor, I. Optimization of material handling system through material handling equipment selection. *Int. J. Progress. Sci. Technol.* **2019**, *15*, 235–243.
32. Vashist, R. An algorithm for finding the reduct and core of the consistent dataset. *Int. Conf. Comput. Intell. Commun. Netw.* **2015**. [CrossRef]
33. Zhang, L.; Zhan, J. Fuzzy soft β-covering based fuzzy rough sets and corresponding decision making applications. *Int. J. Mach. Learn. Cybern.* **2018**. [CrossRef]
34. Zhang, L.; Zhan, J. Novel classes of fuzzy soft;-coverings-based fuzzy rough sets with applications to multi-criteria fuzzy group decision making. *Soft Comput.* **2018**. [CrossRef]
35. Zhang, L.; Zhan, J.; Xu, Z.X. Covering-based generalized IF rough sets with applications to multi-attribute decision making. *Inf. Sci.* **2019**, *478*, 275–302. [CrossRef]
36. Wang, X.; Triantaphyllou, E. Ranking irregularities when evaluating alternatives by using some ELECTRE methods. *Omega Int. J. Manag. Sci.* **2008**, *36*, 45–63. [CrossRef]
37. Büyüközkan, G.; Çifçi, G. A novel hybrid MCDM approach based on fuzzy DEMATEL, fuzzy ANP and fuzzy TOPSIS to evaluate green suppliers. *Expert Syst. Appl.* **2012** *39*, 3000–3011. [CrossRef]
38. Govindan, K.; Khodaverdi, R.; Vafadarnikjoo, A. Intuitionistic fuzzy based DEMATEL method for developing green practices and performances in a green supply chain. *Expert Syst. Appl.* **2015**, *42*, 7207–7720. [CrossRef]
39. Jeong, J.S.; González-Gómez, D. Adapting to PSTs Pedagogical Changes in Sustainable Mathematics Education through Flipped E-Learning: Ranking Its Criteria with MCDA/F-DEMATEL. *Mathematics* **2020**, *8*, 858. [CrossRef]
40. Wang, R.; Li, Y. A Novel Approach for Green Supplier Selection under a q-Rung Orthopair Fuzzy Environment. *Symmetry* **2018**, *10*, 687. [CrossRef]

41. Xu, Y.; Shang, X.; Wang, J.; Wu, W.; Huang, H. Some q-Rung Dual Hesitant Fuzzy Heronian Mean Operators with Their Application to Multiple Attribute Group Decision-Making. *Symmetry* **2018**, *10*, 472. [CrossRef]
42. Sun, B.; Ma, W. Soft fuzzy rough sets and its application in decision making. *Artif. Intell. Rev.* **2014**, *41*, 67–80.
43. Meng, D.; Zhang, X.; Qin, K. Soft rough fuzzy sets and soft fuzzy rough sets. *Comput. Math. Appl.* **2011**, *62*, 4635–4645. [CrossRef]
44. Hussain, A.; Ali, M.I.; Mahmood, T. Pythagorean fuzzy soft rough sets and their applications in decision making. *J. Taibah Univ. Sci.* **2020**, *14*, 101–113. [CrossRef]
45. Zadeh, L.A. The concept of a linguistic variable and its application to approximate reasoning-I. *Inf. Sci.* **1975**, *8*, 199–249. [CrossRef]
46. Zadeh, L.A. Fuzzy sets. *Inf. Control* **1965**, *8*, 338–353. [CrossRef]
47. Atanassov, K.T. Intuitionistic fuzzy sets. *Fuzzy Sets Ans Syst.* **1986**, *20*, 87–96. [CrossRef]
48. Atanassov, K.T. Geometrical interpretation of the elements of the intuitionistic fuzzy objects. *Int. J. Bioautom.* **2016**, *20*, S27–S42.
49. Yager, R.R. Pythagorean membership grades in multi-criteria decision making. *IEEE Trans. Fuzzy Syst.* **2014**, *22*, 958–965. [CrossRef]
50. Yager, R.R. Pythagorean fuzzy subsets. In Proceedings of the 2013 joint IFSA world congress and NAFIPS annual meeting (IFSA/NAFIPS), Edmonton, AB, Canada, 24–28 June 2013; pp. 57–61.
51. Yager, R.R.; Abbasov, A.M. Pythagorean membership grades, complex numbers, and decision making. *Int. J. Intell. Syst.* **2013**, *28*, 436–452. [CrossRef]
52. Ali, M.I. Another view on q-rung orthopair fuzzy sets. *Int. J. Intell. Syst.* **2018**, *33*, 2139–2153. [CrossRef]
53. Yager, R.R. Generalized orthopair fuzzy sets. *IEEE Trans. Fuzzy Syst.* **2017**, *25*, 1222–1230. [CrossRef]
54. Riaz, M.; Hashmi, M.R. Linear Diophantine fuzzy set and its applications towards multi-attribute decision making problems. *J. Intell. Fuzzy Syst.* **2019**, *37*, 5417–5439. [CrossRef]
55. Pawlak, Z. Rough sets. *Int. J. Comput. Inf. Sci.* **1982**, *2*, 145–172. [CrossRef]
56. Molodtsov, D. Soft set theory-first results. *Comput. Math. Appl.* **1999**, *37*, 19–31. [CrossRef]

symmetry

MDPI

Article

Fuzzy Random Chance-Constrained Programming Model for the Vehicle Routing Problem of Hazardous Materials Transportation

Liying Zhao [1] and Ningbo Cao [2,*]

1 School of Economics and Management, Xi'an University of Technology, Xi'an 710000, China; lyzhao@xaut.edu.cn

2 College of Transportation Engineering, Chang'an University, Xi'an 710000, China;

* Correspondence: caonb@chd.edu.cn

Received: 24 June 2020; Accepted: 20 July 2020; Published: 23 July 2020

Abstract: As an indispensable necessity in daily routine of citizens, hazardous materials (Hazmat) not only plays an increasingly important role, but also brings a series of transportation uncertainty phenomena, the most prominent of which is a safety problem. When it attempts to find the best vehicle route scheme that can possess the lowest risk attribute in a fuzzy random environment for a single warehouse, the influence of cost should also be taken into account. In this study, a new mathematical theory was conducted in the modeling process. To take a full consideration of uncertainty, vehicle travel distance and population density along the road segment were assumed to be fuzzy variables. Meanwhile, accident probability and vehicle speed were set to be stochastic. Furthermore, based on the assumptions, authors established three chance constrained programming models according to the uncertain theory. Model I was used to seek the achievement of minimum risk of the vehicle route scheme, using traditional risk model; the goal of Model II was to obtain the lowest total cost, including the green cost, and the main purpose of Model III was to establish a balance between cost and risk. To settle the above models, a hybrid intelligent algorithm was designed, which was a combination of genetic algorithm and fuzzy random simulation algorithm, which simultaneously proved its convergence. At last, two experiments were designed to illustrate the feasibility of the proposed models and algorithms.

Keywords: hazardous materials; vehicle route model (VRP); uncertainty theory; chance constrained programming model; hybrid intelligent algorithm

---

1. Introduction

With the evolution of industrial society, the demand for the logistics industry, especially hazardous materials, which are different from ordinary goods in physical nature and are considered as moving "hazard source" in the transportation process, is constantly increasing. Huge supply demand causes the inter-regional road transportation to be in short supply status and road flow is close to the maximum capacity for a long time. At the same time, public consciousness responding to danger is gradually strengthened, which forced the world to cope with the challenge that hazmat brings. In this condition, any minor uncertainty factor is likely to give rise to risk increment during transportation, therefore, bringing decision-making changes of vehicle routing arrangement. Especially in a situation where uncertain factors change dramatically, random factors and fuzzy influence can easily endanger safety of humans, the environment and ecology, thus, leading to an ascending tendency of risk and cost.

No matter the existing cost-oriented or risk-oriented traditional vehicle, the routing model cannot fully play its role. In a deterministic environment, in accordance with practice, each factor is treated as a constant variable, the pre-arranged route is unable to deal with the emergency during transportation, in this way it might cause unpredictable consequences. Hence, it is necessary to add uncertain factors in the modeling stage to improve the vehicle routing scheme. Due to the maturity of uncertain theory, deformation period for traditional vehicle routing model must exist for a long time in the process of uncertain theory popularization. Uncertain programming applied to hazmat transportation can be divided into three aspects—random, fuzzy, and fuzzy random programming. If stochastic, it usually refers to accident probability, which follows a particular random distribution, and the solution is focused on how to avoid the occurrence of danger. Whereas, a fuzzy situation uses a fuzzy distribution variable to describe accident consequence concentrating on narrowing the range of influence. Accompanied by the decision makers' risk-averse attitude change and continuous application of uncertainty theory, hazmat transportation accident is considered to be a fuzzy random event, therefore, it is urgent to use new methods to solve fuzzy random programming.

In view of the above requirements, this study will study fuzzy and random factors that occurred in the hazmat transportation, then consider multiple demands of supply chain participants, such as the minimum risk value, which is the ideal state the government hopes to achieve, and the minimum cost, which is the goal enterprise pursued. Hence, exploring and establishing different vehicle routing models through comprehensive cost and risk is of practical value.

The remainder of this study is organized as follows. Related literature on hazardous materials transportation is introduced in Section 2. Section 3 gives a glimpse of preliminaries on uncertain theory. Section 4 describes three models for the vehicle routing problem provided in this study. Section 5 designs an algorithm and its component sub-algorithms. Section 6 discusses the computational experiments and the results. Section 7 contains our final conclusions from the research and provides a set of further research directions.

2. Literature Review

As stated by Zografos [1], most research work focused on modifying versions of optimization objectives [2–4], no matter the minimum risk or cost. In this study, the authors are bent on formulating fuzzy random chance-constrained vehicle routing problems (FRCVRP) for hazmat, with the comprehensive consideration of fuzzy random risk and cost. This section reviews related papers on risk assessment methods and uncertain applications for hazmat, respectively.

2.1. Literature on Risk Assessment

Due to a lack of standard risk value assessment benchmark, some methods were tested by existing various traditional VRP instances [5]. Erkut and Ingolfsson provided a classification for models of risk calculation, laying a foundation for the study of hazmat [6–8], some of the high frequency used models are accident probability (AP) model, population exposure (PE) model, traditional risk (TR) model, and so on. For example, AP model was adopted by Jia, and it used the probability of a worst case accident to define different road categories with the same accident rate [9]. Li and Leung found that different population values led to different optimal paths in PE model. However, the data on basic resident population is difficult to be accurately acquired [10]. Wei innovatively proposed indeterminate TR model to assess risks at different confidence levels [11]. Additionally, an environmental risk (EN) model is put forward according to the actual scenario, and Cordeiro pointed out that potential risk strongly depended on the nature of the hazmat and presented an approach for assessing environmental risk [12].

2.2. Literature on Hazardous Materials Transportation Related to Uncertain Theory

Compared to the classical VRP problem, the research on FRCVRP proposed by Dantzig and Ramser started relatively late (1959) [13]. With uncertain factors becoming the focus of research, simultaneously, the green factor is also getting some attention from researchers. Emrah Demir and Laporte provided a research direction on green road transportation and established a Pollution-Routing

Problem based on VRP [14]. By combining the above two aspects, existing studies on hazardous materials can also be split into three categories—random, fuzzy, and fuzzy random programming.

For the first category, it is assumed that parameters affecting risk or cost are governed by random factors. For instance, Lam explored risk formation mechanism in the liquefied petroleum gas field in Japan, the greatest extent to satisfy consumer acceptable level for incidents, by using a probabilistic network modeling approach [15]. Jabir formulated an integer linear programming model for a capacitated multi-depot green VRP, by integrating economic and emission cost reduction [16]. Bula studied a multi-objective vehicle routing problem and adopted two improved solution methods on the basis of neighborhood search to solve it [17]. The accident probabilities were evaluated according to operators and relevant agencies by Poku-Boansi, from qualitative and quantitative insights, using an instance of Accra–Kumasi Highway (N6) in Ghana [18]. Ghaderi formulated a two-stage stochastic programming model in a multimodal network including transfer spots, with the intention of minimizing transportation cost and risk, considering the location and routing problem [19]. Although it did not distinguish between fuzziness and randomness, Qu pointed out that the risks were relevant to time and route condition, and developed a novel MILP model to build the optimal shipping route with minimal risk [20].

Except for the stochastic parameters used in the modeling process, other research work adopted fuzzy theory, which can describe the transportation scenario more realistically. For example, Ghaleh proposed a pattern of assessing safety risk, by using the Analytical Hierarchy Process, under the fuzzy road fleet transportation scene [21]. Deng addressed fuzzy length between nodes to settle the shortest path problem by using the Dijkstra algorithm [22]. Zero applied triangle fuzzy number to specify cost objective, then expanded this theory to risk objective, and balanced the trade-off between them [23]. Li considered VRP as a nonlinear mono-objective programming rather than a multi-objective programming problem, after dealing with the uncertainty of environment benefits [24]. However, a bi-objective nonlinear integer programming model was established by using triangular fuzzy numbers, to facilitate population exposure from a fuzzy programming prospect by Moon [25]. Hu established a credibility goal programming model aiming at achieving minimum positive deviations value of expected risk and cost from the predefined risk level and cost level, simultaneously [26]. Similarly, in response to multiple depots to customers, Du developed a fuzzy bi-level programming model for the purpose of minimizing the total expected risk and cost under the scenario [27]. He also presented a fuzzy multi-objective programming model that optimizes transportation risk, travel time, and fuel consumption, based on the shortest path mode [28].Triggered by the affected people could be described to be a fuzzy variable, Wei established a chance-constrained programming model, obtaining a balance between risk and cost in the premise of transportation cost, which was also a fuzzy variable [11].

Despite numerous studies related to hazardous materials focusing on stochastic models and fuzzy models separately in the past decade, there are also some studies combining two aspects and proposing a fuzzy random programming model for optimal solutions, with least cost or risk, no matter the route choice problem, the vehicle routing problem, or the location-routing problem. Ma concentrated on how to make uncertain decisions under a different environment of route selection problem, such as fuzzy or stochastic environment, and demonstrated dissimilitude between uncertain and certain scenarios for hazardous materials [29]. Wei firstly assumed that transportation risks were time-dependent fuzzy random variables, and then developed a scheduling optimization model to optimize departure and dwell times for each depot-customer pair [30].

A detailed list and a classification for the hazmat routing problems on uncertain programming are shown in Table 1.

Table 1. A summary of routing problem for hazmat.

No	Author	Stochastic	Fuzzy	Fuzzy Stochastic	Green	R	LR	VRP
1	Jabir [16]	√			√			√
2	Ghaderia [19]						√	
3	Qu [20]					√		
4	Deng [22]					√		
5	Du [28]		√			√		
6	Wei [11]		√				√	
7	Wei [30]			√			√	
8	Ghaffari [31]		√				√	
9	Xu [32]			√				√
10	Hassan-Pour [33]	√					√	
11	Ji [34]		√			√		
12	Hu [35]		√				√	
13	Wang [36]		√					√
14	Contreras [37]	√					√	
15	Mohammadi [38]	√					√	
16	Samanlioglu [39]	√					√	
17	Tas [40]	√						√
18	Bertazzi [41]	√						√
19	Zheng [42]		√					√
20	Meng [43]		√					√
21	Zhou [44]		√					√
22	Present work			√	√			√

2.3. Research Gap

From the Table 1 presented above, it is apparent that models on uncertain theory for hazardous materials have significant research work on VRP, in the literature. Furthermore, there are a few studies on green elements in fuzzy random programming, because the green VRP problem tends to drop gas emissions to the bottom, and the human value is so difficult to measure that it is usually ignored. However, as an integral part of the total cost, it has a certain importance. The length and speed of the driving route are not a constant value and can change easily within a certain range. They are decided by the driver, so it is reasonable to take human role into account.

On the other hand, fuzzy stochastic programming contains double uncertain attributes, which are probability measure and credibility measure, but most researchers would like to do research just from an angle, mainly because of their different emphasis. Stochastic programming tries to reduce the probability of accidents. Fuzzy measure, as a supplement to random measure, prefers to describe the impact of accidents in language. Language processing is difficult to use in mathematical theory to do accurate calculation, so there is less research in this area.

Hence, it is essential to solve the VRP problem by considering risk and total cost, including the green factor in a realistic scenario. The proposed model deals with modeling and analysis for vehicle routing problem under an uncertain environment. To the best of our knowledge, in this regard, this paper is pioneer study on multi-modal VRP, using chance measure, by considering the risks and the total costs including green costs. Two instances of model-orientation were figured out by hybrid intelligence algorithm, which combined genetic algorithm and fuzzy random simulation algorithm. Thus, the establishment and analysis of three models for the vehicle routing problem are the main contributions of the research presented in this paper.

3. Preliminaries

Although both fuzziness and randomness belong to uncertainty, they can easily be confused. They are two distinct concepts. The fuzzy event can be described by credibility measure via a membership function, after being pioneered by Zadeh [45]. However, random events usually use probability measure to calculate the probability of occurrence. Fuzziness works as a complementary role for randomness, there are similarities between the two mathematical terms. The membership function in fuzzy theory is analogous to probability density function in random theory, similarly, credibility measure defined by Li and Liu is parallel to probability measure from a theoretical point of view [46]. As risk and cost happening during hazmat transportation have dual attribute, a VRP model using chance measure was considered in this study; a detailed introduction on fuzzy random theory is first presented.

3.1. Fuzzy Theory

Definition 1 ([47]). *Let Θ be a nonempty set, and $P(\Theta)$ is the power set of Θ, for each $A \in P(\Theta)$, there is a nonnegative number $Pos(A)$, called its possibility, such that*

(i) $\text{Pos}\,\{\emptyset\} = 0$, $\text{Pos}\,\{\Theta\} = 1$ *and,*
(ii) $\text{Pos}\,\{\cup_k A_k\} = sup\,_k\, \text{Pos}(A_k)$ *for any arbitrary collection* $\{A_k\}$ *in* $P(\Theta)$

The triplet $(\Theta, P(\Theta), \text{Pos})$ is called a possibility space, and the function Pos is referred to as a possibility measure.

Definition 2 ([48]). *Let ξ be a fuzzy variable on a possibility space $(\Theta, P(\Theta), Pos)$. Then its membership function is derived from the possibility measure Pos by*

$$\mu(x) = \text{Pos}\{\theta \in \Theta \big| \xi(\theta) = x\}, x \in R$$

Definition 3 ([49]). *Let $(\Theta, P(\Theta), Pos)$ be a possibility space, and A be a set in $P(\Theta)$. Then the necessity measure of A is defined by*

$$Nec\{A\} = 1 - \text{Pos}(A^c)$$

Definition 4 ([50]). *Let $(\Theta, P(\Theta), Pos)$ be a possibility space, and A be a set in $P(\Theta)$. Then the credibility measure of A is defined by*

$$Cr\{A\} = (\text{pos}\{A\} + Nec\{A\})/2$$

If the membership function $\mu()$ of is ξ given as μ, then the possibility, necessity, credibility of the fuzzy event $\{\xi \geq r\}$ can be represented, respectively, by

$$\text{Pos}\{\xi \geq r\} = \sup_{\mu \geq r} \mu(\mu), Nec\{\xi \geq r\} = 1 - \sup_{\mu < r} \mu(\mu)$$

$$Cr\{\xi \geq r\} = \{\text{Pos}(\xi \geq r) + Nec(\xi \geq r)\}/2$$

Definition 5 ([51]). *Let ξ be a fuzzy variable, then the function given below Φ: $(-\infty, +\infty) \to [0,1]$, $\Phi(x) = Cr\{\theta \in \Theta \big| \xi(\theta) \leq x\}$ is called the credibility distribution of fuzzy variables ξ.*

Example 1. *A trapezoidal fuzzy variable $\xi = (r_1, r_2, r_3, r_4)$ is defined by the following membership function (See Figure 1), then credibility distribution function is given as follows. (See Figure 2).*

$$\mu(x)=\begin{cases}\dfrac{x-r_1}{r_2-r_1} & r_1\le x\le r_2\\ 1 & r_2\le x\le r_3\\ \dfrac{x-r_4}{r_3-r_4} & r_3\le x\le r_4\\ 0 & \text{otherwise}\end{cases}$$

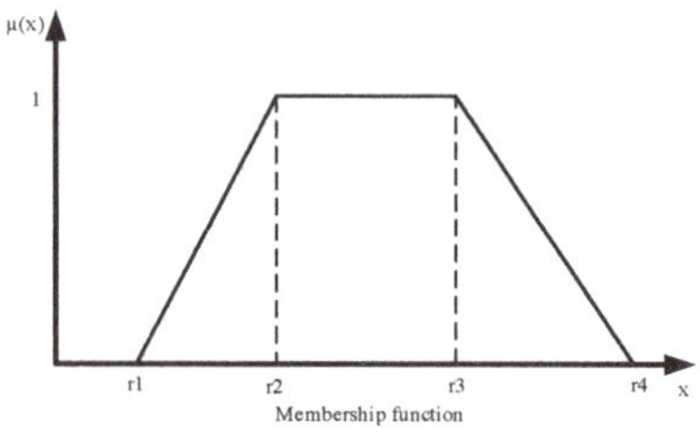

Figure 1. Membership for a trapezoidal fuzzy variable.

$$Cr\{\xi\le x\}=\begin{cases}0 & x\le r_1\\ \dfrac{x-r_1}{2(r_2-r_1)} & r_1\le x\le r_2\\ \dfrac{1}{2} & r_2\le x\le r_3\\ \dfrac{x+r_4-2r_3}{2(r_4-r_3)} & r_3\le x\le r_4\\ 1 & r_4\le x\end{cases}$$

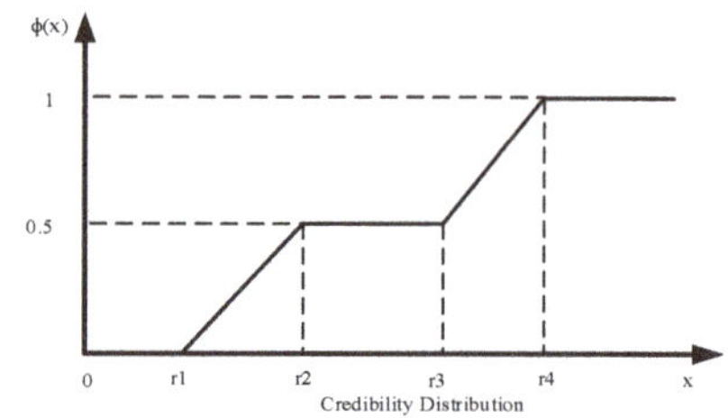

Figure 2. Credibility function for a trapezoidal fuzzy variable.

3.2. Fuzzy Random Theory

Definition 6 ([52]). *Suppose ξ is a function from probability space (Ω, A, Pr) to the fuzzy set of variables, if for any Borel set B, $Pos\{\xi(\omega)\in B\}$ is a measurable function about ω, then ξ is called a fuzzy random variable.*

Example 2. *Suppose (Ω, A, Pr) is set as the probability space, if $\Omega=\{\omega_1,\omega_2,\cdots,\omega_m\}$, and $u_1,u_2,\cdots,u_m$ is a fuzzy variable, then*

$$\xi(\omega)=\begin{cases}u_1 & \omega=\omega_1\\ u_2 & \omega=\omega_1\\ \vdots & \\ u_m & \omega=\omega_1\end{cases}$$

is a fuzzy random variable.

Example 3. *Suppose η is a random variable in probabilistic space (Ω, A, Pr), u is a fuzzy variable, and $\xi(\omega)=\eta(\omega)u, \forall\omega\in\Omega$. If for any Borel set B, $Pos\{\xi(\omega)\in B\}$ is a measurable function about ω, then $\xi=\eta u$ is called a fuzzy random variable.*

Definition 7 ([53,54]). *Suppose ξ is a random variable in a probabilistic space (Ω, A, Pr), B is the Borel set of R, then call the function from $(0,1]$ to $[0,1]$*

$$Ch\{\xi\in B\}(\alpha)=\sup_{\Pr\{A\}\ge\alpha}\ \inf_{\omega\in A} Cr\{\xi(\omega)\in B\}$$

as a chance measure of fuzzy random event $\xi\in B$.

Definition 8 ([55]). *Suppose ξ is a random variable, and $\gamma,\delta\in(0,1]$, then*

$$\xi_{inf}(\gamma,\delta)=inf\{r|Ch\{\xi\le r\}(\gamma)\ge\delta\}$$

is called (γ,δ)-Pessimistic value of ξ.

3.3. Chance-Constrained-Programming Model

Definition 9 ([55]). *Assume that* $\mathbf{x}$ *is a decision vector,* ξ *is a fuzzy random vector,* $f(\mathbf{x}, \xi)$ *is the return function, and* $g_i(\mathbf{x}, \xi)$ *are constraint functions,* $i = 1, 2, \ldots, p$*. It is obvious that the following*

$$\begin{cases} \max \overline{f} \\ \text{subject to} \\ Ch\{f(\mathbf{x}, \xi) \geq \overline{f}\}(\gamma) \geq \delta \\ Ch\{g_i(\mathbf{x}, \xi) \leq 0\}(\alpha_i) \geq \beta_i, i = 1, 2, \ldots, p \end{cases}$$

is a joint chance constraint programming model, where α, β *and* γ, δ *are the predetermined confidence levels. Generally, the authors only considered* values ≥ 0.5.

From the above model, the standard stochastic chance constraint and fuzzy chance constraint programming model could be derived, that is, the chance constraint programming model must contain two measures, a probability measure and a credibility measure, respectively.

4. Vehicle Routing Model Formulation

In this section, three mathematical models are proposed whose object goals are different from each other. An explicit description of unified symbols and assumptions is first presented, followed by a discussion related to model formulation and applicability. From the literature, a chance-constrained programming model was conducted that for the vehicle routing problem with green factor, which had three challenges, listed as follows:

(i) Risk assessment: Due to a series of environmental and human factors, the occurrence of hazardous materials accident is a random event, and the exact consequence of hazardous materials accident was difficult to estimate in advance. Due to the lack of sufficient data, uncertain theory had to be used to solve this intractable problem.
(ii) Cost calculation: This involved determining different components of total cost, especially green cost, and the biggest difference in this study was considering the distance and speed as uncertain factors from a conventional model.
(iii) Vehicle routing assignment: This required arranging sequence serving a set of customers assigned to a vehicle under uncertain environment.

Thus, the comprehensive chance-constrained vehicle routing problem encompassing the above-mentioned three aspects aimed to achieve goals, respectively. In this paper, the following three models subjected to uncertain scenario were formulated as a deformation of classical VRP.

Model I: Vehicle routing model for minimum risk—The objective function was to minimize the risk incurred in all sections of routes.

Model II: Vehicle routing model for cost minimum—Analogous to Model I, the objective function of this model was to minimize total cost consumed along routes.

Model III: Integrated model for risk and cost minimization—The objective function of this model was to minimize the equilibrium value between risk and cost from origin to destination node.

The assumptions, notations and decision variables used in the three mathematical formulations are described below.

Assumptions:

i. The transportation network only has one depot but a set of customers; meanwhile, all vehicles are the same type;
ii. The number of vehicle fleet is decided by the depot; each vehicle has a physical limitation, i.e., capacity, meaning the sum upload amount of all customers shared a path that cannot exceed it;

iii. A customer must be served and visited once and only once, and transportation time can meet all customer's time window limit;
iv. A vehicle routing scheduling must be a loop circle, beginning from the depot and ending at the same depot;
v. A vehicle can visit an uncertain number of customers only if it is within capacity limitation, if not, the vehicle routing scheduling must be abandoned;
vi. The length of arc and population density along the arc are assumed to be fuzzy variables, this work uses triangle fuzzy variables to describe them;
vii. The hazmat accident probability is in a random format, similarly, the speed of the vehicle is adjustable, which is also a random variable.
viii. The customer demands, including time and amount are known, at least, one day earlier.

The notations for the models are described in Table 2.

Table 2. Unified notation for the models.

Set:	
$N = (A,V)$	Transportation network
$A = \{0, 1, 2, \ldots, n\}$	Node set, node 0 denotes single depot
$A_0 = A/\{0\}$	A set of customers waiting for delivery.
$V = \{i, j \mid i, j \in A,\ i \neq j\}$	A collection of arcs that have been connected between customers.
$K = \{1, 2, 3, \ldots k\}$	A collection of vehicles of the same type available in a depot.
Indices:	
i, j	Customer index
m	Depot index
v	Vehicle index
Parameter:	
q_i	Demand of customer i
Q	Capacity of the vehicle.
w	Vehicle weight (empty weight).
F_{fix}	Fixed cost for a vehicle.
F_{fuel}	Variable vehicle operating cost per unit distance.
F_{emi}	CO_2 emission cost per unit weight of vehicle per unit
λ_{ij}	Affected area of the accident on arc (i, j).
Fuzzy parameters:	
$\overline{\xi_{ij}}$	Length of arc (i, j).
$\overline{\rho_{ij}}$	Average population density along arc (i, j).
Random parameters:	
p_{ij}	Probability of accident occurring on arc (i, j).
v_{ij}	Speed of vehicle traveling across arc (i, j).
Decision variables:	
x_{ij}^k	it takes value 1 if arc (i, j) uses vehicle k to travel, it takes value 0, otherwise.
y_i^k	it takes value 1 if customer i uses vehicle to travel, it takes value 0, otherwise.

The three proposed mathematical models adopting the above-mentioned notions are explained from Sections 4.1–4.4.

4.1. Model I-Vehicle Routing Model for Risk Reduction

Minimize total risk

$$\overline{R_{sum}} = \sum_{\forall (i,j) \in N} \sum_{\forall k \in K} \overline{R_{ij}} x_{ij}^k \tag{1}$$

where $\overline{R_{sum}}$ denotes the total risk, $\overline{R_{ij}}$ is risk on arc (i, j).

According to Erkut [8], the risk along arc (i, j) can be demonstrated as Figure 3. The affected area is seen as a circle along arc (i, j), with the radius of r_{ij} and a center dot of k.

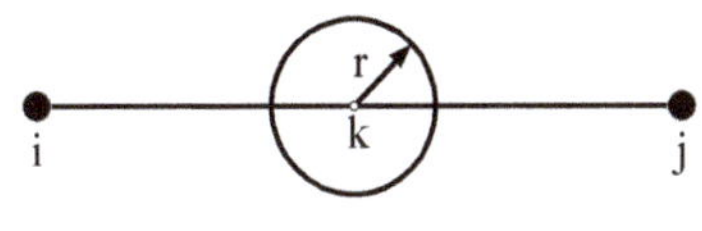

Figure 3. Risk along arc (i, j).

Then, the formulation of hazardous materials risk can be expressed as:

$$\overline{R_{ij}} = p_{ij} \cdot \overline{C_{ij}} \tag{2}$$

where p_{ij} means probability of an incident on road segment (i, j) and $\overline{C_{ij}}$ is population consequence along road segment (i, j), thus, $\overline{C_{ij}}$ can be resulted by the product of population density $\overline{\rho_{ij}}$ and affected area λ_{ij} of accident happening on arc (i, j). Therefore,

$$\begin{aligned} \overline{R_{sum}} &= \sum_{\forall (i,j) \in N} \sum_{\forall k \in K} \overline{R_{ij}} x_{ij}^k = \sum_{\forall (i,j) \in N} \sum_{\forall k \in K} p_{ij} \cdot \overline{C_{ij}}\, x_{ij}^k \\ &= \sum_{\forall (i,j) \in N} \sum_{\forall k \in K} p_{ij} \cdot \overline{\rho_{ij}} \cdot \lambda_{ij}\, x_{ij}^k = \sum_{\forall (i,j) \in N} \sum_{\forall k \in K} p_{ij} \cdot \overline{\rho_{ij}} \cdot \pi {r_{ij}}^2 \cdot x_{ij}^k \end{aligned} \tag{3}$$

From the assumptions and the above equation, the population density is a fuzzy variable. After multiplying area, the number of people affected is still a fuzzy variable. Since accident probability is a stochastic variable, according to Definition 6, the result of risk is a fuzzy random variable.

As we all know, risk ξ is a fuzzy random variable. Suppose Ω denotes the accident probability set, $(\Omega, A, \Pr)$ is probability space, $\overline{C_{ij}} = (200, 250, 280)$ is the accident consequence, then, the risk occurred on arc (i, j), ξ_{ij} can be expressed as follows,

$$\xi_{ij}(\omega) = \begin{cases} (200, 250, 280) & \omega = p_{ij} \\ 0 & \omega = 1 - p_{ij} \end{cases} \tag{4}$$

According to **Definitions 7** and **8**, $\overline{R_{ij}}$ is defined as follows,

$$\begin{aligned} \overline{R_{ij}}\,(\beta, \alpha) &= \left\{ \overline{R} \,\middle|\, Pr\left\{ Cr(p_{ij} \cdot \overline{\rho_{ij}} \cdot \lambda_{ij} \le \overline{R}\,) \ge \beta \right\} \ge \alpha \right\} \\ &= Ch\left\{ p_{ij} \cdot \overline{\rho_{ij}} \cdot \lambda_{ij} \le \overline{R} \right\}(\beta) \ge \alpha \end{aligned} \tag{5}$$

Then the sum risk under the chance measure (β, α) is calculated by

$$\begin{aligned} min\, \overline{R_{sum}}(\beta, \alpha) &= min \sum_{\forall (i,j) \in N} \sum_{\forall k \in K} \overline{R_{ij}}\,(\beta, \alpha) x_{ij}^k \\ &= \sum_{\forall (i,j) \in N} \sum_{\forall k \in K} \left(inf\, Ch\left\{ p_{ij} \cdot \overline{\rho_{ij}} \cdot \lambda_{ij} \le \overline{R} \right\}(\beta) \ge \alpha \right) x_{ij}^k \\ &= \sum_{\forall (i,j) \in N} \sum_{\forall k \in K} \overline{R_{ij(inf)}}(\beta, \alpha) x_{ij}^k \end{aligned} \tag{6}$$

4.2. Model II-Vehicle Routing Model for Cost Reduction

In this section, authors place emphasis on transportation cost of hazmat with the vehicle routing model, the total cost can be broken up into three components, namely fixed cost, fuel cost, and emission cost [20], which can be expressed as Equation (7).

Minimize total cost

$$\overline{F_{sum}} = F_{fix} + F_{fuel} + F_{emi} \tag{7}$$

The first section means expenses that the propritor must pay during a certain period, which is not related to the transportation business volume. It includes the basic salary and fixed allowance of the worker, enterprise management fee and vehicle depreciation, respectively, that is,

$$F_{fix} = c\cdot \sum_{\forall(i,j)\in N} \sum_{\forall k\in K} x_{ij}^k \tag{8}$$

where parameter c denotes the transformed money of using a vehicle one time servicing a customer.

As for the F_{fuel}, in this work, it refers to the following fuel consumption model [28,54],

$$P_t = Mav + Mgvsin\theta + 0.5C_dS\zeta v^3 + MgvC_hcos\theta \tag{9}$$

where P_t represents the total tractive power in watts, M is the total quality of vehicle (curb weight plus carried load). Take gas transportation, for example, explanation and value for parameters used in Equation (9) are listed as follows:

Authors assume that the vehicle travels through a given arc (i,j) at the speed v_{ij}, then the total quantity F_{ij} of energy consumed on arc can be approximated as:

$$\begin{aligned} F_{ij} &= P_t \times (\overline{\xi_{ij}}/v_{ij}) = (M_{ij}av_{ij} + M_{ij}gv_{ij}sin\theta + 0.5C_dS\zeta v_{ij}{}^3 + M_{ij}gv_{ij}C_hcos\theta) \times (\overline{\xi_{ij}}/v_{ij}) \\ &= (M_{ij}a + M_{ij}gsin\theta + 0.5C_dS\zeta v_{ij}{}^2 + M_{ij}gC_hcos\theta)\overline{\xi_{ij}} \\ &= M_{ij}(a + gsin\theta + gC_hcos\theta)\overline{\xi_{ij}} + 0.5C_dS\zeta v_{ij}{}^2\overline{\xi_{ij}} \\ &= (M_{ij}\phi + \varphi v_{ij}{}^2)\overline{\xi_{ij}} \end{aligned} \tag{10}$$

where $\phi = a + gsin\theta + gC_hcos\theta$, $\varphi = 0.5C_dS\zeta$, $M_{ij} = w + q_{ij}$, from the above equation, authors can learn that the fuel consumption is related to two factors, not only the mass, but also victory.

Thus, knowing that the value of unit fuel price will provide some convenient method regarding the value of the total fuel cost, it can be calculated as:

$$F_{fuel} = \sum_{\forall(i,j)\in N} \sum_{\forall k\in K} (M_{ij}\phi + \varphi v_{ij}{}^2)\overline{\xi_{ij}}x_{ij}^k \times \frac{1}{\vartheta} \times P_{fuel} \tag{11}$$

where ϑ is fuel efficiency and P_{fuel} is fuel price per unit, such as $P_{fuel} = 7\,RMB/L$.

Last but not least, the emission cost is greatly affected by the fuel, η_c is fuel conversion factor, t_c is carbon tax, it can define the emission cost as below in Equation (12):

$$F_{emi} = \sum_{\forall(i,j)\in N} \sum_{\forall k\in K} (M_{ij}\phi + \varphi v_{ij}{}^2)\overline{\xi_{ij}}x_{ij}^k \times \frac{1}{\vartheta} \times \eta_c \times t_c \tag{12}$$

According to the above analysis (7)~(12), the total cost of the vehicles can be aggregated as:

$$\begin{aligned} \overline{F_{sum}} &= c\cdot \sum_{\forall(i,j)\in N} \sum_{\forall k\in K} x_{ij}^k + \sum_{\forall(i,j)\in N} \sum_{\forall k\in K} (M_{ij}\phi + \varphi v_{ij}{}^2)\overline{\xi_{ij}}x_{ij}^k \times \tfrac{1}{\vartheta} \times P_{fuel} + \sum_{\forall(i,j)\in N} \sum_{\forall k\in K} (M_{ij}\phi + \varphi v_{ij}{}^2)\overline{\xi_{ij}}x_{ij}^k \times \tfrac{1}{\vartheta} \times \eta_c \times t_c \\ &= c\cdot \sum_{\forall(i,j)\in N} \sum_{\forall k\in K} x_{ij}^k + \sum_{\forall(i,j)\in N} \sum_{\forall k\in K} (M_{ij}\phi + \varphi v_{ij}{}^2)\overline{\xi_{ij}}x_{ij}^k \times \tfrac{1}{\vartheta} \times (P_{fuel} + \eta_c \cdot t_c) \end{aligned} \tag{13}$$

From the assumption, it is known that the length is a fuzzy and the vehicle speed is a random variable. Similar to risk calculations, the sum cost of fuel is also a fuzzy random variable. Then, the sum cost under chance measure (χ,γ) is calculated by,

$$\begin{aligned}\overline{F_{sum}}(\chi,\gamma) &= \left\{Pr\{Cr(\sum_{\forall(i,j)\in N}\sum_{\forall k\in K}\left[(M_{ij}\phi+\varphi v_{ij}{}^2)\overline{\xi_{ij}}x_{ij}^k\times\tfrac{1}{\vartheta}\times(P_{fuel}+\eta_c\cdot t_c)\right]\le\overline{F_{ij}})\ge\chi\}\ge\gamma\right\}+c\cdot\sum_{\forall(i,j)\in N}\sum_{\forall k\in K}x_{ij}^k \\ &= Ch\{\sum_{\forall(i,j)\in N}\sum_{\forall k\in K}\left[(M_{ij}\phi+\varphi v_{ij}{}^2)\overline{\xi_{ij}}\times\tfrac{1}{\vartheta}\times(P_{fuel}+\eta_c\cdot t_c)\le\overline{F_{ij}}\right](\chi)\ge\gamma\}x_{ij}^k+c\cdot\sum_{\forall(i,j)\in N}\sum_{\forall k\in K}x_{ij}^k\end{aligned} \tag{14}$$

Therefore, the objective of Model II is as follows:

$$\begin{aligned}min\ \overline{F_{sum}}(\chi,\gamma) &= min\ Ch\{\sum_{\forall(i,j)\in N}\sum_{\forall k\in K}\left[(M_{ij}\phi+\varphi v_{ij}{}^2)\overline{\xi_{ij}}\times\tfrac{1}{\vartheta}\times(P_{fuel}+\eta_c\cdot t_c)\le\overline{F_{ij}}\right](\chi)\ge\gamma\}x_{ij}^k+c\cdot\sum_{\forall(i,j)\in N}\sum_{\forall k\in K}x_{ij}^k \\ &= \sum_{\forall(i,j)\in N}\sum_{\forall k\in K} inf\ Ch\{\left[(M_{ij}\phi+\varphi v_{ij}{}^2)\overline{\xi_{ij}}\times\tfrac{1}{\vartheta}\times(P_{fuel}+\eta_c\cdot t_c)\le\overline{F_{ij}}\right](\chi)\ge\gamma\}x_{ij}^k+c\cdot\sum_{\forall(i,j)\in N}\sum_{\forall k\in K}x_{ij}^k \\ &= \sum_{\forall(i,j)\in N}\sum_{\forall k\in K}\overline{F_{ij(inf)}}(\chi,\gamma)x_{ij}^k+c\cdot\sum_{\forall(i,j)\in N}\sum_{\forall k\in K}x_{ij}^k\end{aligned} \tag{15}$$

4.3. Model III-Vehicle Routing Model for Risk and Cost Minimization

In order to work out this integrated model, it can take a compromise value by weighting sum of the two aspects. First, the authors perform the normalization operation on risk and cost. Denote $\overline{R_{(inf)max}}(\beta,\alpha)$, $\overline{R_{(inf)min}}(\beta,\alpha)$ as the maximum and minimum values for total risk under the chance measure (β,α), $\overline{F_{(inf)max}}(\chi,\gamma)$, $\overline{F_{(inf)min}}(\chi,\gamma)$, as the maximum and minimum values for total cost, the chance measure (χ,γ), respectively, then the normalized risk and cost are

$$R' = \frac{\overline{R_{(inf)}}(\beta,\alpha)-\overline{R_{(inf)min}}(\beta,\alpha)}{\overline{R_{(inf)max}}(\beta,\alpha)-\overline{R_{(inf)min}}(\beta,\alpha)}\ F' = \frac{\overline{F_{(inf)}}(\chi,\gamma)-\overline{F_{(inf)min}}(\chi,\gamma)}{\overline{F_{(inf)max}}(\chi,\gamma)-\overline{F_{(inf)min}}(\chi,\gamma)} \tag{16}$$

With the given parameter $\tau\in[0,1]$, the compromise objective value is

$$T = \tau F' + (1-\tau)R' \tag{17}$$

4.4. Model Constraints

Equation (18) means that customer j is visited by the vehicle k, and vehicle k must arrive at the customer j from customer i. Equation (19) signifies that customer i can be served by the vehicle k, and the vehicle k must arrive at the customer j, after delivering the materials from the customer i. Equation (20) represents that the load of every vehicle could not exceed the maximum capacity Q. Constraint (21) means that each customer must be served by only one vehicle, and constraint (22) means that all vehicle routing arrangements start from the same depot.

$$\sum_{k=1}^{v} x_{ij}^k = y_j^k\ \forall k = 1,2,\ldots v,\ \forall j = 1,2,\ldots,n \tag{18}$$

$$\sum_{k=1}^{v} x_{ij}^k = y_i^k\ \forall k = 1,2,\ldots v,\ \forall i = 1,2,\ldots,n \tag{19}$$

$$\sum_{i=0}^{n} y_i^k \times q_i \le Q\ \forall k = 1,2,\ldots v \tag{20}$$

$$\sum_{k=1}^{v} y_i^k = \forall i = 1,2,\ldots n \tag{21}$$

$$\sum_{k=1}^{v} y_0^k = v \tag{22}$$

5. Solution Methodology

As stated above, a fuzzy random simulation must be used to acquire the objective value according to the corresponding models. After this, a genetic algorithm on the basis of fuzzy random simulation algorithm is designed to optimize vehicle routing strategy, with the above three models.

5.1. Fuzzy Random Simulation Algorithm

Let ξ be an n-dimensional fuzzy vector with the membership degree u_i for all $i = 1, 2, \ldots, N$, and let $f : R^n \to R$ be a real function. Then, the credibility $Cr\{\xi \le r\}$ value can be obtained by

$$L(r) = \frac{1}{2}\big(\max_{f(\mathbf{y}_i) \le r} u_i + 1 - \max_{f(\mathbf{y}_i) > r} u_i\big)$$

Considering that $L(r)$ is an increasing function, the chance measure value can be calculated by fuzzy random simulation [55], which is the combination of fuzzy simulation and random simulation, after using fuzzy simulation to obtain a series of β-pessimistic value, then taking the α-proportion incremental value to be the approximate cutoff value. The steps of calculating β-pessimistic value by fuzzy simulation invented by Liu is described as follows [54]:

Step 1. Initialize a small real number $\varepsilon > 0$.
Step 2. Randomly generate vectors $\mathbf{y_i}$ with membership degrees u_i for all $i = 1, 2, \ldots, N$.
Step 3. Calculate the minimum and maximum values $a = min\{f(\mathbf{y_i}) | 1 \le i \le N\}$ and $b = max\{f(\mathbf{y_i}) | 1 \le i \le N\}$.
Step 4. Set $r = (a + b)/2$.
Step 5. If $L(r) \ge \alpha$, set $b = r$. Otherwise, set $a = r$.
Step 6. If $b - a \ge \varepsilon$, go to Step 4.
Step 7. Return $(\mathrm{a} + \mathrm{b})/2$ as an approximation of the β-pessimistic value.

Then, the fuzzy random simulation algorithm can be summarized as follows:

Step 1. Generate $\omega_1, \omega_2, \ldots \omega_N$, from space Ω according to the probability measure Pr.
Step 2. Find the smallest values $\overline{f_n}$ such that $Cr\{f(\mathbf{x}, \xi(\omega_n)) \le \overline{f_n}\} \ge \beta$ for $n = 1, 2, \ldots, N$ by fuzzy simulation, respectively.
Step 3. Set NN value, which equals to the integer part of αN.
Step 4. Return the NN th largest element in $\{\overline{f}_1, \overline{f}_2, \ldots, \overline{f}_N\}$.

5.2. Fuzzy Random Simulation Based Genetic Algorithm

The general procedures of genetic algorithm are initialization, evaluation, selection, crossover, and mutation, in turn.

5.2.1. Initialization Operation

In general, the vehicle routing problem is a combinatorial optimization problem, so the chromosomes can be encoded as integers. Their structures can be divided into two parts, Part C and Part V, so the length is decided by the number of customers and vehicles. Part C stands for the information about the customer order, and Part V denotes vehicle information on how to service several customers using a common vehicle (see Figure 4).

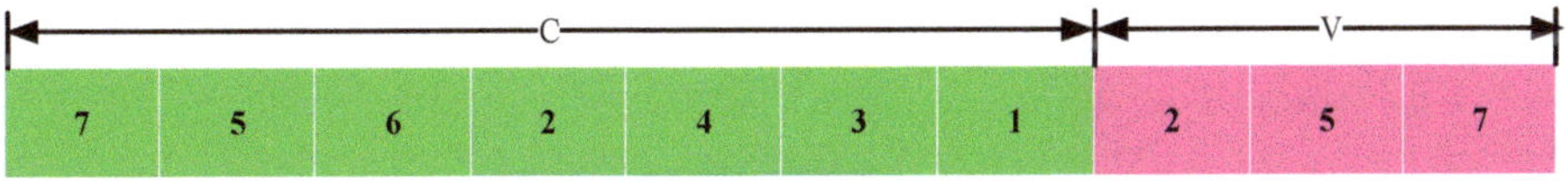

Figure 4. Initialization operation.

For example, Part C is initialized to be 7,5,6,2,4,3,1, which means that the service order is 7,5,6,2,4,3,1 in sequence. The content of Part V is the last customer index of Part C in the transportation loop by a common vehicle. For example, there are three vehicles waiting for transportation, so the length of Part V is 3. If Part V list is 2,5,7, it means that the first vehicle serves two customers—customer 7 and customer 5. The second vehicle serves from the next node to the node that is the second number in Part V, node 5, hence, the customer 6, customer 2, and customer 4 use the second vehicle in common. In the same way, the third vehicle serves from the sixth node to the seventh node, which is customer 3 and customer 1. From the above description, it requests the Part V must be in an ascending form.

5.2.2. Evaluation Function

Let $Y = (C, V)$ be a chromosome from feasible space. By employing fuzzy random simulation, the objective value can be easily obtained for the three models. From the objective values of three models, it seeks for minimum, so $\frac{1}{objective\ value}$ is defined as the evaluation function Eval (Y).

5.2.3. Selection Operation

The aim of selection operation is to select better chromosomes to be parent, and roulette wheel selection method uses fitness-proportions to make choice. This paper adopted this method for the selection operation. First, it calculated the cumulative probability p_k for each chromosome Yk, $k = 1, 2, \ldots, popsize$:

$$p_0 = 0, p_k = \sum_{q=1}^{k} Eval(Y_q),\ k = 1, 2, \ldots, popsize$$

Then, compare the randomly generated number $r \in (0, p_{popsize}]$ with the cumulative probability $[p_{k-1,}p_k]$, if $r \in [p_{k-1,}p_k]$, the select chromosomes Y_k to be the parent chromosome.

5.2.4. Crossover Operation

Repeat the following scheme for $k = 1, 2, \ldots, popsize$: randomly generated number $r \in (0, 1]$, if r is lower than the predefined crossover probability p_c, the corresponding chromosome is chosen to be a parent.

The crossover operation mainly acts on part V, take the chromosome pair (Ya, Yb), for example, it changes the whole Part V, such as the chromosome Ya are coded as 7,5,6,2,4,3,1,2,5,7, Yb are coded as 2,5,4,3,7,1,6,1,4,7, after crossover operation, Ya becomes 7,5,6,2,4,3,1,1,4,7 and Yb becomes 2,5,4,3,7,1,6,2,5,7 (see Figure 5).

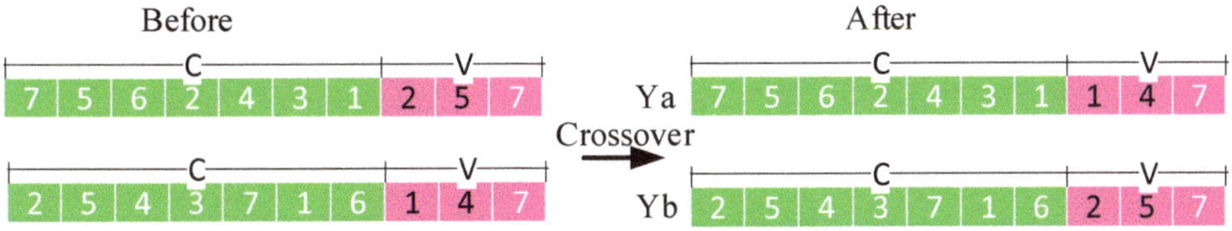

Figure 5. Crossover operation.

5.2.5. Mutation Operation

Define beforehand a parameter p_m, which is regarded as the mutation probability and do the next process for $k = 1, 2, \ldots, popsize$: Generate a random number r in the unit interval [0,1], and select the chromosome Yk to perform the mutation operation if $r < p\_c$.

The mutation operation acts on part C, take the chromosome Yk, for example, randomly generate two integers $a, b \in (0, length(Part\,C)]$ (see red arrows in Figure 6), then exchange the numbers the arrow points to. Before the mutation operation, the chromosome Yk is coded as 7,5,6,2,4,3,1,2,5,7, then it becomes 7,5,3,2,4,6,1,2,5,7, the whole mutation operation is shown in Figure 6.

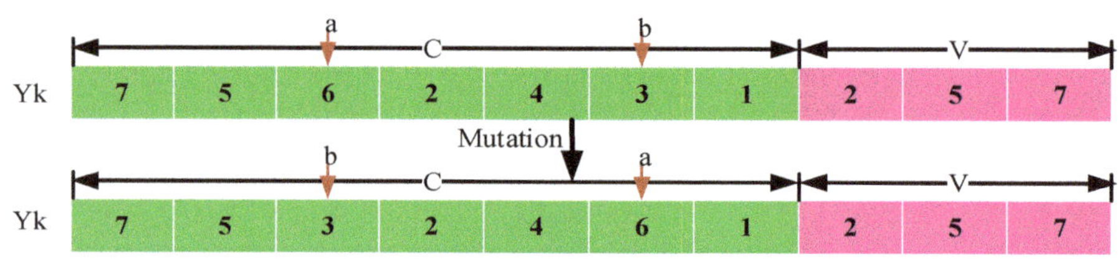

Figure 6. Mutation operation.

Figure 7 shows the whole process to solve the problem. The procedure of aforementioned fuzzy random simulation-based GA is as follows:

Step 1. Set $i = 1$. Initialize relative parameters, such as population size, maximum generation, crossover probability, mutation probability, and so on.

Step 2. Randomly generate *pop_size* feasible chromosomes to be the initial population.

Step 3. According to the models used, calculate the objective values for all chromosomes to obtain evaluation values by fuzzy random simulation.

Step 4. After performing selection, crossover, and mutation operations, update all chromosomes.

Step 5. If $i = max\_gen$, the simulation must be terminated, then choose the best chromosome as the ultimate solution. Otherwise, set $i = i + 1$ and return to Step 3.

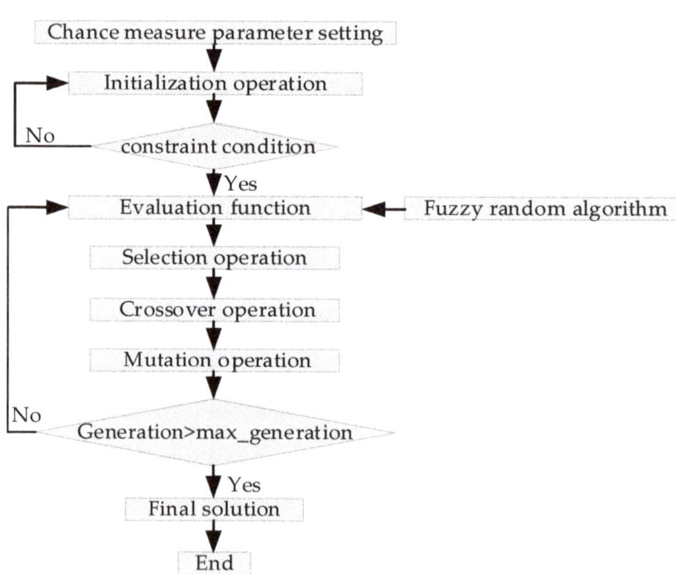

Figure 7. Hybrid intelligent algorithm flow chart.

As can be seen from Figure 7, the calculation process of the three models is the same. The difference lies in the evaluation function acquisition. In order to make the model proposed in this paper more applicable, the design of chromosomes needs to traverse all vehicle path combinations, according to the number of fleets and the load requirements of vehicles. After setting different chance level values, the objective values between each pair of nodes in the path need to be simulated for N times, which was set as 5000 in this study. Therefore, each operation of the genetic algorithm, be it crossover or mutation, needs to be repeated for 5000× N2 times, so the complexity of the algorithm is O(N2). Not only this, it still needs to satisfy the limits of capacity limitation, as shown in Section 4.4, so it is more complex than the model in the deterministic environment.

6. Case Study

In this section, two numerical experiments are presented to illustrate the efficiency of the proposed three models and solution methodology. The first one was a small-size network that consisted of only 10 customers, while the second case considered a practical case which was applied to the Changchun city, Jilin province in China. When calculating the objectives of Model II and III, for the specific values of the parameters of cost refer to Table 3.

Table 3. Explanation and value for parameters in Equation 9.

Parameter	Meaning	Value
M	Total quality	5 t
θ	Road angle of arc	0
a	Acceleration	0
g	Gravitational constant	9.8 m/s^2
C_d	Drag resistance coefficient	0.7
C_h	Rolling resistance coefficient	0.01
ζ	Air density	1.2041 kg/m^2
S	Surface area of vehicle	5 m^2
P_{fuel}	Fuel price	7 RMB/L
η_c	Fuel conversion factor	2.32 kg/L
t_c	carbon tax	0.6 RMB/kg
ϑ	Fuel efficiency	20%

6.1. Case 1: Small Case

In this case, a small-scale network was established, and it contained one deport D0 and 10 customers named C1, ... , C10 are shown as Figure 8. The demand amounts of customers were scheduled to be t = (2.5, 4.0, 4.6, 3.2, 2.8, 3.8, 3.0, 3.0, 3.0, 2.0) t. The capacity of the depot was assumed to be 40 t, the arc length and population density were described in the second and third column of Table 4. Then, the random accident probability and driving speed were shown in the third and fourth column of Table 4. The last column in Table 4 was the affected area, once the accident happened. The length of arc obeyed equipossible fuzzy distribution, while the population density was also a fuzzy triangle variable. Two random variables—accident probability and driving speed, the former was normally distributed, while the latter was uniformly distributed. Here, all fuzzy parameters and random variables were assumed to be independent.

Table 4. The risk and cost in Example 6.1.

Arc	Length (km)	Population Density (pop/km^2)	Pr ($\times10^{-5}$)	Speed (km/h)	Area (km^2)
(0,1)	(70,90)	(80,83,87)	N(1,9)	U(40,60)	24
(0,2)	(100,120)	(185,189,205)	N(1,4)	U(40,60)	32
(0,3)	(90,110)	(200,210,235)	N(2,9)	U(40,60)	18
(0,4)	(75,90)	(70,72,75)	N(2,16)	U(40,60)	27
(0,5)	(150,180)	(140,145,160)	N(3,9)	U(40,60)	56
(0,6)	(200,230)	(65,70,72)	N(1,1)	U(40,60)	60
(0,7)	(40,60)	(260,270,278)	N(1,4)	U(40,60)	19
(0,8)	(120,140)	(262,268,270)	N(4,9)	U(40,60)	45
(0,9)	(220,250)	(205,210,220)	N(1,9)	U(40,60)	52
(0,10)	(120,140)	(150,160,165)	N(1,6)	U(40,60)	38
(1,2)	(100,150)	(78,81,85)	N(1,5)	U(40,60)	29
(1,3)	(220,300)	(65,72,88)	N(2,9)	U(40,60)	41
(1,4)	(150,330)	(210,220,235)	N(3,16)	U(40,60)	37
(1,5)	(210,300)	(270,278,298)	N(1,2)	U(40,60)	87
(1,6)	(180,260)	(68,70,72)	N(2,2)	U(40,60)	34
(1,7)	(110,350)	(130,135,140)	N(2,4)	U(40,60)	15.5
(1,8)	(180,280)	(160,170,180)	N(3,9)	U(40,60)	21.5
(1,9)	(160,300)	(300,310,322)	N(3,1)	U(40,60)	40
(1,10)	(220,300)	(96,100,105)	N(3,2)	U(40,60)	31
(2,3)	(115,135)	(100,105,115)	N(3,4)	U(40,60)	17
(2,4)	(290,340)	(102,110,124)	N(1,16)	U(40,60)	29
(2,5)	(260,300)	(165,175,186)	N(2,16)	U(40,60)	47
(2,6)	(180,240)	(320,336,361)	N(2,9)	U(40,60)	16
(2,7)	(260,380)	(280,295,315)	N(3,5)	U(40,60)	25
(2,8)	(220,235)	(90,95,100)	N(4,9)	U(40,60)	82
(2,9)	(220,380)	(200,205,220)	N(4,1)	U(40,60)	54
(2,10)	(300,360)	(55,60,62)	N(4,2)	U(40,60)	26
(3,4)	(180,380)	(170,175,186)	N(4,3)	U(40,60)	54
(3,5)	(120,280)	(215,222,236)	N(4,4)	U(40,60)	61
(3,6)	(200,260)	(105,108,116)	N(5,9)	U(40,60)	57
(3,7)	(210,290)	(195,203,215)	N(5,1)	U(40,60)	38
(3,8)	(160,390)	(155,162,176)	N(5,2)	U(40,60)	28
(3,9)	(280,360)	(195,202,215)	N(5,4)	U(40,60)	37
(3,10)	(160,420)	(66,68,72)	N(5,6)	U(40,60)	26
(4,5)	(220,270)	(305,315,340)	N(5,16)	U(40,60)	45
(4,6)	(260,350)	(345,350,370)	N(6,9)	U(40,60)	32
(4,7)	(120,210)	(210,215,230)	N(6,1)	U(40,60)	17.5
(4,8)	(180,240)	(75,78,82)	N(6,2)	U(40,60)	47.2
(4,9)	(240,350)	(55,60,64)	N(6,3)	U(40,60)	35
(4,10)	(220,310)	(320,354,376)	N(6,4)	U(40,60)	43
(5,6)	(190,285)	(310,322,340)	N(6,1)	U(40,60)	34
(5,7)	(180,320)	(280,290,312)	N(6,4)	U(40,60)	28
(5,8)	(320,420)	(260,285,320)	N(6,2)	U(40,60)	34
(5,9)	(250,360)	(115,119,128)	N(1,1)	U(40,60)	64
(5,10)	(170,250)	(175,180,192)	N(1,2)	U(40,60)	35
(6,7)	(220,290)	(260,275,292)	N(1,3)	U(40,60)	29
(6,8)	(270,365)	(220,231,245)	N(1,4)	U(40,60)	75
(6,9)	(320,390)	(293,300,321)	N(2,9)	U(40,60)	61
(6,10)	(305,375)	(215,223,236)	N(2,1)	U(40,60)	84
(7,8)	(260,320)	(293,303,324)	N(2,3)	U(40,60)	34
(7,9)	(150,240)	(200,210,225)	N(2,4)	U(40,60)	43
(7,10)	(210,275)	(262,272,286)	N(2,5)	U(40,60)	19
(8,9)	(200,255)	(360,383,405)	N(3,9)	U(40,60)	56
(8,10)	(230,285)	(260,266,282)	N(3,4)	U(40,60)	34
(9,10)	(180,270)	(365,377,400)	N(3,1)	U(40,60)	28

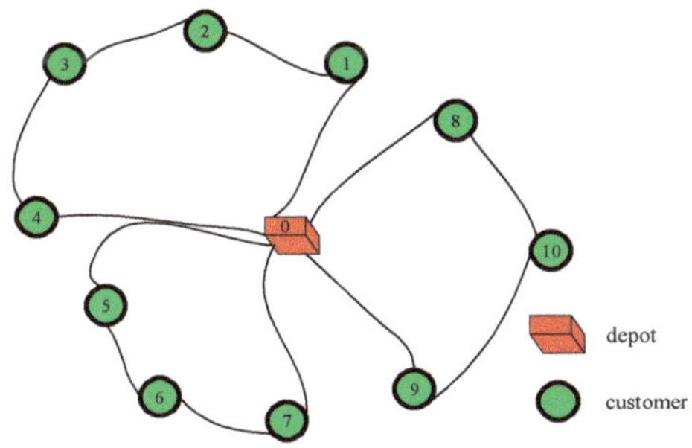

Figure 8. Small case for vehicle routing problem.

First, the authors compared the best solution with different chromosome population, it performed hybrid intelligence GA algorithm with $pop\_size = 3,\ 30,\ 100$ and $max\_generation = 50$, respectively. The crossover probability was set to be 0.8 while the mutation probability was defined as 0.3. To increase the credibility measure of the best solution, the chance level, that is to say, the credibility level (Cr) and the probability level (Pr) were both set to be 0.99. The result generated by the hybrid intelligence algorithm for Model I, Model II, and Model III are presented in Table 5, Table 6, Table 7, respectively. For example, as for Model I, when the *pop size* was 30, the optimum vehicle routing arrangement was:

Vehicle 1: 0-5-2-1-7-8-4-0
Vehicle 2: 0-9-0
Vehicle 3: 0-10-3-6-0

and the sum risk was 7.3103, simulation time was 8197.9 s. The larger the chromosome population, the smaller was the risk, and the more simulation time it consumed. It also showed that the proposed model and algorithm were feasible.

Second, Model II and Model III were simulated under the same conditions, it also conformed to the result that the lower the objective value, the greater the consumption time. It was obvious that this was an important problem that time complexity increased exponentially, which needs to be solved in the long run.

Last but not least, Model III integrates risk and cost, the weight for risk and cost is set to be 0.7 and 0.3, whatever is the weight, the models and algorithm could generate a reasonable solution.

Table 5. Model I result by hybrid intelligence algorithm for case 1.

Genetic Algorithm Parameters			Chance Level	Model I		
pop	Max_Gen	pc pm	Cr Pr	Best Solution	Risk	Consume Time
3	50	0.8 0.3	0.99 0.99	0-1-6-0 0-2-9-5-4-8-10-0 0-7-3-0	8.7891	1203.68 s
30	50	0.8 0.3	0.99 0.99	0-5-2-1-7-8-4-0 0-9-0 0-10-3-6-0	7.3103	8197.9 s
100	50	0.8 0.3	0.99 0.99	0-5-3-10-8-4-0 0-7-9-2-6-1-0	6.6191	24,294.5 s

Table 6. Model II result by hybrid intelligence algorithm for case 1.

Genetic Algorithm Parameters			Chance Level	Model II		
pop	Max gen	pc / pm	Cr / Pr	Best Solution	Cost	Consume Time
3	50	0.8 0.3	0.99 0.99	0-8-9-0 0-10-7-4-3-1-6-0 0-5-2-0	38,393.4	768.761 s
30	50	0.8 0.3	0.99 0.99	0-1-7-8-3-2-1 0-4-5-10-9-0 0-6-0	34,542.4	2882.98 s
100	50	0.8 0.3	0.99 0.99	0-1-6-0 0-2-9-5-4-8-10-0 0-7-3-0	30,799.8	9184.34 s

Table 7. Model III result by hybrid intelligence algorithm for case 1.

Genetic Algorithm Parameters			Chance Level	Model III		
pop	Max gen	pc / pm	Cr / Pr	Best Solution	0.7 Risk + 0.3 Cost	Consume Time
3	50	0.8 0.3	0.99 0.99	0-8-9-10-7-4-0 0-3-1-0 0-6-5-2-0	0.84532	768.761 s
30	50	0.8 0.3	0.99 0.99	0-9-2-6-10-0 0-8-0 0-7-3-5-1-4-0	0.832983	4843.76 s
100	50	0.8 0.3	0.99 0.99	0-1-6-0 0-2-9-5-4-8-10-0 0-7-3-0	0.792522	15824.5 s

6.2. Case 2: Practical Case

In this example, a practical case—gas transportation in the Changchun City, Jilin province, China was considered. The topological graph is shown in Figure 9, and it consisted of 15 customers named from node 1 to node 15 and one depot called depot 0. It was located in the northern part of the city and the main road is shown as the black lines. The length, population density, probability, speed, and affected area are presented from column 2 to column 6 in Table 8. The difference from case 1 was that if the arc length was Inf, it implied that there was no connection between the two customers.

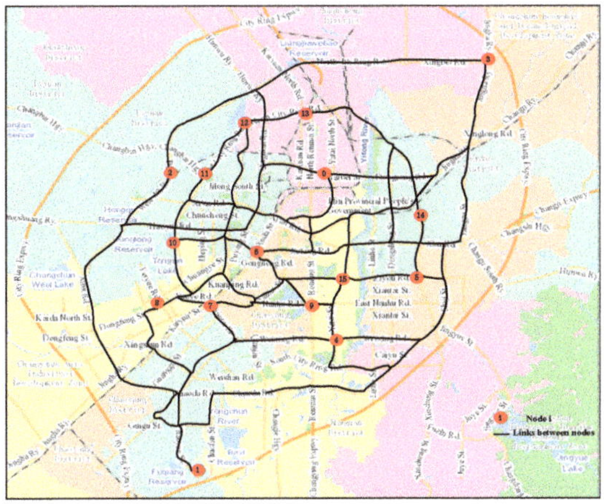

Figure 9. Practical case for vehicle routing problem.

Table 8. The risk and cost in Example 6.2.

Arc	Length (km)	Population Density (pop per km^2)	Probability ($\times 10^{-5}$)	Speed (km/h)	Area (km^2)
(0,1)	Inf	Inf	N(1,2)	U(40,60)	Inf
(0,2)	(10,15)	(15,20,38)	N((1,3)	U(40,60)	2
(0,3)	(15,20)	(20,30,40)	N(2,6)	U(40,60)	5
(0,4)	(30,40)	(20,33,44)	N(1,4)	U(40,60)	6
(0,5)	(15,30)	(22,35,50)	N(1,6)	U(40,60)	3
(0,6)	(10,12)	(18,20,32)	N(2,4)	U(40,60)	1
(0,7)	(8,15)	(26,28,29)	N(1,1)	U(40,60)	3.5
(0,8)	(18,24)	(20,25,30)	N(2,5)	U(40,60)	4.8
(0,9)	(10,13)	(15,20,28)	N(1,3)	U(40,60)	1.6
(0,10)	(10,18)	(15,20,24)	N(2,5)	U(40,60)	1.7
(0,11)	(8,12)	(20,26,27)	N(1,4)	U(40,60)	2.1
(0,12)	(5,10)	(10,16,30)	N(1,1)	U(40,60)	2.3
(0,13)	(6,14)	(30,32,35)	N(2,1)	U(40,60)	2.6
(0,14)	(7,16)	(22,28,40)	N(2,2)	U(40,60)	3
(0,15)	(8,15)	(12,20,26)	N(1,3)	U(40,60)	2.9
(1,2)	(40,42)	(50,60,70)	N(2,6)	U(40,60)	14
(1,3)	(60,62)	(60,70,85)	N(2,8)	U(40,60)	22
(1,4)	(20,25)	(32,38,40)	N(2,3)	U(40,60)	7
(1,5)	(20,30)	(28,29,36)	N(2,4)	U(40,60)	7.5
(1,6)	(25,28)	(40,42,50)	N(3,5)	U(40,60)	8
(1,7)	(15,18)	(20,24,30)	N(1,4)	U(40,60)	3
(1,8)	(8,12)	(20,25,30)	N(2,2)	U(40,60)	2.6
(1,9)	Inf	Inf	Inf	U(40,60)	Inf
(1,10)	(28,32)	(39,45,48)	N(2,5)	U(40,60)	10
(1,11)	(20,26)	(30,36,45)	N(2,6)	U(40,60)	8.2
(1,12)	Inf	Inf	Inf	U(40,60)	Inf
(1,13)	(80,90)	(100,102,110)	N(1,5)	U(40,60)	20
(1,14)	(70,80)	(80,82,88)	N(3,6)	U(40,60)	15
(1,15)	(30,35)	(40,42,48)	N(1,3)	U(40,60)	12.5
(2,3)	(20,25)	(30,38,40)	N(1,1)	U(40,60)	10.2
(2,4)	(40,50)	(42,45,48)	N(3,3)	U(40,60)	14.5
(2,5)	(60,70)	(66,68,70)	N(3,7)	U(40,60)	18
(2,6)	Inf	Inf	Inf	U(40,60)	Inf
(2,7)	Inf	Inf	Inf	U(40,60)	Inf
(2,8)	(50,55)	(65,70,78)	N(5,2)	U(40,60)	22

Table 8. *Cont.*

Arc	Length (km)	Population Density (pop per km^2)	Probability ($\times10^{-5}$)	Speed (km/h)	Area (km^2)
(2,9)	Inf	Inf	Inf	U(40,60)	Inf
(2,10)	(5,8)	(10,15,20)	N(1,2)	U(40,60)	1.2
(2,11)	(10,15)	(12,15,19)	N(2,2)	U(40,60)	1.8
(2,12)	(20,25)	(30,32,37)	N(2,3)	U(40,60)	2.0
(2,13)	(25,30)	(40,46,50)	N(2,4)	U(40,60)	2.3
(2,14)	Inf	Inf	Inf	U(40,60)	Inf
(2,15)	Inf	Inf	Inf	U(40,60)	Inf
(3,4)	(40,50)	(50,55,60)	N(3,2)	U(40,60)	15
(3,5)	(30,40)	(33,38,42)	N(3,5)	U(40,60)	14.6
(3,6)	(30,35)	(32,39,49)	N(2,5)	U(40,60)	13.2
(3,7)	(70,75)	(82,84,90)	N(5,8)	U(40,60)	30
(3,8)	(80,82)	(90,95,105)	N(4,9)	U(40,60)	32
(3,9)	Inf	Inf	Inf	U(40,60)	Inf
(3,10)	(60,70)	(65,70,80)	N(3,5)	U(40,60)	23
(3,11)	(40,50)	(50,62,82)	N(3,3)	U(40,60)	24
(3,12)	(40,42)	(50,62,72)	N(3,6)	U(40,60)	26
(3,13)	(35,40)	(42,50,53)	N(3,5)	U(40,60)	25
(3,14)	(15,22)	(32,38,42)	N(2,3)	U(40,60)	10.2
(3,15)	(25,30)	(30,40,42)	N(3,2)	U(40,60)	20
(4,5)	(15,20)	(20,25,36)	N(1,4)	U(40,60)	16
(4,6)	(30,40)	(42,55,65)	N(2,2)	U(40,60)	25
(4,7)	(10,15)	(20,26,34)	N(1,3)	U(40,60)	6.5
(4,8)	(15,25)	(20,28,35)	N(1,2)	U(40,60)	7.2
(4,9)	(5,8)	(10,20,32)	N(1,1)	U(40,60)	2.5
(4,10)	(50,80)	(65,72,88)	N(3,4)	U(40,60)	19
(4,11)	(60,62)	(80,82,86)	N(4,5)	U(40,60)	28
(4,12)	(50,55)	(62,68,72)	N(2,4)	U(40,60)	24
(4,13)	(40,50)	(44,48,52)	N(1,6)	U(40,60)	20
(4,14)	(15,20)	(20,25,30)	N(2,2)	U(40,60)	13
(4,15)	(4,15)	(10,20,32)	N(1,1)	U(40,60)	2.2
(5,6)	(8,12)	(15,20,25)	N(1,2)	U(40,60)	4.5
(5,7)	(12,15)	(20,23,27)	N(1,3)	U(40,60)	7.2
(5,8)	(13,20)	(20,30,40)	N(1,3)	U(40,60)	7.5
(5,9)	Inf	Inf	Inf	U(40,60)	Inf
(5,10)	(60,70)	(80,90,96)	N(2,5)	U(40,60)	26
(5,11)	(70,72)	(82,88,90)	N(2,6)	U(40,60)	32
(5,12)	Inf	Inf	Inf	U(40,60)	Inf
(5,13)	(30,50)	(36,44,54)	N(2,3)	U(40,60)	15
(5,14)	(8,10)	(20,22,28)	N(1,3)	U(40,60)	4.2
(5,15)	(5,12)	(12,18,28)	N(1,2)	U(40,60)	2.4
(6,7)	(5,8)	(13,18,28)	N(1,1)	U(40,60)	2.2
(6,8)	(8,12)	(20,32,40)	N(1,2)	U(40,60)	4
(6,9)	(8,12)	(20,32,40)	N(1,2)	U(40,60)	4
(6,10)	(8,12)	(20,32,40)	N(1,2)	U(40,60)	4
(6,11)	(10,15)	(25,30,38)	N(1,3)	U(40,60)	4.2
(6,12)	(12,15)	(25,32,42)	N(1,4)	U(40,60)	4.4
(6,13)	(15,18)	(20,30,40)	N(2,2)	U(40,60)	4.8
(6,14)	(16,20)	(22,30,32)	N(2,2)	U(40,60)	5
(6,15)	(8,10)	(15,20,22)	N(1,3)	U(40,60)	3
(7,8)	(5,7)	(12,20,22)	N(1,1)	U(40,60)	1.9
(7,9)	(8,12)	(18,24,35)	N(1,2)	U(40,60)	2.8
(7,10)	(10,14)	(25,30,33)	N(1,3)	U(40,60)	4.3
(7,11)	(15,20)	(22,28,32)	N(2,1)	U(40,60)	4.5
(7,12)	(16,22)	(23,29,35)	N(2,2)	U(40,60)	4.6
(7,13)	(20,22)	(30,36,40)	N(2,3)	U(40,60)	4.8
(7,14)	(20,30)	(30,36,45)	N(2,3)	U(40,60)	5.6
(7,15)	(10,12)	(17,22,25)	N(1,1)	U(40,60)	3.8

Table 8. *Cont.*

Arc	Length (km)	Population Density (pop per km²)	Probability (×10⁻⁵)	Speed (km/h)	Area (km²)
(8,9)	(10,12)	(17,22,25)	N(1,1)	U(40,60)	3.8
(8,10)	(9,12)	(10,15,16)	N(1,2)	U(40,60)	3.6
(8,11)	(15,25)	(12,16,23)	N(2,1)	U(40,60)	5.2
(8,12)	(15,25)	(12,16,23)	N(2,1)	U(40,60)	5.2
(8,13)	(15,30)	(12,18,28)	N(2,3)	U(40,60)	5.6
(8,14)	(35,40)	(50,55,62)	N(2,3)	U(40,60)	28
(8,15)	(10,12)	(20,22,25)	N(1,1)	U(40,60)	4.8
(9,10)	(8,12)	(15,20,25)	N(1,1)	U(40,60)	2.2
(9,11)	(12,15)	(20,28,30)	N(1,2)	U(40,60)	3.3
(9,12)	(15,18)	(25,30,32)	N(1,2)	U(40,60)	3.3
(9,13)	(15,20)	(25,30,36)	N(1,2)	U(40,60)	3.0
(9,14)	(10,12)	(20,22,25)	N(1,1)	U(40,60)	2.6
(9,15)	(4,8)	(10,20,30)	N(0,1)	U(40,60)	1
(10,11)	(4,6)	(10,20,26)	N(0,1)	U(40,60)	0.9
(10,12)	(8,10)	(10,26,32)	N(1,3)	U(40,60)	2.0
(10,13)	(10,15)	(18,28,36)	N(1,2)	U(40,60)	3.2
(10,14)	(18,20)	(20,30,40)	N(2,1)	U(40,60)	3.1
(10,15)	(10,12)	(18,28,32)	N(2,1)	U(40,60)	2.6
(11,12)	(5,8)	(15,20,25)	N(1,1)	U(40,60)	0.8
(11,13)	(8,10)	(18,22,28)	N(1,2)	U(40,60)	1.1
(11,14)	(15,18)	(20,32,38)	N(1,3)	U(40,60)	3.3
(11,15)	(12,14)	(20,24,28)	N(2,3)	U(40,60)	2.8
(12,13)	(6,8)	(10,16,22)	N(1,1)	U(40,60)	0.6
(12,14)	(10,15)	(20,28,32))	N(1,2)	U(40,60)	2.7
(12,15)	(12,18)	(18,26,31)	N(2,1)	U(40,60)	2.8
(13,14)	(12,14)	(16,20,26)	N(2,1)	U(40,60)	2.8
(13,15)	(20,25)	(30,32,38)	N(3,1)	U(40,60)	5.2
(14,15)	(10,12)	(18,22,26)	N(2,2)	U(40,60)	2.0

Similarity with case I, using Algorithm 5.1—Hybrid intelligence algorithm, authors obtained the vehicle routing solution in column 7 from Tables 9–11, for the three models.

Table 9. Model I results by hybrid intelligence algorithm for Case 2.

Genetic Algorithm Parameters			Chance Level	Model I		
pop	Max_gen	pc pm	Cr Pr	Best Solution	Risk	Consume Time
3	50	0.8 0.3	0.99 0.99	0-12-13-15-0 0-10-6-4-5-1-2-11-14-9-8-0 0-7-3-0	0.571448	296.519 s
30	50	0.8 0.3	0.99 0.99	0-4-14-5-13-0 0-10-1-2-6-0 0-7-9-8-11-15-12-2-0	0.372853	2051.57 s
100	50	0.8 0.3	0.99 0.99	0-8-6-11-0 0-10-1-2-13-12-9-15-3-0 0-14-7-0	0.129406	7010.85 s

Table 10. Model II results by hybrid intelligence algorithm for Case 2.

Genetic Algorithm Parameters			Chance Level	Model II		
pop	**Max_gen**	**pc pm**	**Cr Pr**	**Best Solution**	**Cost**	**Consume Time**
3	50	0.8 0.3	0.99 0.99	0-12-13-15-0 0-10-6-4-5-1-2-11-14-9-8-0 0-7-3-0	3658.17	579.293 s
30	50	0.8 0.3	0.99 0.99	0-8-6-0 0-11-10-1-2-0 0-13-12-9-15-3-5-4-14-7-0	834.382	3972.98 s
100	50	0.8 0.3	0.99 0.99	0-8-6-0 0-11-10-1-2-0 0-13-12-9-15-3-5-4-14-7-0	820.419	15,353.4 s

Table 11. Model III results by hybrid intelligence algorithm for Case 2.

Genetic Algorithm Parameters			Chance Level	Model III		
pop	**Max_gen**	**pc pm**	**Cr Pr**	**Best Solution**	**0.7Risk + 0.3 Cost**	**Consume Time**
3	50	0.8 0.3	0.99 0.99	0-1-9-3-0 0-13-8-6-14-12-11-5-2-15-7-0 0-10-4-0	0.982762	901.49 s
30	50	0.8 0.3	0.99 0.99	0-12-15-3-14-13-0 0-10-0 0-4-11-8-2-5-9-1-6-7-0	0.803568	6395.4 s
100	50	0.8 0.3	0.99 0.99	0-9-14-0 0-12-5-6-8-1-10-0 0-4-3-11-7-15-2-13-0	0.778511	20,173 s

As shown by the simulation results, the authors could draw a conclusion that although the size of the case increased, the feasible solution was still obtained. For the sake of demonstrating the efficiency for the proposed algorithm, it selected *pop_size* = 100, *max_gen* = 50 for the three models. To compare and analyze the algorithm convergence, the results are shown in Figure 10.

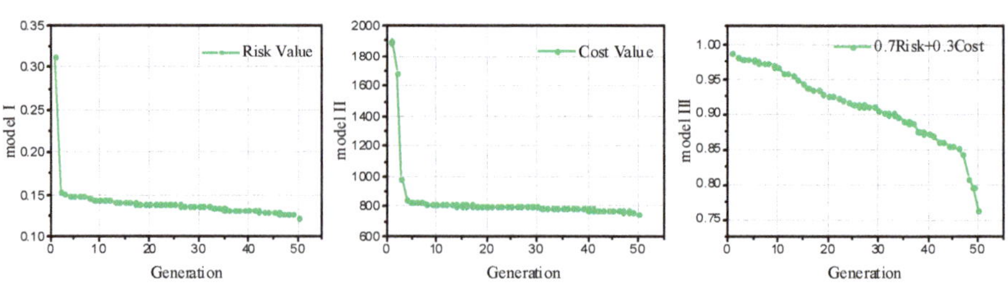

Figure 10. Convergence of GA for the three models.

Note that the convergence curve trend of model I and model II was same, in the first few generations, the decline was rapid, then optimization process was extremely slow from the 5th to 50th generation. This was because, as the number of simulations in each generation was up to 3000, it could get the optimal value. However, for model III, it could be optimized slowly because it calculated the normalized values for risk and cost. The curves demonstrated the algorithm feasibility from the computing angle.

The two cases are coded in C++ language, using software Visual Studio 2012, performed on a personal computer with an Intel(R) core i5 and 12G RAM, the total simulation time of case 1 and case 2 were 19 h and 16 h, respectively. In line with this, with an increase in the chromosome population and customer scale, the simulation time showed a clear exponential growth. Note that no matter what the chance level defined, it could present a reasonable solution in the end. In spite of the proposed algorithm being time-consuming, since it spent most time on the chromosome initialization, it could remarkably bring down objective values, and provide best solutions to participants in the supply chain.

7. Conclusions

Based on the typical characteristics (random and fuzzy) of risk and cost encountered during transportation, three chance-constrained programming models are presented. Additionally, in order to get more accurate simulation results, a hybrid intelligence algorithm integrating the fuzzy random algorithm and GA algorithm was designed. Finally, the model performance was verified by two numerical cases. The major contributions of this study are summarized as follows:

The risk model combining probability measure and credibility measure was developed for hazmat transportation. Most risk assessment models applied to hazmat so far see risk occurring as a stochastic event, which might lead to the prevention of accident, regardless of accident consequence, and might cause a terrible scenario happen. This study considered the ace length and population density as a fuzzy variable, and thus, modified the traditional risk from a practical point of view.

(1) The VRP models using uncertain theory were established by taking risk, cost, risk and cost, as the objective function for hazmat transportation, respectively. According to the risk assessment model, VRP models must be extended to chance-constrained. Different chance level has different solutions for the decision-maker, this can respond to changes in vehicle routing arrangements in time, when an accident occurs.

(2) In order to attain feasible solution for the models proposed by this paper, a hybrid intelligence algorithm integrating the fuzzy random algorithm and GA algorithm was designed. It included mass of simulation calculation; however, two numerical cases showed that the models were efficient, and the hybrid intelligent algorithm was steady, convergent for a small-size, and a middle-size problem.

Despite getting a reasonable optimal solution, it took too long a time, for example, the longest time was up to 30,799.8 s, almost 8.5 h. It is necessary to seek more intelligent and time-saving algorithms to solve the problem. It also takes more time to use this model to solve the vehicle routing problem in large-scale scenarios, which is beyond the acceptance period of the participants. Additionally, when the hazmat transportation is applied to multiple depots scenario, the model in this study would be more complex, new intelligent algorithms might need developing, which are all possible future directions.

Author Contributions: Conceptualization, L.Z. and N.C.; Writing—original draft, methodology, investigation, L.Z.; Writing—review & editing, Funding acquisition, N.C. All authors have read and agreed to the published version of the manuscript.

Funding: This research was funded by Fundamental Research Funds for the Central Universities, under grant number 300102239103 and Young Teachers Research Project for the Xi'an University of Technology, under grant number 256081921.

Conflicts of Interest: The authors declare no conflict of interest.

References

1. Zografos, K.G.; Androutsopoulos, K.N. Solving the bicriterion routing and scheduling problem for hazardous materials distribution. *Transp. Res. Part C Emerg. Technol.* **2010**, *18*, 713–726.
2. Barma, P.S.; Dutta, J.; Mukherjee, A. A 2-opt guided discrete antlion optimization algorithm for multi-depot vehicle problem. *Decis. Mak. Appl. Manag. Eng.* **2019**, *2*, 112–125.
3. Roy, A.; Manna, A.; Malty, S. A novel memetic genetic algorithm for solving traveling salesman problem based on multi-parent crossover technique. *Decis. Mak. Appl. Manag. Eng.* **2019**, *2*, 100–111. [CrossRef]
4. Cam, O.N.; Sezen, H.K. The formulation of a linear programming model for the vehicle routing problem in order to minimize idle time. *Decis. Making Appl. Manag. Eng.* **2020**, *3*, 22–29.
5. Holeczek, N. Hazardous materials truck transportation problems: A classification and state of the art literature review. *Transp. Res. Part D Transp. Environ.* **2019**, *69*, 305–328. [CrossRef]
6. Erkut, E.; Ingolfsson, A. Catastrophe avoidance models for hazardous materials route planning. *Transp. Sci.* **2000**, *34*, 165–179. [CrossRef]
7. Erkut, E.; Ingolfsson, A. Transport risk models for hazardous materials: Revisited. *Oper. Res. Lett.* **2005**, *33*, 81–89. [CrossRef]
8. Erkut, E.; Verter, V. A framework for hazardous materials transport risk assessment. *Risk Anal.* **1995**, *15*, 589–601. [CrossRef]
9. Jia, H.; Zhang, L.; Lou, X.; Cao, H. A fuzzy-stochastic constraint programming model for hazmat road transportation considering terrorism attacking. *Syst. Eng. Proc.* **2011**, *1*, 130–136. [CrossRef]
10. Li, R.; Leung, Y. Multi-objective route planning for dangerous goods using compromise programming. *J. Geogr. Syst.* **2011**, *13*, 249–271. [CrossRef]
11. Wei, M.Y.; Yu, L.; Li, X. Credibilistic Location-Routing Model for Hazardous Materials Transportation. *Int. J. Intell. Syst.* **2015**, *30*, 23–39. [CrossRef]
12. Cordeiro, F.G.; Bezerra, B.S.; Peixoto, A.S.P.; Ramos, R.A.R. Methodological aspects for modeling the environmental risk of transporting hazardous materials by road. *Transp. Res. Part D Transp. Environ.* **2016**, *44*, 105–121. [CrossRef]
13. Dantzig, G.B.; Ramser, J.H. The truck dispatching problem. *Manag. Sci.* **1959**, *6*, 80–91. [CrossRef]
14. Demir, E.; Bektaş, T.; Laporte, G. A review of recent research on green road freight transportation. *Eur. J. Oper. Res.* **2014**, *237*, 775–793. [CrossRef]
15. Lam, C.Y.; Cruz, A.M. Risk analysis for consumer-level utility gas and liquefied petroleum gas incidents using probabilistic network modeling: A case study of gas incidents in Japan. *Reliab. Eng. Syst. Saf.* **2019**, *185*, 198–212. [CrossRef]
16. Jabir, E.; Panicker, V.V.; Sridharan, R. Design and development of a hybrid ant colony-variable neighbourhood search algorithm for a multi-depot green vehicle routing problem. *Transp. Res. Part D Transp. Environ.* **2017**, *57*, 422–457. [CrossRef]
17. Bula, G.A.; Afsar, H.M.; Gonzalez, F.A.; Prodhon, C.; Velasco, N. Bi-objective vehicle routing problem for hazardous materials transportation. *J. Clean. Prod.* **2019**, *206*, 976–986. [CrossRef]
18. Poku-Boansi, M.; Tornyeviadzi, P.; Adarkwa, K.K. Next to suffer: Population exposure risk to hazardous material transportation in Ghana. *J. Transp. Health* **2018**, *10*, 203–212. [CrossRef]
19. Ghaderi, A.; Burdett, R.L. An integrated location and routing approach for transporting hazardous materials in a bi-modal transportation network. *Transp. Res. Part E Logist. Transp. Rev.* **2019**, *127*, 49–65. [CrossRef]
20. Qu, H.; Xu, J.; Wang, S.; Xu, Q. Dynamic Routing Optimization for Chemical Hazardous Material Transportation under Uncertainties. *Ind. Eng. Chem. Res.* **2018**, *57*, 10500–10517. [CrossRef]
21. Ghaleh, S.; Omidvari, M.; Nassiri, P.; Momeni, M.; Lavasani, S.M.M. Pattern of safety risk assessment in road fleet transportation of hazardous materials (oil materials). *Saf. Sci.* **2019**, *116*, 1–12. [CrossRef]
22. Deng, Y.; Chen, Y.; Zhang, Y.; Mahadevan, S. Short communication: Fuzzy Dijkstra algorithm for shortest path problem under uncertain environment. *Appl. Soft Comput.* **2012**, *12*, 1231–1237. [CrossRef]
23. Zero, L.; Bersani, C.; Paolucci, M.; Sacile, R. Two new approaches for the bi-objective shortest path with a fuzzy objective applied to HAZMAT transportation. *J. Hazard. Mater.* **2019**, *375*, 96–106. [CrossRef] [PubMed]

24. Li, G.; Zhai, X.; Li, Y.; Feng, B.; Wang, Z.; Zhang, M. Multi-objective optimization operation considering environment benefits and economy based on ant colony optimization for isolated micro-grids. *Energy Procedia* **2016**, *104*, e26. [CrossRef]
25. Moon, S.; Rosenblum, F.; Tan, Y.H.; Nesset, J.; Waters, K.E.; Finch, J.A. Examination of the United Nations self-heating test for sulphides. *Can. Metall. Q.* **2019**, *58*, 438–444. [CrossRef]
26. Hu, H.; Li, J.; Li, X. A credibilistic goal programming model for inventory routing problem with hazardous materials. *Soft Comput.* **2018**, *22*, 5803–5816. [CrossRef]
27. Du, J.M.; Lia, X.; Yua, L.; Danb, R.; Zhoua, J. Multi-depot vehicle routing problem for hazardous materials transportation: A fuzzy bilevel programming. *Inf. Sci.* **2017**, *399*, 201–218. [CrossRef]
28. Du, J.M.; Yu, L.; Li, X. Fuzzy multi-objective chance-constrained programming model for hazardous materials transportation. *Int. J. Gen. Syst.* **2016**, *45*, 286–310. [CrossRef]
29. Ma, C.; Li, Y.; He, R.; Wu, F.; Qi, B.; Ye, Q. Route optimisation models and algorithms for hazardous materials transportation under different environments. *Int. J. Bio Inspired Comput.* **2013**, *5*, 252–265.
30. Wei, M.Y.; Li, X.; Yu, L. Time-dependent fuzzy random location-scheduling programming for hazardous materials transportation. *Transp. Res. Part C Emerg. Technol.* **2015**, *57*, 146–165.
31. Ghaffari-Nasab, N.; Ahari, S.G.; Ghazanfari, M. A hybrid simulated annealing based heuristic for solving the location-routing problem with fuzzy demands. *Sci. Iran.* **2013**, *20*, 919–930.
32. Xu, J.; Yan, F.; Li, S. Vehicle routing optimization with soft time windows in a fuzzy random environment. *Transp. Res. Part E Logist. Transp. Rev.* **2011**, *47*, 1075–1091. [CrossRef]
33. Hassan-Pour, H.A.; Mosadegh-Khah, M.; Tavakkoli-Moghaddam, R. Solving a multi-objective multi-depot stochastic location-routing problem by a hybrid simulated annealing algorithm. *Proc. Inst. Mech. Eng. Part B J. Eng. Manuf.* **2009**, *223*, 1045–1054. [CrossRef]
34. Ji, X.; Iwamura, K.; Shao, Z. New models for shortest path problem with fuzzy arc lengths. *Appl. Math. Model.* **2007**, *31*, 259–269. [CrossRef]
35. Hua, H.; Libc, X.; Zhang, Y.; Shang, C.; Zhang, S. Multi-objective location-routing model for hazardous material logistics with traffic restriction constraint in inter-city roads. *Comput. Ind. Eng.* **2019**, *128*, 861–876. [CrossRef]
36. Wang, Z.; Zhao, L.; Cao, N.; Yang, L.; Chen, M. Vehicle routing optimum model of hazardous materials transportation under fuzzy environment. *J. Intell. Fuzzy Syst.* **2016**, *31*, 3067–3074. [CrossRef]
37. Contreras, I.; Cordeau, J.F.; Laporte, G. Stochastic uncapacitated hub location. *Eur. J. Oper. Res.* **2011**, *212*, 518–528. [CrossRef]
38. Mohammadi, M.; Jolai, F.; Tavakkoli-Moghaddam, R. Solving a new stochastic multi-mode p-hub covering location problem considering risk by a novel multi-objective algorithm. *Appl. Math. Model.* **2013**, *37*, 10053–10073. [CrossRef]
39. Samanlioglu, F. A multi-objective mathematical model for the industrial hazardous waste location-routing problem. *Eur. J. Oper. Res.* **2013**, *226*, 332–340. [CrossRef]
40. Tas, D.; Dellaert, N.; van Woensel, T.; de Kok, T. Vehicle routing problem with stochastic travel times including soft time windows and service costs. *Comput. Oper. Res.* **2013**, *40*, 214–224. [CrossRef]
41. Bertazzi, L.; Bosco, A.; Guerriero, F.; Lagana, D. A stochastic inventory routing problem with stock-out. *Transp. Res. Part C Emerg. Technol.* **2013**, *27*, 89–107. [CrossRef]
42. Zheng, Y.; Liu, B. Fuzzy vehicle routing model with credibility measure and its hybrid intelligent algorithm. *Appl. Math. Comput.* **2006**, *176*, 673–683. [CrossRef]
43. Meng, Q.; Lee, D.H.; Cheu, R.L. Multiobjective vehicle routing and scheduling problem with time window constraints in hazardous material transportation. *J. Transp. Eng.* **2005**, *131*, 699–707. [CrossRef]
44. Zhou, Z.; Chu, F.; Che, A.; Zhou, M. Constraint and fuzzy logic-based optimization of hazardous material transportation via lane reservation. *IEEE Trans. Intell. Transp. Syst.* **2013**, *14*, 847–857. [CrossRef]
45. La, Z. Fuzzy sets. *Inf. Control* **1965**, *8*, 338–353.
46. Li, X.; Liu, B. A sufficient and necessary condition for credibility measures. *Int. J. Uncertain. Fuzziness Knowl. Based Syst.* **2006**, *15*, 43–52. [CrossRef]
47. Zadeh, L.A. Fuzzy sets as a basis for a theory of possibility. *Fuzzy Sets Syst.* **1978**, *1*, 3–28. [CrossRef]
48. Liu, B. *Uncertain Theory: An Introduction to Its Axiomatic Foundations*; Springer: Berlin, Germany, 2004.
49. Liu, B. Toward Fuzzy Optimization without Mathematical Ambiguity. *Fuzzy Optim. Decis. Mak.* **2002**, *1*, 43–63. [CrossRef]

50. Liu, B.; Liu, Y.K. Expected value of fuzzy variable and fuzzy expected value models. *IEEE Trans. Fuzzy Syst.* **2002**, *10*, 445–450.
51. Liu, B.; Liu, B. *Theory and Practice of Uncertain Programming*; Springer: Berlin, Germany, 2009.
52. Liu, Y.K.; Liu, B. Fuzzy Random Variables: A Scalar Expected Value Operator. *Fuzzy Optim. Decis. Mak.* **2003**, *2*, 143–160. [CrossRef]
53. Bektas, T.; Laporte, G. The Pollution-Routing Problem. *Transp. Res. Part B Methodol.* **2011**, *45*, 1232–1250. [CrossRef]
54. Liu, B.; Iwamura, K. Chance constrained programming with fuzzy parameters. *Fuzzy Sets Syst.* **1998**, *94*, 227–237. [CrossRef]
55. Liu, B.D. Fuzzy random chance-constrained programming. *IEEE Trans. Fuzzy Syst.* **2001**, *9*, 713–720.

symmetry

MDPI

Article

A Robust q-Rung Orthopair Fuzzy Einstein Prioritized Aggregation Operators with Application towards MCGDM

Muhammad Riaz [1], Hafiz Muhammad Athar Farid [1], Humaira Kalsoom [2] and Dragan Pamučar [3] and Yu-Ming Chu [4,*]

[1] Department of Mathematics, University of the Punjab, Lahore P.O. Box No. 54590, Pakistan; mriaz.math@pu.edu.pk (M.R.); hmatharfarid@gmail.com (H.M.A.F.)
[2] School of Mathematical Sciences, Zhejiang University, Hangzhou 310027, China; humaira87@zju.edu.cn
[3] Department of Logistics, University of Defence, 11000 Belgrade, Serbia; dragan.pamucar@va.mod.gov.rs
[4] Department of Mathematics, Huzhou University, Huzhou 313000, China
* Correspondence: chuyuming@zjhu.edu.cn

Received: 9 June 2020; Accepted: 22 June 2020; Published: 26 June 2020

Abstract: A q-rung orthopair fuzzy set (q-ROFS) provides a significant mechanism for managing symmetrical aspects in real life circumstances. The renowned distinguishing feature of q-ROFS is that the sum of the qth powers to each membership degree (MD) and non-membership degree (NMD) is less than or equal 1, and therefore the comprehensive uncertain space for q-ROF information is broader. Numerous researchers have suggested several aggregation operators based on q-ROFSs. In order to discuss prioritized relationship in the criterion and a smooth approximation of q-ROF information, we introduced q-rung orthopair fuzzy Einstein prioritized weighted averaging (q-ROFEPWA) operator and q-rung orthopair fuzzy Einstein prioritized weighted geometric (q-ROFEPWG) operator. Additionally, we presented a multi-criteria group decision making (MCGDM) technique based on q-rung orthopair fuzzy Einstein prioritized aggregation operators. These operators can evaluate the possible symmetric roles of the criterion that express the real phenomena of the problem. In order to investigate characteristic of suggested operators regarding the symmetry of attributes and their symmetrical roles under q-ROF information, we presented an application of Einstein prioritized aggregation operators. Finally, by comparing it with some other established representative MCGDM models, an illustrative example is provided to check the feasibility, efficiency and supremacy of the proposed technique.

Keywords: q-ROFNs; Einstein operators; prioritized aggregation operators; multi-criteria group decision making

1. Introduction

Issues concerning unstable situations typically arise in decision-making, but they are demanding because of the complex and difficult situation of modeling and manipulation that emerges with such uncertainties. In an attempt to solve complex real-world problems, methods widely used in classical mathematics are often not useful due to the different kinds of complexity and lack of clarity in these important issues. To deal with uncertainties and vagueness. Zadeh initiated fuzzy set theory [1], Atanassov [2] introduced intuitionistic fuzzy sets (IFSs) and Yager [3–5] presented the notion of Pythagorean fuzzy sets. Zhang [6] introduced bipolar fuzzy sets and relations.

Several researchers have analyzed implementations of fuzzy sets; Ali et al. [7], Ali [8], Chen et al. [9], Chi and Lui [10], Çağman et al. [11], Eraslan and Karaaslan [12], Feng et al. [13–16] presented some work about soft sets combined with fuzzy sets and rough sets, Garg and Arora [17–19]

introduced some aggregation operators (AOs) related to IFS, soft set and application related to MCDM, Kumar and Garg [20], Karaaslan [21], Liu et al. [22], Naeem et al. [23–25] introduced PFS with m-polar, Peng et al. [26–29] gave some results related to PFS, Riaz and Hashmi [30,31] presented a novel concept of linear diophantine fuzzy set , Riaz et al. [32], Riaz and Tehrim [33,34], Shabir and Naz [35], Wang et al. [36], Xu [37], Xu and Cai [38], Xu [39], Xu developed a number of AOs, based on IFSs [37], Ye [40,41], Zhang and Xu [42], Zhan et al. [43,44] presented some aggregation techniques and Zhang et al. [45–47] presented work of rough set, Riaz et al. [48,49] presented some AOs of q-ROFSs. Sharma et al. [50] and Sinani et al. [51] presented some work related to rough set theory.

Yager initiated the idea of q-ROFS as an extension of PFS [52], in which the sum of membership degree (MD) $\check{\mathfrak{p}}_A(\zeta)$ and non-membership degree (NMD) $\overline{\amalg}_A(\zeta)$ satisfy the condition $0 \leq (\check{\mathfrak{P}}_A(\zeta))^q + (\overline{\amalg}_A(\zeta))^q \leq 1, (q \geq 1)$. The degree of indeterminacy (ID) is given by $\pi_A(\zeta) = \sqrt[q]{(\check{\mathfrak{P}}^q_A(\zeta) + \overline{\amalg}^q_A(\zeta) - \check{\mathfrak{P}}^q_A(\zeta)\overline{\amalg}^q_A(\zeta))}$. There is no condition on q other than $q \geq 1$. Although q is real number, but if q is integral value, it is also very easy to predict the area from which MD and NMD are selected. We can easily check that 99% area is covered when we put $q = 10$ of unit square $[0,1] \times [0,1]$.

Aggregation operators (AOs) are effective tools, particularly in the multi-criteria group decision making (MCGDM) analysis, to merge all input arguments into one completely integrated value. Since Yager introduced the classic OWA operator, different varieties of AOs were studied and applied to various decision-making issues [53]. Yager developed many weighted average, weighted geometric and ordered weighted AOs based on PFSs. Grag [54] and Rahmana et al. [55] introduced some Einstein AOs on PFS. Khan et al. [56] initiated the concept of prioritized AOs and also Einstein prioritized [57] on PFS. However, there has indeed been very few research on AOs in the context of q-ROF. In the available literature, relying on the proposed operation of q-rung orthopair fuzzy numbers (q-ROFNs). Liu and Wang [58] have established several more basic q-ROF AOs. Liu and Liu [59] drawn-out the Bonferroni mean AOs to q-ROF environment. Zhao [60] introduced some hammy mean AOs to aggregate the q-ROFNs. The AOs suggested above for q-ROFNs claiming that the parameters is of the same level of severity. Even so, this assumption may not always be usable in several practical issues. In this article we are specifically exploring the MCGDM issue where a priority relationship occurs over the parameters. The criteria are at different priority stages. Consider the issue in which we pick a new car on the basis of safeness, cost, presence and performance measures. We are not willing to sacrifice safeness for cost-effectiveness. First, we consider the safety requirements, then we consider the cost and finally, we consider appearance and performance. There is a prioritization relationship over the criteria in this situation. Protection has a greater priority than costs. Cost has a higher priority than appearance and performance.

About the question: why have we been developing all this research? If we consider existing aggregation operators, they have not provided us with a smooth approximation. There are several types of groups of t-norms and t-norms that can be chosen to construct intersections and unions. Einstein sums and Einstein products are good alternatives to algebraic sums and algebraic products because they provide a very smooth approximation. If we have a case in which we have a prioritized relationship in criteria and we also have a smooth approximation, we use the proposed aggregation operators.

In the rest of this paper: Section 2 consists of key characteristics for fuzzy sets, IFSs and q-ROFSs. Section 3 introduces some newly aggregation operators (AOs) based on q-ROFSs and their characteristics. Section 4 provides the proposed methodology to deal MCGDM problems. In Section 5 we give a concrete example of the effectiveness and viability of the suggested approach and also present comparison analysis with other techniques. Finally, whole paper is summarized in Section 6.

2. Preliminaries

In 1986, Atanassov developed the concept of IFS as a generalization of Zadeh's fuzzy set, and it should be noted that IFS is an important way of dealing with vagueness and lack of consensus.

Definition 1. *Let $\Psi = (\zeta_1, \zeta_2, \ldots \zeta_n)$ be a finite set, then an IFS, $\check{J}$ in Ψ can described as follows:*

$$\check{J} = \{< \zeta, \check{\mathfrak{P}}_{\check{J}}(\zeta), \overline{\Pi}_{\check{J}}(\zeta) >: \zeta \in \Psi\} \tag{1}$$

where $\check{\mathfrak{P}}_{\check{J}}(\zeta)$ and $\overline{\Pi}_{\check{J}}(\zeta)$ are mappings from Ψ to $[0,1]$, $\check{\mathfrak{P}}_{\check{J}}(\zeta)$ is called MD and $\overline{\Pi}_{\check{J}}(\zeta)$ is called NMD with conditions, $0 \leq \check{\mathfrak{P}}_{\check{J}}(\zeta) \leq 1$, $0 \leq \overline{\Pi}_{\check{J}}(\zeta) \leq 1$ and $0 \leq \check{\mathfrak{P}}_{\check{J}}(\zeta) + \overline{\Pi}_{\check{J}}(\zeta) \leq 1$, $\forall \zeta \in \Psi$. $\pi_{\check{J}}(\zeta) = 1 - (\check{\mathfrak{P}}_{\check{J}}(\zeta) + \overline{\Pi}_{\check{J}}(\zeta))$ is called ID of $\check{J}$ in Ψ. In addition, $0 \leq \pi_{\check{J}}(\zeta) \leq 1 \; \forall \zeta \in \Psi$.

Since IFS meets the limitations that the sum of its MD and NMD would be less than or equal to 1. Fortunately, the DM can handle the scenario in which the sum of MD and NMD is higher than unity in complex decision-making problem. Therefore, Yager introduced the concept of PFS to resolve this situation, which satisfies the constraints that the square sum of its MD and NMD should be less than or equal to 1.

Definition 2. *Let $\Psi = (\zeta_1, \zeta_2, \ldots \zeta_n)$ be a finite set, then an PFS, $\check{P}$ in Ψ can described as follows:*

$$\check{P} = \{< \zeta, \check{\mathfrak{P}}_{\check{P}}(\zeta), \overline{\Pi}_{\check{P}}(\zeta) >: \zeta \in \Psi\} \tag{2}$$

where $\check{\mathfrak{P}}_{\check{P}}(\zeta)$ and $\overline{\Pi}_{\check{P}}(\zeta)$ are mappings from Ψ to $[0,1]$, $\check{\mathfrak{P}}_{\check{P}}(\zeta)$ is called MD and $\overline{\Pi}_{\check{P}}(\zeta)$ is called NMD with conditions, $0 \leq \check{\mathfrak{P}}_{\check{P}}(\zeta) \leq 1$, $0 \leq \overline{\Pi}_{\check{P}}(\zeta) \leq 1$ and $0 \leq \check{\mathfrak{P}}^2_{\check{P}}(\zeta) + \overline{\Pi}^2_{\check{P}}(\zeta) \leq 1$, $\forall \zeta \in \Psi$. $\pi_{\check{P}}(\zeta) = \sqrt{1 - (\check{\mathfrak{P}}^2_{\check{P}}(\zeta) + \overline{\Pi}^2_{\check{P}}(\zeta))}$ is called ID of $\check{P}$ in Ψ. In addition, $0 \leq \pi_{\check{P}}(\zeta) \leq 1 \; \forall \zeta \in \Psi$.

There is still a problem with DM's question as to whether the square sum of MD and NMD is greater than one. To solve this problem, again Yager initiated the idea of q-ROFS in which the sum of qth power of MD and NMD is less or equal to 1.

Definition 3. *Let $\Psi = (\zeta_1, \zeta_2, \ldots \zeta_n)$ be a finite universal set, then a q-ROFS, $\check{H}$ in Ψ can described as follows:*

$$\check{H} = \{< \zeta, \check{\mathfrak{P}}_{\check{H}}(\zeta), \overline{\Pi}_{\check{H}}(\zeta) >: \zeta \in \Psi\} \tag{3}$$

where $\check{\mathfrak{P}}_{\check{H}}(\zeta)$ and $\overline{\Pi}_{\check{H}}(\zeta)$ are mappings from Ψ to $[0,1]$, $\check{\mathfrak{P}}_{\check{H}}(\zeta)$ is called MD and $\overline{\Pi}_{\check{H}}(\zeta)$ is called NMD with conditions, $0 \leq \check{\mathfrak{P}}_{\check{H}}(\zeta) \leq 1$, $0 \leq \overline{\Pi}_{\check{H}}(\zeta) \leq 1$ and $0 \leq \check{\mathfrak{P}}^q_{\check{H}}(\zeta) + \overline{\Pi}^q_{\check{H}}(\zeta) \leq 1 \; q \geq 1$, $\forall \zeta \in \Psi$. $\pi_{\check{H}}(\zeta) = \sqrt[q]{1 - (\check{\mathfrak{P}}^q_{\check{H}}(\zeta) + \overline{\Pi}^q_{\check{H}}(\zeta))}$ is called ID of $\check{H}$ in Ψ. In addition, $0 \leq \pi_{\check{H}}(\zeta) \leq 1 \; \forall \zeta \in \Psi$. For each $\zeta \in \Psi$, a basic element of the form $\langle \check{\mathfrak{P}}_{\check{H}}(\zeta), \overline{\Pi}_{\check{H}}(\zeta) \rangle$ in a q-ROFS, denoted by $\ddot{\mathfrak{S}}$, is called q-ROFN. It could be given as $\ddot{\mathfrak{S}} = \langle \check{\mathfrak{P}}_{\check{H}}, \overline{\Pi}_{\check{H}} \rangle$.

Liu further suggested to aggregate the q-ROFN with the following operational rules.

Definition 4 ([58]). *Let $\ddot{\mathfrak{S}}_1 = \langle \check{\mathfrak{P}}_1, \overline{\Pi}_1 \rangle$ and $\ddot{\mathfrak{S}}_2 = \langle \check{\mathfrak{P}}_2, \overline{\Pi}_2 \rangle$ be q-ROFNs. Then*

$$\overline{\ddot{\mathfrak{S}}_1} = \langle \overline{\Pi}_1, \check{\mathfrak{P}}_1 \rangle \tag{4}$$

$$\ddot{\mathfrak{S}}_1 \vee \ddot{\mathfrak{S}}_2 = \langle max\{\check{\mathfrak{P}}_1, \overline{\Pi}_1\}, min\{\check{\mathfrak{P}}_2, \overline{\Pi}_2\} \rangle \tag{5}$$

$$\ddot{\mathfrak{S}}_1 \wedge \ddot{\mathfrak{S}}_2 = \langle min\{\check{\mathfrak{P}}_1, \overline{\Pi}_1\}, max\{\check{\mathfrak{P}}_2, \overline{\Pi}_2\} \rangle \tag{6}$$

$$\ddot{\mathfrak{S}}_1 \oplus \ddot{\mathfrak{S}}_2 = \langle \sqrt[q]{(\check{\mathfrak{P}}^q_1 + \check{\mathfrak{P}}^q_2 - \check{\mathfrak{P}}^q_1 \check{\mathfrak{P}}^q_2)}, \overline{\Pi}_1 \overline{\Pi}_2 \rangle \tag{7}$$

$$\ddot{\mathfrak{S}}_1 \otimes \ddot{\mathfrak{S}}_2 = \langle \check{\mathfrak{P}}_1 \check{\mathfrak{P}}_2, \sqrt[q]{(\overline{\Pi}^q_1 + \overline{\Pi}^q_2 - \overline{\Pi}^q_1 \overline{\Pi}^q_2)} \rangle \tag{8}$$

$$\sigma \ddot{\mathfrak{S}}_1 = \langle \sqrt[q]{1 - (1 - \check{\mathfrak{P}}^q_1)^\sigma}, \overline{\Pi}^\sigma_1 \rangle \tag{9}$$

$$\ddot{\mathfrak{S}}_1^{\sigma} = \langle \check{\mathfrak{P}}_1^{\sigma}, \sqrt[q]{1-(1-\overline{\Pi}_1^q)^{\sigma}} \rangle \quad (10)$$

Definition 5. *Suppose $\widetilde{\mathfrak{R}} = \langle \check{\mathfrak{P}}, \overline{\Pi} \rangle$ is a q-ROFN, then a score function $\mathfrak{E}$ of $\widetilde{\mathfrak{R}}$ is defined as*

$$\mathfrak{E}(\widetilde{\mathfrak{R}}) = \check{\mathfrak{P}}^q - \overline{\Pi}^q$$

$\mathfrak{E}(\widetilde{\mathfrak{R}}) \in [-1, 1]$. *The score of a q-ROFN defines its ranking i.e., high score defines high preference of q-ROFN. However, score function is not useful in many cases of q-ROFN. For example, let us consider $\ddot{\mathfrak{S}}_1 = \langle 0.6138, 0.2534 \rangle$ and $\ddot{\mathfrak{S}}_2 = \langle 0.7147, 0.4453 \rangle$ are two q-ROFN, if we take value of q is 2. Then $\mathfrak{E}(\ddot{\mathfrak{S}}_1) = 0.3125 = \mathfrak{E}(\ddot{\mathfrak{S}}_2)$ i.e., score function of $\ddot{\mathfrak{S}}_1$ and $\ddot{\mathfrak{S}}_2$ are same. Therefore, to compare the q-ROFNs, it is not necessary to rely on the score function. We add a further method, the accuracy function, to solve this issue.*

Definition 6. *Suppose $\widetilde{\mathfrak{R}} = \langle \check{\mathfrak{P}}, \overline{\Pi} \rangle$ is a q-ROFN, then an accuracy function $\mathfrak{R}$ of $\widetilde{\mathfrak{R}}$ is defined as*

$$\mathfrak{R}(\widetilde{\mathfrak{R}}) = \check{\mathfrak{P}}^q + \overline{\Pi}^q$$

$\mathfrak{R}(\widetilde{\mathfrak{R}}) \in [0, 1]$. *The high value of accuracy degree $\mathfrak{R}(\widetilde{\mathfrak{R}})$ defines high preference of $\widetilde{\mathfrak{R}}$.*

Again consider $\ddot{\mathfrak{S}}_1 = \langle 0.6138, 0.2534 \rangle$ and $\ddot{\mathfrak{S}}_2 = \langle 0.7147, 0.4453 \rangle$ two q-ROFNs. Then their accuracy functions are $\mathfrak{R}(\ddot{\mathfrak{S}}_1) = 0.4410$ and $\mathfrak{R}(\ddot{\mathfrak{S}}_2) = 0.4410$, so by accuracy function we have $\ddot{\mathfrak{S}}_1 < \ddot{\mathfrak{S}}_2$.

Definition 7. *Let $¥ = \langle \check{\mathfrak{P}}_{¥}, \overline{\Pi}_{¥} \rangle$ and $\mathfrak{M} = \langle \check{\mathfrak{P}}_{\mathfrak{M}}, \overline{\Pi}_{\mathfrak{M}} \rangle$ are q-ROFNs, and $\mathfrak{E}(¥), \mathfrak{E}(\mathfrak{M})$ are the score function of ¥ and $\mathfrak{M}$, and $\mathfrak{R}(¥), \mathfrak{R}(\mathfrak{M})$ are the accuracy function of ¥ and $\mathfrak{M}$, then*

(1) If $\mathfrak{E}(¥) > \mathfrak{E}(\mathfrak{M})$, then $¥ > \mathfrak{M}$
(2) If $\mathfrak{E}(¥) = \mathfrak{E}(\mathfrak{M})$, then

if $\mathfrak{R}(¥) > \mathfrak{R}(\mathfrak{M})$ then $¥ > \mathfrak{M}$,
if $\mathfrak{R}(¥) = \mathfrak{R}(\mathfrak{M})$, then $¥ = \mathfrak{M}$.

It should always be noticed that the value of score function is between –1 and 1. We introduce another score function, to support the following research, $\breve{\Xi}(\mathfrak{R}) = \frac{1+\check{\mathfrak{P}}_{\mathfrak{R}}^q - \overline{\Pi}_{\mathfrak{R}}^q}{2}$. We can see that $0 \le \breve{\Xi}(\mathfrak{R}) \le 1$. This new score function satisfies all properties of score function defined by Yager [52].

2.1. The Study's Motivation and Intense Focus

In this subsection, we put a light on the scope, motivation and novelty of proposed work.

1. This article covers two main issues: the theoretical model of the problem and the application of decision-making.
2. The proposed models of aggregated operators are credible, valid, versatile and better than the rest to others because they will be based on the generalized q-ROFN structure. If the suggested operators are used in the context of IFNs or PFNs, the results will be ambiguous leading to the decrease of information in the inputs. This loss is due to restrictions on membership and non-membership of IFNs and PFNs. (see Figure 1). The IFNs and PFNs become special cases of q-ROFNs when $q = 1$ and $q = 2$ respectively.
3. The main objective is to establish strong relationships with the multi-criteria decision-making issues between the proposed operators. The application shall communicate the effectiveness, interpretation and motivation of the proposed aggregated operators.
4. This research fills the research gap and provides us a wide domain for the input data selection in medical, business, artificial intelligence, agriculture, and engineering. We can tackle those problems which contain ambiguity and uncertainty due to its limitations. The results obtained by using proposed operators and q-ROFNs will be superior and profitable in decision-making techniques.

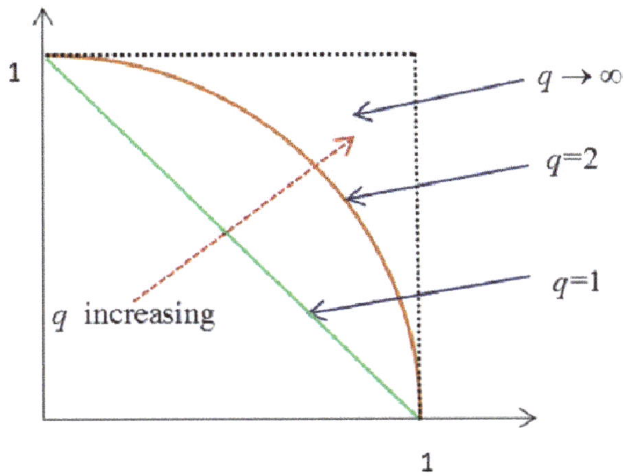

Figure 1. Graphical comparison between IF-value, PF-value and q-ROF-value.

For q-ROFNs, Riaz et al. [48] introduced the Einstein operation and studied the desirable properties of these operations. with the help of these operation they developed q-ROFEWA and q-ROFEWG operators.

Definition 8 ([48]). *Let $\ddot{\mathfrak{S}}_1 = \langle \check{\mathfrak{P}}_1, \overline{\Pi}_1 \rangle$ and $\ddot{\mathfrak{S}}_2 = \langle \check{\mathfrak{P}}_2, \overline{\Pi}_2 \rangle$ be q-ROFNs, $\mathfrak{w} > 0$ be real number, then*

$$\overline{\ddot{\mathfrak{S}}_1} = \langle \overline{\Pi}_1, \check{\mathfrak{P}}_1 \rangle \tag{11}$$

$$\ddot{\mathfrak{S}}_1 \vee_\epsilon \ddot{\mathfrak{S}}_2 = \langle max\{\check{\mathfrak{P}}_1, \check{\mathfrak{P}}_2\}, min\{\overline{\Pi}_1, \overline{\Pi}_2\} \rangle \tag{12}$$

$$\ddot{\mathfrak{S}}_1 \wedge_\epsilon \ddot{\mathfrak{S}}_2 = \langle min\{\check{\mathfrak{P}}_1, \check{\mathfrak{P}}_2\}, max\{\overline{\Pi}_1, \overline{\Pi}_2\} \rangle \tag{13}$$

$$\ddot{\mathfrak{S}}_1 \otimes_\epsilon \ddot{\mathfrak{S}}_2 = \left\langle \frac{\check{\mathfrak{P}}_1 ._\epsilon \check{\mathfrak{P}}_2}{\sqrt[q]{1 + (1 - \check{\mathfrak{P}}_1^q) ._\epsilon (1 - \check{\mathfrak{P}}_2^q)}}, \sqrt[q]{\frac{\overline{\Pi}_1^q + \overline{\Pi}_2^q}{1 + \overline{\Pi}_1^q ._\epsilon \overline{\Pi}_2^q}} \right\rangle \tag{14}$$

$$\ddot{\mathfrak{S}}_1 \oplus_\epsilon \ddot{\mathfrak{S}}_2 = \left\langle \sqrt[q]{\frac{\check{\mathfrak{P}}_1^q + \overline{\Pi}_2^q}{1 + \check{\mathfrak{P}}_1^q ._\epsilon \check{\mathfrak{P}}_2^q}}, \frac{\overline{\Pi}_1 ._\epsilon \overline{\Pi}_2}{\sqrt[q]{1 + (1 - \overline{\Pi}_1^q) ._\epsilon (1 - \overline{\Pi}_2^q)}} \right\rangle \tag{15}$$

$$\mathfrak{w} ._\epsilon \ddot{\mathfrak{S}}_1 = \left\langle \sqrt[q]{\frac{(1 + (\check{\mathfrak{P}}_1)^q)^{\mathfrak{w}} - (1 - (\check{\mathfrak{P}}_1)^q)^{\mathfrak{w}}}{(1 + (\check{\mathfrak{P}}_1)^q)^{\mathfrak{w}} + (1 - (\check{\mathfrak{P}}_1)^q)^{\mathfrak{w}}}}, \frac{\sqrt[q]{2}(\overline{\Pi}_1)^{\mathfrak{w}}}{\sqrt[q]{(2 - (\check{\mathfrak{P}}_1)^q)^{\mathfrak{w}} + ((\overline{\Pi}_1)^q)^{\mathfrak{w}}}} \right\rangle \tag{16}$$

$$\ddot{\mathfrak{S}}_1^{\mathfrak{w}} = \left\langle \frac{\sqrt[q]{2}(\check{\mathfrak{P}}_1)^{\mathfrak{w}}}{\sqrt[q]{(2 - (\check{\mathfrak{P}}_1)^q)^{\mathfrak{w}} + ((\check{\mathfrak{P}}_1)^q)^{\mathfrak{w}}}}, \sqrt[q]{\frac{(1 + (\overline{\Pi}_1)^q)^{\mathfrak{w}} - (1 - (\overline{\Pi}_1)^q)^{\mathfrak{w}}}{(1 + (\overline{\Pi}_1)^q)^{\mathfrak{w}} + (1 - (\overline{\Pi}_1)^q)^{\mathfrak{w}}}} \right\rangle \tag{17}$$

Theorem 1 ([48]). *Let $\ddot{\mathfrak{S}}_1$ and $\ddot{\mathfrak{S}}_2$ be q-ROFNs and $\mathfrak{w}, \mathfrak{w}_1, \mathfrak{w}_2 \geq 0$ be any real number, then*

(i) $\ddot{\mathfrak{S}}_2 \otimes_\epsilon \ddot{\mathfrak{S}}_1 = \ddot{\mathfrak{S}}_1 \otimes_\epsilon \ddot{\mathfrak{S}}_2$
(ii) $\ddot{\mathfrak{S}}_2 \oplus_\epsilon \ddot{\mathfrak{S}}_1 = \ddot{\mathfrak{S}}_1 \oplus_\epsilon \ddot{\mathfrak{S}}_2$
(iii) $(\ddot{\mathfrak{S}}_2 \otimes_\epsilon \ddot{\mathfrak{S}}_1)^{\mathfrak{w}} = \ddot{\mathfrak{S}}_2^{\mathfrak{w}} \otimes_\epsilon \ddot{\mathfrak{S}}_1^{\mathfrak{w}}$
(iv) $\mathfrak{w} ._\epsilon (\ddot{\mathfrak{S}}_1 \oplus_\epsilon \ddot{\mathfrak{S}}_2) = \mathfrak{w} ._\epsilon \ddot{\mathfrak{S}}_1 \oplus_\epsilon \mathfrak{w} ._\epsilon \ddot{\mathfrak{S}}_2$
(v) $\ddot{\mathfrak{S}}_1^{\mathfrak{w}_1} \otimes_\epsilon \ddot{\mathfrak{S}}_1^{\mathfrak{w}_2} = \ddot{\mathfrak{S}}_1^{\mathfrak{w}_1 + \mathfrak{w}_2}$
(vi) $\mathfrak{w}_1 ._\epsilon (\mathfrak{w}_2 ._\epsilon \ddot{\mathfrak{S}}_1) = (\mathfrak{w}_1 ._\epsilon \mathfrak{w}_2) ._\epsilon \ddot{\mathfrak{S}}_1$
(vii) $(\ddot{\mathfrak{S}}_1^{\mathfrak{w}_1})^{\mathfrak{w}_2} = (\ddot{\mathfrak{S}}_1)^{\mathfrak{w}_1 ._\epsilon \mathfrak{w}_2}$
(viii) $\mathfrak{w}_1 ._\epsilon \ddot{\mathfrak{S}}_1 \oplus_\epsilon \mathfrak{w}_2 = (\mathfrak{w}_1 + \mathfrak{w}_2) ._\epsilon \ddot{\mathfrak{S}}_1$

Definition 9 ([48]). *Let $\ddot{\mathfrak{S}}_p = \langle \check{\mathfrak{P}}_p, \overline{\text{II}}_p \rangle$ be the family of q-ROFNs and (q-ROFEWA): $\Lambda^n \rightarrow \Lambda$ if,*

$$\begin{aligned} q\text{-}ROFEWA(\ddot{\mathfrak{S}}_1, \ddot{\mathfrak{S}}_2, \ldots, \ddot{\mathfrak{S}}_n) &= \sum_{s=1}^{n} \check{\mathcal{Z}}_s \ddot{\mathfrak{S}}_s \\ &= \check{\mathcal{Z}}_{1 \cdot \epsilon} \ddot{\mathfrak{S}}_1 \oplus_\epsilon \check{\mathcal{Z}}_{2 \cdot \epsilon} \ddot{\mathfrak{S}}_2 \oplus_\epsilon \ldots \oplus_\epsilon \check{\mathcal{Z}}_{n \cdot \epsilon} \ddot{\mathfrak{S}}_n \end{aligned}$$

where Λ is the assemblage q-ROFNs, and $\check{\mathcal{Z}} = (\check{\mathcal{Z}}_1, \check{\mathcal{Z}}_2, \ldots, \check{\mathcal{Z}}_n)^T$ is weight vector (WV) of $(\ddot{\mathfrak{S}}_1, \ddot{\mathfrak{S}}_2, \ldots, \ddot{\mathfrak{S}}_n)$, s.t $0 \leqslant \check{\mathcal{Z}}_s \leqslant 1$ and $\sum_{s=1}^{n} \check{\mathcal{Z}}_s = 1$. Then, the q-ROFEWA is called the q-rung orthopair fuzzy Einstein weighted averaging operator.

We can also consider q-ROFEWA by the following theorem by Einstein's operational laws of q-ROFNs.

Theorem 2 ([48]). *Let $\ddot{\mathfrak{S}}_p = \langle \check{\mathfrak{P}}_p, \overline{\text{II}}_p \rangle$ be the family of q-ROFNs, we can also find q-ROFEWA by*

$$q\text{-}ROFEWA(\ddot{\mathfrak{S}}_1, \ddot{\mathfrak{S}}_2, \ldots, \ddot{\mathfrak{S}}_n) = \left(\sqrt[q]{\frac{\prod_{s=1}^{n}(1+(\check{\mathfrak{P}}_s)^q)^{\check{\mathcal{Z}}_s} - \prod_{s=1}^{n}(1-(\check{\mathfrak{P}}_s)^q)^{\check{\mathcal{Z}}_s}}{\prod_{s=1}^{n}(1+(\check{\mathfrak{P}}_s)^q)^{\check{\mathcal{Z}}_s} + \prod_{s=1}^{n}(1-(\check{\mathfrak{P}}_s)^q)^{\check{\mathcal{Z}}_s}}}, \frac{\sqrt[q]{2}\prod_{s=1}^{n} \overline{\text{II}}_s^{\check{\mathcal{Z}}_s}}{\sqrt[q]{\prod_{s=1}^{n}(2-(\overline{\text{II}}_s)^q)^{\check{\mathcal{Z}}_s} + \prod_{s=1}^{n}((\overline{\text{II}}_s)^q)^{\check{\mathcal{Z}}_s}}} \right) \quad (18)$$

where $\check{\mathcal{Z}} = (\check{\mathcal{Z}}_1, \check{\mathcal{Z}}_2, \ldots, \check{\mathcal{Z}}_n)^T$ is WV of $(\ddot{\mathfrak{S}}_1, \ddot{\mathfrak{S}}_2, \ldots, \ddot{\mathfrak{S}}_n)$, s.t $0 \leqslant \check{\mathcal{Z}}_s \leqslant 1$ and $\sum_{s=1}^{n} \check{\mathcal{Z}}_s = 1$.

Definition 10 ([48]). *Let $\ddot{\mathfrak{S}}_p = \langle \check{\mathfrak{P}}_p, \overline{\text{II}}_p \rangle$ be the family of q-ROFNs and (q-ROFEWG): $\Lambda^n \rightarrow \Lambda$ if,*

$$\begin{aligned} q\text{-}ROFEWG(\ddot{\mathfrak{S}}_1, \ddot{\mathfrak{S}}_2, \ldots, \ddot{\mathfrak{S}}_n) &= \sum_{s=1}^{n} \ddot{\mathfrak{S}}_s^{\check{\mathcal{Z}}_s} \\ &= \ddot{\mathfrak{S}}_1^{\check{\mathcal{Z}}_1} \otimes_\epsilon \ddot{\mathfrak{S}}_2^{\check{\mathcal{Z}}_2} \otimes_\epsilon \ldots \otimes_\epsilon \ddot{\mathfrak{S}}_n^{\check{\mathcal{Z}}_n} \end{aligned}$$

where Λ is the set of q-ROFNs, and $\check{\mathcal{Z}} = (\check{\mathcal{Z}}_1, \check{\mathcal{Z}}_2, \ldots, \check{\mathcal{Z}}_n)^T$ is WV of $(\ddot{\mathfrak{S}}_1, \ddot{\mathfrak{S}}_2, \ldots, \ddot{\mathfrak{S}}_n)$, s.t $0 \leqslant \check{\mathcal{Z}}_s \leqslant 1$ and $\sum_{s=1}^{n} \check{\mathcal{Z}}_s = 1$. Then, the q-ROFEWG is called the q-rung orthopair fuzzy Einstein weighted geometric operator.

We can also consider q-ROFEWG by the following theorem by Einstein's operational laws of q-ROFNs.

Theorem 3 ([48]). *Let $\ddot{\mathfrak{S}}_p = \langle \check{\mathfrak{P}}_p, \overline{\text{II}}_p \rangle$ be the family of q-ROFNs. Then*

$$q\text{-}ROFEWG(\ddot{\mathfrak{S}}_1, \ddot{\mathfrak{S}}_2, \ldots, \ddot{\mathfrak{S}}_n) = \left(\frac{\sqrt[q]{2}\prod_{s=1}^{n} \check{\mathfrak{P}}_s^{\check{\mathcal{Z}}_s}}{\sqrt[q]{\prod_{s=1}^{n}(2-(\check{\mathfrak{P}}_s)^q)^{\check{\mathcal{Z}}_s} + \prod_{s=1}^{n}((\check{\mathfrak{P}}_s)^q)^{\check{\mathcal{Z}}_s}}}, \sqrt[q]{\frac{\prod_{s=1}^{n}(1+(\overline{\text{II}}_s)^q)^{\check{\mathcal{Z}}_s} - \prod_{s=1}^{n}(1-(\overline{\text{II}}_s)^q)^{\check{\mathcal{Z}}_s}}{\prod_{s=1}^{n}(1+(\overline{\text{II}}_s)^q)^{\check{\mathcal{Z}}_s} + \prod_{s=1}^{n}(1-(\overline{\text{II}}_s)^q)^{\check{\mathcal{Z}}_s}}} \right) \quad (19)$$

where $\check{\mathcal{Z}} = (\check{\mathcal{Z}}_1, \check{\mathcal{Z}}_2, \ldots, \check{\mathcal{Z}}_n)^T$ is WV of $(\ddot{\mathfrak{S}}_1, \ddot{\mathfrak{S}}_2, \ldots, \ddot{\mathfrak{S}}_n)$, s.t $0 \leqslant \check{\mathcal{Z}}_s \leqslant 1$ and $\sum_{s=1}^{n} \check{\mathcal{Z}}_s = 1$.

Definition 11 ([49]). *Let $\ddot{\mathfrak{S}}_p = \langle \check{\mathfrak{P}}_p, \overline{\text{II}}_p \rangle$ be the family of q-ROFNs, and $q - ROFPWA : \Lambda^n \rightarrow \Lambda$, be an n dimension mapping. If*

$$q\text{-}ROFPWA(\ddot{\mathfrak{S}}_1, \ddot{\mathfrak{S}}_2, \ldots \ddot{\mathfrak{S}}_n) = \left(\frac{\grave{\beth}_1}{\sum_{s=1}^{n} \grave{\beth}_s} \ddot{\mathfrak{S}}_1 \oplus \frac{\grave{\beth}_2}{\sum_{s=1}^{n} \grave{\beth}_s} \ddot{\mathfrak{S}}_2 \oplus \ldots, \oplus \frac{\grave{\beth}_n}{\sum_{s=1}^{n} \grave{\beth}_s} \ddot{\mathfrak{S}}_n \right) \quad (20)$$

then the mapping q-ROFPWA is called q-rung orthopair fuzzy prioritized weighted averaging (q-ROFPWA) operator, where $\grave{\beth}_j = \prod_{k=1}^{j-1} \breve{\Xi}(\ddot{\mathfrak{S}}_k)$ $(j = 2 \ldots, n)$, $\grave{\beth}_1 = 1$ and $\breve{\Xi}(\ddot{\mathfrak{S}}_k)$ is the score of kth q-ROFN.

Definition 12 ([49]). *Let $\ddot{\mathfrak{S}}_p = \langle \check{\mathfrak{P}}_p, \overline{\text{II}}_p \rangle$ be the family of q-ROFNs, and $q - ROFPWG : \Lambda^n \rightarrow \Lambda$, be an n dimension mapping. If*

$$q\text{-}ROFPWG(\ddot{\mathfrak{S}}_1, \ddot{\mathfrak{S}}_2, \ldots \ddot{\mathfrak{S}}_n) = \left(\ddot{\mathfrak{S}}_1^{\frac{\grave{\beth}_1}{\sum_{s=1}^{n} \grave{\beth}_s}} \otimes \ddot{\mathfrak{S}}_2^{\frac{\grave{\beth}_2}{\sum_{s=1}^{n} \grave{\beth}_s}} \otimes \ldots, \otimes \ddot{\mathfrak{S}}_n^{\frac{\grave{\beth}_n}{\sum_{s=1}^{n} \grave{\beth}_s}} \right) \quad (21)$$

then the mapping q-ROFPWG is called q-rung orthopair fuzzy prioritized weighted geometric (q-ROFPWG) operator, where $\breve{\beth}_j = \prod_{k=1}^{j-1} \breve{\Xi}(\ddot{\mathfrak{S}}_k)$ $(j = 2\ldots, n)$, $\breve{\beth}_1 = 1$ *and* $\breve{\Xi}(\ddot{\mathfrak{S}}_k)$ *is the score of* k^{th} *q-ROFN.*

2.2. Superiority and Comparison of q-ROFNs with Some Existing Theories

In this section , we discuss the supremacy and comparative analysis of q-ROFNs with several existing systems, such as fuzzy numbers (FNs), IFNs and PFNs. In the decision-making problem of using input data using FNs, we could never talk about the dissatisfaction of part of the alternative or DM's opinion. If we use IFNs and PFNs, then we can not take the MD and NMD with an open choice of the actual working situation. Constraints restricted them to limited criteria. For example $0.75 + 0.85 = 1.60 > 1$ and $0.75^2 + 0.85^2 = 1.285 > 1$, which contradicts the conditions of IFNs and PFNs. If we select $q = 3$ then for 3-ROFN the constraint implies that $0.75^3 + 0.85^3 = 0.614 < 1$. This criteria satisfy the fuzzy criteria and we can handle the decision-making input with wide domain. The Table 1 represents the brief comparison with advantages and limitations of q-ROFN with some exiting theories.

Table 1. Comparison of q-rung orthopair fuzzy set (q-ROFS) with some existing theories.

Set Theory	Truth Information	Falsity Information	Advantages	Limitations
Fuzzy sets [1]	✓	×	can handle uncertainty using fuzzy interval	do not give any information about the NMD in input data
Intuitionistic Fuzzy sets [2]	✓	✓	can handle uncertainty using MD and NMD	cannot deal with the problems satisfying $0 \leq \text{MD} + \text{NMD} > 1$
Pythagorean Fuzzy sets [4,5]	✓	✓	larger valuation space than IFNs	cannot deal with the problems satisfying $0 \leq \text{MD}^2 + \text{NMD}^2 > 1$
q-rung orthopair Fuzzy sets [52]	✓	✓	larger valuation space than IFNs and PFNs	cannot deal with the problems when MD = 1 and NMD = 1

3. q-Rung Orthopair Fuzzy Einstein Prioritized Aggregation Operators

Within this section, we present the notion of q-rung orthopair fuzzy Einstein prioritized weighted average (q-ROFEPWA) operator and q-rung orthopair fuzzy Einstein prioritized weighted geometric (q-ROFEPWG) operator. Then we discuss other attractive properties of proposed operators.

3.1. q-ROFEPWA Operator

Definition 13. *Let* $\ddot{\mathfrak{S}}_p = \langle \check{\mathfrak{P}}_p, \overline{\amalg}_p \rangle$ *be the family of q-ROFNs, and q-ROFEPWA:* $\Lambda^n \to \Lambda$, *be an n dimension mapping. If*

$$q\text{-}ROFEPWA(\ddot{\mathfrak{S}}_1, \ddot{\mathfrak{S}}_2, \ldots \ddot{\mathfrak{S}}_n) = \left(\frac{\breve{\beth}_1}{\sum_{j=1}^{n} \breve{\beth}_j} \cdot_\epsilon \ddot{\mathfrak{S}}_1 \oplus_\epsilon \frac{\breve{\beth}_2}{\sum_{j=1}^{n} \breve{\beth}_j} \cdot_\epsilon \ddot{\mathfrak{S}}_2 \oplus_\epsilon \ldots, \oplus_\epsilon \frac{\breve{\beth}_n}{\sum_{j=1}^{n} \breve{\beth}_j} \cdot_\epsilon \ddot{\mathfrak{S}}_n \right) \tag{22}$$

then the mapping q-ROFEPWA is called q-rung orthopair fuzzy Einstein prioritized weighted averaging (q-ROFEPWA) operator, where $\breve{\beth}_j = \prod_{k=1}^{j-1} \breve{\Xi}(\ddot{\mathfrak{S}}_k)$ $(j = 2\ldots, n)$, $\breve{\beth}_1 = 1$ *and* $\breve{\Xi}(\ddot{\mathfrak{S}}_k)$ *is the score of* k^{th} *q-ROFN.*

Based on Einstein operational rules, we can also consider q-ROFEPWA by the theorem below.

Theorem 4. *Let $\ddot{\mathfrak{S}}_p = \langle \check{\mathfrak{P}}_p, \overline{\amalg}_p \rangle$ be the family of q-ROFNs, we can also find q-ROFEPWA by*

$$\text{q-ROFEPWA}(\ddot{\mathfrak{S}}_1, \ddot{\mathfrak{S}}_2, \ldots, \ddot{\mathfrak{S}}_n) = \left(\sqrt[q]{\frac{\prod_{j=1}^{n}(1+(\check{\mathfrak{P}}_j)^q)^{\frac{\check{\beth}_j}{\sum_{j=1}^{n}\check{\beth}_j}} - \prod_{j=1}^{n}(1-(\check{\mathfrak{P}}_j)^q)^{\frac{\check{\beth}_j}{\sum_{j=1}^{n}\check{\beth}_j}}}{\prod_{j=1}^{n}(1+(\check{\mathfrak{P}}_j)^q)^{\frac{\check{\beth}_j}{\sum_{j=1}^{n}\check{\beth}_j}} + \prod_{j=1}^{n}(1-(\check{\mathfrak{P}}_j)^q)^{\frac{\check{\beth}_j}{\sum_{j=1}^{n}\check{\beth}_j}}}}, \frac{\sqrt[q]{2}\prod_{j=1}^{n}\overline{\amalg}_j^{\frac{\check{\beth}_j}{\sum_{j=1}^{n}\check{\beth}_j}}}{\sqrt[q]{\prod_{j=1}^{n}(2-(\overline{\amalg}_j)^q)^{\frac{\check{\beth}_j}{\sum_{j=1}^{n}\check{\beth}_j}} + \prod_{j=1}^{n}((\overline{\amalg}_j)^q)^{\frac{\check{\beth}_j}{\sum_{j=1}^{n}\check{\beth}_j}}}} \right) \tag{23}$$

where $\check{\beth}_j = \prod_{k=1}^{j-1} \check{\Xi}(\check{\ddot{\mathfrak{S}}}_k)$ $(j = 2 \ldots, n)$, $\check{\beth}_1 = 1$ and $\check{\Xi}(\check{\ddot{\mathfrak{S}}}_k)$ is the score of kth q-ROFN.

Proof. This theorem is proven using mathematical induction.

For $n = 2$

$$\text{q-ROFEPWA}(\ddot{\mathfrak{S}}_1, \ddot{\mathfrak{S}}_2) = \frac{\check{\beth}_1}{\sum_{j=1}^{n}\check{\beth}_j} \cdot_\epsilon \ddot{\mathfrak{S}}_1 \oplus_\epsilon \frac{\check{\beth}_2}{\sum_{j=1}^{n}\check{\beth}_j} \cdot_\epsilon \ddot{\mathfrak{S}}_2$$

As we know that both $\frac{\check{\beth}_1}{\sum_{j=1}^{n}\check{\beth}_j} \cdot_\epsilon \ddot{\mathfrak{S}}_1$ and $\frac{\check{\beth}_2}{\sum_{j=1}^{n}\check{\beth}_j} \cdot_\epsilon \ddot{\mathfrak{S}}_2$ are q-ROFNs, and also $\frac{\check{\beth}_1}{\sum_{j=1}^{n}\check{\beth}_j} \cdot_\epsilon \ddot{\mathfrak{S}}_1 \oplus_\epsilon \frac{\check{\beth}_2}{\sum_{j=1}^{n}\check{\beth}_j} \cdot_\epsilon \ddot{\mathfrak{S}}_2$ is q-ROFN.

$$\frac{\check{\beth}_1}{\sum_{j=1}^{n}\check{\beth}_j} \cdot_\epsilon \ddot{\mathfrak{S}}_1 = \left(\sqrt[q]{\frac{(1+(\check{\mathfrak{P}}_1)^q)^{\frac{\check{\beth}_1}{\sum_{j=1}^{n}\check{\beth}_j}} - (1-(\check{\mathfrak{P}}_1)^q)^{\frac{\check{\beth}_1}{\sum_{j=1}^{n}\check{\beth}_j}}}{(1+(\check{\mathfrak{P}}_1)^q)^{\frac{\check{\beth}_1}{\sum_{j=1}^{n}\check{\beth}_j}} + (1-(\check{\mathfrak{P}}_1)^q)^{\frac{\check{\beth}_1}{\sum_{j=1}^{n}\check{\beth}_j}}}}, \frac{\sqrt[q]{2}(\overline{\amalg}_1)^{\frac{\check{\beth}_1}{\sum_{j=1}^{n}\check{\beth}_j}}}{\sqrt[q]{(2-(\check{\mathfrak{P}}_1)^q)^{\frac{\check{\beth}_1}{\sum_{j=1}^{n}\check{\beth}_j}} + ((\overline{\amalg}_1)^q)^{\frac{\check{\beth}_1}{\sum_{j=1}^{n}\check{\beth}_j}}}} \right)$$

$$\frac{\check{\beth}_2}{\sum_{j=1}^{n}\check{\beth}_j} \cdot_\epsilon \ddot{\mathfrak{S}}_2 = \left(\sqrt[q]{\frac{(1+(\check{\mathfrak{P}}_2)^q)^{\frac{\check{\beth}_2}{\sum_{j=1}^{n}\check{\beth}_j}} - (1-(\check{\mathfrak{P}}_2)^q)^{\frac{\check{\beth}_2}{\sum_{j=1}^{n}\check{\beth}_j}}}{(1+(\check{\mathfrak{P}}_2)^q)^{\frac{\check{\beth}_2}{\sum_{j=1}^{n}\check{\beth}_j}} + (1-(\check{\mathfrak{P}}_2)^q)^{\frac{\check{\beth}_2}{\sum_{j=1}^{n}\check{\beth}_j}}}}, \frac{\sqrt[q]{2}(\overline{\amalg}_2)^{\frac{\check{\beth}_2}{\sum_{j=1}^{n}\check{\beth}_j}}}{\sqrt[q]{(2-(\check{\mathfrak{P}}_2)^q)^{\frac{\check{\beth}_2}{\sum_{j=1}^{n}\check{\beth}_j}} + ((\overline{\amalg}_2)^q)^{\frac{\check{\beth}_2}{\sum_{j=1}^{n}\check{\beth}_j}}}} \right)$$

Then q-ROFEPWA$(\ddot{\mathfrak{S}}_1, \ddot{\mathfrak{S}}_2)$

$$
\begin{aligned}
&= \frac{\check{\beth}_1}{\sum_{j=1}^{n}\check{\beth}_j} \cdot_\epsilon \ddot{\mathfrak{S}}_1 \oplus_\epsilon \frac{\check{\beth}_2}{\sum_{j=1}^{n}\check{\beth}_j} \cdot_\epsilon \ddot{\mathfrak{S}}_2 \\
&= \left(\sqrt[q]{\frac{(1+(\check{\mathfrak{P}}_1)^q)^{\frac{\check{\beth}_1}{\sum_{j=1}^{n}\check{\beth}_j}} - (1-(\check{\mathfrak{P}}_1)^q)^{\frac{\check{\beth}_1}{\sum_{j=1}^{n}\check{\beth}_j}}}{(1+(\check{\mathfrak{P}}_1)^q)^{\frac{\check{\beth}_1}{\sum_{j=1}^{n}\check{\beth}_j}} + (1-(\check{\mathfrak{P}}_1)^q)^{\frac{\check{\beth}_1}{\sum_{j=1}^{n}\check{\beth}_j}}}}, \frac{\sqrt[q]{2}(\overline{\amalg}_1)^{\frac{\check{\beth}_1}{\sum_{j=1}^{n}\check{\beth}_j}}}{\sqrt[q]{(2-(\check{\mathfrak{P}}_1)^q)^{\frac{\check{\beth}_1}{\sum_{j=1}^{n}\check{\beth}_j}} + ((\overline{\amalg}_1)^q)^{\frac{\check{\beth}_1}{\sum_{j=1}^{n}\check{\beth}_j}}}} \right) \\
&\oplus_\epsilon \left(\sqrt[q]{\frac{(1+(\check{\mathfrak{P}}_2)^q)^{\frac{\check{\beth}_2}{\sum_{j=1}^{n}\check{\beth}_j}} - (1-(\check{\mathfrak{P}}_2)^q)^{\frac{\check{\beth}_2}{\sum_{j=1}^{n}\check{\beth}_j}}}{(1+(\check{\mathfrak{P}}_2)^q)^{\frac{\check{\beth}_2}{\sum_{j=1}^{n}\check{\beth}_j}} + (1-(\check{\mathfrak{P}}_2)^q)^{\frac{\check{\beth}_2}{\sum_{j=1}^{n}\check{\beth}_j}}}}, \frac{\sqrt[q]{2}(\overline{\amalg}_2)^{\frac{\check{\beth}_2}{\sum_{j=1}^{n}\check{\beth}_j}}}{\sqrt[q]{(2-(\check{\mathfrak{P}}_2)^q)^{\frac{\check{\beth}_2}{\sum_{j=1}^{n}\check{\beth}_j}} + ((\overline{\amalg}_2)^q)^{\frac{\check{\beth}_2}{\sum_{j=1}^{n}\check{\beth}_j}}}} \right)
\end{aligned}
$$

$$
= \left(\sqrt[q]{\frac{\frac{(1+(\check{\mathfrak{P}}_1)^q)^{\frac{\check{\beth}_1}{\sum_{j=1}^{n}\check{\beth}_j}} - (1-(\check{\mathfrak{P}}_1)^q)^{\frac{\check{\beth}_1}{\sum_{j=1}^{n}\check{\beth}_j}}}{(1+(\check{\mathfrak{P}}_1)^q)^{\frac{\check{\beth}_1}{\sum_{j=1}^{n}\check{\beth}_j}} + (1-(\check{\mathfrak{P}}_1)^q)^{\frac{\check{\beth}_1}{\sum_{j=1}^{n}\check{\beth}_j}}} + \frac{(1+(\check{\mathfrak{P}}_2)^q)^{\frac{\check{\beth}_2}{\sum_{j=1}^{n}\check{\beth}_j}} - (1-(\check{\mathfrak{P}}_2)^q)^{\frac{\check{\beth}_2}{\sum_{j=1}^{n}\check{\beth}_j}}}{(1+(\check{\mathfrak{P}}_2)^q)^{\frac{\check{\beth}_2}{\sum_{j=1}^{n}\check{\beth}_j}} + (1-(\check{\mathfrak{P}}_2)^q)^{\frac{\check{\beth}_2}{\sum_{j=1}^{n}\check{\beth}_j}}}}{1 + \left(\frac{(1+(\check{\mathfrak{P}}_1)^q)^{\frac{\check{\beth}_1}{\sum_{j=1}^{n}\check{\beth}_j}} - (1-(\check{\mathfrak{P}}_1)^q)^{\frac{\check{\beth}_1}{\sum_{j=1}^{n}\check{\beth}_j}}}{(1+(\check{\mathfrak{P}}_1)^q)^{\frac{\check{\beth}_1}{\sum_{j=1}^{n}\check{\beth}_j}} + (1-(\check{\mathfrak{P}}_1)^q)^{\frac{\check{\beth}_1}{\sum_{j=1}^{n}\check{\beth}_j}}} \right) \cdot_\epsilon \left(\frac{(1+(\check{\mathfrak{P}}_2)^q)^{\frac{\check{\beth}_2}{\sum_{j=1}^{n}\check{\beth}_j}} - (1-(\check{\mathfrak{P}}_2)^q)^{\frac{\check{\beth}_2}{\sum_{j=1}^{n}\check{\beth}_j}}}{(1+(\check{\mathfrak{P}}_2)^q)^{\frac{\check{\beth}_2}{\sum_{j=1}^{n}\check{\beth}_j}} + (1-(\check{\mathfrak{P}}_2)^q)^{\frac{\check{\beth}_2}{\sum_{j=1}^{n}\check{\beth}_j}}} \right)}}, \right.
$$

$$
\left. \frac{\left(\frac{\sqrt[q]{2}(\overline{\amalg}_1)^{\frac{\check{\beth}_1}{\sum_{j=1}^{n}\check{\beth}_j}}}{\sqrt[q]{(2-(\overline{\amalg}_1)^q)^{\frac{\check{\beth}_1}{\sum_{j=1}^{n}\check{\beth}_j}} + ((\overline{\amalg}_1)^q)^{\frac{\check{\beth}_1}{\sum_{j=1}^{n}\check{\beth}_j}}}} \right) \cdot_\epsilon \left(\frac{\sqrt[q]{2}(\overline{\amalg}_2)^{\frac{\check{\beth}_2}{\sum_{j=1}^{n}\check{\beth}_j}}}{\sqrt[q]{(2-(\check{\mathfrak{P}}_2)^q)^{\frac{\check{\beth}_2}{\sum_{j=1}^{n}\check{\beth}_j}} + ((\overline{\amalg}_2)^q)^{\frac{\check{\beth}_2}{\sum_{j=1}^{n}\check{\beth}_j}}}} \right)}{\sqrt[q]{1 + \left(1 - \frac{2((\overline{\amalg}_1)^q)^{\frac{\check{\beth}_1}{\sum_{j=1}^{n}\check{\beth}_j}}}{(2-(\overline{\amalg}_1)^q)^{\frac{\check{\beth}_1}{\sum_{j=1}^{n}\check{\beth}_j}} + ((\overline{\amalg}_1)^q)^{\frac{\check{\beth}_1}{\sum_{j=1}^{n}\check{\beth}_j}}} \right) \cdot_\epsilon \left(1 - \frac{2((\overline{\amalg}_2)^q)^{\frac{\check{\beth}_2}{\sum_{j=1}^{n}\check{\beth}_j}}}{(2-(\overline{\amalg}_2)^q)^{\frac{\check{\beth}_2}{\sum_{j=1}^{n}\check{\beth}_j}} + ((\overline{\amalg}_2)^q)^{\frac{\check{\beth}_2}{\sum_{j=1}^{n}\check{\beth}_j}}} \right)}} \right)
$$

$$
\begin{aligned}
= &\left(\sqrt[q]{\frac{(1+(\check{\mathfrak{P}}_1)^q)^{\frac{\check{\beth}_1}{\sum_{j=1}^{n}\check{\beth}_j}} \cdot_\epsilon (1+(\check{\mathfrak{P}}_2)^q)^{\frac{\check{\beth}_2}{\sum_{j=1}^{n}\check{\beth}_j}} - (1-(\check{\mathfrak{P}}_1)^q)^{\frac{\check{\beth}_1}{\sum_{j=1}^{n}\check{\beth}_j}} \cdot_\epsilon (1-(\check{\mathfrak{P}}_2)^q)^{\frac{\check{\beth}_2}{\sum_{j=1}^{n}\check{\beth}_j}}}{(1+(\check{\mathfrak{P}}_1)^q)^{\frac{\check{\beth}_1}{\sum_{j=1}^{n}\check{\beth}_j}} \cdot_\epsilon (1+(\check{\mathfrak{P}}_2)^q)^{\frac{\check{\beth}_2}{\sum_{j=1}^{n}\check{\beth}_j}} + (1-(\check{\mathfrak{P}}_1)^q)^{\frac{\check{\beth}_1}{\sum_{j=1}^{n}\check{\beth}_j}} \cdot_\epsilon (1-(\check{\mathfrak{P}}_2)^q)^{\frac{\check{\beth}_2}{\sum_{j=1}^{n}\check{\beth}_j}}}}, \right. \\
&\left. \frac{\sqrt[q]{2}\left(\overline{\amalg}_1^{\frac{\check{\beth}_1}{\sum_{j=1}^{n}\check{\beth}_j}} \overline{\amalg}_2^{\frac{\check{\beth}_2}{\sum_{j=1}^{n}\check{\beth}_j}}\right)}{\sqrt[q]{(2-(\overline{\amalg}_1)^q)^{\frac{\check{\beth}_1}{\sum_{j=1}^{n}\check{\beth}_j}} \cdot_\epsilon (2-(\overline{\amalg}_2)^q)^{\frac{\check{\beth}_2}{\sum_{j=1}^{n}\check{\beth}_j}} + ((\overline{\amalg}_1)^q)^{\frac{\check{\beth}_1}{\sum_{j=1}^{n}\check{\beth}_j}} \cdot_\epsilon ((\overline{\amalg}_2)^q)^{\frac{\check{\beth}_2}{\sum_{j=1}^{n}\check{\beth}_j}}}} \right)
\end{aligned}
$$

which proves for $n = 2$.

Suppose the result is true for $n = k$, we have

$$
\begin{aligned}
q-ROFEWA(\ddot{\mathfrak{S}}_1, \ddot{\mathfrak{S}}_2, \ldots, \ddot{\mathfrak{S}}_k) &= \left(\frac{\check{\beth}_1}{\sum_{j=1}^{n}\check{\beth}_j} \cdot_\epsilon \ddot{\mathfrak{S}}_1 \oplus_\epsilon \frac{\check{\beth}_2}{\sum_{j=1}^{n}\check{\beth}_j} \cdot_\epsilon \ddot{\mathfrak{S}}_2 \oplus_\epsilon \ldots, \oplus_\epsilon \frac{\check{\beth}_k}{\sum_{j=1}^{n}\check{\beth}_j} \cdot_\epsilon \ddot{\mathfrak{S}}_k \right) \\
&= \left(\sqrt[q]{\frac{\prod_{j=1}^{k}(1+(\check{\mathfrak{P}}_j)^q)^{\frac{\check{\beth}_j}{\sum_{j=1}^{n}\check{\beth}_j}} - \prod_{j=1}^{k}(1-(\check{\mathfrak{P}}_j)^q)^{\frac{\check{\beth}_j}{\sum_{j=1}^{n}\check{\beth}_j}}}{\prod_{j=1}^{k}(1+(\check{\mathfrak{P}}_j)^q)^{\frac{\check{\beth}_j}{\sum_{j=1}^{n}\check{\beth}_j}} + \prod_{j=1}^{k}(1-(\check{\mathfrak{P}}_j)^q)^{\frac{\check{\beth}_j}{\sum_{j=1}^{n}\check{\beth}_j}}}}, \frac{\sqrt[q]{2}\prod_{j=1}^{k}\overline{\amalg}_j^{\frac{\check{\beth}_j}{\sum_{j=1}^{n}\check{\beth}_j}}}{\sqrt[q]{\prod_{j=1}^{k}(2-(\overline{\amalg}_j)^q)^{\frac{\check{\beth}_j}{\sum_{j=1}^{n}\check{\beth}_j}} + \prod_{j=1}^{k}((\overline{\amalg}_j)^q)^{\frac{\check{\beth}_j}{\sum_{j=1}^{n}\check{\beth}_j}}}} \right)
\end{aligned}
$$

Now we will prove for $n = k+1$,

$$
\begin{aligned}
q-ROFEPWA(\ddot{\mathfrak{S}}_1, \ddot{\mathfrak{S}}_2, \ldots, \ddot{\mathfrak{S}}_{k+1}) &= q-ROFEPWA(\ddot{\mathfrak{S}}_1, \ddot{\mathfrak{S}}_2, \ldots, \ddot{\mathfrak{S}}_k) \oplus_\epsilon \frac{\beth_{k+1}}{\sum_{j=1}^{k+1}\beth_j} \cdot_\epsilon \ddot{\mathfrak{S}}_{k+1} \\
&= \left(\frac{\beth_1}{\sum_{j=1}^{n}\beth_j} \cdot_\epsilon \ddot{\mathfrak{S}}_1 \oplus_\epsilon \frac{\beth_2}{\sum_{j=1}^{n}\beth_j} \cdot_\epsilon \ddot{\mathfrak{S}}_2 \oplus_\epsilon \ldots, \oplus_\epsilon \frac{\beth_k}{\sum_{j=1}^{n}\beth_j} \cdot_\epsilon \ddot{\mathfrak{S}}_k \right) \oplus_\epsilon \frac{\beth_{k+1}}{\sum_{j=1}^{k+1}\beth_j} \cdot_\epsilon \ddot{\mathfrak{S}}_{k+1} \\
&= \left(\sqrt[q]{\frac{\prod_{j=1}^{k}(1+(\breve{\mathfrak{P}}_j)^q)^{\frac{\beth_j}{\sum_{j=1}^{n}\beth_j}} - \prod_{j=1}^{k}(1-(\breve{\mathfrak{P}}_j)^q)^{\frac{\beth_j}{\sum_{j=1}^{n}\beth_j}}}{\prod_{j=1}^{k}(1+(\breve{\mathfrak{P}}_j)^q)^{\frac{\beth_j}{\sum_{j=1}^{n}\beth_j}} + \prod_{j=1}^{k}(1-(\breve{\mathfrak{P}}_j)^q)^{\frac{\beth_j}{\sum_{j=1}^{n}\beth_j}}}}, \frac{\sqrt[q]{2}\prod_{j=1}^{k}\overline{\amalg}_j^{\frac{\beth_j}{\sum_{j=1}^{n}\beth_j}}}{\sqrt[q]{\prod_{j=1}^{k}(2-(\overline{\amalg}_j)^q)^{\frac{\beth_j}{\sum_{j=1}^{n}\beth_j}} + \prod_{j=1}^{k}((\overline{\amalg}_j)^q)^{\frac{\beth_j}{\sum_{j=1}^{n}\beth_j}}}} \right) \\
&\oplus_\epsilon \left(\sqrt[q]{\frac{(1+(\breve{\mathfrak{P}}_{k+1})^q)^{\frac{\beth_{k+1}}{\sum_{j=1}^{k+1}\beth_j}} - (1-(\breve{\mathfrak{P}}_{k+1})^q)^{\frac{\beth_{k+1}}{\sum_{j=1}^{k+1}\beth_j}}}{(1+(\breve{\mathfrak{P}}_{k+1})^q)^{\frac{\beth_{k+1}}{\sum_{j=1}^{k+1}\beth_j}} + (1-(\breve{\mathfrak{P}}_{k+1})^q)^{\frac{\beth_{k+1}}{\sum_{j=1}^{k+1}\beth_j}}}}, \frac{\sqrt[q]{2}(\overline{\amalg}_{k+1})^{\frac{\beth_{k+1}}{\sum_{j=1}^{k+1}\beth_j}}}{\sqrt[q]{(2-(\breve{\mathfrak{P}}_{k+1})^q)^{\frac{\beth_{k+1}}{\sum_{j=1}^{k+1}\beth_j}} + ((\overline{\amalg}_{k+1})^q)^{\frac{\beth_{k+1}}{\sum_{j=1}^{k+1}\beth_j}}}} \right)
\end{aligned}
$$

$$
= \left(\sqrt[q]{\frac{\prod_{j=1}^{k}(1+(\breve{\mathfrak{P}}_j)^q)^{\frac{\beth_j}{\sum_{j=1}^{n}\beth_j}}(1+(\breve{\mathfrak{P}}_{k+1})^q)^{\frac{\beth_{k+1}}{\sum_{j=1}^{k+1}\beth_j}} - \prod_{j=1}^{k}(1-(\breve{\mathfrak{P}}_j)^q)^{\frac{\beth_j}{\sum_{j=1}^{n}\beth_j}}(1-(\breve{\mathfrak{P}}_{k+1})^q)^{\frac{\beth_{k+1}}{\sum_{j=1}^{k+1}\beth_j}}}{\prod_{j=1}^{k}(1+(\breve{\mathfrak{P}}_j)^q)^{\frac{\beth_j}{\sum_{j=1}^{n}\beth_j}}(1+(\breve{\mathfrak{P}}_{k+1})^q)^{\frac{\beth_{k+1}}{\sum_{j=1}^{k+1}\beth_j}} + \prod_{j=1}^{k}(1-(\breve{\mathfrak{P}}_j)^q)^{\frac{\beth_j}{\sum_{j=1}^{n}\beth_j}}(1-(\breve{\mathfrak{P}}_{k+1})^q)^{\frac{\beth_{k+1}}{\sum_{j=1}^{k+1}\beth_j}}}}, \right.
$$

$$
\left. \frac{\sqrt[q]{2}\prod_{j=1}^{k}\overline{\amalg}_j^{\frac{\beth_j}{\sum_{j=1}^{n}\beth_j}}(\overline{\amalg}_{k+1})^{\frac{\beth_{k+1}}{\sum_{j=1}^{k+1}\beth_j}}}{\sqrt[q]{\prod_{j=1}^{k}(2-(\overline{\amalg}_j)^q)^{\frac{\beth_j}{\sum_{j=1}^{n}\beth_j}}(2-(\overline{\amalg}_j)^q)^{\frac{\beth_{k+1}}{\sum_{j=1}^{k+1}\beth_j}} + \prod_{j=1}^{k}((\overline{\amalg}_j)^q)^{\frac{\beth_j}{\sum_{j=1}^{n}\beth_j}}((\overline{\amalg}_j)^q)^{\frac{\beth_{k+1}}{\sum_{j=1}^{k+1}\beth_j}}}} \right)
$$

$$
= \left(\sqrt[q]{\frac{\prod_{j=1}^{k+1}(1+(\breve{\mathfrak{P}}_j)^q)^{\frac{\beth_j}{\sum_{j=1}^{n}\beth_j}} - \prod_{j=1}^{k+1}(1-(\breve{\mathfrak{P}}_j)^q)^{\frac{\beth_j}{\sum_{j=1}^{n}\beth_j}}}{\prod_{j=1}^{k+1}(1+(\breve{\mathfrak{P}}_j)^q)^{\frac{\beth_j}{\sum_{j=1}^{n}\beth_j}} + \prod_{j=1}^{k+1}(1-(\breve{\mathfrak{P}}_j)^q)^{\frac{\beth_j}{\sum_{j=1}^{n}\beth_j}}}}, \frac{\sqrt[q]{2}\prod_{j=1}^{k+1}\overline{\amalg}_j^{\frac{\beth_j}{\sum_{j=1}^{n}\beth_j}}}{\sqrt[q]{\prod_{j=1}^{k+1}(2-(\overline{\amalg}_j)^q)^{\frac{\beth_j}{\sum_{j=1}^{n}\beth_j}} + \prod_{j=1}^{k+1}((\overline{\amalg}_j)^q)^{\frac{\beth_j}{\sum_{j=1}^{n}\beth_j}}}} \right)
$$

thus the result holds for $s = k+1$. This proves the required result. □

Theorem 5. *Let $\ddot{\mathfrak{S}}_p = \langle \breve{\mathfrak{P}}_p, \overline{\amalg}_p \rangle$ be the family of q-ROFNs. Aggregated value using q-ROFEPWA operator is q-ROFN.*

Proof. Suppose $\mathcal{G}_s = \langle \breve{\mathfrak{P}}_s, \overline{\amalg}_s \rangle$ family of q-ROFNs. By definition of q-ROFN,

$$0 \le (\breve{\mathfrak{P}}_s)^q + (\overline{\amalg}_s)^q \le 1.$$

Therefore,

$$
\begin{aligned}
\frac{\prod_{s=1}^{n}(1+(\breve{\mathfrak{P}}_s)^q)^{\frac{\beth_s}{\sum_{s=1}^{n}\beth_s}} - \prod_{s=1}^{n}(1-(\breve{\mathfrak{P}}_s)^q)^{\frac{\beth_s}{\sum_{s=1}^{n}\beth_s}}}{\prod_{s=1}^{n}(1+(\breve{\mathfrak{P}}_s)^q)^{\frac{\beth_s}{\sum_{s=1}^{n}\beth_s}} + \prod_{s=1}^{n}(1-(\breve{\mathfrak{P}}_s)^q)^{\frac{\beth_s}{\sum_{s=1}^{n}\beth_s}}} &= 1 - \frac{2\prod_{s=1}^{n}(1-(\breve{\mathfrak{P}}_s)^q)^{\frac{\beth_s}{\sum_{s=1}^{n}\beth_s}}}{\prod_{s=1}^{n}(1+(\breve{\mathfrak{P}}_s)^q)^{\frac{\beth_s}{\sum_{s=1}^{n}\beth_s}} + \prod_{s=1}^{n}(1-(\breve{\mathfrak{P}}_s)^q)^{\frac{\beth_s}{\sum_{s=1}^{n}\beth_s}}} \\
&\le 1 - \prod_{s=1}^{n}(1-(\breve{\mathfrak{P}}_s)^q)^{\frac{\beth_s}{\sum_{s=1}^{n}\beth_s}} \le 1
\end{aligned}
$$

and

$$
\begin{aligned}
(1+(\check{\mathfrak{P}}_s)^q)^{\frac{\beth_s}{\sum_{s=1}^n \beth_s}} &\geq (1-(\check{\mathfrak{P}}_s)^q)^{\frac{\beth_s}{\sum_{s=1}^n \beth_s}} \\
\prod_{s=1}^{n}(1+(\check{\mathfrak{P}}_s)^q)^{\frac{\beth_s}{\sum_{s=1}^n \beth_s}} &\geq \prod_{s=1}^{n}(1-(\check{\mathfrak{P}}_s)^q)^{\frac{\beth_s}{\sum_{s=1}^n \beth_s}} \\
\prod_{s=1}^{n}(1+(\check{\mathfrak{P}}_s)^q)^{\frac{\beth_s}{\sum_{s=1}^n \beth_s}} - \prod_{s=1}^{n}(1-(\check{\mathfrak{P}}_s)^q)^{\frac{\beth_s}{\sum_{s=1}^n \beth_s}} &\geq 0 \\
\frac{\prod_{s=1}^{n}(1+(\check{\mathfrak{P}}_s)^q)^{\frac{\beth_s}{\sum_{s=1}^n \beth_s}} - \prod_{s=1}^{n}(1-(\check{\mathfrak{P}}_s)^q)^{\frac{\beth_s}{\sum_{s=1}^n \beth_s}}}{\prod_{s=1}^{n}(1+(\check{\mathfrak{P}}_s)^q)^{\frac{\beth_s}{\sum_{s=1}^n \beth_s}} + \prod_{s=1}^{n}(1-(\check{\mathfrak{P}}_s)^q)^{\frac{\beth_s}{\sum_{s=1}^n \beth_s}}} &\geq 0
\end{aligned}
$$

So, we get $0 \leq \check{\mathfrak{P}}_{\text{q-ROFEPWA}} \leq 1$.
For $\overline{\text{II}}_{\text{q-ROFEPWA}}$, we have

$$
\begin{aligned}
\frac{2\prod_{s=1}^{n}((\overline{\text{II}}_s)^q)^{\frac{\beth_s}{\sum_{s=1}^n \beth_s}}}{\prod_{s=1}^{n}(1+(\check{\mathfrak{P}}_s)^q)^{\frac{\beth_s}{\sum_{s=1}^n \beth_s}} + \prod_{s=1}^{n}(1-(\check{\mathfrak{P}}_s)^q)^{\frac{\beth_s}{\sum_{s=1}^n \beth_s}}} &\leq \frac{2\prod_{s=1}^{n}(1-(\check{\mathfrak{P}}_s)^q)^{\frac{\beth_s}{\sum_{s=1}^n \beth_s}}}{\prod_{s=1}^{n}(1+(\check{\mathfrak{P}}_s)^q)^{\frac{\beth_s}{\sum_{s=1}^n \beth_s}} + \prod_{s=1}^{n}(1-(\check{\mathfrak{P}}_s)^q)^{\frac{\beth_s}{\sum_{s=1}^n \beth_s}}} \\
&\leq \prod_{s=1}^{n}(1-(\check{\mathfrak{P}}_s)^q)^{\frac{\beth_s}{\sum_{s=1}^n \beth_s}} \\
&\leq 1
\end{aligned}
$$

Also,

$$
\frac{2\prod_{s=1}^{n}((\overline{\text{II}}_s)^q)^{\frac{\beth_s}{\sum_{s=1}^n \beth_s}}}{\prod_{s=1}^{n}(1+(\check{\mathfrak{P}}_s)^q)^{\frac{\beth_s}{\sum_{s=1}^n \beth_s}} + \prod_{s=1}^{n}(1-(\check{\mathfrak{P}}_s)^q)^{\frac{\beth_s}{\sum_{s=1}^n \beth_s}}} \geq 0 \Longleftrightarrow \prod_{s=1}^{n}((\overline{\text{II}}_s)^q)^{\frac{\beth_s}{\sum_{s=1}^n \beth_s}} \geq 0
$$

Moreover,

$$
\begin{aligned}
\check{\mathfrak{P}}^q_{\text{q-ROFEPWA}} + \overline{\text{II}}^q_{\text{q-ROFEPWA}} &= \frac{\prod_{s=1}^{n}(1+(\check{\mathfrak{P}}_s)^q)^{\frac{\beth_s}{\sum_{s=1}^n \beth_s}} - \prod_{s=1}^{n}(1-(\check{\mathfrak{P}}_s)^q)^{\frac{\beth_s}{\sum_{s=1}^n \beth_s}}}{\prod_{s=1}^{n}(1+(\check{\mathfrak{P}}_s)^q)^{\frac{\beth_s}{\sum_{s=1}^n \beth_s}} + \prod_{s=1}^{n}(1-(\check{\mathfrak{P}}_s)^q)^{\frac{\beth_s}{\sum_{s=1}^n \beth_s}}} + \\
&\quad \frac{2\prod_{s=1}^{n}((\overline{\text{II}}_s)^q)^{\frac{\beth_s}{\sum_{s=1}^n \beth_s}}}{\prod_{s=1}^{n}(2-(\overline{\text{II}}_s)^q)^{\frac{\beth_s}{\sum_{s=1}^n \beth_s}} + \prod_{s=1}^{n}((\overline{\text{II}}_s)^q)^{\frac{\beth_s}{\sum_{s=1}^n \beth_s}}} \\
&\leq 1 - \frac{2\prod_{s=1}^{n}(1-(\check{\mathfrak{P}}_s)^q)^{\frac{\beth_s}{\sum_{s=1}^n \beth_s}}}{\prod_{s=1}^{n}(1+(\check{\mathfrak{P}}_s)^q)^{\frac{\beth_s}{\sum_{s=1}^n \beth_s}} + \prod_{s=1}^{n}(1-(\check{\mathfrak{P}}_s)^q)^{\frac{\beth_s}{\sum_{s=1}^n \beth_s}}} + \\
&\quad \frac{2\prod_{s=1}^{n}(1-(\check{\mathfrak{P}}_s)^q)^{\frac{\beth_s}{\sum_{s=1}^n \beth_s}}}{\prod_{s=1}^{n}(1+(\check{\mathfrak{P}}_s)^q)^{\frac{\beth_s}{\sum_{s=1}^n \beth_s}} + \prod_{s=1}^{n}(1-(\check{\mathfrak{P}}_s)^q)^{\frac{\beth_s}{\sum_{s=1}^n \beth_s}}} \\
&\leq 1
\end{aligned}
$$

Thus, q-ROFEPWA $\in [0,1]$. Consequently, q-ROFNs gathered by the q-ROFEPWA operator also are q-ROFNs. □

Theorem 6. *Let $\ddot{\mathfrak{S}}_p = \langle \breve{\mathfrak{P}}_p, \overline{\Pi}_p \rangle$ be the family of q-ROFNs and let*

$$\breve{\mathcal{Z}} = \left(\frac{\breve{\beth}_1}{\sum_{s=1}^{n} \breve{\beth}_s}, \frac{\breve{\beth}_2}{\sum_{s=1}^{n} \breve{\beth}_s}, \ldots, \frac{\breve{\beth}_n}{\sum_{s=1}^{n} \breve{\beth}_s} \right)^T \tag{24}$$

be the WV of $\ddot{\mathfrak{S}}_p = \langle \breve{\mathfrak{P}}_p, \overline{\Pi}_p \rangle$. Then,

$$q\text{-}ROFEPWA(\ddot{\mathfrak{S}}_1, \ddot{\mathfrak{S}}_2, \ldots, \ddot{\mathfrak{S}}_n) \leq q\text{-}ROFPWA(\ddot{\mathfrak{S}}_1, \ddot{\mathfrak{S}}_2, \ldots, \ddot{\mathfrak{S}}_n) \tag{25}$$

where $\breve{\beth}_j = \prod_{k=1}^{j-1} \breve{\Xi}(\breve{\ddot{\mathfrak{S}}}_k)$ $(j = 2\ldots, n)$, $\breve{\beth}_1 = 1$ and $\breve{\Xi}(\breve{\ddot{\mathfrak{S}}}_k)$ is the score of kth q-ROFN.

Proof. Let q-ROFEPWA$(\ddot{\mathfrak{S}}_1, \ddot{\mathfrak{S}}_2, \ldots, \ddot{\mathfrak{S}}_n) = (\mathfrak{Y}_p^E, \mathcal{F}_p^E)$ and q-ROFPWA$(\ddot{\mathfrak{S}}_1, \ddot{\mathfrak{S}}_2, \ldots, \ddot{\mathfrak{S}}_n) = (\mathfrak{Y}_p, \mathcal{F}_p)$, we have

$$\begin{aligned}
\sqrt[q]{\prod_{s=1}^{n} \left(1 - (\breve{\mathfrak{P}}_s)^q\right)^{\frac{\breve{\beth}_s}{\sum_{s=1}^{n}\breve{\beth}_s}} + \prod_{s=1}^{n} \left((\breve{\mathfrak{P}}_s)^q\right)^{\frac{\breve{\beth}_s}{\sum_{s=1}^{n}\breve{\beth}_s}}} &\leq \sqrt[q]{\frac{\breve{\beth}_s}{\sum_{s=1}^{n}\breve{\beth}_s} \prod_{s=1}^{n} \left(1 - (\breve{\mathfrak{P}}_s)^q\right) + \frac{\breve{\beth}_s}{\sum_{s=1}^{n}\breve{\beth}_s} \prod_{s=1}^{n} \left((\breve{\mathfrak{P}}_s)^q\right)} \\
&= \sqrt[q]{2}
\end{aligned}$$

From above theorem,

$$\sqrt[q]{\frac{\prod_{s=1}^{n}\left(1 + (\breve{\mathfrak{P}}_s)^q\right)^{\frac{\breve{\beth}_s}{\sum_{s=1}^{n}\breve{\beth}_s}} - \prod_{s=1}^{n}\left(1 - (\breve{\mathfrak{P}}_s)^q\right)^{\frac{\breve{\beth}_s}{\sum_{s=1}^{n}\breve{\beth}_s}}}{\prod_{s=1}^{n}\left(1 + (\breve{\mathfrak{P}}_s)^q\right)^{\frac{\breve{\beth}_s}{\sum_{s=1}^{n}\breve{\beth}_s}} + \prod_{s=1}^{n}\left(1 - (\breve{\mathfrak{P}}_s)^q\right)^{\frac{\breve{\beth}_s}{\sum_{s=1}^{n}\breve{\beth}_s}}}} \leq \sqrt[q]{1 - \prod_{s=1}^{n}\left(1 - (\breve{\mathfrak{P}}_s)^q\right)^{\frac{\breve{\beth}_s}{\sum_{s=1}^{n}\breve{\beth}_s}}} \tag{26}$$

$$\leftrightarrow \breve{\mathfrak{P}}_p \geq \breve{\mathfrak{P}}_p^E$$

These are equal iff $\breve{\mathfrak{P}}_1 = \breve{\mathfrak{P}}_2 = \ldots = \breve{\mathfrak{P}}_n$

Additionally,

$$\sqrt[q]{\prod_{s=1}^{n}\left(2 - (\overline{\Pi}_s)^q\right)^{\breve{\mathcal{Z}}_s} + \prod_{s=1}^{n}\left((\overline{\Pi}_s)^q\right)^{\breve{\mathcal{Z}}_s}} \leq \sqrt[q]{\breve{\mathcal{Z}}_s \prod_{s=1}^{n}\left(2 - (\overline{\Pi}_s)^q\right) + \breve{\mathcal{Z}}_s \prod_{s=1}^{n}\left((\overline{\Pi}_s)^q\right)} = \sqrt[q]{2}$$

Thus,

$$\begin{aligned}
\frac{\sqrt[q]{2\prod_{s=1}^{n}\left((\overline{\Pi}_s)^q\right)^{\frac{\breve{\beth}_s}{\sum_{s=1}^{n}\breve{\beth}_s}}}}{\sqrt[q]{\frac{\breve{\beth}_s}{\sum_{s=1}^{n}\breve{\beth}_s}\prod_{s=1}^{n}\left(2-(\overline{\Pi}_s)^q\right) + \frac{\breve{\beth}_s}{\sum_{s=1}^{n}\breve{\beth}_s}\prod_{s=1}^{n}\left((\overline{\Pi}_s)^q\right)}} &\geq \frac{\sqrt[q]{2\prod_{s=1}^{n}\left((\overline{\Pi}_s)^q\right)^{\frac{\breve{\beth}_s}{\sum_{s=1}^{n}\breve{\beth}_s}}}}{\sqrt[q]{\prod_{s=1}^{n}\left(2-(\overline{\Pi}_s)^q\right)^{\frac{\breve{\beth}_s}{\sum_{s=1}^{n}\breve{\beth}_s}} + \prod_{s=1}^{n}\left((\overline{\Pi}_s)^q\right)^{\frac{\breve{\beth}_s}{\sum_{s=1}^{n}\breve{\beth}_s}}}} \\
&\geq \prod_{s=1}^{n}\left((\overline{\Pi}_s)^q\right)^{\frac{\breve{\beth}_s}{\sum_{s=1}^{n}\breve{\beth}_s}}
\end{aligned}$$

$$\leftrightarrow \overline{\Pi}_p \leq \overline{\Pi}_p^E \tag{27}$$

These are equal iff $\overline{\Pi}_1 = \overline{\Pi}_2 = \ldots = \overline{\Pi}_n$.

Equations (26) and (27) imply,

$$\breve{\mathfrak{P}}_p^E - \overline{\Pi}_p^E \leq \breve{\mathfrak{P}}_p - \overline{\Pi}_p$$
$$\mathfrak{E}(\breve{\mathfrak{P}}_p^E, \overline{\Pi}_p^E) \leq \mathfrak{E}(\breve{\mathfrak{P}}_p, \overline{\Pi}_p)$$

Thus we have the following relationship by defining the score function of q-ROFS.

$$\text{q-ROFEPWA}(\mathcal{G}_1, \mathcal{G}_2, \ldots, \mathcal{G}_n) \leq \text{q-ROFPWA}(\mathcal{G}_1, \mathcal{G}_2, \ldots, \mathcal{G}_n)$$

□

Example 1. *Let* $\ddot{\mathfrak{S}}_1 = (0.7908, 0.2786)$, $\ddot{\mathfrak{S}}_2 = (0.2086, 0.6315)$, $\ddot{\mathfrak{S}}_3 = (0.4966, 0.2182)$, $\ddot{\mathfrak{S}}_4 = (0.3298, 0.5559)$, $\ddot{\mathfrak{S}}_5 = (0.6107, 0.2364)$ *and* $\ddot{\mathfrak{S}}_6 = (0.3797, 0.4850)$ *be the q-ROFNs* $q = 3$ *then we have,*

$$\sqrt[q]{\frac{\prod_{j=1}^{6}(1+(\breve{\mathfrak{P}}_j)^q)^{\frac{\beth_j}{\sum_{j=1}^{n}\beth_j}} - \prod_{j=1}^{6}(1-(\breve{\mathfrak{P}}_j)^q)^{\frac{\beth_j}{\sum_{j=1}^{n}\beth_j}}}{\prod_{j=1}^{6}(1+(\breve{\mathfrak{P}}_j)^q)^{\frac{\beth_j}{\sum_{j=1}^{n}\beth_j}} + \prod_{j=1}^{6}(1-(\breve{\mathfrak{P}}_j)^q)^{\frac{\beth_j}{\sum_{j=1}^{n}\beth_j}}}} = 0.638318$$

$$\frac{\sqrt[q]{2}\prod_{j=1}^{6}\overline{\Pi}_j^{\frac{\beth_j}{\sum_{j=1}^{n}\beth_j}}}{\sqrt[q]{\prod_{j=1}^{6}(2-(\overline{\Pi}_j)^q)^{\frac{\beth_j}{\sum_{j=1}^{n}\beth_j}} + \prod_{j=1}^{6}((\overline{\Pi}_j)^q)^{\frac{\beth_j}{\sum_{j=1}^{n}\beth_j}}}} = 0.373708$$

and

$$\begin{aligned} q\text{-}ROFEPWA(\ddot{\mathfrak{S}}_1, \ddot{\mathfrak{S}}_2, \ddot{\mathfrak{S}}_3, \ddot{\mathfrak{S}}_4, \ddot{\mathfrak{S}}_5, \ddot{\mathfrak{S}}_6) &= \left(\sqrt[q]{\frac{\prod_{j=1}^{6}(1+(\breve{\mathfrak{P}}_j)^q)^{\frac{\beth_j}{\sum_{j=1}^{n}\beth_j}} - \prod_{j=1}^{6}(1-(\breve{\mathfrak{P}}_j)^q)^{\frac{\beth_j}{\sum_{j=1}^{n}\beth_j}}}{\prod_{j=1}^{6}(1+(\breve{\mathfrak{P}}_j)^q)^{\frac{\beth_j}{\sum_{j=1}^{n}\beth_j}} + \prod_{j=1}^{6}(1-(\breve{\mathfrak{P}}_j)^q)^{\frac{\beth_j}{\sum_{j=1}^{n}\beth_j}}}}, \right. \\ &\quad \left. \frac{\sqrt[q]{2}\prod_{j=1}^{6}\overline{\Pi}_j^{\frac{\beth_j}{\sum_{j=1}^{n}\beth_j}}}{\sqrt[q]{\prod_{j=1}^{6}(2-(\overline{\Pi}_j)^q)^{\frac{\beth_j}{\sum_{j=1}^{n}\beth_j}} + \prod_{j=1}^{6}((\overline{\Pi}_j)^q)^{\frac{\beth_j}{\sum_{j=1}^{n}\beth_j}}}} \right) \\ &= (0.638318, 0.373708) \end{aligned}$$

Below we define some of q-ROFEPWA operator's appealing properties.

Theorem 7. *(Idempotency) Assume that* $\ddot{\mathfrak{S}}_j = \langle \breve{\mathfrak{P}}_j, \overline{\Pi}_j \rangle$ *is the family of q-ROFNs, where* $\beth_j = \prod_{k=1}^{j-1} \breve{\Xi}(\ddot{\mathfrak{S}}_k)$ $(j = 2\ldots, n)$, $\beth_1 = 1$ *and* $\breve{\Xi}(\ddot{\mathfrak{S}}_k)$ *is the score of* k^{th} *q-ROFN. If all* $\ddot{\mathfrak{S}}_j$ *are equal, i.e.,* $\ddot{\mathfrak{S}}_j = \ddot{\mathfrak{S}}$ *for all j, then*

$$q\text{-}ROFEPWA(\ddot{\mathfrak{S}}_1, \ddot{\mathfrak{S}}_2, \ldots \ddot{\mathfrak{S}}_n) = \ddot{\mathfrak{S}}$$

Proof.

$$\begin{aligned}
\text{q-ROFEPWA}(\ddot{\mathfrak{S}}_1, \ddot{\mathfrak{S}}_2, \ldots \ddot{\mathfrak{S}}_n) &= \text{q-ROFEPWA}(\ddot{\mathfrak{S}}, \ddot{\mathfrak{S}}, \ldots \ddot{\mathfrak{S}}) \\
&= \left(\frac{\check{\beth}_1}{\sum_{j=1}^{n} \check{\beth}_j} \cdot_\epsilon \ddot{\mathfrak{S}} \oplus_\epsilon \frac{\check{\beth}_2}{\sum_{j=1}^{n} \check{\beth}_j} \cdot_\epsilon \ddot{\mathfrak{S}} \oplus_\epsilon \ldots, \oplus_\epsilon \frac{\check{\beth}_n}{\sum_{j=1}^{n} \check{\beth}_j} \cdot_\epsilon \ddot{\mathfrak{S}} \right) \\
&= \left(\sqrt[q]{\frac{\prod_{j=1}^{n} (1 + (\check{\mathfrak{P}})^q)^{\frac{\check{\beth}_j}{\sum_{j=1}^{n} \check{\beth}_j}} - \prod_{j=1}^{n} (1 - (\check{\mathfrak{P}})^q)^{\frac{\check{\beth}_j}{\sum_{j=1}^{n} \check{\beth}_j}}}{\prod_{j=1}^{n} (1 + (\check{\mathfrak{P}})^q)^{\frac{\check{\beth}_j}{\sum_{j=1}^{n} \check{\beth}_j}} + \prod_{j=1}^{n} (1 - (\check{\mathfrak{P}})^q)^{\frac{\check{\beth}_j}{\sum_{j=1}^{n} \check{\beth}_j}}}}, \right. \\
&\qquad \left. \frac{\sqrt[q]{2} \prod_{j=1}^{n} \text{II}^{\frac{\check{\beth}_j}{\sum_{j=1}^{n} \check{\beth}_j}}}{\sqrt[q]{\prod_{j=1}^{n} (2 - (\overline{\text{II}})^q)^{\frac{\check{\beth}_j}{\sum_{j=1}^{n} \check{\beth}_j}} + \prod_{j=1}^{n} ((\overline{\text{II}})^q)^{\frac{\check{\beth}_j}{\sum_{j=1}^{n} \check{\beth}_j}}}} \right) \\
&= \left(\sqrt[q]{\frac{(1 + (\check{\mathfrak{P}})^q) - (1 - (\check{\mathfrak{P}})^q)}{(1 + (\check{\mathfrak{P}})^q) + (1 - (\check{\mathfrak{P}})^q)}}, \frac{\sqrt[q]{2}\text{II}}{\sqrt[q]{2}} \right) = (\check{\mathfrak{P}}, \overline{\text{II}}) = \ddot{\mathfrak{S}}
\end{aligned}$$

□

Corollary 1. *If $\ddot{\mathfrak{S}}_j = \langle \check{\mathfrak{P}}_j, \overline{\text{II}}_j \rangle$ is the family of largest q-ROFNs, i.e., $\ddot{\mathfrak{S}}_j = (1, 0)\ \forall j$, then*

$$\textit{q-ROFEPWA}(\ddot{\mathfrak{S}}_1, \ddot{\mathfrak{S}}_2, \ldots \ddot{\mathfrak{S}}_n) = (1, 0)$$

Proof. We can easily obtain a Corollary similar to the Theorem 7. □

Corollary 2. *(Non-compensatory) If $\ddot{\mathfrak{S}}_1 = \langle \check{\mathfrak{P}}_1, \overline{\text{II}}_1 \rangle$ is the smallest q-ROFN, i.e., $\ddot{\mathfrak{S}}_1 = (0, 1)$, then*

$$\textit{q-ROFEPWA}(\ddot{\mathfrak{S}}_1, \ddot{\mathfrak{S}}_2, \ldots \ddot{\mathfrak{S}}_n) = (0, 1)$$

Proof. Here, $\ddot{\mathfrak{S}}_1 = (0, 1)$ then by implication of the score function, we have got,

$$\check{\Xi}(\ddot{\mathfrak{S}}_1) = 0$$

Since,

$$\check{\beth}_j = \prod_{k=1}^{j-1} \check{\Xi}(\ddot{\mathfrak{S}}_k) \qquad (j = 2 \ldots, n), \quad \text{and} \quad \check{\beth}_1 = 1$$

$\check{\Xi}(\ddot{\mathfrak{S}}_k)$ is the score of kth q-ROFN.

We have,
$\check{\beth}_j = \prod_{k=1}^{j-1} \check{\Xi}(\ddot{\mathfrak{S}}_k) = \check{\Xi}(\ddot{\mathfrak{S}}_1) \times \check{\Xi}(\ddot{\mathfrak{S}}_2) \times \ldots \times \check{\Xi}(\ddot{\mathfrak{S}}_{j-1}) = 0 \times \check{\Xi}(\ddot{\mathfrak{S}}_2) \times \ldots \times \check{\Xi}(\ddot{\mathfrak{S}}_{j-1}) \qquad (j = 2 \ldots, n)$

$$\prod_{k=1}^{j} \check{\beth}_j = 1$$

From Definition 14, we have

$$\begin{aligned} \text{q-ROFEPWA}(\ddot{\mathfrak{S}}_1, \ddot{\mathfrak{S}}_2, \ldots \ddot{\mathfrak{S}}_n) &= \frac{\beth_1}{\sum_{j=1}^{n} \beth_j} \ddot{\mathfrak{S}}_1 \oplus \frac{\beth_2}{\sum_{j=1}^{n} \beth_j} \ddot{\mathfrak{S}}_2 \oplus \ldots, \oplus \frac{\beth_n}{\sum_{j=1}^{n} \beth_j} \ddot{\mathfrak{S}}_n \\ &= \frac{1}{1} \ddot{\mathfrak{S}}_1 \oplus \frac{0}{1} \ddot{\mathfrak{S}}_2 \oplus \ldots \frac{0}{1} \ddot{\mathfrak{S}}_n \\ &= \ddot{\mathfrak{S}}_1 = (0, 1) \end{aligned}$$

□

Corollary 2 meant that, if the higher priority criteria are met by the smallest q-ROFN, rewards will not be received by other criteria even though they are fulfilled.

Theorem 8. *(Monotonicity) Assume that* $\ddot{\mathfrak{S}}_j = \langle \check{\mathfrak{P}}_j, \overline{\amalg}_j \rangle$ *and* $\ddot{\mathfrak{S}}_{j^*} = \langle \check{\mathfrak{P}}_{j^*}, \overline{\amalg}_{j^*} \rangle$ *are the families of q-ROFNs, where* $\beth_j = \prod_{k=1}^{j-1} \breve{\Xi}(\ddot{\mathfrak{S}}_k)$, $\beth_{j^*} = \prod_{k=1}^{j-1} \breve{\Xi}(\ddot{\mathfrak{S}}_{k^*})$ $(j = 2 \ldots, n)$, $\beth_1 = 1$, $\beth_{1^*} = 1$, $\breve{\Xi}(\ddot{\mathfrak{S}}_k)$ *is the score of* $\ddot{\mathfrak{S}}_k$ *q-ROFN, and* $\breve{\Xi}(\ddot{\mathfrak{S}}_{k^*})$ *is the score of* $\ddot{\mathfrak{S}}_{k^*}$ *q-ROFN. If* $\check{\mathfrak{P}}_{j^*} \geq \check{\mathfrak{P}}_j$ *and* $\overline{\amalg}_{j^*} \leq \overline{\amalg}_j$ *for all j, then*

$$q\text{-ROFPWA}(\ddot{\mathfrak{S}}_1, \ddot{\mathfrak{S}}_2, \ldots \ddot{\mathfrak{S}}_n) \leq q\text{-ROFPWA}(\ddot{\mathfrak{S}}_{1^*}, \ddot{\mathfrak{S}}_{2^*}, \ldots \ddot{\mathfrak{S}}_{n^*})$$

Proof. Let $f(y) = \sqrt[q]{\frac{2-y^q}{y^q}}$, $y \in (0,1]$ and $q \geq 1$. Then $f'(y) < 0$. So, $f(y)$ is a decreasing function on $(0,1]$. If $\check{\mathfrak{P}}_j^* \geq \check{\mathfrak{P}}_j$ for all j. Then $f(\check{\mathfrak{P}}_j^*) \leq f(\check{\mathfrak{P}}_j)$, i.e.,

$$\sqrt[q]{\frac{2 - \check{\mathfrak{P}}_{s^*}^q}{\check{\mathfrak{P}}_{s^*}^q}} \quad \leq \quad \sqrt[q]{\frac{2 - \check{\mathfrak{P}}_{s}^q}{\check{\mathfrak{P}}_{s}^q}} \quad (j = 1, 2, \ldots, n)$$

Let

$$\check{\mathcal{Z}} \quad = \quad \left(\frac{\beth_1}{\sum_{s=1}^{n} \beth_s}, \frac{\beth_2}{\sum_{s=1}^{n} \beth_s}, \ldots, \frac{\beth_n}{\sum_{s=1}^{n} \beth_s} \right)^T$$

and

$$\check{\mathcal{Z}}_* \quad = \quad \left(\frac{\beth_{1^*}}{\sum_{s=1}^{n} \beth_{s^*}}, \frac{\beth_{2^*}}{\sum_{s=1}^{n} \beth_{s^*}}, \ldots, \frac{\beth_{n^*}}{\sum_{s=1}^{n} \beth_{s^*}} \right)^T$$

be the prioritized WVs of $\ddot{\mathfrak{S}}_j = \langle \check{\mathfrak{P}}_j, \overline{\amalg}_j \rangle$ and $\ddot{\mathfrak{S}}_{j^*} = \langle \check{\mathfrak{P}}_{j^*}, \overline{\amalg}_{j^*} \rangle$ respectively, s.t

$$\sum_{s=1}^{n} \frac{\beth_s}{\sum_{s=1}^{n} \beth_s} = 1$$

and

$$\sum_{s=1}^{n} \frac{\beth_{s^*}}{\sum_{s=1}^{n} \beth_{s^*}} = 1$$

Now,

$$
\begin{aligned}
&\leftrightarrow \sqrt[q]{\left(\frac{2-\breve{\mathfrak{P}}^q_{s*}}{\breve{\mathfrak{P}}^q_{s*}}\right)^{\frac{\breve{\beth}_{s*}}{\sum_{s=1}^{n}\breve{\beth}_{s*}}}} \le \sqrt[q]{\left(\frac{2-\breve{\mathfrak{P}}^q_{s}}{\breve{\mathfrak{P}}^q_{s}}\right)^{\frac{\breve{\beth}_{s}}{\sum_{s=1}^{n}\breve{\beth}_{s}}}} \\
&\leftrightarrow \sqrt[q]{\prod_{s=1}^{n}\left(\frac{2-\breve{\mathfrak{P}}^q_{s*}}{\breve{\mathfrak{P}}^q_{s*}}\right)^{\frac{\breve{\beth}_{s*}}{\sum_{s=1}^{n}\breve{\beth}_{s*}}}} \le \sqrt[q]{\prod_{s=1}^{n}\left(\frac{2-\breve{\mathfrak{P}}^q_{s}}{\breve{\mathfrak{P}}^q_{s}}\right)^{\frac{\breve{\beth}_{s}}{\sum_{s=1}^{n}\breve{\beth}_{s}}}} \\
&\leftrightarrow \sqrt[q]{\prod_{s=1}^{n}\left(\frac{2-\breve{\mathfrak{P}}^q_{s*}}{\breve{\mathfrak{P}}^q_{s*}}\right)^{\frac{\breve{\beth}_{s*}}{\sum_{s=1}^{n}\breve{\beth}_{s*}}}+1} \le \sqrt[q]{\prod_{s=1}^{n}\left(\frac{2-\breve{\mathfrak{P}}^q_{s}}{\breve{\mathfrak{P}}^q_{s}}\right)^{\frac{\breve{\beth}_{s}}{\sum_{s=1}^{n}\breve{\beth}_{s}}}+1} \\
&\leftrightarrow \frac{1}{\sqrt[q]{\prod_{s=1}^{n}\left(\frac{2-\breve{\mathfrak{P}}^q_{s}}{\breve{\mathfrak{P}}^q_{s}}\right)^{\frac{\breve{\beth}_{s}}{\sum_{s=1}^{n}\breve{\beth}_{s}}}+1}} \le \frac{1}{\sqrt[q]{\prod_{s=1}^{n}\left(\frac{2-\breve{\mathfrak{P}}^q_{s*}}{\breve{\mathfrak{P}}^q_{s*}}\right)^{\frac{\breve{\beth}_{s*}}{\sum_{s=1}^{n}\breve{\beth}_{s*}}}+1}} \\
&\leftrightarrow \frac{\sqrt[q]{2}}{\sqrt[q]{\prod_{s=1}^{n}\left(\frac{2-\breve{\mathfrak{P}}^q_{s}}{\breve{\mathfrak{P}}^q_{s}}\right)^{\frac{\breve{\beth}_{s}}{\sum_{s=1}^{n}\breve{\beth}_{s}}}+1}} \le \frac{\sqrt[q]{2}}{\sqrt[q]{\prod_{s=1}^{n}\left(\frac{2-\breve{\mathfrak{P}}^q_{s*}}{\breve{\mathfrak{P}}^q_{s*}}\right)^{\frac{\breve{\beth}_{s*}}{\sum_{s=1}^{n}\breve{\beth}_{s*}}}+1}} \\
&\leftrightarrow \frac{\sqrt[q]{2}}{\sqrt[q]{\frac{\prod_{s=1}^{n}\left(2-\breve{\mathfrak{P}}^q_{s}\right)^{\frac{\breve{\beth}_{s}}{\sum_{s=1}^{n}\breve{\beth}_{s}}}}{\prod_{s=1}^{n}\left(\breve{\mathfrak{P}}^q_{s}\right)^{\frac{\breve{\beth}_{s}}{\sum_{s=1}^{n}\breve{\beth}_{s}}}}+1}} \le \frac{\sqrt[q]{2}}{\sqrt[q]{\frac{\prod_{s=1}^{n}\left(2-\breve{\mathfrak{P}}^q_{s*}\right)^{\frac{\breve{\beth}_{s*}}{\sum_{s=1}^{n}\breve{\beth}_{s*}}}}{\prod_{s=1}^{n}\left(\breve{\mathfrak{P}}^q_{s*}\right)^{\frac{\breve{\beth}_{s*}}{\sum_{s=1}^{n}\breve{\beth}_{s*}}}}+1}} \\
&\leftrightarrow \frac{\sqrt[q]{2}}{\sqrt[q]{\frac{\prod_{s=1}^{n}\left(2-\breve{\mathfrak{P}}^q_{s}\right)^{\frac{\breve{\beth}_{s}}{\sum_{s=1}^{n}\breve{\beth}_{s}}}+\prod_{s=1}^{n}\left(\breve{\mathfrak{P}}^q_{s}\right)^{\frac{\breve{\beth}_{s}}{\sum_{s=1}^{n}\breve{\beth}_{s}}}}{\prod_{s=1}^{n}\left(\breve{\mathfrak{P}}^q_{s}\right)^{\frac{\breve{\beth}_{s}}{\sum_{s=1}^{n}\breve{\beth}_{s}}}}}} \le \frac{\sqrt[q]{2}}{\sqrt[q]{\frac{\prod_{s=1}^{n}\left(2-\breve{\mathfrak{P}}^q_{s*}\right)^{\frac{\breve{\beth}_{s*}}{\sum_{s=1}^{n}\breve{\beth}_{s*}}}+\prod_{s=1}^{n}\left(\breve{\mathfrak{P}}^q_{s*}\right)^{\frac{\breve{\beth}_{s*}}{\sum_{s=1}^{n}\breve{\beth}_{s*}}}}{\prod_{s=1}^{n}\left(\breve{\mathfrak{P}}^q_{s*}\right)^{\frac{\breve{\beth}_{s*}}{\sum_{s=1}^{n}\breve{\beth}_{s*}}}}}} \\
&\leftrightarrow \frac{\sqrt[q]{2}\sqrt[q]{\prod_{s=1}^{n}\left(\breve{\mathfrak{P}}^q_{s}\right)^{\frac{\breve{\beth}_{s}}{\sum_{s=1}^{n}\breve{\beth}_{s}}}}}{\sqrt[q]{\prod_{s=1}^{n}\left(2-\breve{\mathfrak{P}}^q_{s}\right)^{\frac{\breve{\beth}_{s}}{\sum_{s=1}^{n}\breve{\beth}_{s}}}+\prod_{s=1}^{n}\left(\breve{\mathfrak{P}}^q_{s}\right)^{\frac{\breve{\beth}_{s}}{\sum_{s=1}^{n}\breve{\beth}_{s}}}}} \le \frac{\sqrt[q]{2}\sqrt[q]{\prod_{s=1}^{n}\left(\breve{\mathfrak{P}}^q_{s*}\right)^{\frac{\breve{\beth}_{s*}}{\sum_{s=1}^{n}\breve{\beth}_{s*}}}}}{\sqrt[q]{\prod_{s=1}^{n}\left(2-\breve{\mathfrak{P}}^q_{s*}\right)^{\frac{\breve{\beth}_{s*}}{\sum_{s=1}^{n}\breve{\beth}_{s*}}}+\prod_{s=1}^{n}\left(\breve{\mathfrak{P}}^q_{s*}\right)^{\frac{\breve{\beth}_{s*}}{\sum_{s=1}^{n}\breve{\beth}_{s*}}}}} \\
&\leftrightarrow \frac{\sqrt[q]{2\prod_{s=1}^{n}\left(\breve{\mathfrak{P}}^q_{s}\right)^{\frac{\breve{\beth}_{s}}{\sum_{s=1}^{n}\breve{\beth}_{s}}}}}{\sqrt[q]{\prod_{s=1}^{n}\left(2-\breve{\mathfrak{P}}^q_{s}\right)^{\frac{\breve{\beth}_{s}}{\sum_{s=1}^{n}\breve{\beth}_{s}}}+\prod_{s=1}^{n}\left(\breve{\mathfrak{P}}^q_{s}\right)^{\frac{\breve{\beth}_{s}}{\sum_{s=1}^{n}\breve{\beth}_{s}}}}} \le \frac{\sqrt[q]{2\prod_{s=1}^{n}\left(\breve{\mathfrak{P}}^q_{s*}\right)^{\frac{\breve{\beth}_{s*}}{\sum_{s=1}^{n}\breve{\beth}_{s*}}}}}{\sqrt[q]{\prod_{s=1}^{n}\left(2-\breve{\mathfrak{P}}^q_{s*}\right)^{\frac{\breve{\beth}_{s*}}{\sum_{s=1}^{n}\breve{\beth}_{s*}}}+\prod_{s=1}^{n}\left(\breve{\mathfrak{P}}^q_{s*}\right)^{\frac{\breve{\beth}_{s*}}{\sum_{s=1}^{n}\breve{\beth}_{s*}}}}}
\end{aligned} \tag{28}
$$

Again, let $q(t) = \sqrt[q]{\frac{(1-t^q)}{(1+t^q)}}$, $t \in [0,1]$ and $q \ge 1$. Then $q'(y) < 0$. So, $q(y)$ is a decreasing function on $(0,1]$. If $\overline{\text{II}}_j^* \le \overline{\text{II}}_j$ for all j. Then $f(\overline{\text{II}}_j^*) \ge f(\overline{\text{II}}_j)$, i.e.,

$$\sqrt[q]{\frac{1-\overline{\text{II}}^q_{s*}}{1+\overline{\text{II}}^q_{s*}}} \ge \sqrt[q]{\frac{1-\overline{\text{II}}^q_{s}}{1+\overline{\text{II}}^q_{s}}} \quad (j = 1,2,\ldots,n)$$

Let

$$\breve{z} = \left(\frac{\breve{\beth}_1}{\sum_{s=1}^{n}\breve{\beth}_s}, \frac{\breve{\beth}_2}{\sum_{s=1}^{n}\breve{\beth}_s}, \ldots, \frac{\breve{\beth}_n}{\sum_{s=1}^{n}\breve{\beth}_s}\right)^T$$

and

$$\breve{\mathcal{Z}}_* = \left(\frac{\breve{\beth}_{1^*}}{\sum_{s=1}^n \breve{\beth}_{s^*}}, \frac{\breve{\beth}_{2^*}}{\sum_{s=1}^n \breve{\beth}_{s^*}}, \ldots, \frac{\breve{\beth}_{n^*}}{\sum_{s=1}^n \breve{\beth}_{s^*}}\right)^T$$

be the prioritized WVs of $\ddot{\mathfrak{S}}_j = \langle \breve{\mathfrak{P}}_j, \overline{\Pi}_j \rangle$ and $\ddot{\mathfrak{S}}_{j^*} = \langle \breve{\mathfrak{P}}_{j^*}, \overline{\Pi}_{j^*} \rangle$, respectively, s.t

$$\sum_{s=1}^n \frac{\breve{\beth}_s}{\sum_{s=1}^n \breve{\beth}_s} = 1$$

and

$$\sum_{s=1}^n \frac{\breve{\beth}_{s^*}}{\sum_{s=1}^n \breve{\beth}_{s^*}} = 1$$

Now,

$$\begin{aligned}
\leftrightarrow \sqrt[q]{\left(\frac{1-\overline{\Pi}^q_{s^*}}{1+\overline{\Pi}^q_{s^*}}\right)^{\frac{\breve{\beth}_{s^*}}{\sum_{s=1}^n \breve{\beth}_{s^*}}}} &\geq \sqrt[q]{\left(\frac{1-\overline{\Pi}^q_{s}}{1+\overline{\Pi}^q_{s}}\right)^{\frac{\breve{\beth}_{s}}{\sum_{s=1}^n \breve{\beth}_{s}}}} \\
\leftrightarrow \sqrt[q]{\prod_{s=1}^n \left(\frac{1-\overline{\Pi}^q_{s^*}}{1+\overline{\Pi}^q_{s^*}}\right)^{\frac{\breve{\beth}_{s^*}}{\sum_{s=1}^n \breve{\beth}_{s^*}}}} &\leq \sqrt[q]{\prod_{s=1}^n \left(\frac{1-\overline{\Pi}^q_{s}}{1+\overline{\Pi}^q_{s}}\right)^{\frac{\breve{\beth}_{s}}{\sum_{s=1}^n \breve{\beth}_{s}}}} \\
\leftrightarrow \sqrt[q]{1+\prod_{s=1}^n \left(\frac{1-\overline{\Pi}^q_{s^*}}{1+\overline{\Pi}^q_{s^*}}\right)^{\frac{\breve{\beth}_{s^*}}{\sum_{s=1}^n \breve{\beth}_{s^*}}}} &\geq \sqrt[q]{1+\prod_{s=1}^n \left(\frac{1-\overline{\Pi}^q_{s}}{1+\overline{\Pi}^q_{s}}\right)^{\frac{\breve{\beth}_{s}}{\sum_{s=1}^n \breve{\beth}_{s}}}} \\
\leftrightarrow \frac{1}{\sqrt[q]{1+\prod_{s=1}^n \left(\frac{1-\overline{\Pi}^q_{s^*}}{1+\overline{\Pi}^q_{s^*}}\right)^{\frac{\breve{\beth}_{s^*}}{\sum_{s=1}^n \breve{\beth}_{s^*}}}}} &\leq \frac{1}{\sqrt[q]{1+\prod_{s=1}^n \left(\frac{1-\overline{\Pi}^q_{s}}{1+\overline{\Pi}^q_{s}}\right)^{\frac{\breve{\beth}_{s}}{\sum_{s=1}^n \breve{\beth}_{s}}}}} \\
\leftrightarrow \frac{\sqrt[q]{2}}{\sqrt[q]{1+\prod_{s=1}^n \left(\frac{1-\overline{\Pi}^q_{s^*}}{1+\overline{\Pi}^q_{s^*}}\right)^{\frac{\breve{\beth}_{s^*}}{\sum_{s=1}^n \breve{\beth}_{s^*}}}}} &\leq \frac{\sqrt[q]{2}}{\sqrt[q]{1+\prod_{s=1}^n \left(\frac{1-\overline{\Pi}^q_{s}}{1+\overline{\Pi}^q_{s}}\right)^{\frac{\breve{\beth}_{s}}{\sum_{s=1}^n \breve{\beth}_{s}}}}} \\
\leftrightarrow \frac{\sqrt[q]{2}}{\sqrt[q]{1+\frac{\prod_{s=1}^n \left(1-\overline{\Pi}^q_{s^*}\right)^{\frac{\breve{\beth}_{s^*}}{\sum_{s=1}^n \breve{\beth}_{s^*}}}}{\prod_{s=1}^n \left(1+\overline{\Pi}^q_{s^*}\right)^{\frac{\breve{\beth}_{s^*}}{\sum_{s=1}^n \breve{\beth}_{s^*}}}}}} &\leq \frac{\sqrt[q]{2}}{\sqrt[q]{1+\frac{\prod_{s=1}^n \left(1-\overline{\Pi}^q_{s}\right)^{\frac{\breve{\beth}_{s}}{\sum_{s=1}^n \breve{\beth}_{s}}}}{\prod_{s=1}^n \left(1+\overline{\Pi}^q_{s}\right)^{\frac{\breve{\beth}_{s}}{\sum_{s=1}^n \breve{\beth}_{s}}}}}} \\
\leftrightarrow \frac{\sqrt[q]{2}}{\sqrt[q]{\frac{\prod_{s=1}^n \left(1+\overline{\Pi}^q_{s^*}\right)^{\frac{\breve{\beth}_{s^*}}{\sum_{s=1}^n \breve{\beth}_{s^*}}} + \prod_{s=1}^n \left(1-\overline{\Pi}^q_{s^*}\right)^{\frac{\breve{\beth}_{s^*}}{\sum_{s=1}^n \breve{\beth}_{s^*}}}}{\prod_{s=1}^n \left(1+\overline{\Pi}^q_{s^*}\right)^{\frac{\breve{\beth}_{s^*}}{\sum_{s=1}^n \breve{\beth}_{s^*}}}}}} &\leq \frac{\sqrt[q]{2}}{\sqrt[q]{\frac{\prod_{s=1}^n \left(1+\overline{\Pi}^q_{s}\right)^{\frac{\breve{\beth}_{s}}{\sum_{s=1}^n \breve{\beth}_{s}}} + \prod_{s=1}^n \left(1-\overline{\Pi}^q_{s}\right)^{\frac{\breve{\beth}_{s}}{\sum_{s=1}^n \breve{\beth}_{s}}}}{\prod_{s=1}^n \left(1+\overline{\Pi}^q_{s}\right)^{\frac{\breve{\beth}_{s}}{\sum_{s=1}^n \breve{\beth}_{s}}}}}} \\
\leftrightarrow \frac{\sqrt[q]{2\prod_{s=1}^n \left(1+\overline{\Pi}^q_{s^*}\right)^{\frac{\breve{\beth}_{s^*}}{\sum_{s=1}^n \breve{\beth}_{s^*}}}}}{\sqrt[q]{\prod_{s=1}^n \left(1+\overline{\Pi}^q_{s^*}\right)^{\frac{\breve{\beth}_{s^*}}{\sum_{s=1}^n \breve{\beth}_{s^*}}} + \prod_{s=1}^n \left(1-\overline{\Pi}^q_{s^*}\right)^{\frac{\breve{\beth}_{s^*}}{\sum_{s=1}^n \breve{\beth}_{s^*}}}}} &\leq \frac{\sqrt[q]{2\prod_{s=1}^n \left(1+\overline{\Pi}^q_{s}\right)^{\frac{\breve{\beth}_{s}}{\sum_{s=1}^n \breve{\beth}_{s}}}}}{\sqrt[q]{\prod_{s=1}^n \left(1+\overline{\Pi}^q_{s}\right)^{\frac{\breve{\beth}_{s}}{\sum_{s=1}^n \breve{\beth}_{s}}} + \prod_{s=1}^n \left(1-\overline{\Pi}^q_{s}\right)^{\frac{\breve{\beth}_{s}}{\sum_{s=1}^n \breve{\beth}_{s}}}}} \\
\leftrightarrow \sqrt[q]{\frac{2\prod_{s=1}^n \left(1+\overline{\Pi}^q_{s^*}\right)^{\frac{\breve{\beth}_{s^*}}{\sum_{s=1}^n \breve{\beth}_{s^*}}}}{\prod_{s=1}^n \left(1+\overline{\Pi}^q_{s^*}\right)^{\frac{\breve{\beth}_{s^*}}{\sum_{s=1}^n \breve{\beth}_{s^*}}} + \prod_{s=1}^n \left(1-\overline{\Pi}^q_{s^*}\right)^{\frac{\breve{\beth}_{s^*}}{\sum_{s=1}^n \breve{\beth}_{s^*}}}} - 1} &\leq \sqrt[q]{\frac{2\prod_{s=1}^n \left(1+\overline{\Pi}^q_{s}\right)^{\frac{\breve{\beth}_{s}}{\sum_{s=1}^n \breve{\beth}_{s}}}}{\prod_{s=1}^n \left(1+\overline{\Pi}^q_{s}\right)^{\frac{\breve{\beth}_{s}}{\sum_{s=1}^n \breve{\beth}_{s}}} + \prod_{s=1}^n \left(1-\overline{\Pi}^q_{s}\right)^{\frac{\breve{\beth}_{s}}{\sum_{s=1}^n \breve{\beth}_{s}}}} - 1}
\end{aligned}$$

$$\leftrightarrow \sqrt[q]{\frac{\prod_{s=1}^{n}(1+\overline{\amalg}^{q}_{s*})^{\frac{\breve{\beth}_{s*}}{\sum_{s=1}^{n}\breve{\beth}_{s*}}}-\prod_{s=1}^{n}(1-\overline{\amalg}^{q}_{s*})^{\frac{\breve{\beth}_{s*}}{\sum_{s=1}^{n}\breve{\beth}_{s*}}}}{\prod_{s=1}^{n}(1+\overline{\amalg}^{q}_{s*})^{\frac{\breve{\beth}_{s*}}{\sum_{s=1}^{n}\breve{\beth}_{s*}}}+\prod_{s=1}^{n}(1-\overline{\amalg}^{q}_{s*})^{\frac{\breve{\beth}_{s*}}{\sum_{s=1}^{n}\breve{\beth}_{s*}}}}} \leq \sqrt[q]{\frac{\prod_{s=1}^{n}(1+\overline{\amalg}^{q}_{s})^{\frac{\breve{\beth}_{s}}{\sum_{s=1}^{n}\breve{\beth}_{s}}}-\prod_{s=1}^{n}(1-\overline{\amalg}^{q}_{s})^{\frac{\breve{\beth}_{s}}{\sum_{s=1}^{n}\breve{\beth}_{s}}}}{\prod_{s=1}^{n}(1+\overline{\amalg}^{q}_{s})^{\frac{\breve{\beth}_{s}}{\sum_{s=1}^{n}\breve{\beth}_{s}}}+\prod_{s=1}^{n}(1-\overline{\amalg}^{q}_{s})^{\frac{\breve{\beth}_{s}}{\sum_{s=1}^{n}\breve{\beth}_{s}}}}} \tag{29}$$

Let,

$$\text{q-ROFPWA}(\ddot{\mathfrak{S}}_1, \ddot{\mathfrak{S}}_2, \ldots \ddot{\mathfrak{S}}_n) = \ddot{\mathfrak{S}}$$

and

$$\text{q-ROFPWA}(\ddot{\mathfrak{S}}_{1^*}, \ddot{\mathfrak{S}}_{2^*}, \ldots \ddot{\mathfrak{S}}_{n^*}) = \ddot{\mathfrak{S}}_*$$

Equations (28) and (29) can be written as $\breve{\mathfrak{P}}_{\ddot{\mathfrak{S}}} \leq \breve{\mathfrak{P}}_{\ddot{\mathfrak{S}}_*}$ and $\overline{\amalg}_{\ddot{\mathfrak{S}}} \geq \overline{\amalg}_{\ddot{\mathfrak{S}}_*}$. Thus $\mathfrak{E}(\ddot{\mathfrak{S}}) = (\breve{\mathfrak{P}}_{\ddot{\mathfrak{S}}})^q - (\overline{\amalg}_{\ddot{\mathfrak{S}}})^q \leq (\breve{\mathfrak{P}}_{\ddot{\mathfrak{S}}_*})^q - (\overline{\amalg}_{\ddot{\mathfrak{S}}_*})^q = \mathfrak{E}(\ddot{\mathfrak{S}}_*)$ Therefore, $\mathfrak{E}(\ddot{\mathfrak{S}}) \leq \mathfrak{E}(\ddot{\mathfrak{S}}_*)$. If $\mathfrak{E}(\ddot{\mathfrak{S}}) < \mathfrak{E}(\ddot{\mathfrak{S}}_*)$ then

$$\text{q-ROFPWA}(\ddot{\mathfrak{S}}_1, \ddot{\mathfrak{S}}_2, \ldots \ddot{\mathfrak{S}}_n) < \text{q-ROFPWA}(\ddot{\mathfrak{S}}_{1^*}, \ddot{\mathfrak{S}}_{2^*}, \ldots \ddot{\mathfrak{S}}_{n^*}) \tag{30}$$

If $\mathfrak{E}(\ddot{\mathfrak{S}}) = \mathfrak{E}(\ddot{\mathfrak{S}}_*)$, i.e., $(\breve{\mathfrak{P}}_{\ddot{\mathfrak{S}}})^q - (\overline{\amalg}_{\ddot{\mathfrak{S}}})^q = (\breve{\mathfrak{P}}_{\ddot{\mathfrak{S}}_*})^q - (\overline{\amalg}_{\ddot{\mathfrak{S}}_*})^q$, then we get, $(\breve{\mathfrak{P}}_{\ddot{\mathfrak{S}}})^q = (\breve{\mathfrak{P}}_{\ddot{\mathfrak{S}}_*})^q$ and $(\overline{\amalg}_{\ddot{\mathfrak{S}}})^q = (\overline{\amalg}_{\ddot{\mathfrak{S}}_*})^q$.

$\mathfrak{R}(\ddot{\mathfrak{S}}) = (\breve{\mathfrak{P}}_{\ddot{\mathfrak{S}}})^q + (\overline{\amalg}_{\ddot{\mathfrak{S}}})^q = (\breve{\mathfrak{P}}_{\ddot{\mathfrak{S}}_*})^q + (\overline{\amalg}_{\ddot{\mathfrak{S}}_*})^q = \mathfrak{R}(\ddot{\mathfrak{S}}_*)$. So we have

$$\text{q-ROFPWA}(\ddot{\mathfrak{S}}_1, \ddot{\mathfrak{S}}_2, \ldots \ddot{\mathfrak{S}}_n) = \text{q-ROFPWA}(\ddot{\mathfrak{S}}_{1^*}, \ddot{\mathfrak{S}}_{2^*}, \ldots \ddot{\mathfrak{S}}_{n^*}) \tag{31}$$

By Equations (30) and (31), we get

$$\text{q-ROFPWA}(\ddot{\mathfrak{S}}_1, \ddot{\mathfrak{S}}_2, \ldots \ddot{\mathfrak{S}}_n) \leq \text{q-ROFPWA}(\ddot{\mathfrak{S}}_{1^*}, \ddot{\mathfrak{S}}_{2^*}, \ldots \ddot{\mathfrak{S}}_{n^*}) \tag{32}$$

□

Theorem 9. *(Boundary) Assume that $\ddot{\mathfrak{S}}_j = \langle \breve{\mathfrak{P}}_j, \overline{\amalg}_j \rangle$ be the family of q-ROFNs, where $\breve{\beth}_j = \prod_{k=1}^{j-1} \breve{\Xi}(\ddot{\mathfrak{S}}_k)$, $(j = 2 \ldots, n)$, $\breve{\beth}_1 = 1$ and $\breve{\Xi}(\ddot{\mathfrak{S}}_k)$ is the score of $\ddot{\mathfrak{S}}_k$ q-ROFN, then*

$$\ddot{\mathfrak{S}}_{min} \leq \textit{q-ROFPWA}(\ddot{\mathfrak{S}}_1, \ddot{\mathfrak{S}}_2, \ldots \ddot{\mathfrak{S}}_n) \leq \ddot{\mathfrak{S}}_{max} \tag{33}$$

where,

$$\ddot{\mathfrak{S}}_{min} = min(\ddot{\mathfrak{S}}_j), \quad \ddot{\mathfrak{S}}_{max} = max(\ddot{\mathfrak{S}}_j)$$

Proof. Let $f(y) = \sqrt[q]{\frac{2-y^q}{y^q}}$, $y \in (0,1]$ and $q \geq 1$. Then $f'(y) < 0$. So, $f(y)$ is a decreasing function on $(0,1]$. Since $\breve{\mathfrak{P}}_{\ddot{\mathfrak{S}}_{min}} \leq \breve{\mathfrak{P}}_{\ddot{\mathfrak{S}}_j} \leq \breve{\mathfrak{P}}_{\ddot{\mathfrak{S}}_{max}}$, then $f(\breve{\mathfrak{P}}_{\ddot{\mathfrak{S}}_{max}}) \leq f(\breve{\mathfrak{P}}_{\ddot{\mathfrak{S}}_j}) \leq f(\breve{\mathfrak{P}}_{\ddot{\mathfrak{S}}_{min}})$, i.e.,

$$\sqrt[q]{\frac{2-\breve{\mathfrak{P}}^q_{\ddot{\mathfrak{S}}_{max}}}{\breve{\mathfrak{P}}^q_{\ddot{\mathfrak{S}}_{max}}}} \leq \sqrt[q]{\frac{2-\breve{\mathfrak{P}}^q_{\ddot{\mathfrak{S}}_j}}{\breve{\mathfrak{P}}^q_{\ddot{\mathfrak{S}}_j}}} \leq \sqrt[q]{\frac{2-\breve{\mathfrak{P}}^q_{\ddot{\mathfrak{S}}_{min}}}{\breve{\mathfrak{P}}^q_{\ddot{\mathfrak{S}}_{min}}}} \quad (j = 1, 2, \ldots, n)$$

Let

$$\check{\mathcal{Z}} = \left(\frac{\breve{\beth}_1}{\sum_{s=1}^{n} \breve{\beth}_s}, \frac{\breve{\beth}_2}{\sum_{s=1}^{n} \breve{\beth}_s}, \ldots, \frac{\breve{\beth}_n}{\sum_{s=1}^{n} \breve{\beth}_s} \right)^T$$

be the prioritized WVs of $\ddot{\mathfrak{S}}_j = \langle \breve{\mathfrak{P}}_j, \overline{\amalg}_j \rangle$, s.t

$$\sum_{s=1}^{n} \frac{\breve{\beth}_s}{\sum_{s=1}^{n} \breve{\beth}_s} = 1$$

Now,

$$
\begin{aligned}
& \sqrt[q]{\prod_{s=1}^{n}\left(\frac{2-\mathfrak{P}^{q}_{\ddot{\mathfrak{S}}_{max}}}{\check{\mathfrak{P}}^{q}_{\ddot{\mathfrak{S}}_{max}}}\right)^{\frac{\beth_s}{\sum_{s=1}^{n}\beth_s}}} \le \sqrt[q]{\prod_{s=1}^{n}\left(\frac{2-\check{\mathfrak{P}}^{q}_{\ddot{\mathfrak{S}}_{s}}}{\check{\mathfrak{P}}^{q}_{\ddot{\mathfrak{S}}_{s}}}\right)^{\frac{\beth_s}{\sum_{s=1}^{n}\beth_s}}} \le \sqrt[q]{\prod_{s=1}^{n}\left(\frac{2-\check{\mathfrak{P}}^{q}_{\ddot{\mathfrak{S}}_{min}}}{\check{\mathfrak{P}}^{q}_{\ddot{\mathfrak{S}}_{min}}}\right)^{\frac{\beth_s}{\sum_{s=1}^{n}\beth_s}}} \\
\leftrightarrow\ & \sqrt[q]{\left(\frac{2-\check{\mathfrak{P}}^{q}_{\ddot{\mathfrak{S}}_{max}}}{\check{\mathfrak{P}}^{q}_{\ddot{\mathfrak{S}}_{max}}}\right)^{\sum_{s=1}^{n}\frac{\beth_s}{\sum_{s=1}^{n}\beth_s}}} \le \sqrt[q]{\prod_{s=1}^{n}\left(\frac{2-\check{\mathfrak{P}}^{q}_{\ddot{\mathfrak{S}}_{s}}}{\check{\mathfrak{P}}^{q}_{\ddot{\mathfrak{S}}_{s}}}\right)^{\frac{\beth_s}{\sum_{s=1}^{n}\beth_s}}} \le \sqrt[q]{\left(\frac{2-\check{\mathfrak{P}}^{q}_{\ddot{\mathfrak{S}}_{min}}}{\check{\mathfrak{P}}^{q}_{\ddot{\mathfrak{S}}_{min}}}\right)^{\sum_{s=1}^{n}\frac{\beth_s}{\sum_{s=1}^{n}\beth_s}}} \\
\leftrightarrow\ & \sqrt[q]{\left(\frac{2-\check{\mathfrak{P}}^{q}_{\ddot{\mathfrak{S}}_{max}}}{\check{\mathfrak{P}}^{q}_{\ddot{\mathfrak{S}}_{max}}}\right)} \le \sqrt[q]{\prod_{s=1}^{n}\left(\frac{2-\check{\mathfrak{P}}^{q}_{\ddot{\mathfrak{S}}_{s}}}{\check{\mathfrak{P}}^{q}_{\ddot{\mathfrak{S}}_{s}}}\right)^{\frac{\beth_s}{\sum_{s=1}^{n}\beth_s}}} \le \sqrt[q]{\left(\frac{2-\check{\mathfrak{P}}^{q}_{\ddot{\mathfrak{S}}_{min}}}{\check{\mathfrak{P}}^{q}_{\ddot{\mathfrak{S}}_{min}}}\right)} \\
\leftrightarrow\ & \sqrt[q]{\left(\frac{2-\check{\mathfrak{P}}^{q}_{\ddot{\mathfrak{S}}_{max}}}{\check{\mathfrak{P}}^{q}_{\ddot{\mathfrak{S}}_{max}}}\right)+1} \le \sqrt[q]{\prod_{s=1}^{n}\left(\frac{2-\check{\mathfrak{P}}^{q}_{\ddot{\mathfrak{S}}_{s}}}{\check{\mathfrak{P}}^{q}_{\ddot{\mathfrak{S}}_{s}}}\right)^{\frac{\beth_s}{\sum_{s=1}^{n}\beth_s}}+1} \le \sqrt[q]{\left(\frac{2-\check{\mathfrak{P}}^{q}_{\ddot{\mathfrak{S}}_{min}}}{\check{\mathfrak{P}}^{q}_{\ddot{\mathfrak{S}}_{min}}}\right)+1} \\
\leftrightarrow\ & \frac{\sqrt[q]{2}}{\sqrt[q]{\check{\mathfrak{P}}^{q}_{\ddot{\mathfrak{S}}_{max}}}} \le \sqrt[q]{\prod_{s=1}^{n}\left(\frac{2-\check{\mathfrak{P}}^{q}_{\ddot{\mathfrak{S}}_{s}}}{\check{\mathfrak{P}}^{q}_{\ddot{\mathfrak{S}}_{s}}}\right)^{\frac{\beth_s}{\sum_{s=1}^{n}\beth_s}}+1} \le \frac{\sqrt[q]{\check{\mathfrak{P}}^{q}_{\ddot{\mathfrak{S}}_{min}}}}{\sqrt[q]{2}} \\
\leftrightarrow\ & \frac{\sqrt[q]{\check{\mathfrak{P}}^{q}_{\ddot{\mathfrak{S}}_{min}}}}{\sqrt[q]{2}} \le \frac{1}{\sqrt[q]{\prod_{s=1}^{n}\left(\frac{2-\check{\mathfrak{P}}^{q}_{\ddot{\mathfrak{S}}_{s}}}{\check{\mathfrak{P}}^{q}_{\ddot{\mathfrak{S}}_{s}}}\right)^{\frac{\beth_s}{\sum_{s=1}^{n}\beth_s}}+1}} \le \frac{\sqrt[q]{\check{\mathfrak{P}}^{q}_{\ddot{\mathfrak{S}}_{max}}}}{\sqrt[q]{2}} \\
\leftrightarrow\ & \sqrt[q]{\check{\mathfrak{P}}^{q}_{\ddot{\mathfrak{S}}_{min}}} \le \frac{\sqrt[q]{2}}{\sqrt[q]{\prod_{s=1}^{n}\left(\frac{2-\check{\mathfrak{P}}^{q}_{\ddot{\mathfrak{S}}_{s}}}{\check{\mathfrak{P}}^{q}_{\ddot{\mathfrak{S}}_{s}}}\right)^{\frac{\beth_s}{\sum_{s=1}^{n}\beth_s}}+1}} \le \sqrt[q]{\check{\mathfrak{P}}^{q}_{\ddot{\mathfrak{S}}_{max}}} \\
\leftrightarrow\ & \mathfrak{P}_{\ddot{\mathfrak{S}}_{min}} \le \frac{\sqrt[q]{2}}{\sqrt[q]{\prod_{s=1}^{n}\left(\frac{2-\check{\mathfrak{P}}^{q}_{\ddot{\mathfrak{S}}_{s}}}{\check{\mathfrak{P}}^{q}_{\ddot{\mathfrak{S}}_{s}}}\right)^{\frac{\beth_s}{\sum_{s=1}^{n}\beth_s}}+1}} \le \mathfrak{P}_{\ddot{\mathfrak{S}}_{max}} \\
\leftrightarrow\ & \check{\mathfrak{P}}_{\ddot{\mathfrak{S}}_{min}} \le \frac{\sqrt[q]{2}}{\sqrt[q]{\frac{\prod_{s=1}^{n}\left(2-\check{\mathfrak{P}}^{q}_{\ddot{\mathfrak{S}}_{s}}\right)^{\frac{\beth_s}{\sum_{s=1}^{n}\beth_s}}}{\prod_{s=1}^{n}\left(\check{\mathfrak{P}}^{q}_{\ddot{\mathfrak{S}}_{s}}\right)^{\frac{\beth_s}{\sum_{s=1}^{n}\beth_s}}}+1}} \le \check{\mathfrak{P}}_{\ddot{\mathfrak{S}}_{max}}
\end{aligned}
$$

$$\leftrightarrow \quad \check{\mathfrak{P}}_{\ddot{\mathfrak{S}}_{min}} \leq \frac{\sqrt[q]{2}}{\sqrt[q]{\frac{\prod_{s=1}^{n}\left(2-\check{\mathfrak{P}}^{q}_{\ddot{\mathfrak{S}}_s}\right)^{\frac{\check{\beth}_s}{\sum_{s=1}^{n}\check{\beth}_s}}+\prod_{s=1}^{n}\left(\check{\mathfrak{P}}^{q}_{\ddot{\mathfrak{S}}_s}\right)^{\frac{\check{\beth}_s}{\sum_{s=1}^{n}\check{\beth}_s}}}{\prod_{s=1}^{n}\left(\check{\mathfrak{P}}^{q}_{\ddot{\mathfrak{S}}_s}\right)^{\frac{\check{\beth}_s}{\sum_{s=1}^{n}\check{\beth}_s}}}}} \leq \check{\mathfrak{P}}_{\ddot{\mathfrak{S}}_{max}}$$

$$\leftrightarrow \quad \check{\mathfrak{P}}_{\ddot{\mathfrak{S}}_{min}} \leq \frac{\sqrt[q]{2}}{\frac{\sqrt[q]{\prod_{s=1}^{n}\left(2-\check{\mathfrak{P}}^{q}_{\ddot{\mathfrak{S}}_s}\right)^{\frac{\check{\beth}_s}{\sum_{s=1}^{n}\check{\beth}_s}}+\prod_{s=1}^{n}\left(\check{\mathfrak{P}}^{q}_{\ddot{\mathfrak{S}}_s}\right)^{\frac{\check{\beth}_s}{\sum_{s=1}^{n}\check{\beth}_s}}}}{\sqrt[q]{\prod_{s=1}^{n}\left(\check{\mathfrak{P}}^{q}_{\ddot{\mathfrak{S}}_s}\right)^{\frac{\check{\beth}_s}{\sum_{s=1}^{n}\check{\beth}_s}}}}} \leq \check{\mathfrak{P}}_{\ddot{\mathfrak{S}}_{max}}$$

$$\leftrightarrow \quad \check{\mathfrak{P}}_{\ddot{\mathfrak{S}}_{min}} \leq \frac{\sqrt[q]{2\prod_{s=1}^{n}\left(\check{\mathfrak{P}}^{q}_{\ddot{\mathfrak{S}}_s}\right)^{\frac{\check{\beth}_s}{\sum_{s=1}^{n}\check{\beth}_s}}}}{\sqrt[q]{\prod_{s=1}^{n}\left(2-\check{\mathfrak{P}}^{q}_{\ddot{\mathfrak{S}}_s}\right)^{\frac{\check{\beth}_s}{\sum_{s=1}^{n}\check{\beth}_s}}+\prod_{s=1}^{n}\left(\check{\mathfrak{P}}^{q}_{\ddot{\mathfrak{S}}_s}\right)^{\frac{\check{\beth}_s}{\sum_{s=1}^{n}\check{\beth}_s}}}} \leq \check{\mathfrak{P}}_{\ddot{\mathfrak{S}}_{max}} \tag{34}$$

Let $M(t) = \sqrt[q]{\frac{1-t^q}{1+t^q}}$, $t \in [0,1]$ and $q \geq 1$. Then $M'(t) < 0$. So, $M(t)$ is a decreasing function on $(0,1]$. Since $\overline{\Pi}_{\ddot{\mathfrak{S}}_{max}} \leq \overline{\Pi}_{\ddot{\mathfrak{S}}_j} \leq \overline{\Pi}_{\ddot{\mathfrak{S}}_{min}}$, then $M(\overline{\Pi}_{\ddot{\mathfrak{S}}_{min}}) \leq M(\overline{\Pi}_{\ddot{\mathfrak{S}}_j}) \leq M(\overline{\Pi}_{\ddot{\mathfrak{S}}_{max}})$, i.e.,

$$\sqrt[q]{\frac{1-\overline{\Pi}^{q}_{\ddot{\mathfrak{S}}_{min}}}{1+\overline{\Pi}^{q}_{\ddot{\mathfrak{S}}_{min}}}} \leq \sqrt[q]{\frac{1-\overline{\Pi}^{q}_{\ddot{\mathfrak{S}}_j}}{1+\overline{\Pi}^{q}_{\ddot{\mathfrak{S}}_j}}} \leq \sqrt[q]{\frac{1-\overline{\Pi}^{q}_{\ddot{\mathfrak{S}}_{max}}}{1+\overline{\Pi}^{q}_{\ddot{\mathfrak{S}}_{max}}}} \quad (j = 1, 2, \ldots, n)$$

Let

$$\check{\mathcal{Z}} = \left(\frac{\check{\beth}_1}{\sum_{s=1}^{n}\check{\beth}_s}, \frac{\check{\beth}_2}{\sum_{s=1}^{n}\check{\beth}_s}, \ldots, \frac{\check{\beth}_n}{\sum_{s=1}^{n}\check{\beth}_s}\right)^T$$

be the prioritized WV of $\ddot{\mathfrak{S}}_j = \langle \check{\mathfrak{P}}_j, \overline{\Pi}_j \rangle$, s.t

$$\sum_{s=1}^{n} \frac{\check{\beth}_s}{\sum_{s=1}^{n}\check{\beth}_s} = 1$$

Now,

$$\sqrt[q]{\left(\frac{1-\overline{\Pi}^{q}_{\ddot{\mathfrak{S}}_{min}}}{1+\overline{\Pi}^{q}_{\ddot{\mathfrak{S}}_{min}}}\right)^{\frac{\check{\beth}_s}{\sum_{s=1}^{n}\check{\beth}_s}}} \leq \sqrt[q]{\left(\frac{1-\overline{\Pi}^{q}_{\ddot{\mathfrak{S}}_s}}{1+\overline{\Pi}^{q}_{\ddot{\mathfrak{S}}_s}}\right)^{\frac{\check{\beth}_s}{\sum_{s=1}^{n}\check{\beth}_s}}} \leq \sqrt[q]{\left(\frac{1-\overline{\Pi}^{q}_{\ddot{\mathfrak{S}}_{max}}}{1+\overline{\Pi}^{q}_{\ddot{\mathfrak{S}}_{max}}}\right)^{\frac{\check{\beth}_s}{\sum_{s=1}^{n}\check{\beth}_s}}}$$

$$\leftrightarrow \sqrt[q]{\prod_{s=1}^{n}\left(\frac{1-\overline{\Pi}^{q}_{\ddot{\mathfrak{S}}_{min}}}{1+\overline{\Pi}^{q}_{\ddot{\mathfrak{S}}_{min}}}\right)^{\frac{\check{\beth}_s}{\sum_{s=1}^{n}\check{\beth}_s}}} \leq \sqrt[q]{\prod_{s=1}^{n}\left(\frac{1-\overline{\Pi}^{q}_{\ddot{\mathfrak{S}}_s}}{1+\overline{\Pi}^{q}_{\ddot{\mathfrak{S}}_s}}\right)^{\frac{\check{\beth}_s}{\sum_{s=1}^{n}\check{\beth}_s}}} \leq \sqrt[q]{\prod_{s=1}^{n}\left(\frac{1-\overline{\Pi}^{q}_{\ddot{\mathfrak{S}}_{max}}}{1+\overline{\Pi}^{q}_{\ddot{\mathfrak{S}}_{max}}}\right)^{\frac{\check{\beth}_s}{\sum_{s=1}^{n}\check{\beth}_s}}}$$

$$\leftrightarrow \sqrt[q]{\left(\frac{1-\overline{\Pi}^{q}_{\ddot{\mathfrak{S}}_{min}}}{1+\overline{\Pi}^{q}_{\ddot{\mathfrak{S}}_{min}}}\right)^{\sum_{s=1}^{n}\frac{\check{\beth}_s}{\sum_{s=1}^{n}\check{\beth}_s}}} \leq \sqrt[q]{\prod_{s=1}^{n}\left(\frac{1-\overline{\Pi}^{q}_{\ddot{\mathfrak{S}}_s}}{1+\overline{\Pi}^{q}_{\ddot{\mathfrak{S}}_s}}\right)^{\frac{\check{\beth}_s}{\sum_{s=1}^{n}\check{\beth}_s}}} \leq \sqrt[q]{\left(\frac{1-\overline{\Pi}^{q}_{\ddot{\mathfrak{S}}_{max}}}{1+\overline{\Pi}^{q}_{\ddot{\mathfrak{S}}_{max}}}\right)^{\sum_{s=1}^{n}\frac{\check{\beth}_s}{\sum_{s=1}^{n}\check{\beth}_s}}}$$

$$\leftrightarrow \quad \sqrt[q]{\left(\frac{1-\overline{\Pi}^q_{\ddot{\mathfrak{S}}_{min}}}{1+\overline{\Pi}^q_{\ddot{\mathfrak{S}}_{min}}}\right)^{\sum_{s=1}^{n}\frac{\beth_s}{\sum_{s=1}^{n}\beth_s}}} \leq \sqrt[q]{\prod_{s=1}^{n}\left(\frac{1-\overline{\Pi}^q_{\ddot{\mathfrak{S}}_s}}{1+\overline{\Pi}^q_{\ddot{\mathfrak{S}}_s}}\right)^{\frac{\beth_s}{\sum_{s=1}^{n}\beth_s}}} \leq \sqrt[q]{\left(\frac{1-\overline{\Pi}^q_{\ddot{\mathfrak{S}}_{max}}}{1+\overline{\Pi}^q_{\ddot{\mathfrak{S}}_{max}}}\right)^{\sum_{s=1}^{n}\frac{\beth_s}{\sum_{s=1}^{n}\beth_s}}}$$

$$\leftrightarrow \quad \sqrt[q]{\left(\frac{1-\overline{\Pi}^q_{\ddot{\mathfrak{S}}_{min}}}{1+\overline{\Pi}^q_{\ddot{\mathfrak{S}}_{min}}}\right)} \leq \sqrt[q]{\prod_{s=1}^{n}\left(\frac{1-\overline{\Pi}^q_{\ddot{\mathfrak{S}}_s}}{1+\overline{\Pi}^q_{\ddot{\mathfrak{S}}_s}}\right)^{\frac{\beth_s}{\sum_{s=1}^{n}\beth_s}}} \leq \sqrt[q]{\left(\frac{1-\overline{\Pi}^q_{\ddot{\mathfrak{S}}_{max}}}{1+\overline{\Pi}^q_{\ddot{\mathfrak{S}}_{max}}}\right)}$$

$$\leftrightarrow \quad \sqrt[q]{\left(\frac{1-\overline{\Pi}^q_{\ddot{\mathfrak{S}}_{min}}}{1+\overline{\Pi}^q_{\ddot{\mathfrak{S}}_{min}}}\right)+1} \leq \sqrt[q]{\prod_{s=1}^{n}\left(\frac{1-\overline{\Pi}^q_{\ddot{\mathfrak{S}}_s}}{1+\overline{\Pi}^q_{\ddot{\mathfrak{S}}_s}}\right)^{\frac{\beth_s}{\sum_{s=1}^{n}\beth_s}}+1} \leq \sqrt[q]{\left(\frac{1-\overline{\Pi}^q_{\ddot{\mathfrak{S}}_{max}}}{1+\overline{\Pi}^q_{\ddot{\mathfrak{S}}_{max}}}\right)+1}$$

$$\leftrightarrow \quad \frac{\sqrt[q]{2}}{\sqrt[q]{1+\overline{\Pi}^q_{\ddot{\mathfrak{S}}_{min}}}} \leq \sqrt[q]{\prod_{s=1}^{n}\left(\frac{1-\overline{\Pi}^q_{\ddot{\mathfrak{S}}_s}}{1+\overline{\Pi}^q_{\ddot{\mathfrak{S}}_s}}\right)^{\frac{\beth_s}{\sum_{s=1}^{n}\beth_s}}+1} \leq \frac{\sqrt[q]{2}}{\sqrt[q]{1+\overline{\Pi}^q_{\ddot{\mathfrak{S}}_{max}}}}$$

$$\leftrightarrow \quad \sqrt[q]{1+\overline{\Pi}^q_{\ddot{\mathfrak{S}}_{max}}} \leq \frac{\sqrt[2]{q}}{\sqrt[q]{\prod_{s=1}^{n}\left(\frac{1-\overline{\Pi}^q_{\ddot{\mathfrak{S}}_s}}{1+\overline{\Pi}^q_{\ddot{\mathfrak{S}}_s}}\right)^{\frac{\beth_s}{\sum_{s=1}^{n}\beth_s}}+1}} \leq \sqrt[q]{1+\overline{\Pi}^q_{\ddot{\mathfrak{S}}_{min}}}$$

$$\leftrightarrow \quad \sqrt[q]{1+\overline{\Pi}^q_{\ddot{\mathfrak{S}}_{max}}} \leq \frac{\sqrt[q]{2}}{\sqrt[q]{\frac{\prod_{s=1}^{n}\left(1-\overline{\Pi}^q_{\ddot{\mathfrak{S}}_s}\right)^{\frac{\beth_s}{\sum_{s=1}^{n}\beth_s}}}{\prod_{s=1}^{n}\left(1+\overline{\Pi}^q_{\ddot{\mathfrak{S}}_s}\right)^{\frac{\beth_s}{\sum_{s=1}^{n}\beth_s}}}+1}} \leq \sqrt[q]{1+\overline{\Pi}^q_{\ddot{\mathfrak{S}}_{min}}}$$

$$\leftrightarrow \quad \sqrt[q]{1+\overline{\Pi}^q_{\ddot{\mathfrak{S}}_{max}}} \leq \frac{\sqrt[q]{2}}{\sqrt[q]{\frac{\prod_{s=1}^{n}\left(1-\overline{\Pi}^q_{\ddot{\mathfrak{S}}_s}\right)^{\frac{\beth_s}{\sum_{s=1}^{n}\beth_s}}+\prod_{s=1}^{n}\left(1+\overline{\Pi}^q_{\ddot{\mathfrak{S}}_s}\right)^{\frac{\beth_s}{\sum_{s=1}^{n}\beth_s}}}{\prod_{s=1}^{n}\left(1+\overline{\Pi}^q_{\ddot{\mathfrak{S}}_s}\right)^{\frac{\beth_s}{\sum_{s=1}^{n}\beth_s}}}}} \leq \sqrt[q]{1+\overline{\Pi}^q_{\ddot{\mathfrak{S}}_{min}}}$$

$$\leftrightarrow \quad \sqrt[q]{1+\overline{\Pi}^q_{\ddot{\mathfrak{S}}_{max}}} \leq \frac{\sqrt[q]{2\prod_{s=1}^{n}\left(1+\overline{\Pi}^q_{\ddot{\mathfrak{S}}_s}\right)^{\frac{\beth_s}{\sum_{s=1}^{n}\beth_s}}}}{\sqrt[q]{\prod_{s=1}^{n}\left(1-\overline{\Pi}^q_{\ddot{\mathfrak{S}}_s}\right)^{\frac{\beth_s}{\sum_{s=1}^{n}\beth_s}}+\prod_{s=1}^{n}\left(1+\overline{\Pi}^q_{\ddot{\mathfrak{S}}_s}\right)^{\frac{\beth_s}{\sum_{s=1}^{n}\beth_s}}}} \leq \sqrt[q]{1+\overline{\Pi}^q_{\ddot{\mathfrak{S}}_{min}}}$$

$$\leftrightarrow \quad \sqrt[q]{1+\overline{\Pi}^q_{\ddot{\mathfrak{S}}_{max}}} \leq \sqrt[q]{\frac{2\prod_{s=1}^{n}\left(1+\overline{\Pi}^q_{\ddot{\mathfrak{S}}_s}\right)^{\frac{\beth_s}{\sum_{s=1}^{n}\beth_s}}}{\prod_{s=1}^{n}\left(1-\overline{\Pi}^q_{\ddot{\mathfrak{S}}_s}\right)^{\frac{\beth_s}{\sum_{s=1}^{n}\beth_s}}+\prod_{s=1}^{n}\left(1+\overline{\Pi}^q_{\ddot{\mathfrak{S}}_s}\right)^{\frac{\beth_s}{\sum_{s=1}^{n}\beth_s}}}} \leq \sqrt[q]{1+\overline{\Pi}^q_{\ddot{\mathfrak{S}}_{min}}}$$

$$\leftrightarrow \quad \sqrt[q]{1+\overline{\Pi}^q_{\ddot{\mathfrak{S}}_{max}}} \leq \sqrt[q]{\frac{2\prod_{s=1}^{n}\left(1+\overline{\Pi}^q_{\ddot{\mathfrak{S}}_s}\right)^{\frac{\beth_s}{\sum_{s=1}^{n}\beth_s}}}{\prod_{s=1}^{n}\left(1-\overline{\Pi}^q_{\ddot{\mathfrak{S}}_s}\right)^{\frac{\beth_s}{\sum_{s=1}^{n}\beth_s}}+\prod_{s=1}^{n}\left(1+\overline{\Pi}^q_{\ddot{\mathfrak{S}}_s}\right)^{\frac{\beth_s}{\sum_{s=1}^{n}\beth_s}}}} \leq \sqrt[q]{1+\overline{\Pi}^q_{\ddot{\mathfrak{S}}_{min}}}$$

$$\begin{aligned}
&\leftrightarrow \sqrt[q]{1+\overline{\text{П}}^q_{\ddot{\mathfrak{S}}_{max}}}-1 \leq \sqrt[q]{\frac{2\prod_{s=1}^{n}(1+\overline{\text{П}}^q_{\ddot{\mathfrak{S}}_s})^{\frac{\beth_s}{\sum_{s=1}^{n}\beth_s}}}{\prod_{s=1}^{n}(1-\overline{\text{П}}^q_{\ddot{\mathfrak{S}}_s})^{\frac{\beth_s}{\sum_{s=1}^{n}\beth_s}}+\prod_{s=1}^{n}(1+\overline{\text{П}}^q_{\ddot{\mathfrak{S}}_s})^{\frac{\beth_s}{\sum_{s=1}^{n}\beth_s}}}-1} \leq \sqrt[q]{1+\overline{\text{П}}^q_{\ddot{\mathfrak{S}}_{min}}}-1 \\
&\leftrightarrow \sqrt[q]{\overline{\text{П}}^q_{\ddot{\mathfrak{S}}_{max}}} \leq \sqrt[q]{\frac{2\prod_{s=1}^{n}(1+\overline{\text{П}}^q_{\ddot{\mathfrak{S}}_s})^{\frac{\beth_s}{\sum_{s=1}^{n}\beth_s}}-\prod_{s=1}^{n}(1-\overline{\text{П}}^q_{\ddot{\mathfrak{S}}_s})^{\frac{\beth_s}{\sum_{s=1}^{n}\beth_s}}-\prod_{s=1}^{n}(1+\overline{\text{П}}^q_{\ddot{\mathfrak{S}}_s})^{\frac{\beth_s}{\sum_{s=1}^{n}\beth_s}}}{\prod_{s=1}^{n}(1-\overline{\text{П}}^q_{\ddot{\mathfrak{S}}_s})^{\frac{\beth_s}{\sum_{s=1}^{n}\beth_s}}+\prod_{s=1}^{n}(1+\overline{\text{П}}^q_{\ddot{\mathfrak{S}}_s})^{\frac{\beth_s}{\sum_{s=1}^{n}\beth_s}}}} \leq \sqrt[q]{\overline{\text{П}}^q_{\ddot{\mathfrak{S}}_{min}}} \quad (35)\\
&\leftrightarrow \overline{\text{П}}_{\ddot{\mathfrak{S}}_{max}} \leq \sqrt[q]{\frac{\prod_{s=1}^{n}(1+\overline{\text{П}}^q_{\ddot{\mathfrak{S}}_s})^{\frac{\beth_s}{\sum_{s=1}^{n}\beth_s}}-\prod_{s=1}^{n}(1-\overline{\text{П}}^q_{\ddot{\mathfrak{S}}_s})^{\frac{\beth_s}{\sum_{s=1}^{n}\beth_s}}}{\prod_{s=1}^{n}(1+\overline{\text{П}}^q_{\ddot{\mathfrak{S}}_s})^{\frac{\beth_s}{\sum_{s=1}^{n}\beth_s}}+\prod_{s=1}^{n}(1-\overline{\text{П}}^q_{\ddot{\mathfrak{S}}_s})^{\frac{\beth_s}{\sum_{s=1}^{n}\beth_s}}}} \leq \overline{\text{П}}_{\ddot{\mathfrak{S}}_{min}}
\end{aligned}$$

Assume,

$$\text{q-ROFPWA}(\ddot{\mathfrak{S}}_1, \ddot{\mathfrak{S}}_2, \dots \ddot{\mathfrak{S}}_n) = \ddot{\mathfrak{S}}$$

By Equations (34) and (35), we can write $\overline{\text{П}}_{\ddot{\mathfrak{S}}_{max}} \leq \overline{\text{П}}_{\ddot{\mathfrak{S}}} \leq \overline{\text{П}}_{\ddot{\mathfrak{S}}_{min}}$ and $\check{\mathfrak{P}}_{\ddot{\mathfrak{S}}_{min}} \leq \check{\mathfrak{P}}_{\ddot{\mathfrak{S}}} \leq \check{\mathfrak{P}}_{\ddot{\mathfrak{S}}_{max}}$. Thus $\mathfrak{E}(\ddot{\mathfrak{S}}) = \check{\mathfrak{P}}^q_{\ddot{\mathfrak{S}}} - \overline{\text{П}}^q_{\ddot{\mathfrak{S}}} \leq \check{\mathfrak{P}}^q_{\ddot{\mathfrak{S}}_{max}} - \overline{\text{П}}^q_{\ddot{\mathfrak{S}}_{max}} = \mathfrak{E}(\ddot{\mathfrak{S}}_{max})$, similarly $\mathfrak{E}(\ddot{\mathfrak{S}}) = \check{\mathfrak{P}}^q_{\ddot{\mathfrak{S}}} - \overline{\text{П}}^q_{\ddot{\mathfrak{S}}} \geq \check{\mathfrak{P}}^q_{\ddot{\mathfrak{S}}_{min}} - \overline{\text{П}}^q_{\ddot{\mathfrak{S}}_{min}} = \mathfrak{E}(\ddot{\mathfrak{S}}_{min})$. If $\mathfrak{E}(\ddot{\mathfrak{S}}) \leq \mathfrak{E}(\ddot{\mathfrak{S}}_{\mathbf{max}})$ and $\mathfrak{E}(\ddot{\mathfrak{S}}) \geq \mathfrak{E}(\ddot{\mathfrak{S}}_{\mathbf{min}})$, we have

$$\ddot{\mathfrak{S}}_{min} \leq \text{q-ROFPWA}(\ddot{\mathfrak{S}}_1, \ddot{\mathfrak{S}}_2, \dots \ddot{\mathfrak{S}}_n) \leq \ddot{\mathfrak{S}}_{max} \quad (36)$$

If $\mathfrak{E}(\ddot{\mathfrak{S}}) = \mathfrak{E}(\ddot{\mathfrak{S}}_{max})$, i.e., $\check{\mathfrak{P}}^q_{\ddot{\mathfrak{S}}} - \overline{\text{П}}^q_{\ddot{\mathfrak{S}}} = \check{\mathfrak{P}}^q_{\ddot{\mathfrak{S}}_{max}} - \overline{\text{П}}^q_{\ddot{\mathfrak{S}}_{max}}$. Then we have $\check{\mathfrak{P}}^q_{\ddot{\mathfrak{S}}} = \check{\mathfrak{P}}^q_{\ddot{\mathfrak{S}}_{max}}$ and $\overline{\text{П}}^q_{\ddot{\mathfrak{S}}} = \overline{\text{П}}^q_{\ddot{\mathfrak{S}}_{max}}$. So, $\mathfrak{R}(\ddot{\mathfrak{S}}) = \check{\mathfrak{P}}^q_{\ddot{\mathfrak{S}}} + \overline{\text{П}}^q_{\ddot{\mathfrak{S}}} = \check{\mathfrak{P}}^q_{\ddot{\mathfrak{S}}_{max}} + \overline{\text{П}}^q_{\ddot{\mathfrak{S}}_{max}} = \mathfrak{R}(\ddot{\mathfrak{S}}_{max})$. Hence,

$$\text{q-ROFPWA}(\ddot{\mathfrak{S}}_1, \ddot{\mathfrak{S}}_2, \dots \ddot{\mathfrak{S}}_n) = \ddot{\mathfrak{S}}_{max} \quad (37)$$

If $\mathfrak{E}(\ddot{\mathfrak{S}}) = \mathfrak{E}(\ddot{\mathfrak{S}}_{min})$, i.e.,. $\check{\mathfrak{P}}^q_{\ddot{\mathfrak{S}}} - \overline{\text{П}}^q_{\ddot{\mathfrak{S}}} = \check{\mathfrak{P}}^q_{\ddot{\mathfrak{S}}_{min}} - \overline{\text{П}}^q_{\ddot{\mathfrak{S}}_{min}}$. Then we have $\check{\mathfrak{P}}^q_{\ddot{\mathfrak{S}}} = \check{\mathfrak{P}}^q_{\ddot{\mathfrak{S}}_{min}}$ and $\overline{\text{П}}^q_{\ddot{\mathfrak{S}}} = \overline{\text{П}}^q_{\ddot{\mathfrak{S}}_{min}}$. So, $\mathfrak{R}(\ddot{\mathfrak{S}}) = \check{\mathfrak{P}}^q_{\ddot{\mathfrak{S}}} + \overline{\text{П}}^q_{\ddot{\mathfrak{S}}} = \check{\mathfrak{P}}^q_{\ddot{\mathfrak{S}}_{min}} + \overline{\text{П}}^q_{\ddot{\mathfrak{S}}_{min}} = \mathfrak{R}(\ddot{\mathfrak{S}}_{min})$. Hence

$$\text{q-ROFPWA}(\ddot{\mathfrak{S}}_1, \ddot{\mathfrak{S}}_2, \dots \ddot{\mathfrak{S}}_n) = \ddot{\mathfrak{S}}_{min} \quad (38)$$

From Equations (36)–(38), we get

$$\ddot{\mathfrak{S}}_{min} \leq \text{q-ROFPWA}(\ddot{\mathfrak{S}}_1, \ddot{\mathfrak{S}}_2, \dots \ddot{\mathfrak{S}}_n) \leq \ddot{\mathfrak{S}}_{max}$$

□

3.2. q-ROFEPWG Operator

Definition 14. *Let $\ddot{\mathfrak{S}}_p = \langle \check{\mathfrak{P}}_p, \overline{\text{П}}_p \rangle$ be the family of q-ROFNs, and q-ROFEPWG: $\Lambda^n \to \Lambda$, be a n dimension mapping. If*

$$\text{q-ROFEPWG}(\ddot{\mathfrak{S}}_1, \ddot{\mathfrak{S}}_2, \dots \ddot{\mathfrak{S}}_n) = \left(\ddot{\mathfrak{S}}_1^{\frac{\beth_1}{\sum_{j=1}^{n}\beth_j}} \otimes_\epsilon \ddot{\mathfrak{S}}_2^{\frac{\beth_2}{\sum_{j=1}^{n}\beth_j}} \otimes_\epsilon \dots, \otimes_\epsilon \ddot{\mathfrak{S}}_n^{\frac{\beth_n}{\sum_{j=1}^{n}\beth_j}} \right) \quad (39)$$

then the mapping q-ROFEPWG is called q-rung orthopair fuzzy Einstein prioritized weighted geometric (q-ROFEPWG) operator, where $\beth_j = \prod_{k=1}^{j-1} \breve{\Xi}(\ddot{\mathfrak{S}}_k)$ $(j = 2\dots, n)$, $\beth_1 = 1$ and $\breve{\Xi}(\ddot{\mathfrak{S}}_k)$ is the score of kth q-ROFN.

Based on Einstein operational rules, we can also consider q-ROFEPWG by the theorem below.

Theorem 10. *Let $\ddot{\mathfrak{S}}_p = \langle \breve{\mathfrak{P}}_p, \overline{\Pi}_p \rangle$ be the family of q-ROFNs, we can also find q-ROFEPWG by*

$$q\text{-ROFEPWG}(\ddot{\mathfrak{S}}_1, \ddot{\mathfrak{S}}_2, \ldots, \ddot{\mathfrak{S}}_n)$$

$$= \left(\frac{\sqrt[q]{2} \prod_{j=1}^{n} \breve{\mathfrak{P}}_j^{\frac{\beth_j}{\sum_{j=1}^{n} \beth_j}}}{\sqrt[q]{\prod_{j=1}^{n} (2-(\breve{\mathfrak{P}}_j)^q)^{\frac{\beth_j}{\sum_{j=1}^{n} \beth_j}} + \prod_{j=1}^{n} ((\breve{\mathfrak{P}}_j)^q)^{\frac{\beth_j}{\sum_{j=1}^{n} \beth_j}}}}, \sqrt[q]{\frac{\prod_{j=1}^{n} (1+(\overline{\Pi}_j)^q)^{\frac{\beth_j}{\sum_{j=1}^{n} \beth_j}} - \prod_{j=1}^{n} (1-(\overline{\Pi}_j)^q)^{\frac{\beth_j}{\sum_{j=1}^{n} \beth_j}}}{\prod_{j=1}^{n} (1+(\overline{\Pi}_j)^q)^{\frac{\beth_j}{\sum_{j=1}^{n} \beth_j}} + \prod_{j=1}^{n} (1-(\overline{\Pi}_j)^q)^{\frac{\beth_j}{\sum_{j=1}^{n} \beth_j}}}} \right) \quad (40)$$

where $\beth_j = \prod_{k=1}^{j-1} \breve{\Xi}(\breve{\ddot{\mathfrak{S}}}_k)$ $(j = 2 \ldots, n)$, $\beth_1 = 1$ and $\breve{\Xi}(\breve{\ddot{\mathfrak{S}}}_k)$ is the score of kth q-ROFN.

Proof. This theorem is proven using mathematical induction.

For $n = 2$

$$\text{q-ROFEPWG}(\ddot{\mathfrak{S}}_1, \ddot{\mathfrak{S}}_2) = \ddot{\mathfrak{S}}_1^{\frac{\beth_1}{\sum_{j=1}^{n} \beth_j}} \otimes_\epsilon \ddot{\mathfrak{S}}_2^{\frac{\beth_2}{\sum_{j=1}^{n} \beth_j}}$$

As we know that both $\ddot{\mathfrak{S}}_1^{\frac{\beth_1}{\sum_{j=1}^{n} \beth_j}}$ and $\ddot{\mathfrak{S}}_2^{\frac{\beth_2}{\sum_{j=1}^{n} \beth_j}}$ are q-ROFNs, and also $\ddot{\mathfrak{S}}_1^{\frac{\beth_1}{\sum_{j=1}^{n} \beth_j}} \otimes_\epsilon \ddot{\mathfrak{S}}_2^{\frac{\beth_2}{\sum_{j=1}^{n} \beth_j}}$ is q-ROFN.

$$\ddot{\mathfrak{S}}_1^{\frac{\beth_1}{\sum_{j=1}^{n} \beth_j}} = \left(\frac{\sqrt[q]{2} (\breve{\mathfrak{P}}_1)^{\frac{\beth_1}{\sum_{j=1}^{n} \beth_j}}}{\sqrt[q]{(2-(\overline{\Pi}_1)^q)^{\frac{\beth_1}{\sum_{j=1}^{n} \beth_j}} + ((\breve{\mathfrak{P}}_1)^q)^{\frac{\beth_1}{\sum_{j=1}^{n} \beth_j}}}}, \sqrt[q]{\frac{(1+(\overline{\Pi}_1)^q)^{\frac{\beth_1}{\sum_{j=1}^{n} \beth_j}} - (1-(\overline{\Pi}_1)^q)^{\frac{\beth_1}{\sum_{j=1}^{n} \beth_j}}}{(1+(\overline{\Pi}_1)^q)^{\frac{\beth_1}{\sum_{j=1}^{n} \beth_j}} + (1-(\overline{\Pi}_1)^q)^{\frac{\beth_1}{\sum_{j=1}^{n} \beth_j}}}} \right)$$

$$\ddot{\mathfrak{S}}_2^{\frac{\beth_2}{\sum_{j=1}^{n} \beth_j}} = \left(\frac{\sqrt[q]{2} (\breve{\mathfrak{P}}_2)^{\frac{\beth_2}{\sum_{j=1}^{n} \beth_j}}}{\sqrt[q]{(2-(\overline{\Pi}_2)^q)^{\frac{\beth_2}{\sum_{j=1}^{n} \beth_j}} + ((\breve{\mathfrak{P}}_2)^q)^{\frac{\beth_2}{\sum_{j=1}^{n} \beth_j}}}}, \sqrt[q]{\frac{(1+(\overline{\Pi}_2)^q)^{\frac{\beth_2}{\sum_{j=1}^{n} \beth_j}} - (1-(\overline{\Pi}_2)^q)^{\frac{\beth_2}{\sum_{j=1}^{n} \beth_j}}}{(1+(\overline{\Pi}_2)^q)^{\frac{\beth_2}{\sum_{j=1}^{n} \beth_j}} + (1-(\overline{\Pi}_2)^q)^{\frac{\beth_2}{\sum_{j=1}^{n} \beth_j}}}} \right)$$

Then q-ROFEPWG$(\ddot{\mathfrak{S}}_1, \ddot{\mathfrak{S}}_2)$

$$
\begin{aligned}
&= \ddot{\mathfrak{S}}_1^{\frac{\beth_1}{\sum_{j=1}^{n}\beth_j}} \otimes_\epsilon \ddot{\mathfrak{S}}_2^{\frac{\beth_2}{\sum_{j=1}^{n}\beth_j}} \\
&= \left(\frac{\sqrt[q]{2}(\check{\mathfrak{P}}_1)^{\frac{\beth_1}{\sum_{j=1}^{n}\beth_j}}}{\sqrt[q]{(2-(\bar{\Pi}_1)^q)^{\frac{\beth_1}{\sum_{j=1}^{n}\beth_j}} + ((\check{\mathfrak{P}}_1)^q)^{\frac{\beth_1}{\sum_{j=1}^{n}\beth_j}}}}, \sqrt[q]{\frac{(1+(\bar{\Pi}_1)^q)^{\frac{\beth_1}{\sum_{j=1}^{n}\beth_j}} - (1-(\bar{\Pi}_1)^q)^{\frac{\beth_1}{\sum_{j=1}^{n}\beth_j}}}{(1+(\bar{\Pi}_1)^q)^{\frac{\beth_1}{\sum_{j=1}^{n}\beth_j}} + (1-(\bar{\Pi}_1)^q)^{\frac{\beth_1}{\sum_{j=1}^{n}\beth_j}}}} \right) \\
&\otimes_\epsilon \left(\frac{\sqrt[q]{2}(\check{\mathfrak{P}}_2)^{\frac{\beth_2}{\sum_{j=1}^{n}\beth_j}}}{\sqrt[q]{(2-(\bar{\Pi}_2)^q)^{\frac{\beth_2}{\sum_{j=1}^{n}\beth_j}} + ((\check{\mathfrak{P}}_2)^q)^{\frac{\beth_2}{\sum_{j=1}^{n}\beth_j}}}}, \sqrt[q]{\frac{(1+(\bar{\Pi}_2)^q)^{\frac{\beth_2}{\sum_{j=1}^{n}\beth_j}} - (1-(\bar{\Pi}_2)^q)^{\frac{\beth_2}{\sum_{j=1}^{n}\beth_j}}}{(1+(\bar{\Pi}_2)^q)^{\frac{\beth_2}{\sum_{j=1}^{n}\beth_j}} + (1-(\bar{\Pi}_2)^q)^{\frac{\beth_2}{\sum_{j=1}^{n}\beth_j}}}} \right)
\end{aligned}
$$

$$
= \left(\frac{\left(\frac{\sqrt[q]{2}(\check{\mathfrak{P}}_1)^{\frac{\beth_1}{\sum_{j=1}^{n}\beth_j}}}{\sqrt[q]{(2-(\check{\mathfrak{P}}_1)^q)^{\frac{\beth_1}{\sum_{j=1}^{n}\beth_j}} + ((\check{\mathfrak{P}}_1)^q)^{\frac{\beth_1}{\sum_{j=1}^{n}\beth_j}}}} \right) \cdot_\epsilon \left(\frac{\sqrt[q]{2}(\check{\mathfrak{P}}_2)^{\frac{\beth_2}{\sum_{j=1}^{n}\beth_j}}}{\sqrt[q]{(2-(\bar{\Pi}_2)^q)^{\frac{\beth_2}{\sum_{j=1}^{n}\beth_j}} + ((\check{\mathfrak{P}}_2)^q)^{\frac{\beth_2}{\sum_{j=1}^{n}\beth_j}}}} \right)}{\sqrt[q]{1 + \left(1 - \frac{2((\check{\mathfrak{P}}_1)^q)^{\frac{\beth_1}{\sum_{j=1}^{n}\beth_j}}}{(2-(\check{\mathfrak{P}}_1)^q)^{\frac{\beth_1}{\sum_{j=1}^{n}\beth_j}} + ((\check{\mathfrak{P}}_1)^q)^{\frac{\beth_1}{\sum_{j=1}^{n}\beth_j}}}\right) \cdot_\epsilon \left(1 - \frac{2((\check{\mathfrak{P}}_2)^q)^{\frac{\beth_2}{\sum_{j=1}^{n}\beth_j}}}{(2-(\check{\mathfrak{P}}_2)^q)^{\frac{\beth_2}{\sum_{j=1}^{n}\beth_j}} + ((\check{\mathfrak{P}}_2)^q)^{\frac{\beth_2}{\sum_{j=1}^{n}\beth_j}}}\right)}}, \right.
$$

$$
\left. \sqrt[q]{\frac{\frac{(1+(\bar{\Pi}_1)^q)^{\frac{\beth_1}{\sum_{j=1}^{n}\beth_j}} - (1-(\bar{\Pi}_1)^q)^{\frac{\beth_1}{\sum_{j=1}^{n}\beth_j}}}{(1+(\bar{\Pi}_1)^q)^{\frac{\beth_1}{\sum_{j=1}^{n}\beth_j}} + (1-(\bar{\Pi}_1)^q)^{\frac{\beth_1}{\sum_{j=1}^{n}\beth_j}}} + \frac{(1+(\bar{\Pi}_2)^q)^{\frac{\beth_2}{\sum_{j=1}^{n}\beth_j}} - (1-(\bar{\Pi}_2)^q)^{\frac{\beth_2}{\sum_{j=1}^{n}\beth_j}}}{(1+(\bar{\Pi}_2)^q)^{\frac{\beth_2}{\sum_{j=1}^{n}\beth_j}} + (1-(\bar{\Pi}_2)^q)^{\frac{\beth_2}{\sum_{j=1}^{n}\beth_j}}}}{1 + \left(\frac{(1+(\bar{\Pi}_1)^q)^{\frac{\beth_1}{\sum_{j=1}^{n}\beth_j}} - (1-(\bar{\Pi}_1)^q)^{\frac{\beth_1}{\sum_{j=1}^{n}\beth_j}}}{(1+(\bar{\Pi}_1)^q)^{\frac{\beth_1}{\sum_{j=1}^{n}\beth_j}} + (1-(\bar{\Pi}_1)^q)^{\frac{\beth_1}{\sum_{j=1}^{n}\beth_j}}} \right) \cdot_\epsilon \left(\frac{(1+(\bar{\Pi}_2)^q)^{\frac{\beth_2}{\sum_{j=1}^{n}\beth_j}} - (1-(\bar{\Pi}_2)^q)^{\frac{\beth_2}{\sum_{j=1}^{n}\beth_j}}}{(1+(\bar{\Pi}_2)^q)^{\frac{\beth_2}{\sum_{j=1}^{n}\beth_j}} + (1-(\bar{\Pi}_2)^q)^{\frac{\beth_2}{\sum_{j=1}^{n}\beth_j}}} \right)}} \right)
$$

$$
= \left(\frac{\sqrt[q]{2}\left(\check{\mathfrak{P}}_1^{\frac{\beth_1}{\sum_{j=1}^{n}\beth_j}} \check{\mathfrak{P}}_2^{\frac{\beth_2}{\sum_{j=1}^{n}\beth_j}}\right)}{\sqrt[q]{(2-(\check{\mathfrak{P}}_1)^q)^{\frac{\beth_1}{\sum_{j=1}^{n}\beth_j}} \cdot_\epsilon (2-(\check{\mathfrak{P}}_2)^q)^{\frac{\beth_2}{\sum_{j=1}^{n}\beth_j}} + ((\check{\mathfrak{P}}_1)^q)^{\frac{\beth_1}{\sum_{j=1}^{n}\beth_j}} \cdot_\epsilon ((\check{\mathfrak{P}}_2)^q)^{\frac{\beth_2}{\sum_{j=1}^{n}\beth_j}}}}, \right.
$$

$$
\left. \sqrt[q]{\frac{(1+(\bar{\Pi}_1)^q)^{\frac{\beth_1}{\sum_{j=1}^{n}\beth_j}} \cdot_\epsilon (1+(\bar{\Pi}_2)^q)^{\frac{\beth_2}{\sum_{j=1}^{n}\beth_j}} - (1-(\bar{\Pi}_1)^q)^{\frac{\beth_1}{\sum_{j=1}^{n}\beth_j}} \cdot_\epsilon (1-(\bar{\Pi}_2)^q)^{\frac{\beth_2}{\sum_{j=1}^{n}\beth_j}}}{(1+(\bar{\Pi}_1)^q)^{\frac{\beth_1}{\sum_{j=1}^{n}\beth_j}} \cdot_\epsilon (1+(\bar{\Pi}_2)^q)^{\frac{\beth_2}{\sum_{j=1}^{n}\beth_j}} + (1-(\bar{\Pi}_1)^q)^{\frac{\beth_1}{\sum_{j=1}^{n}\beth_j}} \cdot_\epsilon (1-(\bar{\Pi}_2)^q)^{\frac{\beth_2}{\sum_{j=1}^{n}\beth_j}}}} \right)
$$

which proves for $n = 2$.

Assume that result is true for $n = k$, we have

$$\begin{aligned}\text{q-ROFEPWG}(\ddot{\mathfrak{S}}_1,\ddot{\mathfrak{S}}_2,\ldots,\ddot{\mathfrak{S}}_k) &= \left(\breve{\mathfrak{S}}_1^{\frac{\beth_1}{\sum_{j=1}^n \beth_j}} \otimes_\epsilon \breve{\mathfrak{S}}_2^{\frac{\beth_2}{\sum_{j=1}^n \beth_j}} \otimes_\epsilon \ldots, \otimes_\epsilon \breve{\mathfrak{S}}_k^{\frac{\beth_k}{\sum_{j=1}^n \beth_j}}\right) \\ &= \left(\frac{\sqrt[q]{2}\prod_{j=1}^k \breve{\mathfrak{P}}_j^{\frac{\beth_j}{\sum_{j=1}^n \beth_j}}}{\sqrt[q]{\prod_{j=1}^k (2-(\breve{\mathfrak{P}}_j)^q)^{\frac{\beth_j}{\sum_{j=1}^n \beth_j}} + \prod_{j=1}^k ((\breve{\mathfrak{P}}_j)^q)^{\frac{\beth_j}{\sum_{j=1}^n \beth_j}}}}, \sqrt[q]{\frac{\prod_{j=1}^k (1+(\overline{\amalg}_j)^q)^{\frac{\beth_j}{\sum_{j=1}^n \beth_j}} - \prod_{j=1}^k (1-(\overline{\amalg}_j)^q)^{\frac{\beth_j}{\sum_{j=1}^n \beth_j}}}{\prod_{j=1}^k (1+(\overline{\amalg}_j)^q)^{\frac{\beth_j}{\sum_{j=1}^n \beth_j}} + \prod_{j=1}^k (1-(\overline{\amalg}_j)^q)^{\frac{\beth_j}{\sum_{j=1}^n \beth_j}}}}\right)\end{aligned}$$

Now we will prove for $n = k+1$,

$$\begin{aligned}\text{q-ROFEPWG}(\ddot{\mathfrak{S}}_1,\ddot{\mathfrak{S}}_2,\ldots,\ddot{\mathfrak{S}}_{k+1}) &= \text{q-ROFEPWG}(\ddot{\mathfrak{S}}_1,\ddot{\mathfrak{S}}_2,\ldots,\ddot{\mathfrak{S}}_k) \otimes_\epsilon \ddot{\mathfrak{S}}_{k+1}^{\frac{\beth_{k+1}}{\sum_{j=1}^{k+1} \beth_j}} \\ &= \left(\breve{\mathfrak{S}}_1^{\frac{\beth_1}{\sum_{j=1}^n \beth_j}} \otimes_\epsilon \breve{\mathfrak{S}}_2^{\frac{\beth_2}{\sum_{j=1}^n \beth_j}} \otimes_\epsilon \ldots, \otimes_\epsilon \breve{\mathfrak{S}}_k^{\frac{\beth_k}{\sum_{j=1}^n \beth_j}}\right) \otimes_\epsilon \ddot{\mathfrak{S}}_{k+1}^{\frac{\beth_{k+1}}{\sum_{j=1}^{k+1} \beth_j}} \\ &= \left(\frac{\sqrt[q]{2}\prod_{j=1}^k \breve{\mathfrak{P}}_j^{\frac{\beth_j}{\sum_{j=1}^n \beth_j}}}{\sqrt[q]{\prod_{j=1}^k (2-(\breve{\mathfrak{P}}_j)^q)^{\frac{\beth_j}{\sum_{j=1}^n \beth_j}} + \prod_{j=1}^k ((\breve{\mathfrak{P}}_j)^q)^{\frac{\beth_j}{\sum_{j=1}^n \beth_j}}}}, \sqrt[q]{\frac{\prod_{j=1}^k (1+(\overline{\amalg}_j)^q)^{\frac{\beth_j}{\sum_{j=1}^n \beth_j}} - \prod_{j=1}^k (1-(\overline{\amalg}_j)^q)^{\frac{\beth_j}{\sum_{j=1}^n \beth_j}}}{\prod_{j=1}^k (1+(\overline{\amalg}_j)^q)^{\frac{\beth_j}{\sum_{j=1}^n \beth_j}} + \prod_{j=1}^k (1-(\overline{\amalg}_j)^q)^{\frac{\beth_j}{\sum_{j=1}^n \beth_j}}}}\right) \\ &\otimes_\epsilon \left(\frac{\sqrt[q]{2}(\breve{\mathfrak{P}}_{k+1})^{\frac{\beth_{k+1}}{\sum_{j=1}^{k+1} \beth_j}}}{\sqrt[q]{(2-(\overline{\amalg}_{k+1})^q)^{\frac{\beth_{k+1}}{\sum_{j=1}^{k+1} \beth_j}} + ((\breve{\mathfrak{P}}_{k+1})^q)^{\frac{\beth_{k+1}}{\sum_{j=1}^{k+1} \beth_j}}}}, \sqrt[q]{\frac{(1+(\overline{\amalg}_{k+1})^q)^{\frac{\beth_{k+1}}{\sum_{j=1}^{k+1} \beth_j}} - (1-(\overline{\amalg}_{k+1})^q)^{\frac{\beth_{k+1}}{\sum_{j=1}^{k+1} \beth_j}}}{(1+(\overline{\amalg}_{k+1})^q)^{\frac{\beth_{k+1}}{\sum_{j=1}^{k+1} \beth_j}} + (1-(\overline{\amalg}_{k+1})^q)^{\frac{\beth_{k+1}}{\sum_{j=1}^{k+1} \beth_j}}}}\right)\end{aligned}$$

$$\begin{aligned} &= \left(\frac{\sqrt[q]{2}\prod_{j=1}^k \breve{\mathfrak{P}}_j^{\frac{\beth_j}{\sum_{j=1}^n \beth_j}} (\breve{\mathfrak{P}}_{k+1})^{\frac{\beth_{k+1}}{\sum_{j=1}^{k+1} \beth_j}}}{\sqrt[q]{\prod_{j=1}^k (2-(\breve{\mathfrak{P}}_j)^q)^{\frac{\beth_j}{\sum_{j=1}^n \beth_j}} (2-(\breve{\mathfrak{P}}_j)^q)^{\frac{\beth_{k+1}}{\sum_{j=1}^{k+1} \beth_j}} + \prod_{j=1}^k ((\breve{\mathfrak{P}}_j)^q)^{\frac{\beth_j}{\sum_{j=1}^n \beth_j}} ((\breve{\mathfrak{P}}_j)^q)^{\frac{\beth_{k+1}}{\sum_{j=1}^{k+1} \beth_j}}}}\right. \\ &\left.\sqrt[q]{\frac{\prod_{j=1}^k (1+(\overline{\amalg}_j)^q)^{\frac{\beth_j}{\sum_{j=1}^n \beth_j}} (1+(\overline{\amalg}_{k+1})^q)^{\frac{\beth_{k+1}}{\sum_{j=1}^{k+1} \beth_j}} - \prod_{j=1}^k (1-(\overline{\amalg}_j)^q)^{\frac{\beth_j}{\sum_{j=1}^n \beth_j}} (1-(\overline{\amalg}_{k+1})^q)^{\frac{\beth_{k+1}}{\sum_{j=1}^{k+1} \beth_j}}}{\prod_{j=1}^k (1+(\overline{\amalg}_j)^q)^{\frac{\beth_j}{\sum_{j=1}^n \beth_j}} (1+(\overline{\amalg}_{k+1})^q)^{\frac{\beth_{k+1}}{\sum_{j=1}^{k+1} \beth_j}} + \prod_{j=1}^k (1-(\overline{\amalg}_j)^q)^{\frac{\beth_j}{\sum_{j=1}^n \beth_j}} (1-(\overline{\amalg}_{k+1})^q)^{\frac{\beth_{k+1}}{\sum_{j=1}^{k+1} \beth_j}}}},\right)\end{aligned}$$

$$= \left(\frac{\sqrt[q]{2}\prod_{j=1}^{k+1} \breve{\mathfrak{P}}_j^{\frac{\beth_j}{\sum_{j=1}^n \beth_j}}}{\sqrt[q]{\prod_{j=1}^{k+1} (2-(\breve{\mathfrak{P}}_j)^q)^{\frac{\beth_j}{\sum_{j=1}^n \beth_j}} + \prod_{j=1}^{k+1} ((\breve{\mathfrak{P}}_j)^q)^{\frac{\beth_j}{\sum_{j=1}^n \beth_j}}}}, \sqrt[q]{\frac{\prod_{j=1}^{k+1} (1+(\overline{\amalg}_j)^q)^{\frac{\beth_j}{\sum_{j=1}^n \beth_j}} - \prod_{j=1}^{k+1} (1-(\overline{\amalg}_j)^q)^{\frac{\beth_j}{\sum_{j=1}^n \beth_j}}}{\prod_{j=1}^{k+1} (1+(\overline{\amalg}_j)^q)^{\frac{\beth_j}{\sum_{j=1}^n \beth_j}} + \prod_{j=1}^{k+1} (1-(\overline{\amalg}_j)^q)^{\frac{\beth_j}{\sum_{j=1}^n \beth_j}}}}\right)$$

thus the result holds for $s = k+1$. This proves the required result. □

Theorem 11. *Let $\breve{\mathfrak{S}}_p = \langle \breve{\mathfrak{P}}_p, \overline{\amalg}_p \rangle$ be the family of q-ROFNs. Aggregated value using q-ROFEPWG operator is q-ROFN.*

Proof. Proof is similar to Theorem 5. □

Theorem 12. *Let $\ddot{\mathfrak{S}}_p = \langle \breve{\mathfrak{P}}_p, \overline{\amalg}_p \rangle$ be the family of q-ROFNs and let*

$$\breve{\mathcal{Z}} = \left(\frac{\beth_1}{\sum_{s=1}^n \beth_s}, \frac{\beth_2}{\sum_{s=1}^n \beth_s}, \ldots, \frac{\beth_n}{\sum_{s=1}^n \beth_s}\right)^T \quad (41)$$

be the WV of $\ddot{\mathfrak{S}}_p = \langle \check{\mathfrak{P}}_p, \overline{\amalg}_p \rangle$. *Then,*

$$q\text{-ROFEPWG}(\mathcal{G}_1, \mathcal{G}_2, \ldots, \mathcal{G}_n) \geq q\text{-ROFPWG}(\mathcal{G}_1, \mathcal{G}_2, \ldots, \mathcal{G}_n) \tag{42}$$

where $\beth_j = \prod_{k=1}^{j-1} \Xi(\ddot{\mathfrak{S}}_k)$ $(j = 2 \ldots, n)$, $\beth_1 = 1$ *and* $\Xi(\ddot{\mathfrak{S}}_k)$ *is the score of* k^{th} *q-ROFN.*

Proof. Proof is similar to Theorem 6. □

Example 2. *Let* $\ddot{\mathfrak{S}}_1 = (0.7908, 0.2786)$, $\ddot{\mathfrak{S}}_2 = (0.2086, 0.6315)$, $\ddot{\mathfrak{S}}_3 = (0.4966, 0.2182)$, $\ddot{\mathfrak{S}}_4 = (0.3298, 0.5559)$, $\ddot{\mathfrak{S}}_5 = (0.6107, 0.2364)$ *and* $\ddot{\mathfrak{S}}_6 = (0.3797, 0.4850)$ *be the q-ROFNs* $q = 3$ *then we have,*

$$\frac{\sqrt[q]{2}\prod_{j=1}^{6} \check{\mathfrak{P}}_j^{\frac{\beth_j}{\sum_{j=1}^{n}\beth_j}}}{\sqrt[q]{\prod_{j=1}^{6}(2-(\check{\mathfrak{P}}_j)^q)^{\frac{\beth_j}{\sum_{j=1}^{n}\beth_j}} + \prod_{j=1}^{6}((\check{\mathfrak{P}}_j)^q)^{\frac{\beth_j}{\sum_{j=1}^{n}\beth_j}}}} = 0.475915$$

$$\sqrt[q]{\frac{\prod_{j=1}^{6}(1+(\overline{\amalg}_j)^q)^{\frac{\beth_j}{\sum_{j=1}^{n}\beth_j}} - \prod_{j=1}^{6}(1-(\overline{\amalg}_j)^q)^{\frac{\beth_j}{\sum_{j=1}^{n}\beth_j}}}{\prod_{j=1}^{6}(1+(\overline{\amalg}_j)^q)^{\frac{\beth_j}{\sum_{j=1}^{n}\beth_j}} + \prod_{j=1}^{6}(1-(\overline{\amalg}_j)^q)^{\frac{\beth_j}{\sum_{j=1}^{n}\beth_j}}}} = 0.458739$$

and

$$\begin{aligned} q\text{-ROFEPWG}(\ddot{\mathfrak{S}}_1, \ddot{\mathfrak{S}}_2, \ddot{\mathfrak{S}}_3, \ddot{\mathfrak{S}}_4, \ddot{\mathfrak{S}}_5, \ddot{\mathfrak{S}}_6) &= \left(\frac{\sqrt[q]{2}\prod_{j=1}^{6} \check{\mathfrak{P}}_j^{\frac{\beth_j}{\sum_{j=1}^{n}\beth_j}}}{\sqrt[q]{\prod_{j=1}^{6}(2-(\check{\mathfrak{P}}_j)^q)^{\frac{\beth_j}{\sum_{j=1}^{n}\beth_j}} + \prod_{j=1}^{6}((\check{\mathfrak{P}}_j)^q)^{\frac{\beth_j}{\sum_{j=1}^{n}\beth_j}}}}, \right. \\ &\left. \sqrt[q]{\frac{\prod_{j=1}^{6}(1+(\overline{\amalg}_j)^q)^{\frac{\beth_j}{\sum_{j=1}^{n}\beth_j}} - \prod_{j=1}^{6}(1-(\overline{\amalg}_j)^q)^{\frac{\beth_j}{\sum_{j=1}^{n}\beth_j}}}{\prod_{j=1}^{6}(1+(\overline{\amalg}_j)^q)^{\frac{\beth_j}{\sum_{j=1}^{n}\beth_j}} + \prod_{j=1}^{6}(1-(\overline{\amalg}_j)^q)^{\frac{\beth_j}{\sum_{j=1}^{n}\beth_j}}}} \right) \\ &= (0.475915, 0.458739) \end{aligned}$$

Below we define some of q-ROFEPWG operator's appealing properties.

Theorem 13. *(Idempotency) Assume that* $\ddot{\mathfrak{S}}_j = \langle \check{\mathfrak{P}}_j, \overline{\amalg}_j \rangle$ *is the family of q-ROFNs, where* $\beth_j = \prod_{k=1}^{j-1} \Xi(\ddot{\mathfrak{S}}_k)$ $(j = 2 \ldots, n)$, $\beth_1 = 1$ *and* $\Xi(\ddot{\mathfrak{S}}_k)$ *is the score of* k^{th} *q-ROFN. If all* $\ddot{\mathfrak{S}}_j$ *are equal, i.e.,* $\ddot{\mathfrak{S}}_j = \ddot{\mathfrak{S}}\ \forall j$, *then*

$$q\text{-ROFEPWG}(\ddot{\mathfrak{S}}_1, \ddot{\mathfrak{S}}_2, \ldots \ddot{\mathfrak{S}}_n) = \ddot{\mathfrak{S}}$$

Proof.

$$\begin{aligned}
\text{q-ROFEPWG}(\ddot{\mathfrak{S}}_1, \ddot{\mathfrak{S}}_2, \ldots \ddot{\mathfrak{S}}_n) &= \text{q-ROFEPWG}(\ddot{\mathfrak{S}}, \ddot{\mathfrak{S}}, \ldots \ddot{\mathfrak{S}}) \\
&= \left(\ddot{\mathfrak{S}}^{\frac{\beth_1}{\sum_{j=1}^n \beth_j}} \otimes_\epsilon \ddot{\mathfrak{S}}^{\frac{\beth_2}{\sum_{j=1}^n \beth_j}} \otimes_\epsilon \ldots, \otimes_\epsilon \ddot{\mathfrak{S}}^{\frac{\beth_n}{\sum_{j=1}^n \beth_j}} \right) \\
&= \left(\frac{\sqrt[q]{2} \prod_{j=1}^n \check{\mathfrak{P}}^{\frac{\beth_j}{\sum_{j=1}^n \beth_j}}}{\sqrt[q]{\prod_{j=1}^n (2 - (\check{\mathfrak{P}})^q)^{\frac{\beth_j}{\sum_{j=1}^n \beth_j}} + \prod_{j=1}^n ((\check{\mathfrak{P}})^q)^{\frac{\beth_j}{\sum_{j=1}^n \beth_j}}}}, \right. \\
&\quad \left. \sqrt[q]{\frac{\prod_{j=1}^n (1 + (\overline{\Pi})^q)^{\frac{\beth_j}{\sum_{j=1}^n \beth_j}} - \prod_{j=1}^n (1 - (\overline{\Pi})^q)^{\frac{\beth_j}{\sum_{j=1}^n \beth_j}}}{\prod_{j=1}^n (1 + (\overline{\Pi})^q)^{\frac{\beth_j}{\sum_{j=1}^n \beth_j}} + \prod_{j=1}^n (1 - (\overline{\Pi})^q)^{\frac{\beth_j}{\sum_{j=1}^n \beth_j}}}} \right) \\
&= \left(\frac{\sqrt[q]{2}\check{\mathfrak{P}}}{\sqrt[q]{2}}, \sqrt[q]{\frac{(1 + (\overline{\Pi}^q)) - (1 - (\overline{\Pi})^q)}{(1 + (\overline{\Pi})^q) + (1 - (\overline{\Pi})^q)}} \right) = (\check{\mathfrak{P}}, \overline{\Pi}) = \ddot{\mathfrak{S}}
\end{aligned}$$

□

Corollary 3. *If* $\ddot{\mathfrak{S}}_j = \langle \check{\mathfrak{P}}_j, \overline{\Pi}_j \rangle$ $j = (1, 2, \ldots n)$ *is the family of largest q-ROFNs, i.e.,* $\ddot{\mathfrak{S}}_j = (1, 0)$ $\forall j$, *then*

$$q\text{-}ROFEPWG(\ddot{\mathfrak{S}}_1, \ddot{\mathfrak{S}}_2, \ldots \ddot{\mathfrak{S}}_n) = (1, 0)$$

Proof. We can easily obtain a Corollary similar to the Theorem 13. □

Corollary 4. *(Non-compensatory) If* $\ddot{\mathfrak{S}}_1 = \langle \check{\mathfrak{P}}_1, \overline{\Pi}_1 \rangle$ *is the smallest q-ROFN, i.e.,* $\ddot{\mathfrak{S}}_1 = (0, 1)$, *then*

$$q\text{-}ROFEPWG(\ddot{\mathfrak{S}}_1, \ddot{\mathfrak{S}}_2, \ldots \ddot{\mathfrak{S}}_n) = (0, 1)$$

Proof. Here, $\ddot{\mathfrak{S}}_1 = (0, 1)$ then by score function, we have,

$$\breve{\Xi}(\ddot{\mathfrak{S}}_1) = 0$$

Since,

$$\beth_j = \prod_{k=1}^{j-1} \breve{\Xi}(\ddot{\mathfrak{S}}_k) \qquad (j = 2 \ldots, n), \quad \text{and} \quad \beth_1 = 1$$

$\breve{\Xi}(\ddot{\mathfrak{S}}_k)$ is the score of kth q-ROFN.

We have,
$\beth_j = \prod_{k=1}^{j-1} \breve{\Xi}(\ddot{\mathfrak{S}}_k) = \breve{\Xi}(\ddot{\mathfrak{S}}_1) \times \breve{\Xi}(\ddot{\mathfrak{S}}_2) \times \ldots \times \breve{\Xi}(\ddot{\mathfrak{S}}_{j-1}) = 0 \times \breve{\Xi}(\ddot{\mathfrak{S}}_2) \times \ldots \times \breve{\Xi}(\ddot{\mathfrak{S}}_{j-1}) \qquad (j = 2 \ldots, n)$

$$\prod_{k=1}^{j} \beth_j = 1$$

From Definition 14, we have

$$\begin{aligned} \text{q-ROFEPWG}(\ddot{\mathfrak{S}}_1, \ddot{\mathfrak{S}}_2, \ldots \ddot{\mathfrak{S}}_n) &= \ddot{\mathfrak{S}}_1^{\frac{\beth_1}{\sum_{j=1}^n \beth_j}} \otimes \ddot{\mathfrak{S}}_2^{\frac{\beth_2}{\sum_{j=1}^n \beth_j}} \otimes \ldots, \otimes \ddot{\mathfrak{S}}_n^{\frac{\beth_n}{\sum_{j=1}^n \beth_j}} \\ &= \ddot{\mathfrak{S}}_1^{\frac{1}{1}} \otimes \ddot{\mathfrak{S}}_2^{\frac{0}{1}} \otimes \ldots \ddot{\mathfrak{S}}_n^{\frac{0}{1}} \\ &= \ddot{\mathfrak{S}}_1 = (0,1) \end{aligned}$$

□

Corollary 4 meant that, if the higher priority criteria are met by the smallest q-ROFN, rewards will not be received by other criteria even though they are fulfilled.

Theorem 14. *(Monotonicity) Assume that $\ddot{\mathfrak{S}}_j = \langle \check{\mathfrak{P}}_j, \overline{\Pi}_j \rangle$ and $\ddot{\mathfrak{S}}_{j^*} = \langle \check{\mathfrak{P}}_{j^*}, \overline{\Pi}_{j^*} \rangle$ are the families of q-ROFNs, where $\beth_j = \prod_{k=1}^{j-1} \breve{\Xi}(\ddot{\mathfrak{S}}_k)$, $\beth_{j^*} = \prod_{k=1}^{j-1} \breve{\Xi}(\ddot{\mathfrak{S}}_{k^*})$ $(j = 2 \ldots, n)$, $\beth_1 = 1$, $\beth_{1^*} = 1$, $\breve{\Xi}(\ddot{\mathfrak{S}}_k)$ is the score of $\ddot{\mathfrak{S}}_k$ q-ROFN, and $\breve{\Xi}(\ddot{\mathfrak{S}}_{k^*})$ is the score of $\ddot{\mathfrak{S}}_{k^*}$ q-ROFN. If $\check{\mathfrak{P}}_{j^*} \geq \check{\mathfrak{P}}_j$ and $\overline{\Pi}_{j^*} \leq \overline{\Pi}_j$ for all j, then*

$$\text{q-ROFPWG}(\ddot{\mathfrak{S}}_1, \ddot{\mathfrak{S}}_2, \ldots \ddot{\mathfrak{S}}_n) \leq \text{q-ROFPWG}(\ddot{\mathfrak{S}}_{1^*}, \ddot{\mathfrak{S}}_{2^*}, \ldots \ddot{\mathfrak{S}}_{n^*})$$

Proof. Proof is same as Theorem 8. □

Theorem 15. *(Boundary) Assume that $\ddot{\mathfrak{S}}_j = \langle \check{\mathfrak{P}}_j, \overline{\Pi}_j \rangle$ be the assemblage of q-ROFNs, where $\beth_j = \prod_{k=1}^{j-1} \breve{\Xi}(\ddot{\mathfrak{S}}_k)$, $(j = 2 \ldots, n)$, $\beth_1 = 1$ and $\breve{\Xi}(\ddot{\mathfrak{S}}_k)$ is the score of $\ddot{\mathfrak{S}}_k$ q-ROFN,then*

$$\ddot{\mathfrak{S}}_{min} \leq \text{q-ROFPWG}(\ddot{\mathfrak{S}}_1, \ddot{\mathfrak{S}}_2, \ldots \ddot{\mathfrak{S}}_n) \leq \ddot{\mathfrak{S}}_{max} \tag{43}$$

where,

$$\ddot{\mathfrak{S}}_{min} = min(\ddot{\mathfrak{S}}_j) \quad \text{and} \quad \ddot{\mathfrak{S}}_{max} = max(\ddot{\mathfrak{S}}_j)$$

Proof. Proof is same as Theorem 9. □

4. Proposed Methodology

Consider a set of alternatives $\ddot{\mathfrak{X}} = \{\ddot{\mathfrak{X}}_1, \ddot{\mathfrak{X}}_2, \ldots, \ddot{\mathfrak{X}}_m\}$ with m elements and $\bar{\mathsf{T}} = \{\bar{\mathsf{T}}_1, \bar{\mathsf{T}}_2, \ldots, \bar{\mathsf{T}}_n\}$ is the finite set of criterions with n elements and prioritization is given between the criteria presented by the linear order $\bar{\mathsf{T}}_1 \succ \bar{\mathsf{T}}_2 \succ \bar{\mathsf{T}}_3 \cdots \bar{\mathsf{T}}_n$ indicates criteria $\bar{\mathsf{T}}_J$ has a higher priority than $\bar{\mathsf{T}}_i$ if $j > i$. $\mathfrak{K} = \{\mathfrak{K}_1, \mathfrak{K}_2, \ldots, \mathfrak{K}_p\}$ is the group of decision makers and decision makers (DMs) do not have the equal importance. Prioritization given between the DMs presented by the linear order $\mathfrak{K}_1 \succ \mathfrak{K}_2 \succ \mathfrak{K}_3 \ldots \mathfrak{K}_p$ indicates DM $\mathfrak{K}_\zeta$ has a higher priority than $\mathfrak{K}_\varrho$ if $\zeta > \varrho$. Decision makers provide a matrix of their own opinion $D^{(p)} = (\mathscr{B}_{ij}^{(p)})_{m \times n}$, where $\mathscr{B}_{ij}^{(p)}$ is given for the alternatives $\ddot{\mathfrak{X}}_i \in \ddot{\mathfrak{X}}$ with respect to the criteria $\bar{\mathsf{T}}_j \in \bar{\mathsf{T}}$ by $\mathfrak{K}_p$ decision maker in the form of q-ROFNs. If all Criterions are the same types, there is no need for normalization, but there are two types of Criterions (benefit type attributes τ_b and cost type attributes τ_c) in MCGDM, in this case using the normalization formula, the matrix $D^{(p)}$ has been changed into normalized matrix $Y^{(p)} = (\mathscr{P}_{ij}^{(p)})_{m \times n}$,

$$(\mathscr{P}_{ij}^{(p)})_{m \times n} = \begin{cases} (\mathscr{B}_{ij}^{(p)})^c; & j \in \tau_c \\ \mathscr{B}_{ij}^{(p)}; & j \in \tau_b. \end{cases} \tag{44}$$

where $(\mathscr{B}_{ij}^{(p)})^c$ show the compliment of $\mathscr{B}_{ij}^{(p)}$.

We then use the q-ROFPWA operator or q-ROFPWA operator to implement a MCGDM approach in an q-ROF circumstances.

The proposed operators will be applied to the MCGDM, which is defined in Algorithm 1.

Algorithm 1

Step 1:

Acquire a decision matrix $D^{(p)} = (\mathscr{B}_{ij}^{(p)})_{m\times n}$ in the form of q-ROFNs from the decision makers.

$$
\begin{array}{lllllll}
 & & & & & \bar{\text{T}}_1 \quad \bar{\text{T}}_2 \quad \bar{\text{T}}_n \\
\mathfrak{K}_1 & \ddot{\mathfrak{X}}_1 & (\breve{\mathfrak{P}}_{11}^1, \overline{\amalg}_{11}^1) & (\breve{\mathfrak{P}}_{12}^1, \overline{\amalg}_{12}^1) & \cdots\cdots & (\breve{\mathfrak{P}}_{1n}^1, \overline{\amalg}_{1n}^1)[t] \\
 & \ddot{\mathfrak{X}}_2 & (\breve{\mathfrak{P}}_{21}^1, \overline{\amalg}_{21}^1) & (\breve{\mathfrak{P}}_{22}^1, \overline{\amalg}_{22}^1) & \cdots\cdots & (\breve{\mathfrak{P}}_{2n}^1, \overline{\amalg}_{2n}^1) \\
 & & \vdots & \vdots & \ddots\ddots & \vdots \\
 & \ddot{\mathfrak{X}}_m & (\breve{\mathfrak{P}}_{m1}^1, \overline{\amalg}_{m1}^1) & (\breve{\mathfrak{P}}_{m2}^1, \overline{\amalg}_{m2}^1) & \cdots\cdots & (\breve{\mathfrak{P}}_{mn}^1, \overline{\amalg}_{mn}^1)[b] \\
\mathfrak{K}_2 & \ddot{\mathfrak{X}}_1 & (\breve{\mathfrak{P}}_{11}^2, \overline{\amalg}_{11}^2) & (\breve{\mathfrak{P}}_{12}^2, \overline{\amalg}_{12}^2) & \cdots\cdots & (\breve{\mathfrak{P}}_{1n}^2, \overline{\amalg}_{1n}^2)[t] \\
\vdots & \ddot{\mathfrak{X}}_2 & (\breve{\mathfrak{P}}_{21}^2, \overline{\amalg}_{21}^2) & (\breve{\mathfrak{P}}_{22}^2, \overline{\amalg}_{22}^2) & \cdots\cdots & (\breve{\mathfrak{P}}_{2n}^2, \overline{\amalg}_{2n}^2) \\
 & & \vdots & \vdots & \ddots\ddots & \vdots \\
 & \ddot{\mathfrak{X}}_m & (\breve{\mathfrak{P}}_{m1}^2, \overline{\amalg}_{m1}^2) & (\breve{\mathfrak{P}}_{m2}^2, \overline{\amalg}_{m2}^2) & \cdots\cdots & (\breve{\mathfrak{P}}_{mn}^2, \overline{\amalg}_{mn}^2)[b] \\
\mathfrak{K}_p & \ddot{\mathfrak{X}}_1 & (\breve{\mathfrak{P}}_{11}^p, \overline{\amalg}_{11}^p) & (\breve{\mathfrak{P}}_{12}^p, \overline{\amalg}_{12}^p) & \cdots\cdots & (\breve{\mathfrak{P}}_{1n}^p, \overline{\amalg}_{1n}^p)[t] \\
 & \ddot{\mathfrak{X}}_2 & (\breve{\mathfrak{P}}_{21}^p, \overline{\amalg}_{21}^p) & (\breve{\mathfrak{P}}_{22}^p, \overline{\amalg}_{22}^p) & \cdots\cdots & (\breve{\mathfrak{P}}_{2n}^p, \overline{\amalg}_{2n})^p \\
 & & \vdots & \vdots & \ddots\ddots & \vdots \\
 & \ddot{\mathfrak{X}}_m & (\breve{\mathfrak{P}}_{m1}^p, \overline{\amalg}_{m1}^p) & (\breve{\mathfrak{P}}_{m2}^p, \overline{\amalg}_{m2}^p) & \cdots\cdots & (\breve{\mathfrak{P}}_{mn}^p, \overline{\amalg}_{mn}^p)[b]
\end{array}
$$

Step 2:

Two types of criteria are specified in the decision matrix, namely cost type criteria (τ_c) and benefit type criteria (τ_b). If all Criterions are the same type, there is no need for normalization, but there are two types of Criterions in MCGDM. In this case, using the normalization formula Equation (44) the matrix has been changed into transformed response matrix $Y^{(p)} = (\mathscr{P}_{ij}^{(p)})_{m\times n}$

Step 3:

Calculate the values of $\beth_{ij}^{(p)}$ by following formula.

$$\beth_{ij}^{(p)} = \prod_{k=1}^{p-1} \breve{\Xi}(\mathscr{P}_{ij}^{(k)}) \quad (p = 2\ldots, n), \tag{45}$$

$$\beth_{ij}^{(1)} = 1$$

Step 4:

Use one of the suggested aggregation operators.

$$\mathscr{W}_{ij} = \text{q-ROFEPWA}(\mathscr{P}_{ij}^{(1)}, \mathscr{P}_{ij}^{(2)}, \ldots \mathscr{P}_{ij}^{(p)}) = \left(\sqrt[q]{\frac{\prod_{z=1}^{p}(1+((\breve{\mathfrak{P}}_{ij}^{q})^z)^{\frac{\beth_j^z}{\sum_{j=1}^{n}\beth_j^z}} - \prod_{z=1}^{p}(1-((\breve{\mathfrak{P}}_{ij}^{q})^z)^{\frac{\beth_j^z}{\sum_{j=1}^{n}\beth_j^z}}}{\prod_{z=1}^{p}(1+((\breve{\mathfrak{P}}_{ij}^{q})^z)^{\frac{\beth_j^z}{\sum_{j=1}^{n}\beth_j^z}} + \prod_{z=1}^{p}(1-((\breve{\mathfrak{P}}_{ij}^{q})^z)^{\frac{\beth_j^z}{\sum_{j=1}^{n}\beth_j^z}}}}, \frac{\sqrt[q]{2}\prod_{z=1}^{p}\overline{\amalg}_j^{\frac{\beth_j^z}{\sum_{j=1}^{n}\beth_j^z}}}{\sqrt[q]{\prod_{z=1}^{p}(2-((\overline{\amalg}_{ij}^{q})^z)^{\frac{\beth_j^z}{\sum_{j=1}^{n}\beth_j^z}} + \prod_{z=1}^{p}(((\overline{\amalg}_{ij}^{q})^z)^{\frac{\beth_j^z}{\sum_{j=1}^{n}\beth_j^z}}}} \right) \tag{46}$$

Algorithm 1 *Cont.*

or

$$\mathscr{W}_{ij} = \text{q-ROFEPWG}(\mathscr{P}_{ij}^{(1)}, \mathscr{P}_{ij}^{(2)}, \ldots \mathscr{P}_{ij}^{(p)}) = \left(\frac{\sqrt[q]{2}\prod_{z=1}^{p} \mathfrak{P}_{j}^{\frac{\beth_j^z}{\sum_{j=1}^{n}\beth_j^z}}}{\sqrt[q]{\prod_{z=1}^{p}(2-((\mathfrak{P}_{ij}^q)^z))^{\frac{\beth_j^z}{\sum_{j=1}^{n}\beth_j^z}} + \prod_{z=1}^{p}(((\mathfrak{P}_{ij}^q)^z)^{\frac{\beth_j^z}{\sum_{j=1}^{n}\beth_j^z}}}}, \sqrt[q]{\frac{\prod_{z=1}^{p}(1+((\Pi_{ij}^q)^z))^{\frac{\beth_j^z}{\sum_{j=1}^{n}\beth_j^z}} - \prod_{z=1}^{p}(1-((\Pi_{ij}^q)^z))^{\frac{\beth_j^z}{\sum_{j=1}^{n}\beth_j^z}}}{\prod_{z=1}^{p}(1+((\Pi_{ij}^q)^z))^{\frac{\beth_j^z}{\sum_{j=1}^{n}\beth_j^z}} + \prod_{z=1}^{p}(1-((\Pi_{ij}^q)^z))^{\frac{\beth_j^z}{\sum_{j=1}^{n}\beth_j^z}}}} \right) \quad (47)$$

To aggregate all individual q-ROF decision matrices $Y^{(p)} = (\mathscr{P}_{ij}^{(p)})_{m\times n}$ into one cumulative assessments matrix of the alternatives $W^{(p)} = (\mathscr{W}_{ij})_{m\times n}$

Step 5:

Calculate the values of $\beth_{ij}$ by the following formula.

$$\beth_{ij} = \prod_{k=1}^{j-1} \Xi(\mathscr{W}_{ik}) \quad (j = 2\ldots, n), \quad (48)$$

$$\beth_{i1} = 1$$

Step 6:

Aggregate the q-ROF values $\mathscr{W}_{ij}$ for each alternative $\ddot{\mathfrak{X}}_i$ by the q-ROFEPWA (or q-ROFEPWG) operator:

$$\mathscr{W}_i = \text{q-ROFEPWA}(\mathscr{P}_{i1}, \mathscr{P}_{i2}, \ldots \mathscr{P}_{in}) = \left(\sqrt[q]{\frac{\prod_{j=1}^{n}(1+(\mathfrak{P}_{ij})^q)^{\frac{\beth_j}{\sum_{j=1}^{n}\beth_j}} - \prod_{j=1}^{n}(1-(\mathfrak{P}_{ij})^q)^{\frac{\beth_j}{\sum_{j=1}^{n}\beth_j}}}{\prod_{j=1}^{n}(1+(\mathfrak{P}_{ij})^q)^{\frac{\beth_j}{\sum_{j=1}^{n}\beth_j}} + \prod_{j=1}^{n}(1-(\mathfrak{P}_{ij})^q)^{\frac{\beth_j}{\sum_{j=1}^{n}\beth_j}}}}, \frac{\sqrt[q]{2}\prod_{j=1}^{n} \Pi_{ij}^{\frac{\beth_j}{\sum_{j=1}^{n}\beth_j}}}{\sqrt[q]{\prod_{j=1}^{n}(2-(\Pi_{ij})^q)^{\frac{\beth_j}{\sum_{j=1}^{n}\beth_j}} + \prod_{j=1}^{n}((\Pi_{ij})^q)^{\frac{\beth_j}{\sum_{j=1}^{n}\beth_j}}}} \right) \quad (49)$$

or

$$\mathscr{W}_i = \text{q-ROFPWG}(\mathscr{P}_{i1}, \mathscr{P}_{i2}, \ldots \mathscr{P}_{in}) = \left(\frac{\sqrt[q]{2}\prod_{j=1}^{n} \mathfrak{P}_{ij}^{\frac{\beth_j}{\sum_{j=1}^{n}\beth_j}}}{\sqrt[q]{\prod_{j=1}^{n}(2-(\mathfrak{P}_{ij})^q)^{\frac{\beth_j}{\sum_{j=1}^{n}\beth_j}} + \prod_{j=1}^{n}((\mathfrak{P}_{ij})^q)^{\frac{\beth_j}{\sum_{j=1}^{n}\beth_j}}}}, \sqrt[q]{\frac{\prod_{j=1}^{n}(1+(\Pi_{ij})^q)^{\frac{\beth_j}{\sum_{j=1}^{n}\beth_j}} - \prod_{j=1}^{n}(1-(\Pi_{ij})^q)^{\frac{\beth_j}{\sum_{j=1}^{n}\beth_j}}}{\prod_{j=1}^{n}(1+(\Pi_{ij})^q)^{\frac{\beth_j}{\sum_{j=1}^{n}\beth_j}} + \prod_{j=1}^{n}(1-(\Pi_{ij})^q)^{\frac{\beth_j}{\sum_{j=1}^{n}\beth_j}}}} \right) \quad (50)$$

Step 7:

Evaluate the score of the all cumulative alternative assessments.

Step 8:

Ranked the alternatives by the score function and ultimately choose the most appropriate alternative.

5. Illustrative Example

We provide a numerical illustration to explain the approach suggested below.

Let us assume an inviting bid process whereby the investor is trying to find out the optimal biding scheme. In order to catch up with the advancement of modern manufacturing industries and to enhance the city's ecosystem equality, steel and iron works are planning to build a palletizing plant in its primary iron ore production area with a production capacity of more than 1.45 million tons per year. The builder will request bidding for the construction project, taking into account the project regulations, and will choose from five bidders as per six attributes as follows:

Example 3. *Consider a set of alternatives* $\ddot{\mathfrak{X}} = \{\ddot{\mathfrak{X}}_1, \ddot{\mathfrak{X}}_2, \ddot{\mathfrak{X}}_3, \ddot{\mathfrak{X}}_4, \ddot{\mathfrak{X}}_5\}$ *and* $\bar{\mathrm{T}} = \{\bar{\mathrm{T}}_1, \bar{\mathrm{T}}_2, \bar{\mathrm{T}}_3, \bar{\mathrm{T}}_4, \bar{\mathrm{T}}_5, \bar{\mathrm{T}}_6\}$ *is the finite set of criterions given in Table 2. Prioritization is given between the criteria presented by the linear order* $\bar{\mathrm{T}}_1 \succ \bar{\mathrm{T}}_2 \succ \bar{\mathrm{T}}_3 \cdots \bar{\mathrm{T}}_6$ *indicates criteria* $\bar{\mathrm{T}}_J$ *has a higher priority than* $\bar{\mathrm{T}}_i$ *if* $j > i$. $\mathfrak{K} = \{\mathfrak{K}_1, \mathfrak{K}_2, \mathfrak{K}_3\}$ *is the group of decision makers and decision makers (DMs) do not have the equal importance. Prioritization given between the DMs presented by the linear order* $\mathfrak{K}_1 \succ \mathfrak{K}_2 \succ \mathfrak{K}_3$ *indicates DM* $\mathfrak{K}_\zeta$ *has a higher priority than* $\mathfrak{K}_\varrho$ *if* $\zeta > \varrho$. *Decision makers provide a matrix of their own opinion* $D^{(p)} = (\mathscr{B}_{ij}^{(p)})_{m\times n}$, *where* $\mathscr{B}_{ij}^{(p)}$ *is given for the alternatives* $\ddot{\mathfrak{X}}_i \in \ddot{\mathfrak{X}}$ *with respect to the criteria* $\bar{\mathrm{T}}_j \in \bar{\mathrm{T}}$ *by* $\mathfrak{K}_p$ *decision maker in the form of q-ROFNs. We take* $q = 3$.

Table 2. Criterions for evaluating the best alternative.

	Criterions
$\bar{\mathrm{T}}_1$	Rich portfolios
$\bar{\mathrm{T}}_2$	Timely project delivery
$\bar{\mathrm{T}}_3$	Goodwill and reputation
$\bar{\mathrm{T}}_4$	Quality of construction
$\bar{\mathrm{T}}_5$	Credentials
$\bar{\mathrm{T}}_6$	Expertise

Step 1:

Acquire a decision/assessment matrix $D^{(p)} = (\mathscr{B}_{ij}^{(p)})_{m\times n}$ *in the form of q-ROFNs from the decision makers. Assessment matrix acquired from* $\mathfrak{K}_1$ *is given in Table 3.*

Table 3. Assessment matrix acquired from $\mathfrak{K}_1$.

	$\bar{\mathrm{T}}_1$	$\bar{\mathrm{T}}_2$	$\bar{\mathrm{T}}_3$	$\bar{\mathrm{T}}_4$	$\bar{\mathrm{T}}_5$	$\bar{\mathrm{T}}_6$
$\ddot{\mathfrak{X}}_1$	(0.90, 0.00)	(0.65, 0.35)	(0.75, 0.15)	(0.95, 0.15)	(0.75, 0.00)	(0.45, 0.25)
$\ddot{\mathfrak{X}}_2$	(0.95, 0.25)	(0.80, 0.30)	(0.55, 0.25)	(0.75, 0.15)	(0.45, 0.45)	(0.35, 0.15)
$\ddot{\mathfrak{X}}_3$	(0.85, 0.15)	(0.35, 0.55)	(0.75, 0.25)	(0.55, 0.00)	(0.65, 0.35)	(0.45, 0.00)
$\ddot{\mathfrak{X}}_4$	(0.75, 0.35)	(0.81, 0.25)	(0.65, 0.15)	(0.35, 0.25)	(0.75, 0.25)	(0.35, 0.75)
$\ddot{\mathfrak{X}}_5$	(0.80, 0.25)	(0.60, 0.00)	(0.25, 0.15)	(0.15, 0.65)	(0.65, 0.15)	(0.25, 0.65)

Assessment matrix acquired from $\mathfrak{K}_2$ *is given in Table 4.*

Table 4. Assessment matrix acquired from $\mathfrak{K}_2$.

	$\bar{\mathrm{T}}_1$	$\bar{\mathrm{T}}_2$	$\bar{\mathrm{T}}_3$	$\bar{\mathrm{T}}_4$	$\bar{\mathrm{T}}_5$	$\bar{\mathrm{T}}_6$
$\ddot{\mathfrak{X}}_1$	(0.75, 0.25)	(0.55, 0.30)	(0.85, 0.15)	(0.95, 0.15)	(0.80, 0.25)	(0.90, 0.15)
$\ddot{\mathfrak{X}}_2$	(0.55, 0.15)	(0.60, 0.35)	(0.45, 0.15)	(0.75, 0.35)	(0.65, 0.30)	(0.75, 0.00)
$\ddot{\mathfrak{X}}_3$	(0.90, 0.60)	(0.65, 0.20)	(0.25, 0.55)	(0.65, 0.55)	(0.15, 0.25)	(0.70, 0.30)
$\ddot{\mathfrak{X}}_4$	(0.50, 0.00)	(0.55, 0.40)	(0.15, 0.10)	(0.50, 0.60)	(0.10, 0.15)	(0.60, 0.35)
$\ddot{\mathfrak{X}}_5$	(0.85, 0.35)	(0.70, 0.30)	(0.65, 0.55)	(0.25, 0.50)	(0.50, 0.30)	(0.50, 0.25)

Assessment matrix acquired from $\mathfrak{K}_3$ *is given in Table 5.*

Table 5. Assessment matrix acquired from $\mathfrak{K}_3$.

	$\bar{T}_1$	$\bar{T}_2$	$\bar{T}_3$	$\bar{T}_4$	$\bar{T}_5$	$\bar{T}_6$
$\ddot{x}_1$	(0.90, 0.15)	(0.85, 0.25)	(0.80, 0.00)	(0.70, 0.35)	(0.80, 0.20)	(0.70, 0.30)
$\ddot{x}_2$	(0.80, 0.25)	(0.55, 0.15)	(0.60, 0.25)	(0.50, 0.30)	(0.60, 0.30)	(0.60, 0.30)
$\ddot{x}_3$	(0.75, 0.15)	(0.65, 0.25)	(0.35, 0.00)	(0.50, 0.35)	(0.75, 0.30)	(0.35, 0.25)
$\ddot{x}_4$	(0.35, 0.35)	(0.50, 0.35)	(0.45, 0.25)	(0.55, 0.45)	(0.25, 0.25)	(0.65, 0.00)
$\ddot{x}_5$	(0.65, 0.25)	(0.65, 0.25)	(0.60, 0.15)	(0.65, 0.25)	(0.65, 0.55)	(0.45, 0.40)

Step 2:

Normalize the decision matrixes acquired by DMs using Equation (44). In Table 2, there are two types of criterions. $\bar{T}_2$ is cost type criteria and others are benefit type criterions.
Normalized assessment matrix acquired from $\mathfrak{K}_1$ is given in Table 6.

Table 6. Normalized assessment matrix acquired from $\mathfrak{K}_1$.

	$\bar{T}_1$	$\bar{T}_2$	$\bar{T}_3$	$\bar{T}_4$	$\bar{T}_5$	$\bar{T}_6$
$\ddot{x}_1$	(0.90, 0.00)	(0.35, 0.65)	(0.75, 0.15)	(0.95, 0.15)	(0.75, 0.00)	(0.45, 0.25)
$\ddot{x}_2$	(0.95, 0.25)	(0.30, 0.80)	(0.55, 0.25)	(0.75, 0.15)	(0.45, 0.45)	(0.35, 0.15)
$\ddot{x}_3$	(0.85, 0.15)	(0.55, 0.35)	(0.75, 0.25)	(0.55, 0.00)	(0.65, 0.35)	(0.45, 0.00)
$\ddot{x}_4$	(0.75, 0.35)	(0.25, 0.81)	(0.65, 0.15)	(0.35, 0.25)	(0.75, 0.25)	(0.35, 0.75)
$\ddot{x}_5$	(0.80, 0.25)	(0.00, 0.60)	(0.25, 0.15)	(0.15, 0.65)	(0.65, 0.15)	(0.25, 0.65)

Normalized assessment matrix acquired from $\mathfrak{K}_2$ is given in Table 7.

Table 7. Normalized assessment matrix acquired from $\mathfrak{K}_2$.

	$\bar{T}_1$	$\bar{T}_2$	$\bar{T}_3$	$\bar{T}_4$	$\bar{T}_5$	$\bar{T}_6$
$\ddot{x}_1$	(0.75, 0.25)	(0.30, 0.55)	(0.85, 0.15)	(0.95, 0.15)	(0.80, 0.25)	(0.90, 0.15)
$\ddot{x}_2$	(0.55, 0.15)	(0.35, 0.60)	(0.45, 0.15)	(0.75, 0.35)	(0.65, 0.30)	(0.75, 0.00)
$\ddot{x}_3$	(0.90, 0.60)	(0.20, 0.65)	(0.25, 0.55)	(0.65, 0.55)	(0.15, 0.25)	(0.70, 0.30)
$\ddot{x}_4$	(0.50, 0.00)	(0.40, 0.55)	(0.15, 0.10)	(0.50, 0.60)	(0.10, 0.15)	(0.60, 0.35)
$\ddot{x}_5$	(0.85, 0.35)	(0.30, 0.70)	(0.65, 0.55)	(0.25, 0.50)	(0.50, 0.30)	(0.50, 0.25)

Normalized assessment matrix acquired from $\mathfrak{K}_3$ is given in Table 8.

Table 8. Normalized assessment matrix acquired from $\mathfrak{K}_3$.

	$\bar{T}_1$	$\bar{T}_2$	$\bar{T}_3$	$\bar{T}_4$	$\bar{T}_5$	$\bar{T}_6$
$\ddot{x}_1$	(0.90, 0.15)	(0.25, 0.85)	(0.80, 0.00)	(0.70, 0.35)	(0.80, 0.20)	(0.70, 0.30)
$\ddot{x}_2$	(0.80, 0.25)	(0.15, 0.55)	(0.60, 0.25)	(0.50, 0.30)	(0.60, 0.30)	(0.60, 0.30)
$\ddot{x}_3$	(0.75, 0.15)	(0.25, 0.65)	(0.35, 0.00)	(0.50, 0.35)	(0.75, 0.30)	(0.35, 0.25)
$\ddot{x}_4$	(0.35, 0.35)	(0.35, 0.50)	(0.45, 0.25)	(0.55, 0.45)	(0.25, 0.25)	(0.65, 0.00)
$\ddot{x}_5$	(0.65, 0.25)	(0.25, 0.65)	(0.60, 0.15)	(0.65, 0.25)	(0.65, 0.55)	(0.45, 0.40)

Step 3:

Calculate the values of $\beth_{ij}^{(p)}$ by Equation (45).

$$\beth_{ij}^{(1)} = \begin{pmatrix} 1 & 1 & 1 & 1 & 1 & 1 \\ 1 & 1 & 1 & 1 & 1 & 1 \\ 1 & 1 & 1 & 1 & 1 & 1 \\ 1 & 1 & 1 & 1 & 1 & 1 \\ 1 & 1 & 1 & 1 & 1 & 1 \end{pmatrix}$$

$$\breve{\beth}_{ij}^{(2)} = \begin{pmatrix} 0.8645 & 0.3841 & 0.7093 & 0.9270 & 0.7109 & 0.5378 \\ 0.9209 & 0.2575 & 0.5754 & 0.7093 & 0.5000 & 0.5198 \\ 0.8054 & 0.5618 & 0.7031 & 0.5832 & 0.6159 & 0.5456 \\ 0.6895 & 0.2421 & 0.6356 & 0.5136 & 0.7031 & 0.3105 \\ 0.7482 & 0.3920 & 0.5061 & 0.3644 & 0.6356 & 0.3705 \end{pmatrix}$$

$$\breve{\beth}_{ij}^{(3)} = \begin{pmatrix} 0.6078 & 0.1653 & 0.5629 & 0.8593 & 0.5319 & 0.4640 \\ 0.5355 & 0.1065 & 0.3062 & 0.4891 & 0.3119 & 0.3695 \\ 0.6092 & 0.2060 & 0.2985 & 0.3232 & 0.3042 & 0.3590 \\ 0.3878 & 0.1087 & 0.3186 & 0.2334 & 0.3507 & 0.1821 \\ 0.5878 & 0.1341 & 0.2804 & 0.1623 & 0.3489 & 0.3526 \end{pmatrix}$$

Step 4:
Use q-ROFEPWA to aggregate all individual q-ROF decision matrices $Y^{(p)} = (\mathscr{P}_{ij}^{(p)})_{m \times n}$ into one cumulative assessments matrix of the alternatives $W^{(p)} = (\mathscr{W}_{ij})_{m \times n}$ using Equation (46) given in Table 9.

Table 9. Collective q-ROF assessment matrix.

	$\bar{T}_1$	$\bar{T}_2$	$\bar{T}_3$	$\bar{T}_4$	$\bar{T}_5$	$\bar{T}_6$
$\ddot{\mathfrak{X}}_1$	(0.8622, 0.0000)	(0.3303, 0.6444)	(0.7985, 0.0000)	(0.9129, 0.2587)	(0.7792, 0.0000)	(0.7117, 0.2274)
$\ddot{\mathfrak{X}}_2$	(0.8590, 0.2065)	(0.3042, 0.7404)	(0.5334, 0.2139)	(0.7119, 0.1751)	(0.5479, 0.3759)	(0.5720, 0.0000)
$\ddot{\mathfrak{X}}_3$	(0.8510, 0.2408)	(0.4627, 0.4619)	(0.6148, 0.0000)	(0.5780, 0.0000)	(0.5997, 0.3068)	(0.5397, 0.0000)
$\ddot{\mathfrak{X}}_4$	(0.6384, 0.0000)	(0.2981, 0.7340)	(0.5416, 0.1429)	(0.4375, 0.3524)	(0.6023, 0.2099)	(0.4767, 0.0000)
$\ddot{\mathfrak{X}}_5$	(0.7908, 0.2786)	(0.2086, 0.6314)	(0.4966, 0.2182)	(0.3298, 0.5559)	(0.6107, 0.2364)	(0.3797, 0.4849)

Step 5:
Evaluate the values of $\breve{\beth}_{ij}$ by using Equation (48).

$$\breve{\beth}_{ij} = \begin{pmatrix} 1 & 0.8205 & 0.3152 & 0.2378 & 0.2073 & 0.1527 \\ 1 & 0.8125 & 0.2529 & 0.1444 & 0.0978 & 0.0544 \\ 1 & 0.8011 & 0.4007 & 0.2469 & 0.1473 & 0.0874 \\ 1 & 0.6301 & 0.1988 & 0.1149 & 0.0597 & 0.0361 \\ 1 & 0.7365 & 0.2788 & 0.1550 & 0.0669 & 0.0407 \end{pmatrix}$$

Step 6:
Aggregate the q-ROF values $\mathscr{W}_{ij}$ for each alternative $\ddot{\mathfrak{X}}_i$ by the q-ROFPWA operator using Equation (49) given in Table 10.

Table 10. q-ROF Aggregated values $\mathscr{W}_i$.

$\mathscr{W}_1$	(0.7733, 0.0000)
$\mathscr{W}_2$	(0.7111, 0.0000)
$\mathscr{W}_3$	(0.7063, 0.0000)
$\mathscr{W}_4$	(0.5496, 0.0000)
$\mathscr{W}_5$	(0.6383, 0.3737)

Step 7:
Calculate the score of all q-ROF aggregated values $\mathscr{W}_i$.

$$\breve{\Xi}(\mathscr{W}_1) = 0.7312$$

$$\breve{\Xi}(\mathscr{W}_2) = 0.6798$$

$$\breve{\Xi}(\mathscr{W}_3) = 0.6761$$
$$\breve{\Xi}(\mathscr{W}_4) = 0.5830$$
$$\breve{\Xi}(\mathscr{W}_5) = 0.6039$$

Step 8:

Ranks by score function values.

$$\mathscr{W}_1 \succ \mathscr{W}_2 \succ \mathscr{W}_3 \succ \mathscr{W}_5 \succ \mathscr{W}_4$$

So,

$$\ddot{x}_1 \succ \ddot{x}_2 \succ \ddot{x}_3 \succ \ddot{x}_5 \succ \ddot{x}_4$$

Comparison Analysis

The proposed q-ROFEPWA operator is compared as shown in the Table 11 below, which lists the comparative results in the completed ranking of top five alternatives. The best selection made by the proposed operator and current operators supports the efficiency and validity of the suggested methods, can be found in the comparison Table 11. Comparison analysis represented that our top alternative is not changed when we use our proposed AOs. This show the feasibility and consistency of results.

Table 11. Comparison analysis of the proposed operators and existing operators in the given numerical example.

Method	Ranking of Alternatives	The Optimal Alternative
q-ROFEWA (Riaz et al. [48])	$\ddot{x}_1 \succ \ddot{x}_2 \succ \ddot{x}_3 \succ \ddot{x}_5 \succ \ddot{x}_4$	$\ddot{x}_1$
q-ROFEOWA (Riaz et al. [48])	$\ddot{x}_1 \succ \ddot{x}_2 \succ \ddot{x}_5 \succ \ddot{x}_3 \succ \ddot{x}_4$	$\ddot{x}_1$
q-ROFEWG (Riaz et al. [48])	$\ddot{x}_1 \succ \ddot{x}_2 \succ \ddot{x}_3 \succ \ddot{x}_5 \succ \ddot{x}_4$	$\ddot{x}_2$
q-ROFEOWG (Riaz et al. [48])	$\ddot{x}_1 \succ \ddot{x}_2 \succ \ddot{x}_3 \succ \ddot{x}_5 \succ \ddot{x}_4$	$\ddot{x}_2$
q-ROFWA (Liu & Wang [58])	$\ddot{x}_1 \succ \ddot{x}_2 \succ \ddot{x}_3 \succ \ddot{x}_5 \succ \ddot{x}_4$	$\ddot{x}_1$
q-ROFWG (Liu & Wang [58])	$\ddot{x}_1 \succ \ddot{x}_3 \succ \ddot{x}_2 \succ \ddot{x}_5 \succ \ddot{x}_4$	$\ddot{x}_1$
q-ROFWBM (Liu & Liu [59])	$\ddot{x}_1 \succ \ddot{x}_2 \succ \ddot{x}_3 \succ \ddot{x}_4 \succ \ddot{x}_5$	$\ddot{x}_1$
q-ROFWGBM (Liu & Liu [59])	$\ddot{x}_1 \succ \ddot{x}_5 \succ \ddot{x}_3 \succ \ddot{x}_2 \succ \ddot{x}_4$	$\ddot{x}_1$
q-ROFHM (Zhao et al. [60])	$\ddot{x}_1 \succ \ddot{x}_2 \succ \ddot{x}_3 \succ \ddot{x}_5 \succ \ddot{x}_4$	$\ddot{x}_1$
q-ROFWHM (Zhao et al. [60])	$\ddot{x}_1 \succ \ddot{x}_2 \succ \ddot{x}_5 \succ \ddot{x}_3 \succ \ddot{x}_4$	$\ddot{x}_1$
q-ROFHM (Liu et al. [61])	$\ddot{x}_1 \succ \ddot{x}_2 \succ \ddot{x}_3 \succ \ddot{x}_5 \succ \ddot{x}_4$	$\ddot{x}_1$
q-ROFWHM (Liu et al. [61])	$\ddot{x}_1 \succ \ddot{x}_5 \succ \ddot{x}_3 \succ \ddot{x}_2 \succ \ddot{x}_4$	$\ddot{x}_1$
q-ROFPHM (Liu et al. [61])	$\ddot{x}_1 \succ \ddot{x}_2 \succ \ddot{x}_3 \succ \ddot{x}_5 \succ \ddot{x}_4$	$\ddot{x}_1$
q-ROFWPHM (Liu et al. [61])	$\ddot{x}_1 \succ \ddot{x}_2 \succ \ddot{x}_3 \succ \ddot{x}_5 \succ \ddot{x}_4$	$\ddot{x}_1$
q-ROFEPWA (Proposed)	$\ddot{x}_1 \succ \ddot{x}_2 \succ \ddot{x}_3 \succ \ddot{x}_5 \succ \ddot{x}_4$	$\ddot{x}_1$

6. Conclusions

We introduced q-rung orthopair fuzzy Einstein prioritized weighted averaging (q-ROFEPWA) operator and q-rung orthopair fuzzy Einstein prioritized weighted geometric (q-ROFEPWG) operator. The proposed operators are more efficient and flexible for information fusion and superior than existing aggregation operators (AOs) for decision-making process under q-ROF information. Einstein sums and Einstein products are good alternatives to algebraic sums and algebraic products because they provide a very smooth approximation. So the suggested operators are suitable for prioritized relationship in the criterion and a smooth approximation of q-ROF information. The significant contribution of the defined q-ROF prioritized AOs is that they take into account prioritization between attributes and DMs. We addressed many of the basic characteristics of the defined operators, namely idempotency, non-compensatory, boundary and monotonicity. A novel approach for MCGDM issues with q-ROFNs is also provided on the basis of the proposed operators. After this, an illustrative example is presented to demonstrate the effectiveness of the suggested approach. Additionally, the Einstein prioritized aggregation operators are used to discuss the symmetry of attributes and their symmetrical roles under q-ROF information. The MCGDM process has been designed to study the prioritization relationship between parameters and DMs, which have become necessary to obtain symmetrical aspects in decision analysis. For further studies, taking into account the advanced simulation capabilities of q-ROFSs, in the q-ROF context we may further examine different kinds of AOs and apply them to realistic decision-making situations. Moreover, the methodological advances for many fields like machine learning, robotics, green supply chain management (GSCM), medical diagnosis, weather forecasting, intelligence, informatics and sustainable energy planning decision making are promising areas for future studies. We believe that there are substantial growth and opportunities to understand our world in the convergence of these key climate-centric organizational research fields.

Author Contributions: M.R., D.P. and Y.-M.C. conceived and worked together to achieve this manuscript, M.R. and D.P. construct the ideas and algorithms for data analysis and design the model of the manuscript, H.M.A.F. and H.K. processed the data collection and wrote the paper. Finally all authors have read and agreed to the published version of the manuscript.

Conflicts of Interest: The authors declare that they have no conflict of interest.

Acknowledgments: The authors are highly thankful to editor-in-chief and referees for their valuable comments and suggestions for the improvement of our manuscript.

References

1. Zadeh, L.A. Fuzzy sets. *Inf. Control* **1965**, *8*, 338–353. [CrossRef]
2. Atanassov, K.T. Intuitionistic fuzzy sets. *Fuzzy Sets Syst.* **1986**, 20, 87–96. [CrossRef]
3. Yager, R.R. Pythagorean fuzzy subsets. In Proceedings of the 2013 Joint IFSA World Congress and NAFIPS Annual Meeting (IFSA/NAFIPS), Edmonton, Canada, 24–28 June 2013; pp. 57–61.
4. Yager, R.R.; Abbasov, A.M. Pythagorean membership grades, complex numbers, and decision making. *Int. J. Intell. Syst.* **2013**, *28*, 436–452. [CrossRef]
5. Yager, R.R. Pythagorean membership grades in multi-criteria decision making. *IEEE Trans. Fuzzy Syst.* **2014**, *22*, 958–965. [CrossRef]
6. Zhang, W.R. Bipolar fuzzy sets and relations: A computational framework for cognitive modeling and multiagent decision analysis. In Proceedings of the First International Joint Conference of The North American Fuzzy Information Processing Society Biannual Conference, San Antonio, TX, USA, 18–21 December 1994; pp. 305–309.
7. Ali, M.I. A note on soft sets, rough soft sets and fuzzy soft sets. *Appl. Soft Comput.* **2011**, *11*, 3329–3332.
8. Ali, M.I. Another view on *q*-rung orthopair fuzzy sets. *Int. J. Intell. Syst.* **2018**, *33*, 2139–2153. [CrossRef]
9. Chen, J.; Li, S.; Ma, S.; Wang, X. m-Polar Fuzzy Sets: An Extension of Bipolar Fuzzy Sets. *Sci. World J.* **2014**, *2014*. [CrossRef]
10. Chi, P.P.; Lui, P.D. An extended TOPSIS method for the multiple ttribute decision making problems based on interval neutrosophic set. *Neutrosophic Sets Syst.* **2013**, *1*, 63–70.
11. Çağman, N.; Enginoglu, S.; Çitak, F. Fuzzy soft set theory and its applications. *Iran. J. Fuzzy Syst.* **2011**, *8*, 137–147.
12. Eraslan, S.; Karaaslan, F. A group decision making method based on topsis under fuzzy soft environment. *J. New Theory* **2015**, *3*, 30–40.
13. Feng, F.; Jun, Y.B.; Liu, X.; Li, L. An adjustable approach to fuzzy soft set based decision making. *J. Comput. Appl. Math.* **2010**, *234*, 10–20. [CrossRef]
14. Feng, F.; Li, C.; Davvaz, B.; Ali, M.I. Soft sets combined with fuzzy sets and rough sets; A tentative approach. *Soft Comput.* **2010**, *14*, 899–911. [CrossRef]
15. Feng, F.; Liu, X.Y.; Leoreanu-Fotea, V.; Jun, Y.B. Soft sets and soft rough sets. *Inf. Sci.* **2011**, *181*, 1125–1137. [CrossRef]
16. Feng, F.; Fujita, H.; Ali, M.I.; Yager, R.R.; Liu, X. Another view on generalized intuitionistic fuzzy soft sets and related multi-attribute decision making methods. *IEEE Trans. Fuzzy Syst.* **2019**, *27*, 474–488. [CrossRef]
17. Garg, H.; Arora, R. Generalized intuitionistic fuzzy soft power aggregation operator based on t-norm and their application in multicriteria decision-making. *Int. J. Intell. Syst.* **2019**, *34*, 215–246. [CrossRef]

18. Garg, H.; Arora, R. Dual hesitant fuzzy soft aggregation operators and their applicatio in decision-making. *Cogn. Comput.* **2018**, *10*, 769–789. [CrossRef]
19. Garg, H.; Arora, R. A nonlinear-programming methodology for multi-attribute decision-making problem with interval-valued intuitionistic fuzzy soft sets information. *Appl. Intell.* **2018**, *48*, 2031–2046. [CrossRef]
20. Kumar, K.; Garg, H. TOPSIS method based on the connection number of set pair analysis under interval-valued intuitionistic fuzzy set environment. *Comput. Appl. Math.* **2018**, *37*, 1319–1329. [CrossRef]
21. Karaaslan, F. Neutrosophic Soft Set with Applications in Decision Making. *Int. J. Inf. Sci. Intell. Syst.* **2015**, *4*, 1–20.
22. Liu, Y.; Zhang, H.; Wu, Y.; Dong, Y. Ranking range based approach to MADM under incomplete context and its application in venture investment evaluation. *Technol. Econ. Dev. Econ.* **2019**, *25*, 877–899. [CrossRef]
23. Naeem, K.; Riaz, M.; Peng, X.D.; Afzal, D. Pythagorean fuzzy soft MCGDM methods based on TOPSIS, VIKOR and aggregation operators. *J. Intell. Fuzzy Syst.* **2019**, *37*, 6937–6957. [CrossRef]
24. Naeem, K.; Riaz, M.; Afzal, D. Pythagorean m-polar fuzzy sets and TOPSIS method for the selection of advertisement mode. *J. Intell. Fuzzy Syst.* **2019**, *37*, 8441–8458. [CrossRef]
25. Naeem, K.; Riaz, M.; Afzal, D. Fuzzy neutrosophic soft σ-algebra and fuzzy neutrosophic soft measure with applications. *J. Intell. Fuzzy Syst.* **2020**, 1–12. [CrossRef]
26. Peng, X.D.; Yang, Y. Some results for Pythagorean fuzzy sets. *Int. J. Intell. Syst.* **2015**, *30*, 1133–1160. [CrossRef]
27. Peng, X.D.; Selvachandran, G. Pythagorean fuzzy set: State of the art and future directions. *Artif. Intell. Rev.* **2019**, *52*, 1873–1927. [CrossRef]
28. Peng, X.D.; Yang, Y.Y.; Song, J.; Jiang, Y. Pythagorean fuzzy soft set and its application. *Comput. Eng.* **2015**, *41*, 224–229.
29. Peng, X.D.; Dai, J. Approaches to single-valued neutrosophic MADM based on MABAC, TOPSIS and new similarity measure with score function. *Neural Comput. Appl.* **2018**, *29*, 939–954. [CrossRef]
30. Riaz, M.; Hashmi, M.R. MAGDM for agribusiness in the environment of various cubic m-polar fuzzy averaging aggregation operators. *J. Intell. Fuzzy Syst.* **2019**, *37*, 3671–3691. [CrossRef]
31. Riaz, M.; Hashmi, M.R. Linear Diophantine Fuzzy Set and its Applications towards Multi-Attribute Decision Making Problems. *J. Intell. Fuzzy Syst.* **2019**, *37*, 5417–5439. [CrossRef]
32. Riaz, M.; Çağman, N.; Zareef, I.; Aslam, M. N-Soft Topology and its Applications to Multi-Criteria Group Decision Making. *J. Intell. Fuzzy Syst.* **2019**, *36*, 6521–6536. [CrossRef]
33. Riaz, M.; Tehrim, S.T. Cubic bipolar fuzzy set with application to multi-criteria group decision making using geometric aggregation operators. *Soft Comput.* **2020**. [CrossRef]
34. Tehrim, S.T.; Riaz, M. A novel extension of TOPSIS to MCGDM with Bipolar Neutrosophic soft topology. *J. Intell. Fuzzy Syst.* **2019**, *37*, 5531–5549. [CrossRef]
35. Shabir, M.; Naz, M. On soft topological spaces. *Comput. Math. Appl.* **2011**, *61*, 1786–1799. [CrossRef]
36. Wang, H.; Smarandache, F.; Zhang, Y.Q.; Sunderraman, R. Single valued neutrosophic sets. *Multispace Multistruct.* **2010**, *4*, 410–413.
37. Xu, Z.S. Intuitionistic fuzzy aggregation operators. *IEEE Trans. Fuzzy Syst.* **2007**, *15*, 1179–1187.
38. Xu, Z.S.; Cai, X.Q. *Intuitionistic Fuzzy Information Aggregation: Theory and Applications*; Science Press: Beijing, China; Springer: Berlin/Heidelberg, Germany, 2012.
39. Xu, Z.S. *Studies in Fuzziness and Soft Computing: Hesitant Fuzzy Sets Theory*; Springer: Basel, Switzerland, 2014.
40. Ye, J. Interval-valued hesitant fuzzy prioritized weighted aggregation operators for multi attribute decision-making. *J. Algorithms Comput. Technol.* **2013**, *8*, 179–192. [CrossRef]
41. Ye, J. Linguistic neutrosophic cubic numbers and their multiple attribute decision-making method. *Information* **2017**, *8*, 110. [CrossRef]
42. Zhang, X.L.; Xu, Z.S. Extension of TOPSIS to multiple criteria decision making with Pythagorean fuzzy sets. *Int. J. Intell. Syst.* **2014**, *29*, 1061–1078. [CrossRef]
43. Zhan, J.; Liu, Q.; Davvaz, B. A new rough set theory: Rough soft hemirings. *J. Intell. Fuzzy Syst.* **2015**, *28*, 1687–1697. [CrossRef]
44. Zhan, J.; Alcantud, J.C.R. A novel type of soft rough covering and its application to multi-criteria group decision-making. *Artif. Intell. Rev.* **2019**, *52*, 2381–2410. [CrossRef]
45. Zhang, L.; Zhan, J. Fuzzy soft β-covering based fuzzy rough sets and corresponding decision-making applications. *Int. J. Mach. Learn. Cybern.* **2018**, *10*, 1487–1502. [CrossRef]

46. Zhang, L.; Zhan, J. Novel classes of fuzzy soft β-coverings-based fuzzy rough sets with applications to multi-criteria fuzzy group decision-making. *Soft Comput.* **2018**, *23*, 5327–5351. [CrossRef]
47. Zhang, L.; Zhan, J.; Xu, Z.S. Covering-based generalized IF rough sets with applications to multi-attribute decision-making. *Inf. Sci.* **2019**, *478*, 275–302. [CrossRef]
48. Riaz, M.; Salabun, W.; Farid, H.M.A.; Ali, N.; Watróbski, J. A robust q-rung orthopair fuzzy information aggregation using Einstein operations with application to sustainable energy planning decision management. *Energies* **2020**, *13*, 2155. [CrossRef]
49. Riaz, M.; Pamucar, D.; Farid, H.M.A.; Hashmi, M.R. q-Rung Orthopair Fuzzy Prioritized Aggregation Operators and Their Application Towards Green Supplier Chain Management. *Symmetry* **2020**, *13*, 976. [CrossRef]
50. Sharma, H.K.; Kumari, K.; Kar, S. A rough set approach for forecasting models. *Decis. Mak. Appl. Manag. Eng.* **2020**, *3*, 1–21. [CrossRef]
51. Sinani, F.; Živko, E.; Vasiljevic, M. An evaluation of a third-party logistics provider: The application of the rough Dombi-Hamy mean operator. *Decis. Mak. Appl. Manag. Eng.* **2020**, *3*, 92–107.
52. Yager, R.R. Generalized Orthopair Fuzzy sets. *IEEE Trans. Fuzzy Syst.* **2017**, *25*, 1220–1230. [CrossRef]
53. Yager, R.R. On ordered weighted averaging aggregation operators in multicriteria decision making. *IEEE Trans. Syst. Man Cybern.* **1988**, *18*, 183–190. [CrossRef]
54. Garg, H. Generalized Pythagorean Fuzzy Geometric Aggregation Operators Using Einstein t-Norm and t-Conorm for Multicriteria Decision-Making Process. *Int. J. Intell. Syst.* **2017**, *32*, 597–630. [CrossRef]
55. Rahmana, K.; Abdullah, S.; Ahmedc, R.; Ullahd, M. Pythagorean fuzzy Einstein weighted geometric aggregation operator and their application to multiple attribute group decision making. *J. Intell. Fuzzy Syst.* **2017**, *33*, 635–647. [CrossRef]
56. Khan, M.S.A.; Abdullah, S.; Ali, A.; Amin, F. Pythagorean fuzzy prioritized aggregation operator and their application to multiple attribute group decision making. *Granul. Comput.* **2019**, *4*, 249–263. [CrossRef]
57. Khan, M.S.A.; Abdullah, S.; Ali, A. Multiattribute group decision-making based on Pythagorean fuzzy Einstein prioritized aggregation operators. *Int. J. Intell. Syst.* **2019**, *34*, 1001–1033. [CrossRef]
58. Liu, P.; Wang, P. Some q-rung orthopair fuzzy aggregation operator and their application to multi-attribute decision making. *Int. J. Intell. Syst.* **2018**, *33*, 2259–2280.
59. Liu, P.; Liu, J. Some q-Rung Orthopai Fuzzy Bonferroni Mean Operators and Their Application to Multi-Attribute Group Decision Making. *Int. J. Intell. Syst.* **2018**, *33*, 315–347. [CrossRef]
60. Zhao, H.; Zhang, R.; Xu, Y.; Wang, J. Some q-Rung Orthopair Fuzzy Hamy Mean Aggregation Operators with Their Application. In Proceedings of the 2019 IEEE International Conference on Systems, Man and Cybernetics (SMC), Bari, Italy, 6–9 October 2019.
61. Liu, Z.; Wang, S.; Liu, P. Multiple attribute group decision making based on q-rung orthopair fuzzy Heronianmean operators. *Int. J. Intell. Syst.* **2018**, *33*, 2341–2363. [CrossRef]

symmetry

MDPI

Article

A Multicriteria Decision Aid-Based Model for Measuring the Efficiency of Business-Friendly Cities

Mihailo Jovanović [1], Slobodan Nedeljković [2], Milan Ranđelović [3], Gordana Savić [4], Vladica Stojanović [5], Vladimir Stojanović [6] and Dragan Ranđelović [7,*]

1 Office for Information Technologies and e-Government, Government of the Republic of Serbia, 11221 Belgrade, Serbia; mihailo.jovanovic@gov.rs
2 Ministry of Interior, Government of the Republic of Serbia, 11221 Belgrade, Serbia; slobodan.nedeljkovic@mup.gov.rs
3 Science Technology Park, 18000 Niš, Serbia; milan.randjelovic@ntp.rs
4 Faculty of Organizational Sciences, University of Belgrade, 11221 Belgrade, Serbia; goca@fon.bg.ac.rs
5 Faculty of Sciences and Mathematics, University of Criminal Investigation and Police Studies, 11221 Belgrade, Serbia; vladica.stojanovic@kpa.edu.rs
6 Academy for National Security, 11221 Belgrade, Serbia; vladastjnvc@sbb.rs
7 Faculty of Diplomacy and Security, University Union-Nikola Tesla, 11221 Belgrade, Serbia
* Correspondence: dragan.randjelovic@kpa.edu.rs; Tel.: +381-604666486

Received: 26 May 2020; Accepted: 14 June 2020; Published: 17 June 2020

Abstract: Local self-government has the task of enabling stable economic development, in addition to enabling a normal quality of life for citizens. This is why the state government should provide guidelines that will improve the local business climate, and by doing so enable local economic development. This can be done through the introduction of a business-friendly certification procedure, which is influenced by uncertain inputs and influences many output factors. Each local government has the important task of determining its rank of efficiency in this process. A number of methodologies developed to solve this problem are generally divided into two groups: Parametric and non-parametric. These two groups of methodologies could provide quite different results. Therefore, the purpose of this paper was to create a model using both approaches to achieve a balanced symmetrical approach that produces better results than each approach individually. For this purpose, the paper describes a multicriteria decision aid-based model of optimization to evaluate the effectiveness of this process, integrating classification, data envelopment analysis, and stochastic frontier analysis, as well as its application in a case study of business-friendly certification in the Republic of Serbia.

Keywords: MCDA; efficiency; DEA; SFA; classification; dimensionality reduction

1. Introduction

The constant monitoring and quantification of the effects of a job in modern society is a necessary element of its successful implementation, no matter what type of process it is and from which field of human activity it originates from. Logistics processes are crucial for achieving this, and the basic indicator is the definition of the relationship between the results achieved and the resources invested, which is called efficiency [1]. Measuring and increasing efficiency is a necessary prerequisite for the implementation of efficient logistics systems, which is why it is a significant scientific discipline represented in the world literature and practice [2–4].

Depending on the criteria defined, efficiency in logistics can be divided in different ways. In this respect, it is possible to distinguish between logistics efficiency at the strategic, tactical, and operational levels. Depending on the type of indicators used to describe efficiency, several types of efficiency emerge. When it comes to logistics efficiency, the most commonly referred to is operational efficiency or operations efficiency. In addition to operational efficiency, the most commonly encountered are cost (financial) efficiency, environmental or eco-efficiency, energy efficiency, qualitative efficiency, city efficiency, etc. From the type of logistics system and process point of view, as one of the most important criteria, it is possible to distinguish several types of efficiency: Distributive efficiency, transport efficiency, warehouse efficiency, efficiency of the picking process, efficiency of the inventory management process, etc. [5].

The main problem of monitoring efficiency in practice is the misunderstanding and use of partial indicators that often, for example, do not represent an appropriate measure of efficiency. In most logistics systems, the emphasis is on costs and financial indicators that do not provide sufficient information on efficiency, so corrective action is taken to determine appropriate indicators. This problem can be solved both through the use of expert knowledge and the discovery of knowledge from data by the use of appropriate artificial intelligence methods, one of which is a well-known classification, which can provide the selection of essential criteria and thus optimize the procedure to ensure its better performance.

For the purpose of measuring the efficiency of a process, four methodologies are available [6]: Econometric average response estimation, index numbers, data wrapping analysis (for example, data envelopment analysis, DEA), and stochastic boundary analysis (for example, stochastic frontier analysis, SFA). Today, with the advent of artificial intelligence, machine learning methods can also be used to measure efficiency.

All the above-mentioned methodologies belong to a broad group of so-called multi-criteria decision aid (MCDA) methodologies [7,8], which primarily address the solution of four underlying multi-criteria decision problems: Problem description, the choice of the best alternative, the ranking of alternatives, and the classification of alternatives [9]. Therefore, we aimed to address two main research questions in this paper: 1. Is it possible to successfully integrate the efficiency evaluation parametric of non-parametric methods with machine learning? 2. Does problem dimensionality reduction by a machine learning method have an effect on the quality of the efficiency evaluation results?

We propose the integration of the efficiency evaluation methods DEA and SFA, with a machine learning method, classification into the procedure of efficiency measurement, which we have not encountered in the literature. Namely, it is generally known and evident from the content of this introduction and literature review that the most commonly used methods for determining different types of efficiency are the non-parametric DEA method and the parametric SFA method. Symmetry in the approach of using those two methods, and their complementary advantages and disadvantages were the starting points for their simultaneous application. The integration of DEA and SFA with classification methods is done while having in mind the possibilities of the dimensionality reduction, which might lead to more suitable results being obtained.

The aforementioned new procedure was applied for solving the univariate problem of determining the efficiency of the business-friendly certification (BFC) process of local governments in the Republic of Serbia, considering the amount of investment per capita as an output performance indicator. The proposed model for determining the process efficiency of BFC cities determines not only the competitiveness of local self-governments in attracting direct investment as an essential precondition for competitiveness in the market but also improves the efficiency of the planning of their local economic development (LED) [10]. The efficiency determination of the BFC process incorporates the effects of the selected criteria and their individual importance, defined by the appropriate professional organization in the Republic of Serbia, the National Alliance for Local Economic Development (NALED) [11]. This process belongs to a group of problems with the input factors burdened with uncertainty, imprecision, and subjective influence. The fulfillment of conditions related to the established criteria is a prerequisite for obtaining the certificate. The efficiency of the BFC process can be evaluated by different performance, such as the aforementioned average investment per capita, the number of new employees, the average salary of employees, etc. In the general case, solving the described real-world problem leads a complex multivariate problem being solved. Consequently, we decided to deal with a specific but very indicative output indicator: The average amount of investment per capita.

In order to present the subject and achieve the set goal, the paper is organized into the following chapters: In addition to this introduction, the second chapter is an overview of the published studies related to the subject of this work; the third chapter describes the BFC process; the fourth chapter, in the three subchapters of the DEA, classification, and SFA method, describes three methods whose integration addresses the problem of process efficiency evaluation; The fifth chapter is organized in two subchapters which discusses motivation and integration of the DEA, classification and SFA method. Sixth chapter describes the new proposed integrated method in two subchapters, through the case study and seventh chapter is discussion of obtained results. The eight chapter provides the conclusion. In the end, the references chapter provides the literature used in the paper.

2. Literature Review

The multi-criteria decision aid-based model for measuring efficiency as well as the methods used in it are represented in the world literature primarily because of the importance of problem solving and its global representation in many areas of human life.

As we outlined in the introduction, the most commonly used methodologies for determining efficiency are DEA and SFA, and they all belong to a broad group of so-called MCDA methodologies. The papers [12,13] discuss DEA as an MCDA methodology and [14] discusses SFA as an MCDA methodology. The authors of [15] provide evidence of DEA and SFA as MCDA methodology, and [16] discusses two MCDA classifiers. MCDA has been applied in many different fields of human activities [17], which can be found in the literature, such as healthcare [18,19], finance and banking [20], environmental protection [21], construction and manufacturing [22], computer science [23], tourism [24], emergency management [25], logistics [26], electricity supply [27] and others [28,29].

When it comes to efficiency and its measurement, there are widespread applications in the same areas of human activity, such as healthcare [30], finance and banking [31], environmental conservation [32], construction and manufacturing [33], computer science and robotics [34], tourism [35], emergency management [36], logistics [37], electricity supply [38] and others [39,40].

As far as the BFC process is concerned, it is not specific for the Republic of Serbia, in which, as we have already stated in the introduction, it is implemented by NALED. It should be noted that more than 90 local governments from Bosnia and Herzegovina, Montenegro, Croatia, Macedonia, and Serbia are improving their business environment by up to 70% through the BFC South-East Europe (SEE) certification program [41].

Specifically, with the support of the German Agency for International Cooperation (GIZ) and the Open Regional Fund for the Modernization of Municipal Services, the BFC SEE program was launched and implemented through the regional network of institutions in order to establish a unique standard of business environment quality for the SEE local self-governments. The regional network brings together various governmental and non-governmental institutions [11,41].

The literature on the evaluation of LED in the Republic of Serbia can be found in [42,43] and on the NALED BFC process in the Republic of Serbia in [44].

Different aggregations of individual MCDA methodologies for assessing the importance of individual criteria have been discussed in [45,46]. When it comes to evaluating the efficiency of local governments, classical approaches, such as parametric DEA or non-parametric SFA methods, are most commonly used. The parametric SFA method was used for the analysis of the efficiency expenditure indicators in the Republic of Serbia's local governments [47]. The conclusion was that local self-governments could not effectively resolve issues, such as demographic and socioeconomic constraints. The efficiency of municipalities in Portugal was evaluated in two phases: SFA and Tobit regression [48]. DEA has been also used for the regions efficiency evaluation [49,50]. The comparative analysis of the cost-effectiveness of Belgian local governments was performed by FDH, DEA, and econometric approaches in [51] while authors in [52] dealt with the public sector's efficiency in German municipalities. Another technical efficiency evaluation of major Italian municipalities by the DEA method can be found in [53]. Furthermore, a cost efficiency evaluation of Australian local governments was conducted by using mathematical programming and econometric approaches [54] while DEA was also used in the case of South African local government's efficiency measurement [55].

In his book, Rao [56] provides a comprehensive description of the DEA methodological approach and Cooper, Seiford, and Zhu provide an overview of the DEA in their articles [57–59]. The DEA methodology was also used to create a meaningful multiple criteria decision-making platform that was used for evaluating the performance of engineering schools, but in [60], a user-written data envelopment analysis command for the Stata software tool is presented. In the literature, different integrations of DEA with other MCDA methods also exist, such as for, example, with the analytical hierarchy process (AHP) [61,62]. An overview of the SFA methodology can be found in [63–65]. User-written SFA commands for the Stata software tool are given in [66]. SFA has been integrated with other MCDA methods, such as TOPSIS, in order to obtain a method with better characteristics [67].

We should note that in the literature review, there are many attempts to integrate SFA and DEA methods [68–71], as well as integrate them with some other methods from the MCDA group [72,73], especially in order to obtain better quality methods for evaluating the efficiency of different processes. Finally, it should be noted that there are a number of SFA and DEA integrations with data mining methods in the literature [74–77].

3. BFC Process Efficiency

Considering today's level of development of human society, it can be said that when it comes to the city, or local self-government, two of the main functions are service and production. The product group of functions can be classified as crafts, industry, construction, etc. while the service group should cover all service activities that take place in the city or local government area. Of great importance for the development of the city are the so-called basic functions, which include the functions of those services and production activities directly used by the population inside and outside the city, including the population of the wider local government, including the functions of providing and planning the economic basis for the functioning of the city and its future development. These basic functions influence the creation and planning of appropriate city infrastructure, job creation, etc. However, for the life of the people in the city, it is necessary to provide additional social functions, such as information, education, recreation, and so on. The above two types of functions of one city and the local government indicate that they are in fact a conglomerate of several basic and social functions exercised in the area. As for the competitiveness of cities and local governments, the basic functions are the ones that are of greater importance and there is a need to evaluate their value in that domain.

Local self-governments and cities must provide the best possible environment in which the realization of bigger direct investments will provide conditions for job creation and an improvement of salaries of already employed people and thus better overall life of the population. Local governments must create LED plans that allow them to compete competitively in the local through to regional and national context to the global environment.

As it is well known, uneven regional development is one of the biggest problems Serbia faces. Investments represent one of the indicators of these regional differences between cities and local governments in Serbia.

Namely, investors are interested in cities and local self-governments, having in mind several important characteristics starting from the geographical location, infrastructure of the existing production, personnel profiles, and work of the local self-government to successful examples of implemented investments. For this reason, local governments must constantly improve their investment conditions and thus increase their competitiveness.

Following the best practices of the European Union, in 2007, NALED launched a program for the certification of municipalities, cities and local governments with a favorable business environment in order to a create positive business environment and increase the level of investment in local governments, the number of employees, the average salary of employees, etc. The project was made possible with the institutional support of the Ministry of Economy and Regional Development of the Republic of Serbia, with the aim of familiarizing local self-governments with the standards they need to meet in order to be eligible and certified.

BFC is a procedure that introduces rules and enables tools for assessing the quality of services to businesses by municipalities. The certification is intended for all municipalities, cities and local governments in the Republic of Serbia who want to improve the conditions for business in their communities, attract new investments, and stimulate the development of the local economy.

In addition to the financial benefits, communication with the local administration, professional and accurate behavior, as well as a positive expectation of partnership in the future are also important for business. Investors appreciate the most realistic picture of the environment in cities and municipalities, which implies predictability of the duration and cost of all individual procedures, starting from the construction of facilities and its traffic and energy connections for general infrastructure supply through to labor employment and company registration to the payment of all duties.

Twelve criteria were established as a basis for evaluation of whether and to what extent a municipality [78], i.e., the city, met the standards of a favorable business environment. These twelve criteria, which are used in BFC process in the Republic in Serbia, are as follows [79]:

1. C1: A strategic approach in development planning.
2. C2: Organizational capacity for support of the local economy.
3. C3: Involvement of the economy in the work of the local government (economic council).
4. C4: An effective system for issuing building permits.
5. C5: Availability of information for investment.
6. C6: Promotion of investment.
7. C7: Creditworthiness and financial stability.
8. C8: Promotion of employment and development.
9. C9: Encouraging private–public partnerships.
10. C10: Adequate infrastructure.
11. C11: Transparent policy of taxes and incentives.
12. C12: Application of information technologies.

A favorable business environment is provided by those municipalities, i.e., cities, that meet 75% of the above criteria. The official certificate is issued by NALED and the Ministry of Economy and Regional Development of the Republic of Serbia, as a document that investors use, like a proof, showing that a particular local government offers everything for a successful start-up.

Today, more than one-third of all local self-governments in the Republic of Serbia are improving their business environment and participating in NALED's certification program, and more than 20 municipalities have earned the Certificate of Favorable Business Environment.

The certification criteria give clear guidance to municipalities and cities on the type and quality of services they should offer well as recommendations on what reforms they need to implement. The ultimate goal of the certification is to strengthen the competitiveness, promote investments, increase employment, and, as a final goal, raise the standard of living in the Republic of Serbia.

The establishment of the criteria is a process that takes place in real time and involves upgrading them both in quality and quantity. Given the rapid development of human society at the beginning of the 21st century in the era of the fourth industrial revolution, the BFC certification process itself is therefore subject to constant evaluation and mandatory recertification every two years.

The certification program for municipalities with a positive business environment is unique in the Republic of Serbia and includes several activities.

In the BFC process, at the beginning of each current year, NALED defines the significance of the criteria as the average score of the previous levels of assessment, which is often referred to as the relative importance of the observed criteria C_i (i = 1, ... ,12) [10,44,45,61]. It is given in Table 1 by NALED's criterion validity rating.

Table 1. NALED's evaluation criteria importance of the BFC process in Republic of Serbia.

	C_1	C_2	C_3	C_4	C_5	C_6	C_7	C_8	C_9	C_{10}	C_{11}	C_{12}
Evaluation of the criteria by Naled's experts (w_i)	1.250	0.900	0.670	1.190	0.660	0.710	1.000	0.750	1.080	1.210	1.500	0.830

Using the assessment of the fulfillment of the criteria of each local government in certification by experts and the established formula that it is necessary to meet at least 75% for each criterion, it is possible to determine which city, i.e., local government, deserves certification. Additionally, since it is very useful to plan the intensity of investment required for local economic development and to achieve this in the coming period, the evaluation of the criteria by the NALED experts given in Table 1 is useful in determining the rank of each local government, which can be done using some of the known methods of MCDM.

As it is mentioned in this introduction, this paper aimed to evaluate the efficiency of this BFC process, considering the amount of investment per capita as an output criterion. The investment per capita is one of the most important attributes in measuring local economic development success. In our case, this output was chosen in order to make a comparative analysis of the ability of local governments to attract direct investment as well as to determine whether efficiency is related to the level of fulfillment of defined input criteria.

4. Background

As we already indicated in the introduction, we will consider the integration of different multicriteria methods in order to evaluate the efficiency of the BFC certification process of cities and local governments in the Republic of Serbia. The integration procedure of the DEA, SFA, and classification method is proposed to improve the features of the individual methods. The case study of the efficiency evaluation of BFC process in the Republic of Serbia cities is used to verify the goodness of the proposed procedure. However, it could be generally applied in other cases of evaluating the efficiency of a univariate or multivariate process, aforementioned in Section 3 (BFC process).

Namely, it is known that within the MCDA, we generally identify at least one decision maker (DM), who is solely responsible for making the decision, whatever it may be. The DM chooses one of several alternative decisions, judging them by a set of criteria, attributes, or points of view, and which are most often opposed to each other. The DM may express some preferences regarding the alternatives and criteria offered and use the MCDA algorithms as parameters to find a solution to the problem. These problems, as the ultimate implication of a decision, fall into various possible categories:

- Choice (determining the "best" alternative);
- Ranking (ranking the alternatives); and
- Sorting (assigning alternatives to predefined and ordered classes).

MCDA is applied in many different fields of human activity as we already stated in Section 2 [17–29].

The process of MCDA is often complex and depends on the specific area where it is applied and whether it has and what are the preferences of the decision maker. As a result, many different algorithms and their implementations have arisen [80,81]. Several papers have dealt with more or less successful attempts to simplify decision-making by choosing the best algorithm for MCDA problems [82].In one of them [83], this procedure is divided into several steps. We look at inputs and outputs as attributes or criteria for evaluating the decision-making unit (DMU), while minimizing inputs and/or maximizing results as associated goals. With this approach, we can practically consider this process as one ranking that leads to a classification of basically two possible groups, MCDA and DEA formulations [12,13,84].Additionally, the classification of basically two possible efficient and inefficient groups and SFA coincides if we consider the input and output attributes as single function variables [14]. Luckily, in the literature, classifications can be encountered using DEA and SFA together with other MCDA methodologies, such as Promethee's multicriteria decision-making (MCDM) [23].

The DEA and SFA methods can be used to solve the problem of determining the efficiency of the BFC process of cities and municipalities in the Republic of Serbia. For this purpose, a synthetic summary indicator should be created, taking into account all input and output attributes used to accomplish the BFC process itself. The DEA efficiency measure is defined as the ratio of the weighted output t to the weighted input. The efficiency measure enables the aggregation of all the observed inputs (outputs) into one virtual input (output) representing the sum of the product of the coefficients and values of the inputs or outputs, which is necessary, which implies solving the problem of expressing the input and output data in ranges of values that are mutually comparable.

4.1. DEA

As it is aforementioned, the DEA has been widely used for assessing the relative efficiency of decision-making units (DMUs)in an observing set. All DMUs use the same multiple commensurate inputs to produce multiple commensurate outputs. The original efficiency definition is given in [85] and it generalizes single-input to single-output ratios in the definition of efficiency, as the ratio of the sum of weighted outputs to the sum of weighted inputs. Let us suppose that we have a set of n DMU$_s$ (DMUj, j = 1, … ,n), which uses inputs x_{ij} (i = 1, … ,m) to produce outputs y_{rj} (r = 1, … ,s). The absolute efficiency measure model is as follows [86]:

$$E_j = \frac{\sum\limits_{r=1}^{s} u_r y_{rj}}{\sum\limits_{i=1}^{m} v_i x_{ij}}, \tag{1}$$

where v_i (i = 1, … ,m) are input multipliers and u_r (r = 1, … ,s) are output multipliers (weights). The above definition corresponds to a discrete MCDM. The determination of weights is a very sensitive and complicated process. The idea behind the DEA model is to avoid a priori weights determination. The authors of the DEA model in Charnes et al. [87] allowed each DMU to choose the most appropriate set of weights, with the goal of becoming as efficient as possible compared with the other units in the observing set. The linear programming (LP) weighted form of the basic constant return to scale model (DEA CCR or DEA CRS) with output orientation [87] is as follows:

$$(\min) h_k = \sum_{i=1}^{m} v_i x_{ij}, \tag{2}$$

such that:

$$\sum_{r=1}^{s} u_r y_{rk} = 1, \tag{3}$$

$$\sum_{i=1}^{m} v_i x_{ij} - \sum_{r=1}^{s} u_r y_{rj} \geq 0,\ j = 1, \ldots, n, \tag{4}$$

$$v_i \geq 0,\ i = 1, \ldots, m\ ;\ u_r \geq 0,\ r = 1, \ldots, s. \tag{5}$$

The optimal efficiency scores h_k are obtained by solving the linear model of Equations (1)–(5) n—times (once for each DMU with the goal of comparing it with other DMUs). As a solution of basic Charnes, Cooper, and Rhodes (CCR) DEA models [87], all efficient units are assessed with the even efficiency scores h_k(k = 1, … ,n) equal to 1 while the other inefficient ones are assessed with a score greater than 1 (it is usually calculated as the reciprocal value less than one). All inefficient units are enveloped by the production frontier, consisting of efficient DMUs. The efficient DMUs are composed of real-efficient or virtual-composite peer units(lying on the efficient frontier) for each of the inefficient DMUS. This model is transformed into the so-called Banker, Charnes and Cooper (BCC) model, which is described in [88], to incorporate the variable return to scale assumption. Namely, with respect to the DEA CRS model, the DEA BCC or DEA VRS model has an additional variable u^* that defines the position of the auxiliary hyperplane lying above or at each DMU included in the analysis and checks that the specified DMU has reached the desired output level with minimum input engagement and that all possible overlapping hyperplanes of all DMUs are selected from the one that has the least horizontal distance from the observed DMU to this hyperplane. For $u^* = 0$, the BCC model is reduced to the CCR model:

$$(\min)h_k = \sum_{i=1}^{m} v_i x_{ij} - u*, \tag{6}$$

such that:

$$\sum_{i=1}^{m} v_i x_{ij} = 1, \tag{7}$$

$$\sum_{i=1}^{m} v_i x_{ij} - \sum_{r=1}^{s} u_r y_{rj} - u* \geq 0,\ j = 1, \ldots, n, \tag{8}$$

$$v_i \geq 0,\ i = 1, \ldots, m\ ;\ u_r \geq 0,\ r = 1, \ldots, s. \tag{9}$$

It must be noted on this place that, from these two basic DEA CCR and DEA BCC models, many other variants and extensions of DEA have been developed to solve real-world problems.

4.2. SFA

Stochastic frontier analysis is a parametric approach to efficiency measurement introduced by Aigner, Lovell, and Schmidt [89] and Meeusen and Van den Broeck [90]. It takes into account the error of measurement in estimating the efficiency of the firm under observation.

Let us assume that firm j (j = 1, … ,n) produces the output level y_j by using inputs given as a vector $\mathbf{x}_j$. The production function is given as $f(\mathbf{x}_j, \beta)$, where β is a parameter vector to be estimated. The output level is also under the effect of the efficiency ξ_j and random error v_j. Finally, output production for the firm j is given by the form:

$$y_j = f(\mathbf{x}_j, \beta)\xi_j v_j \tag{10}$$

Since u_j represents the level of efficiency for firm i, it must be in the (0; 1]. The firm is efficient if $\xi_j = 1$; otherwise, it is inefficient. The aim is to estimate the vector parameters β, ξ_j and v_j, so as to maximize the ξ_j of the firm under observation. For this purpose, the natural logs of Equation (11) together with the assumption that the production function of k inputs is linear in logs are taken as:

$$\ln(y_j) = \beta_0 + \sum_{i=1}^{m} \beta_{ij} \ln(x_{ij}) + v_j - u_i, \tag{11}$$

where $u_j = -\ln \xi_j$ represents the level of inefficiency, while v_j represents identically and independently the distributed random error. A stochastic frontier is given by $\beta_0 + \sum_{i=1}^{m} \beta_{ij} \ln(x_{ij}) + v_j$, while u_j indicates the inefficiency level.

After estimating the parameters [91] for the given Equation (11), the technical efficiency of firm i can easily be calculated as a relative distance of the actual output to the estimated stochastic frontier:

$$TE_j = -e^{u_j} \tag{12}$$

4.3. Classification

Classification is an important technique, commonly used in expert systems in order to support the domain experts to identify knowledge within the large volume of data.

Classification is considered the task of supervised learning of data mining (DM) and machine learning (ML), where the dataset is divided into classes (two and more) and each instance of the set has a tag identifying the class to which it belongs. Supervised machine learning algorithms are used to induce a classifier from a set of properly classified instances, i.e., expensive training. The test set, as a set of properly classified data instances, is used to measure the quality of a classifier obtained through the training process. Different types of models are used to represent classifiers and there are numerous algorithms available to induce classifiers from data: Logistic regression, decision trees, neuron network, k-nearest neighbor, and support vector machines, usually named neural networks [92–94]. For our case study, we chose naïve Bayes.

Bayesian classifiers imply that the knowledge of an event is described by the probability of its occurrence. The naïve Bayes classifier requires a small amount of training data, so this classifier could be easy implemented, and experience to date shows that in the case if independent predictors, better results are provided as compared to other classifiers [95–97].

The basic measure of classifier success is the confusion matrix, which is given in Figure 1. Additionally, apart from the confusion matrix, it is useful to define several other measures of classification success, such as the accuracy, precision, recall, F measure and area under the receiver operating characteristics (ROC) curve.

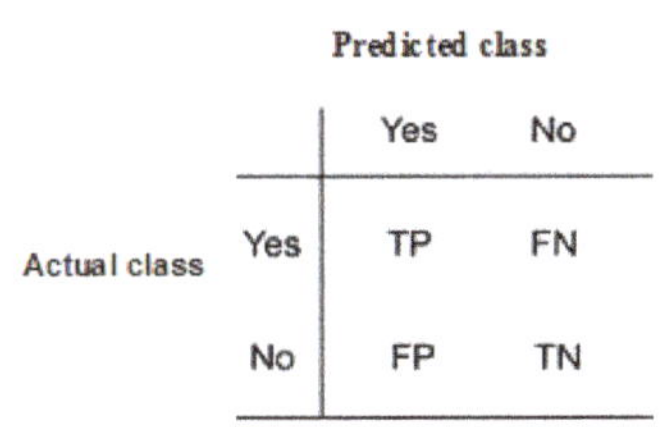

Figure 1. Confusion matrix for the classification process.

Accuracy = (TP + TN)/N, Precision = TP/(TP + FP), Recall = TP/(TP + FN), wherein TP-True Positive; TN-True Negative and N-total number of samples (instances) in a dataset.

The accuracy measure is unreliable in the case of a very unequal distribution of instances between classes (so-called skewed classes). Therefore, it is necessary to make a compromise between the measures of precision and recall in practice. The F measure combines precision and recall measures and the so-called F1 is an F measure, which gives equal importance to both of these two measures so F1 measure = 2 × Precision × Recall/(Precision + Recall).

The ROC curve illustrates the diagnostic ability of a binary classifier system using a comparison of recall (sensitivity) and FPR(specificity) = TN/(TN + FP).

Algorithms for the selection of the optimal feature subset perform a search within the space of feasible solutions. Most of the commonly used classification methods are very sensitive to the dimension of dataset and the instance/feature ratio [98].

The selection algorithm searches for a subset of attributes that provide the best result. The concept of feature ranking is limited and oriented to those classifiers that are very sensitive to the initial ordering of the input features. We proposed a ranker evaluation approach for the detection of attributes because it ranks the attributes by its importance. Weka is software that reduces the information volume [99], reducing it by the application of various algorithms and techniques, respectively, that could be suggested as the ranking approach in the previous sentence.

Ranking methods for optimal feature selection evaluate a single feature by using various metrics and assign a rank, based on its performance. The evaluation metrics are commonly founded on features 'statistical properties or their expected potential. The reduction of the dimensionality of data is based on those properties [100]. Attribute selection algorithms can be broken down into filters and prior learning methods. In this paper, we chose to use three algorithms from the filter group, the measure gain ratio, which is practically derived from the measure information gain (InfoGain) and Relief-F, which perform the individual attribute ranking and was originally intended to be classified into only two classes, which is the case that we solve in this paper and the case because we are interested in whether the BFC process is effective or not.

The complexity of group correlation analysis derives from the huge number of combinations of the attributes in which interactions should be taken into consideration O(2N), where N is the number of attributes in the model [98]. The entropy commonly used in the information theory [101], which represents the "purity" of an arbitrary collection of examples. The entropy measures the system's unpredictability. The entropy of Y is given by Equation (13):

$$H(Y) = -\sum_{y \subset Y} p(y) \log_2(p(y)), \tag{13}$$

where *p(y)* is defined as the marginal probability density function for the random variable Y. Let us assume that Y and X are random variables in the training set S. If the entropy of Y with respect to the partitions induced by X is less than the entropy of Y prior to partitioning, the conditional entropy function is given by Equation(14):

$$H(Y|X) = -\sum_{x \subset X} p(x) \sum_{y \subset Y} p(y|x) \log_2(p(y|x)), \tag{14}$$

where $p(y|x)$ is the conditional probability of y conditional to the knowledge of x.

The entropy can be considered as a criterion of impurity in thetraining set S. Therefore, we can define a measure of the amount by which the entropy of attribute decreases to gain additional information about the attribute provided by the class [102]. This measure is known as information gain: InfoGain. InfoGain evaluates the worth of an attribute by measuring the information gain with respect to the class, according to Equation (15):

$$\text{InfoGain (Class,Attribute)} = \text{H(Class)} - \text{H(Class | Attribute)}, \tag{15}$$

where H represents the information entropy.

The information gain ratio or GainRatio is the non-symmetrical measure, introduced to compensate for the bias of the InfoGain [103] by reducing it on high-branch attributes. GainRatio should be more significant when data is evenly spread or smaller when all data belong to one branch. GainRatio, which takes the number and size of branches into account when choosing an attribute, is given by Equation (16):

$$\text{GainRatio} = \frac{\text{InfoGain}}{\text{H(Class)}} \tag{16}$$

Equation (16) represents the normalization of the InfoGain, by dividing it with the entropy of class. Due to normalization, the GainRatio values fall in the range [0, 1]. The knowledge of the class fully predicts the attribute if the GainRatio is equal to 1. On the other hand, if the GainRatio is equal to 0, one can conclude that there is no relation between attribute and class. The decision tree classification methods C4.5 [104] and ID3 [105] employ the GainRatio as a criterion of the attribute selection at every node.

One of the possible filtering methods with the proceedings of the attribute ranking is ReliefF, based on the procedure of the nearest neighbors (*k*-nearest neighbors or k-NN).

The algorithm estimates and ranks each attribute with the global grade function [−1, ... , 1]. Weight calculation is based on the probability of the nearest neighbors form two different classes with different values for the attributes and probability that form two neighbors from the same class with the same value of attributes.

The function diff(Attribute; Instance1; Instance2) computes the difference of the attribute's values obtained in two instances. For discrete attributes, the difference is either 1 (different values) or 0 (the same values), while for continuous attributes the differences are normalized on the interval [0, 1]. Kononenko [106] notes that the higher the number of instances, the more reliable ReliefF's estimates but the running time also increases. The ReliefF algorithm is given in Figure 2. We used Weka software [99] to perform the feature selection algorithms.

set all weights $W[A] = 0.0$
for $i = 1$ *to* m *do*
begin
randomly select an instance R
find k *nearest hits* H_j
for each class $C \neq class(R)$ *do*
find k *nearest misses* $M_j(C)$
for $A = 1$ *to* #*attributes do*

$$W[A] = W[A] - \sum_{j=1}^{k} diff(A,R,H_j)/(m \times k) + \sum_{C \neq class(R)} [\frac{P(C)}{1 - P(class(R))} \sum_{j=1}^{k} diff(A,R,M_j(C))]/(m \times k)$$

end

Figure 2. Relief algorithm.

5. Methodology

According to Stewart [13], the MCDA formulation corresponds to the DEA formulation. The inputs and outputs are seen as attributes or criteria for DMUs' efficiency evaluation, where the associated objective is to minimize the inputs and/or to maximize the outputs. Practically, we can consider DEA as a non-parametric method, which leads to classification in basically two groups of efficient and inefficient decision-making units. Another option is to use a parametric SFA method, which considers inputs and outputs as variables of the production function.

Classification is a methodology for dividing the dataset into two or more classes. The ReliefF is a classifier for attribute ranking, which enables future selection and reduction of the dimensionality of the database by selecting the only necessary attributes. The future selection process offers the following positive effects:

- Fulfillment of the necessary condition for DEA application, i.e., strong relation between the number of input and outputs and DMUs. According to the literature [107], the general rule of thumb is as follows: ((number of inputs + number of outputs) × 3 <Number of DMUs. There are also milder conditions, set by authors in [107], which requires two DMUs for each input and output;
- Eliminating the noise in the data;
- Increases the readability of the results; and
- Speeds up the calculation.

These are the reasons for proposing an algorithm that integrates efficiency assessment methods with classification methods into a framework that shows better characteristics than each of the methods used individually.

5.1. Basic Motivation for Integrating DEA and SFA with Classification

This paper attempts to optimize the process of solving the considered univariate problem of determining the efficiency of certification (BFC) of local governments in the Republic of Serbia. The authors had in mind four underlying motives, i.e., reasons for building one model that integrates

DEA, SFA, and classification methods to obtain a method with better characteristics than each model individually:

1. The results obtained with the group of DEA methods and with the group of SFA methods very often differ significantly. In our case, we classified the efficiency of BFC processes into two classes, Efficient and inefficient cities, which implies using one type of informational n-redundancy ($n \geq 3$). This means using at least three different methods from the mandatory groups of DEA and SFA methods (in our case DEA CCR, DEA BCC and SFA) and classifying as efficient only those DMUs that are evaluated as efficient by at least two out of these three methods.

2. Classification algorithms can be useful to assess the essential parameters, before and after the attribute selection, to determine and assess the improvement of classification obtained by reducing attributes. In our case, the naïve Bayes classifier was chosen as the most suitable for the set of a small number of training units.

3. The fact that DEA as one of the most commonly used methods requires that the ratio of the total number of DMUs and input and output attributes should be at least 3 (milder condition is 2). This classification can be useful in the case of the necessity of problem dimensionality reduction.

4. Using a well-known attribute selection procedure might be helpful in the reduction of the number of attributes, which solves the previously mentioned limitations of the DEA, as well as the problem of reducing noise in the data. The ReliefF algorithm, as one from the group of Relief algorithms, is selected to estimate the weights of attributes and rank them. In addition, for example, in [108], one can find a number of conclusions that justify using the ReliefF algorithm.

5.2. Integration of the Classification and Efficiency Evaluation

The proposed new model for evaluating the efficiency of the certification process involves the integration of non-parametric DEA and parametric SFA models with the classification into the following algorithm shown in Figure 3.

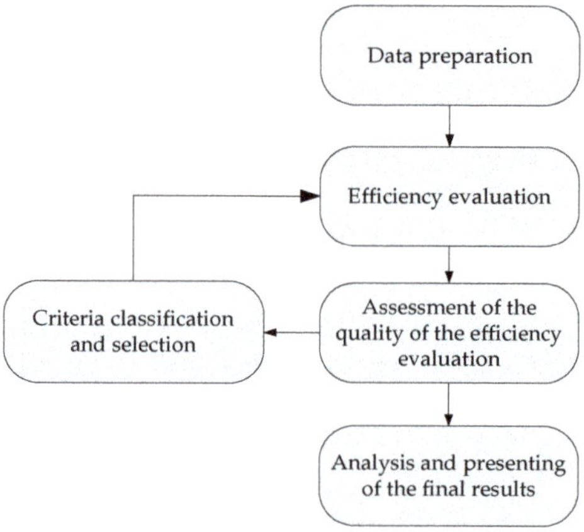

Figure 3. Efficiency evaluation model that integrates three methods: DEA, classification and SFA.

According to Figure 3, the algorithm's steps in the proposed frameworks are:

1. Data preparations assume defining DMUs and criteria of the efficiency evaluation, collecting and cleaning necessary data and handling missing values.

2. Determining the efficiency scores using the three models (DEA CRS, DEA VRS and SFA). Using models with different assumptions allows deeper insight into inefficiency sources and result verifications. The DMUs are classified into two classes (efficient and inefficient subsets) and partially ranked within the class of inefficient ones.

3. Using the obtained efficiency scores as a two-class classification attribute (efficient and inefficient) for the assessment of the essential parameters characterizing the quality of classification, precision, and accuracy by the F-measure [109]. The naive Bayes classification model is selected, like the most appropriate one for the small-set classification [110]. If the quality measures are satisfactory, go to step 5; otherwise, go to step 4.

4. The attribute selection process uses the ReliefF classifier, as the one that individually evaluates each of the attributes and rank them. This ranking provides a base for selecting a subset of parameters that are relevant and checks the eligibility conditions for applying DEA methods by checking the allowed ratio of the number of attributes and units. Go to step 2.

Steps 2, 3 and 4 can be repeated until satisfactory results have been obtained.

5. The definitive ranking of DMUs and analyzing the final results.

6. Case Study: Evaluating of the Effectiveness of the BFC Process

As we mentioned, the authors aimed to propose one new model for determining the efficiency of a successful BFC process in attracting foreign direct investments. The BFC process has been carried out since 2007. It was completed successfully in 21 cities and municipalities in the Republic of Serbia until 2013. The main idea was to evaluate the efficiency of the BFC process in those cities and municipalities using the model given in Figure 3. The efficiency was assessed as the success of attracting investments taking into account the achieved level of the 12 certification criteria given in Section 3.

6.1. Data

The cities and municipalities that completed the BFC process, excluding one outlier, are considered as 20 DMUs in the efficiency evaluation ($j = 1, \ldots ,20$). The 12 relevant BFC criteria, according to NALED's methodology and their importance, are given in Table 1 in Section 3. In the efficiency evaluation, the average values of these 12 criteria (C1–C12) are used as inputs (x_{ij}, $i = 1, \ldots\ 12, j = 1, \ldots\ 20$), while the amount of investment per capita is used as an output (y_j, $j = 1, \ldots\ 20$). The case study of the efficiency evaluation of the BFC process of cities and local governments in the Republic of Serbia uses data, provided by NALED. The input and output criteria database together with BFC scores and ranking according to NALED's methodology (normalized value of $C_i \times w_i$, $i = 1, \ldots ,12$) are presented in Table 2.

Table 2. Descriptive statistics on data and NALED's evaluation.

	Inputs												*Output*	*NALED's Evaluation*	
	C_1	C_2	C_3	C_4	C_5	C_6	C_7	C_8	C_9	C_{10}	C_{11}	C_{12}	*Investment*	*Score*	*Ranking*
Municipality 1	0.80	1.06	1.00	0.73	0.88	1.00	1.00	0.73	0.64	0.83	1.00	1.00	520.02	0.88	10
Municipality 2	1.00	0.82	0.75	1.00	0.93	1.00	1.00	0.93	1.00	0.88	1.00	1.00	686.57	0.95	3
Municipality 3	0.63	0.95	0.80	0.94	0.86	1.00	0.90	0.75	0.67	0.94	0.93	1.00	580.64	0.86	14
Municipality 4	0.90	0.82	0.88	1.00	0.95	1.00	1.00	0.70	0.68	0.76	1.00	0.75	464.16	0.87	12
Municipality 5	1.00	0.62	1.00	0.78	0.60	0.67	1.00	0.60	0.59	0.98	0.83	1.00	315.94	0.82	19
Municipality 6	1.00	1.06	0.75	0.94	0.90	0.94	1.00	0.87	0.91	0.79	1.00	1.00	942.36	0.94	4
Municipality 7	1.00	0.94	1.00	0.78	0.70	0.78	1.00	0.57	0.73	0.70	1.00	0.50	879.20	0.82	18
Municipality 8	1.00	0.82	1.00	0.89	1.00	1.00	1.00	0.83	0.55	0.88	1.00	1.00	415.97	0.91	7
Municipality 9	1.00	0.82	1.00	0.67	0.65	1.00	1.00	0.87	0.96	0.81	0.83	1.00	622.95	0.88	11
Municipality 10	1.00	0.94	0.75	0.81	0.63	0.94	1.00	0.67	0.91	0.79	1.00	1.00	754.09	0.89	8
Municipality 11	1.00	0.77	0.75	0.83	0.73	1.00	1.00	0.53	0.64	0.76	0.83	1.00	687.33	0.83	17
Municipality 12	0.80	1.00	0.75	0.89	0.90	1.00	1.00	0.53	0.73	0.73	0.83	0.75	200.01	0.83	16
Municipality 13	0.80	1.00	1.00	0.74	0.73	1.00	1.00	0.77	0.46	0.77	1.00	1.00	111.78	0.85	15
Municipality 14	1.00	0.94	1.00	0.87	0.73	1.00	1.00	0.83	0.55	0.68	1.00	0.88	368.21	0.87	13
Municipality 15	1.00	0.94	1.00	1.00	0.90	1.00	1.00	1.00	1.00	0.94	1.00	0.62	995.82	0.96	2
Municipality 16	1.00	0.82	1.00	0.89	0.78	1.00	1.00	0.80	0.91	0.78	1.00	1.00	208.68	0.92	5
Municipality 17	1.00	0.82	1.00	0.78	0.88	0.89	1.00	0.67	0.55	0.83	0.67	0.75	306.58	0.81	20
Municipality 18	1.00	0.88	1.00	1.02	0.90	0.94	1.00	0.87	1.09	0.93	1.00	1.00	295.83	0.98	1
Municipality 19	1.00	0.95	0.60	0.97	0.93	1.00	1.00	0.85	0.58	0.94	1.00	1.00	432.21	0.91	6
Municipality 20	1.00	0.77	0.88	0.81	0.80	1.00	1.00	0.73	0.82	0.77	1.00	1.00	697.12	0.89	9
Max	1	1.06	1	1.024	1	1	1	1	1.09	0.98	1	1	995.82	0.98	
Min	0.63	0.62	0.60	0.67	0.60	0.67	0.90	0.53	0.46	0.68	0.67	0.50	111.78	0.81	
Average	0.95	0.89	0.90	0.87	0.82	0.96	1.00	0.76	0.75	0.82	0.95	0.91	524.27	0.88	
SD	0.10	0.11	0.13	0.10	0.11	0.09	0.02	0.13	0.18	0.08	0.09	0.15	248.77	0.05	

The descriptive statistics show that the input criteria values drop into a relatively small range of 0.46 to 1.09, with a standard deviation from 0.02 to 0.15. Therefore, the BFC process accomplishment is evaluated with scores 0.81 to 0.98. The municipalities are expected to attract a relatively even amount of investments considering the BFC process evaluation. However, the investments per capita range from 111.78 to 995.82, which is expected to make an impact on the efficiency evolution.

6.2. Efficiency Evaluation: Preliminary Results and Classification

The preliminary results of the efficiency evaluation of BFC process in the 20 municipalities, according to the criteria given in Table 2, are given in Table 3. The second and third columns show the efficiency results obtained using the DEA model of Equations (2)–(5) with the assumption of a constant to return (CRS) economy. The CRS assumption is stricter than a variable to return economy assumption imposed in the DEA VRS model (Equations (6)–(9)), with the results given in the fourth and fifth columns. The results of the parametric SFA model are given in the last two columns of Table 3.

Table 3. Scores, ranks and descriptive statistics (12 input criteria).

Municipality	DEA CRS		DEA VRS		SFA	
	Score	Rank	Score	Rank	SFA	Rank
Municipality 1	0.716	10	1.000	1	1.000	1
Municipality 2	0.845	8	0.929	18	0.878	10
Municipality 3	0.933	6	1.000	1	1.000	1
Municipality 4	0.588	13	0.999	15	1.000	1
Municipality 5	0.505	15	1.000	1	1.000	1
Municipality 6	1.000	1	1.000	1	1.000	1
Municipality 7	1.000	1	1.000	1	0.582	15
Municipality 8	0.631	12	1.000	1	0.649	14
Municipality 9	0.838	9	1.000	1	0.883	9
Municipality 10	1.000	1	1.000	1	0.676	12
Municipality 11	0.960	5	1.000	1	1.000	1
Municipality 12	0.277	18	0.999	17	0.419	19
Municipality 13	0.203	20	0.999	15	0.505	16
Municipality 14	0.559	14	1.000	1	1.000	1
Municipality 15	1.000	1	1.000	1	1.000	1
Municipality 16	0.245	19	0.269	20	0.358	20
Municipality 17	0.501	16	1.000	1	0.658	13
Municipality 18	0.324	17	0.339	19	0.451	17
Municipality 19	0.674	11	1.000	1	0.425	18
Municipality 20	0.885	7	1.000	1	0.759	11
Average	0.684		0.927		0.762	
Max	1.000		1		1.000	
Min	0.203		0.270		0.358	
St Dev	0.275		0.011		0.241	

As we already mentioned, all three methods provide classification into subsets of efficient and inefficient municipalities. Nevertheless, the size of the subsets varies depending on the used methodology. The DEA CCR model produces the subset of four efficient municipalities (municipality 6, 7, 10 and 15), with an average efficiency score of 0.684 and standard deviation of 0.275. On the other hand, only 6 out of 20 municipalities are assessed as inefficient, with a mean value of 0.927. All municipalities assessed as inefficient according to the DEA CRS model exhibit increasing returns to scale. The size of the SFA efficient subset lies between the two obtained by DEA. It consists of nine municipalities, while the average efficiency score of the whole set is 0.759 (stdev = 0.241).

The most unrealistic results are obtained using the DEA VRS model, which allows the highest degrees of freedom among the three used efficiency evaluation methods. Those results are expected, taking into account that the number of 13 criteria (inputs and outputs) is too big in comparison with 20 DMUs. The optimal number of DMUs for DEA efficiency evaluation should be greater or equal to (12+1) × 3 = 39 according to the rule of thumb given in the literature [107]. On the contrary, the number of criteria for the 20 DMUs should be a maximum of 7. Therefore, in step two, we performed the classification using the naive Bayes algorithm in order to check the data model's validity and the results are given in Table 4.

Table 4. Bayes classification results based on the DEA CRS score (four efficient DMUs).

	TP Rate	FP Rate	Precision	Recall	F-measure	ROC Area	Class
	0.875	1	0.778	0.875	0.824	0.438	No
	0	0.125	0	0	0	0.438	Yes
Weighted Avg.	0.7	0.825	0.622	0.7	0.659	0.438	

Instep three, we performed feature selection using only the Belief classifier because the InfoGain and GainRatio classifiers give only one attribute as important: C12. The results, which are given in Table 5, show that only five attributes, i.e., the input criteria, are in the group of important ones: C12, C6, C2, C8 and C9, respectively. In this procedure of criteria selection, all those criteria that have a value of at least an order of magnitude lower than the previous one were rejected and treated as insignificant.

Table 5. Feature selection using the Belief classifier.

Value	Rank	Attribute
0.1783	1	C12
0.1070	2	C6
0.0601	3	C2
0.0505	4	C8
0.0500	5	C9
0.0019	6	C3
0.0017	7	C5
0.0016	8	C10
−0.0003	9	C11
−0.01	10	C7
−0.015	11	C1
−0.022	12	C4

In step four, we reapplied the three redundant methodology for efficiency evolution (DEA CRS, DEA VRS, and SFA). Based on the obtained results, given in Table 6, we conclude that now we have only two municipalities (7 and 15) that belong to the efficient subset according to the DEA CRS model, while the DEA VRS model classifies six municipalities into the efficient subset. Once again, SFA proves the middle way, with a subset of five efficient municipalities.

Table 6. Scores, ranks and descriptive statistics (5 attributes).

Municipality	DEA CRS		DEA VRS		SFA	
	Score	Rank	Score	Rank	SFA	Rank
Municipality 1	0.676	10	0.757	17	0.795	10
Municipality 2	0.787	7	0.861	12	0.751	11
Municipality 3	0.720	8	0.771	16	0.897	6
Municipality 4	0.588	13	0.652	18	0.687	15
Municipality 5	0.505	15	1.000	1	0.743	12
Municipality 6	0.919	4	0.985	10	1.000	1
Municipality 7	1.000	1	1.000	1	1.000	1
Municipality 8	0.631	11	1.000	1	1.000	1
Municipality 9	0.716	9	0.782	15	0.691	14
Municipality 10	0.832	6	0.832	13	0.707	13

Table 6. *Cont.*

Municipality	DEA CRS Score	DEA CRS Rank	DEA VRS Score	DEA VRS Rank	SFA SFA	SFA Rank
Municipality 11	0.937	3	1.000	1	1.000	1
Municipality 12	0.242	19	0.999	7	0.199	20
Municipality 13	0.203	20	0.999	7	0.295	17
Municipality 14	0.559	14	0.974	11	0.808	9
Municipality 15	1.000	1	1.000	1	1.000	1
Municipality 16	0.245	18	0.262	20	0.234	19
Municipality 17	0.465	16	0.999	7	0.635	16
Municipality 18	0.324	17	0.34	19	0.267	18
Municipality 19	0.613	12	0.817	14	0.886	8
Municipality 20	0.885	5	1	1	0.890	7
Average	0.642		0.852		0.724	
Max	1.000		1		1.000	
Min	0.203		0.262		0.199	
St Dev	0.254		0.218		0.271	

In this step, we also repeated classification using the naïve Bayes algorithm. The results and parameters for classification with five input criteria, given in Table 7, clearly show better values are achieved for all parameters than in the case of the efficiency evaluation with 12 criteria. The precision at this stage is 0.9 (in comparison to 0.778), recall is equal to 1 (former value was 0.875), and consequently the F-measure is almost 1 (0.978 in comparison to 0.824). Those results are obvious indications that attribute (criteria) selection and reduction of the problem dimensionality led to a positive improvement.

Table 7. Bayes classification results based on the DEA CRS score (two efficient DMUs).

	TP Rate	FP Rate	Precision	Recall	F-Measure	ROC Area	Class
	1	1	0.9	1	0.947	0.444	No
	0	0	0	0	0	0.056	Yes
Weighted Avg.	0.9	0.9	0.81	0.9	0.853	0.406	

The results presented in Table 6 might be considered as the final.

7. Results Discussion

The subset of five criteria selection is justified by the increased parameters of quality evaluation after problem dimensionality reduction. The correlation between the ranks obtained before and after reduction shows that the DEA CRS model is the most robust (correlation coefficient is equal to 97.47% at the significance level of 0.001). The correlations for the other two models (DEA VRS and SFA) are 46.79% and 49.39% with no statistical significance. The degrees of freedom together with criteria values are important factors for DEA efficiency evaluation (less criteria led to less efficient DMUs as proven by the obtained results). On the other hand, SFA as a measure of the central tendency also relies also on the criteria values and it is very sensitive to their selection.

To analyze the rank similarity between the final individual efficiency scores obtained by using the three models (Table 6), we computed Spearman's rank correlation between them. We found a DEA rank correlation of 59.96% with no statistical significance at 0.01levels due to different economy of scale assumptions. Actually, all efficient municipalities under the constant return to scale (CRS) assumption remain efficient under the variable return to scale (VRS) assumptions, but the number of efficient DMUs increased. The diversity in the ranks of the individual DMUs might be better explained by introducing the NELED's ranks given in Table 3. For example, municipality 5 is ranked in 19th place according to NALED. It is efficient under VRS but ranked in 15th place under the CRS assumption. By comparing it with municipality 18 (NALEDs top-ranked DMU), we can conclude that municipality 5 attracted more investment per capita (315.95) than municipality 18 295.83. Therefore, municipality 5 is a benchmark DMU for municipality 18. At the same time, NALED's bottom-ranked municipality 17 attracted a smaller amount of investments per capita and cannot be benchmark for municipality 5 if the model considers scale of economy as an important factor in the efficiency evaluation.

When it comes to the correlation between the parametric and nonparametric rankings, there is a correlation of 48.58% between the DEA CRS and SFA ranks and a correlation of 50.79% between the DEA VRS and SFA ranks with no statistical significance, which is in line with a previous study [111]. The authors of [112] stressed that the contradictory results obtained by DEA and SFA might be expected since they have different degrees of dispersion and perform rankings differently. The former one is a frontier deterministic method while the latter one is a central tendency stochastic method, which takes statistical errors into account. The implication of this divergence is given in [113], where the authors stated that the application of only one methodology for ranking may lead to misuse, especially in the case when there is no significant correlation between different models.

8. Conclusions

The initial hypothesis from which the main goal of this paper arose was it is possible to construct an efficiency assessment model that integrates different methods and produces better characteristics than any of the methods involved? This paper proposed a framework for integrating the efficiency assessment non-parametric DEA CRS and DEA VRS and parametric SFA models with the machine learning algorithm for classification and quality evaluation. It was checked and justified by implementing it on the real-world case study of BFC certification of cities in the Republic of Serbia.

Having in mind the existence of the real-world problem of efficiency evaluation, such as evaluation of the BFC process, which includes a large number of influencing factors in comparison with the number of units of local governments, there is an expressed need to reduce the problem dimensions in order to obtain better results. In such a case, the classification method in synergy with the future selection of attributes is realistically the right choice.

In this paper, we successfully integrated representative methods of the two most commonly used approaches in assessing efficiency, DEA as non-parametric and SFA as parametric, with a machine learning classification method to reduce the number of criteria. Therefore, the novel model takes advantage of the excellent characteristics of each of employed method and eliminates the bad ones using dimension optimization:

- Enables proper use of the DEA methodology with appropriate degrees of freedom;
- Reduces noise in the data; and
- Provides better quality results as proved by naïve Bayes classification.

The suggestion is to use the DEA CRS model as the most robust and strict one for result verification. DEA, as a non-parametric model with no a priori weight assignment, is a very suitable method for efficiency evaluation in the presence of multiple inputs and outputs [81]. It is also a primary choice if there is a lack of some input and output criteria, which might be compensated by the advantages of another one. Therefore, criteria classification and selection are essential. SFA is the method of choice for when numerous criteria exist and in the case of the necessity of inclusion of the stochastic nature of the parameters. All in all, these two methodologies (DEA and SFA) might be imposed as corrective factors to one another.

It is important to remark on the possible uncertainty, imprecision, and subjectivity of input data determination, which is the case in the considered BFC process, and implies the necessity of adding methodologies, which decreases the impact of this deficiency on the results obtained with the proposed methodology. This is, for example, the case with the methodologies based on the fuzzy, interval rough set and interval neutrosophic rough set theory, which are considered in the papers [114–120]. This could be the subject of future work of the authors.

Author Contributions: Conceptualization: M.J.; Project administration: S.N.; Writing—original draft, Validation: M.R.; Writing—review and editing, Formal analysis: G.S.; Software: V.S.; Investigation: V.S.; Supervision, Methodology: D.R. All authors have read and agreed to the published version of the manuscript.

Funding: This research was funded by the Ministry of Education, Science and Technological Development, Republic of Serbian, grants number III44007.

Conflicts of Interest: The authors declare no conflict of interest.

References

1. Verbruggen, F.; Sutherland, J.; Werf, J.M.; Brinkkemper, S.; Sutherland, A. Process Efficiency—Adapting Flow to the Agile Improvement Effort. In Proceedings of the 52nd Hawaii International Conference on System Sciences (HICSS), Grand Wailea, Maui, 8–11 January 2019; pp. 1–7.
2. Farell, M.J. The Measurement of Productive Efficiency. *J. R.Stat. Soc. Ser. A Stat.Soc.* **1957**, *120*, 253–290. [CrossRef]
3. Office of the Finanacial Managemnet, State of the Washington. Performance Measure Guide. Available online: http://www.ofm.wa.gov/budget/instructions/other/2009performancemeasureguide.pdf (accessed on 1 June 2020).
4. Kaplan, R.S.; Norton, D.P. *Translating Strategy into Action—The Balanced ScoreCard*; Harward Bussines School Press: Boston, MA, USA, 1996.
5. Dario, C.; Simar, L. *Advaced Robust and Nonparametric Methods in Efficiency Analysis Methodology and Applications*; Springer: New York, NY, USA, 2007; ISBN 987-0-387-35155-1.
6. Coelli, T.J.; Rao, D.S.P.; O'Donnell, C.J.; Battese, G.E. *An Introduction to Efficiency and Productivity Analysis*; Springer: New York, NY, USA, 2005; ISBN 978-0-387-25895-9.
7. Doumpos, M.; Zouponidis, C. *Multicriteria Decision Aid Classification Methods (Applied Optimization)*; Springer: New York, NY, USA, 2002; ISBN 1402008058 (ISBN13: 9781402008054).
8. Zopounidis, C.; Doumpos, M. Multicriteria classification and sorting methods: A literature review. *Eur. J. Oper. Res.* **2002**, *138*, 229–246. [CrossRef]
9. Yeveyeva, I. Solving Classification Problems with Multicriteria Decision Aiding Approaches. Ph.D. Thesis, Faculty of Information Technology, University of Jyvaskyla, Jyväskylä, Finland, 2007.
10. Ranđelović, M.; Stanković, J.; Savić, G.; Kuk, K.; Ranđelović, D. An Approach to Determining the Importance of Criteria in the Process of Certifying a City as a Business-Friendly Environment. *Interfaces* **2018**, *48*, 156–165. [CrossRef]
11. NALED. Business Friendly Certification BFC SEE. Available online: https://naled.rs/certifikacija-opstina-bfc-see (accessed on 1 June 2020).
12. Sarkis, J. A comparative analysis of DEA as a discrete alternative multiplecriteria decision tool. *Eur. J. Oper. Res.* **2000**, *123*, 543–557. [CrossRef]
13. Stewart, T.J. Relationships between data envelopment analysis and multicriteria decision analysis. *J. Oper. Res. Soc.* **1996**, *47*, 654–665. [CrossRef]
14. Prado, J.; Heijungs, R. Implementation of stochastic multi attribute analysis (SMAA) in comparative environmental assessments. *Environ. Model. Softw.* **2018**, *109*, 223–231. [CrossRef]
15. Ploskas, N.; Stiakakis, E.; Fouliras, P. Assessing Computer Network Efficiency Using Data Envelopment Analysis and Multicriteria Decision Analysis Techniques. *J. Multi-Criteria Decis. Anal.* **2014**, *22*. [CrossRef]
16. Bigaret, S.; Hodgett, R.E.; Meyer, P. Supporting the Multi-Criteria Decision Aiding process: R and the MCDA package. *EURO J. Decis. Process.* **2017**, *5*, 169–194. [CrossRef]
17. Brasil, A.T.; Pinheiro, R.P.; Coelho, L.V.A.; Costa, C.N. Comparison of Two MCDA Classification Methods over the Diagnosis of Alzheimer's Disease. In *Rough Sets and Knowledge Technology. RSKT 2009*; Wen, P., Li, Y., Polkowski, L., Yao, Y., Tsumoto, S., Wang, G., Eds.; Springer: Berlin/Heidelberg, Germany, 2009; Volume 5589, pp. 334–341.
18. Longaray, A.; Ensslin, L.; Ensslin, S.; Alves, G.; Dutra, A.; Munhoz, P. Using MCDA to evaluate the performance of the logistics process in public hospitals: The case of a Brazilian teaching hospital. *Int. Trans. Oper. Res.* **2018**, *25*, 133–156. [CrossRef]
19. Roy, J.; Adhikary, K.; Kar, S.; Pamucar, D. A rough strength relational DEMATEL model for analysing the key success factors of hospital service quality. *Decis. Mak. Appl. Manag. Eng.* **2018**, *1*, 121–142. [CrossRef]

20. Figueira, J.; Greco, S.; Ehrgott, M. (Eds.) *Multiple Criteria Decision Analysis: State of the Art Surveys*; International Series in Operations Research & Management Science; Springer: Boston, MA, USA, 2005.
21. Lahdelma, R.; Salminen, P.; Hokkanen, J. Using Multicriteria Methods in Environmental Planning and Management. *Environ. Manag.* **2014**, *26*, 595–605. [CrossRef] [PubMed]
22. Coutinho-Rodrigues, J.; Simao, A.; Antunes, C.H. A gis-based multicriteriaspatial decision support system for planning urban infrastructures. *Decis. Support Syst.* **2011**, *51*, 720–726. [CrossRef]
23. Bagherikahvarin, M.; De Stem, Y. Using the A ranking method based on DEA and PROMETHEE II (a rank based on DEA & PR.II). *Measurement* **2016**, *89*, 333–342.
24. Botti, L.; Peypoch, N. Multi-criteria ELECTRE method and destination competitiveness. *Tour. Manag. Perspect.* **2013**, *6*, 108–113. [CrossRef]
25. Papamichail, K.N.; French, S. 25 years of MCDA in nuclear emergency management. *IMA J. Manag. Math.* **2013**, *24*, 481–503. [CrossRef]
26. Sawicka, H.; Węglinski, S.; Witort, P. Application of multiple criteria decision aid methods in logistic systems. *LogForum* **2010**, *6*, 3–10.
27. Biswas, P.; Pal, B.B. A fuzzy goal programming method to solve congestion management problem using genetic algorithm. *Decis. Mak. Appl. Manag. Eng.* **2019**, *2*, 36–53. [CrossRef]
28. Belacel, N. Multicriteria assignment method PROAFTN: Methodology and medical applications. *Eur. J. Oper. Res.* **2000**, *125*, 175–183. [CrossRef]
29. Brasil, A.T.; Pinheiro, P.R.; Coelho, A.L.V. The impact of the prototype selectionon a multicriteria decision aid classification algorithm. In *Innovations and Advances in Computer Sciences and Engineering*; Springer: New York, NY, USA, 2010; Volume 1, pp. 379–382.
30. Jacobs, R.; Smith, P.; Street, A. *Measuring Efficiency in Health Care*; Cambridge University Press: Cambridge, UK, 2006.
31. Berger, A.N.; Hunter, W.C.; Timme, S.G. The Efficiency of Financial Institutions: AReview and Preview of Research Past, Present, and Future. *J. Bank. Financ.* **1993**, *17*, 221–249. [CrossRef]
32. Sarkis, J.; Talluri, S. Eco-efficiency measurement using data envelopment analysis: Research data practitioner issues. *Integr. Environ. Assess. Manag.* **2004**, *6*, 91–123. [CrossRef]
33. Carlsson, B. The Measurement of Efficiency in Production: An Application to Swedish Manufacturing Industries 1968. *Swedish J. Econ.* **1972**, *74*, 468–485. [CrossRef]
34. Klimchik, A.; Ambiehl, A.; Garnier, S.; Furet, B.; Pashkevich, A. Efficiency evaluation of robots in machining applications using industrial performance measure. *Robot. Comput.-Integr Manuf.* **2017**, *48*, 12–29. [CrossRef]
35. Peypoch, N.; Solonandrasana, B. Research note: Technical efficiency in the tourism industry. *Tour. Econ.* **2006**, *12*, 653–657. [CrossRef]
36. Haar, S.; Segers, R.M.; Jehn, K. Measuring the effectiveness of emergency management teams: Scale development and validation. *Int. J. Emerg. Manag.* **2013**, *9*, 258. [CrossRef]
37. Andrejić, M.; Kilibarda, M. The problems of measuring efficiency in logistics. *Vojnotehnicki glasnik* **2013**, *61*. [CrossRef]
38. Filippini, M.; Farsi, M. Regulation and Measuring Cost-Efficiency with Panel Data Models: Application to Electricity Distribution Utilities. *Rev. Ind. Organ.* **2004**, *25*, 1–19.
39. Ferrera, J.; Pedraja-Chaparro, F.; Salinas-Jimenez, J. Measuring Efficiency in Education: An Analysis of Different Approaches for Incorporating Non-discretionary Inputs. *Appl. Econ.* **2008**, *40*, 1323–1339. [CrossRef]
40. Liket, K.C.; Maas, K. Nonprofit organizational effectiveness: Analysis of best practices. *Nonprofit Volunt. Sect. Q.* **2015**, *44*, 268–296. [CrossRef]
41. BFC SEE Network. Available online: http://bfc-see.org/about-bfc-see-network (accessed on 1 June 2020).
42. Radukić, S.; Stanković, J. Evaluation of Local Business Environment in the Republic of Serbia. *ProcediaEcon. Financ.* **2015**, *19*, 353–363. [CrossRef]
43. Stojanović, B.; Stanković, J.; Ranđelović, M. The City of Niš Competitiveness Analysis in the Field of Foreign Direct Investment. *Econ. Enterp.* **2012**, *60*, 167–178. [CrossRef]
44. Ranđelović, D.; Stanković, J.; Anđelković, M.; Ranđelović, M. Application of AHP method in cities certification process. *Management* **2014**, *69*, 75–84.
45. Ranđelović, M.; Stanković, J.; Ranđelović, D.; Suknović, M. Methods for determination weights in multi-criteria model of cities certification methods for determination weights in multi-criteria model of cities certification. *Tech. Technol. Educ. Manag.* **2013**, *8*, 1404–1412.

46. Randjelović, D.; Janjić, J.; Stanković, J.; Randjelović, M.; Pešić, M. Weights determination in MCDM model combining the techniques of mathematical and statistical analysis. *Metal. Int.* **2013**, *XVIII*, 217–221.
47. Radulovic, B.; Dragutinovic, S. Efficiency of local self-governments in Serbia: An SFA approach. *Industrija* **2015**, *43*, 123–142. [CrossRef]
48. Afonso, A.; Fernandes, S. Assessing and Explaining the Relative Efficiency of Local Government. *J. Socio-Econ.* **2008**, *37*, 1946–1979. [CrossRef]
49. Balaguer, M.T.; Prior, D.; Tortosa, E. On the determinants of local government performance: A two-stage nonparametric approach. *Eur. Econ. Rev.* **2007**, *51*, 425–451. [CrossRef]
50. Sousa, M.D.C.S.D.; Stošić, B. Technical Efficiency of the Brazilian Municipalities: Correcting Nonparametric Frontier Measurements for Outliers. *J. Product. Anal.* **2005**, *24*, 157–181. [CrossRef]
51. De Borger, B.; Kerstens, K. Cost Efficiency of Belgian Local Governments: A Comparative analysis of FDH, DEA, and econometric approaches. *Reg. Sci. Urban Econ.* **1996**, *26*, 145–170. [CrossRef]
52. Geys, B.; Heinemann, F.; Kalb, A. Voter involvement, fiscal autonomy and public sector efficiency: Evidence from German municipalities. *Eur. J. Political Econ.* **2010**, *26*, 265–278. [CrossRef]
53. Lo Storto, C. Evaluating technical efficiency of Italian major municipalities: A data envelopment analysis model. *Procedia Soc. Behav. Sci.* **2013**, *81*, 346–350. [CrossRef]
54. Worthington, A.C. Cost Efficiency in Australian Local Government: A Comparative Analysis of Mathematical Programming and Econometric Approaches. *Financ. Account. Manag.* **2000**, *16*, 201–223. [CrossRef]
55. Westhuizen, G.; Dollery, B. *South African Local Government Efficiency Measurement*; Working Paper Series 4.1-19; Centre for Local Government, School of Business, Economics and Public Policy, University of New England: Armidale, Australia, 2009.
56. Ray, S. *Data Envelopment Analysis*; Cambridge University Press: Cambridge, UK, 2004; ISBN 0-521-80256-3.
57. Charnes, A.; Cooper, W.; Lewin, A.Y.; Seiford, L.M. Data Envelopment Analysis Theory, Methodology and Applications. *J. Oper. Res. Soc.* **1997**, *48*, 332–333. [CrossRef]
58. Cooper, W.W.; Seiford, L.M.; Zhu, J. *Data Envelopment Analysis, Handbook on Data Envelopment Analysis*; Springer: Boston, MA, USA, 2004; ISBN 978-1-4020-7798-2.
59. Kongar, E.; Pallis, J.; Sobh, T. Non-parametric Approach for Evaluating the Performance of Engineering Schools. *Int. J. Eng. Educ.* **2010**, *26*, 1210–1219.
60. Ji, Y.; Lee, C. Data envelopment analysis. *Stata J.* **2010**, *2*, 267–280. [CrossRef]
61. Stanković, J.; Radenković;-Jocić, D. The role of business environment in the promotion of investment activities: Case study and municipalities in the Republic of Serbia. *Teme* **2017**, *XLI*, 457–473.
62. Beiragh, R.; Alizadeh, R.; Shafiei Kaleibari, S.; Cavallaro, F.; Zolfani, S.; Bausys, R.; Mardani, A. An integrated Multi-Criteria Decision Making Model for Sustainability Performance Assessment for Insurance Companies. *Sustainability* **2020**, *12*, 789. [CrossRef]
63. Kumbhakar, S.; Parmeter, C.; Zelenyuk, V. *Stochastic Frontier Analysis: Foundations and Advances*; Working Papers 2017-10; Department of Economics, University of Miami: Coral Gables, FL, USA, 2017.
64. Seale, J., Jr. Stochastic Frontier Analysis. *J. Econ. Lit.* **2000**, *38*, 936–938.
65. Battese, G.; Corra, G. Estimation of a production frontier model: With application to the pastoral zone of eastern Australia. *Aust. J. Agric. Resour. Econ.* **1977**, *21*, 169–179. [CrossRef]
66. Belotti, F.; Daidone, S.; Ilardi, G.; Atella, V. Stochastic Frontier Analysis Using Stata. *Stata J.* **2012**, *13*, 719–758. [CrossRef]
67. Chitnis, A.; Vaidya, O. Efficiency ranking method using SFA and TOPSIS (ERM-ST): Case of Indian banks. *Benchmarking Int. J. Res.* **2018**, *25*, 471–488. [CrossRef]
68. Johnson, A.; Kuosmanen, T. An Introduction to CNLS and StoNED Methods for Efficiency Analysis: Economic Insights and Computational Aspects and Formulations. In *Benchmarking for Performance Evaluation: A Production Frontier Approach*; Ray, S., Kumbhakar, S., Dua, P., Eds.; Springer: Berlin/Heidelberg, Germany, 2014.
69. Thoraneenitiyan, N.; Avkiran, K.N. Measuring the impact of restructuring and country-specific factors on the efficiency of post-crisis East Asian banking systems:Integrating DEA with SFA. *Socio.-Econ. Plan. Sci.* **2009**, *43*, 240–252. [CrossRef]
70. Bezat-Jarzebowska, A. A concept of technical efficiency measurement based on the integrated use of the SFA and DEA methods. *Sci. Works Wrocław University Econ.* **2012**, *261*, 11–24.

71. François-Seck, F.; Al-Mouksit, A.; Wassongma, H. DEA and SFA research on the efficiency of microfinance institutions: A meta-analysis. *World Dev.* **2018**, *107*, 176–188.
72. Bogetoft, P.; Otto, L. Stochastic Frontier Analysis SFA. In *Benchmarking with DEA, SFA, and R*; Operations Research Management Science Series 157; Springer: Berlin/Heidelberg, Germany, 2011; pp. 197–231. [CrossRef]
73. Azadeh, A.; Ghaderi, S.F.; Omrani, H.; Eivazy, H. An integrated DEA-COLS-SFA algorithm for optimization and policy making of electricity distribution units. *Energy Policy* **2009**, *37*, 2605–2618. [CrossRef]
74. Anouze, A.L.; Bou-Hamad, I. Data envelopment analysis and data mining to efficiency estimation and evaluation. *Int. J. Islamic Middle East. Financ. Manag.* **2019**, *12*, 169–190. [CrossRef]
75. Azadeh, A.; Saberi, M.; Moghaddam, R.; Javanmardi, L. An integrated data envelopment analysis-artificial neural network-rough set algorithm for assessment of personnel efficiency. *Expert Syst. Appl.* **2011**, *38*, 1364–1373. [CrossRef]
76. Antonuccia, L.; Crocettaa, C.; D'Ovidio, F. Evaluation of Italian Judicial System. *Procedia Econ. Financ.* **2014**, *17*, 121–130. [CrossRef]
77. Fethi, M.; Pasiouras, F. Assessing bank efficiency and performance with operational research and artificial intelligence techniques: A survey. *Eur. J. Oper. Res.* **2010**, *204*, 189–198. [CrossRef]
78. Swinburn, G.; Goga, S.; Murphy, F. *Local Economic Development: A Primer Developing and Implementing Local Economic Development Strategies and Action Plan*; The World Bank: Washington, DC, USA, 2006. Available online: http://siteresources.worldbank.org/INTLED/423069-1099670772921/20738133/led_primer.pdf (accessed on 1 June 2020).
79. Ranđelović, M.; Nedeljković, S.; Jovanović, M.; Čabarkapa, M.; Stojanović, V.; Aleksić, A.; Ranđelović, D. Use of Determination of the Importance of Criteria in Business-Friendly Certification of Cities as Sustainable Local Economic Development Planning Tool. *Symmetry* **2020**, *12*, 425. [CrossRef]
80. Keeney, R.; Raiffa, H. *Decisions with Multiple Objectives: Preferences and Value Tradeoffs*; J. Wiley: New York, NY, USA, 1976.
81. Koksalan, M.; Wallenius, J.; Zionts, S. *Multiple Criteria Decision Making: _From Early History to 21th Century*; World Scientific: Singapore, 2011; ISBN 978-981-4335-58-4.
82. Ishizaka, A.; Nemery, P. *Multi-Criteria Decision Analysis: Methods and Software*; J. Wiley: New York, NY, USA, 2013.
83. Tsoukiàs, A. From decision theory to decision aiding methodology. *Eur. J. Oper. Res.* **2008**, *187*, 138–161. [CrossRef]
84. Belton, V.; Vickers, S.P. Demystifying DEA—A visual interactive approach based on multi criteria analysis. *J. Oper. Res. Soc.* **1993**, *44*, 883–896.
85. Cooper, W.W.; Seiford, L.M.; Tone, K. *Data Envelopment Analysis: A Comprehensive Text with Models, Applications, References and DEA-Solver Software*; Kluwer Academic Publishers: Boston, MA, USA, 2000.
86. Podinovski, V.V. Side effects of absolute weight bounds in DEA models. *Eur. J. Oper. Res.* **1999**, *115*, 583–595. [CrossRef]
87. Charnes, A.; Cooper, W.W.; Rhodes, E. Measuring the efficiency of decision making units. *Eur. J. Oper. Res.* **1978**, *2*, 429–444. [CrossRef]
88. Banker, R.D.; Charnes, A.; Cooper, W.W. Some Models for Estimating Technical and Scale Inefficiencies in Data Envelopment Analysis. *Manag. Sci.* **1984**, *30*, 1078–1092. [CrossRef]
89. Aigner, D.; Lovell, C.A.K.; Schmidt, P. Formulation and estimation of stochastic frontier production function models. *J. Econ.* **1977**, *6*, 21–37. [CrossRef]
90. Meeusen, W.; Van Den Broeck, J. Efficiency estimation from Cobb–Douglas production functions with composed error. *Int.Econ. Rev.* **1977**, *18*, 435–444. [CrossRef]
91. Kumbhakar, S.C.; Lovell, C.A.K. *Stochastic Frontier Analysis*; Cambridge University Press: Cambridge, UK, 2000.
92. MacKay, D. *Information Theory, Inference, and Learning Algorithms*; CambridgeUniversity Press: Cambridge, UK, 2003.
93. Mitchell, T. *Machine Learning*; McGraw-Hill Science/Engineering/Math: New York, NY, USA, 1997.
94. Haykin, S. *Neural Networks. A Comprehensive Foundation*, 2nd ed.; Prentice Hall: Upper Saddle River, NJ, USA, 2005.

95. Russell, S.; Norvig, P. *Artificial Intelligence: A Modern Approach*; Prentice Hall: Upper Saddle River, NJ, USA, 2003.
96. Langley, P.; Iba, W.; Thompson, K. An analysis of Bayesian classifiers. In Proceedings of the Tenth National Conference on Artificial Intelligence, San Jose, CA, USA, 12–16 July 1992; pp. 399–406.
97. Friedman, N.; Geiger, D.; Goldszmidt, M. Bayesian network classifiers. *Mach. Learn.* **1997**, *29*, 131–163. [CrossRef]
98. Almuallim, H.; Dietterich, T.G. Learning with many irrelevant features. In Proceedings of the Ninth National Conference on Artificial Intelligence, Anaheim, CA, USA, 14–19 July 1991; pp. 547–552.
99. Weka (University of Waikato: New Zealand). Available online: http://www.cs.waikato.ac.nz/ml/weka (accessed on 1 June 2020).
100. Liu, H.; Motoda, H. *Feature Selection for Knowlegde Discovery and Data Mining*; Kluwer Academic Publishers: London, UK, 1998.
101. Abe, N.; Kudo, M. Entropy criterion for classifier-independent feature selection. *Lect. Notes Comput. Sci.* **2005**, *3684*, 689–695.
102. Hall, M.A.; Smith, L.A. Practical feature subset selection for machine learning. In Proceedings of the 21st Australian Computer Science Conference (ACSC'98), Perth, Australia, 4–6 February1998; pp. 181–191.
103. Moriwal, R.; Prakash, V. An efficient info-gain algorithm for finding frequent sequential traversal patterns from web logs based on dynamic weight constraint. In Proceedings of the CUBE International Information Technology Conference (CUBE'12), Pune, India, 3–5 September2012; pp. 718–723.
104. Quinlan, J.R. *C4.5: Programs for Machine Learning*; Morgan Kaufmann Publishers: San Francisco, CA, USA, 1993.
105. Thakur, D.; Markandaiah, N.; Raj, D.S. Re optimization of ID3 and C4.5 decision tree. Proceedingsof the International Conference on Computer and Communication Technology (ICCCT), Allahabad, India, 17–19 September 2010; pp. 448–450.
106. Kononenko, I. Estimating attributes: Analysis and extensions of relief. In *Machine Learning: ECML-94*; Springer: Berlin/Heidelberg, Germany, 1994; pp. 171–182.
107. Cooper, W.; Seiford, L.; Tone, K. *Data Envelopment Analysis*; Springer: New York, NY, USA, 2000.
108. Urbanowicz, R.; Meeker, M.; La Cava, W.; Olson, R.; Moore, J. Relief-based feature selection: Introduction and review. *J. Biomed. Inform.* **2018**, *85*, 189–203. [CrossRef]
109. Powers, D. Evaluation: From precision, recall and F-measure to ROC, informedness, markedness & correlation. *J. Mach. Learn. Technol.* **2011**, *2*, 2229–3981. [CrossRef]
110. Domingos, P.; Pazzani, M. On the optimality of the simple Bayesian classifier under zero-one loss. *Mach. Learn.* **1997**, *29*, 103–130. [CrossRef]
111. Silva, T.C.; Tabak, B.M.; Cajueiro, D.O.; Dias, M.V.B. A comparison of DEA and SFA using micro-and macro-level perspectives: Efficiency of Chinese local banks. *Phys. A* **2017**, *469*, 216–223. [CrossRef]
112. Popović, M.; Savić, G.; Kuzmanović, M.; Martić, M. Using Data Envelopment Analysis and Multi-Criteria Decision-Making Methods to Evaluate Teacher Performance in Higher Education. *Symmetry* **2020**, *12*, 563.
113. Dong, Y.; Hamilton, R.; Tippett, M. Cost efficiency of the Chinese banking sector: A comparison of stochastic frontier analysis and data envelopment analysis. *Econ. Model.* **2014**, *36*, 298–308. [CrossRef]
114. Shumaiza, A.M.; Alcantud, J.C.R. An m-Polar Fuzzy PROMETHEE Approach for AHP-Assisted Group Decision-Making. *Math. Comput. Appl.* **2020**, *25*, 26.
115. Đalić, I.; Stević, Ž.; Karamasa, C.; Puška, A. A novel integrated fuzzy PIPRECIA—Interval rough SAW model: Green supplier selection. *Decis. Mak. Appl. Manag. Eng.* **2020**, *3*, 126–145. [CrossRef]
116. Pamučar, D. Fuzzy-dea model for measuring the efficiency of the transport quality. *Mil. Tech. Cour.* **2011**, *LIX*, 40–61. [CrossRef]
117. Stojić, G.; Sremac, S.; Vasiljković, I. A fuzzy model for determining the justifiability of investing in a road freight vehicle fleet. *Oper. Res. Eng. Sci. Theory Appl.* **2018**, *1*, 62–75. [CrossRef]
118. Liu, F.; Aiwu, G.; Lukovac, V.; Vukic, M. A multicriteria model for the selection of the transport service provider: A single valued neutrosophic DEMATEL multicriteria model. *Decis. Mak. Appl. Manag. Eng.* **2018**, *1*, 121–130. [CrossRef]

119. Kevkić, T.S.; Odalović, M.T.; Petković, D.M. A stochastic model of gamma-ray induced oxide charge distribution and threshold voltage shift of MOS transistors. *Nucl. Technol. Radiat.* **2012**, *27*, 33–39. [CrossRef]
120. Kevkić, T.; Stojanović, V.; Joksimović, D. Application of the Generalized Logistic Functions in the Surface Potential Based MOSFET Modeling. *J. Comput. Electron.* **2017**, *16*, 90–97. [CrossRef]

symmetry

MDPI

Article

q-Rung Orthopair Fuzzy Prioritized Aggregation Operators and Their Application Towards Green Supplier Chain Management

Muhammad Riaz [1,*], Dragan Pamucar [2], Hafiz Muhammad Athar Farid [1] and Masooma Raza Hashmi [1]

1 Department of Mathematics, University of the Punjab, Lahore 54590, Pakistan; hmatharfarid@gmail.com (H.M.A.F.); masoomaraza25@gmail.com (M.R.H.)

2 Department of Logistics, University of Defence, 11000 Belgrade, Serbia; dragan.pamucar@va.mod.gov.rs

* Correspondence: mriaz.math@pu.edu.pk

Received: 2 May 2020; Accepted: 1 June 2020; Published: 8 June 2020

Abstract: Supply management and environmental concerns are becoming increasingly relevant to scientific decision analysis around the world. Several companies have implemented the green supply chain management (GSCM) approach for attaining economic advantages while retaining sustainable growth for the environment. Green supplier selection has also been analyzed in many literary works as an important part of GSCM, which is considered an important multi-criteria group decision making (MCGDM) problem. The lack of consideration of the relationships of alternatives to the uncertain environment will be the main reason for weak conclusions in some MCGDM problems. To address these drawbacks, we introduce a new approach for selecting green suppliers with the q-rung orthopair fuzzy information, in which the input assessment is considered by using q-rung orthopair fuzzy numbers (q-ROFNs). A q-ROFN is extremely valuable in representing vague information that occurs in these real-world circumstances. The priority relationship of the alternatives to q-rung orthopair fuzzy information is very helpful to deal with GSCM. Consequently, we develop some prioritized operators with q-ROFNs named the q-rung orthopair fuzzy prioritized weighted average (q-ROFPWA) operator and q-rung orthopair fuzzy prioritized weighted geometric (q-ROFPWG) operator. Several important characteristics of these operators such as idempotents, boundary, and monotonicity are also well proven. Finally, an application of the proposed operators is presented for green supplier selection in GSCM. The scientific nature of the proposed methodology is illustrated by a numerical example to validate its rationality, symmetry, and superiority.

Keywords: q-rung orthopair fuzzy numbers; q-rung orthopair fuzzy prioritized weighted average operator; q-rung orthopair fuzzy prioritized weighted geometric operator; green supply chain management

---

1. Introduction and Literature Review

Several researchers have now adopted the GSCM approach to greening their supply chains and are willing to learn more about the key performance measures that are accountable for their implementation. In view of environmental legislation and the increasing demand from overseas consumers for many environmentally friendly products, many companies around the world are adopting environmentally friendly products as their business strategy for future sustainability is gaining a competitive advantage over others. Government companies and some non-governmental organizations are working in a number of countries to buy eco-products that would eventually support the world and thus civilization. Limiting environmental degradation will be the biggest challenge facing society in the coming years [1]. In recent decades, more attention has been paid to environmental concerns; some industries, in particular in emerging countries, have taken great care to cope with environmental constraints in the area of green growth and pollution reduction. Government rules and regulations have been enacted to restrict the conduct of business; consumers can take into account the environmental impacts of different firms when making their choice [2]. More and more organizations are now using the new GSCM environmental sustainability mode to reduce emissions during supply chain operations. GSCM covers many facets of the supply chain, such as product design, vendor selection, processing, storage, shipping, marketing, and recycling. The initial linkage of the supply chain and the impact on the productivity and environmental performance of the supply chain are between the different segments. Green suppliers therefore play a crucial role in selecting a green supplier from GSCM. In general, the selection of green suppliers can be seen as a question of a variety of MCGDM evaluating different possible green suppliers with respect to other requirements in order to decide the best option. The assessment details can in practice be ambiguous and incomplete. Green architecture, green construction, green production, green transport, and reverse logistics are the main pursuits involved in GSCM.

The remaining article is structured in the following manner. In Section 2, the basic definitions of the q-ROFN score function, q-ROFN accuracy function, and basic aggregation operators are presented. In Section 3, some q-rung orthopair fuzzy prioritized aggregation operators are developed. We present an MCGDM approach related to the proposed operators in Section 4. The case study of GSCM is discussed in Section 5, and a numerical example is given as well. Section 6 summarizes the main results of the current research work.

1.1. Green Supplier Selection Approaches

Throughout recent years, GSCM's cross-disciplinary research area has included both academia and industry. This trend is attested by the preponderance of special issues devoted exclusively to this subject in leading operations and supply chain management (SCM) journals. The ongoing academic development and further advancement in this inchoate field include developing new ideas and awareness. Suppliers deliver raw materials, products, or services, which cannot be offered by a company. The manufacturer is an integral aspect of the modern business process for supply chains, and the best manufacturer should provide the client with the correct quality and quantity of goods at fair prices and at the required time. In the past few years, environmental factors have been dramatically reemerging as an important problem for decision makers. Waste electrical and electronic equipment (WEEE), restriction of hazardous substances (RoHS), and eco-design requirements for energy using products (EUP) are the three main European Union directives that concern the electronic businesses. The three guidelines demonstrate EU concern for recycling, no-hazardous pollutants, low energy, and resource waste. Rao [3] defined GSCM as involving environmental performance based screening providers and complying with environmental regulations and standards. The selection of suppliers in GSCM is clearly a crucial purchasing practice, since its suppliers can demonstrate environmental and ecological efficiency. As an enterprise becomes completely dependent on suppliers, an effective approach to the evaluation of the performance of suppliers is necessary. The selection of suppliers needs several goals to be considered; hence, the choice of suppliers suggested by Bhutta and Huq [4] in 2002 can be seen as an MCDM.

As the MCGDM issue has become more complex, a number of new approaches have been explored purely on the basis of MCGDM and soft computing techniques. Comparably, owing to the characteristics of GSM, many scientists have considered the green supplier selection process to be a complicated MCGDM problem; therefore, a number of MCGDM methods have been used in GSCM research under fuzzy circumstances. Lee et al. [5] developed the GSCM analytical hierarchy process (AHP). Both Chen et al. [6] and Yazdani [7] developed an integrated MCDM strategy to get the best green supplier (BGS) consisting of fuzzy AHP and the technique for order performance by similarity to ideal solution (TOPSIS). By using the data envelopment analysis (DEA) process, Dobos and Vörösmarty [8] decided on BGS. Kuo et al. [9] utilized the decision making trial and evaluation laboratory (DEMATEL) process and the VIKOR (vlse kriterijumska optimizacija Kompromisno Resenje) technique to examine the relationships among criteria and calculate criteria weights, then select BGS. Banaeian et al. [10] analyzed green providers in the agri-food industry using TOPSIS and VIKOR to address the applications of fuzzy green suppliers. Govindan et al. [11] suggested a method of selecting the BGS based on the revised Simos procedure and preference ranking organization method for enrichment evaluation (PROMETHEE) technique. Quan et al. [12] analyzed BGS selection with a broad decision maker community and established an integrated process combined with ant colony algorithms and multi-objective optimizations by ratio analysis plus the full multiplicative form (MULTIMOORA) method. Young and Kielkiewicz [13] investigated the sustainable supply network management systems. Wang and Li [14] introduced a novel approach for green supplier selection using q-rung orthopair fuzzy numbers (q-ROFNs). Wang et al. [15,16] established models for green supplier selection with some two-tuple linguistic neutrosophic number Bonferroni mean operators and q-rung interval-valued orthopair fuzzy information. Srivastava [17] presented green supply chain management and introduced a brief literature review. Sharfman et al. [18] established the supply-chain environmental management strategies. Rath [19] described GSCM as a catalyst of organizational sustainable growth. Min and Galle [20] with Murphy and Poist [21] presented some modified green purchasing strategies. Curz and Matsypura [22] presented supply chain networks with corporate social responsibility through integrated environmental decision making. Khan et al. [23] worked on measuring the performance of green supply chain management. Mangla et al. [24] presented the analysis of flexible decision strategies for a sustainability focused green product recovery system.

1.2. Indicators for Green Supplier Selection

First, we discuss the indicators for common supplier selection, in order to carry out an appropriate company performance assessment. Dickson [25] performed a survey and provided 23 specific attributes. Quality, delivery, and performance history were the top three indicators. While Dickson introduced the 23 parameters 20 years ago, the majority of them in the literature to date are still covered [26]. In a new analysis, Hu [27] reviewed 24 published papers after 1991. The most important criteria for vendor assessment approaches include cost, quality, production capability, and production. Çelebi and Bayraktar [28] proposed 37 criteria to be more realistic in selecting suppliers and advanced the theory of the integration of neural network and data envelopment analysis for provider evaluation on the basis of inadequate assessment criteria details. The fourdimensions of the criterion were classified. These are cost, quality, service, and delivery. When we talk about indicators for green supplier selection, Seuring and Müller [29] reviewed 191 articles and established two specific strategies, supplier risk management and supply chain management for sustainable products. In addition, a number of researchers analyzed renewable supplier assessment indicators in order to comply with environmental standards. Noci [30] applied the AHP model to help decision makers choose the most efficient vendor from an environmental perspective. In addition, Handfield et al. [31,32] used the Delphi approach to obtain the point of view of professionals from IBM, Ford, Mascotech, Cone Drive, and Herman Miller Company to determine the structure of the criteria and used the AHP method to determine the efficiency of the supplier. That structure was applied to three kinds of factories. The findings showed that the automotive industry and the ready-made garment industry would select the most desirable suppliers. Humphreys et al. [33] thought environmental costs had little emphasis; therefore, they suggested other more established selection criteria. ANPwas used by Sarkis [34] to develop a six-dimensional strategic GSCM decision making system. Sarkis et al. [35] established an organizational theoretic review of green supply chain management literature. The relevant criteria proposed by each researcher are listed in Table 1.

Table 1. The relevant criteria proposed by different researchers.

Researchers and References	Criteria
Noci [30]	Green competencies, the green picture of the manufacturer, efficiency at the current location, and cost of the net life-cycle.
Handfield et al. [31]	Logistics for packaging, managing waste, brand attributes' certification, environmental policy, and rules and regulations of government.
Haumphreys et al. [33]	Production of environmental impacts, environmental planning, eco-friendly, systems of environmental protection, skills in management, and eco-friendly skills green pic.
Sarkis [34]	Enhance procedures of GSC, quality standards for the company, organizational practices that are socially positive, and GSC's program substitutes.
Hsu and Hu [36]	Control of procurement, controlling inbound price, management of research and development, systems of management, and control of procedures.

1.3. MCDM Based Uncertain Data Modeling

For many years, the issue of vague and imperfect information has been at the forefront. Information aggregation is the key factor for the decision management in the areas of business, management, engineering, psychology, social sciences, medical sciences, and artificial intelligence. Traditionally, the information about an alternative has been believed to be considered as a crisp number or linguistic number. Nevertheless, information cannot be aggregated in a simple form due to its uncertainty. It is very important to address this problem, in order to deal with uncertainty. Zadeh [37] initiated the notion of fuzzy set theory. After Zadeh, Atanassov [38] introduced intuitionistic fuzzy sets (IFSs) as an extension of fuzzy sets. Consequently, Yager [39,40] introduced Pythagorean fuzzy sets (PFSs) as an extension of IFS. After that, he introduced [41,42] another generalization of IFSs and PFSs named q-rung orthopair fuzzy sets (q-ROFSs). Additionally, a Pythagorean fuzzy number (PFN) is superior to an intuitionistic fuzzy number (IFN) towards uncertainty. A q-ROFN is superior to both IFN and PFN because both are q-ROFN, but not conversely (see [40–43]). Many works have researched the TOPSIS approach for the problem of decision making: Li and Nan [44], Boran et al. [45], Zhang and Xu [46], and Selvachandran and Peng [47]. Xu et al. [48] established some q-rung dual hesitant fuzzy Heronian mean operators with their application to MAGDM.

Xu et al. [49–51] introduced weighted averaging operators, geometric operators, and induced generalized operators based on intuitionistic fuzzy numbers (IFNs). Hashmi et al. [52] introduced the notion of the m-polar neutrosophic set and m-polar neutrosophic topology and their applications to multi-criteria decision making (MCDM) in medical diagnosis and clustering analysis. Hashmi and Riaz [53] introduced a novel approach to the census process by using Pythagorean m-polar fuzzy Dombi aggregation operators. Riaz and Hashmi [54,55] introduced the notion of linear Diophantine fuzzy Set (LDFS) and its applications to the MCDM problem. The linear Diophantine fuzzy set (LDFS) is superior to IFSs, PFSs, and q-ROFSs. The novel concepts of soft rough Pythagorean m-polar fuzzy sets and Pythagorean m-polar fuzzy soft rough sets with application to decision making problems were introduced. Riaz et al. [56] presented a robust q-rung orthopair fuzzy information aggregation using Einstein operations with applications to sustainable energy planning decision management. Riaz and Tehrim [57] established the idea of a cubic bipolar fuzzy set and cubic bipolar fuzzy ordered weighted geometric aggregation operators and their application using internal and external cubic bipolar fuzzy data. Naeem et al. [58] established Pythagorean fuzzy soft MCGDM methods based on TOPSIS, VIKOR, and aggregation operators.

Feng et al. [59] introduced MADM models in the environment of generalized IFsoft sets. Ye [60] introduced prioritized aggregation operators in the context of IVHFSand worked on its MAGDM. Zhang et al. [61] introduced aggregation operators with MCDM by using interval-valued FNS(IVFNS). Zhao et al. [62] worked on generalized aggregation operators in the context of IFS. Wang and Liu [63] introduced the Einstein operators on IFSs. Garg [64] introduced Pythagorean Einstein operators and presented their applications. Liu and Wang [65] established some q-rung orthopair fuzzy aggregation operators and presented their application to multi-attribute decision making. Yager [66] introduced several prioritized aggregation operators. According to Yager, when considering the situation in which we choose a bicycle for a child based on safety and cost attributes, we should not allow a cost-related advantage to compensate for a safety loss. Then, we have a sort of relationship of prioritization over these two attributes, and protection is of higher importance. This situation can be called a problem of aggregation, where the relationship of priority exists over the attributes. Since we want to consider the satisfaction of the higher priority attributes, such as safety in the example above, it is no longer feasible for the aggregation operators in question, such as the weighted average operator and the weighted geometric operator. In such a case, Yager [66] provided the prioritized aggregation operators by modeling attribute prioritization regarding the weights associated with the attributes based on the satisfaction of the higher priority attributes. Si et al. [67] presented a novel approach for the ranking of picture fuzzy numbers. Yusifov et al. [68] established multi-criteria evaluations and a positional ranking approach for candidate selection in E-voting.

1.4. Motivation, Highlights, and Focus of the Study

In this subsection, we put a light on the scope, motivation, and novelty of the proposed work.

1. This article includes two major issues: a theoretical model of the problem and decision making application.
2. The proposed models of aggregated operators are authentic, valid, flexible, and superior to others because they are based on the generalized structure of q-ROFNs. If we apply the proposed operators in the context of IFNs or PFNs, then the results will be imprecise due to the loss of information in the input data. This loss is due to the constraints based on the membership and non-membership grades of IFNs and PFNs (see Figure 1). The IFNs and PFNs become special cases of q-ROFNs when $q = 1$ and $q = 2$, respectively.

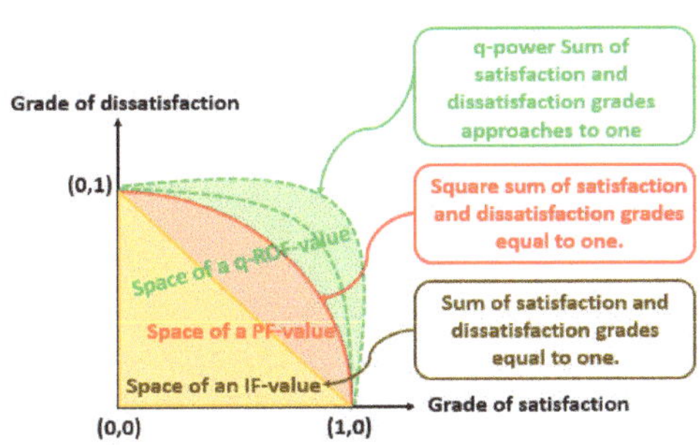

Figure 1. Graphical comparison between the IF-value, PF-value, and q-ROF-value.

3. The vital objective is to construct a strong relationship between the proposed operators with the multi-criteria decision making problems. The application based on the green supplier selection in GSCM communicates the effectiveness, interpretation, and motivation of the proposed aggregated operators.

4. This research fills the research gap and provides us a wide domain for the input data selection in medical, business, artificial intelligence, agriculture, and engineering. We can tackle those problems that contain ambiguity and uncertainty due to its limitations. The results obtained by using proposed operators and q-ROFNs will be superior and profitable in decision making techniques.

2. Some Basic Concepts

We keep in mind a few fundamentals of q-ROFS, the operational laws of q-ROFNs, and score and accuracy functions in this section.

Definition 1 ([42,43]). *Let $q \geq 1$. A q-rung orthopair fuzzy set $\mathcal{O}$ in $\mathcal{Q}$ is defined as:*

$$\mathcal{O} = \{\langle \varsigma, \mathscr{Y}_{\mathcal{O}}(\varsigma), \mathscr{X}_{\mathcal{O}}(\varsigma)\rangle : \varsigma \in \mathcal{Q}\}$$

where $\mathscr{Y}_{\mathcal{O}}, \mathscr{X}_{\mathcal{O}} : \mathcal{Q} \to [0,1]$ defines the membership and non-membership of the alternative $\varsigma \in \mathcal{Q}$, and for every ς, we have:

$$0 \leq \mathscr{Y}^q_{\mathcal{O}}(\varsigma) + \mathscr{X}^q_{\mathcal{O}}(\varsigma) \leq 1.$$

Furthermore, $\pi_{\mathcal{O}}(\varsigma) = (1 - \mathscr{Y}^q_{\mathcal{O}}(\varsigma) - \mathscr{X}^q_{\mathcal{O}}(\varsigma))^{1/q}$ is called the indeterminacy degree of ς to $\mathcal{O}$.

Liu further suggested to combine the q-ROFN information with the following operational rules.

Definition 2 ([65]). *Let $\mathcal{G}_1 = \langle \mathscr{Y}_1, \mathscr{X}_1\rangle$ and $\mathcal{G}_2 = \langle \mathscr{Y}_2, \mathscr{X}_2\rangle$ be q-ROFNs. Then,*
(1) $\bar{\mathcal{G}}_1 = \langle \mathscr{X}_1, \mathscr{Y}_1\rangle$
(2) $\mathcal{G}_1 \vee \mathcal{G}_2 = \langle max\{\mathscr{Y}_1, \mathscr{X}_1\}, min\{\mathscr{Y}_2, \mathscr{X}_2\}\rangle$
(3) $\mathcal{G}_1 \wedge \mathcal{G}_2 = \langle min\{\mathscr{Y}_1, \mathscr{X}_1\}, max\{\mathscr{Y}_2, \mathscr{X}_2\}\rangle$
(4) $\mathcal{G}_1 \oplus \mathcal{G}_2 = \langle (\mathscr{Y}_1^q + \mathscr{Y}_2^q - \mathscr{Y}_1^q\mathscr{Y}_2^q)^{1/q}, \mathscr{X}_1\mathscr{X}_2\rangle$
(5) $\mathcal{G}_1 \otimes \mathcal{G}_2 = \langle \mathscr{Y}_1\mathscr{Y}_2, (\mathscr{X}_1^q + \mathscr{X}_2^q - \mathscr{X}_1^q\mathscr{X}_2^q)^{1/q}\rangle$
(6) $\sigma\mathcal{G}_1 = \langle (1-(1-\mathscr{Y}_1^q)^\sigma)^{1/q}, \mathscr{X}_1^\sigma\rangle$
(7) $\mathcal{G}_1^\sigma = \langle \mathscr{Y}_1^\sigma, (1-(1-\mathscr{X}_1^q)^\sigma)^{1/q}\rangle$

Definition 3. *Suppose $\widetilde{\mathfrak{R}} = \langle \mathscr{Y}, \mathscr{X}\rangle$ is a q-ROFN, then a score function $\mathfrak{E}$ of $\widetilde{\mathfrak{R}}$ is defined as:*

$$\mathfrak{E}(\widetilde{\mathfrak{R}}) = \mathscr{Y}^q - \mathscr{X}^q$$

$\mathfrak{E}(\widetilde{\mathfrak{R}}) \in [-1,1]$. The score of a q-ROFN defines its ranking, i.e., a high score defines the high preference of q-ROFN. However, the score function is not useful in many cases of q-ROFN. For example, let us consider $\mathcal{G}_1 = \langle 0.6138, 0.2534\rangle$ and $\mathcal{G}_2 = \langle 0.7147, 0.4453\rangle$ to be two q-ROFNs, if we take the value of q to be two. Then, $\mathfrak{E}(\mathcal{G}_1) = 0.3125 = \mathfrak{E}(\mathcal{G}_2)$, i.e, the score functions of $\mathcal{G}_1$ and $\mathcal{G}_2$ are the same. Therefore, to compare the q-ROFNs, it is not necessary to rely on the score function. We add a further method, the accuracy function, to solve this issue.

Definition 4. *Suppose $\widetilde{\mathfrak{R}} = \langle \mathscr{Y}, \mathscr{X}\rangle$ is a q-ROFN, then an accuracy function $\mathfrak{N}$ of $\widetilde{\mathfrak{R}}$ is defined as:*

$$\mathfrak{N}(\widetilde{\mathfrak{R}}) = \mathscr{Y}^q + \mathscr{X}^q$$

$\mathfrak{N}(\widetilde{\mathfrak{R}}) \in [0,1]$. The high value of accuracy degree $\mathfrak{N}(\widetilde{\mathfrak{R}})$ defines the high preference of $\widetilde{\mathfrak{R}}$.

Again, consider $\mathcal{G}_1 = \langle 0.6138, 0.2534\rangle$ and $\mathcal{G}_2 = \langle 0.7147, 0.4453\rangle$ to be two q-ROFNs. Then, their accuracy functions are $\mathfrak{N}(\mathcal{G}_1) = 0.4410$ and $\mathfrak{N}(\mathcal{G}_2) = 0.4410$, so by the accuracy function, we have $\mathcal{G}_1 < \mathcal{G}_2$.

Definition 5. *Let $\mathcal{Y} = \langle \mathscr{Y}_{\mathcal{Y}}, \mathscr{X}_{\mathcal{Y}}\rangle$ and $\mathfrak{M} = \langle \mathscr{Y}_{\mathfrak{M}}, \mathscr{X}_{\mathfrak{M}}\rangle$ be any two q-ROFN and $\mathfrak{E}(\mathcal{Y}), \mathfrak{E}(\mathfrak{M})$ be the score function of $\mathcal{Y}$ and $\mathfrak{M}$, while $\mathfrak{N}(\mathcal{Y}), \mathfrak{N}(\mathfrak{M})$ are the accuracy functions of $\mathcal{Y}$ and $\mathfrak{M}$, respectively, then:*

(1) If $\mathfrak{E}(\mathcal{Y}) > \mathfrak{E}(\mathfrak{M})$, *then* $\mathcal{Y} > \mathfrak{M}$
(2) If $\mathfrak{E}(\mathcal{Y}) = \mathfrak{E}(\mathfrak{M})$, *then*

if $\mathfrak{R}(\mathcal{Y}) > \mathfrak{R}(\mathfrak{M})$, *then* $\mathcal{Y} > \mathfrak{M}$,
if $\mathfrak{R}(\mathcal{Y}) = \mathfrak{R}(\mathfrak{M})$, *then* $\mathcal{Y} = \mathfrak{M}$.

It should always be noticed that the value of score function is between –1 and one. We introduce another score function, to support the following research, $\mathscr{H}(\Re) = \frac{1+\mathscr{Y}_{\Re}^{q} - \mathscr{X}_{\Re}^{q}}{2}$. We can see that $0 \leq \mathscr{H}(\Re) \leq 1$. This new score function satisfies all properties of the score function defined by Yager [41].

2.1. q-rung Orthopair Fuzzy Aggregation Operators

Definition 6 ([65]). *Assume that* $\check{\mathcal{G}}_k = \langle \mathscr{Y}_k, \mathscr{X}_k \rangle$ *is a family of q-ROFNs, and q-ROFWA:* $\Lambda^n \to \Lambda$, *if:*

$$\begin{aligned} q - ROFWA(\check{\mathcal{G}}_1, \check{\mathcal{G}}_2, \ldots, \check{\mathcal{G}}_n) &= \sum_{k=1}^{n} \mathfrak{F}_k \check{\mathcal{G}}_k \\ &= \mathfrak{F}_1 \check{\mathcal{G}}_1 \oplus \mathfrak{F}_2 \check{\mathcal{G}}_2 \oplus, \ldots, \mathfrak{F}_n \check{\mathcal{G}}_n \end{aligned}$$

where Λ^n *is the set of all q-ROFNs, and* $\mathfrak{F} = (\mathfrak{F}_1, \mathfrak{F}_2, \ldots,, \mathfrak{F}_n)^T$ *is the weight vector of* $(\check{\mathcal{G}}_1, \check{\mathcal{G}}_2, \ldots, \check{\mathcal{G}}_n)$, *such that* $0 \leqslant \mathfrak{F}_k \leqslant 1$ *and* $\sum_{k=1}^{n} \mathfrak{F}_k = 1$. *Then, the q-ROFWA is called the q-rung orthopair fuzzy weighted average operator.*

Based on q-ROFNs operational rules, we can also consider q-ROFWA by the theorem below.

Theorem 1 ([65]). *Let* $\check{\mathcal{G}}_k = \langle \mathscr{Y}_k, \mathscr{X}_k \rangle$ *be the family of q-ROFNs; we can find* $q - ROFWA$ *by:*

$$q - ROFWA(\check{\mathcal{G}}_1, \check{\mathcal{G}}_2, \ldots, \check{\mathcal{G}}_n) = \left\langle \sqrt[q]{(1 - \prod_{k=1}^{n}(1 - \mathscr{Y}_k^{q})^{\mathfrak{F}_k})}, \prod_{k=1}^{n} \mathscr{X}_k^{\mathfrak{F}_k} \right\rangle$$

Definition 7 ([65]). *Assume that* $\check{\mathcal{G}}_k = \langle \mathscr{Y}_k, \mathscr{X}_k \rangle$ *is the family of* $q - ROFN$, *and* $q - ROFWG : \Lambda^n \to \Lambda$, *if:*

$$\begin{aligned} q - ROFWG(\check{\mathcal{G}}_1, \check{\mathcal{G}}_2, \ldots, \check{\mathcal{G}}_n) &= \sum_{k=1}^{n} \check{\mathcal{G}}_k^{\mathfrak{F}_k} \\ &= \check{\mathcal{G}}_1^{\mathfrak{F}_1} \otimes \check{\mathcal{G}}_2^{\mathfrak{F}_2} \otimes, \ldots, \check{\mathcal{G}}_n^{\mathfrak{F}_n} \end{aligned}$$

where Λ^n *is the set of all* $q - ROFNs$ *and* $\mathfrak{F} = (\mathfrak{F}_1, \mathfrak{F}_2, \ldots,, \mathfrak{F}_n)^T$ *is the weight vector of* $(\check{\mathcal{G}}_1, \check{\mathcal{G}}_2, \ldots, \check{\mathcal{G}}_n)$, *such that* $0 \leqslant \mathfrak{F}_k \leqslant 1$ *and* $\sum_{k=1}^{n} \mathfrak{F}_k = 1$. *Then, the* $q - ROFWG$ *is called the q-rung orthopair fuzzy weighted geometric operator.*

Based on q-ROFNs operational rules, we can also consider q-ROFWG by the theorem below.

Theorem 2 ([65]). *Let* $\check{\mathcal{G}}_k = \langle \mathscr{Y}_k, \mathscr{X}_k \rangle$ *be the family of q-ROFNs; we can find* $q - ROFWG$ *by:*

$$q - ROFWG(\check{\mathcal{G}}_1, \check{\mathcal{G}}_2, \ldots, \check{\mathcal{G}}_n) = \left\langle \prod_{k=1}^{n} \mathscr{Y}_k^{\mathfrak{F}_k}, \sqrt[q]{(1 - \prod_{k=1}^{n}(1 - \mathscr{X}_k^{q})^{\mathfrak{F}_k})} \right\rangle$$

2.2. Superiority and Comparison of q-ROFNs with Some Existing Theories

In this part, we discuss the superiority and comparison of q-ROFNs with some existing structures such as fuzzy numbers (FNs), IFNs, and PFNs. In the decision making problem, if we take the input information by using FNs, then we cannot talk about the dissatisfaction part of the alternatives or decision makers' opinion. If we use IFNs and PFNs, then we cannot take the membership and nonmembership values with the open choice of the real world situation. The constraints restrict them to limited criteria. For example, $0.8 + 0.7 = 1.5 > 1$ and $0.8^2 + 0.7^2 = 1.13 > 1$, which contradicts the conditions of IFNs and PFNs. However, if we select $q = 3$, then for 3-ROFN, the constraint implies that $0.8^3 + 0.7^3 = 0.855 < 1$. This criteria satisfies the fuzzy criteria, and we can handle the decision making input with a wide domain. Table 2 represents the brief comparison of the advantages and limitations of q-ROFN with some exiting theories.

Table 2. Comparison of q-ROFS with some existing theories.

Set Theory	Truth Information	Falsity Information	Advantages	Limitations
Fuzzy sets [37]	✓	×	can handle uncertainty using fuzzy interval	do not give any information about the non-membership grades in input data
Intuitionistic Fuzzy sets [38]	✓	✓	can handle uncertainty using membership and non-membership grades	cannot deal with the problems satisfying $0 \leq$ membership+non-membership > 1
Pythagorean Fuzzy sets [39–41]	✓	✓	larger valuation space than IFNs	cannot deal with the problems satisfying $0 \leq \text{membership}^2 + \text{non-membership}^2 > 1$
q-rung orthopair Fuzzy sets [42,43]	✓	✓	larger valuation space than IFNs and PFNs	cannot deal with the problems when membership=1 and nonmembership=1

3. q-Rung Orthopair Fuzzy Prioritized Aggregation Operators

Within this section, we present the notion of the q-rung orthopair fuzzy prioritized weighted average (q-ROFPWA) operator and q-rung orthopair fuzzy prioritized weighted geometric (q-ROFPWG) operator. Then, we discuss other attractive properties of the proposed operators like idempotency, boundary, and monotonicity in detail.

3.1. q-ROFPWA Operator

Definition 8. *Assume that $\check{\mathcal{G}}_j = \langle \mathscr{Y}_j, \mathscr{X}_j \rangle$ is the family of q-ROFNs, and $q - ROFPWA : \Lambda^n \to \Lambda$, being a n-dimensional mapping. If:*

$$\text{q-ROFPWA}(\check{\mathcal{G}}_1, \check{\mathcal{G}}_2, \ldots, \check{\mathcal{G}}_n) = \frac{\check{\mathscr{T}}_1}{\sum_{j=1}^n \check{\mathscr{T}}_j}\check{\mathcal{G}}_1 \oplus \frac{\check{\mathscr{T}}_2}{\sum_{j=1}^n \check{\mathscr{T}}_j}\check{\mathcal{G}}_2 \oplus, \ldots, \oplus \frac{\check{\mathscr{T}}_n}{\sum_{j=1}^n \check{\mathscr{T}}_j}\check{\mathcal{G}}_n \tag{1}$$

then the mapping q-ROFPWA is called the q-rung orthopair fuzzy prioritized weighted averaging (q-ROFPWA) operator, where $\check{\mathscr{T}}_j = \prod_{k=1}^{j-1} \mathscr{H}(\check{\mathcal{G}}_k)$ $(j = 2, \ldots, n)$, $\check{\mathscr{T}}_1 = 1$, and $\mathscr{H}(\check{\mathcal{G}}_k)$ is the score of the kth q-ROFN.

Based on q-ROFN operational rules, we can also consider q-ROFPWA by the theorem below.

Theorem 3. *Assume that $\check{\mathcal{G}}_j = \langle \mathscr{Y}_j, \mathscr{X}_j \rangle$ is the family of q-ROFNs; we can find q-ROFPWA by:*

$$\text{q-ROFPWA}(\check{\mathcal{G}}_1, \check{\mathcal{G}}_2, \ldots, \check{\mathcal{G}}_n) = \left\langle \sqrt[q]{(1 - \prod_{j=1}^n (1 - \mathscr{Y}_j^q)^{\frac{\check{\mathscr{T}}_j}{\sum_{j=1}^n \check{\mathscr{T}}_j}}}, \prod_{j=1}^n \mathscr{X}_j^{\frac{\check{\mathscr{T}}_j}{\sum_{j=1}^n \check{\mathscr{T}}_j}} \right\rangle \tag{2}$$

Proof. See Appendix A. □

Below, we define some of q-ROFPWA's appealing properties.

Theorem 4. *(Idempotency) Assume that $\check{\mathcal{G}}_j = \langle \mathscr{Y}_j, \mathscr{X}_j \rangle$ is the family of q-ROFNs, where $\check{\mathscr{T}}_j = \prod_{k=1}^{j-1} \mathscr{H}(\check{\mathcal{G}}_k)$ $(j = 2, \ldots, n)$, $\check{\mathscr{T}}_1 = 1$, and $\mathscr{H}(\check{\mathcal{G}}_k)$ is the score of the kth q-ROFN. If all $\check{\mathcal{G}}_j$ are equal, i.e., $\check{\mathcal{G}}_j = \check{\mathcal{G}}$ for all j, then:*

$$q\text{-}ROFPWA(\check{\mathcal{G}}_1, \check{\mathcal{G}}_2, \ldots, \check{\mathcal{G}}_n) = \check{\mathcal{G}}$$

Proof. See Appendix A.1. □

Corollary 1. *If $\check{\mathcal{G}}_j = \langle \mathscr{Y}_j, \mathscr{X}_j \rangle$ $j = (1, 2, \ldots, n)$ is the family of the largest q-ROFNs, i.e., $\check{\mathcal{G}}_j = (1, 0)$ for all j, then:*

$$q\text{-}ROFPWA(\check{\mathcal{G}}_1, \check{\mathcal{G}}_2, \ldots, \check{\mathcal{G}}_n) = (1, 0)$$

Proof. We can easily obtain the corollary similar to Theorem 4. □

Corollary 2. *(Non-compensatory) If $\check{\mathcal{G}}_1 = \langle \mathscr{Y}_1, \mathscr{X}_1 \rangle$ is the smallest q-ROFN, i.e., $\check{\mathcal{G}}_1 = (0, 1)$, then:*

$$q\text{-}ROFPWA(\check{\mathcal{G}}_1, \check{\mathcal{G}}_2, \ldots, \check{\mathcal{G}}_n) = (0, 1)$$

Proof. See Appendix A.2. □

Corollary 4 means that, if the higher priority criteria are met by the smallest q-ROFN, rewards will not be received by other criteria even though they are fulfilled.

Theorem 5 (Monotonicity). *Assume that $\check{\mathcal{G}}_j = \langle \mathscr{Y}_j, \mathscr{X}_j \rangle$ and $\check{\mathcal{G}}_j^* = \langle \mathscr{Y}_j^*, \mathscr{X}_j^* \rangle$ are the families of q-ROFNs, where $\check{\mathscr{T}}_j = \prod_{k=1}^{j-1} \mathscr{H}(\check{\mathcal{G}}_k)$, $\check{\mathscr{T}}_j^* = \prod_{k=1}^{j-1} \mathscr{H}(\check{\mathcal{G}}_k^*)$ $(j = 2, \ldots, n)$, $\check{\mathscr{T}}_1 = 1$, $\check{\mathscr{T}}_1^* = 1$, $\mathscr{H}(\check{\mathcal{G}}_k)$ is the score of $\check{\mathcal{G}}_k$ q-ROFN, and $\mathscr{H}(\check{\mathcal{G}}_k^*)$ is the score of $\check{\mathcal{G}}_k^*$ q-ROFN. If $\mathscr{Y}_j^* \geq \mathscr{Y}_j$ and $\mathscr{X}_j^* \leq \mathscr{X}_j$ for all j, then:*

$$q\text{-}ROFPWA(\check{\mathcal{G}}_1, \check{\mathcal{G}}_2, \ldots, \check{\mathcal{G}}_n) \leq q\text{-}ROFPWA(\check{\mathcal{G}}_1^*, \check{\mathcal{G}}_2^*, \ldots, \check{\mathcal{G}}_n^*)$$

Proof. See Appendix A.3. □

Theorem 6. *(Boundary) Assume that $\check{\mathcal{G}}_j = \langle \mathscr{Y}_j, \mathscr{X}_j \rangle$ is the family of q-ROFNs, and:*

$$\check{\mathcal{G}}^- = (min_j\,(\mathscr{Y}_j), max_j\,(\mathscr{X}_j)) \quad and \quad \check{\mathcal{G}}^+ = (max_j\,(\mathscr{Y}_j), min_j\,(\mathscr{X}_j))$$

Then,

$$\check{\mathcal{G}}^- \leq q\text{-}ROFPWA(\check{\mathcal{G}}_1, \check{\mathcal{G}}_2, \ldots, \check{\mathcal{G}}_n) \leq \check{\mathcal{G}}^+$$

where $\check{\mathscr{T}}_j = \prod_{k=1}^{j-1} \mathscr{H}(\check{\mathcal{G}}_k)$ $(j = 2, \ldots, n)$, $\check{\mathscr{T}}_1 = 1$, and $\mathscr{H}(\check{\mathcal{G}}_k)$ is the score of the kth q-ROFN.

Proof. See Appendix A.4. □

Theorem 7. *Assume that $\check{\mathcal{G}}_j = \langle \mathscr{Y}_j, \mathscr{X}_j \rangle$ and $\beta_j = \langle \phi_j, \varphi_j \rangle$ are two families of q-ROFNs, where $\check{\mathscr{T}}_j = \prod_{k=1}^{j-1} \mathscr{H}(\check{\mathcal{G}}_k)$ $(j = 2, \ldots, n)$, $\check{\mathscr{T}}_1 = 1$, and $\mathscr{H}(\check{\mathcal{G}}_k)$ is the score of the kth q-ROFN. If $r > 0$ and $\beta = \langle \mathscr{Y}_\beta, \mathscr{X}_\beta \rangle$ is an q-ROFN, then,*

1. *$q\text{-}ROFPWA(\check{\mathcal{G}}_1 \oplus \beta, \check{\mathcal{G}}_2 \oplus \beta, \ldots, \check{\mathcal{G}}_n \oplus \beta) = q\text{-}ROFPWA(\check{\mathcal{G}}_1, \check{\mathcal{G}}_2, \ldots, \check{\mathcal{G}}_n) \oplus \beta$*
2. *$q\text{-}ROFPWA(r\check{\mathcal{G}}_1, r\check{\mathcal{G}}_2, \ldots, r\check{\mathcal{G}}_n) = r\ q\text{-}ROFPWA(\check{\mathcal{G}}_1, \check{\mathcal{G}}_2, \ldots, \check{\mathcal{G}}_n)$*
3. *$q\text{-}ROFPWA(\check{\mathcal{G}}_1 \oplus \beta_1, \check{\mathcal{G}}_2 \oplus \beta_2, \ldots, \check{\mathcal{G}}_n \oplus \beta_n) = q\text{-}ROFPWA(\check{\mathcal{G}}_1, \check{\mathcal{G}}_2, \ldots, \check{\mathcal{G}}_n) \oplus q\text{-}ROFPWA\ (\beta_1, \beta_2, \ldots, \beta_n)$*
4. *$q\text{-}ROFPWA(r\check{\mathcal{G}}_1 \oplus \beta \oplus r\check{\mathcal{G}}_2 \oplus \beta, \ldots, \oplus r\check{\mathcal{G}}_n \oplus \beta) = r\ q\text{-}ROFPWA(\check{\mathcal{G}}_1, \check{\mathcal{G}}_2, \ldots, \check{\mathcal{G}}_n) \oplus \beta$*

Proof. See Appendix A.5. □

3.2. q-ROFPWG Operator

Definition 9. *Assume that $\check{\mathcal{G}}_j = \langle \mathscr{Y}_j, \mathscr{X}_j \rangle$ is the family of q-ROFNs, and $q-ROFPWG : \Lambda^n \to \Lambda$, being an n-dimensional mapping. If:*

$$\text{q-ROFPWG}(\check{\mathcal{G}}_1, \check{\mathcal{G}}_2, \ldots, \check{\mathcal{G}}_n) = \check{\mathcal{G}}_1^{\frac{\mathscr{T}_1}{\sum_{j=1}^n \mathscr{T}_j}} \otimes \check{\mathcal{G}}_2^{\frac{\mathscr{T}_2}{\sum_{j=1}^n \mathscr{T}_j}} \otimes, \ldots, \otimes \check{\mathcal{G}}_n^{\frac{\mathscr{T}_n}{\sum_{j=1}^n \mathscr{T}_j}} \tag{3}$$

then the mapping q-ROFPWG is called the q-rung orthopair fuzzy prioritized weighted geometric (q-ROFPWG) operator, where $\mathscr{T}_j = \prod_{k=1}^{j-1} \mathscr{H}(\check{\mathcal{G}}_k)$ $(j = 2, \ldots, n)$, $\mathscr{T}_1 = 1$, and $\mathscr{H}(\check{\mathcal{G}}_k)$ is the score of the kth q-ROFN.

Based on q-ROFNs operational rules, we can also consider q-ROFPWG by the theorem below.

Theorem 8. *Assume that $\check{\mathcal{G}}_j = \langle \mathscr{Y}_j, \mathscr{X}_j \rangle$ is the family of q-ROFNs; we can find q-ROFPWG by:*

$$\text{q-ROFPWG}(\check{\mathcal{G}}_1, \check{\mathcal{G}}_2, \ldots, \check{\mathcal{G}}_n) = \left\langle \prod_{j=1}^n \mathscr{Y}_j^{\frac{\mathscr{T}_j}{\sum_{j=1}^n \mathscr{T}_j}}, \sqrt[q]{(1 - \prod_{j=1}^n (1 - \mathscr{X}_j^q)^{\frac{\mathscr{T}_j}{\sum_{j=1}^n \mathscr{T}_j}}} \right\rangle \tag{4}$$

Proof. See Appendix B. □

Below, we define some of the q-ROFPWG operator's appealing properties.

Theorem 9 (Idempotency). *Assume that $\check{\mathcal{G}}_j = \langle \mathscr{Y}_j, \mathscr{X}_j \rangle$ is the family of q-ROFNs, where $\mathscr{T}_j = \prod_{k=1}^{j-1} \mathscr{H}(\check{\mathcal{G}}_k)$ $(j = 2, \ldots, n)$, $\mathscr{T}_1 = 1$, and $\mathscr{H}(\check{\mathcal{G}}_k)$ is the score of the kth q-ROFN. If all $\check{\mathcal{G}}_j$ are equal, i.e., $\check{\mathcal{G}}_j = \check{\mathcal{G}}$ for all j, then:*

$$\text{q-ROFPWG}(\check{\mathcal{G}}_1, \check{\mathcal{G}}_2, \ldots, \check{\mathcal{G}}_n) = \check{\mathcal{G}}$$

Proof. See Appendix B.1. □

Corollary 3. *If $\check{\mathcal{G}}_j = \langle \mathscr{Y}_j, \mathscr{X}_j \rangle$ $j = (1, 2, \ldots, n)$ is the family of the largest q-ROFNs, i.e., $\check{\mathcal{G}}_j = (1, 0)$ for all j, then:*

$$\text{q-ROFPWG}(\check{\mathcal{G}}_1, \check{\mathcal{G}}_2, \ldots, \check{\mathcal{G}}_n) = (1, 0)$$

Proof. We can easily obtain the corollary similar to Theorem 4. □

Corollary 4 (Non-compensatory). *If $\check{\mathcal{G}}_1 = \langle \mathscr{Y}_1, \mathscr{X}_1 \rangle$ is the smallest q-ROFN, i.e., $\check{\mathcal{G}}_1 = (0, 1)$, then:*

$$\text{q-ROFPWG}(\check{\mathcal{G}}_1, \check{\mathcal{G}}_2, \ldots, \check{\mathcal{G}}_n) = (0, 1)$$

Proof. See Appendix B.2. □

Corollary 4 means that, if the higher priority criteria are met by the smallest q-ROFN, rewards will not be received by other criteria even though they are fulfilled.

Theorem 10 (Monotonicity). *Assume that $\check{\mathcal{G}}_j = \langle \mathscr{Y}_j, \mathscr{X}_j \rangle$ and $\check{\mathcal{G}}_j^* = \langle \mathscr{Y}_j^*, \mathscr{X}_j^* \rangle$ are the families of q-ROFNs, where $\mathscr{T}_j = \prod_{k=1}^{j-1} \mathscr{H}(\check{\mathcal{G}}_k)$, $\mathscr{T}_j^* = \prod_{k=1}^{j-1} \mathscr{H}(\check{\mathcal{G}}_k^*)$ $(j = 2, \ldots, n)$, $\mathscr{T}_1 = 1$, $\mathscr{T}_1^* = 1$, $\mathscr{H}(\check{\mathcal{G}}_k)$ is the score of $\check{\mathcal{G}}_k$ q-ROFN, and $\mathscr{H}(\check{\mathcal{G}}_k^*)$ is the score of $\check{\mathcal{G}}_k^*$ q-ROFN. If $\mathscr{Y}_j^* \geq \mathscr{Y}_j$ and $\mathscr{X}_j^* \leq \mathscr{X}_j$ for all j, then:*

$$\text{q-ROFPWG}(\check{\mathcal{G}}_1, \check{\mathcal{G}}_2, \ldots, \check{\mathcal{G}}_n) \leq \text{q-ROFPWG}(\check{\mathcal{G}}_1^*, \check{\mathcal{G}}_2^*, \ldots, \check{\mathcal{G}}_n^*)$$

Proof. See Appendix B.3. □

Theorem 11 (Boundary). *Assume that $\check{\mathcal{G}}_j = \langle \mathscr{Y}_j, \mathscr{X}_j \rangle$ is the family of q-ROFNs, and:*

$$\check{\mathcal{G}}^- = (min_j\,(\mathscr{Y}_j), max_j\,(\mathscr{X}_j)) \quad and \quad \check{\mathcal{G}}^+ = (max_j\,(\mathscr{Y}_j), min_j\,(\mathscr{X}_j))$$

Then,

$$\check{\mathcal{G}}^- \leq q\text{-}ROFPWG(\check{\mathcal{G}}_1, \check{\mathcal{G}}_2, \ldots, \check{\mathcal{G}}_n) \leq \check{\mathcal{G}}^+$$

where $\mathscr{T}_j = \prod_{k=1}^{j-1} \mathscr{H}(\check{\mathcal{G}}_k)$ $(j = 2, \ldots, n)$, $\mathscr{T}_1 = 1$, and $\mathscr{H}(\check{\mathcal{G}}_k)$ is the score of the kth q-ROFN.

Proof. The proof of this theorem is the same as Theorem 6. □

Theorem 12. *Assume that $\check{\mathcal{G}}_j = \langle \mathscr{Y}_j, \mathscr{X}_j \rangle$ and $\beta_j = \langle \phi_j, \varphi_j \rangle$ are two families of q-ROFNs, where $\mathscr{T}_j = \prod_{k=1}^{j-1} \mathscr{H}(\check{\mathcal{G}}_k)$ $(j = 2, \ldots, n)$, $\mathscr{T}_1 = 1$, and $\mathscr{H}(\check{\mathcal{G}}_k)$ is the score of the kth q-ROFN. If $r > 0$ and $\beta = \langle \mathscr{Y}_\beta, \mathscr{X}_\beta \rangle$ is an q-ROFN, then,*

1. *$q\text{-}ROFPWG(\check{\mathcal{G}}_1 \oplus \beta, \check{\mathcal{G}}_2 \oplus \beta, \ldots, \check{\mathcal{G}}_n \oplus \beta) = q\text{-}ROFPWG(\check{\mathcal{G}}_1, \check{\mathcal{G}}_2, \ldots, \check{\mathcal{G}}_n) \oplus \beta$*

2. *$q\text{-}ROFPWG(r\check{\mathcal{G}}_1, r\check{\mathcal{G}}_2, \ldots, r\check{\mathcal{G}}_n) = r\ q\text{-}ROFPWG(\check{\mathcal{G}}_1, \check{\mathcal{G}}_2, \ldots, \check{\mathcal{G}}_n)$*

3. *$q\text{-}ROFPWG(\check{\mathcal{G}}_1 \oplus \beta_1, \check{\mathcal{G}}_2 \oplus \beta_2, \ldots, \check{\mathcal{G}}_n \oplus \beta_n) = q\text{-}ROFPWG(\check{\mathcal{G}}_1, \check{\mathcal{G}}_2, \ldots, \check{\mathcal{G}}_n) \oplus q\text{-}ROFPWG(\beta_1, \beta_2, \ldots, \beta_n)$*

4. *$q\text{-}ROFPWG(r\check{\mathcal{G}}_1 \oplus \beta \oplus r\check{\mathcal{G}}_2 \oplus \beta, \ldots, \oplus r\check{\mathcal{G}}_n \oplus \beta) = r\ q\text{-}ROFPWG(\check{\mathcal{G}}_1, \check{\mathcal{G}}_2, \ldots, \check{\mathcal{G}}_n) \oplus \beta$*

Proof. The proof of this theorem is the same as Theorem 7. □

4. Proposed Methodology

Consider a set of alternatives $\mathscr{A} = \{\mathscr{A}_1, \mathscr{A}_2, \ldots, \mathscr{A}_m\}$ with m elements; $\mathfrak{O} = \{\mathfrak{O}_1, \mathfrak{O}_2, \ldots, \mathfrak{O}_n\}$ is the finite set of criteria with n elements; and prioritization is given between the criteria presented by the linear order $\mathfrak{O}_1 \succ \mathfrak{O}_2 \succ \mathfrak{O}_3 \ldots \mathfrak{O}_n$ indicating that criteria $\mathfrak{O}_J$ have a higher priority than $\mathfrak{O}_i$ if $j > i$. $\mathfrak{K} = \{\mathfrak{K}_1, \mathfrak{K}_2, \ldots, \mathfrak{K}_p\}$ is the group of decision makers, and decision makers (DMs) do not have equal importance. Prioritization is given between the DMs presented by the linear order $\mathfrak{K}_1 \succ \mathfrak{K}_2 \succ \mathfrak{K}_3 \ldots \mathfrak{K}_p$ indicating DM $\mathfrak{K}_\zeta$ has a higher priority than $\mathfrak{K}_\varrho$ if $\zeta > \varrho$. Decision makers provide a matrix of their own opinion $D^{(p)} = (\mathscr{B}_{ij}^{(p)})_{m \times n}$, where $\mathscr{B}_{ij}^{(p)}$ is given for the alternatives $\mathscr{A}_i \in \mathscr{A}$ with respect to the criteria $\mathfrak{O}_j \in \mathfrak{O}$ by the $\mathfrak{K}_p$ decision maker in the form of q-ROFNs. If all criteria are the same types, there is no need for normalization, but there are two types of criteria (benefit type attributes τ_b and cost type attributes τ_c) in MCGDM; in this case, using the normalization formula the matrix $D^{(p)}$ has been changed into normalizing matrix $Y^{(p)} = (\mathscr{P}_{ij}^{(p)})_{m \times n}$,

$$(\mathscr{P}_{ij}^{(p)})_{m \times n} = \begin{cases} (\mathscr{B}_{ij}^{(p)})^c; & j \in \tau_c \\ \mathscr{B}_{ij}^{(p)}; & j \in \tau_b. \end{cases} \tag{5}$$

where $(\mathscr{B}_{ij}^{(p)})^c$ show the compliment of $\mathscr{B}_{ij}^{(p)}$.

We then use the q-ROFPWA operator or q-ROFPWA operator to implement an MCGDM approach in q-ROF circumstances.

The proposed operators will be applied to the MCGDM, which involves the following steps given in Algorithm 1.

Algorithm 1 Selection of green supplier chain management.

Input:

Step 1:

Acquire a decision matrix $D^{(p)} = (\mathscr{B}_{ij}^{(p)})_{m\times n}$ in the form of q-ROFNs from the decision makers.

$$
\begin{array}{cc}
 & \\
\mathfrak{K}_1 & \mathscr{A}_1 \\
 & \mathscr{A}_2 \\
 & \\
 & \mathscr{A}_m \\
\mathfrak{K}_2 & \mathscr{A}_1 \\
\vdots & \mathscr{A}_2 \\
 & \\
 & \mathscr{A}_m \\
\mathfrak{K}_p & \mathscr{A}_1 \\
 & \mathscr{A}_2 \\
 & \\
 & \mathscr{A}_m
\end{array}
\begin{array}{c}
\begin{array}{cccc} \quad\mathfrak{O}_1 \quad & \quad\mathfrak{O}_2\quad & & \quad\mathfrak{O}_n\quad \end{array} \\
\begin{bmatrix}
(\mathscr{Y}_{11}^1, \mathscr{X}_{11}^1) & (\mathscr{Y}_{12}^1, \mathscr{X}_{12}^1) & \cdots\cdots & (\mathscr{Y}_{1n}^1, \mathscr{X}_{1n}^1) \\
(\mathscr{Y}_{21}^1, \mathscr{X}_{21}^1) & (\mathscr{Y}_{22}^1, \mathscr{X}_{22}^1) & \cdots\cdots & (\mathscr{Y}_{2n}^1, \mathscr{X}_{2n}^1) \\
\vdots & \vdots & \ddots\ddots & \vdots \\
(\mathscr{Y}_{m1}^1, \mathscr{X}_{m1}^1) & (\mathscr{Y}_{m2}^1, \mathscr{X}_{m2}^1) & \cdots\cdots & (\mathscr{Y}_{mn}^1, \mathscr{X}_{mn}^1) \\
(\mathscr{Y}_{11}^2, \mathscr{X}_{11}^2) & (\mathscr{Y}_{12}^2, \mathscr{X}_{12}^2) & \cdots\cdots & (\mathscr{Y}_{1n}^2, \mathscr{X}_{1n}^2) \\
(\mathscr{Y}_{21}^2, \mathscr{X}_{21}^2) & (\mathscr{Y}_{22}^2, \mathscr{X}_{22}^2) & \cdots\cdots & (\mathscr{Y}_{2n}^2, \mathscr{X}_{2n}^2) \\
\vdots & \vdots & \ddots\ddots & \vdots \\
(\mathscr{Y}_{m1}^2, \mathscr{X}_{m1}^2) & (\mathscr{Y}_{m2}^2, \mathscr{X}_{m2}^2) & \cdots\cdots & (\mathscr{Y}_{mn}^2, \mathscr{X}_{mn}^2) \\
(\mathscr{Y}_{11}^p, \mathscr{X}_{11}^p) & (\mathscr{Y}_{12}^p, \mathscr{X}_{12}^p) & \cdots\cdots & (\mathscr{Y}_{1n}^p, \mathscr{X}_{1n}^p) \\
(\mathscr{Y}_{21}^p, \mathscr{X}_{21}^p) & (\mathscr{Y}_{22}^p, \mathscr{X}_{22}^p) & \cdots\cdots & (\mathscr{Y}_{2n}^p, \mathscr{X}_{2n})^p \\
\vdots & \vdots & \ddots\ddots & \vdots \\
(\mathscr{Y}_{m1}^p, \mathscr{X}_{m1}^p) & (\mathscr{Y}_{m2}^p, \mathscr{X}_{m2}^p) & \cdots\cdots & (\mathscr{Y}_{mn}^p, \mathscr{X}_{mn}^p)
\end{bmatrix}
\end{array}
$$

Step 2:

Two types of criteria are specified in the decision matrix, namely cost type criteria (τ_c) and benefit type criteria (τ_b). If all criteria are the same types, there is no need for normalization, but there are two types of criteria in MCGDM. In this case, using the normalization formula Equation (5), the matrix is changed into transformed response matrix $Y^{(p)} = (\mathscr{P}_{ij}^{(p)})_{m\times n}$.

Calculations:

Step 3:

Calculate the values of $\mathscr{T}_{ij}^{(p)}$ by the following formula.

$$
\mathscr{T}_{ij}^{(p)} = \prod_{k=1}^{p-1} \mathscr{H}(\mathscr{P}_{ij}^{(k)}) \quad (p = 2, \ldots, n), \tag{6}
$$

$$
\mathscr{T}_{ij}^{(1)} = 1
$$

Step 4:

Use one of the suggested aggregation operators.

$$
\mathscr{W}_{ij} = \text{q-ROFPWA}(\mathscr{P}_{ij}^{(1)}, \mathscr{P}_{ij}^{(2)}, \ldots, \mathscr{P}_{ij}^{(p)}) = \left\langle \sqrt[q]{(1 - \prod_{z=1}^{p}(1 - ((\mathscr{Y}_{ij}^{q})^{z})^{\frac{\mathscr{T}_j^z}{\sum_{j=1}^{n}\mathscr{T}_j^z}}}, \prod_{z=1}^{p}((\mathscr{X}_{ij}^{q})^{z})^{\frac{\mathscr{T}_j^z}{\sum_{j=1}^{n}\mathscr{T}_j^z}} \right\rangle \tag{7}
$$

or:

$$
\mathscr{W}_{ij} = \text{q-ROFPWA}(\mathscr{P}_{ij}^{(1)}, \mathscr{P}_{ij}^{(2)}, \ldots, \mathscr{P}_{ij}^{(p)}) = \left\langle \prod_{z=1}^{p}((\mathscr{Y}_{ij}^{q})^{z})^{\frac{\mathscr{T}_j^z}{\sum_{j=1}^{n}\mathscr{T}_j^z}}, \sqrt[q]{(1 - \prod_{z=1}^{p}(1 - ((\mathscr{X}_{ij}^{q})^{z})^{\frac{\mathscr{T}_j^z}{\sum_{j=1}^{n}\mathscr{T}_j^z}}} \right\rangle \tag{8}
$$

to aggregate all individual q-ROF decision matrices $Y^{(p)} = (\mathscr{P}_{ij}^{(p)})_{m\times n}$ into one cumulative assessments matrix of the alternatives $W^{(p)} = (\mathscr{W}_{ij})_{m\times n}$

Step 5:
Calculate the values of $\mathscr{T}_{ij}$ by the following formula.

$$\mathscr{T}_{ij} = \prod_{k=1}^{j-1} \mathscr{H}(\mathscr{W}_{ik}) \quad (j = 2, \ldots, n), \tag{9}$$

$$\mathscr{T}_{i1} = 1$$

Step 6:
Aggregate the q-ROF values $\mathscr{W}_{ij}$ for each alternative $\mathscr{A}_i$ by the q-ROFPWA (or q-ROFPWG) operator:

$$\mathscr{W}_i = \text{q-ROFPWA}(\mathscr{P}_{i1}, \mathscr{P}_{i2}, \ldots, \mathscr{P}_{in}) = \left\langle \sqrt[q]{(1 - \prod_{j=1}^{n}(1 - (\mathscr{Y}_{ij}^q)^{\frac{\mathscr{T}_j}{\Sigma_{j=1}^n \mathscr{T}_j}}}, \prod_{j=1}^{n}(\mathscr{X}_{ij}^q)^{\frac{\mathscr{T}_j}{\Sigma_{j=1}^n \mathscr{T}_j}} \right\rangle \tag{10}$$

or:

$$\mathscr{W}_i = \text{q-ROFPWG}(\mathscr{P}_{i1}, \mathscr{P}_{i2}, \ldots, \mathscr{P}_{in}) = \left\langle \prod_{j=1}^{n}(\mathscr{Y}_{ij}^q)^{\frac{\mathscr{T}_j}{\Sigma_{j=1}^n \mathscr{T}_j}}, \sqrt[q]{(1 - \prod_{j=1}^{n}(1 - (\mathscr{X}_{ij}^q)^{\frac{\mathscr{T}_j}{\Sigma_{j=1}^n \mathscr{T}_j}}} \right\rangle \tag{11}$$

Output:
Step 7:
Evaluate the score of all cumulative alternative assessments.

Step 8:
Rank the alternatives by the score function and ultimately choose the most appropriate alternative.

5. Case Study

Environmental problems have grown and spread faster in recent decades, such forest fires, with respect to country by area and worldwide territory, which are a leading cause of weather change and world wide warming. In addition, environmental scarcity and air and water pollution have serious implications for flora and fauna and human life, with various diseases, such as ischemic cardiovascular disease, lung cancer, pulmonary chronic obstruction, stroke, dracunculiasis, cholera, tuberculosis, and typhoid. These are also of serious concern. The green supply chain definition aims to mitigate environmental degradation and to regulate air, water, and waste pollution through green business practices. The core philosophy behind the green concept is certainly one of improved environmental protection. However, companies adopt the green concept of "killing two birds with one stone" because the green supply chains will minimize environmental pollution and manufacturing costs and thus promote economic growth. Sustainability or the green supply chain relates to the notion that sustainable practices should be integrated into the conventional supply chain [24]. This involves the procurement, order, design, production, assembly, distribution, and end-of-life management of the supplier. Figure 2 shows an example of a GSCM for a vendor of baby cribs.

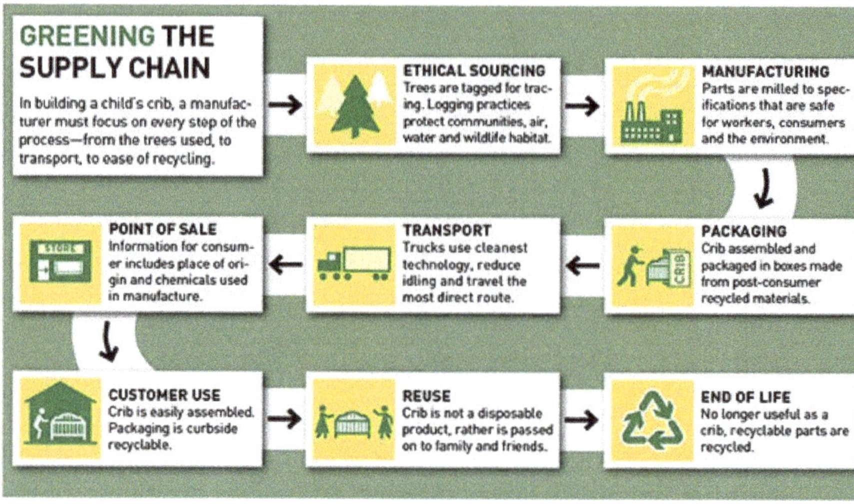

Figure 2. GSCM of a baby crib vendor.

In the world, as environmental consciousness grows, businesses face intense pressure on their damaging impact on the environment from various stakeholders, including governments and clients. Indeed, the industry sector must consider incorporating its operating practices with sustainability into the service and manufacturing industry and rising end-to-end supply chain costs in order for it to have a competitive advantage. During the past few decades, the growing effects of global warming, climate change, waste, and air pollution have driven experts around the world to think more environmentally friendly [69]. Rath [19] described GSCM as a catalyst of organizational sustainable growth. GSCM needs a permanent collective interest in developing nations, as environmental issues continue to grow. In addition, the developing countries have recently become part of the green movement. Administrators of the green supply chain shall be incorporated into the management of the supply chain, including the design, procurement, and selection of goods, the production process, the distribution of the finished product to customers, and the end of the product's life.

The model of reverse logistic activities plays a major role in enhancing green supply chain environmental, social, and economic performance. However, incorporating reverse logistics into the GSCM strategy is not a trivial task. Reverse logistics is characterized as the process of moving goods for things like reutilization, capture, or proper disposal outside their typical destination. Products flow from suppliers to end users in supply chain networks. The efficiency of the flow is calculated by the time delivery metric by supply chain managers. This is a standard metric of the supply chain aimed at ensuring a fast and efficient distribution to the end customer from the moment he/she places an order. Reverse logistics are more complex and are more of a concern than forward-looking logistics, which are more coordinated and also part of the scheduled methodologies of any company in the manufacturing, sales, storage, distribution, and servicing of its goods. Historically, reverse logistics has been one field that is often disorganized and disregarded by any manufacturing company. However, this is no longer so. For a company that does not have a planned reverse logistics strategy, the trends in its financial performance and market share may be a gloomy picture. Figure 3 shows the short summary of reverse logistics.

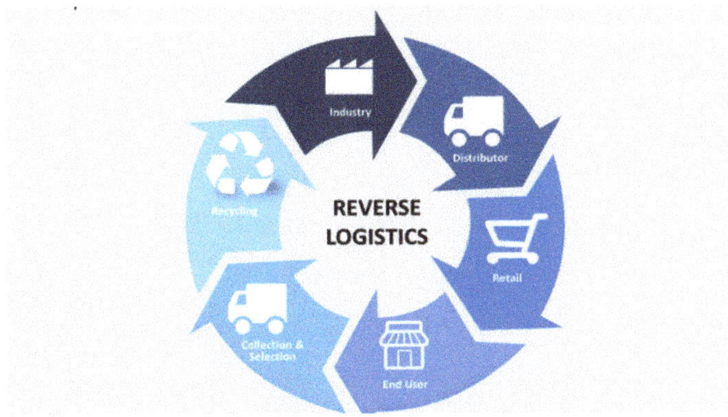

Figure 3. Reverse logistics.

The implementation of ecological management values is necessary across the entire client order cycle, such as design, procurement, manufacture and assembly, packaging, transport, and delivery [32]. GSCM integrates eco-friendly concepts into supply chain management to improve environmental sustainability through a variety of green practices, including green purchasing, green distribution and storage, green transport using biofuels, green manufacturing processes, and end-of-life products [23]. There are several differences in its definition and terminology over the years [35], as we see in the definition of GSCM. Some words characterizing this definition are included in a detailed list below.

- Sustainable management of the supply network [13].
- Sustainability of supply and requirement across corporate social responsibility networks [22].
- Environmental supply chain management [18].
- Green purchasing [20].
- Green logistics [21].

A comprehensive definition of GSCM was given by Srivastava [17], "The GSCM is a aspect of environmental thought into the management of the supply chain including product design and material procurement, selection, manufacturing processes, the distribution and end-of-life management of the product to the customer".

For an enterprise, GSCM has many advantages. The myth that greening would lead to lower sales and higher operating costs has vanished as many companies have now recognized that it will not be terrible and have been able to satisfy customers' desires to incorporate environmental initiatives in their supply chains and turn them into higher profits. There is a connection between better environmental sustainability and financial incentives established by a number of businesses. Firms have gained an insight into their supply chains and found places where changes in the way they work can lead to increased income. Green logistics helps to reduce the emissions of many kinds such as CO_2 and CO. The use of non-fossil fuels such as for electric cars helps to reduce air pollution that affects human health when breathing the air. Various forms of fossil fuel are destroying the atmosphere because of pollution. For example, for marine life, aviation impacts the air quality due to diesel consumption. The same occurs on land using various types of transportation. Collectively, this impacts the environment, agriculture, and human health. Green logistics does help with these problems, however. In a company, green logistics, depending on the sector, is very beneficial. For example, trucks are used to transport products from A to B. The final destination will take days to get to. For the whole journey, the motorists and the cases of idling are more detrimental than driving the trucks. It costs much money to use petrol at the same time. Fuel consumption and energy costs will be reduced as trucks receive alternative or additional power for critical things such as lights and AC while idling. As less energy use = renewable resources, the company or organization will not invest in sustainability.

In the literature review, we discussed criteria for green supplier selection according to different researchers. In this paper, the criteria for the selection of green suppliers are considered as in Table 3.

Table 3. Criteria for evaluating the best alternative. WEEE, waste electrical and electronic equipment; RoHS, restriction of hazardous substances.

	Criteria	Definition
$\mathfrak{O}_1$	Quality	Reject rate, commitment to excellence in leadership, process improvement, warranty coverage and claims, and quality assurance.
$\mathfrak{O}_2$	Cost	Value for price performance, compliance with demand, actions in the sector, and transportation cost.
$\mathfrak{O}_3$	Delivery	Order fulfill rate, lead time, and order frequency.
$\mathfrak{O}_4$	Service	Responsibility, inventory management, willingness, and design capability.
$\mathfrak{O}_5$	Environment	Eco-design specifications, ozone depleting chemicals (ODC), WEEE, and RoHS.
$\mathfrak{O}_6$	Corporate social responsibility	Employee privileges and rights, stakeholder rights, information disclosure, and respect for the policy.

5.1. Numerical Example

Consider a set of alternatives $\mathscr{A} = \{\mathscr{A}_1, \mathscr{A}_2, \mathscr{A}_3, \mathscr{A}_4, \mathscr{A}_5\}$, and $\mathfrak{O} = \{\mathfrak{O}_1, \mathfrak{O}_2, \mathfrak{O}_3, \mathfrak{O}_4, \mathfrak{O}_5, \mathfrak{O}_6\}$ is the finite set of criteria given in Table 3. Prioritization is given between the criteria presented by the linear order $\mathfrak{O}_1 \succ \mathfrak{O}_2 \succ \mathfrak{O}_3 \ldots \mathfrak{O}_6$ indicating criteria $\mathfrak{O}_J$ have a higher priority than $\mathfrak{O}_i$ if $j > i$. $\mathfrak{K} = \{\mathfrak{K}_1, \mathfrak{K}_2, \mathfrak{K}_3\}$ is the group of decision makers, and decision makers (DMs) do not have equal importance. Prioritization is given between the DMs presented by the linear order $\mathfrak{K}_1 \succ \mathfrak{K}_2 \succ \mathfrak{K}_3$ indicating DM $\mathfrak{K}_\zeta$ has a higher priority than $\mathfrak{K}_\varrho$ if $\zeta > \varrho$. Decision makers provide a matrix of their own opinion $D^{(p)} = (\mathscr{B}_{ij}^{(p)})_{m\times n}$, where $\mathscr{B}_{ij}^{(p)}$ is given for the alternatives $\mathscr{A}_i \in \mathscr{A}$ with respect to the criteria $\mathfrak{O}_j \in \mathfrak{O}$ by the $\mathfrak{K}_p$ decision maker in the form of q-ROFNs. We take $q = 3$.

Step 1: Acquire a decision matrix $D^{(p)} = (\mathscr{B}_{ij}^{(p)})_{m\times n}$ in the form of q-ROFNs from three decision makers given as Tables 4–6.

Table 4. q-ROF decision matrix for $\mathfrak{K}_1$.

	$\mathfrak{O}_1$	$\mathfrak{O}_2$	$\mathfrak{O}_3$	$\mathfrak{O}_4$	$\mathfrak{O}_5$	$\mathfrak{O}_6$
$\mathscr{A}_1$	(0.90, 0.00)	(0.65, 0.35)	(0.75, 0.15)	(0.95, 0.15)	(0.75, 0.00)	(0.45, 0.25)
$\mathscr{A}_2$	(0.95, 0.25)	(0.80, 0.30)	(0.55, 0.25)	(0.75, 0.15)	(0.45, 0.45)	(0.35, 0.15)
$\mathscr{A}_3$	(0.85, 0.15)	(0.35, 0.55)	(0.75, 0.25)	(0.55, 0.00)	(0.65, 0.35)	(0.45, 0.00)
$\mathscr{A}_4$	(0.75, 0.35)	(0.81, 0.25)	(0.65, 0.15)	(0.35, 0.25)	(0.75, 0.25)	(0.35, 0.75)
$\mathscr{A}_5$	(0.80, 0.25)	(0.60, 0.00)	(0.25, 0.15)	(0.15, 0.65)	(0.65, 0.15)	(0.25, 0.65)

Table 5. q-ROF decision matrix for $\mathfrak{K}_2$.

	$\mathfrak{O}_1$	$\mathfrak{O}_2$	$\mathfrak{O}_3$	$\mathfrak{O}_4$	$\mathfrak{O}_5$	$\mathfrak{O}_6$
$\mathscr{A}_1$	(0.75, 0.25)	(0.55, 0.30)	(0.85, 0.15)	(0.95, 0.15)	(0.80, 0.25)	(0.90, 0.15)
$\mathscr{A}_2$	(0.55, 0.15)	(0.60, 0.35)	(0.45, 0.15)	(0.75, 0.35)	(0.65, 0.30)	(0.75, 0.00)
$\mathscr{A}_3$	(0.90, 0.60)	(0.65, 0.20)	(0.25, 0.55)	(0.65, 0.55)	(0.15, 0.25)	(0.70, 0.30)
$\mathscr{A}_4$	(0.50, 0.00)	(0.55, 0.40)	(0.15, 0.10)	(0.50, 0.60)	(0.10, 0.15)	(0.60, 0.35)
$\mathscr{A}_5$	(0.85, 0.35)	(0.70, 0.30)	(0.65, 0.55)	(0.25, 0.50)	(0.50, 0.30)	(0.50, 0.25)

Table 6. q-ROF decision matrix for $\mathfrak{K}_3$.

	$\mathfrak{O}_1$	$\mathfrak{O}_2$	$\mathfrak{O}_3$	$\mathfrak{O}_4$	$\mathfrak{O}_5$	$\mathfrak{O}_6$
$\mathscr{A}_1$	(0.90, 0.15)	(0.85, 0.25)	(0.80, 0.00)	(0.70, 0.35)	(0.80, 0.20)	(0.70, 0.30)
$\mathscr{A}_2$	(0.80, 0.25)	(0.55, 0.15)	(0.60, 0.25)	(0.50, 0.30)	(0.60, 0.30)	(0.60, 0.30)
$\mathscr{A}_3$	(0.75, 0.15)	(0.65, 0.25)	(0.35, 0.00)	(0.50, 0.35)	(0.75, 0.30)	(0.35, 0.25)
$\mathscr{A}_4$	(0.35, 0.35)	(0.50, 0.35)	(0.45, 0.25)	(0.55, 0.45)	(0.25, 0.25)	(0.65, 0.00)
$\mathscr{A}_5$	(0.65, 0.25)	(0.65, 0.25)	(0.60, 0.15)	(0.65, 0.25)	(0.65, 0.55)	(0.45, 0.40)

Step 2: Normalize the decision matrices acquired by DMs using Equation (5). In Table 3, there are two types of criteria. $\mathfrak{O}_2$ is the cost type criteria, and the other is the benefit type criteria. The normalized Tables for all the decision-makers are represented as Tables 7–9.

Table 7. Normalized q-ROF decision matrix from $\mathfrak{K}_1$.

	$\mathfrak{O}_1$	$\mathfrak{O}_2$	$\mathfrak{O}_3$	$\mathfrak{O}_4$	$\mathfrak{O}_5$	$\mathfrak{O}_6$
$\mathscr{A}_1$	(0.90, 0.00)	(0.35, 0.65)	(0.75, 0.15)	(0.95, 0.15)	(0.75, 0.00)	(0.45, 0.25)
$\mathscr{A}_2$	(0.95, 0.25)	(0.30, 0.80)	(0.55, 0.25)	(0.75, 0.15)	(0.45, 0.45)	(0.35, 0.15)
$\mathscr{A}_3$	(0.85, 0.15)	(0.55, 0.35)	(0.75, 0.25)	(0.55, 0.00)	(0.65, 0.35)	(0.45, 0.00)
$\mathscr{A}_4$	(0.75, 0.35)	(0.25, 0.81)	(0.65, 0.15)	(0.35, 0.25)	(0.75, 0.25)	(0.35, 0.75)
$\mathscr{A}_5$	(0.80, 0.25)	(0.00, 0.60)	(0.25, 0.15)	(0.15, 0.65)	(0.65, 0.15)	(0.25, 0.65)

Table 8. Normalized q-ROF decision matrix from $\mathfrak{K}_2$.

	$\mathfrak{O}_1$	$\mathfrak{O}_2$	$\mathfrak{O}_3$	$\mathfrak{O}_4$	$\mathfrak{O}_5$	$\mathfrak{O}_6$
$\mathscr{A}_1$	(0.75, 0.25)	(0.30, 0.55)	(0.85, 0.15)	(0.95, 0.15)	(0.80, 0.25)	(0.90, 0.15)
$\mathscr{A}_2$	(0.55, 0.15)	(0.35, 0.60)	(0.45, 0.15)	(0.75, 0.35)	(0.65, 0.30)	(0.75, 0.00)
$\mathscr{A}_3$	(0.90, 0.60)	(0.20, 0.65)	(0.25, 0.55)	(0.65, 0.55)	(0.15, 0.25)	(0.70, 0.30)
$\mathscr{A}_4$	(0.50, 0.00)	(0.40, 0.55)	(0.15, 0.10)	(0.50, 0.60)	(0.10, 0.15)	(0.60, 0.35)
$\mathscr{A}_5$	(0.85, 0.35)	(0.30, 0.70)	(0.65, 0.55)	(0.25, 0.50)	(0.50, 0.30)	(0.50, 0.25)

Table 9. Normalized q-ROF decision matrix from $\mathfrak{K}_3$.

	$\mathfrak{O}_1$	$\mathfrak{O}_2$	$\mathfrak{O}_3$	$\mathfrak{O}_4$	$\mathfrak{O}_5$	$\mathfrak{O}_6$
$\mathscr{A}_1$	(0.90, 0.15)	(0.25, 0.85)	(0.80, 0.00)	(0.70, 0.35)	(0.80, 0.20)	(0.70, 0.30)
$\mathscr{A}_2$	(0.80, 0.25)	(0.15, 0.55)	(0.60, 0.25)	(0.50, 0.30)	(0.60, 0.30)	(0.60, 0.30)
$\mathscr{A}_3$	(0.75, 0.15)	(0.25, 0.65)	(0.35, 0.00)	(0.50, 0.35)	(0.75, 0.30)	(0.35, 0.25)
$\mathscr{A}_4$	(0.35, 0.35)	(0.35, 0.50)	(0.45, 0.25)	(0.55, 0.45)	(0.25, 0.25)	(0.65, 0.00)
$\mathscr{A}_5$	(0.65, 0.25)	(0.25, 0.65)	(0.60, 0.15)	(0.65, 0.25)	(0.65, 0.55)	(0.45, 0.40)

Step 3: Calculate the values of $\mathscr{T}_{ij}^{(p)}$ by Equation (6).

$$\mathscr{T}_{ij}^{(1)} = \begin{pmatrix} 1 & 1 & 1 & 1 & 1 & 1 \\ 1 & 1 & 1 & 1 & 1 & 1 \\ 1 & 1 & 1 & 1 & 1 & 1 \\ 1 & 1 & 1 & 1 & 1 & 1 \\ 1 & 1 & 1 & 1 & 1 & 1 \end{pmatrix}$$

$$\mathscr{T}_{ij}^{(2)} = \begin{pmatrix} 0.8645 & 0.3841 & 0.7093 & 0.9270 & 0.7109 & 0.5378 \\ 0.9209 & 0.2575 & 0.5754 & 0.7093 & 0.5000 & 0.5198 \\ 0.8054 & 0.5618 & 0.7031 & 0.5832 & 0.6159 & 0.5456 \\ 0.6895 & 0.2421 & 0.6356 & 0.5136 & 0.7031 & 0.3105 \\ 0.7482 & 0.3920 & 0.5061 & 0.3644 & 0.6356 & 0.3705 \end{pmatrix}$$

$$\mathscr{T}_{ij}^{(3)} = \begin{pmatrix} 0.6078 & 0.1653 & 0.5629 & 0.8593 & 0.5319 & 0.4640 \\ 0.5355 & 0.1065 & 0.3062 & 0.4891 & 0.3119 & 0.3695 \\ 0.6092 & 0.2060 & 0.2985 & 0.3232 & 0.3042 & 0.3590 \\ 0.3878 & 0.1087 & 0.3186 & 0.2334 & 0.3507 & 0.1821 \\ 0.5878 & 0.1341 & 0.2804 & 0.1623 & 0.3489 & 0.3526 \end{pmatrix}$$

Step 4: Use q-ROFPWA to aggregate all individual q-ROF decision matrices $Y^{(p)} = (\mathscr{P}_{ij}^{(p)})_{m\times n}$ into one cumulative assessments matrix of the alternatives $W^{(p)} = (\mathscr{W}_{ij})_{m\times n}$ using Equation (7) given in Table 10.

Table 10. Collective q-ROF decision matrix.

	$\mathfrak{O}_1$	$\mathfrak{O}_2$	$\mathfrak{O}_3$	$\mathfrak{O}_4$	$\mathfrak{O}_5$	$\mathfrak{O}_6$
$\mathscr{A}_1$	(0.8648, 0.0000)	(0.3304, 0.6417)	(0.7997, 0.0000)	(0.9171, 0.1948)	(0.7796, 0.0000)	(0.7312, 0.2273)
$\mathscr{A}_2$	(0.8611, 0.2064)	(0.3044, 0.7359)	(0.5343, 0.2138)	(0.7153, 0.2300)	(0.5512, 0.3752)	(0.5835, 0.0000)
$\mathscr{A}_3$	(0.8600, 0.2382)	(0.3048, 0.7192)	(0.6288, 0.0000)	(0.5794, 0.0000)	(0.6081, 0.3474)	(0.5470, 0.0000)
$\mathscr{A}_4$	(0.6472, 0.0000)	(0.2988, 0.7269)	(0.5491, 0.1429)	(0.4394, 0.3498)	(0.6184, 0.2099)	(0.4825, 0.0000)
$\mathscr{A}_5$	(0.7936, 0.2784)	(0.2091, 0.6309)	(0.5051, 0.2167)	(0.3400, 0.5516)	(0.6124, 0.2353)	(0.3821, 0.4793)

Step 5: Evaluate the values of $\mathscr{T}_{ij}$ by using Equation (9).

$$\mathscr{T}_{ij} = \begin{pmatrix} 1 & 0.8234 & 0.3178 & 0.2402 & 0.2118 & 0.1561 \\ 1 & 0.8149 & 0.2565 & 0.1466 & 0.0992 & 0.0553 \\ 1 & 0.8113 & 0.2663 & 0.1663 & 0.0993 & 0.0587 \\ 1 & 0.6356 & 0.2042 & 0.1187 & 0.0618 & 0.0379 \\ 1 & 0.7391 & 0.2801 & 0.1567 & 0.0683 & 0.0415 \end{pmatrix}$$

Step 6: Aggregate the q-ROF values $\mathscr{W}_{ij}$ for each alternative $\mathscr{A}_i$ by the q-ROFPWA operator using Equation (10) given in Table 11.

Table 11. q-ROF aggregated values $\mathscr{W}_i$.

$\mathscr{W}_1$	(0.7899, 0.0000)
$\mathscr{W}_2$	(0.7319, 0.0000)
$\mathscr{W}_3$	(0.7299, 0.0000)
$\mathscr{W}_4$	(0.5614, 0.0000)
$\mathscr{W}_5$	(0.6576, 0.3704)

Step 7: Calculate the score of all q-ROF aggregated values $\mathscr{W}_i$.

$$\mathscr{H}(\mathscr{W}_1) = 0.7464$$

$$\mathscr{H}(\mathscr{W}_2) = 0.6960$$

$$\mathscr{H}(\mathscr{W}_3) = 0.6944$$

$$\mathscr{H}(\mathscr{W}_4) = 0.5885$$

$$\mathscr{H}(\mathscr{W}_5) = 0.6168$$

Step 8: Rank by the score function values.

$$\mathscr{W}_1 \succ \mathscr{W}_2 \succ \mathscr{W}_3 \succ \mathscr{W}_5 \succ \mathscr{W}_4$$

Therefore,

$$\mathscr{A}_1 \succ \mathscr{A}_2 \succ \mathscr{A}_3 \succ \mathscr{A}_5 \succ \mathscr{A}_4$$

5.2. Discussion and Symmetrical Analysis

In this part, we discuss the final results obtained from the calculations of green supplier selection by using the proposed aggregation operators. Table 12 represents the ranking of alternatives via the q-ROFPWA and q-ROFPWG aggregation operators. The beauty of the proposed algorithm and operators is that both produce the same results. These operators show the symmetry in the results and provide us an appropriate optimal solution for the decision making problem.

Table 12. Results obtained via the proposed aggregation operators.

Alternatives	Ranking Order	Final Decision
q-ROFPWA	$\mathscr{A}_1 \succ \mathscr{A}_2 \succ \mathscr{A}_3 \succ \mathscr{A}_5 \succ \mathscr{A}_4$	$\mathscr{A}_1$
q-ROFPWG	$\mathscr{A}_1 \succ \mathscr{A}_2 \succ \mathscr{A}_3 \succ \mathscr{A}_4 \succ \mathscr{A}_5$	$\mathscr{A}_1$

For the worst alternatives, we can observe some changes in the ranking results of both operators. This change is due to different formulating strategies and operations in the aggregation operators. Otherwise, the final optimal decision remains the same. This phenomenon represents the validity, flexibility, authenticity, and symmetry of proposed operators.

6. Conclusions

This manuscript proposed a novel approach to the selection of green suppliers under the q-ROF framework to address the complexities of the problems of the selection of green suppliers in practice. The lack of consideration of the relationships of attributes to an uncertain environment may affect the conclusions in some MCGDM problems. To address these drawbacks, we introduced a new approach for selecting green suppliers with the q-ROF information, in which the decision makers' assessment was considered by the q-rROFNs. The q-ROFNs were used to express the assessment of decision makers, and the vagueness and incompleteness of the information were effectively addressed. Meanwhile, we developed prioritized aggregation operators named the q-ROFPWA and q-ROFPWG aggregation operators. Based on these operators, we developed an important MCGDM approach for GSCM. Moreover, a practical example was illustrated for choosing green suppliers to demonstrate the feasibility of the proposed operators. In the case of numerous complicated issues in the selection of green suppliers, the proposed approach could effectively address many areas, such as providing decision makers with a comfortable climate of assessment, fostering a comparatively high level of consensus among decision makers, and fully assessing the weights of decision makers. This paper, therefore, provided a more practical and efficient approach for selecting green suppliers for the companies in practice.

In further research, considering the superiority of new q-ROFNs, one can extend them to some other aggregation operators, such as power mean aggregation operators, Dombi's aggregation operators, Bonferroni mean operators, Heronian mean operators, and so on. We hope our findings will be fruitful for the researchers working in supply chain and GSCM analysis, information aggregation, decision analysis, supply management, and environmental science. The methodological advances for supply chain and GSCM analysis are promising areas for future studies. We believe that there are substantial growth and opportunities to understand our world in the convergence of these key climate-centric organizational research fields.

Author Contributions: M.R., D.P., H.M.A.F. and M.R.H. conceived and worked together to achieve this manuscript, M.R. and D.P. construct the ideas and algorithms for data analysis and design the model of the manuscript, H.M.A.F. and M.R.H. processed the data collection and wrote the paper. All authors have read and agreed to the published version of the manuscript.

Conflicts of Interest: The authors declare no conflict of interest.

Acknowledgments: The authors are highly thankful to editor-in-chief and refress for their valuable comments and suggestions for the improvement of our manuscript.

Abbreviations

FSs	Fuzzy sets
IFSs	Intuitionistic fuzzy sets
IFNs	Intuitionistic fuzzy numbers
PFSs	Pythagorean fuzzy sets
PFNs	Pythagorean fuzzy numbers
q-ROFSs	q-rung orthopair fuzzy sets
q-ROFNs	q-rung orthopair fuzzy numbers
GSCM	Green supply chain management
MCGDM	Multi-criteria group decision making
q-ROFWA	q-rung orthopair fuzzy weighted average
q-ROFWG	q-rung orthopair fuzzy weighted geometric
q-ROFPWA	q-rung orthopair fuzzy prioritized weighted average
q-ROFPWG	q-rung orthopair fuzzy prioritized weighted geometric

Appendix A

The first statement is easily followed by Definition 8 and Theorem 3. In the following, we prove this:

$$\begin{aligned} &\text{q-ROFPWA}(\breve{\mathcal{G}}_1, \breve{\mathcal{G}}_2, \ldots, \breve{\mathcal{G}}_n) \\ &= \left(\frac{\breve{\mathscr{T}}_1}{\sum_{j=1}^{n} \breve{\mathscr{T}}_j} \breve{\mathcal{G}}_1 \oplus \frac{\breve{\mathscr{T}}_2}{\sum_{j=1}^{n} \breve{\mathscr{T}}_j} \breve{\mathcal{G}}_2 \oplus, \ldots, \frac{\breve{\mathscr{T}}_n}{\sum_{j=1}^{n} \breve{\mathscr{T}}_j} \breve{\mathcal{G}}_n \right) \\ &= \left\langle \sqrt[q]{1 - \prod_{j=1}^{n} (1 - \mathscr{Y}_j^{q})^{\frac{\breve{\mathscr{T}}_j}{\sum_{j=1}^{n} \breve{\mathscr{T}}_j}}}, \prod_{j=1}^{n} \mathscr{X}_j^{\frac{\breve{\mathscr{T}}_j}{\sum_{j=1}^{n} \breve{\mathscr{T}}_j}} \right\rangle \end{aligned}$$

To prove this theorem, we use mathematical induction.
For $n = 2$:

$$\frac{\breve{\mathscr{T}}_1}{\sum_{j=1}^{n} \breve{\mathscr{T}}_j} \breve{\mathcal{G}}_1 = \left\langle \sqrt[q]{1 - (1 - \mathscr{Y}_1^{q})^{\frac{\breve{\mathscr{T}}_1}{\sum_{j=1}^{n} \breve{\mathscr{T}}_j}}}, \mathscr{X}_1^{\frac{\breve{\mathscr{T}}_1}{\sum_{j=1}^{n} \breve{\mathscr{T}}_j}} \right\rangle$$

$$\frac{\breve{\mathscr{T}}_2}{\sum_{j=1}^{n} \breve{\mathscr{T}}_j} \breve{\mathcal{G}}_2 = \left\langle \sqrt[q]{1 - (1 - \mathscr{Y}_2^{q})^{\frac{\breve{\mathscr{T}}_1}{\sum_{j=1}^{n} \breve{\mathscr{T}}_j}}}, \mathscr{X}_2^{\frac{\breve{\mathscr{T}}_1}{\sum_{j=1}^{n} \breve{\mathscr{T}}_j}} \right\rangle$$

Then:

$$\frac{\mathcal{F}_1}{\sum_{j=1}^{n}\mathcal{F}_j}\check{\mathcal{G}}_1 \oplus \frac{\mathcal{F}_2}{\sum_{j=1}^{n}\mathcal{F}_j}\check{\mathcal{G}}_2$$

$$= \left\langle \sqrt[q]{1-(1-\mathcal{Y}_1^q)^{\frac{\mathcal{F}_1}{\sum_{j=1}^{n}\mathcal{F}_j}}}, \mathcal{X}_1^{\frac{\mathcal{F}_1}{\sum_{j=1}^{n}\mathcal{F}_j}} \right\rangle \oplus \left\langle \sqrt[q]{1-(1-\mathcal{Y}_2^q)^{\frac{\mathcal{F}_1}{\sum_{j=1}^{n}\mathcal{F}_j}}}, \mathcal{X}_2^{\frac{\mathcal{F}_1}{\sum_{j=1}^{n}\mathcal{F}_j}} \right\rangle$$

$$= \left\langle \sqrt[q]{(1-(1-\mathcal{Y}_1^q)^{\frac{\mathcal{F}_1}{\sum_{j=1}^{n}\mathcal{F}_j}} + 1-(1-\mathcal{Y}_2^q)^{\frac{\mathcal{F}_1}{\sum_{j=1}^{n}\mathcal{F}_j}} - \left((1-(1-\mathcal{Y}_1^q)^{\frac{\mathcal{F}_1}{\sum_{j=1}^{n}\mathcal{F}_j}}\right)\left((1-(1-\mathcal{Y}_2^q)^{\frac{\mathcal{F}_1}{\sum_{j=1}^{n}\mathcal{F}_j}}\right)}, \right.$$
$$\left. \mathcal{X}_1^{\frac{\mathcal{F}_1}{\sum_{j=1}^{n}\mathcal{F}_j}} . \mathcal{X}_2^{\frac{\mathcal{F}_1}{\sum_{j=1}^{n}\mathcal{F}_j}} \right\rangle$$

$$= \left\langle \sqrt[q]{1-(1-\mathcal{Y}_1^q)^{\frac{\mathcal{F}_1}{\sum_{j=1}^{n}\mathcal{F}_j}} + 1-(1-\mathcal{Y}_2^q)^{\frac{\mathcal{F}_1}{\sum_{j=1}^{n}\mathcal{F}_j}} - \left(1-(1-\mathcal{Y}_2^q)^{\frac{\mathcal{F}_1}{\sum_{j=1}^{n}\mathcal{F}_j}} - (1-\mathcal{Y}_1^q)^{\frac{\mathcal{F}_1}{\sum_{j=1}^{n}\mathcal{F}_j}} + \right.}$$
$$\left. \overline{(1-\mathcal{Y}_2^q)^{\frac{\mathcal{F}_1}{\sum_{j=1}^{n}\mathcal{F}_j}}(1-\mathcal{Y}_1^q)^{\frac{\mathcal{F}_1}{\sum_{j=1}^{n}\mathcal{F}_j}}\Big)}, \mathcal{X}_1^{\frac{\mathcal{F}_1}{\sum_{j=1}^{n}\mathcal{F}_j}} . \mathcal{X}_2^{\frac{\mathcal{F}_1}{\sum_{j=1}^{n}\mathcal{F}_j}} \right\rangle$$

$$= \left\langle \sqrt[q]{1-(1-\mathcal{Y}_1^q)^{\frac{\mathcal{F}_1}{\sum_{j=1}^{n}\mathcal{F}_j}}(1-\mathcal{Y}_2^q)^{\frac{\mathcal{F}_1}{\sum_{j=1}^{n}\mathcal{F}_j}}}, \mathcal{X}_1^{\frac{\mathcal{F}_1}{\sum_{j=1}^{n}\mathcal{F}_j}} . \mathcal{X}_2^{\frac{\mathcal{F}_1}{\sum_{j=1}^{n}\mathcal{F}_j}} \right\rangle$$

$$= \left\langle \sqrt[q]{1-\prod_{j=1}^{2}(1-\mathcal{Y}_j^q)^{\frac{\mathcal{F}_j}{\sum_{j=1}^{n}\mathcal{F}_j}}}, \prod_{j=1}^{2}\mathcal{X}_j^{\frac{\mathcal{F}_j}{\sum_{j=1}^{n}\mathcal{F}_j}} \right\rangle$$

This shows that Equation (2) is true for $n = 2$. Now, let Equation (2) hold for $n = k$, i.e.,

$$\text{q-ROFPWA}(\check{\mathcal{G}}_1, \check{\mathcal{G}}_2, \ldots, \check{\mathcal{G}}_k) = \left\langle \sqrt[q]{1-\prod_{j=1}^{k}(1-\mathcal{Y}_j^q)^{\frac{\mathcal{F}_j}{\sum_{j=1}^{n}\mathcal{F}_j}}}, \prod_{j=1}^{k}\mathcal{X}_j^{\frac{\mathcal{F}_j}{\sum_{j=1}^{n}\mathcal{F}_j}} \right\rangle$$

Now, $n = k+1$, and by the operational laws of q-ROFNs, we have,

$$\text{q-ROFPWA}(\check{\mathcal{G}}_1, \check{\mathcal{G}}_2, \ldots, \check{\mathcal{G}}_{k+1}) = \text{q-ROFPWA}(\check{\mathcal{G}}_1, \check{\mathcal{G}}_2, \ldots, \check{\mathcal{G}}_k) \oplus \check{\mathcal{G}}_{k+1}$$

$$= \left\langle \sqrt[q]{1 - \prod_{j=1}^{k} (1 - \mathscr{Y}_j^q)^{\frac{\check{\mathscr{T}}_j}{\sum_{j=1}^n \check{\mathscr{T}}_j}}}, \prod_{j=1}^{k} \mathscr{X}_j^{\frac{\check{\mathscr{T}}_j}{\sum_{j=1}^n \check{\mathscr{T}}_j}} \right\rangle \oplus \left\langle \sqrt[q]{1 - (1 - \mathscr{Y}_{k+1}^q)^{\frac{\check{\mathscr{T}}_{k+1}}{\sum_{j=1}^n \check{\mathscr{T}}_j}}}, \mathscr{X}_{k+1}^{\frac{\check{\mathscr{T}}_{k+1}}{\sum_{j=1}^n \check{\mathscr{T}}_j}} \right\rangle$$

$$= \left\langle \sqrt[q]{1 - \prod_{j=1}^{k} (1 - \mathscr{Y}_k^q)^{\frac{\check{\mathscr{T}}_j}{\sum_{j=1}^n \check{\mathscr{T}}_j}} + 1 - (1 - \mathscr{Y}_{k+1}^q)^{\frac{\check{\mathscr{T}}_{k+1}}{\sum_{j=1}^n \check{\mathscr{T}}_j}} - \left(1 - \prod_{j=1}^{k} (1 - \mathscr{Y}_k^q)^{\frac{\check{\mathscr{T}}_j}{\sum_{j=1}^n \check{\mathscr{T}}_j}}\right)\left(1 - (1 - \mathscr{Y}_{k+1}^q)^{\frac{\check{\mathscr{T}}_{k+1}}{\sum_{j=1}^n \check{\mathscr{T}}_j}}\right)}, \right.$$
$$\left. \prod_{j=1}^{k} \mathscr{X}_k^{\frac{\check{\mathscr{T}}_j}{\sum_{j=1}^n \check{\mathscr{T}}_j}} . \mathscr{X}_{k=1}^{\frac{\check{\mathscr{T}}_{k+1}}{\sum_{j=1}^n \check{\mathscr{T}}_j}} \right\rangle$$

$$= \left\langle \sqrt[q]{1 - \prod_{j=1}^{k} (1 - \mathscr{Y}_k^q)^{\frac{\check{\mathscr{T}}_j}{\sum_{j=1}^n \check{\mathscr{T}}_j}} (1 - \mathscr{Y}_{k+1}^q)^{\frac{\check{\mathscr{T}}_{k+1}}{\sum_{j=1}^n \check{\mathscr{T}}_{k+1}}}}, \prod_{j=1}^{k} \mathscr{X}_k^{\frac{\check{\mathscr{T}}_j}{\sum_{j=1}^n \check{\mathscr{T}}_j}} . \mathscr{X}_{k+1}^{\frac{\check{\mathscr{T}}_{k+1}}{\sum_{j=1}^n \check{\mathscr{T}}_j}} \right\rangle$$

$$= \left\langle \sqrt[q]{1 - \prod_{j=1}^{k+1} (1 - \mathscr{Y}_j^q)^{\frac{\check{\mathscr{T}}_j}{\sum_{j=1}^{k+1} \check{\mathscr{T}}_j}}}, \prod_{j=1}^{k+1} \mathscr{X}_j^{\frac{\check{\mathscr{T}}_j}{\sum_{j=1}^n \check{\mathscr{T}}_j}} \right\rangle$$

This shows that for $n = k + 1$, Equation (2) holds. Then,

$$\text{q-ROFPWA}(\check{\mathcal{G}}_1, \check{\mathcal{G}}_2, \ldots, \check{\mathcal{G}}_n) = \left\langle \sqrt[q]{(1 - \prod_{j=1}^{n} (1 - \mathscr{Y}_j^q)^{\frac{\check{\mathscr{T}}_j}{\sum_{j=1}^n \check{\mathscr{T}}_j}}}, \prod_{j=1}^{n} \mathscr{X}_j^{\frac{\check{\mathscr{T}}_j}{\sum_{j=1}^n \check{\mathscr{T}}_j}} \right\rangle$$

Appendix A.1

From Definition 8, we have:

$$\begin{aligned}
\text{q-ROFPWA}(\check{\mathcal{G}}_1, \check{\mathcal{G}}_2, \ldots, \check{\mathcal{G}}_n) &= \frac{\widetilde{\check{\mathscr{T}}}_1}{\sum_{j=1}^n \check{\mathscr{T}}_j} \check{\mathcal{G}}_1 \oplus \frac{\check{\mathscr{T}}_2}{\sum_{j=1}^n \check{\mathscr{T}}_j} \check{\mathcal{G}}_2 \oplus, \ldots, \oplus \frac{\check{\mathscr{T}}_n}{\sum_{j=1}^n \check{\mathscr{T}}_j} \check{\mathcal{G}}_n \\
&= \frac{\check{\mathscr{T}}_1}{\sum_{j=1}^n \check{\mathscr{T}}_j} \check{\mathcal{G}} \oplus \frac{\check{\mathscr{T}}_2}{\sum_{j=1}^n \check{\mathscr{T}}_j} \check{\mathcal{G}} \oplus, \ldots, \oplus \frac{\check{\mathscr{T}}_n}{\sum_{j=1}^n \check{\mathscr{T}}_j} \check{\mathcal{G}} \\
&= \frac{\sum_{j=1}^n \check{\mathscr{T}}_j}{\sum_{j=1}^n \check{\mathscr{T}}_j} \check{\mathcal{G}} \\
&= \check{\mathcal{G}}
\end{aligned}$$

Appendix A.2

Here, $\check{\mathcal{G}}_1 = (0, 1)$, then by definition of the score function, we have,

$$\mathscr{H}(\check{\mathcal{G}}_1) = 0$$

Since,

$$\check{\mathscr{T}}_j = \prod_{k=1}^{j-1} \mathscr{H}(\check{\mathcal{G}}_k) \qquad (j = 2, \ldots, n), \quad \text{and} \quad \check{\mathscr{T}}_1 = 1$$

$\mathscr{H}(\check{\mathcal{G}}_k)$ is the score of the kth q-ROFN.

We have
$\mathscr{T}_j = \prod_{k=1}^{j-1} \mathscr{H}(\check{\mathcal{G}}_k) = \mathscr{H}(\check{\mathcal{G}}_1) \times \mathscr{H}(\check{\mathcal{G}}_2) \times \ldots \times \mathscr{H}(\check{\mathcal{G}}_{j-1}) = 0 \times \mathscr{H}(\check{\mathcal{G}}_2) \times \ldots \times \mathscr{H}(\check{\mathcal{G}}_{j-1}) \quad (j = 2, \ldots, n)$:

$$\prod_{k=1}^{j} \mathscr{T}_j = 1$$

From Definition 8, we have:

$$\begin{aligned} \text{q-ROFPWA}(\check{\mathcal{G}}_1, \check{\mathcal{G}}_2, \ldots, \check{\mathcal{G}}_n) &= \frac{\mathscr{T}_1}{\sum_{j=1}^n \mathscr{T}_j} \check{\mathcal{G}}_1 \oplus \frac{\mathscr{T}_2}{\sum_{j=1}^n \mathscr{T}_j} \check{\mathcal{G}}_2 \oplus, \ldots, \oplus \frac{\mathscr{T}_n}{\sum_{j=1}^n \mathscr{T}_j} \check{\mathcal{G}}_n \\ &= \frac{1}{1} \check{\mathcal{G}}_1 \oplus \frac{0}{1} \check{\mathcal{G}}_2 \oplus \ldots \frac{0}{1} \check{\mathcal{G}}_n \\ &= \check{\mathcal{G}}_1 = (0, 1) \end{aligned}$$

Appendix A.3

Here, $\mathscr{Y}_j^* \geq \mathscr{Y}_j$ and $\mathscr{X}_j^* \leq \mathscr{X}_j$ for all j, if $\mathscr{Y}_j^* \geq \mathscr{Y}_j$.

$\Leftrightarrow (\mathscr{Y}_j^*)^q \geq (\mathscr{Y}_j)^q \Leftrightarrow \sqrt[q]{(\mathscr{Y}_j^*)^q} \geq \sqrt[q]{(\mathscr{Y}_j)^q} \Leftrightarrow \sqrt[q]{1 - (\mathscr{Y}_j^*)^q} \leq \sqrt[q]{1 - (\mathscr{Y}_j)^q}$

$\Leftrightarrow \sqrt[q]{(1 - (\mathscr{Y}_j^*)^q)^{\frac{\mathscr{T}_j}{\sum_{j=1}^n \mathscr{T}_j}}} \leq \sqrt[q]{(1 - (\mathscr{Y}_j)^q)^{\frac{\mathscr{T}_j}{\sum_{j=1}^n \mathscr{T}_j}}}$

$\Leftrightarrow \sqrt[q]{\prod_{j=1}^n (1 - (\mathscr{Y}_j^*)^q)^{\frac{\mathscr{T}_j}{\sum_{j=1}^n \mathscr{T}_j}}} \leq \sqrt[q]{\prod_{j=1}^n (1 - (\mathscr{Y}_j)^q)^{\frac{\mathscr{T}_j}{\sum_{j=1}^n \mathscr{T}_j}}}$

$\Leftrightarrow \sqrt[q]{1 - \prod_{j=1}^n (1 - (\mathscr{Y}_j)^q)^{\frac{\mathscr{T}_j}{\sum_{j=1}^n \mathscr{T}_j}}} \leq \sqrt[q]{1 - \prod_{j=1}^n (1 - (\mathscr{Y}_j^*)^q)^{\frac{\mathscr{T}_j}{\sum_{j=1}^n \mathscr{T}_j}}}$

Now,
$\mathscr{X}_j^* \leq \mathscr{X}_j$.

$\Leftrightarrow (\mathscr{X}_j^*)^{\frac{\mathscr{T}_j}{\sum_{j=1}^n \mathscr{T}_j}} \leq (\mathscr{X}_j)^{\frac{\mathscr{T}_j}{\sum_{j=1}^n \mathscr{T}_j}}$

$\Leftrightarrow \prod_{j=1}^n (\mathscr{X}_j^*)^{\frac{\mathscr{T}_j}{\sum_{j=1}^n \mathscr{T}_j}} \leq \prod_{j=1}^n (\mathscr{X}_j)^{\frac{\mathscr{T}_j}{\sum_{j=1}^n \mathscr{T}_j}}$

Let

$$\overline{\check{\mathcal{G}}} = \text{q-ROFPWA}(\check{\mathcal{G}}_1, \check{\mathcal{G}}_2, \ldots, \check{\mathcal{G}}_n)$$

and:

$$\overline{\check{\mathcal{G}}^*} = \text{q-ROFPWA}(\check{\mathcal{G}}_1^*, \check{\mathcal{G}}_2^*, \ldots, \check{\mathcal{G}}_n^*)$$

We get that $\overline{\check{\mathcal{G}}^*} \geq \overline{\check{\mathcal{G}}}$. Therefore,

$$\text{q-ROFPWA}(\check{\mathcal{G}}_1, \check{\mathcal{G}}_2, \ldots, \check{\mathcal{G}}_n) \leq \text{q-ROFPWA}(\check{\mathcal{G}}_1^*, \check{\mathcal{G}}_2^*, \ldots, \check{\mathcal{G}}_n^*)$$

Appendix A.4

Since,

$$min_j\,(\mathscr{Y}_j) \leq \mathscr{Y}_j \leq max_j\,(\mathscr{Y}_j) \tag{A1}$$

and:

$$min_j\,(\mathscr{X}_j) \leq \mathscr{X}_j \leq max_j\,(\mathscr{X}_j) \tag{A2}$$

From Equation (A1), we have,

$$min_j\left(\mathscr{Y}_j\right) \leq \mathscr{Y}_j \leq max_j\left(\mathscr{Y}_j\right)$$

$$\Leftrightarrow \sqrt[q]{min_j\left(\mathscr{Y}_j\right)^q} \leq \sqrt[q]{\left(\mathscr{Y}_j\right)^q} \leq \sqrt[q]{max_j\left(\mathscr{Y}_j\right)^q}$$

$$\Leftrightarrow \sqrt[q]{1 - max_j\left(\mathscr{Y}_j\right)^q} \leq \sqrt[q]{1 - \left(\mathscr{Y}_j\right)^q} \leq \sqrt[q]{1 - min_j\left(\mathscr{Y}_j\right)^q}$$

$$\Leftrightarrow \sqrt[q]{\left(1 - max_j\left(\mathscr{Y}_j\right)^q\right)^{\frac{\mathscr{T}_j}{\sum_{j=1}^{n}\mathscr{T}_j}}} \leq \sqrt[q]{\left(1 - \left(\mathscr{Y}_j\right)^q\right)^{\frac{\mathscr{T}_j}{\sum_{j=1}^{n}\mathscr{T}_j}}} \leq \sqrt[q]{\left(1 - min_j\left(\mathscr{Y}_j\right)^q\right)^{\frac{\mathscr{T}_j}{\sum_{j=1}^{n}\mathscr{T}_j}}}$$

$$\Leftrightarrow \sqrt[q]{\prod_{j=1}^{n}\left(1 - max_j\left(\mathscr{Y}_j\right)^q\right)^{\frac{\mathscr{T}_j}{\sum_{j=1}^{n}\mathscr{T}_j}}} \leq \sqrt[q]{\prod_{j=1}^{n}\left(1 - \left(\mathscr{Y}_j\right)^q\right)^{\frac{\mathscr{T}_j}{\sum_{j=1}^{n}\mathscr{T}_j}}} \leq \sqrt[q]{\prod_{j=1}^{n}\left(1 - min_j\left(\mathscr{Y}_j\right)^q\right)^{\frac{\mathscr{T}_j}{\sum_{j=1}^{n}\mathscr{T}_j}}}$$

$$\Leftrightarrow \sqrt[q]{1 - max_j\left(\mathscr{Y}_j\right)^q} \leq \sqrt[q]{\prod_{j=1}^{n}\left(1 - \left(\mathscr{Y}_j\right)^q\right)^{\frac{\mathscr{T}_j}{\sum_{j=1}^{n}\mathscr{T}_j}}} \leq \sqrt[q]{1 - min_j\left(\mathscr{Y}_j\right)^q}$$

$$\Leftrightarrow \sqrt[q]{-1 + min_j\left(\mathscr{Y}_j\right)^q} \leq \sqrt[q]{-\prod_{j=1}^{n}\left(1 - \left(\mathscr{Y}_j\right)^q\right)^{\frac{\mathscr{T}_j}{\sum_{j=1}^{n}\mathscr{T}_j}}} \leq \sqrt[q]{-1 + max_j\left(\mathscr{Y}_j\right)^q}$$

$$\Leftrightarrow \sqrt[q]{1 - 1 + min_j\left(\mathscr{Y}_j\right)^q} \leq \sqrt[q]{1 - \prod_{j=1}^{n}\left(1 - \left(\mathscr{Y}_j\right)^q\right)^{\frac{\mathscr{T}_j}{\sum_{j=1}^{n}\mathscr{T}_j}}} \leq \sqrt[q]{1 - 1 + max_j\left(\mathscr{Y}_j\right)^q}$$

$$\Leftrightarrow \sqrt[q]{min_j\left(\mathscr{Y}_j\right)^q} \leq \sqrt[q]{1 - \prod_{j=1}^{n}\left(1 - \left(\mathscr{Y}_j\right)^q\right)^{\frac{\mathscr{T}_j}{\sum_{j=1}^{n}\mathscr{T}_j}}} \leq \sqrt[q]{max_j\left(\mathscr{Y}_j\right)^q}$$

$$\Leftrightarrow min_j\left(\mathscr{Y}_j\right)^q \leq \sqrt[q]{1 - \prod_{j=1}^{n}\left(1 - \left(\mathscr{Y}_j\right)^q\right)^{\frac{\mathscr{T}_j}{\sum_{j=1}^{n}\mathscr{T}_j}}} \leq max_j\left(\mathscr{Y}_j\right)^q$$

From Equation (A2), we have,

$$min_j(\mathscr{X}_j) \leq \mathscr{X}_j \leq max_j(\mathscr{X}_j) \Leftrightarrow min_j(\mathscr{X}_j)^{\frac{\mathscr{F}_j}{\sum_{j=1}^{n}\mathscr{F}_j}} \leq (\mathscr{X}_j)^{\frac{\mathscr{F}_j}{\sum_{j=1}^{n}\mathscr{F}_j}} \leq max_j(\mathscr{X}_j)^{\frac{\mathscr{F}_j}{\sum_{j=1}^{n}\mathscr{F}_j}}$$

$$\Leftrightarrow \prod_{j=1}^{n} min_j(\mathscr{X}_j)^{\frac{\mathscr{F}_j}{\sum_{j=1}^{n}\mathscr{F}_j}} \leq \prod_{j=1}^{n}(\mathscr{X}_j)^{\frac{\mathscr{F}_j}{\sum_{j=1}^{n}\mathscr{F}_j}} \leq \prod_{j=1}^{n} max_j(\mathscr{X}_j)^{\frac{\mathscr{F}_j}{\sum_{j=1}^{n}\mathscr{F}_j}}$$

$$\Leftrightarrow min_j(\mathscr{X}_j)^{\frac{\mathscr{F}_j}{\sum_{j=1}^{n}\mathscr{F}_j}} \leq \prod_{j=1}^{n}(\mathscr{X}_j)^{\frac{\mathscr{F}_j}{\sum_{j=1}^{n}\mathscr{F}_j}} \leq max_j(\mathscr{X}_j)^{\frac{\mathscr{F}_j}{\sum_{j=1}^{n}\mathscr{F}_j}}$$

Let:

$$\text{q-ROFPWA}(\check{\mathcal{G}}_1, \check{\mathcal{G}}_2, \ldots, \check{\mathcal{G}}_n) = \check{\mathcal{G}} = (\mathscr{Y}, \mathscr{X})$$

Then, $\mathscr{H}(\check{\mathcal{G}}) = \mathscr{Y}^q - \mathscr{X}^q \leq max_j(\mathscr{Y})^q - min_j(\mathscr{X})^q = \mathscr{H}(\check{\mathcal{G}}_{max})$. Therefore, $\mathscr{H}(\check{\mathcal{G}}) \leq \mathscr{H}(\check{\mathcal{G}}_{max})$.

Again, $\mathscr{H}(\check{\mathcal{G}}) = \mathscr{Y}^q - \mathscr{X}^q \geq min_j(\mathscr{Y})^q - max_j(\mathscr{X})^q = \mathscr{H}(\check{\mathcal{G}}_{min})$. Therefore, $\mathscr{H}(\check{\mathcal{G}}) \geq \mathscr{H}(\check{\mathcal{G}}_{min})$.

If, $\mathscr{H}(\check{\mathcal{G}}) \leq \mathscr{H}(\check{\mathcal{G}}_{max})$ and $\mathscr{H}(\check{\mathcal{G}}) \geq \mathscr{H}(\check{\mathcal{G}}_{min})$, then:

$$\check{\mathcal{G}}_{min} \leq \text{q-ROFPWA}(\check{\mathcal{G}}_1, \check{\mathcal{G}}_2, \ldots, \check{\mathcal{G}}_n) \leq \check{\mathcal{G}}_{max} \tag{A3}$$

If $\mathscr{H}(\check{\mathcal{G}}) = \mathscr{H}(\check{\mathcal{G}}_{max})$, then $\mathscr{Y}^q - \mathscr{X}^q = max_j(\mathscr{Y})^q - min_j(\mathscr{X})^q$:

$$\Leftrightarrow \mathscr{Y}^q - \mathscr{X}^q = max_j(\mathscr{Y})^q - min_j(\mathscr{X})^q$$
$$\Leftrightarrow \mathscr{Y}^q = max_j(\mathscr{Y})^q, \quad \mathscr{X}^q = min_j(\mathscr{X})^q$$
$$\Leftrightarrow \mathscr{Y} = max_j\,\mathscr{Y}, \quad \mathscr{X} = min_j\,\mathscr{X}$$

Now, $H(\check{\mathcal{G}}) = \mathscr{Y}^q + \mathscr{X}^q = max_j(\mathscr{Y})^q + min_j(\mathscr{X})^q = H(\check{\mathcal{G}}_{max})$:

$$\text{q-ROFPWA}(\check{\mathcal{G}}_1, \check{\mathcal{G}}_2, \ldots, \check{\mathcal{G}}_n) = \check{\mathcal{G}}_{max} \tag{A4}$$

If $\mathscr{H}(\check{\mathcal{G}}) = \mathscr{H}(\check{\mathcal{G}}_{min})$, then $\mathscr{Y}^q - \mathscr{X}^q = min_j(\mathscr{Y})^q - max_j(\mathscr{X})^q$:

$$\Leftrightarrow \mathscr{Y}^q - \mathscr{X}^q = min_j(\mathscr{Y})^q - max_j(\mathscr{X})^q$$
$$\Leftrightarrow \mathscr{Y}^q = min_j(\mathscr{Y})^q, \quad \mathscr{X}^q = max_j(\mathscr{X})^q$$
$$\Leftrightarrow \mathscr{Y} = min_j\,\mathscr{Y}, \quad \mathscr{X} = max_j\,\mathscr{X}$$

Now, $H(\check{\mathcal{G}}) = \mathscr{Y}^q + \mathscr{X}^q = min_j(\mathscr{Y})^q + max_j(\mathscr{X})^q = H(\check{\mathcal{G}}_{max})$:

$$\text{q-ROFPWA}(\check{\mathcal{G}}_1, \check{\mathcal{G}}_2, \ldots, \check{\mathcal{G}}_n) = \check{\mathcal{G}}_{min} \tag{A5}$$

Thus, from Equations (A3)–(A5), we get:

$$\check{\mathcal{G}}^{-} \leq \text{q-ROFPWA}(\check{\mathcal{G}}_1, \check{\mathcal{G}}_2, \ldots, \check{\mathcal{G}}_n) \leq \check{\mathcal{G}}^{+}$$

Appendix A.5

Here, we just prove Theorems 1 and 3.

Proof of Theorem 1. Since,

$$\check{\mathcal{G}}_j \oplus \beta = \left(1 - (1 - (\mathscr{Y}_j)^q)(1 - (\mathscr{Y}_\beta)^q), \mathscr{X}_j \mathscr{X}_\beta\right)$$

By Theorem 3,

q-ROFPWA$(\check{\mathcal{G}}_1 \oplus \beta, \check{\mathcal{G}}_2 \oplus \beta, \ldots, \check{\mathcal{G}}_n \oplus \beta)$:

$$= \left\langle \sqrt[q]{(1 - \prod_{j=1}^{n} \left((1 - \mathscr{Y}_j^q)(1 - (\mathscr{Y}_\beta)^q)\right)^{\frac{\mathscr{T}_j}{\sum_{j=1}^n \mathscr{T}_j}}}, \prod_{j=1}^{n} \left(\mathscr{X}_\beta \mathscr{X}_j\right)^{\frac{\mathscr{T}_j}{\sum_{j=1}^n \mathscr{T}_j}} \right\rangle$$

$$= \left\langle \sqrt[q]{(1 - \left(1 - (\mathscr{Y}_\beta)^q\right)^{\frac{\mathscr{T}_j}{\sum_{j=1}^n \mathscr{T}_j}} \prod_{j=1}^{n} \left(1 - (\mathscr{Y}_j)^q\right)^{\frac{\mathscr{T}_j}{\sum_{j=1}^n \mathscr{T}_j}}}, \left(\mathscr{X}_\beta\right)^{\frac{\mathscr{T}_j}{\sum_{j=1}^n \mathscr{T}_j}} \prod_{j=1}^{n} \left(\mathscr{X}_j\right)^{\frac{\mathscr{T}_j}{\sum_{j=1}^n \mathscr{T}_j}} \right\rangle$$

$$= \left\langle \sqrt[q]{(1 - \left(1 - (\mathscr{Y}_\beta)^q\right) \prod_{j=1}^{n} \left(1 - (\mathscr{Y}_j)^q\right)^{\frac{\mathscr{T}_j}{\sum_{j=1}^n \mathscr{T}_j}}}, \left(\mathscr{X}_\beta\right) \prod_{j=1}^{n} \left(\mathscr{X}_j\right)^{\frac{\mathscr{T}_j}{\sum_{j=1}^n \mathscr{T}_j}} \right\rangle$$

Now, by the operational laws of q-ROFNs,

$$\text{q-ROFPWA}(\check{\mathcal{G}}_1, \check{\mathcal{G}}_2, \ldots, \check{\mathcal{G}}_n) \oplus \beta$$

$$= \left\langle \sqrt[q]{(1 - \prod_{j=1}^{n} (1 - \mathscr{Y}_j^q)^{\frac{\mathscr{T}_j}{\sum_{j=1}^n \mathscr{T}_j}}}, \prod_{j=1}^{n} \mathscr{X}_j^{\frac{\mathscr{T}_j}{\sum_{j=1}^n \mathscr{T}_j}} \right\rangle \oplus \langle \mathscr{Y}_\beta, \mathscr{X}_\beta \rangle$$

$$= \left\langle \sqrt[q]{(1 - \left(1 - (\mathscr{Y}_\beta)^q\right) \prod_{j=1}^{n} \left(1 - (\mathscr{Y}_j)^q\right)^{\frac{\mathscr{T}_j}{\sum_{j=1}^n \mathscr{T}_j}}}, \left(\mathscr{X}_\beta\right) \prod_{j=1}^{n} \left(\mathscr{X}_j\right)^{\frac{\mathscr{T}_j}{\sum_{j=1}^n \mathscr{T}_j}} \right\rangle$$

Thus,

$$\text{q-ROFPWA}(\check{\mathcal{G}}_1 \oplus \beta, \check{\mathcal{G}}_2 \oplus \beta, \ldots, \check{\mathcal{G}}_n \oplus \beta) = \text{q-ROFPWA}(\check{\mathcal{G}}_1, \check{\mathcal{G}}_2, \ldots, \check{\mathcal{G}}_n) \oplus \beta$$

□

Proof of Theorem 3. According to Theorem 3,

q-ROFPWA$(\check{\mathcal{G}}_1 \oplus \beta_2, \check{\mathcal{G}}_2 \oplus \beta_2, \ldots, \check{\mathcal{G}}_n \oplus \beta_n)$

$$= \left\langle \sqrt[q]{(1 - \prod_{j=1}^{n} \left((1 - \mathscr{Y}_j^q)(1 - (\phi_j)^q)\right)^{\frac{\mathscr{T}_j}{\sum_{j=1}^{n} \mathscr{T}_j}}}, \prod_{j=1}^{n} \left(\varphi_j \mathscr{X}_j\right)^{\frac{\mathscr{T}_j}{\sum_{j=1}^{n} \mathscr{T}_j}} \right\rangle$$

$$= \left\langle \sqrt[q]{(1 - \prod_{j=1}^{n} \left(1 - (\phi_j)^q\right)^{\frac{\mathscr{T}_j}{\sum_{j=1}^{n} \mathscr{T}_j}} \prod_{j=1}^{n} \left(1 - \mathscr{Y}_j^q\right)^{\frac{\mathscr{T}_j}{\sum_{j=1}^{n} \mathscr{T}_j}}}, \prod_{j=1}^{n} \left(\varphi_j\right)^{\frac{\mathscr{T}_j}{\sum_{j=1}^{n} \mathscr{T}_j}} \prod_{j=1}^{n} \left(\mathscr{X}_j\right)^{\frac{\mathscr{T}_j}{\sum_{j=1}^{n} \mathscr{T}_j}} \right\rangle$$

Now,

q-ROFPWA$(\check{\mathcal{G}}_1, \check{\mathcal{G}}_2, \ldots, \check{\mathcal{G}}_n) \oplus$ q-ROFPWA$(\beta_1, \beta_2, \ldots, \beta_n)$:

$$= \left\langle \sqrt[q]{(1 - \prod_{j=1}^{n} (1 - \mathscr{Y}_j^q)^{\frac{\mathscr{T}_j}{\sum_{j=1}^{n} \mathscr{T}_j}}}, \prod_{j=1}^{n} \mathscr{X}_j^{\frac{\mathscr{T}_j}{\sum_{j=1}^{n} \mathscr{T}_j}} \right\rangle \oplus \left\langle \sqrt[q]{(1 - \prod_{j=1}^{n} (1 - \mathscr{Y}_j^q)^{\frac{\mathscr{T}_j}{\sum_{j=1}^{n} \mathscr{T}_j}}}, \prod_{j=1}^{n} \mathscr{X}_j^{\frac{\mathscr{T}_j}{\sum_{j=1}^{n} \mathscr{T}_j}} \right\rangle$$

$$= \left\langle \sqrt[q]{(1 - \prod_{j=1}^{n} \left(1 - (\phi_j)^q\right)^{\frac{\mathscr{T}_j}{\sum_{j=1}^{n} \mathscr{T}_j}} \prod_{j=1}^{n} \left(1 - \mathscr{Y}_j^q\right)^{\frac{\mathscr{T}_j}{\sum_{j=1}^{n} \mathscr{T}_j}}}, \prod_{j=1}^{n} \left(\varphi_j\right)^{\frac{\mathscr{T}_j}{\sum_{j=1}^{n} \mathscr{T}_j}} \prod_{j=1}^{n} \left(\mathscr{X}_j\right)^{\frac{\mathscr{T}_j}{\sum_{j=1}^{n} \mathscr{T}_j}} \right\rangle$$

Thus,

q-ROFPWA$(\check{\mathcal{G}}_1 \oplus \beta_2, \check{\mathcal{G}}_2 \oplus \beta_2, \ldots, \check{\mathcal{G}}_n \oplus \beta_n) =$ q-ROFPWA$(\check{\mathcal{G}}_1, \check{\mathcal{G}}_2, \ldots, \check{\mathcal{G}}_n) \oplus$q-ROFPWA$(\beta_1, \beta_2, \ldots, \beta_n)$

□

Appendix B

The first statement is easily followed by Definition 9 and Theorem 8. In the following, we prove this:

$$\text{q-ROFPWG}(\check{\mathcal{G}}_1, \check{\mathcal{G}}_2, \ldots, \check{\mathcal{G}}_n) = \check{\mathcal{G}}_1^{\frac{\widetilde{\mathscr{T}}_1}{\sum_{j=1}^{n} \mathscr{T}_j}} \otimes \check{\mathcal{G}}_2^{\frac{\mathscr{T}_2}{\sum_{j=1}^{n} \mathscr{T}_j}} \otimes, \ldots, \otimes \check{\mathcal{G}}_n^{\frac{\mathscr{T}_n}{\sum_{j=1}^{n} \mathscr{T}_j}} = \left\langle \prod_{j=1}^{n} \mathscr{Y}_j^{\frac{\mathscr{T}_j}{\sum_{j=1}^{n} \mathscr{T}_j}}, \sqrt[q]{(1 - \prod_{j=1}^{n} (1 - \mathscr{X}_j^q)^{\frac{\mathscr{T}_j}{\sum_{j=1}^{n} \mathscr{T}_j}}} \right\rangle$$

To prove this theorem, we use mathematical induction.

For $n = 2$:

$$\check{\mathcal{G}}_1^{\frac{\mathscr{T}_1}{\sum_{j=1}^{n} \mathscr{T}_j}} = \left\langle \mathscr{Y}_1^{\frac{\mathscr{T}_1}{\sum_{j=1}^{n} \mathscr{T}_j}} \right\rangle, \sqrt[q]{1 - (1 - \mathscr{X}_1^q)^{\frac{\mathscr{T}_1}{\sum_{j=1}^{n} \mathscr{T}_j}}}$$

$$\check{\mathcal{G}}_2^{\frac{\mathcal{F}_2}{\sum_{j=1}^n \mathcal{F}_j}} = \left\langle \mathcal{Y}_2^{\frac{\mathcal{F}_1}{\sum_{j=1}^n \mathcal{F}_j}}, \sqrt[q]{1-(1-\mathcal{X}_2^q)^{\frac{\mathcal{F}_1}{\sum_{j=1}^n \mathcal{F}_j}}} \right\rangle$$

Then,

$\check{\mathcal{G}}_1^{\frac{\mathcal{F}_1}{\sum_{j=1}^n \mathcal{F}_j}} \otimes \check{\mathcal{G}}_2^{\frac{\mathcal{F}_2}{\sum_{j=1}^n \mathcal{F}_j}}$:

$$= \left\langle \mathcal{Y}_1^{\frac{\mathcal{F}_1}{\sum_{j=1}^n \mathcal{F}_j}} \sqrt[q]{1-(1-\mathcal{X}_1^q)^{\frac{\mathcal{F}_1}{\sum_{j=1}^n \mathcal{F}_j}}} \right\rangle \otimes \left\langle \mathcal{Y}_2^{\frac{\mathcal{F}_1}{\sum_{j=1}^n \mathcal{F}_j}}, \sqrt[q]{1-(1-\mathcal{X}_2^q)^{\frac{\mathcal{F}_1}{\sum_{j=1}^n \mathcal{F}_j}}} \right\rangle$$

$$= \left\langle \mathcal{Y}_1^{\frac{\mathcal{F}_1}{\sum_{j=1}^n \mathcal{F}_j}} . \mathcal{Y}_2^{\frac{\mathcal{F}_1}{\sum_{j=1}^n \mathcal{F}_j}}, \sqrt[q]{(1-(1-\mathcal{X}_1^q)^{\frac{\mathcal{F}_1}{\sum_{j=1}^n \mathcal{F}_j}} + 1-(1-\mathcal{X}_2^q)^{\frac{\mathcal{F}_1}{\sum_{j=1}^n \mathcal{F}_j}} - \left((1-(1-\mathcal{X}_1^q)^{\frac{\mathcal{F}_1}{\sum_{j=1}^n \mathcal{F}_j}}\right)\left((1-(1-\mathcal{X}_2^q)^{\frac{\mathcal{F}_1}{\sum_{j=1}^n \mathcal{F}_j}}\right)} \right\rangle$$

$$= \left\langle \mathcal{Y}_1^{\frac{\mathcal{F}_1}{\sum_{j=1}^n \mathcal{F}_j}} . \mathcal{Y}_2^{\frac{\mathcal{F}_1}{\sum_{j=1}^n \mathcal{F}_j}}, \sqrt[q]{1-(1-\mathcal{X}_1^q)^{\frac{\mathcal{F}_1}{\sum_{j=1}^n \mathcal{F}_j}} + 1-(1-\mathcal{X}_2^q)^{\frac{\mathcal{F}_1}{\sum_{j=1}^n \mathcal{F}_j}} - \left(1-(1-\mathcal{X}_2^q)^{\frac{\mathcal{F}_1}{\sum_{j=1}^n \mathcal{F}_j}} - (1-\mathcal{X}_1^q)^{\frac{\mathcal{F}_1}{\sum_{j=1}^n \mathcal{F}_j}} + (1-\mathcal{X}_2^q)^{\frac{\mathcal{F}_1}{\sum_{j=1}^n \mathcal{F}_j}}(1-\mathcal{X}_1^q)^{\frac{\mathcal{F}_1}{\sum_{j=1}^n \mathcal{F}_j}}\right)} \right\rangle$$

$$= \left\langle \mathcal{Y}_1^{\frac{\mathcal{F}_1}{\sum_{j=1}^n \mathcal{F}_j}} . \mathcal{Y}_2^{\frac{\mathcal{F}_1}{\sum_{j=1}^n \mathcal{F}_j}}, \sqrt[q]{1-(1-\mathcal{X}_1^q)^{\frac{\mathcal{F}_1}{\sum_{j=1}^n \mathcal{F}_j}}(1-\mathcal{X}_2^q)^{\frac{\mathcal{F}_1}{\sum_{j=1}^n \mathcal{F}_j}}} \right\rangle$$

$$= \left\langle \prod_{j=1}^{2} \mathcal{Y}_j^{\frac{\mathcal{F}_j}{\sum_{j=1}^n \mathcal{F}_j}}, \sqrt[q]{1-\prod_{j=1}^{2}(1-\mathcal{X}_j^q)^{\frac{\mathcal{F}_j}{\sum_{j=1}^n \mathcal{F}_j}}} \right\rangle$$

This shows that Equation (4) is true for $n = 2$. Now, assume that Equation (4) holds for $n = k$, i.e.,

$$\text{q-ROFPWG}(\check{\mathcal{G}}_1, \check{\mathcal{G}}_2, \ldots, \check{\mathcal{G}}_k) = \left\langle \prod_{j=1}^{k} \mathcal{Y}_j^{\frac{\mathcal{F}_j}{\sum_{j=1}^n \mathcal{F}_j}}, \sqrt[q]{1-\prod_{j=1}^{k}(1-\mathcal{X}_j^q)^{\frac{\mathcal{F}_j}{\sum_{j=1}^n \mathcal{F}_j}}} \right\rangle$$

Now, $n = k + 1$. By operational laws of q-ROFNs, we have

q-ROFPWG$(\breve{\mathcal{G}}_1, \breve{\mathcal{G}}_2, \ldots, \breve{\mathcal{G}}_{k+1})$ = q-ROFPWG$(\breve{\mathcal{G}}_1, \breve{\mathcal{G}}_2, \ldots, \breve{\mathcal{G}}_k) \otimes \breve{\mathcal{G}}_{k+1}$:

$$= \left\langle \prod_{j=1}^{k} \mathscr{Y}_j^{\frac{\mathscr{T}_j}{\sum_{j=1}^n \mathscr{T}_j}}, \sqrt[q]{1 - \prod_{j=1}^{k}(1 - \mathscr{X}_j^q)^{\frac{\mathscr{T}_j}{\sum_{j=1}^n \mathscr{T}_j}}} \right\rangle \otimes \left\langle \mathscr{Y}_{k+1}^{\frac{\mathscr{T}_{k+1}}{\sum_{j=1}^n \mathscr{T}_j}}, \sqrt[q]{1 - (1 - \mathscr{X}_{k+1}^q)^{\frac{\mathscr{T}_{k+1}}{\sum_{j=1}^n \mathscr{T}_j}}} \right\rangle$$

$$= \left\langle \prod_{j=1}^{k} \mathscr{Y}_k^{\frac{\mathscr{T}_j}{\sum_{j=1}^n \mathscr{T}_j}} . \mathscr{Y}_{k=1}^{\frac{\mathscr{T}_{k+1}}{\sum_{j=1}^n \mathscr{T}_j}}, \sqrt[q]{1 - \prod_{j=1}^{k}(1 - \mathscr{X}_k^q)^{\frac{\mathscr{T}_j}{\sum_{j=1}^n \mathscr{T}_j}} + 1 - (1 - \mathscr{X}_{k+1}^q)^{\frac{\mathscr{T}_{k+1}}{\sum_{j=1}^n \mathscr{T}_j}} - \left(1 - \prod_{j=1}^{k}(1 - \mathscr{X}_k^q)^{\frac{\mathscr{T}_j}{\sum_{j=1}^n \mathscr{T}_j}}\right)\left(1 - (1 - \mathscr{X}_{k+1}^q)^{\frac{\mathscr{T}_{k+1}}{\sum_{j=1}^n \mathscr{T}_j}}\right)} \right\rangle$$

$$= \left\langle \prod_{j=1}^{k} \mathscr{Y}_k^{\frac{\mathscr{T}_j}{\sum_{j=1}^n \mathscr{T}_j}} . \mathscr{Y}_{k+1}^{\frac{\mathscr{T}_{k+1}}{\sum_{j=1}^n \mathscr{T}_j}}, \sqrt[q]{1 - \prod_{j=1}^{k}(1 - \mathscr{X}_k^q)^{\frac{\mathscr{T}_j}{\sum_{j=1}^n \mathscr{T}_j}} (1 - \mathscr{X}_{k+1}^q)^{\frac{\mathscr{T}_{k+1}}{\sum_{j=1}^n \mathscr{T}_{k+1}}}} \right\rangle$$

$$= \left\langle \prod_{j=1}^{k+1} \mathscr{Y}_j^{\frac{\mathscr{T}_j}{\sum_{j=1}^n \mathscr{T}_j}}, \sqrt[q]{1 - \prod_{j=1}^{k+1}(1 - \mathscr{X}_j^q)^{\frac{\mathscr{T}_j}{\sum_{j=1}^{k+1} \mathscr{T}_j}}} \right\rangle$$

This shows that for $n = k + 1$,Equation (2) holds. Then,

$$\text{q-ROFPWG}(\breve{\mathcal{G}}_1, \breve{\mathcal{G}}_2, \ldots, \breve{\mathcal{G}}_n) = \left\langle \prod_{j=1}^{n} \mathscr{Y}_j^{\frac{\mathscr{T}_j}{\sum_{j=1}^n \mathscr{T}_j}}, \sqrt[q]{(1 - \prod_{j=1}^{n}(1 - \mathscr{X}_j^q)^{\frac{\mathscr{T}_j}{\sum_{j=1}^n \mathscr{T}_j}}} \right\rangle$$

Appendix B.1

From Definition 8, we have:

$$\begin{aligned} \text{q-ROFPWG}(\breve{\mathcal{G}}_1, \breve{\mathcal{G}}_2, \ldots, \breve{\mathcal{G}}_n) &= \breve{\mathcal{G}}_1^{\frac{\widetilde{\mathscr{T}}_1}{\sum_{j=1}^n \mathscr{T}_j}} \otimes \breve{\mathcal{G}}_2^{\frac{\mathscr{T}_2}{\sum_{j=1}^n \mathscr{T}_j}} \otimes, \ldots, \otimes \breve{\mathcal{G}}_n^{\frac{\mathscr{T}_n}{\sum_{j=1}^n \mathscr{T}_j}} \\ &= \breve{\mathcal{G}}^{\frac{\widetilde{\mathscr{T}}_1}{\sum_{j=1}^n \mathscr{T}_j}} \otimes \breve{\mathcal{G}}^{\frac{\mathscr{T}_2}{\sum_{j=1}^n \mathscr{T}_j}} \otimes, \ldots, \otimes \breve{\mathcal{G}}^{\frac{\mathscr{T}_n}{\sum_{j=1}^n \mathscr{T}_j}} \\ &= \breve{\mathcal{G}}^{\frac{\sum_{j=1}^n \mathscr{T}_j}{\sum_{j=1}^n \mathscr{T}_j}} \\ &= \breve{\mathcal{G}} \end{aligned}$$

Appendix B.2

Here, $\breve{\mathcal{G}}_1 = (0, 1)$, then by the definition of the score function, we have,

$$\mathscr{H}(\breve{\mathcal{G}}_1) = 0$$

Since,

$$\mathscr{T}_j = \prod_{k=1}^{j-1} \mathscr{H}(\breve{\mathcal{G}}_k) \qquad (j = 2, \ldots, n), \quad \text{and} \quad \mathscr{T}_1 = 1$$

$\mathscr{H}(\breve{\mathcal{G}}_k)$ is the score of kth q-ROFN.

We have
$\mathscr{T}_j = \prod_{k=1}^{j-1} \mathscr{H}(\check{\mathcal{G}}_k) = \mathscr{H}(\check{\mathcal{G}}_1) \times \mathscr{H}(\check{\mathcal{G}}_2) \times \ldots \times \mathscr{H}(\check{\mathcal{G}}_{j-1}) = 0 \times \mathscr{H}(\check{\mathcal{G}}_2) \times \ldots \times \mathscr{H}(\check{\mathcal{G}}_{j-1})$ $(j = 2, \ldots, n)$:

$$\prod_{k=1}^{j} \mathscr{T}_j = 1$$

From Definition 8, we have:

$$\begin{aligned}\text{q-ROFPWG}(\check{\mathcal{G}}_1, \check{\mathcal{G}}_2, \ldots, \check{\mathcal{G}}_n) &= \check{\mathcal{G}}_1^{\frac{\mathscr{T}_1}{\sum_{j=1}^n \mathscr{T}_j}} \otimes \check{\mathcal{G}}_2^{\frac{\mathscr{T}_2}{\sum_{j=1}^n \mathscr{T}_j}} \otimes, \ldots, \otimes \check{\mathcal{G}}_n^{\frac{\mathscr{T}_n}{\sum_{j=1}^n \mathscr{T}_j}} \\ &= \check{\mathcal{G}}_1^{\frac{1}{1}} \otimes \check{\mathcal{G}}_2^{\frac{0}{1}} \otimes \ldots \check{\mathcal{G}}_n^{\frac{0}{1}} \\ &= \check{\mathcal{G}}_1 = (0, 1)\end{aligned}$$

Appendix B.3

Here, $\mathscr{X}_j^* \geq \mathscr{X}_j$ and $\mathscr{Y}_j^* \leq \mathscr{Y}_j$ for all j. If $\mathscr{X}_j^* \geq \mathscr{X}_j$.
$\Leftrightarrow (\mathscr{X}_j^*)^q \geq (\mathscr{X}_j)^q \Leftrightarrow \sqrt[q]{(\mathscr{X}_j^*)^q} \geq \sqrt[q]{(\mathscr{X}_j)^q} \Leftrightarrow \sqrt[q]{1 - (\mathscr{X}_j^*)^q} \leq \sqrt[q]{1 - (\mathscr{X}_j)^q}$

$$\Leftrightarrow \sqrt[q]{(1 - (\mathscr{X}_j^*)^q)^{\frac{\mathscr{T}_j}{\sum_{j=1}^n \mathscr{T}_j}}} \leq \sqrt[q]{(1 - (\mathscr{X}_j)^q)^{\frac{\mathscr{T}_j}{\sum_{j=1}^n \mathscr{T}_j}}}$$

$$\Leftrightarrow \sqrt[q]{\prod_{j=1}^n (1 - (\mathscr{X}_j^*)^q)^{\frac{\mathscr{T}_j}{\sum_{j=1}^n \mathscr{T}_j}}} \leq \sqrt[q]{\prod_{j=1}^n (1 - (\mathscr{X}_j)^q)^{\frac{\mathscr{T}_j}{\sum_{j=1}^n \mathscr{T}_j}}}$$

$$\Leftrightarrow \sqrt[q]{1 - \prod_{j=1}^n (1 - (\mathscr{X}_j)^q)^{\frac{\mathscr{T}_j}{\sum_{j=1}^n \mathscr{T}_j}}} \leq \sqrt[q]{1 - \prod_{j=1}^n (1 - (\mathscr{X}_j^*)^q)^{\frac{\mathscr{T}_j}{\sum_{j=1}^n \mathscr{T}_j}}}.$$

Now,
$\mathscr{Y}_j^* \leq \mathscr{Y}_j$.

$$\Leftrightarrow (\mathscr{Y}_j^*)^{\frac{\mathscr{T}_j}{\sum_{j=1}^n \mathscr{T}_j}} \leq (\mathscr{Y}_j)^{\frac{\mathscr{T}_j}{\sum_{j=1}^n \mathscr{T}_j}}$$

$$\Leftrightarrow \prod_{j=1}^n (\mathscr{Y}_j^*)^{\frac{\mathscr{T}_j}{\sum_{j=1}^n \mathscr{T}_j}} \leq \prod_{j=1}^n (\mathscr{Y}_j)^{\frac{\mathscr{T}_j}{\sum_{j=1}^n \mathscr{T}_j}}.$$

Let

$$\overline{\check{\mathcal{G}}} = \text{q-ROFPWG}(\check{\mathcal{G}}_1, \check{\mathcal{G}}_2, \ldots, \check{\mathcal{G}}_n)$$

and:

$$\overline{\check{\mathcal{G}}^*} = \text{q-ROFPWG}(\check{\mathcal{G}}_1^*, \check{\mathcal{G}}_2^*, \ldots, \check{\mathcal{G}}_n^*)$$

We get that $\overline{\check{\mathcal{G}}^*} \geq \overline{\check{\mathcal{G}}}$. Therefore,

$$\text{q-ROFPWG}(\check{\mathcal{G}}_1, \check{\mathcal{G}}_2, \ldots, \check{\mathcal{G}}_n) \leq \text{q-ROFPWG}(\check{\mathcal{G}}_1^*, \check{\mathcal{G}}_2^*, \ldots, \check{\mathcal{G}}_n^*)$$

References

1. Sharma, V.; Chandna, P.; Bhardwaj, A. Green supply chain management related performance indicators in agro industry: A review. *J. Clean. Prod.* **2016**, *141*, 1194–1208. [CrossRef]
2. Sahu, N.K.; Datta, S.; Mahapatra, S.S. Establishing green supplier appraisement plat formu singgrey concepts. *J. Grey Syst.* **2012**, *2*, 395–418.

3. Rao, P. Green the supply chain a new initiative in south East Asia. *Int. J. Oper. Prod. Manag.* **2002**, *22*, 632–655. [CrossRef]
4. Bhutta, K.S.; Huq, F. Supplier selection problem: A comparison of the total cost of ownership and analytic hierarchy process approaches. *Supply Chain Manag. Int. J.* **2002**, *7*, 126–135. [CrossRef]
5. Lee, A.H.I.; Kang, H.Y.; Hsu, C.F.; Hung, H.C. A green supplier selection model for high-tech industry. *Expert Syst. Appl.* **2009**, *36*, 7917–7927. [CrossRef]
6. Chen, H.M.W.; Chou, S.Y.; Luu, Q.D.; Yu, H.K. A fuzzy MCDM approach for green supplier selection from the economic and environmental aspects. *Math. Probl. Eng.* **2016**, *2016*, 1–10.
7. Yazdani, M. An integrated MCDM approach to green supplier selection. *Int. J. Ind. Syst. Eng.* **2014**, *5*, 443–458. [CrossRef]
8. Dobos, I.; Vörösmarty, G. Green supplier selection and evaluation using DEA-type composite indicators. *Int. J. Prod. Econ.* **2014**, *157*, 273–278. [CrossRef]
9. Kuo, T.C.; Hsu, C.W.; Li, J.Y. Developing a green supplier selection model by using the DANP with VIKOR. *Sustainability* **2015**, *7*, 1661–1689. [CrossRef]
10. Banaeian, N.; Mobli, H.; Fahimnia, B.; Nielsen, I.E.; Omid, M. Green supplier selection using fuzzy group decision making methods: A case study from the agri-food industry. *Comput. Oper. Res.* **2017**, *89*, 337–347. [CrossRef]
11. Govindan, K.; Kadzinski, M.; Sivakumar, R. Application of a novel PROMETHEE-based method for construction of a group compromise ranking to prioritization of green suppliers in food supply chain. *Omega* **2016**, *71*, 129–145. [CrossRef]
12. Quan, M.Y.; Wang, Z.L.; Liu, H.C.; Shi, H.A. Hybrid MCDM approach for large group green supplier selection with uncertain linguistic information. *IEEE Access* **2018**, *6*, 50372–50383. [CrossRef]
13. Young, A.; Kielkiewicz-Young, A. Sustainable supply network management. *Corp. Environ. Strategy.* **2001**, *8*, 260–268. [CrossRef]
14. Wang, R.; Li, Y. A Novel Approach for Green Supplier Selection under a q-Rung Orthopair Fuzzy Environment. *Symmetry* **2018**, *10*, 687. [CrossRef]
15. Wang, J.; Gao, H.; Wei, G.; Wei, Y. Methods for Multiple-Attribute Group Decision Making with q-Rung Interval-Valued Orthopair Fuzzy Information and Their Applications to the Selection of Green Suppliers. *Symmetry* **2019**, *11*, 56. [CrossRef]
16. Wang, J.; Wei, G.; Wei, Y. Models for Green Supplier Selection with Some 2-Tuple Linguistic Neutrosophic Number Bonferroni Mean Operators. *Symmetry* **2018**, *10*, 131. [CrossRef]
17. Srivastava, S. Green supply chain management A state of the art literature review. *Int. J. Mang. Rev.* **2007**, *9*, 53–80. [CrossRef]
18. Sharfman, M.; Shaft, T.; Anex, R. The road to cooperative supply-chain environmental management: Trust and uncertainty among proactive firms. *Bus. Strategy Environ.* **2009**, *18*, 1–13. [CrossRef]
19. Rath, R.C. An impact of green marketing on practices of supply chain mangement in Asia: Emerging economic ppportunities and challanges. *Int. J. Supply Chain Manag.* **2013**, *2*, 78–86.
20. Min, H.; Galle, W.P. Green purchasing strategies: Trends and implication. *J. Supply Chain Manag.* **1997**, *33*, 10–17. [CrossRef]
21. Murphy, P.R.; Poist, R.F. Green logistics strategies: An analysis of usage patterns. *Transp. J.* **2000**, *40*, 5–16.
22. Cruz, J.M.; Matsypura, D. Supply chain networks with corporate social responsibility through integrated environmental decision making. *Int. J. Prod. Res.* **2009**, *47*, 621–648. [CrossRef]
23. Khan, S.A.R.; Dong, Q.L.; Yu, Z. Research on the measuring performance of green supply chain management: In the perspective of China. *Int. J. Eng. Res. Afr.* **2016**, *27*, 167–178. [CrossRef]
24. Mangla, S.; Madaan, J.; Chen, F.T. Analysis of flexible decision strategies for sustainability focused green product recovery system. *Int. J. Prod. Res.* **2013**, *51*, 3428–3442. [CrossRef]
25. Dickson, G. An analysis of vendor selections systems and decisions. *J. Purchasing* **1966**, *2*, 5–17. [CrossRef]
26. Weber, C.; Current, J.; Benton, W. Vender selection criteria and methods. *Eur. J. Oper. Res.* **1991**, *50*, 2–18. [CrossRef]
27. Hu, J. Supplier Selection Determination and Centralized Purchasing Decisions. Ph.D. Thesis, Washington State University, Pullman, WA, USA, 2004.
28. Çelebi, D.; Bayraktar, D. An integrated neural network and data envelopment analysis for supplier evaluation under incomplete information. *Expert Syst. Appl.* **2008**, *35*, 1698–1710. [CrossRef]

29. Seuring, S.; Müller, M. From a literature review to a conceptual framework for sustainable supply chain management. *J. Clean. Prod.* **2008**, *16*, 1699–1710. [CrossRef]
30. Noci, G. Designing green vendor rating systems for the assessment of a supplier's environmental performance. *Eur. J. Purch. Supply Manag.* **1997**, *3*, 103–114. [CrossRef]
31. Handfield, R.; Walton, S.V.; Sroufe, R.; Melnyk, S.A. Applying environmental criteria to supplier assessment: A study in the application of the analytical hierarchy process. *Eur. J. Oper. Res.* **2002**, *141*, 70–87. [CrossRef]
32. Handfield, R.; Walton, S.; Seegers, L.; Melnyk, S. Green value chain practices in the furniture industry. *J. Oper. Manag.* **1997**, *15*, 293–315. [CrossRef]
33. Humphreys, P.K.; Wong, Y.K.; Chan, F.T.S. Integrating environmental criteria into the supplier selection process. *J. Mater. Process. Technol.* **2013**, *138*, 349–356. [CrossRef]
34. Sarkis, J. A strategic decision framework for green supply chain management. *J. Clean. Prod.* **2003**, *11*, 397–409. [CrossRef]
35. Sarkis, J.; Zhu, Q.; Lai, K.H. An organizational theoretic review of green supply chain management literature. *Int. J. Prod. Econ.* **2011**, *130*, 1–15. [CrossRef]
36. Hsu, C.W.; Hu, A.H. Applying hazardous substance management to supplier selection using analytic network process. *J. Clean. Prod.* **2009**, *17*, 255–264. [CrossRef]
37. Zadeh, L.A. Fuzzy sets. *Inf. Control.* **1965**, *8*, 338–353. [CrossRef]
38. Atanassov, K.T. Intuitionistic fuzzy sets. *Fuzzy Sets Syst.* **1986**, *20*, 87–96. [CrossRef]
39. Yager, R.R.; Abbasov, A.M. Pythagorean membership grades, complex numbers, and decision making. *Int. J. Intell. Syst.* **2013**, *28*, 436–452. [CrossRef]
40. Yager, R.R. Pythagorean fuzzy subsets. In Proceedings of the IFSA World Congress and NAFIPS Annual Meeting (IFSA/NAFIPS), Edmonton, AB, Canada, 24–28 June 2013, pp. 57–61.
41. Yager, R.R. Pythagorean membership grades in multi criteria decision making. *IEEE Trans. Fuzzy Syst.* **2014**, *22*, 958–965. [CrossRef]
42. Yager, R.R. Generalized orthopair fuzzy sets. *IEEE Trans. Fuzzy Syst.* **2017**, *25*, 1222–1230. [CrossRef]
43. Ali, M.I. Another view on q-rung orthopair fuzzy sets. *Int. J. Fuzzy Syst.* **2018**, *33*, 2139–2153. [CrossRef]
44. Li, D.F.; Nan, J.X. Extension of the TOPSIS for muti-attribute group decision making under Atanassov IFS environments. *Int. J. Fuzzy Syst. Appl.* **2011**, *1*, 47–61. [CrossRef]
45. Boran, F.E.; Genc, S.; Kurt, M.; Akay, D. A multi-criteria intuitionistic fuzzy group decision making for supplier selection with TOPSIS method. *Expert Syst. Appl.* **2009**, *36*, 11363–11368. [CrossRef]
46. Zhang, X.; Xu, Z.S. Extension of TOPSIS to multiple criteria decision making with pythagorean fuzzy sets. *Int. J. Intell. Syst.* **2014**, *29*, 1061–1078. [CrossRef]
47. Selvachandran, G.; Peng, X.D. A modified TOPSIS method based on vague parameterized vague soft sets and its application to supplier selection problems. *Neural Comput. Appl.* **2018**, 1–16. [CrossRef]
48. Xu, Y.; Shang, X.; Wang, J.; Wu, W.; Huang, H. Some q-Rung Dual Hesitant Fuzzy Heronian Mean Operators with Their Application to Multiple Attribute Group Decision-Making. *Symmetry* **2018**, *10*, 472. [CrossRef]
49. Xu, Z.S. Intuitionistic fuzzy aggregation operators. *IEEE Trans. Fuzzy Syst.* **2007**, *15*, 1179–1187.
50. Xu, Z.S.; Yager, R.R. Some geometric aggregation operators based on intuitionistic fuzzy sets. *Int. J. Gen. Syst.* **2006**, *35*, 417–433. [CrossRef]
51. Xu, Z.S.; Xia, M.M. Induced generalized intuitionitic fuzzy operators. *Knowl.-Based Syst.* **2011**, *24*, 197–209. [CrossRef]
52. Hashmi, M.R.; Riaz, M.; Smarandache, F. m-polar Neutrosophic Topology with Applications to Multi-Criteria Decision-Making in Medical Diagnosis and Clustering Analysis. *Int. J. Fuzzy Syst.* **2020**, *22*, 273–292. [CrossRef]
53. Hashmi, M.R.; Riaz, M. A Novel Approach to Censuses Process by using Pythagorean m-polar Fuzzy Dombi's Aggregation Operators. *J. Intell. Fuzzy Syst.* **2020**, *38*, 1977–1995. [CrossRef]
54. Riaz, M.; Hashmi, M.R. Linear Diophantine fuzzy set and its applications towards multi-attribute decision making problems. *J. Intell. Fuzzy Syst.* **2019**, *37*, 5417–5439. [CrossRef]
55. Riaz, M.; Hashmi, M.R. Soft rough Pythagorean m-polar fuzzy sets and Pythagorean m-polar soft rough fuzzy sets with application to decision making. *Comput. Appl. Math* **2020**, *39*, 1–36. [CrossRef]
56. Riaz, M.; Salabun, W.; Farid, H.M.A.; Ali, N.; Watróbski, J. A robust q-rung orthopair fuzzy information aggregation using Einstein operations with applications to sustainable energy planning decision management. *Energies* **2020**, *13*, 2155. [CrossRef]

57. Riaz, M.; Tehrim, S.T. Cubic bipolar fuzzy ordered weighted geometric aggregation operators and their application using internal and external cubic bipolar fuzzy data. *Comput. Appl. Math* **2019**, *38*, 1–25. [CrossRef]
58. Naeem, K.; Riaz, M.; Peng, X.D.; Afzal, D. Pythagorean Fuzzy Soft MCGDM Methods Based on TOPSIS, VIKOR and Aggregation Operators. *J. Intell. Fuzzy Syst.* **2019**, *37*, 6937–6957. [CrossRef]
59. Feng, F.; Fujita, H.; Ali, M.I.; Yager, R.R. Liu, X. Another view on generalized intuitionistic fuzzy soft sets and related multi-attribute decision making methods. *IEEE Trans. Fuzzy Syst.* **2019**, *27*, 474–488. [CrossRef]
60. Ye, J. Interval-valued hesitant fuzzy prioritized weighted aggregation operators for multi attribute decision making. *J. Algorithms Comput. Technol.* **2013**, *8*, 179–192. [CrossRef]
61. Zhang, H.Y.; Wang, J.Q.; Chen, X.H. Interval neutrosophic sets and their applications in multi-criteria decision making problems. *Sci. World J.* **2014**, *2014*, 1–15. [CrossRef]
62. Zhao, H.; Xu, Z.S.; Ni, M.F.; Lui, S.S. Generalized aggregation operators for intuitionistic fuzzy sets. *Int. J. Intell. Syst.* **2010**, *25*, 1–30. [CrossRef]
63. Wang, W.; Liu, X. Intuitionistic fuzzy information aggregation using Einstein operators. *IEEE Trans. Fuzzy Syst.* **2012**, *20*, 923–938. [CrossRef]
64. Garg, H. A new generalized Pythagorean fuzzy information aggregation using Einstein operators and its applications to decision making. *Int. J. Intell. Syst.* **2016**, 1–35.
65. Liu, P.; Wang, P. Some q-rung orthopair fuzzy aggregation operator and their application to multi-attribute decision making. *Int. J. Intell. Syst.* **2018**, *33*, 259–280. [CrossRef]
66. Yager, R.R. Prioritized aggregation operators. *Int. J. Approx. Reason.* **2008**, *48*, 263–274. [CrossRef]
67. Si, A.; Das, S.; Kar, S. An approach to rank picture fuzzy numbers for decision making problems. *Decision-Mak. Appl. Manag. Eng.* **2019**, *2*, 54–64. [CrossRef]
68. Yusifov, F.; Alguliyev, R.; Aliguliyev, R. Multi-criteria Evaluation + Positional Ranking Approach for Candidate Selection in E-voting. *Decision-Making: Appl. Manag. Eng.* **2019**, *2*, 65–80.
69. Rostamzadeh, R.; Govindan, K.; Esmaeili, A.; Sabaghi, M. Application of fuzzy VIKOR for evaluation of green supply chain mangemennt practices. *Ecol. Indic.* **2015**, *49*, 188–203. [CrossRef]

symmetry

MDPI

Article

Multi-Criteria Decision Model for the Selection of Suppliers in the Textile Industry

Chia-Nan Wang [1,*], Van Tran Hoang Viet [1,*], Thanh Phong Ho [2], Van Thanh Nguyen [2] and Viet Tinh Nguyen [2]

1 Department of Industrial Engineering and Management, National Kaohsiung University of Science and Technology, Kaohsiung 80778, Taiwan

2 Department of Logistics and Supply Chain Management, Hong Bang International University, Ho Chi Minh 723000, Vietnam; phonght@hiu.vn (T.P.H.); thanhnv@hiu.vn (V.T.N.); tinhnv@hiu.vn (V.T.N.)

* Correspondence: cn.wang@nkust.edu.tw (C.-N.W.); vanviet@tnut.edu.vn (V.T.H.V.)

Received: 22 May 2020; Accepted: 5 June 2020; Published: 8 June 2020

Abstract: In recent years, the market of textile and garment materials has been volatile, and the ongoing US-China trade war is creating good opportunities for other markets such as Vietnam, Bangladesh and Mexico to continue to expand their market share in the United States. Vietnam is expected to have great advantages thanks to cheap labor cost and strong production capacity. Raw material supplier selection in a volatile competitive environment is crucial for a company to succeed, and supplier selection is a complicate process in which decision-makers must consider multiple quantitative and qualitative features, along with their symmetrical impact, in order to achieve an optimal result. The purpose of selecting the right supplier is to improve competitiveness and product quality, while satisfying customer demand at a minimum production cost. The aim of this paper is to propose a multicriteria decision making model (MCDM) for garment and textile supplier selection. In the first stage, all criteria affecting this process are defined by using the supply chain operations reference model (SCOR) and experts' opinion. Incorporating hybrid fuzzy set theory into the analytical network process (ANP) model is the most effective tool for addressing complex problems of decision-making, which has a connection with various qualitative criteria; thus, the Fuzzy Analytical Hierarchy Process (FAHP) was applied for determining the weight of all potential suppliers, and the preference ranking organization method for enrichment of evaluations (PROMETHEE II) was used for ranking the supplier. The results of this research will assist researchers and decision makers in identifying, adapting and applying appropriate methods to identify the optimal material suppliers in the textile and garment industry. This research can also be used to support supplier selection decisions in other industries.

Keywords: fuzzy theory; sustainable development; SCOR model; FAHP; PROMETHEE II; textile and garments industry; sustainable supplier selection; MCDM

1. Introduction

At present, the textile and garment industry plays an increasingly important role in the national economy. It not only serves the increasing and diverse needs of the people but also creates many jobs and significantly contributes to the national budget to create conditions for economic development. In Vietnam, the textile and garment industry has made great strides. The average growth rate of the industry is about 30%/year; in the export sector, the average growth rate is 24.8%/year and accounts for 20% of the country's total export turnover [1].

However, according to aggregate data of the Vietnam Textile and garment and Apparel Association (Vitas), the US-China trade conflict has made the total textile and garment demand on the world market increase by only 3.3% in 2019, compared to the up to 7.4% from the previous year [2]. When Vietnam joins the Trans-Pacific Strategic Partnership Agreement (TPP), textile and garment enterprises will enjoy a tax rate of 0%. However, the TPP stipulates that all input materials of this industry must be from the TPP to be eligible for preferential tax rates, while Vietnam's textile and garment and garment industry is still heavily dependent on foreign material supply, accounting for nearly 88% of total demand; most of the countries where Vietnam imports raw materials are not part of the TPP [3]. Thus, raw materials supplier selection in a volatile competitive environment is crucial for a company to succeed.

The selection of material suppliers is an extremely important decision that can enhance a company's competitive advantage significantly by enabling the success of subsequence processes within the production chain. The main objective of a supplier selection process is to reduce purchasing risks, maximize overall value for buyers and develop proximity and long-term relationships between buyers and suppliers. Any supply chain activity begins with sourcing raw materials and ends with product delivery to consumers [4]. A perfect supply chain helps businesses gain many benefits, such as cost savings, competitive product prices. Therefore, choosing the right supplier plays an essential role in determining the success or failure in an organization [5]. Supplier selection is a multicriteria decision process and involves many quantitative and qualitative criteria. Thus, this study aims to develop a multicriteria decision making model (MCDM) for the supplier selection process within Vietnam textile and garments industry, by using the supply chain operations reference model (SCOR), Fuzzy Analytical Hierarchy Process (FAHP) and the preference ranking organization method for enrichment of evaluations (PROMETHEE II). The combination of these decision-making methods is an effective tool for supplier selection and evaluation [6,7].

The contribution of this study is to propose a multi-criteria decision-making model to use in supplier selection, which is considered a useful tool for companies operating to increase competitiveness and minimum production costs in the textile and garment industry.

2. Literature Review

As customers' expectations grow year after year, global companies are facing serious challenges in improving and optimizing their supply chains to satisfy consumers. These challenges are further increased with pressures from global competitions and the dissemination of enterprise information systems and shorter product life cycles, which lead to increasingly complex supply chains and requires more sophisticate management methods [8].

There are many different methods for identifying suppliers' criteria, assessments and selection that have been published in prestigious scientific journals. Govindan et al. [9] successfully applied a multi-criteria decision-making model in the evaluation and selection of environmentally-friendly suppliers. Therefore, it is possible to realize that the problem of supplier selection is an important topic in both scientific research and practical applications.

Choosing a supplier is a multifaceted strategic decision, but few studies have looked at factors such as sustainability and risks. Especially when the selection criteria are subjective and require the judgment of decision makers, and since for each supplier candidate a separate selection criterion dominates, the supplier selection process can become very complicate [10]. To address decision-related issues of sustainability, Multi Criteria Decision Analysis (MCDA) models are often applied to support the decision makers in these processes. However, from the methodological and practical perspective of sustainability assessment, the MCDA method has some shortcomings. To limit decision making errors, researchers have used more methods to reduce decision making errors, such as by combining the PROMETHEE and FAHP method [11,12]. Safari et al. [13] developed an integrated MCDM model for supplier evaluation and selection process. In this research, the weights of the evaluation criteria were determined using Shannon's Entropy, while PROMETHEE was used to rank the potential suppliers in the final stage. Senvar et al. [14] proposed a multi criteria supplier selection model based on a fuzzy PROMETHEE model. The proposed methodology can be used assist decision makers within supply chains in solving similar selection problems.

Chen et al. [15] presented a hybrid framework for third-party logistics service supplier selection process. The authors developed a hybrid decision making model by using linguistic PROMETHEE in combination with maximum deviation method to rank potential logistics service providers, based on criteria from industry experts, customers, and operational data. Dağdeviren [16] integrated an approach based on both AHP and PROMETHEE to solve an equipment selection problem. According to Pan et al. [17], multi-criteria decision-making (MCDM) has not been fully utilized to vendor selection processes. An approach based on AHP and PROMETHEE takes into account the characteristics of strategic sourcing, the index for selection focuses on cooperation and long-term character of suppliers and the method of supplier selection.

Bansal et al. [18] suggested that an AHP-PROMETHEE hybrid model is an effective tool for third-party logistics service supplier selection processes. AHP is employed to calculate the weights of criteria, whereas PROMETHEE ranks potential suppliers according to their performance based on these criteria. Shakey [19] introduced a hybrid AHP-PROMETHEE-2 multicriteria decision making model to support supplier selection processes. The result suggests that the hybrid model can calculate the optimum distribution of order quantities among the selected supplier, which maximizes total purchase value. Sari et al. [20] presented a plausible solution for complex selection problems, by comparing traditional and non-traditional methods. In this research, the authors identified a group of main criteria; including quality, delivery, price, environmental health, financial status, managerial capabilities and working conditions; then, they investigated their interrelations and determined each criterion importance degree. Wang et al. [21] applied a hybrid fuzzy analytical hierarchy process and green data envelopment analysis for the sustainable supplier selection process in edible oil production. Wang et al. [22] proposed an MCDM approach, including the fuzzy analytic network process (FANP) and The Technique for Order of Preference by Similarity to Ideal Solution (TOPSIS) model for solid waste to energy plant location selection in Vietnam. Wang et al. [23] applied the MCDM model for supplier selection in the rice supply chain.

As literature review shows, the amount of studies that have applied the MCDM approach to various fields of science and engineering has been increasing in number over the past years. Supplier selection is one of the fields where the MCDM model has been employed, especially in the garment and textile industry, where decision makers must evaluate both qualitative and quantitative factors. Although some studies have reviewed applications of MCDM approaches in garment supplier selection, very few works have focused on this problem in a fuzzy environment. This is a reason why we proposed a fuzzy MCDM model in this study.

3. Methodology

In this paper, the MCDM model for supplier selection is built through a number of steps, as shown in Figure 1.

3.1. *Theorical Basis*

3.1.1. Supply Chain Operations Reference (SCOR) Model

The problem of analyzing and assessing the current state of the selection process of the company needs to be identified. The criteria evaluated and used in the proposed model are built based on the SCOR model. The SCOR model, also known as the Supply Chain Operations Reference Model, was approved in 1996 and recognized by the Supply Chain Council (SCC) [24]. This model enables corporations to conduct a thorough analysis of their supply chains based on the information of various aspects of the supply chains by providing a set of process details and performance metrics.

As Theeranuphattana et al. [25] stated, the SCOR Model criteria set can be utilized as a business process reference model, providing a specific set of analysis tools for supply chain business processes, best practice metrics. The SCOR model is also an appropriate reference for industrial supply chains. Furthermore, the implementation of the SCOR model enables a common language between partners in a supply chain, as it standardizes definitions, process elements and metrics. The main performance attributes of the SCOR model are shown in Table 1.

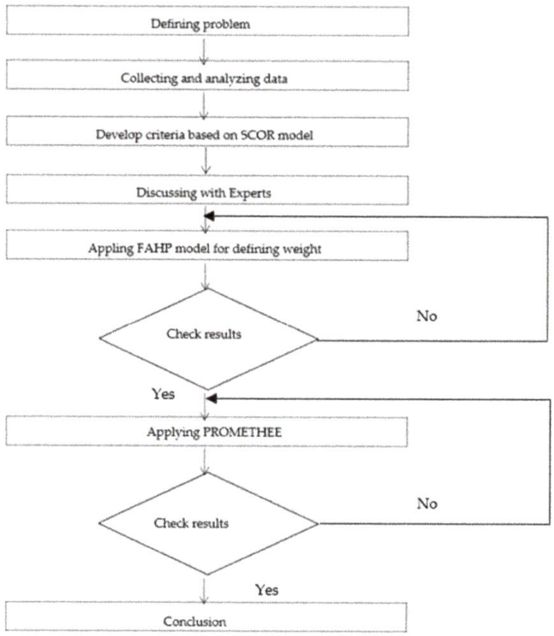

Figure 1. Research graph. SCOR: Supply Chain Operations Reference; FAHP: Fuzzy Analytical Hierarchy Process; PROMETHEE: preference ranking organization method for enrichment of evaluations.

Table 1. The performance attributes of the SCOR model.

Performance Attributes	Definition
Reliability	Capable of fulfilling orders in the best way. With confidence, the focus is on the ability to predict results. For example, delivery on time, high quality and appropriate quantity.
Responsiveness	Express the speed of execution of requests for customers. For example, cycle time.
Flexibility	Able to respond quickly; high speed to increase competitive advantage.
Cost	Costs include operating costs, particularly costs of materials, labor and transportation.
Assets	The ability to use financial resources effectively; being able to quickly execute requests from customers. The ability to use funds, including inventory days and financial uses.

3.1.2. Fuzzy Analytical Hierarchy Process (FAHP)

AHP is a Multiple Criteria Decision Making (MCDM) method that simplifies complex and unclear structured issues by using pairwise comparison matrix to sort criteria [24]. AHP has the main advantage of ranking alternatives in order of effectiveness.

In the AHP model, there are many pairwise comparison metric assembled based on the nine levels of the standardized comparison scale [24]. The AHP method is applied to select the priority level at all levels of the hierarchy according to the pairwise comparison matrix, measured using a scale of 1 to 9 [24].

The Analytical Hierarchy Process, which uses fuzzy theory, is further developed based on AHP. In 1965, Zadeh proposed a theory for use in uncertain environmental conditions [25]. With the application of fuzzy set theory, it can help us better understand and better estimate uncertainty. The degree of dependence of a fuzzy number on certain sets are shown using a fuzzy set. The value of the member function is within the range [0; 1] [26,27]. The Triangular Fuzzy Number (TFN) can be defined as (o, g, p), respectively, with o, g and p ($o \le g \le p$) as parameters, indicating the smallest, most promising TFN and corresponding maximum values. Each degree of membership includes $M^{o(y)}$ (left) and $M^{i(y)}$ (right), which represent the two sides of a fuzzy number:

$$\widetilde{M} = (M^{o(y)}, M^{i(y)}) = [\mathbf{o} + (\mathbf{g} - \mathbf{o})y,\ \mathbf{p} + (\mathbf{g} - \mathbf{p})y], y \in [\mathbf{0}, \mathbf{1}]$$

TFN is shown in Figure 2.

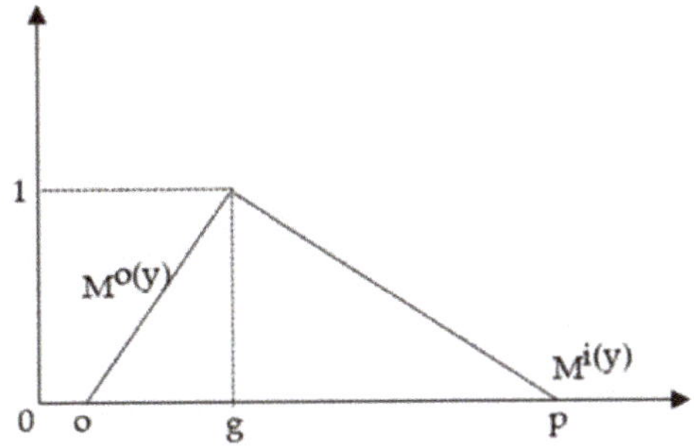

Figure 2. Triangular Fuzzy Number.

3.1.3. Preference Ranking Organization Method for Enrichment of Evaluations (PROMETHEE)

Preference ranking organization method for enrichment of evaluations (PROMETHEE) was introduced by Brans and Vincke in 1985 [28]. PROMETHEE I can enable a partial review of alternative decisions, while PROMETHEE II can evaluate the overall rankings of the alternatives. In this research, the PROMETHEE II was utilized to calculate the ranking of potential suppliers. PROMETHEE II was performed according to these followed steps [29,30]:

Step 1: Normalize the decision matrix:

$$R_{ij} = \frac{[x_{ij} - \min(x_{ij})]}{[\max(x_{ij}) - \min(x_{ij})]}. \quad (1)$$

where x_{ij} is the performance indicator of the ith alternative with reference to the jth criterion. For non-beneficial criteria, Equation (1) can be rearranged as follows:

$$\boldsymbol{R_{ij}} = \frac{[\mathbf{max}(x_{ij}) - x_{ij}]}{[\mathbf{max}(x_{ij}) - \mathbf{min}(x_{ij})]}. \quad (2)$$

Step 2: Determine the differences of the ith alternative in comparison to other alternatives by calculating the pairwise differences in criteria values between the alternatives

Step 3: Determine the preference function, P_j (i,i'). Bran and Mareschal [21] proposed six main type of generalized reference functions [28]. However, these functions require some preferential parameters to be well defined, which, in real world cases, may cause unnecessary difficulties and complexities to the decision makers. Therefore, a simplified preference function is adopted in this study:

$$\begin{gathered} P_j(i, i') = 0 \ \mathit{if}\ R_{ij} \leq R_{i'j}\,, \\ P_j(i, i') = (R_{ij},\ R_{i'j})\ \mathit{if}\ R_{ij} > R_{i'j} \end{gathered} \quad (3)$$

Step 4: Determine the aggregated preference function with respect to the weights of the criteria. The aggregated preference function is as follows:

$$\pi(i,i') = \frac{\left[\sum_{j-1}^{m} w_j \times p_{j(i,i')}\right]}{\sum_{j-1}^{m} w_j \times p_{j(i,i')}}. \tag{4}$$

where w_j is the weight of the j_{th} criterion.

Step 5: Calculate the leaving and entering outranking flows:

$$\begin{aligned} \Phi^+(i) &= \tfrac{1}{n-1} \times \sum_{i'=1}^{n} \pi(i,i') with\ i \neq i' \\ \Phi^-(i) &= \tfrac{1}{n-1} \times \sum_{i'=1}^{n} \pi(i',i) with\ i \neq i'. \end{aligned} \tag{5}$$

where n is the number of alternatives.

In this step, each alternative is compared with $(n-1)$ other alternatives. The leaving flow shows how much the alternative outranks others, whereas the entering flow show how much the alternative is outranked by others. Then, a partial preorder of the alternative can be obtained using PROMETHEE I, or, a complete preorder can be obtained using PROMETHEE II by using a net flow. However, using PROMETHEE II can lead to loss of preference relations information.

Step 6: Determine the net outranking flow for individual alternative:

$$\Phi(i) = \Phi^+(i) - \Phi^-(i). \tag{6}$$

Step 7: Calculate the ranking of all potential alternatives based the value of $\Phi(i)$. The higher value of $\Phi(i)$, the better is the alternative. Thus, the best alternative is the one with the highest $\Phi(i)$ value.

4. Case Study

Vietnam's textile and garment in the international market is said to be currently competitive because of its abundant labor force, high skilled skills and low labor costs when compared to the productivity. However, facing these advantages, Vietnam's textile and garment and garment industry in 2020, besides opportunities and prospects, still faces significant challenges in selecting raw material suppliers. In addition to the tax reduction in the provisions of the EVFTA Agreement, Vietnam's textile and garment products must comply closely with the standards committed in the Agreement such as standards of the origin of raw materials. Thus, the purpose of selecting the right supplier is to improve a company's competitiveness and product quality, while satisfying customer demand at a lower cost.

This study aimed to develop a multicriteria decision making model (MCDM) for the supplier selection process within the Vietnam textile and garments industry, by using the supply chain operations reference model (SCOR), Fuzzy Analytical Hierarchy Process (FAHP) and the preference ranking organization method for enrichment of evaluations (PROMETHEE II). To verify the proposed model, the model will be used to select an optimal supplier from 10 potential suppliers, which is provided by industry experts and head of the purchasing department of a Vietnamese textile company. Ten industry experts were consulted and interviewed to obtain suitable criteria for the model. All criteria affecting to supplier selection process are show in Table 2.

Table 2. Criteria for evaluating supplier define based on the SCOR model.

No.	Main Criteria	Sub-Criteria	Symbol
1	**Reliability (A)**	Delivered the right quantity	A1
		Fulfill an order request	A2
		Delivery performance	A3
2	**Responsiveness (B)**	Order Fulfillment Cycle Time	B1
		Delivery time	B2
		Return processing time	B3
3	**Flexibility (C)**	Order fulfillment lead time	C1
		Production flexibility	C2
4	**Cost (D)**	Transportation cost	D1
		Returns processing cost	D2
		Materials cost	D3
5	**Assets (E)**	Cash to cash cycle time	E1
		Asset turns	E2
		Inventory days of supply	E3
		Inventory value	E4

The industry experts also discussed and provided their inputs based on a 1–9 Saaty scale (Table 3).

Table 3. 1–9 Saaty Scale of Importance Intensities.

Importance Intensity	Definition
1	Equal importance
3	Moderate importance of one over another
5	Essential importance
7	Demonstrated importance
9	Extremely importance
2,4,6,8	Intermediate values

Based on the inputs from the consulted industry experts, the fuzzy comparison matrix of the main criteria from the AHP model are calculated as in Table 4.

Table 4. Fuzzy comparison matrix for the main criteria.

Main Criteria	A	B	C	D	E
A	(1,1,1)	(1,2,3)	(1/5,1/4,1/3)	(1/4,1/3,1/2)	(1,2,3)
B	(1/3,1/2,1/1)	(1,1,1)	(1/3,1/2,1/1)	(1/4,1/3,1/2)	(1,2,3)
C	(3,4,5)	(1,2,3)	(1,1,1)	(1,2,3)	(2,3,4)
D	(2,3,4)	(2,3,4)	(1/3,1/2,1/1)	(1,1,1)	(3,4,5)
E	(1/3,1/2,1/1)	(1/3,1/2,1/1)	(1/4,1/3,1/2)	(1/5,1/4,1/3)	(1,1,1)

The values in Table 5 were converted to real numbers by using the TFN. During the defuzzification, the authors obtained the coefficients $\alpha = 0.5$ and $\beta = 0.5$. Here, α represents the uncertain environment conditions, and β represents the attitude of the evaluator is fair.

Table 5. Real number priority of the main criteria.

Main Criteria	A	B	C	D	E
A	1	2	1/4	1/3	2
B	1/2	1	1/2	1/3	2
C	4	2	1	2	3
D	3	3	1/2	1	4
E	1/2	1/2	1/3	1/4	1

The individual maximum value λ_{max} and weight w of the matrix are calculated as follows:

$$GM1 = (1\times 2\times \frac{1}{4}\times \frac{1}{3}\times 2)^{\frac{1}{5}} = 0.8$$

$$GM2 = (\frac{1}{2}\times 1\times \frac{1}{2}\times \frac{1}{3}\times 2)^{\frac{1}{5}} = 0.7$$

$$GM3 = (4\times 2\times 1\times 2\times 3)^{\frac{1}{5}} = 2.17$$

$$GM4 = (3\times 3\times \frac{1}{2}\times 1\times 4)^{\frac{1}{5}} = 1.78$$

$$GM5 = (\frac{1}{2}\times \frac{1}{2}\times \frac{1}{3}\times \frac{1}{4}\times 1)^{\frac{1}{5}} = 0.46$$

$$\sum GM = 5.91$$

The weights of individual main criteria are calculated as follows:

$$\omega_1 = \frac{0.8027}{5.9140} = 0.14$$

$$\omega_2 = \frac{0.6988}{5.9140} = 0.12$$

$$\omega_3 = \frac{2.6189}{5.9140} = 0.37$$

$$\omega_4 = \frac{1.7826}{5.9140} = 0.3$$

$$\omega_5 = \frac{0.4610}{5.9140} = 0.08$$

$$\begin{bmatrix} 1 & 2 & 1/4 & 1/3 & 2 \\ 1/2 & 1 & 1/2 & 1/3 & 2 \\ 4 & 2 & 1 & 2 & 3 \\ 3 & 3 & 1/2 & 1 & 4 \\ 1/2 & 1/2 & 1/3 & 1/4 & 1 \end{bmatrix} x \begin{bmatrix} 0.14 \\ 0.12 \\ 0.37 \\ 0.30 \\ 0.08 \end{bmatrix} = \begin{bmatrix} 0.72 \\ 0.63 \\ 1.98 \\ 1.56 \\ 0.40 \end{bmatrix}$$

$$\begin{bmatrix} 0.72 \\ 0.63 \\ 1.98 \\ 1.56 \\ 0.40 \end{bmatrix} / \begin{bmatrix} 0.14 \\ 0.12 \\ 0.37 \\ 0.30 \\ 0.08 \end{bmatrix} = \begin{bmatrix} 5.30 \\ 5.30 \\ 5.41 \\ 5.17 \\ 5.16 \end{bmatrix}$$

Based on number of main criteria, the authors found that n = 5; λ_{max} and CI are calculated as follows:

$$\lambda_{max} = \frac{5.30 + 5.30 + 5.41 + 5.17 + 5.16}{5} = 5.27$$

$$CI = \frac{\lambda_{max} - n}{n - 1} = \frac{5.27 - 5}{5 - 1} = 0.07$$

To calculate the CR value, we found that RI = 1.12, with n = 5.

$$CR = \frac{CI}{RI} = \frac{0.07}{1.12} = 0.06$$

Since CR = 0.06 ≤ 0.1, there is no need to re-evaluate. The weights of the main criteria are shown in Table 6.

Table 6. The weights of the main criteria.

Main Criteria	A	B	C	D	E	Weight
A	1	2	1/4	1/3	2	0.14
B	1/2	1	1/2	1/3	2	0.12
C	4	2	1	2	3	0.37
D	3	3	1/2	1	4	0.30
E	1/2	1/2	1/3	1/4	1	0.08
Total						1
CR = 0.06						

The weight of each sub criteria can be calculated based on the weights of main criteria. The calculated weight of each sub criteria using FAHP is shown in Table 7.

Table 7. The weight of the sub criteria.

No	Symbol	Weight
1	A1	0.07
2	A2	0.05
3	A3	0.01
4	B1	0.08
5	B2	0.03
6	B3	0.01
7	C1	0.28
8	C2	0.09
9	D1	0.22
10	D2	0.06
11	D3	0.02
12	E1	0.05
13	E2	0.00
14	E3	0.02
15	E4	0.01

In the next stage, PROMETHEE II was implemented to evaluate and rank the potential suppliers. The results of PROMETHEE II is shown in Table 8.

Table 8. Final ranking from PROMETHEE II.

Supplier	Φ^+(i)	Φ^-(i)	Φ(i)	Ranking
S1	1.46	2.2	-0.74	8
S2	1.04	2.99	-1.95	10
S3	2.23	1.75	0.48	5
S4	1.94	2.55	-0.61	7
S5	2.25	1.71	0.54	4
S6	1.41	1.96	-0.55	6
S7	1.68	2.49	-0.81	9
S8	2.27	1.32	0.95	3
S9	**2.82**	**1.33**	**1.49**	**1**
S10	2.58	1.38	1.20	2

Discussion

Textile enterprises have started to spend a large amount of investment in modern technologies to catch up with the trend of Industry 4.0. There have been many factories investing in public equipment modern technology and robots. Enterprises have been providing solutions to change the product structure and promote exports of high value goods. The selection of material suppliers is an extremely important decision that can enhance a company's competitive advantage significantly by enabling the success of subsequence processes within the production chain. The main objective of a supplier selection process is to reduce purchasing risks, maximize overall value for buyers and develop proximity and long-term relationships between buyers and suppliers.

In this paper, the proposed model was built through three phases as described in Section 3. In the first stage, all criteria affecting to raw material are defined based on SCOR model. FAHP was applied to evaluate weights for the criteria. In the second stage, the criteria will be assessed on a fuzzy scale through experts in the textile and garment industry. In final stage, the authors continue to apply the PROMETHEE II method to enrich the selection, rank the suppliers and help select the most appropriate supplier. Based on the results of PROMETHEE II presented in Table 8, supplier ranking list is S9, S10, S8, S5, S3, S6, S4, S1, S7 and finally S2. With the above results, we can determine that the optimal supplier is supplier 9 (S9).

5. Conclusions

In modern supply chains, supplier performance is evaluated using multiple criteria rather than just cost factors. The selection optimal suppliers nowadays incorporate new viewpoints towards better resource allocation, minimizing risks associated with purchasing and reducing costs by saving time, money and effort.

In this study, the authors proposed a multi-criteria decision-making model for supplier selection in the textile industry in Vietnam. SCOR model helps to build a set of criteria, as a prerequisite for the next stage, using the FAHP model to determine the weight of these criteria. Finally, PROMETHEE II provided the ranking of potential suppliers and identified the optimal alternative. PROMETHEE II helped utilizing the exact weight set of FAHP after converting fuzzy numbers, while reducing the subjectivity of the assessor when developing the FAHP model. In addition, PROMETHEE II is easy to understand, easy to perform calculations and give clear results. Quantitative research also helps to model, analyze data and statistics and produce clear results.

The research has implemented SCOR, FAHP and PROMETHEE II models for selecting the most suitable supplier and the implementation using a case study has shown that the proposed model is feasible. However, while the proposed model provides important criteria for supplier selection processes in garment and textile industry, decision makers can alter the number of criteria to better fit their organizations' specific needs and situations.

The combined model can also be studied in conjunction with other models to diversify options. Not only that, this research can also be applied to many other fields such as financial assessment and measuring the level of risk in construction engineering.

Author Contributions: Conceptualization, C.-N.W., V.T.H.V, T.P.H., V.T.N. (Van Thanh Nguyen) and V.T.N. (Viet Tinh Nguyen); Data curation, C.-N.W., V.T.H.V., V.T.N. (Van Thanh Nguyen) and V.T.N. (Viet Tinh Nguyen); Formal analysis, T.P.H. and V.T.N. (Viet Tinh Nguyen); Funding acquisition, V.T.H.V., T.P.H., V.T.N. (Van Thanh Nguyen) and V.T.N. (Viet Tinh Nguyen); Investigation, C.-N.W., V.T.H.V. and V.T.N. (Viet Tinh Nguyen); Methodology, C.-N.W., V.T.H.V., T.P.H., V.T.N. (Van Thanh Nguyen) and V.T.N. (Viet Tinh Nguyen); Project administration, T.P.H., V.T.N. (Van Thanh Nguyen) and V.T.N. (Viet Tinh Nguyen); Resources, C.-N.W.; Software, V.T.N. (Van Thanh Nguyen); Validation, V.T.N. (Van Thanh Nguyen); Visualization, T.P.H.; Writing—original draft, V.T.H.V. and V.T.N. (Viet Tinh Nguyen); Writing—review and editing, C.-N.W., T.P.H. and V.T.N. (Van Thanh Nguyen). All authors have read and agreed to the published version of the manuscript.

Funding: This research was partly supported by National Kaohsiung University of Science and Technology, and project number 108-2622-E-992-017-CC3 from the Ministry of Sciences and Technology in Taiwan.

Acknowledgments: The authors appreciate the support from Taiwan National Kaohsiung University of Science and Technology, Philippines Technological University of the Philippines Taguig, and Taiwan Ministry of Sciences and Technology.

Conflicts of Interest: The authors declare no conflict of interest.

References

1. Nhu, H. Khái quát về xuất khẩu hàng dệt may ở Việt Nam và vai trò của nó đối với nền kinh tế. Available online: https://voer.edu.vn/m/khai-quat-ve-xuat-khau-hang-det-may-o-viet-nam-va-vai-tro-cua-no-doi-voi-nen-kinh-te/ebe05f9f (accessed on 12 March 2020).
2. Luu, D. Dệt may Việt Nam trông chờ tín hiệu sáng 2020. Available online: https://tinnhanhchungkhoan.vn/thuong-truong/det-may-viet-nam-trong-cho-tin-hieu-sang-2020-308761.html (accessed on 12 March 2020).
3. Nang, D. Ngành dệt may sẽ gặp khó khăn khi Việt Nam tham gia TPP. Available online: http://www.hoatho.com.vn/tin-tuc/thong-tin-trong-nganh/nganh-det-may-se-gap-kho-khan-khi-viet-nam-tham-gia-tpp (accessed on 12 March 2020).
4. Gencer, C.; Gürpinar, D. Analytic network process in supplier selection: A case study in an electronic firm. *Appl. Math. Model.* **2007**, *31*, 2475–2486. [CrossRef]
5. Rouyendegh, B.D.; Erol, S. The dea—Fuzzy anp department ranking model applied in iran amirkabir university. *Acta Polytech. Hung.* **2010**, *7*, 103–114.
6. Taherdoost, H.; Brard, A. Analyzing the process of supplier selection criteria and methods. *Procedia Manuf.* **2019**, *32*, 1024–1034. [CrossRef]
7. Gul, M.; Guven, B.; Guneri, A.F. A new Fine-Kinney-based risk assessment framework using FAHP-FVIKOR incorporation. *J. Loss Prev. Process Ind.* **2018**, *53*, 3–16. [CrossRef]
8. Yu, X.; Chen, H.; Ji, Z. Combination of probabilistic linguistic term sets and PROMETHEE to evaluate meteorological disaster risk: Case study of southeastern China. *Sustainability* **2019**, *11*, 1405. [CrossRef]
9. Govindan, K.; Rajendran, S.; Sarkis, J.; Murugesan, P. Multi criteria decision making approaches for green supplier evaluation and selection: A literature review. *J. Clean. Prod.* **2015**, *98*, 66–83. [CrossRef]
10. Alikhani, R.; Torabi, S.A.; Altay, N. Strategic supplier selection under sustainability and risk criteria. *Int. J. Prod. Econ.* **2019**, *208*, 69–82. [CrossRef]
11. Liao, H.; Wu, D.; Huang, Y.; Ren, P.; Xu, Z.; Verma, M. Green logistic provider selection with a hesitant fuzzy linguistic thermodynamic method integrating cumulative prospect theory and PROMETHEE. *Sustainability* **2018**, *10*, 1291. [CrossRef]
12. Wang, C.N.; Huang, Y.F.; Cheng, I.; Nguyen, V.T. A multi-criteria decision-making (MCDM) approach using hybrid SCOR metrics, AHP, and TOPSIS for supplier evaluation and selection in the gas and oil industry. *Processes* **2018**, *6*, 252. [CrossRef]
13. Safari, H.; Fagheyi, M.S.; Ahangari, S.S.; Fathi, M.R. Applying PROMETHEE method based on entropy weight for supplier selection. *Bus. Manag. Strategy* **2012**, *3*, 97–106. [CrossRef]

14. Senvar, O.; Tuzkaya, G.; Kahraman, C. Multi Citeria Supplier Selection Using Fuzzy PROMETHEE Method. In *Supply Chain Management under Fuzziness*; Springer: Berlin/Heidelberg, Germany, 2014; pp. 21–34.
15. Chen, C.T.; Pai, P.F.; Hung, W.Z. An integrated methodology using linguistic PROMETHEE and maximum deviation method for third-party logistics supplier selection. *Int. J. Comput. Intell. Syst.* **2010**, *3*, 438–451. [CrossRef]
16. Dağdeviren, M. Decision making in equipment selection: An integrated approach with AHP and PROMETHEE. *J. Intell. Manuf.* **2008**, *19*, 397–406. [CrossRef]
17. Pan, W.H.; Li, J.Q. Application of AHP-PROMETHEE Method for Supplier Selection in Strategic Sourcing. *Oper. Res. Manag. Sci.* **2009**, *2*, 008.
18. Bansal, A.; Kumar, P. 3PL selection using hybrid model of AHP-PROMETHEE. *Int. J. Serv. Oper. Manag.* **2013**, *14*, 373–397. [CrossRef]
19. Shakey, B.K. Supplier selection using AHP and promethee-2. *Int. J. Sci. Res.* **2006**, *6*, 156–160. [CrossRef]
20. Sari, T.; Timor, M. Integrated supplier selection model using ANP, Taguchi loss function and PROMETHEE methods. *J. Appl. Quant. Methods* **2016**, *11*, 19–34.
21. Brans, J.; Vincke, P.; Mareschal, B. How to select and how to rank projects: The Promethee method. *Eur. J. Oper. Res.* **1986**, *24*, 228–238. [CrossRef]
22. Wang, C.N.; Nguyen, V.T.; Duong, D.H.; Thai, H.T.N. A hybrid fuzzy analysis network process (FANP) and the technique for order of preference by similarity to ideal solution (TOPSIS) approaches for solid waste to energy plant location selection in Vietnam. *Appl. Sci.* **2018**, *8*, 1100. [CrossRef]
23. Wang, C.N.; Nguyen, V.T.; Duong, D.H.; Do, H.T. A hybrid fuzzy analytic network process (FANP) and data envelopment analysis (DEA) approach for supplier evaluation and selection in the rice supply chain. *Symmetry* **2018**, *10*, 221. [CrossRef]
24. Jamehshooran, B.G.; Shaharoun, M.; Haron, H.N. Assessing supply chain performance through applying the SCOR model. *Int. J. Supply Chain Manag.* **2015**, *4*, 1–11.
25. Theeranuphattana, A.; Tang, J.C. A conceptual model of performance measurement for supply chains. *J. Manuf. Technol. Manag.* **2008**, *7*, 41. [CrossRef]
26. Rezaie, K.; Byat, M.; Shirkouhi, S.N. Evaluating effective factors of implementing knowledge management based on FAHP method. In Proceedings of the IEEE 2009 Third Asia International Conference on Modelling & Simulation, Bali, Indonesia, 25–29 May 2009; pp. 398–403.
27. Wang, C.-N.; Nguyen, V.T.; Thai, H.T.N.; Duong, D.H. Multi-Criteria Decision Making (MCDM) Approaches for Solar Power Plant Location Selection in Viet Nam. *Energies* **2018**, *11*, 1504. [CrossRef]
28. Brans, J.; Vincke, P. A Preference Ranking Organisation Method (The PROMETHEE Method for Multiple Criteria Decision-Making). *Manag. Sci.* **1985**, *31*, 647–656. [CrossRef]
29. Ningsih, S.R.; Windarto, A.P. Penerapan Metode Promethee II Pada Dosen Penerima Hibah P2M Internal. *InfoTekJar: Jurnal Nasional Informatika dan Teknologi Jaringan* **2018**, *3*, 20–25. [CrossRef]
30. Adelia, F.; Wahyuli, D.; Sari, T.I.; Windarto, A.P. Analisis Promethee II Pada Faktor Penyebab Mahasiswa Sulit Menemukan Judul Artikel Ilmiah. *Jurnal Ilmiah KOMPUTASI* **2018**, *17*, 131–136.

symmetry

MDPI

Article

An Integrated Multi-Criteria Approach for Planning Railway Passenger Transport in the Case of Uncertainty

Svetla Stoilova

Faculty of Transport, Technical University of Sofia, 8 Kl. Ohridski Blvd., 1000 Sofia, Bulgaria; stoilova@tu-sofia.bg

Received: 11 May 2020; Accepted: 2 June 2020; Published: 4 June 2020

Abstract: The aim of this study is to elaborate on an integrated approach for transport planning in railway passenger transport in the case of uncertainty. The methodology consists of four stages. In the first stage, the parameters of a multi-criteria model in the case of uncertainty were determined. This includes defining the criteria for selection of a transport plan; formulation of the alternatives of the transport plan; formulation of the strategies and probability variants of passenger flow variation for each strategy. In the second stage, the weights of the probability variants of the strategies for change in passenger flow were determined using the analytic hierarchy process (AHP) method. The alternatives of the transport plan were ranked by applying the sequential interactive modeling for urban systems (SIMUS) method based on linear programming. The results for the values of the criterion of ranking obtained through the SIMUS method and the weights of the variants of passenger flow variation calculated with the AHP method were used as input in the expected values in the decision tree. The selection of a suitable alternative in the case of uncertainty was conducted in the third stage by applying the decision tree method. In the fourth stage, verification of the results was made using Laplace's criterion and Hurwitz's criterion. The integrated multi-criteria approach was applied for Bulgaria's railway network. The multi-criteria approach elaborated herein could be used for decision-making in the case of uncertainty about passenger flow; to investigate different strategies of passenger flow variation and to make decisions in case of instability of passenger flow or lack of sufficient travel data.

Keywords: SIMUS; AHP; decision tree; transport plan; Laplace's criterion; Hurwitz's criterion

---

1. Introduction

Successful transport planning depends on the possibilities of symmetry, on the one hand, between passenger satisfaction and the capabilities of the railway operators, and on the other hand, between the subjectivism of the decision maker and the importance of the criteria for assessment of the transport process. The elaboration of a new integrated approach to decision-making allows for the symmetry principles to be considered also in cases of uncertainty about passenger flow. Thus, a balance should be established between the probabilities for changes in passenger flow and the sustainability of the transport plan.

The number of trains, their categories, routes, and stops are the elements of the transport plan, which need to be determined. Passenger flow and transport demand have to be the subject of preliminary studies in order to establish the optimal organization of the transport process. Various criteria related to passenger transport service and the capabilities of railway operators influence transport planning. When passenger flow is pre-defined on the basis of statistics from sold tickets or counting of the passengers, the situation of decision-making concerning the transport plan is a situation of certainty. Passenger flow may change according to various factors, such as repairs to railway infrastructure; competitive modes of transport; change in the conditions of travel; increase of train operating speeds or other reasons. In such cases, the determination of an appropriate transport plan is carried out in a state of uncertainty. The uncertainty is a situation where there is not adequate data about the distribution of the demand or probabilities of different events. When the demand is not known but there is some information about the probabilities of the events, the situation of decision-making is under risk. The successful planning of passenger services requires a complex view not only when the demand for transport services has been established in advance, but also in cases where the size of passenger flow is uncertain. It is necessary to increase the effectiveness of the decision-making in case of risk and uncertainty, by studying the impact of variation in passenger flow and criteria related to the transport process.

The hypothesis of the study is that transport planning in railway passenger transport depends on technological and economic criteria; the uncertainty of passenger flow impacts the choice of a suitable alternative of the transport plan; the railway transport service could be improved by taking into account both the above criteria and the state of uncertainty.

The research questions that have to be solved to address the following issues: how to determine the probabilities of changes in passenger traffic to be used by the decision maker in transport planning; how the uncertainty in the change of the passenger flow affects the transport plan of passenger trains in the railway network; whether a stable solution can been established that is favorable for both passengers and the railway operator.

In the present study, the sequential interactive model for urban systems method (SIMUS), analytic hierarchy process method (AHP), the decision tree method, and the decision-making criteria—Laplace's criterion and Hurwitz' criterion—are proposed to assess railway passenger transport plan under uncertainty. The SIMUS method based on linear programming makes it possible to rank the alternatives of the transport plan according to multiple objectives, and does not use experts' assessment of the criteria. The decision tree allows for decision-making in the case of uncertainty on the basis of profits and probabilities for variation of passenger flow. The AHP method helps to determine the probabilities of variation of passenger flow.

The integration of the SIMUS method on the one hand and the AHP method on the other hand with the decision tree method allows for the development of an appropriate transport plan with given probabilities of change in passenger flow. The SIMUS method allows for decision-making in a state of certainty where different variants can be studied and compared at a predetermined known size of passenger flow. When the size of passenger flow is not known in advance, or the probabilities of its change are known, then decision-making is in a state of uncertainty and risk. The aim of the decision-maker is to be able to develop a transport plan in a state of uncertainty. The determination of the probabilities of changes in passenger flow can be done on the basis of expert assessments or by an analysis of statistical data about previous periods. Both approaches were used in this study, and on the basis of a study of the size of passenger traffic for a 10-year period, its tendency to decrease or increase compared to the previous year was established, and thus the strategies for changing the passenger flow were determined. The probabilities for the implementation of the strategies for change in passenger flow are determined by expert assessments. In the research, the AHP method is chosen, using expert assessment by an established scale. In this way, the probabilities are established and are used in the decision tree method.

The purpose of this paper is to elaborate on an integrated approach based on the multi-criteria methods and the decision tree method to select the suitable transport plan that takes into account the uncertainty of passenger flow, the needs of the passengers, and the capabilities of the railway operator.

The novelty of the proposed approach and its main contribution refers to the integration of the multi-criteria analysis, which defines the importance of the criteria and ranks the alternatives, and the decision tree method to determine the suitable transport plan for railway networks taking uncertainty into account. The output of the multi-criteria analysis serves as an input to the decision tree technique.

The paper is structured as follows. Section 2 is the literature review. Section 3 presents the methodology. Section 4 shows the experimentation and results. Section 5 gives the conclusions. The elaborated methodology is applied for transport planning in Bulgaria's railway network.

2. Literature Review

Various authors applied multi-criteria decision-making methods to assess the criteria related to transport planning. Different multi-criteria methods used in transport systems and railway engineering were analyzed in [1,2]. The analytic hierarchy process (AHP) method was applied to investigate rail transit networks [3]. Financial, economic, system planning, and policy criteria were assessed. The model was experimented for Istanbul. The quality of passenger transportation by railway transport was analyzed by using the AHP method [4–6]. Lithuanian railways were analyzed using questionnaires referring to four groups of criteria: price of ticket, trip process planning and technology, train elements and the technical state of rails, safety. Forty-nine sub-criteria were investigated. The criteria of costs, comfort, accessibility to the stop, waiting time, riding time, maintenance and renewal of route were used in [7] to investigate the choice of the means of urban passenger transport. Two multi-criteria methods were used— ELimination Et Choice Translating Reality (ELECTRE) and AHP. Multi-criteria analysis was used in [8] to assess transportation investments. The AHP method and best worst method (BWM) are used for problem solving. Passenger services, environment, economics, urban planning, and architecture were determined as the main criteria. Travel cost, travel time, waiting time, suitability, accessibility, and safety were determined in [9] to assess public transport systems. An integrated multi-criteria approach based on the Delphi method, AHP, and Preference Ranking Organization METHod for Enrichment of Evaluations (PROMETHEE) method was applied in [9]. It was found out that the safety and suitability criteria were most important. The safety, rapidity, time, and comfort criteria were used in [10] to analyze the operation efficiency of the passenger transport. The integrated DEA-AHP model was studied. The multi-criteria methods analytic network process (ANP) and technique for order preference by similarity to ideal solution (TOPSIS) were used in [11] to evaluate alternative monorail routes. The economic, social, engineering, environmental impacts were applied to assess the alternatives. In [12], the authors assessed railway route planning based on the investment, costs, and number of trains criteria. The multi-criteria optimization and compromise solution (VIKOR) method was used.

Regression models were examined in [13] to assess the criteria affecting high-speed train services. The authors studied the criteria related to physical conditions, advertisements and information services, food service, personnel. Integer linear programming model and light robustness were proposed in [14] to investigate train timetabling and stop planning. The fuzzy AHP and rough AHP method were applied to investigate traffic accessibility [15]. The authors studied four groups of main criteria, such as transport, space, quality of service, system quality. The capacity utilization in the railway network was studied in [16]. The authors used criteria such as the length of railway network, number of trains per day, passenger and freight kilometers, punctuality of the trains to assess a ten-year period. An integrated neutrosophic set and the decision-making trial and evaluation laboratory (DEMATEL) multi-criteria method was elaborated on in [17] to choose the transport service provider.

The criteria for the quality of passenger rail transport were assessed using the full consistency method elaborated in [18]. The following importance of the defined criteria was established—accessibility, availability, security, time, customer care, information, comfort, and environmental impact. In [19], the authors applied the criteria for evaluation of transport planning such as costs, travel time, safety, profitability, environmental friendliness. The ELECTRE III and AHP methods were applied. The criteria of comfort and cleanness, service accessibility, information availability, service organization, staff behavior, behavior of inspectors, and costs were applied in [20] to establish the service quality of public transport. Factor analysis, segmentation analysis, and cluster analysis were used to study the customers and their quality perception.

Some authors used fuzzy sets and multi-objective optimization for decision-making under uncertainty. The fuzzy AHP method makes it possible to take into account the uncertainty in decision-making. This approach was applied in [21] to determine a transport plan. The criteria of transport costs and car fleet were taken into account. The multi-criteria approach was applied to investigate a transportation system under uncertainty [22]. The authors defined social, environmental, and economic indicators and used the fuzzy AHP method to calculate the weights. The fuzzy AHP method was used to evaluate the railway timetable, [23]. The uncertain demand in passenger rail service was studied in [24]. A revenue-maximization model including operating costs for the rail operator and the value of time for passengers was studied by the authors. The authors used dynamic programming in the research. The fuzzy AHP method and Hurwitz method were applied to choose the best location of parking lots, taking into account the uncertainty of the investigated system [25]. Ranking of locations was done by means of the Hurwitz method.

The fuzzy PIvot Pairwise RElative Criteria Importance Assessment (F-PIPRECIA) and fuzzy evaluation based on distance from average solution (F-EDAS) methods were elaborated on in [26] with the purpose to select the best variant which allows the operator to make a profit. The model was tested for the organization of passenger railway traffic. The authors used the following criteria to assess variants for the organization of passenger traffic: budget, the capability of the operator, the effect, and the period of realization.

The decision tree technique allows for decision-making in the state of uncertainty when the selection of the best variant of action depends on the set of available possibilities. This method was applied to solve the alternative choice problem, to determine the important criteria for the mode of choice, to study public transport planning [27–31]. In [27], two methods were developed for the transportation planning process and mode choice analysis, one based on the decision tree and other based on a multinomial logit model. It was found out that the model based on decision tree was of higher accuracy compared to the multinomial logit models. In [28], the authors studied an expected-value-maximizing strategy and experimented with two types of probabilities in a decision tree, the first type can be modified independently; the second type are interrelated. The decision tree technique was used in [29] to investigate Izmir Transportation Master Plan. Twenty-five variables were selected which were divided into four groups: house information, person information, information of vehicle in trip, trip information. In [30], the authors studied an alternative choice problem on the basis of fuzzy decision trees. The decision tree method was applied to study public transport planning [31]. The following criteria were applied: safety, heading way, people comfort in the queue line, quality of the road in the busway corridor, and nonsterile bus lane. The decision tree approach was applied in [32] to assess urban transport. Criteria such as travel information, wayfinding information, time and movement, access, comfort and convenience, station attractiveness, safety and security, emergency situation handling, and overall satisfaction were studied. The decision tree method was applied in [33] to find the factors in regard to the delay of the trains.

It could be said that the main criteria that influence transport planning in related research are: travel time, traffic safety [7,10,18,19,24,31]; transport costs [3,10,12,18,24]; number of trains [12].

Different techniques were applied in the case of uncertainty, such as fuzzy sets and multi-objective optimization, fuzzy AHP method [21–23,25], fuzzy–PIPRECIA and fuzzy–EDAS method [26]; decision tree [27,29,31–33]. The decision tree approach was successfully used by the authors to select the best variant when the probabilities of the studied events are known.

Table 1 presents the methods used in literature sources on transport planning in the case of uncertainty. The main problems solved in related research concern transport planning, railway timetable planning, urban transport, public transport, railway passenger transport.

The multi-criteria methods using the fuzzy technique in the event of uncertainty are based on fuzzy numbers and complex computational procedures. The probabilities of passenger flow variation are not used in these methods.

Table 1. Some of the methods used in literature sources on transport planning in the case of uncertainty.

Methods Used	Area of Evaluation	Criteria Used	Author
Fuzzy AHP	Transport planning	Transport costs; car fleet	[21]
		Social, environmental, and economic indicators	[22]
	Railway timetable planning	Weighted waiting times, average of waiting time; ratio of waiting time to journey time	[23]
	Assessment location of parking	Population, size, cost, distances	[25]
Fuzzy PIPRECIA and Fuzzy EDAS	Railway passenger transport planning	Budget, ability of the operator, effect of realization, period of realization	[26]
Decision tree	Transport planning	House information, person information, information of vehicle in trip, trip information	[29]
	Urban transport planning	Household size, number of vehicles, income, age and of gender of traveller, education level, type of employment, trip purpose, travel time, cost	[27]
		Travel information, wayfinding information, time and movement, access, comfort and convenience, station attractiveness, safety and security, emergency situation handling, and overall satisfaction	[32]
	Public transport planning	Safety, heading way, people's comfort, quality of the road	[31]
	Assessment delay of the trains	Manner of driving	[33]
Dynamic programming	Railway passenger transport planning	Operating costs, value of time	[24]

In most studies, the efforts of the authors were focused on issues related to uncertainty in the evaluation of criteria by experts, and for this reason, fuzzy models are preferred [21–23,25,26]. It could be concluded that the cases of uncertainty of passenger flow were not sufficiently studied.

The differences between the present study and other studies in related areas lies in the decision-making approach. This study combines the SIMUS method based on linear programming and weighted sum method to determine the appropriate alternative in a state of certainty for given parameters, the AHP method to determine the probabilities and the decision tree method for decision-making in the case of uncertainty. This research deploys a combination of three completely different methods, and thus introduces a new paradigm in multi-criteria decision-making. The probability-based decision-making approach allows for different transport demands to be taken into account. The appropriate alternative in this case is determined on the basis of the profit for each alternative in the different probability states.

In this paper, the SIMUS method was preferred since it does not use expert assessments, in order to evaluate the importance of criteria and rank the alternatives in the case of certainty.

3. Materials and Methods

Figure 1 illustrates the scheme of the methodology.

The proposed methodology consists of the following stages:

Stage 1. Forming the multi-criteria model taking into account uncertainty and risk.

Step 1. Determination of the criteria to assess the railway transport plan.

Step 2. Defining of the alternatives of the transport plan.

Step 3. Formulation the strategies of variation of passenger flow; determination of the probability variants of the strategies for change of passenger flow.

Stage 2: Determination of the input for the decision tree model.

Step 1. Determination of the probabilities of each event. In this step, the weights of each variant of passenger flow variation are calculated by applying the AHP method.

Step 2. Determination of the profit of each alternative. The SIMUS method is used to rank the alternatives. The values of the criterion of the ranking are used as the profits.

Stage 3: Selection of suitable alternative applying the decision tree method. The criterion is the maximum of the expected value. The expected values are determined by using the results of the SIMUS and AHP method.

Stage 4: Verification of the results obtained by the decision tree method. A comparative analysis, using Laplace's criterion and Hurwitz's criterion, is performed.

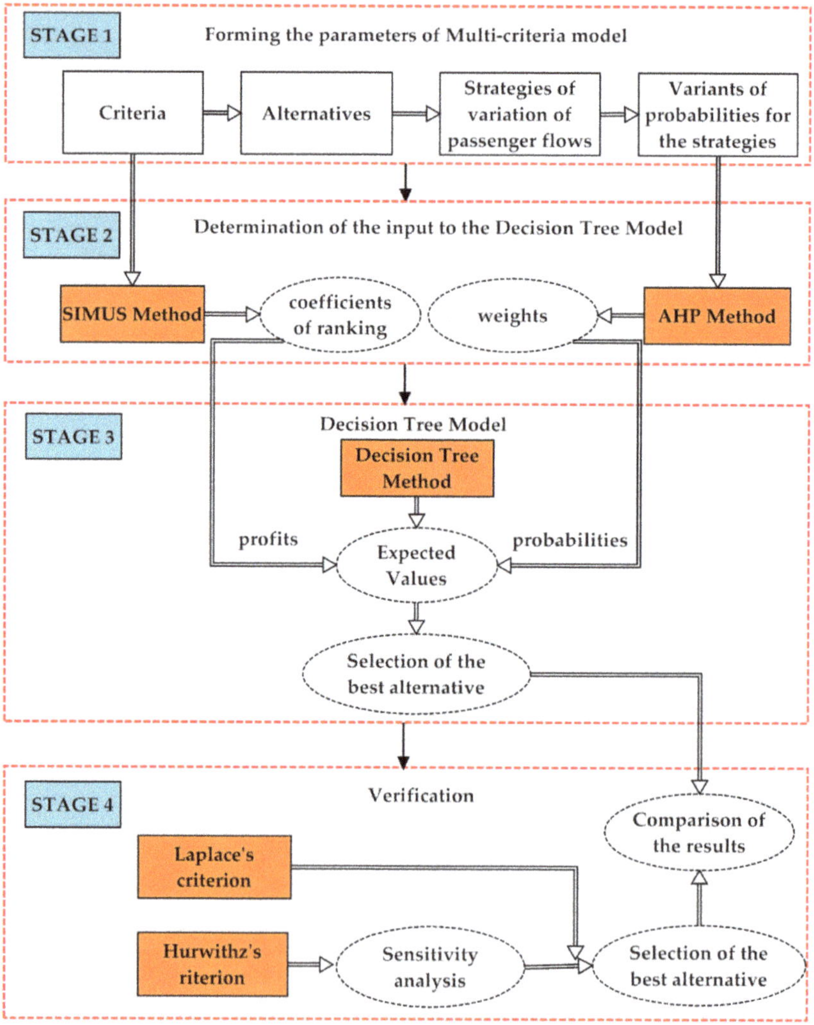

Figure 1. Scheme of methodology.

3.1. *First Stage: Parameters of the Multi-Criteria Model*

3.1.1. Step 1: Defining the Criteria

The first step defines the criteria to evaluate alternatives of the transport plan of intercity trains. The criteria were selected on the basis of an analysis of criteria used to assess transport in similar studies. The important criteria that influence transport planning in related research are: travel time [7,10,18,19,24,31]; transport costs [3,10,12,18,24]; number of trains [12]. Transport costs are an important indicator for the railway operator. Travel time and the number of trains are technological factors significant for passengers. The first indicator is related to the speed of transport; the second one shows the frequency of service. In this study, additional technological criteria related to passenger satisfaction are proposed. The aim of the passengers is to arrive at the final destination in the shortest possible time. This is achieved, for example, by direct trains with reduced stops, with an increase in operating speed. Passengers' expectations are for regular trains service throughout the day with sufficient capacity.

Taking into account the factors listed above the following criteria to assess the railway transport plan were determined in this research:

C_1—Frequency of services, pair trains/day. This criterion represents transport satisfaction of the passengers with railway services.

C_2—Frequency of train stops. This criterion represents the average number of train stops.

C_3—Average distance travelled, km. This criterion represents the capability of the railway operator to offer long itineraries in the transport plan.

C_4—Average operating speed, km/h. This criterion is a measure of the capability of the railway operator to provide fast transport services.

C_5—Reliability. This criterion is presented by a coefficient accounting for the average delay of trains. The coefficient is determined by dividing the number of delayed trains by the total number of trains. In this study, the delays are studied with a duration of up to 30 min.

C_6—Directness. It is represented the availability of direct service. The trains operate between big cities of over 100 thousand inhabitants without intermediate stops. The value of C_6 is 0 or 1. If the alternative includes direct service: $C_6 = 1$, otherwise: $C_6 = 0$.

C_7—Train capacity, seats/day. This criterion is determined by the number of seats in train composition per day.

C_8 Direct operational costs, EUR/day. This factor shows the economic capabilities of the railway operator.

These criteria present two sides of the transport process: the capabilities of the railway operator and the requirements of passengers. The main criterion for railway operators, when they determine the transport plan, is operating costs. Speed, direct journey, frequency of service, and reliability are important factors for the quality of the transport service.

3.1.2. Step 2: Determination of the Alternatives

To determine the appropriate transport plan, it is necessary to compare the pre-defined alternatives. The number of alternatives is $i = 1, \ldots, I$. The category of the trains, the number of wagons in the train, number of trains, and the routes are the parameters of the transport plan.

3.1.3. Step 3: Determination of the Strategies and the Variants of Change in Passenger Flow

The strategies are formed by the decision maker by setting the percentage change in passenger flow (reduction, preservation, or increase). This paper studies the following strategies: pessimistic strategy—reducing passenger traffic by 10%; realistic strategy—keeping the flow of passengers; optimistic strategy—increase of passenger flow by 10%. The reduction of the number of passengers could be, for example, due to various reasons, such as repair of the railway track, competitive road transport, reduced frequency, poor service. The increase in passenger traffic may be, for example, the result of increased frequency, improved attractiveness of rail transport, introduction of additional services, increased speed. The number of strategies is $k = 1, \ldots, K$.

The variants of change of passenger flow are formed by setting probabilities for change of the passenger flow for the respective strategy. Since the strategies are three, each variant contains three numbers, the sum of which is equal to 1. The variants and the strategies are presented as a matrix whose rows are equal to the number of strategies, and the number of columns is equal to the number of variants. The number of variants is $j = 1, \ldots, J$. The variants of probabilities of passenger flow variation for each strategy are set by experts.

3.2. Second Stage: Input for the Decision Tree Model

3.2.1. Step 1. Determination of the Weights of the Variants

This study uses the AHP method to determine the weights of the variants of passenger flow variation. The AHP is a commonly used technique for multi-criteria analysis in decision-making. This method uses expert assessment. The weights are calculated based on the pair-wise comparison of the criteria by using a scale for assessing (Saaty's scale). Table A1 in Appendix A shows Saaty's scale [34,35].

The result of the pairwise comparison of n criteria can be summarized in an (n, n) evaluation matrix where every element is the quotient of weights of the criteria.

The AHP method calculates the consistency ratio CR, as a measure of the expert assessments. Generally, if the CR is less than 0.10, the consistency of the decision-maker is considered satisfactory.

3.2.2. Step 2: Ranking the Alternatives

This study applies the SIMUS technique for ranking the alternatives of transport planning and for assessing the criteria. The SIMUS method uses linear programming, weighted sum, and outranking [36–38]. That method does not use experts to assess the criteria.

The application of the SIMUS starts with the formation of the decision matrix of criteria and alternatives. This matrix is normalized. The type of optimization, the type of restrictive conditions and their limits (RHS) are determined for each criterion This information is set at the end of the normalized matrix. The value of RHS could be determined in two ways: by the decision maker or according to the maximum or the minimum normalized value of the row. The maximum value of the row is chosen in case of a maximum of the objective function; the minimum value of the row is chosen in case of a minimum of objective function.

The linear optimization models for each criterion are formed and calculated. Each row of the decision matrix consistently is used as the objective functions. The restrictive conditions are formed by using the other rows of the matrix. The results of the optimization models represent the score of each alternative. They form the efficient results matrix (ERM).

The ranking of the alternatives is made on the basis of ERM. The criterion of ranking is determined according to the sum of all elements in each column (SC) of normalized ERM and the normalized values of the participation factor (PF). The PF represents the number of participations of each alternative in each column of the normalized ERM. The normalized values of PF are determined according to the number of criteria. The highest value of the criterion of ranking indicates the best alternative.

3.3. Third Stage: Decision Tree Model

The process of decision-making using a decision tree is multi-stage one where each stage is linked to the previous one and affects the next one. Through this method, management decisions can be made if the probabilities of achieving one or another result and the values of the different alternatives are known in advance.

The decision tree method uses a graphical representation of alternatives, probabilities, and profits, [39,40]. The probabilities of different events are determined in advance. In this paper, they are defined by the AHP method and are used as input to the decision tree. The concept of expected value is an integral part of the method of decision trees. In this study, the values of the criterion of ranking by the SIMUS method are used as input in expected values in the decision tree.

The criterion for choosing the best alternative by means of the decision tree method is the maximum of the expected value, depending on the type of explored criteria.

In this study, the weights of passenger flow variation calculated with the AHP method represent the probabilities of the events. The values of the criterion of ranking by the SIMUS method represent the profit.

The expected value for each event showing the variants of passenger flow variation is calculated as follows:

$$EV_{ij} = w_j \sum\nolimits_{i=1}^{I} C_{ERM_{ik}} P_{jk}, \tag{1}$$

where $i = 1, \ldots, I$ are the number of alternatives; $k = 1, \ldots, K$ are the number of strategies of variation of passenger flow; $j = 1, \ldots, J$ are the variants of probabilities of passenger flow variation for each strategy; P_{jk} are the probabilities of passenger flow variation for variant j and strategy k; w_j are the weights of the variants of passenger flow variation determined by the AHP method; $C_{ERM_{ik}}$ are the values of criterion of ranking by the SIMUS method for alternative j and strategy k; w_j are the weights of the variants determined by using the AHP method; P_{jk} are the probabilities for variant j and strategy k for variation of passenger flow.

The following conditions are met:

$$\sum_{j=1}^{J} w_j = 1, \tag{2}$$

$$\sum\nolimits_{k=1}^{K} P_{jk} = 1, \text{ for } \forall j. \tag{3}$$

The Expected value for each alternative is determined as follows:

$$EV_i = \max_i EV_{ij}. \tag{4}$$

The optimal alternative is determined according to the maximal value of the expected value of all alternatives:

$$EV_{opt} = \max_i EV_i. \tag{5}$$

3.4. Fourth Stage: Verification of the Results

The verification of the results was conducted using Laplace's and Hurwitz's criteria [40]. The decision matrix includes the number of alternatives and the number of variants of passenger flow variation for the strategies. The elements of the decision matrix are calculated by the Equation (1):

$$L_i = \frac{\sum_{j=1}^{J} EV_{ij}}{J}. \tag{6}$$

The best alternative is determined through the maximum value of Laplace's criterion as EV_{ij} presents the benefits:

$$L_{opt} = \max_i L_i. \tag{7}$$

Hurwitz's criterion uses an additional coefficient α. This coefficient permits making a decision in the different situations. The value of α has a value between 0 and 1. Generally, $\alpha = 0.5$. While $\alpha = 1$ represents an optimistic approach, $\alpha = 0$ represents a pessimistic approach. Using α, in a decision-making situation, the profit for each alternative is calculated.

The best alternative is determined by the maximum value of Hurwitz's criterion as EV_{ij} presents the benefits:

$$H_i = \alpha \max_i EV_{ij} + (1 - \alpha) \min_i EV_{ij}. \tag{8}$$

The alternative having maximum value of Hurwitz's criterion is selected, as EV_{ij} presents the benefits:

$$H_{opt} = \max_i H_i. \tag{9}$$

4. Results and Discussion

The approach presented here was applied to Bulgaria's railway network. The transport plan of intercity trains was studied.

This research was conducted under the following limitations:

The number of wagons in the train can be three or four. This limitation is determined by the current situation in the Bulgarian railway network.

The reduction and increase of passengers is 10%. In this way, the strategies are formed.

The variants of passenger flow variation are formed on the basis of the assumption that the realistic strategy can have a probability between 20% and 50%.

4.1. Multi-Criteria Model

4.1.1. Alternatives

The approach presented here was applied to Bulgaria's railway network. The transport plan of intercity trains was studied. This research investigates three types of passenger trains: Category 1—express; the passengers must have a reservation; Category 2—intercity trains, reservation is needed; Category 3—fast trains; reservation is not needed. Category 1 serves big transport and administrative centers. Category 2 serves big transport and administrative centers and also additionally big cities. Category 3 operates between additional intermediate stations.

Nine alternatives of a transport plan were studied. The alternatives were chosen taking into account train categories and also the number of wagons in the train compositions.

Table 2 shows the alternatives. Alternatives 1–3 include three categories of trains, Alternatives 4–9 include two categories of trains. For example, Alternative 1 contains the following parameters:

- Category 1 trains are formed of 4 wagons. These trains serve 3 itineraries in the railway network.
- Category 2 trains are formed of 4 wagons too. These trains serve 7 itineraries in the railway network.
- Category 3 trains are formed of 4 wagons too. These trains serve 17 itineraries in the railway network.

Table 2. Alternatives of transport plan.

Alternative	Category of train	Number of wagons	Number of itineraries	Alternative	Category of train	Number of wagons	Number of itineraries	Alternative	Category of train	Number of wagons	Number of itineraries
	1	4	3		1	4	3		1	0	0
1	2	4	7	4	2	0	0	7	2	4	7
	3	4	17		3	4	17		3	4	17
	1	3	3		1	3	3		1	0	0
2	2	3	7	5	2	0	0	8	2	3	7
	3	3	17		3	3	17		3	3	17
	1	3	3		1	3	3		1	0	0
3	2	4	7	6	2	0	0	9	2	3	7
	3	4	17		3	4	17		3	4	17

4.1.2. Strategies and Variants of Passenger Flow Variations

The strategies for changing the passenger flow were determined on the basis of an analysis of the passengers transported on Bulgaria's railway network for a ten-year period (2009–2019). Figure 2 shows the percentage change in passenger traffic compared to the previous year. For example, the reduction in passenger traffic in 2010 compared to 2009 is about 4%; the increase in passenger traffic in 2019 compared to 2018 is also about 4%. Figure 2 shows that the maximum decrease in the transported passengers is about 10%.

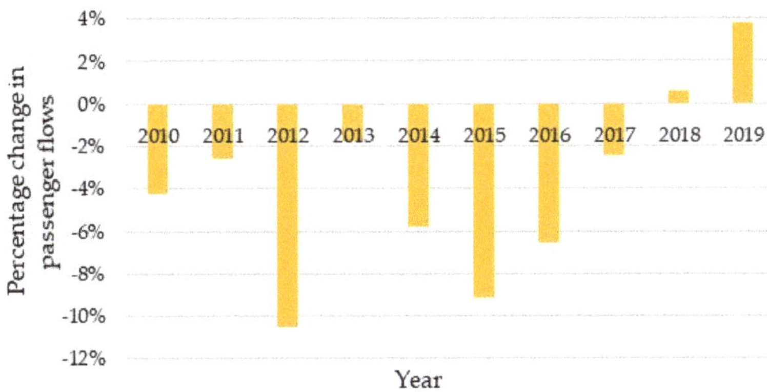

Figure 2. Percentage change in passenger traffic compared to the previous year.

The best transport plan was determined in the case of uncertainty of passenger flow.

This paper studies the following strategies: pessimistic strategy (k = 1)—reducing passenger traffic by 10%; realistic strategy (k = 2)—keeping the flow of passengers; optimistic strategy (k = 3)—increase passenger flow by 10%.

Table 3 presents the variants investigated in this study. For example, variant 1 indicates that the probability of reduction in passenger flow by 10% is 0.4; the probability of preservation of passenger flow is 0.5; and the probability of increase in passenger flow by 10% is 0.1. The variants are formed on the assumption that the realistic strategy can have a probability between 20% and 50%.

Table 3. Variants of variation of passenger flow.

Variant j	Probabilities of Change in Passenger Flow			Variant j	Probabilities of Change in Passenger Flow		
	Strategy, k				Strategy, k		
	1	2	3		1	2	3
1	0.40	0.50	0.10	12	0.50	0.30	0.20
2	0.10	0.50	0.40	13	0.20	0.30	0.50
3	0.30	0.50	0.20	14	0.60	0.30	0.10
4	0.20	0.50	0.30	15	0.10	0.30	0.60
5	0.10	0.40	0.50	16	0.30	0.20	0.50
6	0.50	0.40	0.10	17	0.50	0.20	0.30
7	0.20	0.40	0.40	18	0.40	0.20	0.40
8	0.40	0.40	0.20	19	0.60	0.20	0.20
9	0.30	0.40	0.30	20	0.20	0.20	0.60
10	0.30	0.30	0.40	21	0.70	0.20	0.10
11	0.40	0.30	0.30	22	0.10	0.20	0.70

4.2. Decision Tree Model

4.2.1. Weights of the Variants of Passenger Flow Variation

The weights of passenger flow variation variants were determined by using the AHP method. For this purpose, six experts including three specialists from academia and three specialists from BDZ Passengers service LTD, made a group assessment of the variants using Saaty's scale 1–9, (Table A1 in the Appendix A). Table 4 presents the pairwise comparisons. The end column of Table 4 shows the weights of the variants.

Table 4. Variants of passenger flow variation. Consistency $CR = 0.03$.

j	Variants of Passenger Flow Variation for the Strategies																						w_j
	1	2	3	4	5	6	7	8	9	10	11	12	13	14	15	16	17	18	19	20	21	22	
1	1	1	1	1	1	2	2	1	1	2	1	2	2	2	2	2	3	2	2	2	2	1	0.065
2	1	1	1	1	1	2	1	1	1	2	1	2	2	2	2	2	3	2	2	2	2	2	0.063
3	1	1	1	1	2	1	1	2	1	2	1	1	2	2	2	2	3	2	2	2	2	2	0.063
4	1	1	1	1	2	2	2	1	2	1	2	2	2	2	2	2	3	2	2	2	2	2	0.070
5	1	1	0.5	0.5	1	0.5	1	0.5	0.33	1	1	0.5	1	1	1	1	2	1	1	2	2	1	0.039
6	0.5	0.5	1	0.5	2	1	0.5	1	2	1	1	1	0.5	1	0.5	0.5	1	1	1	0.5	1	2	0.040
7	0.5	1	1	0.5	1	2	1	2	0.5	0.5	1	2	1	2	2	2	2	1	2	2	2	2	0.056
8	1	1	0.5	1	2	1	0.5	1	1	2	1	1	2	2	2	2	1	2	2	2	2	2	0.057
9	1	1	1	0.5	3	0.5	2	1	1	2	2	2	2	2	2	2	2	2	2	2	2	2	0.067
10	0.5	0.5	0.5	1	1	1	2	0.5	0.5	1	1	1	1	2	2	2	2	2	2	2	2	2	0.052
11	1	1	1	0.5	1	1	1	1	0.5	1	1	3	3	3	3	1	2	1	1	1	1	2	0.054
12	0.5	0.5	1	0.5	2	1	0.5	1	0.5	1	0.33	1	2	2	2	2	2	2	2	2	2	2	0.050
13	0.5	0.5	0.5	0.5	1	2	1	0.5	0.5	1	0.33	0.5	1	1	0.5	0.5	1	1	1	0.5	0.5	1	0.031
14	0.5	0.5	0.5	0.5	1	1	0.5	0.5	0.5	0.5	0.33	0.5	1	1	0.5	0.5	1	1	1	0.5	0.5	1	0.027
15	0.5	0.5	0.5	0.5	1	2	0.5	0.5	0.5	0.5	0.33	0.5	2	2	1	1	2	2	2	2	2	2	0.042
16	0.5	0.5	0.5	0.5	1	2	0.5	0.5	0.5	0.5	1	0.5	2	2	1	1	2	2	1	1	2	1	0.038
17	0.5	0.33	0.33	0.33	0.5	1	0.5	1	0.5	0.5	0.5	0.5	1	1	0.5	0.5	1	1	1	0.5	1	0.5	0.028
18	0.5	0.5	0.5	0.5	1	1	0.5	0.5	0.5	0.5	1	0.5	1	1	0.5	0.5	1	1	1	0.5	1	0.5	0.029
19	0.5	0.5	0.5	0.5	1	1	0.5	0.5	0.5	0.5	1	0.5	1	1	0.5	1	1	1	1	1	1	1	0.030
20	0.5	0.5	0.5	0.5	0.5	2	0.5	0.5	0.5	0.5	1	0.5	2	2	0.5	1	2	2	1	1	1	2	0.037
21	0.5	0.5	0.5	0.5	0.5	1	0.5	0.5	0.5	0.5	1	0.5	2	2	0.5	0.5	1	1	1	1	1	0.5	0.029
22	1	0.5	0.5	0.5	1	0.5	0.5	0.5	0.5	0.5	0.5	0.5	1	1	0.5	1	2	2	1	0.5	2	1	0.033

4.2.2. Ranking of the Alternatives

The SIMUS method was applied consistently to rank the alternatives for each of the strategies. Table 5 shows the decision matrices containing criteria values for realistic strategy. Tables A2 and A3 in the Appendix A present the decision matrices for pessimistic and optimistic strategies.

Table 6 presents the way of formation of optimization models. It is formed of two parts. The first part consists of the normalized decision matrix for realistic strategy—keeping the flow of passengers. The second part presents the type of optimization (minimum or maximum), type of operator, and the upper limits to each criterion (RHS).

Table 5. Values of criteria for alternatives. Realistic Strategy ($k = 2$).

Criterion		Alternative, j								
i		1	2	3	4	5	6	7	8	9
C_1	trains/day	38	48	40	35	43	38	37	46	39
C_2	number	15.45	14.94	14.68	16.17	16.79	15.55	16.19	15.72	15.62
C_3	km	336.47	342.1	333.88	347.17	357.63	349.16	330.14	333.72	330.82
C_4	km/h	63	64	63	63	63	63	63	63	63
C_5	coef.	0.132	0.135	0.134	0.133	0.142	0.132	0.125	0.130	0.124
C_6	coef.	1	1	1	1	1	1	0	0	0
C_7	seats/day	10,640	10,080	10,850	9800	9030	10,010	10,360	9660	10,150
C_8	EUR/day	26,374	29,263	26,902	24,937	27,425	26,157	25,419	27,647	25,683

Table 6. Normalized decision matrix for realistic strategy ($k = 2$).

Criterion	Alternative i									Action	Operator	RHS
	1	2	3	4	5	6	7	8	9			
	x_1	x_2	x_3	x_4	x_5	x_6	x_7	x_8	x_9			
C_1	0.10	0.13	0.11	0.10	0.12	0.10	0.10	0.13	0.11	max	$\leq$	0.13
C_2	0.11	0.11	0.10	0.11	0.12	0.11	0.11	0.11	0.11	min	$\geq$	0.10
C_3	0.11	0.11	0.11	0.11	0.12	0.11	0.11	0.11	0.11	max	$\leq$	0.12
C_4	0.11	0.11	0.11	0.11	0.11	0.11	0.11	0.11	0.11	max	$\leq$	0.12
C_5	0.11	0.11	0.11	0.11	0.12	0.11	0.11	0.11	0.10	min	$\geq$	0.10
C_6	0.17	0.17	0.17	0.17	0.17	0.17	0.00	0.00	0.00	max	$\leq$	0.17
C_7	0.12	0.11	0.12	0.11	0.10	0.11	0.11	0.11	0.11	max	$\leq$	0.12
C_8	0.11	0.12	0.11	0.10	0.11	0.11	0.11	0.12	0.11	min	$\geq$	0.10

$x_1, \ldots, x_9$ are the score of alternatives

The value of RHS depends on the type of optimization. The maximum or the minimum normalized value of the row is used. In the first case, the objective of the criterion is a maximum; in the second case, it is a minimum.

The type of optimization is set for each objective. The data for compiling the optimization models are given in Table 5.

For example, the first model is made for the criterion C_1. The objective function is:

$$0.10x_2 + 0.13x_2 + 0.11x_3 + 0.10x_4 + 0.12x_5 + 0.10x_6 + 0.10x_7 + 0.13x_8 + 0.11x_9 \rightarrow \text{Max}, \quad (10)$$

where x_i are the scores of the alternatives.

The other rows of the matrix (C_2 to C_8) serve to form the restrictive conditions. For example, the restrictive condition for C_2 is:

$$0.11x_2 + 0.11x_2 + 0.10x_3 + 0.11x_4 + 0.12x_5 + 0.11x_6 + 0.11x_7 + 0.11x_8 + 0.11x_9 \geq 0.10. \quad (11)$$

The restrictive conditions for the other criteria are similarly formed.

For all variables, the following condition applies:

$$0 \leq x_1, x_2, x_3, x_4, x_5, x_6, x_7, x_8, x_9 \leq 1. \quad (12)$$

The optimization models are performed for all other criteria.

Table 7 demonstrates the normalized efficient results matrix by using the sum of the row method and the results of ERM ranking. $Z_1, \ldots, Z_8$ presents the target functions equivalent to criteria $C_1, \ldots, C_8$ for the linear optimization models in the SIMUS method. Each row presents the values of the scores of the alternatives according to the optimization model. For example, the results show that the second alternative has a score of 1. The scores for all other alternatives are equal to zero. The objective that impacts the ranking the most are criteria: C_1 (frequency of services), C_3 (average distance travelled); C_7 (train's capacity), C_2 (frequency of train stops), and C_8(direct operational costs). They are presented in bold in Table 7.

Table 7. Normalized efficient results matrix for realistic strategy ($k = 2$).

Objective	Alternative *i*								
	1	2	3	4	5	6	7	8	9
Z_1	0.00	**1.00**	0.00	0.00	0.00	0.00	0.00	0.00	0.00
Z_2	0.00	0.03	**0.97**	0.00	0.00	0.00	0.00	0.00	0.00
Z_3	0.00	0.00	0.00	0.00	**0.98**	0.00	0.00	0.02	0.00
Z_4	0.00	0.00	0.00	0.00	0.00	0.00	0.00	0.20	0.80
Z_5	0.00	0.00	0.00	0.00	0.00	0.00	0.00	0.47	0.53
Z_6	0.00	0.00	0.24	0.00	0.76	0.00	0.00	0.00	0.00
Z_7	0.00	0.00	**0.98**	0.00	0.00	0.00	0.02	0.00	0.00
Z_8	0.00	0.00	0.00	**1.00**	0.00	0.00	0.00	0.00	0.00
SC	0.00	1.03	2.18	1.00	1.75	0.00	0.02	0.69	1.33
PF	0	2	3	1	2	0	1	3	2
NPF	0.00	0.25	0.38	0.13	0.25	0.00	0.13	0.38	0.25
$C_{ERM_{ik}}$ = SC × NPF	0.00	0.26	0.82	0.13	0.44	0.00	0.00	0.26	0.33
Ranking	8	5	1	7	2	9	7	4	3

SC—sum of all scores in each column, PF—participation factor, or how many times each alternative satisfies each objective, NPF—normalized participation factor, obtained as a ratio between the PF and total number of objectives; $C_{ERM_{ik}}$—criterion of the ranking; The most important criteria are in bold.

The results indicate that Alternative 3 is the most suitable one for a realistic strategy. The ranking for the pessimistic strategy and the optimistic strategy is determined in a similar way using the SIMUS method. Tables A4 and A5 in the Appendix A present the results of the ranking for the pessimistic and optimistic strategies.

Figure 3 illustrates the ranking of the alternatives for the strategies on the basis of the SIMUS criterion ($C_{ERM_{ik}}$). It could be seen that the best alternative for the studied strategies is different.

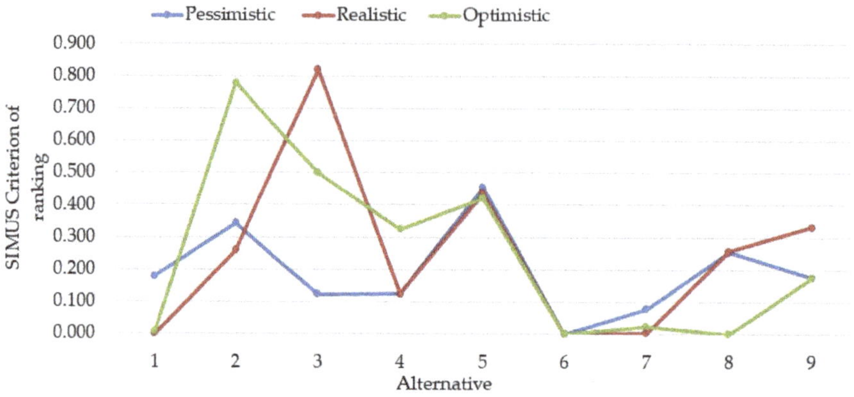

Figure 3. Ranking of the alternatives according the strategy.

Alternative 5 is the best for the pessimistic strategy; Alternative 2 is the best for the optimistic strategy; Alternative 3 is the best for the realistic strategy. These results are valid in a state of certainty. The number of trains, the categories, and the routes are different for each of the strategies. In this situation, the transport operator must change the organization of the trains in the railway network when passenger flow changes. This leads to instability in the transport plan and inconvenience for the users of the train services.

The uncertainty in transport planning is related to the fact that the decision maker cannot predict the probability of a change in passenger flow (10% reduction, saving, or 10% increase). For this purpose, this research deploys a combination of three completely different methods, and thus introduces a new paradigm in the multi-criteria decision-making process. The aim is to obtain a sustainable transport plan solution.

The values of the SIMUS ranking criterion are obtained on the basis of the scores of the objective function for each criterion. In this case, they could be accounted for as profits for each of the alternatives. This allows the values of the criterion of the ranking by the SIMUS method to be used as input to the decision tree in the case of uncertainty. The weights of the passenger flow variation variants determined using the AHP method are interpreted as probabilities and are also the input to the decision tree.

4.2.3. Decision Tree

The process of drawing a decision tree consists of three steps.

First, the tree starts in a chorological order. All the alternatives start marked in branches from the decision-making element denoted with a square. A decision event node, marked with a circle, is placed at the end of each alternative. The variants of variation of passenger flow for each strategy are connected with branches from each decision event node. At the end of each variant are placed additional nodes which denote the strategies. Each strategy is presented by a branch and is connected to the relevant node.

Second, once the tree is drawn, the final profits for each branch are determined and are placed at the end of each branch. The probability for the event is indicated. The values of the ranking criterion obtained using the SIMUS method for each alternative and strategy represents the possibilities.

Third, the tree is evaluated from right to left. The decision tree starts with a decision box having nine branches representing the nine alternatives of the transport plan. Each branch has twenty-two events or possibilities representing the number of variants of change of passenger flow. All the events are illustrated by circles. Each event has three branches representing the strategies of change in passenger flow. The probability of each strategy is indicated in the end of the branch. The values of the ranking criterion calculated by the SIMUS approach are presented on each of branches representing the strategies. The values of the weights of the variant determined using the AHP method are presented in the end of the branches.

Figure 4 presents the decision tree for the problem under study.

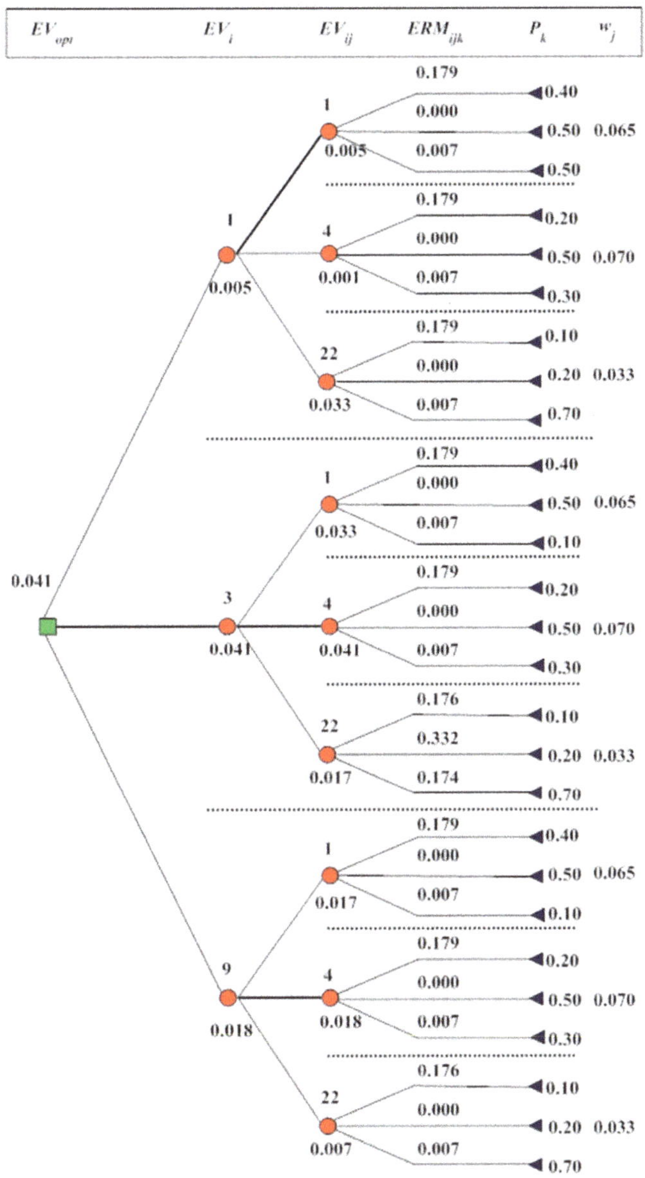

Figure 4. Decision tree.

The selection of the best alternative is performed in the following sequence. First, the values of expected values EV_{ij} for each variant are calculated. The results are placed next to the event node presenting the variants. Second, for each alternative is determined the expected value and it is placed next to event node. Third, the optimal alternative is selected, according to the criterion maximum value of the expected value. The branch of the selected alternative that is connected with the decision-making element is marked with a thick line.

Table A6 in the Appendix A shows the value of the expected value for each variant of passenger flow variation and the alternative determined by Equation (4).

Figure 5 illustrates the comparison of the expected value for all alternatives according to the variants of passenger flow variation. It can be seen that the competing strategies are Alternatives 2, Alternative 3, and Alternative 5. Alternative 3 has the maximum value of the criterion for most of the variants. Alternative 2 is also the best for variants 15–22. Alternative 3, Alternative 2, and Alternative 5 have close results for variants 10 and 14. Alternative 6 has a value equal to zero for all variants. This is due to the value of the ranking criterion obtained using the SIMUS method which is equal to 0.

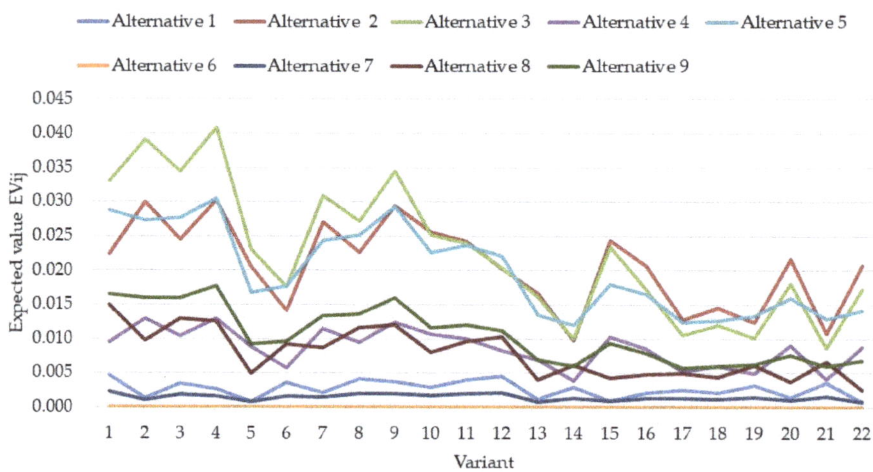

Figure 5. Expected value for each variant of passenger flow variation.

Figure 6 presents the expected value for alternatives, EV_i. The optimal solution is chosen according the maximum expected value. The results show that Alternative 3 is the best.

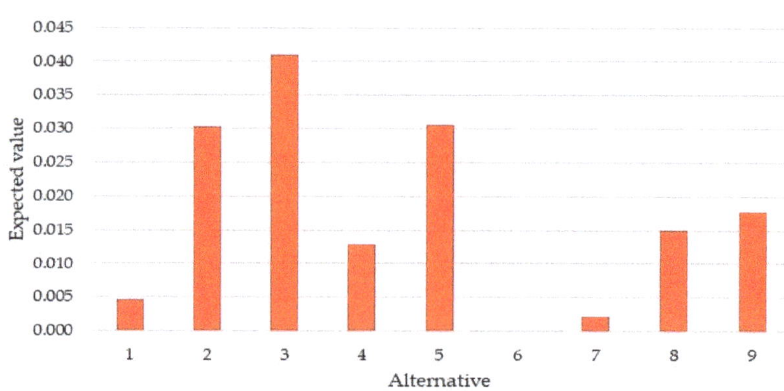

Figure 6. Expected value for alternatives.

The obtained solution makes it possible for the transport plan to be sustainable in the case of uncertainty with specified limitations and probabilistic change in passenger flow. The organization of passenger rail transport according to Alternative 3 includes express, intercity, and fast trains. The number of trains with decreasing and increasing passenger traffic is different. It can be seen in Table 5, Tables A2 and A3 in the Appendix A. In the case of keeping the passengers, the number of trains is 40 pairs per day; when there is a decrease in passengers, the number of trains is 38 pairs per day; when passengers increase, the number of trains is 42 pairs per day. The routes for all categories of trains remain unchanged.

Figure 7 illustrates the difference in operating costs for the best alternatives in the case of certainty or uncertainty. The first row below the abscissa shows the best alternatives for the state of certainty for the studied strategies; the second row indicates the best alternatives for the state of uncertainty for the strategies, and the third row represents the corresponding strategy for which the decision was made. It could be seen that obtained results for the case of uncertainty show a reduction in operating costs for the transport plan compared to the case of certainty. The obtained results make it possible for the transport operators to take not only planning decisions but also operational ones.

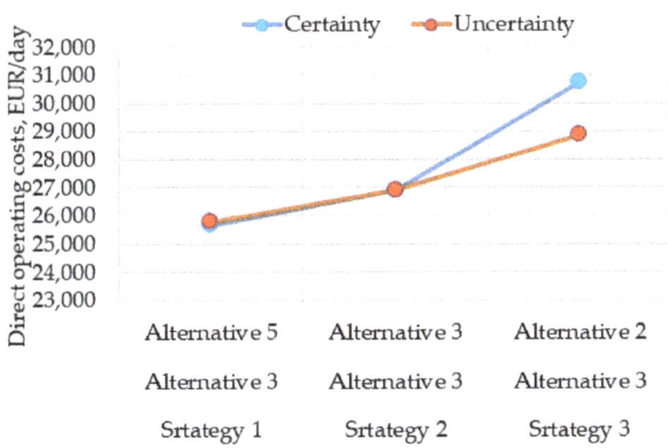

Figure 7. Direct operating costs in the case of certainty and uncertainty, EUR/day.

4.3. *Verification of the Results*

Laplace's criterion and Hurwitz's criterion were used to verify the results obtained through the decision tree method. Both criteria use data of the expected values determined by Equation (4) which are given in Table 8. Hurwitz's approach uses coefficient α to assess the best alternative in different preferences of decision-making. Alternative 3 is selected by means of Laplace's criterion as the best. Alternative 5 is in the second position with close values of Laplace's criterion.

Table 8. Parameters of Laplace's criterion and Hurwitz's criterion.

Alternative i	Laplace's Criterion	$\max_i EV_{ij}$	$\min_i EV_{ij}$	Hurwitz's Criterion									
				Coefficient α									
				0.1	0.2	0.3	0.4	0.5	0.6	0.7	0.8	0.9	1
1	0.003	0.005	0.001	0.001	0.002	0.002	0.002	0.003	0.003	0.004	0.004	0.004	0.005
2	0.021	0.030	0.010	0.012	0.014	0.016	0.018	0.020	0.022	0.024	0.026	0.028	0.030
3	**0.022**	0.041	0.009	0.012	0.015	**0.018**	**0.022**	**0.025**	**0.028**	**0.031**	**0.034**	**0.038**	**0.041**
4	0.009	0.013	0.004	0.005	0.006	0.007	0.008	0.008	0.009	0.010	0.011	0.012	0.013
5	0.020	0.031	0.012	**0.014**	**0.016**	**0.018**	0.019	0.021	0.023	0.025	0.027	0.029	0.031
6	0.000	0.000	0.000	0.000	0.000	0.000	0.000	0.000	0.000	0.000	0.000	0.000	0.000
7	0.001	0.002	0.001	0.001	0.001	0.001	0.002	0.002	0.002	0.002	0.003	0.003	0.003
8	0.008	0.015	0.003	0.004	0.006	0.007	0.009	0.010	0.012	0.013	0.015	0.016	0.017
9	0.011	0.018	0.006	0.008	0.009	0.011	0.013	0.015	0.016	0.018	0.020	0.022	0.024

The optimal values are shown in bold.

The results are similar to those obtained using the decision tree method.

Figure 8 illustrates Hurwitz's criterion according to coefficient α for all alternatives. Hurwitz's criterion gives the opportunity to investigate the sensitivity of the results.

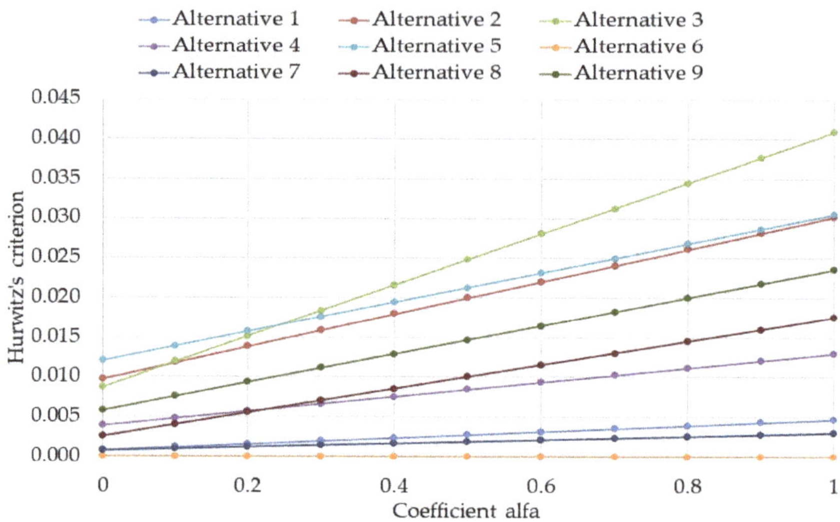

Figure 8. Hurwitz's criterion according to coefficient α.

The value of coefficient α has been set between zero and one, with a step of 0.1. The value of coefficient $\alpha = 0$ coincides with the minimum values of expected value EV_{ij}. The value of coefficient $\alpha = 1$ represents the maximum values of expected value EV_{ij}. The value of $\alpha = 0.5$ could be taken as representing a balanced approach. It could be seen that Alternative 3 is the suitable one for most of the coefficient α values (from 0.26 to 1). Alternative 5 is the best for values of coefficient α from 0 to 0.24. Both alternatives have equal results for value of the coefficient $\alpha = 0.25$. The results obtained with Hurwitz's criterion are similar to those obtained through the decision tree method. On the basis of the analysis performed, the implementation of Alternative 3 is recommended as the most acceptable solution.

5. Conclusions

This paper proposes an integrated model for planning railway passenger transport in the case of uncertainty based on SIMUS, AHP, and decision tree methods. This research introduces a new paradigm in multi-criteria decision-making

Eight quantitative and qualitative criteria accounting for passenger satisfaction and the capabilities of the transport company were defined to assess the transport plan. Nine alternatives for the Bulgarian railway network have been tested. The uncertainty of passenger flow was studied. Pessimistic, realistic, and optimistic strategies of variation of passenger flow were investigated. An increase or a decrease of 10% in passenger flow was established on the basis of an analysis of passengers transported for a ten-year period. This shows the actual state of transport demand and also the practicability of the obtained results. The SIMUS method based on linear programming was applied to rank the alternatives of the transport plan for each of the strategies. It was found out that the criteria that impact the ranking the most are frequency of services, average distance travelled, train's capacity, frequency of train stops, and direct operational costs. The twenty-two variants of probability of change in passenger flow under the respective strategy were studied. Their weights were determined by experts' assessments using the AHP method and were applied as input to the decision tree model.

The best strategy was selected by using the decision tree method. A verification was performed by comparing the results with Laplace's criterion and Hurwitz's criterion. It was found out that the ranking based on both criteria was similar to that of the decision tree method. The sensitivity analysis based on Hurwitz's criterion has been met. It was found out the stability of the choice of suitable alternative.

The theoretical contributions of this paper are based on the elaboration of the integration of multi-criteria methods with the decision tree method to account for uncertainty of passenger flow.

The practical contribution of this study involves the determination of a suitable transport plan (presented by Alternative 3) for the Bulgarian railway network. This alternative offers a transport plan including express intercity trains, intercity trains, and fast trains. This transport scheme includes 27 routes in the railway network. It was found out that the obtained results for the case of uncertainty show a reduction in operating costs for the transport plan compared to the one in the case of certainty.

The results could be used to compare different alternatives in the case of various variations in passenger flow. The proposed integrated approach could be used to investigate some areas or sections of a railway network and also transport corridors. By applying this elaborated approach, it is possible to achieve a benefit for passengers and carriers as well as to improve the quality of transport and the effectiveness of operating costs in the case of uncertainty.

The novelty of this study and its main advantage is the establishment of important objectives for the ranking; the integration of the SIMUS method and AHP method with the decision tree method is a complex approach for decision-making in a state of uncertainty. The methodology makes it possible to study different strategies and variants of variation of passenger flow.

The elaborated integrated approach could serve for making decisions about passenger trains planning in the case of uncertainty in passenger flow and about route planning; to study additional routes; to investigate different strategies of passenger flow variation; to make decisions in case of instability of passenger flow or lack of sufficient travel data.

Future research will expand the scope of the studied strategies of variation of passenger flow; analyze the uncertainty of passenger traffic on railway sections in case of traffic interruption due to repair works; investigate other parameters of the transport process under uncertainty, such as the capacity of trains and implementation of the proposed alternative.

Funding: This work was supported by the National Science Fund of the Ministry of Education and Science of Bulgaria [project numbers No.KП-06-H27/12 of 11.12.2018 "Modelling and elaboration of complex system for selection of transport technology in transport network"].

Acknowledgments: The author expresses her gratitude to "BDZ Passenger Services" Ltd. for providing the data used in this study.

Conflicts of Interest: The author declares no conflict of interest

Appendix A

Table A1. Saaty's scale for pair-wise comparison.

Explanation	Intensity of Importance	Reciprocal Values
Equal importance	1	1
Moderate importance	3	1/3
Strong importance	5	1/5
Very strong importance	7	1/7
Extreme importance	9	1/9
Average intermediate values	2; 4; 6; 8	1/2; 1/4; 1/6; 1/8

Table A2. Values of criteria for alternatives. Pessimistic strategy ($k = 1$).

Criterion i		Alternative, j								
		1	2	3	4	5	6	7	8	9
C_1	trains/day	36	42	38	31	40	35	34	41	37
C_2	number	15.36	14.88	15.21	15.94	16.3	15.63	16.32	16.02	15.62
C_3	km	327	344	335	350	361	355	335	335	331
C_4	km/h	63	64	63	63	63	63	63	62	63
C_5	coef.	0.132	0.135	0.134	0.133	0.142	0.132	0.125	0.130	0.124
C_6	coef.	1	1	1	1	1	1	0	0	0
C_7	seats/day	10,080	8820	10360	8680	8400	9240	9520	8610	9660
C_8	EUR/day	24,404	25,672	25,777	22,198	25,664	24,436	23,603	24,806	24,522

Table A3. Values of criteria for alternatives. Optimistic strategy ($k = 3$).

Criterion i		Alternative, j								
		1	2	3	4	5	6	7	8	9
C_1	trains/day	40	51	42	36	48	41	38	47	40
C_2	number	14.85	15.08	14.36	16.21	16.18	15.63	16.23	15.78	15.79
C_3	km	339.95	337.22	344.33	349.92	354.33	358.61	335.82	336.11	336.2
C_4	km/h	64	64	64	63	63	64	63	63	63
C_5	coef.	0.132	0.135	0.134	0.133	0.142	0.132	0.125	0.130	0.124
C_6	coef.	1	1	1	1	1	1	0	0	0
C_7	seats/day	11,200	10,710	11410	10,080	10,080	10,780	10,640	9870	10,430
C_8	EUR/day	27,782	30,751	28,874	25,916	30,257	28,930	26,571	28,473	26,835

Table A4. Normalized efficient results matrix for pessimistic strategy ($k = 1$).

Objective	Alternative i								
	1	2	3	4	5	6	7	8	9
Z_1	0.00	0.00	0.00	0.00	0.00	0.00	0.00	**1.00**	0.00
Z_2	0.00	**1.00**	0.00	0.00	0.00	0.00	0.00	0.00	0.00
Z_3	0.00	0.00	0.00	0.00	**0.98**	0.00	0.00	0.02	0.00
Z_4	0.55	0.37	0.00	0.00	0.00	0.00	0.00	0.00	0.08
Z_5	0.00	0.00	0.00	0.00	0.00	0.00	0.62	0.00	0.38
Z_6	0.17	0.00	0.00	0.00	0.83	0.00	0.00	0.00	0.00
Z_7	0.00	0.00	**0.98**	0.00	0.00	0.00	0.00	0.00	0.02
Z_8	0.00	0.00	0.00	**1.00**	0.00	0.00	0.00	0.00	0.00
SC	0.72	1.37	0.98	1.00	1.82	0.00	0.00	1.02	0.47
PF	2	2	1	1	2	0	1	2	3
NPF	0.25	0.25	0.13	0.13	0.25	0.00	0.13	0.25	0.38
$C_{ERM_{ik}}$ = SC × NPF	0.18	0.34	0.12	0.13	0.45	0.00	0.08	0.25	0.18
Ranking	4	2	7	6	1	9	8	3	5

SC—sum of all scores in each column, PF—participation factor, or how many times each alternative satisfies each objective, NPF—normalized participation factor, obtained as a ratio between the PF and total number of objectives; $C_{ERM_{ik}}$—criterion of the ranking; The most important criteria are in bold.

Table A5. Normalized efficient results matrix for optimistic strategy ($k = 3$).

Objective	Alternative i								
	1	2	3	4	5	6	7	8	9
Z_1	0.00	**1.00**	0.00	0.00	0.00	0.00	0.00	0.00	0.00
Z_2	0.00	0.00	**1.00**	0.00	0.00	0.00	0.00	0.00	0.00
Z_3	0.00	0.00	0.00	0.00	**0.98**	0.00	0.00	0.00	0.02
Z_4	0.06	0.76	0.00	0.00	0.00	0.00	0.18	0.00	0.00
Z_5	0.00	0.32	0.00	0.00	0.00	0.00	0.00	0.00	0.68
Z_6	0.00	0.00	0.00	0.30	0.70	0.00	0.00	0.00	0.00
Z_7	0.00	0.00	**1.00**	0.00	0.00	0.00	0.00	0.00	0.00
Z_8	0.00	0.00	0.00	**1.00**	0.00	0.00	0.00	0.00	0.00

Table A5. *Cont.*

Objective	Alternative *i*								
	1	**2**	**3**	**4**	**5**	**6**	**7**	**8**	**9**
SC	0.06	2.08	2.00	1.30	1.68	0.00	0.18	0.00	0.70
PF	1	3	2	2	2	0	1	0	2
NPF	0.13	0.38	0.25	0.25	0.25	0.00	0.13	0.00	0.25
$C_{ERM_{ik}}$ = SC × NPF	0.01	0.78	0.50	0.33	0.42	0.00	0.02	0.00	0.17
Ranking	7	1	2	4	3	8	6	9	5

SC—sum of all scores in each column, PF —participation factor, or how many times each alternative satisfies each objective, NPF—normalized participation factor, obtained as a ratio between the PF and total number of objectives; $C_{ERM_{ik}}$—criterion of the ranking; The most important criteria are in bold.

Table A6. Expected value for each variant, EV_{ij}.

Alternative *i*	Variant *j*										
	1	**2**	**3**	**4**	**5**	**6**	**7**	**8**	**9**	**10**	**11**
1	0.005	0.001	0.003	0.003	0.001	0.004	0.002	0.004	0.004	0.003	0.004
2	0.022	0.030	0.024	0.030	0.021	0.014	0.027	0.023	0.029	0.026	0.024
3	0.033	0.039	0.034	0.041	0.023	0.018	0.031	0.027	0.034	0.025	0.024
4	0.009	0.013	0.010	0.013	0.009	0.006	0.011	0.009	0.012	0.011	0.010
5	0.029	0.027	0.028	0.031	0.017	0.018	0.024	0.025	0.029	0.023	0.024
6	0.000	0.000	0.000	0.000	0.000	0.000	0.000	0.000	0.000	0.000	0.000
7	0.002	0.001	0.002	0.002	0.001	0.002	0.001	0.002	0.002	0.002	0.002
8	0.015	0.010	0.013	0.013	0.005	0.009	0.009	0.012	0.012	0.008	0.010
9	0.017	0.016	0.016	0.018	0.009	0.010	0.013	0.014	0.016	0.012	0.012

Alternative *i*	Variant *j*										
	12	**13**	**14**	**15**	**16**	**17**	**18**	**19**	**20**	**21**	**22**
1	0.005	0.001	0.003	0.001	0.002	0.003	0.002	0.003	0.001	0.004	0.001
2	0.020	0.017	0.010	0.024	0.021	0.013	0.015	0.012	0.022	0.011	0.021
3	0.020	0.016	0.010	0.023	0.017	0.011	0.012	0.010	0.018	0.009	0.017
4	0.008	0.007	0.004	0.010	0.009	0.005	0.006	0.005	0.009	0.004	0.009
5	0.022	0.013	0.012	0.018	0.017	0.012	0.013	0.013	0.016	0.013	0.014
6	0.000	0.000	0.000	0.000	0.000	0.000	0.000	0.000	0.000	0.000	0.000
7	0.002	0.001	0.001	0.001	0.001	0.001	0.001	0.002	0.001	0.002	0.001
8	0.010	0.004	0.006	0.004	0.005	0.005	0.004	0.006	0.004	0.007	0.003
9	0.011	0.007	0.006	0.009	0.008	0.006	0.006	0.006	0.008	0.006	0.007

References

1. Djordjević, B.; Krmac, E. Application of Multicriteria Decision-Making Methods in Railway Engineering: A Case Study of Train Control Information Systems (TCIS). In *Modern Railway Engineering*; IntechOpen: London, UK, 2018.
2. Mardani, A.; Zavadskas, E.K.; Khalifah, Z.; Jusoh, A.; Nor, K.M. Multiple Criteria Decision-Making Techniques in Transportation Systems: A Systematic Review of the State of the Art Literature. *Transport* **2015**, *31*, 359–385. [CrossRef]
3. Gerçek, H.; Karpak, B.; Kılınçaslan, T. A multiple criteria approach for the evaluation of the rail transit networks in Istanbul. *Transportation* **2004**, *31*, 203–228. [CrossRef]
4. Sivilevičius, H.; Maskeliūnaitė, L. The Criteria for Identifying the Quality of Passengers' Transportation by Railway and Their Ranking Using Ahp Method. *Transport* **2010**, *25*, 368–381. [CrossRef]
5. Maskeliūnaite, L.; Sivilevičius, H.; Podvezko, V. Research on the Quality of Passenger Transportation by Railway. *Transport* **2009**, *24*, 100–112. [CrossRef]
6. Sivileviäius, H.; Maskelinaite, L. The numerical example for evaluating the criteria describing the quality of the trip by international train. *Econ. Manag.* **2014**, *7*, 74–86. [CrossRef]
7. Dudek, M.; Solecka, K.; Richter, M. A multi-criteria appraisal of the selection of means of urban passenger transport using the Electre and AHP methods. *Czas. Tech.* **2018**, *6*, 79–93. [CrossRef]
8. Yücel, N.; Taşabat, S.E. The Selection of Railway System Projects with Multi Creteria Decision Making Methods: A Case Study for Istanbul. *Procedia Comput. Sci.* **2019**, *158*, 382–393. [CrossRef]

9. Nassereddine, M.; Eskandari, H. An integrated MCDM approach to evaluate public transportation systems in Tehran. *Transp. Res. Part A: Policy Pr.* **2017**, *106*, 427–439. [CrossRef]
10. Wen, H.-Y.; Lin, S. Performance evaluation of highway passenger transport enterprises' operation based on the model of AHP-DEA. In Proceedings of the 2011 IEEE 18th International Conference on Industrial Engineering and Engineering Management, Changchun, China, 3–5 September 2011; Institute of Electrical and Electronics Engineers (IEEE): Piscataway, NJ, USA, 2011; pp. 811–815.
11. Hamurcu, M.; Eren, T. An Application of Multicriteria Decision-making for the Evaluation of Alternative Monorail Routes. *Mathematics* **2018**, *7*, 16. [CrossRef]
12. Ivić, M.; Marković, M.; Belošević, I.; Kosijer, M. Multicriteria decision-making in railway route planning and design. *J. Croat. Assoc. Civ. Eng.* **2012**, *64*, 195–205. [CrossRef]
13. Alpu, Özlem A methodology for evaluating satisfaction with high-speed train services: A case study in Turkey. *Transp. Policy* **2015**, *44*, 151–157. [CrossRef]
14. Qi, J.; Cacchiani, V.; Yang, L. Robust Train Timetabling and Stop Planning with Uncertain Passenger Demand. *Electron. Notes Discret. Math.* **2018**, *69*, 213–220. [CrossRef]
15. Stanković, M.; Gladović, P.; Popović, V. Determining the importance of the criteria of traffic accessibility using fuzzy AHP and rough AHP method. *Decis. Making: Appl. Manag. Eng.* **2019**, *2*, 86–104. [CrossRef]
16. Krmac, E.; Djordjević, B. Evaluation of the TCIS Influence on the capacity utilization using the TOPSIS method: Case studies of Serbian and Austrian railways. *Oper. Res. Eng. Sci. Theory Appl.* **2019**, *2*, 27–36. [CrossRef]
17. Liu, F.; Aiwu, G.; Lukovac, V.; Vukić, M. A multicriteria model for the selection of the transport service provider: A single valued neutrosophic DEMATEL multicriteria model. *Decis. Making: Appl. Manag. Eng.* **2018**, *1*, 121–130. [CrossRef]
18. Đorđević, D.; Stojic, G.; Stević, Ž.; Pamučar, D.; Vulevic, A.; Mišić, V. A New Model for Defining the Criteria of Service Quality in Rail Transport: The Full Consistency Method Based on a Rough Power Heronian Aggregator. *Symmetry* **2019**, *11*, 992. [CrossRef]
19. Zak, J.; Fierek, S.; Kruszyński, M. Evaluation of Different Transportation Solutions with the Application of Macro Simulation tools and Multiple Criteria Group Decision Making/Aiding Methodology. *Procedia-Soc. Behav. Sci.* **2014**, *111*, 340–349. [CrossRef]
20. D'Ovidio, F.D.; Leogrande, D.; Mancarella, R.; Schinzano, A.; Viola, D. A Multivariate Analysis of the Quality of Public Transport Services. *Procedia Econ. Financ.* **2014**, *17*, 238–247. [CrossRef]
21. Banaś, J.; Tomaszewska, K. Support in multi-criteria decision-making under uncertainty in a transport company. *Oper. Res. Decis.* **2013**, *2*, 11–23. [CrossRef]
22. Ngossaha, J.M.; Ngouna, R.H.; Archimède, B.; Nlong, J. Sustainability assessment of a transportation system under uncertainty: An integrated multicriteria approach. *IFAC-PapersOnLine* **2017**, *50*, 7481–7486. [CrossRef]
23. Isaai, M.T.; Kanani, A.; Tootoonchi, M.; Afzali, H.R. Intelligent timetable evaluation using fuzzy AHP. *Expert Syst. Appl.* **2011**, *38*, 3718–3723. [CrossRef]
24. Zhang, X.; Li, L.; Le Vine, S.; Liu, X. An integrated pricing/planning strategy to optimize passenger rail service with uncertain demand. *J. Intell. Fuzzy Syst.* **2019**, *36*, 435–448. [CrossRef]
25. Arsovski, S.; Todorovic, G.; Lazić, Z.; Arsovski, Z.; Ljepava, N.; Aleksic, A. Model for Selection of the Best Location Based on Fuzzy AHP and Hurwitz Methods. *Math. Probl. Eng.* **2017**, *2017*. [CrossRef]
26. Vesković, S.; Stević, Ž.; Karabašević, D.; Rajilić, S.; Milinković, S.; Stojić, G. A New Integrated Fuzzy Approach to Selecting the Best Solution for Business Balance of Passenger Rail Operator: Fuzzy PIPRECIA-Fuzzy EDAS Model. *Symmetry* **2020**, *12*, 743. [CrossRef]
27. Sekhar, C.R.; Minal; Madhu, E. Mode Choice Analysis Using Random Forrest Decision Trees. *Transp. Res. Procedia* **2016**, *17*, 644–652. [CrossRef]
28. Kaminski, B.; Jakubczyk, M.; Szufel, P. A framework for sensitivity analysis of decision trees. *Cent. Eur. J. Oper. Res.* **2017**, *26*, 135–159. [CrossRef]
29. Oral, L.O.; Tecim, V. Using Decision Trees for Estimating Mode Choice of Trips in Buca-Izmir. *ISPRS Int. Arch. Photogramm. Remote. Sens. Spat. Inf. Sci.* **2013**, 139–145. [CrossRef]
30. Dorokhov, O.; Chernov, V. Application of the fuzzy decision trees for the tasks of alternative choices. *Transp. Telecommun.* **2011**, *12*, 4–11.

31. Safitri, D.M.; Surjandari, I. Travel mode switching prediction using decision tree in Jakarta greater area. In Proceedings of the 2017 International Conference on Information Technology Systems and Innovation (ICITSI), Bandung, Indonesia, 23–24 October 2017; Institute of Electrical and Electronics Engineers (IEEE): Piscataway, NJ, USA, 2017; pp. 246–250.
32. Tsami, M.; Adamos, G.; Nathanail, E.; Budiloviča, E.B.; Jackiva, I.Y.; Magginas, V. A Decision Tree Approach for Achieving High Customer Satisfaction at Urban Interchanges. *Transp. Telecommun. J.* **2018**, *19*, 194–202. [CrossRef]
33. Ochiai, Y.; Masuma, Y.; Tomii, N. Improvement of timetable robustness by analysis of drivers' operation based on decision trees. *J. Rail Transp. Plan. Manag.* **2019**, *9*, 57–65. [CrossRef]
34. Saaty, T. Fundamentals of the Analytic network process—Dependence and feedback in decision-making with a single network. *J. Syst. Sci. Syst. Eng.* **2004**, *13*, 129–1577. [CrossRef]
35. Saaty, T. *Fundamentals of Decision—Making and Priority Theory with the Analytic Hierarchy Process*, 1st ed.; RWS: New York, NY, USA, 2000.
36. Munier, N. A new approach to the rank reversal phenomenon in MSDM with the SIMUS method. *Mult. Criteria Decis. Mak.* **2016**, *11*, 137–152. [CrossRef]
37. Munier, N. *A Strategy for Using Multi-Criteria Analysis in Decision-Making*; Springer: Berlin/Heidelberg, Germany, 2011.
38. Munier, N.; Hontoria, E.; Jiménez-Sáez, F. Strategic Approach in Multi-Criteria Decision Making. In *International Series in Operations Research & Management Science*; Springer International Publishing: Cham, Switzerland, 2019.
39. Taha, H.A. *Operations Research: An Introduction*, 9th ed.; University of Arkansas: Fayetteville, AR, USA, 2011.
40. Srivastava, T.N. *Shailaja Rego. Statistics for Management*; Tata McCraw-Hill Publishing Company: New York, NY, USA, 2008.

symmetry

MDPI

Article

Synergies of Text Mining and Multiple Attribute Decision Making: A Criteria Selection and Weighting System in a Prospective MADM Outline

Sarfaraz Hashemkhani Zolfani * and Arman Derakhti

School of Engineering, Catholic University of the North, Larrondo 1281, Coquimbo 1780000, Chile; derakhti.arman@ucn.cl

* Correspondence: sarfaraz.hashemkhani@ucn.cl

Received: 21 April 2020; Accepted: 19 May 2020; Published: 25 May 2020

Abstract: In this study, a new way of criteria selection and a weighting system will be presented in a multi-disciplinary framework. Weighting criteria in Multi-Attribute Decision Making (MADM) has been developing as the most attractive section in the field. Although many ideas have been developed during the last decades, there is no such great diversity that can be mentioned in the literature. This study is looking from outside the box and is presenting something totally new by using big data and text mining in a Prospective MADM outline. PMADM is a hybrid interconnected concept between the Futures Studies and MADM fields. Text mining, which is known as a useful tool in Futures Studies, is applied to create a widespread pilot system for weighting and criteria selection in the PMADM outline. Latent Semantic Analysis (LSA), as an influential method inside the general concept of text mining, is applied to show how a data warehouse's output, which in this case is Scopus, can reach the final criteria selection and weighting of the criteria.

Keywords: text mining; Multi-Attribute Decision Making (MADM), criteria selection; weighting; Prospective MADM; Latent Semantic Analysis (LSA)

---

1. Definition of the Current Study in the MADM Outline

Multiple Criteria Decision Making (MCDM) is a multidisciplinary area and field that is working actively in interdisciplinary atmospheres of such fields like management science, operations research and decision science [1,2]. MCDM has two separated parts, which are Multi-Attribute Decision Making (MADM) and Multi-Objective Decision Making (MODM), and it can be described shortly as follows: MADM problems can be considered as discrete problems and MODM problems as continuous problems [3,4]. The MADM structure is linked to the theory of Rational Choice, which is acting rationally with given information, constraints and conditions. Decisions can be made based on alternatives, criteria and the relative importance of them. On the other hand, the MODM framework is designed for non-predetermined alternatives, in which decision makers are involved in to find one of a set of appropriate answers for their models. Generally, the number of alternatives for a MODM problem is infinite [5,6].

At the present time, MADM models and methods are reflected and applied for decision-making problems in different majors and fields, which is not limited to the any special area or structure [7–13]. In the next section, all MADM methods will be introduced in Table 1. The main point about all common MADM methods is they can be categorized in certain sections that are usually predictable. It means all new contributions could be classified in common sections, which can be comparable as well. The four main contributions as categories are as follows:

Category 1:

Concentrate on criteria and their analysis and weighting, such as AHP [14], ANP [15,16], SWARA [17], Extended SWARA [18], FARE [19], BWM [20] and FUCOM [21]. The newest methods are BWM and FUCOM, and this part still has enough motivation from researchers to be worked on. Except for SWARA, they can evaluate alternatives but the key point about them is the analyzing of criteria.

Category 2:

Concentrate on analyzing for prioritizing and ranking of the alternatives that is really active these days. In comparison to the previous section, so many new methods (later than 2010) have been introduced lately, such as ARAS [22], WASPAS [23], EDAS [24], CODAS [2], CoCoSo [25] and MARCOS [26]. There is a trend, and we predict more and more methods will be introduced.

Category 3:

Hybrid new models that is really common and it can be mentioned, such as SWARA–COPRAS [27], SWARA–WASPAS [28], SWARA–VIKOR [29], SWARA–EDAS [30], BWM–WASPAS [31], BWM–MAIRCA [32], etc. With a new method, so many hybrid models can be developed, and this is a really common trend among researchers. This combination is imaginable between the two previous sections, in which one method applies for weighting criteria and another one for the evaluating and prioritizing of criteria.

Category 4:

The main aim is a comparison between methods with the basic and same logic, like VIKOR and TOPSIS [33], EDAS and TOPSIS [34] and SWARA and BWM [35], etc.

Category 5:

The combination of logics with MADM methods, such as fuzzy and grey, is another trend that is so common among researchers and it is the most active part of studies, somehow. It is so common to find different combinations of methods with the same logic but different details, such as interval type-2 fuzzy WASPAS and TOPSIS [36], Fuzzy BWM [37], Fuzzy EDAS, Fuzzy SWARA and Fuzzy CRITIC [38], Fuzzy ANP, Fuzzy TOPSIS and Fuzzy VIKOR [39], Fuzzy AHP and Fuzzy MAIRCA [40], Grey COPRAS and Fuzzy COPRAS [41], Fuzzy FUCOM [42] and Fuzzy group BWM–MULTIMOORA [43].

Table 1. Primary model of Prospective Multi-Attribute Decision Making (PMADM) based on limiters and boosters [44].

		C_1		C_{n+1}		C_n
Weights						
Limiters (L) /Boosters (B)		$L_{1-1} \cdots L_{1-n}$		$L_{n+1-1} \cdots L_{n+1-n}$		$L_{n-1} \cdots L_{n-n}$
	Based on C_1	**Average**	**Based on C_{n+1}**	**Average**	**Based on C_n**	**Average**
A_1 without L						
A_1 based on L_{1-1}						
A_1 based on …						
A_1 based on L_{1-n}						
A_{n+1} without L						
A_{n+1} based on L_{n+1-1}						
A_{n+1} based on …						
A_{n+1} based on L_{n+1-n}						
A_n without L						
A_n based on L_{n-1}						
A_n based on …						
A_n based on L_{n-n}						

The main idea of the current study is to present a new way to weigh criteria based on something more scientific. Although using experts' opinions have had a great position in the decision-making history, results would not necessarily be accurate and robust [18]. Furthermore, one step backward is the criteria selection strategies usually conducted by researchers based on limited previous studies.

Criteria selection, itself, can be an essential part of defining an MADM model and MADM problem in reality. Accordingly, this study can be classified as in Section 1, and even as something newer that has not yet been added as a category of innovation in the MADM field. Text mining and its analysis can be a really powerful tool for finding the most critical criteria based on the entire data base, and then weighting the criteria based on the majority of existing reports and analysis of similar studies.

2. Definition of the Current Study in the Prospective MADM Outline

PMADM is a new approach and model for decision-making about the future in practice. Since introducing this new approach, a new sub-branch has been imaginable in the MADM framework, which can be developed more and more in reality. As can be analyzed from the literature of the MADM framework, some studies have been working since 1988 about the MADM structure and its framework in decision-making for future matters and topics [45–56]. Time (time period) consideration has been developed in decision-making problems and Dynamic MADM with different definitions could be considered as the last contribution regarding time consideration in MADM models.

The MADM and classic methods used to consider a decision in a stable and fixed state that could not be flexibly measured. Dynamic MADM (DMADM) has developed since around one decade ago but could not meet and support all necessities, needs and requirements. By developing "Futures Studies" and "Foresight" perspectives, imaginations and thoughts about the decision process about the future have changed. Classic decision-making structures could not meet such ideas like explorative and descriptive perspectives, so new paradigms and ideas have shaped since then. PMADM was introduced to cover and support all new aspects of needs and necessities of decision making about the future with a flexible idea.

PMADM as a new sub-branch in the MADM field, which is also a multidisciplinary area, and it can be considered as an approach in "Futures Studies" as well. PMADM is not limited to the classic dimensions of MADM and it can be developed in a really new space. Due to needs, new items can be added to the classic model and make that more applicable with more reliable and accurate outputs and decisions. In the first step, Limiters (L) and Boosters (B) are presented [44]. Limiters and Boosters as new items that will be considered in cases in which different scenarios can happen with different possibilities. Mostly it considers alternatives that will have a different quality in different scenarios. Hashemkhani Zolfani et al. [57,58] discussed the importance of considering the future in MADM models. Another new model has discussed about MADM framework and future scenarios in different states and situations [59].

PMADM has this potential to be developed in both concept and for introducing new methods that have the same framework. New items and rules can be added and considered in evaluating criteria and their weights, alternatives and the general concept. New methods with the basic structure of PMADM also can be developed for application in the future in a better way in real-world cases. Here, the main point is methods can be developed the same, original PMADM structure.

All the latest contributions of Prospective MADM are based on new items:

- Limiters/Boosters:

Hashemkhani Zolfani et al. [57] released the first contribution and definition of the PMADM outline, which can be explained as Limiters/Boosters. Limiters/Boosters can have the role of pay-offs of future scenarios for the evaluated alternatives in their positions. This fact can be demonstrated by examining where they are located in the structure of a classic MADM structure; for example, as shown in Table 1. Limiters and Boosters can be outputs of some future scenarios or just some future possibilities and can have a direct influence on the alternatives' analysis and expectations.

- Multi-Aspect Criterion

Multi-Aspect Criterion is a new item in the classic structure of MADM in the PMADM area. It contains two main shapes: "Hybrid criteria as a new criterion" and "a lately defined concept for the other criteria as a criterion". The importance of time will be showed with this new item to control the definitions during the period of time. In future definitions, criteria can be mixed or developed in different aspects and approaches. It is really important to have an explicit definition about a certain time in the future while the decision-making process is happening [60].

- Supportive-backup criteria

"Supportive-backup criteria" is another additive item to the PMADM outline. While different future scenarios are considered, this new item can be really useful. It shapes all future decision-making matrices into one matrix that decision-makers can shape to whatever they want and make their decisions better and more effective [61]. For instance, an example is illustrated in Table 2. "Supportive-backup criteria" gives great possibility to the researchers to consider a set of different future-possible scenarios for their calculations and evaluations. Decision-makers can have a back-up system for possible ways of managing and leading probable future scenarios in their decision models in advance.

Table 2. Position of the "Supportive-backup criteria" [61].

	C_1	C_2	$C_{n\text{-}1}$	C_n
Supportive/Backup Criteria	C_{s1-1}	C_{2*-s1}	$C_{s1-n-1-sb1}$	…
	C_{s2-1}	C_{s1-2}	$C_{n-1*-s2}$	…
	$C_{u1\text{-}1}$	…	…	…
A_1	…	…	…	…
Reserved A_1	…	…	…	…
Reserved A_1	…	…	…	…
Reserved A_1	…	…	…	…
…	…	…	…	…
…	…	…	…	…
…	…	…	…	…
A_n	…	…	…	…

- Sensitivity analysis of the experts based on Causal Layered Analysis (CLA)

Applying CLA as a qualitative "Futures Studies" field can give a great opportunity to the researchers of the MCDM field to evaluate many things, including analysis of experts who are going to be invited as a part of panel teams. This study showed how experts can be finally selected for cooperation in a study [62].

3. Research Gap and Case Study: "Machine Tool Selection"

Text mining has been accepted as a powerful and useful tool in foresight exercises [63]. Saritas & Burmaoglu [64] presented Text Mining as a method or tool in the field of Futures Studies, which includes Foresight as well. Prospective MADM is the output and interconnection of two multidisciplinary fields, namely Futures Studies and Multiple Criteria Decision Making. As a matter of fact, this research has a connection between three fields of study and can develop more possibilities for doing better studies in the future.

Making a critical decision for the future is so challenging and all the procedures can be really vital. Similar to the Multi-Aspect criterion, the procedure of defining criteria is a big challenge; therefore, reliability of selecting the most important criteria should be the core of an MADM problem and challenge. If researchers cannot define the best set of criteria, a logical, useful output would be out of reach.

Text Mining can help researchers to use big data to find the most important criteria and relative importance of each of them. The common way of defining a set of criteria in the MADM field is only a limited study field, and in a related literature review, a maximum of some interviews with limited accessible experts are available. Indeed, in numerous studies there is no need to use some older MADM methods (Category 1) for weighting criteria if we are working on future-based decisions in a big level of the study.

Machine tool selection has always been an important issue for decision-makers in different industries in order to make the most efficient and effective decisions. Over the past decades, many researchers studied, with various methodologies, which MCDM is the most well-known methodology that has been used several times. In all the past articles, the criteria and methodologies were selected based on the author's opinion; however, in this investigation we would like to implement a new way in order to classify the most relevant studies and the most significant themes. More specifically, we try to answer the following question: What are the main criteria and topics of current machine tool selection research?

To answer this question, the literature items or literature positions were analyzed by Latent Semantic Analysis (LSA), which revealed five important criteria on machine tool selection: size and precision, cost and serviceability, flexibility, productivity as well as technical features and safety. This study contributes to the machine tool selection literature by providing a comprehensive review of current machine tool selection studies and recognizing its primary research topics, which provides guideline for future studies. This new approach is a unique way to gather data and determine criteria by using text mining based on previous studies and this study would be able to serve as a research map for future MCDM articles.

4. Method

4.1. Data Collection

In order to attain all the related articles in the machine tool selection research landscape and identify the research area, we first searched for the "machine selection" and "MCDM" phrases—for all peer-reviewed academic publications—in their titles, abstract or author-supplied keywords in the SCOPUS database. This database presents the largest abstract and citation of peer-reviewed literature in scientific, technical, medical and social sciences. This process resulted in 107 articles, which means 107 publications exactly used the terms "machine selection" and "MCDM" in their titles, abstract or keywords. Then, the authors read all 107 publications in order to find out the most relevant studies. After reading all 107 abstracts, 28 publications were chosen to be considered as machine tool selection by the MCDM technique research. These 28 articles explain how to select the best machine tool by different MCDM techniques, in which most of the authors used hybrid techniques in order to find the best choice. The abstracts of these articles turned into a new raw data set for analyzing in Latent Semantic Analysis.

4.2. Data Analysis

With help of RapidMiner [65] a text mining approach was implemented that is a part of data mining tools. Distinct techniques form the text mining structure, such as natural language processing (NLP), machine learning, information extraction, information retrieval and statistics. This idea derives from "the machine supported analysis of text" [66]. Since this era is famous for data science, there have been many studies that investigated the use of text mining in the literature [67,68]. Latent Semantic Analysis is used in this study to extract the most significant and relevant criteria from the previous studies, which was implemented in different contributions [69,70]. In comparison to other text mining techniques that are only able to analyze textual data and count the occurrences of particular words,

LSA can extract the contextual-usage meaning of words and estimates of similarities among words with the information at the semantic level [71]. Thus, the intuitive application of LSA has been growing in different sorts of text mining classifications, containing library indexing, search engine and natural language processing, and so on [72].

This study follows the text mining procedures that was used in previous studies [67,68,71,72]. The following steps explain all processes of the LSA, from the pre-processing term reduction and term frequency matrix transformation to the singular value decomposition.

First, we consider all abstracts as input data in this text mining technique; however, it did not work out very well because usually abstracts do not contain criteria and mostly discuss methodologies and their achievements. Therefore, we read all 28 publications in order to pull out the specific part that has the criteria in its context and then consolidated it in a spreadsheet, finally loading it into RapidMiner. It might form a doubt why we did not consider all parts of the publication as our input data: all the sections of an academic publication together may contain many different contexts and ideas, such as methodologies, literature, mathematic formulas, etc. Thus, we thought it would not a good decision to consider each article completely.

4.2.1. Pre-Processing and Term Reduction

In the first step, every record (the specific part pulled out of the publications) in the dataset is defined as a unique document. This function lets authors trace the results of the LSA back to a specific article to find out which one is of more significance. Secondly, in RapidMiner, the data were imported and called to the procedure by the retrieve operator. Each record was converted into a document object before it could be analyzed. Next, all the words were recognized as tokens and each token was diagnosed by space or a non-letter separator. Then, all tokens were transformed into the lower case, because it is essential to integrate all tokens in a unit format. For instance, "Machine Tool Selection" was considered to "machine tool selection". After that, the "stopwords English" operator removed all stopwords, such as "the", "is", "and", "a", "an", etc., in the English language. The presence of these stopwords do not make any valuable meaning and increases dimensionality. Afterwards, all the tokens that were less than two letters or more than twenty-five letters were removed because in none of both situations the tokens do not make sense. Then, the "stem porter" operator, which is one of the stemming techniques, was applied in order to decrease the number of words that has the same root. For example, "contribute", "contribution", "contributed" and "contributions" were considered as a single token, the "contribut". With the stemming process, plenty of similar words were decreased and this issue helps the dimensionality from a further increment. The result of these processes was concluded at 224 tokens. In this step, we realized that there are some common academic words that are used in academic publications. In order to eliminate these common academic tokens, we searched and selected an academic phrase bank [73]. This academic phrase bank specifically discusses phrases that are used in academic publications. In this step, we considered this book as a discrete input in another procedure and implemented the previous steps containing the tokenization, transforming to lower case, filtering English stopwords, filtering tokens by length and stemming, from where we took the result of 1907 tokens to a new dictionary in order to eliminate all the common academic words in the main process. After this reduction, the number of tokens decreased to 101.

4.2.2. Term Frequency Matrix Transformation

In this study, the technique of calculating the relatively rare weighting called Term Frequency-Inverse Document Frequency (TF-IDF) is used. The TF-IDF technique is a new approach of term frequency matrix transformation and is a fundamental procedure in different types of text mining techniques [68]. Such transformation promotes the occurrence of rare terms and decreases the impact of more common non-stopwords. TF-IDF is separated in two parts: first, TF explains the ratio of the number of times a keyword emerges in a given document, n_k (where k is keyword), to the total number of terms in the document, n:

$$TF = n_k/n$$

and IDF is defined as follows:

$$IDF = log_2\ (N/N_k)$$

where N is the number of documents and N_k is the number of documents that contain the keyword, K [74]. Then, TF-IDF is illustrated as follows:

$$TF\text{-}IDF = (n_k/n) * log_2\ (N/N_k)$$

4.2.3. Singular Value Decomposition (SVD)

Singular Value Decomposition (SVD) plays the most important role in the latent semantic analysis. SVD is a linear algebra technique, which is a factorization of a complex matrix. More information about computation of the SVD is presented in previous literature [75,76]. The major idea is to make a rectangular matrix A be broken down into the product of three matrices, an orthogonal matrix U, a diagonal matrix S and the transpose of an orthogonal matrix V, as follows:

$$A_{mn} = U_{mm} S_{mn} V^{T}{}_{nn}$$

where $U^T U = I$; $V^T V = I$; the columns of V are orthonormal eigen-vectors of $A^T A$; the columns of U are orthonormal eigenvectors of AA^T; and S is a diagonal m × n matrix containing the square roots of the eigenvalues from V or U in descending order. These eigenvalues indicate the variance of the linearly independent components along each dimension (factor).

Singular value decomposition gets the TF-IDF weighted term matrix and converts it into three matrices containing the term-by-factor matrix, document-by-factor matrix and singular value matrix (square roots of eigenvalues). The term-by-factor matrix describes the term loading to a specific latent factor. The document-by-factor describes the document loadings to a specific latent factor. The singular value illustrates the significance of a specific factor.

The performance of singular value decomposition in LSA in terms of simulation is almost similar to the way the human brain distills meaning in text [68]. It comes from the notion that some different words can have the same meaning or vice versa; one word in distinct contexts can have a different meaning. The words that have the same meaning will load to their common underlying concepts. This explains that one word might load multiple latent concepts in comparison to its main underlying concept. This is a key that empowers LSA in distinguishing the underlying concepts within textual data [68]. The more detailed mathematics can be found in prior studies [68,75].

4.2.4. Factor Determination

Singular Value Decomposition (SVD) can be calculated in different dimensions by eliminating the less important factors in the matrix. In addition, LSA can explain different levels of abstraction by decreasing the number of factors. In SVD there is a possibility to analyze data with different factors, which is usually is related to how much variance in the term vector is cumulatively explained by the factor [68,72]. However, the number of tokens in our study is too small to consider the variance and there are more specific tokens that need to be classified by the LSA. We calculated different dimensions to reach the ideal number of factors; in our study, the ideal number of the factors for the top level LSA analysis is five (Table 3).

Table 3. The five most important factors for machine tool selection and the high-loading terms.

Factors	High-Loading Terms
Factor 1	Rock, diamet, economi, weight, load, max, altern, kw, divers, secondary, conform
Factor 2	Consumpt, compat, energi, service, price, install, wast, multi, rel, power, technic, environment, space
Factor 3	Setup, product, custom. Integr, sub, eas, property, user
Factor 4	Mm, fig, shift, labor, rework, scrap, capit, pallet depreci, axi
Factor 5	Etc, cnc, rotary, adapt, tool, machin, deform, spindle, drive, failure, thermal, taper, environ, extinguish, fire

These five factors distinguish 57 tokens among 101 tokens in the word vector that specifically explain which words have been applied more.

4.2.5. Term Loadings and Cross-Loadings

As it is possible in exploratory factor analysis for one item to load multiple factors, in the LSA, one token might also load multiple factors. This comes from human language, in that one word may have different meanings according to context. For instance, the token "spindl" load from Factor 1 to Factor 5, respectively, as follows: 0.0295, 0.0045, −0.1682, 0.0547 and 0.1890. It shows that the token "spindl" were used in all factors but with different meanings or purposes, which made us decide to choose the high-loading term for each token in the five factors. Therefore, the token "spindl" was added to Factor 5 and the other loadings were named cross-loadings. Table 1 shows the high-loading terms after omitting the cross-loading terms (Appendix A shows all high-loading and cross-loading terms).

5. Results

5.1. Factor Interpretation and Labels

The meaning of each factor in Table 1 is explained by the terms and documents loaded to it. We created a new table (Table 4) that shows how these tokens describe sub-criteria in the MCDM framework. Now it is essential to label the factors and interpret the tokens. As it was mentioned in previous studies [68,72], labeling factors in LSA can be a challenging task, as usually there are no corresponding explanations or phrases in order to match to a specific factor. Labeling the criteria was decided by the authors. In addition, the authors read all the articles separately in order to realize the relation of each token and the previous literature. In this step, the authors read each token and found it in the literature in order to find out the most fitted sub-criterion, because each token does not make sense alone, and most of the sub-criteria are a mixture of some words. In some cases, making two or more tokens up concluded a sub-criterion; but, in some cases, merging a token and some other words out of Table 1 showed us the best and the most fitting sub-criterion. The first factor category or criterion is called "Size and Precision" because the tokens are referring to the previous studies that discussed the details. For example, ultimate load capacity, which is an important sub-criterion in machine tool selection, is considered as Precision. The second sub-criterion "diversity of materials and structure" discusses the changeability of a tool in terms of choosing materials or structure. Moreover, weight machine dimensions, maximum speed, maximum tool diameter and product conformance discus the size and precision at the same time. In some previous studies [77], Size and Precision were considered as two different criteria; however, in this study we show that they are meaningfully related to each other interchangeably. The second criterion is "Cost and Serviceability". Unlike the previous studies [77–79] that considered cost and serviceability as two different criteria, in this we demonstrate that these two criteria are somehow cause and effect elements. Price, energy consumption, maintenance cost, waste amount, operation cost, quality of technical service, service training and repair service are sub-criteria of the Cost and Serviceability criterion. The tool's flexibility has always been an important criterion in order to select an optimum choice. In machine tool selection, the literature setup time, installation easiness, ease of learning, ease of use, integration, properties and user friendliness fitted very well with the third classification of the tokens. "Productivity" is a well-known criterion in choosing all different type of machines and technologies. In this study, the best fitted tokens in the productivity classification are as follows: depreciation quality, scrap and rework reliability, pallet changer and fixture, labor cost as well as operation shifts. The last criterion, which is also is a mixture of two distinct criteria in prior studies, is called "Technical Features and Safety". These two criteria are straightly related to each other and it is better to consider them in a unique criterion. Because they are cause and effect criteria, the better and high-quality the technical features are, the higher the safety is, and vice versa. The most fitted tokens in the fifth classification and sub-criteria in the literature are as follows: capacity of rotary table, thermal deformation, spindle speed, spindle power, adaptability, failure rate, tool changer time, fire extinguisher, number of tappers and reliability of the drive system. These sub-criteria show that the most discussed type of machine tool was Computer Numerical Control (CNC). Regarding the literature, the previous studies that discussed the sub-criteria are displayed in Table 2. These references were concluded by SVD output in RapidMiner 9.6, and the results were classified based on high-term loadings in each factor; the related methodologies in each reference are demonstrated in Table 4.

Table 4. Criteria, sub-criteria, methodology and representative articles, according to the high-loading terms.

Criteria or Factors	Sub-Criteria or Sub Factor	Methodology	Representative Articles
Size and Precision	Ultimate load capacity, Diversity of materials and structure, Weight, Machine dimensions, Maximum speed, Maximum tool diameter, Product conformance,	Fuzzy DEMATEL and entropy weighting and later defuzzification VIKOR, fuzzy AHP and grey relational analysis, SWARA and COPRAS-G methods AHP Fuzzy ANP	[80] [79] [77] [81] [82]
Cost and Serviceability	Price, Energy consumption, Maintenance cost, Waste amount, Operation cost, Quality of technical service, Service training, Repair Service	ANP and grey relational analysis Fuzzy ANP and PROMETHEE AHP AHP TOPSIS and fuzzy ANP	[83] [84] [85] [86] [87]
Flexibility	Setup time, Installation easiness, Ease of learning, Ease of use, Integration, Properties, User friendliness,	Fuzzy ANP VIKOR AHP TOPSIS and fuzzy ANP Fuzzy ANP	[88] [89] [85] [87] [90]
Productivity	Depreciation quality, Scrap and rework reliability, Pallet changer and fixture, Labor cost, Operation shifts,	ANP and grey relational analysis Fuzzy ANP and PROMETHEE Fuzzy ANP AHP	[83] [84] [82] [91]
Technical Features and Safety	Capacity of rotary table, Thermal deformation, Spindle speed, Spindle power, Adaptability, Failure rate, Tool changer time, Fire extinguisher, Number of tapers, Reliability of drive system,	AHP and TOPSIS SWARA and COPRAS-G TOPSIS and fuzzy ANP Fuzzy ANP AHP	[92] [77] [87] [90] [85]

5.2. Confluence of PMADM and Text mining

As mentioned above, the application of text mining in PMADM is novel and has space to grow. The innovation in our results is that the prior studies presented each criterion separately, but the text mining approach shows that some criteria are interchangeably connected to each other based on prior literature containing Size and Precision, Cost and Serviceability, and Technical Features and Safety. The following Table 4 demonstrates the results of the Latent Semantic Analysis in finding the most discussed criteria in previous studies, which allow us to anticipate future research. In order to adjust the obtained tokens and sub-criteria, the authors needed to read all prior studies in detail to understand the relation between them.

6. Final Proposed Weighting Structure

In this section, each criterion and sub-criterion's weight will be calculated. As a result of the last section, sub-criteria were obtained based on a text-mining approach. With help of the LSA methodology, the most significant tokens were classified into five different categories, which are called the machine tool selection criteria. In the first step, the authors found the number of occurrences of each sub-criterion in the literature. For example, the phrase "Ultimate load capacity" were repeated in three different documents in the literature; thus, the number of occurrences were counted for each criterion and are shown in Table 5. In order to acquire each sub-criterion weight, the number of occurrences is summed in each criterion, and then every number of occurrences is divided by summation. This procedure is concluded by a decimal number that illustrates the sub-criterion weight. This procedure carries on for all criteria. For instance, the wight of the sub-criterion "Ultimate load capacity" is 0.11, which is obtained by the division of 3 by 27. To find out the criteria's weight, the last procedure was implemented in a higher level. The number of occurrences of each criterion was divided by the summation of all criteria. For example, the "Size and Precision" occurrences were 27, which was divided by the summation of all criteria, 149, with the result being 0.18. The other results are shown in Table 5.

The obtained results show us the importance of criteria in machine tool selection literature. Cost and Serviceability has the highest priority among the criteria, with 0.34 as the weight. The classification of criteria considering high priorities is identified as follows: (1) Cost and Serviceability; (2) Technical Features and Safety; (3) Size and Precision; (4) Flexibility; and (5) Productivity. Therefore, Table 5 displays the importance of each sub-criterion with its weight in order to find out the importance priority.

Generally, it is common to have a comparison between MADM methods to analyze the advantages and disadvantage of similar methods of weighting or ranking. This study presented a unique way of criteria selection and weighting, which is not based raw experts' opinions about a subject or topic.

Table 5. Criteria weighting based on the high-term loading in the Singular Decomposition Value.

Criteria	Sub-Criteria	Number of Occurrences	Sub-Criteria Weight	Criteria Weight
Size and Precision	Ultimate load capacity	3	0.11	0.18
	Diversity of materials and structure	2	0.07	
	Weight	6	0.22	
	Machine dimensions	6	0.22	
	Maximum speed	4	0.15	
	Maximum tool diameter	4	0.15	
	Product conformance	2	0.07	
Sum		27	1	

Table 5. *Cont.*

Criteria	Sub-Criteria	Number of Occurrences	Sub-Criteria Weight	Criteria Weight
Cost and Serviceability	Price	5	0.10	0.34
	Energy Consumption	5	0.10	
	Maintenance Cost	14	0.28	
	Waste amount	2	0.04	
	Operation Cost	8	0.16	
	Quality of Technical Service	1	0.02	
	Service training	10	0.20	
	Repair Service	5	0.10	
Sum		50	1	
Flexibility	Setup Time	4	0.18	0.15
	Installation easiness	6	0.27	
	Ease of Learning	3	0.14	
	Ease of Use	2	0.09	
	Integration	1	0.05	
	Properties	2	0.09	
	User Friendliness	4	0.18	
Sum		22	1	
Productivity	Depreciation Quality	3	0.23	0.1
	Scrap & Rework Reliability	3	0.23	
	Pallet Changer & Fixture	2	0.15	
	Labor Cost	3	0.23	
	Operation Shifts	2	0.15	
Sum		13	1	
Technical Features and Safety	Capacity of Rotary Table	5	0.14	0.25
	Thermal Deformation	5	0.14	
	Spindle Speed	4	0.11	
	Spindle Power	2	0.05	
	Adaptability	5	0.14	
	Failure Rate	4	0.11	
	Tool Changer Time	1	0.03	
	Fire Extinguisher	3	0.08	
	Number of Taper	4	0.11	
	Reliability of Drive System	4	0.11	
Sum		37	1	

7. Conclusions

As can be seen in Tables 4 and 5, the criteria selection andf weighting system was presented in a special case study, which was "Machine Tool Selection". This study showed how other researchers can apply text mining for the process of criteria selection and weighting in MADM and Prospective MADM. This new approach and model can be applied in many other cases and topics with bigger data bases. There are many proper data bases, such as Scopus, that can help to have more reliable answers and outputs for solving complicated decision-making problems. RapidMiner 9.6 is really powerful software in data and text mining, and as it was illustrated in the study, can be a convenient way to apply test mining methods for criteria selection and their weighting procedure.

In order to illustrate the importance of criteria selection and the weighting the criteria (referring to the MADM field), this study can be introduced as a new perspective in the literature review of weighting criteria, far from pairwise comparisons and policy-based decision-making models. This new approach can be applied with other newer contributions in the PMADM outline, such as "Multi-Aspect Criterion" or "Supportive-backup criteria", and still can be developed more with other tools and methods in text mining, or by adding newer items to the classic scheme of MADM in the wider area of the PMADM items and models.

Researchers in the field of MCDM can use this new framework as a new method for criteria selection and as a novel weighting system. Formerly, the MCDM field did not have any special way of criteria selection and many researchers tried to use social science methodologies to propose a proper way. From now on, this new proposed method can be applied in other decision-making problems, especially future-based ones like Prospective MADM models.

Author Contributions: Main idea, conceptualization, methodology, editing, discussion, and writing—original, S.H.Z.; conceptualization, text mining evaluation, case study, and writing—original, A.D. All authors have read and agreed to the published version of the manuscript.

Funding: Proyecto N° 11190104: New approaches to the future-based decision making based on Prospective Multiple Attribute Decision Making (PMADM) outline; Programa Fodecyt, Conicyt, Ministrio de Educacion, Chile.

Conflicts of Interest: The authors declare no conflict of interest.

Appendix A

Table A1. High-loading and cross-loading terms.

Tokens	Factor 1	Factor 2	Factor 3	Factor 4	Factor 5
accuraci	−0.07544	−0.02045	−0.11645	−0.02227	0.019636
adapt	0.05399	−0.04528	0.003571	−0.14157	0.199365
administr	−0.02739	−0.04876	−0.00882	0.016549	−0.00983
altern	0.035358	−0.07187	−0.01185	−0.20609	0.014524
axi	−0.02261	0.00917	−0.16617	0.035082	0.095056
calibr	0.010538	−0.18789	0.004858	−0.04542	−0.03483
capabl	0.017671	0.005341	0.001862	−0.10701	0.049956
capit	−0.01365	−0.3049	0.01159	0.03833	−0.03655
choos	−0.03783	−0.00694	0.0011	−0.02371	0.018954
cnc	−0.01822	0.023044	−0.0021	0.026414	0.271168
collector	−0.00613	0.009799	0.005666	0.008668	0.123106
compani	−0.1016	0.002902	−0.01972	−0.10697	0.004729
compat	−0.21839	0.073125	0.010751	−0.07765	0.003632
conform	0.021347	−0.23393	0.00796	0.026274	−0.0212
consumpt	−0.13604	0.087801	−0.09374	−0.24513	−0.09154
cost	−0.17724	−0.29611	−0.0384	−0.14504	−0.05739
creat	−0.03566	−0.01711	−0.0005	−0.01023	−0.01453
custom	−0.02544	0.009187	0.014583	−0.02641	0.061236
deform	0.008177	0.017282	0.014448	0.005093	0.189623
depreci	0.019106	−0.30184	0.00804	0.035376	−0.02536
desir	−0.06595	0.008115	−0.00911	0.02126	0.063925
diamet	0.099029	−0.0026	−0.16178	−0.15385	0.015298

Table A1. *Cont.*

Tokens	Factor 1	Factor 2	Factor 3	Factor 4	Factor 5
divers	0.022183	−0.00125	0.001156	−0.10511	−0.00081
door	0.00085	0.000514	−0.00049	0.015471	0.080006
drive	0.011075	0.02959	0.021017	−0.04859	0.187868
durabl	−0.09892	0.016209	0.009514	−0.12024	−0.05007
eas	−0.10411	0.000595	0.013019	−0.03576	0.01473
economi	0.097927	−0.03463	−0.00437	−0.18764	0.026237
energi	−0.09209	0.071298	−0.00312	−0.22761	−0.07012
environ	−0.04275	0.0179	0.011725	−0.0469	0.160445
environment	−0.0535	0.029703	−0.00172	−0.19527	−0.03063
etc	0.15136	−0.04217	−0.03988	0.052489	0.471026
extinguish	0.001812	0.010433	0.004893	0.017118	0.156383
failur	−0.0148	0.011944	0.011471	−0.00073	0.178497
fig	−0.12019	−0.06003	−0.00246	0.062841	−0.01877
fire	0.001812	0.010433	0.004893	0.017118	0.156383
fixtur	−0.10158	−0.0179	−0.03705	−0.01674	−0.02785
gener	0.01332	−0.00645	−0.01385	0.004389	0.047838
imag	−0.05945	0.026555	0.004708	−0.08376	−0.0285
instal	−0.19012	0.04396	0.022779	−0.09798	0.042728
integr	−0.02544	0.009187	0.014583	−0.02641	0.061236
intend	−0.05033	0.005145	−0.005	0.012282	0.037751
inventori	−0.05286	−0.06489	−0.00272	0.014498	0.012564
invest	−0.11431	−0.03194	0.008617	−0.04711	−0.04063
kw	0.024839	−0.00395	−0.16872	0.025859	−0.02441
labor	−0.11883	−0.08484	0.013301	0.047077	−0.00877
length	0.016347	−0.00252	−0.15699	−0.03902	−0.0261
load	0.055425	−0.00905	0.001524	−0.12312	0.071062
lot	−0.06024	−0.06781	−0.00899	0.02154	0.001898
machin	−0.34665	−0.15065	−0.02262	0.033575	0.191764
manufactur	0.003534	−0.33313	−0.00022	0.013707	−0.00348
market	−0.06512	−0.03902	0.01068	−0.01209	−0.01693
max	0.053809	−0.01321	−0.15942	0.0453	0.078574
mcdm	−0.00424	0.011741	−0.00546	−0.10385	−0.01076
mist	−0.00613	0.009799	0.005666	0.008668	0.123106
mm	0.081566	−0.00395	−0.81775	0.097339	−0.14824
multi	−0.05101	0.040368	−0.00491	−0.14251	−0.04423
oper	−0.18888	−0.10804	0.003421	−0.02289	0.032413
pallet	−0.09463	−0.02823	−0.00904	0.036023	0.065802
paramet	0.001408	−0.02892	0.009004	−0.11643	0.017664
physic	−0.03349	−0.00185	−0.03829	0.006777	0.030456
power	0.004777	0.032131	−0.13564	−0.05492	0.110604

Table A1. *Cont.*

Tokens	Factor 1	Factor 2	Factor 3	Factor 4	Factor 5
previou	−0.04542	0.011221	0.002405	−0.07085	0.003702
price	−0.01604	0.052631	−0.12576	−0.20072	−0.04932
product	−0.17811	−0.13235	0.014905	−0.10792	0.050977
properti	0.003185	−0.02044	0.01204	−0.08363	0.0051
purchas	−0.05033	0.005145	−0.005	0.012282	0.037751
recycl	−0.02378	0.026506	0.011101	−0.06907	0.051117
rel	−0.01033	0.035153	0.015351	−0.13575	0.016411
rework	0.011429	−0.33022	0.007266	0.040113	−0.02494
rock	0.463096	−0.23186	−0.03155	−0.44445	0.130465
rotari	−0.00274	0.013883	−0.00411	0.023967	0.211357
safe	−0.05033	0.005145	−0.005	0.012282	0.037751
scrap	0.011429	−0.33022	0.007266	0.040113	−0.02494
secondari	0.022183	−0.00125	0.001156	−0.10511	−0.00081
secur	−0.05206	0.000298	0.00651	−0.01788	0.007365
servic	−0.20497	0.060389	−0.05111	−0.07789	0.149842
setup	−0.13246	−0.04561	0.022969	−0.15475	−0.05275
shape	−0.05785	0.017883	−0.03902	−0.03418	−0.01467
shift	−0.13133	−0.06672	0.01663	0.050026	−0.01085
space	−0.04351	0.027589	−0.04554	−0.05652	0.15348
spindl	0.0295	0.0045	−0.1682	0.0547	0.1890
standard	−0.06674	−0.01489	−0.11931	0.00499	−0.04856
stroke	−0.02433	0.014644	−0.14311	−0.01087	−0.03614
sub	0.007558	−0.24063	0.014101	0.004916	−0.02523
suppli	−0.02739	−0.04876	−0.00882	0.016549	−0.00983
taper	0.014388	0.005333	−0.00691	0.024307	0.171176
technic	−0.1124	0.030998	0.010576	−0.22095	−0.05604
technolog	−0.03303	0.013566	0.01132	−0.08502	−0.01854
thermal	−0.02329	0.012514	0.007474	0.005213	0.175115
tool	−0.26426	−0.04665	−0.23164	0.032951	0.197688
travers	0.009275	0.005969	−0.00797	0.00751	0.112826
unit	−0.05183	−0.0385	0.004586	0.000737	−0.01226
us	−0.10535	0.015706	−0.00151	0.005064	0.123736
user	−0.22003	0.049804	−0.05291	−0.08046	−0.03492
util	−0.06063	−0.22188	−0.0083	0.029607	−0.00313
variou	−0.04542	0.011221	0.002405	−0.07085	0.003702
volum	−0.00642	0.025635	0.008904	−0.13559	0.009527
warranti	−0.04616	0.027072	−0.00139	−0.07093	−0.02382
wast	−0.04027	0.042821	0.005618	−0.20761	−0.04861
weight	0.063673	0.014336	−0.04865	−0.22286	0.035649

References

1. Ho, W.; Xu, X.; Dey, P.K. Multi-criteria decision making approaches for supplier evaluation and selection: A literature review. *Eur. J. Oper. Res.* **2010**, *202*, 16–24. [CrossRef]
2. Keshavarz Ghorabaee, M.; Zavadskas, E.K.; Turskis, Z.; Antucheviciene, J. A new combinative distance-based assessment (CODAS) method for multi-criteria decision-making. *Econ. Comput. Econ. Cybern. Stud. Res.* **2016**, *50*, 25–44.
3. Zavadskas, E.K.; Turskis, Z. Multiple criteria decision making (MCDM) methods in economics: An overview. *Technol. Econ. Dev. Econ.* **2011**, *17*, 397–427. [CrossRef]
4. Kabir, G.; Sadiq, R.; Tesfamariam, S. A Review of Multi-criteria Decision-making Methods for Infrastructure Management. *Struct. Infrastruct. Eng.* **2014**, *10*, 1176–1210. [CrossRef]
5. Jahan, A.; Edwards, K.L. VIKOR method for material selection problems with interval numbers and target-based criteria. *Mater. Des.* **2013**, *47*, 759–765. [CrossRef]
6. Zavadskas, E.K.; Turskis, Z.; Kildiene, S. State of art surveys of overviews on MCDM/MADM methods. *Technol. Econ. Dev. Econ.* **2014**, *20*, 165–179. [CrossRef]
7. Ishizaka, A.; Labib, A. Review of the main developments in the analytic hierarchy process. *Expert Syst. Appl.* **2011**, *38*, 14336–14345. [CrossRef]
8. Scott, J.A.; Ho, W.; Dey, P.K. A review of multi-criteria decision-making methods for bioenergy systems. *Energy* **2012**, *42*, 146–156. [CrossRef]
9. Wang, Y.; Shi, X.; Sun, J.; Qian, W. A grey interval relational degree-based dynamic multi-attribute decision making method and its application in investment decision making. *Math. Probl. Eng.* **2014**. [CrossRef]
10. Aguezzoul, A. Third-party logistics selection problem: A literature review on criteria and methods. *Omega* **2014**, *49*, 69–87. [CrossRef]
11. Mardani, A.; Jusoh, A.; Zavadskas, E.K. Fuzzy multiple criteria decision-making techniques and applications – two decades review from 1994 to 2014. *Expert Syst. Appl.* **2015**, *42*, 4126–4148. [CrossRef]
12. Mardani, A.; Zavadskas, E.K.; Khalifah, Z.; Jusoh, A.; Nor, K.M.D. Multiple criteria decision-making techniques in transportation systems: A systematic review of the state of the art literature. *Transport* **2016**, *31*, 359–385. [CrossRef]
13. Zavadskas, E.K.; Mardani, A.; Turskis, Z.; Jusoh, A.; Nor, K.M.D. Development of TOPSIS Method to Solve Complicated Decision-Making Problems—An Overview on Developments from 2000 to 2015. *Int. J. Inf. Technol. Decis. Mak.* **2016**, *15*, 645–682. [CrossRef]
14. Saaty, T.L. *The Analytical Hierarchy Process*; McGraw-Hill: New York, NY, USA, 1980.
15. Saaty, T.L. *Decision making in Complex. Environments, the Analytical Hierarchy Process. for decision Making with Dependence and Dependence and Feedback*; RWS Publications: Pittsburgh, PA, USA, 1996.
16. Saaty, T.L. Fundamentals of analytic network process. In Proceedings of the The International Symposium on the Analytic Hierarchy Process, Cobe, Japan, 12–14 August 1999; pp. 348–379.
17. Keršulienė, V.; Zavadskas, E.K.; Turskis, Z. Selection of rational dispute resolution method by applying new step-wise weight assessment ratio analysis (SWARA). *J. Bus. Econ. Manag.* **2010**, *11*, 243–258. [CrossRef]
18. Hashemkhani Zolfani, S.; Yazdani, M.; Zavadskas, E.K. An extended stepwise weight assessment ratio analysis (SWARA) method for improving criteria prioritization process. *Soft Comput.* **2018**, *22*, 7399–7405. [CrossRef]
19. Ginevicius, R. A New Determining Method for the Criteria Weights in Multi-Criteria Evaluation. *Int. J. Inf. Technol. Decis. Mak.* **2011**, *10*, 1067–1095. [CrossRef]
20. Rezaei, J. Best-worst multi-criteria decision-making method. *Omega* **2015**, *53*, 49–57. [CrossRef]
21. Pamučar, D.; Stević, Z.; Sremac, S. A new model for determining weight coefficients of criteria in MCDM models: Full consistency method (FUCOM). *Symmetry* **2018**, *10*, 393. [CrossRef]
22. Zavadskas, E.K.; Turskis, Z.; Vilutiene, T. Multiple criteria analysis of foundation instalment alternatives by applying additive ratio assessment (ARAS) method. *Arch. Civil. Mech. Eng.* **2010**, *10*, 123–141. [CrossRef]
23. Zavadskas, E.K.; Turskis, Z.; Antucheviciene, J.; Zakarevicius, A. Optimization of weighted aggregated sum product assessment. *Electron. Electr. Eng.* **2012**, *6*, 3–6. [CrossRef]
24. Keshavarz Ghorabaee, M.; Zavadskas, E.K.; Olfat, R.; Turskis, Z. Multi-Criteria Inventory Classification Using a New Method of Evaluation Based on Distance from Average Solution (EDAS). *INFORMATICA* **2015**, *26*, 435–451. [CrossRef]

25. Yazdani, M.; Zarate, P.; Zavadskas, E.K.; Turskis, Z. A combined compromise solution (CoCoSo) method for multi-criteria decision-making problems. *Manag. Decis.* **2019**, *57*, 2501–2519. [CrossRef]
26. Stević, Z.; Pamucar, D.; Puska, A.; Chatterjee, P. Sustainable supplier selection in healthcare industries using a new MCDM method: Measurement of alternatives and ranking according to COmpromise solution (MARCOS). *Comput. Ind. Eng.* **2020**, *120*, 106231. [CrossRef]
27. Hashemkhani Zolfani, S.; Bahrani, M. Investment prioritizing in high tech industries based on SWARA-COPRAS approach. *Technol. Econ. Dev. Econ.* **2014**, *20*, 534–553. [CrossRef]
28. Hashemkhani Zolfani, S.; Aghdaie, M.H.; Derakhti, A.; Zavadskas, E.K.; Morshed Varzandeh, M.H. Decision making on business issues with foresight perspective; An application of new hybrid MCDM model in shopping mall locating. *Expert Syst. Appl.* **2013**, *40*, 7111–7121. [CrossRef]
29. Hashemkhani Zolfani, S.; Esfahani, M.H.; Bitarafan, M.; Zavadskas, E.K.; Lale Arefi, S. Developing a new hybrid MCDM method for selection of the optimal alternative of mechanical longitudinal ventilation of tunnel pollutants during automobile accidents. *Transport* **2013**, *28*, 89–96. [CrossRef]
30. Chini, M.; Lale Arefi, S.; Hashemkhani Zolfani, S.; Ustinovicius, L. Choosing a proper method for strengthening WPC beams with grooving method using SWARA-EDAS. *Arch. Civ. Eng.* **2018**, *64*, 161–174. [CrossRef]
31. Hashemkhani Zolfani, S.; Mosharafiandehkordi, S.; Kutut, V. A pre-planning for hotel locating according to the sustainability perspective based on BWM-WASPAS approach. *Int. J. Strateg. Prop. Manag.* **2019**, *23*, 405–419. [CrossRef]
32. Hashemkhani Zolfani, S.; Ecer, F.; Pamucar, D.; Raslanas, S. Neighborhood selection for a newcomer via a novel BWM-based revised MAIRCA integrated model: A case from the Coquimbo-La Serena conurbation, Chile. *Int. J. Strateg. Prop. Manag.* **2020**, *24*, 102–118. [CrossRef]
33. Opricovic, S.; Tzeng, G.H. Compromise solution by MCDM methods: A comparative analysis of VIKOR and TOPSIS. *Eur. J. Oper. Res.* **2004**, *156*, 445–455. [CrossRef]
34. Keshavarz Ghorabaee, M.; Amiri, M.; Zavadskas, E.K.; Turskis, Z.; Antucheviciene, J. A Comparative Analysis of the Rank Reversal Phenomenon in the EDAS and TOPSIS Methods. *Econ. Comput. Econ. Cybern. Stud. Res.* **2018**, *52*, 121–134. [CrossRef]
35. Hashemkhani Zolfani, S.; Chatterjee, P. Comparative Evaluation of Sustainable Design Based on Step-Wise Weight Assessment Ratio Analysis (SWARA) and Best Worst Method (BWM) Methods: A Perspective on Household Furnishing Materials. *Symmetry* **2019**, *11*, 74. [CrossRef]
36. Deveci, M.; Canitez, F.; Gokasar, I. WASPAS and TOPSIS based interval type-2 fuzzy MCDM method for a selection of a car sharing station. *Sustain. Cities Soc.* **2018**, *41*, 777–791. [CrossRef]
37. Zhao, H.; Guo, S.; Zhao, H. Comprehensive assessment for battery energy storage systems based on fuzzy-MCDM considering risk preferences. *Energy* **2019**, *168*, 450–461. [CrossRef]
38. Keshavarz Ghorabaee, M.; Amiri, M.; Zavadskas, E.K.; Turskis, Z.; Antucheviciene, J. A new hybrid fuzzy MCDM approach for evaluation of construction equipment with sustainability considerations. *Arch. Civ. Mech. Eng.* **2018**, *18*, 32–49. [CrossRef]
39. Dincer, H.; Yuksel, S. An integrated stochastic fuzzy MCDM approach to the balanced scorecard-based service evaluation. *Math. Comput. Simul.* **2019**, *166*, 93–112. [CrossRef]
40. Boral, S.; Howard, I.; Chaturvedi, S.K.; McKee, K.; Naikan, V.N.A. An integrated approach for fuzzy failure modes and effects analysis using fuzzy AHP and fuzzy MAIRCA. *Eng. Fail. Anal.* **2020**, *108*, 104195. [CrossRef]
41. Roozbahani, A.; Ghased, H.; Hashemi Shahedany, M. Inter-basin water transfer planning with grey COPRAS and fuzzy COPRAS techniques: A case study in Iranian Central Plateau. *Sci. Total Environ.* **2020**, 138499. [CrossRef]
42. Pamučar, D.; Deveci, M.; Canitez, F.; Bozanic, D. A fuzzy Full Consistency Method-Dombi-Bonferroni model for prioritizing transportation demand management measures. *Appl. Soft Comput.* **2020**, *87*, 105952. [CrossRef]
43. Rahimi, S.; Hafezalkotob, A.; Monavari, S.M.; Hafezalkotob, A.; Rahimi, R. Sustainable landfill site selection for municipal solid waste based on a hybrid decision-making approach: Fuzzy group BWM-MULTIMOORA-GIS. *J. Clean. Prod.* **2020**, *248*, 119186. [CrossRef]
44. Hashemkhani Zolfani, S.; Maknoon, R.; Zavadskas, E.K. An introduction to Prospective Multiple Attributes Decision Making (PMADM). *Technol. Econ. Dev. Econ.* **2016**, *22*, 309–326. [CrossRef]
45. Ozernoy, V.M. Multiple criteria decision making in the USSR: A survey. *Nav. Res. Logist.* **1988**, *35*, 543–566. [CrossRef]

46. Leong, T.Y. Multiple perspective dynamic decision making. *Artif. Intell.* **1998**, *105*, 209–261. [CrossRef]
47. Salo, A.; Gustafsson, T.; Ramanathan, R. Multi-criteria methods for technology foresight. *J. Forecast.* **2003**, *22*, 235–255. [CrossRef]
48. Xu, Z.; Yager, R. Dynamic intuitionistic fuzzy multi-attribute decision making. *Int. J. Approx. Reason.* **2008**, *48*, 246–262. [CrossRef]
49. Campanella, G.; Ribeiro, R.A. A framework for dynamic multiple-criteria decision making. *Decis. Support Syst.* **2011**, *52*, 52–60. [CrossRef]
50. Trutnevyte, E.; Stauffacher, M.; Scholz, R.W. Linking stakeholder visions with resource allocation scenarios and multi-criteria assessment. *Eur. J. Oper. Res.* **2012**, *219*, 762–772. [CrossRef]
51. Arms, H.; Wiecher, M.; Kleiderman, V. Dynamic models for managing big decisions. *Strategy Leadersh.* **2012**, *40*, 39–46. [CrossRef]
52. Zhang, Z. An approach to dynamic multi-attribute decision making for choosing green supplier. *J. Converg. Inf. Technol.* **2012**, *7*, 261–269.
53. Tadic, S.R.; Zecevic, S.M.; Krstic, M.D. Ranking of logistics system scenarios for central business district. *Promet Traffic Transp.* **2014**, *26*, 159–167.
54. Gonzalez-Prida, V.; Viveros, P.; Barbera, L.; Crespo Marquez, A. Dynamic analytic hierarchy process: AHP method adapted to a changing environment. *J. Manuf. Technol. Manag.* **2014**, *24*, 457–475. [CrossRef]
55. Ondrus, J.; Bui, T.; Pigneur, Y. A Foresight Support System Using MCDM Methods. *Group Decis. Negot.* **2014**, *24*, 333–358. [CrossRef]
56. Jassbi, J.J.; Ribeiro, R.A.; Varela, L.R. Dynamic MCDM with future knowledge for supplier selection. *J. Decis. Syst.* **2014**, *23*, 232–248. [CrossRef]
57. Hashemkhani Zolfani, S.; Maknoon, R.; Zavadskas, E.K. Multiple Attribute Decision Making (MADM) based scenarios. *Int. J. Strateg. Prop. Management* **2016**, *20*, 101–111. [CrossRef]
58. Hashemkhani Zolfani, S.; Dehnavieh, R.; Poursheikhali, A.; Prentkovskis, O.; Khazaelpour, P. Foresight Based on MADM-Based Scenarios' Approach: A Case about Comprehensive Sustainable Health Financing Models. *Symmetry* **2020**, *12*, 61. [CrossRef]
59. Hashemkhani Zolfani, S.; Maknoon, R.; Zavadskas, E.K. MADM and Futures Studies; A necessity. In Proceedings of the 9th International Scientific Conference "Business and Management 2016", Vilnius Gediminas Technical University Vilnius, Lithuania, 12–13 May 2016; pp. 1–7. [CrossRef]
60. Hashemkhani Zolfani, S.; Zavadskas, E.K.; Khazaelpour, P.; Cavallaro, F. The Multi-Aspect Criterion in the PMADM Outline and Its Possible Application to Sustainability Assessment. *Sustainability* **2018**, *10*, 4451. [CrossRef]
61. Hashemkhani Zolfani, S.; Masaeli, R. *From Past to Present and into the Sustainable Future; PMADM Approach in Shaping Regulatory Policies of the Medical Device Industry in the New Sanction Period*; Sustainability Modeling in Engineering; A multi-Criteria Perspective; Chatterjee, P., Yazdani, M., Chakraborty, S., Eds.; Word Scientific: Singapore, 2019.
62. Hashemkhani Zolfani, S.; Yazdani, M.; Zavadskas, E.K.; Hasheminasab, H. Prospective MADM and sensitivity analysis of the experts based on Causal Layered Analysis (CLA). *Ekon. a Manag.* **2020**. In press.
63. De Miranda Santo, M.; Massari Coelho, G.; Maria dos Santos, D.; Fellos Filho, L. Text mining as a valuable tool in foresight exercises: A study on nanotechnology. *Technol. Forecast. Soc. Chang.* **2006**, *73*, 1013–1027. [CrossRef]
64. Saritas, O.; Burmaoglu, S. The evolution of the use of Foresight methods: A scientometric analysis of global FTA research output. *Scientometrics* **2015**, *105*, 497–508. [CrossRef]
65. Jungermann, F.; Information Extraction with RapidMiner. GSCL Symposium Sprachtechnologie Und EHumanities. 2009, p. 1. Available online: http://citeseerx.ist.psu.edu/viewdoc/download?doi=10.1.1.184.1826&rep=rep1&type=pdf#page=59 (accessed on 19 May 2020).
66. Hotho, A.; Nürnberger, A.; Paaß, G. A Brief Survey of Text Mining. *Gldv J. Comput. Linguist. Lang. Technol.* **2005**, *20*, 19–62.
67. Delen, D.; Crossland, M.D. Seeding the survey and analysis of research literature with text mining. *Expert Syst. Appl.* **2008**, *34*, 1707–1720. [CrossRef]
68. Sidorova, A.; Evangelopoulos, N.; Valacich, J.S.; Ramakrishnan, T. Uncovering the Intellectual Core of the Information Systems Discipline. *Mis Q.* **2008**, *32*, 467–482. [CrossRef]
69. Han, J.; Kamber, M.; Pei, J. *Data Mining Techniques*, 3rd ed.; Elsevier: New York, NY, USA, 2011.

70. Li, Y.; Joshi, K.D. The state of social computing research: A literature review and synthesis using the latent semantic analysis approach. In Proceedings of the 18th Americas Conference on Information Systems 2012, Seattle, DC, USA, 9–11 August 2012; Volume 1, pp. 33–40.
71. Hossain, M.M.; Prybutok, V.; Evangelopoulos, N. Causal Latent Semantic Analysis (cLSA): An Illustration. *Int. Bus. Res.* **2011**, *4*, 38–50. [CrossRef]
72. Lin, X.; Li, Y.; Wang, X. Social commerce research: Definition, research themes and the trends. *Int. J. Inf. Manag.* **2017**, *37*, 190–201. [CrossRef]
73. Morley, J. The Academic Phrasebank_ An Academic Writing Resource for Students and Researchers. The University of Manchester: Manchester, UK, 2017.
74. Kotu, V.; Deshpande, B. *Data Science 2nd Edition Concepts and Practice*; Elsevier: New York, NY, USA, 2018.
75. Baker, K. *Singular Value Decomposition Tutorial*; Working Paper; Ohio State University: Columbus, OH, USA, 2013; pp. 1–24.
76. Klema, V.; Laub, A. The singular value decomposition: Its computation and some applications. *IEEE Trans. Autom. Control* **1980**, *25*, 164–176. [CrossRef]
77. Aghdai, M.H.; Hashemkhani Zolfani, S.; Zavaskas, E.K. Decision making in machine tool selection: An integrated approach with SWARA nad COPRAS-G method. *Inz. Ekon. Eng. Econ.* **2014**, *24*, 5–17. [CrossRef]
78. Önüt, S.; Kara, S.S.; Efendigil, T. A hybrid fuzzy MCDM approach to machine tool selection. *J. Intell. Manuf.* **2008**, *19*, 443–453. [CrossRef]
79. Samvedi, A.; Jain, V.; Chan, F.T.S. An integrated approach for machine tool selection using fuzzy analytical hierarchy process and grey relational analysis. *Int. J. Prod. Res.* **2012**, *50*, 3211–3221. [CrossRef]
80. Hai, L.; Wang, W.; Fan, L.; Li, Q.; Chen, X. A novel hybrid MCDM model for machine tool selection using fuzzy DEMATEL, entropy weighting and later defuzzification VIKOR. *Appl. Soft Comput. J.* **2020**, *91*, 106207. [CrossRef]
81. Yurdakul, M. AHP as a strategic decision-making tool to justify machine tool selection. *J. Mater. Process. Technol.* **2004**, *146*, 365–376. [CrossRef]
82. Myint, S.; Tabucanon, M.T. A multiple-criteria approach to machine selection for flexible manufacturing systems. *Int. J. Prod. Econ.* **1994**, *33*, 121–131. [CrossRef]
83. Matijevi&#x107, M.; Mrvac, N.; Mikota, M. The effect of expansion and simultaneous contrast in modificated figural dotted and groundal dotted illusions. *Teh. Vjesn.* **2014**, *21*, 1297–1301. [CrossRef]
84. Özceylan, E.; Kabak, M.; Dadeviren, M. A fuzzy-based decision making procedure for machine selection problem. *J. Intell. Fuzzy Syst.* **2016**, *30*, 1841–1856. [CrossRef]
85. Arslan, M.Ç. A Decision Support System for Machine Tool Selection. Master's Thesis, Sabanci University, Istanbul, Turkey, 2002.
86. Çimren, E.; Çatay, B.; Budak, E. Development of a machine tool selection system using AHP. *Int. J. Adv. Manuf. Technol.* **2007**, *35*, 363–376. [CrossRef]
87. Ayag, Z.; Gürcan Özdemir, R. Evaluating machine tool alternatives through modified TOPSIS and alpha-cut based fuzzy ANP. *Int. J. Prod. Econ.* **2012**, *140*, 630–636. [CrossRef]
88. Kumru, M.; Kumru, P.Y. A fuzzy ANP model for the selection of 3D coordinate-measuring machine. *J. Intell. Manuf.* **2015**, *26*, 999–1010. [CrossRef]
89. Hafezalkotob, A.; Hafezalkotob, A. Interval target-based VIKOR method supported on interval distance and preference degree for machine selection. *Eng. Appl. Artif. Intell.* **2017**, *57*, 184–196. [CrossRef]
90. Ayağ, Z.; Özdemir, R.G. An intelligent approach to machine tool selection through fuzzy analytic network process. *J. Intell. Manuf.* **2011**, *22*, 163–177. [CrossRef]
91. Lin, Z.C.; Yang, C.B. Evaluation of machine selection by the AHP method. *J. Mater. Process. Technol.* **1996**, *57*, 253–258. [CrossRef]
92. Xia, Y.M.; Lin, L.K.; Wu, D.; Jia, L.H.; Chen, Z.; Bian, Z.K. Geological adaptability matching design of disc cutter using multicriteria decision making approaches. *J. Cent. South. Univ.* **2018**, *25*, 843–854. [CrossRef]

symmetry

MDPI

Article

Application of Six Sigma Model on Efficient Use of Vehicle Fleet

Tatjana Stanivuk [1], Tamara Gvozdenović [2], Jelena Žanić Mikuličić [1,*] and Vesko Lukovac [3]

[1] University of Split, Faculty of Maritime Studies, 21000 Split, Croatia; tstanivu@pfst.hr
[2] Hydro Power Plants on the river Trebisnjica; 89104 Trebinje, Bosnia & Herzegovina; tgvozdenovic@henatrebisnjici.com
[3] Traffic Engineering-Transportation and Labour Organization, University of Defence; Military Academy-Chair of Logistics, 11000 Belgrade, Serbia; vesko.lukovac@va.mod.gov.rs
* Correspondence: jzanic@pfst.hr

Received: 24 March 2020; Accepted: 7 May 2020; Published: 22 May 2020

Abstract: Each business faces large competition in the market, and it is necessary to adopt the most effective methodology as possible in order to obtain the best solution. Six Sigma (6σ) is a set of techniques and tools for process improvement. The tools of Six Sigma apply within a simple improvement model known as Define–Measure–Analyze–Improve–Control (DMAIC). This paper shows that implementing Six Sigma can be more effective in managing the vehicle fleet. The combination of mathematical, i.e., statistical basis and practice makes Six Sigma so successful. The Six Sigma project, implemented to reduce costs and increase the availability of a vehicle fleet in a selected company, can be widely applied in other similar enterprises.

Keywords: Six Sigma (6σ); DMAIC; vehicle fleet; optimization

1. Introduction

Today, in a time of technological progress, and in dynamic market, it is important to be adaptive to change, and to use new models in order to remain competitive in the market. To respond to these needs, various industrial engineering and quality management strategies such as series of standards ISO 9000, Total Quality Management, Kaizen, just-in-time manufacturing, Enterprise Resource Planning, Business Process Reengineering, Lean Management, etc., have been developed [1]. A new paradigm in this area of strategies is Six Sigma (6σ). The Six Sigma strategy is not just a quality management system. Its philosophy and vision has increased the profits of many organizations. The greatest news issued by Six Sigma concept is the quantification of indicators related to quality. The main benefit of a Six Sigma program is the elimination of subjectivity in decision making by creating a system where everyone in the organization collects, analyzes, and displays data in a consistent way [2]. This paper deals with application of Six Sigma Define–Measure–Analyze–Improve–Control (DMAIC) methodology on the optimization of the vehicle fleet of an enterprise. Any fleet within transport can optimize the use and enforcement of the model, whether in the case of cars, as in this paper, or in the case of various vessels in maritime transport.

2. The Concept of Six Sigma

2.1. Background of the Research

Six Sigma is a set of techniques and tools for process improvement. This statistical method is used in many companies whether they are manufacturing or giving services. Six Sigma methodology involves finding and eliminating the causes of errors or deficiencies. The focus is on the outputs that are of major importance to consumers. Six Sigma was developed in the early and mid 1980s by the

Motorola Company. The company's aim was to achieve business excellence. Thanks to the strategy, Motorola gained the leading position in the area of quality and was awarded the Malcolm National Quality Award [3]. In 1986, the engineers of Motorola, Bill Smith and Mikel J Harry, concluded that the previous method was not enough for measuring defects. After implementing the new methodology, better results were evident. Many companies like Toyota, Ford, BMW, Hilti, Shell, General Electric, Honey International, Caterpillar, Raytheon and Merrill Lynch also applied it successfully [3].

Sigma "σ" is a symbol for standard deviation that describes the degree of variation in a given set, i.e., the degree of product quality, services or processes [4]. The aim of Six Sigma is to reduce waste to the lowest possible level, as well as cost and time of production to increase business productivity. The basic measurement unit of Six Sigma is Defects per Million Opportunities (DPMO). Six Sigma is an indicator of the frequency of error/deviation occurrence. According to this model 3.4 errors per million are acceptable, which means a process shift of 1.5 σ [5,6]. Therefore, the goal of all companies is to accomplish that each process has an index value of $Cp \geq 2$ [7]. In Figure 1, this condition corresponds to the main curve. The range between the Upper Specification Limit (USL) and the Lower Specification Limit (LSL) is named the specification range. The Six Sigma methodology is part of Statistical Process Control (SPC). A variational reduction in processes leads to higher profits and increases the quality of products and services [5].

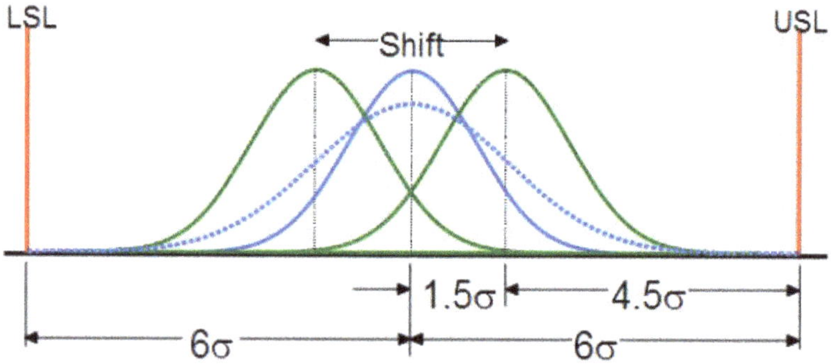

Figure 1. Six Sigma curve [8].

Six Sigma is a system for quality management, metrics and methodology, wherein quality indicators could be quantified [9]. Six Sigma methodology is basically focused on [7]:

- improving user satisfaction (customers);
- decreasing the product-making time (cycle time reduction);
- reducing the number of defects (errors) in products and services.

Improvements in these areas provide high levels of quality, large savings and high profits to companies, gaining new markets for the company and raising the company's image. The application of Six Sigma reduces the cost of waste (from 20%-30% to less than 0.1%), the cycle-time, the cost and need for control, and increases the quality of products and customer satisfaction [10–13].

In recent years, there has been a renewed trend in the rise of Six Sigma methodology. It is associated with Lean Methodology and is called Lean Six Sigma. This package represents a set of tools within the structures set up under the name of Business excellence management. Its main purpose is achieving the highest possible financial and other benefits. The increased use of Six Sigma has contributed significantly to industrial expansion areas. The concept finds its application in high technology, the transport industry, machinery production and general purpose equipment.

2.2. Six Sigma Model

The Six Sigma strategy is not based solely on statistics and high technology, but also on proven methods and measurements that focus on improving processes and cost savings. It is currently one of the most popular quality management systems in the world [14].

DMAIC and Define–Measure–Analyze–Design–Verify (DMADV) are two models that use Six Sigma methodology. The tools of Six Sigma are often applied within a simple performance improvement model known as Define–Measure–Analyze–Improve–Control (DMAIC). DMAIC is used when the aim is to improve an existing product, process or service. Another approach, used for developing a new product, process or service is Define–Measure–Analyze–Design–Verify (DMADV) [15].

The major differences between DMAIC and DMADV are in the goals and outcomes of the completed project. The DMADV project has a more tangible outcome, but in reality, both methods give better quality, efficiency, more production and profits, and higher customer satisfaction [16]. The DMAIC model is used in this paper.

DMAIC has a Plan-Do-Check-Act (PDCA) model for the base, and is concerned with the life cycle of the project (exclusive orientation on projects). PDCA, as a tool, is used specifically in the management phase. DMAIC is an integral part of Six Sigma, but in general can be implemented as a standalone quality improvement procedure or as a part of other process improvement activities. In Figure 2, the letters in the acronym DMAIC represent five phases of the process.

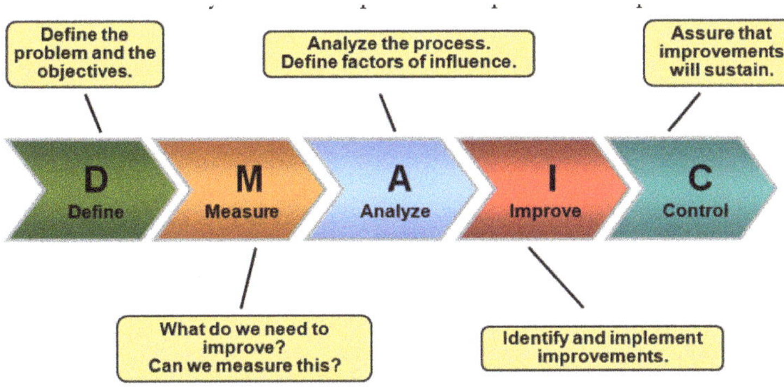

Figure 2. Six Sigma Define–Measure–Analyze–Improve–Control (DMAIC) roadmap [17].

The Define Phase is the first phase of the Lean Six Sigma improvement process. This phase finishes with signing a complete project assignment (Project Charter). Measurement is critical throughout the life of the project. There are two focuses: determining the starting point of the process and trying to understand the root cause of the process [18]. In the Analyze stage, the project team use data analysis tools and process analysis techniques to identify and verify the main causes of the problem [19]. The Improve phase consists of developing and selecting the optimal solutions for the best results and most robust performance [20]. The Control phase controls the solution implementation, and monitors the process and its operation.

DMAIC contains a number of various tools used by certain phases (Table 1). The method offers rough guidelines how to use tools at certain phases. Process owners and the team may use the tools they find to be the most responsive.

Table 1. Six Sigma tools commonly used in each phase of a project [15].

Project Phase	Candidate Six Sigma Tools
Define	Project charter; VOC tools (surveys, focus groups, letters, comment cards); Process map; QFD; SIPOC; Benchmarking; Project planning and management tools; Pareto analysis
Measure	Measurement system analysis; Process behavior charts (SPC); Exploratory data analysis; Descriptive statistics; Data mining; Run charts; Pareto analysis
Analysis	Cause-and-effect diagrams; Tree diagrams; Brainstorming; Process behavior charts (SPC); Process maps; Design of experiments; Enumerative statistics (hypothesis tests); Inferential statistics (Xs and Ys); Simulations
Improve	Force field diagrams; FMEA; 7M tools; Project planning and management tools; Prototype and pilot studies; Simulations
Control	SPC; FMEA; ISO 900x; Change budgets, bid models, cost estimating models; Reporting system

3. Solution Approaches for Vehicle Fleet by DMAIC Method

This part of paper presents the process of applying the DMAIC model to the fleet in one selected profitable (successful) firm.

3.1. Problem Presentation

The selected company is one of the largest organizations, but its primary activity is not transport. It has a transport service, which includes a large number of passenger cars, buses, and other vehicles. It deals with heavy maintenance costs, low availability and a long process of purchasing spare parts. Two key processes are identified within DMAIC application: vehicle approval and vehicle fleet maintenance. The research data is from 2018. The research began in August 2019 and ended in February 2020.

3.2. Methodology

The suppliers, inputs, process, outputs, and customers (SIPOC) method was used to determine the process steps, customers (suppliers), as well as the inputs/outputs of the project [21]. By using another quality tool, Voice of the Customer (VOC), a transfer from the required to quantifiable specifications was made [22]. When analyzing interested parties, the following stakeholders are identified: management, internal and external users, and transport servicers.

The project goal is to reduce total costs by 20%.

A Swim lane map was a process map that separates process into lanes. The Swim lane workflow map also shows what performs each part of the process and the resources used in the performance [23]. The following areas are of utmost importance:

- non-defined vehicle class;
- reports (local order—a travel warrant for the narrow geographical area within facilities Q) on the use of the vehicle;
- procedures for updating the vehicle fleet;
- procedures for maintenance and use of official vehicles should include: travel plan (approval), the number of passengers per vehicle (optimal), report and maintenance plan, fault books;
- technical booklets.

The improvement process was measured by the total costs (Y). The total costs consist of the following: regular maintenance, replacement parts, vehicle registration and third-party services.

During the sampling, the following vehicle data was collected for all vehicles: type of vehicle, model of vehicle, registration number, year of production, total costs, kilometers travelled, fuel consumption in liters, consumption per 100 kilometers, fuel costs and maintenance costs.

3.3. Results and Discussion

Statistical data analysis was performed by using Minitab 17 (Minitab Inc., State College, PA, USA). A normality test for response variable (Y) was carried out. Figure 3 shows that the data for maintenance costs do not follow a normal distribution (Anderson–Darling test, $p < 0.005$).

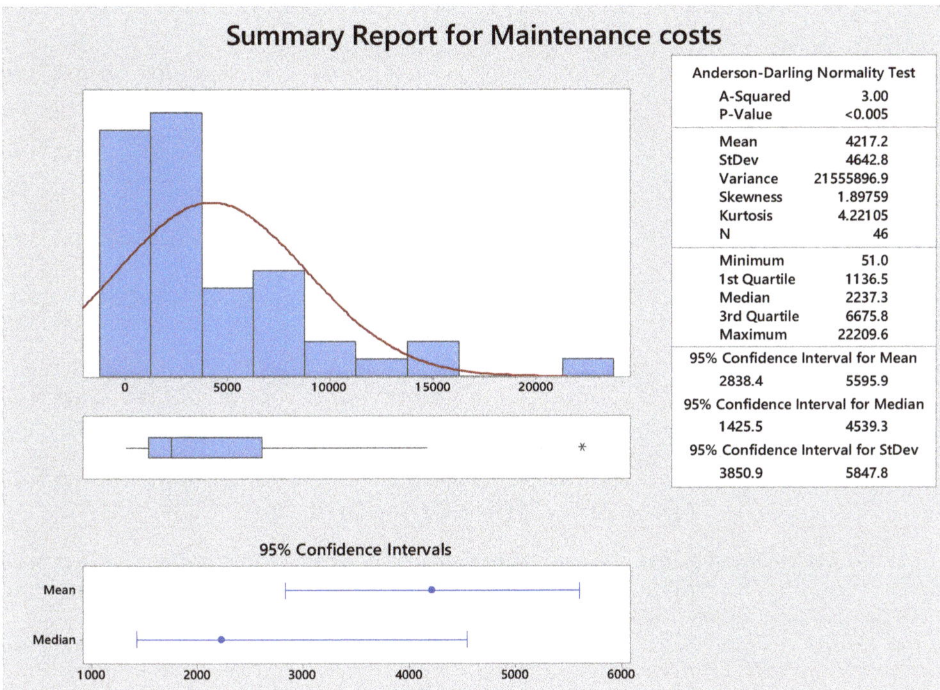

Figure 3. Normality test for maintenance costs.

Moving average and moving range control charts in Figure 4 show that the process is unstable/out of control. There are also ten points in the line (more than seven) emerging from the same side of the line, which are the mean values. It shows that there are variations in a specific cause, which should be removed [24]. Specific causes should not be ignored, but it is necessary to:

- detect variations in specific causes quickly;
- stop activities until the process is rectified (reactively);
- identify and permanently eliminate specific causes (preventively);
- adjust the process if specific causes cannot be eliminated.

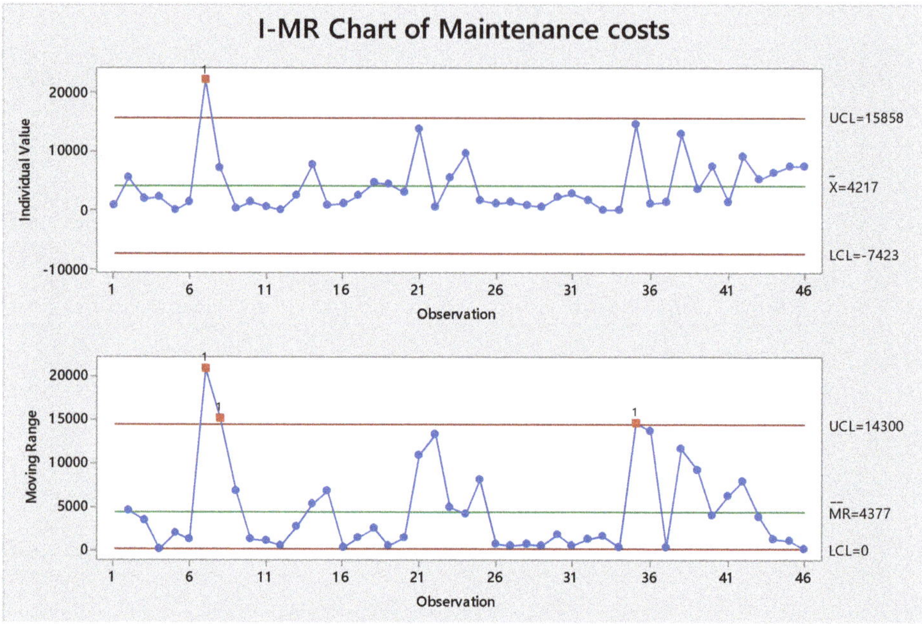

Figure 4. Stability of the maintenance costs process.

The Cause and Effect Matrix (Table 2) helped to prioritize the most important process inputs, i.e., Causes (X), which affect most (the highest rated) key process outputs (Y). Based on this Cause and Effect Matrix, Pareto analysis was performed (Figure 5).

Table 2. Cause and Effect Matrix. Rating of importance to customer (1 = not important, 10 = very important). Key process outputs (Y): maintenance costs.

Process Input (X)		Total
nonexistence of a technical book	9	90
too many external requirements	9	90
oversized exploitation	9	90
type of vehicle	9	90
distance travelled in km	9	90
inadequate procedures for maintenance	9	90
vehicle age	9	90
irresponsibility of driver toward vehicle	9	90
model vehicle	9	90
failing to write in the book of registered defects	3	30
lack of procedure for upgrading vehicle park	3	30
undefined vehicle class	3	30
lack of loco reports	1	10
failing to follow legally binding procedure	1	10

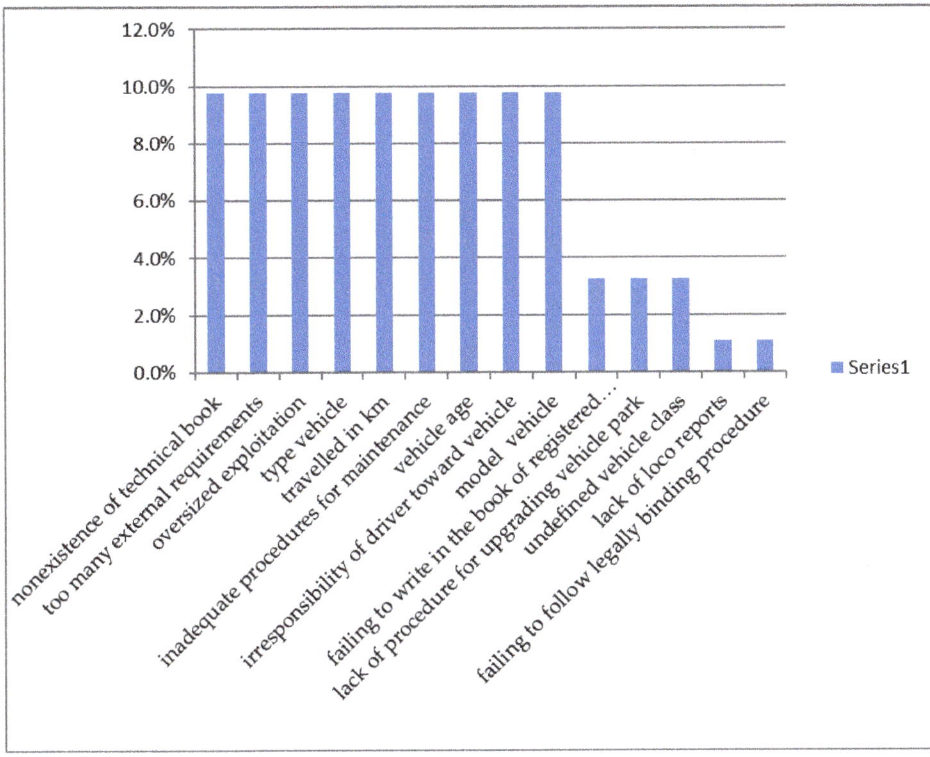

Figure 5. Pareto chart.

The most important (critical) causes (X) were identified. They lead to 80% of the cost problems of the vehicle fleet, namely:

- the nonexistence of a technical book;
- too many external requirements;
- oversized exploitation;
- the type of the vehicle;
- kilometers travelled;
- inadequate procedures for maintenance;
- the age of the vehicle (year of production);
- the irresponsibility of the driver;
- the model of the vehicle.

Failure Mode and Effects Analysis (FMEA) applies in order to reduce the circle of potential causes. FMEA is a systematic method of identifying and preventing system, product and process problems before they occur [25]. The aim of FMEA analysis is to:

- detect errors and prevent them before they occur;
- reduce costs by identifying potential improvements early in the development cycle;
- evaluate the process/product from a new perspective.

The concept of FMEA analysis implies determining the ways in which errors can occur in the process or in the product. Therefore, it is necessary to plan how to avoid them.

Risk priority number (RPN) is an indicator of certain problems within FMEA analysis, consisting of the severity of the problem, the likelihood of occurrence and the probability of problem detection [26]:

$$\text{RPN} = \text{Severity} \times \text{Occurrence} \times \text{Detection}. \quad (1)$$

The higher the RPN is, the more likely it is concerned with a single error.

The FMEA contains a plan of activities/corrective measures that will prevent the occurrence of an error, i.e., reduce the RPN.

Following the proposed measures of FMEA analysis, (Tables 3 and 4) risk reduction is expected. The recommended measures affected the risk reduction.

Table 3. Failure Mode and Effects Analysis (FMEA).

Process Inputs	Potential Failure Mode	Potential Effect(s) of Failure	Severity	Potential Cause(s)/Mechanisms of Failure	Occurrence	Current Process Controls Detection
Data on maintenance costs	Unreliable information	Difficulties in spare parts planning	10	Lack of technical booklet	10	There is none
Fuel consumption	Incorrect information on consumption	Increased fuel costs	10	Non-existence of device for control of reported consumption (e.g., sonde)	9	Travel order
Operating time of machine	Lack of adequate information	Increased costs of fuel, lubricants and parts	10	Machines lack mechanical counter (mileage) or it is incorrigible	9	Travel order
Vehicle	Inadequate number of people per vehicle	Increased costs	9	Lack of rulebook for usage of official company cars	9	Dispatcher
Vehicle	Inadequate number of people per vehicle	Decreased vehicle availability	7	Lack of rulebook for usage of official company cars	5	Dispatcher
Vehicle	Bad vehicle condition (due to multi years of exploitation)	Increased maintenance costs	9	Lack of rulebook for renovation of vehicle fleet	8	There is none
Driver	Driver irresponsibility relating to vehicle	Increased maintenance costs	5	Lack of control at writing in travel order	4	Technical rectitude officer

Table 4. Recommended actions and responsibilities.

Detection	RPN	Recommended Action (s)	Responsible Person	Responsibility	Target Completion Date	SEV	OCC	DET	RPN
10	1000	Create technical booklet for each vehicle	Office worker in transport service	Design and make a form of technical booklet	Implemented	10	2	1	20
9	810	Install sondes for big consumers	Management, transport service chief, specialized firm for sondes installation	Upon proposal by transport service chief, management makes decision, expert from Firm installs sondes	In agreement with management of the company	10	1	1	10
9	810	Installation/repair of mechanical counter	Transport service	Repair and installation of mechanical counter	In agreement with management of the company	10	1	1	10
2	162	Make rulebook for usage by official company	Management	Management appoints board for making Rulebook	In agreement with management of the company	9	3	2	54
2	70	Make rulebook for usage by official company	Management	Management appoints board for making Rulebook	In agreement with management of the company	7	2	2	28
10	720	Make a rulebook on transport fleet renewal	Management, transport service	Management makes decision upon suggestion by transport service	In agreement with management of the company	9	2	1	18
9	180	Dispatcher issues new order upon delivery of old order and its control	Dispatcher	Control of old order	In agreement with management of the company	5	1	1	5

After identifying all inputs X that affect output Y (maintenance costs), collecting data and narrowing the circle of potential causes, the validation of critical causes is done. Validation takes the form of a tool that confirms critical causes. Figure 6 shows that the vehicle models 11, 12, 3 and 6 cause major maintenance costs.

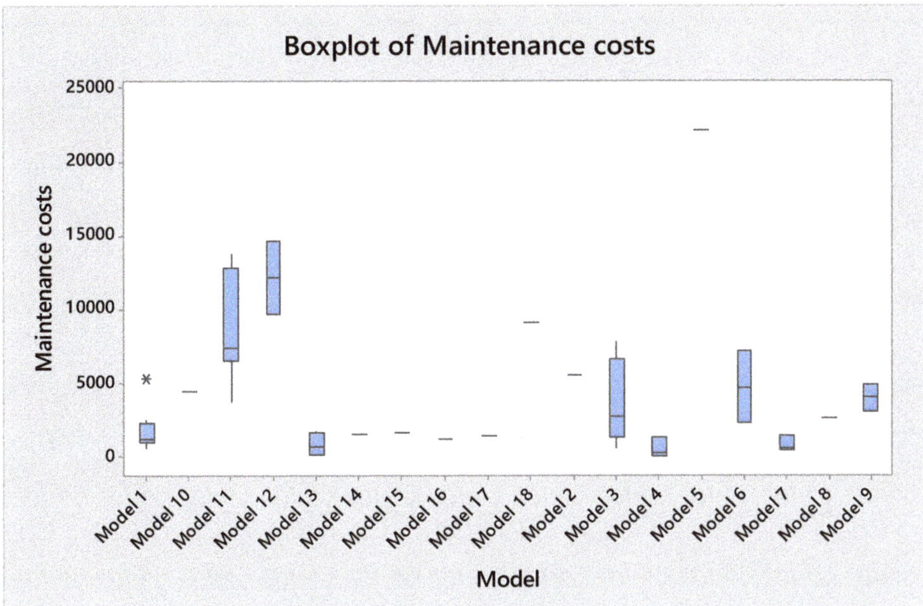

Figure 6. Boxplot of maintenance costs.

An analysis of variance (ANOVA) was used to test the effect or impact of X, which is an attribute data (vehicle model), on Y, which is a variable data (maintenance cost). Despite the non-normality of maintenance costs (Figure 3), the sample size is large (>30) and the ANOVA is "acceptable" [24]. Statistical software MINITAB has techniques for process capability measuring even in the case of non-normal distribution. How much a particular X affects Y is seen on R-sq (adj). Figure 7 shows that the P-value is 0.000. It is clear that the vehicle model affects maintenance costs of 75.17%.

A regression analysis was performed to test whether the maintenance costs are affected by the kilometers travelled and the year of production (age of the vehicle). Figure 8 shows that kilometers travelled affect maintenance costs (Regression ANOVA, $p < 0.001$). It was also expected that the age of the vehicle would affect the maintenance costs (Regression ANOVA, $p = 0.788$) (Figure 9). However, these results are unexpected and introducing/applying all identified procedures is needed.

In Figure 10, the Pareto chart shows the total number of kilometers per vehicle model. It can be concluded that six vehicle models make up almost 80% of all kilometers travelled. In this regard, the vehicle fleet should be balanced in order to reduce maintenance costs, the number of training drivers and technicians and to increase the availability of spare parts.

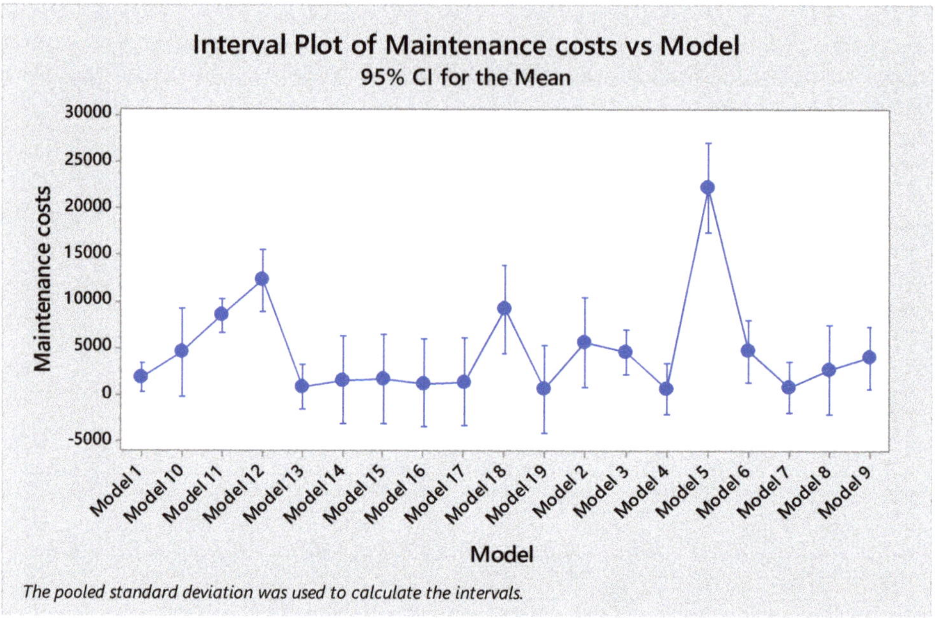

Figure 7. Interval plot of maintenance costs vs. model.

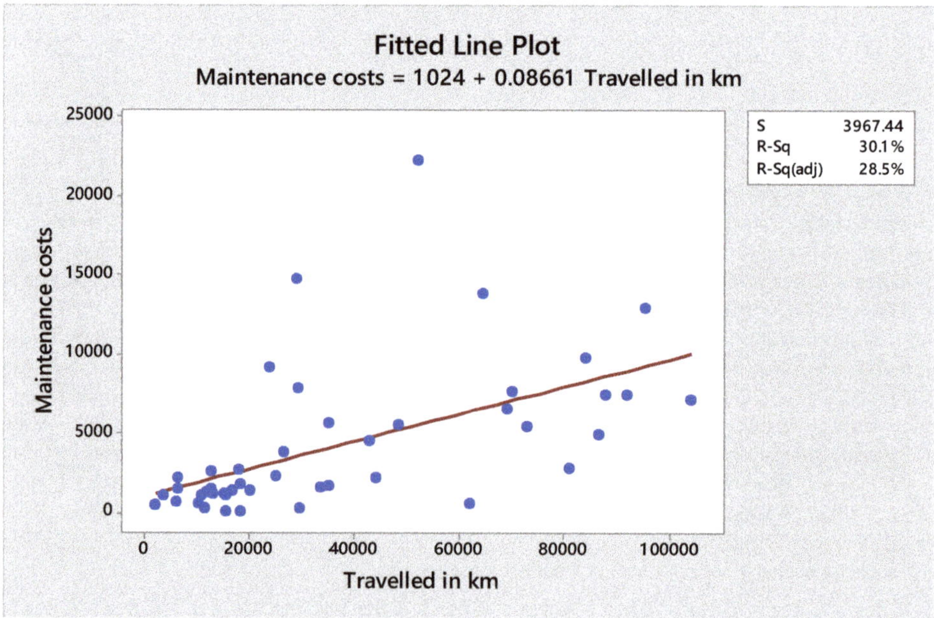

Figure 8. Regression analysis: maintenance costs vs. travelled in km.

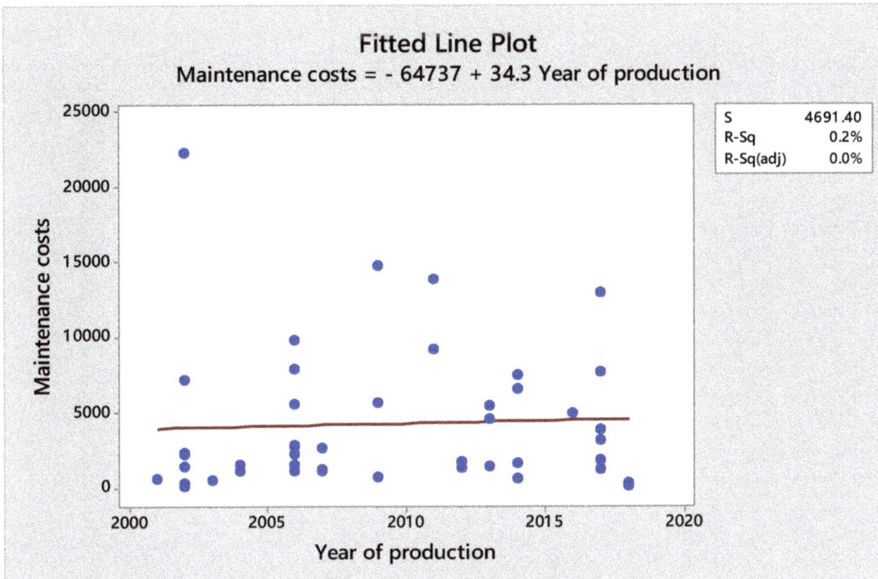

Figure 9. Regression analysis: maintenance costs vs. year of production.

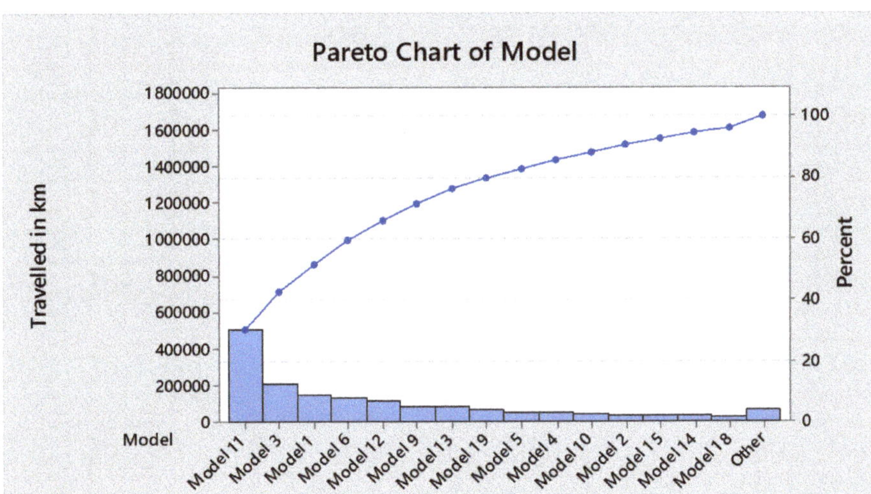

Figure 10. Pareto chart of model.

Tables 5 and 6 explain the Improvement Plan for all samples identified (X). The improvement phase starts with brainstorming process that will accomplish further activity plans.

Tables 7 and 8 show the Control Plan. Phase Control provides the transition from the state of the project into a stable condition. The Control plan is mandatory to ensure:

- documents are updated;
- the training required due to the changes in the processes is carried out;
- an audit plan is created for control activities.

Table 5. Improvement plan.

No.	Critical Xs	Problem Caused by This Critical X	Action Plan to Eliminate/Reduce the Problem
1	Untimely filling in travel order	Incorrect fuel consumption	Dispatcher issues new order upon delivery and control of old order
2	Inadequate and untimely filling in local order	Increased fuel consumption; Reduction of vehicle availability (lack of fleet information)	Dispatcher compares travel order to daily evidence with inputs–outputs of gatekeeper
3	Technical booklet	Increased maintenance costs; Unreliable data on technical rectitude of vehicle; Not detailed plan of spare parts	Make technical booklet, make decision on way of filling in and usage of technical booklet
4	Nonexistence of procedures for repair by third party	Not defined who initiates procedure; Increased maintenance costs; long repair time	Create procedure for repair by third party
5	Nonexistence of procedures for regular maintenance	Untimely services (checks); increased maintenance costs (failure on parts); Unconscientious acting of driver	Create procedure for regular maintenance
6	Inefficient exploitation of vehicle fleet	Increased costs (bad distribution of travelers per vehicle); Decreased availability of vehicle	Rule book on cost-effective usage of vehicle park
7	Non-existence of motor hour counter	Not specified: operating time of machine, consumption of fuel, lubricant and parts	Install or repair motor hour counter; specify fuel consumption per motor-hour counter for each machine; create monthly reports on consumption of fuel, lubricants and parts for each vehicle
		Uncontrolled costs of vehicle exploitation and maintenance	
8	Sondes for big consumers	Unreliable data on fuel consumption	Installation of sondes for trucks, construction machines, buses
9	Lack of buses	Large costs for hiring out buses	Procurement of new bus
10	Nonuniformity of vehicles	Higher costs of maintenance; inconstant fuel consumption; Workman not trained for various vehicle types	To form a work team with task to make a suggestion, e.g., about the projection of the structure of a vehicle park
11	Nonexistence of rule book for renewal of vehicle park	Age vehicle; increased maintenance costs; Increased costs for engagement of third parties' services	Write a rule book for renewal of the vehicle park

Table 6. Improvement plan effects.

Improvement Effects	Response Person	Remark	Target Completion Data
Decrease of fuel consumption, increased control of drivers	Dispatcher, driver		In agreement with management
Decrease number of unnecessary "outgoings", fuel costs decrease and maintenance, greater availability of vehicle	Dispatcher, porter, driver		In agreement with management
Detailed data on consumption, repair history, equipment ascribed to vehicle, detailed plan of spare parts procurement, decreased maintenance costs	Administrative worker in transport service		Implemented: technical booklet designed
Decreased maintenance costs, shorter time of repair, defined reliability, more settled business doing	Quality management representative	The procedure has to contain the following: Reason for sending vehicle repair by third party; Report signed by contractor; Broken (unrepaired) part returned	In agreement with management
Decreased maintenance costs, greater reliability of vehicle	Quality management representative		In agreement with management
Better vehicle availability, decreased costs of maintenance and fuel	Management	Instructions for the rational use of a particular type of vehicle by number of passengers, mileage, the number of vehicles	In agreement with management
Reliable information on consumption of fuel and operating time of machine for each vehicle/machine Better control of exploitation costs	The drill crew manager		In agreement with management
Reliable data on fuel consumption	Management		In agreement with management
Decreased costs of hiring out bus, increased availability of bus for own needs	Management		In agreement with management
Reduce maintenance costs; constant fuel consumption; reduced number of trainings for workmen	Commission on proposal of management		In agreement with management
Recent and reliable vehicle park with reduced costs of maintenance	Commission on proposal of management		In agreement with management

Table 7. Control plan.

PROCESS IDENTIFICATION		SPECIFICATION & MEASUREMENTS	
What is Controlled?	**Input or Output?**	**Spec. Limits/Requirements**	**Measurement Method**
Travel order	Input	Accurately filled in travel order according to rule book on reasonable usage of vehicle park	By insight to travel order and check list by dispatcher
Travel order	Output	Accurate information in travel order on average consumption and/or operating time of working machine/vehicle	On insight in sound readings and vehicle motor hour counter
Local order	Input	Local order filled in in a timely manner	On insight into local order by dispatcher
Technical booklet	Input	Regular and accurate filling in of technical booklet	On insight into technical booklet
Request for repair by third parties	Input	Precise and justified reason for condition	Chief of transport service on insight into signature of workshop chief
Report by a third party who performs repair of vehicle (contractor)	Output	Accurately filled in report in accordance with performed repair	"Domestic" person compares report to actual conditions

Table 8. Control plan strategy.

	SAMPLING STRATEGY		ACTION & DOCUMENTATION
Frequency	**Who/What Measures**	**Where Recorded**	**Decision Rule/Corrective Action**
On occasion of closing each Travel Order	Dispatcher	Book (dispatcher)	If travel order is not duly filled in, dispatcher sends it back for driver to correct/ament it and does not issue a new one without a duly filled in previous one.
On occasion of closing each Travel order	Dispatcher	Book (dispatcher)	If travel order is not duly filled in, dispatcher sends it back for driver to correct/ament it and does not issue a new one without a duly filled in previous one.
On occasion of closing each local order	Dispatcher	Book (dispatcher)	If local order is not filled in in a timely manner, dispatcher acts according to the Role book on usage of business vehicle.
After each intervention on the vehicle	Administrative worker in transport service	In technical booklet by signature	If technical booklet is filled in in an adequate and timely manner, the administrative worker in transport service writes his signature. Otherwise, he does not write his signature and acts in accordance with the rule book on the usage of business vehicles.
Before each intervention by third parties	Chief of transport service	In request for repair by third parties	Chief of transport service, after the workman, signs the same request and continues the procedure of repair by third parties. Otherwise, he does not sign it and returns the request to workshop chief.
Upon each intervention on vehicle by third parties	"Domestic" person delegated by transport service	In the report	"Domestic" person taker over broken part, then signs the report.

4. Conclusions

The Six Sigma methodology is based primarily on quantifiable data that aims to eliminate losses and improve the quality of products. The main purpose of the Six Sigma methodology is to implement strategies based on measurements that focus on improving processes and reducing variation. Six Sigma uses the process improvement methodology DMAIC, which has five phases: Define, Measure, Analyze, Improve and Control.

The optimization of the vehicle fleet in a profitable (successful) company in this paper precisely shows the application of the DMAIC model and the maintenance costs for 2018 were measured. The project started in 2019 and the available data for 2018 were taken into consideration. The Six Sigma (6σ) model was expected to reduce costs by 20%. The goal of a 20% reduction in costs was not attained, but the activities shown in the Improvement and Control Plans will reduce these costs by more than 20%.

By implementing the FMEA analysis, the following statistics were obtained. The vehicle model affects the maintenance costs by 75.17%, but the age of the vehicle was found not to affect maintenance costs.

Direct improvement measures were implemented due to the lack of technical booklets, procedures on vehicle maintenance and non-timely completion of the travel order. The expectations regarding the project relate to the implementation of recommended measures. This will lead to a reduction in the maintenance costs in general.

The advantages of the more efficient use of the vehicle fleet should be reducing maintenance and fuel costs, increasing the reliability and availability of the vehicle, defining responsibilities, etc. Accurate information about the history of repairs, shorter vehicle repair time and better control of exploitation costs may also be taken into consideration. The work on this project showed the remarkable importance of the existence of historical data. In addition, this project can also be applied in other similar enterprises. Moreover, the methods of fuzzy linear and dynamic programming combined with heuristic and metaheuristic methods find their place of application [27–30].

Author Contributions: T.S., T.G., J.Ž.M. and V.L. carried out research and methodology in the manuscript. T.S. and T.G. wrote original draft, interpreted the results, created tables and figures. T.S., T.G. and J.Ž.M. reviewed, edited and corrected the paper. All authors have read and agreed to the published version of the manuscript.

Funding: This article is funded by University of Split, Faculty of Maritime Studies, R. Boškovića 37, 21000 Split, Croatia.

Conflicts of Interest: The authors declare no conflicts of interest.

References

1. Desai, T.N.; Shrivastava, R.L. Six Sigma A New Direction to Quality and Productivity Management. In Proceedings of the World Congress on Engineering and Computer Science WCECS 2008, San Francisco, CA, USA, 22–24 October 2008; ISBN 978-988-98671-0-2. Available online: http://www.iaeng.org/publication/WCECS2008/WCECS2008_pp1047-1052.pdf (accessed on 1 March 2020).
2. Kumar, S.; Satsangi, P.S.; Prajapati, D.R. Six Sigma an excellent tool for process improvement—A case study. *Int. J. Scie. Eng. Res.* **2011**, *2*, 1–10.
3. Sujova, A.; Simanova, L.; Marcinekova, K. Sustainable Process Performance by Application of Six Sigma Concepts: The Research Study of Two Industrial Cases, Sustainability, Sustainable Business Models, Printed Edition of the Special Issue Published in Sustainability. *Sustainability* **2016**, *8*, 260. [CrossRef]
4. Habul, A.; Pilav-Velić, A.; Kremić, E. Improvements of Business Process by Implementing Six Sigma Model. In Proceedings of the Scientific Conference with International Participation "Quality 2011", Neum, Bosnia & Herzegovina, 01–04 June 2011; pp. 7–12. Available online: http://www.quality.unze.ba/zbornici/QUALITY%202011/002-Q11-017.pdf (accessed on 3 March 2020).
5. Bratić, D.; Optimizing the Printing Concept on Six Sigma Principles. Ph. D. Thesis, University of Zagreb, Faculty of Graphic Arts, Zagreb, Croatia, 2015; p. 15. Available online: https://eprints.grf.unizg.hr/2249/1/Doktorski%20rad%20Bratic%20Diana.pdf (accessed on 15 January 2020).

6. Kwak, Y.H.; Anbari, F.T. Benefits, obstacles, and future of six sigma approach. *Technovation* **2006**, *26*, 708–715. Available online: https://www.researchgate.net/publication/222518320_Benefits_obstacles_and_future_of_SixSigmaapproach (accessed on 14 March 2020). [CrossRef]
7. Lazić, M. Six sigma—Methodology for quality improvement, Festival of quality 2011. In Proceedings of the National Conference on Quality, Faculty of Mechanical Engineering, Center for Quality, Kragujevac, Serbia, 19–21 May 2011; pp. 213–220, ISBN 978-86-86663-69-6. Available online: http://www.cqm.rs/2011/FQ2011/pdf/38/34.pdf (accessed on 12 March 2020).
8. Gustafsson, V.; Davidsson, S. Streamlining the Invisible Value Chain Reduction of Losses within Administrative Processes: A Case Study. Bachelor's Thesis, Linnaeus University, School of Engineering, Växjö, Sweden, 2011. Available online: http://www.diva-portal.org/smash/get/diva2:433853/FULLTEXT01.pdf (accessed on 14 February 2020).
9. Lazibat, T.; Baković, T. Six Sigma System for Quality Management, Business Excellence, Zagreb, 2007; Volume 1, pp. 55–66. Available online: https://hrcak.srce.hr/38522 (accessed on 12 March 2020).
10. Rajković, V. Lean Six Sigma Concept, Festival of quality 2012. In Proceedings of the National Conference on Quality, Faculty of Mechanical Engineering, Center for Quality, Kragujevac, Serbia, 07–09 June 2012; pp. 39–43, ISBN 978-86-86663-83-2. Available online: http://www.cqm.rs/2012/cd1/pdf/39/05.pdf (accessed on 10 March 2020).
11. Anthony, P.; Behnoee, B.; Hassanpour, M.; Pamucar, D. Financial performance evaluation of seven Indian chemical companies. *Decis. Mak. Appl. Manag. Eng.* **2019**, *2*, 81–99. [CrossRef]
12. Biswas, S.; Bandyopadhyay, G.; Guha, B.; Bhattacharjee, M. An ensemble approach for portfolio selection in a multi-criteria decision making framework. *Decis. Mak. Appl. Manag. Eng.* **2019**, *2*, 138–158. [CrossRef]
13. Jankovic, A.; Popovic, M. Methods for assigning weights to decision makers in group AHP decision-making. *Decis. Mak. Appl. Manag. Eng.* **2019**, *2*, 147–165. [CrossRef]
14. Russell, R.; Taylor, B. *Operations Management—Creating Value along the Supply Chain*; John Wiley & Sons, Inc.: Hoboken, NJ, USA, 2011; Available online: http://jtelen.free.fr/0MARINE%20bouquins/%5BRoberta_S._Russell,_Bernard_W._Taylor%5D_Operations(Bookos.org).pdf (accessed on 15 January 2020).
15. Pyzdek, T.; Keller, P. *The Six Sigma Handbook: A Complete Guide for Green Belts, Black Belts and Managers at all Levels*, 3rd ed.; The McGraw-Hill Companies, Inc.: New York, NY, USA, 2009; ISBN 978-0-07-162337-7.
16. The Council for Six Sigma Certification. *Six Sigma—A Complete Step-by-Step Guide: A Complete Training & Reference Guide for White Belts, Yellow Belts, Green Belts, and Black Belts*; The Council for Six Sigma Certification: Buffalo, WY, USA, 2018; ISBN 978-1732592650. Available online: https://www.sixsigmacouncil.org/wp-content/uploads/2018/08/Six-Sigma-A-Complete-Step-by-Step-Guide.pdf (accessed on 15 January 2020).
17. Fung, P. Design for Six Sigma, Power Point Presentation. 2015. Available online: http://www.hksq.org/DFSS-STP-150124-Peter.pdf (accessed on 18 February 2020).
18. Krishnan, R.; Prasath, A. Six Sigma Concept and DMAIC Implementation. *IJBMR* **2013**, *3*, 111–114.
19. Sindha, N.; Suthar, K. Review on Implementation of Six Sigma DMAIC Methodology in Manufacturing Industries. *IJSTE* **2017**, *3*. Available online: http://www.ijste.org/articles/IJSTEV3I8064.pdf (accessed on 20 February 2020).
20. Kaid, H.; Noman, M.; Nasr, E.; Alkahtani, M. Six Sigma DMAIC phases application in Y company: A case study. *Int. J. Collab. Enterp.* **2016**, *5*, 181–197. [CrossRef]
21. Miski, A. Improving Customers Service at IKEA Using Six Sigma Methodology. *Int. J. Sci. Eng. Res.* **2014**, *5*, 1712–1720. Available online: https://www.ijser.org/researchpaper/Improving-Customers-Service-at-IKEA-Using-Six-Sigma-Methodology.pdf (accessed on 16 February 2020).
22. Griffin, A.; Hauser, J. The Voice of the Customer. *Mark. Sci.* **1993**, *12*, 1–27. [CrossRef]
23. Ezeonwumelu, E.P.; Ozuomba, S.; Kalu, C. Development of Swim Lane Workflow Process Map for Enterprise Workflow Management Information System (Wfmis): A Case Study of Comsystem Computer and Telecommunication Ltd (Cctl) Eket. *Eur. J. Eng. Technol.* 2015, 3. Available online: https://pdfs.semanticscholar.org/49fa/9f7f3585c2bf7223b6d334256b4d868eac0a.pdf (accessed on 20 January 2020).
24. DaimlerChrysler Corporation, Ford Motor Company, and General Motors Corporation. Statistical Process Control (SPC) Reference Manual. 2005. Available online: https://www.academia.edu/7829906/AIAG_Statistical_Process_Control_SPC_2nd_Edition (accessed on 20 January 2020).

25. Sharma, K.D.; Srivastava, S. Failure Mode and Effect Analysis (FMEA) Implementation: A Literature Review. *J. Adv. Res. Aeronaut. Space Sci.* **2018**, *5*, 1–17. Available online: https://www.researchgate.net/publication/333209894_Failure_Mode_and_Effect_Analysis_FMEA_Implementation_A_Literature_Review (accessed on 18 February 2020).
26. Liu, H.; Deng, X.; Jiang, W. Risk Evaluation in Failure Mode and Effects Analysis Using Fuzzy Measure and FuzzyIntegral. *Symmetry* **2017**, *9*, 162. [CrossRef]
27. Dobrosavljević, A.; Urošević, S. Analysis of Business Process Management Defining and Structuring Activities in Micro, Small and Medium—Sized Enterprises. *Oper. Res. Eng. Sci. Appl.* **2019**, *2*, 40–54. [CrossRef]
28. Badi, I.; Shetwan, A.; Hemeda, A. A Grey-Based Assessment Model to Evaluate Health-Care Waste Treatment Alternatives in Libya. *Oper. Res. Eng. Sci. Appl.* **2019**, *2*, 92–106. [CrossRef]
29. Petrovic, G.; Mihajlovic, J.; Cojbasic, Z.; Madic, M.; Marinkovic, D. Comparison of three fuzzy MCDM methods for solving the supplier selection problem. *Facta Univ. Ser. Mech. Eng.* **2019**, *17*, 455–469. [CrossRef]
30. Sunny Diyaley, S.; Chakraborty, S. Optimization of multi-pass face milling parameters using metaheuristic algorithms. *Facta Univ. Ser. Mech. Eng.* **2019**, *17*, 365–383.

symmetry

MDPI

Article

A New Integrated Fuzzy Approach to Selecting the Best Solution for Business Balance of Passenger Rail Operator: Fuzzy PIPRECIA-Fuzzy EDAS Model

Slavko Vesković [1], Željko Stević [2,*], Darjan Karabašević [3], Snježana Rajilić [4], Sanjin Milinković [1] and Gordan Stojić [5]

1 Faculty of Transport and Traffic Engineering, University of Belgrade, Vojvode Stepe 305, 11000 Belgrade, Serbia; veskos@sf.bg.ac.rs (S.V.); s.milinkovic@sf.bg.ac.rs (S.M.)

2 Faculty of Transport and Traffic Engineering, University of East Sarajevo, Vojvode Mišića 52, 74000 Doboj, Bosnia and Herzegovina

3 Faculty of Applied Management, Economics and Finance, University Business Academy in Novi Sad, Jevrejska 24, 11000 Belgrade, Serbia; darjan.karabasevic@mef.edu.rs

4 Bosnia and Herzegovina Railways Public Corporation, Kneza Miloša 105, 74000 Doboj, Bosna and Hercegovina; snjezana_rajilic@yahoo.com

5 Faculty of Technical sciences, University of Novi Sad, Trg Dositeja Obradovića 6, 21000 Novi Sad, Serbia; gordan@uns.ac.rs

* Correspondence: zeljkostevic88@yahoo.com or zeljko.stevic@sf.ues.rs.ba

Received: 21 March 2020; Accepted: 12 April 2020; Published: 5 May 2020

Abstract: The analysis of operations of the passenger traffic operator in the Republic of Srpska (RS) showed that the volume of passenger transport has, for the last fifteen years, been in constant decline. It is of particular importance that the operator has, year after year, recorded a negative balance of business. The way out of the current unfavorable situation in the sector of passenger traffic is based on the application of Public Service Obligation (PSO) based on the Regulation 1370/2007. In order to solve the problems, seven realistically possible variants have been identified. This paper defines the criteria for selecting the best variant, as well as a new integrated fuzzy model for the selection of the best variant that will enable the operator to make a profit. To define the weights of criteria in this paper, we have used the fuzzy PIvot Pairwise RElative Criteria Importance Assessment (F-PIPRECIA) method, while for ranking and selection of the best variant, we have used the Fuzzy Evaluation based on Distance from Average Solution (F-EDAS) method. Results show that the seventh variant: "Increase in revenue from ticket sales and PSO services and reduction in costs" is the best solution in current conditions. Validation tests are performed with different scenarios and approaches and show that the model is stable. A validity test was created consisting of variations in the significance of model input parameters, testing of reverse rank, applying the fuzzy Measurement Alternatives and Ranking according to the COmpromise Solution (F-MARCOS), fuzzy Simple Additive Weighing (F-SAW) method, and fuzzy Technique for Order of Preference by Similarity to Ideal Solution (F-TOPSIS). As a part of the validation tests, Spearman's coefficient of correlation (SCC) in some scenarios is performed and weights of the criteria have been obtained using the Fuzzy Analytic Hierarchy Process (F-AHP) and Full Consistency Method (FUCOM).

Keywords: fuzzy PIPRECIA; fuzzy EDAS; railway; multi-criteria decision-making; transport policy

1. Introduction

One of the most important factors for the functioning and development of cities and regions according to Stojić et al. [1] is the public transport of passengers. The transport policy developed by the European Union (EU) has one of the main goals of overcoming the undesirable "modal split," in which road transport has a dominant position, strengthening the role of the railway, thus establishing the possibility of developing a transport system in the spirit of sustainable development. In fact, the Public Service Obligation (PSO) system represents a model for financing unprofitable transport services of a common interest of the country, the region, or the city and local community. Since the end of the 1960s, the EU has tried to improve and develop the concept of PSO in a number of sub-legal acts and regulations in all modes of transport, especially in rail and road public passenger transport (PPT). The basic idea of this concept was that the competent authority (state or local) should provide PPT on lines where the operator (transport company) cannot profitably operate practically, the public authority (ordering party) "buys" (negotiates) the transport service on the "open" market publicly and without discrimination. The volume and service quality, the number of lines and transportation units, the model of determining the amount of compensation for the execution of the service, as well as other mutual rights and obligations, are regulated by the contract. The operator is awarded a Public Service Compensation (PSC) for public transport. According to Regulation (EC) No 1370/2007 [2], the fee for covering the costs arising from the performance of the PSO should, therefore, be determined to prevent over-compensation, and it must be determined so that it does not exceed the amount corresponding to the net financial effect of an equal amount of effects, either positive or negative. The two basic terms that are contained in the new PPT system are: Public Service Obligation (PSO) and Public Service Compensation (PSC). For definition and details of these terms, see (Regulation (EC) No 1370/2007 [2]. By optimizing the PSO system in the PPT process, it is possible to achieve a number of effects, the most significant of which are: Increasing the volume of passenger transport (especially regional and suburban) and, in the worst case, a stoppage in the volume of transport, higher and more stable quality of transport services, reduction in travel costs, better and more efficient cost control, achieve the preconditions for the stabilization and reliability of the operation of railway companies that carry out the transport of passengers (operators). There is no universal and generally accepted model for defining the PSO and the PSC. For example, socio-economic and transport data for PPT services in European cities [3] show the ratio between subventions and operating costs, as well as the ratio of total revenue from the sale of tickets and total operating costs of PPT services in selected cities. According to the mentioned study, the revenues from the sale of tickets cover an average of 44% of the total operating costs of public transport companies. The second indicator shows the percentage of subventions in total operating costs of transport. On average, 48% of the total operating costs of transport are covered by subventions. This means that one-half of the total operating costs of transport is covered by sales revenues, while the other half comes from different subventions from the local, municipal, or national level.

The first aim of the paper refers to the development of a new integrated fuzzy PIvot Pairwise RElative Criteria Importance Assessment (F-PIPRECIA)—Fuzzy Evaluation based on Distance from Average Solution (F-EDAS)—model for solving the business balance of a passenger rail operator, which is harmonized with the EU transport policy. The second aim of the paper is the possibility to overcome the gap between different variants of solving concrete problems in, often, very different demographic, infrastructural, economic, and level-of-service quality levels. The design of the new integrated fuzzy model for the solution business balance of the passenger rail operator allows, within a reasonable time, the non-operational balance sheet of the passenger operator and even the possibility of achieving a rational profit. In order to solve the problem, seven realistic variants based on the combination of procedures, which, in different ways, lead to a defined goal, have been identified. In addition, the criteria for selecting the most favorable variant are defined, and the integrated model for selecting the most favorable variant should provide a positive balance.

This paper is structured as follows. Section 2 shows some brief backgrounds, while Section 3 shows the material and methods, the basic characteristics of railway transport in the Republic of Srpska (RS), its organization, and its current and future role. In addition, in this section, the proposed methodology is explained in detail. Section 4 shows the obtained results, applying a new developed fuzzy model, while Section 5 shows the extent of the validation tests. Section 6 presents the discussion and conclusions.

2. Brief Background

In the paper about public suburban transport in Germany, Beck [4] analyzes the state of the so-called commercial and non-commercial transport. In doing so, he notes that, after a decade of stagnation due to non-commercial transport, in the performance of the PSO, there is a positive change and the intensification of competition. The methodology for assessment of the future transport needs in PPT by Rojo et al. [5] is upgraded by the inclusion of the subjective value of time and readiness users pay for the improvement of services in order to determine the optimal concept of PSO. The system is optimized in two ways: With and without considering the economic business of the company in the function of the goal. Vesković et al. [6] used fuzzy logic for the assessment of the liberalization of rail passenger traffic on the example of Serbia, and one of the criteria in the model for assessment is PSO. Nash et al. [7] used quantitative and qualitative methods to investigate the impact on the cost of the vertical separation of railways in cases of a radical approach to restructuring. They are suspicious that reforming the railways through vertical and horizontal separation leads to cost savings. They state that precisely determining the methods and control of the distribution "of state money," subventions (PSO, maintenance and infrastructure development) have primarily led to cost reductions. In order to achieve the aims defined by the overall transport policy according to Ibarra-Rojas and Rios-Solis [8], cities and municipalities choose to subsidize PPT. These aims are different and range from providing transport options to all social categories to increase mobility for all residents. As a special advantage of these systems, Tirachini and Hensher [9] and Kim and Schonfeld [10] point out that the implementation of such a transport policy reduces the need for the use of personal vehicles. This, in turn, offers the opportunity to better manage urban space and transform the environment for the sustainable development of urban communities. In his paper, Van Reeven [11] developed a model aiming to demonstrate that the costs on the principle of consumer spending time do not provide justification for public transport subventions. PPT subventions are common in developing countries and are often justified by the availability of traffic accessibility, but not efficiency. In view of this justification, it is of interest to know how to use and distribute transport subventions.

To understand the idea behind public transport subsidies, Vuchic [12] and Hanson and Giuliano [13] emphasize that cities and municipalities do not subsidize operators, but the actual public transport service offered to citizens. In the absence of a subsidy, carriers are forced to charge the full cost of transportation for passengers through the price of tickets, which would lead to a significant reduction in transport demand and thus a decrease in traffic supply. Such a transport strategy implies, on the one hand, reduced mobility and, on the other, increased citizen dissatisfaction.

3. Materials and Methods

3.1. Proposed Methodology

The multi-criteria decision-making (MCDM) methods are widely used for the facilitation of the decision-making process in various fields [14–16]. The original developed MCDM methodology shown in Figure 1 was applied for selection of the best solution for the business balance of the passenger rail operator.

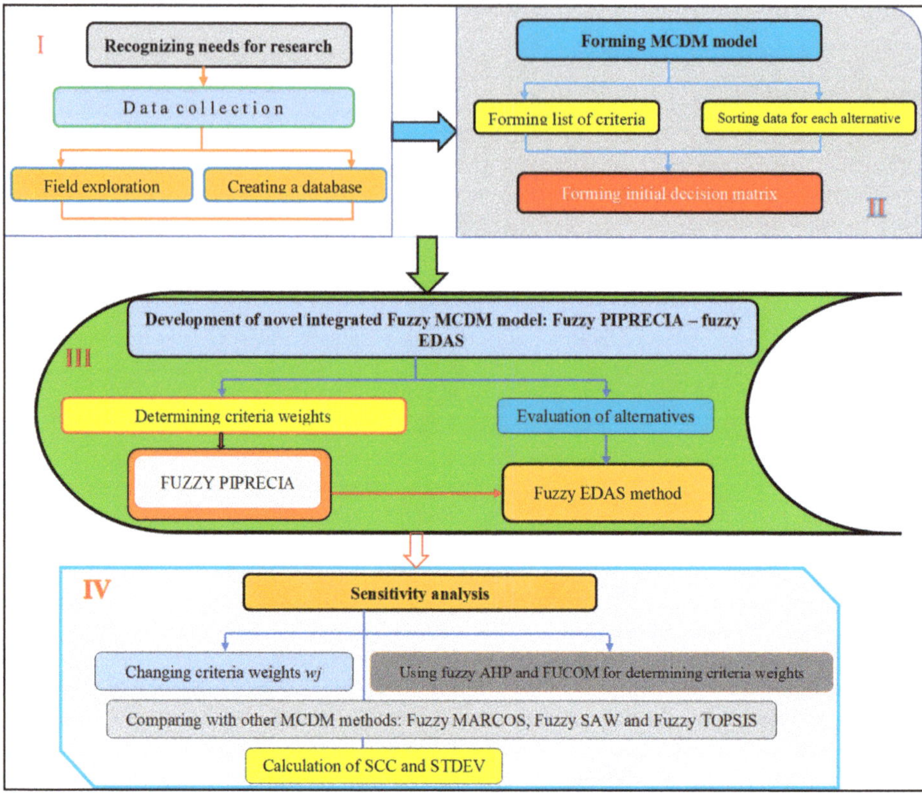

Figure 1. Proposed methodology.

As part of the first phase of the research, data were collected. After that, an adequate database on transport policy was created in order to obtain and to analyze their effects on the business operators. Based on the collected data and created base, the forming of the MCDM model represents the second phase of the proposed methodology. Five most important criteria, explained in detail in the further text, were considered, while seven different variants were identified. Based on such parameters, an initial fuzzy decision matrix was formed. The third part of the methodology represents the most important part of the research and consists of two steps that are causally linked both to each other and to the elements of the following phase. These steps represent the development of an original integrated fuzzy MCDM model. First, the significance of the criteria was determined using the F-PIPRECIA method [17] according to the assessment of three decision-makers. Evaluation of various variants for selecting the best solution for the business balance of the passenger rail operator was performed using the F-EDAS method [18]. The fourth phase of the methodology involves the validation and sensitivity analysis of the proposed model. It is implemented throughout a few steps, where the first step relates to variations in the significance of the criteria. All individual approaches are individually included in the calculation of the F-EDAS method and a comparative analysis is given with respect to the proposed model. Testing the influence of dynamic factors—of the reverse rank and calculation of the criteria weights using the Fuzzy Analytic Hierarchy Process (F-AHP) [19] and Full Consistency Method (FUCOM) [20] methods—is also a part of the validity test. The next step includes the comparison of the developed model with three other fuzzy MCDM methods: fuzzy Measurement Alternatives and Ranking according to the COmpromise Solution (F-MARCOS) [21], fuzzy Simple

Additive Weighing (F-SAW) [22], and fuzzy Technique for Order of Preference by Similarity to Ideal Solution (F-TOPSIS) [23].

Finally, the Spearman's correlation coefficient (SCC) was calculated to determine the correlation of all obtained ranks across previously formed scenarios. As the F-PIPRECIA [17,24–26], F-EDAS [18,27–29], FUCOM [30,31], F-MARCOS [21], F-SAW [22,32], and F-AHP [23,33,34] methods have been exploited in the literature, their detailed algorithms are not presented.

3.2. The Position of Public Transport Services (PTS) for Passengers by Rail in the Transportation System of the Republic of Srspka

The Railways of the Republic of Srpska (RRS) have been established as a public transport company, and it is important to emphasize that by "under the railway traffic of interest for the Republic of Srpska," we mean "railway public passenger transport." Irrespective of commercial interest, RRS must have at their disposal adequate capacity (material and human) and organizational conditions for the provision of public transport services (PTS) for passengers. Therefore, the authorities of the Republic of Srpska exert significant impact on the results of operations and the balance sheet of the company. RRS, and the segment of the company that deals with passenger transport (passenger transport operations) in particular, must establish an original system of determining results (revenues, expenses, profit-loss) on the grounds of the public transport of passengers. The opening of the railways to competition in the market of transport services brought about a separation of management and accounts (balance sheet) of infrastructure and transport. Consistent realization of this process means that "RRS shall—through a special type of bookkeeping—present to its founder the state and the railway infrastructure costs compared to the costs of operators." Separate reporting of costs is aimed at expressing the impact of business segments upon the operating results, which are determined by the balance sheet. Therefore, it is necessary to separately determine the balance of infrastructure and the balance of transport (assets, debts, obligations, liabilities, equity, revenues, expenses, results), as well as the consolidated balance of the corporation. In its efforts to provide for the traffic of interest for the Republic of Srpska, the government participates through partial financing. This means that RRS provide funding for a part of the public transport system that is of interest for the Republic of Srpska. According to Gangwar and Raghuram [35], one of the options is structuring public private partnerships. The volume of passenger transport is in a constant downward trend, and the largest volume of transport was recorded in 1996, amounting to 1,648,000 of transported passengers, while in 2009, the RRS transported no more than 368,289 passengers. The negative trend has continued in the years to come, so in the last two years, the annual number was at the level of about 150,000 passengers. Financial results regarding passenger traffic have been made according to the planning documents: Annual report of RRS for 2014, and business plan for the period 2012 to 2014.

The revenue and expenditure plan in passenger traffic is projected at the level of the financial loss of over −19,000,000 KM for each considered year, which is why the plan of inflows and outflows of funds remains at the level of loss of −26,869,280 KM in 2012 to −38,616,384 KM in 2014. The increase in expenditure in 2012 was by 67% higher compared to 2011, amounting to 10,371,589 KM, and the revenues were lower by about 30%, i.e., by 2,559,281 KM. The increase in expenditure in the said amount was the result of an increase in the following: Cost of fees for access and use of railway infrastructure in the amount of KM + 5,458,404 (+52%); cost of wages, salaries, and other employee benefits in the amount of KM +2,996,647 (+29%), cost of materials for the work in the amount of KM + 1,020,676 (+10%), and costs of production services in the amount of + 966,014 (9%) (Figure 2).

The problem with the above, i.e., the problem with the operations in the reported period with a huge financial loss, lies in reduced business competitiveness of RRS as the operator at a future liberalized market of transport services, and, therefore, its uncertain business future. In this sense, the "experts" of the Railways of the Republic of Srpska have reduced passenger traffic for the 2008/2009 timetable by eliminating 22 passenger trains that were, by internal calculations, within the area of unprofitable business.

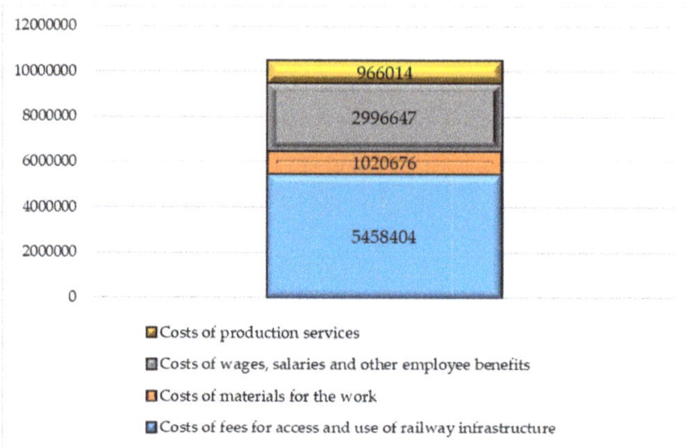

Figure 2. Increase in expenditures of Railways of the Republic of Srpska (RRS) for 2011–2012 years.

Reactions of passengers to this move were completely understandable, so the reduction in the number of trains by 25% (from 76 to 54 trains a day) led to a reduction in the number of passengers for close to 50%, or to be more exact, by 45% in that same (first) year when they implemented the reduction in the number of trains (from 635,000 annually to 368,000). This trend of reducing the number of passengers due to an unsatisfactory timetable and reduced frequency of trains was carried out on almost all routes. The authorities of the Republic of Srpska noted that by this move, they achieved a reduction in operating costs of about 2,000,000 KM but failed to note the loss and reduction in income due to a drastic reduction in the number of passengers.

The downward trend in train numbers has led to an increase in the company's financial losses. It is true that the cost of doing business has been somewhat reduced (Figure 2), but revenue has fallen significantly, leading to greater financial losses (Figure 3). The financial loss of the company in 2011 amounted to 6,969,205 KM. In 2012, expenditures of KM 10,441,741 were still high, although they were somewhat reduced, but revenues were significantly lower and decreased by over KM 2.5 million so that the company's negative balance in fiscal 2012 increased to 19,970,227 million KM.

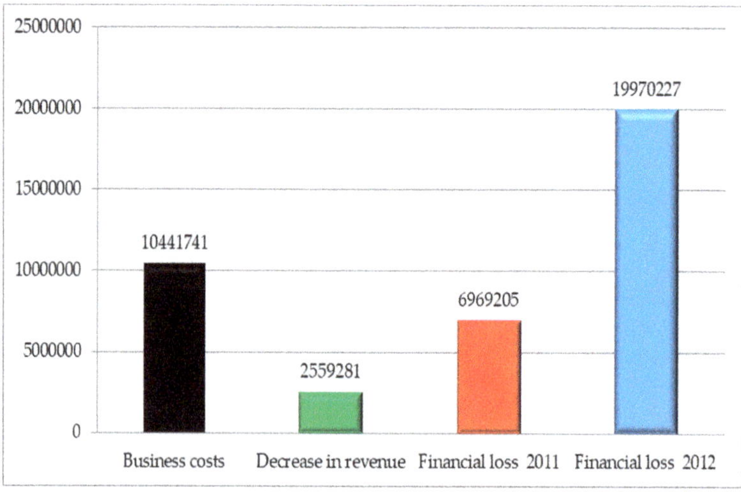

Figure 3. Financial loss of RRS 2011–2012.

3.3. Problem Identification and Solving Methodology

The analysis of the passenger traffic subsystem showed the following characteristics: From 1996 until today, the number of passengers has been in constant decline, the number of passenger trains has decreased in domestic traffic by 28 trains, in inter-entity transport by 18 trains, and by 8 trains in international transport. The railway fee for the infrastructure in domestic services amounts to 4,176,295 KM, in inter-entity transport amounts to 601,836 KM, and in international transport amounts to 1,603,022 KM. The other elements of the RRS business operations are shown in [36]. The problem-solving methodology is based on:

1. increase in revenue from direct ticket sales and increase in revenue from agreements on PSO,
2. reduction in expensing, i.e., operating costs.

The expected result of the mentioned activities according to the given methodology should be sustainable business operations. Figure 4 shows the cost realization plan for the next fiscal year, as well as the perception of cost coverage by government revenues and government subsidies (PSOs), and a model of the long-term business stabilization goal (Figure 5).

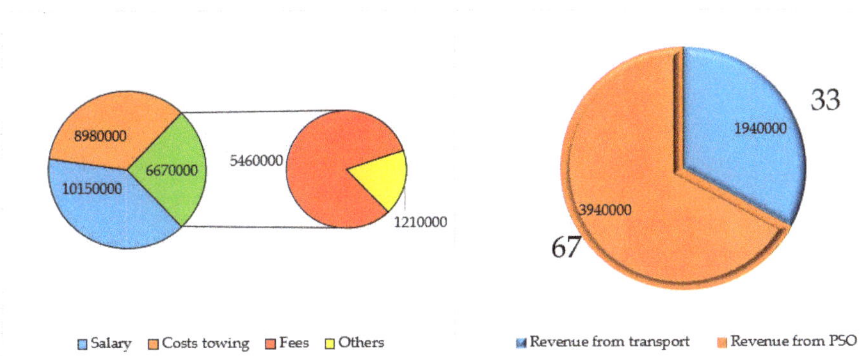

Figure 4. Business plan for the period of 2013 year (costs and revenue).

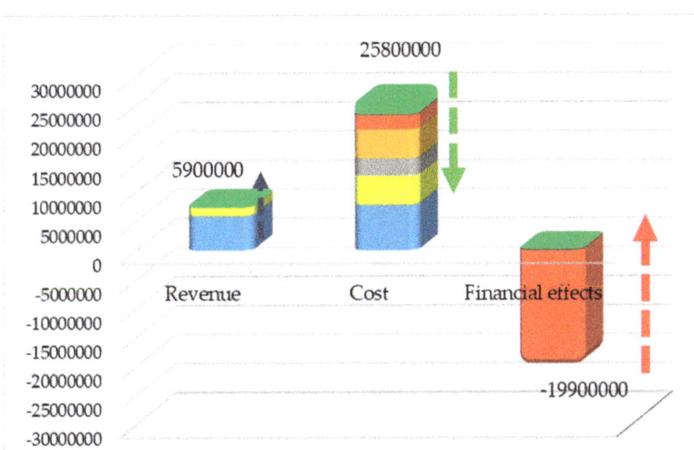

Figure 5. Problem-solving methodology.

The aim of the problem solving is to bring RRS as the operator in passenger traffic into the domain of positive operations, thus providing the necessary conditions for successful operation at a liberalized transport market. In [6], details about the model for liberalization in Serbia can be found.

In this paper, a new integrated F-PIPRECIA-F-EDAS model is created for solving problems. Multi-criteria methods for decision-making are used to resolve a large number of problems in all spheres of business, and they represent an area that is developing rapidly, primarily due to a large number of methods that have been developed, particularly within the last decade. The combination of these methods with fuzzy logic gives excellent results because classical methods cannot, with such precision, perform the required quantification, and this is where fuzzy logic shows all its advantages [37,38].

3.4. Forming a MCDM Model

3.4.1. Possible Solutions

In order to resolve the problem, seven realistically possible variants (V) have been identified. All variants are described in [36]:

- V1: Reduction in operating costs (Figure 6 left):

$$T = f(T_1, T_2, T_3, \dots, T_n) \rightarrow \text{min} \tag{1}$$

where T denotes costs.

- V2: Increase in revenue from ticket sales (Figure 6 right):

$$P_1 = f(P_{11}, P_{12}, P_{13}, \dots, P_{1n}) \rightarrow \text{max} \tag{2}$$

where P denotes revenue.

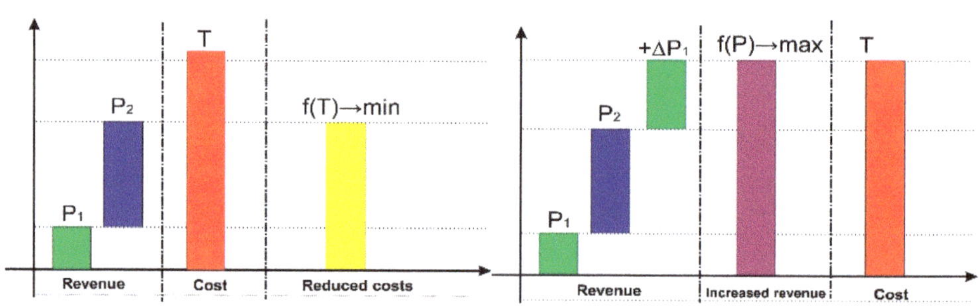

Figure 6. V1—reduction in operating costs, V2—increase in revenue from ticket sales.

- V3: Increase in ticket revenue and reduction in operating costs (Figure 7 left):

$$P_1 = f(P_{11}, P_{12}, P_{13}, \dots, P_{1n}) \rightarrow \text{max}. \wedge T = f(T_1, T_2, T_3, \dots, T_n) \rightarrow \text{min} \tag{3}$$

- V4: Increase in revenue from PSO services (Figure 7 right):

$$P_2 = f(P_{21}, P_{22}, P_{23}, \dots, P_{1n}) \rightarrow \text{max} \tag{4}$$

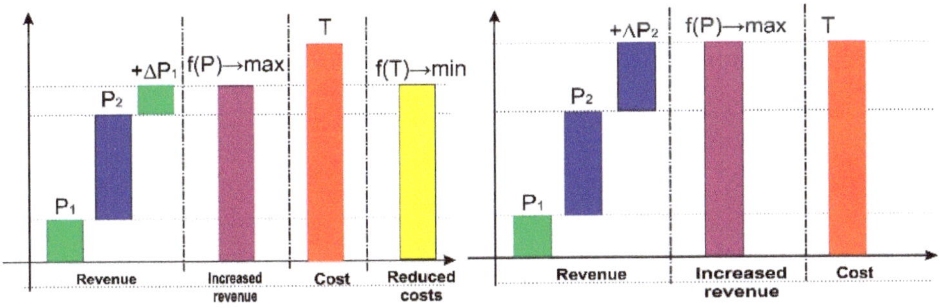

Figure 7. V3—increase in ticket revenue and reduction in operating costs, V4—increase in revenue from Public Service Obligation (PSO) services.

- V5: Increase in revenue from PSO services and reduction in operating costs (Figure 8 left):

$$P_2 = f(P_{21}, P_{22}, P_{23}, \ldots, P_{2n}) \rightarrow \text{max.} \wedge T = f(T_1, T_2, T_3, \ldots, T_n) \rightarrow \text{min} \quad (5)$$

- V6: Increase in revenue from ticket sales and PSO services (Figure 8 right):

$$P_1 + P_2 = f(P_{11}, P_{12}, P_{13}, \ldots, P_{1n}) + = f(P_{21}, P_{22}, P_{23}, \ldots, P_{2n}) \rightarrow \text{max} \quad (6)$$

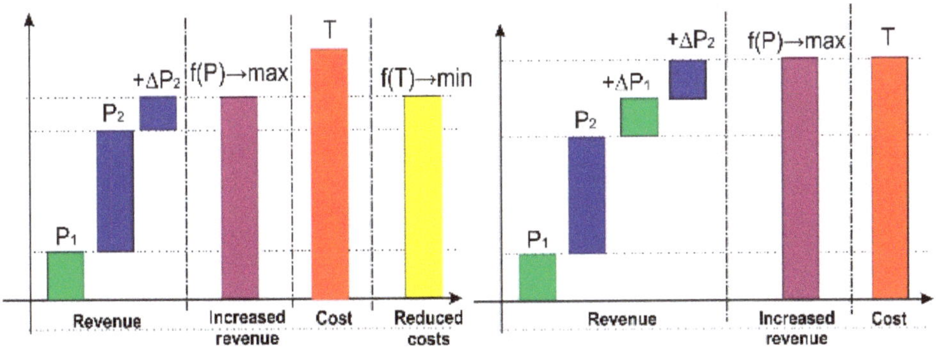

Figure 8. V5—increase in revenue from PSO services and reduction in operating costs, V6—increase in revenue from ticket sales and PSO services.

- V7: Increase in revenue from ticket sales and PSO services and reduction in costs (Figure 9):

$$P_1 + P_2 = f(P_{11}, P_{12}, P_{13}, \ldots, P_{1n}) + = f(P_{21}, P_{22}, P_{23}, \ldots, P_{2n}) \rightarrow \text{max} \quad (7)$$

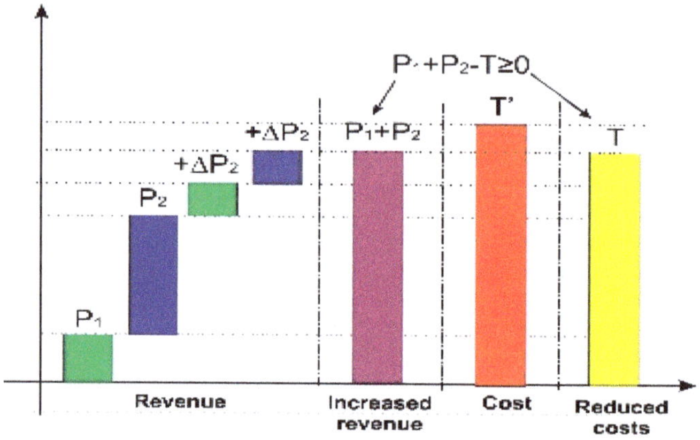

Figure 9. V7—increase in revenue from ticket sales and PSO services and reduction in costs.

3.4.2. Identification of Evaluation Criteria

Identification and quantification of the criteria for evaluating the manner of implementing the principles and concluding a PSO contract were carried out over four steps: Defining the required level or volume of service, reduction in business costs, increase in revenues from ticket sales, and increase in revenues under the PSO contract.

The selection of an optimal variant depends on many factors. Therefore, in the proposed methodology, as the criteria, the following values have been adopted: The reality of the feasibility of the proposed variant, means available to the public authority - budget, the ability of the operator, the effect of realization, and the period of realization (Table 1).

Table 1. Criteria for evaluation of identified variants.

Mark	Title of Criterion	Type
C_1	variant feasibility	profit-type
C_2	public authorities–the budget size	profit-type
C_3	operators' ability	profit-type
C_4	the effect of realization	profit-type
C_5	Period of realization	loss-type

4. Results

As for obtaining the weight value of criteria, we have used the F-PIPRECIA method; after identifying the criteria on which the ranking of potential variants will be made, it is required that we compare the criteria by using the scale presented in [17]. In order to derive the relative importance of the criteria, a team of three experts had been established; for many years, they have been performing managerial functions in the field of railway transport. As this is an already exploited method, detailed procedures for calculating the values of criteria will not be shown, but rather the summed results by each step (Table 2).

Table 2. Calculation and results of applying the fuzzy PIvot Pairwise RElative Criteria Importance Assessment (F-PIPRECIA) method for determining the criteria weights.

	$\overline{s_j}$	$\overline{k_j}$	$\overline{q_j}$	$\overline{w_j}$	DF
C1		(1,1,1)	(1,1,1)	(0.288,0.323,0.364)	0.324
C2	(0.356,0.433,0.556)	(1.444,1.567,1.644)	(0.608,0.638,0.692)	(0.175,0.206,0.252)	0.209
C3	(0.262,0.302,0.356)	(1.644,1.698,1.738)	(0.35,0.376,0.421)	(0.101,0.121,0.153)	0.123
C4	(1.3,1.45,1.5)	(0.5,0.55,0.7)	(0.5,0.683,0.842)	(0.144,0.22,0.307)	0.222
C5	(0.262,0.302,0.356)	(1.644,1.698,1.738)	(0.288,0.402,0.512)	(0.083,0.13,0.187)	0.131
SUM			(2.745,3.1,3.467)		
	$\overline{s'_j}$	$\overline{k'_j}$	$\overline{q'_j}$	$\overline{w'_j}$	DF
C1	(1.333,1.5,1.55)	(0.45,0.5,0.667)	(2.276,7.36,11.54)	(0.088,0.399,1.45)	0.523
C2	(1.233,1.35,1.4)	(0.6,0.65,0.767)	(1.517,3.68,5.193)	(0.059,0.2,0.653)	0.252
C3	(0.28,0.328,0.395)	(1.605,1.672,1.72)	(1.163,2.392,3.116)	(0.045,0.13,0.392)	0.159
C4	(1.5,1.75,1.8)	(0.2,0.25,0.5)	(2,4,5)	(0.077,0.217,0.628)	0.262
C5		(1,1,1)	(1,1,1)	(0.039,0.054,0.126)	0.064
SUM			(7.956,18.432,25.848)		

Where $\overline{s_j}$ represents the group matrix obtained by expert's assessment, starting from the second criterion, and $\overline{k_j}$ is the coefficient obtained when $\overline{s_j}$ is subtracted from number 2, except for $\overline{s_1}$. $\overline{q_j}$ is the fuzzy weight, $\overline{w_j}$ is the relative weight of the criterion, and DF is the defuzzified value.

Based on the aggregation of the values wj shown in Table 2, the final criterion values are obtained:$w_1 = 0.423$; $w_2 = 0.230$; $w_3 = 0.141$; $w_4 = 0.242$; $w_5 = 0.098$. After calculating the weight value of criteria, we then begin the selection of the optimal variant by using the F-EDAS method. On the basis of the linguistic scale, the experts evaluate variants according to each criterion individually (Table 3).

Table 3. Evaluation of variants according to the criteria expressed in trapezoidal fuzzy numbers.

Expert Rating	Variant	Criterion				
		C_1	C_2	C_3	C_4	C_5
E_1	V_1	(1,2,2,3)	(4,5,5,6)	(8,9,10,10)	(8,9,10,10)	(0,0,1,2)
	V_2	(0,0,1,2)	(5,6,7,8)	(8,9,10,10)	(5,6,7,8)	(0,0,1,2)
	V_3	(2,3,4,5)	(5,6,7,8)	(7,8,8,9)	(8,9,10,10)	(5,6,7,8)
	V_4	(1,2,2,3)	(8,9,10,10)	(4,5,5,6)	(7,8,8,9)	(0,0,1,2)
	V_5	(5,6,7,8)	(7,8,8,9)	(7,8,8,9)	(7,8,8,9)	(7,8,8,9)
	V_6	(7,8,8,9)	(7,8,8,9)	(7,8,8,9)	(8,9,10,10)	(5,6,7,8)
	V_7	(8,9,10,10)	(7,8,8,9)	(5,6,7,8)	(8,9,10,10)	(7,8,8,9)
E_2	V_1	(2,3,4,5)	(5,6,7,8)	(8,9,10,10)	(7,8,8,9)	(1,2,2,3)
	V_2	(1,2,2,3)	(7,8,8,9)	(8,9,10,10)	(7,8,8,9)	(0,0,1,2)
	V_3	(4,5,5,6)	(7,8,8,9)	(8,9,10,10)	(8,9,10,10)	(5,6,7,8)
	V_4	(2,3,4,5)	(8,9,10,10)	(4,5,5,6)	(8,9,10,10)	(0,0,1,2)
	V_5	(5,6,7,8)	(8,9,10,10)	(7,8,8,9)	(7,8,8,9)	(5,6,7,8)
	V_6	(7,8,8,9)	(7,8,8,9)	(8,9,10,10)	(7,8,8,9)	(7,8,8,9)
	V_7	(8,9,10,10)	(7,8,8,9)	(7,8,8,9)	(8,9,10,10)	(8,9,10,10)
E_3	V_1	(1,2,2,3)	(4,5,5,6)	(8,9,10,10)	(7,8,8,9)	(0,0,1,2)
	V_2	(0,0,1,2)	(5,6,7,8)	(7,8,8,9)	(8,9,10,10)	(0,0,1,2)
	V_3	(4,5,5,6)	(7,8,8,9)	(8,9,10,10)	(8,9,10,10)	(7,8,8,9)
	V_4	(0,0,1,2)	(7,8,8,9)	(4,5,5,6)	(7,8,8,9)	(1,2,2,3)
	V_5	(7,8,8,9)	(8,9,10,10)	(7,8,8,9)	(8,9,10,10)	(7,8,8,9)
	V_6	(5,6,7,8)	(8,9,10,10)	(8,9,10,10)	(7,8,8,9)	(7,8,8,9)
	V_7	(7,8,8,9)	(7,8,8,9)	(5,6,7,8)	(8,9,10,10)	(8,9,10,10)

Table 4 also shows, apart from the values of the average decision matrix, the values of an average solution according to all the criteria.

Table 4. The elements of the average decision-matrix and the average solution matrix.

	V_1	V_2	V_3	V_4
C_1	(0.13,0.23,0.27,0.37)	(0.03,0.07,0.13,0.23)	(0.33,0.43,0.47,0.57)	(0.1,0.17,0.23,0.33)
C_2	(0.43,0.53,0.57,0.67)	(0.57,0.67,0.73,0.83)	(0.63,0.73,0.77,0.87)	(0.77,0.87,0.93,0.97)
C_3	(0.8,0.9,1.0,1.0)	(0.77,0.87,0.93,0.97)	(0.77,0.87,0.93,0.97)	(0.4,0.5,0.5,0.6)
C_4	(0.73,0.83,0.87,0.93	(0.67,0.77,0.83,0.9)	(0.8,0.9,1.0,1.0)	(0.73,0.83,0.87,0.93
C_5	(0.03,0.07,0.13,0.23)	(0,0,0.1,0.2)	(0.57,0.67,0.73,0.83)	(0.03,0.07,0.13,0.23)
	V_5	V_6	V_7	AV
C_1	(0.57,0.67,0.73,0.83)	(0.63,0.73,0.77,0.87)	(0.77,0.87,0.93,0.97)	(0.37,0.45,0.50,0.60)
C_2	(0.77,0.87,0.93,0.97)	(0.73,0.83,0.87,0.93	(0.7,0.8,0.8,0.9)	(0.66,0.76,0.80,0,88)
C_3	(0.7,0.8,0.8,0.9)	(0.77,0.87,0.93,0.97)	(0.57,0.67,0.73,0.83)	(0.68,0.78,0.83,0.89)
C_4	(0.73,0.83,0.87,0.93)	(0.73,0.83,0.87,0.93)	(0.8,0.9,1.0,1.0)	(0.74,0.84,0.90,0.95)
C_5	(0.63,0.73,0.77,0.87)	(0.63,0.73,0.77,0.87)	(0.77,0.87,0.93,0.97)	(0.38,0.45,0.51,0.60)

Next, we need to calculate positive distances (PDA) and negative distances (NDA) from the average solutions depending on the criteria type. In this case, only the fifth criterion is useless, while the others are useful criteria. First, we obtain the values of the positive distance (PDA) and the values of the negative distance from the average solution. In order to obtain the values shown in Table 5, it is necessary to first apply step 5 of the F-EDAS method, and this represents the sum of the weighted matrix for positive $\widetilde{sp_i}$ and negative distance $\widetilde{sn_i}$ for all variants. Further, it is necessary to normalize previous values in order to obtain $\widetilde{nsp_i}$ and $\widetilde{nsn_i}$. Finally, it is necessary to calculate the assessment of the results, the appraisal score ($\widetilde{as_i}$), and make the defuzzification appraisal score ($\widetilde{as_i}$) (Table 5).

Table 5. The weighted sum of distances, the normalized values of them, and the appraisal scores.

	$\widetilde{sp_i}$	$\widetilde{sn_i}$	$\widetilde{nsp_i}$	
V_1	(0.01,0.08,0.13,0.17)	(−0.06,0.21,0.34,0.61)	(0.04,0.20,0.33,0.45)	
V_2	(0.01,0.08,0.13,0.17)	(0.02,0.30,0.46,0.67)	(0.04,0.20,0.34,0.45)	
V_3	(−0.06,0.01,0.07,0.12)	(−0.25,−0.01,0.14,0.40)	(−0.16,0.02,0.19,0.33)	
V_4	(0.00,0.08,0.14,0.21)	(−0.01,0.24,0.37,0.59)	(0.00,0.22,0.37,0.54)	
V_5	(−0.09,0.16,0.30,0.54)	(−0.05,0.04,0.08,0.16)	(−0.23,0.42,0.78,1.42)	
V_6	(−0.04,0.21,0.34,0.58)	(−0.05,0.04,0.08,0.16)	(−0.09,0.56,0.89,1.51)	
V_7	(0.06,0.32,0.48,0.68)	(0.01,0.08,0.13,0.18)	(0.16,0.84,1.25,1.78)	
	$\widetilde{nsn_i}$	$\widetilde{as_i}$	$k(\widetilde{as_i})$	Rank
V_1	(−0.69,0.04,0.42,1.17)	(−0.33,0.12,0.37,0.81)	0.244	5
V_2	(−0.86,−0.28,0.17,0.94)	(−0.41,−0.04,0.26,0.69)	0.127	7
V_3	(−0.11,0.60,0.96,1.70)	(−0.14,0.31,0.57,1.01)	0.439	4
V_4	(−0.63,−0.04,0.33,1.02)	(−0.32,0.09,0.35,0.78)	0.227	6
V_5	(0.56,0.76,0.90,1.13)	(0.16,0.59,0.84,1.28)	0.718	3
V_6	(0.56,0.76,0.90,1.13)	(0.23.0.66,0.89,1.32)	0.778	2
V_7	(0.51,0.65,0.77,0.98)	(0.33,0.75,1.01,1.38)	0.865	1

Based on the performed analysis, and in accordance with the task, implementation of Variant A_7 is recommended as the most acceptable solution. As good enough solutions, we might accept variants A_6 and A_5; Variant A_3 could possibly represent a satisfactory solution. Thus, it is evident that the most acceptable variant is essentially the scenario in which the positive result stems from joint "efforts" of the operator (decreased costs and increased revenues from the ticket sales) and public authorities through increased subsidies for PSO. Another acceptable variant is a scenario where, because of the limitations of the market (low flow and low purchasing power of the population-passengers), there lacks any significant increase in revenue from ticket sales; the solution is then sought through reduction in costs and increase in PSO subsidies. The variants where the problem is solved only by increased PSO subsidies by the public authorities and the combined approach based on the increase in revenues from ticket sales and operator's cost reduction are not favorable.

5. Validation Tests

5.1. Changing the Significance of Criteria

In this phase of validation test, the impact of changing the three most important criteria C_1, C_2, and C_4 on the ranking results was analyzed. Using Equation (8), a total of 18 scenarios were formed.

$$W_{n\beta} = (1 - W_{n\alpha})\frac{W_\beta}{(1 - W_n)} \tag{8}$$

In scenarios S_1–S_6, the first criterion was changed, criterion C_2 was changed in scenarios S_7–S_{12}, and criterion C_4 was changed in scenarios S_{13}–S_{18}. In Equation (8), $\widetilde{W}_{n\beta}$ represents the new value of criteria C_2–C_5 for scenarios S_1–S_6; then, C_1, C_3–C_5 for scenarios S_7–S_{12}, i.e., C_1–C_3, and C_5 for scenarios S_{13}–S_{18}. $\widetilde{W}_{n\alpha}$ represents the corrected value of criteria C_1, C_2, and C_3 respectively by groups of scenarios, $\widetilde{W}_\beta$ represents the original value of the criterion considered, and $\widetilde{W}_n$ represents the original value of the criterion whose value is reduced, in this case, C_1, C_2, and C_4.

In all scenarios, the value of criteria was reduced by 15%, while the values of the remaining criteria were proportionally corrected by applying Equation (8). After forming 18 new vectors of the weight coefficients of the criteria (Table 6), new model results were obtained, as presented in Figure 10.

Table 6. New criterion values across 18 scenarios.

	w_1	w_2	w_3	w_4	w_5
S_1	0.360	0.255	0.157	0.269	0.108
S_2	0.296	0.281	0.172	0.296	0.119
S_3	0.233	0.306	0.188	0.322	0.130
S_4	0.169	0.331	0.203	0.349	0.140
S_5	0.106	0.357	0.219	0.376	0.151
S_6	0.042	0.382	0.235	0.402	0.162
S_7	0.442	0.196	0.148	0.253	0.102
S_8	0.461	0.161	0.154	0.264	0.106
S_9	0.480	0.127	0.160	0.275	0.111
S_{10}	0.499	0.092	0.167	0.286	0.115
S_{11}	0.518	0.058	0.173	0.297	0.119
S_{12}	0.537	0.023	0.179	0.307	0.124
S_{13}	0.444	0.241	0.148	0.206	0.102
S_{14}	0.464	0.252	0.155	0.170	0.107
S_{15}	0.484	0.263	0.162	0.133	0.112
S_{16}	0.504	0.274	0.168	0.097	0.116
S_{17}	0.525	0.285	0.175	0.061	0.121
S_{18}	0.545	0.296	0.182	0.024	0.126

In most scenarios, there is no change in initial rank, as shown in Figure 10. However, it is important to emphasize that the model is very sensitive to the change in the most important criterion, and in scenarios S1–S6, significant changes occur. With a slight decrease in the value of the first criterion, the ranks slightly change; for example, variants V_1 and V_4 change their positions in the second scenario. As the value of the first criterion decreases drastically, the ranks also change drastically. In the fourth scenario, V_7 loses the first position, while in the sixth scenario, it comes in last place. Practically, the most important role is played by the first criterion in the set decision conditions. In accordance with the rank changes in the mentioned scenarios, a statistical check of the rank correlation was performed using Spearman's correlation coefficient, as shown in Figure 11.

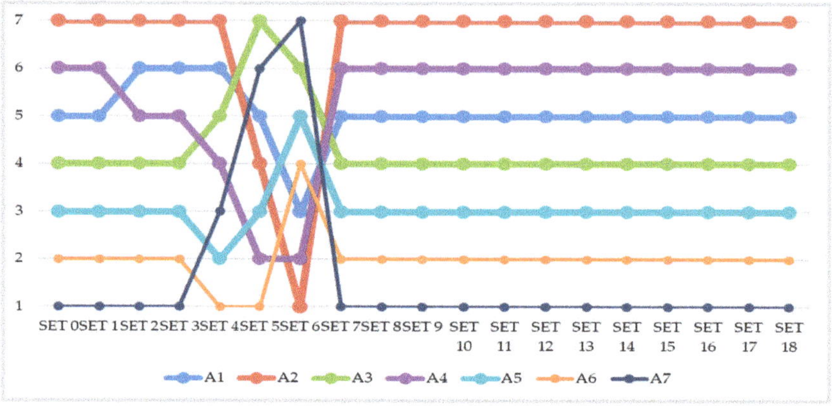

Figure 10. Comparison of obtained results by F-PIPRECIA-Fuzzy Evaluation based on Distance from Average Solution (F-EDAS) model with all formed scenarios S1–S18.

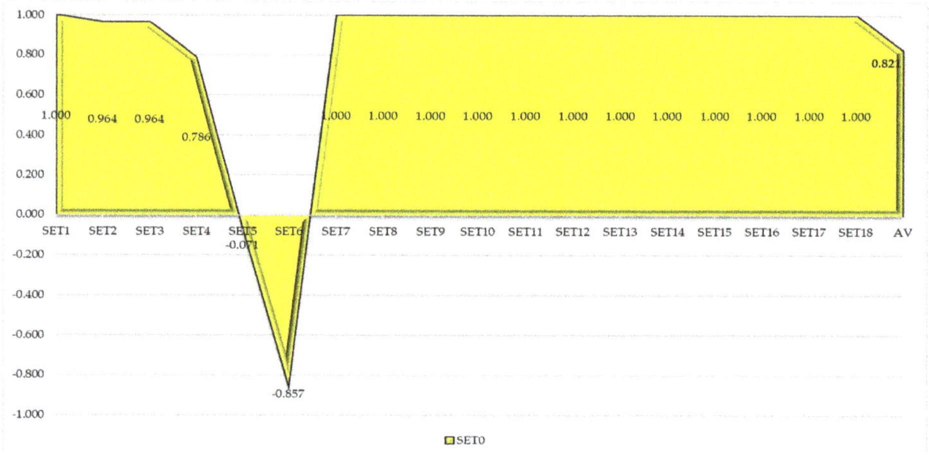

Figure 11. Spearman's correlation coefficient (SCC) through 18 formed scenarios.

The calculated Spearman's correlation coefficient (Figure 11), despite significant deviations in some scenarios, shows a high correlation of ranks in total, 0.821. Generally, in 13 out of 18 scenarios, variants have a full correlation. The correlation between the initial results obtained by the F-PIPRECIA-F-EDAS model and the S_2 and S_3 scenarios is 0.964, while in the S_4 scenario, it is 0.786. The biggest deviation in the rankings is in the fifth and sixth scenarios when the negative correlations are −0.071 and −0.857, respectively.

5.2. *Impact of Reverse Rank Matrices*

One of the ways to test the validity of the obtained results is to construct dynamic matrices that analyze the solutions that the model provides under new conditions. A change in the number of variants is made for each scenario, eliminating the worst variant from further consideration. In the test, six scenarios are formed in which the change in elements of the decision matrix is simulated.

As can be seen in Figure 12, there is no change in ranks for any variant. That means that the proposed F-PIPRECIA-F-EDAS model is stable and gives good results.

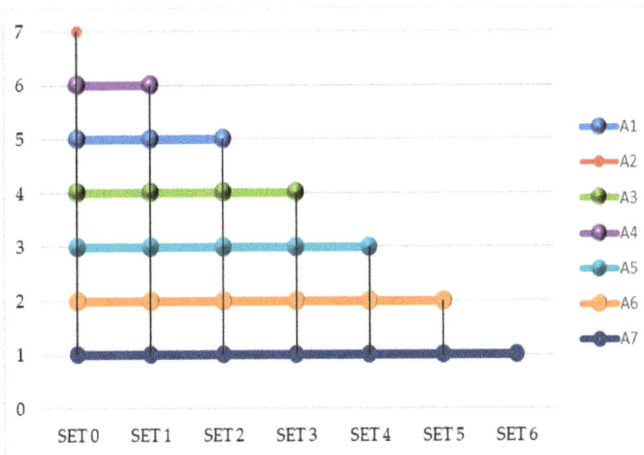

Figure 12. Results of the test of reverse rank matrix.

5.3. Comparison with other Fuzzy MCDM Methods

In this part, a validation test is performed, including comparison with three other fuzzy methods: F-MARCOS, F-SAW, and the F-TOPSIS method. Obtained results are presented in Figure 13.

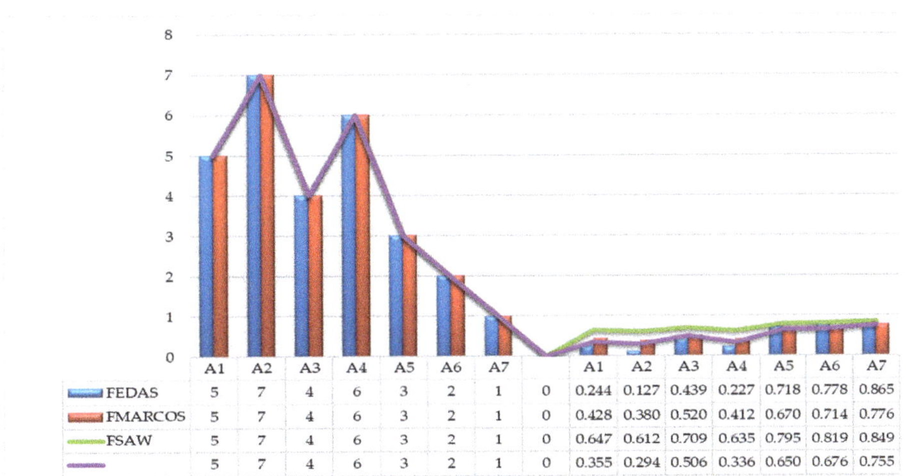

Figure 13. Results of comparison with fuzzy Measurement Alternatives and Ranking according to the COmpromise Solution (F-MARCOS), fuzzy Simple Additive Weighing (F-SAW), and fuzzy Technique for Order of Preference by Similarity to Ideal Solution (F-TOPSIS) methods.

As can be seen in Figure 13, there is no change in ranks for any variant. In Figure 13, in addition to the rankings of variants, values for each variant are given so that a cross-sectional comparison can be made.

5.4. Determining Criteria Weights with F-AHP and FUCOM Methods

In this part of the paper, the criteria weights were re-determined using the F-AHP and FUCOM methods, and the results compared to the original F-PIPRECIA-F-EDAS model are shown in Figure 14.

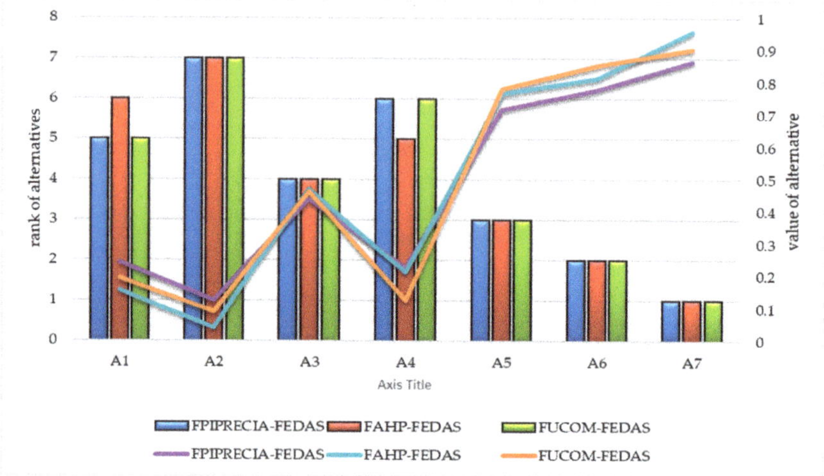

Figure 14. Results obtained using different methods for determining criteria weights.

Applying the above methods for determining the significance of the criteria and including them into the F-EDAS method yield the results presented in Figure 14. In addition to the ranks shown on the left, values of variants on the right are defined. It can be observed that F-PIPRECIA and FUCOM give identical ranks, while, applying F-AHP, there are deviations in the ranks of the first and fourth variants.

5.5. Additional Correction of Criteria Weights Obtained Using F-AHP

After presenting the previous results, the stability of the model is additionally determined as changing the significance of particular criteria. Therefore, a sensitivity analysis has been performed, which is presented throughout two parts in this subsection. Figure 15 shows the ranking of variants in all ten scenarios, while Figure 16 shows Spearman's coefficient of correlation for the ranking of variants. In the first set, the three most important criteria reduced the values by 10%, while the others increased by 15%. In the second set, the two most important criteria reduced the values by 15%, while the others increased by 10%. In the third set, the first criterion reduced by 20%, while the others increased by 5%. In next set, the second criterion reduced by 20%, while the others increased by 5%. In the fifth set, the fourth criterion reduced by 20%, while the others increased by 5%. In the next set, the first three criteria have values of 0.25, the fourth has 0.15, and the fifth has 0.1. In the seventh set, the criteria have values as follows: $C_1 = C_2 = C_4 = 0.30$, $C_3 = 0.10$, and the last criterion has a value of zero. In set 8: $C_1 = C_2 = C_4 = 0.30$, $C_5 = 0.10$, and the third criterion has a value of zero. In set 9: $C_1 = 0.34$, $C_2 = 0.27$, $C_3 = 0.20$, $C_4 = 0.13$, $C_5 = 0.06$. In the last set, $C_1 = 0.30$, $C_2 = 0.20$, $C_3 = 0.15$, $C_4 = 0.20$, $C_5 = 0.15$.

As it can be seen in Figure 15, the seventh variant in seven, from ten formed sets, represents the best solution, while in the other scenarios, the best solution is variant six. The fifth variant is stable in all formed scenarios and has a third position. Variant three and two are also very stable and, only in the first and sixth sets, changing the position. Variant three has position five in the first set, while variant two has position six in the first and sixth sets. The ranking of the first variant varies from the fourth to seventh position in different scenarios, while the fourth variant varies from the fifth to seventh position. We can conclude that with the decrease, the three most important criteria by the 10% results and ranking of variants are very sensitive.

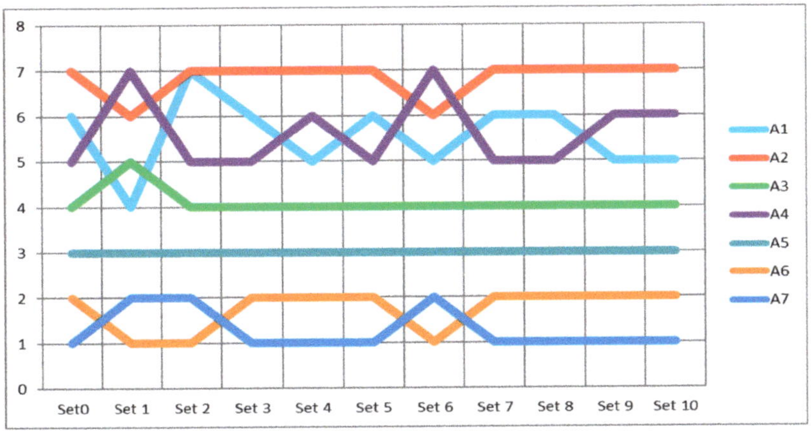

Figure 15. Results of sensitivity analysis of Fuzzy Analytic Hierarchy Process (F-AHP)-F-EDAS changing the significance of criteria.

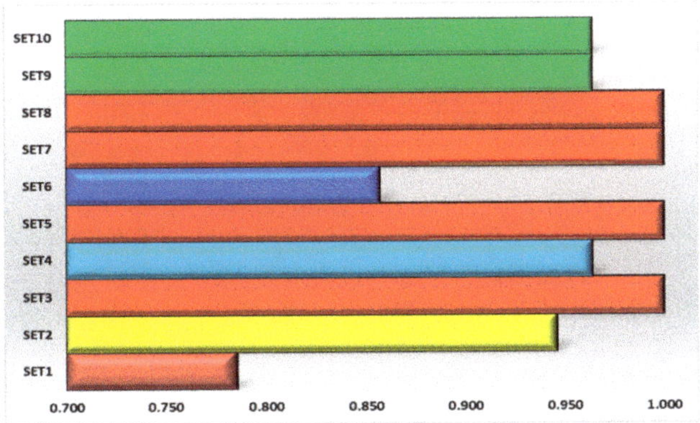

Figure 16. SCC through ten formed scenarios of F-AHP-F-EDAS model.

Figure 16 shows the SCC throughout all scenarios. From Figure 15, it can be seen that the model is sensitive to changes in the weight of the criteria and that each criterion can play an important role in the variant ranking. Spearman's coefficient of correlation has the range of 0.786–1.00, which represents a high degree of correlation, and the results obtained using the integrated fuzzy model are considered stable. The average SCC value for all ten formed scenarios in relation to the initial rank is 0.948.

6. Discussion and Conclusions

In certain cases, there is risk of insufficient financial resources for the execution of the PSO. The costs for the realization of PSO by the operators that are in a state or local ownership may also affect the possibility of implementing the model. Within the framework of the realization of this model, there are several possible sensitive situations that can appear from the moment of planning to the realization: Poor implementation of "business cost reduction" activities, especially with operators owned by government authorities; the lack of interest in "increasing revenue" in the gross contract, especially with operators owned by the authorities, regardless of whether they are revenue from the sale of tickets or other effects; incomplete and untimely realization of the fee for the execution of the PSO; lack of sufficient financial resources from the authorities to increase the fee for the execution of the PSO; the weakness of the state operators in the realization of other effects that can be realized on the basis of the granted right to perform PSO.

In this paper, a dynamic model for optimal application of the PSO system in the PPT process is proposed, which can contribute to the development of appropriate systems for the implementation of PPT services. In addition, it contributes to raising the service quality with the achievement of minimal costs of the functioning of these systems from the aspect of state and local government. By applying this model, it is possible to achieve a large number of effects (increase in passenger transport volume, higher and more stable quality of transport services, reduction in travel costs, better and more efficient cost control, etc.) and achieve significant savings in the functioning of the PPT system. Optimization of the PPT system has an indirect influence on the optimization of transport capacities and improvement in the quality of the transport service with economic quantification and cost savings.

The model was tested in the case of the organization of passenger traffic in the RRS (B&H). Based on the performed analysis, and in accordance with the task, the implementation of Variant V_7 is recommended as the most acceptable solution. As good enough solutions, we might accept variants V_6 and V_5. The contribution of this research represents the possibility for rationalization of the PTT system in RRS. The new F-PIPRECIA-F-EDAS model developed in this research uses the strengths of fuzzy logic and multicriteria decision-making methods. One of the reasons for the F-PIPRECIA method application is its ability to equally handle quantitative and qualitative criteria. One of the reasons for using the F-EDAS method is a mathematical apparatus that assumes the evaluation of variants on the basis of positive and negative deviations from the average solution. The development of the new F-PIPRECIA-F-EDAS model based on TFNs represents the main scientific novelty of this paper. Future research related to this paper should be the implementation of the best variant and post-analysis of PPT systems.

Author Contributions: Conceptualization, S.V. and D.K.; methodology, Ž.S. and D.K.; validation, G.S. and S.M.; investigation, S.V. and S.R.; data curation, S.R.; writing—original draft preparation, Ž.S. and S.M.; writing—review and editing, S.V. and G.S. All authors have read and agreed to the published version of the manuscript.

Funding: This research received no external funding.

Conflicts of Interest: The authors declare no conflict of interest.

References

1. Stojić, G.; Mladenović, D.; Prentkovskis, O.; Vesković, S. A Novel model for determining public service compensation in integrated public transport systems. *Sustainability* **2018**, *10*, 2969. [CrossRef]
2. The European Parliament and the Council of the European Union. *On Public Passenger Transport Services by Rail and by Road and Repealing Council Regulations (EEC) Nos 1191/69 and 1107/70, Regulation (EC) No 1370/2007*; L 315/1; Official Journal of the European Union; The European Parliament and the Council of the European Union: Brussels, Belgium, 2007.
3. EMTA Barometer of Public Transport in European Metropolitan Areas in 2006. Available online: https://www.emta.com/IMG/pdf/Barometer_2006_full_Report.pdf (accessed on 17 February 2020).
4. Beck, A. Commercial public bus transport services in Germany: How a market in motion struggles with its regulatory framework. *Res. Transp. Econ.* **2010**, *29*, 183–194. [CrossRef]
5. Rojo, M.; dell'Olio, L.; Gonzalo-Orden, H.; Ibeas, A. Inclusion of quality criteria in public bus service contracts in metropolitan areas. *Transp. Policy* **2015**, *42*, 52–63. [CrossRef]
6. Vesković, S.; Raičević, V.; Stojić, G.; Milinković, S. A model to estimate the passenger rail liberalisation: The case of serbia. *Int. J. Traffic Transp. Eng.* **2012**, *1*, 202–220. [CrossRef]
7. Nash, C.A.; Smith, A.S.J.; van de Velde, D.; Mizutani, F.; Uranishi, S. Structural reforms in the railways: Incentive misalignment and cost implications. *Res. Transp. Econ.* **2014**, *48*, 16–23. [CrossRef]
8. Ibarra-Rojas, O.J.; Rios-Solis, Y.A. Synchronization of bus timetabling. *Transp. Res. Part B Methodol.* **2012**, *46*, 599–614. [CrossRef]
9. Tirachini, A.; Hensher, D.A. Bus congestion, optimal infrastructure investment and the choice of a fare collection system in dedicated bus corridors. *Transp. Res. Part B Methodol.* **2011**, *45*, 828–844. [CrossRef]

10. Kim, M.; Schonfeld, P. Conventional, flexible, and variable-type bus services. *J. Transp. Eng.* **2011**, *138*, 263–273. [CrossRef]
11. Van Reeven, P. Subsidisation of urban public transport and the mohring effect. *J. Transp. Econ. Policy (JTEP)* **2008**, *42*, 349–359.
12. Vuchic, V. *Urban Transport Operation, Planning and Economics*; John Viley & Sons Inc.: Hoboken, NJ, USA, 2005.
13. Hanson, S.; Giuliano, G. *The Geography of Urban Transportation*, 3rd ed.; Guilford Press: New York, NY, USA, 2004.
14. Karabašević, D.; Popović, G.; Stanujkić, D.; Maksimović, M.; Sava, C. An approach for hotel type selection based on the single-valued intuitionistic fuzzy numbers. *Int. Rev.* **2019**, 7–14. [CrossRef]
15. Naeini, A.B.; Mosayebi, A.; Mohajerani, N. A hybrid model of competitive advantage based on Bourdieu capital theory and competitive intelligence using fuzzy Delphi and ism-gray Dematel (study of Iranian food industry). *Int. Rev.* **2019**, 21–35. [CrossRef]
16. Zhou, Y.; Xu, L.; Muhammad Shaikh, G. Evaluating and prioritizing the green supply chain management practices in pakistan: Based on delphi and fuzzy AHP approach. *Symmetry* **2019**, *11*, 1346. [CrossRef]
17. Stević, Ž.; Stjepanović, Ž.; Božičković, Z.; Das, D.K.; Stanujkić, D. Assessment of conditions for implementing information technology in a warehouse system: A novel fuzzy piprecia method. *Symmetry* **2018**, *10*, 586. [CrossRef]
18. Keshavarz Ghorabaee, M.; Zavadskas, E.K.; Amiri, M.; Turskis, Z. Extended EDAS method for fuzzy multi-criteria decision-making: An application to supplier selection. *Int. J. Comput. Commun. Control* **2016**, *11*, 358–371. [CrossRef]
19. Chang, D.Y. Applications of the extent analysis method on fuzzy AHP. *Eur. J. Oper. Res.* **1996**, *95*, 649–655. [CrossRef]
20. Pamučar, D.; Stević, Ž.; Sremac, S. A new model for determining weight coefficients of criteria in mcdm models: Full consistency method (fucom). *Symmetry* **2018**, *10*, 393. [CrossRef]
21. Stanković, M.; Stević, Ž.; Das, D.K.; Subotić, M.; Pamučar, D. A new fuzzy marcos method for road traffic risk analysis. *Mathematics* **2020**, in press.
22. Fauzi, N.; Nungsiyati, T.; Noviarti, M.; Muslihudin, R.; Irviani, R.; Maseleno, A. Optimal dengue endemic region prediction using fuzzy simple additive weighting based algorithm. *Int. J. Pure Appl. Math.* **2018**, *118*, 473–478.
23. Chatterjee, P.; Stević, Ž. A two-phase fuzzy AHP-fuzzy TOPSIS model for supplier evaluation in manufacturing environment. *Oper. Res. Eng. Sci. Theory Appl.* **2019**, *2*, 72–90. [CrossRef]
24. Đalić, I.; Stević, Ž.; Karamasa, C.; Puška, A. A novel integrated fuzzy PIPRECIA – interval rough SAW model: Green supplier selection. *Decis. Mak. Appl. Manag. Eng.* **2020**, *3*, 126–145. [CrossRef]
25. Marković, V.; Stajić, L.; Stević, Ž.; Mitrović, G.; Novarlić, B.; Radojičić, Z. A novel integrated subjective-objective mcdm model for alternative ranking in order to achieve business excellence and sustainability. *Symmetry* **2020**, *12*, 164. [CrossRef]
26. Vesković, S.; Milinković, S.; Abramović, B.; Ljubaj, I. Determining criteria significance in selecting reach stackers by applying the fuzzy PIPRECIA method. *Oper. Res. Eng. Sci. Theory Appl.* **2020**, *3*, 72–88. [CrossRef]
27. Stević, Ž.; Vasiljević, M.; Zavadskas, E.K.; Sremac, S.; Turskis, Z. Selection of carpenter manufacturer using fuzzy EDAS method. *Eng. Econ.* **2018**, *29*, 281–290. [CrossRef]
28. Stević, Ž.; Vasiljević, M.; Puška, A.; Tanackov, I.; Junevičius, R.; Vesković, S. Evaluation of suppliers under uncertainty: A multiphase approach based on fuzzy AHP and fuzzy EDAS. *Transport* **2019**, *34*, 52–66. [CrossRef]
29. Ecer, F. Third-party logistics (3PLs) provider selection via Fuzzy AHP and EDAS integrated model. *Technol. Econ. Dev. Econ.* **2018**, *24*, 615–634. [CrossRef]
30. Durmić, E. Evaluation of criteria for sustainable supplier selection using FUCOM method. *Oper. Res. Eng. Sci. Theory Appl.* **2019**, *2*, 91–107. [CrossRef]
31. Badi, I.; Abdulshahed, A. Ranking the Libyan airlines by using full consistency method (FUCOM) and analytical hierarchy process (AHP). *Oper. Res. Eng. Sci. Theory Appl.* **2019**, *2*, 1–14. [CrossRef]
32. Roszkowska, E.; Kacprzak, D. The fuzzy SAW and fuzzy TOPSIS procedures based on ordered fuzzy numbers. *Inf. Sci.* **2016**, *369*, 564–584. [CrossRef]
33. Bojanić, D.; Kovač, M.; Bojanic, M.; Ristic, V. Multi-criteria decision making in defensive operation of guided anti-tank missile battery: An example of hybrid model fuzzy AHP-MABAC. *Decis. Mak. Appl. Manag. Eng.* **2018**, *1*, 51–66. [CrossRef]

34. Božanić, D.; Tešić, D.; Milićević, J. A hybrid fuzzy AHP-MABAC model: Application in the Serbian Army—The selection of the location for deep wading as a technique of crossing the river by tanks. *Decis. Mak. Appl. Manag. Eng.* **2018**, *1*, 143–164. [CrossRef]
35. Gangwar, R.; Raghuram, G. Framework for structuring public private partnerships in railways. *Case Stud. Transp. Policy* **2015**, *3*, 295–303. [CrossRef]
36. Vesković, S.; Stević, Ž.; Stojić, G.; Rajilić, S.; Vasiljević, M. Application of fuzzy AHP method for profit analysis of railway operators with PSO. In Proceedings of the XVII International Scientific-Expert Conference on Railways -RAILCON, Niš, Serbia, 13–14 October 2016; pp. 105–108.
37. Puška, A.; Kozarević, S.; Stević, Ž.; Stovrag, J. A new way of applying interval fuzzy logic in group decision making for supplier selection. *Econ. Comput. Econ. Cybern. Stud. Res.* **2018**, 52. [CrossRef]
38. Rezaei, P.; Rezaie, K.; Nazari-Shirkouhi, S.; Tajabadi, M.R. Application of fuzzy multi-criteria decision making analysis for evaluating and selecting the best location for construction of underground dam. *Acta Polytech. Hung.* **2013**, *10*, 187–205.

symmetry

MDPI

Article

Robust Multi-Objective Sustainable Reverse Supply Chain Planning: An Application in the Steel Industry

Jurgita Antucheviciene [1,*], Ahmad Jafarnejad [2], Hannan Amoozad Mahdiraji [2,3], Seyed Hossein Razavi Hajiagha [4] and Amir Kargar [5]

1 Department of Construction Management and Real Estate, Vilnius Gediminas Technical University, LT-10223 Vilnius, Lithuania
2 Faculty of Management, University of Tehran, Tehran 1417466191, Iran; jafarnjd@ut.ac.ir (A.J.); h.amoozad@ut.ac.ir (H.A.M.)
3 School of Strategy and Leadership, Faculty of Business and Law, Coventry University, Coventry CV1 5FB, UK
4 Faculty of Management, Khatam University, Tehran 1417466191, Iran; h.razavi@khatam.ac.ir
5 Alborz Campus, University of Tehran, Tehran 1417466191, Iran; amirkargar@ut.ac.ir
* Correspondence: jurgita.antucheviciene@vgtu.lt; Tel.: +370-52-74-5233

Received: 4 March 2020; Accepted: 3 April 2020; Published: 8 April 2020

Abstract: In the design of the supply chain, the use of the returned products and their recycling in the production and consumption network is called reverse logistics. The proposed model aims to optimize the flow of materials in the supply chain network (SCN), and determine the amount and location of facilities and the planning of transportation in conditions of demand uncertainty. Thus, maximizing the total profit of operation, minimizing adverse environmental effects, and maximizing customer and supplier service levels have been considered as the main objectives. Accordingly, finding symmetry (balance) among the profit of operation, the environmental effects and customer and supplier service levels is considered in this research. To deal with the uncertainty of the model, scenario-based robust planning is employed alongside a meta-heuristic algorithm (NSGA-II) to solve the model with actual data from a case study of the steel industry in Iran. The results obtained from the model, solving and validating, compared with actual data indicated that the model could optimize the objectives seamlessly and determine the amount and location of the necessary facilities for the steel industry more appropriately.

Keywords: multi-objective planning; reverse supply chain; robust optimization; uncertainty; meta-heuristic algorithm; steel making industry

1. Introduction

With the expansion of the competitive environment, optimal supply chain (SC) design has become one of the fundamental issues business communities are facing [1]. This has affected all of the organization's activities to produce products, improve quality, reduce costs and provide the required services. On the other hand, with increasing greenhouse gas emissions and pollutants, managers of organizations and researchers are planning to set up networks that, in addition to considering economic optimization, have a special focus on environmental factors and the reduction of pollutants in all sectors [2].

The reverse logistics network, as part of the SC, means the accurate, correct and timely transmission of materials and the kinds of goods that are usable and unusable from the endpoint (last consumer or end-user) through the SC to the appropriate plant. In other words, reverse logistics is the process of moving and transferring goods and products that can be returned through the SC [3]. In this regard, the most important factor that is recognized in technical and economic studies of supply chains is the demand parameter, which should be considered in the design of forward or reverse supply chain networks (SCNs) [4–7].

Moreover, many countries have an increasing interest in protecting the environment and applying environmental laws. Hence, industry owners and manufacturers have turned their attention to the design and development of the SC, taking into account environmental factors [8–12]. Green SC Design, integrating SC management with environmental requirements at all stages of product design, the selection and delivery of raw materials, production and manufacturing, distribution and transfer processes, delivery to the customer, and the management of recycling and reuse after consumption to maximize energy efficiency and the efficient use of resources are associated with improving the performance of the entire SC [8,13–20].

Several reasons justify the notion of reverse logistics and using recycled material in a reverse supply chain. The steel industry, with more than 2.5 trillion dollars worth of products, is important [21]. Usually, different economic, cost reduction, governmental regulatory, and social responsibility motivations encourage organizations to follow reverse logistic notions. Generally, the steel industry supply chain includes several stages of mining, processing, distributing and recycling. The concern of sustainability is very important in this industry. For instance, directly producing reduced iron instead of scrap requires 1120 cubic meters of water, 300,000 cubic meters of natural gas and 130,000 kilowatt-hours of electricity. This potential amount of saving has led to the introduction of a reverse logistic supply chain in the steel industry.

In this research, scenario planning was used to deal with uncertainty in the demand parameter due to unpredictable changes that have occurred during the research period in the studied case. To realize the economic, environmental and social effects of the reverse SCN and to optimize the model, three objectives were laid out, including maximizing operating profit, minimizing adverse environmental impacts and maximizing the level of service to suppliers and customers. To consider uncertainty, the multi-echelon supply chain, reverse logistics, and green supply design, the logistics network presented in this study consisted of four levels. The first level was the waste providers, considered as returning product suppliers, which could be the customers of previous periods who have returned their remaining products or can be new suppliers of scrap supplies. The second level was the gathering centers of the returned products, being responsible for supplying the scrap from the first-level suppliers of the chain, and in particular, being responsible for supplying the returned product, inspection, sorting, storage, and transferring the product to the recycling plants (product factories). The third level was the recycling plants for the production of new products, based on the received scrap from the gathering centers, which were responsible for producing new products. Finally, the fourth level was the customers. According to the given explanation, the proposed network is shown as a framework in Figure 1.

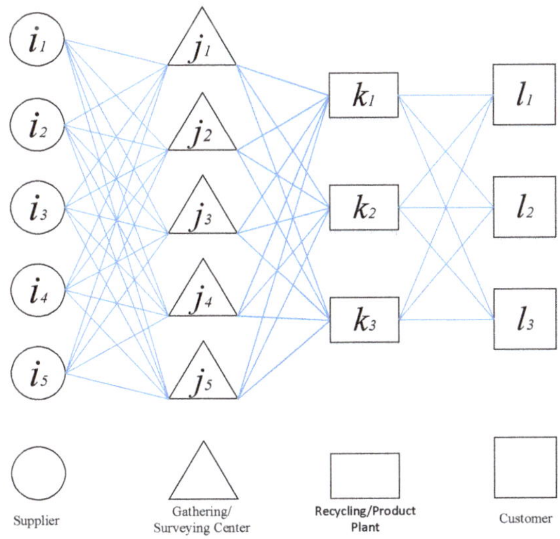

Figure 1. The considered supply chain (SC) scheme.

The overall aim of this study was to design a sustainable reverse logistics integrated model in conditions of demand uncertainty, to optimize the flow of materials throughout the SC, and to determine the number and location of facilities and the planning of SC transportation. In this regard, the following objectives were considered in this research:

1. Identifying and categorizing the necessary processes to implement the reverse logistics network of the steel industry;
2. Maximizing the operating profit of the SC so as to meet economic requirements;
3. Minimizing the adverse environmental impacts to meet environmental requirements;
4. Maximizing the satisfaction of suppliers and customers to meet social requirements.

This study presents a multi-objective mathematical model for reverse SC design. The proposed model allows the NSGA-II algorithm to plan the recycling of products in the Iranian steel industry based on the modified approach of Feito Cespon et al. (2017) with their model. The proposed model has the following features [22]:

1. Using a robust optimization approach and NSGA-II algorithm for the multi-objective modeling of the reverse SCN, including the flows of materials and transportation planning in conditions of uncertain demand;
2. Evaluating environmental indicators based on CO_2 emissions as one of the most important greenhouse gas emissions in the environment;
3. Evaluating customer service levels (CSLs) based on maximizing the received products returned from suppliers/previous customers and selling new products to customers;
4. Defining different scenarios for dealing with uncertainty of demand and quantifying them according to expert opinion.

A reverse logistics network as part of the SC means the accurate, correct and timely transmission of materials and the types of goods that are usable and unusable from the endpoint (last consumer or end-user) through the SC to the appropriate plant. In this regard, many types of research have been previously illustrated. Table 1 compares the illustrated pieces of research with the proposed method, from different perspectives.

Table 1. Previous related research.

Solution Method	Network Flow		Network Design					Attributes of the Mathematical Model				Objective Function			Researcher
	Reverse	Forward	Collecting and Distribution	Transport	Facilities	Repair and Recovery	Recycling	Limited Capacity	Multi-Period	Multi-Product	Uncertainty	Customer Service Level	Environmental Issues	Minimizing the Cost	
Mathematical Programming		✓				✓					✓			✓	[23]
New Optimization Model	✓					✓	✓		✓				✓		[24]
Mathematical Programming and Goal Programming Technique		✓					✓		✓				✓	✓	[25]
Genetic Algorithm		✓		✓										✓	[26]
Multi-Objective Programming		✓		✓									✓	✓	[27]
Metaheuristic Method		✓	✓	✓									✓	✓	[28]
Multi-Objective Linear Fuzzy Programming		✓									✓		✓	✓	[29]
Multi-Objective Genetic Algorithm		✓	✓			✓			✓			✓	✓	✓	[30]
Fuzzy Optimization		✓							✓	✓	✓			✓	[31]
Mixed Integer Nonlinear Programming Model	✓	✓	✓		✓					✓	✓			✓	[32]
Column Generation Paradigm	✓		✓		✓	✓	✓			✓				✓	[33]
Robust Optimization	✓			✓			✓				✓		✓	✓	[22]
Mathematical Programming	✓				✓					✓		✓	✓	✓	[34]
Two-Stage Stochastic Programming		✓			✓					✓	✓			✓	[20]
Mathematical Programming and Lagrange Algorithm	✓					✓			✓		✓			✓	[35]
Mathematical Programming	✓							✓		✓		✓	✓	✓	[36]
Complex Integer Nonlinear Programming, HGA and HHS	✓										✓	✓		✓	[37]
Single Objective Programming, Genetic and Neighborhood Search		✓						✓						✓	[38]
Mathematical Programming	✓			✓			✓				✓			✓	[39]
Mathematical Programming	✓				✓					✓		✓	✓	✓	[40]
Mathematical Programming, Two-Phase Stochastic Programming		✓		✓	✓			✓			✓			✓	[41]
Mathematical Programming, Lp-Metric Based Method	✓	✓	✓		✓	✓		✓	✓	✓		✓	✓	✓	[42]
Multi-Objective		✓	✓	✓						✓	✓		✓	✓	[43]
Queueing Network Model	✓	✓	✓		✓					✓	✓		✓	✓	[44]
De Novo Programming Method	✓	✓	✓	✓		✓				✓		✓		✓	[45]
Robust Optimization	✓	✓	✓	✓			✓	✓		✓	✓		✓	✓	Current Study

According to previous research, although many studies and articles have focused on the issue of sustainable SCN, there are some knowledge gaps in this area that are briefly summarized as follows:

1. Most research focuses on the design of a new SC, and there exists a shortage of network redesign;
2. The impact of the number and location of facilities on the environment is not considered;
3. There are very few models that consider reconstructing reverse SC with a simultaneous analysis of social, economic, and environmental goals;
4. Uncertainty about the number of resources and demand for recycled products, along with the management of diverse materials, are issues that require investigation in the future.

Based on the above-mentioned gaps, the present study expresses a multi-objective mathematical model for redesigning the reverse SC network. The proposed model allows the use of a robustness approach to recycling multiple products. The proposed model has the following features:

- The use of a robust optimization approach for redesigning a recycling SC network, including multiple flows of materials and uncertainties regarding the waste products used as raw materials, and the final demand for recycled products;
- The structure of the expected functional index for evaluating a configuration for a new SC considering the economic and environmental objectives in different scenarios.

2. Methods and Materials

Based on the above mentioned theoretical background and defined problem, to resolve the uncertainty of the model parameters, a scenario-based robust optimization by the augmented epsilon constraint method was developed using the General Algebraic Modeling System (GAMS) software. An augmented epsilon constraint method was used for cases of multi-objective optimization in which one of the objective functions was more important than the other functions, and based on this, the optimization of other functions was performed. In this study, due to the greater importance of the first objective function compared to the others, this method was used. Since the main model with the network and the actual data of the case study by the GAMS cannot be solved, the objectives were defined based on an initial model on a smaller scale; they were solved by a scenario-based robust optimization, and the comparison and validation of the model were investigated by the NSGA-II algorithm in MATLAB.

2.1. Assumptions

- Uncertainty in the demand parameter has been considered;
- The studied SC consists of four levels when acting in a single period;
- The capacity of the gathering centers is unlimited, and the capacity of the recycling plants is limited;
- The numbers of gathering centers and recycling plant candidates are limited;
- Fixed and variable costs (gathering, recycling and transportation) and the number and capacity of the transportation modes are determined;
- The flow of material between two non-consecutive levels is not allowed;
- The numbers of suppliers and customers are fixed and are five and three, respectively;
- The nominated locations for selecting gathering centers and recycling plants are five and three, respectively. These will determine the exact number of centers during the process of solving the model [22].

2.2. Model Notations

Based on the SC structure shown in Figure 1, the problem is formulated as a multi-objective optimization model. The list of indices, parameters and decision variables of the model are presented in this section. This proposed model is based upon the work of Feito Cespon et al. 2017 [22] by using different objective functions, and case study and solving approaches, to compare the results.

The notations used in the paper are as follows.

Indexes

$i \in I$	A set of renewable waste suppliers
$j \in J$	A set of location candidates for gathering centers
$k \in K$	A set of location candidates for recycling plants
$l \in L$	A set of customers
$m \in M$	A set of transportation modes
$p \in P$	A set of final products
$s \in S$	A set of scenarios

Parameters

G_{ip}	The amount of product supply (p) by the supplier (i), in tons per month
CT_{mp}	The capacity of the transportation mode (m) for the transfer of product (p), in tons, on the trip
C_{kp}	The capacity of the recycling plant (k) to produce the product (p), in tons per month
D_{lps}	The amount of product (p) which is demanded by the customer (l) under the scenario (s), in tons per month
NV_m	Total number of trips available for each mode (m)
IT_m	The environmental impact of moving materials in the transportation mode (m) on the environmental index, per ton-km
IE	The environmental effect of the total gas consumption of the system on the environmental index, per normal cubic meter per hour
IP	The environmental impact of infrastructure in the environmental index
IA	The environmental impact generated by water consumption on the whole system in the environmental index, per cubic meter
Cfe_k	Stable gas consumption at the recycling plant (k) in relation to normal condtions, in cubic meters per hour
Cfe_j	Fixed gas consumption of the gathering center (j) in normal conditions, in cubic meters per hour
Cve_p	Variable gas consumption to produce a unit of product (p) in normal conditions, in cubic meters per hour
Cvap	Variable water consumption to obtain a unit of product (p), in cubic meters
$\alpha_k \cdot \beta_j$	Gathering center (j) and recycling plant (k) capacity ratio
d_{ij}^{SR}	Distance between supplier (i) and the gathering center (j), in km
d_{jk}^{RP}	Distance between gathering center (j) and recycling plant (k), in km
d_{kl}^{PC}	Distance between recycling plant (k) and customer (l), in km
CUR_{jp}	The cost of production (p) in the gathering center (j), in rials per ton
CUP_{kp}	The cost of production (p) in the recycling plant (k), in rials per ton
CUT_m	The variable cost of the transport mode (m), in rials per km
CFR_j	Fixed cost of using the gathering center (j), in rials
CFP_k	Fixed cost of using a recycling plant (k), in rials
PS_s	Probability of scenario (s)
PRI_p	Product sales price (p)

Variables

QSR_{ijmps}	The amount of product supply (p) that is transmitted in the transportation mode (m) between the waste supplier (i) and the gathering center (j) under the scenario (s), in tons
QRP_{jkmps}	The amount of product (p) that is transmitted in the transportation mode (m) between the gathering center (j) and the recycling plant (k) under the scenario (s), in tons
QPC_{klmps}	The amount of product (p) transmitted in the transportation mode (m) between the recycling plant (k) and customer (l) under the scenario (s), in tons
VSR_{ijms}	The number of trips between the waste supplier (i) and the gathering center (j) using the transportation mode (m) under the scenario (s)
VRP_{jkms}	The number of trips between the gathering center (j) and the recycling plant (k) using the transportation mode (m) under the scenario (s)
VPC_{klms}	The number of trips between the recycling plant (k) to the customer (l) using the transportation mode (m) under the scenario (s)
HSR_{ijms} HRP_{jkms} HPC_{klms}	Variables that indicate the number of trips (excess or defect) to balance between the transportation modes
R_j	Variable; 1 if the gathering center (j) is used, otherwise it is zero
P_k	Variable; 1 if the recycling plant (k) is used, otherwise it is zero

2.3. Model Objective Functions

Equation (1) maximizes the operating profit of the SC.

$$\begin{aligned}\max f_1 \ &= \sum_s PS_s(\sum_k \sum_p PRI_p \sum_l \sum_m QPC_{klmps} \\ &- (\sum_m CUT_m \cdot (\sum_j \sum_k VRP_{jkms} d_{jk}^{PC} \\ &+ \sum_k \sum_l VPC_{klms} d_{kl}^{PC} \\ &+ \sum_i \sum_j VSR_{ijms} d_{ij}^{SR})) \\ &- \sum_k CFP_k P_k - \sum_k \sum_p CUP_{kp} \sum_l \sum_m QPC_{klmps} \\ &- \sum_j CFR_j R_j - \sum_j \sum_p CUR_{jp} \sum_k \sum_m QRP_{jkmps}\end{aligned} \tag{1}$$

Equation (2) minimizes the adverse environmental impacts of the SC.

$$\begin{aligned}\min f_2 \ &= \sum_s PS_s(\\ &\sum_m IT_m (\sum_i \sum_j \sum_p QSR_{ijmps} d_{ij}^{SR} \\ &+ \sum_j \sum_k \sum_p QRP_{jkmps} d_{jk}^{RP} \\ &+ \sum_k \sum_l \sum_p QPC_{klmps} d_{kl}^{PC}) \\ &+ IE(\sum_k Cfe_k P_k + \sum_j Cfe_j R_j + \sum_p Cve_p \sum_k \sum_l \sum_m QPC_{klmps}) \\ &+ IP(\sum_k \alpha_k P_k + \sum_j \beta_j R_j) + IA \sum_p Cva_p \sum_k \sum_l \sum_m QPC_{klmps})\end{aligned} \tag{2}$$

Equation (3) maximizes the supplier's and customers' service levels, being different from that in the work of Feito Cespon et al. 2017 [22]:

$$\max f_3 = \sum_s P_s\left(\frac{\left[\sum_k \sum_l \sum_m \sum_p QPC_{klmps} + \sum_i \sum_j \sum_m \sum_p QSR_{ijmps}\right]}{\left[\sum_l \sum_p D_{lps} + \sum_i \sum_p G_{ip}\right]}\right) \quad (3)$$

2.4. Model Constraints

The model constraints are shown in Equations (4) to (19). Each constraint has been discussed below [22]:

- Equations (4) to (6) guarantee the flow of materials through the SCN. The output from each center is, at most, equal to the inputs from different centers at the previous level of the SC;

$$\sum_j \sum_m QSR_{ijmps} \leq G_{ip} \ \forall i,p,s \quad (4)$$

$$\sum_k \sum_m QRP_{jkmps} \leq \sum_i \sum_m QSR_{ijmps} \ \forall j,p,s \quad (5)$$

$$\sum_l \sum_m QPC_{klmps} \leq \sum_j \sum_m QRP_{jkmps} \ \forall k,p,s \quad (6)$$

- Equations (7) and (8) respectively guarantee that the flow of materials rate does not exceed the maximum capacity of the recycling plants and the product demand;

$$\sum_l \sum_m QPC_{klmps} \leq C_{kp} \ \forall k,p,s \quad (7)$$

$$\sum_k \sum_m QPC_{klmps} \leq D_{lps} \ \forall l,p,s \quad (8)$$

- Equations (9) to (11) maintain the balance between two facilities concerning the number of transportation. Since the number of transport must be an integer value, a series of inactive variables have been suggested to maintain the model's probability;

$$\sum_p \frac{QSR_{ijmps}}{CT_{mp}} + HSR_{ijms} = VSR_{ijms} \ \forall i,j,m,s \quad (9)$$

$$\sum_p \frac{QRP_{jkmps}}{CT_{mp}} + HRP_{jkms} = VRP_{jkms} \ \forall j,k,m,s \quad (10)$$

$$\sum_p \frac{QPC_{klmps}}{CT_{mp}} + HPC_{klms} = VPC_{klms} \ \forall k,l,m,s \quad (11)$$

- Equations (12) to (14) guarantee that ineffective variables focus only on differences in the number of transport;

$$VSR_{ijms} + HSR_{ijms} \geq 0 \quad \begin{array}{l} \forall i,j,m,s, \\ (-1 < HSR_{ijms} < 1) \end{array} \quad (12)$$

$$VRP_{jkms} + HRP_{jkms} \geq 0 \quad \begin{array}{l} \forall j,k,m,s, \\ (-1 < HRP_{jkms} < 1) \end{array} \tag{13}$$

$$VPC_{klms} + HPC_{klms} \geq 0 \quad \begin{array}{l} \forall k,l,m,s, \\ (-1 < HPC_{klm} < 1) \end{array} \tag{14}$$

- Equation (15) limits the number of trips per transportation mode [21];

$$\sum_i \sum_j VSR_{ijms} + \sum_j \sum_k VRP_{jkms} + \sum_k \sum_l VPC_{klms} \leq NV_m \ \forall m,s \tag{15}$$

- According to Equations (16) and (17), binary variables should be assumed, such that if a gathering center or recycling plant is used in the model, then the value is 1, and otherwise it is zero;

$$\sum_k \sum_m \sum_p QRP_{jkmps} \leq M\, R_j \ \forall j,s \tag{16}$$

$$\sum_l \sum_m \sum_p QPC_{klmps} \leq MP_k \ \forall k,s \tag{17}$$

- Finally, Equations (18) and (19) show the nature of the variables.

$$\begin{array}{l} QRP_{jkmps}, QPC_{klmps}, QSR_{ijmps}, VPC_{klms}, \\ VRP_{jkms}, VSR_{ijms} \geq 0 \end{array} \tag{18}$$

$$R_j, P_k \in \{0,1\} \tag{19}$$

3. Results

This proposed model is based upon the work of Feito Cespon et al. 2017 [22] by using a different objective function and case study and different solving approaches to compare the results. This is due to the main model (real-world case study) not being solvable with mathematical programming methods. At first, a smaller scale research model with fewer data called the "Initial Model" can be solved by an augmented epsilon constraint method, and subsequently, it is solved by the NSGA-II algorithm [46,47]. Furthermore, the performance of the NSGA-II algorithm is evaluated by solving several examples in the proposed research model, and the corresponding criteria are calculated. Afterwards, with the confidence of the model's validity, and since the main problem is Np-hard, the model of the real-world case study called "Main Model" is solved by the NSGA-II algorithm and will be analyzed at the end. Note that sensitivity analysis will be implemented on the initial model. Before solving the model, the method for determining the chromosome in the NSGA-II algorithm is presented. The algorithmic scheme of this section is illustrated in Figure 2.

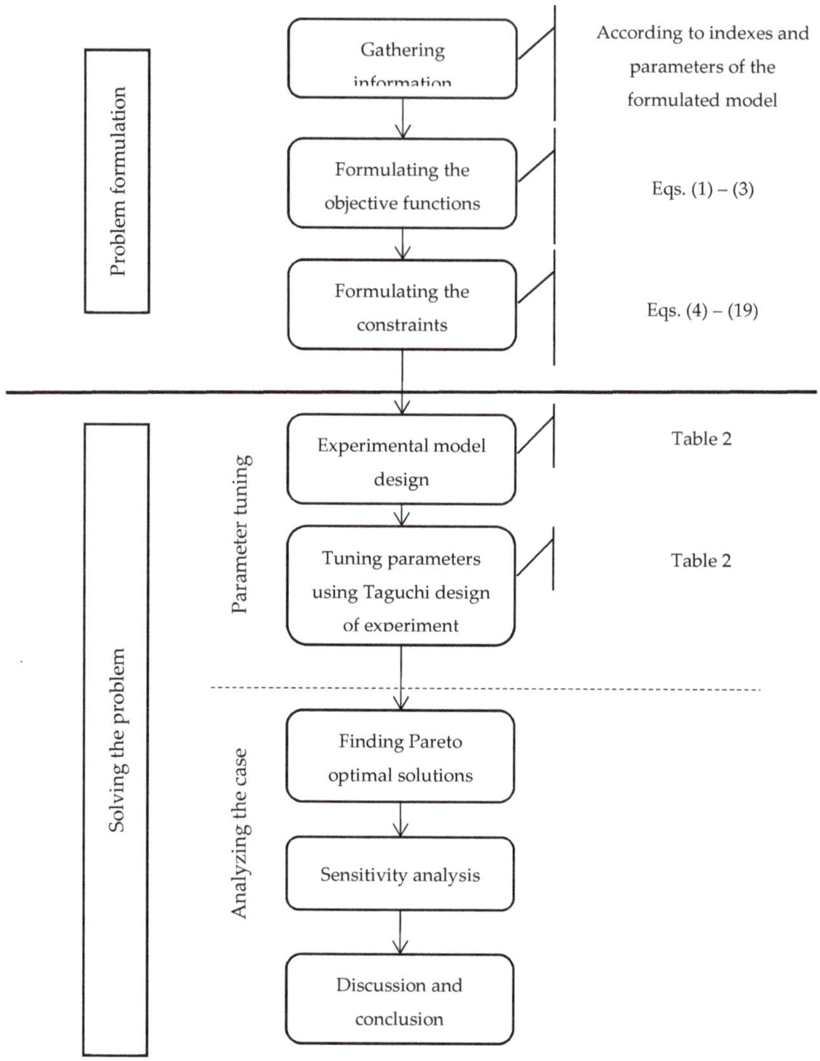

Figure 2. The algorithmic scheme of empirical research.

3.1. Definition of Chromosomes in the NSGA-II Algorithm

The matrix of the answer in the model has two sections, called allocation and assignment. The allocation section has two parts, the first part of which is the location of the gathering centers (J), and the second part is the location of the recycling plants (K). The cells of the matrix are filled with numbers 0 or 1, for example, if J = 5 and K = 3; an example of this matrix is given in Table 2.

According to Table 2, gathering center No. 5 has been constructed, and gathering centers No. 1, 2, 3 and 4 have not been constructed. Moreover, the recycling plant No.1 has been constructed and the recycling centers No. 2 and 3 have not been constructed. Each set is the answer that is called a chromosome. The assignment section shows the flow rate from the waste supplier to the gathering centers, from the gathering centers to the recycling plants and from the recycling plants to the customers. In Table 3, the assignment section is shown. As a case in point, in the first part of the following table, which is a K ∗ L dimensional matrix, the flow rates from the recycling plants (k) to the customer (l) for the transportation mode (m), that is m = 1, p = 1 and s = 1, are shown.

Table 2. The allocation matrix.

	J1	J2	J3	J4	J5
X1	0	0	0	0	1

	K1	K2	K3
X2	1	0	0

Based on Table 3, it is obvious that the flow rate of product 1 from the recycling plant 1 to customer 1 by transportation mode 1 in scenario 1 is 3. In this regard, each answer set is called a chromosome, and each cell is a gene.

Table 3. The assignment matrix.

X3	L1	L2	L3
K1	3	2	1
K2	0	0	0
K3	0	0	0

X4	K1	K2	K3
J1	0	0	0
J2	0	0	0
J3	0	0	0
J4	0	0	0
J5	4	0	0

X5	J1	J2	J3	J4	J5
I1	0	0	0	0	3
I2	0	0	0	0	2
I3	0	0	0	0	5
I4	0	0	0	0	1
I5	0	0	0	0	1

3.2. NSGA-II Operator Selection

Achieving a high performance of genetic algorithms is highly dependent on the performance of the genetic operators. One of the main operators in genetic algorithms is crossover. The crossover operator is used to generate a new chromosome by crossing over two selected chromosomes. Different crossover operators are represented in previous studies. Here in this paper, the single point crossover is used. The next important operator is a mutation to assure diversity. Beyond the mutation probability that is tuned in Section 3.6, in this study, the reverse and replace operators are used randomly to mutate the selected chromosomes. In reverse mutation, two genes are selected in the considered chromosome, and the values of remaining genes between these two selected genes are reversed from right to left. In the replacement mutation, two genes are selected, and their positions are swapped with one another's.

3.3. Initial Model Solving Results

Table 4 indicates SC characteristics in the initial model. Furthermore, the probability of the occurrence of each scenario is obtained using the analytical hierarchical process (hereafter AHP) method, which for scenarios 1 to 2, is 52.4% and 47.6%, respectively. Moreover, in the initial model, a big M value is 10,000.

Table 4. The specifications and parameters of the initial model.

Number of Suppliers	2	Number of Gathering Center	2	Number of products	2
Number of Recycling Plant	2	Number of Customers	2		
Number of Transportation modes	2	Number of Scenarios	2		

The Pareto result according to the GAMS and NSGA-II algorithm of five sets of answers derived from the initial model solving is shown in Tables 5 and 6. Figures 3 and 4 show these Pareto points. It is conceivable that the results obtained for the small scale problems by GAMS will outperform the NSGA-II results, as this can be seen in similar studies [48–50]; however, as it is illustrated in the next sections, the main advantage of NSGA-II is in its ability to solve large scale and real-world problems. The time of the GAMS solving in this model, although the problem dimensions are low, is 326 seconds, which is increased sharply by increasing the dimensions of the problem.

Table 5. Pareto points set by the GAMS for the initial model.

Answer No.	The Value of the First Objective Function	The Value of the Second Objective Function	The Value of the Third Objective Function
1	−128.17	2271.64	0.8
2	−247.05	1135.82	0.6
3	−92.47	801.17	0.41
4	67.78	1135.82	0.2
5	87.77	2271.64	0.6

Table 6. Pareto points set by the NSGA-II algorithm for the initial model.

Answer No.	The Value of the First Objective Function	The Value of the Second Objective Function	The Value of the Third Objective Function
1	−21.51	1961.65	0.4876
2	−8.1	1944.2	0.4819
3	3.65	1920.59	0.46
4	3.85	1896.37	0.4706
5	13.4	1860.68	0.4607

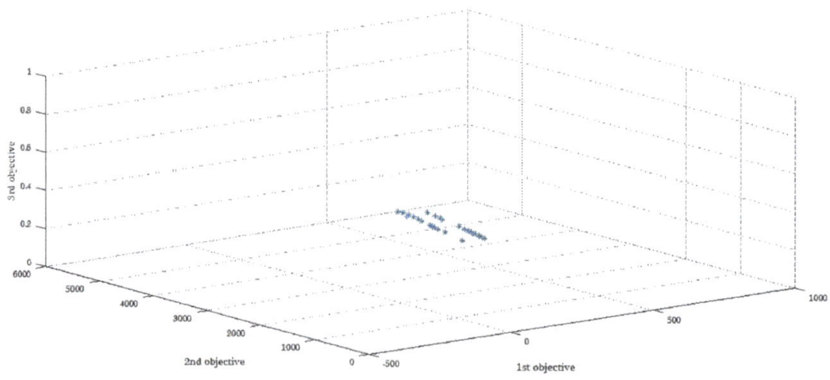

Figure 3. Pareto points obtained by the NSGA-II algorithm in the initial model.

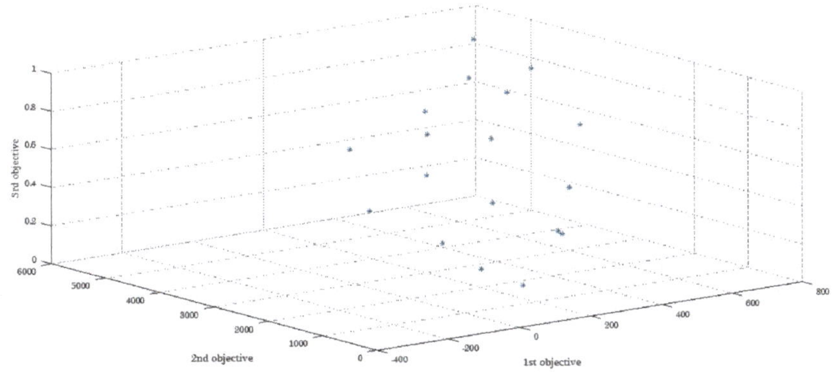

Figure 4. Pareto points obtained by solving the GAMS in the initial model.

Figures 3 and 4 show that when the values of the first objective function deteriorate, the values of the other objectives function do not. In other words, these values remain either constant or close to their optimal values, which is the expected process that the multi-objective models suggest.

3.4. Model Validation

To evaluate the performance of the model and to compare the performance of the NSGA-II algorithm with the augmented epsilon constraint method, five examples with different dimensions randomly compiled on the research model, and the criteria for comparing the efficiency of the multi-objective algorithms, are calculated, the results of which are shown in Table 7. The results are obtained by running the proposed algorithm in a single trial with a population size of 10,000 and 250 repetitions. As the results indicate, it can be seen that using the NSGA-II algorithm has the necessary validity to solve the main model.

In this table, five measures are reported. Mean Idear Distance (MID) measures the convergence of an algorithm by averaging the distances of solutions from the best feasible solution [51,52]. Spacing measures the standard deviation of the distances among the Pareto front solution [52]. Diversity evaluates the spread of the Pareto front [52]. The Number of solutions (NoS) is the number of different Pareto solutions [53,54]. Time(s) is the time for which the algorithm needs to be run to reach the near-optimal solution [53,54].

The lower the index MID, the better the research results. As can be seen, the performance of the Epsilon Constraint (E.C). method in two sets of responses is better than that of the NSGA-II algorithm; however, with increasing dimensions of the problem, the method of E.C. loses its effectiveness. Since this difference is not very high, both indicators have shown good performance.

The lower the index spacing, the better the research results. According to Table 7, the performance of the NSGA-II algorithm is better than that of the E.C. method. The higher the index (diversity), the better the research results. Based on the results, it can be seen that the proposed E.C method is better than the NSGA-II algorithm.

The higher the index NoS, the better the research results. Based on the results, the NSGA-II algorithm obtained a greater number of Pareto members. It is logical to increase the solution time of the algorithms by increasing the dimensions of the problem.

Table 7. Comparison of indices for five examples with NSGA-II algorithms and the Epsilon Constraint method.

Item	Epsilon Constraint					NSGA-II				
	MID	Spacing	Diversity	NoS	Time(s)	MID	Spacing	Diversity	NoS	Time(s)
1	8556.59	51.73	2562.22	14	8	7283.27	13.05	2858.35	96	55.96
2	7574.8	73.37	3820.57	16	13	7749.36	79.91	2247.99	97	63.73
3	5383.46	181.73	6709.34	23	48	6720.7	30.82	3616.23	98	58.43
4	6317.78	181.41	5209.74	16	93	7150.89	28.77	2423.52	99	57.68
5	7109.71	242.98	5219.62	18	407	7903.34	13.88	1650.52	95	58.53

Therefore, according to the results, the same trend is observed; with an increase in the dimensions of the problems, the time taken to solve by the method of E.C. increases exponentially, and this method loses its efficiency in high-dimensional issues. However, it is almost constant for the NSGA-II algorithm.

3.5. The Parameter Adjustment of the NSGA-II Algorithm

Under the meta-heuristic algorithms that do not guarantee an exact optimal solution, the algorithm may be followed by a different response at any time by solving it. Therefore, a meta-heuristic algorithm is good when used, with almost identical answers each time. The most influential parameters in the NSGA-II algorithm are the number of initial population (nPop), the number of repetitions (MaxIt), the intersection rate (Pc) and the rate of mutation (Pm). With using the Taguchi design of experiments method, the parameters of this algorithm are based on comparative criteria for nine exams that have been determined under the following steps.

3.6. Taguchi Design of Experiment

In the NSGA-II algorithm, the four factors/parameters MaxIt, nPop, Pc, and Pm should be set to optimal levels. For this purpose, at first, for each parameter, three levels of low (1), medium (2) and high (3) are considered, as shown in Table 8. The proposed Taguchi experiments for four factors at three levels are shown in Table 9 for nine experiments. These experiments are designed based on Taguchi methods [55].

Table 8. The setting up NSGA-II parameters at three levels.

NSGA-II Parameters	Low Level (1)	Middle Level (2)	High Level (3)
MaxIt	60	80	100
nPop	50	70	100
Pc	0.7	0.8	0.9
Pm	0.15	0.25	0.35

Table 9. Taguchi designed experiments to adjust the parameters of the NSGA-II algorithm.

Exam No.	MaxIt	nPop	Pc	Pm
1	1	1	1	1
2	1	2	2	2
3	1	3	3	3
4	2	1	2	3
5	2	2	3	1
6	2	3	1	2
7	3	1	3	2
8	3	2	1	3
9	3	3	2	1

Table 8 reveals the levels of the NSGA-II parameters, for each parameter considering three different levels. Table 9 demonstrates the experiments designed to adjust the parameters of the NSGA-II algorithm. In Table 10, the results of the NSGA-II algorithm for nine independent experiments are presented.

Table 10. Results from the experiments of the NSGA-II algorithm.

No.	MID	Spacing	Diversity	NoS	Time(s)
1	7636.4	23.4	1869.3	50	27.4
2	7725.7	19.6	2329.9	68	48.4
3	7677.5	22.4	2453.4	100	130.4
4	7745.1	70.8	2677.1	49	42.7
5	7615.1	58.1	3041.4	69	69.5
6	7801.7	91.8	3019.3	97	125.9
7	7640.1	32.1	1924.5	48	48.7
8	7670.5	39.2	2856.5	70	85.5
9	7678.4	30.6	2598.7	98	152.9

According to Table 10, to create an output from each test and for five criteria, using the fuzzy unambiguous technique and the ideal planning approach, all indicators become responses after normalization. The normalization of the results and the calculation of the response variable are shown in Table 11.

Table 11. Normalized results and the calculation of responses for setting the parameter of the NSGA-II algorithm.

No.	MID	Spacing	Diversity	Nos	Time(s)	Response
1	0. 11	0.05	1.00	0.96	0.00	22.46
2	0.59	0.00	0.61	0.62	0.17	65.89
3	0.33	0.04	0.5	0.00	0.82	39.22
4	0.7	0.71	0.31	0.98	0.12	81.30
5	0.00	0.53	0.00	0.6	0.34	6.24
6	1.00	1.00	0.02	0.06	0.79	111.05
7	0.13	0.17	0.95	1.00	0.17	25.37
8	0.3	0.26	0.16	0.58	0.46	35.24
9	0.34	0.15	0.38	0.04	1.00	40.34

In the last step, based on the calculated response variable in the previous step, the S/N rate is calculated, and the optimal levels of the input parameters are determined. This operation is performed by the MINITAB software, and the results are illustrated in Figure 5. This figure illustrates the main effect plot of different algorithm parameters. The plots are plotted by fixing parameters at their three levels, and then comparing the means of the S/N ratios against those at different levels.

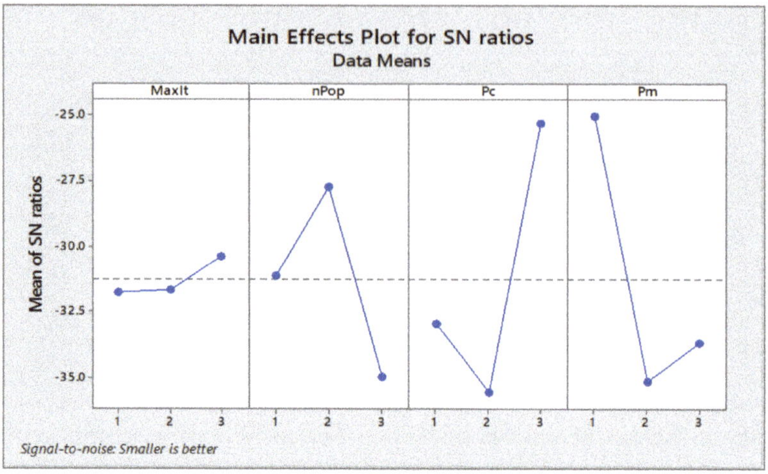

Figure 5. MINITAB output to adjust the parameter of the NSGA-II algorithm.

The optimal levels for the parameters of the algorithm examined according to Figure 5 and the above tables are shown in Table 12.

Table 12. Optimized levels for the NSGA-II algorithm.

	MaxIt	nPop	Pc	Pm
NSGA-II	Level 3 100	Level 2 70	Level 3 0.9	Level 1 0.15

3.7. Results of Solving the Main Model (Case Study)

Table 13 shows the main model of the case study. The case study is related to a steel production company with 8.1 million tons of yearly capacity in Iran. The company produced a set of intermediate and final products. The considered network includes suppliers, recycling plants, transportation modes and gathering centers. Additionally, five types of product are identified to be delivered to three types of customer. The problem parameters are gathered from the company's databases, which are not presented due to their large magnitude. The problem specification and its parameters are illustrated in Table 13.

Table 13. The specifications and parameters of the model in a case study.

Number of Suppliers	5	Number of Gathering Centers	5	Number of Products	5
Number of Recycling Plants	3	Number of Customers	3		
Number of Transportation Modes	225	Number of Scenarios	5		

According to the requirements of the considered organization as the case study, five incidental conditions are defined for these conditions, which are considered as a scenario for each mode, providing different data. Moreover, the probabilities of occurrence of each scenario are obtained using the AHP method, which are—for scenarios 1 to 5—16%, 22%, 48%, 9% and 5%, respectively. Furthermore, in the main model, a big M value of 10,000 is considered.

As stated above, since the size of the case study is high and the GAMS software is not able to solve it at an acceptable time, the original model in the MATLAB software is solved based on the NSGA-II algorithm, the Pareto points from which are presented in Table 14 and Figure 6.

Table 14. A set of the Pareto points generated by algorithm NSGA-II for the case study.

Answer No.	The Value of the First Objective Function	The Value of the Second Objective Function	The Value of the Third Objective Function
1	1,168,678,032,301	17,570,971,633	0.4738
2	1,535,360,428,421	18,258,944,734	0.5864
3	1,532,610,197,259	18,179,813,506	0.5912
4	1,226,611,751,948	17,585,580,845	0.3662
5	1,534,765,140,449	18,251,470,312	0.5337

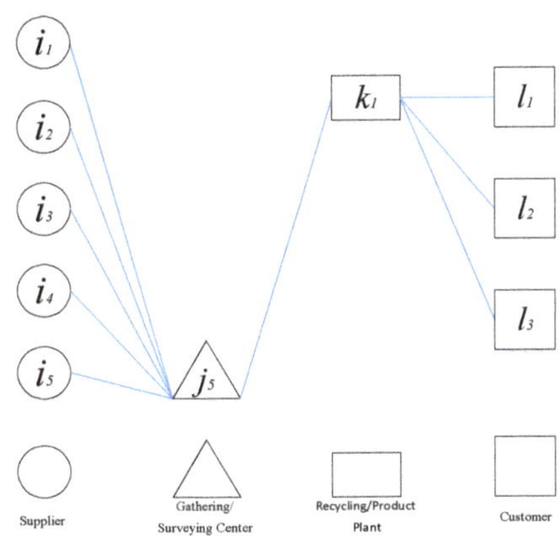

Figure 6. The reverse supply chain (SC) after a solution.

As expected, due to the high cost of constructing facilities in the steel industry, one center (center number 5) of the five candidates was selected, and one factory (factory number 1) of the three nominated recycling/production plants for construction is calculated, and it provides an excellent answer to the case study. In this way, the schematic of the reverse SC model is changed after the solution, as shown in Figure 6.

Besides, the values of the parameters of the NSGA-II algorithm are described in Table 15 in the main model.

Table 15. The values of the algorithm NSGA-II operators for the case study.

	MaxIt	nPop	Pc	Pm
NSGA-II	100	100	0.6	0.3

For any Pareto optimal solution, the optimal values of decision variables are obtained(see Figure 7). For instance, the magnitudes of some decision variables for the first Pareto solution in Table 14 are represented in Table 16. According to this table, under the first scenario, a magnitude of 2.4605 of the first product type should be transported from the first supplier to the fifth gathering center. Other values can be interpreted similarly. For each Pareto optimal solution, a similar set of optimal decision variables is obtained.

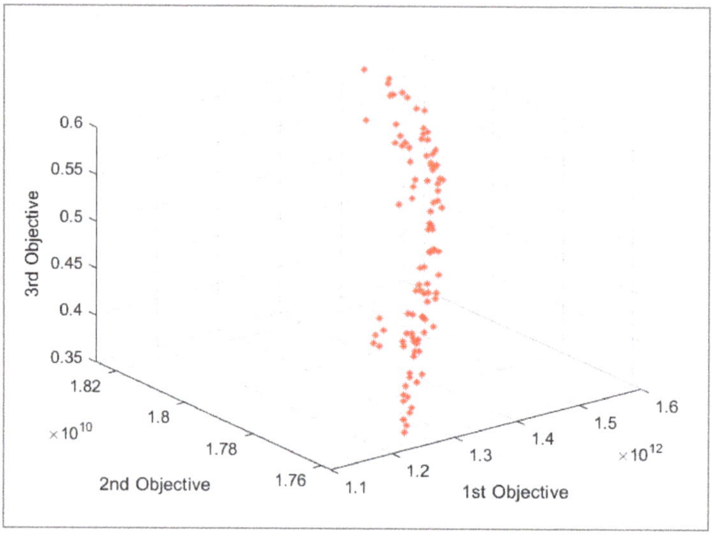

Figure 7. A set of the Pareto points for the case study.

Table 16. A sample of optimal decision variables for the first Pareto solution of Table 14.

Variable	Value	Variable	Value
$QSR_{1,5,1,1,1}$	2.4605	$QSR_{1,5,2,1,1}$	7.9593
$QSR_{2,5,1,1,1}$	2.9064	$QSR_{2,5,2,1,1}$	7.7476
$QSR_{3,5,1,1,1}$	6.1607	$QSR_{3,5,2,1,1}$	11.3636
$QSR_{4,5,1,1,1}$	8.0460	$QSR_{4,5,2,1,1}$	7.8387
$QSR_{5,5,1,1,1}$	4.5488	$QSR_{5,5,2,1,1}$	6.7933

To assure the convergence of the proposed algorithm, with its tuned parameters, the above problem is repetitively solved 100 times. Figure 8 illustrates the obtained results of the solutions for different objectives. According to this figure, it is clear that the algorithm-proposed solution in all of the objectives represents a controllable variance, and it can be considered as the proposed algorithm reliability. No outlier solutions can be detected in repetitions.

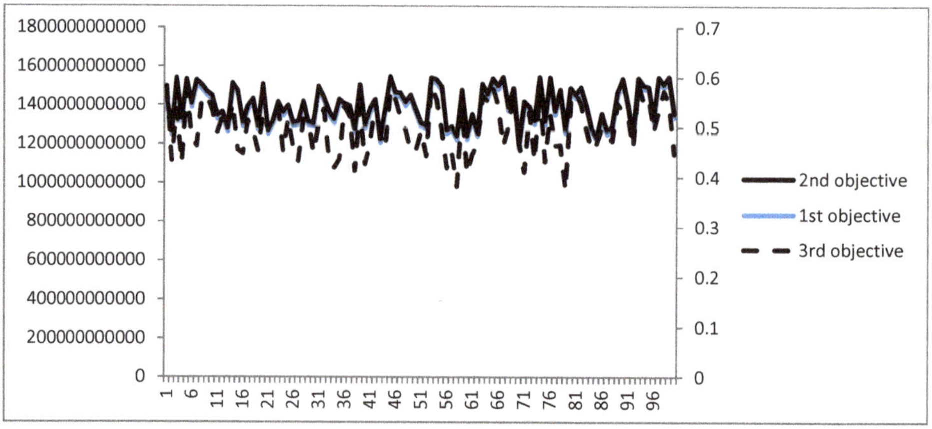

Figure 8. Algorithm consistency over repetitions.

3.8. Sensitivity Analysis

To investigate how the values of the objective functions varied, sensitivity analysis should be performed on some of the parameters. Regarding the multiplicity of the model, two types of analysis are performed. The first type is the change in Pareto's values relative to the change in one of the parameters. In the present study, this type of analysis—as compared to the change in the demand parameter in the initial model, which decreased by 10%—and the results of this sensitivity analysis are shown in Table 17 and Figure 9.

Table 17. Changes in Pareto points for the initial model induced by changing the value of demand.

No.	Before Changing the Demand Parameter			After Changing the Demand Parameter		
	Amount of 1st O.F.	Amount of 2nd O.F.	Amount of 3rd. O.F.	Amount of 1st O.F.	Amount of 2nd O.F.	Amount of 3rd. O.F.
1	−128.17	2271.64	0.8	−170.57	2117.32	0.8
2	−247.05	1135.82	0.6	−92.47	801.17	0.41
3	−92.47	801.17	0.41	42.57	1058.66	0.2
4	67.78	1135.82	0.2	49.15	2117.32	0.6
5	87.77	2271.64	0.6	158.82	1058.66	0.08

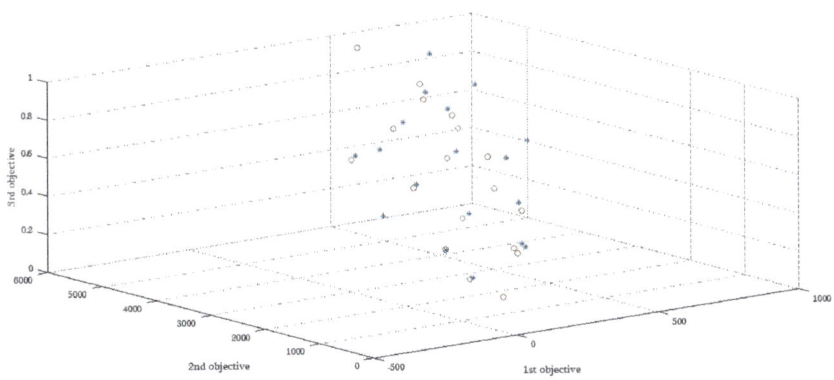

Figure 9. A set of the Pareto points for the initial model from changing the value of demand.

As demonstrated, with the decrease in the average demand, the value of the objective function decreased. By virtue of shipping costs, other items are reduced by decreasing demand. In Figure 4, the stars represent the Pareto before the change, and the circles represent the Pareto after the change.

The second type of sensitivity analysis is employed for one Pareto point (here, for the tenth Pareto point), which is done for the demand parameter. The variability of the value of the objective function concerning demand in the initial model is shown in Table 18 and Figure 10.

Table 18. Changes to the first objective function for the initial model induced by changing the amount of demand.

Item	The Amount of Demand Average	The Amount of First Objective Function
1	9.57	459.08
2	17.76	423.237
3	30.765	369.45
4	51.994	276.155
5	82.643	90.683

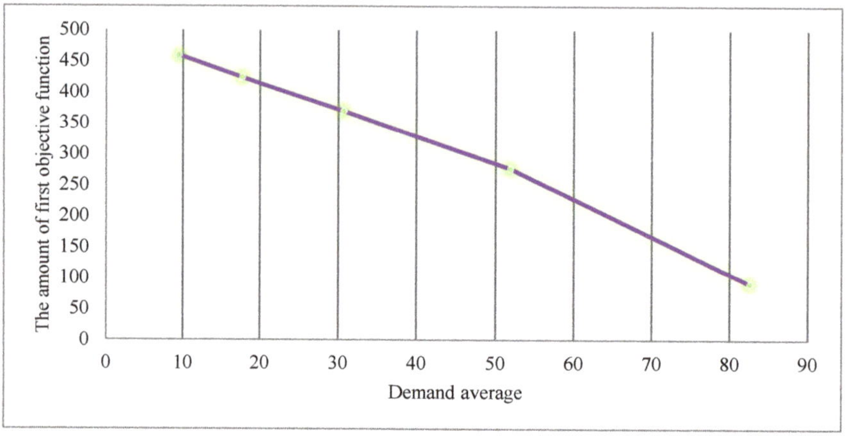

Figure 10. Sensitivity analysis of the first objective function in terms of the demand average.

In Table 18, by assuming that the second and third objective functions are fixed, and that only the changes in the first objective function have been investigated, it is seen that with increasing average demand, the first objective function is reduced. In fact, with increasing demand, the amount of cost is higher than the amount of income.

4. Discussion and Conclusions

In the present study, the model was defined as multi-objective functions based on the conditions of the uncertainty of demand and five scenarios; the model was solved by an augmented epsilon constraint method and the NSGA-II algorithm, and finally analyzed. This proposed model is based upon the work of Feito Cespon et al. 2017 [22] by using a different objective function and case study and different solving approaches to compare the results. Because the number of levels and actual data of the model would be Np-hard by solving the GAMS, and it would not be able to achieve the optimal response, model validation and sensitivity analysis were done on a smaller scale. The results of the comparative indices showed that solving the model with the NSGA-II algorithm yielded acceptable results, and the main model was solved accordingly. Additionally, the optimal levels of the NSGA-II algorithm parameters were adjusted in the original model, based on the Taguchi design of experiments method. In analyzing the results, as expected, in the locating facility, one gathering center was selected from five candidates, and one recycling plant was selected from three candidate plants. The number of objective functions in different Pareto points has been obtained with a suitable and acceptable dispersion criterion. The model showed that it could be integrated into optimizing the objectives, determining the number and location of necessary facilities and planning the transportation between different levels of the steel industry. Some of the assumptions implied in the current study can be adjusted in future studies. First, there are some general assumptions including the uncertainty of demand parameter, the determinedness of costs, the number and capacity of transportation modes and the number of supply chain levels. These assumptions can be generalized straightforwardly, by considering the uncertainty of other parameters and extending the model into more levels. Additionally, in the current paper, it is assumed that the number of suppliers, customers, gathering centers and recycling plants are determined. However, in some cases, the problem can be formulated to select different markets, suppliers, and gathering and recycling centers in a broader scope. These extensions will not change the structure of the proposed method drastically. However, altering some assumptions requires fundamental changes in the proposed model. Among these assumptions, reference to transshipment among levels (ignoring the sixth assumption) and limiting the capacity of gathering centers and recycling plants can be made. Further research can be done on the above-mentioned problems by changing the current model's assumptions.

Author Contributions: J.A.—conceptualization, formal analysis, writing—review and editing; A.J.—conceptualization, methodology, writing—original draft preparation, supervision; H.A.M.—conceptualization, formal analysis, resources, writing—review and editing, visualization; S.H.R.H.—conceptualization, methodology, software, validation, resources, writing—original draft preparation; A.K.—conceptualization, methodology, software, validation, investigation, data curation, writing—original draft preparation, project administration. All authors have read and agreed to the published version of the manuscript.

Funding: This research received no external funding.

Conflicts of Interest: The authors declare no conflict of interest.

References

1. Beamon, B.M. Supply chain design and analysis: Models and methods. *Int. J. Prod. Econ.* **1998**, *55*, 281–294. [CrossRef]
2. Elzen, B.; Geels, F.W.; Green, K.E. *System Innovation and the Transition to Sustainability: Theory, Evidence, and Policy*; Edward Elgar Publishing: Cheltenham, UK, 2004; pp. 154–160.
3. Fleischmann, M.; Bloemhof-Ruwaard, J.M.; Dekker, R.; Van Der Laan, E.; Van Nunen, J.A.E.E.; Van Wassenhove, L.N. Quantitative models for reverse logistics: A review. *Eur. J. Oper. Res.* **1997**, *103*, 1–17. [CrossRef]
4. Santoso, T.; Ahmed, S.; Goetschalckx, M.; Shapiro, A. A stochastic programming approach for supply chain network design under uncertainty. *Eur. J. Oper. Res.* **2005**, *167*, 96–115. [CrossRef]
5. Pishvaee, M.S.; Rabbani, M.; Torabi, S.A. A robust optimization approach to closed-loop supply chain network design under uncertainty. *Appl. Math. Modell.* **2011**, *35*, 637–649. [CrossRef]
6. Razavi Hajiagha, S.H.; Mahdiraji, H.A.; Zavadskas, E.K.; Hashemi, S.S. Fuzzy multi-objective linear programming based on compromise VIKOR method. *Int. J. Inf. Technol. Decis. Mak.* **2014**, *13*, 679–698. [CrossRef]
7. Mahdiraji, H.A.; Zavadskas, E.K.; Razavi Hajiagha, S.H. Game-theoretic approach for coordinating unlimited multi-echelon supply chains. *Transf. Bus. Econ.* **2015**, *14*, 35.
8. Pishvaee, M.S.; Razmi, J. Environmental supply chain network design using multi-objective fuzzy mathematical programming. *Appl. Math. Modell.* **2012**, *36*, 3433–3446. [CrossRef]
9. Jia, P.; Mahdiraji, H.A.; Govindan, K.; Meidutė, I. Leadership selection in an unlimited three-echelon supply chain. *J. Bus. Econ. Manag.* **2013**, *14*, 616–637. [CrossRef]
10. Mahdiraji, H.; Arabzadeh, M.; Ghaffari, R. Supply chain quality management. *Manag. Sci. Lett.* **2012**, *2*, 2463–2472. [CrossRef]
11. Mahdiraji, H.A.; Govindan, K.; Zavadskas, E.K.; Razavi Hajiagha, S.H. Coalition or decentralization: A game-theoretic analysis of a three-echelon supply chain network. *J. Bus. Econ. Manag.* **2014**, *15*, 460–485. [CrossRef]
12. Beheshti, M.; Mahdiraji, H.A.; Zavadskas, E.K. Strategy portfolio optimisation: A COPRAS G-MODM hybrid approach. *Transf. Bus. Econ.* **2016**, *15*, 500–519.
13. Wang, F.; Lai, X.; Shi, N. Multi-Objective optimization for green supply chain network design. *Decis. Support Syst.* **2011**, *51*, 262–269. [CrossRef]
14. Jamalnia, A.; Mahdiraji, H.A.; Sadeghi, M.R.; Razavi Hajiagha, S.H.; Feili, A. An integrated fuzzy QFD and fuzzy goal programming approach for global facility location-allocation problem. *Int. J. Inf. Technol. Decis. Mak.* **2014**, *13*, 263–290. [CrossRef]
15. Garg, K.; Kannan, D.; Diabat, A.; Jha, P.C. A multi-criteria optimization approach to manage environmental issues in a closed-loop supply chain network design. *J. Clean. Prod.* **2015**, *100*, 297–314. [CrossRef]
16. Razavi Hajiagha, S.H.; Akrami, H.; Hashemi, S.S.; Amoozad, H. An integer grey goal programming for project time, cost and quality trade-off. *Inzinerine Ekon.-Eng. Econ.* **2015**, *26*, 93–100. [CrossRef]
17. Razavi Hajiagha, S.H.; Hashemi, S.S.; Mahdiraji, H.A.; Azaddel, J. Multi-period data envelopment analysis based on Chebyshev inequality bounds. *Expert Syst. Appl.* **2015**, *42*, 7759–7767. [CrossRef]

18. Razavi Hajiagha, S.H.; Mahdiraji, H.A.; Hashemi, S.S.; Turskis, Z. Determining weights of fuzzy attributes for multi-attribute decision-making problems based on a consensus of expert opinions. *Technol. Econ. Dev. Econ.* **2015**, *21*, 738–755. [CrossRef]
19. Azadfallah, M.; Azizi, M. A new approach in group decision-making based on pairwise comparisons. *J. Int. Bus. Entrep. Dev.* **2016**, *8*, 159–165. [CrossRef]
20. Rezaee, A.; Dehghanian, F.; Fahimnia, B.; Beamon, B. Green supply chain network design with stochastic demand and carbon price. *Ann. Oper. Res.* **2017**, *250*, 463–485. [CrossRef]
21. World Steel Association. *World Steel in Figures*; World Steel Association: Brussels, Belgium, 2019.
22. Feitó-Cespón, M.; Sarache, W.; Piedra-Jimenez, F.; Cespón-Castro, R. Redesign of a sustainable reverse supply chain under uncertainty: A case study. *J. Clean. Prod.* **2017**, *151*, 206–217. [CrossRef]
23. Guo, S.; Aydin, G.; Souza, G.C. Dismantle or remanufacture? *Eur. J. Oper. Res.* **2014**, *233*, 580–583. [CrossRef]
24. Niknejad, A.; Petrovic, D. Optimization of integrated reverse logistics networks with different product recovery routes. *Eur. J. Oper. Res.* **2014**, *238*, 143–154. [CrossRef]
25. Boukherroub, T.; Ruiz, A.; Guinet, A.; Fondrevelle, J. An integrated approach for sustainable supply chain planning. *Comput. Oper. Res.* **2015**, *54*, 180–194. [CrossRef]
26. Sarrafha, K.; Rahmati, S.H.A.; Niaki, S.T.A.; Zaretalab, A. A bi-objective integrated procurement, production, and distribution problem of a multi-echelon supply chain network design: A new tuned MOEA. *Comput. Oper. Res.* **2015**, *54*, 35–51. [CrossRef]
27. Santibanez-Gonzalez, E.D.; Diabat, A. Modeling logistics service providers in a non-cooperative supply chain. *Appl. Math. Modell.* **2016**, *40*, 6340–6358. [CrossRef]
28. Inderfurth, K. Impact of uncertainties on recovery behavior in a remanufacturing environment. A numerical analysis. *Int. J. Phys. Distrib. Logist. Manag.* **2005**, *35*, 318–336. [CrossRef]
29. Azadeh, A.; Raoofi, Z.; Zarrin, M. A multi-objective fuzzy linear programming model for optimization of the natural gas supply chain through a greenhouse gas reduction approach. *J. Nat. Gas Sci. Eng.* **2015**, *26*, 702–710. [CrossRef]
30. Memari, A.; Rahim, A.R.A.; Ahmad, R.B. An integrated production-distribution planning in the green supply chain: A multi-objective evolutionary approach. *Procedia Corp.* **2015**, *26*, 700–705. [CrossRef]
31. Pishvaee, M.S.; Khalaf, M.F. Novel robust fuzzy mathematical programming methods. *Appl. Math. Modell.* **2016**, *40*, 407–418. [CrossRef]
32. Mirmajlesi, S.R.; Shafaei, R. An integrated approach to solve a robust forward/reverse supply chain for short lifetime products. *Comput. Ind. Eng.* **2016**, *97*, 222–239. [CrossRef]
33. Dondo, R.G.; Méndez, C.A. Operational planning of forwarding and reverse logistics activities on multi-echelon supply-chain networks. *Comput. Chem. Eng.* **2016**, *88*, 170–184. [CrossRef]
34. Musavi, M.; Rayat, F. A bi-objective green truck routing and scheduling problem in a cross dock with the learning effect. *Iranian J. Oper. Res.* **2017**, *8*, 2–14. [CrossRef]
35. Rafie-Majd, Z.; Pasandideh, S.H.R.; Naderi, B. Modeling and solving the integrated inventory-location-routing problem in a multi-period and multi-perishable product supply chain with uncertainty: Lagrangian relaxation algorithm. *Comput. Chem. Eng.* **2018**, *109*, 9–22. [CrossRef]
36. Mogale, D.G.; Kumar, M.; Kumar, S.K.; Tiwari, M.K. Grain silo location-allocation problem with dwell time for optimization of food grain supply chain network. *Transp. Res. Part E Logist. Transp. Rev.* **2018**, *111*, 40–69. [CrossRef]
37. Dai, Z.; Aqlan, F.; Zheng, X.; Gao, K. A location-inventory supply chain network model using two heuristic algorithms for perishable products with fuzzy constraints. *Comput. Ind. Eng.* **2018**, *119*, 338–352. [CrossRef]
38. Seifbarghy, M.; Hasanzadeh, H. Designing a three-layer supply chain considering different transportation channels and delivery time-dependent demand. *Int. J. Ind. Eng. Theory Appl. Pract.* **2018**, *253*, 370–386.
39. Khodaparasti, S.; Bruni, M.E.; Beraldi, P.; Maleki, H.R.; Jahedi, S. A multi-period location-allocation model for nursing home network planning under uncertainty. *Oper. Res. Health Care* **2018**, *18*, 4–15. [CrossRef]
40. Doolun, I.S.; Ponnambalam, S.G.; Subramanian, N.; Kanagaraj, G. The data-driven hybrid evolutionary analytical approach for multi-objective location-allocation decisions: Automotive green supply chain empirical evidence. *Comput. Oper. Res.* **2018**, *98*, 265–283. [CrossRef]
41. Tsao, Y.C.T.; Thanh, V.V.; Lu, J.C.L.; Yu, V. Designing sustainable supply chain networks under uncertain environments: Fuzzy multi-objective programming. *J. Clean. Prod.* **2018**, *174*, 1550–1565. [CrossRef]

42. Sadeghi Rad, R.; Nahavandi, N. A novel multi-objective optimization model for the integrated problem of green closed-loop supply chain network design and quantity discount. *J. Clean. Prod.* **2018**, *196*, 1549–1565. [CrossRef]
43. Shen, J. An environmental supply chain network under uncertainty. *Phys. A Stat. Mech. Appl.* **2019**, *12*, 12–34. [CrossRef]
44. Falsafi, M.; Fornasiero, R.; Terkaj, W. Performance evaluation of stochastic forward and reverse supply networks. *Procedia CIRP* **2019**, *81*, 1342–1347. [CrossRef]
45. Alizadeh, M.; Makui, A.; Paydar, M.M. Forward and reverse supply chain network design for consumer medical supplies considering biological risk. *Comput. Ind. Eng.* **2020**, *140*, 106229. [CrossRef]
46. Debb, K.; Agrawal, S.; Pratap, A.; Meyarivan, T. A Fast Elitist Non-dominated Sorting Genetic Algorithm for Multi-objective Optimization: NSGA-II. In Proceedings of the International Conference on Parallel Problem Solving from Nature, Paris, France, 18–20 September 2000; pp. 849–858.
47. Deb, K.; Pratap, A.; Agrawal, S.; Meyarivan, T. A fast and elitist multiobjective genetic algorithm: NSGA-II. *IEEE Trans. Evol. Comput.* **2002**, *6*, 182–197. [CrossRef]
48. Gao, X.; Chen, B.; He, X.; Qiu, T.; Li, J.; Wang, C.; Zhang, L. Multi-objective optimization for periodic operation of the naphta pyrolysis process using a new parallel hybrid algorithm combining NSGA-II with SQP. *Comput. Chem. Eng.* **2008**, *32*, 2801–2811. [CrossRef]
49. Rabbani, M.; Farrokhi-Asl, H.; Asgarian, B. Solving a bi-objective location routing problem by a NSGA-II combined with clustering approach: Application in waste collection problem. *J. Ind. Eng. Int.* **2017**, *13*, 13–27. [CrossRef]
50. Wang, Y.; Zhang, S.; Guan, X.; Peng, S.; Wang, H.; Liu, Y.; Xu, M. Collaborative multi-depot logistic network design with time window assignment. *Expert Syst. Appl.* **2020**, *140*, 112910. [CrossRef]
51. Karimi, N.; Zandieh, M.; Karamooz, H.R. Bi-objective group scheduling in hybrid flexible flowshop: A multi-phase approach. *Expert Syst. Appl.* **2010**, *37*, 4024–4032. [CrossRef]
52. Zitzler, E.; Thiele, L. Multi-objective optimization using evolutionary algorithms a comparative case study. In Proceedings of the Fifth International Conference on Parallel Problem Solving from Nature (PPSN-V), Amsterdam, The Netherlands, 27–30 September 1998; pp. 292–293.
53. Sarrafha, K.; Kazemi, A.; Alinezhad, A. A multi-objective evolutionary approach for integratd production-distribution planning problem in a supply chain network. *J. Optim. Ind. Eng.* **2014**, *14*, 89–102.
54. Sharifi, M.; Pourkarim Guilani, P.; Shahriari, M. Using NSGA-II algorithm for a three-objective redundancy allocation problem with k-out-of-n sub-systems. *J. Optim. Ind. Eng.* **2016**, *19*, 87–95.
55. Peace, G.S. *Taguchi Methods*; Addison-Wesley Publishing Company: Boston, MA, USA, 1993.

symmetry

MDPI

Article

Using Data Envelopment Analysis and Multi-Criteria Decision-Making Methods to Evaluate Teacher Performance in Higher Education

Milena Popović *, Gordana Savić, Marija Kuzmanović and Milan Martić

Faculty of Organizational Sciences, University of Belgrade, 11000 Belgrade, Serbia;
gordana.savic@fon.bg.ac.rs (G.S.); marija.kuzmanovic@fon.bg.ac.rs (M.K.); milan.martic@fon.bg.ac.rs (M.M.)
* Correspondence: milena.popovic@fon.bg.ac.rs

Received: 14 February 2020; Accepted: 11 March 2020; Published: 5 April 2020

Abstract: This paper proposes an approach that combines data envelopment analysis (DEA) with the analytic hierarchy process (AHP) and conjoint analysis, as multi-criteria decision-making methods to evaluate teachers' performance in higher education. This process of evaluation is complex as it involves consideration of both objective and subjective efficiency assessments. The efficiency evaluation in the presence of multiple different criteria is done by DEA and results heavily depend on their selection, values, and the weights assigned to them. Objective efficiency evaluation is data-driven, while the subjective efficiency relies on values of subjective criteria usually captured throughout the survey. The conjoint analysis helps with the selection and determining the relative importance of such criteria, based on stakeholder preferences, obtained as an evaluation of experimentally designed hypothetical profiles. An efficient experimental design can be either symmetric or asymmetric depending on the structure of criteria covered by the study. Obtained importance might be a guideline for selecting adequate input and output criteria in the DEA model when assessing teachers' subjective efficiency. Another reason to use conjoint preferences is to set a basis for weight restrictions in DEA and consequently to increase its discrimination power. Finally, the overall teacher's efficiency is an AHP aggregation of subjective and objective teaching and research efficiency scores. Given the growing competition in the field of education, a higher level of responsibility and commitment is expected, and it is therefore helpful to identify weaknesses so that they can be addressed. Therefore, the evaluation of teachers' efficiency at the University of Belgrade, Faculty of Organizational Sciences illustrates the usage of the proposed approach. As results, relatively efficient and inefficient teachers were identified, the reasons and aspects of their inefficiency were discovered, and rankings were made.

Keywords: data envelopment analysis; conjoint analysis; experimental design; criteria importance; weight restrictions; subjective and objective teacher efficiency; AHP

1. Introduction

The sector of higher education and development, faced with competitive pressure, carries a great responsibility to increase the efficiency of its activities continuously. Obviously, higher education productivity has a multidimensional character as it relates to knowledge production and dissemination through both teaching and scientific research. Therefore, the evaluation of teachers' performance is a more challenging issue because it involves multiple criteria as objectives.

Following the standards for assessing the quality of teachers' work, one of the measuring instruments is student satisfaction [1]. An important factor affecting the satisfaction of the students, as the users of higher education services, with the education process, is the professional and practical knowledge of the teachers and their academic assessment [2–4]. Therefore, at many higher education institutions, students are offered some kind of evaluation in which they rate the teaching process and the competencies of the teachers for each course [5–7].

Data envelopment analysis (DEA) is an approach to measure the relative efficiency of decision-making units (DMUs) that are characterized by multiple incommensurate inputs and outputs. Its results rely heavily on the set of criteria used in the analysis. Therefore, one of the most important stages in the DEA is the selection of criteria, especially as the effort of evaluation increases significantly with the increase in the amount of data available. In a number of studies, researchers treat inputs and outputs simply as "givens" and then proceed to deal with the DEA methodology [8]. On the other hand, the analytic hierarchy process (AHP) and conjoint analysis are multi-criteria decision-making methods (MCDM) that can provide a priori information about the significance of inputs and outputs.

Although the theoretical foundations and methodological frameworks of conjoint analysis and AHP methods are different, they can be used independently and comparatively in similar or even the same studies [9–15]. Both methods can be used to measure respondents' preferences as well as to determine the relative importance of attributes, but still the choice of the appropriate one depends on the particular problem and aspects of the research [16].

DEA models can be combined with AHP in numerous ways [17]. According to the literature, the AHP method is used in cases when the following are necessary: complete ranking in a two-stage process [18–21]; estimating missing data [22]; imposing weight restrictions [23–27]; reducing the number of input or output criteria [28–30], and converting qualitative data to quantitative [31–41]. The only paper published so far that has had the idea of combining the DEA method with conjoint analysis is by Salhieh and Al-Harris [42]. They suggested combining these methods for selecting new products on the market.

This paper presents a new approach for measuring the overall teachers' efficiency as a weighted sum of subjective and objective efficiency scores. The approach integrates DEA with the AHP and conjoint analysis as multi-criteria decision-making methods. The AHP enables the creation of a hierarchical structure used to configure the problem of the overall efficiency evolution. Furthermore, the weights of all efficiency measures at the highest level of the hierarchy are obtained using AHP. The procedure of assessing subjective efficiency consists of the conjoint analysis and DEA. The conjoint analysis is finding out the relative importance of each criterion, based on stakeholder preferences, afterwards used as guidelines for the DEA criteria selection. Another reason to use conjoint preferences is to set a basis for weight restrictions imposed in DEA models. The objective teaching and research efficiency scores are assessed by applying traditional DEA models. The proposed approach provides the determination of scores and ranking of relatively efficient and inefficient teachers as well as strong and weak aspects of their teaching and research work.

The paper is structured as follows: Section 2 describes the DEA basics and the implementation process, followed by a literature survey concerning criteria (input and output) selection. Conjoint analysis and the AHP method, including an approach for determining the importance of the criteria considered, are also presented in this section. A new methodological framework for combining conjoint analysis, AHP, and DEA are presented in Section 3. An illustration of the proposed methodology and real-world test results are given in Section 4. Section 5 provides the main conclusions and directions of future research.

2. Background

2.1. Data Envelopment Analysis

The creators of DEA, Charnes, Cooper, and Rhodes [43], introduced the basic DEA model (the so-called CCR DEA model) in 1978 as a new way to measure the efficiency of DMUs using multiple inputs and outputs. Since then, many variations of DEA models have been developed. Some of them are: the BCC DEA model proposed by Banker, Charnes, and Cooper [44], which assumes variable return to scale; the additive model [45], which is non-radial; the Banker and Morey [46] model that involves qualitative inputs and outputs; and the Golany and Roll [47] model, with restricted input and/or output weights to specific ranges of values. DEA empirically identifies the data-driven frontier of efficiency, which envelopes inefficient DMUs while efficient DMUs lie on the frontier. Let us assume that there are n DMUs, and the jth DMUs produce s outputs ($y_{ij}, \ldots, y_{sj}$) by using m inputs ($x_{ij}, \ldots, x_{mj}$). The basic output-oriented CCR DEA model is as follows:

$$
\begin{array}{l}
(\max)h_k = \sum\limits_{r=1}^{s} u_r y_{rk} \\
st \\
\sum\limits_{i=1}^{m} v_i x_{ik} = 1 \\
\sum\limits_{r=1}^{s} u_r y_{rj} - \sum\limits_{i=1}^{m} v_i x_{ij} \leq 0, \ j = 1, \ldots, n \\
u_r \geq 0; \ r = 1, 2, \ldots, s, \\
v_i \geq 0; \ i = 1, 2, \ldots, m,
\end{array} \quad . \tag{1}
$$

where u_r, $(r = 1, 2, \ldots, s)$, are weights assigned to the rth outputs, and v_i, $(i = 1, 2, \ldots, m)$, are weights assigned to the ith inputs, in order to assess maximal possible efficiency score. The score h_k shows relative efficiency of DMU$_k$, obtained as the maximum possible achievement in comparison with the other DMUs under the evaluation.

Emrouznejad and Witte [48] proposed a complete procedure for assessing DEA efficiency in large-scale projects, a so-called COOPER-framework, which can be further modified and adapted to the specific requirements of a particular study. The COOPER-framework consists of six phases: (1) Concepts and objectives, (2) On structuring data, (3) Operational models, (4) Performance comparison model, (5) Evaluation, and (6) Results and deployment. The first two phases involve defining the problem and understanding how the DMU works, while the last two phases involve producing a summary of the results and reporting.

In this paper, attention is paid to phases 1, 2, 3, and 4, since the objective definition in the model (1) obviously indicates that the efficiency of DMU$_k$ is crucially related to the criteria selected. Jenkins and Anderson [49] claim that the more criteria there are, the less constrained weights are assigned to the criteria and the less discriminating the DEA scores are. The number of criteria may be substantial, and it may not be clear which one to choose. Moreover, the selection of different criteria can lead to different efficiency evaluation results. Of course, it is possible to consider all the criteria for evaluation. Still too many of them may lead to too many efficient units, and it may give rise to difficulties in distinguishing efficient units from inefficient ones. For this reason, the problem of selecting adequate criteria becomes an essential issue for improving the discrimination power of DEA.

There is no consensus on how to limit the number of criteria in the best way even though it is very advantageous. Banker et al. [44] suggest that the number of DMUs being evaluated should be at least three times the number of criteria. As noted by Golani and Roll [47], several studies emphasize the importance of the process of selecting data variables in addition to the DEA methodology itself. One approach is to select those criteria that are low-correlated. However, studies have shown that removing highly correlated criteria can still have a significant effect on DEA results [50]. Morita and Avkiran [51] used a three-level orthogonal layout experiment to select an appropriate combination of inputs and outputs based on external information. Edirisinghe and Zhang [52] proposed a two-step heuristic algorithm for criteria selection in DEA based on maximizing the correlation between DEA score and the external performance index.

Regardless of the method of criteria selection and the criteria, DEA does not allow discrimination between efficient DMUs because of their maximal efficiency. Several attempts to fully rank DMUs have been made, including modifying basic DEA models and connecting them to multi-criteria approaches [53]. The discrimination power of the DEA method can also be improved by promoting symmetric weight selection [54] by imposing penalizing differences in the values of each combination of two inputs or outputs. Other options are using cross-efficiency evolution [55] or imposing weight restrictions on models. A well-known assurance region DEA model (AR DEA) [56] imposes lower and upper boundaries on the weight ratio, as follows:

$$L_{1,2} \leq \frac{v_2}{v_1} \leq U_{1,2}. \tag{2}$$

An important consideration in the weight restrictions is setting realistic boundaries. In most cases, they are set on the basis of expert opinions and experience. Another direction can be DEA's combination with other statistical methods to get data or evidence-driven boundaries [57]. In this paper, the results of the conjoint analysis are used to help determine the boundaries.

2.2. Conjoint Analysis

Conjoint analysis is a class of multivariate techniques used to understand individuals' preferences better. A key goal of conjoint analysis is to identify which criteria most affects individuals' choices or decisions, but also to find out how they make trade-offs between conflicting criteria.

The first step in conjoint analysis involves determining the set of key features (attributes, criteria) that describe an object (entity) and the levels of attributes that differentiate objects from one another. Sets of attribute levels that describe single alternatives are referred to as profiles. Depending on the number of attributes included in the study, a list of profiles that are presented to the respondent to evaluate can be either full factorial (all possible combinations of attribute levels) or fractional factorial (subset of all possible combinations) experimental design. Furthermore, fractional factorial designs could be either symmetric, if all attributes are assigned an equal number of levels, or asymmetric otherwise [58]. Both the ranking and rating approach can be used to evaluate profiles from the experimental design.

After collecting individuals' responses, a model should be specified that relates those responses to the utilities of the attribute levels that are included in the certain profiles. The most commonly used model is the linear additive model of part-worth utilities. In the conjoint experiment with K attributes, each with L_k levels, model implies that the overall utility of the profile j ($j = 1, \ldots, J$) for the respondent i ($i = 1, \ldots, I$) can be expressed as follows [59]:

$$U_{ij} = \sum_{k=1}^{K} \sum_{l=1}^{L_k} \beta_{ikl} x_{jkl} + \varepsilon_{ij} \tag{3}$$

where x_{jkl} is a (0,1) variable that equals 1 if profile j contains lth level of attribute k, otherwise it equals 0. β_{ikl} is respondent i's utility (part-worth) assigned to the level l of the attribute k; ε_{ij} is a stochastic error term.

Part-worths are estimated using the least square method and reflect the extent to which the selection of a particular profile is affected by these levels. The larger the variations of part-worths within an attribute, the more important the attribute is. Therefore, the relative importance of attribute k ($k = 1, \ldots, K$) for respondent i ($i = 1, \ldots, I$) can be expressed as the ratio of the utility range for a particular attribute and the sum of the utility ranges for all attributes [60]:

$$FI_{ik} = \frac{\max_{l} \hat{\beta}_{ikl} - \min_{l} \hat{\beta}_{ikl}}{\sum_{k=1}^{K} \left(\max_{l} \hat{\beta}_{ikl} - \min_{l} \hat{\beta}_{ikl} \right)}. \tag{4}$$

The resulting importance scores can be further used to calculate aggregated importance values. Estimated part-worth utilities can also be used as input parameters of the simulation models to predict how individuals will choose between competing alternatives, but also to examine how their choices change as the characteristics of the alternatives vary.

2.3. The Analytic Hierarchy Process (AHP)

The AHP is a MCDM method proposed by Saaty [61], which allows experts to prioritize decision criteria through a series of pairwise comparisons. There are three basic principles that AHP relies on: (1) the hierarchy principle, which involves constructing a hierarchical tree with criteria, sub-criteria, and alternative solutions; (2) the priority-establishing principle; and (3) the consistency principle [62].

In order to establish the various criteria weights, the AHP method uses their pairwise comparisons recorded a square matrix A. All elements on diagonal of matrix are 1. A decision maker compares elements in pairs at the same level of hierarchical structure using the Satie scale of relative importance. The same procedure is applied throughout the downward hierarchy until comparisons of all alternatives with respect to the parent sub-criteria at the (k-1) level are made at the last k-th level. The resulting elements at this stage are referred to as "local" weights. The mathematical model performs the aggregation of weights from different levels and gives the final result of the priorities of the alternatives in relation to the set goal.

3. Methodological Framework

The following methodological framework is designed with the intention to make an aggregated efficiency assessment of the DMUs under consideration. The first step is to define the concepts and aims of the analysis, followed by the selection of the units under the evaluations. Afterwards, the efficiency scores are evaluated in an independent phase following the procedure proposed for subjective or objective efficiency assessment, shown in Figure 1.

Phase I of the methodological framework is an assessment of subjective efficiencies, which strongly depends on respondents' opinions and preferences. Consequently, this efficiency is evaluated throughout two steps (Step 1—Conjoint preference analysis and Step 2—DEA efficiency assessment). Step 1 firstly defines the objectives of preference analysis and stakeholders as a starting point of this phase. Afterwards, the set of K key attributes (criteria) and their levels are selected based on the defined objectives. Secondly, experimental design is generated. It is the most sensitive stage of the conjoint analysis as the levels of the selected criteria should be combined to create different hypothetical profiles for the survey. The respondents (stakeholders) need to assign preference ratings towards each of the profiles from the generated experimental design. After making the most suitable experimental layout, conducting the survey, and collecting the data, the next stage assumes the estimating of the model's parameters using statistical techniques and calculating the importance of the attributes FI_k, $k = 1, \ldots,$ K. The starting set of K criteria together with obtained importance values FI_k will be used as inputs for the next step.

Step II (Phase I), assumes the DEA efficiency evaluation. There are two possibilities for the analysis in the second step (DEA), depending on the total number (K) of criteria selected during Step I. In the first case, an analyst reduces the set of criteria to a suitable number ($n \leq 3 \times K$), by selecting them in descending order of stockholder's preference FI_k, $k = 1, \ldots, K$. In the second case, when the number of criteria is not too high, importance values FI_k are used for the weight restrictions to better discriminate between DMUs. This decision leads to the classification of selected criteria into the subsets of m inputs and n outputs depending on their nature, data collection, and DEA model selection. Finally, in this step, the chosen DEA model is solved to obtain the efficiency scores for each DMU in the observing set.

Phase II of the framework includes the objective DEA efficiency assessment. Unlike the subjective efficiency evaluation based on the stakeholders' opinion, data-driven DEA efficiency is measured objectively, using the explicit data on the behavior of the system. Main steps are similar to the steps defined in the first phase: selecting input and outputs, collecting data, selecting the appropriate DEA model, and evaluation of the efficiency score.

Finally, the overall efficiency is calculated as a sum of products of all partial efficiency scores, subjective and objective, and their weights. The weights obtained using the AHP method, define the importance of all efficiency measures included in analysis.

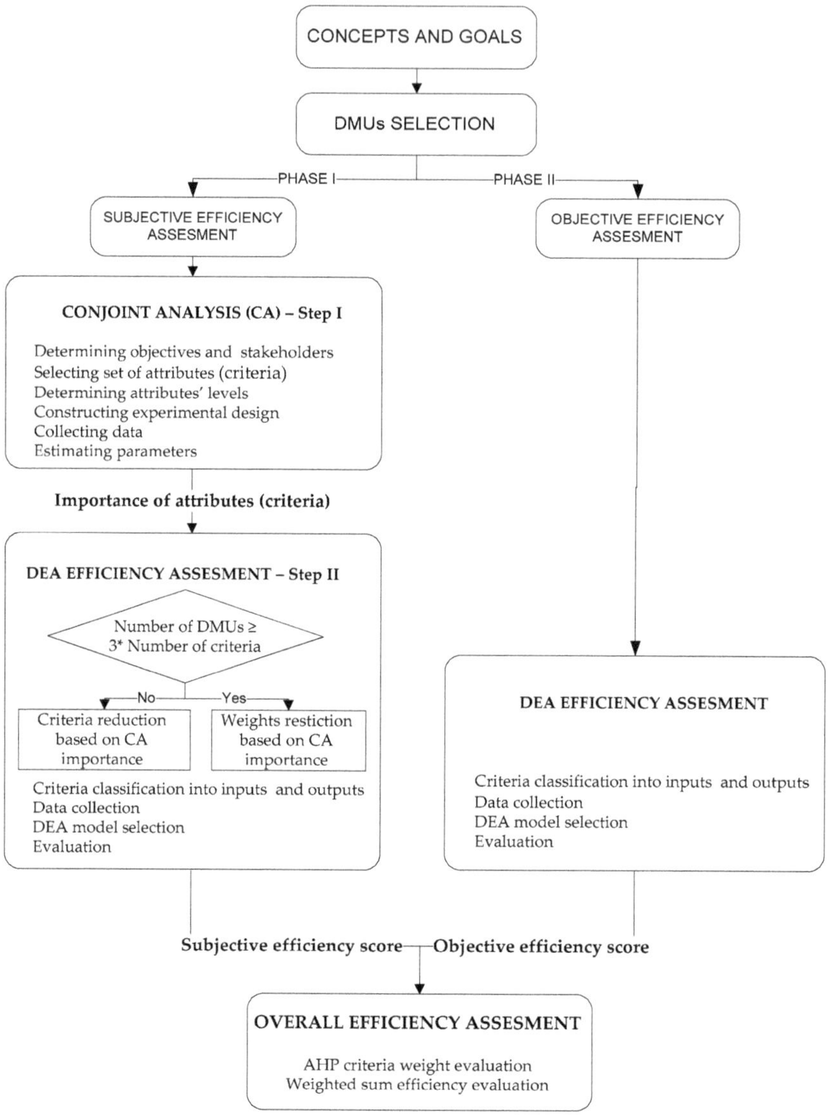

Figure 1. Methodological framework.

The proposed procedure allows the combination of the subjective (Phase I) and objective efficiency measures (Phase II) obtained by DEA. The obtained measures are relative and data-driven. The subjective efficiency is made to be objective by using DEA for efficiency assessment and conjoint analysis for criteria importance evaluation. The main advantages and disadvantages of such a procedure come from DEA characteristics. On the one hand, there is no need for a priori weight imposing, data normalization, or production frontier determination. On the other hand, a small range of criteria values or a large number of criteria can lead to untrustworthy efficiency evaluation using the basic CCR DEA model. Step II (Phase I) tackles this issue. The conjoint preference analysis among stakeholders provides values of criteria importance that can be used for either criteria number reduction or criteria weight restrictions incorporated into DEA models. Both scenarios should lead to improved discrimination power based on DEA efficiency, which is the advantage of the proposed procedure. The procedure described above is illustrated in the next section using real data.

4. Empirical Study

Considering the importance of measuring and monitoring the performance of academic staff in both the teaching and research process, university teachers from the Faculty of Organizational Sciences were selected as DMUs in this study. Their overall efficiency should be measured from different aspects. Based on the proposed methodological framework the aggregated assessment of teacher's efficiency was considered from two aspects: a subjective (assessment of teaching) and objective (teaching and research efficiency) aspect (see Figure 2). The AHP hierarchical structure is used for defining the problem of overall teachers' efficiency, with overall teachers' efficiency as a goal at the top level. The first and second levels of the hierarchy comprise subjective efficiency and two types of objective efficiencies, needed to be aggregated into overall efficiency. The second level of the hierarchy represents sub-criteria used as inputs and outputs in DEA efficiency assessment.

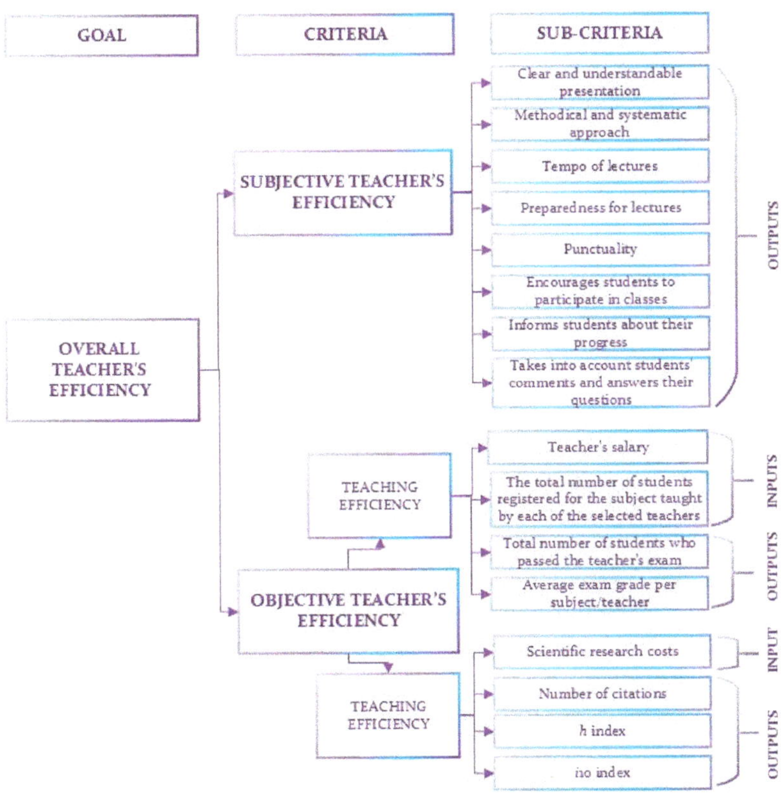

Figure 2. The aggregated assessment of teachers' efficiency.

4.1. *Subjective Assessment of Teacher's Efficiency*

The evaluation was carried out following the proposed methodological framework throughout Step I and Step II.

Step I. Students' preferences toward eight criteria pre-set by university authorities were determined using conjoint analysis (see Table 1). An efficient experimental design of 16 profiles was constructed using the statistical package SPSS 16.0 (Orthoplan component). As all attributes did not have the same number of levels, the resulting design was asymmetric but orthogonal. In order to verify the consistency of students' responses, two holdout profiles were added to the given design. A total of 106 third-year students from the Faculty of Organizational Sciences expressed their preferences for each of the 18 hypothetical teacher profiles in a nine-point Likert scale, with 1 referring to absolutely undesirable, and 9 to absolutely desirable profiles. An example of the hypothetical teacher profile evaluation task is given in Figure 3.

Table 1. A set of criteria considered in the conjoint analysis survey, and the resulting utilities and importance values.

No	Criteria (Attributes)	Attribute Levels	Part-Worths (β)	Relative Importance Values (*FI*)
C1	Clear and understandable presentation of teaching content	Yes No	0.865 −0.865	22.98%
C2	Methodical and systematic approach to teaching	Yes No	0.73 −0.73	18.96%
C3	Tempo of lectures	Too slow Optimal Too fast	0.451 −0.117 −0.334	14.92%
C4	Preparedness for lectures	Good Poor	0.266 −0.266	7.96%
C5	Punctuality	On time Late	0.303 −0.303	9.00%
C6	Encouraging students to actively participate in classes	Yes No	0.28 −0.28	8.14%
C7	Informing students about their progress	Yes No	0.324 −0.324	9.08%
C8	Takes into account students' comments and answers their questions	Yes No	0.293 −0.293	8.95%
	Constant		4.046	

Correlations
Pearson's R = 0.966 (sig. = 0.000)
Kendall's tau = 0.933 (sig. = 0.000)
Kendall's tau (for two holdouts) = 1.000

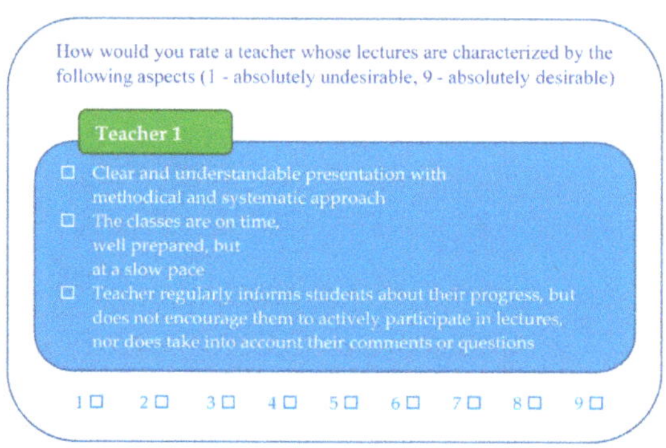

Figure 3. An example of the hypothetical teacher-profile evaluation task.

After removing the incomplete responses, 98 acceptable surveys remained, yielding a total of 1568 observations. The parameters were estimated for each student in the sample individually, and the sample as a whole. The averaged results and model fit statistics are shown in Table 1, indicating that the estimated parameters are highly significant.

The conjoint data presented in Table 1 indicate wide variations in the relative importance of the criteria considered. The most important criterion is the one concerning the clarity and comprehensibility of the teacher's presentation (C1), followed by the criteria relating to the methodical and systematic approach to lectures (C2), and the tempo of lectures (C3). The three criteria listed cover more than 50% of the total importance, and these results were further used for the efficiency evaluation in step II.

Step II. DEA analyses were carried out in order to compare teachers, make a distinction between their performances, and find out advantages and disadvantages. The official database consists of student evaluation of teaching according to criteria C1 to C8 (1-5) for all teachers. We have selected 27 teachers (DMUs) who hold classes for students that participated in the conjoint research. This sample is representative because it includes professors and teaching assistants in all academic positions (full professor, associate professor, assistant professor, and teaching assistants); they are equally represented across the departments, and there is an almost equal ratio of male to female. Teachers' average scores on each of the eight criteria obtained as a result of the students' evaluations are treated as DEA outputs to be as high as possible since the single input is a dummy value of 1. The number of teachers observed as DMUs (27) is more than three times the number of criteria considered (8), which means that the rule of thumb suggested by Banker et al. [44] is satisfied. Descriptive statistics of the criteria values (DEA outputs) are given in Table 2.

Table 2. Subjective criteria descriptive statistics.

Criteria	Min	Max	Mean	Std. Dev.
C1	2.17	5.00	4.400	0.535
C2	2.22	5.00	4.369	0.559
C3	2.17	5.00	4.302	0.565
C4	2.67	4.95	4.527	0.470
C5	1.72	4.92	4.380	0.652
C6	2.00	4.85	4.194	0.624
C7	1.83	4.85	4.127	0.643
C8	1.78	5.00	4.375	0.632

The directions of the methodology proposed in the previous section were implemented as Scenario A (criteria reduction) and Scenario B (weights restriction). Prior to this, the following marks and teacher ranks were calculated: the EWSM mark (equal weighted sum method), the WSM-Conjoint (weighted sum method with conjoint criteria importance values used as weights [63]), and the basic CCR DEA efficiency score (1). The CCR DEA model was chosen since the data range is small, and there is only one dummy input. Therefore, constant return to scale is expected. The descriptive statistics of these values are shown in Table 3.

Table 3. Results' descriptive statistics.

	EWSM-Original	WSM-Conjoint	DEA
Min	2.073	2.098	0.539
Max	4.944	4.960	1.000
Mean	4.335	4.344	0.941
Std. Dev	0.544	0.541	0.090
	Spearman's rho correlations		
EWSM-Original	1	0.993 **	0.809 **
WSM-Conjoint	0.993 **	1	0.797 **
DEA	0.809 **	0.797 **	1

** Significant at the 0.01 level (2-tailed).
3 efficient teachers,
$h_k \geq 0.95$ for 18 out of 27 DMUs

The results of the Spearman's test show that the correlation between the EWSM-Original and WSM-Conjoint ranks is almost complete, due to the accumulation of an average rate of teachers between 4 and 5. These results were expected since all mean values were higher than 4 (Table 2). On the other hand, the DEA ranks were correlated with the other ranks with a value of 0.803. Furthermore, the results show that three out of 27 teachers are efficient, but it is interesting that two-thirds of teachers have efficiency indexes greater or equal to 0.95. This is due to criteria value accumulation as well as a flexible choice of weights. The weight assignment scheme is not forced to be symmetric [54] and results in the existence of many zeros in the weight matrix. For example, in the matrix for three teachers, there are just four nonzero weights (Table 4).

Table 4. Teachers' ranks and DEA weights.

DMU	Ranks			DEA	Weights							
	EWSM-Original	WSM-Conjoint	DEA	θk	C1	C2	C3	C4	C5	C6	C7	C8
1	6	6	14	0.982	0	0	0	0.82	0	0.18	0	0
2	13	13	4	0.996	0	0	0	1	0	0	0	0
17	20	20	5	0.996	0	0	0	0	0	1	0	0

Extreme differences in the ranks of the teachers shown in Table 4 are just a consequence of the DEA weight assignment. In the case of teacher DMU 1, only two of the criteria are taken into account for calculating her/his efficiency score. These are criteria C4 and C6, whose relative importance are less than 10% according to the conjoint results. Therefore, the rank is lower than the ranks obtained by the EWSM-Original and WSM-Conjoint methods. On the other hand, in the cases of teachers DMU 2 and DMU 17, just one criterion, with the highest average rate, was weighted and their DEA ranks are therefore better than the ranks according to two other methods. Obviously, the evaluation method has an impact on the final result.

To overcome the above problems, the conjoint analysis data were used to increase the discriminatory power of the DEA method as proposed in the methodological framework.

SCENARIO A: Reducing the number of criteria

In a real-world application, it is often necessary to choose adequate outputs from a set consisting of a large number of criteria. For that purpose, it was possible to use a multivariate correlation analysis. However, since almost all correlations are higher than 0.95, which means that only one output would remain, we suggest using criteria importance values from conjoint analysis. The most important criteria C1, C2, and C3 were selected since they cover 56.87% of the total criteria importance (see Table 1). The descriptive statistics of the results obtained by the DEA method, based on criteria C1, C2, and C3 are given in the column "Conjoint & DEA" in Table 5. It is evident that the discriminatory power significantly increased, as only one professor and two teaching assistants were assessed as efficient by the three major output criteria. The number of teachers with efficiency indexes over 0.95 also decreased.

SCENARIO B: Imposing weights restriction

In a situation where stakeholders believe that all criteria are significant and should be included in the analysis, weight restrictions can be imposed in DEA models to cover stakeholders' opinions and to reduce the number of zero weights. Here we propose a procedure with the following steps:

1. Set f as an index of criterion with the lowest importance FI according to results of the conjoint analysis
2. Impose boundaries for all criteria evaluated by the conjoint analysis. AR DEA constraints presented as Equation (2) in Section 2.1, are defined here as follows:

$$\frac{FI_r}{\min\limits_r(FI_r)} \leq \frac{v_r}{v_f} \leq \frac{\max\limits_r(FI_r)}{\min\limits_r(FI_r)}, r = 1, \ldots, s. \quad (5)$$

For example, C4 is the criterion with the lowest importance value ($v_f = v_4, \min_r(FI_r) = 0.0796$) and C1 is the criterion with the highest importance value ($\max_r(FI_r) = 0.2298$). So, the upper bound is $\max_r(FI_r)/\min_r(FI_r) = 2.89$ and it is the same for each criterion, which means that the upper bounds are symmetric [64]. On the other hand, the lower bound differs depending on the FI_r value (Table 1) and varies from 1.12 for C8 to 2.89 for C1. That indicates that the lower bounds are asymmetric.

The descriptive statistics of the results obtained by the AR DEA method are given in the column "Conjoint AR DEA". With restricted weights, the discrimination power of DEA is increased. Obviously the full ranking, according to all output criteria, is provided for the set all teachers (T) who are classified into subsets of professors (P) and teaching assistants (TA).

The Spearman's rank correlation analysis of all the ranks for all 27 teachers is given in Table 6. The results obtained by the last analysis are highly correlated with the original ranks and with the DEA ranks based on three criteria selected conjointly.

Table 5. Results of teacher efficiency evaluation.

Method	DEA			Conjoint & DEA (Scenario A)			Conjoint AR DEA (Scenario B)		
$m + s$		8			3 (C1, C2, C3)			8	
Teachers	T	P	T + A	T	P	T + A	T	P	T + A
No. of DMUs	27	17	10	27	17	10	27	17	10
Average	0.941	0.955	0.943	0.895	0.914	0.900	0.884	0.909	0.895
SD	0.088	0.131	0.055	0.105	0.149	0.069	0.107	0.152	0.074
Max	1.000	0.996	1.000	1.000	0.985	1.000	1.000	0.982	1.000
Min	0.539	0.539	0.866	0.445	0.445	0.824	0.425	0.425	0.747
$h_k = 1$	3	0	3	1	0	1	1	0	1
$h_k \geq 0.95$	18	12	6	11	7	4	7	4	3

Table 6. Spearman's rho correlations.

	EWSM-Original	WSM-Conjoint	DEA	Conjoint & DEA (Scenario A)	Conjoint AR DEA (Scenario B)
Original	1.000	0.993	0.809	0.933	0.997
Conjoint		1.000	0.797	0.939	0.991
DEA			1.000	0.777	0.820
Conjoint & DEA				1.000	0.941
Conjoint AR DEA					1.000

Verification of the DEA Results

The descriptive statistics for the data used in the example (Table 2) indicate low heterogeneity among the criteria values. Therefore, according to Spearman's rank correlation analysis, there are no big differences between the results for the original method (EWSM) and the WSM Conjoint and Conjoint DEA results. This conclusion is consistent with Buschken's claim [65] that the naive model almost perfectly replicates the DEA efficiency scores for constant return-to-scales and low input–output data heterogeneity. Therefore, it can be concluded that the heterogeneity of input–output data is essential to take advantage of the DEA capability. In order to verify the methodology, we invented two artificial datasets (one with 27 and one with 1000 DMUs) in which the values of the inputs were generated from a uniform distribution over the interval [1, 5]. The simulated inputs were less correlated (0.34–0.81) than in the original data (0.75–0.998). The results of the analyses for both datasets are given in Table 7.

Table 7. DEA results for simulated data.

Method	DEA		Conjoint & DEA (Scenario A)		Conjoint AR DEA (Scenario B)	
$m+s$	8		3		8	
No. of DMUs	27	1000	27	1000	27	1000
Average	0.971	0.948	0.827	0.800	0.889	0.861
SD	0.061	0.055	0.179	0.069	0.100	0.110
Max	1.000	1.000	1.000	1.000	1.000	1.000
Min	0.760	0.637	0.390	0.577	0.672	0.507
$h_k = 1$	23 (85.19%)	153 (15.3%)	5 (18.52%)	3 (0.30%)	5 (18.52%)	18 (1.8%)
$h_k \geq 0.95$	23 (85.19%)	613 (61.3%)	9 (33.33%)	11(1.10%)	9 (33.33%)	261 (26.1%)

According to the results obtained by solving the CCR DEA model for the first data set, there are more efficient DMUs (23 out of 27) than in the original dataset (Table 5). In the second, bigger data set there are 153 efficient DMUs and 613 DMUs with efficiency greater than or equal to 0.95. Due to the heterogeneity of the simulated data and the possibility of each DMU to find a good enough criterion and to prefer it with a sizeable optimal weight value, while putting minimal weights on the other criteria [48], the discrimination power of the DEA method is feeble. However, the DEA results obtained by incorporating using conjoint weights, either for a reduced number of criteria or for weights restrictions, are much more realistic, with a lower percentage of efficient DMUs. There are just five efficient DMUs out of 27 in both scenarios and nine with an efficiency score greater than or equal to 0.95. Furthermore, for the set of 1000 DMUs, just three DMUs were evaluated as efficient in Scenario A since there are fewer criteria (just three) for selecting a preference with maximal weight. Scenario B, with imposed weights restrictions and compressed feasible set, evaluates only 18 out of 1000 as an efficient DMUs. All this proves that imposing conjoint analysis results into the model contributes to the distinction between efficient and inefficient DMUs.

4.2. Objective Assessment of Teacher's Efficiency

4.2.1. Objective Assessment of Teaching Efficiency

Assessing the efficiency of the teaching process ensures continuous monitoring of whether the teacher achieves the prescribed objectives, outcomes, and standards. This is a continuous activity that expresses the relationship between the evaluation criteria. In the proposed methodological framework, a classical output-oriented CCR model was used for the objective assessment of the teaching efficiency, the parameters of which are:

Inputs:

1. The total number of students registered for the listening subject by each of the selected teachers, over one academic year (I1)
2. Annual salary of the teacher (I2)

Outputs:

1. Total number of students who passed the exam with the chosen subject teacher in one academic year (O1)
2. Average exam grade per subject/teacher (O2)

Data on the number of students who registered for exams (I1), as well as those who passed them in one school year (O1) and the average grade per subject/teacher, were taken from the student services at the faculty. Teacher salaries (I2) are determined according to their position, years of service, and the variable part of the salary relating to workload.

When it comes to an objective assessment of the efficiency of the teaching process, five teachers have an efficiency index of 1. A satisfactory 29% of the teachers have an efficiency index of greater than 0.9, which means that based on this objective efficiency assessment criterion, almost a third of the teachers are efficient.

4.2.2. Assessment of the Research Efficiency

Teacher ranking has become increasingly objective over the past few years thanks to new methods, a systematic approach and well-developed, organized academic networks and databases [65]. Mester [66] states that the leading indicators for the metric of teachers' scientific research work are: number of citations, *h*-index, and *i*10 index. The *h*-index (Hirsch's index) of researchers was introduced in 2005 by German physicist Hirsch [67], and it represents the highest *h* number, when *h* number of citations agrees with *h* number of published papers to which the citations refer. The *i*10 index was introduced in 2004 by Google Scholar and it represents the total number of published papers with ten or more citations [68]. The total number of citations is an excellent indicator since the data are publicly available, reliable, objective, and collected quickly.

According to the results achieved over five-year period, the researcher is classified into one of six categories predefined by the Ministry of Science and Technological Development of the Republic of Serbia: A1–A6; T1–T6. Depending on which category they belong to, and their academic position, teachers are paid an additional monthly amount. In addition to these earnings, by expert decision at a professional meeting, the university approves a quota (annual) which teachers can use to co-finance participation in scientific gatherings in the country and abroad. The total value of the earnings (scientific research costs) received by a teacher for scientific research work is equal to the extra earnings. In further analysis, scientific research costs will be taken as input values.

When formulating the DEA model, which is used to analyze the efficiency of teachers' research efficiency, it is required that the functional dependence of the output and input has the mathematical characteristic of isotonicity. A correlation analysis between the inputs and outputs was performed in order to prove the character of isotonicity. The results of the descriptive statistics are given in Table 8.

Table 8. Descriptive statistics for the parameter of scientific research work.

Parameters	Scientific Research Costs	Number of Citations	*h* Index	*i*10 Index
Min	58419.00	683	14	17
Max	91666.70	20	3	1
Average value	32153.10	205.18	6.81	5.25
Standard deviation	16368.70	161.16	2.74	4.14
		Correlation		
Scientific research costs	1	0.646	0.624	0.616
Number of citations		1	0.925	0.892
h index			1	0.944
*i*10 index				1

The data in Table 8 show that the correlation coefficient is positive and that the isotonicity is not broken. The EMS software tool was used to solve the output-oriented CCR model, and the results obtained are shown in Table 9.

Table 9. Aggregated assessment of teacher efficiency and final rank.

DMU	Subjective Teachers' Efficiency	Objective Teachers' Efficiency		Overall Teachers' Efficiency	Rank
	Conjoint & DEA (Scenario A)	Teaching	Research		
1	0.9581	0.989	0.7941	0.9055	9
2	0.9571	0.696	1	0.9177	5
3	0.7913	0.991	1	0.9083	8
4	0.4444	0.742	0.8037	0.6362	27
5	0.8769	0.955	1	0.9376	3
6	0.9857	0.755	0.6334	0.8104	22
7	0.9429	0.979	0.8478	0.9162	7
8	0.8552	1	0.7262	0.8391	18
9	0.9165	0.769	0.8439	0.8593	15
10	0.9765	1	1	0.9898	1
11	0.9586	0.739	0.7649	0.8427	16
12	0.8424	0.991	0.8889	0.8903	11
13	0.95	0.692	0.6071	0.7723	26
14	0.9091	0.761	0.6524	0.7855	25
15	0.8409	0.955	1	0.9221	4
16	0.8667	0.937	0.6655	0.8090	23
17	0.8345	0.947	0.7697	0.8347	19
18	0.95	0.767	0.6877	0.8171	21
19	0.9238	0.767	0.6877	0.8058	24
20	0.86	1	0.9373	0.9172	6
21	0.8211	0.992	0.8877	0.8809	14
22	0.8248	1	0.9065	0.891	10
23	1	1	0.9683	0.9885	2
24	0.8267	1	0.7692	0.8423	17
25	0.9789	0.948	0.7252	0.8810	13
26	0.9733	0.767	0.6877	0.8271	20
27	0.9833	0.889	0.769	0.8863	12
Average	0.8907	0.8899	0.8157	0.8635	
SD	0.1092	0.1168	0.1285	0.07245	
Max	1	1	1	0.9898	
Min	0.4444	0.692	0.6071	0.6362	
$h_k = 1$	1	6	5	0	
$h_k \geq 0.95$	11	13	6	2	

4.3. Aggregated Assessment of Overall Teacher's Efficiency

Based on the proposed methodological framework (Figure 2), the aggregated score of teacher efficiency was obtained as the sum of the subjective and objective scores multiplied by the weight coefficients obtained by the AHP method. The weight coefficients are evaluated as average values of efficiency indices' importance, given by 72 teachers from the Faculty of Organizational Sciences who are familiar with the AHP method. The evaluation was conducted in September 2017 and March 2018. The final values of the weight coefficients were obtained as the average value of all 72 vectors of the eigenvalues of the matrix, which are: $w_1 = 0.43$ (subjective teachers' efficiency), $w_2 = 0.21$ (objective teaching efficiency), and $w_3 = 0.36$ (research efficiency). The values obtained for the weight coefficients show that the subjective assessment of teaching has double the significance of the objective assessment of teaching. The teachers also considered that the importance of research work is 36% in the aggregated assessment of efficiency.

The final result for the efficiency indexes of the teachers and their rank are shown in Table 9.

The teachers were ranked based on the aggregated assessment of efficiency. Only two teachers had an aggregated efficiency index over 0.95. Rank 1 was assigned to DMU 10 (assistant professor); he/she was ranked first based on the objective assessment of efficiency. Rank 2 was assigned to DMU 23 (teaching assistant), given the slightly lower score of research efficiency, although he/she was first-ranked in teaching efficiency.

The lowest-ranked was DMU 4 (full professor), whose lectures were rated lowest by the students. His research efficiency was significantly higher than the results of the teacher ranked last but one (DMU 13), for whom the priorities were to improve the objective assessment both of teaching and scientific research work. This indicates the advantage of applying the proposed model for assessing the overall teachers' efficiency.

Two teachers (DMU 8 and DMU 22) have practically the same rating for teaching efficiency; however, DMU 22 dominates over DMU 8 based on scientific research work and acts as an exemplary model for it.

The importance of the results obtained by the AHP method confirms the use of only DEA. The input was a dummy and the output was three ratings. Twenty-one teachers had an efficiency index greater than 0.95, while 10 teachers had an efficiency index of 1. However, the AHP method enables comprehensive DMU ranking. Descriptive statistics (Table 9) show the research efficiency has the lowest average value of 0.81, while only six teachers were evaluated with a score higher or equal to 0.95. The average subjective and objective teaching efficiency are relatively balanced, around 0.89. Furthermore, 11 teachers might be considered as subjectively and 13 teachers as objectively good performers ($h_k \geq 0.95$). Accordingly, the potential for efficiency growth can be found in the improvements of research and publishing quality, which will have a positive impact on the citation. The improvement can be achieved by upgrading subjective teaching efficiency, since it is considered as the most important one ($w_1 = 0.43$). Particular focus should be on a methodical approach to teaching, a more understandable presentation of teaching content, and a slower lecture tempo as criteria of particular relevance to students.

5. Conclusions

Each entity aims to provide the most reliable, useful, and inexpensive business analysis. One of these entities is DEA, which can help managers make processes easier and focus on the key business competencies. DEA is an effective tool for evaluating and managing operational performances in a wide variety of settings. Since DEA gives different indexes of efficiencies with varying combinations of criteria, the selection of inputs and outputs is one of the essential steps in DEA.

The DEA efficiency index is a relative measure, depending on the number of DMUs and the number and structure of the criteria included in the analysis. It requires more considerable effort to determine the efficiency index of each DMU when there are a number of criteria. The criteria number is usually reduced using statistical methods such as regression and correlation analysis.

This paper suggests the use of conjoint analysis to select more relevant teaching criteria based on student preferences. The criteria importance values derived from stakeholder preferences are the basis for selection of the most appropriate set of criteria to be used in the DEA efficiency measurement phase. Applying the framework to the evaluation of teachers from the students' perspective shows that (a) not all criteria are equally important to stakeholders, and (b) the results vary depending on the method employed and the criteria selected for the evaluation. For this reason, this paper combines conjoint analysis as a method for revealing stakeholder preferences, and DEA as an "objective" method for evaluating performance, which does not require a priori weight determination. Additionally, DEA makes it possible to incorporate stakeholder preferences, either as weight restrictions or adequate criteria selection. The AHP method provides the ability to decompose the decision-making problems hierarchically and allows the DMU to be thoroughly ranked.

The methodological framework proposed in this paper has several advantages that can be summarized as follows:

- It allows subjective and objective efficiency assessment, as well as determining an overall efficiency score by considering the weights associated with the various aspects of efficiency;
- It provides better criteria selection that is well-matched for the stakeholders and allows the selection of different criteria combinations suitable for different objectives and numbers of DMUs;
- It incorporates students' preferences by selecting a meaningful and desirable set of criteria or imposing weight restrictions;
- It identifies key aspects of teaching that affect student satisfaction;

- It increases the discriminative power of the DEA and thus enables a more realistic ranking of teachers.

The value and validity of applying this original methodological framework are illustrated through the evaluation of teachers at the Faculty of Organizational Sciences. The significance of the proposed framework is particularly seen in its adaptability and flexibility. It also enables a straightforward interpretation of teachers' efficiency, of all the criteria that describe teaching and research, and provides a clear insight into which assessment is weak and which criterion is causing it. Therefore, teachers are suggested to improve teaching efficiency by observing their efficient colleagues and digging deep into content knowledge. At the institutional level, quality of research and publishing on one hand, and enhancement of presentation, methodical, and systematic approaches to lectures on the other hand, are the main drivers of teachers' efficiency augmentation.

Further research can be directed towards procedures for improving the assessment of universities, their departments, and staff, taking into account other relevant criteria such as the total number of publications and/or number of publications published in the last three years, the number of publications in journals indexed in the WoS and Scopus databases, average number of citations per publication, etc. The study can also be directed to other fields, including measuring the satisfaction of service users, where the proposed methodology would represent the general paradigm for measuring efficiency according to all the relevant criteria.

Author Contributions: Conceptualization, G.S. and M.K.; methodology, M.P., G.S. and M.K.; validation, M.P., G.S., M.K. and M.M.; formal analysis, M.P., G.S. and M.K.; investigation, M.P., G.S. and M.K.; writing—original draft preparation, M.P., G.S. and M.K.; visualization, M.P., G.S., M.K. and M.M.; writing—review and editing, M.P., G.S, M.K. and M.M. All authors have read and agreed to the published version of the manuscript.

Funding: This research was funded by the Ministry of Education, Science and Technological Development, Republic of Serbian, grants number TR33044 and III44007. The APC was partially funded by the Faculty of Organizational Sciences.

Conflicts of Interest: The authors declare no conflicts of interest.

References

1. Letcher, D.W.; Neves, J.S. Determinant of undergraduate business student satisfaction. *Res. High. Educ.* **2010**, *6*, 1–26.
2. Venesaar, U.; Ling, H.; Voolaid, K. Evaluation of the Entrepreneurship Education Programme in University: A New Approach. *Amfiteatru Econ.* **2011**, *8*, 377–391.
3. Johnes, G. Scale and technical efficiency in the production of economic research. *Appl. Econ. Lett.* **1995**, *2*, 7–11. [CrossRef]
4. Despotis, D.K.; Koronakos, G.; Sotiros, D. A multi-objective programming approach to network DEA with an application to the assessment of the academic research activity. *Procedia Comput. Sci.* **2015**, *55*, 370–379. [CrossRef]
5. Dommeyer, C.J.; Baum, P.; Chapman, K.; Hanna, R.W. Attitudes of Business Faculty Towards two Methods of Collecting Teaching Evaluations: Paper vs. Online. *Assess. Eval. High. Edu.* **2002**, *27*, 455–462. [CrossRef]
6. Zabaleta, F. The use and misuse of student evaluation of teaching. *Teach. High. Edu.* **2007**, *12*, 55–76. [CrossRef]
7. Onwuegbuzie, J.; Daniel, G.; Collins, T. A meta-validation model for assessing the score-validity of student teacher evaluations. *Qual. Quant.* **2009**, *43*, 197–209. [CrossRef]
8. Mazumder, S.; Kabir, G.; Hasin, M.; Ali, S.M. Productivity Benchmarking Using Analytic Network Process (ANP) and Data Envelopment Analysis (DEA). *Big Data Cogn. Comput.* **2018**, *2*, 27. [CrossRef]
9. Mulye, R. An empirical comparison of three variants of the AHP and two variants of conjoint analysis. *J. Behav. Decis. Mak.* **1998**, *11*, 263–280. [CrossRef]
10. Helm, R.; Scholl, A.; Manthey, L.; Steiner, M. Measuring customer preferences in new product development: Comparing compositional and decompositional methods. *Int. J. Product Developm.* **2004**, *1*, 12–29. [CrossRef]
11. Scholl, A.; Manthey, L.; Helm, R.; Steiner, M. Solving multiattribute design problems with analytic hierarchy process and conjoint analysis: An empirical comparison. *Eur. J. Oper. Res.* **2005**, *164*, 760–777. [CrossRef]

12. Helm, R.; Steiner, M.; Scholl, A.; Manthey, L. A Comparative Empirical Study on common Methods for Measuring Preferences. *Int. J. Manag. Decis. Mak.* **2008**, *9*, 242–265. [CrossRef]
13. Ijzerman, M.J.; Van Til, J.A.; Bridges, J.F. A comparison of analytic hierarchy process and conjoint analysis methods in assessing treatment alternatives for stroke rehabilitation. *Patient* **2012**, *5*, 45–56. [CrossRef] [PubMed]
14. Kallas, Z.; Lambarraa, F.; Gil, J.M. A stated preference analysis comparing the analytical hierarchy process versus choice experiments. *Food Qual. Prefer.* **2011**, *22*, 181–192. [CrossRef]
15. Danner, M.; Vennedey, V.; Hiligsmann, M.; Fauser, S.; Gross, C.; Stock, S. Comparing Analytic Hierarchy Process and Discrete-Choice Experiment to Elicit Patient Preferences for Treatment Characteristics in Age-Related Macular Degeneration. *Value Health* **2017**, *20*, 1166–1173. [CrossRef]
16. Popović, M.; Kuzmanović, M.; Savić, G. A comparative empirical study of Analytic Hierarchy Process and Conjoint analysis: Literature review. *Decis. Mak. Appl. Manag. Eng.* **2018**, *1*, 153–163. [CrossRef]
17. Pakkar, M.S. A hierarchical aggregation approach for indicators based on data envelopment analysis and analytic hierarchy process. *Systems* **2016**, *4*, 6. [CrossRef]
18. Sinuany-Stern, Z.; Mehrez, A.; Hadad, Y. An AHP/DEA methodology for ranking decision making units. *Int. Trans. Oper. Res.* **2000**, *7*, 109–124. [CrossRef]
19. Martić, M.; Savić, G. An application of DEA for comparative analysis and ranking of regions in Serbia with regards to social-economic development. *Eur. J. Oper. Res.* **2001**, *132*, 343–356. [CrossRef]
20. Feng, Y.J.; Lu, H.; Bi, K. An AHP/DEA method for measurement of the efficiency of R&D management activities in university. *Int. Trans. Oper. Res.* **2004**, *11*, 181–191. [CrossRef]
21. Tseng, Y.F.; Lee, T.Z. Comparing appropriate decision support of human resource practices on organizational performance with DEA/AHP model. *Expert Syst. Appl.* **2009**, *36*, 6548–6558. [CrossRef]
22. Saen, R.F.; Memariani, A.; Lotfi, F.H. Determining relative efficiency of slightly non-homogeneous decision making units by data envelopment analysis: A case study in IROST. *Appl. Math. Comput.* **2005**, *165*, 313–328. [CrossRef]
23. Zhu, J. DEA/AR analysis of the 1988–1989 performance of the Nanjing Textiles Corporation. *Ann. Oper. Res.* **1996**, *66*, 311–335. [CrossRef]
24. Seifert, L.M.; Zhu, J. Identifying excesses and deficits in Chinese industrial productivity (1953–1990): A weighted data envelopment analysis approach. *Omega* **1998**, *26*, 279–296. [CrossRef]
25. Premachandra, I.M. Controlling factor weights in data envelopment analysis by incorporating decision maker's value judgement: An approach based on AHP. *J. Inf. Manag. Sci.* **2001**, *12*, 1–12.
26. Lozano, S.; Villa, G. Multi-objective target setting in data envelopment analysis using AHP. *Comp. Operat. Res.* **2009**, *36*, 549–564. [CrossRef]
27. Kong, W.; Fu, T. Assessing the Performance of Business Colleges in Taiwan Using Data Envelopment Analysis and Student Based Value-Added Performance Indicators. *Omega* **2012**, *40*, 541–549. [CrossRef]
28. Korhonen, P.J.; Tainio, R.; Wallenius, J. Value efficiency analysis of academic research. *Eur. J. Oper. Res.* **2001**, *130*, 121–132. [CrossRef]
29. Cai, Y.Z.; Wu, W.J. Synthetic Financial Evaluation by a Method of Combining DEA with AHP. *Int. Trans. Oper. Res.* **2001**, *8*, 603–609. [CrossRef]
30. Johnes, J. Data envelopment analysis and its application to the measurement of efficiency in higher education. *Econ. Educ. Rev.* **2006**, *25*, 273–288. [CrossRef]
31. Yang, T.; Kuo, C.A. A hierarchical AHP/DEA methodology for the facilities layout design problem. *Eur. J. Oper. Res.* **2003**, *147*, 128–136. [CrossRef]
32. Ertay, T.; Ruan, D.; Tuzkaya, U.R. Integrating data envelopment analysis and analytic hierarchy for the facility layout design in manufacturing systems. *Inf. Sci.* **2006**, *176*, 237–262. [CrossRef]
33. Ramanathan, R. Data envelopment analysis for weight derivation and aggregation in the analytical hierarchy process. *Comput. Oper. Res.* **2006**, *33*, 1289–1307. [CrossRef]
34. Korpela, J.; Lehmusvaara, A.; Nisonen, J. Warehouse operator selection by combining AHP and DEA methodologies. *Int. J. Prod. Econ.* **2007**, *108*, 135–142. [CrossRef]
35. Jyoti, T.; Banwet, D.K.; Deshmukh, S.G. Evaluating performance of national R&D organizations using integrated DEA-AHP technique. *Int. J. Product. Perform. Manag.* **2008**, *57*, 370–388. [CrossRef]
36. Sueyoshi, T.; Shang, J.; Chiang, W.C. A decision support framework for internal audit prioritization in a rental car company: A combined use between DEA and AHP. *Eur. J. Oper. Res.* **2009**, *199*, 219–231. [CrossRef]

37. Mohajeri, N.; Amin, G. Railway station site selection using analytical hierarchy process and data envelopment analysis. *Comput. Ind. Eng.* **2010**, *59*, 107–114. [CrossRef]
38. Azadeh, A.; Ghaderi, S.F.; Mirjalili, M.; Moghaddam, M. Integration of analytic hierarchy process and data envelopment analysis for assessment and optimization of personnel productivity in a large industrial bank. *Expert Syst. Appl.* **2011**, *38*, 5212–5225. [CrossRef]
39. Raut, R.D. Environmental performance: A hybrid method for supplier selection using AHP-DEA. *Int. J. Bus. Insights Transform.* **2011**, *5*, 16–29.
40. Thanassoulis, E.; Dey, P.K.; Petridis, K.; Goniadis, I.; Georgiou, A.C. Evaluating higher education teaching performance using combined analytic hierarchy process and data envelopment analysis. *J. Oper. Res. Soc.* **2017**, *68*, 431–445. [CrossRef]
41. Wang, C.; Nguyen, V.T.; Duong, D.H.; Do, H.T. A Hybrid Fuzzy Analytic Network Process (FANP) and Data Envelopment Analysis (DEA) Approach for Supplier Evaluation and Selection in the Rice Supply Chain. *Symmetry* **2018**, *10*, 221. [CrossRef]
42. Salhieh, S.M.; All-Harris, M.Y. New product concept selection: An integrated approach using data envelopment analysis (DEA) and conjoint analysis (CA). *Int. J. Eng. Technol.* **2014**, *3*, 44–55. [CrossRef]
43. Charnes, A.; Cooper, W.W.; Rhodes, E. Measuring Efficiency of Decision Making Units. *Eur. J. Oper. Res.* **1978**, *2*, 429–444. [CrossRef]
44. Banker, R.D.; Charnes, A.; Cooper, W.W. Some models for estimating technical and scale inefficiencies in data envelopment analysis. *Manag. Sci.* **1984**, *30*, 1078–1092. [CrossRef]
45. Ahn, T.; Charnes, A.; Cooper, W.W. Efficiency characterizations in different DEA models. *Socio-Econ. Plan. Sci.* **1988**, *22*, 253–257. [CrossRef]
46. Banker, R.D.; Morey, R.C. The use of categorical variables in data envelopment analysis. *Manag. Sci.* **1986**, *32*, 1613–1627. [CrossRef]
47. Golany, B.; Roll, Y. An application procedure for DEA. *Omega* **1989**, *17*, 237–250. [CrossRef]
48. Emrouznejad, A.; Witte, K. COOPER-framework: A unified process for non-parametric projects. *Eur. J. Oper. Res.* **2010**, *207*, 1573–1586. [CrossRef]
49. Jenkins, L.; Anderson, M. A multivariate statistical approach to reducing the number of variables in data envelopment analysis. *Eur. J. Oper. Res.* **2003**, *147*, 51–61. [CrossRef]
50. Nunamaker, T.R. Using data envelopment analysis to measure the efficiency of non-profit organizations: A critical evaluation. *MDE Manag. Decis. Econ.* **1985**, *6*, 50–58. [CrossRef]
51. Morita, H.; Avkiran, K.N. Selecting inputs and outputs in data envelopment analysis by designing statistical experiments. *J. Oper. Res. Soc. Jpn.* **2009**, *52*, 163–173. [CrossRef]
52. Edirisinghe, N.C.; Zhang, X. Generalized DEA model of fundamental analysis and its application to portfolio optimization. *J. Bank. Financ.* **2007**, *31*, 3311–3335. [CrossRef]
53. Jablonsky, J. Multicriteria approaches for ranking of efficient units in DEA models. *Cent. Eur. J. Oper. Res.* **2011**, *20*, 435–449. [CrossRef]
54. Dimitrov, S.; Sutton, W. Promoting symmetric weight selection in data envelopment analysis: A penalty function approach. *Eur. J. Oper. Res.* **2010**, *200*, 281–288. [CrossRef]
55. Shi, H.; Wang, Y.; Zhang, X. A Cross-Efficiency Evaluation Method Based on Evaluation Criteria Balanced on Interval Weights. *Symmetry* **2019**, *11*, 1503. [CrossRef]
56. Thompson, R.G.; Singleton, F.D.; Thrall, M.R.; Smith, A.B. Comparative Site Evaluation for Locating a High-Energy Physics Lab in Texas. *Interfaces* **1986**, *16*, 35–49. [CrossRef]
57. Radojicic, M.; Savic, G.; Jeremic, V. Measuring the efficiency of banks: The bootstrapped I-distance GAR DEA approach. *Technol. Econ. Dev. Econ.* **2018**, *24*, 1581–1605. [CrossRef]
58. Addelman, S. Symmetrical and asymmetrical fractional factorial plans. *Technometrics* **1962**, *4*, 47–58. [CrossRef]
59. Popović, M.; Vagić, M.; Kuzmanović, M.; Labrović Anđelković, J. Understanding heterogeneity of students' preferences towards English medium instruction: A conjoint analysis approach. *Yug. J. Op. Res.* **2016**, *26*, 91–102. [CrossRef]
60. Kuzmanovic, M.; Makajic-Nikolic, D.; Nikolic, N. Preference Based Portfolio for Private Investors: Discrete Choice Analysis Approach. *Mathematics* **2020**, *8*, 30. [CrossRef]
61. Saaty, R.W. The analytic hierarchy process—What it is and how it is used. *J. Math. Model.* **1987**, *9*, 161–176. [CrossRef]

62. Stankovic, M.; Gladovic, P.; Popovic, V. Determining the importance of the criteria of traffic accessibility using fuzzy AHP and rough AHP method. *Decis. Mak. Appl. Manag. Eng.* **2019**, *2*, 86–104. [CrossRef]
63. Kuzmanović, M.; Savić, G.; Popović, M.; Martić, M. A new approach to evaluation of university teaching considering heterogeneity of students' preferences. *High. Educ.* **2013**, *66*, 153–171. [CrossRef]
64. Basso, A.; Funari, S. Introducing weights restrictions in data envelopment analysis models for mutual funds. *Mathematics* **2018**, *6*, 164. [CrossRef]
65. Buschken, J. When does data envelopment analysis outperform a naive efficiency measurement model? *Eur. J. Oper. Res.* **2009**, *192*, 647–657. [CrossRef]
66. Mester, G.L. Measurement of results of scientific work. *Tehnika* **2015**, *70*, 445–454. [CrossRef]
67. Hirsch, J.E. An index to quantify an individual's scientific research output. *Proc. Natl. Acad. Sci. USA* **2005**, *102*, 16569–16572. [CrossRef]
68. Available online: https://scholar.google.com/intl/en/scholar/citations.html (accessed on 9 January 2020.).

symmetry

MDPI

Article

Assessing Factors for Designing a Successful B2C E-Commerce Website Using Fuzzy AHP and TOPSIS-Grey Methodology

Ran Li [1,2,*] and Tao Sun [1]

1 College of Economics and Management, Nanjing University of Aeronautics and Astronautics, Nanjing 211106, Jiangsu, China; suntaonuaa@163.com

2 Jincheng College, Nanjing University of Aeronautics and Astronautics, Nanjing 211156, Jiangsu, China

* Correspondence: Li-ran@nuaa.edu.cn

Received: 23 January 2020; Accepted: 27 February 2020; Published: 2 March 2020

Abstract: The recent hype in online purchasing has skyrocketed the importance of the electronic commerce (e-commerce) industry. One of the core segments of this industry is business-to-consumer (B2C) where businesses use their websites to sell products and services directly to consumers. Thus, it must be taken care of that B2C websites are designed in a way which can build a trustworthy and long-term relationship between businesses and consumers. Thus, this study assesses and prioritizes factors for designing a successful B2C e-commerce website. The study employs multi-criteria decision making (MCDM), and to minimize any ambiguity and greyness in the decision-making, it integrates fuzzy and grey respectively with the Analytical Hierarchy Process (AHP) and Technique for Order of Preference by Similarity to Ideal Solution (TOPSIS) to form FAHP and TOPSIS-Grey. Initially, the study conducts a thorough literature survey to screen important factors reported in past studies. Five main factors and nineteen sub-factors were selected for further prioritization. Later, FAHP prioritized factors based on their importance. Finally, based on the FAHP results, TOPSIS-Grey ranked five alternatives (e-commerce websites). FAHP revealed "service quality" as the most successful website designing factor, while TOPSIS-Grey reported "Website-3" as the most successful website, having incorporated the factors required to design a successful website.

Keywords: B2C e-commerce factors; website; MCDM; Fuzzy AHP; TOPSIS-Grey; China

1. Introduction

The essence of marketing has changed with contemporary advancement and the development of the internet world, which have positively boosted the e-commerce trend [1]. E-commerce enables both consumers and companies to buy or sell products and offers varieties of services online, easily accessible quality products, and services that do not just save time but that also maximize profit or bargaining for both consumers and companies [2]. In this digital era, the e-commerce trend is increasing among people who want to buy and sell any products or services; and therefore, many researchers are interested to know in which way the success of e-commerce businesses inspires the consumers to buy and sell online. Researchers have determined that various important factors enhance the success of e-commerce businesses, and many companies or business owners are investing a gigantic amount of money on e-commerce websites. Many companies are trying hard to design a B2C e-commerce website that attracts their customers to buy and sell any product or service [3]. However, it is still very hard for many business owners to assess the success of B2C e-commerce websites, since various factors are involved. Moreover, the performance of B2C e-commerce depends upon the efficiency and success of the B2C e-commerce website. Therefore, it is important to assess and prioritize the B2C e-commerce websites since this is very vital for both customers and companies.

Moreover, the continuous development in e-commerce has expanded into five known categories: Business to Consumer (B2C), Business to Business (B2B), Consumer to Business (C2B), Consumer to Consumer (C2C), and Business-to-Government (B2G) [4]. Amazon is the best example of a B2C commerce which sells products and services to final consumers. Alibaba, a top-rated online platform, is an example of B2B commerce where companies deal only with companies. Upwork, formally known as Elance, is a C2B commerce where consumers post their project online and let companies bid for these projects. After that, consumers decide to select companies. A perfect example of C2C is eBay, where consumers find consumers to sell their products online. Upwork is an example of B2G, where businesses deal with the government and the government agencies to offer information, products, and services through online marketing. Business-to-Government (B2G) e-commerce offers competition among different companies to bid for government projects, products, and services that can later be acquired by the government from their organizations.

These are the popular categories of e-commerce; however, B2C happens to be a dominant form of e-commerce in today's online market matching with traditionally giant brink-and-mortar outlets. The currently most famous and top B2C e-commerce companies are Amazon, Alibaba, Walmart, Otto, JD.com, Priceline, eBay, and Rakuten [5]. These are the leading and most influential B2C e-commerce companies in the world. The popularity of B2C opens the business door for online companies to enjoy the high volume of sales every year. However, the rapid success and development of internet-based commerce also cause the sensitivity and vulnerability of consumers' privacy on B2C online platforms [6]. Therefore, this study focuses on the reliability of B2C online platforms to provide better services to final consumers.

Many marketing researchers apply multiple criteria decision making (MCDM) and several other approaches to B2C e-commerce related problems, such as Analytical Network Process (ANP) [7], Analytical Hierarchy Process (AHP) [8], Decision-Making Trial and Evaluation Laboratory (DEMATEL) [9], Technique for Order Performance by Similarity to Ideal Solution (TOPSIS) [10], Data Envelopment Analysis (DEA) [11], Grey Relational Analysis (GRA) [7], Preference Ranking Organisation METHod for Enrichment Evaluation (PROMETHEE) [12], and Vlse Kriterijumska Optimizacija Kompromisno Resenje (VIKOR) [13]. The PROMETHEE for Sustainability Assessment (PROSA) is also a very suitable method for determining any multi-faceted decision problem [14]. However, prior studies mainly focused on B2C e-commerce assessment; practical limitations should also be paid equal attention to. First, the evaluation of the B2C e-commerce platform primarily advances in terms of service quality [15]. Many marketing researchers believe that the level of the perceived service cannot just define the service quality, and they described the difference between the level of the perceived service and the level of the expected service [16,17].

Therefore, this study further contributes to the literature by integrating the Fuzzy AHP and TOPSIS-Grey methodology to assess the B2C e-commerce critical factors for designing a website. To the best of the author's knowledge, there is no such study conducted to evaluate B2C e-commerce factors using Fuzzy AHP and TOPSIS-Grey methodology. The Fuzzy AHP method deals with the hierarchical structure between main-factors (criteria) and sub-factors (sub-criteria). The fuzzy set theory was adopted to enhance the incapability of deterministic evaluation information in modeling the real problem. Furthermore, the TOPSIS-Grey method was utilized to determine the best-suited B2C e-commerce website in China. The proposed decision method is based on symmetric principal targets to evaluate the usability of the consumer information about the perceived reputation of the quality service of the B2C e-commerce platform. Additionally, practical applicability regarding making a decision under a complicated situation is a specific strength of this technique while assessing the B2C e-commerce platform.

This research paper is formatted as follows. Section 2 highlights the literature review on MCDM. Section 3 discusses the proposed methods of this paper. Section 4 broadens the understanding of the proposed method through results and a discussion. Finally, Section 5 sums up the paper with a conclusion, implications, and future directions.

2. Literature Review

Over the last twenty years, the usage of the internet has largely increased. In this era of modernization, the internet has become a key channel for powerful communication mechanisms to facilitate the processing of business and trade transactions effectively. Nowadays, business dealings mostly rely on e-commerce channels because they provide a fast and reliable quality service to the customer. The term e-commerce is defined as any form of business transaction in which the parties contact each other electronically rather than exchanging physically [18]. E-commerce refers to business activities containing manufacturers, consumers, intermediaries, and service providers using the internet [19]. E-commerce activities reduce the costs of business transactions and save time, which makes business efficient and practicable.

The B2C e-commerce evaluation is a crucial problem where complex trajectories are involved in making a final decision. Since the decision problems are complex, it is important to structure the problems to avoid any difficulty in accomplishing the task. Therefore, in this context, the MCDM approaches are considered significant to minimize the decision problem to some extent. The MCDM methods help decision-makers to assess and rank the alternative based on the evaluation of several criteria of a decision problem.

2.1. Application of MCDM Approaches in B2C E-Commerce Evaluation

The MCDM are widely used techniques in evaluating the B2C e-commerce critical factors for the successful designing of a website. Mardani et al. [20] investigated the MCDM method used in various decision problem studies. Here, Table 1 displays the MCDM methods used in previous studies related to the development of B2C e-commerce websites.

Table 1. Multi-criteria studies based on the assessment of B2C e-commerce websites.

Study Focus	Findings	Method	Year	Reference
An integrated model for the performance evaluation of e-commerce web sites	In the study, four criteria were undertaken, and the findings show that information quality is a more important criterion for evaluating e-commerce websites.	AHP and Intuitionistic Fuzzy TOPSIS (IFT)	2018	[21]
Assessing the websites of academic departments	In the research, 21 criteria were analyzed for 70 Turkish industrial engineering department websites. The results show that trust flow is a feasible criterion for assessing the websites.	Hesitant fuzzy AHP and TOPSIS	2019	[22]
Analyzing the museum websites known worldwide	The results present that usability is the most significant criteria for evaluating the five known museum websites of the world.	AHP and TOPSIS	2019	[23]
Evaluating and prioritizing the B2C e-commerce websites	The findings show that security, ease use, and appearance are the most important factors for successfully implementing e-commerce websites.	AHP and Fuzzy TOPSIS	2011	[10]
Assessment of website quality in the Turkish E-business market	In this research, nine sub-criteria under four main-criteria were undertaken. The results present that price saving, awareness, and security are the best-suited evaluated criteria for developing the B2C online shopping website.	Fuzzy AHP and Fuzzy TOPSIS	2010	[24]

Table 1. *Cont.*

Study Focus	Findings	Method	Year	Reference
An integrated approach for the assessment of e-commerce websites	The findings of this study reveal that system availability is a very crucial criteria, followed by privacy, fulfillment, and efficiency for assessing the e-commerce websites.	Single-Valued Trapezoidal Neutrosophic (SVTN) and DEMATEL	2017	[25]
Prioritization of B2C e-commerce website	In this study, the results present that content quality is ranked as the first factor, followed by usage and service quality for analyzing the B2C e-commerce websites.	AHP and TOPSIS	2018	[26]
Assessing and improving the e-store business	The findings show creatively and innovatively improved strategies to optimize each dimension and criterion at a high level for B2C e-commerce business.	DANP and GRA	2013	[27]
Assessment of five-star hotel websites in Mashhad	The findings of this study show that customer orientation is an important criterion for the assessment of hotel websites, followed by marketing, security, and technology.	PROMETHEE	2019	[12]
Evaluation of e-commerce security	This study focuses on B2C e-commerce website security. It is very critical to have complete security of e-commerce because of complex security issues and cybersecurity limitations to acquire control over threats possessed by hackers.	AHP and Evidential Reasoning	2012	[8]

It is identified in the literature that numerous studies relate to the evaluation of B2C e-commerce websites by determining the critical factors. These studies used numerous MCDM methods to assess the decision problem. This research further contributes to the state-of-the-art methods by developing an integrated decision framework comprising of Fuzzy AHP and TOPSIS-Grey methodology to assess the B2C e-commerce websites in the context of China. The Fuzzy AHP is widely recognized as one of the effective techniques for the weight allocation of criteria and sub-criteria. It has the advantage of simplicity and ease of use, but it is not sufficient to take into account the uncertainty related to the mapping of one's perception to a number. Moreover, the qualitative assessment of respondent judgement is vague, and it is not reasonable to represent it in terms of precise numbers. As such, in order to address this apprehension, the TOPSIS-Grey concept was proposed in this study to compensate for the insufficiency of Fuzzy AHP regarding the uncertainty problem, to identify the ideal alternative solutions.

2.2. *Proposed B2C E-Commerce Factors*

This research identifies and evaluates several key factors for the designing of a B2C e-commerce website. These factors are very important and are considered as a supporting mechanism for evaluating a feasible e-commerce website. In the present study, a detailed literature review was analyzed to determine the most feasible factors for a B2C e-commerce website. Thus, in the study, five factors and 19 sub-factors were identified through the set of the literature review. These main e-commerce factors are design (D), information (I), service quality (Q), security/privacy (S), and customer support and service (C). Table 2 presents the B2C e-commerce website factors.

Table 2. B2C e-commerce website factors, sub-factors, and their description.

Main Factor	Sub-Factor	Factor-Type	Description	Reference
Design (D)	Attractiveness (D-1)	Benefit	The information and appearance on the B2C e-commerce website should be well-organized and should appear in such a way as to attract its customers or website users.	[10,25,26]
	Easy navigation (D-2)	Benefit	The B2C e-commerce website must be easy to navigate so that the visitors may quickly find the related information that interests them.	[8,13,25]
	Content (D-3)	Benefit	The web content refers to the aural, visual, or textual content available on the website. The content means the website must be creative in the sense of applications, text, images, e-service, and data.	[10,12]
	Speed (D-4)	Benefit	The speed refers to the website that runs immediately after opening, and it means the average response time should be fast.	[10,25,26]
	Mobile-friendly (D-5)	Benefit	A B2C e-commerce website that has a mobile-friendly site or application is considered to be more appropriate for users because it can be displayed on mobile devices such as smartphones or tablets.	[28,29]
Information (I)	Effective search tool (I-1)	Benefit	The effective search tool in the website refers to a web-search engine that is designed to carry advanced features for users to find out the product by defining keywords.	[22,25]
	Availability of information to compare across alternatives (I-2)	Benefit	This sub-factor is defined as the availability of item stocks or accurate information on the website that is claimed as being available. The website which has accurate information is considered feasible for users.	[8,25]
	Contact information (I-3)	Benefit	The contact information refers to the standard web page on an e-commerce website, which allows users to contact the website company for any information, query, or problem.	[30,31]
	FAQs (I-4)	Benefit	In the B2C e-commerce websites, the frequently asked questions (FAQs) option is very important, since it provides useful information relating to the business and answers to a question on a particular topic.	[32,33]
Service Quality (Q)	Trust (Q-1)	Benefit	Trust refers to the truthfulness about the product or service on the website. Additionally, a trusted website does not harm the computer. Therefore, the website should be well trusted.	[10,22]
	Payment alternatives (Q-2)	Benefit	The payment alternative on a B2C e-commerce website offers various payment options or billing solutions for its users to buy any product or service very easily.	[26,34]
	On-time delivery (Q-3)	Benefit	The on-time delivery of products or items when promised. The B2C e-commerce website that delivers items to its users timely is considered as being important in the e-market.	[8,25,35]
	Easy returns (Q-4)	Benefit	B2C e-commerce must have a flexible policy for the exchange or return of any product or item to avoid disputes between its consumer and the owner of the business.	[26,36]
Security/Privacy (S)	Account security (S-1)	Benefit	Account security refers to the ability to provide protection and safety to a customer or online user account, since customers take the risk of providing personal and financial information on the website.	[6,25]
	Secure payment (S-2)	Benefit	B2C e-commerce websites must have secure payment options to protect the information of a customer's credit card. Therefore, the website should have well-established privacy for online payments.	[6,25,26]
	Non-sharing personal information (S-3)	Cost	A B2C e-commerce website does not share its user's or customers' information with other websites or databases. This is considered crucial for e-business success.	[8,25]

Table 2. *Cont.*

Main Factor	Sub-Factor	Factor-Type	Description	Reference
Customer service and support (C)	Feedback mechanism (C-1)	Benefit	A B2C e-commerce website should have a feedback mechanism where customers can provide feedback about the positive or negative aspects of the product or service.	[7,26,37]
	Order tracking (C-2)	Benefit	Order tracking refers to the current time tracking, on a website, of a product or item which has been ordered by its customer. This is also a vital sub-factor for B2C e-commerce websites.	[10,26,35]
	Assisting in solving delivery dispute (C-3)	Benefit	A B2C e-commerce website provides or helps its customers in solving delivery disputes which sometimes arise due to the return of funds or products.	[36,38]

It is observed that MCDM methods are comprehensively utilized in analyzing the critical factors for evaluating the successful implementation of e-commerce websites. The MCDM methods have been considered as very effective and efficient in solving multi-faceted decision problems. To the best of our knowledge, this is the very first study that analyzes the B2C e-commerce factors of websites using the Fuzzy AHP and TOPSIS-Grey methodology in the context of China.

3. Research Methodology

Many decision problems are too multifaceted to be solved quantitatively. In such cases, the use of MCDM proves to be the best choice due to their ability to deal with the multidimensionality of decision-making problems [39,40]. However, while solving such problems qualitatively, people tend to use imprecise knowledge rather than precise knowledge. Therefore, MCDM methods are integrated with fuzzy set theory and grey theory to minimize uncertainty and greyness in people's feedback. So, this study combines Fuzzy AHP, TOPSIS and Grey theory to rank e-commerce websites. We firstly define Fuzzy AHP, TOPSIS, and Grey theory individually and then introduce and present the procedure of the proposed Fuzzy AHP and TOPSIS-Grey methodology.

3.1. Fuzzy AHP Method

Fuzzy AHP applies for triangular fuzzy numbers (TFNs) to construct a pairwise matrix of decision-makers' preference [41,42]. This study has followed [43] to apply FAHP. The steps of FAHP are given as:

Step 1: The initial step of FAHP transforms the problem into a hierarchal structure.

Step 2: Construct a pairwise matrix of attributes using TFNs provided in Table 3.

Table 3. Fuzzy Scale using TFNs.

Linguistic Preference	TFNs
Equally-preferred	(1,1,1)
Moderately-preferred	(2/3,1,3/2)
Strongly-preferred	(3/2,2,5/2)
Very strongly-preferred	(5/2,3,7/2)
Extremely-preferred	(7/2,4,9/2)

TFNs define relative significance values to incorporate human judgement. For an inverse comparison, reciprocal values are assigned, for example, $x_{ji} = \frac{1}{x_{ij}}$, where x_{ji} denotes the significance of ith element to jth element. Subsequently, a fuzzy matrix $\widetilde{D}$ can be given as:

$$\widetilde{D} = \begin{bmatrix} 1 & \widetilde{x}_{12} & \cdots & \widetilde{x}_{1n} \\ \widetilde{x}_{21} & 1 & \cdots & \widetilde{x}_{2n} \\ \cdots & \cdots & \cdots & \cdots \\ \widetilde{x}_{n1} & \widetilde{x}_{n2} & \cdots & 1 \end{bmatrix} \tag{1}$$

where $(\widetilde{x}_{ij} = 1)$, if $(i = j)$; and $(\widetilde{x}_{ij} = \widetilde{1}, \widetilde{3}, \widetilde{5}, \widetilde{7}, \widetilde{9})$ or $(\widetilde{x}_{ij} = \widetilde{1}^{-1}, \widetilde{3}^{-1}, \widetilde{5}^{-1}, \widetilde{7}^{-1}, 9^{-1})$ if $(i \neq j)$.

Step 3: The third step aggregates the judgement of individuals and then generates priority vectors of the group. Two common aggregation approaches are provided in the literature. The first one involves aggregating individual priorities (AIP), and the second one involves aggregating individual judgements (AIJ). AIP is proficient for aggregating when group members unite for decision while AIJ is applicable when group members make a decision individually. This study applies AIJ because it addresses experts' judgements earlier and avoids re-evaluation if inconsistencies arise while ranking the alternatives. Subsequently, we express the TFN score assigned by i expert on j component as $\widetilde{w}_{ij} = \left(x_{ij}, y_{ij}, z_{ij}\right)$, where $(i = 1,2,3,\ldots,n)$ and $(j = 1,2,3,\ldots,m)$. The aggregate judgement $\widetilde{w}_{ij} = (x_i, y_i, z_i)$, where $(j = 1,2,3,\ldots,m)$ of a group is given by $x_j = \underset{i}{Min}\left\{x_{ij}\right\}$, $y_j = \frac{1}{n}\sum_{i=1}^{n} y_{ij}$, and $z_j = \underset{i}{Max}\left\{z_{ij}\right\}$. The crisp value of TFN $\widetilde{w}_{ij} = (x_i, y_i, z_i)$, where $(j = 1,2,3,\ldots,m)$, is computed by $w_j = \left[\frac{x_j + (4 \times y_j) + z_j}{6}\right]$.

Step 4: The consistency index CI given in Equation (2) is used to check the consistency of the matrix:

$$CI = \frac{\lambda_{max} - n}{n - 1} \tag{2}$$

where n denotes the matrix's size.

The consistency ratio CR provided in Equation (3) has been applied to check the consistency of judgement:

$$CR = \frac{CI}{RI} \tag{3}$$

where RI represents the random index, whose values are given in Table 4. Only if the value of CR is less than 0.1 is the judgment matrix considered as consistent.

Table 4. *RI*.

n	1	2	3	4	5	6	7	8
RI	0	0	0.52	0.89	1.11	1.25	1.35	1.40

3.2. TOPSIS Method

TOPSIS is one of the most famous approaches of the MCDM techniques [41]. The method was proposed by Hwang and Yoon for the first time in 1981 [44]. According to the TOPSIS method, the optimal solution point is nearest to the "positive ideal solution" and farthest from the "negative ideal solution." The positive ideal solution is the one that maximizes (minimizes) benefit criteria (cost criteria). Conversely, the negative ideal solution minimizes (maximizes) benefit criteria (cost criteria) [45,46]. The following are the seven steps involved in a typical procedure of the TOPSIS method:

Step 1: Construct a decision matrix.

Let us define a decision matrix D as:

$$D = \begin{bmatrix} x_{11} & x_{12} & x_{13} & \cdots & x_{1m} \\ x_{21} & x_{22} & x_{23} & \cdots & x_{2m} \\ x_{31} & x_{32} & x_{33} & \cdots & x_{3m} \\ \cdots & \cdots & \cdots & \cdots & \cdots \\ x_{n1} & x_{n2} & x_{n3} & \cdots & x_{nm} \end{bmatrix} \quad (4)$$

where the decision matrix D has n alternatives and m criteria; x_{ij} evaluates the ith alternative with respect to the jth criteria.

Step 2: Normalize the decision matrix D using Equation (5) as given below:

$$g_{ij} = \frac{x_{ij}}{\sqrt{\sum_{j=1}^{m} x_{ij}^2}}, \ (j = 1,2,3,\ldots,m), \ (i = 1,2,3,\ldots,n) \quad (5)$$

Step 3: Transform the normalized matrix into a weighted normalized matrix using Equation (6):

$$q_{ij} = w_j g_{ij}, \ (j = 1,2,3,\ldots,m), \ (i = 1,2,3,\ldots,n) \quad (6)$$

where w_j is the criteria weight of the jth criteria, and the sum of weights of all the criteria is equal to 1.

Step 4: Find out the ideal positive solution (A^+) and ideal negative solution (A^-) using Equations (7) and (8), respectively:

$$A^+ = \left\{ \left(\max_i q_{ij} \middle| j \in J \right), \left(\min_i q_{ij} \middle| j \in J' \right) \middle| i \in n \right\} = \left[q_1^+, q_2^+, q_3^+, \ldots, q_m^+ \right] z \quad (7)$$

$$A^- = \left\{ \left(\min_i q_{ij} \middle| j \in J \right), \left(\max_i q_{ij} \middle| j \in J' \right) \middle| i \in n \right\} = \left[q_1^-, q_2^-, q_3^-, \ldots, q_m^- \right] \quad (8)$$

where J denotes the benefit-type criteria (larger the better), while J' represents the cost-type criteria (smaller the better).

Step 5: Calculate the distance between the optimal point and ideal positive and ideal negative solutions using the Euclidean distance [47]. For a benefit-type criterion, the distance can be calculated using Equation (9), and for a cost-type criterion, Equation (10) can be used to find the distance:

$$d_i^+ = \left[\sum_{j=1}^{m} \left(q_{ij} - q_j^+ \right)^2 \right]^{1/2}, \ (i = 1,2,3,\ldots,n) \quad (9)$$

$$d_i^- = \left[\sum_{j=1}^{m} \left(q_{ij} - q_j^- \right)^2 \right]^{1/2}, \ (i = 1,2,3,\ldots,n) \quad (10)$$

Step 6: Compute the relative closeness (C_i^+) to the ideal solution using Equation (11):

$$C_i^+ = \frac{d_i^-}{d_i^+ + d_i^-}, \ (i = 1,2,3,\ldots,n) \quad (11)$$

Step 7: Rank the alternatives based on the C_i^+ score; the larger score of C_i^+ indicates the better alternative.

3.3. Grey Theory

The Grey theory is a mathematical theory proposed by Professor Deng in 1982. The theory was founded on the concept of a grey set. The theory introduces a grey number that can effectively solve problems that involve uncertainty and have insufficient or incomplete data [48]. Let us define a grey number $\otimes X = [\underline{x}, \overline{x}]$, where $\underline{x}$, and $\overline{x}$ are real numbers showing lower and upper limits, respectively. If the values of both $\underline{x}$, and $\overline{x}$ are known, then the number is called a white number, which translates the availability of complete information. In the case where both $\underline{x}$, and $\overline{x}$ are unknown, then the number is called a black number, which means the information is not meaningful. A grey number $\otimes X$ means that the exact value of a number is unknown; however, it is certain that the value is not lower than $\underline{x}$ and not greater than $\overline{x}$. We can define the value of a grey number as $\underline{x} \leq \otimes X \leq \overline{x}$. Mathematical operations on grey numbers $\otimes a + \otimes b$ can be done as below [49]:

$$\otimes a + \otimes b = \left[\underline{a} + \underline{b}; \overline{a} + \overline{b}\right] \tag{12}$$

$$\otimes a - \otimes b = \left[\underline{a} - \underline{b}; \overline{a} - \overline{b}\right] \tag{13}$$

$$\otimes a * \otimes b = \left[\min(\underline{a}\underline{b}, \overline{a}\overline{b}, \overline{a}\underline{b}, \underline{a}\overline{b}); \max(\underline{a}\underline{b}, \overline{a}\overline{b}, \overline{a}\underline{b}, \underline{a}\overline{b})\right] \tag{14}$$

$$\otimes a : \otimes b = \otimes a * \left[\frac{1}{\overline{b}}, \frac{1}{\underline{b}}\right]; 0 \notin \otimes b \tag{15}$$

Since grey numbers are a special case of fuzzy numbers, we can therefore transform TFNs $\widetilde{a} = (a_1, a_2, a_3)$ and $\widetilde{b} = (b_1, b_2, b_3)$ into the grey numbers $\otimes a = [a_1, a_2]$ and $\otimes b = [b_1, b_2]$ using the Euclidean distance between the grey numbers ($\otimes a$, $\otimes b$), as given in Equation (16):

$$d(\otimes a, \otimes b) = \sqrt{\frac{1}{2}\left[\left(\underline{a} - \underline{b}\right)^2 + \left(\overline{a} - \overline{b}\right)^2\right]} \tag{16}$$

3.4. Proposed Integrated Fuzzy AHP and TOPSIS-Grey Methodology

The proposed integrated method combines two widely used MCDM techniques, i.e., AHP and TOPSIS, with fuzzy theory and grey theory to form the integrated Fuzzy AHP and TOPSIS-Grey method. The method starts by developing the hierarchal structure of the problem and then computing weights of the criteria. Later, TOPSIS-Grey is applied to rank the alternatives. Figure 1 presents the structure of how the model is executed.

The following are the steps involved in ranking the alternatives using the Fuzzy AHP and TOPSIS-Grey approach:

Step 1: Develop the hierarchal structure of the problem by defining the goal, criteria, and alternatives to be evaluated.

Step 2: Compute the weights of criteria using Fuzzy AHP.

Step 3: Rate alternatives with respect to each criterion using the linguistic values given in Table 5.

Table 5. Grey scale for rating alternatives with respect to criteria.

Linguistic	$\otimes$X
Very low (VL)	[0, 1]
Low (L)	[1, 3]
Moderate Low (ML)	[3, 4]
Moderate (M)	[4, 5]
Moderate High (MH)	[5, 6]
High (H)	[6, 9]
Very High (VH)	[9, 10]

Step 4: Define the TOPSIS-Grey decision matrix D^k as:

$$\mathrm{D}^k = \begin{bmatrix} \otimes x^k_{11} & \otimes x^k_{12} & \otimes x^k_{13} & \cdots & \otimes x^k_{1m} \\ \otimes x^k_{21} & \otimes x^k_{22} & \otimes x^k_{23} & \cdots & \otimes x^k_{2m} \\ \otimes x^k_{31} & \otimes x^k_{32} & \otimes x^k_{33} & \cdots & \otimes x^k_{3m} \\ \cdots & \cdots & \cdots & \cdots & \cdots \\ \otimes x^k_{n1} & \otimes x^k_{n2} & \otimes x^k_{n3} & \cdots & \otimes x^k_{nm} \end{bmatrix} \tag{17}$$

where $\otimes x^k_{\mathrm{ij}}$ represents a grey evaluation of the ith alternative with respect to the jth criteria by the decision-maker k ($k = 1, 2, 3, \ldots, K$); $\otimes x^k_i = [\otimes x^k_{i1}, \otimes x^k_{i2}, \otimes x^k_{i3}, \ldots, \otimes x^k_{im}]$ represents an evaluation of the ith alternative by the kth decision-maker.

Step 5: Normalize D^k using Equation (18) (for the benefit-type criteria) and Equation (19) (for the cost-type criteria):

$$\otimes g_{ij} = \frac{\otimes x_{ij}}{\max_i(\overline{x}_{ij})} = \left(\frac{\underline{x}_{ij}}{\max_i(\overline{x}_{ij})}; \frac{\overline{x}_{ij}}{\max_i(\overline{x}_{ij})}\right) \tag{18}$$

$$\otimes g_{ij} = 1 - \frac{\otimes x_{ij}}{\max_i(\overline{x}_{ij})} = \left(1 - \frac{\overline{x}_{ij}}{\max_i(\overline{x}_{ij})}; 1 - \frac{\underline{x}_{ij}}{\max_i(\overline{x}_{ij})}\right) \tag{19}$$

where $\underline{x}_{ij}$ denotes the interval's lower value, and $\overline{x}_{ij}$ denotes the interval's upper value.

Step 6: Compute a positive ideal alternative A^{k+}_i and a negative ideal alternative A^{k-}_i using Equations (20) and (21), respectively:

$$A^{k+}_i = \left\{\left(\max_i \overline{g}_{ij} \middle| j \in J\right), \left(\min_i \underline{g}_{ij} \middle| j \in J'\right) \middle| i \in n\right\} = \left[g^+_1, g^+_2, g^+_3, \ldots, g^+_m\right] \tag{20}$$

$$A^{k-}_i = \left\{\left(\min_i \underline{g}_{ij} \middle| j \in J\right), \left(\max_i \overline{g}_{ij} \middle| j \in J'\right) \middle| i \in n\right\} = \left[g^+_1, g^+_2, g^+_3, \ldots, g^+_m\right] \tag{21}$$

where J denotes the benefit-type criteria (larger the better), while J' represents the cost-type criteria (smaller the better).

Step 7: Compute the alternatives' positive ideal solution distance d^{k+}_i and negative ideal solution distance d^{k-}_i using Equations (22) and (23), respectively:

$$d^{k+}_i = \left\{\frac{1}{2\sum w_j\left[\left|g^{k+}_j - \underline{g}^k_{ij}\right|^p + \left|g^{k+}_j - \overline{g}^k_{ij}\right|^p\right]}\right\}^{1/p} \tag{22}$$

$$d^{k-}_i = \left\{\frac{1}{2\sum w_j\left[\left|g^{k-}_j - \underline{g}^k_{ij}\right|^p + \left|g^{k-}_j - \overline{g}^k_{ij}\right|^p\right]}\right\}^{1/p} \tag{23}$$

In Equations (22) and (23), $p = 2$ (Euclidean distance function), and w_j is the weight of the jth criteria determined using Fuzzy AHP.

Step 8: Obtain the relative closeness (C^+_i) to the ideal solution using Equation (24):

$$\mathrm{C}^+_i = \frac{d^-_i}{d^+_i + d^-_i}, \ (i = 1, 2, 3, \ldots, n) \tag{24}$$

Step 9: Rank the alternatives based on the C_i^+ score; the larger score of C_i^+ indicates the better alternative.

The steps of the above proposed Fuzzy AHP and TOPSIS-Grey methods would provide meaningful results to determine this decision problem.

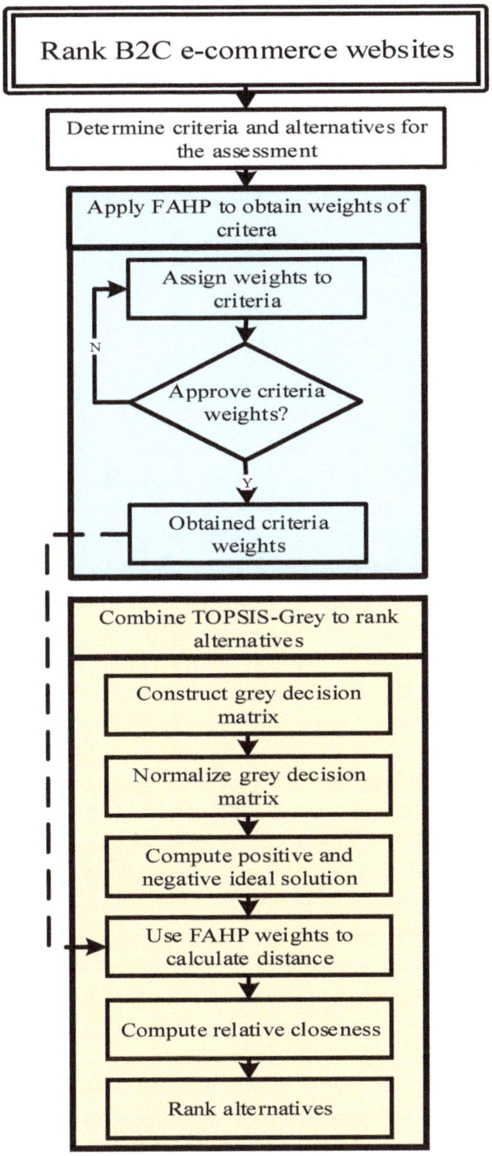

Figure 1. Schematic of the model formulation.

4. Results and Discussion

In the present research, the Fuzzy AHP and TOPSIS-Grey methodology has been presented in a real-life case study. This integrated decision framework outlines a feasible and systemic approach for government and managers toward assessing and prioritizing the B2C e-commerce factors for designing a website. The case analysis of the study is shown in the following sub-section.

4.1. Case Analysis

This case study is from the B2C e-commerce shopping websites in China, which sell various products to the consumers. These companies operate their e-commerce websites and simultaneously plan to introduce B2C e-commerce websites in order to expand their market. Meanwhile, each B2C e-commerce business has different requirements, processes, and related costs. Therefore, it is significant to understand the role of B2C e-commerce to implement the website in the electronic market successfully. In this study, five B2C e-commerce websites were evaluated and ranked based on the identified factors and sub-factors. The information or names of the websites are not exposed, and we define them as Website-1, Website-2, Website-3, Website-4, and Website-5. To evaluate feasible websites, the present study implemented the Fuzzy AHP and TOPSIS-Grey approach with respect to the proposed B2C e-commerce factors.

4.2. Fuzzy AHP Results

The results of this study are divided into two parts. The first part presents the result and analysis of Fuzzy AHP, which is used to assign the weights of main-factors and sub-factors. The second part presents the ranking of alternatives computed by applying TOPSIS-Grey. The study involved 15 experts to rate each factor (criteria) and sub-factor (sub-criteria) using linguistic values which were converted into crisp values. Initially, Fuzzy AHP transformed the problem into a hierarchal structure that is provided in Figure 2.

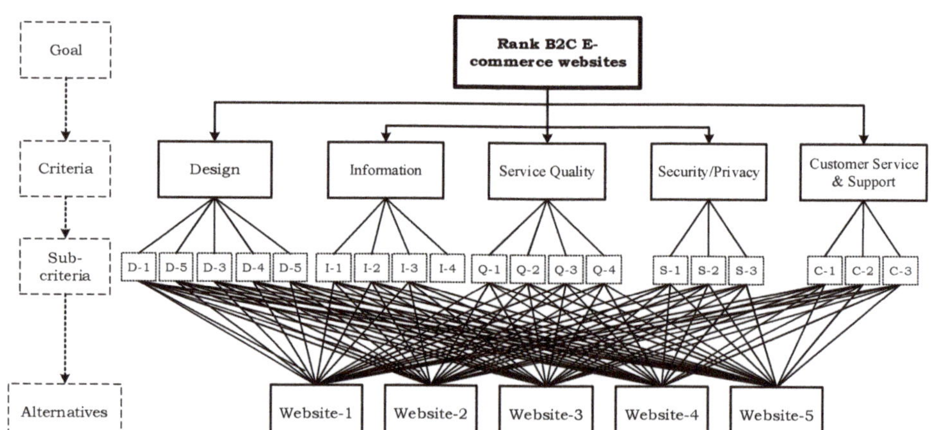

Figure 2. The hierarchical structure of the decision problem.

4.3. Main-Factors Weights

After transforming the problem into a hierarchal structure, the Fuzzy AHP computed the weight of the main factor (Design, Information, Service Quality, Security/Privacy, and Customer Support & Services). The pairwise matrix of the main factor is given in the Appendix A section. By solving the pairwise matrix, we obtained the main factor weights, which are presented in Figure 3. It can be seen that the Service Quality criterion was rated as the most critical successful factor in designing a B2C e-commerce website by receiving a 25.8% weight. The Security/Privacy criterion obtained the second-highest weight of 24.5%, which is nearly 5% lower than the weight of the Service Quality criterion. Thus, it can be said that both factors hold significant importance and must be given due consideration while designing the website. The third criterion in the row is Design, which received a

17.9% weight, followed respectively by the Information criterion (16.4%) and the Customer Service & Support criterion (15.4%).

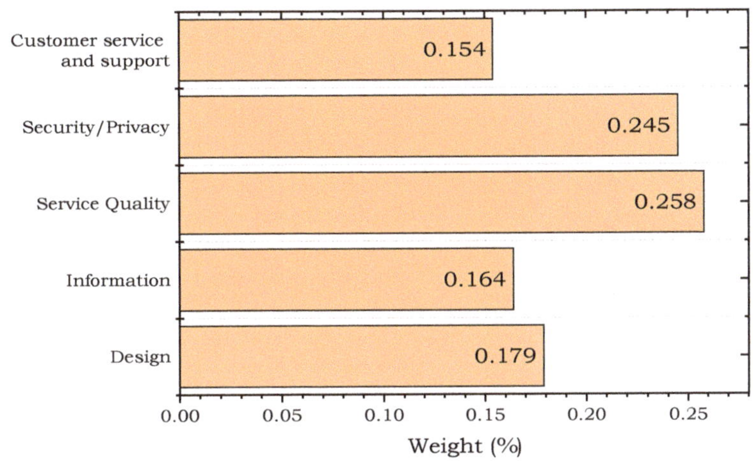

Figure 3. The B2C e-commerce factor (criteria) results with respect to the goal.

4.4. *Weights of Sub-Factors (Design)*

After computing the main factor's weights, the Fuzzy AHP computed the weights of sub-factors with respect to the main factor using similar steps to those used for calculating the weights of the main factor. A total of five pairwise matrices were constructed (one for each main criteria), which are given in Appendix A (Tables A2–A6). By solving these matrices, we get the sub-factor weights with respect to their respective main factor. Figure 4 presents the weights of sub-factors with respect to the Design criterion. Under this criterion, the sub-criterion Attractiveness (D-1) received the highest weights of 22.8%, followed respectively by Speed (D-4) 22.1%, Content (D-3) 22.4%, Easy Navigation (D-2) 17.4%, and Mobile-friendly (D-5) 16.3%.

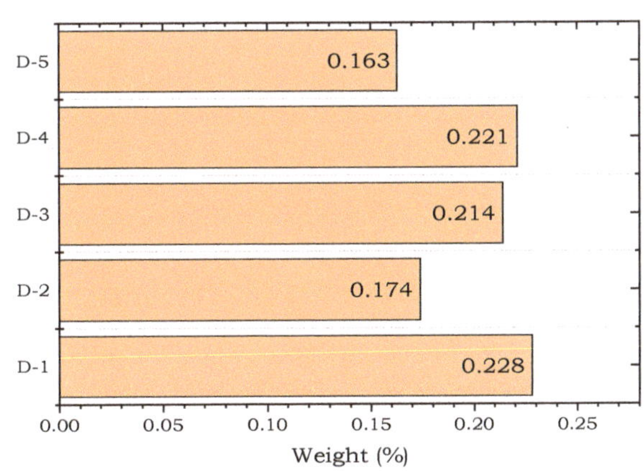

Figure 4. The sub-factor results with respect to the design.

4.5. *Weights of Sub-Factors (Information)*

Figure 5 contains the weights of sub-factors with respect to Information. It shows that the Effective search tool (I-1) criterion obtained the highest weight of 28.3%, followed respectively by

Availability of information to compare across alternatives (I-2) 27% and Contact Information (I-3) 23.1%. The sub-criterion FAQs (I-4) received the least weight of 21.6%, under the Information criterion.

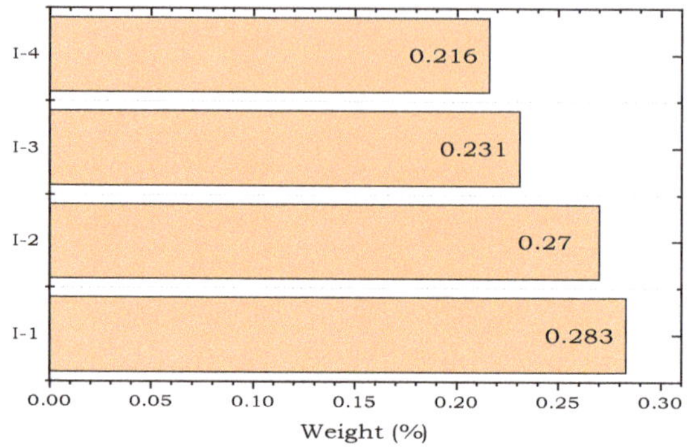

Figure 5. The sub-factor results with respect to the information.

4.6. Weights of Sub-Factors (Service Quality)

Figure 6 shows the sub-factor weights with respect to the Service Quality criterion. It can be seen that the sub-criterion Trust (Q-1) received the highest weight of 33.2%. The sub-criterion Easy Returns (Q-4) got the second-highest weight of 30.6%. The On-time delivery (Q-3) and Payment Alternatives (Q-2) sub-factors obtained the second lowest and lowest weights of 22% and 14.2%, respectively.

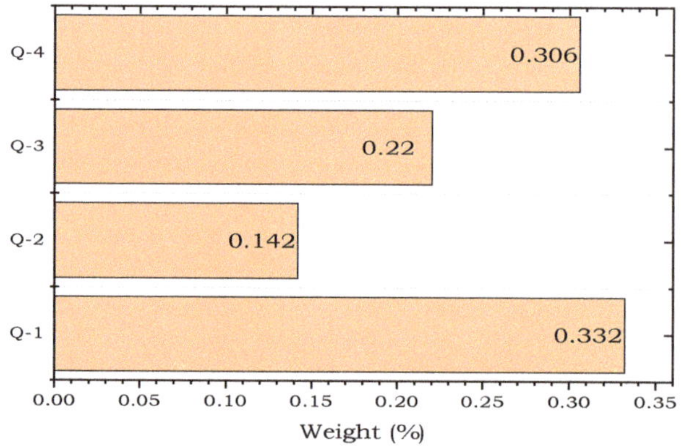

Figure 6. The sub-factor results with respect to the service quality.

4.7. Weights of Sub-Factors (Security/Privacy)

Figure 7 displays the weights of the sub-factors with respect to the Security/Privacy criterion. The Secure Payment (S-2) sub-criterion achieved 51.6% of the weight, which is the highest weight received under the Security/Privacy criterion. The Account Security (S-1) sub-criterion received 30.9%, while Non-sharing personal information (S-3) got the lowest weight of 17.5%.

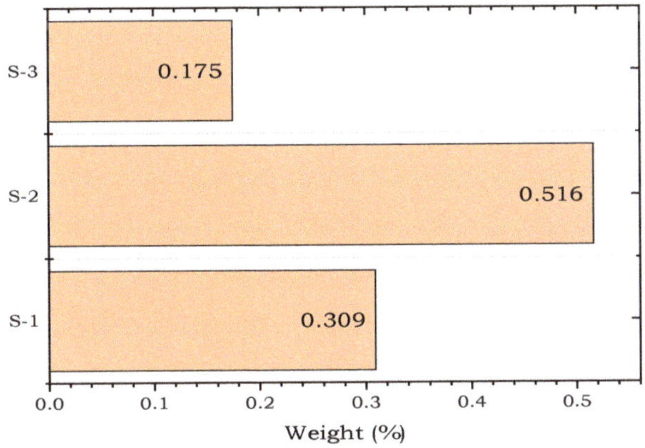

Figure 7. The sub-factor results with respect to the security/privacy.

4.8. Weights of Sub-Factors (Customer Service & Support)

Figure 8 provides the weights of the sub-factors under the Customer Service & Support criterion. Order Tracking (C-2) received the highest weight of 38.6% under this criterion, followed respectively by Assisting in solving delivery issues (C-3) 33.1% and Feedback mechanism (C-1) 28.3%.

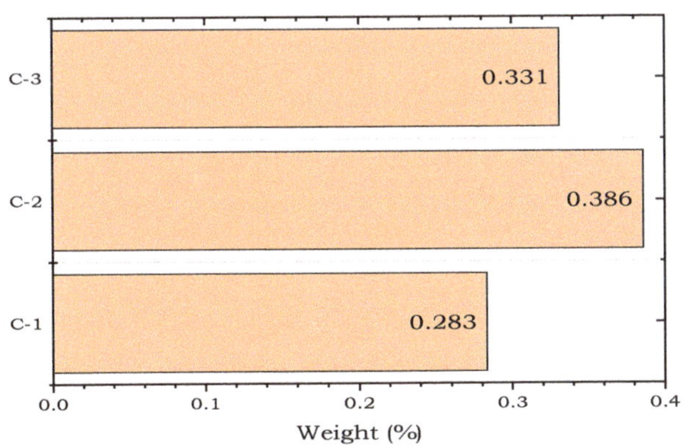

Figure 8. The sub-factors result with respect to the Customer Service & Support.

4.9. Final Ranking of Overall Factors

After obtaining the main factor weights and sub-factor weights (with respect to the main criteria), we finally computed the final weights of sub-factors, which shall be employed in TOPSIS-Grey to rank the alternatives. The final weights of sub-factors were calculated by multiplying the initial weights of sub-factors with weights of their respective main factor. Table 6 lists the final weights of sub-factors and their overall ranking. The Secure payment (S-2) sub-factor ranked as the most important among the 19 sub-factors. In contrast, the Mobile-friendly (D-5) sub-factor was the least significant factor. A rationale behind the low ranking of the D-5 sub-factor is perhaps because people tend to use mobile apps instead of browsing online on shopping websites, and most of the famous online stores already have mobile apps for online shopping.

Table 6. Final weights of overall B2C e-commerce factors.

Main Factor	Main Factor Weight	Sub-Factor	Sub-Factor Code	Sub-Factor Initial Weights	Sub-Factor Final Weights
Design (D)	0.179	Attractiveness	D-1	0.228	0.041
		Easy Navigation	D-2	0.174	0.031
		Content	D-3	0.214	0.038
		Speed	D-4	0.221	0.04
		Mobile-friendly	D-5	0.163	0.029
Information (I)	0.164	Effective search tool	I-1	0.283	0.046
		Availability of information to compare across alternatives	I-2	0.270	0.044
		Contact Information	I-3	0.231	0.038
		FAQs	I-4	0.216	0.035
Service Quality (Q)	0.258	Trust	Q-1	0.332	0.086
		Payment alternatives	Q-2	0.142	0.037
		On-time delivery	Q-3	0.220	0.057
		Easy returns	Q-4	0.306	0.079
Security/Privacy (S)	0.245	Account Security	S-1	0.309	0.076
		Secure Payment	S-2	0.516	0.126
		Non-Sharing personal information	S-3	0.175	0.043
Customer service and support (C)	0.154	Feedback mechanism	C-1	0.283	0.044
		Order tracking	C-2	0.386	0.059
		Assisting in solving a delivery dispute	C-3	0.331	0.051

4.10. TOPSIS-Grey Method

The integrated TOPSIS-Grey method was used to rank five B2C e-commerce websites based on five main factors (main-criteria) and 19 sub-factors (sub-criteria). During this phase, experts were asked to rate alternatives with respect to the sub-factors. To compile the experts' feedback, a grey decision matrix was constructed which was later normalized. Tables A7 and A8 in the Appendix B provide the grey decision and grey normalized matrices, respectively. Table A9 in the Appendix B shows the values of the positive ideal and negative ideal solutions. Tables A10 and A11 contain the values of the positive ideal distance and negative ideal distance, respectively. Finally, the relative closeness of each alternative was obtained, and the alternatives were ranked according to their relative closeness values. Table 7 lists the relative closeness and a final ranking of websites. It can be seen that Website-3 received the highest relative closeness score (0.631), which translates that Website-3 is the most successful website among all the five websites analyzed in this study. Website-1 ranked second by obtaining a 0.622 relative closeness. Website-2 received the third-highest relative closeness value of 0.498, followed by Website-4, which received a second-lowest score of 0.44 and was ranked fourth. Website-5 got the least score (0.344), and thus it can be said that Website-5 has the lowest implementation of critical successful factors required for an effective B2C e-commerce website.

Table 7. The relative closeness and a final ranking of B2C E-commerce websites (alternatives).

	d_i^{k+}	d_i^{k-}	C+	Rank
Website-1	0.19	0.313	0.622	2
Website-2	0.255	0.253	0.498	3
Website-3	0.19	0.325	0.631	1
Website-4	0.282	0.222	0.44	4
Website-5	0.338	0.177	0.344	5

4.11. Sensitivity Analysis

A sensitivity analysis was performed to check if the results received using the integrated methodology are robust and reliable. To know the impact of changes in the criteria and sub-criteria weights on the final ranking of the website, we developed 6 more cases with different weights. In Case-2, all the main criteria were given equal weights (0.20 weight to each main criterion). For Case-3, we assigned a 0.40 weight to the design criteria, and the rest of each criterion was given 0.15. In Case-4, the Information criterion was given a 0.40 weight, and each of the others were given 0.15. In Cases-5, 6, and 7, service quality, security/privacy, and customer support center were respectively given a 0.40 weight, while the others were assigned 0.15. The subsequent changes in the final weights of the sub-criteria for all the seven cases are provided in Table 8. These different weights of the sub-criteria were used in the integrated TOPSIS-Grey methodology to check any variance in the final ranking. Figure 9 depicts the results of changes in weights on the final ranking. It can be seen that the final rankings remained the same in almost every case except Case-4 and Case-5, where the effect only changed the rankings of Website-1 and Website-3 while the others remained the same.

Table 8. Different sub-criteria weights.

Sub-Criteria.	Case-1 (FAHP Weights)	Case-2	Case-3	Case-4	Case-5	Case-6	Case-7
D-1	0.041	0.046	0.091	0.034	0.034	0.034	0.034
D-2	0.031	0.035	0.07	0.026	0.026	0.026	0.026
D-3	0.038	0.043	0.086	0.032	0.032	0.032	0.032
D-4	0.04	0.044	0.088	0.033	0.033	0.033	0.033
D-5	0.029	0.033	0.065	0.024	0.024	0.024	0.024
I-1	0.046	0.057	0.042	0.113	0.042	0.042	0.042
I-2	0.044	0.054	0.041	0.108	0.041	0.041	0.041
I-3	0.038	0.046	0.035	0.092	0.035	0.035	0.035
I-4	0.035	0.043	0.032	0.086	0.032	0.032	0.032
Q-1	0.086	0.066	0.05	0.05	0.133	0.05	0.05
Q-2	0.037	0.028	0.021	0.021	0.057	0.021	0.021
Q-3	0.057	0.044	0.033	0.033	0.088	0.033	0.033
Q-4	0.079	0.061	0.046	0.046	0.122	0.046	0.046
S-1	0.076	0.062	0.046	0.046	0.046	0.124	0.046
S-2	0.126	0.103	0.077	0.077	0.077	0.206	0.077
S-3	0.043	0.035	0.026	0.026	0.026	0.07	0.026
C-1	0.044	0.057	0.042	0.042	0.042	0.042	0.113
C-2	0.059	0.077	0.058	0.058	0.058	0.058	0.154
C-3	0.051	0.066	0.05	0.05	0.05	0.05	0.132

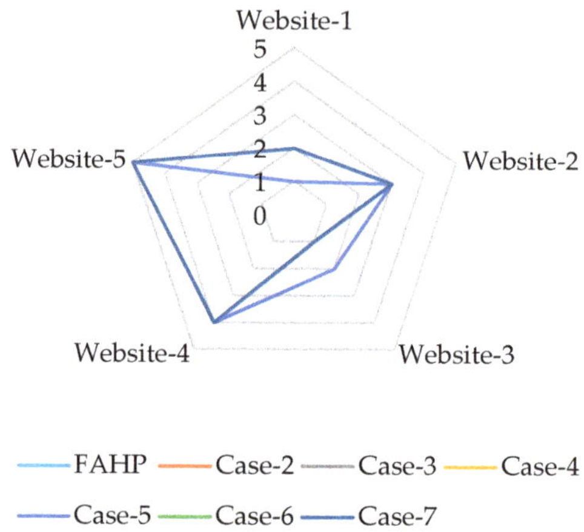

Figure 9. Sensitivity analysis.

4.12. Discussion

In the present research, five B2C e-commerce websites of China were selected as a case analysis. Each of the websites was assessed based on proposed e-commerce website factors and sub-factors. In the study, an integrated decision methodology comprised of Fuzzy AHP and TOPSIS-Grey was applied to determine this decision problem. The Fuzzy AHP results showed that service quality (Q) is the favorite factor when implementing a B2C e-commerce website, followed by security/privacy (S), design (D), information (I), and customer service and support (C). The TOPSIS-Grey analysis presents that Website-3 is the most successful in running a B2C e-business because this website significantly follows crucial factors when compared to the other four websites. Website-1 was identified as the second most important B2C e-commerce website, followed by Website-2, Website-4, and Website-5.

This research is the very first that has identified and evaluated the B2C e-commerce factors and sub-factors based on the Fuzzy AHP and TOPSIS-Grey approach. However, there are many studies that are available in the existing literature that have evaluated websites by determining e-commerce factors with different goals and objectives. In the literature review section, the authors provided previous studies with their research findings. In these studies, the authors used different types of MCDM methods to significantly determine the decision problem. The AHP [21,23,50], TOPSIS [22–24], DEMATEL [25], and ANP [27] methods have been used for assessing the performance of e-commerce websites. In this study, we identified that none of the researchers utilized a Fuzzy AHP and TOPSIS-Grey model to assess the B2C e-commerce factors and sub-factors when assessing e-commerce websites in the context of China.

The proposed Fuzzy AHP and TOPSIS-Grey approach is validated through this case study for China. The determined e-commerce websites were evaluated in a fuzzy environment, and it was not easy to determine the problem since it had various uncertainties and vagueness. Therefore, this study utilized the Fuzzy AHP method to analyze the e-commerce factors and sub-factors, and the TOPSIS-Grey approach was used to evaluate the B2C e-commerce websites based on identified factors and sub-factors. This research could help the government and managers to determine this decision problem for the feasible performance of B2C e-commerce websites.

5. Conclusions

The evaluation of B2C e-commerce factors constitutes the crucial notion of the current research, and we applied integrated Fuzzy AHP and TOPSIS-Grey techniques, which have never been used in any previous studies before. This decision framework was further categorized into three sections. In the first section, a problem statement was observed and explained; for evaluating websites (alternatives), the B2C e-commerce websites were chosen, and we also identified successful assessment factors and sub-factors. In the second section, the Fuzzy AHP method was used to determine the B2C e-commerce factors and sub-factors using TFNs. Then, the TOPSIS-Grey method was utilized to assess the B2C e-commerce websites (alternatives) based on identified factors and sub-factors.

To implement the proposed methodology of the study, we highly recommend that one consider these factors for successfully designing a website on the e-commerce platform. Therefore, analysts are suggested to conduct further investigations regarding this decision problem. Moreover, it is essential to consider the main-factors' and their sub-factors' importance weight information. There are three leading potential areas of utility and contributions to this work. First, the previous studies on the assessment of B2C e-commerce websites only focused on a single or a hybrid MCDM method. However, this study suggested new integrated Fuzzy AHP and TOPSIS-Grey techniques. The strength of this decision-making approach is the fundamental idea of Fuzzy AHP, which provides meaningful and accurate explanations regarding the B2C e-commerce factors (and their sub-factors) of the hierarchical structure. Second, empirical work shows that TOPSIS-Grey was found to be an efficient and practical instrument of the B2C e-commerce websites' ranking based on various factors. This technique has the potential to evaluate the performance of service sectors in relation to those with similar B2C e-commerce platform characteristics. Finally, the advantages of this technique are not just limited and applicable to B2C e-commerce websites' evaluation but also enhance different specific operations and services via potential applications.

Although the proposed method offers numerous advantages and potentials, some limitations can lead to suggestions for future work. First, the current research did not consider the existing relationship with B2C e-commerce websites. Thus, we suggest that it be included for future work for better results. This study can be extended further by applying the Fuzzy DEMATEL technique to capture interrelationships graphically among defined criteria. Second, the proposed method would be useful for decision-making in other related areas.

In this study, we presented a Fuzzy AHP and TOPSIS-Grey methodology to evaluate B2C e-commerce factors for improving the website quality. In the study, the authors believe that an integrated decision model helps in minimizing the complexity and fuzziness of the decision problem. For future research directions, the results of this study could be compared with findings of other fuzzy MCDM approaches such as VIKOR, SAW, DEA, ANP, and PROMETHEE. Moreover, the proposed B2C e-commerce factors for designing the websites can be applied to other sectors like health, banking, music, and aviation.

Author Contributions: Conceptualization, R.L.; methodology, T.S.; software, T.S.; validation, R.L. and T.S.; formal analysis, R.L.; investigation, T.S.; data curation, R.L.; writing—original draft preparation, R.L.; writing—review and editing, T.S.; supervision, T.S. All authors have read and agreed to the published version of the manuscript.

Funding: This research received funding from outstanding young backbone teachers of the "Blue Project" in the Department of Education, Jiangsu Province, 2019.

Conflicts of Interest: The authors declare no conflict of interest.

Appendix A. Results of Fuzzy AHP

Table A1. Main-factors Pairwise matrix.

	Design (D)	Information (I)	Service Quality (Q)	Security/Privacy (S)	Customer Service and Support (C)
Design (D)	1, 1, 1	0.874, 1.236, 1.693	0.46, 0.616, 0.871	0.558, 0.752, 1.027	0.791, 1.105, 1.551
Information (I)	0.591, 0.809, 1.144	1, 1, 1	0.473, 0.645, 0.912	0.503, 0.657, 0.894	0.813, 1.18, 1.637
Service Quality (Q)	1.149, 1.624, 2.173	1.097, 1.551, 2.115	1, 1, 1	0.785, 1.076, 1.463	1.163, 1.551, 2.013
Security/Privacy (S)	0.973, 1.33, 1.792	1.118, 1.521, 1.989	0.684, 0.929, 1.273	1, 1, 1	1.218, 1.726, 2.296
Customer service and support (C)	0.645, 0.905, 1.264	0.611, 0.847, 1.231	0.497, 0.645, 0.86	0.436, 0.579, 0.821	1, 1, 1
CR = 0.0026 (Consistent)					

Table A2. Pairwise matrix of Sub-factor (Design).

	D-1	D-2	D-3	D-4	D-5
D-1	1, 1, 1	0.874, 1.236, 1.693	0.985, 1.366, 1.826	0.816, 1.097, 1.467	0.791, 1.105, 1.551
D-2	0.591, 0.809, 1.144	1, 1, 1	0.591, 0.809, 1.144	0.503, 0.657, 0.894	0.813, 1.18, 1.637
D-3	0.547, 0.732, 1.015	0.874, 1.236, 1.693	1, 1, 1	0.785, 1.076, 1.463	1.163, 1.551, 2.013
D-4	0.681, 0.912, 1.225	1.118, 1.521, 1.989	0.684, 0.929, 1.273	1, 1, 1	0.985, 1.393, 1.857
D-5	0.645, 0.905, 1.264	0.611, 0.847, 1.231	0.497, 0.645, 0.86	0.538, 0.718, 1.015	1, 1, 1
CR = 0.0096 (Consistent)					

Table A3. Pairwise matrix of Sub-factor (Information).

	I-1	I-2	I-3	I-4
I-1	1, 1, 1	0.741, 0.988, 1.35	1.055, 1.499, 2.044	0.858, 1.149, 1.503
I-2	0.741, 1.012, 1.35	1, 1, 1	0.858, 1.149, 1.503	0.898, 1.236, 1.648
I-3	0.489, 0.667, 0.948	0.665, 0.871, 1.166	1, 1, 1	0.912, 1.26, 1.678
I-4	0.665, 0.871, 1.166	0.607, 0.809, 1.113	0.596, 0.794, 1.097	1, 1, 1
CR =0.0093 (Consistent)				

Table A4. Pairwise matrix of Sub-factor (Service Quality).

	Q-1	Q-2	Q-3	Q-4
Q-1	1, 1, 1	2.319, 3.033, 3.852	1.055, 1.499, 2.044	0.611, 0.858, 1.231
Q-2	0.26, 0.33, 0.431	1, 1, 1	0.596, 0.794, 1.097	0.356, 0.471, 0.66
Q-3	0.489, 0.667, 0.948	0.912, 1.26, 1.678	1, 1, 1	0.665, 0.871, 1.166
Q-4	0.813, 1.166, 1.637	1.514, 2.124, 2.812	0.858, 1.149, 1.503	1, 1, 1
CR = 0.0213 (Consistent)				

Table A5. Pairwise matrix of Sub-factor (Security/Privacy).

	S-1	S-2	S-3
S-1	1, 1, 1	0.422, 0.558, 0.747	1.446, 1.908, 2.465
S-2	1.339, 1.792, 2.372	1, 1, 1	2.058, 2.79, 3.608
S-3	0.406, 0.524, 0.692	0.277, 0.358, 0.486	1, 1, 1
	CR = 0.0047 (Consistent)		

Table A6. Pairwise matrix of Sub-factor (Customer Service & Support).

	C-1	C-2	C-3
C-1	1, 1, 1	0.569, 0.782, 1.076	0.608, 0.787, 1.051
C-2	0.929, 1.279, 1.758	1, 1, 1	0.938, 1.255, 1.629
C-3	0.952, 1.27, 1.646	0.614, 0.797, 1.066	1, 1, 1
	CR = 0.0055 (Consistent)		

Appendix B. Results of TOPSIS-Grey

Table A7. Decision matrix.

	D-1	D-2	D-3	D-4	D-5	I-1	I-2	I-3	I-4	Q-1	Q-2	Q-3	Q-4	S-1	S-2	S-3	C-1	C-2	C-3
W-1	4.5, 6.2	4.9, 6.5	3, 4.2	5.9, 7.3	3.7, 5	4.1, 5.2	4.8, 6.2	4.7, 6.1	4.2, 5.5	4.2, 5.6	2.9, 4.2	3.8, 5.2	4.1, 5.4	6, 7.7	4.2, 5.3	4.4, 5.5	5, 6.4	4.5, 6.1	4.3, 5.5
W-2	4.5, 5.8	4.8, 6.4	2.8, 3.9	5, 6.4	3.5, 4.8	3.6, 4.8	4.9, 6.1	4.5, 5.8	3.7, 5	3.7, 5.2	3.1, 4.2	2.8, 4.2	3.9, 5.5	5.3, 6.8	3.6, 4.6	4.4, 6	4.6, 6.1	4.5, 5.6	3.5, 4.8
W-3	4.5, 6.3	4.9, 6.5	3.4, 4.6	5.2, 6.6	4.3, 5.7	3.6, 5	4.9, 6.3	4.6, 6.2	3.9, 5.2	3.9, 5.5	3, 4.2	3.7, 5	3.9, 5.4	6, 7.9	4.5, 5.9	4.5, 5.8	5.2, 6.5	5, 6.5	4.4, 5.6
W-4	4.4, 5.7	4.5, 5.9	2.1, 3.5	4.4, 5.7	3.1, 4.5	2.5, 4	4.2, 5.6	3.9, 5.4	3.5, 4.6	3.1, 4.6	2.9, 4.2	3, 4.3	3.5, 4.8	5.7, 7.3	4, 5.3	4, 5.3	3.9, 5.5	4.5, 6	3.6, 5.2
W-5	4, 5.3	4.1, 5.4	1.6, 3.1	3.9, 5	2.7, 4	2.2, 3.5	4.2, 5.5	3.5, 4.9	3.6, 5	2.8, 4	2.6, 4	3.1, 4.3	3.5, 4.8	5.1, 6.8	3, 4.4	3.7, 5.3	3.5, 4.9	4.4, 5.8	3.7, 5

Table A8. Normalized matrix.

	D-1	D-2	D-3	D-4	D-5	I-1	I-2	I-3	I-4	Q-1	Q-2	Q-3	Q-4	S-1	S-2	S-3	C-1	C-2	C-3
W-1	0.7, 1	0.8, 1	0.6, 0.9	0.8, 1	0.7, 0.9	0.8, 1	0.8, 1	0.8, 1	0.8, 1	0.7, 1	0.7, 1	0.7, 1	0.8, 1	0.8, 1	0.7, 0.9	0.1, 0.3	0.8, 1	0.7, 0.9	0.8, 1
W-2	0.7, 0.9	0.7, 1	0.6, 0.8	0.7, 0.9	0.6, 0.8	0.7, 0.9	0.8, 1	0.7, 0.9	0.7, 0.9	0.7, 0.9	0.7, 1	0.5, 0.8	0.7, 1	0.7, 0.9	0.6, 0.8	0, 0.3	0.7, 0.9	0.7, 0.9	0.6, 0.9
W-3	0.7, 1	0.8, 1	0.7, 1	0.7, 0.9	0.7, 1	0.7, 1	0.8, 1	0.8, 1	0.7, 1	0.7, 1	0.7, 1	0.7, 1	0.7, 1	0.8, 1	0.8, 1	0, 0.3	0.8, 1	0.8, 1	0.8, 1
W-4	0.7, 0.9	0.7, 0.9	0.5, 0.7	0.6, 0.8	0.5, 0.8	0.5, 0.8	0.7, 0.9	0.6, 0.9	0.7, 0.9	0.5, 0.8	0.7, 1	0.6, 0.8	0.6, 0.9	0.7, 0.9	0.7, 0.9	0.1, 0.3	0.6, 0.8	0.7, 0.9	0.6, 0.9
W-5	0.6, 0.8	0.6, 0.8	0.4, 0.7	0.5, 0.7	0.5, 0.7	0.4, 0.7	0.7, 0.9	0.6, 0.8	0.7, 0.9	0.5, 0.7	0.6, 1	0.6, 0.8	0.7, 0.9	0.6, 0.9	0.5, 0.7	0.1, 0.4	0.5, 0.8	0.7, 0.9	0.7, 0.9

Table A9. Positive ideal alternative A_i^{k+} and negative ideal alternative A_i^{k-}.

	D-1	D-2	D-3	D-4	D-5	I-1	I-2	I-3	I-4	Q-1	Q-2	Q-3	Q-4	S-1	S-2	S-3	C-1	C-2	C-3
A_i^{k+}	1	1	1	1	1	1	1	1	1	1	1	1	1	1	1	0	1	1	1
A_i^{k-}	0.638	0.625	0.353	0.538	0.476	0.421	0.667	0.574	0.65	0.5	0.63	0.544	0.633	0.644	0.508	0.379	0.542	0.667	0.629

Table A10. Alternatives' positive ideal solution distance d_i^{k+}.

	D-1	D-2	D-3	D-4	D-5	I-1	I-2	I-3	I-4	Q-1	Q-2	Q-3	Q-4	S-1	S-2	S-3	C-1	C-2	C-3	d_i^{k+}
Website-1	0.003	0.002	0.005	0.001	0.004	0.002	0.002	0.002	0.002	0.006	0.003	0.004	0.005	0.004	0.012	0.004	0.002	0.006	0.003	0.19
Website-2	0.004	0.002	0.007	0.005	0.005	0.004	0.002	0.003	0.004	0.01	0.003	0.014	0.006	0.01	0.025	0.007	0.004	0.007	0.008	0.255
Website-3	0.003	0.002	0.003	0.004	0.002	0.004	0.002	0.002	0.003	0.008	0.003	0.005	0.006	0.004	0.007	0.006	0.002	0.003	0.003	0.19
Website-4	0.004	0.003	0.014	0.008	0.008	0.014	0.005	0.006	0.005	0.02	0.003	0.012	0.012	0.006	0.015	0.003	0.008	0.006	0.007	0.282
Website-5	0.006	0.005	0.02	0.012	0.011	0.021	0.006	0.009	0.004	0.029	0.005	0.011	0.011	0.011	0.039	0.003	0.012	0.007	0.007	0.338

Table A11. Alternatives' negative ideal solution distance d_i^{k-}.

	D-1	D-2	D-3	D-4	D-5	I-1	I-2	I-3	I-4	Q-1	Q-2	Q-3	Q-4	S-1	S-2	S-3	C-1	C-2	C-3	d_i^{k-}
Website-1	0.005	0.005	0.015	0.012	0.005	0.022	0.005	0.008	0.005	0.027	0.005	0.014	0.011	0.009	0.024	0.003	0.01	0.004	0.007	0.313
Website-2	0.004	0.004	0.012	0.005	0.004	0.016	0.005	0.006	0.003	0.017	0.006	0.004	0.011	0.004	0.011	0.003	0.008	0.002	0.003	0.253
Website-3	0.006	0.005	0.021	0.007	0.01	0.017	0.005	0.008	0.003	0.022	0.005	0.012	0.01	0.011	0.039	0.003	0.012	0.007	0.008	0.325
Website-4	0.003	0.003	0.006	0.003	0.003	0.006	0.002	0.003	0.001	0.009	0.005	0.005	0.005	0.006	0.022	0.005	0.004	0.004	0.004	0.222
Website-5	0.002	0.001	0.004	0.001	0.001	0.003	0.002	0.002	0.003	0.004	0.004	0.005	0.005	0.004	0.007	0.007	0.002	0.003	0.003	0.177

References

1. Hoffman, D.L.; Novak, T.P. A New Marketing Paradigm for Electronic Commerce. *Inf. Soc.* **1997**, *13*, 43–54.
2. E-Commerce and E-Business. In *Information and Communication Technology in Organizations: Adoption, Implementation, Use and Effects*; Sage Publications: London, UK, 2012; pp. 139–162.
3. Oliveira, T.; Alhinho, M.; Rita, P.; Dhillon, G. Modelling and Testing Consumer Trust Dimensions in E-Commerce. *Comput. Human Behav.* **2017**, *71*, 153–164. [CrossRef]
4. Shaw, M.J. Electronic Commerce: State of the Art. In *Handbook on Electronic Commerce*; Springer: Berlin/Heidelberg, Germany, 2000; pp. 3–24.
5. Bhasin, H. *Top E-Commerce Companies in the World*; Marketing91: Mumbai, India, 2019.
6. Gurung, A.; Raja, M.K. Online Privacy and Security Concerns of Consumers. *Inf. Comput. Secur.* **2016**, *24*, 348–371. [CrossRef]
7. Chiu, W.Y.; Tzeng, G.H.; Li, H.L. Developing E-Store Marketing Strategies to Satisfy Customers' Needs Using a New Hybrid Gray Relational Model. *Int. J. Inf. Technol. Decis. Mak.* **2014**, *13*, 231–261. [CrossRef]
8. Zhang, Y.; Deng, X.; Wei, D.; Deng, Y. Assessment of E-Commerce Security Using AHP and Evidential Reasoning. *Expert Syst. Appl.* **2012**, *39*, 3611–3623. [CrossRef]
9. Abdullah, L.; Ramli, R.; Bakodah, H.O.; Othman, M. Developing a Causal Relationship among Factors of E-Commerce: A Decision Making Approach. *J. King Saud Univ.-Comput. Inf. Sci.* **2019**, in press. [CrossRef]
10. Yu, X.; Guo, S.; Guo, J.; Huang, X. Rank B2C E-Commerce Websites in e-Alliance Based on AHP and Fuzzy TOPSIS. *Expert Syst. Appl.* **2011**, *38*, 3550–3557. [CrossRef]
11. Jurado, E.B.; Moral, A.M.; Viruel, M.J.M.; Uclés, D.F. Evaluation of Corporate Websites and Their Influence on the Performance of Olive Oil Companies. *Sustainability* **2018**, *10*, 1274. [CrossRef]
12. Ostovare, M.; Shahraki, M.R. Evaluation of Hotel Websites Using the Multicriteria Analysis of PROMETHEE and GAIA: Evidence from the Five-Star Hotels of Mashhad. *Tour. Manag. Perspect.* **2019**, *30*, 107–116. [CrossRef]
13. Aydin, S.; Kahraman, C. Evaluation of E-Commerce Website Quality Using Fuzzy Multi-Criteria Decision Making Approach. *IAENG Int. J. Comput. Sci.* **2012**, *39*, 64–70.
14. Ziemba, P. Towards Strong Sustainability Management-a Generalized PROSA Method. *Sustainability* **2019**, *11*, 1555. [CrossRef]
15. Nisar, T.M.; Prabhakar, G. What Factors Determine E-Satisfaction and Consumer Spending in e-Commerce Retailing? *J. Retail. Consum. Serv.* **2017**, *39*, 135–144. [CrossRef]
16. Lin, Y.; Luo, J.; Cai, S.; Ma, S.; Rong, K. Exploring the Service Quality in the E-Commerce Context: A Triadic View. *Ind. Manag. Data Syst.* **2016**, *116*, 388–415. [CrossRef]
17. Zameer, H.; Wang, Y.; Yasmeen, H. Reinforcing Green Competitive Advantage through Green Production, Creativity and Green Brand Image: Implications for Cleaner Production in China. *J. Clean. Prod.* **2020**, *247*, 119119. [CrossRef]
18. Chesher, M.; Kaura, R. *Introduction to Electronic Commerce*; Springer: London, UK, 1998; pp. 69–87.
19. Liang, T.P.; Turban, E. Introduction to the Special Issue Social Commerce: A Research Framework for Social Commerce. *Int. J. Electron. Commer.* **2011**, *16*, 5–13. [CrossRef]
20. Mardani, A.; Jusoh, A.; Zavadskas, E.K. Fuzzy Multiple Criteria Decision-Making Techniques and Applications—Two Decades Review from 1994 to 2014. *Expert Syst. Appl.* **2015**, *42*, 4126–4148. [CrossRef]
21. Rouyendegh, B.D.; Topuz, K.; Dag, A.; Oztekin, A. An AHP-IFT Integrated Model for Performance Evaluation of E-Commerce Web Sites. *Inf. Syst. Front.* **2019**, *21*, 1345–1355. [CrossRef]
22. Özkan, B.; Özceylan, E.; Kabak, M.; Dağdeviren, M. Evaluating the Websites of Academic Departments through SEO Criteria: A Hesitant Fuzzy Linguistic MCDM Approach. *Artif. Intell. Rev.* **2020**, *53*, 875–905. [CrossRef]
23. Kabassi, K. Evaluating Museum Websites Using a Combination of Decision-Making Theories. *J. Herit. Tour.* **2019**, *14*, 544–560. [CrossRef]
24. Kaya, T. Multi-Attribute Evaluation of Website Quality in e-Business Using an Integrated Fuzzy AHPTOPSIS Methodology. *Int. J. Comput. Intell. Syst.* **2010**, *3*, 301–314. [CrossRef]

25. Liang, R.; Wang, J.; Zhang, H. Evaluation of E-Commerce Websites: An Integrated Approach under a Single-Valued Trapezoidal Neutrosophic Environment. *Knowl. -Based Syst.* **2017**, *135*, 44–59. [CrossRef]
26. Aggarwal, A.G.; Aakash, N.A. Multi-Criteria-Based Prioritisation of B2C e-Commerce Website. *Int. J. Soc. Syst. Sci.* **2018**, *10*, 201. [CrossRef]
27. Chiu, W.Y.; Tzeng, G.H.; Li, H.L. A New Hybrid MCDM Model Combining DANP with VIKOR to Improve E-Store Business. *Knowl. -Based Syst.* **2013**, *37*, 48–61. [CrossRef]
28. Makki, E.; Chang, L.-C. Understanding the Effects of Social Media and Mobile Usage on E-Commerce: An Exploratory Study in Saudi Arabia. *Int. Manag. Rev.* **2015**, *11*, 98.
29. Bezhovski, Z. The Future of the Mobile Payment as Electronic Payment System, European Journal of Business and Management. *Eur. J. Bus. Manag.* **2016**, *8*, 127–132.
30. Zhou, L.; Wang, W.; Xu, J.; Liu, T.; Gu, J. Perceived Information Transparency in B2C E-Commerce: An Empirical Investigation. *Inf. Manag.* **2018**, *55*, 912–927. [CrossRef]
31. Ilbahar, E.; Cebi, S. Classification of Design Parameters for E-Commerce Websites: A Novel Fuzzy Kano Approach. *Telemat. Inform.* **2017**, *8*, 34. [CrossRef]
32. Muneer, A.; Samreen, R.; Zaineb, F. Data Privacy Issues and Possible Solutions in E-Commerce. *J. Account. Mark.* **2018**, *3*, 7. [CrossRef]
33. Thepsuparungsikul, W.; Rattanawicha, P. A Study of E-Service Applications in e-Commerce Websites. In Proceedings of the International Conference on Electronic Business (ICEB), Bangkok, Thailand, 29 November–2 December 2011; pp. 279–284.
34. Halaweh, M. Implementation of the COD Payment Method on E-Commerce Websites in the Arab Region. *Int. J. Bus. Inf. Syst.* **2019**, *32*, 145–160.
35. Leung, K.H.; Choy, K.L.; Siu, P.K.Y.; Ho, G.T.S.; Lam, H.Y.; Lee, C.K.M. A B2C E-Commerce Intelligent System for Re-Engineering the e-Order Fulfilment Process. *Expert Syst. Appl.* **2018**, *91*, 386–401. [CrossRef]
36. Ong, C.E.; Teh, D. Redress Procedures Expected by Consumers during a Business-to-Consumer e-Commerce Dispute. *Electron. Commer. Res. Appl.* **2016**, *17*, 150–160. [CrossRef]
37. Lin, H.F. The Impact of Website Quality Dimensions on Customer Satisfaction in the B2C E-Commerce Context. *Total Qual. Manag. Bus. Excell.* **2007**, *18*, 363–378. [CrossRef]
38. Abedi, F.; Zeleznikow, J.; Bellucci, E. Universal Standards for the Concept of Trust in Online Dispute Resolution Systems in E-Commerce Disputes. *Int. J. Law Inf. Technol.* **2019**, *27*, 209–237. [CrossRef]
39. Xu, L.; Shah, S.A.A.; Zameer, H.; Solangi, Y.A. Evaluating Renewable Energy Sources for Implementing the Hydrogen Economy in Pakistan: A Two-Stage Fuzzy MCDM Approach. *Environ. Sci. Pollut. Res.* **2019**, *26*, 33202–33215. [CrossRef]
40. Shah, S.A.A.; Solangi, Y.A.; Ikram, M. Analysis of Barriers to the Adoption of Cleaner Energy Technologies in Pakistan Using Modified Delphi and Fuzzy Analytical Hierarchy Process. *J. Clean. Prod.* **2019**, *235*, 1037–1050. [CrossRef]
41. Solangi, Y.A.; Shah, S.A.A.; Zameer, H.; Ikram, M.; Saracoglu, B.O. Assessing the Solar PV Power Project Site Selection in Pakistan: Based on AHP-Fuzzy VIKOR Approach. *Environ. Sci. Pollut. Res.* **2019**, *26*, 30286–30302. [CrossRef]
42. Wang, Y.; Xu, L.; Solangi, Y.A. Strategic Renewable Energy Resources Selection for Pakistan: Based on SWOT-Fuzzy AHP Approach. *Sustain. Cities Soc.* **2020**, *52*, 101861. [CrossRef]
43. Shah, S.A.A. Feasibility Study of Renewable Energy Sources for Developing the Hydrogen Economy in Pakistan. *Int. J. Hydrog. Energy* **2019**, in press. [CrossRef]
44. Tzeng, G.H.; Huang, J.J. *Multiple Attribute Decision Making: Methods and Applications*; Taylor and Francis: New York, NK, USA, 2011; pp. 1–333.
45. Wang, X.; Zameer, S.; Siyal, S.W. Economic Viability and Environmental Efficiency Analysis of Hydrogen Production Processes for the Decarbonization of Energy Systems. *Processes* **2019**, *7*, 494.
46. Solangi, Y.A.; Tan, Q.; Mirjat, N.H.; Valasai, G.D.; Khan, M.W.A.; Ikram, M. An Integrated Delphi-AHP and Fuzzy TOPSIS Approach toward Ranking and Selection of Renewable Energy Resources in Pakistan. *Processes* **2019**, *7*, 118. [CrossRef]
47. Zavadskas, E.K.; Vilutienė, T.; Turskis, Z.; Tamosaitienė, J. Contractor Selection for Construction Works by Applying Saw-G and Topsis Grey Techniques. *J. Bus. Econ. Manag.* **2010**, *11*, 34–55. [CrossRef]
48. Deng, J. Introduction to Grey System. *J. Grey Syst.* **1989**, *1*, 1–24.

49. Oztaysi, B. A Decision Model for Information Technology Selection Using AHP Integrated TOPSIS-Grey: The Case of Content Management Systems. *Knowl. -Based Syst.* **2014**, *70*, 44–54. [CrossRef]
50. Musaad, O.; Sultan, A.; Zhuo, Z.; Musaad, O.; Otaibi, A.; Siyal, Z.A.; Hashmi, H.; Shah, S.A.A. A Fuzzy Multi-Criteria Analysis of Barriers and Policy Strategies for Small and Medium Enterprises to Adopt Green Innovation. *Symmetry* **2020**, *12*, 116. [CrossRef]

symmetry

MDPI

Article

Implementing a Novel Use of Multicriteria Decision Analysis to Select IIoT Platforms for Smart Manufacturing

Roberto Contreras-Masse [1,2,*,†], Alberto Ochoa-Zezzatti [1], Vicente García [1], Luis Pérez-Dominguez [1] and Mayra Elizondo-Cortés [3]

1 Universidad Autonoma de Ciudad Juárez (UACJ), Ciudad Juárez 32310, Mexico; alberto.ochoa@uacj.mx (A.O.-Z.); vicente.jimenez@uacj.mx (V.G.); luis.dominguez@uacj.mx (L.P.-D.)
2 Instituto Tecnológico de Ciudad Juárez (ITCJ), Ciudad Juárez 32500, Mexico
3 Departamento de Ingeniería en Sistemas DIMEI-FI, Universidad Nacional Autonoma de Mexico (UNAM), Ciudad de México 04510, Mexico; mayra.elizondo@comunidad.unam.mx
* Correspondence: rcontreras@itcj.edu.mx
† Current address: Av. Tecnológico No. 1340 Fracc. El Crucero C.P. 32500 Ciudad Juárez, Chih, Mexico.

Received: 4 February 2020; Accepted: 27 February 2020 ; Published: 2 March 2020

Abstract: Industry 4.0 is having a great impact in all smart efforts. This is not a single product but is composed of several technologies, one of them being Industrial Internet of Things (IIoT). Currently, there are very varied implementation options offered by several companies, and this imposes a new challenge to companies that want to implement IIoT in their processes. This challenge suggests using multi-criteria analysis to make a repeatable and justified decision, requiring a set of alternatives and criteria. This paper proposes a new methodology and comprehensive criteria to help organizations to take an educated decision by applying multi-criteria analysis. Here, we suggest a new original use of PROMETHEE-II with a full example from weight calculation up to IIoT platform selection, showing this methodology as an effective study for other organizations interested in selecting an IIoT platform. The criteria proposed stands out from previous work by including not only technical aspects, but economic and social criteria, providing a full view of the problem analyzed. A case of study was used to prove this proposed methodology and finds the minimum subset to reach the best possible ranking.

Keywords: IoT; platform selection; multi criteria decision analysis (MCDA); AHP; PROMETHEE-II; Industry 4.0

---

1. Introduction

Industry 4.0 is having a high impact in all industries. This is not a unique product, but it is composed of several technologies. Boston Consulting Group has defined nine technological pillars for Industry 4.0: cloud, additive manufacturing, simulation, big data and analysis, autonomous robots, augmented reality, integration of horizontal and vertical systems, cybersecurity and industrial internet of things (IIOT) [1]. IIOT has been used not only in the manufacturing industry, but has expanded to other industries such as health, travel and transportation, energy, gas and oil, etc. This is one of the main reasons that IIOT is known as the Internet of Things (IoT) [2]. IIoT is a key intelligent factor that allows factories to act intelligently. By adding sensors and actuators to objects, the object becomes intelligent because it can interact with people, other objects, generate data, generate transactions, and react to environmental data [3,4]. Cities do not ignore this trend, since there is a plan to turn cities into smart cities in certain countries [5].

The decision processes that companies must follow should be supported by methods that consider pros and cons of plural points of view that affect the decision process. Researchers and practitioners have developed over time the techniques that today are part of the domain of Multiple Criteria Decision Analysis (MCDA), which, very simplistically, requires three basic elements: a finite set of actions or alternatives, at least two criteria, and at least one decision making method. [6]. The MCDA has been the object of study and nowadays there are a lot of methods for decision-making in disciplines such as waste management, industrial engineering, strategies, manufacturing, even natural resource management and environmental impact [7].The purpose of this manuscript is precisely to propose a method of MCDA with the corresponding criteria for the selection of an IIoT(Industria Internet of Things) platform, which can serve as a starting point to companies and individuals embarked on implementation projects of Industry 4.0. Our conceptual model to solve the problem is shown in Figure 1.

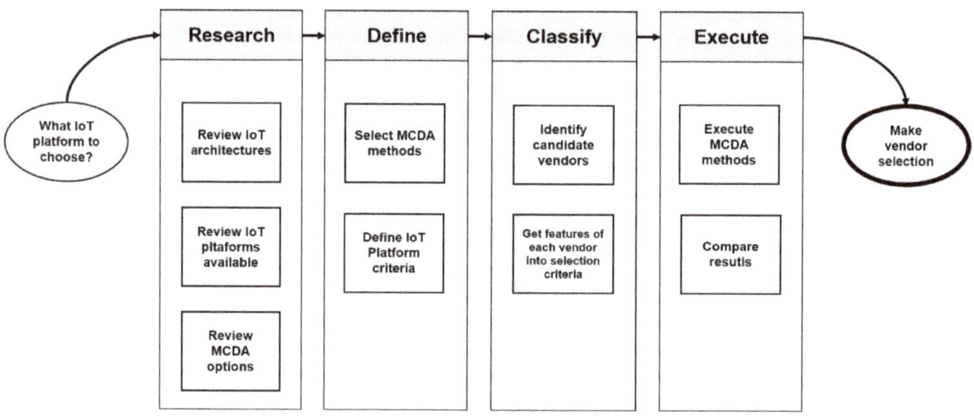

Figure 1. Conceptual model to select IIoT platforms.

1.1. Literature Review

Industria Internet of Things (IIoT) continues to evolve. Due to the instrinsic complexity, it is good practice to look at architectural references. IIoT have five main requirements on a general basis [8]: (1) Enable communication and connectivity between devices and data processing; (2) Establish a mechanism to manage devices, including tasks such as adding or deleting devices, updating software and configurations; (3) Gather all the data produced by the devices and then analyze them to provide a meaningful perspective to the companies or users; (4) Facilitate scalability to handle the increased flow of "data pipes" (hereinafter referred to as data pipelines) and the flow of data, and handle an increasing number of devices; (5) Protect the data by adding the necessary functions to provide privacy and trust between the devices and the users. Table 1 shows the summary of the various multi-layer architectures found in the literature.

Table 1. IIoT architectures.

Num.	Layers	References
2	Devices and Communication	[9]
3	Devices, Communication and Application	[10–12]
4	Devices, Communication, Transport and Application	[9,12–16]
5	Devices, Local processing, Communication, Transport and Applications	[12]
7	Business, Management, Communication, Processing, Acquisition, User interaction and Security	[15,17]
8	Physical devices, Communication, Edge or Fog processing, Data storage, Applications, Collaboration and process, Security	[18]

Technical architecture provides an extreme value to users because it can be implemented with different products. Therefore, it is understandable that several companies offer IIoT platforms that can be useful for our architectures. Commercial providers aim for flexible options offered, and consumers are responsible for using each component in the best way they consider. The main commercial players identified are, in alphabetical order: Amazon Web Services, Bosch IoT Suite, Google Cloud Platform, IBM Blue Mix (now Watson IoT), Microsoft Azure IoT, and Oracle Integrated Cloud [19]. The leading players identified in 2014 by Gartner Group were AWS and Microsoft, but, in 2018, Google enters the leaders quadrant. IBM, for its commercial relevance, is considered, although it has become a niche player, along with Oracle. Although Bosch IoT does not appear in the panorama detected by Gartner, we include it for being used in several industries. Each of these suppliers has similar characteristics among them but have different value propositions.

1.1.1. MCDA as a Tool to Select an IIoT Platform

Making a decision introduces problems to individuals. One of the problems is the integration of heterogeneous data and the uncertainty factor surrounding a decision, and the criteria that usually conflict with each other [7,20]. To carry out a MCDA process, a series of tasks is proposed, based on the three generic steps suggested by [21]: (i) identify the objective or goal, (ii) select the criteria, parameters, factors, and attributes, (iii) selection of alternatives, (iv) association of attributes with the criteria, (v) selection of weight methods to represent the importance of each criterion, and (vi) the method of aggregation. Ref. [21] included a step that is left out of these proposed tasks, but which should be considered in the discussion before executing the selected action. This step is to understand and compare the preferences of the person making the decision.

The MCDA can be classified according to the basis of the problem, by type, by category, or by the methods used to make the analysis. Figure 2 shows a taxonomy adapted from [22]; the methods included in this taxonomy are not exhaustive. The MCDA is a collection of systematic methodologies for comparisons, classification, and selection of multiple alternatives, each one with multiple attributes and is dependent on an evaluation matrix. Generally, it used to detect and quantify the decisions and considerations from interested parties (stakeholders) about various monetary factors and non-monetary factors to compare an alternative course of action [7,22]. The major division that exists in MCDA lies in the category of methodologies. First, the group considers discrete values with a limited number of known alternatives that involve some compensation or trade-off. This group is called Multiple Attributes Decision Making (MADM). The other group is the Multiple Objectives Decision Making (MODM), and its variable decision values are within a continuous domain with infinite or very numerous options that satisfy the restrictions, preferences, or priorities [20]. In addition, there is another classification according to the way of adding criteria, and it is divided into the American school, which aggregates into a single criterion, and into the European or French school that uses outranking methods. It can be considered a mixture of both schools and they are indirect approaches, such as the Peer Criteria Comparison methods (PCCA) [23].

1.1.2. Use of MCDA to Select IIoT Platforms or Technology Platforms—Related Work

When finding the available alternatives of the market, a new question will arise to find the method that helps to select the appropriate option. To answer this last question, a review of the literature is made looking for: (a) MCDA methods applied to the selection of IIoT platforms and (b) knowing the criteria taken into account.

In the literature, there is little information on the subject in recent years. Table 2 shows the summary of the work found. The selected methods are focused on AHP, TOPSIS, and Fuzzy logic in AHP and TOPSIS. The outranking methods were not implemented but were considered as an option or for future work by some authors [24,25]. The selection of an IIoT platform is neither dominated by a single criterion nor is there a single alternative. Ref. [26] considered AWS, Azure, Bosch, IBM Watson, and Google Cloud within their options, which coincide with some of the alternatives considered in this manuscript. Therefore, it is interesting to review the criteria they included for MCDA, as summarized in Table 2.

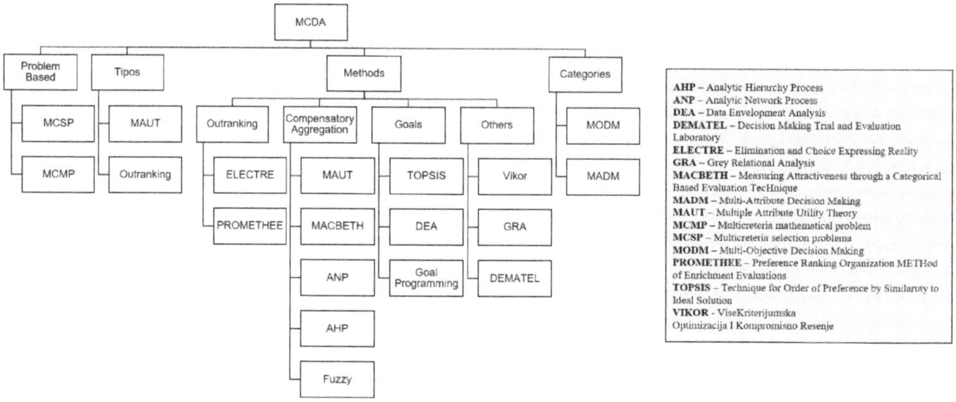

Figure 2. Taxonomy of MCDA (adapted from [22]).

Table 2. Previous work related to select technology.

Year	Application	MCDA	Criteria	Ref.
2019	IoT Challenges	AHP, ANP	Communication, Technology, Privacy and security, Legal regulations, Culture	[27]
2018	Cloud service for IoT	FAHP, FTOPSIS	Availability, Privacy, Capacity, Speed, Cost	[28]
2018	Platform IoT	Fuzzy	Security, Device management, Integration level, Processing level, Database functionality, Data collection protocols, Visualization, Analytics variety	[26]
2018	IaaS	TOPSIS	Cost, Computing required, Storage capacity, Operating system	[25]
2018	Distributed IoT Databases	AHP	Usability, Prtability, Support	[29]
2017	IoT Device	AHP	Energy consumption, Implementation time, Difficulty of implementation, Cost, Clock device	[24]
2017	IoT Platform	AHP	Energy, Cost, Computing speed, Data memory, Program memory, device weight	[30]
2013	Ranking cloud services	AHP	Responsibility, Agility, Service assurance, Cost, Performance, Security and privacy, Usability	[31]

Analytic Hierarchy Process (AHP), Fuzzy Analytic Hierarchy Process (FAHP), Analytic Network Process (ANP), Technique for Order of Preference by Similarity to Ideal Solution (TOPSIS), Fuzzy TOPSIS (FTOPSIS), Internet of Things (IoT), Infrastructure as a Service (IaaS).

Criteria found in literature are purely technical with some hints of economy, and can be found as part of the characteristics of IIoT architecture [32]. However, when implementing an IIoT platform, non-technical aspects should also be considered. As the platform to be considered has its foundation in the cloud, it is valid to review the criteria included in previous MCDA exercises to select a cloud provider, looking for non-technical aspects.

The criteria for selecting a cloud proposed in the CSMIC Framework v 2.1 of 2014 (Cloud Services Measurement Initiative Consortium (CSMIC) was created by Carnegie Mellon University to develop Service Measurement Index (SMI). it can be found at https://spark.adobe.com/page/PN39b/) as the Index of Measure of Service (SMI) includes topics of interest to the organization, financial, and usability, together with the technical issues [31]. Some of these criteria can be included to complement the analysis having the technical point of view and the business point of view.

Finally, there is a question about which methods are suitable for these types of problems, noting that the previous work includes AHP, ANP, TOPSIS, and Fuzzy Logic, but they are left aside for future research methods such as PROMETHEE and ELECTRE. There are many more methods available in MCDA scope. Following the decision tree to select an MCDA method written by [23], which considers 56 methods, the number of options can be easily reduced. In the case of selecting an IIoT platform that has different criteria, the problem has the characteristics of classification or ranking, ordering the options from best to worst. This technique is useful in real life, since they hardly conform and subject themselves to a single option, but they have to consider their primary option and another option as backup, assuming that the first option is not viable.

The candidate methods found are COMET, NAIADE II, EVAMIX, MAUT, MAVT, SAW, SMART, TOPSIS, UTA, VIKOR, Fuzzy SAW, Fuzzy TOPSIS, Fuzzy VIKOR, PROMETHEE I, PAMSSEM II, Fuzzy PROMETHEE II, AHP + TOPSIS, AHP + VIKOR, fuzzy AHP + TOPSIS, AHP + Fuzzy TOPSIS, Fuzzy ANP + Fuzzy TOPSIS, AHP, ANP, MACBETH, DEMATEL, REMBRANDT, Fuzzy AHP, and Fuzzy ANP.

Of the 29 methods suggested by the decision tree, those used in the literature are included for this type of problem. However, although it would be a very interesting exercise to compare the 29 methods with each other, it is beyond the scope of this article. We propose to use PROMETHEE II, which has been widely used in different industries: stock exchange assets, selecting electric vehicles, biology growth models, drainage models, to mention few, but it has not been used in IIoT platform selection [33–35]. The fact that this prodigious method has not yet been used in the field of IIoT encourages us to explore the use of this method, which will be novel. Furthermore, PROMETHEE methods are recognized as one of the best and most popular methods for outrank, allowing the experts who evaluate the alternatives to possibly not have complete and thorough knowledge of all the criteria and also allow them to express the importance of their preferences clearly [34]. These characteristics cover in a good way the aspect that the roles of experts involved in a decision of IIoT platform are multidisciplinary, having in several occasions roles that are not experts in the field of technology, but experts in another area, such as social or economic.

2. Materials and Methods

In our experience, companies that want to implement IIoT show great enthusiasm for the initiative, but, on several occasions, they have a misconception of what IIoT entails. IIoT concepts are technical and of great interest to engineers and systems architects, but the business factors, cost aspects, methods of payment, and commercial conditions, and all of them are of great interest for senior management represented by the Chief Officers, referred to often as the CxO Level. In addition, the wide offer that exists in the market where suppliers have different prices and service schemes makes it difficult to compare one between the other, or at least difficult to do a linear comparison.

Our proposal identifies and suggests the criteria required for IIoT Platform selection for a MCDA exercise with PROMETHEE-II method, enabling organizations to compare results and make a well-founded decision. This work does not provide a universal and definitive solution, but, rather, it proposes the methodology that any organization, be it small or large, can use to decide on the IIoT platform that best suits their circumstances and needs. Following the general MCDA process depicted in Figure 3, the decision objective is the selection of an IIoT platform.

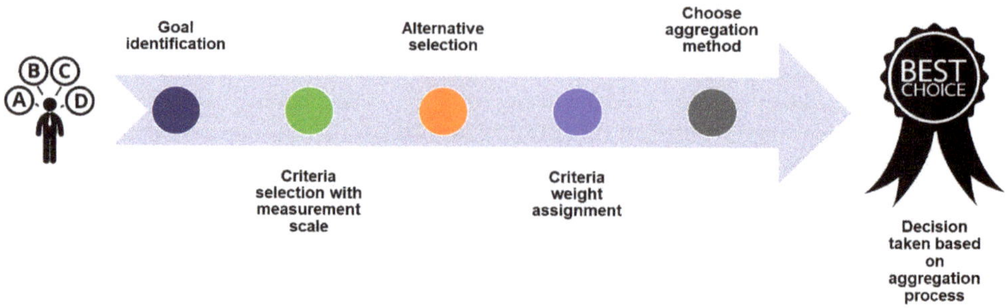

Figure 3. Process for multiple criteria analysis.

The selection of criteria must be consistent with the decision and each criterion must be independent of one another. Each criterion must also be measured on the same scale and applicable to all alternatives. Table 3 summarizes the criteria to be used together with its definition. Criteria that are qualitative, i.e., based on expert judgement, can be measured by text to number scale. For calculating criteria weights, we propose to use the Analytic Hierarchy Process and the Saaty scale [24,27]. Criteria that are quantitative should consider equal scenarios, such as the cost of data transmission, which for all alternatives should be calculated with the same number of devices, same message size, and same number of messages per day.

The selected criteria are divided into three major areas of interest: technical, economic, and social. This is a major enhancement over previous works found in the literature. To identify to what area each criterion belongs, we use a relationship matrix, where we identify if the criterion has a high, medium, or low relationship with each of the areas. The selected criteria are also classified as quantitative and qualitative according to their nature, and are summarized in Table 3.

Table 3. Criteria for IIoT Platform selection process.

Area	**Criterion** (Abbreviation)	**Definition** (Qualitative (Q) or Quantitative (C). All are maximization except when noted Minimization (min))	**Type**
Technical (T)	Available region (TAr)	In cloud-based solutions, it is important to identify the regions where the provider is present and that are suited to the geographical situation of the industry.	C
	Managed Integration (TMi)	The platform has the ability to offer an integration engine with services and applications.	Q
	Communication Protocols (TCp)	IoT devices can communicate telemetry and receive messages with different protocols such as HTTP, MQTT, AMQP, CoAP, or even private.	C
	Security (TS)	The security of the platform must include security for the transmission, registration of devices, avoiding apocryphal devices, authentication and authorization, preferably from start to finish.	Q
	Device Management (TDm)	Devices that can be connected, device identification, device monitoring , send software updates to devices and specify alert conditions. The digital twin refers to the digital replica of the physical asset.	Q

Table 3. *Cont.*

Area	Criterion (Abbreviation)	Definition (Qualitative (Q) or Quantitative (C). All are maximization except when noted Minimization (min))	Type
	Display (TD)	It allows that the data and the behavior of the devices can be seen by humans. It is better if a native and customizable dashboard is offered to show the relevant data to each person.	Q
	Variety of Data Analytics (TAi)	The data collected must be analyzed in different ways. It is important to consider the data flow, real-time analysis, batch, and machine learning algorithms available on the platform.	Q
Economic (E)	Longevity in market (EM)	Years that the provider has in the market. It is expected that the reputation of a supplier will increase over the years.	Q
	Cost (EC)	Calculate the monthly cost (30 days average) for the devices that will be connected. Use constant message size and the frequency of constant message sending.	C(Min)
	Free Cost (EFc)	The providers offer a free amount of messages that are subtracted from the monthly consumption.	Q
	Training Cost (ETc)	Providers can offer access to training with cost or free, and staff certification plans.	C(Min)
Social (S)	Community support (SCs)	Informative resources about the platform, including the available documentation of the provider and external resources of the expert community (blogs, tutorials, discussion forums, etc.)	Q
	Available Resources (SHr)	Availability of human resources with expert knowledge in the platform.	Q
	Training (ST)	Providers offer training and certifications, which can be complicated to follow and hinder the learning curve. One measure may be the estimated time to complete the courses and certifications.	C

The existing alternatives for the IIoT platform considered in this paper appear in the literature, or are widely used in the industry and are recognized as market leaders of cloud providers, such Gartner's Magic Quadrant. Figure 4 shows how in 2014 there were 15 competitors, while, in 2018, only six remained. However, it is easy to observe the leaders, dominated by AWS, Microsoft and the recently newcomer, Google. Thus, the alternatives included in this exercise are: AWS IoT Platform, Microsoft Azure IoT Platform, and Google Cloud IoT Platform. The alternatives and criteria is arranged in a matrix style, as shown in Table 4.

Our proposal includes profiles of people who must participate in the expert judgement exercise, something that has not been found in literature. It is important that they are not only dedicated to technology in order to enrich the exercise. The Table 5 lists the desirable profiles of people we suggest, who should be involved in a MCDA exercise as experts. It is important to note that not all roles must necessarily be participating, as these positions may vary between organizations.

Methods

Our proposed methodology, shown in Figure 5, consists of several tasks in order to found the best alternative. The first task (Activity 1) is to define a decision matrix, taking in consideration sub tasks. It is required to find the alternatives available in the market (Activity 1.1). A good source of information is to rely in recognized entities such as Gartner Consulting (Activity 1.1.1), which has been recognized as a trusted source of information to perform studies to find who are the leaders, challengers, niche players, and visionaries; other sources may be Forrester and IDC, but, for our study, we took Gartner. In next activity, criteria is defined (Activity 1.2) supported by elaborating a relationship matrix (Activity 1.2.1) as presented in Figure 6 using the defined criteria proposed in

Table 3. It consists of fourteen items available, named C_i, where $i = 1, 2, ..., n$, and $n = 14$, arranged in the three main areas.

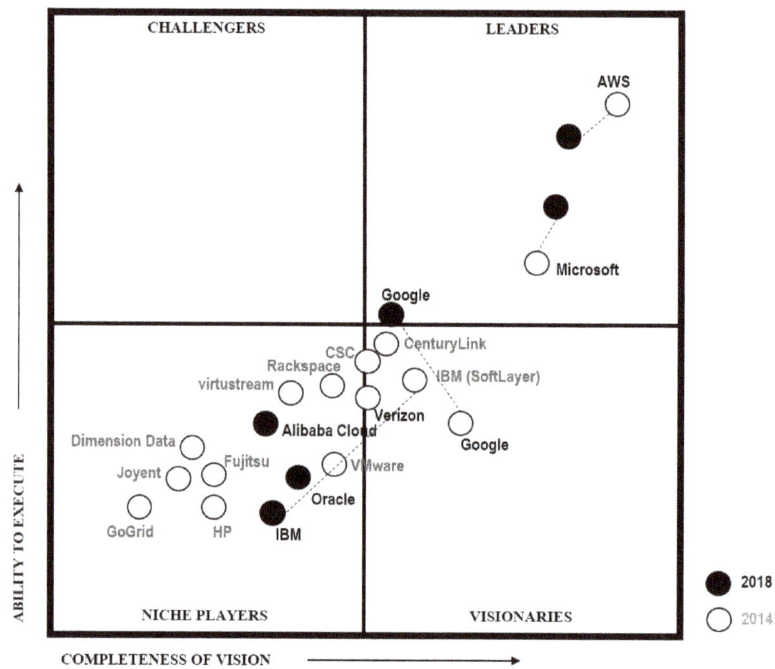

Figure 4. Gartner Cloud Providers Leaders Magic Quadrant 2014 vs. 2018 (adapted from [36,37], own creation).

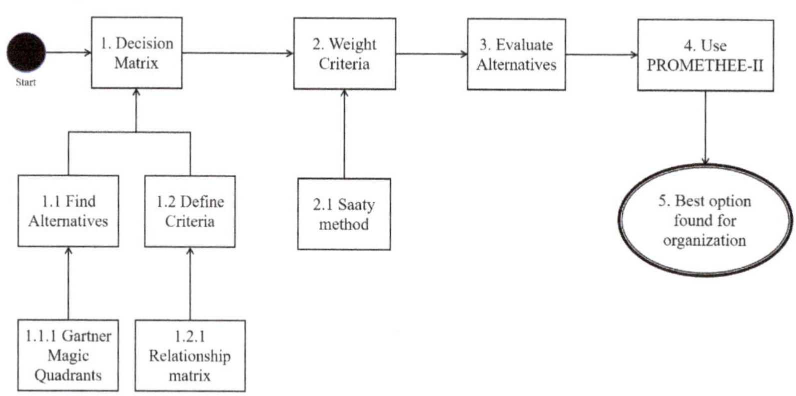

Figure 5. Methodology proposed to select an IIoT Platform.

Each criterion was marked with the level of relationship it has with each group proposed in Low, Medium, and High. It may happen that a criterion has a high relationship with two or more groups. This indicates that the criterion could be classified in any group, or it needs to be broken down in finer criteria.

When evaluating the relationship each of the criteria proposed has with the three groups suggested, it is clear that the technical group will have {Available Regions, Communication Protocols, Device Management, Display, Managed Integration, Security, and Variety of Data Analytics}. The same treatment occurs for economic and social groups. The criterion having high and medium relationship could be argued to have a certain degree of impact in the related groups, but the highest relationship is taken to classify the criterion. It was found that there is no criterion with a high relationship in two or more groups. In addition, the relationship matrix suggests which group may have more impact during decisions, which has to be verified later. In this relationship matrix, the technical group is the one with the most elements (seven), then Economic group with four elements, and, finally, the social group got three elements.

Proposed groups	Available Regions	Available Resources	Communication Protocols	Community Support	Cost	Device Management	Display	Free Cost	Longevity in Market	Managed Integration	Security	Training Available	Training cost	Variety of Data Analytics
Technical	H	L	H	M	L	H	H	M	L	H	H	M	L	H
Economic	L	M	L	M	H	L	L	H	H	L	L	L	H	L
Social	L	H	L	H	L	L	L	L	M	L	L	H	L	L

Figure 6. Relationship matrix to find the criteria and area belonging.

The resulting decision matrix will have 14 criteria, grouped in three categories (technical, economic and social) with three alternatives presented in Table 4, as we are considering as feasible alternatives only the leaders from Figure 4. The structure of the criteria broken down into groups is presented in Figure 7.

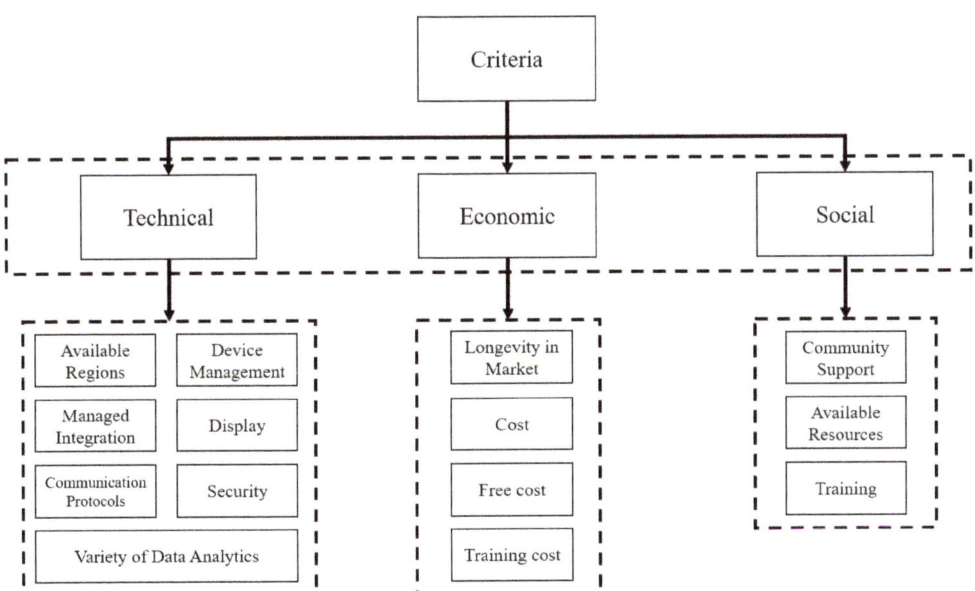

Figure 7. Criteria breakdown into groups.

Table 4. Our resulting decision matrix (activity 1).

Alternative	Criterion C_1	Criterion C_2	...	Criterion C_14
AWS (S_1)				
Azure (S_2)				
GCP (S_3)				

Table 5. Roles involved in the IIoT Platform selection.

Role	Description	Interest
CIO	**Chief Information Officer** In terms usually is, it is the most important person responsible for technology in any company. Their tasks range from buying IT equipment to directing the workforce to the use of technology.	T, E, S
CTO	**Chief Technology Officer** The technology director reports to the CIO, which means that it acts as support for IIoT projects. That said, in larger organizations, the work may be too much for just one person, so the CTO has this responsibility.	T
CInO	**Chief Innovation Officer** This role has been recently created and is the one that can counteract the wild instinct oriented to sales of the business units of a company and design an organizational environment more favorable to innovation.	T, S
CSO	**Chief Security Officer** He is the main person responsible for the information security program of an organization and should be consulted before any deployment of technology.	T
COO	**Chief Operations Officer** Oversees the business operations of an organization and work to create an operations strategy and communicate it to employees. He is very involved in the day to day of the company and will be one of the main impacted in an IIoT project.	E
CMO	**Chief Marketing Officer** The technology and the business aspects of the company are converging. This convergence of technology and marketing reflects the need for the traditional Commercial Director to adapt to a digital world and, therefore, participates in any IIoT project in which they are working, to express their opinion so as to obtain commercial benefit for the company.	E
CFO	**Chief Financial Officer** In all the projects of the company, there must be the support of the Finance Director, who controls the economic resources of the company. In an IIoT project, he is interested in the investment required, and especially in the return of investment to exercise.	E
HRO	**Human Resources Officer** It is the person who needs to know if the necessary skills to the project exist in the market, how easy it is to obtain them, and the sources where they can be obtained. Among his responsibilities are the personnel development plans and the recruitment of human resources.	S
BUL	**Business Unit Leaders** The deputy directors and managers who report within each hierarchy are key personnel that can provide good opinions and issue a more tactical than strategic judgement. By being more focused on specific projects, their knowledge and sensitivity also become specific, giving value to expert judgements.	T, E, S

Then, Activity 2 starts, where experts will need to grade each criterion in pairwise fashion, using Saaty scale [38] (Activity 2.1) for pairwise comparison (Table 6) to assign a level of importance of C_i over C_j. Experts' answers are recorded in a square matrix $x = [n \times n]$. Each element x_{ij} will have a numeric value translated from Saaty scale and, as it is pairwise, the reciprocal $x_{ji} = 1/x_{ij}$ when $i \neq j$; when $i = j$, then $x_{ij} = 1$. In other words, x_{ij} corresponds to the importance of C_i over C_j.

Table 6. Saaty scale for pairwise comparison (adapted from [38]).

Intensity of Importance	Definition	Explanation
1	Equal importance	Two elements contribute equally to the objective
3	Moderate importance	Experience and judgement slightly favor one element over another
5	Strong importance	Experience and judgement strongly favor one element over another
7	Very strong importance	One element is favored very strongly over another, its dominance is demonstrated in practice
9	Extreme importance	The evidence favoring one activity over another is of the highest possible order of affirmation
2, 4, 6, 8	Intermediate values	Importance between above and below value

When designing the tool to grab expert's answers, consider the number of pairwise comparisons required. These can be easily calculated by

$$NumComparisons = \frac{n^2 - n}{2} \tag{1}$$

After having recorded all answers, it is required to calculate weights w, for each C_i. To proceed, the matrix values need to first be normalized by obtaining the sum of each column and then dividing each cell by the sum of its corresponding column.

From this normalized matrix, criteria weights w are obtained by the sum on each row element $\sum_{i=1}^{n} x_{ij}$, when $j = 1, 2, ..., n$. However, it is important to verify if weights found are trustworthy and can be applied later. This is achieved by calculating the Consistency Ratio (CR). CR will measure how consistent the judgements are relative to a large sample of pure random judgements, known as Random Index (RI). When $CR < 0.1$, then the weights are acceptable. In the case $CR > 0.1$, it indicates that the judgements are untrustworthy because they are closer to random distribution and the exercise must be repeated. Random distribution, also known as Saaty random consistency index, is well documented by Saaty [38] and widely used in literature. As a reference, Table 7 shows values for RI, based on a number of criteria [39].

CR is found by

$$CR = \frac{CI}{RI} \tag{2}$$

where CI is Consistency Index and RI is the Random Index. CI is calculated as

$$CI = \frac{\lambda_{max} - n}{n - 1} \tag{3}$$

It is required to multiply each value for its corresponding criteria weight and then sum each row to obtain a weighted sum value (WSM). Then, each of this weighted sum values is divided by the corresponding criteria weight (CW). The result is a new column with $\lambda_i = \frac{WSM_i}{CW_i}$ values.

To calculate λ_{max}, just sum up the results of each λ and divide it by the number of rows in the matrix

$$\lambda_{max} = \frac{\sum_{i=1}^{n}(\lambda_i)}{\text{num of rows}} \tag{4}$$

Table 7. Random index [39].

N	Random Index (RI)
1	0.00
2	0.00
3	0.58
4	0.90
5	1.12
6	1.24
7	1.32
8	1.41
9	1.45
10	1.49
11	1.51
12	1.48
13	1.56
14	1.57
15	1.59

If $CR < 0.1$, then calculated weights are accepted (trustworthy) and experts can proceed to grade each alternative S_k for each C_i. We propose a qualitative criterion to use qualitative conversion from 1 to 5. Each word from low, below low, average, good, and excellent has a corresponding value, in this case $\{1, 2,3,4,5\}$.

Activity 3 consists of evaluating the alternatives using the decision matrix with the weights found and validated. It is required to define a criterion goal. They can be Maximize (also known as direct criteria, or beneficial criteria) or Minimize (also known as indirect criteria or non beneficial criteria). This goal setting is important as it will define the normalization method in Activity 4.

A quantitative criterion just needs to enter the value as it is found. For a qualitative criterion, the expert enters a perception of the criterion that in turn will be translated into a numeric value. We propose to use 1 to 5 values, as shown in Table 8.

Table 8. Perception to value.

Perception	Value
Excellent	5
Good	4
Average	3
Below Average	2
Low	1

After all decision matrix is evaluated, a PROMETHEE-II method can be applied. PROMTHEE-II stands for a Preference Ranking Organization Method for Enrichment Evaluations. Version I is just a partial ranking, reason enough not to use it in our methodology, while version II is a full ranking. PROMETHEE-II is an extensively documented method, and the reader can find information about this method in [40,41].

Finally, all alternatives are ranked, and the best option for the organization (Activity 5) can be obtained.

3. Results

Calculating weights, consistency, and selecting the best alternative can be difficult to follow. It is better to show an example. In our work, we follow our proposed methodology to obtain the best option to select an IIoT platform calculating the weighted criteria with the three platform vendors located in the leader quadrant from Gartner's magic quadrant (Figure 4). Those are: AWS, Azure, and GCP.

3.1. Weight Criteria Calculation

The first step in our methodology says to calculate the weights required for platform selection. In order to achieve this, there are two things to do: (1) Weight calculation coming from experts judgement (participants came from Table 5) and (2) Validate consistency.

Each expert must answer how important is $criterion_i$ over $criterion_j$. Using Saaty scale [38] for pairwise comparison (Table 6), experts can express the importance between two criteria. In our proposed methodology, each expert consulted should answer $[(14^2) - 14]/2 = 91$ comparisons, as there are 14 criteria. This is 91 items.

By following criteria abbreviations proposed in Table 3, and having recorded experts' judgement for each pairwise comparison, Table 9 shows the matrix with answers given.

Table 9. Expert's judgement pairwise comparison recorded.

	TAr	TMi	TCp	TS	TDm	D	TAi	EM	EC	EFc	ETc	SCs	SHr	ST
TAr	**1**	1/2	1/2	1/5	1/2	1/5	1/2	2	1/2	1	1/2	1/2	1/2	1/2
TMi	2	**1**	1	1	1	1	1	5	1	3	3	5	1	3
TCp	2	1	**1**	1	3	1	1	5	1	3	5	5	3	5
TS	5	1	1	**1**	1	5	5	2	1	5	3	5	5	5
TDm	2	1	1/3	1	**1**	3	3	3	1	3	3	2	1	1
D	5	1	1	1/5	1/3	**1**	1	3	1	3	4	3	2	3
TAi	2	1	1	1/5	1/3	1	**1**	3	1	2	1	2	1	2
EM	1/2	1/5	1/5	1/2	1/3	1/3	1/3	**1**	1/2	1	1/3	1/3	1/3	1/3
EC	2	1	1	1	1	1	1	2	**1**	1	2	2	2	3
EFc	1	1/3	1/3	1/5	1/3	1/3	1/2	1	1	**1**	1/2	1/3	1/2	1/3
ETc	2	1/3	1/5	1/3	1/3	1/55	1	3	1/2	2	**1**	1	1/2	1
SCs	2	1/5	1/5	1/5	1/2	1/3	1/2	3	1/2	3	1	**1**	1	1
SHr	2	1	1/3	1/5	1	1/2	1	3	1/2	2	2	1	**1**	1
ST	2	1/3	1/5	1/5	1	1/3	1/2	3	1/3	3	1	1	1	**1**
$\sum x_{ij}$	30.5	9.9	8.3	7.23	11.67	15.283	17.33	39	10.83	33	27.33	29.167	19.83	27.167

We need to obtain the sum of each column. The sum of each column will be used to normalize Table 9 resulting in Table 10. Then, in Table 11 are shown the weighted values for all criteria.

Table 10. Normalized matrix.

	TAr	TMi	TCp	TS	TDm	TD	TAi	EM	EC	EFc	ETc	SCs	SHr	ST
TAr	0.033	0.051	0.060	0.028	0.043	0.013	0.029	0.051	0.046	0.030	0.018	0.017	0.025	0.018
TMi	0.066	0.101	0.120	0.138	0.086	0.065	0.058	0.128	0.092	0.091	0.110	0.171	0.050	0.110
TCp	0.066	0.101	0.120	0.138	0.257	0.065	0.058	0.128	0.092	0.091	0.183	0.171	0.151	0.184
TS	0.164	0.101	0.120	0.138	0.086	0.327	0.288	0.051	0.092	0.152	0.110	0.171	0.252	0.184
TDm	0.066	0.101	0.040	0.138	0.086	0.196	0.173	0.077	0.092	0.091	0.110	0.069	0.050	0.037
TD	0.164	0.101	0.120	0.028	0.029	0.065	0.058	0.077	0.092	0.091	0.146	0.103	0.101	0.110
TAi	0.066	0.101	0.120	0.028	0.029	0.065	0.058	0.077	0.092	0.061	0.037	0.069	0.050	0.074
EM	0.016	0.020	0.024	0.069	0.029	0.022	0.019	0.026	0.046	0.030	0.012	0.011	0.017	0.012
EC	0.066	0.101	0.120	0.138	0.086	0.065	0.058	0.051	0.092	0.030	0.073	0.069	0.101	0.110
EFc	0.033	0.034	0.040	0.028	0.029	0.022	0.029	0.026	0.092	0.030	0.018	0.011	0.025	0.012
ETc	0.066	0.034	0.024	0.046	0.029	0.016	0.058	0.077	0.046	0.061	0.037	0.034	0.025	0.037
SCs	0.066	0.020	0.024	0.028	0.043	0.022	0.029	0.077	0.046	0.091	0.037	0.034	0.050	0.037
SHr	0.066	0.101	0.040	0.028	0.086	0.033	0.058	0.077	0.046	0.061	0.073	0.034	0.050	0.037
ST	0.066	0.034	0.024	0.028	0.086	0.022	0.029	0.077	0.031	0.091	0.037	0.034	0.050	0.037

Table 11. Weights w_i calculated for each criterion.

Criterion C_i	Weight Calculated w_i
TAr	0.033054398
TMi	0.099114871
TCp	0.129047676
TS	0.159817455
TDm	0.094698157
TD	0.091812783
TAi	0.066103106
EM	0.025301927
EC	0.082932622
EFc	0.030639156
ETc	0.042044181
SCs	0.043080184
SHr	0.056348976
ST	0.046004508

To determine if weights are trustworthy, we calculated Consistency Index and Consistency ratio. In order to achieve this, calculation of weighted values need to be found by $(x_{ij} \times w_i)$, as is shown in Table 12. The Table 13 shows the values obtained when calculating WVS, the ratio of each $\frac{WVS}{w_i}$, λ_{max} and Equation (5) shows Consistency Index CI calculation.

Table 12. Computed weighted values.

	TAr	TMi	TCp	TS	TDm	TD	TAi	EM	EC	EFc	ETc	SCs	SHr	ST
TAr	0.033	0.050	0.065	0.032	0.047	0.018	0.033	0.051	0.041	0.031	0.021	0.022	0.028	0.023
TMi	0.066	0.099	0.129	0.160	0.095	0.092	0.066	0.127	0.083	0.092	0.126	0.215	0.056	0.138
TCp	0.066	0.099	0.129	0.160	0.284	0.092	0.066	0.127	0.083	0.092	0.210	0.215	0.169	0.230
TS	0.165	0.099	0.129	0.160	0.095	0.459	0.331	0.051	0.083	0.153	0.126	0.215	0.282	0.230
TDm	0.066	0.099	0.043	0.160	0.095	0.275	0.198	0.076	0.083	0.092	0.126	0.086	0.056	0.046
TD	0.165	0.099	0.129	0.032	0.032	0.092	0.066	0.076	0.083	0.092	0.168	0.129	0.113	0.138
TAi	0.066	0.099	0.129	0.032	0.032	0.092	0.066	0.076	0.083	0.061	0.042	0.086	0.056	0.092
EM	0.017	0.020	0.026	0.080	0.032	0.031	0.022	0.025	0.041	0.031	0.014	0.014	0.019	0.015
EC	0.066	0.099	0.129	0.160	0.095	0.092	0.066	0.051	0.083	0.031	0.084	0.086	0.113	0.138
EFc	0.033	0.033	0.043	0.032	0.032	0.031	0.033	0.025	0.083	0.031	0.021	0.014	0.028	0.015
ETc	0.066	0.033	0.026	0.053	0.032	0.023	0.066	0.076	0.041	0.061	0.042	0.043	0.028	0.046
SCs	0.066	0.020	0.026	0.032	0.047	0.031	0.033	0.076	0.041	0.092	0.042	0.043	0.056	0.046
SHr	0.066	0.099	0.043	0.032	0.095	0.046	0.066	0.076	0.041	0.061	0.084	0.043	0.056	0.046
ST	0.066	0.033	0.026	0.032	0.095	0.031	0.033	0.076	0.028	0.092	0.042	0.043	0.056	0.046

Table 13. Computed consistency.

Criterion C_i	Weight Value $\sum$ (WVS)	Ratio WVS/w_i
TAr	0.494310596	14.95445755
TMi	1.543958531	15.57746603
TCp	2.022150174	15.66979151
TS	2.577562734	16.12816779
TDm	1.501905104	15.85991904
TD	1.413764592	15.39834154
TAi	1.012396031	15.31540793
EM	0.386173129	15.26259755
EC	1.291838682	15.57696654
EFc	0.454059119	14.81956987
ETc	0.636805226	15.14609676
SCs	0.651477099	15.12243086
SHr	0.855083138	15.17477683
ST	0.69821939	15.17719502
		$\lambda_{max} = 15.37023$

Consistency Index in our experiment is calculated as

$$CI = \frac{\lambda_{max} - n}{n-1} = \frac{15.37023 - 14}{(14-1)} = 0.105402 \quad (5)$$

Using the random index for $N = 14$ from Table 7, Consistency ratio is computed as

$$CR = \frac{CI}{RI(n)} = \frac{0.105402}{1.59} = 0.06671 \quad (6)$$

As CR < 0.1, the weights for each criterion are consistent and trustworthy; therefore, they are accepted to use in our decision process.

3.2. IIoT Platform Selection

Among the three cloud platform vendors considered for this excercise: AWS, Azure, and Google Cloud Platform (GCP), listed in alphabetical order. Each vendor brings IIoT capacity, different services, and price schema not directly comparable among vendors. Each organization must have their goals, and will answer the weight criteria process differently, so it is not possible to determine which vendor is better than another in an absolute fashion. For that reason, this scenario is a good fit for our methodology.

Each alternative (let us call them S_i) needs to be graded on each of the criterion proposed. It is convenient to have it on a table, with criteria identified (in this case, we use abbreviations suggested in our methodology) and specify if criterion is qualitative, i.e., requires a numeric value contained in criterion domain, or it is qualitative and requires converting the appreciation of expert grading into a pre-established numeric value, as shown in Table 14.

Table 14. Pre-define values for qualitative labels.

Qualitative Label	Pre-Defined Value
Low	1
Below Avg	2
Average	3
Good	4
Excellent	5

For criterion, "Available regions (TAr), AWS has 22 available regions worldwide (https://aws.amazon.com/about-aws/global-infrastructure/?p=ngi&loc=1), Azure offers 55 regions (https://azure.microsoft.com/en-us/global-infrastructure/regions/), and GCP offers 21 (https://cloud.google.com/about/locations/). Criterion Communication ports (TCp), AWS offers three options (HTTP, Websockets, MQTT), Azure offers four (HTTP, AMQP, MQTT, Websockets), and GCP offers two (HTTP, MQTT). Criterion Cost (EC) is the most cumbersome to compare and calculate. AWS uses a mix schema to estimate IIoT costs. Azure is based on messages, and GCP has a traffic consumption schema. As it can be seen, this is not comparable directly, so we estimated costs based on a same scenario for all three vendors.

The scenario consists of 1000 devices, sending a message of 8 Kb with a rate of two messages per minute. All estimations are per month. Our compared estimations using each vendor calculator are summarized in Table 15.

Table 15. Cost estimations by vendor.

AWS	Azure	GCP
$ 3.46 Connectivity $86.40 of messaging $36.00 device shadow $ 4.32 rules triggered $ 8.64 rules actions	2880 meessages/device 2,880,000 msg/day S1 node provides 400,00 msg/day unlimited access Need 8 X S1 nodes	675,000 MB/month $0.0045/MB
Total Cost: $138.32	Total Cost: $180.00	Total Cost: $3,037.50

Training cost (ETc) takes into consideration the cost of certification, being AWS $150.00, Azure $165.00, and GCP $200.00 (at the time of writing this paper). The rest of the criteria are evaluated from a qualitative form. Table 16 contains the grades provided and $Max(x_{ij})$ and $Min(x_{ij})$. In order to save space, we use S_1 as AWS, S_2 as Azure, and S_3 as GCP.

Table 16. Graded alternatives.

S_i	TAr	TMi	TCp	TS	TDm	TD	TAi	EM	EC	EFc	ETc	SCs	SHr	ST
S_1 AWS	22	4	3	5	3	4	5	5	138.82	3	150	4	5	4
S_2 Azure	55	5	4	4	4	5	5	4	182.53	5	165	5	5	3
S_3 GCP	21	3	3	3	3	5	4	3	3037.5	4	200	3	3	3
$Max(x_{ij})$	55	5	4	5	4	5	5	5	3037.5	5	200	5	5	4
$Min(x_{ij})$	21	3	3	3	3	4	4	3	138.82	3	150	3	3	3

To normalize the table, we need to consider if we are maximizing or minimizing. The resulting normalized matrix is in Table 17. As a courtesy to the reader, we exemplify the operation using the first cell of the matrix. The operation executed to normalize values (Maximizing) is

$$\frac{X_{1,1} - Min(x_{ij})}{Max(x_{ij}) - Min(x_{ij})} = \frac{22-21}{55-21} = 0.023$$

For criterion looking for minimization, the equation changes, such as EC calculation (top row):

$$\frac{Max(x_{ij} - X_{1,1}}{Max(x_{ij}) - Min(x_{ij})} = \frac{3037.5-138.82}{3037.5-138.82} = 1$$

Table 17. Normalized table.

S_i	TAr	TMi	TCp	TS	TDm	TD	TAi	EM	EC	EFc	ETc	SCs	SHr	ST
S_1	0.029	0.5	0	1	0	0	1	1	1	0	1	0.5	1	1
S_2	1	1	1	0.5	1	1	1	0.5	0.985	1	0.7	1	1	0
S_3	0	0	0	0	0	1	0	0	0	0.5	0	0	0	0

The next step is to calculate differences from normalized Table 17 using a pairwise comparison as shown in Table 18. The sample operation is

$$S_1 - S_2 = (0.029 - 1) = -0.971$$

Table 18. Calculated differences from normalized matrix.

$S_a - S_b$	TAr	TMi	TCp	TS	TDm	TD	TAi	EM	EC	EFc	ETc	SCs	SHr	ST
$S_1 - S_2$	−0.971	−0.5	−1	0.5	−1	−1	0	0.5	0.015	−1	0.3	−0.5	0	1
$S_1 - S_3$	0.029	0.5	0	1	0	−1	1	1	1	−0.5	1	0.5	1	1
$S_2 - S_1$	0.971	0.5	1	−0.5	1	1	0	−0.5	−0.015	1	−0.3	0.5	0	−1
$S_2 - S_3$	1	1	1	0.5	1	0	1	0.5	0.985	0.5	0.7	1	1	0
$S_3 - S_1$	−0.029	−0.5	0	−1	0	1	−1	−1	−1	0.5	−1	−0.5	−1	−1
$S_3 - S_2$	−1	−1	−1	−0.5	−1	0	−1	−0.5	−0.985	−0.5	−0.7	−1	−1	0

Next, calculate preference function values, resulting in Table 19. The operation is

$$P_i(a,b) \leq 0 \text{ then } P_i(a,b) = 0; \; -0.971 \leq 0 \text{ then } = 0$$

Table 19. Preference function computation results.

$S_a - S_b$	TAr	TMi	TCp	TS	TDm	TD	TAi	EM	EC	EFc	ETc	SCs	SHr	ST
$S_1 - S_2$	0	0	0	0.5	0	0	0	0.5	0.0151	0	0.3	0	0	1
$S_1 - S_3$	0.023	0.5	0	1	0	0	1	1	1	0	1	0.5	1	1
$S_2 - S_1$	0.971	0.5	1	0	1	1	0	0	0	1	0	0.5	0	0
$S_2 - S_3$	1	1	1	0.5	1	0	1	0.5	0.985	0.5	0.7	1	1	0
$S_3 - S_1$	0	0	0	0	0	1	0	0	0	0.5	0	0	0	0
$S_3 - S_2$	0	0	0	0	0	0	0	0	0	0	0	0	0	0

Next, we calculate the weighted preferences, using preference function and weights found in Table 11. Each cell has the value $wP(a,b)$ and results are in Table 20 by doing

$$w_i P_i(a,b) = 0.033 \times 0 = 0$$

Table 20. Weighted preferences.

	TAr	TMi	TCp	TS	TDm	TD	TAi	EM	EC	EFc	ETc	SCs	SHr	ST
w_i	0.033	0.099	0.129	0.160	0.095	0.092	0.066	0.025	0.083	0.031	0.042	0.043	0.056	0.046
$S_1 - S_2$	0.000	0.000	0.000	0.080	0.000	0.000	0.000	0.013	0.001	0.000	0.013	0.000	0.000	0.046
$S_1 - S_3$	0.001	0.050	0.000	0.160	0.000	0.000	0.066	0.025	0.083	0.000	0.042	0.022	0.056	0.046
$S_2 - S_1$	0.032	0.050	0.129	0.000	0.095	0.092	0.000	0.000	0.000	0.031	0.000	0.022	0.000	0.000
$S_2 - S_3$	0.033	0.099	0.129	0.080	0.095	0.000	0.066	0.013	0.082	0.015	0.029	0.043	0.056	0.000
$S_3 - S_1$	0.000	0.000	0.000	0.000	0.000	0.092	0.000	0.000	0.000	0.015	0.000	0.000	0.000	0.000
$S_3 - S_2$	0.000	0.000	0.000	0.000	0.000	0.000	0.000	0.000	0.000	0.000	0.000	0.000	0.000	0.000

The aggregated preference is shown in Table 21.

Table 21. Aggregated preference.

$S_q - S_b$	$\pi(a,b)$
$S_1 - S_2$	0.152428017
$S_1 - S_3$	0.55062249
$S_2 - S_1$	0.44937751
$S_2 - S_3$	0.740439621
$S_3 - S_1$	0.107132361
$S_3 - S_2$	0

Next, using the aggregated preference values, we calculate the entering and leaving flows. Table 22 has the arranged values; the right-most column contains the leaving flow (φ^+), and the bottom row shows the entering flow (φ^-).

Table 22. Entering and leaving flows.

	AWS	Azure	GCP	φ^+
AWS		0.152428017	0.55062249	0.351525254
Azure	0.44937751		0.740439621	0.594908565
GCP	0.107132361	0		0.053566181
φ^-	0.278254935	0.076214009	0.645531056	

Leaving flow φ^+ and entering flow φ^- are calculated as follows:

$$\varphi^+ = \frac{1}{n-1}\sum_{b=1}^{n}\pi(a,b) = \frac{(0.152428017 + 0.55062249)}{3-1} = 0.351525254$$

$$\varphi^- = \frac{1}{n-1}\sum_{b=1}^{n}\pi(b,a) = \frac{(0.44937751 + 0.107132361)}{3-1} = 0.278254935$$

As we are using PROMETHEE-II, we need to calculate net flow Φ. The best way to do it is to build another table with each alternative and its corresponding leaving and entering flows. Add the column for net flow ($\Phi = \varphi^+ - \varphi^-$) and order the net flows from highest to lowest to rank all alternatives available. Table 23 shows the results.

Table 23. Ranking of alternatives.

	Leaving flow φ^+	Entering flow φ^-	Net Flow Φ	Rank
AWS	0.351525254	0.278254935	0.073270318	2
Azure	0.594908565	0.076214009	0.518694557	**1**
GCP	0.053566181	0.645531056	−0.591964875	3

4. Discussion

The methodology proposed to find the best alternative within a decision matrix, using all criteria, and applied to an example, finds the best solution. However, as part of this research, we decided to execute two validations. The first one uses the proposed methodology with criteria subsets. The second consists of running the full criteria (14 elements) with three different methods: TOPSIS, and its use has been reported in literature for similar problems, MOORA and Dimensional Analysis (DA), using the same alternatives and values in decision matrix.

Our proposed methodology with criteria subsets shows a good consistency in the alternative selected, except when we used five criteria. When use seven or ten criteria, the result is exactly the same, as shown in Table 24 and Figure 8.

Table 24. Ranking with our proposed methodology with criteria subsets (1 is highest).

	5 Criteria	7 Criteria	10 Criteria	Full Criteria (14)
AWS	1	2	2	2
Azure	2	1	1	1
GCP	3	3	3	3

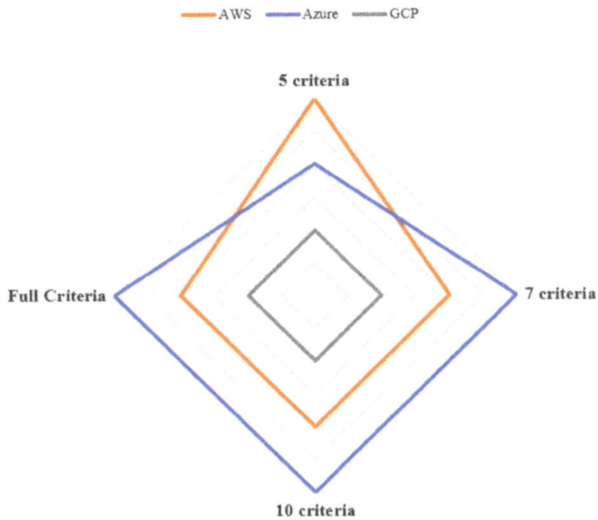

Figure 8. Comparison of results using different criteria subsets with the same methodology.

In addition, we found that there is a change of index values when adding criteria. Figure 9 depicts how alternative AWS lowers when adding criteria, and alternative GCP increases. It can be observed also how alternative Azure remains not only as the best alternative, but also consistent in the index value.

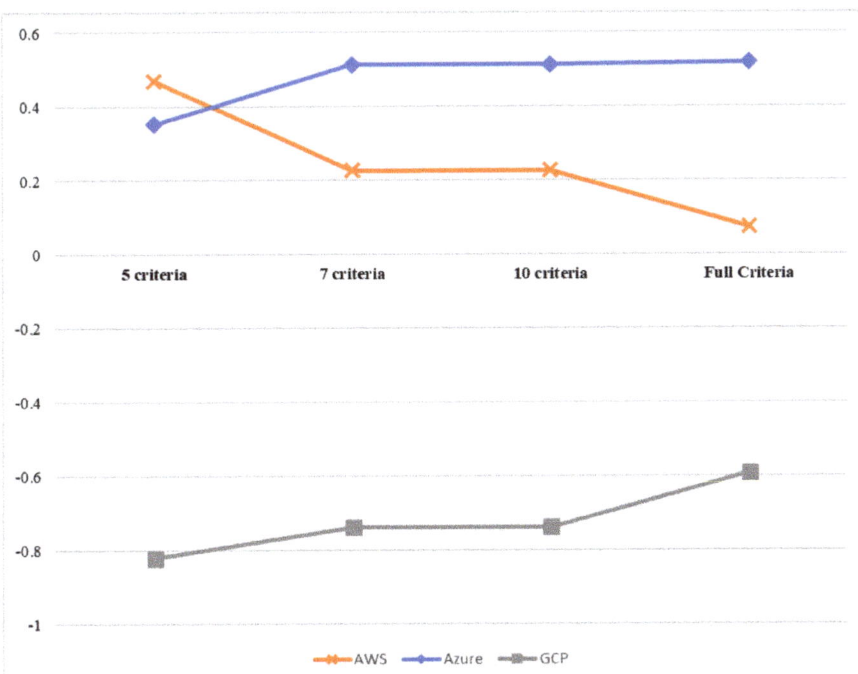

Figure 9. Comparison of resulting indexes in the proposed methodology.

Now, comparing TOPSIS, MOORA, and DA against our proposed methodology, the results are consistent, as all algorithms selected the same alternative with same number of criteria considered. Table 25 and Figure 10 show that all three other methods selected the same alternative as our methodology.

Table 25. Proposed methodology validation with three more algorithms using full criteria.

	Ours	TOPSIS	MOORA	AD
AWS	2	2	2	3
Azure	1	1	1	1
GCP	3	3	3	2

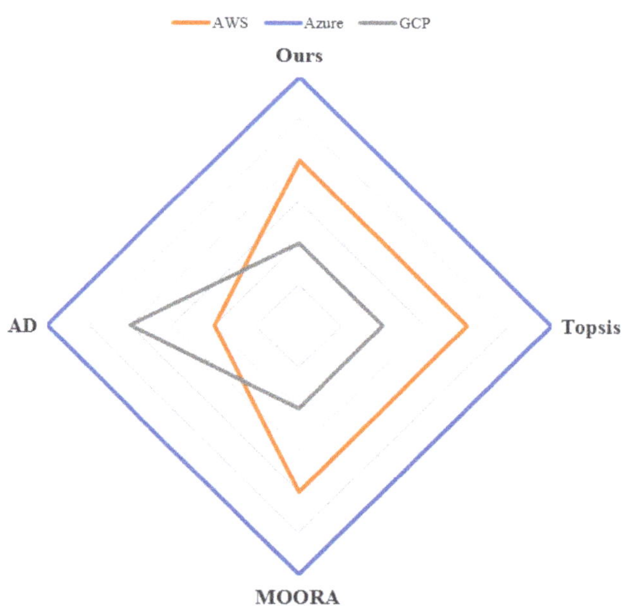

Figure 10. Comparing different methodologies against our proposed methodology.

Becasue TOPSIS has been used in similar problems, we decided to do an additional comparison. By running TOPSIS against the same criteria subsets, we can observe that the selected alternative is the same for all cases, as shown in Table 26.

Table 26. Ranking with our proposed methodology with criteria subsets (1 is highest).

	5 Criteria	7 Criteria	10 Criteria	Full Criteria (14)
AWS	1	2	2	2
Azure	2	1	1	1
GCP	3	3	3	3

As it can be observed, when the number of criteria varies, only in one case, the one with fewest criteria subset, the result changes while the rest remains constant. This suggests that there should be a criteria subset that could provide the best selection option. We analyzed another set of scenarios, in order to identify the minimum criteria subset. To achieve this, it is interesting to take a look at resulting indexes, to identify: 1) where is the major gap among alternatives ranked, and 2) what is the trend by expanding the number of criteria. Ordering the criteria weights, it can be found that some criteria provide a very low percentage in the mix (we assume for every scenario $\sum(w_i) = 1$) (Table 27).

Table 27. Ordered weighted preferences.

TS	TCp	TMi	TDm	TD	EC	TAi
0.1598	0.1290	0.0991	0.0947	0.0918	0.0829	0.0661
SHr	**ST**	**SCs**	**ETc**	**TAr**	**EFc**	**EM**
0.0563	0.0460	0.0431	0.0420	0.0331	0.0306	0.0253

If all criteria weights were equally important (baseline), for each criterion, its deviation from that baseline is identified. Positive deviation means more importance, while a negative deviation means lower importance. By using this reasoning, we found six criteria candidates that could lead us to the minimum subset. Figure 11 shows the subset chosen {Security, Communication Protocols, Managed Integration, Device Management, and Display and Cost}

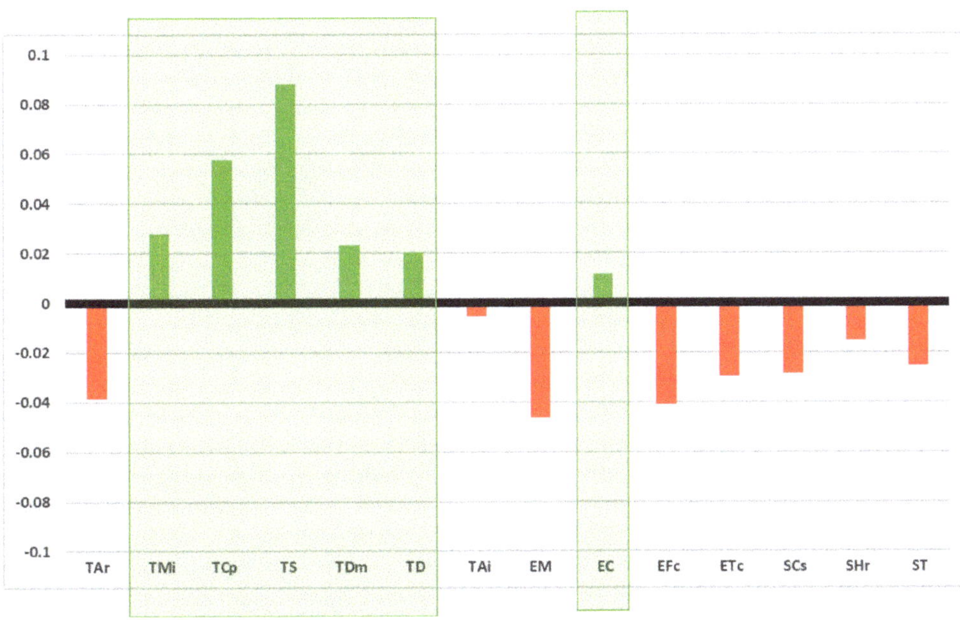

Figure 11. Importance comparison based on distance to baseline.

To verify that this is a significant subset, this subset called "Top" is evaluated in PROMETHEE-II, and, to double check our selection, we add three more scenarios: top subset with equal weights (TopEq), bottom criteria (Bot), and bottom criteria with equal weights (BotEq). The results in Figure 12 show an extremely well performance selecting the alternative S_2 (Azure) with the largest separation from the other two alternatives, being AWS and GCP with negative numbers, in both Top and TopEq scenarios. In comparison with our full criteria set (weighted in the graph), Top and TopEq scenarios show the largest distance between alternative S_2 and S_1 (AWS). In addition, it can be observed that Bot and BotEq scenarios are very close each other, with less separation between S_2 and S_1. Finally, the criteria subset labeled Top provides the highest rank index, suggesting that the selected subset is feasible to be the minimum set required.

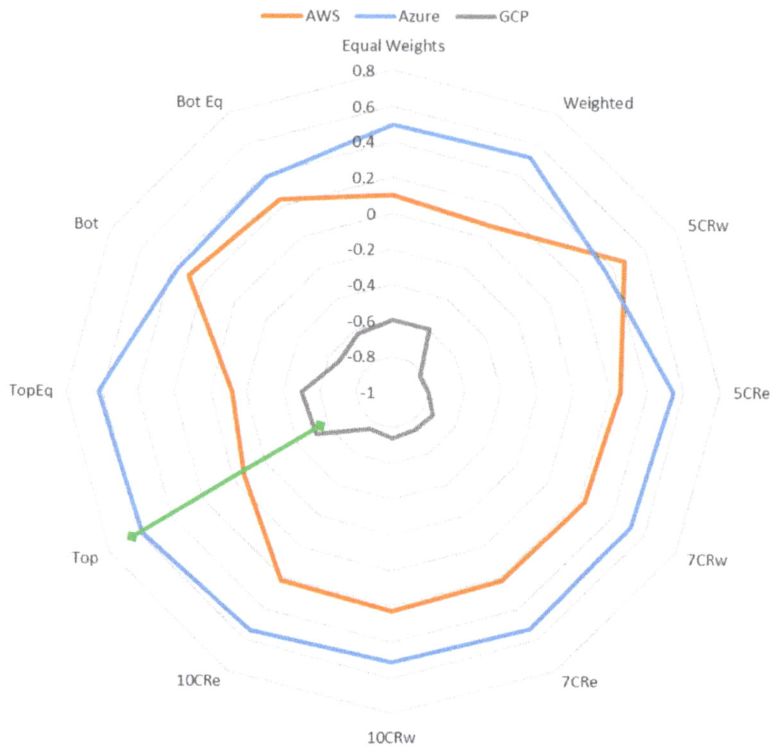

Figure 12. Comparison of results with different criteria subsets.

5. Conclusions

As technology in IIoT and the cloud advances, there will be new options available in the market for the organizations. In addition, there are aspects that are relevant, not only technical, but economical and social. The three alternatives evaluated for this paper are aligned to leaders identified by Gartner up to 2018; however, it doesn't assure they will be the only ones in the near-, mid- or long-term.

The criteria proposed follows and adapt for today's vision. People must have double deep abilities—which are technical and business. This is one of the reasons to add to technical criteria the angles of economics and social view. As per our literature review, economics and social views have not been considered. Our contribution to industry provides these two missing aspects.

Cost is one of the most difficult and confusing comparisons, if there is not a good scenario to run against each price schema. However, as it is shown in Table 11, cost is not the main driver to take a decision in IIoT. Security has the highest weight and this is understandable as an organization's IIoT implementations and solutions will transmit sensitive data. Communication protocols are the second most important criterion, and the reasoning behind is the flexibility required for different sensors available in the market. Device management and display are very close in importance, which is logical as organizations need to deploy from dozens to thousands of devices for a solution, and having a dashboard to locate and get information about devices is important.

Of economic and social criteria, the most significant are cost and available resources, respectively; longevity in the market was the least important criterion. This can be read as organizations possibly being open to experiments and learning with newcomers.

It is the best to have different experts from different backgrounds or responsibility within the organization. The roles suggested in this methodology (Table 5) cover a large part of main organization areas. We decided to include not only the IT department, but operations, financial, human resources, and business unit leaders. This proves to be aligned with the criteria suggested. By inviting the ability to participate in different roles, the weighting criteria become more accurate; therefore, the selection process will be better. We do not suggest to have a single expert to provide an opinion on criteria weighting. As people may have different understanding or could be biased towards a specific criteria, having more than one expert is preferred, and our proposed set of roles provides the options to select the experts.

Use of Saaty scale and method to evaluate criteria importance was proven to be effective. However, we discover that the validation of opinions is even more important, in order to provide trustworthy weights for the selection criteria. In our experiment, consistency ratio was 0.06, which is acceptable and allows for continuing with the process. Organizations must use these kinds of validations when choosing what would be more important over other criteria.

As it was discovered in the literature review (Table 2), most work related to cloud and IIoT has focused on AHP and TOPSIS. However, selecting an IIoT platform cannot have a single alternative winner; it is better to have all alternatives ranked. Our experience states, in some cases, that the vendor selected cannot deliver or does not meet other organizations' requirements such as terms, legal contracts, conditions, or timing. When this happens, it would be a waste of time to redo the whole MCDA process again. This is why PROMETHEE-II has been proven to be effective as it can rank from top to bottom the alternatives available. In our exercise, Azure was the first option, followed by AWS and GCP.

It is important to notice that PROMETHEE-II and our methodology will not say which platform or technology is better, from an absolute standpoint, but which platform or technology is better suited for the organization based on the weights and grades provided by experts within the organization.

The paper demonstrated that our proposed methodology is effective at finding the best alternative to select an IIoT platform vendor as it has been performed consistently with five, seven, and ten criteria subsets, as well as comparing results against other methods. In addition, it contributes to the field of IIoT, as it provides a novel method to solve the problem many organizations are or will face at any time. Combining Saaty weight method and PROMEHEE-II, decision makers have a good tool to perform the selection. However, if it is limited to the technical aspects, the result may be biased and miss important aspects of the market. For example, if the technology is very good, the platform is the most complete and least expensive, but if there are not engineers or developers available, or training classes cost a fortune, implementing this platform will be a difficult and expensive project, with hidden costs not detected since inception. This is the reason and justification to include economic and social aspects in the criteria, as our methodology proposes.

IIoT platform selection should not be left to IT departments or CIO or CTO. Doing that will miss the point of view of other important leaders that will use, maintain or benefit from the selected platform. The Chief Operation Officer, leaders from business units, interdisciplinary teams, and even human resources and finance should participate in the MCDA process, as they bring ideas and considerations that sometimes are ignored unintentionally. Our proposed methodology provides a suggested list of key persons that should participate, something that was not found in the literature, and is very valuable for the decision process.

As a side discovery, comparing price schemes among vendors is not an easy task. We saw it as very useful to have a common scenario to run against the price schemes. To build a common scenario, it is required to have a close to reality idea of usage, number of devices, message size, and frequency of communication. Trying to compare price schemes without this scenario could lead to incorrect information entered into the grading matrix of the PROMETHEE-II part (Table 16).

The process of doing calculations and operations is laborious, due to the nature of algorithms used in our proposed methodology. This inspires us to continue the future work enhancing the methodology, creating a software to facilitate the computation. Another key aspect is the importance grading from Saaty's process. Filling the matrix with reciprocal values could lead to human error easily. This also highlights, as part of our future work, to develop a graphical user interface that experts can use in a friendly fashion to enter the importance between criteria and fully automate our methodology when multiple experts participate in the process.

Future research work will focus on the fact that, by 2047, the year with the greatest incidence of a paradigm change in Generation Z in Industry 4.0, each tender that will require detailing the side effect of environmental impact can be carried out by an intelligent system using multi-criteria analysis to determine the best option for an alternative in a set of parts supplying resolution possibilities, where decision-making is decisive for its adequate solution, as can be seen in the following Figure 13.

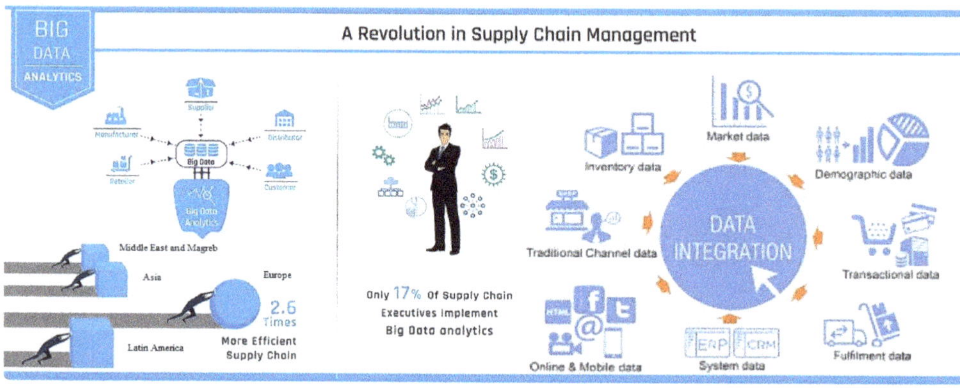

Figure 13. Conceptual diagram of an Intelligent Model that can adequately determine the best multi-criteria selection of a component supply model associated with Industry 4.0.

The decision-making in this century will allow for extending in the Z generation to societies with a specific competitive value such as Bouganville, Brunei, Chuuk, East Timor, Rapa Nui, Sarawak, and Tuva that will have more symbolic capital with a combination of low population and diverse natural resources. Where manual work or traditional manufacturing will generate valuable cultural artifacts such as a French poodle made with balloons, and of which there will be no mass production, something that will be an avant-garde model for the Z generation and their descendants.

Finally, our future work will explore the use and implementation of other techniques to find the minimum criteria required to select the optimum IIoT platform, applying machine learning and data mining techniques. In addition, we plan to expand data acquisition from different experts around the globe in the roles identified previously. This is planned to be achieved by publishing a tool accessed via a web browser to collect the importance of each criterion in pairwise comparison.

Author Contributions: All of the authors jointly contributed to the finalization of the paper: R.C.-M. defined the criteria proposed and provided the MCDA options; A.O.-Z. supervised the overall process and provided resources; M.E.-C. directed the method of ranking; L.P.-D. reviewed the paper; R.C.-M. developed the methodology; V.G. critically reviewed the concept and design of the paper. All authors have read and agreed to the published version of the manuscript.

Funding: This research received no external funding

Conflicts of Interest: The authors declare no conflict of interest. The funders had no role in the design of the study; in the collection, analyses, or interpretation of data; in the writing of the manuscript, or in the decision to publish the results.

Abbreviations

The following abbreviations are used in this manuscript:

IoT	Internet of Things
IIoT	Industrial Internet of Things
MQTT	Message Queue Telemetry Transport
HTTP	Hypertext Transfer Protocol
AMQP	Advanced Message Queuing Protocol
S1	Type of Azure IoT Hub
AWS	Amazon Web Services
GCP	Google Cloud Platform
MCDA	Multiple Criteria Decision Analysis

References

1. Rüßmann, M.; Lorenz, M.; Gerbert, P.; Waldner, M.; Justus, J.; Engel, P.; Harnisch, M. Industry 4.0: The future of productivity and growth in manufacturing industries. *Boston Consult. Group* **2015**, *9*, 54–89.
2. Hatzivasilis, G.; Fysarakis, K.; Soultatos, O.; Askoxylakis, I.; Papaefstathiou, I.; Demetriou, G. The Industrial Internet of Things as an enabler for a Circular Economy Hy- LP: A novel IIoT protocol, evaluated on a wind park's SDN/NFV-enabled 5G industrial network. *Comput. Commun.* **2018**. [CrossRef]
3. Höller, J.; Tsiatsis, V.; Mulligan, C.; Karnouskos, S.; Avesand, S.; Boyle, D. IoT Architecture—State of the Art. In *From Machine-To-Machine to the Internet of Things*; Academic Press: Oxford, UK, 2014. [CrossRef]
4. Lanotte, R.; Merro, M. A semantic theory of the Internet of Things. *Inf. Comput.* **2018**, *259*, 72–101. [CrossRef]
5. Rathore, M.M.; Ahmad, A.; Paul, A.; Rho, S. Urban planning and building smart cities based on the Internet of Things using Big Data analytics. *Comput. Netw.* **2016**, *101*, 63–80. [CrossRef]
6. Figueira, J.; Greco, S.; Ehrgott, M. *Multiple Criteria Decision analysis: State of the Art Surveys*; Springer Science & Business Media: Berlin, Germany, 2005; Volume 78.
7. Huang, I.B.; Keisler, J.; Linkov, I. Multi-criteria decision analysis in environmental sciences: Ten years of applications and trends. *Sci. Total Environ.* **2011**, *409*, 3578–3594. [CrossRef] [PubMed]
8. Weyrich, M.; Ebert, C. Reference architectures for the internet of things. *IEEE Softw.* **2016**, *33*, 112–116. [CrossRef]
9. Vasilomanolakis, E.; Daubert, J.; Luthra, M.; Gazis, V.; Wiesmaier, A.; Kikiras, P. On the Security and Privacy of Internet of Things Architectures and Systems. In Proceedings of the 2015 International Workshop on Secure Internet of Things, SIoT 2015, Vienna, Austria, 21–25 September 2015. [CrossRef]
10. Gironés, T.; Canovas Solbes, J.; Parra-Boronat, A. An Integrated IoT Architecture for Smart Metering. *IEEE Commun. Mag.* **2016**, *54*, 50–57. [CrossRef]
11. Krishnamurthy, R.; Cecil, J.; Perera, D. IMECE2017-72293 an Internet of Things (iot) Based Frameworks for Colloborative Manufacturing. In Proceedings of the International Mechanical Engineering Congress & Exposition, Tampa, FL, USA, 3–9 November 2017.
12. Ray, P.P. A survey on Internet of Things architectures. *J. King Saud Univ. Comput. Inf. Sci.* **2018**, *30*, 291–319. [CrossRef]
13. Ferreira, H.G.C.; Dias Canedo, E.; De Sousa, R.T. IoT architecture to enable intercommunication through REST API and UPnP using IP, ZigBee and arduino. In Proceedings of the International Conference on Wireless and Mobile Computing, Networking and Communications, Lyon, France, 7–9 Octpber 2013. [CrossRef]
14. Gazis, V.; Goertz, M.; Huber, M.; Leonardi, A.; Mathioudakis, K.; Wiesmaier, A.; Zeiger, F. Short paper: IoT: Challenges, projects, architectures. In Proceedings of the IEEE 2015 18th International Conference on Intelligence in Next, Generation Networks, Paris, France, 17–19 Febuary 2015; pp. 145–147.
15. Firdous, F.; Mohd Umair, M.; Alikhan Siddiqui, D.; Mohd Umair, A. IoT Based Home Automation System over the Cloud. *Int. J. Innov. Adv. Comput. Sci. (IJIACS)* **2018**, *7*, 512–517.
16. Nitti, M.; Pilloni, V.; Giusto, D.; Popescu, V. IoT Architecture for a sustainable tourism application in a smart city environment. *Mob. Inf. Syst.* **2017**. [CrossRef]
17. Contreras-Castillo, J.; Zeadally, S.; Guerrero Ibáñez, J.A. A seven-layered model architecture for Internet of Vehicles. *J. Inf. Telecommun.* **2017**. [CrossRef]

18. Rahimi, H.; Zibaeenejad, A.; Safavi, A.A. A Novel IoT Architecture Based on 5G-IoT and Next, Generation Technologies. In Proceedings of the 2018 IEEE 9th Annual Information Technology, Electronics and Mobile Communication Conference (IEMCON), Vancouver, BC, Canada, 1–3 November 2018.
19. Dumitru, R.L. IoT Platforms: Analysis for Building Projects. *Inf. Econ.* **2017**. doi:10.12948/issn14531305/21.2.2017.04. [CrossRef]
20. Zanakis, S.H.; Solomon, A.; Wishart, N.; Dublish, S. Multi-attribute decision-making: a simulation comparison of select methods. *Eur. J. Oper. Res.* **1998**, *107*, 507–529. [CrossRef]
21. Henig, M.I.; Buchanan, J.T. Solving MCDM problems: Process concepts. *J. Multi-Criteria Decis. Anal.* **1996**, *5*, 3–21. [CrossRef]
22. Whaiduzzaman, M.; Gani, A.; Anuar, N.B.; Shiraz, M.; Haque, M.N.; Haque, I.T. Cloud service selection using multicriteria decision analysis. *Sci. World J.* **2014**, *2014*, 459375. [CrossRef]
23. Watrobski, J.; Jankowski, J.; Pawel, Z.; Karczmarczyk, A.; Ziolo, M. Generalised framework for multi-criteria method selection. *Omega* **2018**, *86*, 107–124. [CrossRef]
24. Silva, E.M.; Jardim-Goncalves, R. Multi-criteria analysis and decision methodology for the selection of internet-of-things hardware platforms. In *Doctoral Conference on Computing, Electrical and Industrial Systems*; Springer: Cham, Switzerland, 2017; pp. 111–121.
25. Soltani, S.; Martin, P.; Elgazzar, K. A hybrid approach to automatic IaaS service selection. *J. Cloud Comput.* **2018**, *7*, 12. [CrossRef]
26. Kondratenko, Y.; Kondratenko, G.; Sidenko, I. Multi-criteria decision-making for selecting a rational IoT platform. In Proceedings of the 2018 IEEE 9th International Conference on Dependable Systems, Services and Technologies (DESSERT), Kiev, Ukraine, 24–27 May 2018; pp. 147–152.
27. Uslu, B.; Eren, T.; Gür, S.; Özcan, E. Evaluation of the Difficulties in the Internet of Things (IoT) with Multi-Criteria Decision-Making. *Processes* **2019**, *7*, 164. [CrossRef]
28. Singla, C.; Mahajan, N.; Kaushal, S.; Verma, A.; Sangaiah, A.K. Modelling and Analysis of Multi-objective Service Selection Scheme in IoT-Cloud Environment. In *Cognitive Computing for Big Data Systems Over IoT*; Springer: Berlin, Germany, 2018; pp. 63–77.
29. Alelaiwi, A. Evaluating distributed IoT databases for edge/cloud platforms using the analytic hierarchy process. *J. Parallel Distrib. Comput.* **2019**, *124*, 41–46. [CrossRef]
30. Silva, E.M.; Agostinho, C.; Jardim-Goncalves, R. A multi-criteria decision model for the selection of a more suitable Internet-of-Things device. In Proceedings of the IEEE 2017 International Conference on Engineering, Technology and Innovation (ICE/ITMC), Funchal, Portugal, 27–29 June 2017; pp. 1268–1276.
31. Garg, S.K.; Versteeg, S.; Buyya, R. A framework for ranking of cloud computing services. *Future Gener. Comput. Syst.* **2013**, *29*, 1012–1023. [CrossRef]
32. Guth, J.; Breitenbucher, U.; Falkenthal, M.; Leymann, F.; Reinfurt, L. Comparison of IoT platform architectures: A field study based on a reference architecture. In Proceedings of the 2016 Cloudification of the Internet of Things, CIoT 2016, Paris, France, 23–25 November 2016. [CrossRef]
33. Mitkova, V.; Mlynarovič, V. Investment Opportunities Identification Based on Macroeconomic Development, the Multiple Criteria Decision Approach. *Symmetry* **2019**, *11*, 827. [CrossRef]
34. Wątróbski, J.; Małecki, K.; Kijewska, K.; Iwan, S.; Karczmarczyk, A.; Thompson, R.G. Multi-criteria analysis of electric vans for city logistics. *Sustainability* **2017**, *9*, 1453. [CrossRef]
35. Palevičius, V.; Podviezko, A.; Sivilevičius, H.; Prentkovskis, O. Decision-aiding evaluation of public infrastructure for electric vehicles in cities and resorts of Lithuania. *Sustainability* **2018**, *10*, 904. [CrossRef]
36. Google Cloud Platform breaks into leader category in Gartner's Magic Quadrant. Available online: https://www.zdnet.com/article/google-cloud-platform-breaks-into-leader-category-in-gartners-magic-quadrant/ (accessed on 28 January 2020).
37. Amazon and Microsoft top Gartner's IaaS Magic Quadrant. Available online: https://www.zdnet.com/article/amazon-and-microsoft-top-gartners-iaas-magic-quadrant/ (accessed on 28 January 2020).
38. Saaty, T.L. Decision making with the analytic hierarchy process. *Int. J. Serv. Sci.* **2008**, *1*, 83–98. [CrossRef]
39. Setiawan, A.; Sediyono, E.; Moekoe, D.A. Application of AHP method in determining priorities of conversion of unusedland to food land in Minahasa Tenggara. *Int. J. Comput. Appl.* **2014**, *89*, 8. [CrossRef]

40. Vulević, T.; Dragović, N. Multi-criteria decision analysis for sub-watersheds ranking via the PROMETHEE method. *Int. Soil Water Conserv. Res.* **2017**, *5*, 50–55. [CrossRef]
41. Brans, J.P.; De Smet, Y. PROMETHEE methods. In *Multiple Criteria Decision Analysis*; Springer: Berlin, Germany, 2016; pp. 187–219.

symmetry

MDPI

Article

Integrated Decision-Making Approach Based on SWARA and GRA Methods for the Prioritization of Failures in Solar Panel Systems under Z-Information

Saeid Jafarzadeh Ghoushchi [1], Mohd Nizam Ab Rahman [2,*], Diba Raeisi [1], Elnaz Osgooei [3] and Majid Jafarzadeh Ghoushji [4,*]

[1] Faculty of Industrial Engineering, Urmia University of Technology, Urmia 57166, Iran; s.jafarzadeh@uut.ac.ir (S.J.G.); raeisi.diba69@ine.uut.ac.ir (D.R.)

[2] Department of Mechanical and Manufacturing Engineering, Faculty of Engineering and Built Environment,Universiti Kebangsaan Malaysia, Bangi 43600, Malaysia

[3] Faculty of Science, Urmia University of Technology, Urmia 57166, Iran; e.osgooei@uut.ac.ir

[4] Department of Engineering, Sanmina Corporation, Carrollton, TX 75006, USA

* Correspondence: mnizam@ukm.edu.my (M.N.A.R.); majid.ghoushji@sanmina.com (M.J.G.)

Received: 21 January 2020; Accepted: 17 February 2020; Published: 21 February 2020

Abstract: Encountering a problem or error in the final stages of providing products or services increases costs and delays scheduling. The key task is to ensure quality and reliability in the early stages of the production process and prevent errors from occurring from the beginning. Failure mode and effect analysis (FMEA) is one of the tools for identifying potential problems and their impact on products and services. The conventional FMEA technique has been criticized extensively due to its disadvantages. In this study, the concepts of uncertainty and reliability are considered simultaneously. The processes of weighting risk factors, prioritizing failures by using the stepwise weight assessment ratio analysis (SWARA)–gray relational analysis (GRA) integrated method based on Z-number theory and complete prioritization of failures are implemented. Crucial management indices, such as cost and time, are considered in addition to severity, occurrence and detection factors along with assigning symmetric form of the weights to them. This, in turn, increases the interpretability of results and reduces the decision-maker's subjectivity in risk prioritization. The developed model is implemented on solar panel data with 19 failure modes determined by the FMEA team. Results show that the proposed approach provides a more complete and realistic prioritization of failures than conventional FMEA and fuzzy GRA methods do.

Keywords: failure mode and effects analysis; solar panel systems; step-wise weight assessment ratio analysis; grey relational analysis; Z-number theory

---

1. Introduction

In manufacturing and services, several factors, such as competition, customer expectations and changes and technological developments, encourage producers to increase their commitment to fixing product defects and eliminating performance deficiencies. Otherwise, market share will be lost due to reduced customer satisfaction [1–4]. To maintain market share, companies use different procedures to deliver unflawed products to the market. They use risk evaluation techniques to identify potential risks and determine their causes and effects. Various methods for risk assessment have been developed in recent years [5]. One of these methods is failure mode and effect analysis (FMEA). This method was first used to systematically analyze failure modes and their subsequent effects on military products, especially in the aviation industry [6]. One of the best features of FMEA is adopting proactive measures instead of reactive ones. If an accident occurs, large sums of money will be spent on solving problems and eliminating failures and if a failure occurs during the design process, the damage will be maximized [7]. Design modifications result in changes in production tools, templates and fixtures and additional costs in process and product redesign. FMEA is implemented before the design and process failure factor enters production to maximize work efficiency. Spending time and money on a complete and accurate implementation of FMEA allows for easy modifications during process or product design at a minimal cost. FMEA minimizes the problems associated with implementing such changes [8]. It is a systematic approach that identifies evident and hidden errors, deficiencies and failures in systems, products and processes then applies proper measures to eliminate these problems. Thus, FMEA can be utilized as a tool for the continuous improvement of the quality of products and services in companies.

The main purposes of applying the FMEA technique are to identify potential failure modes in system components, determine their causes, evaluate their effects on system performance, identify ways to reduce the possibility of their occurrence and alleviate consequences and increase the capability to detect failure modes [9]. Risk priority number (RPN) is used in the conventional FMEA technique to calculate the risk of various system failure modes. RPN is the product of three factors, namely, occurrence (O), severity (S) and detection (D) [10]. The higher RPN is, the higher the risk associated with the failure mode is. The purpose of RPN calculation is to prioritize failure modes. Despite the widespread use of FMEA, the technique has major drawbacks that limit its application, especially when used for critical analysis in the calculation of RPNs.

This paper presents a new score to improve the deficiencies of conventional RPNs. This score is obtained by developing an FMEA approach based on gray relational analysis (GRA) and stepwise weight assessment ratio analysis (SWARA) methods. The first section identifies the failure modes. In the second section, the SWARA method is used to determine the weights of RPN factors via the proposed approach to keep symmetrical property of their weights. In the third section, the GRA method is applied to consider the uncertainty in RPN factors and the unreliability in these values by using Z-number theory. Time (T) and cost (C) are considered in addition to S, O and D. In this approach, the identified failures are considered the decision-making alternatives and the SODCT factors weighted by SWARA are considered the criteria for evaluating these failures. The advantages of this theory over conventional fuzzy methods are as follows—it considers the uncertainty in experts' opinions and allocates the credit in their opinions for estimating fuzzy parameters [11]. The following shows the contributions of this study:

- Consideration of crucial management indices, such as cost and time, in the process of prioritizing risks with SOD factors
- Assignation of different weights to risk factors according to the uncertainty of decision-makers' preferences and the symmetric form of the weights with the aim of overcoming the deficiencies of traditional RPN score and making results more interpretable
- Simultaneous consideration of the concepts of uncertainty (U) and reliability (R) in the processes of weighting risk factors and prioritizing failures by using Z-number theory
- Complete prioritization of failures and distinction between failure ranks by using the SWARA–GRA integrated method based on -number theory.

2. Literature Review

This section reviews related literature. The first subsection presents a review of published studies that applied the FMEA technique and hybrid approaches (two or more techniques) based on this method. The second subsection examines GRA and SWARA methods and the research conducted using these methods.

2.1. Hybrid FMEA Approach

The development of multi-criteria decision making (MCDM) methods with the approaches for continuous risk assessment has resulted in the establishment of new quantitative and qualitative tools and methods [12–14]. Among the various techniques for risk assessment, FMEA is one of the most powerful ones in identifying defects. The simplicity and applicability of this technique make it suitable for use in different fields, such as solar energy, automotive, chemical, medical, pharmaceutical and food industries [15–19].

Despite the shortcomings of the FMEA technique, it is still considered one of the most widely used approaches for prioritizing failures. In this technique, failure prioritization is accomplished based on conventional RPN indices, which are a product of three factors, namely, O, S and D [20,21]. Numerous researchers, including Liu [9], attempted to combine this technique with MCDM approaches to resolve the disadvantages of conventional RPN indices. Braglia and Bevilacqua [22] combined the analytic hierarchy process with FMEA and prioritized the failure modes in a refrigerator company. Liu et al. [23] proposed a new risk prioritization model for risk assessment in FMEA on the basis of D-numbers and the improved GRA method and called the model GRP. Safari et al. [24] used the fuzzy VIKOR method to evaluate FMEA and facilitate the deployment of EA in an organization. Emovon et al. [25] proposed an improved FMEA model that uses the VIKOR technique to prioritize the risk of different failures in a marine machinery system. Liu [26] utilized a hybrid GRA-TOPSIS method for risk assessment in FMEA under uncertainty. The author showed that using this integrated approach is superior to other methods in risk assessment and prioritization. Ghoushchi, Yousefi and Khazaeili [5] used Z-MOORA and fuzzy BWM to prioritize and evaluate risks in the FMEA method. They utilized fuzzy BWM to calculate factor weights and the Z-MOORA method to analyze and prioritize failure risks. Table 1 presents several alternative hybrid approaches of the hybrid FMEA approach based on MCDM methods.

2.2. GRA Application

GRA is an MCDM method developed by Deng [47]. This decision-making technique is applied to solve various MCDM problems, such as employment decision-making [48], power distribution system reconstruction planning [49], integrated spiral process inspection [50], quality function modeling [51] and silicon wafer chip defect detection [52]. This method is also used to improve other decision-making methods, such as TOPSIS, VIKOR and ELECTRE, which use only positive and negative criteria to rank alternatives. Certain cases have neither positive nor negative criteria but they are presented as a number or a linguistic variable in the problem. The original GRA method translates the functions of all alternatives in a comparable order. This process is called the gray relation-generating step. Afterward, a set of ideal goals is defined in accordance with this sequence. Then, the gray correlation coefficient between all compatible and target sequences is calculated and the relative gray value between the ideal target and each comparable sequence is calculated based on these coefficients. The alternative with a high gray coefficient degree is selected [53]. The gray decision matrix comprises the following criteria—The larger, the better (positive criteria in TOPSIS and VIKOR techniques); The smaller, the better (negative criteria in TOPSIS and VIKOR techniques); The closer to the desired value, the better (not included in TOPSIS and VIKOR techniques) [53]. In fact, The GRA method distinguishes between different levels of criteria and can thus be used as a powerful decision-making method in MCDM issues. This method is adopted in the result analysis of this study because of its advantage over other decision-making methods, such as TOPSIS, VIKOR and ELECTRE. The GRA MCDM method has been applied to various problems. Among the studies conducted on the GRA method and solar energy data is the work of Kou et al. [54] on the optimization of the collection process of flat plates with multiple qualitative characteristics in the production of solar energy collectors. Acır et al. [55] identified the optimal parameters influencing the energy efficiency of solar air heaters by using the GRA method. Tiwari et al. [56] used GRA to examine the effects of four controllable parameters (fuel blend, boiling point, inlet temperature and bending point temperature) of a solar organic Rankine cycle on energy efficiency. Narendranathan et al. [57] applied GRA to optimize CI engine parameters.

Table 1. Hybrid approaches of the hybrid failure mode and effect analysis (FMEA) approach based on multi-criteria decision making (MCDM) methods.

Author(s)	Approaches	Specification-Characteristics				Author(s)	Approaches	Specification-Characteristics			
		Weighting		Ranking				Weighting		Ranking	
		U	R	U	R			U	R	U	R
Tian et al. [27]	Fuzzy best-worst (BWM), relative entropy, VIKOR	√		√		Melani et al. [28]	ANP	√		√	
Nie et al. [29]	BWM, COPRAS	√		√		Galehdar et al. [30]	ANP and Fuzzy DEMATEL	√			
Nie et al. [31]	GRA–TOPSIS	√		√		Kumar et al. [32]	GRA			√	
Arabsheybani et al. [33]	Fuzzy MOORA			√		Panchal and Srivastava [34]	GRA			√	
Nazeri and Naderikia [35]	ANP and DEMATEL	√				Bian et al. [36]	TOPSIS			√	
Battirola Filho et al. [37]	BPMS and AHP	√				Mangeli, et al. [38]	LFPP method and Fuzzy TOPSIS			√	
Liu [26]	GRA and TOPSIS	√		√		Liu et al. [39]	DEMATEL and AHP	√			
Safari et al. [24]	VIKOR			√		Ak and Gul [40]	AHP and TOPSIS	√		√	
Dorosti et al. [41]	Fuzzy BWM and MOORA	√		√		Liu [42]	ITL-ELECTRE			√	
Lo et al. [43]	R-BWM and R-TOPSIS	√		√		Liu et al. [39], Wang et al. [44]	Regret theory and TODIM	√		√	
Li and Chen [45]	FGRP			√		Ghoushchi et al. [5]	Z-MOORA and Fuzzy BWM	√		√	√
Fattahi and Khalilzadeh [46]	MULTIMOORA and AHP fuzzy	√		√		Proposed approach	Z-GRA and Z-SWARA	√	√	√	√

2.3. SWARA

SWARA is an MCDM method that aims to calculate criterion and sub-criterion weights. The performance of this method in weighing criteria is similar to that of Best-Worst Method (BWM) and the linear programming technique for multidimensional analysis of preference (LINMAP) The linear programming technique for multidimensional analysis of preference (LINMAP) methods. This method was developed by Keršuliene et al. [58]. SWARA is generally used to solve various complicated MCDM problems, such as deciding on machinery tools [59], recruitment [60,61], corporate social responsibility and sustainability [62,63], product design [64], packaging design [65], logistics [66] and utilization of clean technology [67]. The most important criterion in this method is listed as number one and the least important one is listed as the last. Experts (respondents) have an important role in determining criterion weights. This method allows experts to estimate the importance ratio of criteria in the process of determining their weight. It is effective in collecting and coordinating data obtained from experts [68]. Experts also have an important role in assessing the calculated weights. Each expert identifies the importance of each criterion based on his or her tacit knowledge, information and experience. Then, the weight of each criterion is determined in accordance with the average value of group ratings obtained from the experts. Keršuliene, Zavadskas and Turskis [58] suggested using a group of experts and discussing their views as a group; meanwhile, a researcher takes notes, sums up the experts' opinions and determines the relative weights of criteria by ranking them.

The SWARA method is used in determining criterion weights in this study because of this method's capability to rank criteria and determine criterion weights. Research has been conducted on the SWARA method in consideration of solar energy systems. Ijadi Maghsoodi, Ijadi Maghsoodi, Mosavi, Rabczuk and Zavadskas [67] studied the selection of renewable energy technology by applying the SWARA method along with the multi-MOORA approach. Ghasempour et al. [69] employed the SWARA MCDM method in selecting solar cell manufacturers and production technology. Siksnelyte et al. [70] conducted a review of MCDM methods, including SWARA, in the context of sustainable energy development.

3. Methodology

3.1. Fuzzy Sets Theory

The fuzzy theory introduces the concept of membership function to discuss various linguistic variables [71]. There is a certain degree of uncertainty in terms of people's thoughts, deduction and perception. Fuzzy set (fuzzy logic) works with the sources of uncertainty and imprecision which are vague and non-statistical, in nature. Basic definitions for the fuzzy numbers are provided below.

Definition 1. *A fuzzy set A, defined in reference X, is as Equation (1).*

$$\widetilde{A} = \left\{ (x, \mu_{\widetilde{A}}(x)) \middle| x \in X \right\} \tag{1}$$

In Equation (1), $\mu_{\widetilde{A}}(x) : X \rightarrow [0, 1]$ is the membership function of set A. Membership value $\mu_A(x)$ shows the dependence degree $x \in X$ at A. The degree of membership of each element like $x \in R$ to the fuzzy set $\widetilde{A}$, in the form of the degree of our acceptance or belief in accepting x, is defined as a member of the fuzzy set $\widetilde{A}$ or the degree of conformity of member x with the considered concept of set $\widetilde{A}$.

Definition 2. *A symmetric triangular fuzzy number $\widetilde{A}$ is represented as a triplex of (l, m, u) and the membership function is according to Equation (2) and the diagram is as in Figure 1.*

$$\begin{cases} 0 & x < l \\ \frac{x-l}{m-l} & l \leq x \leq m \\ \frac{u-x}{u-m} & m \leq x \leq u \\ 0 & x > u \end{cases} \tag{2}$$

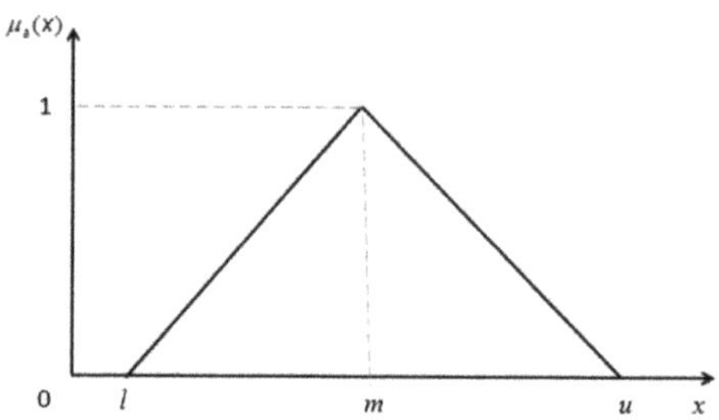

Figure 1. Symmetric triangular Fuzzy Number.

Definition 3. *Assume that $\widetilde{A} = (l_1, m_1, u_1)$, $\widetilde{B} = (l_2, m_2, u_2)$ are symmetric triangular fuzzy numbers. Math operations are done as follow:*

$$\widetilde{A} \oplus \widetilde{B} = (l_1 + l_2, m_1 + m_2, u_1 + u_2) \tag{3}$$

$$\widetilde{A} \otimes \widetilde{B} = (l_1 l_2, m_1 m_2, u_1 u_2) \tag{4}$$

$$\widetilde{A} \ominus \widetilde{B} = (l_1 - u_2, m_1 - m_2, u_1 - l_2) \tag{5}$$

$$\widetilde{A} \oslash \widetilde{B} = (l_1 / u_2, m_1 / m_2, u_1 / l_2) \tag{6}$$

$$\lambda \widetilde{A} = \lambda(l_1, m_1, u_1) = (\lambda l_1, \lambda m_1, \lambda u_1), \lambda > 0 \tag{7}$$

Definition 4. *Assume that $\widetilde{A} = (l_1, m_1, u_1)$, $\widetilde{B} = (l_2, m_2, u_2)$ are two positive triangular fuzzy numbers. The distance between A, B is defined as in Equation (8).*

$$d(A, B) = \sqrt{\frac{\left((l_1 - l_2)^2 + (m_1 - m_2)^2 + (u_1 - u_2)^2\right)}{3}} \tag{8}$$

Definition 5. *Assume that the triangular fuzzy number $\widetilde{A}$ is represented a triplex of (l, m, u). Equation (9) is used to convert it into a crisp number according to the Best Non fuzzy Performance (BNP):*

$$BNP(\widetilde{A}) = \frac{(u - l) + (m - l)}{3} + l \tag{9}$$

3.2. Z-Number Theory

Zadeh [11] defined a Z-number associated with an uncertain variable as an ordered pair of fuzzy numbers denoted as $Z = (A, B)$. A is a fuzzy constraint on values of X and B is defined as a partial reliability of a probability criterion of A. According to Kang, et al. [72], Z-number is to solve problems in controlling, decision making, modeling and other problems. This method is based on the conversion of a Z-number to a fuzzy number on the basis of the expectation of a fuzzy set. However, converting the Z-number to fuzzy numbers will lead to the loss of the original information. Aliev, et al. [73], Aliev, et al. [74], Aliev, et al. [75] presented an effective general and computational approach to calculate the Z-number.

Triple (X, A, B), known as Z-VALUATION, which is equivalent to an assignment statement and is defined as a general constraint on X as in Equation (10).

$$Prob(X\ is\ A)\ is\ B \tag{10}$$

This constraint is referred to as a probability restriction that shows a probability distribution function. In particular, it can be explained in Equation (11).

$$R(X) : X\ is \rightarrow \mathrm{poss(X = u)} = \mu_A(u) \tag{11}$$

where, μ_A is the membership function of A and u is a generic value of X. μ_A may be viewed as a constraint which is associated with $R(X)$. It means that how much the constraint that covers $\mu_A(u)$, can satisfy u. when, X is a random variable, the probability distribution of the X acts as the probabilistic restriction on X. Possible restriction and a probability density function are described in Equations (12) and (13):

$$R(X) : X\ is\ p \tag{12}$$

$$R(X) : X\ is\ p \rightarrow prob(u \leq X \leq u + du) = p(u)du \tag{13}$$

In Equation (13), du shows the components of U derivations.

3.3. Z-SWARA

Keršuliene, Zavadskas and Turskis [58] proposed the step-wise weight assessment ratio analysis (SWARA) method for the first time.

Different factors, such as non-assessable information, incomplete information and non-accessible information cause uncertainty in decision-making. Since conventional MADM methods cannot solve problems with such ambiguous information, fuzzy multi-criteria decision-making methods have been developed because of ambiguity in evaluating the relative importance of criteria and ranking the alternatives according to the criteria. The process of determining the relative weight of criteria using Z-SWARA, like SWARA method, is as following steps:

Step 1. Sort the evaluation factors in descending order of expected importance.

Step 2. Switch Z-numbers linguistic variables to symmetric triangular fuzzy variables.

In this step, the verbal variables for factors, in the form of Z-Numbers, are transformed into triangular fuzzy verbal variables. The process of this transformation is as follows:

Assume that $Z = (A, B)$, which A is the verbal variable presented in Table 2 and B is the verbal variable presented in Table 3 and assume that, $\widetilde{A} = \left\{\left(x, \mu_{\widetilde{A}}(x)\right)\middle| x \in [0,1]\right\}$ and $\widetilde{B} = \left\{\left(x, \mu_{\widetilde{B}}(x)\right)\middle| x \in [0,1]\right\}$ are triangular membership functions. According to Equations (14) and (15), reliability of Z-Number is transferred to crisp number

$$\alpha = \frac{\int x\mu_{\widetilde{B}}(x)dx}{\int \mu_{\widetilde{B}}(x)dx} \tag{14}$$

$$\widetilde{Z}^{\alpha} = \left\{\left(X, \mu_{\widetilde{A}^{\alpha}}\right)\middle|\mu_{\widetilde{A}^{\alpha}}(x) = \alpha\mu_{\widetilde{A}^{\alpha}}, X \in [0,1]\right\} \tag{15}$$

Table 2. Linguistics variable for evaluating the factors.

Linguistics Terms	Membership Function
Equally Important (EI)	(1,1,1)
Moderately less important (MOL)	(2/3,1,3/2)
Less important (LI)	(2/5,1/2,2/3)
Very less Important (VLI)	(2/7,1/3,2/5)
Much less important (MUL)	(2/9,1/4,2/7)

Table 3. Transformation rules of linguistics variables of reliability.

Linguistic Variables	Very Low (VL)	Low (L)	Medium (M)	High (H)	Very High (VH)
TFNs	(0,0,0.35)	(0.2,0.35,0.50)	(0.35,0.50,0.65)	(0.50,0.65,0.80)	(0.65,1.0,1.0)

In these Equations, α expresses the weight of reliability, $\mu_{\widetilde{B}^{\alpha}}(x)$ indicates the degree of dependence $x \in X$ in B and $\mu_{\widetilde{A}^{\alpha}}(x)$ indicates the degree of dependence $x \in X$ in A^{α}. Then, by combining the Linguistics variable for evaluating the factors (see Table 2) and the Transformation rules of linguistics variables of reliability (see Table 3), the roles of transforming verbal variables of decision makers, used for maintaining the symmetry of the response, are obtained for the Z-SWARA method.

For instance, assume that $Z = (A, B)$, which is $\widetilde{A} = (MOL)$ and $\widetilde{R} = (H)$, so it is described as $Z = \left[\left(\frac{2}{3}, 1, \frac{3}{2}\right), (0.50, 0.65, 0.80)\right]$. Firstly, reliability component of Z-Number converts to a crisp number by using Equations (14) and (15). According to Equation (15), the value of α is 0.5, then, this value is used in Equation (14) $\widetilde{Z}^{\alpha} = \left(\frac{2}{3}, 1, \frac{3}{2}; 0.65\right)$. Now, the Z-number weight is converted to the triangular fuzzy number using Equation (15) $\widetilde{Z}' = \left(\frac{2}{3}\sqrt{0.65}, 1 * \sqrt{0.65}, \frac{3}{2} * \sqrt{0.65}\right) = (0.54, 0.81, 1.21)$. Other conversions are presented in Table 4 according to Tables 2 and 3.

Table 4. Transformation rules of linguistics variables to z-number of Z-stepwise weight assessment ratio analysis (SWARA).

Linguistics Terms	Membership Function	Linguistics Terms	Membership Function
(EI,VL)	(1,1,1)	(EI,L)	(1,1,1)
(EI,M)	(1,1,1)	(EI,H)	(1,1,1)
(EI,VH)	(1,1,1)	(MOL,VL)	(0.23,0.35,0.52)
(MOL,L)	(0.40,0.59,0.89)	(MOL,M)	(0.47,0.71,1.06)
(MOL,H)	(0.54,0.81,1.21)	(MOL,VH)	(0.63,0.94,1.41)
(LI,VL)	(0.14,0.17,0.23)	(LI,L)	(0.24,0.30,0.40)
(LI,M)	(0.28,0.35,0.47)	(LI,H)	(0.32,0.40,0.54)
(LI,VH)	(0.38,0.47,0.63)	(VLI,VL)	(0.10,0.11,0.14)
(VLI,L)	(0.17,0.20,0.24)	(VLI,M)	(0.21,0.23,0.28)
(VLI,H)	(0.23,0.27,0.32)	(VLI,VH)	(0.27,0.31,0.38)
(MUL,VL)	(0.08,0.09,0.10)	(MUL,L)	(0.13,0.15,0.17)
(MUL,M)	(0.16,0.18,0.21)	(MUL,H)	(0.18,0.20,0.23)
(MUL,VH)	(0.21,0.23,0.27)		

Step 3. According to Table 4, state the relative importance of the factor j in relation to the previous factor $(j-1)$ according by z-number, which has higher importance and follow to the last factor. After determining all relative importance scores by all experts, the geometric mean of the corresponding scores is obtained, to aggregate their judgments.

Step 4. Obtain the coefficient $\widetilde{k}_j$ as (16):

$$\widetilde{k}_j = \begin{cases} \widetilde{1} & j = 1 \\ \widetilde{s}_j + \widetilde{1} & j > 1 \end{cases} \tag{16}$$

Step 5. Calculate the fuzzy weight $\widetilde{q}_j$ as (17):

$$\widetilde{q}_j = \begin{cases} \widetilde{i} & j = 1 \\ \frac{\widetilde{x}_{j-1}}{\widetilde{k}_j} & j > 1 \end{cases} \quad (17)$$

Step 6. Calculate the relative weights of the evaluation criteria as (18):

$$\widetilde{W}_j = \frac{\widetilde{q}_j}{\sum_{k=1}^{n} \widetilde{q}_k} \quad (18)$$

where $\widetilde{W}_j = \left(w_j^l, w_j^m, w_j^u\right)$ is the relative fuzzy weight of j, the criterion and n shows the number of evaluation criteria.

3.4. Z-GRA

Z-GRA approach, is described as follow steps:

Step 1: Decision-making matrix with Z-Number elements is indicated as a matrix, where m and n, respectively, show the number of alternatives and criteria. Also, x_{ij} and y_{ij}, respectively, indicate the value of the ith criterion for the jth alternative and the ith reliability for the jth alternative.

$$\widetilde{Z} = \begin{bmatrix} \left[\left(x_{11}^l, x_{11}^m, x_{11}^u\right), \left(y_{11}^l, y_{11}^m, y_{11}^u\right)\right] & \left[\left(x_{12}^l, x_{12}^m, x_{12}^u\right), \left(y_{12}^l, y_{12}^m, y_{12}^u\right)\right] & \cdots & \left[\left(x_{1n}^l, x_{1n}^m, x_{1n}^u\right), \left(y_{1n}^l, y_{1n}^m, y_{1n}^u\right)\right] \\ \cdots & \cdots & \cdots & \cdots \\ \cdots & \cdots & \cdots & \cdots \\ \left[\left(x_{m1}^l, x_{m1}^m, x_{m1}^u\right), \left(y_{m1}^l, y_{m1}^m, y_{m1}^u\right)\right] & \left[\left(x_{m2}^l, x_{m2}^m, x_{m2}^u\right), \left(y_{m2}^l, y_{m2}^m, y_{m2}^u\right)\right] & \cdots & \left[\left(x_{mn}^l, x_{mn}^m, x_{mn}^u\right), \left(y_{mn}^l, y_{mn}^m, y_{mn}^u\right)\right] \end{bmatrix} \quad (19)$$

Step 2: Switch Z-numbers linguistic variables to symmetric triangular fuzzy variables.

The elements of above matrix are converted into symmetric triangular fuzzy numbers and a decision-making matrix is obtained with elements of symmetric triangular fuzzy numbers.

Assume that $Z = (A, B)$ where $\widetilde{A} = \left\{\left(x, \mu_{\widetilde{A}}(x)\right) \middle| x \in [0,1]\right\}$ and $\widetilde{B} = \left\{\left(x, \mu_{\widetilde{B}}(x)\right) \middle| x \in [0,1]\right\}$ are triangular membership functions. Equations (20) and (21) show their transformation to the crisp numbers.

$$\alpha = \frac{\int x\mu_{\widetilde{B}}(x)dx}{\int \mu_{\widetilde{B}}(x)dx} \quad (20)$$

$$\widetilde{Z}^{\alpha} = \left\{\left(X, \mu_{\widetilde{A}^{\alpha}}\right) \middle| \mu_{\widetilde{A}^{\alpha}}(x) = \alpha\mu_{\widetilde{A}^{\alpha}}, X \in [0,1]\right\} \quad (21)$$

In the Equations above, α represents the reliability weight, $\mu_{\widetilde{B}}(x)$ indicates the dependence degree of $x \in X$ in B and $\mu_{\widetilde{A}^{\alpha}}(x)$ indicates the dependence degree of $x \in X$ in A^{α}.

Then, by combining linguistic variables presented in Table 5 and the rules of converting linguistic variables, the components of conversion of linguistic variables by decision makers' for Z-GRA method are obtained. For example, assume that $Z = (A, B)$ where $\widetilde{A} = (MH)$ and the $\widetilde{R} = (M)$, then it is converted to $Z = [(5,7,9), (0.35, 0.50, 0.65)]$. According to Equations (20) and (21), $\widetilde{Z}^{\alpha} = \left(5 * \sqrt{0.5}, 7 * \sqrt{0.5}, 9 * \sqrt{0.5}\right) = (3.54, 4.95, 6.36)$. According to the Tables 5 and 6, other conversions are brought in Table 7.

Table 5. Linguistic variables for rating the failure modes.

Linguistic Variables	Very Low (VL)	Low (L)	Medium Low (ML)	Medium (M)	Medium High (MH)	High (H)	Very High (VH)
TFNs	(0,0,1)	(0,1,3)	(1,3,5)	(3,5,7)	(5,7,9)	(7,9,10)	(9,10,10)

Table 6. Transformation rules of linguistics variables of reliability.

Linguistic Variables	Very Low (VL)	Low (L)	Medium (M)	High (H)	Very High (VH)
TFNs	(0,0,0.35)	(0.2,0.35,0.50)	(0.35,0.50,0.65)	(0.50,0.65,0.80)	(0.65,1,1)

Table 7. Transformation rules for Z-number linguistic variables to Z-gray relational analysis (GRA).

Linguistics Terms	Membership Function	Linguistics Terms	Membership Function
(VL,VL)	(0,0,0.35)	(M,H)	(2.42,4.03,5.64)
(VL,L)	(0,0,0.59)	(M,VH)	(2.81,4.69,6.57)
(VL,M)	(0,0,0.71)	(MH,VL)	(1.73,2.42,3.12)
(VL,H)	(0,0,0.81)	(MH,L)	(2.96,4.14,5.32)
(VL,VH)	(0,0,0.94)	(MH,M)	(3.54,4.95,6.36)
(L,VL)	(0,0.35,1.04)	(MH,H)	(4.03,5.64,7.26)
(L,L)	(0,0.59,1.77)	(MH,VH)	(4.69,6.57,8.44)
(L,M)	(0,0.71,2.12)	(H,VL)	(2.42,3.12,3.46)
(L,H)	(0,0.81,2.42)	(H,L)	(4.14,5.32,5.92)
(L,VH)	(0,0.94,2.81)	(H,M)	(4.95,6.36,7.07)
(ML,VL)	(0.35,1.04,1.73)	(H,H)	(5.64,7.26,8.06)
(ML,L)	(0.59,1.77,2.96)	(H,VH)	(6.57,8.44,9.38)
(ML,M)	(0.71,2.12,3.54)	(VH,VL)	(3.12,3.46,3.46)
(ML,H)	(0.81,2.42,4.03)	(VH,L)	(5.32,5.92,5.92)
(ML,VH)	(0.94,2.81,4.69)	(VH,M)	(6.36,7.07,7.07)
(M,VL)	(1.04,1.73,2.42)	(VH,H)	(7.26,8.06,8.06)
(M,L)	(1.77,2.96,4.14)	(VH,VH)	(8.44,9.38,9.38)
(M,M)	(2.12,3.54,4.95)		

Step 3: in this step, the decision-making matrix with symmetric triangular fuzzy numbers is formed and it is normalized. In this matrix, d_{mn} demonstrates the value that the alternative takes in n criteria and m alternative (performance measurement).

$$\widetilde{D} = \begin{bmatrix} \left(d^l_{11}, d^m_{11}, d^n_{11}\right) & \left(d^l_{12}, d^m_{12}, d^n_{12}\right) & \cdots & \left(d^l_{1n}, d^m_{1n}, d^n_{1n}\right) \\ \cdots & \cdots & \cdots & \cdots \\ \cdots & \cdots & \cdots & \cdots \\ \left(d^l_{m1}, d^m_{m1}, d^n_{m1}\right) & \left(d^l_{m2}, d^m_{m2}, d^n_{m2}\right) & \cdots & \left(d^l_{mn}, d^m_{mn}, d^n_{mn}\right) \end{bmatrix} \tag{22}$$

Step 4: In this step, fuzzy GRA works as follows:

Decision matrix (22) is converted into the normalized decision matrix ˜. Given ˜ (23), the normalized performance rating can be calculated as (Gumus et al., 2013; Zhang and Liu, 2011):

$$\begin{aligned} \widetilde{d_{ij}}^* &= \left(\frac{d^{l*}_{ij}}{d^+_j}, \frac{d^{m*}_{ij}}{d^+_j}, \frac{d^{u*}_{ij}}{d^+_j}\right) and\ \forall ij:\ i = 1, 2, \ldots m,\ j = 1, 2, \ldots n \\ d^+_j &= \max_i\{d_{ij}\}\ \forall i\ i = 1, 2, \ldots m \end{aligned} \tag{23}$$

3.5. Proposed Approach

A combination of FMEA, Z-SWARA and Z-GRA is used to evaluate and prioritize failure modes in this study. In the first phase of the research method, the failure modes and reliability of each of mode are determined by the FMEA team. In the second phase, the failure modes are weighted in the symmetric form and the criteria are ranked by decision makers (DMs) via the Z-SWARA method. In the third phase, the primary matrix Z-GRA is formed in consideration of the failure modes identified in the first phase and the final symmetric weights assigned in the second phase of the study. Figure 2 shows the steps in prioritizing the FMs of solar panels.

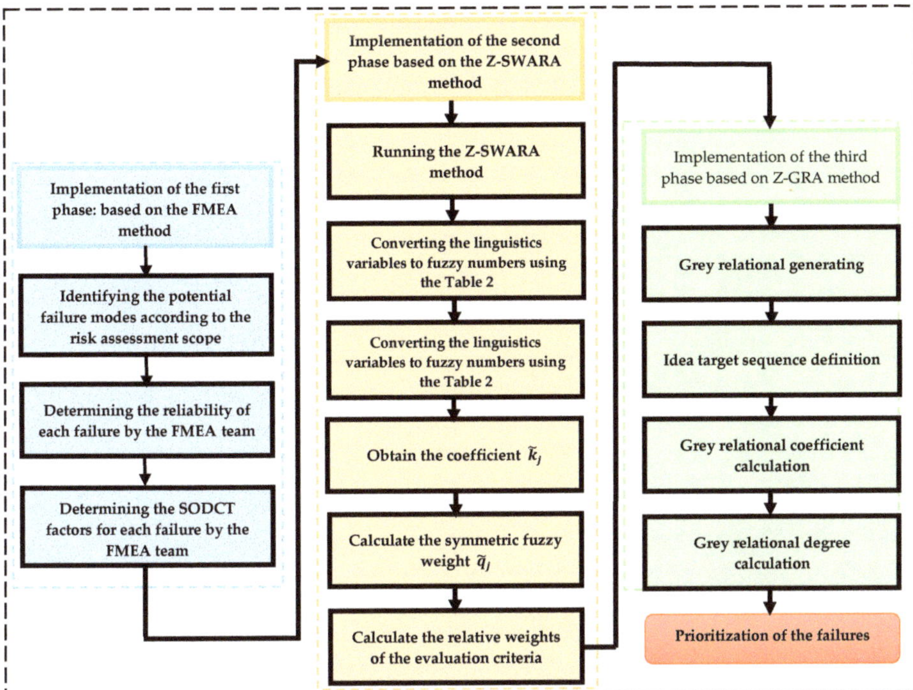

Figure 2. Proposed approach for prioritizing the failures of the solar panels.

4. Analysis of the Results

In accordance with the methodology of this study, 19 failures of solar panels are detected using FMEA and the factor values for each failure are determined by the team. Z-number theory is used to convert uncertain data into fuzzy numbers because of the uncertainty in the factors. The uncertainty in the factors and their reliability values are considered. The Z-number values obtained from the conversion of linguistic numbers based on the team's opinion are indicated in Table 8.

Then, in the second phase of the research method and also according to the SWARA method expressed, the values of coefficient k and the weight of q and w are calculated on the basis of Equations (16) to (18) for each decision-maker in examining the failures of solar panels as in table (10). In this step, the linguistic variables are converted into triangular fuzzy numbers, based on the Equations shown in Tables 2 and 3. For example, the fuzzy numbers corresponding to the linguistic variable MOL-M are $(0.47, 0.71, 1.06)$, respectively. After the conversion of linguistic variables into fuzzy numbers, the coefficient k_j from Equation (16), the fuzzy weight q_j from Equation (17) and the final weight of the factors in the form of fuzzy numbers w_j from Equation (18) are obtained. Final symmetric fuzzy weight of main criteria by each decision maker shown in Table 9.

Table 8. The score of ach failure mode in Z-number format.

Symb-ol	Failure Modes	S			O			D			C			T		
		TM1	TM2	TM3	TM1	TM2	TM3	TM1	TM2	TM3	TM1	TM2	TM3	TM1	TM2	TM3
FM1	Shading	(MH,H)	(M,VH)	(H,VH)	(MH,M)	(M,VH)	(M,VH)	(ML,H)	(L, H)	(M,VH)	(M,H)	(ML,H)	(L,M)	(MH,M)	(M,VH)	(ML,H)
FM2	Dust	(MH, H)	(H,M)	(H,VH)	(VH,VH)	(H,H)	(MH,M)	(H,H)	(MH,H)	(M,M)	(M,H)	(ML,M)	(M,M)	(M,VH)	(MH,H)	(M,M)
FM3	Orientation	(MH,VH)	(H,H)	(M,H)	(ML,VH)	(M,VH)	(MH,VH)	(ML,H)	(MH,VH)	(M,M)	(M,M)	(MH,H)	(H,M)	(H,VH)	(MH,M)	(H,H)
FM4	Corrosion	(M,M)	(L,H)	(ML,VH)	(MH,VH)	(M,H)	(ML,M)	(H,VH)	(MH,H)	(M,M)	(M,M)	(ML,H)	(MH,VH)	(M,M)	(ML,VH)	(L,H)
FM5	fire	(MH,VH)	(MH,H)	(M,M)	(ML,H)	(L,M)	(M,VH)	(ML,M)	(ML,H)	(ML,VH)	(M,H)	(L,VH)	(ML,M)	(M,VH)	(M,H)	(M,VH)
FM6	Incorrect energy yield prediction	(VH,VH)	(H,H)	(MH,M)	(MH,VH)	(M,VH)	(ML,H)	(M,VH)	(ML,M)	(L,H)	(M,H)	(ML,H)	(L,VH)	(H,H)	(M,H)	(MH,H)
FM7	Stability	(H,M)	(M,M)	(MH,H)	(H,M)	(VH,M)	(MH,H)	(M,VH)	(MH,M)	(ML,M)	(ML,VH)	(L,VH)	(M,M)	(H,M)	(M,M)	(MH,M)
FM8	Sizing	(MH,H)	(H,M)	(MH,H)	(M,H)	(MH,VH)	(MH,H)	(M,M)	(MH,H)	(ML,M)	(M,M)	(M,VH)	(M,M)	(H,VH)	(MH,H)	(M,H)
FM9	Electrical connections	(M,M)	(MH,VH)	(H,H)	(H,VH)	(MH,M)	(M,VH)	(ML,H)	(L,VH)	(M,M)	(L,VH)	(ML,H)	(VL,VH)	(MH,M)	(H,H)	(M,H)
FM10	Lightning/ groundi-ng	(MH,M)	(ML,VH)	(M,H)	(ML,H)	(L,H)	(M,VH)	(MH,VH)	(ML,M)	(M,VH)	(ML,M)	(ML,VH)	(L,VH)	(MH,H)	(H,H)	(M,VH)
FM11	grid connection	(H,H)	(H,VH)	(MH,M)	(MH,VH)	(H,H)	(M,M)	(L,H)	(ML,H)	(M,H)	(L,VH)	(ML,H)	(M,H)	(M,M)	(ML,H)	(MH,H)
FM12	not compliant with IEC standard	(M,H)	(ML,VH)	(MH,VH)	(M,M)	(ML,VH)	(L,VH)	(M,VH)	(L,H)	(ML,H)	(MH,H)	(M,M)	(H,H)	(ML,H)	(MH,M)	(M,VH)
FM13	Equipment	(M,H)	(ML,VH)	(MH,H)	(H,VH)	(MH,H)	(M,M)	(M,H)	(L,VH)	(ML,H)	(M,H)	(M,M)	(MH,M)	(M,M)	(ML,VH)	(MH,H)
FM14	Structure Damage	(M,H)	(ML,H)	(M,VH)	(ML,VH)	(L,VH)	(VL,VH)	(ML,M)	(M,H)	(M,VH)	(M,M)	(MH,H)	(H,M)	(ML,H)	(L,M)	(M,VH)
FM15	Wiring	(M,H)	(H,M)	(MH,VH)	(MH,VH)	(M,H)	(ML,M)	(MH,H)	(H,VH)	(M,M)	(MH,M)	(M,H)	(H,VH)	(ML,VH)	(L,H)	(M,M)
FM16	Batteries	(M,M)	(MH,VH)	(H,H)	(MH,VH)	(M,H)	(ML,H)	(M,VH)	(M,H)	(M,M)	(MH,H)	(M,M)	(ML,VH)	(H,H)	(MH,VH)	(M,VH)
FM17	Labelling and warning signs	(L,H)	(VL,VH)	(ML,H)	(MH,M)	(M,VH)	(ML,VH)	(MH,VH)	(ML,H)	(M,M)	(M,VH)	(M,H)	(M,M)	(ML,VH)	(L,M)	(VL,H)
FM18	Sensors	(MH,H)	(M,VH)	(ML,M)	(M,H)	(H,M)	(MH,VH)	(M,M)	(ML,H)	(MH,VH)	(H,VH)	(MH,M)	(M,H)	(M,H)	(ML,VH)	(MH,M)
FM19	Boxes or conduit bodies	(H,VH)	(MH,M)	(M,H)	(M,VH)	(L,VH)	(ML,H)	(MH,VH)	(M,VH)	(ML,H)	(M,VH)	(H,M)	(MH,M)	(ML,H)	(ML,VH)	(L,VH)

Table 9. Symmetric fuzzy weight of main criteria by each decision maker.

DM1					K			q			Wj		
		l	*m*	*u*	*l*	*m*	*u*	*l*	*m*	*u*	*l*	*m*	*u*
S					1	1	1	1.000	1.000	1.000	0.357595	0.418505	0.495377
C	MOL-M	0.47	0.71	1.06	1.47	1.71	2.06	0.485	0.585	0.680	0.17359	0.24474	0.336991
D	MOL-H	0.54	0.81	1.21	1.54	1.81	2.21	0.220	0.323	0.442	0.078547	0.135215	0.218826
O	MUL-VH	0.21	0.23	0.27	1.21	1.23	1.27	0.173	0.263	0.365	0.061848	0.109931	0.180848
T	MUL-H	0.18	0.2	0.23	1.18	1.2	1.23	0.141	0.219	0.309	0.050283	0.091609	0.153261
							Sum	2.019	2.389	2.796			
DM2					K			q			Wj		
		l	*m*	*u*	*l*	*m*	*u*	*l*	*m*	*u*	*l*	*m*	*u*
C					1	1	1	1.000	1.000	1.000	0.329376	0.371481	0.428399
S	MOL-H	0.54	0.81	1.21	1.54	1.81	2.21	0.452	0.552	0.649	0.149039	0.205238	0.278181
D	MUL-M	0.16	0.18	0.21	1.16	1.18	1.21	0.374	0.468	0.560	0.123173	0.17393	0.239811
O	MUL-VH	0.21	0.23	0.27	1.21	1.23	1.27	0.294	0.381	0.463	0.096986	0.141407	0.198191
T	VLI-VH	0.27	0.31	0.38	1.27	1.31	1.38	0.213	0.291	0.364	0.07028	0.107944	0.156056
							Sum	2.334	2.692	3.036			
DM3					K			q			Wj		
		l	*m*	*u*	*l*	*m*	*u*	*l*	*m*	*u*	*l*	*m*	*u*
S					1	1	1	1.000	1.000	1.000	0.327769	0.373165	0.435067
C	MOL-M	0.47	0.71	1.06	1.47	1.71	2.06	0.485	0.585	0.680	0.159111	0.218225	0.295964
D	LI-M	0.28	0.35	0.47	1.28	1.35	1.47	0.330	0.433	0.531	0.108239	0.161648	0.231222
T	VLI-H	0.17	0.2	0.24	1.17	1.2	1.24	0.266	0.361	0.454	0.087289	0.134707	0.197626
O	MUL-H	0.18	0.2	0.23	1.18	1.2	1.23	0.217	0.301	0.385	0.070967	0.112256	0.167479
							Sum	2.298	2.680	3.051			

Table 10 shows the average of the final symmetric weight, obtained from all the opinions of decision-makers for evaluating and prioritizing the risk of failures in FMEA method. This table consists of the average weight W for each factor of FMEA in all decision-makers' opinions.

Table 10. Final symmetric weight of main criteria with Fuzzy SWARA method.

Factor	DM1			DM2			DM3			Final Weight			Crisp
	l	m	u	l	m	u	l	m	u	l	m	u	
S	0.358	0.419	0.495	0.149	0.205	0.278	0.328	0.373	0.435	0.278	0.332	0.403	0.338
C	0.174	0.245	0.337	0.329	0.371	0.428	0.159	0.218	0.296	0.221	0.278	0.354	0.284
D	0.079	0.135	0.219	0.123	0.174	0.240	0.108	0.162	0.231	0.103	0.157	0.230	0.163
O	0.062	0.110	0.181	0.097	0.141	0.198	0.071	0.112	0.167	0.077	0.121	0.182	0.127
T	0.050	0.092	0.153	0.070	0.108	0.156	0.087	0.135	0.198	0.069	0.111	0.169	0.117

According to Table 10, the final symmetric weight, obtained in the form of triangular fuzzy numbers, is for each failure factor in FMEA method. The final factor weight for factors are calculated as $w_s = (0.278, 0.332, 0.403)$, $w_c = (0.221, 0.278, 0.354)$, $w_d = (0.103, 0.157, 0.230)$, $w_o = (0.077, 0.121, 0.182)$ and $w_t = (0.069, 0.111, 0.169)$, respectively. Then the failure modes are prioritized, using the developed Z-GRA method.

Table 11 shows the decision-making matrix Z-GRA in the form of Z-number elements for failure factors of FMEA. The lines in Table 12 show the failure modes identified in the first phase of the research method by the team.

Table 11. Z-GRA initial decision matrix for failure modes of FMEA.

Failure	S			O			D			C			T		
	l	m	u	l	m	u	l	m	u	l	m	u	l	m	u
FM1	4.470	6.257	7.737	3.053	4.777	6.500	1.207	2.640	4.340	1.077	2.150	3.460	2.387	4.020	5.653
FM2	5.183	6.813	7.903	5.873	7.197	7.933	3.930	5.480	6.757	1.750	3.230	4.710	2.987	4.623	6.260
FM3	4.250	5.953	7.380	2.813	4.690	6.567	2.540	4.177	5.807	3.700	5.180	6.427	5.250	6.883	7.933
FM4	1.020	2.387	4.020	2.607	4.240	5.873	4.240	5.873	7.197	2.540	4.177	5.807	1.020	2.387	4.020
FM5	3.613	5.250	6.883	1.207	2.607	4.240	0.820	2.450	4.087	1.043	2.363	3.997	2.680	4.470	6.260
FM6	5.873	7.197	7.933	2.770	4.560	6.347	1.173	2.540	4.177	1.077	2.463	4.160	4.030	5.643	6.987
FM7	3.700	5.180	6.427	5.113	6.357	7.133	2.353	3.920	5.490	1.020	2.430	4.150	3.537	4.950	6.127
FM8	4.337	5.880	7.197	3.713	5.413	7.113	2.287	3.767	5.250	2.350	3.923	5.490	4.340	6.037	7.427
FM9	4.150	5.790	7.150	4.307	6.027	7.437	0.977	2.300	3.930	0.270	1.120	2.593	3.867	5.413	6.687
FM10	2.300	3.930	5.563	1.207	2.640	4.340	2.737	4.460	6.183	0.550	1.957	3.680	4.160	5.863	7.297
FM11	5.250	6.883	7.933	4.150	5.790	7.150	1.077	2.420	4.030	1.077	2.463	4.160	2.320	3.867	5.413
FM12	2.683	4.470	6.257	1.020	2.430	4.150	1.207	2.640	4.340	3.930	5.480	6.757	2.387	4.020	5.653
FM13	2.463	4.160	5.863	4.240	5.873	7.197	1.077	2.463	4.160	2.693	4.173	5.650	2.363	3.997	5.633
FM14	2.013	3.713	5.413	0.313	1.250	2.813	1.980	3.613	5.250	3.700	5.180	6.427	1.207	2.607	4.240
FM15	4.020	5.653	7.050	2.607	4.240	5.873	4.240	5.873	7.197	4.177	5.807	7.127	1.020	2.387	4.020
FM16	4.150	5.790	7.150	2.640	4.340	6.037	2.450	4.087	5.720	2.363	3.997	5.633	4.380	6.173	7.690
FM17	0.270	1.077	2.463	2.430	4.150	5.873	2.540	4.177	5.473	2.450	4.087	5.720	0.313	1.173	2.540
FM18	2.517	4.150	5.790	4.020	5.653	7.050	2.540	4.177	5.807	4.177	5.807	7.127	2.300	3.930	5.563
FM19	4.177	5.807	7.127	1.207	2.683	4.470	2.770	4.560	6.347	3.767	5.333	6.667	0.583	2.057	3.843

Table 12. Normalized weighted matrix.

Failure/Factor	S	O	D	C	T
FM1	0.745	0.555	0.461	0.425	0.517
FM2	0.863	1.000	0.871	0.510	0.579
FM3	0.701	0.543	0.619	0.809	1.000
FM4	0.387	0.505	1.000	0.627	0.405
FM5	0.611	0.398	0.439	0.443	0.560
FM6	1.000	0.532	0.453	0.451	0.715
FM7	0.599	0.782	0.584	0.448	0.612
FM8	0.698	0.630	0.565	0.591	0.787
FM9	0.678	0.711	0.436	0.370	0.677
FM10	0.480	0.400	0.662	0.414	0.754
FM11	0.877	0.678	0.444	0.451	0.503
FM12	0.524	0.390	0.461	0.890	0.517
FM13	0.498	0.690	0.448	0.627	0.515
FM14	0.462	0.341	0.546	0.809	0.417
FM15	0.659	0.505	1.000	1.000	0.405
FM16	0.678	0.513	0.606	0.601	0.812
FM17	0.333	0.497	0.604	0.613	0.349
FM18	0.498	0.659	0.619	1.000	0.509
FM19	0.680	0.403	0.677	0.852	0.387
WEIGHT	0.338	0.127	0.163	0.284	0.117

After the normalization of the primary matrix presented in Table 11, the normalized weighted matrix, considering the weights of the factor used in FMEA method, is obtained for all the failure modes as in Table 12.

Now, after normalizing the final symmetric weights, the identified failures are prioritized based on the Z-GRA approach and also a comparison between the outputs of this approach and conventional methods such as Fuzzy GRA and traditional RPN has been presented in Table 13.

Table 13. New approach results with existing methods.

Failure	RPN	Rank	Fuzzy GRA	Rank	Z-GRA	Rank
FM1	1890	12	0.570	16	0.578	13
FM2	18,144	1	0.815	1	0.773	2
FM3	11,200	2	0.799	2	0.753	3
FM4	2100	11	0.576	15	0.583	12
FM5	1152	14	0.525	17	0.520	18
FM6	2835	8	0.706	6	0.691	6
FM7	7680	4	0.667	8	0.596	11
FM8	7840	3	0.710	5	0.667	7
FM9	2352	10	0.581	14	0.574	14
FM10	1680	13	0.518	18	0.527	17
FM11	4608	5	0.663	9	0.641	9
FM12	840	15	0.645	11	0.615	10
FM13	2625	9	0.593	13	0.567	16
FM14	1152	14	0.610	12	0.567	15
FM15	7840	3	0.797	3	0.781	1
FM16	4200	6	0.661	10	0.659	8
FM17	600	16	0.490	19	0.489	19
FM18	4200	6	0.702	7	0.696	4
FM19	3528	7	0.725	4	0.679	5

Table 13 implies that failures FM2 with a score of 18,144, FM3 with a score of 11,200 and FM8 and FM15 with a score of 7840 are ranked from 1 to 3, respectively. Consideration of the different weights of risk factors (SODET) demonstrates that although failure FM8 with the FGRA approach ranks fifth, it ranks third based on traditional RPN indices. This change indicates the application of the weights of risk factors in the process of prioritizing failures.

FM2 with a score of 0.815, FM3 with a score of 0.799 and FM15 with a score of 0.797 are ranked from 1 to 3 based on fuzzy GRA, respectively. The fuzzy GRA index has a more substantial impact on distinguishing priorities (complete prioritization of failures) compared with the RPN indices.

On the basis of the Z-GRA approach, FM15 with a score of 0.781, FM2 with a score of 0.773 and FM3 with a score of 0.753 are ranked from 1 to 3, respectively. Further investigation of this index shows that the recommended approach not only considers uncertainty and reliability simultaneously in the processes of prioritizing failures and assigning different weights to risk factors but can also prioritize the failures completely and assign distinct ranks to each risk properly.

A simultaneous comparison of critical failures in the two approaches of Z-GRA and traditional RPN shows that although failures FM8 and FM15 share the third rank based on the RPN indices, they have distinct ranks of seventh and first, respectively, based on the suggested approach. The reason for the lower rank of FM8 compared with that of FM15 is the difference in the values of symmetric weights assigned to the risk factors. For example, FM15, which is ranked first based on the Z-GRA approach, assigns large values to crucial risk factors, such as cost and detection (Table 11).

$$C_{FM_{15}} = (4.177, 5.807, 7.127) > C_{FM_8} = (2.35, 3.923, 5.490)$$
$$D_{FM_{15}} = (4.240, 5.873, 7.197) > C_{FM_8} = (2.287, 3.767, 5.250)$$

Figure 3 shows the resolution of ranks assigned to failures based on traditional FMEA, fuzzy GRA and Z-GRA methods. The conventional FMEA performs an incomplete prioritization of failures by placing 19 risks in 15 categories. By contrast, fuzzy GRA and Z-GRA conduct a complete prioritization by assigning distinct ranks to identified failures. The advantage of this ranking over incomplete prioritization is that it can increase the ability of DMs to discern critical failures and plan corrective actions in accordance with the limitations of sources. Although, the fuzzy GRA method provides DMs with a complete ranking, reliability is disregarded in this ranking. Consequently, the results of the

Z-GRA method are more coincident with the FMEA team's opinion compared with those of the fuzzy GRA method.

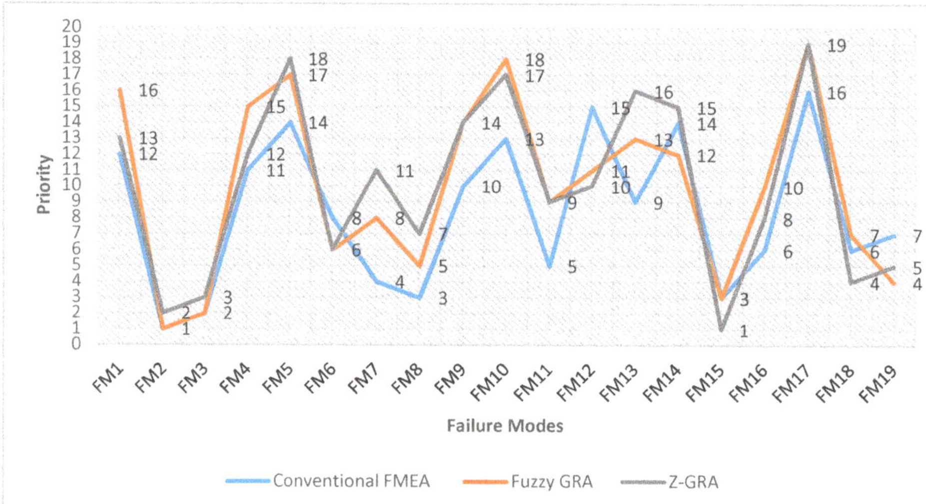

Figure 3. Comparison of failure prioritization based on conventional FMEA, fuzzy GRA, Z-GRA approaches.

5. Sensitivity Analysis

Sensitivity is calculated with the risk factor weights in accordance with the information in Table 14. For example, the original weight values of the risk factors are shown in Case 0. In Case 1, 0.1 is added to the weight of S and 0.025 is deducted from the weight of O, D, C and T. Similarly, 0.1 is added to the weight of O in Case 2, to the weight of D in Case 3, to the weight of C in case 4 and to the weight of T in Case 5; meanwhile, 0.025 is deducted from the initial weight of the others. The results of the rating sensitivity analysis of solar panels are shown in Table 15 and Figure 4. In Case 1, by increasing the weight of S, FM2 (Dust) is upgraded from the second position to the first position, whereas FM15 (Wiring) is downgraded from the first position to the second position. In Case 2, by increasing the weight of O, FM2 (Dust) is upgraded from the second position to the first position, whereas FM15 (Wiring) is downgraded from the first position to the second position. In Case 4, by increasing the weight of C, FM2 (Dust) is downgraded from the second position to the third position. In Case 5, by increasing the weight of T, FM15 (Wiring) is downgraded from the first position to the third position. FM3 (Orientation) is upgraded from the third position to the first one. In all cases, FM17 (Labeling and warning signs) is selected as the last failure mode.

Table 14. Weights of the risk factors with respect to considered cases.

	S	O	D	C	T
Case 0	0.338	0.127	0.163	0.284	0.117
Case 1	0.438	0.102	0.138	0.259	0.092
Case 2	0.313	0.227	0.138	0.259	0.092
Case 3	0.313	0.102	0.263	0.259	0.092
Case 4	0.313	0.102	0.138	0.384	0.092
Case 5	0.313	0.102	0.138	0.259	0.217

Table 15. Ranking results of failure modes with respect to the considered cases.

Failures	Rank					
	Case 0	Case 1	Case 2	Case 3	Case 4	Case 5
FM1	13	11	14	14	15	13
FM2	2	1	1	2	3	2
FM3	3	3	3	3	2	1
FM4	12	16	15	9	12	15
FM5	18	17	17	18	17	18
FM6	6	4	5	6	6	4
FM7	11	12	10	12	13	11
FM8	7	8	6	7	7	5
FM9	14	13	12	15	16	12
FM10	17	18	18	17	18	17
FM11	9	6	8	10	10	9
FM12	10	10	11	11	8	10
FM13	16	15	13	16	14	14
FM14	15	14	16	13	11	16
FM15	1	2	2	1	1	3
FM16	8	9	9	8	9	6
FM17	19	19	19	19	19	19
FM18	4	7	4	4	4	7
FM19	5	5	7	5	5	8

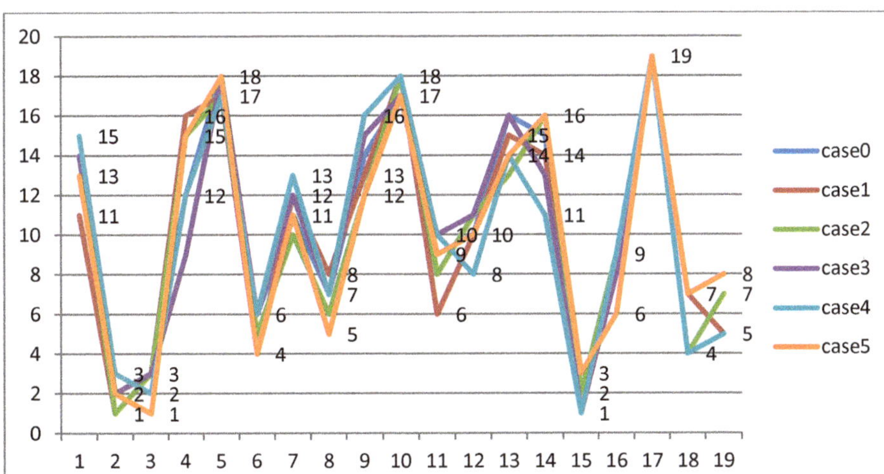

Figure 4. Sensitivity analysis for Z-GRA.

6. Conclusions

The FMEA technique is widely used in various fields but it has deficiencies and limitations, which have pushed researchers to improve the technique. In this study, an FMEA approach is developed using Z-SWARA and Z-GRA. A new approach is recommended to address several of the defects of conventional RPN. After identifying failures via the FMEA technique, the Z-SWARA method is used to weigh RPN determining factors because not considering the symmetric weights of these factors is one of the disadvantages of conventional RPN indices. Applying the Z-GRA method also helps DMs incorporate uncertainty into the determinants of RPN and consider reliability in failure modes in accordance with Z-number theory. Under this condition, prioritization is close to reality because reliability is considered, and a complete prioritization is provided. DMs can thus execute a set of precautionary actions for important failures and re-evaluate the new system condition and the effectiveness of these actions. In general, wiring should be examined and dust should be removed from solar panels. The orientation of panels should be set and sensors and boxes or conduit bodies must be arranged properly; the other components can be controlled based on the prioritization obtained. In the case of failure, the quality control department or laboratory should be informed for repairs. In future studies, the prioritization of failure modes can be evaluated using the G-number.

Author Contributions: Conceptualization, M.N.A.R. and M.J.G.; Data curation, D.R. and M.J.G.; Formal analysis, E.O. and M.J.G.; Funding acquisition, M.N.A.R.; Methodology, E.O., M.N.A.R., D.R. and S.J.G.; Software, S.J.G.; Supervision, E.O., M.N.A.R. and S.J.G.; Validation, E.O., M.N.A.R. and D.R.; Visualization, D.R.; Writing—original draft, S.J.G.; Writing—review & editing, M.J.G. and M.N.A.R. All authors have read and agree to the published version of the manuscript.

Funding: The authors also greatly appreciate the support of the Universiti Kebangsaan Malaysia, Malaysia under grant No. FRGS/2/2014/TK01/UKM/02/2 and FRGS/1/2018/TK08/UKM/02/1 for financing this research.

Acknowledgments: The authors wish to express their sincere thanks to the academic editor and reviewers for their detailed comments and many valuable suggestions that have significantly improved the quality of this paper.

Conflicts of Interest: The authors declare no conflict of interest.

References

1. Jafarzadeh, S.G.; Ab Rahman, M.N.; Wahab, D.A. Forecasting capabilities of spare part production with artificial neural networks model in a supply chain. *World Appl. Sci. J.* **2012**, *20*, 674–678.
2. Jafarzadeh-Ghoushchi, S.; Ab Rahman, M.N. Performance study of artificial neural network modelling to predict carried weight in the transportation system. *Int. J. Logist. Syst. Manag.* **2016**, *24*, 200–212. [CrossRef]
3. Jainury, S.M.; Ramli, R.; Ab Rahman, M.N.; Omar, A. Integrated Set Parts Supply system in a mixed-model assembly line. *Comput. Ind. Eng.* **2014**, *75*, 266–273. [CrossRef]
4. Rose, A.N.M.; Deros, B.M.; Ab Rahman, M.N. Critical success factors for implementing lean manufacturing in Malaysian automotive industry. *Res. J. Appl. Sci. Eng. Technol.* **2014**, *8*, 1191–1200. [CrossRef]
5. Ghoushchi, S.J.; Yousefi, S.; Khazaeili, M. An extended FMEA approach based on the Z-MOORA and fuzzy BWM for prioritization of failures. *Appl. Soft Comput.* **2019**, *81*, 105505. [CrossRef]
6. Bowles, J.B.; Peláez, C.E. Fuzzy logic prioritization of failures in a system failure mode, effects and criticality analysis. *Reliab. Eng. Syst. Saf.* **1995**, *50*, 203–213. [CrossRef]
7. Rezaee, M.J.; Yousefi, S.; Eshkevari, M.; Valipour, M.; Saberi, M. Risk analysis of health, safety and environment in chemical industry integrating linguistic FMEA, fuzzy inference system and fuzzy DEA. *Stoch. Environ. Res. Risk Assess.* **2020**, *34*, 201–218. [CrossRef]
8. Rezaee, M.J.; Salimi, A.; Yousefi, S. Identifying and managing failures in stone processing industry using cost-based FMEA. *Int. J. Adv. Manuf. Technol.* **2017**, *88*, 3329–3342. [CrossRef]
9. Liu, H.-C. FMEA Using Uncertainty Theories and MCDM Methods. In *FMEA Using Uncertainty Theories and MCDM Methods*; Springer: Berlin/Heidelberg, Germany, 2016; pp. 13–27.
10. Rezaee, M.J.; Yousefi, S.; Valipour, M.; Dehdar, M.M. Risk analysis of sequential processes in food industry integrating multi-stage fuzzy cognitive map and process failure mode and effects analysis. *Comput. Ind. Eng.* **2018**, *123*, 325–337. [CrossRef]
11. Zadeh, L.A. A note on Z-numbers. *Inf. Sci.* **2011**, *181*, 2923–2932. [CrossRef]
12. Jafarzadeh Ghoushchi, S.; Khazaeili, M.; Sabri-Laghaie, K. An extended Multi-Criteria Green Supplier Selection based on Z-Numbers for Fuzzy Multi-Objective Linear Programming Problem. *Int. J. Ind. Eng. Manag. Sci.* **2019**, *6*, 74–96.
13. Jafarzadeh Ghoushchi, S.; Khazaeili, M.; Amini, A.; Osgooei, E. Multi-criteria sustainable supplier selection using piecewise linear value function and fuzzy best-worst method. *J. Intell. Fuzzy Syst.* **2019**, *37*, 2309–2325. [CrossRef]
14. Mardani, A.; Jusoh, A.; Zavadskas, E.K. Fuzzy multiple criteria decision-making techniques and applications–Two decades review from 1994 to 2014. *Expert Syst. Appl.* **2015**, *42*, 4126–4148. [CrossRef]
15. Mustaffa, N.F.; Hishamuddin, H.; Ropi, N.M.; Saibani, N.; Ab Rahman, M.N. Assessing Supply Chain Risk Management Practices in Manufacturing Industries in Malaysia. *J. Kejuruter.* **2018**, *6*, 17–22.

16. Baghery, M.; Yousefi, S.; Rezaee, M.J. Risk measurement and prioritization of auto parts manufacturing processes based on process failure analysis, interval data envelopment analysis and grey relational analysis. *J. Intell. Manuf.* **2018**, *29*, 1803–1825. [CrossRef]
17. Yousefi, S.; Alizadeh, A.; Hayati, J.; Baghery, M. HSE risk prioritization using robust DEA-FMEA approach with undesirable outputs: A study of automotive parts industry in Iran. *Saf. Sci.* **2018**, *102*, 144–158. [CrossRef]
18. Leuveano, R.A.C.; Ab Rahman, M.N.; Mahmood, W.M.F.W.; Saleh, C. Integrated Vendor–Buyer Lot-Sizing Model with Transportation and Quality Improvement Consideration under Just-in-Time Problem. *Mathematics* **2019**, *7*, 944. [CrossRef]
19. Ab Rahman, M.N.; Doroodian, M.; Kamarulzaman, Y.; Muhamad, N. Designing and validating a model for measuring sustainability of overall innovation capability of small and medium-sized enterprises. *Sustainability* **2015**, *7*, 537–562. [CrossRef]
20. Mandal, S.; Maiti, J. Risk analysis using FMEA: Fuzzy similarity value and possibility theory based approach. *Expert Syst. Appl.* **2014**, *41*, 3527–3537. [CrossRef]
21. Dabbagh, R.; Yousefi, S. A hybrid decision-making approach based on FCM and MOORA for occupational health and safety risk analysis. *J. Saf. Res.* **2019**, *71*, 111–123. [CrossRef]
22. Braglia, M.; Bevilacqua, M. Fuzzy modelling and analytical hierarchy processing as a means of quantifying risk levels associated with failure modes in production systems. *Technol. Law Insur.* **2000**, *5*, 125–134. [CrossRef]
23. Liu, H.-C.; You, J.-X.; Fan, X.-J.; Lin, Q.-L. Failure mode and effects analysis using D numbers and grey relational projection method. *Expert Syst. Appl.* **2014**, *41*, 4670–4679. [CrossRef]
24. Safari, H.; Faraji, Z.; Majidian, S. Identifying and evaluating enterprise architecture risks using FMEA and fuzzy VIKOR. *J. Intell. Manuf.* **2016**, *27*, 475–486. [CrossRef]
25. Emovon, I.; Norman, R.A.; Alan, J.M.; Pazouki, K. An integrated multicriteria decision making methodology using compromise solution methods for prioritising risk of marine machinery systems. *Ocean Eng.* **2015**, *105*, 92–103. [CrossRef]
26. Liu, H.-C. FMEA Using Uncertain Linguistic GRA-TOPSIS and Its Application to Endotracheal Suctioning. In *Improved FMEA Methods for Proactive Healthcare Risk Analysis*; Springer: Berlin/Heidelberg, Germany, 2019; pp. 173–193.
27. Tian, Z.-P.; Wang, J.-Q.; Wang, J.; Zhang, H.-Y. A multi-phase QFD-based hybrid fuzzy MCDM approach for performance evaluation: A case of smart bike-sharing programs in Changsha. *J. Clean. Prod.* **2018**, *171*, 1068–1083. [CrossRef]
28. Melani, A.H.A.; Murad, C.A.; Netto, A.C.; de Souza, G.F.M.; Nabeta, S.I. Criticality-based maintenance of a coal-fired power plant. *Energy* **2018**, *147*, 767–781. [CrossRef]
29. Nie, R.-X.; Tian, Z.-P.; Wang, X.-K.; Wang, J.-Q.; Wang, T.-L. Risk evaluation by FMEA of supercritical water gasification system using multi-granular linguistic distribution assessment. *Knowl. Based Syst.* **2018**, *162*, 185–201. [CrossRef]
30. Galehdar, E.; Saghih, A.M.F.; Pooya, A. A compilation model for the selection of quality management system based on the benefits of their application in the automotive industry by using dematel fuzzy and analytic network process. *Int. J. Qual. Res.* **2018**, *12*, 317–336.
31. Hu, Y.-P.; You, X.-Y.; Wang, L.; Liu, H.-C. An integrated approach for failure mode and effect analysis based on uncertain linguistic GRA–TOPSIS method. *Soft Comput.* **2019**, *23*, 8801–8814. [CrossRef]
32. Kumar, A.M.; Rajakarunakaran, S.; Pitchipoo, P.; Vimalesan, R. Fuzzy based risk prioritisation in an auto LPG dispensing station. *Saf. Sci.* **2018**, *101*, 231–247. [CrossRef]
33. Arabsheybani, A.; Paydar, M.M.; Safaei, A.S. An integrated fuzzy MOORA method and FMEA technique for sustainable supplier selection considering quantity discounts and supplier's risk. *J. Clean. Prod.* **2018**, *190*, 577–591. [CrossRef]
34. Panchal, D.; Srivastava, P. Qualitative analysis of CNG dispensing system using fuzzy FMEA–GRA integrated approach. *Int. J. Syst. Assur. Eng. Manag.* **2019**, *10*, 44–56. [CrossRef]
35. Nazeri, A.; Naderikia, R. A new fuzzy approach to identify the critical risk factors in maintenance management. *Int. J. Adv. Manuf. Technol.* **2017**, *92*, 3749–3783. [CrossRef]
36. Bian, T.; Zheng, H.; Yin, L.; Deng, Y. Failure mode and effects analysis based on D numbers and TOPSIS. *Qual. Reliab. Eng. Int.* **2018**, *34*, 501–515. [CrossRef]

37. Battirola Filho, J.C.; Piechnicki, F.; Loures, E.d.F.R.; Santos, E.A.P. Process-aware FMEA framework for failure analysis in maintenance. *J. Manuf. Technol. Manag.* **2017**, *28*, 822–848. [CrossRef]
38. Mangeli, M.; Shahraki, A.; Saljooghi, F.H. Improvement of risk assessment in the FMEA using nonlinear model, revised fuzzy TOPSIS and support vector machine. *Int. J. Ind. Ergon.* **2019**, *69*, 209–216. [CrossRef]
39. Liu, H.-C.; You, J.-X.; Shan, M.-M.; Su, Q. Systematic failure mode and effect analysis using a hybrid multiple criteria decision-making approach. *Total Qual. Manag. Bus. Excell.* **2019**, *30*, 537–564. [CrossRef]
40. Ak, M.F.; Gul, M. AHP–TOPSIS integration extended with Pythagorean fuzzy sets for information security risk analysis. *Complex Intell. Syst.* **2019**, *5*, 113–126. [CrossRef]
41. Dorosti, S.; Fathi, M.; Ghoushchi, S.J.; Khakifirooz, M.; Khazaeili, M. Patient waiting time management through fuzzy based failure mode and effect analysis. *J. Intell. Fuzzy Syst.* **2020**, *38*, 1–12. [CrossRef]
42. Liu, H.-C. FMEA Using ITL-ELECTRE Approach and Its Application to Proton Beam Radiotherapy. In *Improved FMEA Methods for Proactive Healthcare Risk Analysis*; Springer: Berlin/Heidelberg, Germany, 2019; pp. 97–124.
43. Lo, H.-W.; Liou, J.J.; Huang, C.-N.; Chuang, Y.-C. A novel failure mode and effect analysis model for machine tool risk analysis. *Reliab. Eng. Syst. Saf.* **2019**, *183*, 173–183. [CrossRef]
44. Wang, L.; Hu, Y.P.; Liu, H.C.; Shi, H. A linguistic risk prioritization approach for failure mode and effects analysis: A case study of medical product development. *Qual. Reliab. Eng. Int.* **2019**, *35*, 1735–1752. [CrossRef]
45. Li, Z.; Chen, L. A novel evidential FMEA method by integrating fuzzy belief structure and grey relational projection method. *Eng. Appl. Artif. Intell.* **2019**, *77*, 136–147. [CrossRef]
46. Fattahi, R.; Khalilzadeh, M. Risk evaluation using a novel hybrid method based on FMEA, extended MULTIMOORA and AHP methods under fuzzy environment. *Saf. Sci.* **2018**, *102*, 290–300. [CrossRef]
47. Deng, J. Introduction to grey system theory. *J. Grey Syst.* **1989**, *1*, 1–24.
48. Olson, D.L.; Wu, D. Simulation of fuzzy multiattribute models for grey relationships. *Eur. J. Oper. Res.* **2006**, *175*, 111–120. [CrossRef]
49. Chen, W.-H.; Tsai, M.-S.; Kuo, H.-L. Distribution system restoration using the hybrid fuzzy-grey method. *IEEE Trans. Power Syst.* **2005**, *20*, 199–205. [CrossRef]
50. Jiang, B.C.; Tasi, S.-L.; Wang, C.-C. Machine vision-based gray relational theory applied to IC marking inspection. *IEEE Trans. Semicond. Manuf.* **2002**, *15*, 531–539. [CrossRef]
51. Wu, H.-H. A comparative study of using grey relational analysis in multiple attribute decision making problems. *Qual. Eng.* **2002**, *15*, 209–217. [CrossRef]
52. Lin, C.-T.; Chang, C.-W.; Chen, C.-B. The worst ill-conditioned silicon wafer slicing machine detected by using grey relational analysis. *Int. J. Adv. Manuf. Technol.* **2006**, *31*, 388–395. [CrossRef]
53. Wei, G.-W. GRA method for multiple attribute decision making with incomplete weight information in intuitionistic fuzzy setting. *Knowl. Based Syst.* **2010**, *23*, 243–247. [CrossRef]
54. Kuo, C.-F.J.; Su, T.-L.; Jhang, P.-R.; Huang, C.-Y.; Chiu, C.-H. Using the Taguchi method and grey relational analysis to optimize the flat-plate collector process with multiple quality characteristics in solar energy collector manufacturing. *Energy* **2011**, *36*, 3554–3562.
55. Acır, A.; Canlı, M.E.; Ata, İ.; Çakıroğlu, R. Parametric optimization of energy and exergy analyses of a novel solar air heater with grey relational analysis. *Appl. Therm. Eng.* **2017**, *122*, 330–338. [CrossRef]
56. Tiwari, D.; Sherwani, A.F.; Asjad, M.; Arora, A. Grey relational analysis coupled with principal component analysis for optimization of the cyclic parameters of a solar-driven organic Rankine cycle. *Grey Syst. Theory Appl.* **2017**, *7*, 218–235. [CrossRef]
57. Narendranathan, S.; Sudhagar, K.; Karthikeyan, R. Optimization of engine operating parameters suitable for punnai oil application in CI engine using Grey relational method. *Energy Environ.* **2019**, *30*, 732–751. [CrossRef]
58. Keršuliene, V.; Zavadskas, E.K.; Turskis, Z. Selection of rational dispute resolution method by applying new step-wise weight assessment ratio analysis (SWARA). *J. Bus. Econ. Manag.* **2010**, *11*, 243–258. [CrossRef]
59. Aghdaie, M.H.; Zolfani, S.H.; Zavadskas, E.K. Decision making in machine tool selection: An integrated approach with SWARA and COPRAS-G methods. *Eng. Econ.* **2013**, *24*, 5–17.
60. Keršulienė, V.; Turskis, Z. Integrated fuzzy multiple criteria decision making model for architect selection. *Technol. Econ. Dev. Econ.* **2011**, *17*, 645–666. [CrossRef]

61. Zolfani, S.H.; Banihashemi, S.S.A. Personnel Selection Based on a Novel Mmodel of Game Theory and MCDM Approaches. In Proceedings of the 8th International Scientific Conference Business and Management, Vilinus, Lithuania, 5–16 May 2014; pp. 15–16.
62. Zolfani, S.H.; Chatterjee, P. Comparative evaluation of sustainable design based on Step-wise Weight Assessment Ratio Analysis (SWARA) and best worst method (BWM) methods: A perspective on household furnishing materials. *Symmetry* **2019**, *11*, 74. [CrossRef]
63. Karabašević, D.; Paunkovic, J.; Stanujkić, D. Ranking of companies according to the indicators of corporate social responsibility based on SWARA and ARAS methods. *Serb. J. Manag.* **2016**, *11*, 43–53. [CrossRef]
64. Zolfani, S.H.; Saparauskas, J. New application of SWARA method in prioritizing sustainability assessment indicators of energy system. *Eng. Econ.* **2013**, *24*, 408–414. [CrossRef]
65. Zolfani, S.H.; Salimi, J.; Maknoon, R.; Kildiene, S. Technology foresight about R&D projects selection; application of SWARA method at the policy making level. *Eng. Econ.* **2015**, *26*, 571–580.
66. Zavadskas, E.K.; Stević, Ž.; Tanackov, I.; Prentkovskis, O. A novel multicriteria approach–rough step-wise weight assessment ratio analysis method (R-SWARA) and its application in logistics. *Stud. Inform. Control* **2018**, *27*, 97–106. [CrossRef]
67. Ijadi Maghsoodi, A.; Ijadi Maghsoodi, A.; Mosavi, A.; Rabczuk, T.; Zavadskas, E. Renewable energy technology selection problem using integrated h-swara-multimoora approach. *Sustainability* **2018**, *10*, 4481. [CrossRef]
68. Shahsavar, S.; Rad, A.J.; Afzal, P.; Nezafati, N.; Aghdam, M.A. Prospecting for polymetallic mineralization using step-wise weight assessment ratio analysis (SWARA) and fractal modeling in Aghkand Area, NW Iran. *Arab. J. Geosci.* **2019**, *12*, 248. [CrossRef]
69. Ghasempour, R.; Nazari, M.A.; Ebrahimi, M.; Ahmadi, M.H.; Hadiyanto, H. Multi-Criteria Decision Making (MCDM) Approach for Selecting Solar Plants Site and Technology: A Review. *Int. J. Renew. Energy Dev.* **2019**, *8*, 15–25. [CrossRef]
70. Siksnelyte, I.; Zavadskas, E.; Streimikiene, D.; Sharma, D. An overview of multi-criteria decision-making methods in dealing with sustainable energy development issues. *Energies* **2018**, *11*, 2754. [CrossRef]
71. Zadeh, L.A. Fuzzy sets. *Inf. Control* **1965**, *8*, 338–353. [CrossRef]
72. Kang, B.; Wei, D.; Li, Y.; Deng, Y. A method of converting Z-number to classical fuzzy number. *J. Inf. Comput. Sci.* **2012**, *9*, 703–709.
73. Aliev, R.A.; Alizadeh, A.V.; Huseynov, O.H. The arithmetic of discrete Z-numbers. *Inf. Sci.* **2015**, *290*, 134–155. [CrossRef]
74. Aliev, R.; Alizadeh, A.; Huseynov, O. An introduction to the arithmetic of Z-numbers by using horizontal membership functions. *Procedia Comput. Sci.* **2017**, *120*, 349–356. [CrossRef]
75. Aliev, R.A.; Huseynov, O.H.; Serdaroglu, R. Ranking of Z-numbers and its application in decision making. *Int. J. Inf. Technol. Decis. Mak.* **2016**, *15*, 1503–1519. [CrossRef]

symmetry

MDPI

Article

Application of Fuzzy Analytic Hierarchy Process to Underground Mining Method Selection

Sanja Bajić *, Dragoljub Bajić, Branko Gluščević and Vesna Ristić Vakanjac

Faculty of Mining and Geology, University of Belgrade, 11000 Belgrade, Serbia; dragoljub.bajic@rgf.bg.ac.rs (D.B.); branko.gluscevic@rgf.bg.ac.rs (B.G.); vesna.ristic@rgf.bg.ac.rs (V.R.V.)

* Correspondence: sanja.bajic@rgf.bg.ac.rs

Received: 30 December 2019; Accepted: 14 January 2020; Published: 23 January 2020

Abstract: The paper proposes a problem-solving approach in the area of underground mining, related to the evaluation and selection of the optimal mining method, employing fuzzy multiple-criteria optimization. The application of fuzzy logic to decision-making in multiple-criteria optimization is particularly useful in cases where not enough information is available about a given system, and where expert knowledge and experience are an important aspect. With a straightforward objective, multiple-criteria decision-making is used to rank various mining methods relative to a set of criteria and to select the optimal solution. The considered mining methods represent possible alternatives. In addition, various criteria and subcriteria that influence the selection of the best available solution are defined and analyzed. The final decision concerning the selection of the optimal mining method is made based on mathematical optimization calculations. The paper demonstrates the proposed approach as applied in a case study.

Keywords: multiple-criteria decision-making; underground mines; mining methods; expert knowledge

---

1. Introduction

It is well-known that in most cases, a large number of criteria and subcriteria for decision-making matrices are uncertain and decision makers are unable to arrive at exact numerical values for comparing decisions. As such, mathematical methods are needed to effectively treat uncertainty, vagueness, and subjectivity. Viewed from that perspective, fuzzy logic is a scientifically based approach that relies on experience and intuition (or expert judgment). The fuzzy analytic hierarchy process (FAHP) enables the evaluation and analysis of criteria using fuzzified evaluation scales based on Saaty's scale [1].

In recent years, scientists worldwide have introduced a number of new theories and procedures for selecting underground mining methods, which generally involve gray correlation and multiple-criteria decision-making (AHP, FAHP, TOPSIS, PROMETHEE, ELECTRE, and VIKOR). Multiple-criteria decision-making (MCDM) methods have been demonstrated as useful problem-solving tools in various fields of engineering [2–4]. FAHP is widely applied. Guo et al. [5] used FAHP to determine evaluation index weights when they assessed the stability of a worksite above an abandoned coalmine, which threatened the safety of a high-speed railroad line. Pipatprapa et al. [6] used structural equation modeling (SEM) and FAHP to investigate factors suitable for assessing the environmental performance of the food industry. Lee et al. [7] proposed an FAHP-based decision-making model for selecting the best location for a frontal solar facility, given that the electric power demand, fossil fuel depletion, and environmental awareness necessitate power supply from renewable sources. Chatterjee & Stević [8] used FAHP for supplier selection in supply chain management. Božanić et al. [9] compare the FAHP method to another method that uses the fuzzy approach in MCDM for ranking the locations for deep wading as a technique of crossing the river by the army tank units. Stanković et al. [10] used FAHP for determining the importance of the traffic accessibility criteria. Mallick et al. [11] applied FAHP in groundwater management of a semi-arid region.

An in-depth literature review revealed that much research has used MCDM techniques to define optimal mining methods for different ores. Özfırat [12] applied FAHP to assess the use of certain machinery in the Amasra coalmine, in order to boost production, downsize the workforce and, consequently, reduce the number of accidents. Chander et al. [13] propose a decision-making technique for the selection of the optimal underground bauxite mining method. Based on AHP and VIKOR multiple-criteria optimization techniques, their results show that the optimal mining method, in that case, was cut-and-fill. Balusa & Gorai [14] compare mining methods using five MCDM models (TOPSIS, VIKOR, ELECTRE, PROMETHEE II, and WPM). They employed AHP to determine the weights of effective criteria for the Tummalapalle uranium mine in India. The results indicate that the selected mining methods were not equally efficient. Balusa & Gorai [15] used FAHP to select suitable underground mining methods. Bogdanovic et al. [16] employed a combination of AHP and PROMETHEE to select the most suitable mining method for the Čoka Marin underground mine in Serbia: AHP to analyze the structure of the problem and determine criteria weights, and PROMETHEE for final ranking and sensitivity analysis. Alpay & Yavuz [17] developed a decision-making support system for the Karaburun underground chromite mine in Eskisehir, Turkey. They applied AHP to find acceptable alternatives. Yazdani-Chamzini et al. [18] proposed a selection model for the optimal mining method at the Angouran mine, one of the main producers of zinc in Iran. They developed the model based on FAHP and FTOPSIS. Then Asadi et al. [19] used a TOPSIS model to select the optimal mining method for the Tazareh coalmine in Iran. Javanshirgiv & Safari [20] applied fuzzy TOPSIS to select the optimal mining method for the Kamar Mahdi mine in Iran. Ataei et al. [21] also used TOPSIS to do the same for the Jajarm mine in Iran. For this mine, Naghadehi et al. [22] proposed a combination of FAHP and AHP: FAHP to determine criteria weights and AHP to rank the mining methods. On the other hand, some researchers have employed MCDM models to address mine dewatering, which is a parallel process in mining operations. Bajić et al. [23] describe the selection of the optimal groundwater control system for the open cast-mine Buvač (Bosnia and Herzegovina), using soft optimization and fuzzy optimization (VIKOR and FAHP) techniques. For the same case study, Polomčić et al. [24] performed mathematical optimization calculations applying fuzzy dynamic TOPSIS.

The present paper describes and tests a decision-making algorithm for the selection of the optimal underground mining method. The algorithm is applied in a real case study to the Borska Reka copper mine (Serbia). First, the relevant alternatives are identified and then the selection criteria are analyzed. This if followed by MCDM, to select the optimal mining method. Finally, the best choice is the method that maximizes the output of useful components and minimizes tailings. In addition, the optimal solution involves the shortest mining time and the lowest consumption of energy and materials, along with full safety at work and no adverse effect on mine development.

2. Case Study

The FAHP-based methodology for decision-making on the optimal underground mining method was applied in a real case study. The study area is the Borska Reka copper mine in eastern Serbia (Figure 1). In terms of regional metallogeny, the Bor ore field and Borska Reka copper mine belong the so-called Bor Zone, which coincides with the Timok igneous complex. In geologic terms, the sediments are composed of volcanites and volcanoclastic rocks, quartz-diorite porphyritic rocks, hydrothermally altered volcanic and volcanoclastic rocks, pelites with tuffs and tuffites, conglomerates, sandstones, Quaternary alluvial sediments, and technogenic deposits.

The mineral composition of the ore from Borska Reka includes chalcopyrite, covellite, chalcosine, rutile, hematite, magnetite, sphalerite, galenite, tetrahedrite, tennantite, digenite, cubanite, and native gold. The prevalent ore is pyrite, the dominant copper mineral is chalcopyrite, and there are covellite, chalcosine, and bornite to a lesser extent. On the other hand, enargite and molybdenite are very rare. However, this ratio of copper minerals is not uniform across the ore body. Certain parts have elevated concentrations of covellite, chalcosine and bornite, but they are rarely dominant. There are also frequent occurrences of rutile, magnetite and hematite, as well as sphalerite and galenite. Tetrahedrite tennantite, digenite, cubanite and native gold are very rare and occur sporadically.

Past exploration has revealed that the Borska Reka ore body is among very large deposits in the geometric sense, with elevated copper concentrations. The ore body is at an angle of 45°–55°. Its maximum length is ~1.410 m and maximum width 635 m. The ore body is deep; the average ultimate depth is ~920 m from the ground surface.

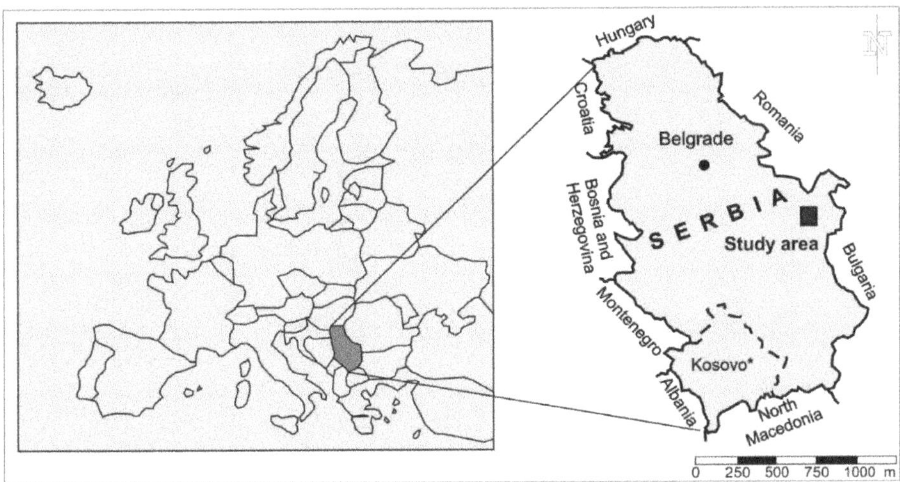

Figure 1. Geographic position of the study area: Borska Reka copper mine.

3. Methodology

The underground mining decision-making algorithm is shown in Figure 2. FAHP is the optimization technique. In general, one of the limiting factors of conventional methods applied to select the optimal mining technology is often a lack of data. Mines are complex geologic systems and mining operations are dynamic as the size and depth of the mine constantly increase (in plain view and elevation). As such, mining requires continual adaptation to new conditions. The contribution to science of decision-making methods based on fuzzy logic is the ability to focus on overcoming uncertainties inherent in mining method selection.

On the other hand, compared to other methods that include the fuzzy approach, FAHP offers certain specific advantages in optimal underground mining method selection. Because of the depth of the ore deposit and imprecise data typical of such a geologic system, which make it impossible to accurately define all the physical, mechanical and geologic conditions, the entire mining process requires constant "learning" and gradual, hierarchical problem-solving, to achieve the set objective. FAHP involves a continual "learning process", along with discussion among experts and prioritizing.

Consequently, the use of FAHP highlighted the quality of this technique based on expert judgment or, in other words, reflected the decision-makers' knowledge and experience in evaluating information, to arrive at an optimal decision concerning multiple alternative underground mining methods.

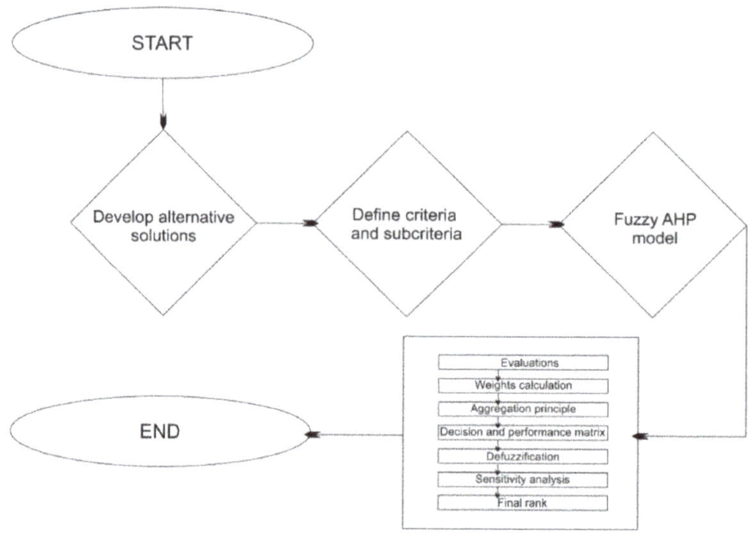

Figure 2. Multiple-criteria decision-making (MCDM) model for the selection of optimal underground mining method.

FAHP is a combination of the conventional AHP method [1] and the fuzzy set theory [25]. It is implemented using triangular fuzzy numbers [26]. *TFN* (Figure 3) in set *R* is a triangular fuzzy number if its membership function $\mu_M(x) : R \to [0,1]$ is defined as follows:

$$\mu_{TFN}(x) = \begin{cases} \frac{x}{s-l} - \frac{l}{s-l}, & x \in [l,s] \\ \frac{x}{s-d} - \frac{d}{s-d}, & x \in [s,d] \\ 0, & x \notin [l,d] \end{cases}$$

where $l \leq s \leq d$.

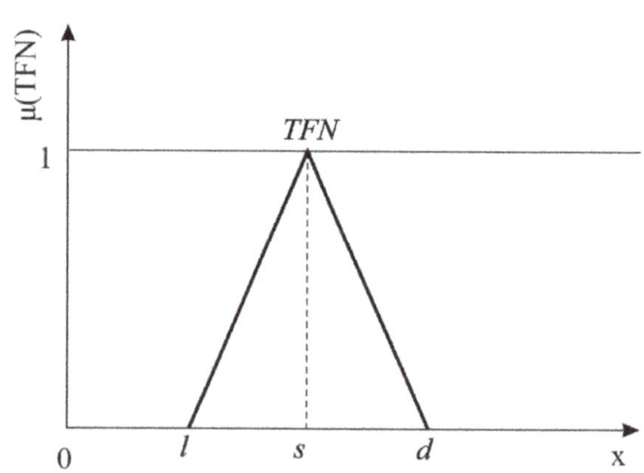

Figure 3. Membership function of triangular fuzzy number (TFN).

The modification of AHP into FAHP is in that the relative importance of the optimality criteria is described by linguistic variables [27], determined by the expert, and modeled by triangular fuzzy numbers (TFN). In other words, fuzzy numbers describe the pairwise comparison matrices of the optimality criteria. The fuzzified Saaty scale, proposed by many authors [26,28–30] is used. One of them is shown in Table 1.

Table 1. Fuzzified scale [26,30].

Linguistic Variable (Definition of Importance)	AHP Scale	FAHP Scale TFN $(0.5 \le \alpha \le 2)$
Equal	1	$(1, 1, 1 + \alpha)$
Weak	3	$(3 - \alpha, 3, 3 + \alpha)$
Strong	5	$(5 - \alpha, 5, 5 + \alpha)$
Proven dominance	7	$(7 - \alpha, 7, 7 + \alpha)$
Absolute dominance	9	$(9 - \alpha, 9, 9)$
Intermediate values	2, 4, 6, 8	$(x - 1, x, x + 1)$ $x = 2, 4, 6,8$

Chang [26] made the first development steps and Deng [30] modified the method. Also, Bajić et al. [23] applied fuzzy optimization to mine hydrogeology. Based on the above, the FAHP analysis was implemented in the following steps:

(a) First the problem relating to the selection of the underground mining method was examined and the alternatives and criteria/subcriteria that influence the selection of the optimal alternative were identified. This involved the selection of a team of experts and the "exploitation" of their knowledge and experience.

(b) Pairs of criteria (Equation (1)), subcriteria (Equation (2)) and alternatives (Equation (3)) were evaluated and compared using the FAHP scale (Table 1):

$$A = \begin{bmatrix} a_{11} & a_{12} & \cdots & a_{1m} \\ a_{21} & a_{22} & \cdots & a_{2m} \\ \cdots & \cdots & \cdots & \cdots \\ a_{m1} & a_{m2} & \cdots & a_{mm} \end{bmatrix} \tag{1}$$

where: $a_{ij} = 1$ for every $i = j, (i, j = 1, 2, \ldots, m)$ and $a_{ij} = \frac{1}{a_{ji}}$

$$A_j = \begin{bmatrix} a_{11} & a_{12} & \cdots & a_{1k_j} \\ a_{21} & a_{22} & \cdots & a_{2k_j} \\ \cdots & \cdots & \cdots & \cdots \\ a_{k_j1} & a_{k_j2} & \cdots & a_{k_jk_j} \end{bmatrix} \tag{2}$$

where criterion C_j is composed of k_j subcriteria,

$$Y_k = \begin{bmatrix} a_{11} & a_{12} & \cdots & a_{1N} \\ a_{21} & a_{22} & \cdots & a_{2N} \\ \cdots & \cdots & \cdots & \cdots \\ a_{N1} & a_{N2} & \cdots & a_{NN} \end{bmatrix} \tag{3}$$

where N is the number of alternatives relative to each of the K subcriteria; $k = 1, 2, \ldots, K$.

(c) The weights of all three matrices from step **b** are determined gradually, using fuzzy extent analysis [26] or fuzzy arithmetic and the extension principle [31]. All the resulting weights are normalized:

$$w_i = \sum_{j=1}^{m} a_{ij} \otimes \left[\sum_{k=1}^{m} \sum_{l=1}^{m} a_{kl} \right]^{-1} \tag{4}$$

where $i = 1,2,\ldots,m$

$$w'_j = \left(\sum_{l=1}^{k_j} a_{il} \otimes \left[\sum_{i=1}^{k_j}\sum_{l=1}^{k_j} a_{il}\right]^{-1}\right) \otimes w_j \tag{5}$$

where $j = 1,2,\ldots,m; p = 1,2,\ldots,k_j$

$$W = \left(w_1^1, w_1^2, \ldots, w_1^{k_1}; w_2^1, w_2^2 \ldots w_2^{k_2}; \ldots; w_j^1, w_j^2, \ldots, w_j^{k_j}; \ldots; w_m^1, w_m^2, \ldots, w_m^{k_m}\right) \tag{6}$$

where W are subcriteria weights, whose total "length" is K

$$W = (W_1, W_2, \ldots, W_K) \tag{7}$$

(d) The next step is the application of the aggregation principle, to reduce two hierarchy tiers (criteria and subcriteria) to a single tier:

$$K = \sum_{j=1}^{m} k_j \tag{8}$$

where $C_1, C_2, \ldots, C_m$ is a set of m criteria, each with its subcriteria; k_j—number of subcriteria of the j-th criterion.

(e) The fuzzy decision matrix and fuzzy performance matrix are now calculated. The fuzzy decision matrix results from calculations of the fuzzy extent analysis from step ***c*** for the alternatives:

$$X = \begin{bmatrix} x_{11} & x_{12} & \cdots & x_{1K} \\ x_{21} & x_{22} & \cdots & x_{2K} \\ \cdots & \cdots & \cdots & \cdots \\ x_{N1} & x_{N2} & \cdots & x_{NK} \end{bmatrix} \tag{9}$$

and the fuzzy performance matrix represents the overall performance of each alternative relative to all the subcriteria:

$$Z = \begin{bmatrix} x_{11} \otimes W_1 & x_{12} \otimes W_2 & \cdots & x_{1K} \otimes W_K \\ x_{21} \otimes W_1 & x_{22} \otimes W_2 & \cdots & x_{2K} \otimes W_K \\ \cdots & \cdots & \cdots & \cdots \\ x_{N1} \otimes W_1 & x_{N2} \otimes W_2 & \cdots & x_{NK} \otimes W_K \end{bmatrix} \tag{10}$$

(f) The ultimate values of the alternatives are calculated in the form of triangular fuzzy numbers:

$$F_i = \sum_{j=1}^{K} x_{ij} \otimes W_j \tag{11}$$

(g) The final step includes defuzzification [32], ranking of alternatives and, in parallel, sensitivity analysis [33,34]. The optimal alternative is the one with the greatest weight. The sum of the weights of all the alternatives is equal to zero:

$$defuzzy(A) = \frac{(d-l)+(s-l)}{3} + l \tag{12}$$

The sensitivity analysis is performed by introducing the optimization index λ. The "total integral"—I is calculated, to express the expert's risk assessment (0—pessimistic, 1—optimistic, and 0.5—moderate):

$$I = \frac{(d\lambda + s + (1-\lambda)l)}{2}, \quad \lambda \in [0,1] \tag{13}$$

where: l, s and d are elements of the triangular fuzzy number.

A special-purpose application, Fuzzy-GWCS2 based on Microsoft Excel, was developed for the above mathematical optimization calculations. The objective was to provide clearer insight into the results and facilitate monitoring of changes in the final calculations during the sensitivity analysis.

4. Results and Discussion

FAHP-aided selection of underground mining methods enables efficient decision-making and facilitates solving of complex problems that involve vagueness and multiple uncertainties, like in the case of the Borska Reka copper mine. The first uncertainty was associated with the identification of all lithostratigraphic units. This copper deposit is highly specific, with occurrences of numerous minerals. On the other hand, there was a lack of information on its geometry and certain physical indicators and parameters pertaining to the ore and surrounding rocks.

Calculations were made using the MCDM model (or the algorithm shown in Figure 2), to determine the best mining alternative for the Borska Reka copper mine. The procedure was gradual, following the above steps ***a–g*** and using the specially developed Fuzzy-GWCS2 application.

The selection of a team of experts and "exploitation" of their knowledge and experience play a key role in decision- making and underground mining method selection. Teamwork ensures technically sustainable, economically viable and, above all, safe mining of copper ore.

Successful underground mining method selection requires substantial knowledge about the geology of the mineral ore deposit. In addition, the depth of the mine necessitates exploratory drilling experience. Because of the specific features of copper deposits, petrologists, mineralogists and geochemists contribute key knowledge and analysis of the minerals and their physical parameters. Hydrogeologists examine groundwater flow to the mine and ways of protecting the mine. Experts in economic geology and mine management assess the technoeconomic viability of mining. Geologists define the characteristics of the ore deposit. As a result, mining experts gain insight into applicable underground mining methods and develop alternative solutions. Engineers then synthesize the information and define and asses the criteria than affect the selection of the preferred underground mining method. The quality of the identification of mining conditions and the experts' knowledge and experience directly influence the selection of the optimal method.

The given problem—selection of the optimal underground mining method—was examined in step ***a***. Then the criteria and subcriteria that influence the selection were defined. Based on literature sources that address the selection of underground mining methods and the governing factors [18,35], the following three criteria were identified: technical, production, and economic.

The criteria were subdivided into subcriteria, in this case 18, as shown in Table 2. Given the different types of essentially opposed criteria, the MCDM approach was a reasonable and justifiable choice.

In addition, five different alternatives (underground mining methods) were defined, including:

Alternative 1—sublevel caving;
Alternative 2—cut and fill;
Alternative 3—shrinkage stoping;
Alternative 4—block caving;
Alternative 5—vertical crater retreat (VCR)

Mining methods depend on the shape, size and depth of the ore body, physical and mechanical properties of the ore and accompanying rocks, hydrologic conditions, sensitivity of ground surface to mining, mineral and chemical composition of the ore, mineral distribution, and value of ore. Consequently, all these characteristics are important and need to be taken into account when a decision is made about the optimal mining method.

In the case of ore bodies of irregular shape, such as that at Borska Reka, priority is usually given to a caving method. The ore body size is often the decisive factor, because it reflects ore reserves. In addition, the thickness of the ore body is important, as are its depth, angle, type of contact and tectonic circumstances. At large depths, the cut-and-fill method should be given priority over block caving.

Table 2. Defining of criteria and subcriteria.

Criterion	Symbol	Subcriteria	Symbol
Technical	T	Depth of ore body	T_1
		Thickness of ore body	T_2
		Shape of ore body	T_3
		Value of ore	T_4
		Ore body slope (angle)	T_5
		Rock hardness and stability	T_6
		Form of ore body and contact with neighboring rocks	T_7
		Mineral and chemical composition of ore	T_8
Production	P	Mining method productivity and output	P_1
		Safety at work	P_2
		Adverse environmental impact	P_3
		Ore dilution	P_4
		Ore impoverishment	P_5
		Ventilation	P_6
		Hydrologic conditions	P_7
Economic	E	Capital expenditure	E_1
		Mining costs	E_2
		Maintenance costs	E_3

In the present case study, the mineral and chemical composition was important because of the presence of pyrite and pyrrhotite. Copper pyrite ore, with more than 40% of sulfur, as well as other sulfide ores with elevated concentrations of pyrite and pyrrhotite, are susceptible to oxidation, self-ignition and sticking. If the ore is left in a crushed state for a long time, it becomes oxidized and warm in contact with air and humidity. This reduces the ore utilization rate. As such, if the ore contains large amounts of pyrite and pyrrhotite, cut-and-fill methods are given priority over shrinkage stoping or block caving methods. If the ore is highly valuable, often the method of choice is less effective but with a much higher ore utilization rate than vice-versa.

Ore impoverishment is the reduction in metal content of the produced ore, relative to that of the excavated block. Shrinkage stoping and caving methods typically lead to greater impoverishment. Also, even cut-and-fill methods, where the ore is loaded by means of mechanical devices (scrapers or shovels) directly from the fill, tend to result in a higher level of impoverishment. In general, however, cut-and-fill and block caving, compared to other methods, cause less impoverishment. In the case of the room-and-pillar methods, secondary cutting invariably leads to impoverishment because the ore is mixed with side or roof gangue.

Physical and mechanical characteristics are also taken into account. Rock hardness and stability tend to be the most important parameters because they affect the span and surface of the tunnels. With regard to hydrologic circumstances, the amount and properties of groundwater need to be known, particularly its effect on "plastic" rocks such as clays. The presence of water-bearing rocks and stagnant groundwater hinder the shrinkage stoping method. The preferred technologies are cut-and- fill (with hydraulic or paste backfill) or room-and-pillar mining methods. If the ore mineral distribution is not uniform, cut-and-fill methods are given priority.

Safety at work is an extremely important factor. The economic advantages of a given mining method should not threaten people's lives, operations or the safety of mine installations. The selected mining method should not be capable of causing fire, inrush of groundwater or surface water, caving of underground or above-ground mine walls or other structural components, or endanger miners and mining. A healthy work environment requires good ventilation (fresh air supply and venting of harmful gases and dust), proper illumination and safe access to work stations, as well as machinery to relieve miners of heavy manual work and measures to ensure health protection. Certain underground mining methods degrade the environment by damaging the soil and potentially causing land subsidence. On the other hand, the productivity of the mining method is important in the technoeconomic assessment of a mine, given that a higher productivity leads to greater output. The productivity of a method is based on the rate of mining of blocks or parts of the ore body, and the capacity of the ore body depends on the ability to mine all active levels. The costs of mining are also examined, because spending is required before there can be a return on investment (such as for shafts or declines, mining equipment, crushers, transporters, and venting and dewatering systems). Also, there are costs associated with excavation (e.g., materials for tunneling and consumables such as ANFO explosives, detonators, drilling tools, diesel fuel, oil, lubricants, loader and transporter tires, steel, steel cables and cement, as well as the preparation and distribution of backfill paste, along with associated labor) and maintenance costs (of machinery and installations, as well as depreciation, overhead, etc.).

In view of the above facts and given that Borska Reka belongs to the group of ore bodies with relatively high copper concentrations, that the ore body is deep and that there are structures and facilities on the land surface, the research warranted the consideration of five high-productivity mining methods, which would ensure economically viable mining.

The criteria, subcriteria and alternatives were evaluated and the scores were input parameters for the MCDA model. Their weights determined in the form of fuzzy numbers per steps ***b*** and ***c***. Equation (1) was used to evaluate the criteria, Equation (2) the subcriteria, and Equation (3) the alternatives. Evaluation was based on pairwise comparison (of criteria, subcriteria and alternatives), using linguistic variables and their numerical values from FAHP scales (Table 1). Table 3 shows the criteria scores in the form of triangular fuzzy numbers and their relative importance. Equations (4) through (7) were used to calculate weights by fuzzy extent analysis.

Table 3. Evaluation of criteria.

	T			P			E		
	TFN			TFN			TFN		
T	1	1	1	0.33	0.5	1	1	2	3
P	1	2	3	1	1	1	1	2	3
E	0.33	0.5	1	0.33	0.5	1	1	1	1

With regard to the selection of the most suitable underground mining method in the present case study, the technical and production criteria were given a slight advantage over the economic criterion. Then the subcriteria were evaluated. Given that each criterion was subdivided into a number of subcriteria (Table 2), this step involved the determination of the importance of all the subcriteria in a group, relative to each of the criteria. Table 4 shows the technical subcriteria scores. The relative weights of the technical subcriteria are presented in Table A1 (Appendix A).

Table 4. Evaluation of technical subcriteria.

	T_1			T_2			T_3			T_4		
	TFN			TFN			TFN			TFN		
T_1	1	1	1	3	4	5	7	8	9	1	3	5
T_2	0.2	0.25	0.33	1	1	1	7	9	9	1	2	3
T_3	0.11	0.125	0.14	0.11	0.11	0.14	1	1	1	1	2	3
T_4	0.2	0.33	1	0.33	0.5	1	0.33	0.5	1	1	1	1
T_5	0.2	0.25	0.33	0.14	0.2	0.33	3	5	7	0.14	0.166	0.2
T_6	0.33	0.5	1	0.2	0.33	1	7	8	9	0.11	0.14	0.2
T_7	0.11	0.14	0.2	0.11	0.14	0.2	7	8	9	0.11	0.14	0.2
T_8	0.14	0.2	0.33	0.33	0.5	1	3	5	7	0.2	0.33	1

Table 4. *Cont.*

	T_5			T_6			T_7			T_8		
	TFN			TFN			TFN			TFN		
T_1	3	4	5	1	2	3	5	7	9	3	5	7
T_2	3	5	7	1	3	5	5	7	9	1	2	3
T_3	0.14	0.2	0.33	0.11	0.125	0.14	0.11	0.125	0.14	0.14	0.2	0.33
T_4	5	6	7	5	7	9	5	7	9	1	3	5
T_5	1	1	1	0.14	0.2	0.33	1	3	5	0.14	0.2	0.33
T_6	3	5	7	1	1	1	7	9	9	1	2	3
T_7	0.2	0.33	1	0.11	0.11	0.14	1	1	1	0.2	0.25	0.33
T_8	3	5	7	0.33	0.5	1	3	4	5	1	1	1

Among the technical subcriteria, the most important were T_1—ore body depth and T_2—ore body thickness, which were given a slight advantage over the other subcriteria, per the FAHP scale.

Table 5 shows the relative scores of the production subcriteria. The relative weight of each subcriterion in the form of a fuzzy number is presented in Table A2 (Appendix A). Among the production subcriteria, a slight advantage, per the FAHP scale, was given to P_2—safety at work, P_3—environmental impact, and P_6—ventilation.

Table 5. Evaluation of production criteria.

Cr.	P1			P2			P3			P4			P_5			P6			P7		
	TFN			TFN			TFN			TFN			TFN			TFN			TFN		
P_1	1	1	1	0.2	0.25	0.33	0.2	0.33	1	0.33	0.5	1	1	3	5	0.33	0.5	1	3	4	5
P_2	3	4	5	1	1	1	3	4	5	3	5	7	1	3	5	1	2	3	3	4	5
P_3	1	3	5	0.2	0.25	0.33	1	1	1	1	3	5	1	2	3	1	3	5	1	2	3
P_4	1	2	3	0.14	0.2	0.33	0.2	0.33	1	1	1	1	0.2	0.33	1	0.2	0.25	0.33	1	2	3
P_5	0.2	0.33	1	0.2	0.33	1	0.33	0.5	1	1	3	5	1	1	1	0.2	0.33	1	1	2	3
P_6	1	2	3	0.33	0.5	1	0.2	0.33	1	3	4	5	1	3	5	1	1	1	1	3	5
P_7	0.2	0.25	0.33	0.2	0.25	0.33	0.33	0.5	1	0.33	0.5	1	0.33	0.5	1	0.2	0.33	1	1	1	1

Table 6 shows the relative scores of the economic subcriteria. The relative weight of each subcriterion in the form of a fuzzy number is presented in Table A3 (Appendix A).

Table 6. Evaluation of economic subcriteria.

Cr.	E_1			E_2			E_3		
	TFN			TFN			TFN		
E_1	1	1	1	0.33	0.5	1	0.2	0.33	1
E_2	1	2	3	1	1	1	1	3	5
E_3	1	3	5	0.2	0.33	1	1	1	1

The alternatives were evaluated in the next step, by pairwise comparison relative to each subcriterion. This involved 18 comparisons. The results are shown in Tables 7–9. The respective calculated weight vectors are presented in Tables A4–A6 (Appendix A), based on the fuzzy extent analysis applying Equation (4) through (7).

Table A7 (Appendix A) shows (per step ***(d)***) the ultimate weights of the subcriteria, calculated applying the aggregation principle according to Equation (8). The triangular fuzzy numbers of the criterion weights were multiplied by the weights of their subcriteria calculated in the previous step ***(c)***. Hence, one tier was eliminated from the criteria-subcriteria-alternatives hierarchy.

Then, using the equations described in step ***e***, the fuzzy decision matrix was calculated for the five alternatives (Equation (5)), as was the fuzzy performance matrix (Equation (10)), which represented the overall performance of each alternative relative to all the subcriteria. It was a result of multiplying all the subcriteria weights by the elements of the decision matrix (Table A8, Appendix A).

Table 7. Evaluation of alternatives relative to technical subcriteria.

T_1	A_1			A_2			A_3			A_4			A_5		
	TFN			TFN			TFN			TFN			TFN		
A_1	1	1	1	0.2	0.33	1	0.2	0.33	1	1	2	3	0.2	0.33	1
A_2	1	3	5	1	1	1	1	2	3	7	9	9	3	4	5
A_3	1	3	5	0.33	0.5	1	1	1	1	5	6	7	1	3	5
A_4	0.33	0.5	1	0.11	0.11	0.14	0.14	0.166	0.2	1	1	1	0.14	0.2	0.33
A_5	1	3	5	0.2	0.25	0.33	0.2	0.33	1	3	5	7	1	1	1

T_2	A_1			A_2			A_3			A_4			A_5		
	TFN			TFN			TFN			TFN			TFN		
A_1	1	1	1	7	9	9	3	4	5	1	3	5	1	2	3
A_2	0.11	0.11	0.14	1	1	1	0.2	0.25	0.33	0.2	0.33	1	0.2	0.25	0.33
A_3	0.2	0.25	0.33	3	4	5	1	1	1	1	3	5	0.2	0.25	0.33
A_4	0.2	0.33	1	1	3	5	0.2	0.33	1	1	1	1	0.2	0.33	1
A_5	0.33	0.5	1	3	4	5	3	4	5	1	3	5	1	1	1

T_3	A_1			A_2			A_3			A_4			A_5		
	TFN			TFN			TFN			TFN			TFN		
A_1	1	1	1	1	3	5	3	4	5	7	9	9	3	4	5
A_2	0.2	0.33	1	1	1	1	1	3	5	3	5	7	1	3	5
A_3	0.2	0.25	0.33	0.2	0.33	1	1	1	1	1	3	5	0.33	0.5	1
A_4	0.11	0.11	0.14	0.14	0.2	0.33	0.2	0.33	1	1	1	1	0.2	0.25	0.33
A_5	0.2	0.25	0.33	0.2	0.33	1	1	2	3	3	4	5	1	1	1

T_4	A_1			A_2			A_3			A_4			A_5		
	TFN			TFN			TFN			TFN			TFN		
A_1	1	1	1	3	5	7	1	3	5	3	4	5	0.33	0.5	1
A_2	0.14	0.2	0.33	1	1	1	0.2	0.33	1	0.33	0.5	1	0.11	0.11	0.14
A_3	0.2	0.33	1	1	3	5	1	1	1	1	3	5	0.2	0.25	0.33
A_4	0.2	0.25	0.33	1	2	3	0.2	0.33	1	1	1	1	0.14	0.2	0.33
A_5	1	2	3	7	9	9	3	4	5	3	5	7	1	1	1

T_5	A_1			A_2			A_3			A_4			A_5		
	TFN			TFN			TFN			TFN			TFN		
A_1	1	1	1	1	3	5	7	9	9	5	6	7	1	2	3
A_2	0.2	0.33	1	1	1	1	3	4	5	1	3	5	1	3	5
A_3	0.11	0.11	0.14	0.2	0.25	0.33	1	1	1	0.2	0.33	1	0.2	0.25	0.33
A_4	0.14	0.166	0.2	0.2	0.33	1	1	3	5	1	1	1	0.2	0.25	0.33
A_5	0.33	0.5	1	0.2	0.33	1	3	4	5	3	4	5	1	1	1

T_6	A_1			A_2			A_3			A_4			A_5		
	TFN			TFN			TFN			TFN			TFN		
A_1	1	1	1	0.2	0.33	1	1	3	5	3	4	5	0.2	0.33	1
A_2	1	3	5	1	1	1	3	5	7	7	9	9	1	2	3
A_3	0.2	0.33	1	0.14	0.2	0.33	1	1	1	1	3	5	0.2	0.25	0.33
A_4	0.2	0.25	0.33	0.11	0.11	0.14	0.2	0.33	1	1	1	1	0.2	0.25	0.33
A_5	1	3	5	0.33	0.5	1	3	4	5	3	4	5	1	1	1

T_7	A_1			A_2			A_3			A_4			A_5		
	TFN			TFN			TFN			TFN			TFN		
A_1	1	1	1	0.2	0.25	0.33	0.2	0.33	1	0.11	0.11	0.14	0.33	0.5	1
A_2	3	4	5	1	1	1	1	2	3	0.33	0.5	1	3	4	5
A_3	1	3	5	0.33	0.5	1	1	1	1	0.2	0.33	1	1	3	5
A_4	7	9	9	1	2	3	1	3	5	1	1	1	3	5	7
A_5	1	2	3	0.2	0.25	0.33	0.2	0.33	1	0.14	0.2	0.33	1	1	1

T_8	A_1			A_2			A_3			A_4			A_5		
	TFN			TFN			TFN			TFN			TFN		
A_1	1	1	1	0.14	0.166	0.2	1	3	5	0.2	0.25	0.33	0.2	0.33	1
A_2	5	6	7	1	1	1	7	9	9	1	2	3	1	3	5
A_3	0.2	0.33	1	0.11	0.11	0.14	1	1	1	0.2	0.25	0.33	0.2	0.25	0.33
A_4	3	4	5	0.33	0.5	1	3	4	5	1	1	1	1	3	5
A_5	1	3	5	0.2	0.33	1	3	4	5	0.2	0.33	1	1	1	1

Table 8. Evaluation of alternatives relative to production subcriteria.

P_1	A_1			A_2			A_3			A_4			A_5		
	TFN			TFN			TFN			TFN			TFN		
A_1	1	1	1	3	4	5	1	3	5	3	4	5	0.33	0.5	1
A_2	0.2	0.25	0.33	1	1	1	0.2	0.25	0.33	0.33	0.5	1	0.11	0.11	0.14
A_3	0.2	0.33	1	3	4	5	1	1	1	1	3	5	0.2	0.25	0.33
A_4	0.2	0.25	0.33	1	2	3	0.2	0.33	1	1	1	1	0.14	0.2	0.33
A_5	1	2	3	7	9	9	3	4	5	3	5	7	1	1	1
P_2	A_1			A_2			A_3			A_4			A_5		
	TFN			TFN			TFN			TFN			TFN		
A_1	1	1	1	1	3	5	3	5	7	5	6	7	0.2	0.33	1
A_2	0.2	0.33	1	1	1	1	1	3	5	3	4	5	0.2	0.25	0.33
A_3	0.14	0.2	0.33	0.2	0.33	1	1	1	1	1	2	3	0.14	0.166	0.2
A_4	0.14	0.166	0.2	0.2	0.25	0.33	0.33	0.5	1	1	1	1	0.11	0.11	0.14
A_5	1	3	5	3	4	5	5	6	7	7	9	9	1	1	1
P_3	A_1			A_2			A_3			A_4			A_5		
	TFN			TFN			TFN			TFN			TFN		
A_1	1	1	1	0.11	0.11	0.14	0.2	0.25	0.33	0.14	0.2	0.33	0.33	0.5	1
A_2	7	9	9	1	1	1	3	4	5	1	2	3	5	6	7
A_3	3	4	5	0.2	0.25	0.33	1	1	1	0.33	0.5	1	1	2	3
A_4	3	5	7	0.33	0.5	1	1	2	3	1	1	1	3	4	5
A_5	1	2	3	0.14	0.166	0.2	0.33	0.5	1	0.2	0.25	0.33	1	1	1
P_4	A_1			A_2			A_3			A_4			A_5		
	TFN			TFN			TFN			TFN			TFN		
A_1	1	1	1	0.14	0.166	0.2	0.2	0.33	1	0.33	0.5	1	0.2	0.33	1
A_2	5	6	7	1	1	1	3	4	5	7	9	9	1	3	5
A_3	1	3	5	0.2	0.25	0.33	1	1	1	3	4	5	0.2	0.33	1
A_4	1	2	3	0.11	0.11	0.14	0.2	0.25	0.33	1	1	1	0.14	0.2	0.33
A_5	1	3	5	0.2	0.33	1	1	3	5	3	5	7	1	1	1
P_5	A_1			A_2			A_3			A_4			A_5		
	TFN			TFN			TFN			TFN			TFN		
A_1	1	1	1	0.11	0.11	0.14	0.2	0.33	1	0.2	0.25	0.33	0.14	0.2	0.33
A_2	7	9	9	1	1	1	5	6	7	1	3	5	1	2	3
A_3	1	3	5	0.14	0.166	0.2	1	1	1	0.33	0.5	1	0.2	0.33	1
A_4	3	4	5	0.2	0.33	1	1	2	3	1	1	1	0.2	0.33	1
A_5	3	5	7	0.33	0.5	1	1	3	5	1	3	5	1	1	1
P_6	A_1			A_2			A_3			A_4			A_5		
	TFN			TFN			TFN			TFN			TFN		
A_1	1	1	1	0.2	0.25	0.33	0.11	0.11	0.14	0.14	0.2	0.33	0.33	0.5	1
A_2	3	4	5	1	1	1	0.2	0.25	0.33	0.2	0.25	0.33	1	2	3
A_3	7	9	9	3	4	5	1	1	1	1	3	5	5	6	7
A_4	3	5	7	3	4	5	0.2	0.33	1	1	1	1	3	4	5
A_5	1	2	3	0.33	0.5	1	0.14	0.166	0.2	0.2	0.25	0.33	1	1	1
P_7	A_1			A_2			A_3			A_4			A_5		
	TFN			TFN			TFN			TFN			TFN		
A_1	1	1	1	0.11	0.11	0.14	0.2	0.25	0.33	0.14	0.166	0.2	0.2	0.33	1
A_2	7	9	9	1	1	1	3	4	5	1	3	5	5	6	7
A_3	3	4	5	0.2	0.25	0.33	1	1	1	0.2	0.33	1	1	3	5
A_4	5	6	7	0.2	0.33	1	1	3	5	1	1	1	3	4	5
A_5	1	3	5	0.14	0.166	0.2	0.2	0.33	1	0.2	0.25	0.33	1	1	1

Table 9. Evaluation of alternatives relative to economic subcriteria.

E_1	A_1			A_2			A_3			A_4			A_5		
	TFN			TFN			TFN			TFN			TFN		
A_1	1	1	1	1	2	3	0.2	0.33	1	0.14	0.166	0.2	0.2	0.33	1
A_2	0.33	0.5	1	1	1	1	0.2	0.25	0.33	0.11	0.11	0.14	0.2	0.25	0.33
A_3	1	3	5	3	4	5	1	1	1	0.2	0.33	1	1	3	5
A_4	5	6	7	7	9	9	1	3	5	1	1	1	3	4	5
A_5	1	3	5	3	4	5	0.2	0.33	1	0.2	0.25	0.33	1	1	1
E_2	A_1			A_2			A_3			A_4			A_5		
	TFN			TFN			TFN			TFN			TFN		
A_1	1	1	1	3	4	5	1	3	5	1	3	5	0.2	0.33	1
A_2	0.2	0.25	0.33	1	1	1	0.2	0.25	0.33	1	2	3	0.11	0.11	0.14
A_3	0.2	0.33	1	3	4	5	1	1	1	1	2	3	0.2	0.25	0.33
A_4	0.2	0.33	1	0.33	0.5	1	0.33	0.5	1	1	1	1	0.14	0.166	0.2
A_5	1	3	5	7	9	9	3	4	5	5	6	7	1	1	1
E_3	A_1			A_2			A_3			A_4			A_5		
	TFN			TFN			TFN			TFN			TFN		
A_1	1	1	1	7	9	9	3	4	5	5	6	7	1	2	3
A_2	0.11	0.11	0.14	1	1	1	0.2	0.25	0.33	0.33	0.5	1	0.14	0.2	0.33
A_3	0.2	0.25	0.33	3	4	5	1	1	1	1	3	5	0.2	0.33	1
A_4	0.14	0.166	0.2	1	2	3	0.2	0.33	1	1	1	1	0.2	0.25	0.33
A_5	0.33	0.5	1	3	5	7	1	3	5	3	4	5	1	1	1

Per steps *f* and *g*, Tables 10 and 11 show the ultimate scores of the five alternatives in the form of fuzzy numbers, obtained by adding the fuzzy numbers—elements of the fuzzy performance matrix, according to Equation (11). Then the ultimate weights of the alternatives are shown in the form of non-fuzzy numbers, after defuzzification employing Equation (12). The final ranking of the alternatives is based on the sensitivity analysis per Equation (13). Figure 4 shows the total integral value of moderate, pessimistic and optimistic experts' risk assessments, or the weights of the alternatives relative to the optimization index parameters. If the decision-maker's inclination is optimistic ($\alpha = 1$), the weights of the alternatives vary over a very narrow range, compared to pessimistic ($\alpha = 0$) and moderate ($\alpha = 0.5$). Based on the sensitivity analysis, the average differences between the weights of the alternatives were in the 0.1–0.73% range for an optimization index of 0.5, and 0.75–7.8% for an optimization index of 0. Defuzzification yielded the weights of the alternatives in the form of "normal" or real numbers. The highest weight is the best score. Based on the results, alternative 5 is the optimal underground mining method, followed in descending order by Alternative 2, Alternative 1, Alternative 3 and Alternative 4.

According to the MCDA model, Alternative 5 (VCR) was proposed as the optimal underground mining method for the Borska Reka copper mine. This method does not require extensive preparations, its productivity is high and the costs of mining are relatively low. There are also other advantages, such as a high ore utilization rate, low ore impoverishment, and a high level of safety at work, which was one of the most important evaluation factors in the case study. For all these reasons, the method proposed for the given copper mine provides optimal mining conditions.

Table 10. Ranking and optimal alternative.

	TFN			Real Number	Ranking
A_1	0.020	0.196	1.955	0.1978	3
A_2	0.023	0.222	2.019	0.2048	2
A_3	0.016	0.173	1.814	0.1833	4
A_4	0.014	0.133	1.407	0.1421	5
A_5	0.028	0.275	2.684	0.2717	1
	Optimal alternative			A_5	

Table 11. Sensitivity analysis.

Alternatives	$\alpha = 0$	$\alpha = 0.5$	$\alpha = 1$
A_1	0.1962	0.1975	0.1977
A_2	0.2220	0.2074	0.2059
A_3	0.1724	0.1817	0.1826
A_4	0.1339	0.1409	0.1416
A_5	0.2752	0.2722	0.2719

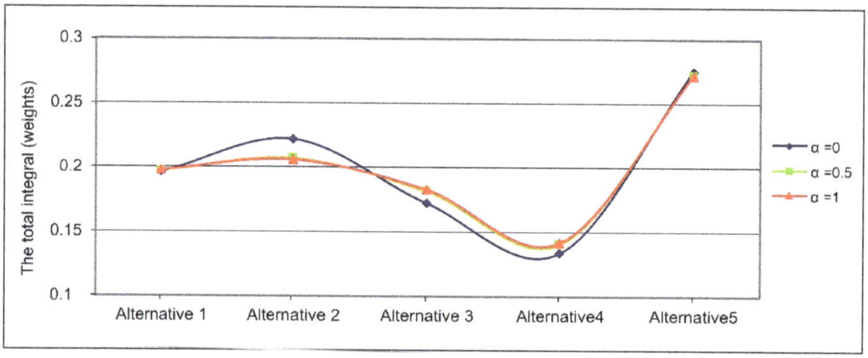

Figure 4. Total integral values of moderate, pessimistic and optimistic expert's risk assessments.

This procedure does not complete the analysis of the mining problem. Management support strategies are developed for the upcoming period of mining. Such strategies enable the management team to assume full professional responsibility for improving development plans. Additional future activities are defined to ensure mining efficiency and high productivity. This also includes the use of the latest technological achievements that help upgrade mining safety. On the one hand, the implementation of solutions and management team's commitment contribute to sustainable development of the entire process of mining operations, while on the other hand, they contribute to long-term stable technical, economic, and production conditions.

5. Conclusions

The paper demonstrated that FAHP is an extremely useful technique in the mining industry, given that the criteria used in the case study were subjective and based on expert judgment (of mining engineers and geologists), which is an important consideration in underground mining.

The research indicated that an interdisciplinary approach connects underground mining with other areas of science. For example, it links mining with fuzzy logic (based on mathematics and psychology) and multiple-criteria decision-making.

The paper described and analyzed in detail the factors that influence the selection of the optimal underground mining method, including (i) technical (ore body depth, ore body thickness, ore body shape, value of ore, ore body slope, rock hardness and stability, type of ore body and contact with neighboring rocks, and the mineral and chemical composition of the ore), (ii) production (productivity, capacity, safety at work, environmental impact, ore dilution, ore impoverishment, ventilation and hydrologic conditions), and (iii) economic (capital expenditure, costs of mining and costs of maintenance). These criteria, along with their subcriteria, are deemed to be universal and applicable to other underground mines.

The practical importance of the proposed methodology was demonstrated in a case study that included the evaluation of criteria, subcriteria and alternatives applying FAHP, and decision-making/selection of the optimal underground mining method. This reflects the primary academic contribution and implications for further research.

In addition, the approach implemented fuzzy logic in multiple-criteria optimization related to underground mining. On the one hand, the objective of applying the fuzzy approach to decision-making and problem-solving in cases where there are several alternatives and analyzing the relevant factors is to arrive at the optimal solution. On the other hand, expert intuition and experience play an important role in the assessment of the ore system and underground mining methods, while fuzzy logic in mathematical calculations enables such a heuristic approach to problem solving. Such an interdisciplinary approach contributes to the quality and sustainable management of underground mining.

Author Contributions: All the authors jointly contributed to the finalization of the paper: S.B. designed the MCDM model and conducted optimization calculations; B.G. and V.R.V., along with S.B., analyzed the criteria and alternatives, and D.B. critically reviewed the concept and design of the paper. All authors have read and agreed to the published version of the manuscript.

Funding: This research received no external funding.

Acknowledgments: We express our gratitude to the Serbian Ministry of Education, Science and Technological Development, for funding projects TR33029, TR33003 and OI176022.

Conflicts of Interest: The authors declare no conflict of interest. The funders had no role in the design of the study; in the collection, analyses, or interpretation of data; in the writing of the manuscript, or in the decision to publish the results.

Appendix A

Table A1. Weights of technical subcriteria.

Subcriteria	Weights (TFN)		
T_1	0.119	0.219	0.403
T_2	0.095	0.188	0.342
T_3	0.013	0.025	0.048
T_4	0.088	0.163	0.312
T_5	0.028	0.064	0.133
T_6	0.097	0.167	0.286
T_7	0.044	0.065	0.111
T_8	0.054	0.106	0.214

Table A2. Weights of production criteria.

Subcriteria	Weights (TFN)		
P_1	0.052	0.112	0.318
P_2	0.128	0.300	0.688
P_3	0.053	0.186	0.495
P_4	0.032	0.079	0.214
P_5	0.033	0.097	0.288
P_6	0.064	0.180	0.466
P_7	0.022	0.043	0.125

Table A3. Weights of economic subcriteria.

Subcriteria	E_1	E_2	E_3
	TFN	TFN	TFN
E_1	0.080	0.150	0.446
E_2	0.158	0.493	1.337
E_3	0.116	0.356	1.040

Table A4. Weights of alternatives relative to technical subcriteria.

T_1	Weights (TFN)			T_5	Weights (TFN)		
A_1	0.039	0.083	0.225	A_1	0.229	0.430	0.758
A_2	0.197	0.395	0.740	A_2	0.095	0.232	0.515
A_3	0.126	0.281	0.612	A_3	0.026	0.039	0.085
A_4	0.026	0.041	0.086	A_4	0.039	0.097	0.228
A_5	0.082	0.199	0.461	A_5	0.115	0.201	0.394
T_2	Weights (TFN)			T_6	Weights (TFN)		
A_1	0.205	0.405	0.741	A_1	0.082	0.181	0.419
A_2	0.027	0.041	0.090	A_2	0.198	0.417	0.807
A_3	0.085	0.181	0.375	A_3	0.039	0.099	0.247
A_4	0.041	0.106	0.290	A_4	0.026	0.040	0.090
A_5	0.131	0.266	0.547	A_5	0.127	0.261	0.548
T_3	Weights (TFN)			T_7	Weights (TFN)		
A_1	0.229	0.438	0.807	A_1	0.029	0.048	0.118
A_2	0.094	0.257	0.613	A_2	0.134	0.254	0.513
A_3	0.042	0.106	0.268	A_3	0.057	0.173	0.444
A_4	0.025	0.039	0.090	A_4	0.209	0.441	0.855
A_5	0.082	0.158	0.333	A_5	0.041	0.083	0.193
T_4	Weights (TFN)			T_8	Weights (TFN)		
A_1	0.127	0.281	0.612	A_1	0.039	0.097	0.228
A_2	0.027	0.044	0.111	A_2	0.229	0.430	0.758
A_3	0.052	0.158	0.397	A_3	0.026	0.039	0.085
A_4	0.039	0.078	0.182	A_4	0.127	0.256	0.515
A_5	0.229	0.437	0.805	A_5	0.082	0.177	0.394

Table A5. Weights of alternatives relative to production subcriteria.

P_1	Weights (TFN)		
A_1	0.132	0.260	0.513
A_2	0.029	0.044	0.084
A_3	0.086	0.179	0.372
A_4	0.040	0.078	0.171
A_5	0.239	0.438	0.755
P_2	Weights (TFN)		
A_1	0.149	0.291	0.569
A_2	0.078	0.163	0.334
A_3	0.036	0.070	0.150
A_4	0.026	0.038	0.072
A_5	0.248	0.437	0.732
P_3	Weights (TFN)		
A_1	0.029	0.042	0.079
A_2	0.280	0.456	0.708
A_3	0.091	0.160	0.292
A_4	0.137	0.259	0.481
A_5	0.044	0.081	0.156

Table A5. *Cont.*

P_4	Weights (TFN)		
A_1	0.028	0.046	0.127
A_2	0.252	0.462	0.820
A_3	0.080	0.172	0.374
A_4	0.036	0.071	0.146
A_5	0.092	0.247	0.577
P_5	**Weights (TFN)**		
A_1	0.025	0.039	0.090
A_2	0.227	0.437	0.805
A_3	0.040	0.104	0.264
A_4	0.082	0.159	0.354
A_5	0.096	0.260	0.612
P_6	**Weights (TFN)**		
A_1	0.028	0.040	0.075
A_2	0.084	0.147	0.260
A_3	0.265	0.452	0.728
A_4	0.159	0.282	0.513
A_5	0.042	0.077	0.149
P_7	**Weights (TFN)**		
A_1	0.024	0.035	0.072
A_2	0.248	0.438	0.734
A_3	0.079	0.163	0.335
A_4	0.149	0.273	0.516
A_5	0.037	0.090	0.204

Table A6. Weights of alternatives relative to economic subcriteria.

E_1	Weights (TFN)			E_2	Weights (TFN)			E_3	Weights (TFN)		
A_1	0.039	0.078	0.188	A_1	0.098	0.236	0.513	A_1	0.263	0.441	0.713
A_2	0.028	0.043	0.085	A_2	0.039	0.075	0.145	A_2	0.027	0.041	0.080
A_3	0.095	0.232	0.515	A_3	0.085	0.158	0.312	A_3	0.083	0.172	0.352
A_4	0.260	0.471	0.818	A_4	0.031	0.052	0.127	A_4	0.039	0.075	0.157
A_5	0.082	0.175	0.374	A_5	0.268	0.479	0.815	A_5	0.129	0.270	0.542

Table A7. Ultimate weights of subcriteria.

Subcriterion	Symbol	Weights (TFN)		
T_1	W_1	0.018	0.073	0.288
T_2	W_2	0.015	0.063	0.245
T_3	W_3	0.002	0.008	0.034
T_4	W_4	0.013	0.054	0.223
T_5	W_5	0.004	0.021	0.095
T_6	W_6	0.015	0.056	0.204
T_7	W_7	0.007	0.021	0.079
T_8	W_8	0.008	0.035	0.153
P_1	W_9	0.010	0.053	0.318
P_2	W_{10}	0.025	0.143	0.689
P_3	W_{11}	0.010	0.088	0.496
P_4	W_{12}	0.006	0.038	0.214
P_5	W_{13}	0.006	0.046	0.289
P_6	W_{14}	0.013	0.086	0.467
P_7	W_{15}	0.004	0.020	0.126
E_1	W_{16}	0.009	0.028	0.191
E_2	W_{17}	0.017	0.094	0.574
E_3	W_{18}	0.013	0.068	0.446

Table A8. Elements of the performance matrix.

Weight	Alt.	Fuzzy Number			Weight	Alt.	Fuzzy Number		
W_1	A_1	0.000728	0.006069	0.065084	W_{10}	A_1	0.003817	0.041651	0.392601
	A_2	0.003641	0.028898	0.213848		A_2	0.002021	0.023312	0.230513
	A_3	0.002333	0.020533	0.176657		A_3	0.000928	0.010042	0.103385
	A_4	0.000482	0.003005	0.024825		A_4	0.000666	0.005505	0.049916
	A_5	0.001512	0.014571	0.133237		A_5	0.006362	0.062491	0.504773
Weight	**Alt.**	**Fuzzy Number**			**Weight**	**Alt.**	**Fuzzy Number**		
W_2	A_1	0.003029	0.025452	0.181489	W_{11}	A_1	0.000311	0.003785	0.039362
	A_2	0.000398	0.002599	0.022094		A_2	0.002971	0.040417	0.351445
	A_3	0.001258	0.011386	0.092007		A_3	0.000966	0.014238	0.145217
	A_4	0.000606	0.006684	0.071018		A_4	0.001456	0.022964	0.238982
	A_5	0.001941	0.016745	0.134144		A_5	0.000467	0.007194	0.07774
Weight	**Alt.**	**Fuzzy Number**			**Weight**	**Alt.**	**Fuzzy Number**		
W_3	A_1	0.00048	0.003662	0.027639	W_{12}	A_1	0.000178	0.001774	0.027396
	A_2	0.000198	0.00215	0.021005		A_2	0.001614	0.017546	0.176119
	A_3	8.74E-05	0.000886	0.009209		A_3	0.000513	0.006545	0.080428
	A_4	5.28E-05	0.00033	0.003096		A_4	0.000233	0.002716	0.03131
	A_5	0.000173	0.001322	0.01142		A_5	0.000589	0.009406	0.123936
Weight	**Alt.**	**Fuzzy Number**			**Weight**	**Alt.**	**Fuzzy Number**		
W_4	A_1	0.001751	0.015312	0.136508	W_{13}	A_1	0.000168	0.001832	0.026059
	A_2	0.000374	0.002427	0.024931		A_2	0.001527	0.020354	0.232674
	A_3	0.000715	0.008597	0.088586		A_3	0.000272	0.004842	0.076317
	A_4	0.000534	0.004287	0.040665		A_4	0.00055	0.007424	0.102377
	A_5	0.003152	0.023818	0.179616		A_5	0.000644	0.012116	0.176832
Weight	**Alt.**	**Fuzzy Number**			**Weight**	**Alt.**	**Fuzzy Number**		
W_5	A_1	0.001019	0.009255	0.072218	W_{14}	A_1	0.000358	0.003486	0.035279
	A_2	0.000421	0.004993	0.049108		A_2	0.001086	0.012693	0.121712
	A_3	0.000116	0.000855	0.008088		A_3	0.00342	0.038926	0.34019
	A_4	0.000172	0.002092	0.021752		A_4	0.002052	0.024253	0.239393
	A_5	0.000511	0.004332	0.037553		A_5	0.000537	0.006628	0.069676
Weight	**Alt.**	**Fuzzy Number**			**Weight**	**Alt.**	**Fuzzy Number**		
W_6	A_1	0.001248	0.010096	0.085902	W_{15}	A_1	0.000107	0.000732	0.009131
	A_2	0.003004	0.023315	0.165196		A_2	0.001098	0.009068	0.092337
	A_3	0.000587	0.005572	0.050616		A_3	0.000349	0.003383	0.042167
	A_4	0.000395	0.002262	0.018502		A_4	0.000659	0.00565	0.064978
	A_5	0.001925	0.014572	0.112333		A_5	0.000164	0.001871	0.025752
Weight	**Alt.**	**Fuzzy Number**			**Weight**	**Alt.**	**Fuzzy Number**		
W_7	A_1	0.000202	0.00105	0.009398	W_{16}	A_1	0.000346	0.002245	0.035966
	A_2	0.000913	0.005516	0.040626		A_2	0.000251	0.001238	0.016243
	A_3	0.000387	0.003756	0.03521		A_3	0.000846	0.006649	0.098616
	A_4	0.001425	0.009593	0.067711		A_4	0.002319	0.013498	0.156626
	A_5	0.000278	0.001813	0.01533		A_5	0.000737	0.005035	0.071526
Weight	**Alt.**	**Fuzzy Number**			**Weight**	**Alt.**	**Fuzzy Number**		
W_8	A_1	0.000329	0.003452	0.03495	W_{17}	A_1	0.001711	0.022177	0.294687
	A_2	0.001945	0.015274	0.116035		A_2	0.000693	0.007066	0.083206
	A_3	0.000222	0.001411	0.012996		A_3	0.00149	0.014837	0.179066
	A_4	0.00108	0.009092	0.078904		A_4	0.000552	0.004886	0.072805
	A_5	0.0007	0.006299	0.060338		A_5	0.004691	0.045019	0.468033
Weight	**Alt.**	**Fuzzy Number**			**Weight**	**Alt.**	**Fuzzy Number**		
W_9	A_1	0.001375	0.013901	0.163554	W_{18}	A_1	0.003369	0.029912	0.318404
	A_2	0.000304	0.002346	0.026938		A_2	0.000353	0.002801	0.035661
	A_3	0.000891	0.009541	0.118625		A_3	0.00107	0.011666	0.157037
	A_4	0.000419	0.004204	0.054454		A_4	0.000503	0.005093	0.070431
	A_5	0.002475	0.023353	0.240521		A_5	0.001651	0.018355	0.241987

References

1. Saaty, T.L. *The Analytic Hierarchy Process: Planning, Priority Setting, Resource Allocation*; McGraw-Hill: New York, NY, USA, 1980.
2. Badi, I.; Abdulshahed, A.; Shetwan, A.; Eltayeb, W. Evaluation of solid waste treatment methods in Libya by using the analytic hierarchy process. *Decis. Mak. Appl. Manag. Eng.* **2019**, *2*, 19–35. [CrossRef]
3. Kovačević, N.; Stojiljković, A.; Kovač, M. Application of the matrix approach in risk assessment. *Oper. Res. Eng. Sci. Theory Appl.* **2019**, *2*, 55–64. [CrossRef]
4. Zhang, H.; Sun, Q. An Integrated MCDM Approach to Train Derailment Risk Response Strategy Selection. *Symmetry* **2020**, *12*, 47. [CrossRef]
5. Guo, Q.; Guo, G.; Li, Y.; Lei, W.; Zhao, X. Stability Evaluation of an Expressway Construction Site above an Abandoned Coal Mine Based on the Overlay and Index Method. *Sustainability* **2019**, *11*, 5163. [CrossRef]
6. Pipatprapa, A.; Huang, H.-H.; Huang, C.-H. A Novel Environmental Performance Evaluation of Thailand's Food Industry Using Structural Equation Modeling and Fuzzy Analytic Hierarchy Techniques. *Sustainability* **2016**, *8*, 246. [CrossRef]
7. Lee, A.H.I.; Kang, H.-Y.; Lin, C.-Y.; Shen, K.-C. An Integrated Decision-Making Model for the Location of a PV Solar Plant. *Sustainability* **2015**, *7*, 13522–13541. [CrossRef]
8. Chatterjee, P.; Stević, Ž. A two-phase fuzzy AHP-fuzzy TOPSIS model for supplier evaluation in manufacturing environment. *Oper. Res. Eng. Sci. Theory Appl.* **2019**, *2*, 72–90. [CrossRef]
9. Bozanić, D.; Tešić, D.; Milićević, J. A hybrid fuzzy AHP-MABAC model: Application in the Serbian Army–The selection of the location for deep wading as a technique of crossing the river by tanks. *Decis. Mak. Appl. Manag. Eng.* **2018**, *1*, 143–164. [CrossRef]
10. Stanković, M.; Gladović, P.; Popović, V. Determining the importance of the criteria of traffic accessibility using fuzzy AHP and rough AHP method. *Decis. Mak. Appl. Manag. Eng.* **2019**, *2*, 86–104. [CrossRef]
11. Mallick, J.; Khan, R.A.; Ahmed, M.; Alqadhi, S.D.; Alsubih, M.; Falqi, I.; Hasan, M.A. Modeling Groundwater Potential Zone in a Semi-Arid Region of Aseer Using Fuzzy-AHP and Geoinformation Techniques. *Water* **2019**, *11*, 2656. [CrossRef]
12. Özfırat, M.K. A fuzzy method for selecting underground coal mining method considering mechanization criteria. *J. Min. Sci.* **2012**, *48*, 533–544. [CrossRef]
13. Chander, B.B.; Gorai, A.K.; Jayantu, S. Design of Decision-Making Techniques Using Improved AHP and VIKOR for Selection of Underground Mining Method. *Recent Find. Intell. Comput. Tech.* **2018**, 495–504. [CrossRef]
14. Balusa, B.C.; Gorai, A.K. A Comparative Study of Various Multi-criteria Decision-Making Models in Underground Mining Method Selection. *J. Inst. Eng. (India) Ser. D* **2018**, *100*, 105. [CrossRef]
15. Balusa, B.C.; Gorai, A.K. Sensitivity analysis of fuzzy-analytic hierarchical process (FAHP) decision making model in selection of underground metal mining method. *J. Sustain. Min.* **2019**, *18*, 8–17. [CrossRef]
16. Bogdanovic, D.; Nikolic, D.; Ilic, I. Mining method selection by integrated AHP and PROMETHEE method. *Ann. Braz. Acad. Sci.* **2012**, *84*, 219–233. [CrossRef]
17. Aplay, S.; Yavuz, M. A Decision Support System for Underground Mining Method Selection. In Proceedings of the 20th International Conference on Industrial, Engineering and Other Applications of Applied Intelligent Systems, Kyoto, Japan, 26–29 June 2007; pp. 334–343.
18. Yazdani-Chamzini, A.; Yakchali, S.H.; Zavadskas, E.K. Using a integrated MCDM model for mining method selection in presence of uncertainty. *Econ. Res.* **2012**, 869–904. [CrossRef]
19. Asadi Ooriad, F.; Yari, M.; Bagherpour, R.; Khoshouei, M. The development of a novel Model for Mining Method Selection in a Fuzzy Environment; Case study: Tazareh Coal Mine, Semnan Province, Iran. *Min. Geol. Pet. Eng. Bull.* **2018**, 45–53. [CrossRef]
20. Javanshirgiv, M.; Safari, M. The selection of an underground mining method using the Fuzzy TOPSIS method: A case study in the Kamar Mahdi II fluorine mine, Iran. *Min. Sci.* **2017**, *24*, 161–181. [CrossRef]
21. Ataei, M.; Sereshki, F.; Jamshidi, M.; Jalali, S.M.E. Suitable mining method for Golbini No. 8 deposit in Jajarm (Iran) using TOPSIS method. *Min. Technol.* **2008**, *117*, 1–5. [CrossRef]
22. Naghadehi, M.Z.; Mikaeil, R.; Ataei, M. The application of fuzzy analytic hierarchy process (FAHP) approach to selection of optimum underground mining method for Jajarm Bauxite Mine, Iran. *Expert Syst. Appl.* **2009**, 8218–8226. [CrossRef]

23. Bajić, D.; Polomčić, D.; Ratković, J. Multi-criteria decision analysis for the purposes of groundwater control system design. *Water Resour. Manag.* **2017**, *31*, 4759–4784. [CrossRef]
24. Polomčić, D.; Gligorić, Z.; Bajić, D.; Gligorić, M.; Negovanović, M. Multi-criteria fuzzy-stochastic diffusion model of groundwater control system selection. *Symmetry* **2019**, *11*, 705. [CrossRef]
25. Zadeh, L.A. Fuzzy sets. *Inf. Control.* **1965**, *8*, 338–353. [CrossRef]
26. Chang, D.Y. Applications of the extent analysis method on fuzzy AHP. *Eur. J. Oper. Res.* **1996**, *95*, 649–655. [CrossRef]
27. Saaty, T.L. How to make a decision: The analytic hierarchy process. *Eur. J. Oper. Res.* **1990**, *48*, 9–26. [CrossRef]
28. Zhu, K.; Jing, Y.; Chang, D. A discussion on extent analysis method and applications of fuzzy AHP. *Eur. J. Oper. Res.* **1999**, *116*, 450–456. [CrossRef]
29. Lamata, M.T. Ranking of alternatives with ordered weighted averaging operators. *Int. J. Intell. Syst.* **2004**, *19*, 473–482. [CrossRef]
30. Deng, H. Multicriteria analysis with fuzzy pair-wise comparison. *Int. J. Approx. Reason.* **1999**, *21*, 215–231. [CrossRef]
31. Zadeh, L.A. The concept of a liguistic variable and its application to approximate reasoning. *Inf. Sci.* **1975**, *8*, 199–249. [CrossRef]
32. Van Broekhoven, E. A comparison of three methods for computing the center of gravity defuzzification. *Proc. Int. Conf. Fuzzy Syst.* **2004**, *3*, 1537–1542.
33. Liou, T.S.; Wang, M.J.J. Ranking fuzzy numbers with integral value. *Fuzzy Sets Syst.* **1992**, *50*, 247–256. [CrossRef]
34. Kwang, H.C.; Lee, H.J. A method for ranking fuzzy numbers and its application to decision making. *IEEE Trans. Fuzzy Syst.* **1999**, *7*, 677–685. [CrossRef]
35. Ataei, M.; Jamshidi, M.; Sereshki, F.; Jalali, S.M.E. Mining method selection by AHP approach. *J. S. Afr. Inst. Min. Metall.* **2008**, *108*, 741–749.

MDPI
St. Alban-Anlage 66
4052 Basel
Switzerland
Tel. +41 61 683 77 34
Fax +41 61 302 89 18
www.mdpi.com

Symmetry Editorial Office
E-mail: symmetry@mdpi.com
www.mdpi.com/journal/symmetry

www.ingramcontent.com/pod-product-compliance
Lightning Source LLC
Chambersburg PA
CBHW061445220926
51850CB00004B/16
* 9 7 8 3 0 3 6 5 1 5 7 4 8 *